The Last Generation of the Roman Republic

WITHDRAWN

The Last Generation of the Roman Republic

ERICH S. GRUEN

UNIVERSITY OF CALIFORNIA PRESS
Berkeley, Los Angeles, London

PARENTIBUS OPTIMIS

University of California Press
Berkeley and Los Angeles, California

University of California Press, Ltd.
London, England

First Paperback Printing 1995

Library of Congress Cataloging-in-Publication Data

Gruen, Erich S.
The last generation of the Roman Republic [by] Erich S. Gruen. Berkeley, University of California Press [1974] With new Introduction [1994]
Includes bibliographical references and index.
ISBN 0-520-20153-1 (pbk.: alk. paper)
1. Rome—Politics and government—265–30 B.C. 2. Public law—Rome—History. I. Title.
DG254.2.G78 320.9'37'05 72-89244
MARC

Printed in the United States of America
Designed by Lloyd Linford

2 3 4 5 6 7 8 9

The paper used in this publication meets the minimum requirements of American National Standard for Information Sciences—Permanence of Paper for Printed Library Materials, ANSI Z39.48–1984. ♾

CONTENTS

INTRODUCTION TO THE PAPERBACK EDITION

THE LAST *Generation of the Roman Republic* was conceived, composed, and revised in Berkeley in the late 1960s and early 1970s. Turbulence and turmoil took prominence in those years, a period of high passion, political strife, moral outrage, ideological conflict, and occasional violence. The atmosphere crackled with tension. The university served simultaneously as staging-ground for dissent, target for spleen, and center for contention. Friction and stress were everywhere evident, dispute and heated debate the standard order of the day. The discord went well beyond liberals vs. conservatives; it involved generational battles, racial differences, cultural and counter-cultural claims, the incipient women's movement and was fueled by issues like civil rights, the Vietnam War, ethnic demands, and a pervasive sense of alienation.

All of this inescapably had an impact upon the inception and evolution of *LGRR*. Yet an equally remarkable feature of the time, far less conspicuous or dramatic, provided stimulus for its orientation: the stability and endurance of institutions in the midst of upheaval. The events of the late 1960s and early 1970s, to be sure, left their mark and wrought important changes or accelerated developments in the university, the community, and the broader society. But the continuities, which captured little public attention, had lessons of their own. Traditional patterns of behavior, conventions, and attitudes subsisted through the turmoil with surprising durability. That aspect of events and outcome prompted reflections that issued in *LGRR:* a search for the bases of stability rather than the seeds of tumult.

LGRR therefore has its place in a special time and special circumstances. To revise it in light of subsequent interpretations, criticisms, or second thoughts would bring little advantage to author or reader, and would even compromise whatever value the book possesses as a period piece. Hence text and notes in this edition remain unchanged.

The subject, however, continues to exercise fascination. A substantial bibliography has accumulated in the two decades since publication of *LGRR*, much of it moving in different directions, applying other emphases, providing variant interpretations, or taking issue with tenets of the book. Neither rebuttal nor apologia would be appropriate here. And space prevents a survey of the vast scholarship that has appeared since 1974. But it may be serviceable to review a small selection of the more important contributions to topics treated in *LGRR* – the gains, advancements, and improvements in our understandings since that time – and to offer some suggestions for the lines of future research.[1]

The role of patronage in Roman social and political life drew attention in *LGRR* and has been much discussed subsequently and fruitfully. N. Rouland's *Pouvoir politique et dépendance personnelle dans l'antiquité romaine* (Brussels, 1979) supplies a far-ranging treatment that traces the institution of clientship in Rome from its purported beginnings through the early Principate. His central thesis projects a breakdown of traditional ties between patron and client in the late Republic. Expansion of the citizenry meant that increasing numbers of persons without links to the established aristocracy put pressure on the political scene. Conventional bonds were further short-circuited by electoral bribery, *popularis* politicking, and the replacement of individual patronage by collective institutions. The earlier networks of clientage largely dissolved in the late Republic, leaving only the display of dependents in one's entourage or their employment as strong-armed retainers to serve as legacy to the Principate. The demise of *clientela,* on this analysis, mirrors the disintegration of the Republic. P. A. Brunt, in the extended essay on *clientela* in *The Fall of the Roman Republic* (Oxford, 1988), 382-442, goes further. Brunt questions the proposition that patronage had much effect at all on the operations of Roman politics. Ascribing this system in its flourishing state to the early or middle Republic is dubious, for the sources are late and unreliable, and testimony to patronage at a political level in the later Republic is conspicuously skimpy. Insofar as the institution existed, on Brunt's analysis, the bonds were loose, supposedly hereditary ties were unenduring, patrons could not reckon on clients' loyalties in the political arena, and overlapping connections render insupportable the hypothesis that individual houses of the nobility owed positions and influence to the control of familial *clientes.* This sustained assault on Gelzer and his *epigoni* has exhibited the fragility of constructs that interpret Roman politics as dependent upon a network of mutual obligations.

The debate, however, too often confines itself to the realm of politics. Links

[1] This endeavor was much facilitated by the assistance of Judy Gaughan, Michael Ierardi, Cecilia Peek, and Beth Severy, who have earned considerable gratitude.

of patronage, viewed as moral responsibilities and social relationships, had wider impact outside the purely political scene. There is evidence to be exploited in this regard. As a fine example one can cite the new work by E. Deniaux, *Cliéntèles et pouvoir à l'époque de Ciceron* (Rome, 1993), which explores in exhaustive detail the corpus of Ciceronian letters of recommendation. They disclose a broad range of associations, reaching into a variety of social levels and involving mutual accommodations that stretch well beyond the stage of high politics. The relative absence of the explicit term *cliens* (generally shunned for obvious reasons of tact), as Deniaux rightly observes, does not in any way signal the demise of the institution. The persistence of patronage networks between Republic and Empire, associating Roman *nobiles* with persons not only in the city but in diverse communities and regions of Italy and the provinces, is amply documented by R. Saller, *Personal Patronage in the early Empire* (Cambridge, 1982). These were not largely means of winning votes, if at all, but, as A. Wallace-Hadrill argues in *Patronage in Ancient Society* (London, 1990), 63-87, a vehicle for social integration and the extension of control from center to periphery. The massive study of J.-M. David, *Le patronat judicaire au dernier siècle de la republique romaine* (Rome, 1992), among other things, illuminates the role of the orator as *patronus,* not just in a limited judicial sense but in the wider social meaning as protector and advocate of established clients, carrying out the obligations of *fides,* reinforcing mutual bonds, and keeping alive a patronage model that goes back to early Roman history – thus, a significant continuity between present and past. The institution served as a vital means to exhibit the distinction of the *patronus* and the allegiance of the client. Future research will profit from skirting the old debate about clients as instruments of politics and instead focusing on practices like *salutatio* and *adsectatio* as displays of the *patronus's* prestige, social status, and beneficent image.

Predominance of the *nobiles* in high office remains an unassailable fact. Dispute over definition of the term has borne little fruit and makes little difference (see the inconclusive arguments of Brunt, *JRS,* 72 [1982], 1-17, and L. Burckhardt, *Historia,* 39 [1990], 80-84). None can gainsay the pattern that men of consular descent, whether near or far, dominated access to the top magistracies. The quantitative analysis of K. Hopkins and G. Burton in K. Hopkins, *Death and Renewal* (Cambridge, 1983), 31-119, has shown that the oligarchy was no impenetrable caste, that new men could enter the ranks of the privileged, and that the prominence of individual families varied over the generations. Nevertheless, the principal continuities prevailed. Even on the findings of Hopkins and Burton, two-thirds of the consuls in the last two centuries of the Republic had immediate consular ancestors. Furthermore, the Republic's final two decades show that more than 80 percent of the consuls had forebears in that office, a statistic reaffirmed in the most recent survey by E. Badian, *Chiron,* 30 (1990), 371-413. The electoral power of the elite can be illustrated from still another direction: the frequency with which defeated candidates from its ranks attained office in subsequent campaigns, a point made in the final work of the great scholar T. R. S. Broughton, *Candidates Defeated in Roman Elections: Some Ancient Roman "Also-Rans"* (Philadelphia, 1991).

How to account for this persistent success? *LGRR* laid stress on "familial ties, connections, wealth, and aristocratic heritage" (p. 133). Current opinion casts doubt upon the strength of inherited bonds and obligations, as discussed above. More attention has now been paid to the claims of the populace, the need to promote popular interests, and the influence that the *populus Romanus* could exercise upon electoral results. A provocative series of articles by F. Millar gave special weight to the "democratic element" in Roman political culture – the importance of publicly appealing to the needs of a broad constituency in order to assure positions of leadership: *JRS,* 74 (1984), 1-19; *JRS,* 76 (1986), 1-11; *JRS,* 79 (1989), 142-149. That feature plays a central role in P. J. J. Vanderbroeck's *Popular Leadership and Collective Behaviour in the Late Roman Republic, ca. 80-50 B.C.* (Amsterdam, 1987), especially 161-173. If one could not win the backing of the electorate through advocacy of its causes, there was always the avenue of bribery. Evidence for the practice accumulates in the late Republic, and increased numbers of laws on *ambitus* attest to its greater conspicuousness. For some it became a determinant factor in electoral outcomes: J. Linderski, *AncWorld,* 11 (1985), 87-94. In the recent interpretation of A. W. Lintott, *JRS,* 80 (190), 1-16, bribery represents an alternative to conventional patronage or indeed a form of patronage itself, a liberating force for the electorate, which could now market its votes. Bribery was objected to more on moral than on political grounds when it became too institutionalized, thus interfering with the association between grandee and beneficiary. A. Yakobson, *JRS,* 82 (1992), 32-52, takes the case to a still further level, arguing that even the *comitia centuriata,* generally regarded as a bastion of privilege, gave considerable scope to the voice of the commons, thereby rendering meaningful the practice of *largitio* to the *plebs* as a route to the election of senior magistrates. The trend of these studies has been salutary and productive, shaking the complacency of earlier scholarship on the smooth and untroubled hold by the *nobiles* on the electorate.

Yet problems still exist and solutions remain elusive. The composition and quantity of the electorate at any given time have to be considered. The voting structures themselves set severe limits, assuring that only a fraction of eligible electors could exercise that privilege, a point rightly emphasized by R. MacMullen, *Athenaeum,* 78 (1980), 454-457. The implementation of voting rights generally and their meaning for the role of a Roman citizen are discussed in the valuable survey by C. Nicolet, *The World of the Citizen in Republican Rome* (Berkeley, 1980), 207-315. Laws designed to effect electoral reform may not signify an opening of the process to wider levels of society, but rather represent an instrument whereby the elite curbed the influence of *novi homines* who sought to encroach upon their nexus of traditional associations; cf. E. S. Gruen, in A. Molho, K. Raaflaub, and J. Emlen, *City-States in Classical Antiquity and Medieval Italy* (Stuttgart, 1991), 251-267. The whole idea of a democratic character in Roman society where the oligarchy enjoyed virtually unchallenged control in political, institutional, and religious life is difficult to defend, as J. North, *Past and Present,* 126 (1990), 3-21, recently reaffirmed. In North's view, the popular will made itself felt only to arbitrate matters in which the oligarchy itself was bitterly divided. The clear consistency with which the electorate returned members of the aristocracy to high office still stands as the dominant datum. It would be productive to investigate this phenomenon not so much through the hold of individual families, but through the projection of the aristocratic image as a collective ideal. That may have had more enduring impact than ties of patronage or distribution of largesse.

With regard to the character and activities of the senatorial class, significant information is now more accessible and serviceable. Two useful works appeared about the time of *LGRR.* I. Shatzman's *Senatorial Wealth and Roman Politics* (Brussels, 1975) sets out the data on the property, other sources of income, and expenditures, where known, for all senators in the middle and late Republic. His findings – that the nobles owned a predominant portion of the available land in the post-Sullan era and also had readier access to other means of securing wealth, thus reinforcing positions of power and authority – have implications for the solidarity and continuity of the privileged order. H. Schneider, *Wirtschaft und Politik: Untersuchungen zur Geschichte der späten römischen Republik* (Erlangen, 1974), supplies parallel information, though not in tabular form, for senatorial possessions, diverse means of enrichment, and the extensive outlays that featured the lifestyle of the elite. In Schneider's interpretative framework, the access to economic power translated into political authority, but also hardened the senate's protection of its own interests and resistance to popular needs or advantage. A third study, that of M. Bonneford-Coudry, *Le senat de la république romaine* (Rome, 1989), provides an exhaustive topographical, calendrical, and procedural examination of the senate's activities. Her detailed analysis also documents fully the deference paid to hierarchy within senatorial ranks, the preponderance of intervention by exconsuls, and their near monopoly in the sponsorship of *senatus consulta.* Bonneford-Coudry's massive work underscores not only continuity in senatorial practice, but also the maintenance of the senate's place in the governmental structure of Rome. Additional support for that stance comes from L. de Libero's *Obstruktion* (Stuttgart, 1992), which approaches the subject from a novel angle. De Libero collects the evidence on senatorial tactics of obstructionism to argue that these maneuvers were part of the *mos maiorum* – conventional behavior built into the structure, a sign of institutional stability rather than disintegration.

The nature of Roman politics continues to provoke debate. Views diverge on the manner and means whereby aristocratic competition was structured. *LGRR* sought to steer a middle course between an older thesis that divided the senate into contending family factions and the notion that political alignments were momentary, makeshift, and inconsequential. It proposed a complex picture in which familial alliances carried political meaning but came under increasing pressure in the late Republic as they splintered or were reshaped by volatile rivalries, forceful personalities, an expanded citizenry, the posturing of leaders, and the interests of various segments of society.

Subsequent studies have, however, raised doubts about the existence of groups formed on the basis of blood ties, marriage alliances, and mutual obligations. T. P. Wiseman, in *Roman Political Life, 90 B.C.-A.D. 69* (Exeter, 1985), 3-19, prefers a simpler model that has political units built around powerful individuals rather than around family groups or wider alliances. Brunt's broader assault in *Fall of the Roman Republic,* 443-502, denies that any political assemblages cohered on the basis of kinship ties, familial connections, or even the leadership of ascendant individuals. This has parallels with an earlier and influential study by C. Meier, *Res Publica Amissa* (Wiesbaden, 1966), whose views are restated in the introduction to a 1980 edition of his book (see, especially, xxxii-xliii). On Brunt's analysis, marriage ties suggest no political union, criminal trials supply evidence only for private enmities, ambition, or a drive for justice, and the absence of Latin terminology for cohesive factions throws the very concept into question. The senate, therefore, did not divide into competitive segments; and figures like Pompey, Caesar, and Crassus never carried or presumably sought much influence in that body. Nor did they command the consistent allegiance of any collection of followers themselves. Personal advantage prevailed.

This notion of individualism and the evanescence of combines has its limits. Brunt concedes the existence of the *optimates,* a loose collection of *principes* united in a broad commitment to senatorial control of the state. The identity and composition of the "*optimates*", however, remain fuzzy. L. A. Burckhardt devoted an entire book to eliciting the methods and tactics of the "*optimates*" in the political arena: *Politische Strategien der Optimaten in der späten römischen Republik* (Stuttgart, 1988). Yet he can provide no clear criteria for discerning the size, makeup, or organization of this shadowy cluster of personages. In fact, the term "*optimates*" in our texts serves only to register approbation, just as "*factio*" generally designates opprobrium – without signifying any political structure.

A different approach to this issue can be recommended. More scholarly energy needs to be applied to an examination of how the Roman aristocracy defined itself and endeavored to promote its solidarity rather than to reanalyzing the mechanisms of friction and division. An admirable start in that direction has now been made by N. Rosenstein, *Imperatores Victi: Military Defeat and Aris-*

tocratic Competition in the Middle and Late Republic (Berkeley, 1990). Although his book deals largely with events prior to the period of *LGRR,* Rosenstein exposes a fundamental feature of the aristocratic mentality: the setting of limits to aristocratic competition, both to assure a fairly wide distribution of *honores* among the political class and to reaffirm the collective interests of that class. He deftly exploits the remarkable phenomenon that defeated commanders pursued political careers with a success rate comparable to that of victorious ones. Such evidence suggests that the ruling elite not only shielded their own members from the consequences of defeat, but presented the image of a unified aristocracy with competent leadership stretched throughout its ranks. Further probes of the bonding values would be welcome.

Criminal trials played a conspicuous role on the public scene of the late Republic. Well over one hundred cases made their way into the extant record during the period under scrutiny—and doubtless many more went unreported. The *iudicia publica* gained widespread attention as highly visible arenas for contests among the influential, the aggressive, the aggrieved, and the aspiring. *LGRR* presented a plethora of motives that prompted battles in the courts: major public issues such as the debate over the *senatus consultum ultimum,* the implications of the Catilinarian movement, or the efforts to restore stable government after the disorders of the mid-50s; intense political contests between Pompey and his detractors; attacks and counterattacks involving allies and opponents of the "triumvirs"; private enmities, familial quarrels, and feuds between houses; personal obligations that influenced lineups for prosecution or defense; the ambitions of the young to reach the limelight by putting their talents on show in a judicial setting. A combination of such incentives and objectives normally characterized criminal trials, which provide a rich harvest of information on the political climate—and also exemplary of the continuities that run through the period.

The subject regularly stimulates discussion. D. F. Epstein, *Personal Enmity in Roman Politics, 218-43* B.C. (London, 1987), expresses discomfort with complexity (pp. 101-102). His treatment finds a preponderance of private motives and a centrality for *inimicitia* in criminal trials, a useful reminder of how frequently this element recurs. But the examination is highly selective for the cases of the Republic's last generation. David, in his *Le patronat judicaire,* rightly discerns a multiplicity of motives that drove Romans repeatedly into the courts: pursuit of personal or familial feuds, protection of clients, establishment or enhancement of reputation, the inducement of tangible rewards, the carrying out of obligations to more powerful personages. But David's extensive analysis goes well beyond the search for motives. He details the social constraints and the social demands that governed appearances at the bar, as well as the different pressures that influenced types of behavior, styles of presentation, and expressed attitudes, gestures, and symbolic acts in judicial contests. A noteworthy distinction between the backgrounds of accusers and those of defendants (the former almost always of lesser status) gives important insight into the role played by the expectations of society: eagerness for advancement on the one side, exhibit of prestige and patronage on the other. David further usefully reminds us that the benches of both prosecutor and defendant swelled with supporters and advocates – a means to demonstrate solidarity and strength, that the physical setting of trials encouraged the indirect participation of the broader public, and that even the proximity of monuments underlined the civic meaning of the trials and their continuity with the past. Here again, symbolic features and the display of status afford avenues for further research. Material on judicial activity in the late Republic is now more readily at hand than before. David supplies a most valuable prosopography of all the persons who appeared in judicial cases in the last century and a half of the Republic, providing full testimony, discussion, and rich bibliographical notes. A most serviceable complement to David's assemblage of data appeared independently: a comprehensive listing of trials, organized by case rather than by individual, and with far more attention to legal matters, in M. C. Alexander, *Trials in the Late Roman Republic, 149 B.C. to 30 B.C.* (Toronto, 1990). These will be advantageous springboards for future work.

The role of the populace has drawn increasing attention and a sharper focus in recent years. To what degree did the needs of the commons divide public sentiments, stimulate *popularis* activity, and generate resistance in the nobility? L. Perelli's *Il movimento populare nell' ultimo secolo della repubblica* (Torino, 1982) portrays a relatively consistent contest between champions of popular interests, however sincere or insincere their motives, and a conservative opposition, at least from the time of the Gracchi. This was no simplistic class struggle in Marxist terms, nor was it a mere battle between reformist and reactionary wings of the senate. A range of issues, recurrent and serious, helped to define a popular movement that reflected genuine stirrings in the *populus Romanus:* increase in the power of assemblies and tribunes, a broadening of the electoral system, extension of the franchise, food subsidies, distribution of land and colonial settlements. Perelli's analysis extends to identification of a complex constituency for this popular tide: a principal base in the dislocated and underemployed rural dwellers, augmented by an urban component that consisted not so much of the "proletariate" as of shopkeepers, small merchants, indebted workers, freedmen, and migrants from the countryside without previous ties to the nobility. The dichotomy of *optimates* and *populares* applies then not to political parties but to divergent positions on the desirability of reform to meet the needs of various groups and levels of society. The "triumvirs" rode the popular tide for a time – Catiline only partially and temporarily, Caesar more consistently, and Clodius more intensely. A clear and vivid picture emerges. But the reductive schematism tends to flatten out frictions within the ruling orders themselves. That drawback exists as well in Schneider's *Wirtschaft und Politik,* a fuller but even starker presentation of conflict between the privileged class and the oppressed poor – a picture repeated in his broader study, *Die Entstehung der römischen Militärdiktatur: Kriese und Niedergang einer antiken Republik* (Köln, 1977). P. Garnsey, *Famine and Food Supply in the Greco-Roman World* (Cambridge, 1988), 198-217, underlines the vulnerability of the *plebs* to grain shortages produced by warfare, piracy, natural calamities, or speculation. Their plight also prompted political struggles and popular advocates, as well as persistent conservative reaction. For Garnsey, any efforts by conservatives to alleviate the situation can only have been designed to deter radical measures and upheaval. Cf. also G. Rickman, *The Corn Supply of Ancient Rome* (Oxford, 1980), 48-58, 166-175.

Vanderbroeck provides a more intricate reconstruction in his *Popular Leadership and Collective Behavior.* He discerns levels of leadership reshaped in the late Republic to mobilize popular opinion and to galvanize collective action. Vanderbroeck meticulously examines the variety of means through which popular sentiments might be elicited and expressed, the forms of communication between the elite and the commons, the symbols and images employed, the organizational structures, and the strategies. A fundamental shift took place in the late Republic, on Vanderbroeck's assessment: vertical ties between patrons and clients loosened as a consequence of population increase, and the slippage of previous channels of intimate communication led to the emergence of a "public clientele" that looked to popular leaders – a more independent, more diverse, and more volatile collectivity. At the same time, however, and most interestingly, Vanderbroeck recognizes that this transformation occurred within a traditional structure. Popular leaders shared the ideology of their peers and produced no innovations in the existing power relations. They employed conventional slogans and built on preexisting organizations. Even the shift in patron-client bonds retained the expectation of mutual responsibilities, only increasing the distance between leader and constituency, and elevating the traditional relationship to a broader, national level. The spokesmen of the *plebs* had no revolutionary aims but rather sought to enhance their own prominence within the conventional structure. Whatever one makes of Vanderbroeck's thesis, his appendix, which assembles all instances of collective behavior in the late Republic, with summary description, sources, and outcome, provides an eminently convenient resource. The recent study of the *plebs* by B. Kühnert, *Die Plebs Urbana der späten römischen Republik: ihre ökonomische Situation und soziale Struktur* (Innsbruck, 1991), dispels some common misconceptions and offers some salutary reminders. The *plebs,* as she rightly recognizes, constituted no monolithic mass; it comprised individuals engaged in a diverse range of occupations and differentiated by socioeconomic conditions, including some who might have attained substantial wealth. She reargues with conviction a number of useful points that have had inadequate acknowledgment in the literature: that the city contained relatively few refugees from the countryside, that the proportion of *libertini* among the *plebs urbana* may have been exaggerated by some scholars, that indebtedness was not a significant problem among urban dwellers, and that neither grain distributions nor bribery nor a combination thereof could have sufficed to sustain the welfare of the *plebs.* Although none of the positions is altogether novel, Kühnert supplies a compact and cogent discussion.

The most effective mobilizer of the *plebs,* of course, was P. Clodius Pulcher. He is now receiving his due as scholarly treatments continue to multiply. Perelli recognized the comprehensive character of his *popularis* program. Vanderbroeck regards him as the most efficient organizer of popular opinion, the one Roman political innovator who created effective channels of communication between a leader and his public clientele. A more detailed, though often speculative, analysis of Clodius's mechanisms for structuring and activating his followers to deliver maximum impact in civic affairs appears in J. M. Flambard, *MEFRA,* 89 (1977), 115-156. The subject obtains fuller study in H. Benner, *Die Politik des P. Clodius Pulcher: Untersuchungen zur Denaturierung des Clientelwesens in der ausgehenden römischen Republik* (Stuttgart, 1987). On Benner's hypothetical reconstruction, Clodius modelled the structure of his popular retinue upon the military *clientelae* of dynasts like Marius, Sulla, and Pompey. The argument is designed to account for the marshalling of what one might characterize as paramilitary forces, constituted for the purpose of organized violence.

Clodius, on any reckoning, counts as a central figure in all discussions of violence in the late Republic. Perelli endeavors to absolve him of blame, seeing a resort to force as a reaction to the violence first employed by Clodius's opponents. Benner sees a somewhat reverse development: Clodius gradually abandoned violent tactics after his tribunate and turned to broader methods of courting popular favor. The impact of violence itself has received an important reassessment now by W. Nippel, *Aufruhr und "Polizei" in der römischen Republik* (Stuttgart, 1988). Nippel decisively refutes the common notion that absence of a police force allowed violence to get out of hand and erode the authority of the state. In fact, social and political stability and flexible institutions allowed the structure to discourage and absorb acts of violence without threatening its foundation. Perpetrators of violence could also find justification through appeal to tradition and history. Nippel's intelligent treatment of Clodius is particularly illuminating. The tribune eschewed violence in the passage of his measures, for they stirred widespread enthusiasm among the *plebs.* And the subsequent use of force represented not lawlessness but significant symbolic activity, adopting the forms and rituals of antique folk-justice, an analysis that also sheds important light on the violence of Clodius's supporters after his death. These very findings, however, stand in tension with Nippel's own conclusion that state authority had broken down in the 50s and that Pompey's sole consulship of 52 signified the collapse of traditional means of maintaining order. The inference remains unproved. And one might still consider the proposition of *LGRR* that the reluctance of the officialdom to stamp out violence acknowledged an outlet for urban dissent that did not threaten the fabric of society.

A far greater threat loomed in the army. The part played by soldiers in weakening the hold of the oligarchy, shifting loyalties from the state to individual commanders, and setting the stage for military dictatorship has long been a staple in interpretations of the Republic's fall. *LGRR* questioned some of the standard presuppositions. The idea of a gradual professionalization of the army since the Marian reforms does not easily meet the facts. Most of the rank and file served only limited terms in the forces, preferring a temporary tour of duty and hoping for some enhancement of economic status after their return. Senior officers, and indeed many junior officers, reckoned time with the military as a stage in one's political career, not an alternative to it. Nor did allegiance to the *res publica* erode while soldiers tied themselves to generals who could promise the benefactions that the state denied them. In fact, even the most successful *imperatores* did not receive—and probably could not expect—enduring loyalties from veterans on the domestic front. Nothing suggests that the soldiery had developed a separatist mentality, let alone that they contemplated toppling the Republic. Even those who crossed the Rubicon responded to appeals on constitutional grounds. Positions taken on these matters in *LGRR* owed much to Brunt's important study, "Army and the Land in the Roman Revolution," subsequently republished in revised form, with updated notes, in *The Fall of the Roman Republic,* 240-280. Brunt argues forcefully that the bulk of military recruits came from the *plebs rustica,* peasants, tenants, and agricultural laborers for whom the acquisition of land after discharge was a preeminent goal, although he perhaps undervalues the possibility that urban dwellers may have had comparable goals. The composition of the post-Marian armies, in Brunt's analysis, did not differ markedly from the past, nor had Rome developed a dual structure of standing armies and emergency forces. Neither personal attachment to generals nor professionalization characterized the late Republican military. Soldiers enlisted to better their economic circumstances, and, in particular, had a yen for land. That reconstruction remains a cogent one.

The subject of the army in the Republic's last generation has sparked no dramatic scholarly turns of late. Two noteworthy German dissertations appeared around the time of *LGRR:* E. H. Erdmann, *Die Rolle des Heeres in der Zeit von Marius bis Caesar* (Neustadt/Aisch, 1972), and H. Aigner, *Die Soldaten als Machtfaktor in der ausgehenden römischen Republik* (Innsbruck, 1974). Each provides a welcome catalogue of actions by the late Republican army outside the battlefield. But the evidence prompts them to divergent conclusions. For Erdmann, the Marian reforms divided army from citizenry. The post-Marian soldiery had become a professional force and, as such, no mere tool of individual commanders. Support by the troops for their *imperator*'s political ends came only when he advanced *their* interests. Aigner arrived at somewhat different verdicts. He found no move toward professionalism, nor any developing bonds of clientage between general and soldiers. Men enlisted for purely economic motives, feeling little sense of allegiance either to their commander or to the *res publica*. They eschewed politics, aiming only for enrichment. Both books, while assembling valuable material, incline to reductive analysis. Land assignations and colonial foundations for veterans receive treatment in H.-C. Schneider, *Das Problem der Veteranversorgung in der späteren römischen Republik* (Bonn, 1977). The frequency of such measures in the late Republic implies, as he recognizes, that most soldiers came from the Italian countryside, sought property as veterans, and had not embraced a professional mentality—although a trend toward career service had emerged. The *imperatores* who sponsored or backed land allocations—with the possible exception of Julius Caesar—did so to appease troops and win their adherence for political ends, rather than to provide enduring socioeconomic reform. And, in fact, the land distributions did not notably raise the economic levels of the veterans. Nor indeed did they do much for the social mobility and political involvement of the ex-soldiers, a point reaffirmed now by J. Patterson, in J. Rich and G. Shipley, *War and Society in the Roman World* (London, 1993), 92-112. The analysis is a cynical but sober one. In a recent study, L. de Blois, *The Roman Army and Politics in the First Century B.C.* (Amsterdam, 1987), unfortunately reverts to a number of conventional positions. His reconstruction has professionalism in the ascendant by the first century B.C., not only in the rank and file but in much of the officer corps, with political grandees as commanders who obtained the personal loyalties of their forces. The result was a split both in the ruling orders and, in society at large, between those committed to a civilian existence and the military careerists. In de Blois's formulation, a decline in "political culture" left the citizenry vulnerable to the army as traditional bonds of *clientela* yielded to the ad hoc allegiance of armies to warlords. De Blois cites all the relevant literature—but seems largely unaffected by it.

The question of continuity or crisis holds center stage in *LGRR*. It emerges at the very outset of the period under scrutiny. The death of Sulla, on the conventional view, issued in a decade of challenges to his system, both internal and external, culminating in a number of reforms that ostensibly caused the Sullan settlement to unravel and heralded the breakdown of the aristocratic order. *LGRR* took a different line: the Sullan senate embraced many of the reforms itself, and it adjusted and shifted to address public concerns and respond to challenges; the advocates of change sought to advance within the system, not to overturn it. That analysis found little favor with Perelli, *Il movimento popolare*, 159-171, who revived the portrait of the 70s as a battleground between Sullani and *populares*, with Pompey carrying a popular banner to triumph over the Sullan system. But the sense of broader concord and a more flexible attitude operating within the traditional structure has been acknowledged by a number of recent studies; e.g., T. N. Mitchell, *Cicero: The Ascending Years* (New Haven, 1979), 107-133; J. Paterson, in T. P. Wiseman, *Roman Political Life, 90 B.C.-A.D. 69* Exeter, 1985), 21-43; B. Marshall-J. L. Beness, *Athenaeum,* 65 (1987), 361-378; T. P. Hillman, *Hermes,* 118 (1990), 444-454. Not that one can discern a consensus-especially when Brunt pronounces that in 70 B.C. "the Sullan system was now in ruins" (*Fall of the Roman Republic,* 472). But a more nuanced picture has taken hold in much of the scholarship.

Events leading to the rupture between Caesar and Pompey and the outbreak of civil war have engendered books and articles by the dozens-but surprisingly little in the past twenty years. *LGRR* endeavored to highlight the contingent character of those events. The dynasts were not hurled into contention by inexorable destiny or purposeful calculation. Neither Caesar nor Pompey desired the split, let alone open warfare. Collaboration continued almost to the end of the decade of the 50s, with the break prompted by others than the principals, a feature of standard senatorial infighting rather than a drive for civil war. Propaganda and pretexts overwhelmed reasoned judgment at the end, and mutual distrust sabotaged negotiations. A convergence of unanticipated circumstances occasioned the calamity. Such an interpretation had not previously attracted many advocates, but the time was evidently ripe. Two other works appeared almost simultaneously with, and independently of, *LGRR.* K. Raaflaub, *Dignitatis Contentio* (Munich, 1974), explored with great subtlety the presentations and justifications put forward by the contending parties before and during the war. He too sought to lift blame off the shoulders of the principal antagonists, stressing the reluctance of each to come to blows-although he does place a heavy load of responsibility upon the "Ultras" headed by Cato, who were prepared to push the conflict into conflagration. Raaflaub's analysis, however, underlines the seriousness and meaningfulness of negotiations down to the Rubicon and beyond. Rather than a hardening of positions, he recognizes the remarkable variety of options that remained open down to the end. D. L. Stockton, *Historia,* 24 (1975), 232-259, working from a different angle, reached similar conclusions: tensions between Caesar and Pompey did not rise until late in the game, triggered by unforeseen circumstances in Gaul and misunderstandings in Rome, not by a determined drive for confrontation. The point was more recently reaffirmed by H. Botermann, *Historia,* 38 (1989), 410-430, who directs attention to Cicero's ruminations as late as the end of December 50, sketching several possible scenarios that might resolve the situation short of military conflict. Misapprehensions played a larger role in bringing about civil war than did the intentions of the individuals or the iron grip of events.

The "fall of the Republic" exercises unbroken fascination upon scholars and students alike. The Republic's failings and the reasons for its collapse are repeatedly excogitated and analyzed. *LGRR* had a different orientation. Its objective was not to search for the weaknesses that brought about the Republic's fall but to examine the practices and conventions that kept it going for so long. Transformation of the state into a monarchical regime can be laid to the charge of a devastating civil war, rather than to the putative disintegration of institutions and morale in the previous decades.

A comparable orientation marks the important and much discussed *Res Publica Amissa* by C. Meier, first published in 1966 and reissued in 1980 with a new introduction that rephrased his conclusions in an even more abstract and theoretical form. Meier too endeavors to elicit the structures and conditions that held the Republic together and postponed its demise. Prominent among them was a complex network of mutual obligations and shared commitments to a sociopolitical system that went unquestioned. The very constellation of elements, however, that sustained the Republic, according to Meier, paradoxically, inevitably, and unwittingly worked toward its demise. The reason for this, in Meier's view, was that when crisis came, no one could conceive or contemplate any alternative system to the Republic. The theme of "Krise ohne Alternative" pervades his work. But the "crisis" itself seems to resist clear articulation. Meier's reformulation in 1980 sees its dynamic as a struggle between the oligarchy and the "great individuals." The growing crisis developed without intentions on any side to topple the Republic, for no other constitutional option was even thinkable. The system resisted any serious change. Efforts at reform only hardened it in place. The very idea of a new order never emerged; the upper classes were incapable of imagining it, the lower classes incapable of building it. The old order was destroyed, without ever having been rejected. Meier's paradoxes, even when not fully comprehensible, stimulate productive thinking.

The concept of "crisis" remains elusive, not by any means clarified by Meier's book. Nor indeed, despite its title, by K. Christ's survey of the later republic in *Krise und Untergang der römischen Republik* (Darmstadt, 1979). Christ restates a number of standard interpretations of the Republic's ruin: the incapacity of a city-state to govern an empire, the growth of client armies, the contest between the Sullan oligarchy and the "triumvirs" who aimed to undermine traditional senatorial rule, the radicalization of urban politics by Clodius, the failure of the nobility to resolve the state's social and economic difficulties. The book offers a lucid representation of the *communis opinio* on the problems and deficiencies of the Republic. But the notion of "crisis" receives no real analysis.

Debate proceeded in the journals over whether the Republic suffered a "crisis" or a "revolution," or some combination of the two. The idea of a "Roman revolution," which stemmed from Mommsen and gained wider notoriety from Syme, has now generally and rightly been judged as inapplicable or anachronistic in treating the experience of the late Republic. Yet in various forms it continues to crop up in discussions. K. E. Petzold, *RSA,* 2 (1972), 229-243, discerned both a crisis and a revolution, the first prompting the second, though without deliberate intent or inevitable result. U. Hackl, *RSA,* 9 (1979), 95-103, shrank from the term "revolution," preferring instead "revolutionary situation"—which does not help much. The usefulness of the term "crisis" is questioned too by K. Bringmann, *Geschichte in Wissenschaft und Unterricht,* 31 (1980), 354-377. And even the old chestnut, owing its original formulation to Montesquieu, that imperial responsibilities created intolerable burdens for the city-state, seemed an inadequate tool for understanding, as properly pointed out by J. Molthagen, in I. Geiss and R. Tamchina, *Ansichten einer künftigen Geschichtswissenschaft* (Munich, 1974), 34ff. A useful review of opinions can be found in R. Rilinger, *Archiv für Kulturgeschichte,* 64 (1982), 279-306, and in J. Ungern-Sternberg, *MH,* 39 (1982), 254-271. Both revert in modified form to a connection between Roman expansionism abroad and the disruption of internal concord. For Rilinger, the creation of overseas *clientelae* and military *clientelae* upset traditional bonds at home, without the substitution of enduring relationships, thereby loosening the structure. And Ungern-Sternberg postulated that the tremendous power wielded by the Roman nobility over imperial holdings rendered them even more impervious to needed internal reform and change—a recipe for crisis. Imperial expansion also supplies a key element in the analysis of Brunt, *Fall of the Roman Republic,* 68-92. He approves Sallust's verdict that the elimination of foreign danger undermined harmony at home, exacerbating divisions between rich and poor. The senate's neglect of social ills and the claims of the poor spawned disloyalty among the army's rank and file and alienated almost all segments of Roman society. The long shadow cast by the civil strife of the 80s left a legacy of tension from which Rome could not escape. And the string of great military commands by the dynasts issued in civil war and the collapse of traditional authority. These and like propositions have all been adumbrated before. None can claim the status of a definitive solution. And controversy over phraseology like "crisis" or "revolution" sheds little light. The search for explanations of the Republic's fall continues to entice—and to tantalize—the seekers.

The proposals advanced by *LGRR* have hardly swept the field. But many of them have stimulated salutary debate as well as sharp dissent, and some have even survived. As an eminent scholar predicted in a critical but balanced review twenty years ago, "I do not think that G's extensive onslaught will capture the citadel of *communis opinio,* though it will certainly leave its mark on parts of the perimeter." (D. R. Shackleton Bailey, *AJP,* 46 [1975], 436-443). A fair forecast.

Erich S. Gruen
July, 1994

PREFACE

A BOOK OF THIS SIZE rightly causes misgivings. The topic is hardly new and the treatment is lengthy. A word of justification seems appropriate. The period under discussion is pivotal in Roman history, endlessly fascinating, and a stimulus for reinterpretation. In an area already well explored, the problem of inclusion or omission is acute. I have elected to err, if error it be, on the side of the former. Much of the material will consequently be familiar to specialists on the Roman Republic. But it is hoped that the book may attract some attention outside specialist circles. The early chapters, in particular, supply matter designed to give a foothold to those not well versed in Republican problems. And, throughout, an effort has been made to see even familiar material in a new light.

The book offers a heterodox viewpoint–and hence summons expansive argumentation. Readers, of course, will form their own judgment. It is to facilitate that process that the information underlying this thesis is presented *in extenso.* For similar reasons the citations of ancient sources have been set out at length, thereby providing more direct access to the evidence than would a host of referrals to *RE* or *MRR.* Some repetition is inevitable. Several items are examined more than once, in different contexts and for different purposes. It seemed preferable to risk repetition than to mire the reader in a maze of cross-references. All this adds bulk to the product–but perhaps affords greater convenience.

My debts are large. Several scholars gave generously of their time to scrutinize various portions of the manuscript, at various stages of completion. Professor J. Linderski's enviable expertise in Roman constitutional matters was brought to bear on chapters VI–VIII. The sections on the *plebs,* the army, and social discontents profited enormously from the careful and extensive comments of Professor P. A. Brunt. His generosity in dispatching advance proofs of his *Italian Manpower* spared me much rewriting at a later stage. I am under similar obligation to Dr. T. P. Wiseman for an early look at his *New Men in the Roman Senate* and for his remarks on chapters IV and V. That we arrived independently at kindred conclusions was a source of relief and gratification. Professor E. Badian also supplied criticism and encouragement on chapters IV and V with his customary acuity. A detailed critique of the remaining chapters came from the pen of Professor G. V. Sumner, to whom particular gratitude is here extended. Those chapters benefited also from the observations of Professor R. J. Rowland, and, not least, from the eloquent counsel of Sir Ronald Syme. The arduous task of reading the entire manuscript was cheerfully undertaken by Professor R. Sealey, with much profit to the author. None of these gentlemen will be found guilty of concurrence with all my opinions.

Grants from the Guggenheim Foundation and the Humanities Research Institute at the University of California afforded the necessary leisure for writing–if leisure it be. Mr. David Thomas provided invaluable assistance in proofreading and in the checking of sources, assistance that went well beyond the mere mechanical. Finally, acknowledgment is due to the stimulation and salutary skepticism furnished by graduates of my seminar on the social history of the Ciceronian age: Jack Cargill, Philip Flowers, Judith Ginsburg, Russell Reinberg, Kenneth Sacks, and David Thomas.

Berkeley
April 1972

E. S. G.

ABBREVIATIONS

AbhLeipz	*Abhandlungen der Sächsichen Akademie der Wissenschaften, Leipzig*
AbhMainz	*Abhandlungen der Akademie der Wissenschaften und der Literatur, Mainz*
AbhMünch	*Abhandlungen der Bayerischen Akademie der Wissenschaften, München*
AHR	*American Historical Review*
AJP	*American Journal of Philology*
AnnPisa	*Annali della R. Scuola Normale Superiore de Pisa, Sezione di Lettere*
Ann. Univ. Cagliari	*Annali della Facoltà di Lettere, Filosofia e Magistero della Università di Cagliari*
Atti Accad. Arch. Nap.	*Atti della Accademia di Archeologia, Lettere, e Belle Arti, Napoli*
Atti Congr. Int. Stud. Cic.	*Atti del I Congresso Internazionale di Studi Ciceroniani*

BICS	*Bulletin of the Institute of Classical Studies, London*
BonnJbb	*Bonner Jahrbücher*
Bull. Mus. Imp. Rom.	*Bulletino del Museo dell' Impero Romano*
CAH	*Cambridge Ancient History*
CJ	*Classical Journal*
ClMed	*Classica et Mediævalia*
CP	*Classical Philology*
CQ	*Classical Quarterly*
CR	*Classical Review*
CSCA	*California Studies in Classical Antiquity*
CW	*Classical World*
GiornItalFilol	*Giornale Italiano di Filologia*
Gött. Gel. Anz.	*Göttingische Gelehrte Anzeigen*
HSCP	*Harvard Studies in Classical Philology*
ILLRP	*Inscriptiones Latinæ Liberæ Rei Publicæ*
ILS	*Inscriptiones Latinæ Selectæ*
JahrbClPhil	*Jahrbücher Classische Philologie*
JP	*Journal of Philology*
JRS	*Journal of Roman Studies*
LEC	*Les Etudes Classiques*

Mem. Am. Acad. Rome	*Memoirs of the American Academy in Rome*
MemIstLomb	*Memorie del Reale Instituto Lombardo di scienze, lettere ed arti, Milan*
MemLinc	*Memorie della R. Academia Nazionale dei Lincei*
MusHelv	*Museum Helveticum*
NAkG	*Nachrichten von der Akademie der Wissenschaften in Göttingen*
PBSR	*Papers of the British School at Rome*
PCPS	*Proceedings of the Cambridge Philological Society*
Phil. Quart.	*Philological Quarterly*
PhilWoch	*Philologische Wochenschrift*
PP	*La Parola del Passato*
RE	*Real-Encyclopädie der Classischen Altertumswissenschaft*
REL	*Revue des Etudes Latines*
RendLinc	*Rendiconti della R. Accademia dei Lincei*
RevBelg	*Revue Belge de philologie et d' histoire*
Rev. Hist. Droit	*Revue d' Histoire du Droit*
RevHistDroitFrEtr	*Revue Historique de Droit Français et Etranger*
RhMus	*Rheinisches Museum für Philologie*

RivFilol	*Rivista di Filologia e d'Istruzione Classica*
Riv. Indo-Grec.-Ital. Filol.	*Rivista Indo-Greco-Italica di Filologia, Lingua, Antichità*
SBBerl	*Sitzungsberichte der Deutschen Akademie der Wissenschaften zu Berlin*
StudClassOrient	*Studi Classici e Orientali*
StudItalFilClass	*Studi Italiani di Filologia Classica*
TAPA	*Transactions and Proceedings of the American Philological Association*
ZSS	*Zeitschrift der Savigny-Stiftung für Rechtsgeschichte, Romanistische Abteilung*

INTRODUCTION

IN JANUARY, 49 B.C., Julius Cæsar crossed the Rubicon—an event of magnitude perhaps unparalleled in Roman history. A ruinous civil war followed. Turmoil and insecurity gripped inhabitants of the Roman world for nearly two decades. Upon conclusion of the contest Rome had been transformed: the proud traditions of the Republic had given way to monarchy and a new imperial order. The long line of Roman emperors had been installed; Republican institutions endured largely as archaisms.

Cæsar's momentous deed constitutes an unquestioned turning point. Therein lies its fascination—and its delusiveness. The fall of the Roman Republic exercises a compelling allurement, undiminished in power through the centuries. The subject already excited the curiosity of ancient commentators, beginning with Sallust and Livy. Even the emperor Claudius indulged in an analysis, prudently suppressed by his advisers and lost to posterity. From Montesquieu to Mommsen, from Thomas Arnold to Eduard Meyer, with their countless *epigoni,* the Republic's calamity has summoned forth speculation on a grand scale. How had it come about? The question is a seductive one, and Cæsar's march on Italy seems the logical vantage point from which to look back. Yet its very seductiveness represents the chief hazard. The temptation to read the past in light of the civil war is difficult to resist. Because one knows what came after, events tend to be refashioned into a pattern pointing inescapably to the final collapse. The closing years of the Roman Republic are frequently described as an era of decay and disintegration: the crumbling of institutions and traditions; the displacement of constitutional procedures by anarchy and force; the shattering of ordered structures, status and privilege; the stage prepared for inevitable autocracy. Hindsight deceives and distorts. That fact is unanimously endorsed in principle and often neglected in practice. In order to explain the Republic's fall, it has seemed appropriate to ransack preceding generations for symptoms of decline and signposts for the future. The portrait is shaped to suit the result–a retrojected prophecy. Yet Cicero's contemporaries did not know what was in store. Nor should their every action be treated as if it conspired to determine the outcome.

A problem in perspective dogs the historian of the late Republic. Cæsar's dramatic triumph casts antecedents in the shade. Hence, earlier events have become precursors and determinants of that denouement–a dangerous fallacy. And perspective can lead us astray in another direction. Information on the late Republic rests heavily upon the pronouncements of Cicero. A figure of no small significance, he looms even larger through the survival of his voluminous writings. But Cicero's attitudes grew out of personal–and atypical–experiences. One cannot understand the history of the late Republic as an extension of Cicero's biography or as an evolving blueprint for Cæsar's dictatorship.

The fall of the Republic may be applauded or lamented. That is not our purpose here. An effort will be made to understand the Ciceronian era in its own terms, without the categories imposed by retrospective judgment.

The last generation of the free state forms the subject under scrutiny–from the age of Sulla to the crossing of the Rubicon. The men who belonged to it did not behave as if they stood under the shadow of impending doom. The era that produced Cæsar, Pompey, Cato, Cicero, Catullus, Lucretius, and Sallust can hardly be reckoned merely as the prelude to disaster. Nor, on the other hand, should it be swallowed up by its dominant figures. A larger canvas is necessary. Institutions as well as personalities call for study, social tensions as well as politics, the *plebs* and the army as well as the aristocracy. The Ciceronian era will here undergo examination in several different aspects. An unexpected portrait emerges: conventions were tenacious; no cascading slide downhill to destruction is evident; links to the past were more conspicuous than heralds of the future; tradition, not "revolution," predominated.

The aftermath of Sulla forms an appropriate starting point. The breakdown of the Sullan constitution, it is often asserted, exposed the weakness of the ruling class, impaired faith in institutions, opened the path for those who would undermine the old order. Yet the "breakdown" itself is in question–or should be. It is possible to contend that Sulla's legislation endured in its essentials; the oligarchic establishment which he sponsored was not lightly toppled. Prudent reform and compromise may have sustained rather than enfeebled the structure.

There follows an assessment of politics in the Republic's final decades. The notion of a *dominatio,* first of Pompey, then of Cæsar, requires serious modification. No single figure could twist events to his own purposes. The aristocratic structure of politics persevered, baffling or subsuming individual machinations. Pompey's burgeoning *clientelae,* Cæsar's *popularis* activities, formation of the "first triumvirate," Cato's ideological posturing–all these injected divisive issues into the political scene. But the enduring features also claim attention; they have too long been soft-pedaled. The great families of the *nobilitas* had not released their grip on public affairs. Pompey aimed for acceptance by them, Cæsar cultivated associations with them, Cato hoped to mobilize them. A bifurcation of conservatives and revolutionaries at no time explains the course of events. Multifarious alignments, with countless overlapping strands, permitted the aristocracy to absorb both ideologues and military heroes.

Scrutiny of electoral results fills out the picture. Rome's highest offices had long been a near private preserve for the hereditary *nobilitas.* The late Republic seems to have altered that situation only slightly, if at all. Occasions can be pointed to when force or bribery exercised an influence on the outcome. But exceptional events should not obscure standard procedures. And standard procedures prevailed. The electorate showed remarkable loyalty to ancestral patrons at the polls. Aristocratic houses of antiquity and pedigree dominated the chief magistracies down to the end of the Republic. And one must search beyond the top offices. Social composition of the senate requires inspection in detail. Sulla expanded that body to double its former size, thereby furnishing opportunity for new men, municipal families, and individuals of equestrian background. But traditional social structure and hierarchy were difficult to dislodge. Analysis of senatorial personnel reveals important continuities. The heritage of the past largely determined the makeup and leadership of Rome's governing class.

A massive amount of legislation secured passage during the years under study–on political, judicial, administrative, social, and economic matters. The process lends itself to varied interpretations. That reform groups or popular leaders foisted legislative change on a reluctant government has often been postulated. But it is rash to assume that Roman legislators adhered to consistent patterns and divisions. Some may detect an ideological split–or a struggle for power. Perhaps the flood of legislation indicates the failure of traditional, informal procedures. An alternative–and more charitable–estimate sees a genuine effort to grapple with problems that the late Republic had brought to the fore. Only careful investigation of the enactments, their sponsors, and the contests which they called forth can supply some answers.

A host of criminal trials mark the Ciceronian age. Information survives on more than one hundred cases of some import. Whether the fact should be taken to imply increased corruption, violations, and disrespect for law is another matter. Criminal trials served varied purposes in the Republic. Politics were generally involved. The courts offered a setting for conflict within the aristocracy, for quarrels between rival personages and political groups–for the playing out of private enmities and political maneuverings. The pattern was familiar also in earlier eras of Roman history. Scrutiny of the trials provides insight into the major issues that run through the period, affecting principal figures and their adherents, stirring discord and bringing to light intrigues within the ruling circles. Bitterness and controversy stand revealed. How far that affected the stability of institutions, however, is a quite different question. Results of judicial hearings might reinforce rather than damage the status quo.

Disorders in the city and the rumblings of the army could pose more serious threats. The claims of the commons played no insignificant role in the late Republic. Incidents of urban unrest are frequent. But there is a difference between popular demonstrations and insurrection, between crowds gathered for a political purpose and lower-class opposition to the system itself. Incidents of turbulence need to be observed in context in order to draw proper distinctions and to elicit possible meanings. The relationship between the armies and their commanders also warrants reexamination. The notion of "private forces" set against the civil machinery may be oversimplified–or false. *Imperatores* were senators and magistrates, not private adventurers; for the rank and file, military service might offer a source of livelihood rather than a vehicle for revolution. Discontent among the soldiery was no new phenomenon in the Ciceronian age. Inferences about alienation from the *res publica* would be hasty. That doctrine invites inquiry–and doubt.

The subject of provincial administration is absent from these pages, which in no way reflects on its significance. The theme is large and can claim a volume unto itself. Administration of overseas holdings created numerous problems that remained unresolved in the late Republic–and much later. Its unsystematic and unprofessional character permitted abuse and oppression. Roman magistrates abroad roused little love or admiration from exploited provincials. But the provinces did not rise against Rome in the Republic. Their situation cannot be dealt with here. Internal matters form the substance of this study: the actions and behavior of Rome's governing elite, the relationship between exceptional leaders and prevailing institutions, the impact of social unrest and military demands upon the old order.

A final chapter provides close and detailed survey of events leading to the civil war itself. The effort is essential. Most have assumed a lengthy and unbroken chain of circumstances drawing inescapably to disaster. The evidence calls for reassessment. Preoccupation with "underlying causes" or abstract explanations can sometimes be the historian's undoing. Accident and irrationality, stubbornness and miscalculation, have more than once helped to shape the course of history. The crossing of the Rubicon was a milestone–for Rome and for her historians. The very magnitude of the event and its implications creates a predisposition to imagine that matters could have been no different. The facts suggest an alternative possibility. Civil war need not be read as a token of the Republic's collapse.

Do the last decades of the Republic constitute a revolutionary era? The formulation is facile–but perhaps misleading. A balance between innovation and continuity may be the more proper designation. What appear to be novelties often turn out, upon reflection, to have roots in a deeper past–when there can be no question of decline and revolution. One must address a slightly different question: how well did the *res publica* absorb and adjust to change? Exceptional personages and dramatic episodes capture the attention of our sources. But Roman traditionalism was not easily shaken. Institutional and behavioral continuities must be accorded their due weight. The following is an effort in that direction.

I

THE AFTERMATH OF SULLA

SULLA THE DICTATOR has left an adverse imprint on the historical record. The ancients remembered him as the purveyor of civil war, the author of proscription and murder, the architect of a repressive regime. Scholarship imposed an even more damaging verdict. Sulla became a convenient starting point for analyses of the "fall" of the Republic. His rigidly ordered system could not arrest social and political change. The structure began to crack after Sulla's death, and when his reforms had been wiped off the books, the Republic's headlong slide to self-destruction went unchecked. The dictator, by intensifying divisions, by exacerbating hostilities, and by instituting a reactionary order, hastened and insured the Republic's end.

That analysis does Sulla considerably less than justice. The background to the dictatorship is more revealing than its consequences. In the previous half-century the Roman political system had undergone numerous vicissitudes. Developments since the era of the Gracchi had fostered an undulating pattern of calm and friction. The conflicts may be perceived on two levels. On the purely political scale, the governing class was divided by internal rivalries, with powerful noble clans jockeying for position within the aristocracy. Contests could be bitter, but not fatal. The stakes were high office, provincial command, a voice in the decisions of the ruling oligarchy. Struggles were fought out through senatorial debate, in elections, and, especially, in the criminal courts. The conflicts, however, usually centered upon the men who were to make or execute policy rather than upon the policy itself. Fluidity of personnel in noble groupings and shifting positions on issues indicate that prestige and power were the principal objects of attention. But there was a social level also, which impinged upon and gradually altered the character of political warfare. In the half-century between the Gracchi and Sulla, numerous pressures built up to challenge the traditional aristocracy. Men of wealth, with business interests and foreign contacts, sought access to political power. Italians, lacking the franchise and its privileges, fought to extort equality from a reluctant ruling class. Burgeoning population in the city of Rome created increased demands and growing political awareness among the *plebs.* A series of foreign wars produced strains at home, military heroes abroad, and a large pool of soldiers and veterans. In Rome ambitious politicians could capitalize on discontents to promote their own careers and to shake the establishment. Conflict became more heated, change more rapid. The process culminated in violence in the 80s. Italy rose in revolt, Roman holdings in Asia were menaced by foreign powers, and a brutal civil war ravaged the Italian peninsula at the close of the decade.

Sulla emerged as victor and dictator. He had ridden the tiae of previous developments, a protégé of aristocrats in factional strife, a military hero, and a leader of loyal troops and land-hungry veterans. He also showed himself capable of applying the lessons of the preceding decades. Concern now focused on stability and structure. Yet it was not a mechanical and an anachronistic system that Sulla imposed.

THE SULLAN BLUEPRINT

Internal struggle within the aristocracy had reached a peak in the 80s. Sulla punished intransigent foes mercilessly. Proscriptions and confiscations lopped off many wealthy adversaries; there were rich spoils for the dictator's loyal supporters and for shrewd speculators. The unrepentant suffered. But Sulla needed the *principes.*

Several leading figures had deserted to the Sullan camp during the civil war; others had maintained a prudent neutrality. After the war they could share in the new establishment. Officers and friends of Sulla, men who had served with him in the East, were naturally conspicuous in the government: L. Lucullus, P. Servilius Vatia, C. Curio, the Cottæ, Cn. Dolabella, Ap. Claudius Pulcher. So also were prominent individuals who had remained neutral or quiescent, and had joined Sulla only when civil war made it profitable to do so: Q. Metellus Pius, M. Crassus, the Lentuli. And most striking, some influential and eloquent leaders, who cooperated actively with Sulla's enemies in the 80s but deserted to him at the last moment, found that belated action wiped out earlier sins. They too could enjoy high office and even profit from the proscriptions: L. Philippus, the Valerii Flacci, M. Lepidus, Cn. Pompeius Magnus. Numerous others could be mentioned.[1]

[1] Cf. E. S. Gruen, *Roman Politics and the Criminal Courts, 149–78* B.C. (Cambridge, Mass., 1968), pp. 236–239, 249–250; *AJP*, 87 (1966); 385–399.

Sulla's policy seems clear. Aristocratic strife, which had weakened the senatorial class and erupted in fratricidal warfare, would now be reduced to less dangerous proportions. The Sullan regime advertised conciliation among hostile factions. Not that rivalry or feuds were banned. But the horrors of civil war ensured a broader consensus within the ruling class and a "gentlemen's agreement" that squabbles were best kept within the family.

That Sulla placed the governing process in the hands of the senatorial class is unquestionably true. But it would be incautious to dismiss this as reactionary or myopic. The dictator sought to soften discontents and avert potential upheavals. His technique has not always received proper analysis. Sulla avoided direct redress of grievances; he preferred to co-opt those who might otherwise exploit the grievances. Periodic rivalry between the senatorial and equestrian orders over control of the judiciary had caused conflict and disruption in the past. Sulla reduced eligibility for juries to the senatorial order. But at the same time he expanded considerably the numbers of the senate. New recruits must have been drawn largely from the *equites* themselves, some of them experienced jurors, others long anxious to join the ranks of the senate. One could expect them now to be grateful and quiescent.

Similar motives can be discerned in the dictator's attitude toward the Italians. Roman franchise had been extended to the entire peninsula as a consequence of the Social War. Sulla knew better than to turn back the clock. Not only were those arrangements retained, but Italian leaders were also brought into the Roman senate, where their talents would be useful and their allegiance to the establishment would be secured. The municipal aristocracy need no longer be tempted into separatist tendencies.

A more well-defined *cursus honorum* guaranteed that magistrates would serve several years in the ranks of the senate, absorbing its traditions and respecting its hierarchy, before they could exercise important military commands. The army, in Sulla's scheme, should be a force for order, not chaos. His discharged veterans were settled in colonial foundations; his junior officers could aim at political careers, and some were enrolled into the new senate.

Of civilian magistracies only the tribunate saw its powers diminished. This was consistent with the Sullan system. Ambitious politicians had recently used the tribunate to make reckless promises and stir the populace against its leaders. Sulla closed higher magistracies to holders of the tribunate. If the post attracted only second-rank individuals, the people would continue to look to their traditional patrons in the rolls of the senate.[2]

[2] For sources on Sulla's reforms, see T. R. S. Broughton, *The Magistrates of the Roman Republic* (New York, 1951–1952), II:74–76; an extended analysis in E. Valgiglio, *Silla e la crisi repubblicana* (Florence, 1956), pp. 76–154. On the Sullan senate, see W. Schur, *BonnJbb,* 134 (1929): 54–66; R. Syme, *PBSR,* 14 (1938): 22–25; E. Gabba, *Athenæum,* 34 (1956): 124–133;

That was Sulla's way. Leaders of groups and classes which had wrought dissension in the past were to be brought into the governing class. The urban populace, the equestrian order, the new citizens, and the soldiers would all find their more prominent representatives co-opted by the government. It was easier now either to ignore social grievances or to deal with them in a paternalistic fashion. The new members of the senatorial order heavily outnumbered the old aristocracy. But they were much less likely to attack an establishment of which they had become a part. *Equites, novi homines,* former Italians, men who rose through the ranks of the army, were now able to reach offices and positions closed to their ancestors. Their principal concern, it might be expected, would be to preserve, not to destroy the system.

Admission to the senatorial order was not the same as admission to the *nobilitas.* The consulship, the censorship, and the top provincial posts would remain, with few exceptions, in the hands of a privileged minority of old families. The latter comprised the men whose voices would dominate senatorial debate, whose names would carry elections, and whose influence could sway the law courts. Sulla had not disturbed their preeminence when he enrolled new men into an enlarged senate. "Back-benchers" were more docile and indeed often more conservative than their social superiors. Fewer *novi homines* reached the consulship in the generation after Sulla than in the generation before. The electorate continued to return the same familiar aristocratic names. Their prestige was only enhanced by additional colleagues who shared the senate house and were willing to follow their lead.

It was not Sulla's intention to make of the senate a sterile monolith. Familial feuds and rivalries constituted a traditional part of aristocratic life. The restoration of the courts, the systematization of the judicial structure, the increased number of magistracies and elections all revived and expanded the institutions that had been standard vehicles for aristocratic infighting. The Sullan system did not enforce total harmony. Its purpose was to assure that political fights would stop short of producing alienated social reformers or ambitious military men whose allegiance and appeal could threaten the establishment. The senatorial class had undergone such threats in the previous half-century. Crises induced it to close ranks against Ti. Gracchus in 133, against C. Gracchus in 121, against Marius and the demagogues at the end of the second century. But the receding of each threat left the oligarchy weaker and more divided than before. The bloody decade of Social and civil wars meant that the major decisions were being made not in the forum,

---

C. Meier, *Res Publica Amissa* (Wiesbaden, 1966), pp. 256–258; C. Nicolet, *L'Ordre Equestre à l'Epoque Republicaine, 312–43 av. J. C.* (Paris, 1966), pp. 581–591; cf. Gruen, *Roman Politics*, pp. 255–258. On the colonies, see now P. A. Brunt, *Italian Manpower, 225* B.C.–A.D. *14* (Oxford, 1971), pp. 304–312.

the *curia,* or the *iudicia,* but on the battlefield. Sulla resolved to put an end to that cycle. Military commanders would be drawn from men who honored the traditions of the aristocracy; soldiers would move through the ranks, receive land upon discharge, and even pursue political careers. Italians possessed Roman franchise, their leaders obtained seats in the Roman senate; *equites,* or former *equites,* sat not only in the courts but also in the *curia.* Conflict would continue, as always, within the establishment; but it would not be sedition against the establishment.

Such was the design. It did not lack intelligence or foresight. Our concern, however, must be to examine how far and how well it was implemented. Scholars have too readily assumed that the Sullan constitution was doomed to failure from the outset, that its institutions were fragile and obsolete, that its personnel was incompetent.[3] The decade of the 70s, so it is frequently argued, was pivotal. After Sulla's death, a contest ensued between supporters of the Sullan constitution and the *populares* who were bent on scrapping it. By the end of the decade, the popular tide, having enlisted the aid of Pompey the Great, succeeded in sweeping away Sulla's system and in setting the stage for radicals and military men to complete the destruction of the Republic.[4]

The analysis, however, will not fit the facts, as scholars have increasingly realized in more recent years. The decade of the 70s warrants careful analysis, not as a prelude to disaster, but in its own terms. The system was challenged after Sulla's death in 78, but without success. Politicians and statesmen in the 70s, it will be seen, worked out the implications of the Sullan scheme, pruning the peripheral and retaining the essential. Examination of that decade sheds important light on the political structure under which Rome operated in the later years of the Republic.

A fundamental distinction must be made at the outset. The struggles manifested after Sulla's death took two quite independent forms which have not hitherto been distinguished. On the one hand, there was a genuine challenge to the system and its ruling class, which had serious social as well as political implications. The consensus which Sulla had sought was not complete. To make room for land allotments and colonial foundations for his supporters,

[3] An exception, it must be noted, is U. Laffi, *Athenæum,* 55 (1967): 177–213, whose emphasis on the continuity of the Sullan system is forceful and persuasive.

[4] See, e.g., T. Mommsen, *Römische Geschichte* (Berlin, 1904), III:3–108; esp. 94–108; W. E. Heitland, *The Roman Republic* (Cambridge, 1923), III:1–22; T. Rice Holmes, *The Roman Republic* (Oxford, 1923), I:133–166; H. Last, *The Cambridge Ancient History* (Cambridge, 1932), IX:313–318, 326–349; J. Carcopino, *Histoire Romaine* (Paris, 1935), II:529–579; R. E. Smith, *The Failure of the Roman Republic* (Cambridge, 1955), pp. 107–111; Valgiglio, *Silla,* pp. 144–154; A. Heuss, *Römische Geschichte* (Braunschweig, 1960), pp. 178–188; H. H. Scullard, *From the Gracchi to Nero* (London, 1970), pp. 86–98.

Sulla had been compelled to dispossess numerous farmers and landowners. Italians, especially Samnites, who had fought against him in the civil war, suffered proscription and confiscation. Intransigent political enemies had been executed or exiled, their sons disenfranchised. These men could not benefit from the new order and had little to lose in revolt against it.[5] Their claims were taken up by Lepidus and Brutus in Italy and by Sertorius in Spain. The demands included recall of exiles, restoration of confiscated property, and cancellation of Sulla's measures. Tactics took the form of armed insurrection. In response to this challenge, the governing class as a whole could unite. Factional differences were overridden, as they had been in previous emergencies against the Gracchi or against Marius. Q. Catulus and Cn. Pompeius Magnus, no lovers of each other, combined to meet the threat of Lepidus and Brutus; Pompey again and Metellus Pius collaborated in Spain against Sertorius. When Pompey sought additional recruits and supplies, his political enemies Lucullus and Cotta made certain that the request was granted. Threat to the established order, as so often, engendered closing of the ranks. Distinctions relevant in the 80s between Sullan supporter, enemy, and neutral did not apply in the 70s, when all had become part of the new order and when that order was challenged by armed force and revolution.[6]

On the other hand, those distinctions remained relevant on a second level. Sulla's program had not foreclosed the aristocratic rivalries which had been a traditional part of Roman political activity. Such contests continued in the 70s, often reviving old feuds of the 80s and before. But they are in no way to be confused with attacks on the ruling class as a whole or on the Sullan constitution. So, for example, young Julius Cæsar could prosecute the Sullan officer and ex-consul Dolabella in the courts and at the same time refuse to join the uprising of Lepidus against the government. Vigorous struggles in the courts, long a central feature of aristocratic life, proceeded in the 70s. Men who had fought together under Sulla's banner in the civil war and who were now prominent members of the governing class did not refrain from conflict with one another in the courts. So a Metellus clashed with a Curio, a Scaurus with a Dolabella, a Claudius with a Terentius Varro. Similarly, Lucullus and Cotta intrigued for provincial commands, but had

[5] For sources on the Sullan proscriptions, see Broughton, *MRR*, II:69; and cf. Brunt, *Italian Manpower*, pp. 300–304; for the disenfranchisement, see Broughton, *MRR*, II:75. But note also that Sulla had brought the proscriptions to an end in 81 and turned his back on the worst offenders like Chrysogonus; cf. Gruen, *Roman Politics*, pp. 265–271. Moreover, a prætor ca. 79, Cn. Octavius, compelled some of the profiteers to restore property gained through force and intimidation; Cic. *Ad Q. Frat.* 1.1.21; cf. *Verr.* 2.3.152; so, rightly, J. M. Kelly, *Roman Litigation* (Oxford, 1966), pp. 15–16; A. W. Lintott, *Violence in Republican Rome* (Oxford, 1968), pp. 129–130. Sulla, evidently, did not stand in the way.

[6] On all these matters, see the fuller discussion below.

their own public differences on other matters. This internal friction coexisted with, but was distinct from, the larger clash over land, civil rights, and the political order. Aristocrats, as always, competed for *dignitas* and power. Their contests formed an accepted part of the system, not an assault upon it. The situation has many parallels with that of the later years of the second century. At that time also internal strife within the aristocracy went on side by side with demagogic pressures and foreign wars. One cannot identify the warring forces in the 70s simply as Sullani vs. democrats, or senate vs. *populares.* The war that Sertorius waged in Spain, as a self-proclaimed government in exile, had little in common with the actions of tribunes in Rome who were advocating reform. Pompey the Great rightly saw no contradiction between supporting constitutional change at home and fighting enemies of the Sullan order abroad. We must determine whether these crosscurrents and strains, brought dramatically to the surface in the 70s, amounted to a serious diminution of the Sullan scheme.

CHALLENGES TO THE SYSTEM

Sulla died in 78. He had resigned the dictatorship somewhat earlier, at least by mid-79.[7] His shadow, it may be presumed, hung over events, even after his retirement. When Sulla died, however, some men hoped to find a vacuum and to fill it.

M. Æmilius Lepidus was consul in 78, having reached that post through money collected in the proscriptions and through the support of Pompey.[8] Lepidus could claim patrician forebears, but his previous career showed only inconsistency and opportunism. A marriage alliance linked him to the demagogue Saturninus and to Marius' supporters. But when the popular movement was shattered in 100, Lepidus defended the status quo and helped to crush the agitators. A similar pattern is evident in the 80s. Lepidus was in Rome, collaborating, no doubt, with the enemies of Sulla. But when civil war came he landed on his feet once again, transferring allegiance to Sulla, profiting from the proscriptions, and securing prætorship and provincial command.[9]

[7] Appian, *BC,* 1.103; Orosius, 5.22.1; cf. Plut. *Sulla,* 34; *Pomp.* 15. Scholarly controversy continues on the exact date of the resignation; cf. esp. Valgiglio, *Silla,* pp. 199–207; E. Badian, *Historia,* 11 (1962): 230; Gabba, *Appiani Bellorum Civilium Liber Primus* (Florence, 1958), pp. 282–283; Syme, *Sallust* (Berkeley and Los Angeles, 1964), p. 180; G. V. Sumner, *JRS,* 54 (1964): 44–45; I. Shatzman, *Athenæum,* 46 (1968): 345–347; E. Badian, *Athenæum,* 48 (1970): 8–14.

[8] Sallust, *Hist.* 1.55.18, 1.77.4, Maur.; Plut. *Sulla,* 34.4–5; *Pomp.* 15.1–2.

[9] For references and analysis of Lepidus' early career, see J. E. Neunheuser, *M. Æmilius Lepidus* (Münster, 1902), pp. 18–24; Gruen, *Roman Politics,* pp. 274–275. The recent study of N. Criniti, *MemIstLomb,* 30 (1969): 324–371, though excessively encumbered with doxographical material, offers the fullest examination, but plays down Lepidus' vagaries and inconsistencies.

Attainment of the consulship had not sated Lepidus' ambitions. When Sulla died in 78, he promptly grasped at opportunity. The grievances of Sulla's victims were real, but they could also be exploited. Lepidus first made a propaganda gesture: he maintained that Sulla deserved no public funeral; he sought to block the proceedings and to damn the dictator's memory.[10] The effort failed, but Lepidus expanded his propaganda and fashioned a program. It was a direct appeal to those elements that had been excluded from the new regime: the restoration of confiscated property, reinstatement of civil and political rights for those who had been disenfranchised, recall of exiles, and repeal of Sulla's decrees.[11] To secure the sympathy of the urban *plebs,* he resorted to a traditional demagogic device: a *lex frumentaria* for the distribution of grain.[12] Lepidus could have retained an honored place within the establishment. He evidently sought preeminence.

Lepidus' colleague in the consulship, Q. Lutatius Catulus, was fashioned from a different mold. Sober, steady, and firm, Catulus enjoyed supreme self-confidence. He could with impunity criticize either the temerity of the populace or the foolishness of the senate. Cicero rarely mentions him without extravagant praise.[13] Catulus survived the Marian terror in the 80s, despite the fact that his father had been slain by a Marian executioner. His was a distinguished consular family, and he predictably received Sulla's favor after the civil war. Catulus prudently advised the dictator to limit the proscriptions and murders, although he had himself gained vengeance upon his father's assassin.[14] In 79 he had been Sulla's personal choice for the consulship and secured the post, running second to Lepidus.[15]

Friction arose between the two consuls right at the outset. Catulus did not approve of the effort to deprive Sulla of burial honors. And there was

[10] Appian, *BC,* 1.105; Plut. *Sulla,* 38.1; *Pomp.* 15.3.

[11] Sallust, *Hist.* 1.77.6, 1.77.14, Maur.; Gran. Licin. 34, Flem.; Appian, *BC,* 1.107; Livy, *Per.* 90; Florus, 2.11.23; Schol. Gronov. 286, Stangl; Exsup. 6.

[12] Gran. Licin. 34, Flem. Cf. Macrob. *Sat.* 3.17.13, with Criniti, *MemIstLomb,* 30 (1969): 399–400. The violently anti-Sullan speech which Sallust puts into Lepidus' mouth, *Hist.* 1.55, Maur., can hardly have been delivered during the dictator's lifetime; cf. Neunheuser, *Lepidus,* pp. 24–25; Syme, *Sallust,* pp. 184–186; *contra*: Criniti, *MemIstLomb,* 30 (1969): 383–396. But it may well be an accurate reflection of Lepidus' espoused views after Sulla's death. On the speech of Lepidus, see further A. La Penna, *Athenæum,* 51 (1963): 212–219.

[13] Cf. Cic. *Pro Sest.* 122: *is enim libere reprehendere et accusare populi non numquam temeritatem solebat aut errorem senatus.* Other references to Catulus collected by F. Münzer, *RE,* 13:2082–2094, "Lutatius," n.8.

[14] Orosius, 5.21.2; Schol. Bern. Lucan, 2.173; cf. Münzer, *RE,* 13:2083, "Lutatius," n.8. On Catulus in the 80s, see Badian, *Studies in Greek and Roman History* (New York, 1964), pp. 216–218.

[15] Plut. *Sulla,* 34.5; *Pomp.* 15.1–2.

some conflict over the appointment of a *præfectus urbis.*[16] But more serious matters were brewing. Lepidus' pronouncements brought results, perhaps even unforeseen results. At Fæsulæ in Etruria citizens attacked the garrisons and colonies of Sullan veterans. Here was open revolt. The senate acted promptly and appropriately: both consuls were dispatched to deal with the emergency.[17] That was an interesting response, not sufficiently stressed in modern accounts. Evidently the senate did not feel that Lepidus' *popularis* pronouncements had compromised him to the point where he could not be sent to stifle an insurrection inspired by his own propaganda. Lepidus was still consul, and it was the chief magistrate's responsibility to maintain order in Italy. It may not be overbold to imagine that Lepidus never intended his program to produce armed revolt. Events in Etruria, however, outstripped his plans and forced his hand.[18] The Etruscan insurgents claimed Lepidus as their spokesman and their inspiration. Lepidus, for want of an alternative or in expectation of *dominatio,* put himself at their head.[19]

The ambiguity of the situation in 78 needs to be stressed. Lepidus had attached to himself the rebels in Etruria, but at the same time he was Rome's official representative. The Roman senate obviously did not leap to the conclusion that he was a rebel. In fact, Lepidus had been awarded the province of Gallia Transalpina and, apparently, Cisalpina as well, in the normal fashion.[20] A good part of the Roman senate was friendly to the consul, and surely not because they approved of revolutionary schemes. The *patres* instructed Catulus and Lepidus not to train their arms on one another. Even when Lepidus began to engage in suspicious activities, they preferred to deal with him through embassies and persuasion rather than by force. Indeed, he was summoned home to assume his proper and official role of presiding over the consular elections.[21]

[16] Sallust, *Hist.* 1.54, Maur.; Appian, *BC,* 1.105; cf. Cic. *Cat.* 3.24; Schol. Gronov. 286, Stangl.

[17] Sallust, *Hist.* 1.65–66, 1.77.6, Maur.; Gran. Licin. 35, Flem.

[18] Cf. Sallust, *Hist.* 1.68, Maur.: *Lepidum pænitentem consili*; perhaps wrongly interpreted by Maurenbrecher, *loc. cit.*

[19] Sallust, *Hist.* 1.67, Maur.: *Tunc vero Etrusci cum ceteris eiusdem causæ ducem se nactos rati maximo gaudio bellum irritare*; also, 1.65, 1.69, Maur.; Exsup., 6; Florus, 2.11.23.

[20] Sallust, *Hist.* 1.77.7, Maur.; Appian, *BC,* 1.107. See Badian, *Foreign Clientelæ, 264–70 B.C.* (Oxford, 1958), p. 275.

[21] On the senatorial decree to keep Lepidus and Catulus from each other's throats, see Gran. Licin. 35, Flem.; Appian, *BC,* 1.107; cf. Sallust, *Hist.* 1.68, 1.77.15, Maur. Lepidus' support within the senate is clear from Philippus' speech in Sallust, *Hist.* 1.77, Maur.; esp. 3–7, 12–13, 17–20; cf. Gran. Licin. 35, Flem. Among his supporters was the devious P. Cornelius Cethegus; Sallust, *Hist.* 1.77.20, Maur. For the recall to hold elections, see Appian, *BC,* 1.107; cf. Sallust, *Hist.* 1.72, Maur.

It was only at this point that Lepidus' decision to side with the insurgents became irrevocable and that senatorial sentiment turned against him. He refused to return to Rome to hold elections and in fact demanded a second consulship, a condition which (he must have known) was unacceptable.[22] Catulus now received authority to operate against him, urged by the considerable oratorical talents of L. Marcius Philippus. Philippus was himself a master of tergiversation. An ex-consul and ex-censor, he had been a senior member of the regime in the 80s that opposed Sulla. But he was to be found later fighting in the Sullan ranks. Philippus secured a distinguished position, befitting his *dignitas,* within the Sullan senate. When it became clear that Lepidus was threatening the supremacy of the new establishment, Philippus came forth as the most ardent spokesman for that establishment. He roused the senate out of its lethargy and its sympathy for Lepidus. The *senatus consultum ultimum* was passed in early 77, instructing the proconsul Catulus, the *interrex* Ap. Claudius Pulcher, and others with *imperium* to defend the state.[23]

Lepidus was not the only *nobilis* who rose in revolt. He was joined by L. Cornelius Cinna the younger, the son of Sulla's fallen foe of the 80s. M. Junius Brutus held Cisalpine Gaul for Lepidus, probably as his legate. The Junii Bruti had been firm enemies of Sulla in the 80s. M. Brutus had held a tribunate in 83, and although this had evidently not precluded promotion by Sulla after the civil war, Brutus returned to anti-Sullan activities in 77. M. Perperna, an ex-prætor and governor of Sicily for the Marians in 82, emerges again as Lepidus' associate in his insurrection. We hear also of a Scipio, son of Lepidus and adopted son of the Scipiones.[24] The aid of Julius Cæsar was solicited by the insurgents. He had been no friend of Sulla's and had rejected his political advances in 81. And he had married Cinna's daughter. But Cæsar shrewdly abjured revolt against the regime.[25] Nonetheless, the government faced serious and dangerous challenge. Lepidus and Brutus had troops under their command, disaffected Etruscans who had joined them, and ancestral connections in the Cisalpina and Transalpina.[26]

The military quality of Catulus did not inspire confidence. Hence the senate had recourse to Cn. Pompeius Magnus, who was awarded an extraordinary

[22] Sallust, *Hist.* 1.77.15, Maur.; Appian, *BC,* 1.107; Plut. *Pomp.* 16.3.

[23] Philippus' speech is given by Sallust, *Hist.* 1.77, Maur. His previous career is summed up in J. Van Ooteghem, *L. Marcius Philippus e sa famille* (Brussels, 1961), pp. 101–149. For the *s.c.u.*, see Florus, 2.11.23; Sallust, *Hist.* 1.77.22, Maur.

[24] For Brutus, see Plut. *Pomp.* 16.2; *Brut.* 4.1; Livy, *Per.* 90; Cinna, Suet. *Iul.* 5; Perperna, Appian, *BC,* 1.107; Exsup. 7; Scipio, Orosius, 5.22.17. On the Junii Bruti in the 80s, cf. Gruen, *Roman Politics,* p. 243.

[25] Suet. *Iul.* 3; cf. 1.2; Plut. *Cæs.* 1.1; Schol. Gronov. 293, Stangl.

[26] Cf. Badian, *For. Client.*, pp. 275–277.

command against the rebels. Young Pompey had already demonstrated his military credentials in dramatic fashion while eliminating Sulla's enemies in the civil war. There had been differences with the dictator over a triumph, but they were resolved, at least in public, through reconciliation. Pompey had supported Lepidus for the consulship in 79, but felt no enduring loyalty. When Lepidus sought to block Sulla's funeral, it was Pompey, along with Catulus, who brought those efforts to naught. Hence a combination of Pompey and Catulus against Lepidus in 77 was in no way anomalous. L. Philippus, who advocated resistance to the rebels, had also supported and eulogized Pompey. He doubtless approved of the extraordinary command.[27] The military details will not concern us here. By mid-77, Pompey and Catulus had soundly defeated the forces menacing the regime, Brutus suffered execution, and Lepidus fled to Sardinia, where he perished. The first genuine threat to the Sullan system had been dispelled.[28]

The affair of Lepidus has here been set out at some length, for its misinterpretation has too often clouded understanding of this pivotal decade. The Livian tradition is largely to blame. By foreshortening events, it adjudges Lepidus to be intent upon revolution from the beginning of his consulship, or even before. Such is the impression left by the telescoped accounts of Florus, Orosius, the Livian *Periocha,* Appian, and Plutarch. But careful attention to the fragments of Sallust and his excerptor Granius Licinianus reveals that Lepidus initially engaged only in political agitation. He expected to widen his support after Sulla's death by appealing to elements of the population that did not benefit from the Sullan system. Such behavior stood in the tradition of previous popular demagogues and did not amount to anything like revolution.[29] The Roman senate, filled as it was with beneficiaries of Sulla's bounty, still preferred to regard Lepidus as a legitimate representative of the constitutional order. He was dispatched to crush revolt in Etruria and retained provincial command in Gaul, awarded through regular channels. But Lepidus was induced, by massive support in Etruria and Gaul, to carry out the implications of his own propaganda and to take command of insurrection

[27] On Pompey's early career and his relations with Sulla, Lepidus, and Philippus, see M. Gelzer, *Pompeius* (Munich, 1949), pp. 25–45; Gruen, *Roman Politics,* pp. 244–246, 272–277.

[28] Sources in Broughton, *MRR,* II:89–90; cf. the accounts in Neunheuser, *Lepidus,* pp. 37–42; T. Rice Holmes, *Roman Republic,* I:134–138, 363–369; and, esp., Criniti, *MemIstLomb,* 30 (1969): 396–450.

[29] It is noteworthy, for example, that in his initial program Lepidus did not regard it as fitting even to advocate restoration of the tribunician powers curtailed by Sulla; Gran. Licin. 33–34, Flem.: *Verum [ubi] convenerant tribuni plebis, consules uti tribuniciam potestatem restituerunt. negavit prior Lepidus, et in contione magna pars adsensa est dicenti non esse utile restitui tribuniciam potestatem.* He changed his mind later; Sallust, *Hist.* 1.73, 1.77.14, Maur; cf. 1.55.22, Maur.

against the government. It was at that point, apparently, that his once considerable support in the *curia* melted away and the state mobilized its resources in opposition. Senators and their clients could tolerate political dissent, but the ranks closed when it appeared that their own position was threatened.

The contrast between the two phases of Lepidus' activity is instructive. It helps to clarify events in the remainder of the decade. Agitation to alter details in the Sullan arrangement or to attack Sulla's former friends and officers became standard political practice. But efforts to disrupt the social order or to undermine the establishment would be treated as a menace to the Sullan constitution.

Another such menace existed in the Iberian peninsula. Q. Sertorius held forth there, defying the government in Rome and building his own following. Adherents came from Romans resident in Spain and from the disenfranchised and disaffected who had fled Italy during the Sullan terror and after the defeat of Lepidus. Sertorius, an Italian from the rugged Sabine country, had made his mark in war from an early age. Valorous service under Marius in the German wars at the end of the second century earned him plaudits and prizes. Further exploits are recorded for the Social War. Sertorius' career was then checked by Sulla, who engineered his defeat in a tribunician election, probably in 88. It was a slight which the proud Sabine did not easily forget. Sertorius combined his talents with those of Marius and Cinna and became a prominent member of the anti-Sullan regime in the 80s. A prætorship was his reward by 83, no mean post for a *novus homo.* But Sertorius found himself an uneasy ally of the men in power during that decade. In 83 he proceeded to a governorship in Spain, where he had earlier seen distinguished service. After initial reverses, the resourceful Sertorius established a firm base and defeated a series of generals sent to the peninsula by Sulla.[30]

Motives and aims of Sertorius have long been debated; and verdicts have ranged from ecstatic praise to denunciation. Some have regarded him as Rome's only true patriot, others as a base betrayer of his country.[31] It will serve little purpose to indulge in speculation on Sertorius' psyche. Of greater relevance is the fact that his political and military successes in Spain represented a clear challenge to the legitimacy of the Roman government. As if to emphasize his stance, Sertorius organized a government in exile, appointing his own

[30] Most of the picture summarized here is contained in Plutarch's biography; *Sert.* 2–12; cf. also the favorable portrait by Sallust, *Hist.* 1.88, Maur. On some chronological questions in Sertorius' career, see now B. Scardigli, *Athenæum,* 49 (1971): 229–270.

[31] On the strongly favorable side, see esp. A. Schulten, *Sertorius* (Leipzig, 1926), *passim*; cf. Schur, *Sallust als Historiker* (Stuttgart, 1934), pp. 222–256; for the opposite judgment, see H. Berve, *Hermes,* 64 (1929): 199–227; cf. Gelzer, *PhilWoch,* 52 (1932): 1129–1136. For more sober analyses, see P. Treves, *Athenæum,* 10 (1932): 127–147; Gabba, *Athenæum.* 32 (1954): 293–317, 323–332; La Penna, *Athenæum,* 41 (1963): 219–232.

senate of resident or expatriate Romans, with magistracies and military commands, in imitation or mockery of the Roman system.[32] With Sertorius originally had come men who could not endure the prospect of Sulla's return from the East; later he was joined by exiles and victims of the Sullan proscriptions; and after the defeat of Lepidus a large number of survivors swelled his ranks under the leadership of M. Perperna. These were all men who had no future under the present regime in Rome and who sought refuge or prospective return under Sertorius' banner. An ancient source rightly described the war against Sertorius as the bitter legacy of the Sullan proscriptions.[33]

The government could not tolerate that hostile presence in Spain. Whether or not Sertorius ever expected or desired to return to Rome, his control of a Roman province was an open sore. Naturally Rome continued to send its own governors of Spain, which meant, in effect, a continual state of warfare. Q. Metellus Pius, head of the powerful Metellan clan, was appointed to deal with Sertorius in 79. Like so many other prominent *nobiles* in the 70s, Metellus could not be reckoned among the original supporters of Sulla. He controlled an army in Africa in the mid 80s, maintaining a firm independence of both the Sullani and their enemies. Only in 83 did he bring his troops over to the Sullan side. Metellus Pius was a man who evinced fierce loyalty to his friends and benefactors–but never, apparently, reckoned Sulla in those categories. The dictator treated him with respect, sharing a joint consulship with him in 80. There had been friction and mutual suspicion, but Metellus fulfilled his official obligations dutifully, and outward harmony prevailed.[34] Whatever his personal feelings toward Sulla, Metellus and his family were long accustomed to being pillars of the Roman aristocracy. He did not hesitate to defend the regime against Sertorius' challenge in Spain.

But the leadership and armies of Metellus Pius were insufficient. He proved to be no match for Sertorius.[35] Reinforcements were needed, and Metellus long awaited them.[36] The consuls of 77, Mam. Æmilius Lepidus and Dec. Junius Brutus, declined the task of bringing assistance to the beleaguered

[32] Plut. *Sert.* 22.3–4; Appian, *BC*, 1.108.

[33] Florus, 2.10.22: *Bellum Sertorianum quid amplius quam Sullanæ proscriptionis hereditas fuit?* Cf. also Sallust, *Hist.* 3.83, Maur., on one of Sertorius' officers: *L. Fabius Hispaniensis senator ex proscriptis.* On the flight of Perperna and the survivors of Lepidus' movement, see Plut. *Sert.* 15.1; Appian, *BC*, 1.107; Orosius, 5.23.12; Exsup. 7. On the men with Sertorius, see further the illuminating prosopographical analysis by Gabba, *Athenæum*, 32 (1954): 305–317, who argues that Sertorius attracted many disaffected Italians who survived the Social War.

[34] Plut. *Sulla*, 6.5. On Metellus' loyalty to genuine friends, see Cic. *Pro Planc.* 69; Val. Max. 5.2.7. For the command against Sertorius, see Broughton, *MRR*, II:83. And see further on Metellus, Münzer, *RE*, 3:1221–1224, "Cæcilius," n.98.

[35] Sources in Broughton, *MRR*, II:83.

[36] Cf. Sallust, *Hist.* 2.32, Maur.: *Et Metello procul agente longo spes auxiliorum.*

governor of Spain. Reasons are obscure and much debated. Perhaps nothing more need be conjectured than a reluctance to engage in the hazardous and difficult enterprise.[37] Pompeius Magnus, however, was available–and eager. After crushing the forces of Lepidus in Italy and Gaul, he retained control of his troops, evading requests for disbandment. The eloquent L. Philippus emerged once again in senatorial debate, resuming his role of 78. Philippus pointed out the obvious: Pompey should be dispatched to Spain *non pro consule sed pro consulibus.* His motion received approval by the House. The armies of Pompey were added to the Roman effort against Sertorius.[38]

The challenge of Sertorius could be neither ignored nor minimized. What about the challenge of Pompey himself? The *imperator*'s role in the 70s was central–and often misconstrued. Was he the true menace to the endurance of Sulla's system? Pompey's *imperia extraordinaria* did, of course, sidestep regulations instituted by the dictator. But the Sullan constitution was not an inflexible document. Emergency situations called for ad hoc adjustments. The senate itself duly authorized Pompey's commands. And his were not the only unusual assignments to be so authorized in that decade. M. Antonius was later to obtain a so-called *imperium infinitum* against Mediterranean pirates, and L. Lucullus received the senate's blessing in taking charge of the Mithridatic war.[39] It had not been the dictator's intention to tie the hands of the government in providing for its own protection. Pompey's position was legitimized by senatorial decrees. He led his forces against the enemies of the established order.

Pompey had his rivals and detractors in the senate. No prominent politician was without them. Catulus had objected to Pompey's retention of his armies; vigorous argumentation by Philippus was required to secure the appointment to Spain. But the senate made a proper decision–and an intelligible one. The consuls of 77, by stepping aside, had left the field clear for Pompey. Political differences did not stand in the way of unity against external threat. Friction between Pompey and Metellus Pius in Spain has been stressed by moderns, but is unattested in the ancient evidence. There was competition, of course, for military distinction. Anything less would be out of keeping with Roman traditions. But their rivalry did not extend to undermining operations against Sertorius. Metellus was Pompey's *adfinis,* and the two co-

[37] Cf. Gruen, *AJP,* 92 (1971): 3–5. For other interpretations, see Badian, *For. Client.*, p. 277; Sumner, *JRS,* 54 (1964): 41–48; Criniti, *MemIstLomb,* 30 (1969): 367–368.

[38] On Philippus' speech, see Cic. *Phil.* 11.18; *De Imp. Pomp.* 62; cf. Plut. *Pomp.* 17.3–4. Additional sources on Pompey's command in Broughton, *MRR,* II:90.

[39] Sources in Broughton, *MRR,* II:101–102. *Imperium infinitum* is not to be taken as a technical phrase. It rests on Ciceronian rhetoric; so, rightly, S. Jameson, *Historia,* 19 (1970): 541–542. But Antonius' command is clearly put in the realm of the *extraordinaria* by Vell. Pat. 2.31.2–4. On *imperia extraordinaria* in general, see below, Appendix III.

operated consistently against the common foe.[40] Support from home was slow and insufficient. Pompey had to write a blistering letter to the senate, complaining of inexcusable neglect. No political implications need be read into that affair. The government's niggardliness may have been due to financial stringency. Pompey wrote for Metellus Pius as well as for himself. And the consuls of 74, L. Lucullus and M. Cotta, no friends of Pompey, saw to the implementation of his requests. The Roman oligarchy backed their proposals with enthusiasm: two new legions, money, and supplies were forthwith dispatched to Spain. Political divisions in the *curia* ceased at the point of national emergency. The ruling class stood in unison against Sertorius. Defeat of the great rebel came through the combined efforts of Metellus and Pompey (plus treachery in the ranks). Senatorial rewards awaited both victors in 71: the celebration of triumphs and the authorization of land grants for their veterans. Closing of the ranks assured survival of the Sullan establishment.[41]

The same unity, of course, prevailed in the face of Spartacus' revolt of slaves and gladiators from 73 to 71. It was not the governing class alone that would react in horror to the prospect of a slave insurrection. Whatever the grievances of men disenfranchised and dispossessed by Sulla, they would have found unthinkable any common enterprise with Thracian or Gallic slaves. It causes no surprise that Marxist historians and writers have idealized Spartacus as a champion of the masses and leader of the one genuine social revolution in Roman history. That, however, is excessive. Spartacus and his companions sought to break the bonds of their own grievous oppression. There is no sign that they were motivated by ideological considerations to overturn the social structure. The sources make clear that Spartacus endeavored to bring his forces out of Italy toward freedom rather than to reform or reverse Roman society. The achievements of Spartacus are no less formidable for that. The courage, tenacity, and ability of the Thracian gladiator who held Roman forces at bay for some two years and built a handful of followers into an assemblage of over 120,000 men can only inspire admiration.[42]

[40] See, esp., Plut. *Pomp.* 19.5; cf. 19.4; *Sert.* 19.6, 21.2; Appian, *BC*, 1.110, 1.112. For Pompey's marriage into the Metellan clan, see Cic. *Ad Fam.* 5.2.6; Dio, 37.49.3; further, W. Drumann-P. Groebe, *Geschichte Roms* (Berlin, 1908), IV:560–561; J. Carcopino, *Sylla ou la Monarchie Manquée* (Paris, 1931), pp. 188–193.

[41] The argument summarized here is elaborated, with full references, in Gruen, *AJP*, 92 (1971): 5–9—in critique of the account in Badian, *For. Client.*, pp. 278–282. Pompey's letter, of course, is fashioned by Sallust—for his own purposes; *Hist.* 2.98, Maur.; cf. Schur, *Sallust als Historiker*, pp. 256–271; Syme, *Sallust*, pp. 200–202. That aid was requested on behalf of both magistrates is clear from Sallust, *Hist.* 2.47.6, 2.98.9, Maur. The enthusiastic response of the *nobilitas*: Sallust, *Hist.* 2.98.fin., Maur.; the triumphs, Broughton, *MRR*, II:123; the land grants, Dio, 38.5.1.

[42] Principal evidence on the revolt in Plut. *Crass.* 8–11; Appian, *BC*, 1.116–120; Florus, 2.8; Sallust, *Hist.* 3.90–106, Maur. Cf. Sallust's judgment of Spartacus, *Hist.* 3.91, Maur.: *ingens*

The Roman reaction was tardy and ineffective. Cohorts under prætorian leadership were routed in 73; then consular armies in 72 proved unequal to the task. When M. Crassus took command in late 72 he added six new legions; even then the senate felt the need to recall Pompey from Spain and M. Lucullus from Macedon with their armies before the revolt was crushed. But no one will imagine that Spartacus had support in high places or that the government was divided. Error of judgment induced the senate to treat the uprising too lightly at the outset.[43] By the time Rome took firm steps, Spartacus' ranks had considerably swelled and the state's finest soldiers were serving abroad. But Crassus' efforts obtained full support, and the revolt was wiped out in 71. It would be superfluous to stress that Spartacus' rebellion had no connection with any popular movement in Rome or any dissent within the political structure. One might note simply in passing that L. Quinctius, the demagogic tribune of 74 who agitated for more tribunician power and attacked senatorial mismanagement of the courts, was to be found in 71 as an officer of Crassus', commanding a cavalry detachment against Spartacus.[44]

It will be useful to sum up the discussion to this point. The state confronted a number of external crises in the decade of the 70s. Tardiness in grappling with them and defeats in the field no doubt damaged the prestige of the *nobiles,* offering a handle to their critics and underlying Sallust's bitter denunciations a generation later. The failure of several prætors and two consuls to contain the servile uprising proved especially embarrassing. Yet there is little sign that the government installed in power by Sulla was inert or on the point of crumbling. One might be tempted to argue that recurrent dangers reflect weakness in the state, that Lepidus, Sertorius, Mithridates, and Spartacus only exploited the feebleness that was already there. But crises faced in the recent past, before the Sullan settlement, had been no less serious. Toward the end of the second century Rome was subjected to the Jugurthine War, to the German invasions, and to internal upheaval. And the decade preceding Sulla's reforms had witnessed Italian revolt, the Mithridatic conflict, and civil war.

The external troubles of the 70s were, if anything, rather milder. The government's failure to deal more sternly with them at the outset stemmed, not from dissension and infirmity, but from miscalculation and delinquency. Action was delayed against Lepidus, for he was the duly constituted repre-

---

ipse virium atque animi. For a summary of recent Soviet scholarship on Spartacus, see E. M. Štærman, *Die Blütezeit der Sklavenwirtschaft der römischen Republik* (Wiesbaden, 1969), pp. 261–269. The view of Z. Rubinsohn, *RivFilol,* 99 (1971): 290–299, that the *bellum Spartacium* was an Italian nationalist rising receives no explicit support in the evidence.

[43] Cf. Appian, *BC,* 1.118: γελώμενος ἐν ἀρχῇ καὶ καταφρονούμενος ὡς μονομάχων.

[44] Frontinus, *Strat.* 2.5.34; Plut. *Crass.* 11.4.

sentative of the state. It did not become clear until later, perhaps not even in Lepidus' own mind, that his political activity would be transformed into armed revolt. Sertorius enjoyed no respite in Spain; Roman commanders were sent against him from 81 on. After Pompey joined Metellus in 77, the senate lapsed into dilatoriness, evidently expecting that forces in the field were sufficient. But they showed no hesitation in shipping additional forces and supplies once Pompey's letter arrived in 74. Similarly, failure to take Spartacus' rebellion seriously enough at its inception allowed it to get out of hand. When the gravity of the threat became manifest, the state's response was correspondingly decisive. Dangers from the East were at no time taken lightly. Lucullus and Cotta received large forces to meet the menace of Mithridates, and M. Antonius acquired *imperium* of broad territorial extent to clear the Mediterranean of piracy. In all of these instances, despite initial difficulties, the tasks were eventually carried through to successful conclusions by representatives of the Roman government. The oft-repeated strictures upon the Sullan senate in the 70s–that it was divided, incompetent, and feeble–do not easily apply in the realm of external affairs and the management of the empire.[45]

[45] Even Badian repeats and exaggerates (something he is not wont to do) the standard arraignment of the Sullan oligarchy: "Sulla's well-planned scheme of reform had handed the government over to a class of proved cowards and open self-seekers"; "Lucius Sulla, The Deadly Reformer" (*7th Todd Memorial Lecture*, Sydney, 1970), p. 32. As evidence he points to the series of consuls from 78 to 59, approximately half of whom (so it is alleged) did not hold provincial commands. Hence the oligarchy was sunk in "inertia and irresponsibility" (pp. 30–31). But Badian's list dwindles sharply upon analysis. Pompey and Crassus are included. The fact that they did not go to provinces immediately after their consulships in 70 is of no consequence; both undertook major military commissions in subsequent years. Cn. Lentulus Clodianus took a post on Pompey's staff in the East five years after his consulship of 72. L. Julius Cæsar, consul in 64, later served with his more illustrious kinsman in Gaul. Q. Catulus fought against Lepidus in 78 and is attested as a proconsul; Sallust, *Hist.* 1.77.22. L. Metellus, consul in 68, died in office, and Q. Metellus Celer, consul in 60, perished before going off to his assigned province in 59. P. Lentulus Sura was evicted from the senate in the year after his consulship. Some consuls, of advanced age when they reached the chief magistracy, were perhaps not suited for provincial posts–like Dec. Brutus (cos. 77) and L. Gellius Publicola (cos. 72). Others had served lengthy and distinguished military careers before attaining consular rank and can hardly be adjudged to be irresponsible and inert: witness L. Murena (cos. 62) and M. Pupius Piso (cos. 61). Cn. Aufidius Orestes had discharged promagisterial duties after his prætorship of 77. For some of the remaining cases only an *argumentum ex silentio* can be invoked against their promagistracies–indecisive, given the state of our evidence. In fact, only six consuls (out of forty) during this period can be said, with some certainty, to have shunned promagisterial or overseas assignments–and one of those, L. Cotta, obtained the censorship in the year after his consulate, thus hardly lapsing into inertia. The others are Q. Hortensius, C. Marcius Figulus, M. Cicero, M. Messalla Niger, and M. Bibulus.

INTERNAL ADJUSTMENTS

One may turn now to internal matters and the alleged challenges to the Sullan constitution. The issue of tribunician powers stands as a persistent theme in the sources and in modern works. Sulla, it is well known, curtailed the prerogatives of the tribunes. Agitation to restore the privileges occurred throughout the decade, usually resisted by conservative senators, until the powers were reinstated in full in 70. That last decision has often been seen as a culminating act which signaled the collapse of the Sullan constitution. The facts and interpretation call for renewed scrutiny.

The nature of the restrictions that Sulla placed on tribunician authority remains obscure. That is probably the fault of the propaganda of the 70s. Agitation for reform may have put a weightier construction on the limitations than was warranted. The one change that Sulla certainly imposed was the closing of higher offices to holders of the tribunate.[46] He obviously wanted to reduce the attractiveness of the office for ambitious politicians. Details of the limitations elude inquiry. Tribunes retained the *ius auxilii,* the right to protect individuals against magisterial action. On the other hand, legislative initiative seems to have been curtailed, possibly abolished. As for the tribunes' veto power, sources are divided, but there were certainly some restrictions.[47] The *tribunicia potestas* was sufficiently modified to provide reformers with ammunition for argument.

The propaganda smokescreen should not be allowed to obscure our vision. How central to the Sullan system really was the curtailment of tribunes? It is noteworthy that when Lepidus in 78 first devised his broad program of reform, he specifically abjured any desire to alter Sulla's arrangement for tribunes; and he carried the populace with him at a *contio.*[48] Tribunician activity in Rome's past had, in fact, more often promoted conservative rather than radical ends. To associate the tribunate with the Gracchi, Saturninus, or Sulpicius Rufus is to forget that ten men held the office every year in Rome, very few of whom are known to have engaged in radical agitation. Veto by a single tribune could cancel any legislation inimical to the ruling class,

[46] Asconius, 78, Clark; Appian, *BC,* 1.100.

[47] For the continued exercise of *ius auxilii,* see Cic. *De Leg.* 3.22. Abolition of legislative prerogative is asserted by Livy, *Per.* 89. Cæsar indicates that the right of *intercessio* was retained under the Sullan program; *BC,* 1.5, 1.7. But the tribune Opimius in 75 must have overstepped some bounds when he issued his veto *contra legem Corneliam*; Cic. *Verr.* 2.1.155. J. Beranger, *Mélanges Piganiol* (1966), II:723–727, argues that Sulla placed no serious restriction upon the tribunes' powers. Unfortunately, he seems unaware of the passage in the *Verrines.*

[48] Gran. Licin. 33-34, Flem. At a later stage in Lepidus' activity, he seems to have reversed himself and supported tribunician reform, or so, at least, Philippus is reported to have charged in his speech. Lepidus advocated the change *concordiæ gratia*; Sallust, *Hist.* 1.77.14; cf. 1.73, Maur. Does this perhaps imply that the issue generated more heat than it was worth?

even if it were sponsored by all nine colleagues. The tribunate was an arm of the aristocracy.[49] Moreover, it had traditionally served other purposes. Young aristocrats, eager to make a name and earn popularity, could use the tribunate to sponsor popular measures. The bills, even if dropped, as they often were, could earn their proposer support for higher elective office in later years.

Sulla, by limiting tribunician initiative, evidently had in mind the actions of Sulpicius Rufus in 88. That tribune had used the office against him and had driven Sulla to inaugurate the civil war.[50] The dictator wanted no repetition of such action. And in the interests of calm, he preferred to hamstring the tribunate and to reduce harangues to the populace. But, whatever Sulla's fears after the conclusion of a brutal civil war, the tribunate as an institution represented no threat to the established order. It could be argued indeed that curtailment of the office violated constitutional precedent and the *mos maiorum.* Its revival would soothe rather than inflame the feelings of the multitude. Competent tribunes would serve as a check on popular passions.[51] The reformers who advocated restoration of tribunician privileges in the 70s were seeking, among other things, to reopen a traditional avenue to prestige and influence for members of the plebeian nobility.

If this analysis carries conviction, one must inquire why the efforts to revive full *tribunicia potestas* met with tenacious resistance on the part of oligarchic leaders. The resistance itself is not in doubt. In 76 the tribune Cn. (or L.) Sicinius ventured to speak out on the restrictions surrounding his office. A sharp-tongued orator, Sicinius laced his speeches with barbed sarcasm and mockery aimed at the consuls Cn. Octavius and C. Curio. But the consuls seem to have retaliated in kind. Sicinius met with intimidation and possibly even with violence.[52] In 75 Q. Opimius challenged the limitations directly by exercising his veto in contravention of the Sullan law. He too punctuated his speech with remarks offensive to several Roman *nobiles,* notably Q. Catulus. Opimius was to suffer grievously for his pains. In the following year Catulus, Q. Hortensius, and others leveled a charge against him for exceeding the bounds of his office. The result was a crushing fine, which entailed the confisca-

[49] Cf. J. Bleicken, *Das Volkstribunat der klassischen Republic* (Munich, 1955), pp. 43–94; R. F. Rossi, *PP*, 20 (1965): 141–143; Laffi, *Athenæum*, 55 (1967): 203–205.

[50] On Sulpicius' tribunate, see Broughton, *MRR*, II:41–42.

[51] Cf. Cic. *De Leg.* 3.23–26.

[52] Sallust, *Hist.* 3.48.8, Maur.: *L. Sicinius primus de potestate tribunicia loqui ausus, mussantibus vobis circumventus erat*; 3.48.10, Maur.: *C. Curio ad exitium usque insontis tribuni dominatus est*; cf. Ps. Ascon. 189, Stangl. *Exitium* here may signify political destruction. For Sicinius' ridiculing of the consuls, see Cic. *Brutus*, 216–217; cf. Quint. *Inst. Orat.* 11.3.129; Plut. *Crass.* 7.9. Curio was evidently a favorite target; someone referred to him by the name of a demented actor; Val. Max. 9.14.5; Sallust, *Hist.* 2.25, Maur.; Pliny, *NH,* 7.55.

tion of Opimius' property and brought him to financial ruin.[53] L. Quinctius, tribune in 74, continued the agitation–with equally abusive language directed at the senatorial oligarchy. This engendered conflict with the consul L. Lucullus, who, with private remonstrances and public attacks, firmly opposed the tribune's activity.[54]

The pattern continues. In 73 C. Licinius Macer took up the cudgels on behalf of tribunician privileges. Sallust accords him a full speech on the subject, in which, among other things, Macer claims the support of Pompeius Magnus for his efforts. The orator notes the resistance of the nobility and condemns the "domination of the few." Catulus, Curio, and Lucullus are named among the reactionary. Macer himself was shouted down. Other evidence attests the opposition of M. Lucullus and Mam. Lepidus to tribunician reform.[55] We are not informed of any activity on this issue in 72. Opposition, however, appears to have receded. M. Lollius Palicanus revived the clamor for reform in 71. The tradition does not find him attractive: an orator more full of words than of eloquence.[56] But Palicanus had persuasive backing. Pompey had returned from Spain and had secured election to the consulship. At his first *contio* as consul-designate, the general joined with Palicanus to announce his endorsement of tribunician reform. He met with enthusiastic response.[57] In the following year, the consuls Pompey and Crassus put the reform into

[53] Cic. *Verr.* 2.1.155–156: *Petita multa est . . . a Q. Opimio; qui adductus est in iudicium, verbo quod cum esset tribunus plebis intercessisset contra legem Corneliam, re vera quod in tribunatu dixisset contra alicuius hominis nobilis voluntatem . . . Q. Opimius, senator populi Romani, bona, fortunas, ornamenta omnia amiserit.* The accusers of Opimius are identified by Ps. Ascon. 255, Stangl; cf. Schol. Gronov. 341, Stangl.

[54] Plutarch, *Luc.* 5.4, recording a tradition favorable to Lucullus, states that the consul dissuaded Quinctius from his purpose by gentle and moderate upbraiding. There is no hint in Cicero, however, that Quinctius yielded gracefully; see esp. Cic. *Pro Cluent.* 110, 136; cf. Ps. Ascon. 189, Stangl. Sallust reports that Lucullus engaged in spirited public attacks on the tribune; *Hist.* 3.48.11, Maur.: *Lucullus superiore anno quantis animis ierit in L. Quintium vidistis.* That there were private negotiations is not impossible. Lucullus may have hoped for Quinctius' assistance in discouraging any successors for his Mithridatic command; Schol. Gronov. 320, 321, Stangl; cf. Sallust, *Hist.* 3.48.5–6, Maur. See, esp., Sallust, *Hist.* 4.71, Maur.: *Lucullus pecuniam Quintio dedit, ne illi succederetur.* The fragment belongs logically in 74, not 68 when Quinctius sought to have Lucullus succeeded; Plut. *Luc.* 33.5. Acknowledgment on this point is due an unpublished thesis by S. Burbank.

[55] On Macer's speech, see esp. Sallust, *Hist.* 3.48.6, Maur.: *omnes concessere iam in paucorum dominationem*; 3.48.11, Maur.: *quantae denique nunc mihi turbae concitantur.* Reference to Pompey is in 3.48.23, Maur.; to Catulus, Curio, and Lucullus, in 3.48.9–11, Maur. For the attitude of M. Lucullus and Lepidus, see Asconius, 79, Clark; cf. Sumner, *JRS*, 54 (1964): 43–44.

[56] Sallust, *Hist.* 4.43, Maur.: *loquax magis quam facundus*; Cic. *Brutus*, 223: *aptior etiam Palicanus auribus imperitorum.*

[57] Cic. *Verr.* 1.45; Ps. Ascon. 220, Stangl; cf. Ps. Ascon. 189, Stangl; Plut. *Pomp.* 21.4–5; Appian, *BC*, 1.121.

effect: the tribunician prerogatives were restored in full.[58]

The recurring struggle is clear. One will not find it surprising, in view of this testimony, that many tend to see the 70s as a contest between the supporters and the opponents of the Sullan system. *Tribunicia potestas* has been judged a pivotal matter at issue, advocated by the *populares,* resisted by the oligarchy. On this interpretation, the enactment of tribunician reform marked the overthrow of the Sullan constitution. Yet, as we have seen, the office of tribune did not represent a genuine threat to the establishment. How then to explain the oligarchy's resistance? A closer look at the evidence shows that the objections were not continuous or uniform. Opposition to change in the early years of the decade is intelligible. Sulla was only recently dead; his arrangements had had little opportunity to meet the test of time. Rome had just survived a new civil war in Lepidus' rebellion, and the menace of Sertorius was still very real in Spain. It would be natural, under those circumstances, for the members of the governing class, especially those who had been newly installed by Sulla's benefactions, to frown upon any agitation that might upset the system. The cry of *tribunicia potestas* had been adopted belatedly by M. Lepidus. Hence, in the minds of some senators, it was now associated with disruption. But the attitude failed to endure.

As early as 75 not all aristocrats looked upon tribunician reform as distasteful or dangerous. C. Aurelius Cotta, consul in that year, sponsored a measure that removed the ban on higher offices for holders of the tribunate.[59] Evidently he, at least, recognized that a yielding on this point was far from opening the door to sedition and upheaval. Sallust describes Cotta as *ex factione media consul.* That does not signify, as was once thought, that Cotta led a "moderate party," situated somewhere between the Sullani and the *populares.* Cotta, in fact, had been closely tied to Sulla from the beginning. Exiled from Rome in 90, he apparently fled to Sulla, and returned to resume his political career after Sulla's victory in the civil war. Cotta was one of the most distinguished of Roman aristocrats, much praised by Cicero as an orator and a statesman. Sallust, however, has a more cynical view. The historian introduces Cotta with a sneer: a man affected by ambition and attracted by gain.[60] Obviously, Sallust did not intend the phrase *ex factione media consul* to signify approbation. *Factio* is never a term of praise in Sallust's vocabulary. C. Cotta was a "consul from the heart of the oligarchy."[61] This makes his bill all the more revealing.

[58] Sources in Broughton, *MRR,* II:126; add also Asconius, 21, Clark.

[59] Sallust, *Hist.* 3.48.8, Maur.; Asconius, 67, 78, Clark; Ps. Ascon. 255, Stangl.

[60] Sallust, *Hist.* 2.42, Maur.: *ambitione tum ingenita largitione cupiens gratiam singulorum.* The description as *ex factione media consul* is in *Hist.* 3.48.8, Maur. For Cotta's previous career, references in Cicero and elsewhere, see Klebs, *RE,* 2:2482–2484, "Aurelius," n. 96; G. Perl, *Philologus,* 109 (1965): 75–82.

[61] So, rightly, Perl, *Philologus,* 109 (1965): 77–78, with references to earlier literature. The

Cotta was a central figure in the Sullan establishment, a friend of Hortensius, Lucullus, and the Metelli. He knew full well that an enhancement of the tribunician office opened no major breach in the Sullan constitution.

The measure was doubtless welcomed by young aristocrats, who could once again employ the tribunate as a stepping-stone for positions of greater prestige within the establishment. Their interest in the office is understandable, not so much as an instrument of power, but as a source of *dignitas.*[62] Asconius suggests that Cotta made himself obnoxious to the *nobilitas* by relieving the tribunate of its stigma.[63] That some *nobiles* objected is, no doubt, true. Their resistance continued, as we have seen, against tribunes in 74 and 73. But Cotta must have carried a majority of the senate with him. The consul would not have presented a bill to the assembly without a *senatus consultum* behind him.

In 73 Sertorius' fortunes were ebbing in Spain, and in the following year he was dead. The dissipation of this external threat must have given the Roman aristocracy greater confidence in its own position and institutions. It was no longer felt necessary to maintain every Sullan enactment for fear that the structure itself might crumble.[64] Repeated motions were now heard in the senate itself to abolish the kind of intimidation that conservatives had imposed in their prosecution of the ill-fated tribune Opimius in 74.[65] When Lollius Palicanus and Pompey revived the issue of full restoration of tribunician powers in 71, opposition was nowhere evident. And the implementation of the policy in the following year occurred, so far as we can tell, without resistance or subsequent upheaval.[66]

The series of tribunes who advocated increase in tribunician authority in

---

conclusion of Rossi, *PP*, 20 (1965): 140–141, that Cotta belonged to the moderate or reformist wing of the *factio nobilitatis* is no better than the older view that he headed a moderate party.

[62] Cic. *Pro Corn. apud* Asconius, 78, Clark: *is consul paulum tribunis plebis non potestatis sed dignitatis addidit.*

[63] Asconius, 67, 78, Clark.

[64] Licinius Macer in 73 complained, according to Sallust, that the *nobiles* were putting off reform until after the return of Pompeius Magnus; *Hist.* 3.48.21, Maur.: *differunt vos in adventum Cn. Pompeii.* This may mean that they wanted to be certain of the defeat of Sertorius. Cf. also the interpretation of the passage by Rossi, *PP*, 20 (1965): 136–140.

[65] Cic. *Verr.* 2.1.156: *cuius propter indignitatem iudicii sæpissime est actum in senatu ut genus hoc totum multarum atque eius modi iudiciorum tolleretur.*

[66] A late Ciceronian scholiast suggests that some were unhappy with the tribunician reform; Ps. Ascon. 220, Stangl: *in invidia tunc Pompeius fuit, quod consul redderet populo tribuniciam potestatem.* Perhaps so. Two of them could still be described as *inimici tribuniciæ potestatis* in 65; Cic. *Pro Corn. apud* Asconius, 79, Clark. Cf. the conservative argument as reconstructed and rebutted by Cic. *De Leg.* 3.19–26. But no source indicates any obstacles in the way of the measure of 70.

the 70s did not form a party. Nor were they committed to a destruction of senatorial privileges. Their efforts were aimed at reform of a particular institution, and each used the office, as was customary, to appeal to the populace and to increase his own popularity. In that sense only does the term *populares* take on any meaning. The tribunes, in fact, show individual connections with some members of the *nobilitas.* Sicinius, who clashed with the consuls of 76, assaulted demagogues and magistrates alike, but consciously avoided training his fire on M. Crassus. Quinctius, the reforming tribune of 74, was later to serve as Crassus' cavalry officer in the war against Spartacus. Opimius in 75 collaborated with C. Cotta and supported the passage of his reform measure. Lollius Palicanus operated as advance guard for Pompey's legislation on the tribunate.[67]

By 70 there was very little argument left. Pompey and Crassus, who agreed on little else and bore no affection for each other, both sponsored the measure that restored tribunician prerogatives. Young Julius Cæsar also spoke up in its behalf. And, most revealing, Q. Catulus, a central figure in the Sullan establishment, delivered a pivotal judgment in the senate. His speech showed small enthusiasm but seems to have acknowledged the inevitability of reform.[68] Pompey had not joined the *populares;* he had simply ridden the tide of inescapable change. The analysis of Cicero and Sallust is close to the mark: Pompey sought to heal any rift between *plebs* and *patres;* the tribunate was indispensable for the state; better that sober statesmen support its revival than that the task be left to demagogues.[69] There was no perpetual confrontation in the 70s between two irreconcilable factions on the issue of tribunician reform. The evidence suggests instead a growing consensus as the dangers of foreign war and civil war receded. In the end, restoration of the *tribunicia potestas* was not only inescapable but innocuous. The establishment could easily live with it; the Sullan constitution and concept suffered no serious damage.[70]

The issue of judicial reform and the courts has also been seen as a continuous source of friction throughout the decade of the 70s. Sulla restricted personnel

[67] For Sicinius and Crassus, see Plut. *Crass.* 7.9; for Quinctius' service in Crassus' ranks, see Frontin. *Strat.* 2.5.34; Plut. *Crass.* 11.4; Opimius' support for Cotta's measure is recorded by Ps. Ascon. 255, Stangl; Palicanus' cooperation with Pompey is clear from Ps. Ascon. 220, Stangl.

[68] For Cæsar's support, see Suet. *Iul.* 5; for Catulus' speech, Cic. *Verr.* 1.44; Ps. Ascon. 220, Stangl. That Crassus and Pompey did not cooperate on other matters during their consulship is stated by Suet. *Iul.* 19.2; cf. Sallust, *Hist.* 4.51, Maur.; Plut. *Crass.* 12.2–4; *Pomp.* 23.1–2.

[69] Sallust, *Hist.* 4.45, Maur.: *si nihil ante adventum suum inter plebem et patres convenisset, coram se daturum operam;* Cic. *De Leg.* 3.26: *sensit enim deberi non posse huic civitati illam potestatem . . . sapientis autem civis fuit causam nec perniciosam et ita popularem, ut non posset obsisti, perniciose populari civi non relinquere.*

[70] Cf. Laffi, *Athenæum,* 55 (1967): 203–205.

of the jury panels to members of the senatorial order. But senatorial jurors, so it might appear, betrayed their incompetence and venality. Indignant *equites* were anxious to recover their place on the *iudicia.* Corruption dominated judicial decisions; pressure for reform increased and eventually prevailed. The *lex Aurelia* of 70 removed the senate's monopoly on the courts. Yet another prop of the Sullan system had been dislodged; reform eliminated judicial control by the establishment. How valid is that analysis?

One may profitably begin at the end, with the *lex Aurelia.* Do the terms of that law indicate that it aimed a blow at the Sullan senate or that it was designed to eliminate judicial corruption? The question is an obvious one, yet rarely asked. L. Aurelius Cotta, prætor in 70 and brother of the consul of 75, was author of the measure. Once more, a member of the ruling class, not an *eques* or a demagogue, sponsored reform.[71] That suggests immediately that his bill involved no important fissure in the Sullan constitution. The *lex Aurelia* divided jury panels into senators, *equites,* and *tribuni ærarii.*[72] Precise definition of the latter two categories has been the subject of much controversy, without definitive solution. The difference may have consisted in census ratings or simply in *dignitas.* The distinction can hardly have been significant. Sources frequently ignore the *tribuni ærarii* and speak of the courts as shared simply between senators and *equites.* It is in any case clear that the new jury panels did not reach into the lower scales of the Roman social ladder.[73]

Nor was the *lex Aurelia* a victory of the *equites* over the senatorial order. To conjure up that dispute is to fall into anachronism. The courts had been a political football, shifting between senators and *equites,* for two generations before Sulla. But the dictator had met that particular issue. His courts were

[71] Cic. *Verr.* 2.2.174; *legem ab homine non nostri generis, non ex equestri loco profecto, sed nobilissimo, promulgatam videmus.* On Cotta, see Klebs, *RE,* 2:2485–2487, "Aurelius," n.102.

[72] Sources in Broughton, *MRR,* II:127; see esp. Asconius, 17, 67, 78, Clark; Schol. Bob. 91, 94, 97, 189, Stangl. There is no good reason to believe that Cotta first intended to transfer the courts exclusively to the *equites* and then switched to a compromise after the conviction of Verres; so Laffi, *Athenæum,* 55 (1967): 195–197. Cicero's language in the *Verrines* would suggest that a threat to remove senators from the juries altogether was in the air; *Verr.* 2.2.174–175, 2.3.168, 2.3.223. But, of course, it was in Cicero's interest to emphasize such a threat at the time and later to exaggerate the importance of the trial; cf. Gelzer, *Kleine Schriften* (Wiesbaden, 1962), II:167–173. The orator uses similar language, deliberately obfuscating, when speaking of the final form of the bill; *Verr.* 2.5.177–178.

[73] Discussions of the *tribuni ærarii* and their relations to the *equites* have been numerous. See, e.g., H. Hill, *The Roman Middle Class in the Republican Period* (Oxford, 1952), pp. 155–156, 212–214; M. I. Henderson, *JRS,* 53 (1963): 61–72; Nicolet, *L'Ordre Equestre,* pp. 593–613. Most recently, T. P. Wiseman, *Historia,* 19 (1970): 71–72, 74, 79–80, revived Mommsen's view that the *tribuni ærarii* comprised all men of equestrian census outside the senate and the eighteen equestrian centuries.

staffed by senators only, in the interests of convenience and efficiency. But his senate was expanded to encompass numerous members of the *equester ordo,* including many of those who had previously served on juries. The late Republic no longer witnessed conflict between the two *ordines* as groups or classes.[74] The *equites* and *tribuni ærarii* who were permitted to sit on the courts by the *lex Aurelia* were of substantially the same social background as much of the Sullan senate: businessmen, tax farmers, municipal aristocrats, military officers. The change was not the product of class struggle. Administrative reasons may have played a role. The judicial docket was large, and senatorial numbers were perhaps insufficient; some members were certainly grumbling at the excessive amount of judicial business.[75] Increasing the pool of eligible jurors would both relieve the administrative burden and extend privileges to men whose origin allowed them to be reckoned as peers of the Sullan senators. The constitution was not adversely affected.[76]

Did the *lex Aurelia* aim at eradication of corruption in the courts? It is not easy to defend that proposition. Some will have it that the men brought into the Sullan senate were poor and venal enough to make corruption into a big business.[77] Yet the *lex Aurelia* allowed the senate to supply one-thrid of the jury panels. The lot would surely fall upon the venal and the honest alike. To be sure, the censors of 70 removed sixty-four men from the Roman senate. But only two of those were expelled because of judicial corruption.[78] If the background of men who sat in the Sullan senate made them susceptible to bribery, it is an odd remedy to create new jurors from similar backgrounds and of perhaps even lower census ratings. A final point, usually ignored in this connection, seems decisive. According to a Sullan enactment, which repeated a law of C. Gracchus, senatorial jurors who conspired to convict a defendant were liable under the homicide statute. But *equites,* not specified in the legislation, remained immune from its provisions.[79] The *lex Aurelia* made no change in that respect. It requires faith to imagine that the purpose of the measure was to eliminate judicial bribery, when it placed on the juries men who could be corrupted without fear of prosecution.[80]

The charge of corruption itself, so frequently leveled against the Sullan

[74] Cf. Brunt, *Int. Conf. Econ. Hist., 1962* (Paris, 1965), pp. 132–137; Nicolet, *L'Ordre Equestre,* pp. 625–630; Laffi, *Athenæum,* 55 (1967): 198–202.

[75] Cic. *Verr.* 2.1.22: *putatis onus esse grave et incommodum iudicare.*

[76] Cf. the cogent arguments of Laffi, *Athenæum,* 55 (1967): 188–203.

[77] Cf. J. R. Hawthorn, *Greece and Rome,* 9 (1962): 53–60.

[78] Cic. *Pro Cluent.* 127: *duos solos video auctoritate censorum adfines ei turpitudini iudicari.* For the censorship of 70, see Broughton, *MRR,* II:126–127.

[79] Cic. *Pro Cluent.* 144, 148–158.

[80] It is not surprising, therefore, to find an instance of judicial corruption recorded already under the year 68; Dio, 36.38.3.

administration, warrants reappraisal. The evidence comes almost exclusively from Cicero's *Verrines* and *Pro Cluentio.* In this, as in much else, the orator's motives for distortion are relevant. In the Verres case of 70 he sought a guilty verdict by dwelling on the consequences of an acquittal: there had been so many instances of malversation in the courts that another unjustifiable acquittal would bring the wrath of the people upon the jurors. In his defense of Cluentius in 66, Cicero stressed the bad odor into which his client had fallen because of his alleged association with judicial bribery in an earlier case; the orator is at pains to shift that odium onto other individuals in order to clear the defendant of suspicion. Given these postures, it is a fair assumption that Cicero did not err on the side of understatement in recounting instances of corruption in the 70s.[81]

Yet Cicero's list, when collected, is not shockingly long. Q. Calidius was convicted of extortion, probably in 77, and lamented that the going rate for convicting a man of prætorian rank was 300,000 sesterces.[82] In 74 Terentius Varro secured acquittal on an extortion charge; the case achieved notoriety because the good faith of bribed jurors was guaranteed by marked ballots.[83] The same year witnessed the celebrated trial of Oppianicus, in consequence of which numerous jurors were charged with corruption by both sides.[84] Only two other attested cases involved suspicions of bribery, and they obviously caused little stir. C. Staienus, one of the jurors in the Oppianicus trial, was also alleged to have taken bribes at another hearing, that of an otherwise unknown Safinius. Only a passing reference informs us of the transaction. And the hearing seems to have been a civil one, hence irrelevant for the Sullan *iudices.*[85] P. Lentulus Sura, the consul of 71 and future Catilinarian, appears, if our evidence can be trusted, to have indulged in judicial bribery. Cicero reports that he had twice secured acquittal in his early career. On the second occasion, Plutarch affirms, Lentulus was indignant that the acquittal came by the margin of two votes: he could have saved his money on the second juror.[86] No dates are recorded, and we cannot be certain even that

[81] L. P. Hoy, "Political Influence in Roman Prosecutions, 78 to 60 BC," (unpub. diss., Bryn Mawr College, 1952), pp. 25–29.

[82] Cic. *Verr.* 1.38: *Q. Calidius damnatus dixerit minoris HS triciens prætorium hominem honeste non posse damnari*; Ps. Ascon. 219, Stangl; cf. Cic. *Verr.* 2.3.63.

[83] Cic. *Verr.* 1.40; *Pro Cluent.* 130; Ps. Ascon. 193, 194, 218, Stangl; Schol. Gronov. 339, 340, 349, Stangl; cf. Cic. *Div. in Cæc.* 24; Schol. Gronov. 337, Stangl; Porphyrio on Hor. *Sat.* 2.1.49.

[84] Cic. *Pro Cluent.* 62–116; *Verr.* 1.29, 1.39, 2.2.79; *Pro Cæc.* 28–29; *Brutus*, 241; Ps. Ascon. 216, 219, 255–256, Stangl; Schol. Gronov. 329, 331, 351, Stangl; Quint. *Inst. Orat.* 5.13.32; Schol. on Persius, *Sat.* 2.19.

[85] Cic. *Pro Cluent.* 68, 99.

[86] Cic. *Ad Att.* 1.16.9; Plut. *Cic.* 17.2–3.

the case occurred in the 70s. The bon mot, clearly, is the reason for its preservation.

That is as far as the evidence will take us. Other instances sometimes cited to show judicial corruption in the 70s carry little weight. Cicero suggests that Verres, in his prætorian campaign of 75, bribed a would-be prosecutor to refrain from charging him with electoral corruption.[87] In 70, as is notorious, Cicero accused Verres of preparing every form of untoward practice to assure his acquittal on a *repetundæ* charge. Among the alleged devices was the fabrication of another extortion case, with an unnamed defendant, to be heard before Verres' own case, thereby postponing the latter until the following year.[88] And one other trial is recorded for 70: a Roman senator of slender means suffered conviction. Cicero suggests that if the defendant had had enough cash he would have gotten off.[89] None of these cases, of course, affords clear evidence for corruption. Where Cicero lacks hard facts, he naturally speaks of attempted bribery, would-be prosecutors, or penurious victims who possessed the will but not the means of bribery.

Apart from the minor case of Lentulus, which cannot even be dated, we are left with only three certain examples of judicial bribery in the 70s, the trials of Calidius, Varro, and Oppianicus, plus a mass of Ciceronian hyperbole. Of these, almost all the testimony and the bulk of the rhetoric concern the *iudicium Iunianum* which heard the case of Oppianicus. And even here, despite countless rumors, only two of the jurors were actually charged with corruption and only one was convicted, the latter as the consequence of a tumultuous mob scene. Other jurors on that case heard corruption charges flung at them later in court, but they were never prosecuted on that count.[90]

By contrast, we know of numerous other trials in the 70s, some politically motivated and some of little consequence, in which there is no suggestion of bribery. It would be pointless to engage in extended analysis of them here. Some will receive fuller discussion in other contexts. Close to twenty

[87] Cic. *Verr.* 2.1.101, 2.4.45.

[88] Cic. *Verr.* 1.6, 1.9, 2.1.30; cf. Ps. Ascon. 207, 208, 236, Stangl; Schol. Gronov. 331, 332, Stangl.

[89] Cic. *Verr.* 1.46; Ps. Ascon. 221, Stangl.

[90] Only C. Junius, the presiding *iudex quæstionis* on Oppianicus' case, was convicted on charges associated with that case; Cic. *Pro Cluent.* 89–96, 108, 113; Ps. Ascon. 255–256, Stangl; Schol. Gronov. 351, Stangl. Fidiculanius Falcula was accused of violating certain regulations in his capacity as juror, but gained acquittal; Cic. *Pro Cluent.* 103–104, 108, 112, 114; Ps. Ascon. 219, Stangl. Suspicions surrounded other jurors, but none was brought to trial for corruption; Cic. *Pro Cluent.* 97–103, 114–116; cf. Cic. *Verr.* 1.29, 1.39, 2.2.79; *Brutus*, 241; Ps. Ascon. 216, 219, 255–256, Stangl; Schol. Gronov. 331, 351, Stangl; Schol. on Persius, *Sat.* 2.19; cf. Hoy, "Political Influence," pp. 12–20. Miss Hoy rightly sees that the actual instances of corruption were few. Yet she still considers these cases to be examples of the "struggle over the Sullan constitution."

are known certainly to have occurred in the 70s, and another six or seven, although undated, probably fell in this decade as well.[91] Corruption was hardly rampant. The *argumentum ex silentio* is never itself decisive. It becomes more telling when coupled with the terms of the *lex Aurelia,* which do not presuppose a background of major judicial abuses. That there was some politics in the courts is only to be expected, for Rome had a long tradition of that. On the whole, however, the evidence on juries in the 70s indicates that they were no more susceptible to bribery and no less subject to politics than their predecessors in the pre-Sullan generation.

The *Verrines* have misled us in more than one way. The impression persists that agitation for judicial reform built steadily throughout the 70s and reached fever pitch at the trial of Verres. The courts, on that view, were a central item in the popular program to wreck the Sullan settlement. In fact, the issue played a surprisingly small role in this decade. It is nowhere mentioned among the catch phrases and demagogic platform of M. Lepidus. Q. Calidius may have complained of excessive bribery when he was convicted in 77, but no politician took up the cry. The popular tribunes of 76 and 75, Sicinius and Opimius, could appeal to the people on the issue of tribunician reform—that always had a *popularis* ring. But the shifting of jury personnel between senators and *equites* made very little difference to the *plebs.* We hear nothing of the matter in the first half of the decade.[92]

A fortuitous circumstance linked judicial reform with popular agitation in 74. The trial of Oppianicus in that year produced scandal. A poisoning charge had been leveled against Oppianicus; he received vigorous defense, but the jury handed down a conviction. Reports were rife about illegal intrigues associated with the trial. The presiding officer, C. Junius, had tampered with the regulations; the whole bench of *iudices* was under suspicion of bribery. No one was more indignant about the verdict and its implications than Oppianicus' defense attorney. That individual happens to have been L. Quinctius, the demagogic tribune of 74. Quinctius clashed with L. Lucullus over the matter of tribunician prerogatives. Now he could add another item to

[91] See Hoy, "Political Influence," pp. 1–51. Her discussions, however, are rarely as full as they might be. In addition to her list, one could cite other cases which may have come in the 70s: L. Varenus (H. Gundel, *RE,* 8A:374–375, "Varenus," n. 3); L. Gellius (Val. Max. 5.9.1); Cn. Sergius Silus (Val. Max. 6.1.8; cf. Gruen, *Roman Politics,* pp. 300–301); Procilius (Ps. Ascon. 236, Stangl); Q. Sergius (Cic. *Pro Cluent.* 21); Pericles (Cic. *Verr.* 2.1.85); M. Seius (Cic. *Pro Planc.* 12); and a trial in 74 (Cic. *Verr.* 1.39).

[92] Some measure on private *iudicia* was sponsored by C. Cotta in 75. No word is preserved on its content and it was repealed in the following year; Asconius, 67, Clark. It is in any event irrelevant for the issue of the criminal courts. Cicero makes reference to Octavius, probably the consul of 76, who instituted a formula for the charge of robbery combined with assault or intimidation; *Verr.* 2.3.152. There is no reason to imagine political implications.

his platform. Quinctius initiated proceedings against the *iudex* Junius and used the opportunity to whip up a riotous mob. The tribune punctuated his prosecution by railing at senatorial mismanagement of the courts. Angry crowds intimidated the hapless Junius, who succumbed without resistance. Quinctius thereupon stepped up his propaganda campaign.[93] The tribune, a *novus homo* who affected elaborate dress, aristocratic haughtiness, and outrage, had seized upon the temporary unpopularity of senatorial jurors in a cause célèbre in order to advance his own name more dramatically before the public.[94] It does not follow that this constituted a general assault on the social structure. The senate itself, in fact, voted to conduct an inquiry into corrupt practices as a consequence of the Oppianicus case. It was the magistrates who were dilatory in executing the decree.[95] Tribunician agitation and the campaign for jury reform had thus come briefly into combination. Both could serve the political ends of L. Quinctius. There was, however, no natural or enduring connection. The years 73 and 72, so far as our evidence goes, saw no proposals or activity for reform of the courts. Obviously this was not a live issue throughout the decade of the 70s.

The political climate changed gradually but perceptibly in the last years of the decade. With regard to tribunician reform, as we have seen, the removal of external threat and its concomitant alleviation of senatorial anxiety brought about a more open attitude. It is reasonable to assume that, with the defeat of Sertorius and the failure of Spartacus, a similarly relaxed posture prevailed on the matter of the courts. At his *contio* as consul-elect in 71, Pompey announced that he would lend his support to a reform of the *iudicia.* That move was greeted by popular acclaim, so Cicero reports.[96] Pompey himself showed no great zeal for the reform. The bill was enacted by L. Cotta in Pompey's consulship of 70; the consul simply avoided standing in Cotta's way.[97] Nothing attests to any political struggle over passage of the measure.

[93] For Quinctius' defense of Oppianicus, see Cic. *Pro Cluent.* 74, 77, 109; Ps. Ascon. 206, 216, Stangl; Schol. Gronov. 329, Stangl; Quint. *Inst. Orat.* 5.13.39; for his prosecution of Junius, see Cic. *Pro Cluent.* 89–96, 108, 113; Schol. Gronov. 351, Stangl; his attacks on the senate, Cic. *Pro Cluent.* 77, 110, 136: *cum tribunus plebis populo concitato rem pæne ad manus revocasset, cum vir optimus et homo innocentissimus pecunia circumventus diceretur, cum invidia flagraret ordo senatorius.* The story reported but not endorsed by Schol. Gronov. 328–329, Stangl, that Quinctius actually proposed dividing juries among senators, *equites*, and *tribuni ærarii,* is an apparent anachronism.

[94] Cic. *Pro Cluent.* 77: *condemnato Oppianico statim L. Quinctius, homo maxime popularis, qui omnes rumorem et contionum ventos colligere consuesset, oblatam sibi facultatem putavit, ut ex invidia senatoria posset crescere.* On Quinctius' habits and character, see Cic. *Pro Cluent.* 110–112.

[95] Cic. *Pro Cluent* 136–137.

[96] Cic. *Verr.* 1.45.

[97] Plut. *Pomp.* 22.3: τὰς δίκας περιεῖδεν αὖθις εἰς τοὺς ἱππέας νόμῳ μεταφερομένας.

Q. Catulus, among others, conceded that there was no point in unnecessarily rousing public antipathy.[98]

Cicero magnifies out of all proportion the significance of the Verres case in the agitation for change. It was his purpose to stress the agitation and thereby to goad senatorial jurors into a conviction, lest they lose control of the courts.[99] The fact is, however, that Cotta's bill was already in the air, perhaps already drafted, before the trial of Verres.[100] The jury had nothing to be ashamed of in that trial; Verres fled into exile after the *actio prima.* No effect, however, was discernible on the *lex Aurelia;* it secured passage despite the trial's outcome. Later, in preparing the *Verrines* for publication, Cicero naturally obscured events and exaggerated the role of the trial. With something less than candor, the orator urged that judicial reform hung on the outcome of Verres' case, and consequently he stressed the infamy of the law courts. But, despite Ciceronian rhetoric, it seems clear that senatorial juries had not spent the 70s wallowing in corruption.

Atmosphere for change was propitious in 70. The *lex Aurelia* could serve more than one purpose. It would provide administrative relief for the senate, give added prestige to respectable groups outside the senatorial class, and short-circuit needless popular discontent. The Sullan system was never dependent upon airtight oligarchy. New judicial arrangements show the self-confidence, not the weakness, of the system.

The notion of continual friction between a conservative Sullan senate and progressive democratic reformers does not fit the facts. A gradual loosening of the system that came with growing security is perhaps a more accurate description of events in the 70s. This was true not only of tribunician and judicial reform; other instances confirm the picture.

Grain distribution was a standard device for popular demagogues. M. Lepidus, as we have seen, made it part of his program in 78, thereby following a long and well-established tradition. But *leges frumentariæ* were by no means a monopoly of the *populares.* Grain shortage reached an acute point in 75; the populace was unhappy, even ugly.[101] Sallust gives the consul C. Cotta a speech: it was gloomy and pessimistic, promising nothing and asking for

[98] Cic. *Verr.* 1.44.

[99] See, e.g., Cic. *Div. in Cæc.* 8–9; *Verr.* 1.1–2, 1.20, 1.47–49, 2.1.5–6, 2.1.20–23, 2.2.174, 2.3.224, 2.5.175–179.

[100] Cic. *Verr.* 1.49, 2.2.174–175, 2.5.177–178; cf. Gelzer, *Cicero, Ein Biographischer Versuch* (Wiesbaden, 1969), pp. 41–42. Schol. Gronov. 328, Stangl, indeed, asserts that the plan enacted by Cotta was already proposed in 71 by Lollius Palicanus. One cannot, of course, guarantee the accuracy of that statement. Ward's view, *Latomus,* 29 (1970): 67–71, that Cicero cooperated with Cotta in passing the law is the height of paradox and altogether fanciful.

[101] Cf. Sallust, *Hist.* 2.44–46, Maur.

patience and endurance. Cotta professed willingness to sacrifice himself, but he also exculpated himself of all blame for the situation: the demands of external wars produced the straitened circumstances.[102] The speech casts Cotta in an unfavorable light; but then that individual was not one of Sallust's favorites. Some relief came from Sicily, where Cicero, serving his quæstorship, secured the shipment of needed grain to Rome.[103] Under the pressure of wartime, with Mithridates threatening bellicose actions in the East and Rome's commanders in Spain clamoring for additional money and supplies, the senate was in no position to remedy the situation altogether.[104] Yet the ædile Q. Hortensius–at the center of the Sullan oligarchy, a friend of Cotta's, and certainly no *popularis*–distributed grain to the populace in 75 at a price considerably below the inflated market rate.[105] In the following year another ædile, M. Seius, also no friend of the people, disarmed public hostility by another distribution below the still prohibitive market price.[106] The foreign situation was rather more favorable in 73. The consuls of that year, M. Lucullus and C. Cassius, on the basis of a senatorial decree, promulgated a measure directing additional purchase of corn in Sicily and renewed distribution to the Roman populace.[107] There is no reason to doubt that distributions continued on senatorial and magisterial initiative in succeeding years. We know that M. Crassus, as consul in 70, engaged in generous food benefactions to the people.[108] It is abundantly clear that the Roman senate did not leave this activity exclusively to popular demagogues.

One may discern liberal measures on the part of the ruling class in other areas as well, especially in the later years of the decade. Many profiteers had enriched themselves during the Sullan proscriptions by purchasing cheaply the property of the proscribed. Sulla had assisted his favorites further by remitting part of the outlays for their purchases. Not surprisingly, no attempt was made to tamper with these arrangements in the early 70s. But in 72, a senatorial decree, duly promulgated into law by the consuls, directed that the profiteers return to the state any funds remitted to them by Sulla.[109] The action rarely receives much notice in modern works. It deserves attention. The ruling class could welcome and, in fact, initiate redress for Sullan inequities without in any sense imperiling its own position. In 72 also the consuls,

[102] Sallust, *Hist.* 2.47, Maur.; cf. Perl, *Philologus,* 109 (1965): 80–82.

[103] Sources on Cicero's quæstorship in Broughton, *MRR,* II:98.

[104] Cf. Sallust, *Hist.* 2.47.6–7, Maur.; Cic. *Pro Balbo,* 40.

[105] Cic. *Verr.* 2.3.215.

[106] Cic. *De Off.* 2.58; cf. Pliny, *NH,* 15.2, 18.16.

[107] Sallust, *Hist.* 3.48.19, Maur.; Cic. *Verr.* 2.3.163, 2.3.173, 2.5.52; cf. Asconius, 8, Clark.

[108] Plut. *Crass.* 12.2; *Comp. Nic. et Crass.* 1.4.

[109] Cic. *Verr.* 2.3.81–82; Sallust, *Hist.* 4.1, Maur.

acting on senatorial instructions, granted the commanders in Spain the right to bestow Roman citizenship on worthy provincials. This was not simply a political move by Pompey's friends to enhance his position. Metellus Pius acquired similar powers, and the grant revived an earlier liberal policy whereby Roman generals had rewarded loyal provincials.[110]

By 70 the wounds opened by Lepidus' revolt had healed sufficiently and the Sertorian episode was over. The government could afford to be generous. A *lex Plautia* granted amnesty to the supporters of Lepidus and Sertorius: the survivors could return to Rome and resume their civil and political rights. The Roman senate had itself set the policy.[111] Finally, a word should be said about agrarian legislation. Land grants for veterans are usually associated with demagogues and military men, and with subversion of aristocratic control in the state. But upon conclusion of the Spanish war and return of Roman forces, it was again the *curia* that authorized legislation to provide land for the soldiers of both Metellus and Pompey.[112]

In all of the instances recounted above, the initiative for reform legislation and liberal measures came from the senate and its representatives. This includes, of course, also the military commissions discussed earlier, those of Pompey, Lucullus, and Antonius. The bulk of them, for reasons already explained, belong in the later part of the 70s.

Sulla had instituted a system whereby the state would be run by an oligarchy buttressed by an expanded governing class and operating within established institutions. Far from lapsing into progressive incompetence and feebleness, the new senate gradually obtained a firmer footing. It is therefore logical and fitting that the elections of 70 returned conservative consuls like Hortensius and Metellus. Those elections were anything but anomalous. The year 70 culminated a process that revealed the resiliency and flexibility of the Sullan constitution.

[110] Cic. *Pro Balbo*, 19, 32, 37, 50; cf. *Pro Arch.* 26. That the measure was carried in accordance with senatorial opinion is clear from Cic. *Pro Balbo*, 19: *ex ea lege, quam L. Gellius Cn. Cornelius ex senatus sententia tulerunt.*

[111] Sallust, *Hist.* 3.47, Maur.: *Post reditum eorum, quibus senatus belli Lepidani gratiam fecerat*; Cic. *Verr.* 2.5.151–152: *ex Hispania fugientes . . . quibus hominibus per senatum, per populum Romanum, per omnes magistratus, in foro, in suffragiis, in hac urbe, in re publica versari liceret.* Neither of these references, unfortunately, is included in Broughton, *MRR*, II:128. Cæsar spoke on behalf of the measure; Suet. *Iul.* 5; Dio, 44.47.4; Gellius, 13.3.5. For the date of the *lex Plautia*, see L. R. Taylor, *CP*, 36 (1941): 121; Broughton, *MRR*, II:130, n.4. It follows that when Pompey judiciously burned the correspondence of Sertorius, which might implicate some of the latter's sympathizers in Rome, he was not engaged in anti-senatorial policy; Plut. *Pomp.* 20.4; *Sert.* 27.3; Appian, *BC*, 1.115.

[112] Dio, 38.5.1; Cic. *Ad Att.* 1.18.6; Plut. *Luc.* 34.3–4; cf. R. E. Smith, *CQ*, 7 (1957): 82–85.

DIVISIONS AND FACTIONALISM

On the matter of institutions and structure, the Roman ruling class stood together. Divisions in the aristocracy operated on other levels. Internal politics involved power and faction: influence within the government was the object of attention. The Sullan system had not precluded aristocratic politics. Participants in the new establishment were an amalgam of men and groups. Some had been loyal Sullan officers in the eastern wars of the 80s and returned with their commander to serve him in the civil war. Others had collaborated with the Marian and Cinnan regime, but reversed their allegiance in time to benefit from Sulla's generosity. Still others had enjoyed a discreet aloofness from both sides in the 80s, but resumed respectable places in the Sullan oligarchy after the conclusion of civil war. The great families of the *nobilitas,* patrician and plebeian, remained the central forces in the new government.[113] But older rivalries were not forgotten. The return of stability also signaled the revival of aristocratic intrigue.

There are some signs of the old bitterness. Sullan officers who had reached positions of authority through closeness to the dictator furnished convenient objects of attack after his death. Several underwent prosecution in the 70s: Cn. Cornelius Dolabella, C. Antonius, A. Terentius Varro, and P. Gabinius.[114] Other Sullani made appearances as defense counsel: Q. Hortensius and C. Cotta for Dolabella, Hortensius again for Varro. But thrusts against Sulla's friends in no sense involved designs on the Sullan constitution. Identity of the prosecutors makes that clear. C. Julius Cæsar, *accusator* of Dolabella and Antonius, whatever his distaste for Sullan profiteers, remained safely within the aristocratic structure. Ap. Claudius Pulcher, who brought Varro to trial, was eldest son of the consul of 79, who had been restored to Rome by Sulla and who was doubtless the dictator's personal choice for the consulship. Nor can L. Piso, the prosecutor of Gabinius, be termed an opponent of the regime. He was a respectable member of the governing class, a prætor in 74, and *propinquus* of C. Piso, the consul of 67, one of the most conservative figures in the Roman senate.[115]

[113] One need glance only at the consular *fasti* of the 70s to see the continued prominence of aristocratic families, especially those connected with Sulla. See below, Chapter 4.

[114] Sources for the trial of Dolabella are in Broughton, *MRR*, II:89; a full discussion in Gruen, *AJP*, 87 (1966): 385–389. On C. Antonius, see Asconius, 84, 88, 92, Clark; Plut. *Caes.* 4.1–2; cf. Cic. *Verr.* 2.1.60; [Q. Cic.] *Comm. Petit.* 8. For the trial of Varro, see above, n.83. On the trial of Gabinius, see Cic. *Div. in Cæc.* 64; cf. *Pro Arch.* 9. Cf. also Badian, *Studies*, pp. 81–82, 99, n.69.

[115] On Cæsar, see below, chap. 2. Evidence on the Claudii is in Münzer, *RE*, 3:2848–2853, "Claudius," nn.296–297. For L. Piso's prætorship, see Cic. *Verr.* 2.1.119, 2.4.56; Ps. Asconius, 250, Stangl. On C. Piso, see Münzer, *RE*, 3:1376–1377, "Calpurnius," n.63.

Feuds and internal contests for power were working themselves out here. In the early 70s, the Sullani still felt the need for unity. So, Cotta and Hortensius collaborated in the defense of Dolabella in 77. Both men again served as defense counsel for M. Canuleius, apparently at about the same time.[116] Dolabella, a faithful Sullan officer, could rely on illustrious defenders. By contrast, another Cn. Dolabella, who had joined Sulla's cause late and only after consorting with his enemies, found no support at his trial and fell to the prosecution of young M. Scaurus, the stepson of Sulla.[117] Cooperation among Sulla's beneficiaries in the years immediately subsequent to his death is plain. The Sullan lieutenants Dolabella and Antonius, despite misbehavior in the provinces, received powerful defense and gained acquittal. By 74, however, A. Varro required devious machinations to escape conviction. And P. Gabinius, in the last part of the decade, had to fight his own battles, and succumbed to his prosecutor.

A cohesion of diverse politicians had been imposed by the exigencies of civil war and dictatorship. But as the need for unity receded in the course of the decade politics once more fragmented. This must have been a period of complex realignments and readjustments, which are now impossible to follow. Clearly, a simple division into "Sullani" and "democrats" does not even remotely describe the situation. Insofar as the scanty evidence discloses any pattern, it is one along the lines already discerned in other contexts: oligarchic solidarity under stress in the early 70s, followed by the gradual opening or reopening of rifts and rivalries within the governing class. The situation has numerous parallels in earlier Roman history, notably in the generation after the Gracchi.

Details are no longer susceptible to reconstruction. But we can pinpoint one of the beneficiaries of the political adjustments. P. Cornelius Cethegus was a master of intrigue and manipulation. A supporter of Marius, he had been expelled from Rome by Sulla in 88. But feigned contrition subsequently brought him back into Sulla's good graces, and he made certain to demonstrate loyalty during the civil war. Cethegus' background and unsavory habits made him obnoxious to others in the establishment. L. Philippus, himself no model of consistency, made reference to Cethegus' treachery and categorized him with M. Lepidus in 77. L. Lucullus, the haughtiest of Roman aristocrats and closest of Sulla's associates, found him unwelcome and unbearable. But Cethegus remained a force to be reckoned with. Politics was his life and he was a supreme practitioner of the art. Men of noble birth and distinction sought his favors when they aimed at office and commands. Express examples are

[116] Cicero, in any event, associates the two cases; *Brutus*, 317: *pro M. Canuleio, pro Cn. Dolabella consulari, cum Cotta princeps adhibitus esset, priores tamen agere partis Hortensium*. Cf. also Cotta's defense of the Sullan system in 79; Cic. *Pro Cæc*. 97.

[117] Full discussion of the two trials in Gruen, *AJP*, 87 (1966): 385–399.

recorded for the year 74. M. Antonius obtained large powers for his commission against the pirates with support of the consul M. Cotta. But the whole affair was managed by the effort of Cethegus. Cotta received the province of Bithynia, probably also through Cethegus' intrigues. And L. Lucullus himself had been awarded Cisalpine Gaul, but wanted Cilicia and command against Mithridates. He swallowed his pride and importuned Cethegus through flattery and gifts for his mistress Præcia.[118] The remarkable effectiveness of that political manipulator reveals how power had shifted within senatorial ranks in the aftermath of Sulla's death. It is also a sober reminder of how little we know of the backstage maneuvers that made such shifts possible.

The era was obviously a congenial one for political machinators. Not the least of these was M. Licinius Crassus, who first emerges into public prominence in this decade. Command against Spartacus in 72 earned him military repute and a consulship for 70. But that was the fruit, not the inception, of Crassus' influence. He had gathered an army in Spain in the 80s, duly brought it into the Sullan camp, and performed signal service during the civil war. Ingenious and unscrupulous real estate deals allowed Crassus to amass a fortune during the proscriptions. His influence expanded in subsequent years.[119] Crassus' attitudes are obscure, his maneuvers closed to view. There is nothing to show cooperation with individuals like Lucullus, Hortensius, Curio, or Catulus. The men who hoped to hold the line, at least temporarily, against tribunician reform would not have found Crassus an ally. He had the respect of Sicinius and of Quinctius, the advocates of reform, and he helped implement the change in his consulship of 70.[120]

At the same time, however, Crassus engaged in intense rivalry with Pompeius Magnus. The friction during their joint consulship and thereafter is well known. But it contains earlier roots. Both men had collected private armies in the 80s; both had watched and waited upon events; both ultimately brought their forces onto Sulla's side and were instrumental in his victory. It is a striking example, though by no means the only one, of cooperation in civil war followed by competition in peacetime. Plutarch reports that Crassus

[118] For Cethegus' earlier Marian associations, see Appian, *BC*, 1.60, 1.62; Plut. *Marius*, 40.2; on his service for Sulla, see Appian, *BC*, 1.80; Val. Max. 9.2.1. Philippus' remark is in Sallust, *Hist.* 1.77.20, Maur.: the friction with Lucullus in Plut. *Luc.* 5.3. The power and influence of Cethegus is clear from Cic. *Parad.* 5.40; *Brutus*, 178: *P. Cethegus cui de re publica satis suppeditabat oratio; totam enim tenebat eam penitusque cognoverat; itaque in senatu consularium auctoritatem assequebatur*; cf. Cic. *Pro Cluent.* 84–85. On his management of Antonius' command, see Ps. Asconius, 259, Stangl: *M. Antonius qui, gratia Cottæ consulis et Cethegi factione in senatu curationem infinitam nactus totius oræ maritimæ.* For Lucullus' soliciting of Cethegus' favor, see Plut. *Luc.* 6.1–3.

[119] Plut. *Crass.* 2.3–8. On Crassus' early career, see A. Garzetti, *Athenæum*, 19 (1941): 3–37; F. E. Adcock, *Marcus Crassus Millionaire* (Cambridge, 1966), pp. 1–20.

[120] See above, pp. 27–28.

was filled with jealousy at Pompey's triumph in 80, the inception of their bitter rivalry.[121] The anecdote may simply be a biographer's fabrication. But there are other minor and neglected bits of information which indicate continued enmity between them in the 70s. At some unknown date Crassus was prosecuted for illicit relations with a certain Licinia, one of the Vestal Virgins. The defendant entered a plausible plea (given his reputation): he had wooed Licinia only in order to purchase her property. That got him an acquittal.[122] The case may have come in 73, in connection with the trial of Fabia to be discussed below. We know that a number of Vestals were under accusation and escaped conviction.[123] In any event, the prosecutor of Crassus rouses some interest. He is identified simply as a "certain Plotius."[124] The sources offer nothing further. But it may not be unreasonable to identify Plotius with the magistrate of the same name whose agrarian bill provided land for Pompey's veterans in 70.[125] And another item points in the same direction. The consuls of 72, Cn. Lentulus Clodianus and L. Gellius Publicola, sponsored the measure that gave Pompey and Metellus authority to enfranchise Spanish provincials. They were also responsible for the legislation, discussed above, that required Sullan profiteers to disgorge some of the cash remitted by the dictator nearly a decade before. One of the intended victims of that bill could well have been M. Crassus, the most successful of Sullan profiteers. The angry senatorial discussion in 72 regarding the command against Spartacus now takes on an added dimension. Lentulus and Gellius had both led forces against the slave uprising and had failed ignominiously. When the senate determined to transfer control of the war to Crassus, they abruptly terminated the consuls' activity.[126] It was fitting irony that Pompey eventually claimed responsibility for crushing the slave revolt by rounding up Spartacus' stragglers, thereby robbing the infuriated Crassus of well-earned credit. The bitterness between them had a long background.

That the concord of senatorial leaders did not endure beyond the mid-70s can be shown in more than one instance. Old Sullan ties were no longer necessarily common bonds. C. Cotta's measure of 75 to permit tribunes to seek higher office would hardly have found favor with men like C. Curio,

[121] Plut. *Crass.* 7.1.

[122] Plut. *Crass.* 1.2; *Ex Inim. Util.* 6; cf. *Comp. Nic. et Crass.* 1.2.

[123] Cic. *Cat.* 3.9; cf. *Brutus*, 236. On Fabia's trial, see below, n.127.

[124] Plut. *Crass.* 1.2: **Πλωτίου τινὸς διώκοντος**.

[125] Cic. *Ad Att.* 1.18.6; see below, chap. 9, n.119. This Plotius or another was a legate of Pompey's in 67; Florus, 1.41.9; Appian, *Mithr.* 95; see Syme, *JRS*, 53 (1963): 57–58.

[126] Plut. *Crass.* 10.1: **ταῦ θ' ἡ βουλὴ πυθομένη τοὺς μὲν ὑπάτους πρὸς ὀργὴν ἐκέλευσεν ἡσυχίαν ἄγειν, Κράσσον δὲ τοῦ πολέμου στρατηγὸν εἵλετο**. Cf. Shatzman, *Athenaeum*, 46 (1968): 347–350. A different–and less plausible–interpretation in Z. Rubinsohn, *Historia*, 19 (1970); 624–627.

Q. Catulus, Q. Hortensius, and L. Lucullus. The prosecution of A. Terentius Varro by Ap. Claudius Pulcher in 74 has already received mention. In the following year, Appius' brother, the erratic and volatile P. Clodius, uncovered or fabricated a scandal involving Vestal Virgins and their alleged paramours. Judicial procedures followed, and among the defendants was L. Sergius Catilina, accused of *incestum* with the Vestal Fabia. The notorious Catiline had been one of the more successful executioners and profiteers in the Sullan proscriptions. Evidently the Claudii, who had reason to remember Sulla fondly, did not scruple to earn reputation by attacking Sullan adherents.[127] The instinct for self-preservation may have entailed a moratorium on family feuds at the time of the dictatorship. By the late 70s that no longer held true. Both the Metelli and the Curiones profited from Sulla's favors. But, at some point, probably in 72, young Q. Metellus Nepos laid a charge against C. Scribonius Curio, the consul of 76. Curio had once been the accuser of Nepos' father. The trial came to naught when Curio filed countercharges and the two men agreed to drop proceedings.[128] If evidence were fuller, similar rivalries among members of the establishment would doubtless be uncovered.

It is by now more than obvious that the common interests which united politicians in the Sullan years dissolved into factionalism in the 70s. To speak simply of the "Sullan oligarchy" as if it were a monolith throughout the decade is to misunderstand the dynamics of Roman politics. It ought not to require reiteration that the internal struggles noted above had nothing to do with differences over the Sullan constitution. Individuals calculated their moves in terms of personal advancement, family ties, and traditional rivalries. An attack on former associates of Sulla did not make one a *popularis,* any more than advocacy of reform made one an enemy of the government.

A final example will suffice to make the point. L. Calpurnius Piso Frugi, the prætor of 74, was heir to a long line of distinguished *nobiles.* He was also an active and energetic politician in the 70s. During his prætorship he made a habit of vetoing the decrees and frustrating the aims of his colleague C. Verres.[129] Verres, of course, was client and supporter of leading Sullan oligarchs, a relative of the Metelli, and friend of Curio, Hortensius, and others. Piso's badgering of Verres parallels his prosecution of P. Gabinius, one of

[127] Clodius' attack on Fabia is recorded by Plut. *Cato,* 19.3; Catiline's involvement in the affair: Asconius, 91, Clark; Orosius, 6.3.1; cf. Sallust, *Cat.* 15.1; [Q. Cic.] *Comm. Petit.* 10. Catiline gained acquittal, through the assistance of Q. Catulus; Orosius, 6.3.1; cf. Sallust, *Cat.* 35.1. On the date of the trial, see Cic. *Cat.* 3.9.

[128] The story is given in full by Asconius, 63–64, Clark. Date of the trial is unrecorded, but it very likely followed Curio's return from a Macedonian proconsulship in 72; for which, see Broughton, *MRR,* II:118.

[129] Cic. *Verr.* 2.1.119.

Sulla's ex-officers.[130] At the same time, however, when the demagogic tribune of 74, L. Quinctius, brought charges against C. Junius and used the occasion to deliver blistering diatribes against senatorial mismanagement of the judiciary, L. Piso stepped up and came to the defense of Junius.[131] There was, of course, no inconsistency: Piso was keeping himself in the public eye. Though some may find it puzzling that the same politician could engage in attacks on Sullan associates and also resist popular demagogues, no Roman would have found it so.

A complex reshuffling of alignments and alliances dominated the political scene of the 70s. The evidence recounted above is sufficient to place that beyond doubt, though insufficient to allow us to follow the process in detail. Amidst the intricacies and complexities, however, one fact stands out: the meteoric rise to prominence and *auctoritas* of Pompey the Great. Pompey had the advantage of being away from Rome and aloof from politics, and of building an extraordinary military reputation while eliminating the enemies of the government. Not surprisingly, many politicians at home made swift to attach themselves to him or to claim his support. But Pompey's *auctoritas* entailed no *dominatio.*[132] Nor did his consulship of 70 mark the irreversible victory of the military over civilian government. Pompey did not extort his consulship by force of arms or even by threat of force. He retained his armies until he could celebrate his triumph. But the armies were dismissed before the end of 71. Pompey entered his consulship as a civilian.[133]

Far from imposing a military regime, Pompey was eager and careful to school himself in proper senatorial procedure–commissioning Terentius Varro to write him a book on the subject.[134] To be sure, a consulship for Pompey was irregular and unprecedented. Constitutional regulations had to be suspended, for Pompey was well under age and he had held no prior magistracy. But it is difficult to imagine that anyone would have questioned the propriety

[130] Cic. *Div. in Cæc.* 64.

[131] Schol. Gronov. 351, Stangl: *Iunium præpositum Quintius accusavit, contra Pisone Frugi posito.*

[132] Sallust's famous judgment of Pompey, *modestus ad alia omnia, nisi ad dominationem* (*Hist.* 2.17, Maur.) is partisan and *post eventum*; cf. *Hist.* 3.88, Maur.

[133] Plut. *Pomp.* 21.3–22.2; *Crass.* 11.8–12.1; cf. Vell. Pat. 2.30.2. According to Plutarch, Pompey campaigned for voters' support at the polls–on his own behalf and that of Crassus. The fact may be reflected in Sallust, *Hist.* 4.48, Maur.: *collegam minorem et sui cultorem expectans.* The account in Appian, *BC,* 1.121, obviously telescopes and misinterprets the events; see Gelzer, *Kleine Schriften,* II:156–165; A. N. Sherwin-White, *JRS,* 46 (1956): 5–6. Pompey also expressed no interest, at least temporarily, in a new provincial command; Vell. Pat. 2.31.1; Plut. *Pomp.* 23.4. On the elections for 70, see further J. Linderski, *Mélanges Michalowski* (1966), pp. 523–526.

[134] Gellius, 14.7.

of a consulship for him. Pompey had commanded Roman legions for over a dozen years, half of that time as *imperator pro consule,* and had celebrated two triumphs. It would have been unthinkable to ask Pompey to begin the *cursus honorum* and sue for the quæstorship! The exemption, in what was obviously a unique case, did not nullify the constitutional structure.

Pompey had made his reputation through military success and ruthlessness in the field. But permanent political eminence required a traditional approach—the building of a faction. Pompey, like Sulla, welcomed support from all angles: from *consulares* like Lentulus Clodianus and Gellius, from reformers like Macer and Palicanus, from *novi homines* like M. Cicero. He had defeated Sertorius, but had ostentatiously burned Sertorius' correspondence, thereby earning the gratitude of men in Rome who might have sympathized with the rebel. Having saved the state from foreign foe and revolution, he could afford to endorse liberal measures, which increased his popularity and widened his support. The consuls of 72, friends of Pompey, were now the censors of 70. They conducted a resolute purge of the senate: sixty-four members were expelled, others were censured. That should not be taken to mean that the censors simply removed opponents of Pompey. Among the victims were *nobiles* of unsavory character, like P. Lentulus Sura and C. Antonius, whose misdeeds had already been broadcast in criminal trials, and jurors like M'. Aquillius and Ti. Gutta, whose alleged corruption was notorious. A rigid censorship, in the traditional style, symbolized conservatism and order. As in so many other instances, Pompey and his friends strengthened rather than weakened the Sullan system and the senatorial leadership.[135]

Enough has been said to show that Pompey was no enemy of the oligarchy. His aim was to be one of them, indeed the best of them.[136] Sponsorship of tribunician *potestas* and acquiescence in judicial reform in no way detracted from that stance. The time was ripe for such adjustments, and Pompey deftly saw them through. Statesmanlike measures would nourish his drive toward a position of leadership within the ruling class. Burgeoning political support for Pompey becomes increasingly discernible. It did not stem only from military veterans, popular tribunes, and *novi homines.* A marriage alliance with

[135] On the censorship of 70, see the sources in Broughton, *MRR*, II:126–127. The censors may also have named Mam. Lepidus, a good conservative, as *princeps senatus*; Val. Max. 7.7.6; cf. Sumner, *JRS*, 54 (1964): 47–48. There is no reason to believe that Sulla had abolished the censorship; see Gabba, *Athenæum*, 34 (1956): 135–138; Laffi, *Athenæum*, 55 (1967): 206–207. Nor need one assume that the censors of 70 expelled men of lowly origin who had been placed in the senate by Sulla, a view revived again by Rossi, *PP*, 20 (1965): 147–149.

[136] Cf. Sallust, *Hist.* 3.48.23, Maur.: *mihi quidem satis spectatum est Pompeium, tantæ gloriæ adulescentem, malle principem volentibus vobis esse quam illis dominationis socium.*

the Metelli gave him access to one of Rome's most powerful senatorial clans.[137] The younger generation of ambitious politicians, including those from families at the heart of the Sullan oligarchy, found attachment to Pompey attractive and profitable. The fruits of this development may be seen clearly in the names on Pompey's staff for the eastern wars beginning in 67.[138] And we may take note of one individual who neatly confirms the picture. L. Cornelius Sisenna was the foremost historian of the Sullan era, and his work was known for its partiality toward the dictator. In 78, the last year of Sulla's life, Sisenna reached the prætorship. He was a friend of Lucullus and Hortensius, and in 70 backed the Metelli in their defense of Verres. Here, if ever, there were solid Sullan credentials. Yet none of this prevented Sisenna from taking a military post three years later in the service of Pompey the Great.[139] Again there is no contradiction or inconsistency.

In an era when political alliances were being shaped anew, Pompey showed himself not only Rome's most successful general, but also her most successful politician. Far from destroying the Sullan system, Pompey had applied Sulla's own lessons. Not that he was without opponents—M. Crassus was only the most potent of them. But even Crassus was induced to cooperate temporarily in order to enjoy a joint consulship in 70. Pompey had assembled an amalgam of influential supporters from several groups. Like Sulla, he turned from the role of military hero to become head of a political faction.

Adjustment, rather than breakdown, was the hallmark of the 70s. An aristocratic government, headed by *consulares* and *nobiles* and supported by a broadened senatorial class, remained in control throughout. Foreign foes and internal revolt were successfully resisted by authorized representatives of the state. As the new aristocracy gained maturity and self-confidence, it could tolerate and even encourage change that, in the long run, allowed its own machinery to operate more smoothly. Tribunician reform and liberal legislation relieved political pressure on the government, and broadening of the judiciary eased

[137] The notion of a political quarrel between Pompeian and Metellan factions in this period does not meet the facts, and should now be banished from the standard accounts. Verres' trial has been used in the reconstruction. The rapacious governor of Sicily was supported in his case by the Metelli, his patrons and kinsmen. But not a scrap of evidence attests to Pompey's involvement or interest in the case. See Gruen, *AJP*, 92 (1971): 9–12, with citations and bibliography.

[138] See Gruen, *Historia*, 18 (1969): 74–77.

[139] On Sisenna's reputation as an historian, see Cic. *Brutus*, 228; *De Leg.* 1.7; his advocacy of a Sullan line: Sallust, *Iug.* 95.2; his prætorship: Broughton, *MRR*, II:86; connection with Lucullus and Hortensius: Plut. *Luc.* 1.5; defense of Verres: Cic. *Verr.* 2.2.110, 2.4.33, 2.4.43; service with Pompey: Appian, *Mithr.* 95; Dio, 36.18–19; cf. Badian, *Studies*, pp. 212–213. It may be noted also that Sisenna, Sullan though he was, enjoyed the friendship of the popular tribune of 73, Licinius Macer, a fellow historian: Cic. *De Leg.* 1.7.

administrative burdens while it brought a larger number of active participants into the realm of public policy.

The second half of the decade witnessed increased aristocratic infighting, reshuffling of alliances, and the emergence of new and potent figures, men like P. Cethegus, M. Crassus, and Cn. Pompeius Magnus. But on the structure of government and the perpetuation of the Sullan system there was no argument. The changes in 70 were only tinkerings with the machinery, designed to make the government more popular, the administration more efficient. Serious social and political problems created by the Sullan dictatorship and punctuated by the revolts of Lepidus and Sertorius were not resolved. Whatever the internal bickering within the establishment, there was agreement on essentials. Citizenship might be extended to some Spanish provincials; but no one advocated the reinstatement of Romans and Italians whose civil and political rights had been removed by Sulla. The government gained popularity and strengthened the treasury by recovering funds from Sullan profiteers; but no one dreamed of redistributing land or restoring confiscated property to rightful owners.[140] Structure and institutions were not at issue. The size and disposition of the senate, the *cursus honorum,* the system of criminal courts and legislation, civilian control over provincial commands–all the fundamental pillars of the aristocratic system remained intact. By 70 the senatorial leadership was more secure and more firmly in control than before. The Sullan constitution had been altered only slightly in form, not at all in intent.

[140] On the endurance of Sullan regulations in Etruria and Umbria, see W. V. Harris, *Rome in Etruria and Umbria* (Oxford, 1971), pp. 267–284.

II

POLITICAL ALLIANCES AND ALIGNMENTS

POLITICS IN Rome had traditionally operated through aristocratic combines. A relatively small number of families occupied key positions and controlled the wellsprings of power. Unlike the workings of modern political parties, Roman coalitions relied largely on family ties, marriage alliances, and unofficial pacts for mutual cooperation. Terminology for such combines varied in accordance with the vantage point of the speaker. The members of a group might style themselves *optimates;* and their cooperation would professedly be founded on *amicitia.* But to their political enemies they were no more than a *factio.*[1] Since the virtue or vice of these coalitions lay in the eye of the beholder, we need not pause over the phraseology. The nature of Roman politics, however, merits attention.

Senatorial coteries were never permanent alliances. Their informal nature precluded rigid organization or "party loyalty." Cooperation among certain noble houses in one generation might dissolve into rivalry and feud in the next, or vice versa. But the forms and structure remained reasonably consistent: dynastic families sought and consolidated power through intermarriage, adoptions, *amicitiae,* and competition for *clientelae.* Political warfare among the *nobiles* was fought out in senatorial debate, electoral contests, criminal trials, and disputes over military commands. *Dignitas* and *gloria* were the ends; they were restricted to a comparatively closed circle.

The era between the Gracchi and Sulla added important new dimensions

[1] Cic. *De Rep.* 3.23: *cum autem certi propter divitias aut genus aut aliquas opes rem publicam tenent, est factio, sed vocantur illi optimates*; Sallust, *Iug.* 31.15: *sed hæc inter bonos amicitia, inter malos factio est.* For discussion of some of these terms, see L. R. Taylor, *Party Politics in the Age of Cæsar* (Berkeley and Los Angeles, 1949), pp. 7–15.

to that traditional pattern. Growing self-consciousness among the *plebs,* a more active business community, and a more mobile social structure injected issues into politics which forced themselves on the attention of the aristocracy. Political forms, however, are tenaciously conservative. The Gracchi were promoted by senatorial leaders, Marius sought cooperation and support from the nobility, and Sulla rose to power through the backing of aristocratic families. The changes are detectable not so much in structure as in dynamics. Traditional allegiances among the *nobiles* came under greater pressure; rivalries took on a more volatile character. The men engaged in politics began to represent a broader spectrum: not only *equites* and representatives of Italian municipalities, but old patrician houses that had long been in a state of eclipse and obscurity. Many of them were individuals without previous ties to the *gentes* that had controlled the government in preceding generations. As a result, political alliances shifted more rapidly and more dramatically as aristocrats reacted to or accommodated themselves to changing circumstances. New groupings could spring up at short notice over new issues. Alignments could gravitate around powerful individuals who made military reputations or promoted the claims of the discontented. The Gracchi began as adherents of a political group, but their activities split older loyalties and created a faction of their own. Sulla too was brought into prominence by a senatorial faction, but ended by molding a new group through force of personality and achievements. The forms persisted. But the speed and frequency of realignments became more marked.[2]

Civil wars in the 80s and the tightened regimen of Sulla's dictatorship brought renewed unity to the senatorial class. The insecurity of the early 70s kept the oligarchy harnessed for a time. But rifts reappeared in the later part of the decade. More men were involved in government, and there were more opportunities for new alliances and new leaders. Hence, the emergence of figures like P. Cethegus, M. Crassus, and Cn. Pompeius Magnus. This fragmentation set the stage for succeeding years. Two critical decades elapsed between the consulship of Crassus and Pompey and the civil war that ruined the Republic. How does one analyze the politics of the period? It can be argued that they were very much as they had always been. The great families continued to maintain control through interlocking marriages and adoptions, a whole network of relationships and *amicitiae* which formed the principal branches of the oligarchy. Behind the more publicized activities of military conquerors and demagogic tribunes lay the subtle manipulations of senatorial factions.[3]

[2] The process is examined in detail in Gruen, *Roman Politics, passim.*

[3] Such is the thesis brilliantly researched and formulated by Münzer, *Röm. Adelsp.*, pp. 283–373; followed by Syme, *Rom. Rev.*, pp. 10–46.

By contrast, however, one can point to numerous instances in the 60s and 50s where reconstruction along customary lines breaks down. Marriage connections between noble houses no longer guarantee political cooperation; members of the same family are found with conflicting interests and policies. Individuals appear to shift public stance indiscriminately. So, it has been said, political arrangements, when they exist, are makeshift and ad hoc. No factional or familial basis is discernible.[4]

It will not be obligatory to select between these two alternatives. The former ignores significant changes which Roman society and politics had undergone since the era of the Gracchi. Links among noble houses cannot by themselves explain the course of politics. Too many other elements, social, economic, and personal, permeated the scene. In a constantly changing political climate, those links did not possess consistency or endurance. The alternative view, however, would appear to deny all structure to Roman politics. Aristocratic families continued to form marriage connections, to adopt relatives and friends, to flaunt their *amici,* and to feud with their *inimici.* It would be foolish to imagine that these maneuvers possessed no political connotations.

What marks the Ciceronian age is a persistent tension between the old categories of political behavior and the onrush of events that appeared to outstrip them. The nobility continued to think in terms of compacts cemented by personal and familial alliance. That attitude was as common to Pompey, Cæsar, and Crassus as it was to the Metelli, the Claudii, and the Luculli. But the fluidity of combines is even more apparent. The process of splintering that had begun in the later 70s accelerated in the following two decades. At the same time, the numbers and types of men engaged in public affairs had considerably increased. Some attached themselves to noble families, others were attracted to individual leaders and formed new groups. Men without long-standing ties to traditional patrons could shift allegiance easily. The units of political combination were now diverse. One must look not only to bonds among *nobiles,* but to individuals who, through force of personality, prestige, or accomplishment, could frame their own alliances and attract their own following. Attitudes overlap and converge. Pompey's remarkable military career brought him numerous adherents, but he also secured connections with dominant houses of the aristocracy. Cæsar won a reputation by espousing popular causes, but he did not lack associations in the nobility. Crassus could claim a much more distinguished family, yet he preferred to accumulate power without cooperating with leading *nobiles.* Although families like the Metelli maintained fierce family pride, they did not operate as a political unit. Individuals like Catulus and the younger Cato were influential figures

[4] For this view, see Meier's important work, *Res Pub., passim*; esp., pp. 174–200.

not so much through a nexus of relationships as through their own personality or vigor. One cannot minimize the complexities. But structure and pattern are recoverable.

TENSIONS IN THE NOBILITAS

Roman politicians did not normally divide on matters of principle. The term *optimates* identified no political group. Cicero, in fact, could stretch the term to encompass not only aristocratic leaders but also Italians, rural dwellers, businessmen, and even freedmen. His criteria demanded only that they be honest, reasonable, and stable. It was no more than a means of expressing approbation.[5] Romans would have even greater difficulty in comprehending the phrase "senatorial party." Virtually all figures of note in the late Republic were members of the senate. The phrase originates in an older scholarship, which misapplied analogies and reduced Roman politics to a contest between the "senatorial party" and the "popular party." Such labels obscure rather than enlighten understanding. But there were certain senatorial leaders, *principes,* who stood out in ability or prestige and who exercised weight in aristocratic circles. Without affixing labels, it will be salutary to note some of them.

Three *principes,* linked by relations and attitudes, held particular prominence in the 60s: Q. Lutatius Catulus, Q. Hortensius, and L. Licinius Lucullus. If Cicero is to be believed, no one carried more prestige and authority than Q. Catulus. His activities in the 70s have already been delineated. He had led the opposition to reform of the tribunate in the middle of that decade. But by 70 he recognized that resistance was no longer necessary. It was doubtless Catulus' acquiescence, above all, which permitted smooth restoration of tribunician powers and reform of the courts. He was the senate's most eminent member and the framer of public policy.[6] In 67 and 66, when debate ensued over Pompey's eastern commands, it was the weight of Catulus' objections which caused greatest hesitation. Gabinius in 67 assumed that a favorable word from Catulus would bring all objectors into line. And when Catulus argued that extraordinary powers should not be concentrated in a single individual, lest he perish in the course of service, the people unanimously shouted that in that event the powers could be bestowed upon Catulus himself. When he withdrew his objection the measure passed.[7] Catulus remained preeminent in the 60s and attained the coveted censorship in 65. His death in 61 or

[5] Cic. *Pro Sest.* 96–98: *qui et integri sunt et sani et bene de rebus domesticis constituti.*

[6] Cic. *In Pis.* 6: *Q. Catulus, princeps huius ordinis et auctor publici consilii.*

[7] Vell. Pat. 2.32.1–2; Dio, 36.36a; Val. Max. 8.15.9; cf. Cic. *De Imp. Pomp.* 59–61.

60 left a noticeable gap. Cicero felt the loss: the sole mainstay of right-mindedness was gone. The obituary by Dio Cassius called Catulus the foremost champion of the public interest. His name was invoked *honoris causa* on numerous occasions in subsequent years.[8]

Associated with him, in more than one important situation, was Q. Hortensius, the husband of Catulus' sister. Hortensius did not have his brother-in-law's reputation for integrity. But if Catulus won admiration for his character, Hortensius secured it through talent and energy. Until Cicero surpassed him, Hortensius was Rome's most celebrated orator. He possessed a prodigious memory, a vibrant, sonorous voice, and boundless industry and enthusiasm. Those qualities catapulted him to the forefront of orators while he was still a youth in the 90s and 80s. He was tireless in the law courts and much sought after as a defense counsel. High principle, to be sure, was not Hortensius' chief characteristic. At times, he might stoop to shady practices; we have already noted his use of marked ballots when defending his cousin Terentius Varro in 74. And there was some suggestion that he had received large bribes from Verres to take his case in 70. The reports did not affect his standing. Hortensius reached the consulship in 69 and joined Catulus in opposing Pompey's military commissions in 67 and 66. Cicero's references to him in that connection make it clear that he was a formidable, eloquent, and powerful opponent. Hortensius' oratory itself was more impressive in his youth than in his riper years, when the ponderous rhetoric fell a little flat. And he began to prefer the luxuries of leisure which his wealth afforded him: vast estates, an art collection, and fish ponds. The fanaticism in care and concern for his bearded mullets became a standing joke. He took to writing: rhetorical treatises, a history, and a good deal of poetry. But Hortensius did not withdraw from the public arena. He continued to be an active voice in the courts until his death in 50. Cicero, who had had his rifts with Hortensius and who knew his failings, could genuinely mourn his loss.[9]

Of this trio, L. Lucullus was the ablest. He was a man of cultivated tastes, with a thorough education in Greek and Latin letters, a devotee of philosophic discussion, a student of philosophy, and a patron of philosophers. Although

[8] Cic. *Ad Att.* 1.20.3: *me hanc viam optimatem post Catuli mortem nec præsidio ullo nec comitatu tenere*; Dio, 37.46.3. Cf. Cic. *Pro Cæl.* 59; *Pro Sest.* 101, 122; *P. Red. in Sen.* 9; *De Domo*, 113.

[9] The fullest description of Hortensius' career and his oratory is in Cic. *Brutus*, 1–6, 228–230, 301–303, 308, 317–330. On the trial of Varro, see above, chap. 1, n.83; for hints of bribery by Verres, see, e.g., Cic. *Verr.* 2.2.192; on Hortensius' opposition to Pompey's commands, see Cic. *De Imp. Pomp.* 51–53. On luxury and fish ponds, see, esp., Varro, *De Re Rust.* 3.13.2, 3.17.5–8; art collection, Pliny, *NH*, 34.48, 35.130. Other references in vonder Mühl, *RE*, 8:2470–2481, "Hortensius," n.13. But his oratorical powers were still undiminished in 56; cf. Cic. *Pro Sest.* 3.

not an orator of any note, Lucullus earned distinction in the literary sphere: his history of the Social War, written in Greek, was still read in Plutarch's day. Sulla showed the utmost confidence in him. The dictator entrusted to Lucullus the execution of his will, the publication of his memoirs, and the education of his son. Intellectual accomplishments did not exhaust his talents; Lucullus was a military man of great capacity. He had already served notice of his abilities in the Social War under Sulla and again in the Mithridatic war of the 80s, once more under Sulla's command. In 74, Lucullus employed dubious means to secure the Mithridatic command himself. But the war he waged for seven years in Asia Minor and Armenia fully justified the appointment. Lucullus not only gained military successes, but also proved to be a sound and forceful administrator. He cracked down hard on the extortionate practices of moneylenders in Asia, and reorganized and revitalized the province. That brought him the gratitude and favor of the Asian cities, but it also called down the wrath of the business community in Rome. His victories fell short of completion. A haughty aristocrat and stern disciplinarian, Lucullus paid insufficient heed to the grievances of his own soldiers. Mutinous activity in the army and the pressures of Lucullus' enemies in Rome brought about his recall and replacement by Pompey in 66. Exploits abroad produced only frustration at home. A triumph was delayed for three years, and Pompey's successes cast Lucullus' important accomplishments into the shade. But Lucullus remained a powerful figure in the senate until 59. After that he preferred the comforts of his own estates and villas, and developed a reputation for luxury and liberality unsurpassed by any of his contemporaries. His gardens, his parks, and his lavish dinners gained notoriety. But Lucullus was also, until his death in 56, a great collector of art, the possessor of a magnificent library, and a tireless organizer of intellectual discussions.[10]

Close relations prevailed among Lucullus, Catulus, and Hortensius. There was cultural camaraderie between Hortensius and Lucullus; both were patrons of the Greek poet Archias.[11] All three shared a political antipathy to Pompeius Magnus. The opposition of Catulus and Hortensius to Pompey's eastern commands had as its principal object the prevention of Lucullus' recall. It is fitting, in view of their collaboration, that Cicero's dialogue the *Hortensius* had as interlocutors Q. Catulus, Q. Hortensius, and L. Lucullus, gathered in the country villa of Lucullus.[12]

[10] On Lucullus' intellectual attainments, see, esp., the flattering comment by Cicero, *Acad. Prior.* 2.4; cf. Plut. *Luc.* 1.3–5, 42.1–4. For sources and discussion of his career, one may consult the biography by J. Van Ooteghem, *Lucius Licinius Lucullus* (Brussels, 1959), *passim.*

[11] Cic. *Pro Arch.* 6. Hortensius and Lucullus were friends from youth; Plut. *Luc.* 1.5.

[12] Cic. *Acad. Prior.* 2.148. Cicero had originally considered making the three men interlocutors in his *Academica*; Cic. *Ad Att.* 13.16.1, 13.19.5.

This group, which had wielded considerable influence in the senate for two decades, faded into the background in the 50s. Catulus perished in 61 or 60, and Lucullus moved into retirement in 59. Hortensius appears to have confined his activities in the 50s largely to the courts. But relatives and sympathizers of these individuals moved into the forefront to take up the slack. The group revolved now around the imposing figure of M. Porcius Cato. One can point to marriage links that cemented Cato's relations to the others. Lucullus, probably in the mid-60s, put away his first wife because of her promiscuity and married Servilia, Cato's half-sister. The choice was not felicitous: Servilia proved to be no more chaste than her predecessor. But Lucullus retained the connection for some time, out of regard for his brother-in-law.[13] Hortensius was Cato's intimate companion and associate. He sought Cato's daughter in marriage and received even better: Cato's wife. Hortensius wanted heirs, and Cato had enough; hence the generous exchange.[14] The relationship went further: Hortensius' daughter, it seems, was the wife of Cato's stepbrother, Q. Servilius Cæpio.[15] No marriage tie is on record between Cato and Q. Catulus, but the two men were close friends, with admiration and respect for each other.[16] Cato pursued the policies of the group, especially in opposition to Pompey and the Pompeians. It was Cato who helped to steel Lucullus' resolve in pressing senatorial rejection of Pompey's eastern arrangements in 60.[17] And Lucullus' withdrawal from the political arena left leadership in the hands of Cato.[18] Other marital alliances can be discerned, linking Cato to families of the nobility, such as the Livii Drusi, the Servilii Cæpiones, the Junii Silani, the Marcii Philippi.

But Cato's career cannot be explained by a nexus of connections. He had already vaulted into prominence in 63 when he was in his early thirties and when he had held no office higher than the quæstorship. At an age when most senators, even of the most noble stock, rarely ventured to utter a sound in the *curia,* Cato's was already a compelling voice. Obviously, strength of personality conveyed him into the front ranks.

It will not be necessary to dwell at length upon Cato's character, about which so much has been written. His suicide at Utica in 46, a dramatic protest against Cæsar's dictatorship, earned him the *cognomen* Uticensis and everlasting repute. For the enemies of Cæsar, and the opponents of monarchy under the emperors, Cato was the very symbol of the Roman Republic. Consequently,

[13] Plut. *Luc.* 38.1; *Cato,* 24.3, 54.1.
[14] Plut. *Cato,* 25.2–5; Appian, *BC,* 2.99; Lucan, 2.325 ff.
[15] See the reconstruction by Münzer, *Röm. Adelsp.,* 342–347.
[16] Plut. *Cato,* 16.4–6.
[17] Dio, 37.50.1; Plut. *Pomp.* 46.3; *Luc.* 42.6; *Cato,* 31.1.
[18] Plut. *Luc.* 42.4–5.

the legend of his steadfastness and foresight grew apace.[19] Shortly after his death, it could already be said that "Cato foresaw what has come to pass and what will be; he struggled to prevent it and perished lest he witness it."[20]

But Cato won the respect also of his contemporaries. He was a resolute Stoic, not only in pursuing the philosophic doctrines of that sect. but in applying them to his political behavior. Cicero twitted him once for inflexible adherence to impossible dogmas. And the orator also could lament, in a private letter, that Cato always spoke as if he lived in the Republic of Plato rather than in the sewer of Romulus.[21] But Cicero's fits of pique need not be taken too seriously. In general, he reserved the utmost praise for Cato: a man of great seriousness, incorruptible, and blessed with a noble spirit; none surpassed him in integrity, wisdom, courage, and patriotism. "Cato was worth a hundred thousand men."[22] Similar sentiments were expressed by Sallust: Cato was preeminent in uprightness. self-control, and austerity; he preferred to be rather than seem virtuous.[23] Moderns have too often written him off as espousing Utopian ideas, as obstinate and uncompromising. But motivation by high principle could coexist with practical politics. Cato was not averse to sponsoring grain laws, thereby outbidding his opponents, or to indulging in bribery, if this could bring supporters into power. And his firm opposition to Cæsar and Pompey, it can be argued, was deliberately calculated to drive them to extreme positions and to undermine their own standing. A series of measures or attempted measures, reformist and progressive, stand to his credit. Politics, administration, the judiciary, foreign policy, legislative activity—all areas felt Cato's presence. He was completely enmeshed in public affairs, not Utopianism. Cato's policies, when properly analyzed, show a shrewdness and penetration which scholars have not always acknowledged.[24]

[19] Lucan's *Pharsalia* is the most eloquent surviving testament to that tradition. On the Cato legend, cf. the remarks of Taylor, *Party Politics,* pp. 162–182; R. MacMullen, *Enemies of the Roman Order* (Cambridge, Mass., 1966), pp. 1–45.

[20] Cic. *Ad Att.* 12.4.2: *quod ille ea quæ nunc sunt et futura viderit et ne fierent contenderit et facta ne viderit vitam reliquerit.*

[21] Cic. *Ad Att.* 2.1.8: *dicit enim tamquam in Platonis* πολιτείᾳ, *non tamquam in Romuli fæce, sententiam.* For Cicero's ridiculing of Cato's rigid Stoicism, see *Pro Mur.* 61–66. The criticism was rhetorical and excessive. Cato disarmed his critic by a quick retort; Plut. *Cato,* 21.5.

[22] Cic. *Ad Att.* 2.5.1: *Cato ille noster qui mihi unus est pro centum milibus; Pro Sest.* 60: *quid gravitas, quid integritas, quid magnitudo animi, quid denique virtus valeret; De Domo,* 21: *sanctissimum, prudentissimum, fortissimum, amicissimum rei publicæ, virtute, consilio, ratione vitæ mirabili ad laudem et prope singulari.*

[23] Sallust, *Cat.* 54.2–6: *huic severitas dignitatem addiderat . . . Catoni studium modestiæ, decoris, sed maxume severitatis erat . . . esse quam videri bonus malebat.*

[24] Note, for example, Cato's calculated obstructionism in 55, designed to multiply grievances

Cato burst into the limelight in 63. His blistering speech in the senate rallied that body to decisive action against the Catilinarian conspirators. Julius Cæsar had counseled moderation, and senatorial opinion appeared to have acquiesced. The *auctoritas* of Q. Catulus, however, interposed itself. And then his young friend delivered the oration that successfully urged the extreme penalty.[25] Cato's reputation was made. He proceeded to block efforts to summon Pompey from the East, lest more military power be gathered into his hands: a strong government at home could handle domestic emergencies. Already by late 63 Cato's influence and reputation were such that the opposing counsel in a criminal case feared that his very presence might be tantamount to conviction of the defendant.[26] After the death of Catulus, Cato became the senate's foremost spokesman and the most fearsome obstacle to the ambitions of certain other politicians.

It would do Cato insufficient justice to label him simply the leader of a faction. Sallust avows that Cato did not compete with the rich in riches or the factious in factional intrigue.[27] Conviction in his own rectitude could induce him to deliver a lesson in virtue even to Q. Catulus or to prosecute for electoral bribery an associate of L. Lucullus.[28] The force and fire of his personality weighed more heavily than familial connections. Cato represented for the aristocracy a nobility of purpose and principle that they liked to associate with their whole order. Therein perhaps lay the attractiveness of his policy.

But Cato did not stand alone. Nor was his circle of *adfines* irrelevant. Cato's firmest associates and supporters were L. Domitius Ahenobarbus, who married his sister, and M. Calpurnius Bibulus, who was the husband of his daughter. Neither man possessed the abilities of Cato. Bibulus received much praise for his courage and tenacity. But less kindly observers adjudged his steadfastness to be stubbornness. In the forum he was dull of speech; in the field he was cruel and irascible. His talent was fitted less for shrewdness

---

against his enemies; Dio, 39.34. Cato's activities will be described in greater detail below. On his career generally, see the articles of Gelzer, *Kleine Schriften,* II:257–285; A. Afzelius, *ClMed,* 4 (1941): 100–203; and Fr. Miltner, *RE,* 22:168–211, "Porcius," n.16. For his policy in the 50s, see the illuminating remarks of Meier, *Res Pub.*, pp. 270–288; and, now, the trenchant article of A. Dragstedt, *Agon,* 3 (1969): 69–96.

[25] The fullest account is in Sallust, *Cat.* 50–55, who gives his own version of Cato's speech. That Catulus was the first to oppose Cæsar's motion is affirmed by Plut. *Cic.* 21.3; cf. *Cæs.* 8.1; Cic. *Ad Att.* 12.21.1.

[26] Cic. *Pro Mur.* 58–60. On Cato's blocking of Pompey's recall, see Meier, *Athenæum,* 40 (1962): 103–125.

[27] Sallust, *Cat.* 54.6: *non divitiis cum divite neque factione cum factioso.*

[28] For the reproof of Catulus, see Plut. *Cato,* 16.4–6. L. Murena, whom Cato prosecuted in 63, was a former officer of Lucullus'; Cic. *Pro Mur.* 20, 34.

than for malevolence.[29] Bibulus was an exact contemporary of Cæsar, sharing magistracies with him, but consistently eclipsed and frustrated by him.[30] The rivalry spilled into hatred and rancor in their joint consulship of 59. Domitius owned greater weight and nobler birth. Cicero could describe him as consul-designate in infancy. He was a cousin of Catulus', as well as Cato's brother-in-law. Inherited property swelled in the Sullan proscriptions: Domitius controlled large estates in Italy. Dogged and proud, he boasted of his influence in the city and of his *dignitas.* That aristocratic pride made him, even in his youth, a fierce opponent of demagogic activities.[31] Domitius had a hereditary feud with Pompey, who had slain his brother in the civil wars of the 80s. And he served notice of his political attitude in the mid-60s, harrying the Pompeian tribune C. Manilius.[32] Domitius and Cato undertook political collaboration in 61 against Pompey's consular candidate. The relationship endured through the 50s against the machinations of Pompey and Cæsar.[33] Bibulus and Domitius could be counted on by Cato for steady cooperation in reducing the influence of Cæsarians and Pompeians in Roman politics.

Other, lesser figures attached themselves to this group. M. Favonius was a zealous admirer and imitator of Cato, though he lacked his friend's stature. The boldness of speech that marked Cato's demeanor became recklessness and impertinence in Favonius. He was impulsive, so the ancients report, almost to the point of frenzy. But Favonius' reputation gives him perhaps less than he deserved. If his speeches were inelegant, they were often effective. And he could display a caustic wit, usually at Pompey's expense. Cato found him a dependable ally. The two men were to be seen shoulder to shoulder on several key political occasions in the 50s. Favonius' name eventually became synonymous with unbending Republicanism.[34] Another of Cato's imitators

[29] [Sallust], *Ep. ad Cæs.* 9.1: *M. Bibuli fortitudo atque animi vis in consulatum erupit; hebes lingua, magis malus quam callidus ingenio*; Cic. *Brutus,* 267: *cum præsertim non esset orator, et egit multa constanter; Phil.* 13.29: *M. Bibulum cuius est in rem publicam semper merito laudata constantia; Inv. in Sall.* 12: *Bibuli patientiam culpavi.* On his cruelty and irascibility, see Cæs. *BC,* 3.14.3, 3.16.3. Cf. on Bibulus, J. H. Collins, *CJ,* 50 (1955): 261–270.

[30] The frustration began already in a joint ædileship of 65; Suet. *Iul.* 10.

[31] On his noble birth, see Cic. *Ad Att.* 4.8a.2: *qui tot annos quot habet designatus consul fuerit.* On his Italian property, Cæs. *BC,* 1.17; Dio, 41.11.1–2. For his character, cf. Cæs. *BC,* 3.83: *Domitius urbanam gratiam dignitatemque iactaret*; Cic. *Pro Mil.* 22: *dederas enim quam contemneres popularis insanias iam ab adulescentia documenta maxima*; Cic. *Brutus,* 267. Cf., on Domitius, A. Burns, *Historia,* 15 (1966): 75–79.

[32] Asconius, 45, Clark; Schol. Bob. 119, Stangl.

[33] For cooperation in 61, see Cic. *Ad Att.* 1.16.12. Activities in the 50s will be discussed below.

[34] For Favonius' aping of Cato, see Plut. *Cato,* 46–1; *Cæs.*.21.4, 41.2; *Pomp.* 60.4; *Brutus,* 12.3, 34.2; Dio, 38.7.1; Suet. *Aug.* 13; cf. Val. Max. 2.10.8; Plut. *Cato,* 32.6. On his excitable character, see Plut. *Cato,* 46.1; *Cæs.* 41.2; *Pomp.* 60.4; *Brutus,* 34.2–4; his jibes at Pompey,

was P. Servilius Isauricus, the future consul of 48. Servilius remained for a long time under the thumb of his father, a harsh disciplinarian who believed in meting out punishment to his children even after they had reached maturity. But the younger Servilius married Cato's niece in or about the year 60 and dutifully pursued the policies and politics of his new *adfinis*. On more than one occasion in 60 and in the 50s, he engaged in public at the side of Cato, of Bibulus, and of Favonius.[35]

The group was cohesive and formidable: Cato, Domitius, Bibulus, Favonius, Servilius. They were all born between ca. 102 and 90, came to public notice by the late 60s, and cooperated prominently in the 50s. And, with the exception of Favonius, they were all related by marriage. This circle of aristocrats inherited a central role in senatorial politics from the coalition of Catulus, Lucullus, and Hortensius. Indeed, Hortensius was still active in conjunction with the Catonian group in the 50s.

But there was a difference, and an important one. Catulus, Lucullus, and Hortensius had begun their political careers in the 90s and had become leading figures in the oligarchy established in power by Sulla. Their acme came in the 70s, when protection of that establishment and their own positions within it was of paramount concern. Hence, their somewhat doctrinaire stands and conservative disposition as senior statesmen in the 60s are explicable.[36] The Catonian group, by contrast, belongs to the post-Sullan generation. They were too young to have engaged in a meaningful way in the civil wars of the 80s or to have felt the insecurities of men in power during the decade after Sulla's death. They inherited a going concern; they could afford the luxury of a more flexible attitude and a more aggressive politics. The notion that Cato and his *amici* represented a rigid, uncompromising conservatism will be shown, in other contexts, to be serious misjudgment. The difference in generations was critical.

It is to this collection of prominent aristocrats, from Catulus to Favonius, that moderns have traditionally applied the epithets *optimates* or "senatorial party." But they do not by any means exhaust the influential personages in the Roman senate. Not all noble families followed their lead, not even families who can be shown to have had marriage connections with them.

Val. Max. 6.2.7; Plut. *Caes.* 41.2; *Pomp.* 60.4; Appian, *BC*, 2.37. For his later reputation for firm Republicanism, see Cic. *Ad Att.* 12.44.3, 15.29.2. The pseudo-Sallustian, *Ep. ad Caes.*, links together Cato, Domitius, Bibulus, Favonius, and L. Postumius as the *factio nobilitatis*; 8.6–9.4. Postumius, unfortunately, is otherwise unknown.

[35] On Servilius' upbringing, see Quint. *Inst. Orat.* 6.3.25, 6.3.48; his cooperation with Cato, Bibulus, and Favonius: Cic. *Ad Att.* 1.19.9, 2.1.10, 4.18.4; *Ad Q. Frat.* 2.3.2, 3.4.6. Cicero describes him as Cato's *aemulator*; *Ad Att.* 2.1.10.

[36] Cf. Catulus' stand in 66; Cic. *De Imp. Pomp.* 60: *ne quid novi fiat contra exempla atque instituta maiorum.*

Several powerful clans of the *nobilitas* played important roles in the Ciceronian age. But those roles were independent and shifting.

The great *gens* of the Cæcilii Metelli remained an imposing force. Its fecundity proved to be a valuable asset: five consulships in the 60s and 50s. The stature of the family in the past had been adorned by calculated alliances. And that policy endured. The Metelli show links by marriage to Lucullus and to P. Servilius Isauricus.[37] At the same time there was double connection to the house of M. Crassus. Crassus' two sons married daughters of Metelli. And, equally significant, Pompeius Magnus was the husband of a half-sister of the Metelli.[38] The bonds with various powerful figures might be expected to keep the Metelli in a pivotal position, manipulating public affairs through their *adfines*. That had been a large factor in Metellan success during previous years. But the results proved now to be very different—and symptomatic. Instead of solidifying their own dominance, the associations with warring political leaders tended to split the family itself. So, for example, Q. Metellus Creticus, the consul of 69, clashed with Pompey over rival military claims in the Ægean and later joined with Lucullus and Cato in undermining Pompey's eastern arrangements. But Metellus Celer and Metellus Nepos, Pompey's brothers-in-law, served with him in those eastern campaigns, and Nepos, in defending Pompey's interests at home, found himself in violent confrontation with Cato. Q. Metellus Pius, the consul of 80, is attested in the mid-60s as cooperating with Hortensius and the Luculli. But his adopted son, Q. Metellus Pius Scipio, contracted a personal feud with Cato and in 60 suffered prosecution at the hands of Favonius.[39]

It does not follow that the Metelli had dissolved as a family unit. On the level of the clan, there could be solidarity still, as Metellus Celer pointedly reminded Cicero in a letter: *familiæ nostræ dignitas*.[40] The Metelli were united also in defense of their *adfinis* and client C. Verres in 70. What one can discern in the next two decades, however, is a growing tension between the claims of the *gens* and the demands of politics. The pull of the former retained its force, but it could not always surmount political exigencies. The tension

[37] Lucullus was the son of a Cæcilia Metella; Cic. *Verr.* 2.4.147; *P. Red. in Sen.* 37; *P. Red. ad Quir.* 6; Plut. *Luc.* 1.1. Servilius was grandson of another Cæcilia Metella; Münzer, *RE*, 2(2):1812, "Servilius," n.93.

[38] For Crassus' sons, see *ILS*, 881; Plut. *Pomp.* 55.1; for Pompey's marriage, see above, chap. 1, n.40.

[39] On Pompey and the Metelli, cf. Gruen, *Historia*, 18 (1969): 75, 82–83. For Metellus Pius' appearance at the trial of Cornelius, with Hortensius and the Luculli, see Asconius, 60, 79, Clark; Val. Max. 8.5.4. For Metellus Scipio's feud with Cato, see Plut. *Cato*, 7.1–2; his prosecution by Favonius, Cic. *Ad Att.* 2.1.9.

[40] Cic. *Ad Fam.* 5.1.1. On this affair, see Ooteghem, *LEC*, 25 (1957): 168–172, who has, however, nothing to say that is new.

warrants emphasis. Perhaps more than any other single element, it distinguishes the politics of this period from earlier eras. Clearly one cannot talk of "Metellan politics" as if membership in that family identified one's political allegiances or attitudes. The *gens* was still an object of loyalty; the marriage alliance was still a political act. But, in the more volatile atmosphere of the late Republic, the marriage alliance often served (however unintentionally) to undermine rather than to consolidate the political unity of the *gens*.

The Metelli represent only one example of this tension. The patrician house of the Cornelii Lentuli was also prominent in the counsels of the aristocracy. Five Lentuli reached the consulship between 72 and 49, and a sixth was a near miss. Family unity could make itself felt on the public scene. At the trial of Clodius in 61 three Lentuli combined their talents as prosecutors. On other occasions, however, extraneous political considerations might divide members of the clan. In 70 the censors were persuaded to take their role as moral reformers seriously; they conducted a purge of the senate. One of the censors was Cn. Cornelius Lentulus Clodianus; one of his victims was P. Cornelius Lentulus Sura. In 56 dispute arose over a prospective military command in Egypt. P. Lentulus Spinther coveted the job and had received senatorial endorsement. But the commission was blocked, and the man chiefly responsible was the consul of 56, Cn. Lentulus Marcellinus.[41]

Similar vicissitudes can be discerned in the patrician family of the Claudii Pulchri. Three brothers from that house, and three sisters, were conspicuous in the Ciceronian age. Their notoriety came both through public affairs and through private licentiousness. Political collaboration among the brothers is attested, particularly in the early 50s. But there were complications. Ap. Claudius Pulcher, the eldest of the three and their provider after his father's death, fostered his political career through important marriage alliances. One sister was married to Lucullus, another to Metellus Celer. One daughter was the wife of M. Brutus, the nephew of Cato; the other was later given in marriage to Pompey's eldest son. The opportunistic Appius followed no consistent political line. His attitudes and his fortunes shifted; none could claim him as a reliable ally. The same was true, doubly, of his brother P. Clodius. That capricious individual served abroad in the 60s with his brother-in-law Lucullus, only to arouse mutiny in the ranks. His activities there presaged the more spectacular demagoguery of the 50s, when Clodius' explosive political stands combined with dramatic transfers of allegiance. The Claudii provide a particularly good example of the changing character of older political categories.[42]

[41] On Lentuli at the trial of Clodius, see Cic. *De Har. Resp.* 37; Val. Max. 4.2.5; Schol. Bob. 89, Stangl; the censorship of 70, Broughton, *MRR*, II:127; on friction between Spinther and Marcellinus, Cic. *Ad Fam.* 1.1.2; cf. Gruen, *Historia*, 18 (1969): 81–82.

[42] On the Claudii, cf. Gruen, *Historia*, 18 (1969): 94–95, 101–103.

The Calpurnii Pisones should be cited as well. Theirs was a distinguished family, long a power in the Roman senate. Three Pisones earned consulships in the Ciceronian period, a fourth gained the prætorship, and two others perished prematurely after their quæstorships. Late Republican politics, however, fragmented the *gens*. C. Piso, the consul of 67, was an associate of Catulus, Hortensius, and Bibulus, and an unrelenting foe of Julius Cæsar. By contrast, his relative, L. Piso Cæsoninus, consul in 58, became Cæsar's father-in-law. The latter endured brutal verbal assault from the tongue of Cicero. But still another Piso, a quæstor in 58, was married to Cicero's daughter. Fragmentation can be documented further. A connection with Crassus, for example, is discovered for Cn. Piso, the quæstor of 65. It is clear that the Pisones formed no cohesive group. But though politics drove members of the clan apart, it could also bring them together. Antipathy toward Pompey provided common ground. The family, certainly as individuals if not as a unit, resisted the ambitions of the general. Their experience reflects once again the complex interplay of personal and political considerations.[43]

One may detect similar elements at play in the attitudes of the Æmilii Lepidi. The consul of 78, the notorious adventurer M. Æmilius Lepidus, had raised insurrection after the death of Sulla. His activities escalated into an attack on the Sullan oligarchy and a threat to the whole system. Yet his cousin Mam. Lepidus, consul in the following year, was a protégé of Sulla's and a dependable member of the oligarchy. He showed no sympathy for Marcus, and his actions in subsequent years reveal growing conservatism. Once more politics caused a parting of the ways. But the post-Sullan generation of Lepidi found that family loyalty could override political considerations. Pompey had been responsible for the demise of M. Lepidus in 77; Lepidus' sons recalled that only too well. Although L. Æmilius Lepidus Paullus and M. Lepidus the younger did not pursue the policies of their father, they perpetuated the feud against Pompey.[44]

Analogous examples could be multiplied. C. Antonius Hybrida, a former officer of Sulla's, suffered prosecution at the hands of Julius Cæsar in the 70s. But his brother, M. Antonius Creticus, married into the Julii Cæsares. And Hybrida's three nephews loyally followed Cæsar in the 50s and 40s. One of them was M. Antonius, the future triumvir. When the latter in 44 drew up a list of exiles to be recalled, he pointedly excluded his uncle.[45] M. Valerius Messalla Niger, the consul of 61, served on the agrarian commis-

[43] For details on the Pisones, see Gruen, *CSCA*, 1 (1968): 155–170.

[44] Cf. Gruen, *Historia*, 18 (1969): 87.

[45] For Cæsar's prosecution of Hybrida, see above, chap. 1, n.114; for the marriage alliance, Plut. *Ant.* 2; on Antony's exclusion of Hybrida, see Cic. *Phil.* 2.55–56; Dio, 46.15.

sion of 59 which distributed land to Pompey's veterans. His cousin, M. Valerius Messalla Rufus, the consul of 53, however, was the nephew of Hortensius and a firm opponent of Pompey.[46]

Other senatorial families carried stature and exercised influence in the late Republic: the Aurelii Cottæ, the Scribonii Curiones, the Cassii Longini, the Claudii Marcelli, the Manlii Torquati. They were aristocrats all, plebeian and patrician. There was no discernible difference in social class or status among them. But political differences did exist, complex and ever changing. The objects of political allegiance varied and, at times, conflicted. Familial pride was no less significant than it had ever been. The *dignitas* of his *gens* always held paramount importance to a Roman aristocrat. His name could win him elections; his inherited clients gave him conspicuous stature. So, the Claudii or the Metelli espoused uncompromising pride in their lineage. So, also, family feuds persisted, whatever the political climate: Luculli and Servilii might agree on policy, but their inherited rivalry brought mutual hostility; the Lepidi, despite political differences, carried familial vengeance against Pompey.

But prestige of the clan might no longer bring as much profit as association with a prominent figure or identification with a popular issue. Such matters could divide families: M. Pupius Piso's loyalty to Pompey isolated him from other Pisones; young C. Scribonius Curio's friendship with M. Antonius incurred the wrath of his father. Expansion of influence through intermarriage or interlocking combines had been a traditional recourse of noble *gentes*. The practice continued, but now it could produce friction rather than unity: the ties of the Metelli to Pompey, to Lucullus, and to Crassus tended to weaken, not strengthen the clan; similarly, the various attachments of the Pisones rendered difficult any cooperation among themselves. Traditional methods of securing alliance were often inconvenient in the face of new political realities. But those traditional methods endured; they formed a counterpoint to the rise of individual leaders, the creation of new groups, and the divisions on issues. Factions can no longer be understood simply in terms of familial relationships. And it is clear that notions like "senatorial party" or "aristocratic party" serve no useful conceptual purpose in understanding the dynamics of late Republican politics. Divergent lines produced the splintering so characteristic of the period. The acceleration of this fragmenting process came in the post-Sullan generation. That is significant. It was precisely because aristocratic control over the governmental machinery was solidified in the decade after Sulla's death that the ruling class could indulge in such divisions without fear of upsetting the structure.

[46] On Niger as an agrarian commissioner, see *ILS*, 46; for Rufus' relation to Hortensius, see Val. Max. 5.9.2; his friction with Pompey, Cic. *Ad Att.* 4.9.1.

POMPEIUS MAGNUS

The most imposing figure to emerge in the aftermath of Sulla was Pompeius Magnus. Ruthlessness and terror had marked his early military years. As defeated foes learned, no mercy could be expected from the man who was termed the "young executioner."[47] But if Pompey's rise to martial prominence had involved considerable carnage, his political career would require different techniques. As we have noted earlier, Pompey demonstrated no small amount of political acumen. It was a standard Pompeian practice to express his own ambitions in terms of the needs and desires of his soldiers.[48] In the field Pompey had emulated the exploits of Alexander the Great.[49] But at home he coveted the reputation of a sober statesman. Senatorial duties were taken seriously; Pompey sought no province after his consulship. He preferred to emphasize his *dignitas* by appearing in public accompanied by large throngs of adherents.[50] He assumed the traditional posture of the aristocrat. Good training in Greek and Latin letters gave him a taste for cultural matters. Pompey became an orator of some distinction and also dabbled in literature.[51] He took pride in his association with and patronage of Greek poets, authors, and intellectuals. Close friends like L. Lucceius, Terentius Varro, and Theophanes were literary figures who served also as political advisers.[52] Pompey desired prestige within the ruling class.

Alliance with houses of the nobility, the customary path to political respectability, was the path which Pompey trod. Indeed, Pompey's gathering of support among aristocrats became the single most important factor in scrambling older senatorial loyalties. His connections were manifold. Not the least of them bound Pompey to the house of Sulla himself. He had divorced his first wife in 81 to marry the stepdaughter of the dictator. Through Sulla's son Faustus, his stepson M. Scaurus, and through the family of the Memmii, related by marriage to both Pompey and Sulla, the connections, reinforced by several strands, persisted at least to the mid-50s. Pompey could regard

[47] Val. Max. 6.2.8: *adulescentulus carnifex.*

[48] Cf. Plut. *Pomp.* 13–14, 17.3, 30; Sallust, *Hist.* 2.98, Maur.

[49] Sallust, *Hist.* 3.88, Maur.: *sed Pompeius a prima adulescentia sermone fautorum similem fore se credens Alexandro regi, facta consultaque eius quidem æmulus erat*; cf. Plut. *Pomp.* 2.1–2, 12.3, 13.5.

[50] Plut. *Pomp.* 23.3–4.

[51] On his oratory, see Cic. *Brutus,* 239; cf. *De Imp. Pomp.* 42; *Pro Sest.* 107; as a writer and intellect, Cic. *Ad Att.* 7.17.2; *Pro Balbo,* 15.

[52] Pompey's literary interests and his associations with intellectuals are admirably discussed by W. S. Anderson, *Pompey, His Friends, and the Literature of the First Century* B.C. (Berkeley and Los Angeles, 1963), pp. 28–82. One should add also T. Ampius Balbus, historian and biographer; Cic. *Ad Fam.* 6.12.5; cf. Suet. *Iul.* 77. But it is too extravagant to compare Pompey's patronage of literature, as Anderson does, with the court of a Hellenistic monarch.

himself as the heir of Sulla in more than one respect. The ever astute clan of the Metelli had helped promote Sulla's career. And when Pompey's star rose, they were swift to form a new tie: the general married Mucia, half-sister to Q. Metellus Celer and Q. Metellus Nepos. Members of other noble clans also saw profit in attaching themselves to a man already covered with laurels. In 67 Pompey was engaged by the state to eliminate the menace of piracy in the Mediterranean; and in the following year he gained supreme command against Mithridates, replacing in that task L. Licinius Lucullus. Lucullus' friends and political allies objected. But a large number of aristocrats from Rome's noblest families either supported the commissions or joined Pompey's staff to serve under him abroad. Four men of distinguished stock who had held consulships in the 70s spoke up on behalf of Pompey's Mithridatic command: P. Servilius Vatia, C. Scribonius Curio, C. Cassius Longinus, and Cn. Lentulus Clodianus. The two consuls of 72 accepted subordinate positions under Pompey abroad. And his staff included numerous patricians and illustrious plebeians: two Lentuli, two Manlii Torquati, two Metelli, Claudius Nero, Aemilius Scaurus, Cornelius Sulla, Valerius Flaccus, Pupius Piso, Octavius, Plautius Hypsæus.[53] Of Pompey's legates several were older than he; most were of more distinguished families. It is evident that the attraction of Pompeius Magnus outweighed for many the older allegiances to family or faction. Pompey, for his part, could gain much from the prestige of contact with Rome's senatorial nobility.

Pompey's following went beyond the confines of the old aristocracy. From his father he inherited loyal clients and a virtual barony in Picenum. Some of his adherents, from lesser families, seem to possess Picene origins. L. Afranius served his chief loyally in Spain and in the East, and eventually received his support for a consulship in 60. T. Labienus, who later earned a place among Rome's finest military men, also stemmed from Picenum and advanced Pompey's interests in the 60s. The veteran soldier M. Petreius spent the bulk of his life in the service, much of it in the entourage of Pompey or Pompeians. A. Gabinius was active in politics as well as war, employing demagoguery and threats in support of Pompey's commission against the pirates. He proved to be an effective politician, gained military experience under Pompey, and ennobled his family with a consulship in 58.[54] Other partisans of humble backgrounds warrant mention. M. Lollius Palicanus, also from Picenum, concerted his efforts with Pompey in securing tribunician reform in 71 and 70,

[53] Sources on Pompey's legates in Broughton, *MRR*, II:148–149. For a fuller discussion, see Gruen, *Historia*, 18 (1969): 74–77.

[54] On Pompey's Picene following, see the discussion by Syme, *Rom. Rev.*, p. 31. On Labienus, see Syme, *JRS*, 28 (1938); 113–125; on Gabinius' early career, see Badian, *Philologus*, 103 (1959): 87–99.

and later combined efforts with Gabinius in 67. C. Cornelius had been Pompey's quæstor in Spain in the 70s and was also an active Pompeian tribune in 67.[55]

Professional military men made reputations as Pompeian officers, and some reached high magisterial posts in Rome as a consequence. Similarly, Pompey attracted men from the Italian municipalities and countryside. In addition to the dynast's supporters from Picenum, there were individuals like his *adfinis* Lucilius Hirrus, who owned estates in Bruttium; T. Annius Milo from Lanuvium; C. Messius, probably of Campanian origin; and the great scholar Terentius Varro, with vast property in the Sabine country.[56] And one cannot neglect the ambitious orator from an equestrian family in Arpinum. M. Tullius Cicero in 66 delivered an encomiastic speech, extolling the virtues of Pompey and urging his fitness for the Mithridatic command. It would be unjust to label the Arpinate simply as a "Pompeian." But Cicero recognized the political value of expressing public praise of the general. In addition to the speech of 66, he defended Pompey's friends, Cornelius and Manilius, in the mid-60s, and sprinkled his consular orations of 63 with laudations of Pompey.[57] There were, no doubt, many other *equites,* especially the moneyed interests, who looked forward to gain from Pompey's clearing-out of the pirates and elimination of the Mithridatic threat to the rich province of Asia.

Pompey was generous also with the franchise. The Spanish magnate L. Cornelius Balbus owed his citizenship to the general, as did Theophanes, a Greek intellectual from Mitylene. Both men went on to play important roles in the Roman political scene. Several lesser individuals are on record as recipients of the franchise through Pompey. He had developed a strong following in Spain through his years of service there. And the number of foreign dependencies was substantially increased during his eastern campaigns of the 60s.[58] Military men, *equites, municipales,* and *provinciales* bolstered the *clientela* of Pompey the Great.[59] And they profited from the association.

[55] On Palicanus, see above, pp. 25–26, and cf. Val. Max. 3.8.3. On Cornelius' service with Pompey, see Asconius, 57, Clark. For his activities as tribune, see below, pp. 250–252.

[56] For Lucilius Hirrus, see Varro, *De Re Rust.* 2.1.2; Milo, Asconius, 31, Clark; Messius, Cic. *Ad Att.* 8.11D.2; Varro, C. Cichorius, *Römische Studien* (Leipzig-Berlin, 1922), pp. 189–241. Note also, among non-senatorial *amici,* the financier M. Cluvius Rufus from Puteoli, who acted as Pompey's business agent in Cappadocia; Cic. *Ad Fam.* 13.56.3.

[57] See, esp., the orations *De Imperio Pompei* of 66 and *De Lege Agraria* of 63. Ward, *Phoenix,* 24 (1970): 119–129, traces a friendship between Pompey and Cicero back to the 80s.

[58] On Balbus, see Cic. *Pro Balbo, passim;* on Theophanes, see Cic. *Pro Arch.* 24. The list of men enfranchised by Pompey is collected by Badian, *For. Client.,* App. B, 302–308. For Pompey's influence in Spain, Sallust, *Cat.* 19; Asconius, 92, Clark.

[59] By 65, Cicero could speak of Pompey's large following and its influence among the voters; Cic. *Ad Att.* 1.1.2: *illam manum . . . Pompei;* cf. [Q. Cic.] *Comm. Petit.* 5, 51.

The rise of Pompeius Magnus points up most strikingly the paradoxical character of politics in this era. Pompey's goal was preeminence within an aristocratic order. To that end he established connections with noble houses and sponsored the careers of young scions of the aristocracy. His attitude is exemplified by his actions upon his triumphant return from the eastern campaigns in 62. Pompey immediately dismissed his vast armies, to demonstrate respect for proper constitutional forms. And, more revealing, he sought marriage alliance with the most influential of his political opponents, the family of Cato.[60] Although the plan did not materialize, it typifies Pompey's traditionalist approach. But not all of Rome's leading *nobiles* saw it that way. Whatever the general's attitude, many aristocrats feared in his following of *equites,* municipal dynasts, and military men a threat to the established order. Worse still was his dispensing of favors to foreign princes and principalities and his enfranchisement of provincials. Further uneasiness doubtless issued from the enormous personal wealth that he was accumulating through conquests in the East.[61] The fear of Pompey in some senatorial circles produced much of the splintering in Roman politics indicated above. Attitudes toward Pompey formed an overriding issue in the post-Sullan years. While many preferred to see him as a political leader in the standard mold, much as he saw himself, others felt that the traditional supremacy of the ruling class was incompatible with so much authority in the hands of a single individual. Decisions on this matter could sever previous ties and even divide families.

The cohesiveness of interests behind Catulus and Cato was exceptional in this period. A large part of the explanation lies in their reaction to Pompey. These were the men foremost in organizing the opposition. Catulus and Hortensius resisted Pompey's eastern posts in 67 and 66, pointing out constitutional dangers if extensive authority were to be conferred on an individual. In 65 both men testified against C. Cornelius, an ex-quæstor of Pompey's, who had advocated popular measures and had been highly critical of the senate during his tribunate. M. Cato came to the fore in 63. When it was proposed that Pompey be recalled with his military force to quell the Catilinarian conspiracy, Cato fought the attempt by veto and physical obstruction. Cato vowed in public that Pompey would enter the city with armed troops only over his dead body.[62] The blunt Stoic rejected with scorn Pompey's offer of marriage in the following year: he was not going to play politics with female intermediaries.[63] Cato's young brother-in-law, L. Domitius Ahenobar-

[60] Plut. *Cato,* 30.2–5, 45.1–2; *Pomp.* 44.2–4.

[61] On Pompey's fortune, see Badian, *Roman Imperialism in the Late Republic* (2nd ed., Oxford, 1968), pp. 80–84.

[62] Plut. *Cato*, 26.4: ζῶντος αὐτοῦ Πομπήιος οὐ παρέσται μεθ' ὅπλων εἰς τὴν πόλιν.

[63] Plut. *Cato*, 30.4.

bus, was conspicuous already in the 60s, attacking the friends of Pompey, Manilius and Afranius.[64] Resistance proceeded in 61 and 60, when Lucullus and Cato blocked approval of Pompey's eastern arrangements. Again the arguments dwelled on the general's authoritarian and arrogant behavior: the eastern settlement had come without the customary consent of a senatorial embassy.[65]

Other aristocrats found themselves persuaded, and contributed to the anti-Pompeian propaganda. Q. Metellus Creticus had experienced Pompey's insatiable desire for military glory. The general sought to reap the harvests of Metellus' victories in Crete, as he had those of Crassus against Spartacus. Embittered and resentful, Metellus joined the chorus in opposition to Pompey's administrative *acta* for the East.[66] The Pisones were even more vociferous. In 69 or 68, young Cn. Piso attacked Pompey in court and charged that the general, if crossed, would engulf the state in civil war. His relative, C. Piso, the consul of 67, engaged in violent resistance to the schemes of Pompey's supporters, the tribunes Cornelius and Gabinius and the consular candidate Lollius Palicanus. It was the pirate command to which he objected most strenuously, branding Pompey as the new Romulus.[67]

The propaganda showed consistency. Pompey was portrayed as a military dynast, a perpetual menace to civil order. His authority abroad, so it was claimed, shattered precedent and bypassed senatorial traditions. His supporters were sprung from lowly families, engaged in demagoguery, and consisted of soldiers or foreigners. The portrait convinced many senators; and it helped to solidify the backing of Cato. It was, however, a distortion, deliberately so. Pompey understood the utilization of hitherto untapped resources: career officers, *equites,* foreign *clientelae.* But he did not aim at military despotism. Association with prominent members of the ruling class was his principal asset. Despite the efforts of Catulus, Lucullus, Cato, and their adherents, the aristocrats who espoused Pompey's cause or marched in his service in the 60s formed an impressive cadre. The conqueror of Sertorius and Mithridates could look forward to a distinguished political career.

M. LICINIUS CRASSUS

The aristocracy was fragmented, and the fragmentation afforded opportunities for individual leaders. As a consummate politician, M. Licinius Crassus stood in the first rank. None, apart from Pompey, could compete with him in

[64] Asconius, 45, Clark; Schol. Bob. 119, Stangl; Cic. *Ad Att.* 1.16.12.

[65] Broughton, *TAPA*, 77 (1946): 40–43.

[66] Plut. *Pomp.* 29; Dio, 36.18–19; Livy, *Per.* 99; Vell. Pat. 2.40.5; Florus, 2.13.9.

[67] References and discussion in Gruen, *CSCA*, 1 (1968): 155–162.

dignitas and *potentia.* His was a dominant figure in the Ciceronian age. The scholarly tradition has not been kind to Crassus: he is the capitalist par excellence, "Mr. Moneybags," consumed by greed, and devoid of real statesmanship.[68] The judgment is superficial and misleading. Crassus was wealthy, to be sure, and ostentatious about his wealth. His oft-repeated boast is notorious: no man can consider himself rich unless he can maintain a legion.[69] But it is a mistake to dwell on his financial resources. The luxurious villas and conspicuous consumption of many of his contemporaries held no attractions for M. Crassus.[70] Money was power. Crassus possessed a single-minded ambition: to exercise political power and to attain unchallenged political stature. His riches were a means to an end.[71]

The preeminence of Crassus was acknowledged by his contemporaries. And there is no reason to question most details preserved by later authors. The biographical tradition on Julius Cæsar is properly suspect. It was convenient and tempting to see the dictator of the 40s as the potential dictator of the 60s and 50s. But for Crassus, who perished ignominiously in 53, there would be little point in inventing an impressive background. That makes all the more striking the frequent references, in a variety of sources, to Crassus as a man of *summa potentia* or as *præpotens* or even *rei publicæ princeps.*[72]

The general phrases may be supported by a number of specific instances which attest to the extraordinary power and influence of M. Crassus. We have had occasion to note already that Sicinius, the volatile tribune of 76, who was fearless in his outspoken attacks on Roman public figures, treated Crassus alone with the utmost respect.[73] A decade later, another demagogic

[68] Cf., e.g., Gelzer, *RE*, 25:330–331, "Licinius," n.68. It is symptomatic that Adcock's recent little book should be entitled *Marcus Crassus, Millionaire.* For a juster appraisal of Crassus, see T. J. Cadoux, *Greece and Rome*, 3 (1956): 153–161.

[69] Pliny, *NH*, 33.134; Cic. *De Off.* 1.25; *Parad.* 6.45; Plut. *Crass.* 2.7; Dio, 40.27.3. For Crassus' public display of his resources, see Plut. *Crass.* 2.2. His great wealth is noted frequently in the sources; Sallust, *Cat.* 48.5; Cic. *De Off.* 3.75; Dio, 37.56.4; 40.27.3; Plut. *Crass.* 2.1–8; *Pomp.* 22.1; *Cic.* 8.4, 25.4.

[70] Plut. *Crass.* 2.5.

[71] Cic. *De Off.* 1.25: *in quibus autem maior est animus, in iis pecuniæ cupiditas spectat ad opes et ad gratificandi facultatem, ut nuper M. Crassus negabat ullam satis magnam pecuniam esse ei, qui in re publica princeps vellet esse, cuius fructibus exercitum alere non posset*; Vell. Pat. 2.46.2: *qui vir* [Crassus] *cetera sanctissimus immunisque voluptatibus neque in pecunia neque in gloria concupiscenda aut modum norat aut capiebat terminum*; Dio, 37.56.4: Κράσσος δὲ ἠξίου τε πάντων ἀπό τε τοῦ γένους καὶ ἀπὸ τοῦ πλούτου περιεῖναι; cf. Vell. Pat. 2.44.2.

[72] Sallust, *Cat.* 48.5: *Crassum nominavit, hominem nobilem maxumis divitiis, summa potentia;* Cic. *De Fin.* 2.57: *non solum callidum . . . verum etiam præpotentem, ut M. Crassus fuit*; Vell. Pat. 2.30.6: *M. Crassum . . . mox rei publicæ omnium* [*consensu*] *principem*; cf. also Plut. *Pomp.* 22.1, 22.3; *Cic.* 15.1.

[73] Plut. *Crass.* 7.9.

tribune, C. Manilius, proposed a measure to enhance the voting privileges of freedmen. The senate rejected it and the populace was furious. Manilius, frightened and insecure, reckoned that there was no better way to calm the objectors than to claim that his bill had the sanction of M. Crassus.[74] In 63, when the machinations of Catiline were threatening disruption, the consul and senate found themselves for a long time unable or reluctant to act. But resolute action followed immediately when Crassus brought information to implicate the conspirators.[75] And after the plot was exposed and its participants apprehended, there emerged even more dramatic proof of the *auctoritas* of Crassus. One of the plotters suggested that Crassus had been engaged in the scheme. Reaction was swift and decisive: the testimony was immediately discredited and the informer placed in chains. Not that the allegation was necessarily incredible. But no one wished to risk the ire of M. Crassus. The slightest suggestion of Crassus' involvement might mean that all the conspirators would be shielded by his immense influence. If Crassus were to take up the cause of the accused, the state could find itself powerless.[76] The affair attests eloquently to Crassus' *potentia.* And further instances demonstrate that his authority continued undiminished. When Cicero in 58 found himself threatened by Clodius and then compelled to seek exile, he knew that the attitude of Crassus could be crucial.[77] Clodius, for his part, realized that the success of his plans would be markedly bolstered if he claimed the support, among others, of Crassus.[78] Again in 56, when Clodius was training his fire on Pompey, he instructed his followers once more to invoke the name of Crassus in order to give greater substance to his attacks.[79] The extraordinary power wielded by Crassus is confirmed again and again by contemporary evidence.

What was the source of Crassus' authority? Money, of course, helped considerably. Crassus lent out cash, not for material profit, but to place men under an obligation. A good number of Roman senators were in his debt.[80] The aim was to expand his faction and solidify his political position.[81] But Crassus

[74] Dio, 36.42.2–3.

[75] Dio, 37.31.1; Plut. *Cic.* 15.1–4.

[76] Sallust, *Cat.* 48.3–9: *in tali tempore tanta vis hominis magis leniunda quam exagitanda videbatur . . . Erant eo tempore qui existumarent indicium illud a P. Autronio machinatum, quo facilius appellato Crasso per societatem periculi reliquos illius potentia tegeret. Alii Tarquinium a Cicerone immissum aiebant, ne Crassus more suo suscepto malorum patrocinio rem publicam conturbaret.*

[77] Cic. *Ad Q. Frat.* 1.3.7; *Ad Fam.* 14.2.2; *Pro Sest.* 41.

[78] Cic. *De Har. Resp.* 47; *Pro Sest.* 39–40; *Pro Planc.* 86.

[79] Cic. *Ad Q. Frat.* 2.3.2.

[80] As is well known, Crassus paid off Julius Cæsar's debts in 61; Plut. *Crass.* 7.6; *Caes.* 11.1. By 63, many senators were obligated to him; Sallust, *Cat.* 48.5. That Crassus' purpose was political, not economic, is shown by the fact that he did not charge interest on the loans; Plut. *Crass.* 3.1.

[81] Cf. Plut. *Crass.* 7.2.

did not rely on his finances alone. He was a tireless pleader in the law courts. Though deficient in oratorical gifts, he worked at the art with great energy and made himself available as advocate for defendants of every rank and station. This added in no small measure to his following.[82] Again the general observations of the sources can be documented further, by a number of known appearances as defense counsel: the trials of C. Licinius Macer, L. Licinius Murena, P. Sestius, M. Cælius, and L. Cornelius Balbus.[83]

Crassus was generous with his time and his efforts, as well as with his resources. His political rivals might grumble and sneer, but Crassus gained much success by catering to the populace. His home was open to all, his entertainments were frequent though frugal, and he made it a point to avoid all aristocratic airs when in the presence of the common man. In this, as in all else, there was deliberate purpose: for his generosity Crassus expected recompense in terms of political support.[84] And, finally, one should not minimize the *clientelæ* who came through Crassus' activities abroad and his military exploits. The disaster at Carrhæ in the Parthian war of 53 dominates the tradition on Crassus' martial reputation. But his previous career on the battlefield earned distinction. As a young man in Spain he had collected 2,500 men and brought them over to Sulla's side. Crassus held the honored post of commanding Sulla's right wing at the Colline Gate in 82; it was his success that determined the issue. In crushing the revolt of Spartacus, he revealed a strong strain of ruthlessness and cruelty, but added appreciably to his military laurels.[85] These operations doubtless swelled his support, at home and abroad. Legates and officers, as well as enlisted men, would remember their commander. At least one foreign *cliens* received Roman citizenship through the patronage of Crassus. And Crassus' efforts as censor in 65 to extend the franchise to Transpadane Gaul belongs in the same context: he was expanding the lists of potential adherents.[86] The sources of Crassus' wide influence were manifold.

The accumulation of influence is clear. But the direction in which it was to be employed is another matter. What were Crassus' politics? Much has been written on the subject; little can be tied to any evidence. The older

[82] Cic. *Brutus,* 233; Sallust, *Cat.* 48.8; Plut. *Crass.* 3.2, 7.2–4.

[83] For the trial of Macer, see Plut. *Cic.* 9.1–2; Murena, Cic. *Pro Mur.* 10; Sestius, Schol. Bob. 125, Stangl; Cælius, Cic. *Pro Cæl.* 18, 23; Balbus, Cic. *Pro Balbo,* 17, 50.

[84] Plut. *Crass.* 3.1, 3.3, 12.2; Dio, 37.56.5; cf. Cic. *De Off.* 1.109: *qui quidvis perpetiantur, cuivis deserviant, dum, quod velint, consequantur, ut Sullam et M. Crassum videbamus.*

[85] On the gathering of an army in Spain, see Plut. *Crass.* 6.1; on the battle of the Colline Gate, see Plut. *Crass.* 6.6; on Crassus' role in defeating Spartacus, see the sources collected in Broughton, *MRR,* II:118, 123; for his cruelty toward his own soldiers and toward the slaves, see Plut. *Crass.* 10.2–3; Appian, *BC,* 1.120. The *gloria* won in the servile war is indicated by Vell. Pat. 2.30.6.

[86] The grant of citizenship: Cic. *Pro Balbo,* 50; the censorial activities: Dio, 37.9.3.

literature transmitted the notion that Crassus headed a "popular party" or that Crassus and Cæsar were dual champions of the popular cause.[87] The concept is fallacious. Crassus can justly be termed a *popularis,* if one understands that word in the proper Roman sense: a man who, at least on occasion, courted popularity and sought to endear himself to the people. But the term, at best, applies only to Crassus' behavior, not to his policy. His career shows no advocacy of measures designed to promote the social or political status of the Roman populace. The coupling of Crassus with Cæsar was the work of propagandists in the 50s and later.[88] Crassus did not rest his authority on any identifiable popular programs.

There are some who would find in Crassus a "middle-of-the-road man." Plutarch and Dio Cassius are invoked as testimony for this analysis.[89] But the relevant passages do not bear the weight placed upon them. Dio makes reference to a specific occasion, the consular elections for 55: Pompey openly sought the office; Crassus was more moderate about it—that is, he hedged. In the two other selections, both Dio and Plutarch examine Crassus' behavior in the light of his relations with Cæsar and Pompey. Their conclusion is proper, but suggests no "middle-of-the-road" policy: Crassus shifted position readily, supporting now the one, now the other, advocating or opposing measures in accordance with his own political interests. In this respect, Crassus was no different from most Roman politicians, only more successful than most. Self-aggrandizement, not conviction, dictated his actions. Similarly, the notion that Crassus represented the capitalist classes or the *equites* constitutes a serious misjudgment. To be sure, he had money tied up in business investments and enterprises, as had many other Roman senators and *nobiles.* But there is only a single known instance in which Crassus openly advocated the cause of the business classes. A tax-farming company in 61 asked reduction of their contract for collection of the Asian revenues; Crassus had urged them to press their claims.[90] The explanation is perhaps no more profound than that Crassus himself had some cash invested in the enterprise. M. Crassus was a *nobilis,* an aristocrat, the most distinguished and potent of Roman senators. The idea that he was in any sense a "representative" of the *equites* would have been entirely unintelligible.

Hence, perhaps in the end, Crassus was simply a conservative aristocrat. Standard senatorial politics required marriage alliances with powerful noble

[87] Cf., e.g., E. G. Hardy, *JRS,* 7 (1917): 155; J. Carcopino, *Hist. Rom.,* II:663; Garzetti, *Athenæum,* 20 (1942): 12–40.

[88] See below, n.117.

[89] Plut. *Crass.* 7.8: Κράσσος δὲ μέσος; Dio, 39.30.2: ὥσπερ εἰώθει διὰ μέσου ἐχώρησεν; cf. Dio, 37.56.5; see Taylor, *Party Politics,* pp. 106, 121.

[90] Cic. *Ad Att.* 1.17.9.

families. One of Crassus' sons married the daughter of Q. Metellus Creticus; his other son took the daughter of Q. Metellus Scipio, adopted heir of Q. Metellus Pius.[91] But the phrase "conservative statesman" misses the point. Crassus' political power did not come about through typical senatorial politics. He was not one to be absorbed into the "Metellan faction" or into anyone else's group. Crassus systematically developed his own faction. For Pompeius Magnus, association with the aristocracy offered a means to achieve political respectability. But Crassus' family was older and more distinguished. For him, close links with houses of the *nobilitas* might tie his hands and limit his maneuverability. The remarkable fact about Crassus' career is that cooperation with prominent *nobiles* is almost nowhere attested. By contrast, the evidence, when collected and examined, shows numerous instances of friction between Crassus and important senatorial politicians.

A few examples should suffice. The rivalry with Pompey needs no further illustration. It persisted throughout their careers, even when they joined forces for mutual benefit.[92] Marriage ties with the Metelli do not appear to have issued in political profit. At least, no positive evidence can be cited. And we know of a clash between Crassus and Metellus Pius in 83, and opposition in the senate between Crassus and Metellus Celer in 61.[93] Crassus' rather unsavory profiteering during the Sullan proscriptions roused the enmity of many of his fellow senators.[94] Q. Catulus was his colleague in the censorship of 65. The two men checkmated each other throughout the year and ended their frustrations by resigning office.[95] More than one senator would have liked to see Crassus implicated in the Catilinarian conspiracy of 63.[96] M. Porcius Cato, the stubborn spokesman of the oligarchy, blocked Crassus' efforts to reduce the Asian tax contract in 61.[97] After formation of the coalition with Pompey and Cæsar, opposition by the nobility naturally increased. Cato and his brother-in-law L. Domitius Ahenobarbus were in the forefront, together with the consul of 56, Lentulus Marcellinus, exerting every effort to stall

[91] For the elder son, see *ILS,* 881; the younger, Plut. *Pomp.* 55.1. The marriages are stressed and the notion of Crassus as a conservative senator is suggested by Syme, *JRS,* 34 (1944): 96-97; *Sallust,* 19.

[92] Cf., e.g., Cic. *Ad Att.* 1.14.2-3; 2.21.3-4; *Ad Q. Frat.* 2.3.2-4.

[93] For Metellus Pius, see Plut. *Crass.* 6.2; for Celer, Cic. *Ad Att.* 1.17.9. Florus, 1.46.3, records a tribune Metellus who uttered hostile imprecations against Crassus in 55. But this may be his own or a copyist's error; the tribune who fits that context is Ateius; sources in Broughton, *MRR,* II:216.

[94] Plut. *Crass.* 6.5-7.

[95] Dio, 37.9.3; Plut. *Crass.* 13.1.

[96] Sallust, *Cat.* 48.3-7.

[97] Cic. *Ad Att.* 1.17.9; 1.18.7; 2.1.8.

the consular candidacies of Crassus and Pompey.[98] Q. Hortensius added his voice in criticism of Crassus in 55, and then Ap. Claudius Pulcher joined Domitius in attacking Crassus in 54.[99] Despite occasional protestations of public support, there was deep-rooted hostility between Crassus and Cicero.[100] The pent-up anger of Crassus once found release in actual fisticuffs with another Roman senator.[101] The instances could be multiplied. It seems abundantly plain that Crassus did not rest his influence on collaboration with the nobility.

Money, favors, and patronage would have little impact on the ancient houses of the aristocracy. But Sulla had greatly increased, perhaps doubled, the ranks of the Roman senate. The new men, from the lists of the *equites* and from the municipal leadership of Italy, were more susceptible to blandishments. It may well have been the rank and file, the *pedarii,* of the senate to whom Crassus turned.[102] In the 70s and 60s these men were making their initial contributions to Roman government: holding the lower magistracies, filling minor offices, serving as junior officers in the army, sitting in the Roman senate. The *consulares* and the older families of the *nobilitas* dominated senatorial debate and formulated policy. But the *pedarii* could vote—or withhold their vote. And, as magistrates and officers, they could exercise important functions and implement decisions. Within a generation or two, it might be foreseen, the new families could escalate into a senatorial majority. M. Crassus may have possessed more foresight than scholars have credited him with. The sources report that he held a dominant position in the *curia;* many senators were in his debt through private business deals.[103] Reference must be to the relatively silent but numerically weighty lower ranks of the senate. Two hundred senators, at least one-third of the senatorial personnel, are said to have traveled to Luca in 56, when Crassus, Pompey, and Cæsar renewed their cooperation. Many of them, we may imagine, were clients and adherents of M. Crassus.[104]

In this connection, it is instructive to examine the lists of legates and officers who served under Crassus in his two major military engagements: the war against Spartacus in 72–71, and the invasion of Parthia in 54–53. In almost every case they came from families of little prior prominence or

[98] Plut. *Crass.* 15.1–4; *Pomp.* 51–52; *Cato,* 41–42; Dio, 39.27–31; Val. Max. 6.2.6.

[99] Dio, 39.37.2–4; Cic. *Ad Fam.* 5.8.1.

[100] Cf., esp., Cic. *Ad Fam.* 1.9.20; *Ad Att.* 4.13.2; Sallust, *Cat.* 48.8–9; Plut. *Crass.* 13.2–4; Dio, 39.10.2.

[101] Plut. *Comp. Nic. et Crass.* 2.2.

[102] For the term *pedarii*, see Cic. *Ad Att.* 1.19.9, 1.20.4.

[103] Sallust, *Cat.* 48.5: *plerique Crasso ex negotiis privatis obnoxii*; Plut. *Pomp.* 22.3: ἐν μὲν τῇ βουλῇ μᾶλλον ἴσχυεν ὁ Κράσσος.

[104] Appian, *BC*, 2.17; Plut. *Pomp.* 51.3; *Cæs.* 21.2.

from new senatorial houses. The known officers of Crassus in the slave war were Q. Marcius Rufus, Mummius, C. Pomptinus, L. Quinctius, and Cn. Tremellius Scrofa.[105] Of these, only the name Mummius had made a substantial mark in Roman history. But it is most unlikely that this Mummius, otherwise unknown, belonged to the same line as the celebrated L. Mummius Achaicus, consul in 146 and conqueror of Corinth, the only Mummius to achieve the consulship.[106] Cn. Tremellius Scrofa's ancestors had included six Roman prætors, but no consuls. He himself, an expert in agriculture and a source for Varro's treatise on the subject, reached a prætorship ca. 58, perhaps with the patronage of Crassus.[107] The family of Q. Marcius Rufus had held no known prior office. The same was true of C. Pomptinus, who himself went on to a prætorship in 63. L. Quinctius, though he occupied a tribunate in 74, possibly with Crassus' support, is specifically said to have been of humble origins.[108]

Most of the men who served with Crassus in the Parthian war show similar undistinguished backgrounds.[109] C. Cassius Longinus and Octavius possessed illustrious names. But Octavius is otherwise unknown. He need not have come from the consular family of the Octavii. Censorinus, if he was a Marcius Censorinus, could look back to a consular ancestor in 149. Alternatively, however, he may be from a municipal family of the same name attested in Aletrium.[110] The remainder of the officers in 54 and 53 belong to, at best, lesser senatorial houses: Coponius, Egnatius, Megabocchus, Petronius, the Roscii, Vargunteius. One of them, Coponius, came from a Latin family that had held Roman citizenship for only two generations.[111] The contrast between this list and the distinguished roster of noble names that accompanied Pompey in his eastern wars of the 60s is striking. Pompey hoped to develop a faction by constructing bonds with prominent houses of the old aristocracy. Crassus' faction would be more tightly controlled: he would be patron and dispenser of favors for families of lesser rank. While Pompey operated along more traditional lines, Crassus looked to the future.

[105] Frontinus, *Strat.* 2.4.7, 2.5.34; Plut. *Crass.* 10.1–3, 11.4.

[106] On L. Mummius Achaicus, see Münzer, *RE,* 16:1195–1206, "Mummius," n.7a. A certain C. Mummius was an officer of Sulla's in the civil war of 88; Plut. *Sulla,* 9.5–6; and a M. Mummius was prætor in 70; Cic. *Verr.* 2.3.123. The latter might conceivably be identified with the officer of Crassus.

[107] Varro, *De Re Rust.* 2.4.2; Cic. *Ad Att.* 6.1.13; cf. Münzer, *RE,* 6(2):2287–2289, "Tremellius," n.5.

[108] Cic. *Pro Cluent.* 112. On Pomptinus, see H. Gundel, *RE,* 21:2421–2424, "Pomptinus."

[109] The names are collected in Broughton, *MRR,* II:229–232. He missed, however, the Roscii brothers; Plut. *Crass.* 31.2.

[110] *ILLRP,* 528 and 529.

[111] Cic. *Pro Balbo,* 53. A certain C. Megabocchus was a promagistrate in Sardinia sometime before 54; Cic. *Pro Scauro,* 40. The date and circumstances are unknown. This too may reflect the patronage of M. Crassus; cf. Cic. *Ad Att.* 2.7.3.

Other men associated with Crassus show a similar pattern. Cn. Sicinius, the tribune of 76 who cooperated with Crassus, could claim (so far as our evidence goes) only a distant prætorian ancestor in the early second century. The family emerges again in the 70s. In addition to the tribune of 76, a promising young orator named C. Sicinius died an untimely death after reaching the quæstorship ca. 70.[112] Even more instructive is the example of Q. Arrius. Of humble birth and obsequious personality, Arrius attached himself to Crassus and catered to his interests. The result was prestige, money, and high office, a prætorship by 63, and hopes for a consulship in 58.[113] Crassus also acted as patron and defense counsel for C. Licinius Macer in 66. Macer was the tribune of 73, a vocal advocate of tribunician reform. Lacking immediate forebears in high office, Macer, a historian, glorified instead the Licinii of the early Republic.[114] Cn. Plancius, son of an equestrian businessman, reached the ædileship in 55, thanks in large part to sponsorship by the house of Crassus. Finally, there is the flamboyant and fun-loving young M. Cælius Rufus. His origins were in municipal Italy; the family had not enjoyed office in Rome. But Cælius aimed at a Roman political career. For that purpose one needed oratorical training and political connections. Cælius' father sent him to the best: to Cicero for the former, to Crassus for the latter.[115]

The evidence is not extensive, but it is consistent. Crassus was not the sort to be swallowed up in other men's political groupings. Like Sulla before him, Crassus fashioned his own following out of individuals dependent upon him and obligated to him. While Pompey sought the dignity of association with noble houses, and Cæsar furthered his career by espousing popular causes, Crassus welded together a coalition of new senatorial families with a stake in the government and an interest in lifting their status under his powerful patronage.

[112] For the tribune, see Cic. *Brutus,* 216–217; Plut. *Crass.* 7.9; the quæstor, Cic. *Brutus,* 263–264.

[113] Cic. *Brutus,* 242–243: *Quod idem faciebat Q. Arrius, qui fuit M. Crassi quasi secundarum. Is omnibus exemplo debet esse quantum in hac urbe polleat multorum obœdire tempori multorumque vel honori vel periculo servire. His enim rebus infimo loco natus et honores et pecuniam et gratiam consecutus.* For the prætorship, see Plut. *Cic.* 15; the consular expectations, Cic. *Ad Att.* 1.17.11, 2.5.2, 2.7.3. Another Q. Arrius was prætor in 73; Broughton, *MRR,* II:109. He may be a cousin and, perhaps, another example of Crassus' patronage. Syme, *CP,* 50 (1955): 133, identifies the two Arrii. That, however, denies the explicit evidence of Schol. Gronov. 324, Stangl.

[114] On Crassus' defense of Macer in 66, see Plut. *Cic.* 9.1–2; on Macer as a historian, see R. M. Ogilvie, *Livy: Books 1–5* (Oxford, 1965), pp. 7–12.

[115] Cic. *Pro Cælio,* 9: *hoc dicam, hunc a patre continuo ad me esse deductum; nemo hunc M. Cælium in illo ætatis flore vidit nisi aut cum patre aut mecum aut in M. Crassi castissima domo, cum artibus honestissimis erudiretur.* For Cælius' municipal origins, see Cic. *Pro Cælio,* 5; cf. Wiseman, *CQ,* 14 (1964): 126. On Crassus and the Plancii, see below, chap. 8, n.41.

THE EMERGENCE OF JULIUS CÆSAR

For C. Julius Cæsar a great future lay ahead. But there were few in 60, and far fewer a decade earlier, who could have predicted that future. In Cæsar's case separation of the man from the myth is extremely difficult. Later authors who looked back upon a Republic that had crumbled and upon Cæsar who had triumphed over it naturally detected signs of the determined and destined monarch from the outset of Cæsar's career.[116] Numerous tales and anecdotes of doubtful validity permeate the story of Cæsar's early years in politics. Some are retrospective anticipations of his later stature; others are the product of anti-Cæsarian propaganda in the 50s.[117] The facts are simpler. In the 70s and 60s Cæsar was a young aristocrat making his way up the regular magisterial ladder. He could not rank with those families who had dominated the top offices for the past several decades, much less with Cn. Pompeius Magnus or M. Crassus. He controlled no faction of his own before the 50s; nor can he be termed "chief of the popular party," even if that phrase contained any meaning. At the same time, however, Cæsar was hardly a typical example of the lower senatorial ranks. His connections in a number of aristocratic camps gave him a wide and varied backing. Natural talent, a winning personality, and shrewd political sense brought him early into the public eye—and kept him there.

Cæsar's father had not held the consulship. Nor had the family been a significant power in previous generations. But Cæsar attached great importance to its antiquity: his maternal lineage could be traced back to the kings of Rome, and the paternal stock claimed descent from Venus herself.[118] Cæsar's *dignitas* was an obsession. Aristocrats from more influential houses could take their station for granted; Cæsar insisted upon his.[119] The portrait drawn by Sallust is justly famous: Cæsar was generous, gentle, compassionate, a friend in need, a solace for the unfortunate, an expansive and open personality. But Sallust does not conceal the driving ambition of the man: Cæsar would hurl

[116] So Cicero, already shortly after Cæsar's death, could say: *multos annos regnare meditatus, magno labore, magnis periculis quod cogitarat effecerat; Phil.* 2.116.

[117] In the latter category must be placed alleged plots by Cæsar and Crassus to murder senators, and Cæsar's supposed effort to secure control of Egypt in the mid-60s; Suet. *Iul.* 9, 11. The tradition on Cæsar's early career has been subjected to rigorous scrutiny by H. Strasburger, *Cæsars Eintritt in die Geschichte* (Munich, 1938), *passim.* His persistent skepticism is, at times, excessive, but a necessary corrective to earlier uncritical acceptance of the tradition. Gelzer, disappointingly, still retails with faith the story of Cæsar's Egyptian escapade: *Cæsar: Politician and Statesman* (Eng. trans., Cambridge, Mass., 1968), pp. 40–41.

[118] Suet. *Iul.* 6.

[119] Cic. *Ad Att.* 7.11.1: *atque hæc ait* [Cæsar] *omnia facere se dignitatis causa*; Cæs. *BC.* 1.7.7: *hortatur . . . ut eius existimationem dignitatemque ab inimicis defendant*; cf. Cæs. *BC.* 1.9.2; Suet. *Iul.* 16.2, 72.

Rome into war in order to provide a stage for his own talents.[120] And Cæsar's bullying pride and arrogance surfaced on more than one occasion, even in his early career.[121] Appeal to personal and familial *dignitas,* however, was not always sufficient in the world of Roman politics. Cæsar's connections were more formidable.

It was of no small significance that Cæsar's aunt Julia had been the wife of C. Marius, Rome's most celebrated general and seven times consul. Cæsar himself perpetuated the association. After a brief initial marriage to a woman of undistinguished birth, he took to wife the daughter of L. Cinna, the accomplice of Marius in the 80s and himself four times consul. Nor did Cæsar let anyone forget those affiliations. He employed the occasion of his aunt's funeral to deliver a ringing eulogy and to display the *imagines* of Marius. A similar propagandistic opportunity was seized at his own wife's funeral. Cæsar defied custom in order to bring signal honor to his family. And in his ædileship of 65, he conspicuously restored to their place the trophies and monuments that commemorated Marius' triumphs over the Germans.[122]

This kind of bravado and the stress on Marian connections naturally produced friction with Sulla and some of the Sullani. The dictator in 81 asked Cæsar to divorce his wife, Cornelia, the daughter of Cinna. But the young patrician refused, thereby braving Sulla's displeasure and retaliation. When Lepidus raised revolt against the Sullan regime in 78, he could hope for the support and participation of Julius Cæsar. That support failed to materialize; Cæsar was not interested in armed revolution. But he showed zeal in prosecuting former officers of Sulla in the courts: Dolabella in 77 and C. Antonius in 76.[123] A dozen years later he was again pressing for the conviction of Sulla's creatures, this time the men who had served as executioners under the dictatorship.[124] Cæsar followed an unambiguous line. It was also in the

[120] Sallust, *Cat.* 54.2–4: *Cæsar beneficiis ac munificentia magnus habebatur . . . ille mansuetudine et misericordia clarus factus . . . Cæsar dando, sublevando, ignoscundo . . . gloriam adeptus est . . . miseris perfugium erat . . . sibi magnum imperium, exercitum, bellum novum exoptabat, ubi virtus enitescere posset;* cf. Suet. *Iul.* 27.

[121] For some examples, see Cic. *Ad Att.* 2.24.3; Suet. *Iul.* 20.4, 22.2.

[122] For the funeral orations over his aunt and his wife, see Suet. *Iul.* 6.1; Plut. *Cæs.* 5.1–2. The marriage alliance between Marius and the Julii is noted also by Vell. Pat. 2.41.2; Suet. *Iul.* 1; Plut. *Marius,* 6.2; *Cæs.* 1.1, 5.1, 5.3. For the restoration of Marius' trophies, see Vell. Pat. 2.43.4; Suet. *Iul.* 11; Plut. *Cæs.* 6.1–4.

[123] Cæsar's conflict with Sulla may be found in Vell. Pat. 2.41.2, 2.43.1; Suet. *Iul.* 1.1–2, 74.1; Plut. *Cæs.* 1.1–3; the offer from Lepidus: Suet. *Iul.* 3; on the trials of Dolabella and Antonius, see above, chap. 1, n.114. Strasburger, *Cæsars Eintritt,* pp. 90–91, suggests that the story of Lepidus' importuning of Cæsar derives from a speech of Cæsar himself.

[124] Suet. *Iul.* 11, suggests that Cæsar served as *iudex quæstionis* or *quæsitor* in those trials, a version accepted by most scholars; cf., e.g., Gelzer, *Cæsar,* p. 42. But Cicero implies that he was an *accusator; Pro Lig.* 12. That is certainly the way in which the scholiast understood

mid-60s, so we are told, that he advocated the restoration of political rights to the sons of men proscribed by Sulla. That too fits the pattern.[125]

Not surprisingly, Cæsar found himself at odds with some of Rome's more conservative senators, in particular with Q. Catulus, the most distinguished of aristocrats. When Cæsar sought to revitalize the memory of Marius, Catulus raised strenuous objection, though in vain. Cæsar's election as *pontifex maximus* in 63 came at the expense of Catulus, who did not forgive or forget. The two men clashed again in senatorial debate on the fate of the Catilinarian plotters. Catulus endeavored even to implicate Cæsar in the conspiracy itself. And the latter retaliated in 62 by charging Catulus with failure to carry out a public commission. The friction and bitterness between them proved implacable.[126] The same hostility expressed itself on more than one occasion in the late 60s between Cæsar and M. Porcius Cato. Like Catulus, Cato contended with Cæsar in senatorial debate and sought to cast suspicion on him for alleged involvement in Catilinarian schemes. In 62, the year of Cæsar's prætorship and Cato's tribunate, the two men engaged in violent confrontation.[127]

So far the pattern is consistent: Cæsar the heir of the Marian tradition and scourge of conservative senators. But that tells only a part of the story, and perhaps not the most important part. For all his emphasis upon his relation to Marius, Cæsar retained close contacts in the oligarchy installed by Sulla. Cæsar's mother was an Aurelia, cousin of the Cottæ who were consuls in 75, 74, and 65. The family had old associations with Sulla.[128] When Cæsar roused the wrath of Sulla by refusing to divorce Cornelia, relatives and friends like Mam. Lepidus and Aurelius Cotta interceded for him, as did some of Rome's most respected leaders.[129] Connections like these enabled him to survive

---

him; Schol. Gronov. 293, Stangl: *multos accusavit et damnavit Sullanos.* The latter analysis is supported by Dio, 37.10.1–2; so Strasburger, *Cæsars Eintritt,* pp. 117–119. There is no ancient evidence for the view, frequently retailed by moderns, that Cæsar effected the acquittal of Catiline on this charge.

[125] Vell. Pat. 2.43.4: *simulque* [65 BC] *revocati ad ius dignitatis proscriptorum liberi.* Velleius is wrong if he means that Cæsar effected this aim in the mid-60s. The effort was successfully resisted: Cic. *In Pis.* 4; *De Leg. Agrar.* 2.10; cf. *Ad Att.* 2.1.3; Quint. *Inst. Orat.* 11.1.85; Dio, 37.25.3, 44.47.4. But that is not sufficient reason to throw his testimony out altogether, as does Strasburger, *Cæsars Eintritt,* p. 11.

[126] For the conflict over restoring Marius' trophies, see Plut. *Cæs.* 6.4; for the election as *pontifex maximus,* see Plut. *Cæs.* 7.1–3; Dio, 37.37.2; Vell. Pat. 2.43.3; Sallust, *Cat.* 49.2; for the debate on the Catilinarians, see Cic. *Ad Att.* 12.21.1; Plut. *Cæs.* 8.1; *Cic.* 21.3; for Catulus' effort to implicate Cæsar, see Sallust, *Cat.* 49.1–2; Plut. *Cæs.* 7.3; for Cæsar's clashes with Catulus in 62, see Cic. *Ad Att.* 2.24.3; Suet. *Iul.* 15; Dio, 37.44.1.

[127] For the sources and a narrative of events, see Gelzer, *Cæsar,* pp. 50–58.

[128] Suet. *Iul.* 1.2, 74.2; Plut. *Cæs.* 9.2; Tac. *Dial.* 28.6; on the Cottæ, see Münzer, *Röm. Adelsp.*, pp. 324–325.

[129] Suet. *Iul.* 1.1–2: *perque Mamercum Æmilium et Aurelium Cottam propinquos et adfines suos veniam impetravit . . . deprecantibus amicissimis et ornatissimis viris.*

the proscriptions. And he did more than survive. In the immediately succeeding years, Cæsar saw military service in Asia under M. Minucius Thermus, who had held a prætorship during Sulla's tenure as dictator, and then under P. Servilius Vatia, Sulla's choice for the consulship of 79.[130] Later in the decade he seems to have been on the staff of M. Antonius Creticus, who had been dispatched by the senate to clear the Mediterranean of piracy.[131] Obviously, Cæsar did not appear to be an outcast or an enemy of the Sullan oligarchy. The fact is decisively confirmed by his co-optation into the prestigious college of pontiffs, probably in 73. Among the priests who effected that election were two Metelli, Mam. Lepidus, Servilius Vatia, and even Q. Lutatius Catulus.[132] In the 60s, Cæsar was calling attention to his Marian heritage. Yet he found it not at all incongruous, after the death of Cornelia, to take as his third wife, in 67, the granddaughter of Sulla himself.[133] It is clear that the labels "Marian" and "Sullan" are no longer meaningful designations in the 60s. Cæsar sedulously cultivated contacts in a number of circles.

Associations like these gave Cæsar security and influence within the aristocracy. It was therefore safe to espouse popular causes and to develop an image as champion of those out of power. Cæsar chose that stance frequently in the 70s and 60s. He was among those who spoke up on behalf of the restoration of tribunician power in the late 70s. He also delivered a speech in support of the *lex Plotia,* which reinstated citizenship to the surviving participants of Lepidus' revolt, probably in 70.[134] Both actions were unobjectionable in the context of those years. For Cæsar's own purposes, we may be sure, their main function was to keep him in the public eye. A similar goal inspired the dramatic funeral orations and displays that resurrected the memory of Marius. Among other things, Marius had been associated with Italian claims and with the expansion of Roman citizenship. The franchise had now been awarded to all Italy south of the Po. Cæsar went further in 68 and urged citizen rights for Latin colonies, presumably those beyond the Po.[135]

In 63 Cæsar escalated his *popularis* activity. Together with the tribune T. Labienus he engineered the prosecution of an aged Roman knight, C. Rabirius.

[130] Suet. *Iul.* 2–3; *Vir. Ill.* 78.1.

[131] *SIG*[3], 748, 22; see Broughton, *MRR*, II:115–116, n.6.

[132] Vell. Pat. 2.43.1; the list of pontiffs is reconstructed by Taylor, *AJP*, 63 (1942): 385–404. On Cæsar's connections with the oligarchy, see also Taylor, *TAPA,* 73 (1942): 1–24.

[133] Suet. *Iul.* 6.2; Plut. *Cæs.* 5.3.

[134] Suet. *Iul.* 5; Gellius, 13.3.5; Dio, 44.47.4.

[135] Suet. *Iul.* 8: *colonias Latinas de petenda civitate agitantes adiit.* Suetonius goes too far, however, in suggesting that Cæsar was stirring revolt. The story is to be dissociated from Crassus' plans to extend the franchise to Transpadani, which did not come until 65; so, rightly, Strasburger, *Cæsars Eintritt,* pp. 96–97. But Strasburger has no warrant for jettisoning the story altogether.

The charge concerned Rabirius' alleged participation in the slaying of the *popularis* tribune Saturninus thirty-seven years before. Cæsar once more proclaimed himself an advocate of due process and a friend of the people.[136] The stance received reinforcement later in the year when Cæsar voiced opposition in the senate to summary execution of the Catilinarian conspirators. And after the executions were carried out, Cæsar led strident criticism of the consul Cicero, who had authorized the deed.[137] It was in 63 also that Cæsar, again in collaboration with T. Labienus, successfully urged the substitution of popular election for co-optation in the college of pontiffs.[138]

The advocacy of such measures may or may not have arisen out of conviction. Cæsar, in any case, designed to win the admiration of the populace. By 63 he had already developed a reputation for pursuing a *popularis via.*[139] As a patrician, he was ineligible for the tribunate, an office which customarily fostered such a posture. His support for popular goals stretched over a longer period of time. Political astuteness was evident throughout. Cæsar's measures were never too radical or ill-timed. In no instance did they threaten the established structure or his own position within it. At the same time they successfully earned him wide popular favor.[140]

But it is well to repeat an earlier warning. Cæsar's stature in the 60s could not bear comparison with that of M. Crassus or Cn. Pompeius Magnus. Careful examination of Cæsar's activities in that decade reveals a consistent thread not always sufficiently stressed. The ambitious patrician advanced his career by attaching himself to the following of Pompey the Great.

The signs are already discernible in the late 70s. Pompey's accumulated victories abroad and his enormous prestige attracted many young aristocrats into his orbit. It may not be mere chance that Julius Cæsar was one of the champions of tribunician reform at about the time when Pompey announced his support for it. And Cæsar's speech for the Plotian law to restore the followers of Lepidus affords a revealing parallel. The author of that measure evidently also sponsored a *lex agraria* to provide land for Pompey's veterans.[141]

[136] On this case, see below, chap. 7.

[137] Cæsar's speech in the senate is reconstructed by Sallust, *Cat.* 51. It is summarized also by Cicero, *Cat.* 4.7–10; cf. *Ad Att.* 12.21.1. The later sources are numerous: Suet. *Iul.* 14.1; Plut. *Cæs.* 7.4–5; *Cic.* 21.2–4; *Cato,* 22.4–5; Dio, 37.36.1–2; Appian, *BC*, 2.6. For Cæsar's attack on Cicero, see Plut. *Cic.* 23.1–3,

[138] Dio, 37.37.1. The measure has no direct connection with Cæsar's own election as *pontifex maximus* in that year. The chief priest, unlike the other pontiffs, was already subject to popular election; Cic. *De Leg. Agrar.* 2.18.

[139] Cic. *Cat.* 4.9: *C. Cæsaris, quoniam hanc is in re publica viam quæ popularis habetur secutus est*; cf. Cic. *De Prov. Cons.* 38: *ex illa iactatione cursuque populari*; also, Cic. *Ad Att.* 2.1.6; *Pro Planc.* 93; *Phil.* 5.49; Plut. *Cæs.* 4.2–3; 5.4–5.

[140] For Cæsar's support among the *plebs* in early 62, see Suet. *Iul.* 16.2; Plut. *Cæs.* 8.3–4.

[141] See below, chap. 9, n.119.

Hence one will not be surprised to find Cæsar speaking in behalf of the *lex Gabinia* of 67 for Pompey's commission against the pirates, or the *lex Manilia* of 66 for the Mithridatic command, or both.[142] In 63, when Pompey's eastern campaigns were pushing to a conclusion, and his return to Rome could be anticipated for the near future, Cæsar stepped up his activities in Pompey's behalf. Two tribunes, T. Labienus and T. Ampius Balbus, proposed measures for extraordinary triumphal honors to celebrate Pompey's victories in the East. According to Dio Cassius, the man who stood behind these measures was Julius Cæsar[143] The report is plausible. Cæsar and Labienus cooperated on more than one occasion in 63. Both men supported popular election for the priesthood and both engaged in the prosecution of Rabirius.[144] Cæsar was stressing his *amicitia* with the friends of Pompey. Common political enemies confirm the fact. Among the most vociferous opponents of Pompey's overseas commands had been Q. Catulus and C. Piso. Cæsar had already clashed openly with Catulus. Now in 63 he delivered a stunning defeat to Catulus in the elections for the chief pontificate.[145] It is therefore no coincidence that in the same year Cæsar brought a *repetundæ* prosecution against Piso. Both Catulus and Piso showed their vindictiveness later in the year: they alleged Cæsar's participation in the conspiracy of Catiline.[146]

Cæsar spared no effort to demonstrate his sympathies toward Pompey. His first official act as prætor at the beginning of 62 was a proposal to deprive Catulus of the task of restoring the Capitol and to confer that honor upon Pompey.[147] Cæsar then joined with the tribune Q. Metellus Nepos, who had recently returned from Pompey's camp; both men insisted that Pompey be summoned from the East to stamp out the remaining embers of the Catilinarian conflagration.[148] In light of all this, Cæsar's startling victory over Catulus in the pontifical elections becomes more intelligible. It need not be ascribed

[142] Plutarch, *Pomp.* 25.4, has Cæsar advocate the *lex Gabinia*; Dio, 36.43.2-4, gives him as a supporter of the *lex Manilia.* Possibly, one of them is confused, and Cæsar spoke up on only one of the two occasions. Cicero, *De Imp. Pomp.* 68, does not include Cæsar among the advocates of the *rogatio Manilia.* But that may simply reflect Cæsar's stature in 66. The support of a *quæstorius* was not worthy of mention.

[143] Vell. Pat. 2.40.4, records only the names of the tribunes; Dio, 37.21.4, gives only Cæsar. Strasburger, *Cæsars Eintritt*, pp. 101-103, therefore, casts doubt on the latter account, unnecessarily. Velleius confines himself properly to the formal proposers.

[144] See above. On Labienus' connection with Pompey and his collaboration with Cæsar, see further Syme, *JRS*, 28 (1938): 113-125.

[145] See above, n.126.

[146] Sallust, *Cat.* 49.1-2.

[147] Suet. *Iul.* 15; Dio, 37.44.1-3.

[148] Plut. *Cato*, 27-29; *Cic.* 23; Suet. *Iul.* 16.1; Schol. Bob. 134, Stangl; cf. Suet. *Iul.* 55.3; Dio, 37.42-43. On this, see Meier, *Athenæum*, 40 (1962): 103-125.

solely to heavy bribery, much less to Cæsar's superior stature. Pompey's supporters and agents doubtless solicited votes to assure the defeat of his *inimicus* Catulus. Cæsar was the fortunate beneficiary. The evidence is overwhelming and consistent throughout. Julius Cæsar, far from being a great power or a potential dictator, was one of those young aristocrats in the 60s who endeavored to bask in the glory of Pompeius Magnus.[149]

Aristocratic politics in the 60s had become exceedingly complex. The psychology of the post-Sullan generation made it inevitable. By 70 there was no longer imminent danger that the social structure might crumble or that the establishment would be toppled. As a consequence, feuds and rivalries among noble houses resumed. Individual leaders emerged and divided older alliances, but only with the aim of framing new ones of their own. The aristocratic basis of the structure remained intact.

Some *principes,* holdovers from the generation of Sulla, were still nervous and hewed to a strictly conservative line. The attitude manifested itself most prominently in the circle of Catulus, Hortensius, and the Luculli, joined by men like Metellus Creticus and C. Piso. All those individuals had held the consulship between 78 and 67. Their friends and political heirs were concentrated in the group around Cato Uticensis: Bibulus, Domitius Ahenobarbus, Servilius Vatia, and Favonius. But these men belonged to a younger generation; none would be eligible for the chief magistracy before the decade of the 50s. The "generation gap" is significant. Cato and his partisans could pursue a more vigorous policy, one concerned with reform and adjusted to a dynamic society.

The reputation and martial successes of Pompeius Magnus attracted many diverse elements into his camp. Professional military men, business leaders, *municipales,* and enfranchised provincials counted among his beneficiaries. But Pompey desired access to the inner citadels of senatorial power. For that purpose he gained alliance through marriage connections or favors with many clans of the *nobilitas.* The process further fragmented Rome's political groupings.

[149] The relation between Pompey and Cæsar in these years was acutely pointed out by Taylor, *TAPA*, 73 (1942): 1–24. One other item has often been exploited to argue Cæsarian hostility to Pompey. In early 63 a tribune, P. Servilius Rullus, proposed a sweeping agrarian law, which Cicero persuaded the people to reject on the grounds that it was aimed against Pompey; Cic. *De Leg. Agrar.* I–III, *passim.* Scholars have sometimes assumed that Cæsar and Crassus were behind the bill. But no ancient evidence specifies the names of either man in this connection and the matter does not warrant further speculation; cf. Strasburger, *Cæsars Eintritt*, pp. 114–117. See below, chap. 9. Cicero's arguments against the proposal are clearly tendentious. A large-scale allotment of land in 63 would surely have been to the benefit of Pompey's veterans themselves. If Cæsar were in fact behind the measure, this would be yet another effort to solicit the favor of Pompey; so Sumner, *TAPA*, 97 (1966): 569–582.

Pompey's great rival M. Crassus also became a potent force in the senate of the 60s. But Crassus preferred to tap the resources of the lower echelons of the senate. He was the patron and benefactor of *novi homines,* men of non-consular families, and men who had entered the senatorial class since the dictatorship of Sulla. Wealth, judicial activity, and patronage enabled him to control votes in the *curia* and bind together a loyal group of dependents.

Finally, the 60s mark the rise to notoriety and influence of Julius Cæsar. When stripped of the embellishments added by later traditions, Cæsar's climb is seen to have been made along conventional routes. A patrician background, coupled with connections in the nobility, fostered his career. Shrewdness led him to vigorous partisan activities on behalf of Pompeius Magnus, which speeded access to higher offices. Relationship to the house of Marius and conspicuous espousal of popular measures kept him in the limelight. The personal following that Cæsar began to amass would enable him eventually to step out of Pompey's shadow. It was the most significant harbinger of the future.

III

THE "FIRST TRIUMVIRATE" AND THE REACTION

THE CAMPAIGNS OF Pompeius Magnus in the East achieved unmitigated success. Rome's most persistent foe, Mithridates of Pontus, was no more. Provinces and client kingdoms had been added to the Roman system, wealth revitalized the treasury, and new opportunities were available for the business classes. Pompey's reputation left him without peer abroad. A loyal and enriched soldiery would accompany him home. Pompey's return, it could already be anticipated, would have a profound impact upon the political constellation in Rome.

That proved indeed to be the case. The contests that followed his return drove the general into a new and even more potent coalition. It will be prudent to avoid the assumption that the "first triumvirate" prefigured the fall of the Republic. But its effect on the political groupings traced above was significant and far-reaching. Not that the fluidity of Roman politics disappeared–rather, the lines were more firmly drawn, and the transfers of allegiance became, in many instances, acts of commitment, not mere expediency.

FORMATION OF THE TRIUMVIRATE

Pompey hoped to cap his Asian victories as he had his Spanish: by wiping out revolutionary elements in Italy. In 71 it had been the remnants of Spartacus' revolt; in 62 the Catilinarian conspirators offered opportunity. As we have seen, Pompey's partisans, the tribune Metellus Nepos and the prætor Julius Cæsar, duly proposed that the general be summoned to crush the Catilinarians. The effort foundered. M. Cato, also tribune in 62, interposed his veto; bitter recriminations followed in the senate, and violence in the forum. Cæsar backed down and Nepos withdrew to Pompey's camp.[1]

The general was not one to press the issue. But the failure had significant implications. The *inimici* of Pompey could now expand their propaganda campaign and make it appear plausible. Cato had already disparaged Pompey's victories over Mithridates: it was a war fought against mere women.[2] The real work, it could be argued, had been done by Lucullus. And Lucullus had pointedly celebrated his triumph, after long delay, in 63. Another indignant and vengeful individual whose accomplishments had been usurped by Pompey did the same. In 62, Q. Metellus Creticus, who had been waiting for four years, finally secured his triumph. Pompey was characterized as a carrion bird that feasts upon prey slain by others.[3] His foes insisted that Pompey awaited only an excuse to march his forces on Rome and install a military despotism. Sulla had done it; who was to say that the idea escaped Sulla's former lieutenant? The abortive proposals of Nepos and Cæsar could now be cited as proof of Pompey's revolutionary intentions. The insinuations of Pompey's enemies received widespread belief.[4] M. Licinius Crassus gave dramatic force to the rumors, conspicuously gathering up his children and his money and departing from Italy. Not that Crassus had any genuine fears. The purpose was to lend credence to the anti-Pompeian gossip and thereby to discredit the general.[5]

Pompey evidently did not entertain the dastardly schemes ascribed to him by his enemies. He sent public dispatches back home promising domestic quiet upon his return. Some were, no doubt, disappointed: in particular, the men who had suffered expropriation in the Sullan era, and the indebted classes, who were frustrated by the failure of the Catilinarian movement. Such groups had nothing to lose and everything to gain by renewed upheaval and civil

[1] See, esp., Dio, 37.43.1–3; Plut. *Cic.* 23.2–3; *Cato*, 26.2–4; Schol. Bob. 134, Stangl; cf. the analyses by Sumner, *CP*, 58 (1963): 215–219, and Meier, *Athenæum*, 40 (1962): 103–125.

[2] Cic. *Pro Mur.* 31: *bellum illud omne Mithridaticum cum mulierculis esse gestum.*

[3] On the triumph of Lucullus, see Broughton, *MRR*, II:169; of Creticus, Broughton, *MRR*, II:176. For Lucullus' bitter comparison of Pompey to the carrion bird, see Plut. *Pomp.* 31.6.

[4] Vell. Pat. 2.40.2: *quippe plerique non sine exercitu venturum in urbem adfirmarant et libertati publicæ statuturum arbitrio suo modum*; Plut. *Pomp.* 43.1; Appian, *Mithr.* 116; Dio, 37.44.3.

[5] The motive is accurately diagnosed by Plut. *Pomp.* 43.1. There is no reason to believe that Crassus really feared that Pompey would return to crush him by force; as, e.g., Meyer, *Cæsars Monarchie*, p. 38; Rice Holmes, *Rom. Rep.* I:467. Crassus left Italy for Asia; Cic. *Pro Flacco*, 32. That was hardly a likely refuge from the power of Pompey. Nor should one imagine that Crassus' trip was actually the first step in effecting reconciliation with his rival; as Adcock, *Marcus Crassus*, pp. 41–42. Crassus was back in Rome in 61 and 60 using his influence to undermine Pompey's position further; Cic. *Ad Att.* 1.14.3; Appian, *BC*, 2.9. Perhaps business interests in Asia influenced Crassus' choice of destination; cf. Cic. *Ad Att.* 1.17.9.

war in Italy.[6] Their hopes had been raised in vain. But the propaganda of Pompey's *inimici* had a telling effect in senatorial circles. Nothing that the general did thereafter would easily erase the suspicions and hostility implanted by the tirades of Cato and the actions of Crassus.

In December of 62, after an absence of nearly six years, Pompey arrived in Brundisium. The general was generous to his forces, conducted a final assemblage on the shores of Italy, and then ostentatiously dismissed every man to his home.[7] Pompey desired full cooperation with the Roman aristocracy. In order to neutralize opposition, he dangled marriage alliance to the house of M. Cato: he and his son were available for wedlock with Cato's two nieces. The offer reveals the attitude of a feudal lord, not of a military despot. But it played perfectly into the hands of Pompey's adversaries. Cato affected indignant scorn and exposed the attempt as a cynical maneuver by Pompey to bribe the opposition into silence. The great man's credit suffered further damage. In the process of rendering himself eligible for marriage, Pompey had divorced his previous wife, Mucia, thereby giving substance to reports of her infidelity. The act raised the hackles of Mucia's brothers, Metellus Celer and Metellus Nepos. An insult to the family name caused the two men, former legates and agents of Pompey, to sever the connection and turn against their benefactor. The *dignitas* of the aristocratic clan remained an item to be taken most seriously. Personal and political elements were combining to undermine Pompey's position.[8]

The years 61 and 60 exacerbated Pompey's discomfiture. His influence could still be felt in the electorate. A legate and friend of many years, M. Pupius Piso, gained one of the consulships for 61, although Pompey's request to have elections postponed long enough to permit a personal canvass for Piso was denied. And in 60 another of Pompey's officers, L. Afranius, a loyal subordinate since the Spanish wars, became the first of his *gens* to reach the consulship.[9] But these men did little to augment the image of their leader.

[6] That may be the proper explanation for the notorious crux in Cicero's letter to Pompey of mid-62; Cic. *Ad Fam.* 5.7.1: *Ex litteris tuis, quæ publice misisti, cepi una cum omnibus incredibilem voluptatem. Tantam enim spem oti ostendisti, quantam ego semper omnibus te uno fretus pollicebar. Sed hoc scito, tuos veteres hostes, novos amicos, vehementer litteris perculsos atque ex magna spe deturbatos iacere.* See Gruen, *Phoenix,* 24 (1970): 237–243.

[7] Sources in Broughton, *MRR,* II:176.

[8] On the divorce of Mucia, see Plut. *Pomp.* 42.7; Cic. *Ad Att.* 1.12.3; cf. Suet. *Iul.* 50.1; Asconius, 19, Clark; M. E. Deutsch, *Phil. Quart.* 8 (1929): 218–222. For Cato's rejection of the marriage alliance, see Plut. *Cato,* 30.2–5, 45.2; *Pomp.* 44.2–4; the indignation of the Metelli, Dio, 37.49.3. Cf. the discussion in Gruen, *Historia,* 18 (1969): 82–83.

[9] Postponement of elections in 62 has been disputed. Plutarch reports that Pompey's request was denied; *Pomp.* 44.1–2; *Cato,* 30.1–2. Dio, 37.44.3, asserts that the *comitia* were delayed to allow Piso's candidacy. There need be no contradiction. The elections were postponed

Piso preferred literature and philosophy to public duties. As consul he proved to be ill-tempered and impatient, drawing the scorn of Cicero and engendering the hostility of the Catonian backers, of his consular colleague Messalla, and even of his kinsman C. Piso.[10] Afranius was a still worse bargain. Idle and incompetent, he was totally lacking in energy, except when it came to dancing. As a public official, so we are told, he had no comprehension of the office he had attained. His entire consulship could be accounted an open sore for Pompey.[11]

The great man also proved to be ineffective on the public podium. Crassus had returned from his brief sojourn in Asia to swing the weight of his followers against Pompey in 61. None could refuse the conqueror of the pirates and of Mithridates the right to a splendid triumph. But the political defeats multiplied. M. Pupius Piso expected appointment to the province of Syria; but that prize plum was denied him. And when trouble threatened in Gaul, one of the men removed by the senate from consideration for a Gallic post was Pompey himself. The tightness of his faction slackened. Cicero had been one of Pompey's warmest supporters. But the orator was offended at Pompey's failure to praise the actions of his consulship. In 61 Cicero crossed swords publicly with M. Piso. And Pompey's choice for the consulship in the following year, L. Afranius, endured daily insult from Lollius Palicanus, a former associate of Pompey's.[12]

The general's difficulties increased. He had promised his veterans land, and his eastern arrangements were still without formal ratification. True to character, he routed his requests through the senate house. But the propaganda of Cato and Crassus had had its effect. Pompey's consul Afranius was of no use. His colleague Metellus Celer had suffered an affront to the family and was now implacably hostile. Lucullus challenged Pompey's *acta* in the East, which had superseded his own. He was backed by Celer and by Cato.

---

long enough to permit Piso's return from the East, but not long enough for his chief to appear in his behalf; cf. P. Stein, *Die Senatssitzungen der Ciceronischen Zeit (68–43)* (Münster, 1930), p. 19.

[10] See, esp., Cic. *Ad Att.* 1.13.2–3, 1.14.5–6, 1.16.8, 1.16.12; cf. Gruen, *CSCA*, 1 (1968): 167–168.

[11] Cic. *Ad Att.* 1.20.5: *eius consulatus non consulatus sit sed Magni nostri ὑπώπιον; Ad Att.* 1.18.5: *quam ignavus ac sine animo miles!; Ad Att.* 1.19.4: *ille alter nihil ita est ut plane quid emerit nesciat.* For his dancing, see Dio, 37.49.3.

[12] On Pompey's failures at the rostra, see Cic. *Ad Att.* 1.13.4, 1.14.1–2; Crassus' maneuvers, Cic. *Ad Att.* 1.14.3. Sources for Pompey's triumph are collected by Broughton, *MRR*, II:181. Piso was denied Syria; Cic. *Ad Att.* 1.16.8; and Pompey was to be kept from a Gallic command; Cic. *Ad Att.* 1.19.3. In public, Pompey's relations with Cicero were close; Cic. *Ad Att.* 1.12.3, 1.13.4, 1.16.11, 1.19.7; but Cicero did not forget the general's reluctance to endorse his actions of 63; Cic. *Ad Fam.* 5.7.2–3; *Ad Att.* 1.13.4, 1.14.3–4. For Cicero's attacks on Piso, see Cic. *Ad Att.* 1.16.8; for the hostility between Afranius and Palicanus, see Cic. *Ad Att.* 1.18.5.

A lengthy filibuster was threatened. M. Crassus, pleased with Pompey's failures, joined the fray. The same individuals led the fight against an agrarian law for veterans of the general's campaigns. Both Pompeian efforts encountered firm rebuff by the *curia.* The bulk of the senate persuaded itself that any new schemes by Pompey's partisans contained hidden powers for their chief.[13] The conqueror of the Mediterranean was reduced to mute contemplation of his triumphal toga.[14]

It was not the style of Pompey the Great to lay his case before the Roman populace. Much less did he consider mobilizing his veterans to crush the opposition. The favor of his discharged troops endured; so also did the favor of much of the electorate, heightened by the splendor of his triumph. But Pompey suffered political defeat at the level of the ruling class. Given his temperament, that was the only level that counted. Cato had welded his coterie into a potent bloc. And M. Crassus, with considerable following in the senate's lower ranks, had mustered votes to effect the eclipse of his rival. A costly miscalculation had lost Pompey the support of such former associates as the brothers Metelli. Anti-Pompeian propaganda had inspired in many senators suspicions about his aims. If Pompey was to resuscitate his position, new alliances among the ruling circles of Roman government would be required. No other route would have been palatable.

An additional fact stands out noticeably in the wrecking of Pompey's endeavors in 61 and 60. No capable confederate sat in the consul's chair. Pompey's choices, Piso and Afranius, were pusillanimous, idle, and ineffective. Piso had lost credit with members of his own clan; Afranius' humble background rendered him incapable of firm leadership. The consul could be a pivotal figure. Presiding officer in the senate, initiator of senatorial motions and comitial legislation, holder of elections—the state's chief executive, by his actions or inaction, could set the tone for a year. Pompey required vigorous and positive leadership in the consulship of 59. Where was a suitable candidate to be found? C. Julius Cæsar arrived in Italy in mid-60, after a successful tenure in Spain, with good prospects for the following year.[15] Cæsar had espoused Pompeian causes for nearly a decade, and he could be expected to pursue an energetic line as consul. More important, Cæsar had won popularity and independent support in previous years. M. Crassus too recognized the

[13] Cic. *Ad Att.* 1.19.4: *huic toti rationi agrariæ senatus adversabatur, suspicans Pompeio novam quandam potentiam quæri.* Further evidence on the agrarian bill and its rejection: Cic. *Ad Att.* 1.18.6, 2.1.6; Dio, 37.49–50; Plut. *Cato,* 31.1; *Luc.* 42.6; on the blocking of Pompey's eastern settlement: Dio, 37.49–50.1; Plut. *Pomp.* 46.3; *Cato*, 31.1; *Luc.* 42.5–6; Vell. Pat. 2.40.5; Appian, *BC*, 2.9: Suet. *Iul.* 19.

[14] Cic. *Ad Att.* 1.18.6: *Pompeius togulam illam pictam silentio tuetur suam.*

[15] Cic. *Ad Att.* 2.1.6: *Cæsarem cuius nunc venti valde sunt secundi.*

talents and promise of Julius Cæsar. In early 61, when Cæsar set out for his province of Spain, Crassus contracted to act as surety for his debts.[16] Like so many other transactions conducted by that individual, it was an investment for the future.

Scholarly debate has been profuse on the date at which the "first triumvirate" was formed. The sources are divided. Hindsight may have predated the compact; ascription of motive has confused the situation. It will suffice to adduce a few relevant comments. There is no reason to doubt that both Crassus and Pompey, each for his own reasons, lent assistance to the candidacy of Cæsar. Crassus cultivated promising adherents, and Pompey needed a strong figure in the consulship. Cæsar conducted his canvass in league with L. Lucceius, a wealthy intellectual and future adviser to Pompey. Lucceius hoped for the other consular position. The intermediary, so we are told, was Q. Arrius, a dutiful partisan of Crassus.[17]

None of this, however, is tantamount to formation of the "first triumvirate."[18] A letter of Cicero's, dated December 60, well after the elections, implies that no union of the trio had taken place. Cæsar requested the support of Cicero: he would promise to follow the counsel of the orator and of Pompey; and he held out hope for a future reconciliation between Crassus and Pompey.[19] The conjoining of forces, therefore, postdates the inception of Cæsar's consulship. Cæsar had skillfully enjoyed the backing of both Pompey and Crassus at a time when the latter two were still very much at odds. It best served his ends not to advertise that endorsement too widely. Overt support from Crassus might alienate some friends of Pompey, and vice versa.

[16] Plut. *Cæs.* 11.1; *Crass.* 7.6.

[17] Cic. *Ad Att.* 1.17.11: *Lucceium scito consulatum habere in animo statim petere. Duo enim soli dicuntur petituri, Cæsar, cum eo coire per Arrium cogitat, et Bibulus, cum hoc se putat per C. Pisonem posse coniungi.* Lucceius opted for the former alternative; Suet. *Iul.* 19.1. For Lucceius' closeness with Pompey, see Cic. *Ad Fam.* 13.41; 13.42. On Arrius and Crassus, see Cic. *Brutus*, 242.

[18] Some sources place the coalition prior to the consular elections of 60; Livy, *Per.* 103; Plut. *Crass.* 14.1–3; *Cæs.* 13.1–2; *Pomp.* 47.1–3; *Cato,* 31.2–5. They are followed by many historians; e.g., Meyer, *Cæsars Monarchie*, pp. 59–60; Taylor, *Party Politics*, p. 132; Rowland, *Historia*, 15 (1966), p. 218. The chronological remarks, however, are inexact and buttressed only by retrospection.

[19] Cic. *Ad Att.* 2.3.3: *is adfirmabat illum omnibus in rebus meo et Pompei consilio usurum daturumque operam ut cum Pompeio Crassum coniungeret.* It will not do to argue that the pact was being deliberately concealed from Cicero; much less that no one knew of it until 56; so H. A. Sanders, *Mem. Am. Acad. Rome*, 10 (1932): 55–68; cf. also G. M. Bersanetti, *Riv. Indo-Grec.-Ital. Filol.*, 11 (1927): 1–20; *ibid.*, 12 (1928): 21–42. Cæsar could have served no purpose in withholding the arrangement from Cicero; indeed he offered hope for its fulfillment to Cicero himself. And the cooperation of the triumvirs was clear and unabashed in 59.

Only after he was safely voted into the consulship would he move to effect reconciliation.[20]

Julius Cæsar had successfully engineered his election to the consulship. But it would require powerful support to render that office effective. The friends of Cato were prepared to emasculate Cæsar as they had M. Piso and Afranius in the two preceding years. Cato had already blocked Cæsar's desire to stand for the consulship *in absentia,* thus compelling him to forfeit a triumph in order to submit his candidacy. And the senate had voted minimal provincial duties for the consuls of 59, ensuring that they would not have large forces under their command.[21] The Catonian group also procured a suitable counterweight in the consulship: Cato's son-in-law M. Calpurnius Bibulus. Bitterly resentful and envious of Cæsar, Bibulus was expected to offer unrelenting opposition. The year 59 promised to be as exasperating for Pompey as the two previous years had been.

These facts lie behind the coalition which moderns have dubbed "the first triumvirate." Pompey had gained an energetic adherent in the consulship. But there was no reason to believe that Cæsar would be any more convincing in promoting Pompey's aims than Piso and Afranius had been. Nor did Cæsar desire a year of frustration to be followed by political obscurity. He would fight Pompey's battles only if more substantial assistance were forthcoming from the *ordo senatorius.* Alliance with the Catonian group had been foreclosed. But Cæsar proffered the hope of bringing together the contingents of Pompey and Crassus. Pompey would have no objections. The votes that Crassus controlled in the senate, and the *clientelæ* that he could muster in the assemblies might bring at last the ratification of Pompey's *acta* and land distribution for his veterans. Cæsar, for his part, would escape the subordinate stature of Pompey's other *amici,* override a weakened opposition, and anticipate a profitable provincial command. The motives of Crassus are, as ever, obscure. He had banded with Cato, Lucullus, and Metellus Celer in blocking Pompey's

[20] The process is accurately described by Dio, 37.54.3–37.56.1; cf. Appian, *BC,* 2.9. Other sources also place the formation of the triumvirate after the elections; Suet. *Iul.* 19; or, more specifically, during Cæsar's consulship; Vell. Pat. 2.44.1: *hoc igitur consule inter eum et Cn. Pompeium et M. Crassum inita potentiæ societas*; Florus, 2.13.11. See the arguments of R. Hanslik, *RhMus,* 98 (1955): 324–334; cf. Rice Holmes, *Rom. Rep.*, I:474–476; Gelzer, *Cæsar*, p. 68. That Crassus was involved seems clear from a passage not usually invoked in this context; Cic. *Ad Att.* 2.4.2: *neque mihi umquam veniet in mentem Crasso invidere neque pænitere quod a me ipso non desciverim.* Cf. also Cicero's reference to *tres homines; Ad Att.* 2.9.2.

[21] On the rejection of Cæsar's candidacy in absence, see Suet. *Iul.* 18; Plut. *Cato*, 31.2–3; *Cæs.* 13.1; Dio, 37.54.1; Appian, *BC*, 2.8; cf. Linderski, *Mélanges Michalowski* (1966), pp. 524–525. On the consular provinces, see Suet. *Iul.* 19.2. Balsdon, *JRS*, 29 (1939): 181–182, takes the latter reference to be to Italy. But see Gelzer, *Cæsar*, p. 65, n.2; Meier, *Res Pub.*, p. 278, n.73.

objectives during 61 and 60. But he would not rebuff an opportunity to lift his prestige and power to the level of his rival. Crassus had recently clashed with Cato over a request by the Asian *publicani* to reduce the terms of their contract.[22] It is myopic to assume, as is often done, that Crassus' investment in a tax-farming company determined his participation in the triumvirate. But the friction with Cato no doubt made it more palatable to lend assistance to Cato's antagonists. Crassus exacted a price. Reduction of the Asian contract was perhaps not the most important concession. If land was to be distributed to veterans of the eastern wars, Crassus wanted to make certain that he would be one of the administrators of that bounty. The distribution of *beneficia* would also bring political gain to the benefactor. When the agrarian commission was instituted in 59, it was under the joint control of Pompey and Crassus.[23] There was, however, a more basic motive. The preeminence which Crassus could not quite attain on his own was within his grasp with the backing of powerful allies.[24]

THE IMPACT OF THE TRIUMVIRATE

The creation of the "first triumvirate" has been seen as a momentous milestone in the crippling of Republican institutions.[25] Asinius Pollio chose to begin his history of the civil wars with the year 60, the year of Cæsar's election to the consulship. Later authorities were eloquent on the constitutional disaster produced by the union of three dynasts to enslave the Republic.[26] But the retrospective lamenting is excessive. The phrase "first triumvirate" itself is a modern construct, unattested in the ancient evidence. It draws on false analogy from the triumvirate of Octavian, Antony, and Lepidus in 43, which possessed formal sanction and received dictatorial authority. By contrast, the union of political cliques in 59 was an informal *amicitia.* That betokened no novelty in Roman politics and simply underlined the mobility of groupings that had been characteristic of previous decades. The three men sought mutual advantage by combining *clientelæ* and influence. In traditional fashion the

[22] Cic. *Ad Att.* 1.17.9, 1.18.7, 2.1.8.

[23] Dio, 38.1.7.

[24] Vell. Pat. 2.44.2: *Crassus, ut quem principatum solus adsequi non poterat, auctoritate Pompei, viribus teneret Cæsaris*; cf. Florus, 2.13.10–11: *Pompeius tamen inter utrumque eminebat; sic igitur Cæsare dignitatem conparare, Crasso augere, Pompeio retinere cupientibus.*

[25] So even Syme, *Rom. Rev.*, pp. 35–36: "This capture of the constitution may fairly be designated as the end of the Free State. From a triumvirate, it was a short step to dictatorship."

[26] Cf. Livy, *Per.* 103: *eoque consulatus candidato et captante rem publicam invadere conspiratio inter tres civitatis principes facta est*; Florus, 2.13.10–11; Lucan, 1.84–86; Vell. Pat. 2.44.1. On Pollio's history, see Horace, *Carm.* 2.1.

pact was sealed by marriage alliance: Pompey wed the daughter of Cæsar. Rape of the Republic was not its aim, nor its effect.

That is not to deny the significance of the political consequences. The gathering of this coalition induced sharp restructuring of alliances and alignments. And much of it did not turn out to the advantage of the triumvirate. Temporary benefit accrued to them, particularly during Cæsar's consulship. But the cooperation was shaky and the disenchantment of former supporters proved in the long run to be debilitating to the league itself. The chief consequence of this pact was not the supremacy of the triumvirate, but the coalescence of aristocratic groups in opposition. Pompeius Magnus counted the most immediate gains. But his was to be the more bitter disillusionment. When erosion of support in the ruling class came, it was principally erosion of Pompey's support. It may not have been beyond the power of M. Crassus to anticipate that result. His influence did not depend on links with houses of the *nobilitas*.

The legislative activities of Cæsar's consulship were full and controversial. A more detailed analysis will be reserved for discussion below. For the moment our concern must be with the political implications. It should be noted that the consul operated initially through standard channels. He hoped for approval of legislation through senatorial decrees. It was only when resistance in the *curia* stiffened that Cæsar brought his bills before the populace, unmasked the support of Pompey and Crassus, and collected sufficient popular votes for passage of the measures. Pompey's eastern settlement now at last received formal ratification. Agrarian measures to provide for land-hungry troops were pushed through, to be administered by Pompey, Crassus, and several subordinates. The desired reduction of contract terms for the Asian *publicani* was also put into effect. And Julius Cæsar, by law of the people, acquired appointment to the provinces of Cisalpine Gaul and Illyricum, thereby overriding earlier senatorial arrangements for the consular provinces.[27] On the surface, the aims of Pompey, baffled for two years, seem to have been implemented. But the manifestations were deceptive. Opposition was congealing, and the gains of 59 were soon to be overbalanced by greater losses in that and subsequent years.

The spearhead of the resistance was, of course, Cato's coterie. Cato's moral position was appreciably augmented by the actions of the dynasts. He could, with some justice, castigate the combine as a cynical alliance for purely personal advantage. The idea that Catonian counteraction was purely negative, obstructive, and mindless does scant justice to its tactical value. Whatever the merits of the triumvirs' proposals, Cato could always call them into question on grounds of the character and aims of their proposers. Cato deftly played the

[27] On the consulship of Cæsar, see, esp., Gelzer, *Cæsar*, pp. 71-101.

role of the martyr. Delaying tactics and combative resistance forced his adversaries into intimidation and even, occasionally, into violence. That, of course, only played into the hands of Cato and made his denunciations appear the more plausible.[28] Cæsar's consular colleague Bibulus steadfastly vetoed his bills and summoned religious objections to declare the legislation invalid. Bibulus' contrariness was no mere empty display. He ostentatiously shut himself up in his home, professing to require its protection. The edicts issuing from his confines failed to impede Cæsar's enactments. No matter: Bibulus' purpose was to discredit the triumvirs, to heighten public indignation, and to render the legislation vulnerable to future repeal.[29] The maneuvers did not lack effect.

The unpopularity of the *tres homines* in 59 was notable. Their public appearances were received coldly or with open antagonism; their adversaries earned conspicuous favor. Bibulus, far from being a pitiable figure, had never enjoyed such high repute. His edicts were read avidly, and his boycotting tactics were regarded as the proper means to rescue the state's honor.[30] The propaganda proved to be potent. Dissatisfaction with the triumvirate spread among all groups: the younger generation, the *equites,* even the Italian municipalities. The compact was described by critics as **τρικάρανον**: "the three-headed monster."[31]

Cæsar was the target of much abuse. But he could look forward to a provincial command and a long tenure abroad whereby to build his following. It was Pompey who was to remain at home, expecting the role of a *princeps* in the senate. And it was he who witnessed most painfully the diminution of his prestige and the dwindling of his influence. Pompey became enraged by Bibulus' edicts, plagued by personal attacks in public, and bitterly downcast at persistent failures. The great man moped about, ineffective in his public appearances and longing for the old days when he could still command some respect. He had paid a large price for the alliance. Crassus, who may have anticipated it all, smiled at the general's miseries. As Cicero properly noted,

[28] Cf. e.g., Dio, 38.3; Plut. *Cæs.* 14.6–7; *Cato*, 33.1–2; Val. Max. 2.10.7; Gellius, 4.10.8. And, esp., Cic. *Ad Att.* 2.21.1: *qui Catoni irati omnia perdiderunt.*

[29] Cf. Appian, *BC*, 2.11: ἐπενόουν δ' ὅμως βύβλον ἐνίστασθαι τοῖς νόμοις καὶ μὴ δόξαν ἀμελείας ἀλλὰ ἥσσης ἐνέγκασθαι. Sources on Bibulus' activity in Broughton, *MRR,* II:187. Cf. the analysis in Meier, *Res Pub.*, pp. 282–285. If there is any truth in the story that Lucullus, after intimidation by Cæsar, fell on his knees to beg mercy from the consul, it may well be another mock demonstration to dramatize the tyrannical behavior of the triumvirs; Suet. *Iul.* 20.

[30] Cic. *Ad Att.* 2.19.2: *Bibulus in cælo est, nec qua re scio, sed ita laudatur quasi 'unus homo nobis cunctando restituit rem'*; *Ad Att.* 2.19.5, 2.20.4, 2.20.6, 2.21.5; cf. Suet. *Iul.* 9.2, 49.2.

[31] For the young men, Cic. *Ad Att.* 2.8.1; the *equites*, 2.19.3; the *municipia* and the countryside, 2.13.2, 2.21.1; for the term Τρικάρανον, see Appian, *BC*, 2.9.

Pompey had brought it all on himself.[32] The strategy of the opposition had taken its toll. Not only had they stirred resentment against the triumvirate; by stressing the illegality of their measures, they had also touched on Pompey's sensitivity. Jealous of his posture as a constitutionalist, he could only feel increasing discomfort at the methods which Cæsar was compelled to adopt. Crassus cooperated politically, but nourished personal hostility. The syndicate was already beginning to crack.[33]

It should be stressed again that the members of this confederacy had united each for his own purposes. There was little sense of permanency or even congeniality. Insofar as it brought unity, it was unity in the opposition. Cæsar's purposes were served. He could claim to have kept faith with Pompey, indeed to have suffered abuse in promulgating the general's measures. But Cæsar did not need to worry. His consulship had left a firm mark, and upon its expiry he would move to Gaul, where supreme command was guaranteed for five years. That offered the desired opportunity to make him a power in his own right. Crassus had lost no repute. As agrarian commissioner he could add to his *clientelæ*. His personal senatorial partisans remained loyal. And he looked with pleasure on the declining stature of Pompey. As so often happened in the past, when abuse was directed against Roman politicians Crassus escaped it. Pompey's allies had entered the triumvirate in order to lift their prestige to his level. Their aims progressed toward fulfillment. It was Pompey who had miscalculated. The alliance with Crassus brought him temporary and grudging cooperation from the latter's supporters. But the most obvious political consequence for Pompey was the gradual desertion of his former associates in the ruling class. For the man who desired, above all, acceptance by the aristocracy this was the most bitter pill.

The process can be illustrated by a number of examples. The alienation of the Metelli has already been noted. Metellus Creticus had fostered enmity toward Pompey since the early 60s. And Pompey's divorce of Mucia activated the fury of her brothers, Celer and Nepos, who had been his officers in the eastern wars. As consul in 60, Celer combated Pompey's schemes, and after the formation of the triumvirate in 59, he cooperated with the Catonians

[32] Cic. *Ad Att.* 2.19.2: *Pompeius, nostri amores, quod mihi summo dolore est, ipse se adflixit.* On Crassus' pleasure at Pompey's discomfiture; see Cic. *Ad Att.* 2.21.3–4. Cf. also, Cic. *Ad Att.* 2.13.2: *quanto in odio noster Magnus!*; 2.22.6: *tædet ipsum Pompeium eumque vehementer pænitet*; 2.23.2: *nostrum amicum, vehementer sui status pænitere restituique in eum locum cupere ex quo decidit*; 2.14.1, 2.17.2, 2.19.2–3, 2.19.5; Val. Max. 6.2.9.

[33] On Pompey's unhappiness with Cæsar's methods, see Cic. *Ad Att.* 2.16.2: *se leges Cæsaris probare, actiones ipsum præstare debere.* On dissension among the triumvirs, see Cic. *Ad Att.* 2.7.3, 2.21.3, 2.23.2. Cicero does put into Pompey's mouth the belligerent statement *'oppressos vos,' inquit, 'tenebo exercitu Cæsaris'*; *Ad Att.* 2.16.2. That, however, is evidence, not for Pompey's attitude, but for the reputation that his enemies had successfully hung upon him.

against the agrarian measure. His brother Nepos, once a firm ally of Pompey's, also found the triumvirate obnoxious, and could be reckoned among Pompey's *inimici* in the mid-50s.

Similar shifts may be ascertained among the Cornelii Lentuli. They had been among the general's most prominent patrician adherents in the 60s. But when Pompey elected to tie his fortunes to Crassus and Cæsar, their support melted away. Lentulus Niger and his son became Pompeian antagonists in 59, and the younger Niger continued his activities through the 50s. A cousin, Lentulus Crus, was lined up with them against the *tres homines* in 59 and 58. By 57 Pompey had to face also the hostility of Lentulus Spinther and Lentulus Marcellinus, who helped to wreck his hopes for a new overseas command.

There can be no doubt that the creation of the triumvirate galvanized the aristocracy into a unity that it had not previously possessed. Some of the old feuds were dispensed with in the light of what seemed a greater peril. The Luculli and the Servilii may be taken as illustrative of the trend. Hereditary rivalry between them endured at least into the early 60s, and probably beyond. Several prosecutions attest to their mutual *inimicitia.* Servilius Isauricus had been among those who espoused Pompey's Mithridatic commission in 66, in part to obtain the eclipse of L. Lucullus. But the events of 59 altered the picture. The two *gentes* combined to withstand the triumvirs. The younger Servilius married into Cato's family and became the Stoic's most ardent admirer. The Servilii, father and son, were active among Pompey's adversaries in the mid-50s. A comparable pattern is detectable among the Scribonii Curiones. The elder Curio had also been a proponent of Pompey's command in 66. But the situation reversed itself sharply after Pompey backed Cæsar's measures of 59. Curio published biting orations and later a polemical dialogue ascribing every iniquity, political and personal, to the dynasts. His son was even more in evidence in 59, developing his public reputation with fierce denunciations of Cæsar, for which he drew thunderous applause. Once again father and son carried their enmity into ensuing years.[34]

More grievous still was the desertion of the Sullæ and the Memmii through whom Pompey had linked himself to the house of Sulla the dictator. Pompey's brother-in-law P. Sulla was in league with his enemies in the mid-50s, and Faustus Sulla, son of the dictator and a former officer of Pompey's, could no longer be depended on in the latter part of the decade. C. Memmius, Sulla's son-in-law and a Pompeian partisan in the 60s, became a vociferous opponent of the triumvirate in 59 and 58. Pompey's own nephew, another C. Memmius, appears among his antagonists in the mid-50s.[35]

[34] Full citation of sources and discussion on these developments may be found in Gruen, *Historia*, 18 (1969): 80–85.

[35] Gruen, *Historia*, 18 (1969): 105–106.

Other figures, of less political note, followed analogous paths. L. Gellius Publicola had been a loyal Pompeian confederate at least since his consulship in 72. Even after reaching the censorship he consented to serve as a subordinate officer under Pompey in the 60s. But the triumvirate was more than the aged Publicola could stomach. He vowed to resist to the death the agrarian measures of 59 and persisted in opposition to Pompey through the mid-50s. L. Valerius Flaccus, a young patrician, had also been among Pompey's legates in the Mithridatic campaign. In 59, however, he too turns up on the other side. Pompey engineered a prosecution of Flaccus in that year, an effort which ended in failure. Finally, there was the military man, M. Petreius, who had served long campaigns under Pompey and who was induced to join him again in 55. Yet in 59, even Petreius, an ex-prætor and proud of senatorial traditions, found the strong-arm tactics of the triumvirs unacceptable. When Cæsar ordered Cato to prison to end his obstruction, Petreius marched off with him, explaining that he preferred Cato's company in prison to Cæsar's in the senate.[36]

There can be no coincidence in the fact that, in almost every case, former *amici* of Pompey are first seen to be ranged with the opposition in the year 59. That development provides eloquent testimony to the effectiveness of propaganda and tactics of the Catonian group. The strategy of filibuster and boycott, practiced particularly by Bibulus and Cato, should no longer be regarded as shallow gesturing. The political gains were marked. By maintaining a consciously moral posture, driving the triumvirs to extreme measures, and parading their own martyrdom, Cato and his associates ruined triumviral credit among the people and assembled aristocratic collaboration in resistance. In addition to the former allies of Pompey who deserted him, there were other leading families included in the opposition: the Pisones, the Lepidi, and the Claudii.[37] Clans that did not usually act in conjunction found common ground.

A strange plot in midsummer or autumn 59 further documents the tensions of that year. An informer of little repute, L. Vettius, announced a conspiracy of leading nobles to murder Pompey. Among those named were Bibulus, the older and younger Curiones, two Lentuli, Æmilius Paullus, and M. Brutus.

[36] On Publicola and Flaccus, see Gruen, *Historia*, 18 (1969): 85–86. On Petreius, overlooked in that article, see Dio, 38.3.2–3; Gellius, 4.10.8. It would be imprudent to include Terentius Varro in this company. He was, to be sure, author of the pamphlet Τρικάρανον; Appian, *BC*, 2.9. However, he had been a loyal Pompeian partisan in the past, and more important, he saw service on Pompey's agrarian commission in 59; Pliny, *NH*, 7.176; cf. Varro, *De Re Rust.* 1.2.10. Varro's treatise may simply have mocked the use of the term by enemies of the triumvirate; so Anderson, *Pompey*, p. 45. The arguments of R. Astbury, *CQ*, 17 (1967): 403–407, which require Varro to have shifted back and forth in 59, are strained and unconvincing.

[37] Cf. Gruen, *Historia*, 18 (1969): 86–89; *CSCA*, 1 (1968): 155–170.

The testimony was garbled and readily discredited. Paullus was not even in Italy; and Bibulus had himself earlier given Pompey warning of the plot. Vettius was chained and imprisoned. But Julius Cæsar and the tribune P. Vatinius dragged him out on the following day to pursue and intensify the questioning. The informer changed his story; Brutus' name was dropped and new ones were added: Lucullus, Domitius Ahenobarbus, C. Fannius, C. Piso, M. Laterensis, and some sly hints about Cicero. Few could be induced to credit the insinuations, no charges were brought against the alleged plotters, and Vettius was soon thereafter found dead in prison.[38]

The meaning and motivation of the affair will probably never be known. Excessive speculation is pointless. At the time, men suspected the machinations of Cæsar: Vettius was suborned to fabricate the plot in order to ruin young Curio and other aristocrats who were giving the consul difficulty. That analysis has won the assent of most commentators. They have added also another motive: Cæsar hoped, by frightening Pompey, to detach him from the aristocracy. The reconstruction is vulnerable and unconvincing. Our preceding discussion has demonstrated that Pompey's relations with the *nobilitas* were already sufficiently strained. And the notion of Vettius as Cæsar's agent is difficult to swallow. Three years before, in 62, Vettius had endeavored to implicate Cæsar in the Catilinarian conspiracy.[39]

Cæsar, it appears, intimidated Vettius and induced him to alter his testimony at the second senatorial hearing: in particular, to drop the name of Brutus, son of Cæsar's mistress Servilia. That itself suggests that Cæsar was not behind Vettius' initial revelations. It is not impossible that Pompey or Pompeian partisans concocted the scheme in order to tarnish the moral image of some of his tormentors. One may note at least that Vettius had once served with Pompey on the staff of Pompey's father and that both men had partaken of the spoils during the Sullan proscriptions.[40] The aims, whatever they were, failed of fulfillment. Vettius' deceitful testimony rebounded only upon himself. Pompey's enemies suffered no prosecution, nor loss of prestige.

[38] Principal evidence on the affair is in Cic. *Ad Att.* 2.24, which stresses Cæsar's role. Three years later Cicero charged the machinations to Vatinius; *In Vat.* 24–26; *Pro Sest.* 132. Later sources provide muddled versions of the same events; Suet. *Iul.* 20.5; Dio, 38.9.2–4; Plut. *Luc.* 42.7–8; Schol. Bob. 139, 148, Stangl. Modern literature is considerable. See, e.g., Rice Holmes, *Rom. Rep.*, I:323–324, 479–482; W. C. McDermott, *TAPA*, 80 (1949): 351–367; L. R. Taylor, *Historia*, 1 (1950): 45–51; W. Allen, *TAPA*, 81 (1950): 153–163; R. Rossi, *Annali Triestini*, 21 (1951): 247–260; Meier, *Historia,* 10 (1961): 68–98; R. Seager, *Latomus*, 24 (1965): 519–531.

[39] Suet. *Iul.* 17; cf. Dio, 37.41.2–4.

[40] On Vettius' service with Pompeius Strabo, see *ILLRP*, II.no.515; cf. N. Criniti, *L'Epigrafe di Asculum di Gn. Pompeo Strabone* (Milan, 1970), pp. 128–131; in the proscriptions, Sallust, *Hist.* 1.55.17. The Sallustian passage reveals a Picene origin for Vettius. Plut. *Luc.* 42.7–8, in fact, affirms that Vettius was instigated by partisans of Pompey.

The year 59 was a pivotal one in Roman politics. Pompey's misguided alliance with Crassus and Cæsar had raised the stature of those two men, but had considerably diminished his own. The artful strategy of the Catonians had drawn most of the pedigreed nobility out of Pompey's orbit and into opposition. But it does not follow that the aristocracy as a whole acknowledged Cato's leadership. Nor was Rome divided into "triumviral" and "optimate" parties. Pompey had been the single most powerful figure in Roman politics for almost two decades. The weakening of his position freed a great many individuals and groups to pursue independent lines and to develop their own following. Having escaped dependency on Pompey, they did not need to seek the shelter of Cato. For the *nobilitas,* in fact, the atmosphere was liberating, not repressive. Aristocratic politics became further fragmented. In the eyes of the aristocracy, that constituted a sign of vigor, not degeneration.

The activities of the Claudii, proud but renegade patricians, provide a revealing case in point. The long history of that ancient family showed several examples of aberrant political activity, including demagoguery and espousal of popular causes. The tradition dates back at least to Ap. Claudius Cæcus, the blustering reformer of the fourth century. One recalls also Ap. Claudius, father-in-law of Ti. Gracchus and sponsor of the Gracchan movement. In the Ciceronian age, as we have seen, three Claudian brothers reached prominence. The *dignitas* of the clan was fiercely proclaimed by the eldest, Ap. Claudius Pulcher: his *Appietas,* so Cicero unkindly termed it. Ambition, however, led Appius on a checkered political career, with unstable loyalties—except to himself. Marital alliances with several *gentes* gave him freedom of movement; the Claudian name and cash acquired by unsavory means made him a power. Consulship and censorship were reached in the late 50s. A second brother, C. Claudius, was less conspicuous though sufficiently prominent to gain a prætorship and to suffer political prosecution. The youngest of the brothers achieved the greatest notoriety. P. Clodius Pulcher was brilliant but unpredictable. An explosive temperament and varied political talents combined to make him a key figure in the early 50s.

The Claudii, it can be claimed, were politically linked to prominent families of the aristocracy. Three sisters of the three brothers married leading *nobiles:* L. Lucullus, Q. Metellus Celer, and Q. Marcius Rex. But actions of the Claudii were rarely determined by their family connections. As was noted earlier, Appius and Publius inaugurated public careers in the 70s by prosecuting *epigoni* of Sulla, though their father had himself been a Sullan beneficiary. Both men served with their brother-in-law Lucullus in Asia. But Clodius' loyalty did not extend beyond his advantage. He postured as champion of the enlisted man, stirred mutiny in Lucullus' army, and moved over to the staff of his other brother-in-law, Q. Marcius. Lucullus did not forgive or forget. The haughty aristocrat terminated relations with a flourish, divorcing his wife, Clodia, and leveling charges of incestuous relations with her brother.[41] The activities of the Claudii already set them apart in fame and scandal by the mid-60s.

P. Clodius' mercurial career kept him in the center of the political stage. Standard aristocratic politics was not his game. The Claudii had their own traditions and could go their own way. Clodius had wantonly betrayed one brother-in-law. He then alienated another: Metellus Celer opposed his unusual effort to secure the tribunate, an office closed to patricians.[42] The flouting of convention was part of Clodius' style. Clodius, it seems, was caught in female garb at the festival of the Bona Dea, a ceremony from which males were excluded. The affair caused opprobrium and brought prosecution in 61. But Clodius escaped conviction. An unorthodox political style had its charm and attractiveness. A Claudian could perhaps be permitted behavior denied to or frowned upon by the plebeian nobility.[43]

Clodius was already a man to be reckoned with. His antics may have been contrived to win support and to demonstrate independence. And Clodius mastered the craft of playing off political groups against one another for his own advantage. In 59 he persuaded the triumvirs that he could be a useful ally against their critics and enemies. Under the auspices of Cæsar and Pompey, Clodius was adopted by a plebeian family and thus became eligible for a tribunate. The aim was in line with what might be regarded as his calculated unorthodoxy. And more important, the tribunate always gave scope for activity that would, in any other office, be regarded as unseemly. The opportunity to ingratiate himself further with the populace supplied the principal attraction.

It should no longer be necessary to refute the older notion that Clodius acted as agent or tool of the triumvirate. Nor were his actions the result of sheer irrationality. When it suited his interests, particularly in his vengeful

[41] For the *Appietas* of Ap. Claudius, see Cic. *Ad Fam.* 3.7.5. On his character, cf. Cic. *Ad Att.* 8.1.3: *nemo . . . inconstantior quam Ap. Claudius.* The family's marriage alliances are perhaps unduly stressed by Syme, *Rom. Rev.*, pp. 20, 23; *Sallust,* 24–25. For Clodius' betrayal of Lucullus, see Cic. *De Har. Resp.* 42; Dio, 36.14.4, 36.17.2; Plut. *Luc.* 34.1–4; Lucullus' divorce of Clodia, Cic. *Pro Mil.* 73; Plut. *Luc.* 38.1; *Cic.* 29.3; *Cæs.* 10.5. On Ap. Claudius, see further the work of L. A. Constans, *Un Correspondant de Ciceron, Ap. Claudius Pulcher* (Paris, 1921).

[42] Cic. *De Har. Resp.* 45; *Ad Att.* 2.1.4; *Pro Cæl.* 60; Dio, 37.51.2.

[43] For the trial, see below, chap. 7. On Clodius' strong support at this time, see Plut. *Cæs.* 10.6; Dio, 37.45.1; cf. Plut. *Cato,* 31.2; and cf. Gruen, *Phoenix,* 20 (1966): 121–122. To the modern references collected in the latter article, add R. Y. Hathorn, *CJ,* 50 (1954): 33–34; I. Trencsényi-Waldapfel, *Athenæum,* 42 (1964): 49–51; Wiseman, *CQ,* 18 (1968): 297–299.

attacks on Cicero, Clodius could flaunt the endorsement of the dynasts and of their military force. But the unpopularity of Cæsar and Pompey also played into Clodius' hands. He paraded himself as the true champion of the people in his tribunate of 58 and denounced the syndicate, which had been formed only to serve its own ends. Popular legislation on a large and striking scale stood to Clodius' credit in 58. Inordinate influence in the assemblies made him for a time Rome's most prominent figure, not only in legislative matters but in manipulation of foreign policy. He succeeded in effecting the temporary elimination of his *inimici* Cicero and Cato. At the same time, he could utilize the propaganda of the Catonians themselves against the triumvirate. Clodius railed against the legislation of Cæsar as having violated religious sanctions and constitutional traditions. But the principal target of his attacks, both physical and verbal, was the unhappy Pompeius Magnus. Clodius picked apart some of the arrangements that Pompey had implemented for the eastern provinces, had him assaulted in public, and compelled him to huddle in the confines of his own home. In those activities he had the sanction also of the consul L. Piso, father-in-law of Cæsar, thereby further weakening the shaky concert of the dynasts. The tribune wielded weighty influence.[44]

P. Clodius is fascinating in his own right. But the vagaries of his career exemplify larger tendencies noted earlier. The triumvirate had instituted no closed corporation. Nor had it divided Rome simply into two warring camps. The Catonian circle took the lead in combating its measures and undermining its appeal. But the success of their efforts led to an opening-up of senatorial politics. Combined with the desertion of many of Pompey's aristocratic allies, this process allowed other individuals and groups to come to the fore, of whom Clodius is only the most obvious example. The fragmenting of alliances gave added opportunities to clever politicians. Clodius' brother, C. Claudius, accepted a post in Cæsar's officer corps, and the tribune could use that fact to suggest the backing of Cæsar's troops, when it was advantageous.[45] He did not, however, let it deter him from questioning Cæsar's legislation or attacking Cæsar's allies. Similarly, earlier marriage connections with Lucullus and Metellus Celer had not deterred him from clashing with those individuals. The enemy at once of both Cato and Pompey, Clodius nevertheless developed a formidable following of his own. His influence endured beyond 58. Pompey

[44] The picture of Clodius presented here is developed in greater detail, with reference to the sources and modern literature, in Gruen, *Phoenix*, 20 (1966): 120–130. Add also A. W. Lintott, *Greece and Rome*, 14 (1967): 157–169; *Violence in Republican Rome* (Oxford, 1968), pp. 190–198. The speculations of Seager, *Latomus*, 24 (1965): 519–531, and Rowland, *Historia*, 15 (1966): 217–223, do not carry conviction.

[45] On C. Claudius' service in Cæsar's army, Cic. *Pro Sest.* 41. On Clodius' flaunting of Cæsar's support, doubtless without substance, see Cic. *Pro Sest.* 39–40; *De Har. Resp.* 47; *Pro Planc.* 86.

somewhat checked his activities in 57 by subsidizing armed bands and securing the recall of Cicero. But the Claudii remained potent and independent figures, dramatizing the splintering of loyalties in the aftermath of the triumvirate.

Mutual suspicion further undermined any effective cooperation among the triumvirs in 57 and 56. Pompey was the favorite object of sniping from almost all groups. Crassus, smug and secure, enjoyed the general's frustrations. While refraining from overt attacks, he allowed activist demagogues, like Clodius and C. Porcius Cato, to use his name while they engaged in attacks on Pompey. C. Cato, though a relative of Cato Uticensis', evidently followed his own line, courting popular favor and being available for any alliance that seemed to promise political advancement. He furnishes yet another illustration of the futility of analyzing politics solely in terms of family or of ideology. Julius Cæsar was accumulating military successes and strengthening his personal contingent in Gaul. Friends of Cæsar, like P. Vatinius, felt free to act in concert with Clodius and to increase the troubles of Pompey the Great. Pompey's hopes for a new military command in early 56 were shattered as the Claudii, the Lentuli, and the Catonians, combined with the aloofness of Crassus and Cæsar, brought his prestige to a new low. His former friends in the aristocracy had already signified their defection. Advocates of Pompey in 57 and 56 seem limited to political small fry: men like Afranius, Milo, Messius, Rutilius Lupus, Scribonius Libo, Caninius Gallus.

Pompey found himself in a constricted situation comparable to the one he had faced in 60. At that time he had salvaged his position temporarily by alliance with Cæsar and Crassus. In 56, channels to the nobility were more effectively closed than ever. Pompey had recourse once more to the triumvirate. He cannot have been unaware of the consequences, after the experiences of 59. Other alliances, however, were not available, and he could no longer endure the role of an eclipsed and maligned figure. Pompey still had some cards to play. He issued an indirect but unmistakable threat to Cæsar. Pompey's partisans were advocating repeal or alteration of the agrarian bill of 59. That might mean loss of prospective landed rewards for Cæsar's soldiers in Gaul. And Domitius Ahenobarbus announced his candidacy for the consulship, expecting victory and a Gallic command that would displace Cæsar. The proconsul of Gaul could not risk Pompey's displeasure when the Catonian group was preparing to remove him from his post. The result was the famed conference of Luca in April 56. A renewal of the triumviral cooperation followed. If the *nobilitas* was implacable, Pompey could now again secure the support of *clientelæ* controlled by Crassus and Cæsar.[46]

[46] Details and references in Gruen, *Historia*, 18 (1969): 87–92; cf. also M. Cary, *CQ*, 17 (1923): 103–107; L. G. Pocock, *CP*, 22 (1927): 301–306; D. Stockton, *TAPA*, 93 (1962): 471–489. Th. N. Mitchell, *TAPA*, 100 (1969): 295–320, properly deflates Cicero's role in

This time the collaboration was closer, the common aims more compatible. Crassus and Pompey determined upon a joint consulship. That also served the interests of Cæsar, for it would postpone the ambitions of Domitius Ahenobarbus. A chief magistracy would lay the foundations as well for new provincial command long desired by Pompey. He could resume his role as commander of armies. And the allure of military glory had not escaped M. Crassus. He would use his allies to secure a major commission in Syria. The combining of *clientelæ* and influence was impressive. Two hundred senators are reported to have gathered at Luca with the triumvirs, most of them probably from the lower registers of the senatorial order. As in 59, so in 56 and 55, the syndicate achieved its immediate ends. Cæsar's tenure was renewed; Pompey and Crassus received consulships and provincial commands.

But the conference of Luca, like the formation of the triumvirate, made no fundamental change in the constitutional structure. There was some switching of sides, as ambitious individuals calculated that their advantage might lie with a coalition that appeared to have new vigor and force. The opportunistic Claudii, Appius and Publius, and C. Cato now transferred allegiance and advanced the aims of the dynasts. M. Cicero, disgruntled and disappointed, but largely dependent upon Pompey, also engaged his oratorical talents on behalf of the syndicate. But the gains were not considerable in personnel. The Claudii and C. Cato proved to be unreliable partners. Cicero did not always conceal his resentment; although he heaped public praise on Cæsar and Pompey, he persisted in attacking some of their *amici,* like Vatinius, Gabinius, and L. Piso.

The vigorous senatorial opposition that the triumvirs had provoked in 59 was evident again in 55 and 54. M. Cato had returned from Cyprus in late 56 to rally his followers to more concerted action. Consulships for Pompey and Crassus in 55 came only with intimidation and dubious maneuvers, costing the triumvirate further supporters in the aristocracy and credit among the populace. The consequences are traceable in the elections and political trials in immediately ensuing years. Most of them went against the triumvirs. Details of these developments will be examined later. But it is clear that the triumvirate could not control Roman politics even after Luca. The political structure did not yield readily to the preeminence of any particular group, much less to strong-arm tactics and unconstitutional activity. And the triumvirs themselves were no revolutionaries. They expected to attain political power by pooling supporters, seeking office, and sponsoring legislation. The aim and

---

these events, but underrates the importance of the Campanian question: *arx illius causæ*; Cic. *Ad Fam.* 1.9.8. Nothing novel is offered in the recent article of C. Luibheid, *CP*, 65 (1970): 88–94.

means were largely traditional. But the dynasts could not escape the stigma of cynicism, self-interest, and despotism imposed by the propaganda of their enemies. Hence their political defeats more than matched their temporary successes. Fragmentation, rather than polarization, remained the rule in Roman politics.[47]

THE OLIGARCHY

The baronial clans of the oligarchy prized their independence. They were not overawed by the triumvirate; nor were they susceptible to being herded into Cato's following. If the constitution was crumbling, that fact escaped the notice of the aristocracy. The decade of the 50s did not inflict upon Roman politicians the necessity of opting between two sides; either submission to military dynasts or enrollment in defense of the Republic. Key families with roots deep in Rome's past continued to provide leaders who held high office and swayed senatorial deliberations. Prestige of the clan, deeds of ancestors, control of hereditary clients and dependencies gave these families autonomous positions. They were not answerable to Cato, much less to Pompey or Cæsar.

The ancient houses of the Claudii Marcelli and the Cornelii Lentuli provide appropriate examples. Links between them had been forged in the previous generation. Adoption of a Claudius Marcellus by a Lentulus produced the line of Lentulus Marcellinus, which included the consul of 56. And the *agnomen* of Cn. Lentulus Clodianus, consul in 72, may suggest that he too was born a Claudius Marcellus and was adopted by the Lentuli.[48] At least six Lentuli and three Marcelli were politically active in the 50s. The collaboration came dramatically to the fore in the consular elections of 50: C. Claudius Marcellus and L. Cornelius Lentulus Crus were chosen to head the government in that critical year.

It was not ideology that motivated those men. The three Marcelli, two brothers and a cousin, held consulships in successive years, 51 through 49, achieving a station that had been denied to their clan for several generations. They were not readily browbeaten by other political figures. M. Marcellus, an imposing consul in 51, castigated Cæsar and openly flogged one of his clients. He also had little use for Pompey, clashing with him in 51 and dissenting from his strategy in 49. This Marcellus was on the Pompeian side in the civil war, perhaps largely through the influence of Lentulus Crus. But

[47] The development summarized here is given, with fuller detail, in Gruen, *Historia*, 18 (1969): 92–108.

[48] For evidence on the adoption of Lentulus Marcellinus, see Cic. *Brutus*, 136; Broughton, *MRR*, II:437. The case for Clodianus cannot be pressed; see Syme, *JRS*, 53 (1963): 55, correcting his own notion in *Rom. Rev.*, p. 44.

he eventually withdrew altogether, finding both sides unacceptable.[49] Anti-Cæsarian activities also marked the consulships of his cousin and brother in 50 and 49. One continued the fight during civil war, the other sat it out in Italy. The Marcelli went their own way.[50]

Intermittent friction within the Lentuli, as was noted earlier, did not prevent them from concerted resistance to the schemes of Pompey the Great. Like most aristocrats, they were avid for office and provincial posts and were more successful than most. Lentulus Spinther, consul in 57, engaged in every kind of maneuver and pressure to secure a commission in Egypt. Lentulus Crus, consul in 49, coveted military command, financial gain, and *gloria,* in open emulation of Sulla. The family could boast still another *consularis* and two other prætorians in the 50s, active particularly in the forum and the law courts. They would hardly acknowledge the overlordship of any figure or group. Family pride was potent. The Lentuli, despite political vicissitudes, all possessed *Lentulitas* in common.[51]

The old aristocratic game of bolstering the strength of a *gens* by prudent marriage alliance was still being played. The patrician Aemilii Lepidi were especially successful. A complicated nexus of connections gave them a central position in the 50s. Not themselves particularly prolific or gifted, they could rely on a glittering array of *adfines.* Three Lepidi were in the senatorial ranks in this decade: M'. Lepidus, the consul of 66, and two men of the younger generation, M. Lepidus and L. Paullus Lepidus, sons of the ill-fated revolutionary of 78. M'. Lepidus made little dent in the tradition; he was a quiet and unobtrusive senator in the 50s, and a hesitant neutral in the civil war. The younger Lepidi, by contrast, were early on display. M. Lepidus, absorbed in vanity and idleness, nonetheless became a *pontifex* by the early 50s, as befitted his family's station, and served as *interrex* in the troubled year of 52. His brother demonstrated oratorical talents by the late 60s, emerged as a prominent politician in the 50s, and advertised the family's *dignitas* by restoration of

[49] For Marcellus' activities as consul, see Broughton, *MRR,* II:241; for his distrust of Pompey and eventual neutrality, see Cic. *Ad Fam.* 4.9.3; cf. 4.7.2; *Pro Marc.* 16; Shackleton Bailey, *CQ,* 10 (1960): 253–254. On the influence of Lentulus Crus, see Cæs. *BC,* 1.2.

[50] On the consul of 50, see Münzer, *RE,* 3:2734–2736, "Claudius," n.216; the consul of 49, Münzer, *RE,* 3:2736–2737, "Claudius," n.217.

[51] On the Lentuli and Pompey, see Gruen, *Historia,* 18 (1969): 80–82; on Lentulus Crus' character and motives, see, esp., Cæs. *BC,* 1.4; cf. Cic. *Ad Att.* 11.6.6; Vell. Pat. 2.49.3. Lentulus Spinther was consul in 57, Marcellinus in 56, and Crus in 49. L. Lentulus Niger's prætorship came in the late 60s; he was a consular candidate in 59; Cic. *In Vat.* 25. His son was already conspicuous in the 50s; Cic. *Ad Att.* 2.24.2, 4.18.1; *Ad Q. Frat.* 3.1.15, 3.4.1; *In Vat.* 25. Finally, Cn. Lentulus Clodianus, son of the consul of 72, was prætor in 59 and a prominent politician; Cic. *Ad Att.* 1.19.2; *In Vat.* 27. On the family's *Lentulitas,* see Cic. *Ad Fam.* 3.7.5.

the Basilica Æmilia as ædile in 55. A consulship awaited Lucius in 50; Marcus would reach that office in 46, under the ægis of Julius Cæsar.[52]

The brothers' hostility to Pompey, conqueror of their father, remained constant; the lure of Cæsar did not come before 50; nor were they to be found in the entourage of Cato. Relatives and connections kept the Lepidi in the forefront of senatorial politics. Ties of *adfinitas,* unspecified but attested, linked them to the Aurelii Cottæ and the Scribonii Curiones, two great houses of the Sullan era. M. Lepidus' first wife, so it seems, was Cornelia, a daughter of the Lentuli, or, perhaps, of the Scipiones. A second marriage brought even more far-reaching associations. He wed Junia, the daughter of Servilia and D. Junius Silanus, who had been consul in 62. Servilia's fecundity had paid dividends. Lepidus was now brother-in-law to M. Junius Brutus, C. Cassius Longinus, and P. Servilius Isauricus, all from families of great esteem in the late Republic. Finally, a marriage bond existed with Q. Metellus Scipio, consul in 52 and scion of the ancient clans of the Metelli and Scipiones. Metellus Scipio took to wife Æmilia Lepida, sister or cousin of the Lepidi, snatching her from the grasp of an exasperated M. Cato himself.[53] That web of interlocking relationships assured the Lepidi an independent and eminent political position.

Paradox dogged the footsteps of the aristocracy. Political ambition dictated the formation of ever-widening ties. Yet the creation of expanding concentric circles meant the inclusion of dissident individuals and groups who strained the unity of the center. We have noted the process earlier, with reference to families like the Metelli and the Pisones and, to a lesser extent, the Antonii and the Valerii Messallæ.[54] The clans just discussed also suffered from this schizophrenia. Lentulus Spinther received electoral backing from Julius Cæsar in 58; but his cousin Lentulus Niger had been defeated by Cæsarian candidates in the previous year.[55] The Marcelli worked fervidly for the removal of Cæsar from Gaul after 52. Yet the stance must have involved some embarrassment

[52] On M'. Lepidus, see Klebs, *RE,* 1:550–551, "Æmilius," n.62; Sumner, *JRS,* 54 (1964): 42–44; M. Lepidus, von Rohden, *RE,* 1:556–561, "Æmilius," n.73; L. Paullus, Klebs, *RE,* 1:564–565, "Æmilius," n.81.

[53] On the connection of the Lepidi with the Aurelii Cottæ, see Suet. *Iul.* 1.2; with the Scribonii Curiones, Dio, 40.63.5. On Lepidus' wife, Cornelia, see Asconius, 43, Clark. The union is not certain; cf. Münzer, *Röm. Adelsp.,* pp. 353–354. Sumner, *JRS,* 54 (1964): 43, n.19, raises the possibility that Cæcilia's husband was M'., not M., Lepidus. That conjecture, however, requires emendation of several different texts and is best shunned. For the widespread associations attained through marriage with Junia, see Münzer, *Röm. Adelsp.,* pp. 347–362. Scipio's wedding of Æmilia Lepida is recorded by Plut. *Cato,* 7.1–2. She may have been daughter of Mam. Lepidus, consul 77; so Münzer, *Röm. Adelsp.,* pp. 282, 314.

[54] See above, chap. 2.

[55] On Spinther, Cæs. *BC,* 1.22; on Niger, Cic. *In Vat.* 25.

for C. Marcellus, consul in 50, whose spouse was Cæsar's grand-niece.[56] Other clans had analogous difficulties. The old patrician house of the Manlii Torquati supplied two legates for Pompey's pirate war. Unlike many others, they continued to cooperate with Pompey in the 50s. Two Torquati were to be found in the general's ranks once more when civil war came in 49. But the Torquati show a link also with the Lentuli, active opponents of Pompey in the 50s. A son of Lentulus Spinther received adoption into the Torquati in order to secure a coveted augurate in 57.[57]

It is not necessary to multiply illustrations. The tension in political combines is clear. The aristocracy could not escape it. As familial alliances spread in the customary fashion, the issues and conflicts of the 50s weakened the bonds and rendered such groupings even more fragile and less cohesive. Cato's efforts to polarize politics had in the end been unsuccessful. The formation of larger groups, in the circumstances of the late Republic, brought only greater atomization. That paradox is, in fact, the most characteristic feature of the politics of the era. It will not do either to postulate ideological bifurcation or to reduce the units to self-contained family factions. While engaging in "politics as usual" the *nobiles* unwittingly but effectively transformed the traditional bases of political cooperation.

The disintegration of Pompey's ties with the nobility after 59 was a contributing factor. His former allies, out of disillusionment or indignation, drifted away. The result could only be new combinations, some of them ad hoc and temporary. Certain aristocrats found themselves with conflicting loyalties, induced to take stands inconsistent with their previous political behavior. As we have seen, Pompey's league with Crassus and Cæsar cost him the support of the Lentuli, the Metelli, the Scribonii, the Servilii, the Sullæ, and the Memmii, among others. Reactions were manifold. Some engaged in concert with the Catonians, others struck out on independent lines, most found their families divided, with overlapping links. The process does not lend itself to artificial structuring. The shifting character of alignments may have puzzled contemporaries no less than it does moderns. It is precisely because aristocrats regarded the traditional system of politics as an unchallengeable assumption that the only possible reaction to events of the 50s was to form new alliances,

[56] Suet. *Iul.* 27.

[57] On the Torquati who served as Pompey's legates, A. Torquatus, prætor ca. 70, and L. Torquatus, consul 65, see Broughton, *MRR*, II:149. L. Torquatus the younger fought for Pompey in 49, as did A. Torquatus; Münzer, *RE*, 14:1203–1207, "Manlius," n.80; Münzer, *RE*, 14:1194–1199, "Manlius," n.76. For the adoption of Lentulus Spinther, possibly by T. Manlius Torquatus, see Dio, 39.17.1–2; cf. Cic. *Pro Planc.* 27. A. Torquatus was also a judicial appointee of Pompey's in 52; Asconius, 39, 54, Clark. On the confusing stemma of the Torquati, see now the article of J. F. Mitchell, *Historia*, 15 (1966): 23–31, itself by no means devoid of confusion.

which inevitably muddied relations and doubtless befuddled the participants themselves. The abandonment of Pompey by his distinguished *amici* played a central role in producing the confusion. Pompey's own discomfiture was matched by that of his former associates.

THE FOLLOWING OF POMPEY

The general's retinue had not, of course, deserted en masse. Catonian propaganda affected pedigreed families, who found the activities of the triumvirate intolerable. Less influential politicians may not have regarded it as profitable to shift allegiance. The men who actively propagated Pompey's interests in the 50s were very different from the distinguished group with whom he had combined in the 60s. The difference goes far in explaining his relative lack of political success.

Four *consulares* may be adjudged promoters of Pompey's ends in the 50s: L. Volcacius Tullus, consul 66, M. Tullius Cicero, consul 63, L. Afranius, consul 60, and A. Gabinius, consul 58. That was not an impressive lot. None of the four offered consular lineage. Two of them, at least, Afranius and Gabinius, reached the chief magistracy only through the backing of Pompey and could not command an independent following. Association with Pompey may help to explain the elections of Volcacius and Cicero as well. Afranius' origins were lowly, perhaps from the Picene *clientela* of Pompeius. His consulship had been an abomination and his weight in the senate minimal. Loyalty to Pompey, however, persisted. Afranius supported a bill for the general's corn commission in 57, advocated his Egyptian command in 56, and sponsored an *ambitus* measure on Pompey's instructions in 55. From 55 on he served as a Pompeian legate in Spain and remained with his chief until his death in the civil war. Afranius was reliable but ineffectual.[58] Gabinius' background gave better promise. The family could show a prætor in the previous generation and was of senatorial stock at least from the second century. Gabinius himself had been a vigorous tribune in 67 and a competent legate of Pompey's in the East. His consulship of 58, however, was consumed in intrigues for provincial command. Unsavory habits, so Cicero reports, stained his reputation: a fondness for dancing, drink, and cosmetics. Gabinius' governorship of Syria spanned the mid-50s. It included military successes and rigorous administration, but fell afoul of Roman financial interests. The event proved to be a grievous embarrassment for Pompey. A *supplicatio* for Gabinius was resoundingly quashed by the senate, and despite Pompey's best endeavors, Gabinius suffered ignominious conviction on an extortion charge in 54.[59]

[58] On Afranius' origins, see Plut. *Rei Pub. Ger.* 11; cf. *ILS*, 878. For his consulship, see above, n.11; support for the corn commission, Cic. *Ad Att.* 4.1.6; the Egyptian command, Cic. *Ad Fam.* 1.1.3; the *ambitus* bill, Cic. *Ad Q. Frat.* 2.9.3; cf. Plut. *Cato*, 42.1–2. For his service in Spain, see Vell. Pat. 2.48.1.

[59] Sources on Gabinius' consulship in Broughton, *MRR*, II: 193–194; his proconsulship,

Volcacius Tullus was a senior consular by the decade of the 50s. But the lack of consular progenitors gave him little *auctoritas.* A motion in 56 proposing Pompey's command in Egypt is Volcacius' only recorded senatorial act in the decade. His support would not have counted for much.[60] Cicero, of course, could be a potent ally. His blistering oratory had in the past been effectively employed in Pompey's behalf. Pompey arranged Cicero's recall from exile in 57, and the orator responded with warm and generous praise. But Cicero did not warm to the triumvirate. His efforts in 56 to divorce Pompey from Cæsar brought only the conference of Luca. Out of loyalty and with no alternative, he duly defended Pompeian adherents in subsequent years. But the efforts were mechanical and disingenuous. Cicero controlled no faction in the senate; his preferences in the later 50s were for withdrawal and literary pursuits.[61]

Only two political *amici* of Pompey's in the 50s could boast a consular ancestor in a previous generation: P. Rutilius Lupus and P. Plautius Hypsæus. Neither of them reached the consulship himself. Lupus makes an appearance as tribune in 56, supporter of the resolution to appoint Pompey to Egypt and advocate of reform of the Campanian land bill, probably also in Pompey's interests. He does not turn up again until his service in the civil war on the Pompeian side. Plautius Hypsæus' contacts with the general went back to the eastern wars of the 60s when he was a faithful quæstor. Lupus' efforts on Pompey's behalf in 56 were dutifully seconded by Hypsæus. A consulship was the goal. Pompey exerted strenuous effort in Hypsæus' campaign for the post in 53–in vain. Riotous disturbances canceled the elections. Hypsæus' career came to an inglorious end in 52: a prosecution *de ambitu* reduced him to groveling at Pompey's feet. Evidently, both Lupus and Hypsæus were lightweights.[62]

Broughton, *MRR,* II:203, 210–211, 218. Cicero's invectives are full and repetitious; cf. vonder Mühll, *RE,* 7:424–430, "Gabinius," n.11. For a juster appraisal, see E. M. Sanford, *TAPA,* 70 (1939): 64–92; Badian, *Philologus,* 103 (1959): 87–99. On the refusal of a *supplicatio,* see Cic. *Ad Q. Frat.* 2.6.1; *De Prov. Cons.* 14–15, 25; *In Pis.* 41–45; *Phil.* 14.24. For the trials of Gabinius, see below, chap. 8.

[60] On Volcacius, see Gundel, *RE,* 9(2):754–756, "Volcacius," n.8; the proposal in 56: Cic. *Ad Fam.* 1.1.3, 1.2.2.

[61] Cicero's actions in the 50s are well known and much discussed; cf. in general, Ciaceri, *Cicerone,* II:63–161; Gelzer, *Cicero,* pp. 145–212; and see Gruen, *HSCP,* 71 (1966): 215–233; *Historia,* 18 (1969): 106–107. Sumner, *JRS,* 54 (1964): 42–43, would tentatively add M'. Lepidus, consul 66, to this list of Pompey's consular supporters. But for that person there is no trace of pro-Pompeian activities in the 50s, and only conjectures for the 60s.

[62] Though of consular family, each had only a single consular forebear. For their activity on Pompey's behalf in 57 and 56, see Cic. *Ad Q. Frat.* 2.1.1; *Ad Fam.* 1.1.3, 1.2.2; Plautius Hypsæus' quæstorship, Asconius, 35, Clark; cf. Cic. *Pro Flacco,* 20; Schol. Bob. 100, Stangl;

Three men of prætorian family may be registered in Pompey's faction in the 50s. One was his *adfinis* and trusted adviser L. Scribonius Libo, who was, among other things, an annalist and a scholar. Libo's daughter was married to a son of Pompey's probably in this decade. Along with Rutilius Lupus, Plautius Hypsæus, and Afranius, he agitated for Pompey's Egyptian commission in 56. The following year saw him hauled before the censors, where Pompey appeared on his behalf, only to be mocked and insulted. Libo was later to be found as a principal consultant on Pompey's staff in the civil war.[63] Q. Terentius Culleo, a tribune in 58, saw the situation more clearly than most. He advised the general to divorce Julia, sever connection with Cæsar, and resume cooperation with the senate. The friendly suggestion was astute. Culleo recognized the evaporation of Pompey's old alliances, which had been provoked by formation of the triumvirate. Pompey, his hands tied and his commitment made, could not comply.[64] Finally, there was A. Plautius, perhaps of prætorian family, a tribune in 56, who pressed Pompey's claim on the Egyptian command by presenting documentation from Ptolemy Auletes. He turns up in the Pompeian forces in 49.[65]

The remaining supporters of Pompey in this decade came from lesser senatorial houses or possessed no known ancestors in the *curia.* Most were from municipal families or of equestrian origin. T. Annius Milo, from Lanuvium, was driven by morbid ambition and addicted to violence, as well as to good food. In 57 he collected armed bands, with the general's sanction, to confront with force the hirelings of Pompey's tormentor P. Clodius. At Milo's trial in 56 Pompey appeared in his defense, only to be abused and shouted down. Milo's tumultuous career showed more success in the streets than in the *curia.*

Pompey's support in his consular campaign, Asconius, 35, Clark; trial, humiliation, and conviction, Val. Max. 9.5.3; Plut. *Pomp.* 55.6; Appian, *BC,* 2.24; Dio, 40.53.1; association with Pompey is suggested also in 58, Cic. *Ad Att.* 3.8.3.

[63] On Libo's marriage alliance, see Münzer, *RE,* 3(2):881–883, "Scribonius," n.20; his literary activities, Cic. *Ad Att.* 13.30.2, 13.32.3; *Acad. Post.* 1.3; the activity in 56, Cic. *Ad Fam.* 1.1.3; the censorial hearing, Val. Max. 6.2.8; service in the civil war, Broughton, *MRR,* II:269, 282; for his closeness to Pompey, see, esp., Cæs. *BC,* 3.18.3. Weinrib, *HSCP,* 72 (1968): 248, dates the marriage alliance to the 40s, but without hard evidence.

[64] Plut. *Pomp.* 49.3: Κουλλέωνι μὲν οὖν κελεύοντι τὴν Ἰουλίαν ἀφεῖναι καὶ μεταβαλέσθαι πρὸς τὴν σύγκλητον ἀπὸ τῆς Καισαρος φιλίας οὐ προσέσχε; Cic. *Ad Att.* 8.12.5.

[65] Dio, 39.16.2; Cic. *Ad Fam.* 13.29.4. Pompeian connections with the Plautii were manifold. In addition to Plautius Hypsæus, discussed above, there was the Plautius who sponsored an agrarian law for Pompey's veterans in 70; see below, chap. 9, n.119. Yet another Plautius or Plotius was an officer of Pompey's in the pirate war; Appian, *Mithr.* 95; Florus, 1.41.9. He is often identified with A. Plautius, the tribune of 56; so Broughton, *MRR,* II:149; Shackleton Bailey, *Cicero's Letters,* III:216. More likely he is C. Plotius, mentioned in 59 as a senator and a former legate in Asia; Cic. *Pro Flacco,* 50.

He was eventually to suffer conviction and exile in 52.[66] Rather more sedate was the writer T. Ampius Balbus. He had spoken up for Pompey since his tribunate of 63. By 55 he was hoping for a consulship and received the general's backing. The result, however, was rejection at the polls and a prosecution; Pompey and Cicero came to his aid as defense counsel. Balbus showed his gratitude later, serving in the Pompeian ranks during the civil war and retailing malicious stories about Cæsar in his histories.[67]

In addition to Q. Terentius Culleo, two other tribunes and one prætor acted for Pompey in 58 against the intimidating tactics of Clodius. L. Flavius had been Pompey's front man in sponsoring an agrarian bill in 60. His efforts to deal with resistance proved abortive and ludicrous. Flavius' prætorship came in 58, with the endorsement of Pompey and Cæsar. Entrusted by Pompey with custody of the Armenian prince Tigranes, Flavius was outwitted by Clodius, and the prisoner escaped. A violent clash ensued, Flavius' attendants were worsted, and Pompey endured further and bitter chagrin. Flavius' prætorship had been as ineffectual as his tribunate.[68] The violence of Clodius and a plot on Pompey's life were reported to the senate by the tribune L. Novius. And another tribune, L. Ninnius Quadratus, probably of Campanian family, withstood Clodius and operated, on Pompey's instructions, to effect the recall of Cicero.[69] None of the three–Flavius, Novius, Ninnius–advanced to higher office.

Two further tribunes, of relatively humble origins, are on record as Pompeian adherents in 57 and 56. C. Messius in 57 pronounced Pompey worthy of a sweeping grain commission, which would encompass control of funds, fleet, an army, and *maius imperium*. L. Caninius Gallus, in the following year,

[66] On Milo's career, see Klebs, *RE*, 1:2271–2276, "Annius," n.67. For Pompey's role in the trial of 56, see Cic. *Ad Q. Frat.* 2.3.1–3; Dio, 39.18–19; Plut. *Pomp.* 48.7.

[67] Balbus' tribunate, Vell. Pat. 2.40.4; his consular defeat, Cic. *Pro Planc.* 25; Schol. Bob. 156, Stangl; his trial, Cic. *De Leg.* 2.6; service with Pompey, Broughton, *MRR*, II:266, 280; literary activities, Cic. *Ad Fam.* 6.12.5; Suet. *Iul.* 77.

[68] For the tribunate, see Cic. *Ad Att.* 1.18.6, 1.19.4; Dio, 37.50.1–4. On his connection with Pompey, see also Cic. *Ad Q. Frat.* 1.2.11. The Tigranes episode is recounted by Asconius, 47, Clark; cf. Dio, 38.30.1–2. Flavius' origin is unknown. He was surely not of noble background. Several other contemporary Flavii are recorded, all *equites* or *municipales*; Münzer, *RE*, 6:2525–2526, 2528, "Flavius," nn.10–13, 16–17. His associate in 58 was also an *eques*, M. Papirius, a tax farmer and a friend of Pompey's; Asconius, 47, Clark.

[69] L. Novius' announcement is given by Asconius, 46–47, Clark. That he is to be identified with Novius Niger who conducted hearings on the Catilinarian conspirators in 62 is by no means certain; Suet. *Iul.* 17. The tribune of 58 would have been too junior a personage for a weighty judicial task in 62. On Ninnius Quadratus, see Münzer, *RE*, 17:632–633, "Ninnius," n.3; cf. Wiseman, *CQ*, 14 (1964); 127. Cooperation with Pompey is attested by Dio, 38.30.3. It did not endure. In 55, he struggled to prevent passage of the *lex Trebonia*; Dio, 39.35.4–5.

joined the chorus in pressing for Pompey's appointment to Egypt. The proposals failed in each instance. Both men were later indicted in the courts, and both were defended by Cicero, doubtless at Pompey's behest.[70] And Pompey could bank on the services of a tribune in 54: D. Lælius, a close family friend. The connection went back at least a generation. Lælius' father had been a Pompeian officer in the Sertorian war, in which he perished. The younger Lælius comes to light as a prosecutor in 59, again serving the interests of Pompey. His tribunate shows similar loyalties: he came to the assistance of Pompey's beleagered *amicus* A. Gabinius.[71] Again, few, if any, senatorial precursors adorned the houses of Messius, Caninius, and Lælius. These were the types whose loyalties endured.

Of Pompey's legates and officers in this decade we are woefully ill informed, an unhappy omission in the evidence. He appointed fifteen *legati* in connection with the grain commission of 57. And the *legati* in Spain after 55 acted as the general's proxies while he remained in Italy. Only two of the appointees in 57 are known: the Cicero brothers from Arpinum, Marcus and Quintus; and two only of the Spanish legates: the trustworthy Picentine L. Afranius and the grizzled old soldier M. Petreius.[72]

Electoral disturbances in 54 brought rumors of an impending dictatorship. Some spread word that Pompey was prepared to assume such a post, though the general himself denied interest.[73] In the following year two tribunes actually proposed a Pompeian dictatorship, only to have the motion rejected. M. Cœlius Vinicianus was the formal sponsor, a relative nonentity, probably from Tusculum, who went on later to become a Cæsarian officer in the civil war.[74]

[70] Messius was very likely of Campanian background; cf. Cic. *Ad Att.* 8.11D.2. For his proposal in 57, see Cic. *Ad Att.* 4.1.7. Caninius' activities in 56 are noted in Cic. *Ad Fam.* 1.2.1, 1.2.4, 1.4.1, 1.7.3; *Ad Q. Frat.* 2.2.3, 2.4.5; Plut. *Pomp.* 49.6; cf. Dio, 39.16.1. The trial of Messius: Cic. *Ad Att.* 4.15.9; cf. Seneca, *Controv.* 7.4.8; Gruen, *HSCP,* 71 (1966): 222; the trial of Caninius: Cic. *Ad Fam.* 7.1.4.

[71] Val. Max. 8.1.abs.3. The close connection with Pompey is affirmed for 59; Cic. *Pro Flacco,* 14: *paterno amico ac pernecessario*; Schol. Bob. 98, Stangl; cf. Front. *Strat.* 2.5.31; Obseq. 58. The family is not to be identified with the consular branch of the Lælii; cf. Cic. *Pro Flacco,* 18. Lælius went on to serve in Pompey's fleet in the civil war; Broughton, *MRR,* II:270, 283.

[72] On the Cicerones, Cic. *Ad Att.* 4.1.7, 4.2.6; *Ad Q. Frat.* 2.1.3; on Afranius and Petreius, see Vell. Pat. 2.48.1. In 59 Petreius had shown a negative reaction to the triumvirate; Dio, 38.3.2–3; Gellius, 4.2.8. But military service was a way of life with him; Sallust, *Cat.* 59.6. It is possible that Pompey's old friend M. Terentius Varro was also appointed to Spain in the 50s; he was certainly there in 49; Broughton, *MRR,* II:269. Pompey did choose a *nobilis,* Q. Cassius Longinus, as his quæstor for Spain, probably in 52; Broughton, *MRR,* II:236. But the connection was brief. Cassius was already under a cloud by 51, perhaps on trial, and suffered remonstrances from Pompey's *amicus* L. Lucceius; Cic. *Ad Att.* 5.20.8; cf. *Ad Fam.* 15.14.4. By 49 he was serving Cæsar's interests against Pompey; Broughton, *MRR,* II:259.

[73] Cic. *Ad Att.* 4.18.3, 4.19.1; *Ad Q. Frat.* 2.15a.5, 3.4.1, 3.8.4, 3.8.6, 3.9.3; Plut. *Pomp.* 54.2.

[74] The proposal is given by Cic. *Ad Fam.* 8.4.3; on Cœlius' career, see *ILLRP,* 402, a Tusculan

He received assistance from C. Lucilius Hirrus, a cousin of Pompey's and descendant of the second-century satirist Lucilius. Hirrus was a man of wealth, with great estates in Bruttium and large expenditures on fishponds. As a politician, however, he proved to be less than effective. Fatuous conceit and an unfortunate lisp made him the butt of Ciceronian ridicule. A "would-be noble," Cicero termed him. Hirrus did not gain further office, suffering rejection at the ædilician and augural elections in the late 50s.[75] The results were symptomatic.

Pompey endured numerous political defeats or failures in the early and middle 50s. The triumvirate had proved to be a liability rather than an asset. The string of frustrations is long: unpopularity and abuse in 59; helplessness before Clodius' attacks in 58; failure to achieve *maius imperium* or an Egyptian command in 57 and 56; a series of prosecutions involving Pompey's *amici* and open attacks on the general, culminating in Gabinius' conviction in 54; consistent defeat of supporters in curule elections; a growing chorus of hostile propaganda; and outright rejection of any dictatorial plans in 53. The tide of success in the previous decade had ebbed away dramatically.

Explanation lies partially in the altered character of the Pompeian faction. The resplendent names that were found in association with Pompey in the 60s were no longer there in the 50s. Most were ranged in opposition. Pompey's supporters were reduced largely to *novi homines,* former *equites,* ambitious Italians. Fidelity endured among relatives like Scribonius Libo and Lucilius Hirrus; among men who owed their careers to Pompey, like Afranius, Gabinius, Ampius Balbus, and the Plautii; and among close friends and admirers, like Lucceius, Lælius, and Terentius Varro. Those were not names with great weight in the *curia.* Their relative ineffectiveness or apparent incompetence is testimony to continued control of the political process by clans of the *nobilitas.*

M. Crassus had escaped the difficulties that Pompey encountered. Himself a *nobilis* of lofty standing and pedigree—a pedigree much older than that of his rival—Crassus could content himself with a close-knit assemblage of *pedarii.* Pompey had pinned his hopes on a more illustrious collection of allies—who proved fickle and deleterious.

---

inscription; his service for Cæsar, *BAlex.* 77.2. The name suggests adoption from the Vinicii, possibly the family from Cales in Campania; cf. Syme, *Rom. Rev.*, p. 194.

[75] Hirrus' wealth and his background: Varro, *De Re Rust.* 2.1.2, 3.17.3; Pliny, *NH*, 9.171; cf. Appian, *BC,* 4.180; Cichorius, *Röm. Stud.*, pp. 67–70; his abortive effort in 53; Cic. *Ad Fam.* 8.4.3; Plut. *Pomp.* 54.2–3; his aspirations: Cic. *Ad Fam.* 8.2.2: *nobilem agentem;* conceit and ineptitude: Cic. *Ad Q. Frat.* 3.6.4; *o di, quam ineptus, quam se ipse amans sine rivali;* cf. *Ad Fam.* 8.9.1. The lisp is mocked by Cicero, *Ad Fam.* 2.10.1; cf. 2.9.1–2. Defeat in the ædilician and augural elections: Cic. *Ad Fam.* 2.9.1–2, 2.10.1, 2.15.1, 8.2.2, 8.3.1, 8.4.3, 8.9.1. Hirrus remained loyal to Pompey in the civil war; Cæs. *BC.* 3.82.4–5. A third tribune in 53, P. Licinius Crassus Junianus, was dissuaded by Cicero from supporting a Pompeian dictatorship; Cic. *Ad Q. Frat.* 3.8.4.

THE FOLLOWING OF CÆSAR

Crassus went to a Parthian war and to death in 53. The faction he had assembled and the following he had gathered dissolved after that fatal miscalculation. Pompey held proconsular *imperium* and legions under command of his lieutenants in Spain, while he himself remained near Rome with an eye on political developments. But his support in the city continued to be a waning asset. By contrast, the most significant political development of the 50s was the startling growth of prestige and power accumulated by Julius Cæsar. In 60, for all his dash and vigor, he was still only one of many ambitious politicians moving in the shadow of Pompey the Great. By the later 50s he possessed reputation and stature that made him the equal of Pompey. Cæsar's rise to eminence proved to be critical for Rome's future, and requires sober analysis without the dangerous pitfalls of hindsight.

Cæsar commanded Roman armies in Gaul for nine successive years. The commission was unprecedented and portentous. No *imperator* in Rome's past had had such an opportunity to amass loyal subordinates and establish preeminent repute. Few would have expected spectacular military exploits from Cæsar, who had had only modest experience in war. But the years in Gaul were long; the victories multiplied and the reputation grew. Strategic brilliance, personal courage, and the charisma of the general transformed the Gallic campaigns into an affair of the first magnitude. A successful commander and a lengthy command attracted ambitious men. Pompey had enjoyed that experience a decade before. Cæsar's was now the greater advantage. His tenure was more continuous, his successes more striking.

It will be best to refrain from ascription of premature motivation. Cæsar's aims of conquest included Gaul and perhaps Britain, but not Italy. Nothing in his past conduct and career, not in his future behavior, would suggest revolutionary schemes. Through agents and friends Cæsar kept in constant touch with affairs in Rome, sending back dispatches and cash, supporting candidates for office, receiving official congratulations and *supplicationes,* all within the customary framework of Roman practice. As we have seen, his response to Domitius' attempt at supersession in Gaul was not to brandish weapons or threaten a march on Rome, but to reinvigorate political alliances and to engineer Domitius' defeat for magisterial office. The methods were conventional. The laurels of the conqueror, of course, enhanced his stature. Stories of Gallic gold and of victories over the barbarian spurred widespread desire to serve under Cæsar. While the *nobiles* quarreled in Rome, Cæsar was welding a powerful entourage abroad.

Enrollment in the service of a proconsul had not always implied political attachment. Some junior officers, like quæstors and military tribunes, were traditionally elected by the people and assigned provincial responsibilities by lot. They could be men who served a brief tenure abroad and returned to proceed on a civilian *cursus honorum.* But the warfare of the late Republic altered the old patterns. Campaigns could be long and complicated. The foes were more widespread, the need for professionalism greater. Generals began to rely more heavily on trusted advisers with military experience. They selected their own legates, who bore responsibility for heading legions; and the number of military tribunes appointed by the commander now exceeded those elected by the assembly; generals exercised influence on the assignment of quæstors, nominally distributed by lot; prefects were, from the beginning, appointees of the commander, and the growing sophistication of the military appreciably increased their number.[76] Loyalty to commander in politics as in war cannot always be assumed. Many of Pompey's legates in the eastern wars abandoned him on the political scene after 59. But Cæsar's officers remained faithful. Almost without exception those who survived the Gallic campaigns continued to follow their chief in the conflict with Pompey. The social background of Cæsar's lieutenants and subordinates needs scrutiny.

Studies are available on Cæsar's following in the civil war after 49. The rhetoric of his enemies, claiming that he attracted only the desperate, the lowborn, and the rabble, has long since been exploded.[77] Distinguished and respectable men can be found in his retinue. The *nobilitas* seems equally divided among Cæsarians and Pompeians. But it is dangerous, indeed futile, to argue back from that situation into the 50s. Civil war compelled men to make unhappy decisions. Neutrality was difficult and hazardous. Families were split, and old loyalties disintegrated. The lines that formed under the pressure of fratricidal strife bear no relation to the circumstances of the previous decade, when no one envisioned civil war and when Cæsar and Pompey were coupled in political alliance. It is the burgeoning following of Cæsar in the 50s which calls for examination. A new officer class would be the backbone of the Cæsarian faction.

Confidence in prosopography can sometimes be misplaced. Lack of caution may produce delusive results. The composition of Cæsar's staff need not be exceptional. We possess no counterpart to the *Gallic Wars* for the campaigns of Pompey or Crassus in the 50s: the officers of those commanders may have been drawn from similar sources. But Cæsar had the advantage of an extraordinarily long command, which called for personnel in larger numbers and, perhaps, of more varied origins. Whence did they come?

[76] See R. E. Smith, *Service in the Post-Marian Army* (Manchester, 1958), pp. 44–69; J. Suolahti, *The Junior Officers of the Roman Army in the Republican Period* (Helsinki, 1955), pp. 35–57, 198–213; J. Harmand, *L'Armée et le Soldat à Rome, de 107 à 50 avant notre ère* (Paris, 1967), pp. 349–407.

[77] Syme, *Rom. Rev.*, pp. 61–96; Shackleton Bailey, *CQ*, 10 (1960): 253–267.

The proconsul of Gaul, to be sure, did not lack *nobiles* among his lieutenants, men of consular family who sought service abroad. They included the two sons of M. Crassus. One of them, P. Crassus, was prefect of Cæsar's cavalry in 58 and continued to exercise important responsibilities in the succeeding two years. Ambition beyond his rank impelled him further. He joined his father for the Parthian wars in 54; high courage and leadership quality marked his service until he perished at Carrhæ in 53. The other son, M. Crassus, was Cæsar's quæstor in 54; after the deaths of his father and brother had dissolved the Crassan *factio,* he elected to rely on Cæsar's patronage. C. Claudius Pulcher saw advantage in a post as Cæsarian legate in 58. But the fickle Claudii were not readily assimilable. C. Claudius' tenure lasted no more than a year and was followed by return to Rome and a prætorship in 56. Q. Tullius Cicero, the orator's brother, an ex-prætor and ex-proconsul, had been a Pompeian legate in 57 and 56. Hot-tempered, vain, and anxious for higher office, Quintus could act as useful surety for his brother's good behavior after Luca. In 54 he transferred to the service of Cæsar. The arrangement was not permanent. In 51 Quintus served under his brother in Cilicia. He had perhaps hoped for the consulship; but Cæsar had other plans. The connection lapsed. Ser. Sulpicius Galba, descendant of distinguished patrician consulars, joined Cæsar for similar reasons. Three years as the proconsul's legate in Gaul brought him sufficient wealth and influence for a prætorship in 54. Friendship with Cæsar, however, could backfire. Galba lost his bid for the consulship in 50 because of concerted effort by the enemies of Cæsar.

In addition, four young *nobiles,* near the beginning of their public careers, are found as *legati* or *præfecti* in Gaul: M. Antonius, D. Junius Brutus Albinus, M. Junius Silanus, and C. Volcacius Tullus. All were born in the 80s; all were in their early thirties when they saw duty in Gaul. The experience and contacts could presage swift advancement in civilian posts later. For at least two of them, Antonius and Brutus, high magisterial office awaited in the 40s under Cæsarian patronage. Only a single legate of aristocratic pedigree was older than the proconsul himself. That was Cæsar's own relative, L. Julius Cæsar, the consul of 64. As a senior statesman in 52 he joined his kinsman and took charge of the province of Gallia Narbonensis.[78]

In general, the contingent of *nobiles* under Cæsar's charge is not conspicuous or imposing. Ten men of consular families fought in Gaul during Cæsar's

[78] Sources on these Cæsarian officers may be found under the relevant years in Broughton, *MRR,* II. Cf. on the legates, Drumann-Groebe, *Geschichte Roms,* III: 696–701; B. Bartsch, *Die Legaten der römischen Republik vom Tode Sullas bis zum Ausbruche des zweiten Bürgerkrieges* (Breslau, 1908), pp. 39–59. And see further, on some of these individuals, the chapter on the senate below. On Q. Cicero's consular aims and his break with Cæsar, see Wiseman, *JRS,* 56 (1966): 108–115. Galba's consular defeat in 50, at the hands of Cæsar's enemies, is recorded by Hirtius, *BG,* 8.50.4. For L. Cæsar's position in 52, see Cæs. *BG,* 7.85.1.

tenure. Two of them barely warrant the designation: the families of Q. Tullius Cicero and C. Volcacius Tullus attained consular distinction only in the previous decade. Two other aristocrats served with Cæsar but briefly and returned to Rome to seek magisterial office. Six, including the two sons of Crassus, were young men in their thirties, hitherto without much weight in Roman politics. Scions of the great families of the nobility were proud, independent, and often unpredictable. The bulk of Cæsar's officer corps was drawn from other sources.

Men of lesser senatorial *gentes* found welcome acceptance in the army of Gaul. The individuals, in most cases, have left little mark on history. Nomenclature is often our only guide. Cæsar, it seems, appointed some officers whose names recall families of distant antiquity. Their forebears, however, had lapsed into obscurity for several generations. In that category fall the legates L. Aurunculeius Cotta, C. Caninius Rebilus, and M. Sempronius Rutilus. Senators of similar name do not appear on record after the early second century.

In rather larger numbers came representatives of new senatorial houses, families that first make an appearance at the beginning of the first century or that were introduced into senatorial ranks only after Sulla's expansion of the *curia.* Among the former may be reckoned legates, quæstors, and other junior officers like C. Antistius Reginus, C. Fabius, L. Minucius Basilus, L. Munatius Plancus, P. Sulpicius Rufus, Q. Titurius Sabinus, and C. Vibius Pansa. The latter category is of even greater interest. It shows that many of the new men who had no pre-Sullan senatorial ancestors were beginning to drift into Cæsar's camp in the 50s. In this group belongs P. Vatinius, the volatile tribune of 59, whose measure gave Cæsar his command, and who went on to serve as legate in Gaul and eventually to reach the consulship with Cæsar's blessing. Of similar background and persuasion was Q. Fufius Calenus. An active tribune in 61, he was a supporter of the triumvirs during his prætorship of 59 and a legate of Cæsar's from 51. Vatinius and Fufius were to become joint consuls under Cæsar's dictatorship in 47. Two tribunes of 57, C. Messius and Q. Numerius Rufus, quarreled in that year over Cicero's recall from exile. Later in the decade, however, both men became Cæsarian legates in Gaul. Still another triumviral tribune of the 50s, C. Trebonius, son of a Roman *eques,* sponsored the bill on long-term provincial commands for Pompey and Crassus in 55. He then proceeded to a post on Cæsar's staff and an eventual consulship in the 40s. A relative, C. Trebonius, is discovered as *præfectus* in Gaul in 53. In the same group one may notice L. Roscius Fabatus, tribune in 55 and co-author of a measure to further Cæsar's plans for agrarian and municipal reform. A legateship in Gaul followed, and subsequently a prætorship in 49. T. Sextius, from an Ostian family, served his commander faithfully and rose to high office in the 40s. Q. Pedius, Cæsar's nephew and his legate in the early 50s, was son of an *eques,* but had attained senatorial rank. He returned to Rome to seek an ædileship in 55, in vain, and later resumed service with Cæsar, eventually ennobling his *gens* with a consulship in 43. Two other junior officers warrant mention: M. Curtius, military tribune in 54, and Q. Attius Varus, prefect in 51. Members of their families turn up in the Roman senate for the first time in the post-Sullan era. The proconsul of Gaul was making a sound investment for the future.[79]

Scholars have, in recent years, pointed to a gradual decline in the social level of junior officers in the late Republic.[80] Descendants of older *gentes* appear less and less frequently in the posts of *tribuni militum* and *præfecti.* The reason cannot have been simply that the positions had lost attractiveness. They served not only as training grounds for military careers, but as vehicles for future civil offices. The exigencies of warfare in the late Republic, the demands for larger armies and greater specialization, required increased numbers of officers, who could not be supplied entirely by the traditional houses of the *nobilitas.* The source of supply came increasingly from the *equester ordo* and from the *municipia.* Men from northern and southern Italy, from rural families, from the Apennines, and even from provincial areas begin to staff the officer ranks of the Roman army. The experience of Julius Cæsar marks acceleration of the process. The Gallic wars were lengthy, arduous, and often complicated. Cæsar's staff took on large proportions. And one need not doubt that he consciously encouraged the recruitment of men from non-senatorial backgrounds.

The geographical origins of Cæsar's legates and junior officers cannot in every case be documented. Occasionally, the literary and epigraphical sources give notice of an individual's home town. More often one is left to conjecture from the *nomen* or *cognomen.* But if the evidence is not always decisive for each individual, the cumulative effect is compelling: Cæsar drew on most of Italy for his officer corps.

It is noteworthy that Latium itself does not loom large in Cæsar's recruitment of non-senatorial officers. A. Hirtius, scholar, writer, and lover of luxury, who undertook the task of completing Cæsar's *Gallic Wars,* apparently derived from a family of Ferentinum in Latium.[81] Hirtius, whose intellectual tastes brought him close friendship with both Cæsar and Cicero, was a useful companion in Gaul, though he does not appear to have exercised military duties.[82] But most of the men trained for war came from areas at a greater distance

[79] References in Broughton, *MRR.* Fufius Calenus may not have been a *novus* if one postulates relation to the tribune of the mid-second century.

[80] See, esp., the extensive research and results compiled by Suolahti, *Junior Officers, passim*; also, R. E. Smith, *Service,* pp. 59–69; Harmand, *L'Armée,* pp. 349–397.

[81] An A. Hirtius, perhaps his father, turns up as a magistrate in Ferentinum; *ILLRP,* 584–586.

[82] On Hirtius, see vonder Mühll, *RE,* 8:1956–1962, "Hirtius," n.2.

from Rome. Campanian origins are attested for Q. Lepta and M. Orfius, the latter from Cales, the former from Atella.[83] The notorious fortune-hunter Mamurra, Cæsar's *præfectus fabrum* since 58 and target of Catullus' jibes, came from the Volscian town of Formiæ.[84] Etruria, it may be conjectured, supplied the *tribuni militum*, M. Aristius and Q. Laberius Durus.[85] Others came from somewhat farther afield. The name T. Terrasidius, a junior officer in 56, suggests a family from the Apennines; Q. Atrius, prefect of the fleet in 54, was apparently of Umbrian origins.[86] Note too the Voluseni, who included a military tribune, C. Volusenus, and a cavalry prefect, C. Volusenus Quadratus.[87] The scholarly lawyer C. Trebatius Testa, recommended to Cæsar by Cicero, spent some years in Gaul, in Cæsar's headquarters rather than in the field. He possessed ancestral holdings in Velia in Lucania.[88] And even Picenum, Pompey's recruiting ground, provided Cæsarian officers. P. Ventidius, from a Picene family of insurgents during the Social War, transcended a dubious background to perform important services for Cæsar.[89] Other junior officers, whose specific geographic origins are untraceable, were also from equestrian families, probably from the Italian countryside: T. Silius, M. Trebius Gallus, and Q. Velanius.[90]

Finally, there were the *provinciales.* L. Cornelius Balbus, the subtle and resourceful financier from Gades, was Cæsar's trusted confidant, shuttling back and forth between Rome and Gaul to serve his chief's political interests. From Gallia Narbonensis came Pompeius Trogus, whose father received Roman citizenship from Pompey and who now handled Cæsar's correspondence and official business. C. Valerius Procillus (or Troucillos), a *princeps* in Gaul, whose family was also enfranchised in the previous generation, became a close friend and an interpreter for Cæsar. Procillus and M. Mettius, another Cæsarian subordinate of Gallic background, were employed by the proconsul in Gaul.[91]

[83] On Lepta, see Cic. *Ad Fam.* 7.5.2, 9.13.1–3; on Orfius, Cic. *Ad Q. Frat.* 2.14.3; cf. Suolahti, *Junior Officers,* p. 129.

[84] Pliny, *NH,* 36.48; Catullus, 29, 57; cf. *ILS,* 5566.

[85] On Aristius and Laberius, see Cæs. *BG,* 5.15, 7.42–43; cf. Suolahti, *Junior Officers,* p. 164.

[86] Klebs, *RE,* 2:2148, "Atrius," n.4; Münzer, *RE,* 5(2):820, "Terrasidius;" Suolahti, *Junior Officers,* p. 129.

[87] They may derive from Sentinum; cf. Wiseman, *New Men in the Roman Senate, 139* B.C.–A.D. *14* (Oxford, 1971), p. 277, no. 512. Syme, *Rom. Rev.*, pp. 70–71, amalgamates the Voluseni; followed by Broughton, *MRR, Supp.*, p. 71. But see now Harmand, *L'Armée,* pp. 356–357.

[88] Cic. *Ad Fam.* 7.20.1; see Sonnet, *RE,* 6(2):2251–2261, "Trebatius," n.7.

[89] On Ventidius, see Syme, *Rom. Rev.*, p. 71; but cf. Badian, *Historia,* 12 (1963): 141–142; Wiseman, *New Men,* pp. 88–89.

[90] Cæs. *BG,* 3.7–8.

[91] On Balbus, see, esp., Cic. *Pro Balbo, passim*; Münzer, *RE,* 4:1260–1268, "Cornelius," n.69. On Valerius Procillus and M. Mettius, see Cæs. *BG,* 1.19, 1.47, 1.53; for Pompeius Trogus, see Justin, 43.11–12.

The quantity of testimony is impressive. Junior officers and lieutenants of Cæsar show a predominance of non-Roman and equestrian families. That does not even take into account the *legati* who had only recently reached senatorial rank and stemmed from municipal or rural Italy. The most accomplished military man among Cæsar's lieutenants, T. Labienus, was from Cingulum. Vatinius derived from the Marsi; T. Sextius' *gens* was Ostian; L. Minucius Basilus was a *patronus agri Piceni et Sabini;* C. Messius and perhaps Q. Pedius possessed Campanian origins; Perusia was the home town of Vibius Pansa; L. Munatius Plancus was born in Tibur, L. Roscius Fabatus in Lanuvium; Q. Numerius Rufus was probably a Picene; and a Sabine background may explain the name of Q. Titurius Sabinus. Finally, there were members of new consular families: Q. Tullius Cicero from Arpinum and C. Volcacius Tullus, an Etruscan from Perusia.[92]

The contrast with Pompey's officers in the pirate and Mithridatic wars could not be greater. Pompey brought with him the cream of Rome's aristocracy, consciously building a faction with *gravitas* and *auctoritas* in the ranks of the senate. Cæsar's company possessed much broader dimensions: not only new senatorial houses, but *equites,* municipal magistrates, the local magnates of Italy. Pompey's illustrious *legati* were infected with antique pride and independence. By the mid-50s most of them had gone their own ways, scorning their former general. Crassus' *factio* did not endure beyond his death in 53, and many of its members may have followed Crassus' sons into Cæsar's circle. The officers who served the proconsul of Gaul, however, remained on their chosen path of political loyalty.

Cæsar was not unaware of the future political benefits in a following that encompassed the leading aristocrats of rural Italy. It was a matter of policy, rather than simply convenience. One need look only at Cæsar's kinsmen by marriage. Links with the Roman nobility might be unstable; not so the ties to Italian houses. Cæsar's sisters provided a means. One was wed to M. Atius Balbus, an entrepreneur and nabob in Aricia, who enjoyed displaying the images of his ancestors. A daughter of that union became the wife of C. Octavius, a wealthy *eques* from Velitræ. It will come as no surprise to learn that Balbus and Octavius were the first of their families to attain Roman magistracies and senatorial rank. Both reached the prætorship by the late 60s.

[92] For the origins of Labienus, see Cæs. *BC,* 1.15; cf. Syme, *JRS,* 28 (1938): 113–125; Vatinius, Cic. *In Vat.* 36; L. R. Taylor, *Voting Districts of the Roman Republic* (Rome, 1960), p. 263; Sextius, Wiseman, *CQ,* 14 (1964): 130–131; Minucius, Cic. *De Off.* 3.74; Messius, Cic. *Ad Att.* 8.11D.2; Pedius, Wiseman, *CQ,* 14 (1964): 129; Pansa, Syme, *Rom. Rev.,* p. 90, and Wiseman, *CQ,* 14 (1964): 131; Munatius Plancus, Porphyr. on Horace, *Carm.* 1.7.21; Roscius Fabatus, Taylor, *Voting Districts,* p. 251; Numerius Rufus, Taylor, *Voting Districts,* p. 238; Volcacius Tullus, Propertius, 1.22.3, and cf. Syme, *JRS,* 53 (1963): 59; but see Wiseman, *New Men,* pp. 276–277, no. 506, who prefers Tusculum.

Cæsar's other sister acquired two husbands of equestrian family, Q. Pedius and Pinarius; her issue are later discovered among Cæsar's heirs.[93] The proconsul could place justifiable faith in associates among the *equites*. The banker C. Oppius was a trusted confidant and agent. And the general's most stalwart friend was C. Matius, a Roman businessman who shunned senatorial politics.[94]

Julius Cæsar, it seems, found confederates and allies among elements of the populace not so fully exploited by rival politicians: men of substance and influence outside aristocratic circles, financiers, rural barons, the patrons of *municipia*. Cæsar anticipated an eventual return and a considerably augmented political role. His faction could call upon dependents who spanned the towns and countryside of peninsular Italy.

The weight of Rome's past hung heavily over the late Republic. On the level of *haute politique* change was minor and barely perceptible. Even in the late 50s few Roman aristocrats would have felt that matters were pushing to a crisis or that they were in the grips of a "revolution." The political structure continually frustrated the aims of particular political figures.

Pompeius Magnus overreached himself, not by threatening the system but by trying to make it his own. When he endeavored to extend his alliances to absorb the principal clans, a reaction set in. Jealously independent *nobiles* broke away to form new groupings. That process was symptomatic: overextension of political alliances brought friction within the ranks of a group and resulted in splintering, rather than cohesiveness. The effective propaganda and posturing of the Catonians separated Pompey's old partisans decisively from their chief. By the mid-50s the general's supporters were reduced to new men, personal friends and *adfines* who were in no position to manipulate senatorial politics.

The system itself resisted overextension. Pompey discovered that, to his cost. So, in a different way, did Cato Uticensis. Cato pressed for a clear division, which could isolate the "revolutionaries" and unite the defenders of the *res publica* under his own leadership. But conventional aristocratic politics proved intractable also to this tactic of assimilation. Noble *gentes* would not accept reduction of the system to an ideological bifurcation. Clans like the Lentuli, the Metelli, the Marcelli, and the Lepidi were not prepared to fall in line behind Cato or Pompey. Their notion of politics was to expand familial influence in customary ways: marriage ties, *amicitiæ*, mutual *beneficia*. This

[93] On Atius Balbus, see Suet. *Aug.* 4; for C. Octavius, father of the future emperor Augustus, see, esp., Vell. Pat. 2.59.1–2; Suet. *Aug.* 2–4; on Pedius and Pinarius, see Suet. *Iul.* 83; Appian, *BC*, 3.23; cf. Münzer, *RE*, 19:38–40, "Pedius," n.1. Note too the young T. Pinarius who was among Cæsar's *comites* in Gaul; Cic. *Ad Q. Frat.* 3.1.22.

[94] On Oppius, see Münzer, *RE*, 18:729–736, "Oppius," n.9; on Matius, Münzer, *RE*, 14:2206–2210, "Matius," n.1.

fundamental behavior pattern, when crossed by Cato's politics of confrontation, produced the patchwork of overlapping and often conflicting obligations so characteristic of the late Republic.

M. Crassus had been more astute and circumspect. He eschewed traditional combines with noble *gentes,* whose jealous autonomy made them unreliable allies. Crassus could weld a tighter faction of dependencies. Pooling resources with Pompey, he gained power while his rival slipped in prestige. In the end, however, Crassus too was done in by traditional aspirations: the triumphal toga and the laurels of the conqueror. The Syrian campaign terminated in disaster, and the aspiring *triumphator* perished in the desert. The dissolution of Crassus' *factio,* combined with the desertion of Pompey's allies, contributed significantly to the confusion of political allegiances in the 50s.

Crassus' fate might also have been Cæsar's. But the proconsul of Gaul survived. A decade of successful warfare abroad gave him a preponderant position. Constant reports of his victories and lavish expenditures of cash kept Cæsar in the center of the Roman stage. More and more younger politicians moved out to Gaul to become Cæsar's legates and junior officers. These were not scions of pedigreed clans, but *novi homines,* new senators, *equites, municipales,* who looked forward to offices and careers not attained by or open to their ancestors. None of them aimed at overthrow of the state, least of all their chief. But the officer ranks of the general were to be the faction of the politician. By the late 50s Cæsar's was the most solid and disciplined of political contingents.

IV

THE CONSULS AND CONSULAR ELECTIONS

A GOVERNING OLIGARCHY ruled the Roman Republic. Its members were conjoined in common enterprise, its ascendancy fixed by self-perpetuation. The drive for power and prestige produced frequent internal struggles. But an unspoken principle cemented the ruling class: leadership and responsibility must devolve upon an elite distinguished by generations of public service. The Roman senate, so it was firmly believed, was the repository of national wisdom and experience. And within the senate lay a smaller group, an inner circle of *nobiles,* who supplied ultimate leadership: the ex-consuls and members of consular families.[1] From that core radiated the unofficial lines of power.

The consulship was the summit of ambition. Only two men could occupy the post in any one year. As principal executive officers of the state, they held the reins of government and symbolized its authority. But the impact of this chief magistracy went well beyond the twelve months' tenure. Ex-consuls comprised the leadership of the senate. Their opinions were voiced first in debate, and their *auctoritas* guided policy. Magistracies were brief, but senatorial membership was lifetime. *Consulares* were the kingpins of a corporate body. Access to the consulship was open in principle, closed in practice. Men without forebears in the office stood little chance of election. The electorate would see to that. They were attracted by resplendent names and by families who had traditionally dispensed patronage. Democratic theory and practice had no place in the system. Voting for the top magistracies, the consuls and prætors, occurred in assemblies structured to the advantage of propertied

[1] On the term *nobiles*, which, at least in the Ciceronian age, seems to have designated *consulares* or their relatives, see Gelzer, *Kleine Schriften*, I:39–50; A. Afzelius, *ClMed*, 1 (1938): 40–94. Evidence on the consular elections from 78 to 49 is collected by A. Neuendorff, *Die römischen Konsulwahlen von 78–49 v. Chr.* (Breslau, 1913).

Romans. Timocratic criteria determined the weight of men's votes. The organization of the electoral system guaranteed a heavy influence for landed and affluent citizens, most of whom had their residences in the *municipia* or the countryside. Ballots of the urban *plebs* carried little weight in the *comitia centuriata.*[2] The system produced an exclusivist corporation.

Tradition, self-interest, and experience perpetuated the structure. Sallust, in bitter retrospect, pilloried the *nobiles*: they passed the consulship from hand to hand within their tight little clique; they paraded portrait busts of ancestors as a substitute for personal merit.[3] The voters, however, did not share Sallust's displeasure. Electoral results consistently returned a small number of prestigious families to the highest offices of the land. The Republic's last generation marked no change in that situation.

THE POST-SULLAN DECADE

The Sullan regime placed a premium on illustrious names at the head of the establishment. That included not only families of distinction in recent generations, but also old patrician houses who had played prominent roles in earlier eras of Roman history. Sulla was sensitive to their claims: his family was numbered among them. The men who had been with him in the East could expect to profit under his ægis. So also could those who had joined the proper side during the civil war or showed themselves willing to cooperate afterwards. Sulla did not indulge in rancor against clans whose distinction would add luster to his government. As dictator he maintained firm control over appointments to high office. But Sulla had retired from the dictatorship by mid-79 and died in the following year. Would the electorate oblige his intentions posthumously? Perusal of the consular lists for the decade of the 70s discloses that they did.

In 79 Sulla was a private citizen. Whether he intervened in the electoral contests of that year is uncertain. There was little need. The *comitia* returned Q. Lutatius Catulus and M. Æmilius Lepidus. Plutarch retails the story that Sulla was pleased with Catulus' success, displeased with Lepidus'. That may be hindsight and anachronism. The split between Catulus and Lepidus came only in 78 after Sulla's death; Lepidus' revolutionary machinations could not

[2] On the *comitia centuriata*, which elected consuls and prætors, see L. R. Taylor, *Party Politics*, pp. 50–62; *Roman Assemblies*, pp. 85–106.

[3] Sallust, *Iug.* 63.6: *consulatum nobilitas inter se per manus tradebat; Iug.* 85.38: *Ceterum homines superbissumi procul errant. Maiores eorum omnia quæ licebat illis reliquere: divitias, imagines, memoriam sui præclaram; virtutem non reliquere, neque poterant.* Cf. also the concentrated contempt in Sallust's reference to the *globus nobilitatis; Iug.* 85.10. And see Cic. *De Leg. Agrar.* 2.3: *eum locum* [consulship] *quem nobilitas præsidiis firmatum atque omni ratione obvallatum tenebat*; cf. *Verr.* 2.5.180.

have been foreseen in the previous year. Both men, it appears, had been awarded prætorships during Sulla's tenure as dictator. Although neither had been in his military service, they seemed safe choices. Catulus had lost his father in the massacres perpetrated by Sulla's enemies in 87. Lepidus' adherence to the new order had been warmly rewarded by profits in the proscriptions; moreover, he received the endorsement of Sulla's most successful lieutenant, Cn. Pompeius Magnus.[4] The electorate was obliging.

The process continued after Sulla's death. Mam. Æmilius Lepidus and D. Junius Brutus held the chief magistracies in 77. The former had contributed notable service for Sulla in the civil war: he was responsible for the subjugation of Norba. Sulla and the Sullani were duly grateful. Mam. Lepidus missed the consulship once, but C. Curio, who had been with Sulla since the eastern campaigns, postponed his own candidacy and eased Mamercus' path for 77.[5] Conservative in temperament, with solid military and familial background, Mamercus was a natural choice.[6] His colleague D. Brutus has left little imprint on the record. Brutus' career lay primarily in the civil sphere, as an active participant in the courts and a man of respected learning in both Greek and Latin letters.[7] Another particular gave him strong claim for office in the 70s. Brutus was identified, along with Catulus and Lepidus, as a dedicated adherent of Sulla's.[8]

Former Sullan officers did well for themselves in the elections of that decade. C. Scribonius Curio stepped aside for Mam. Lepidus in 77; the gesture earned him consular office in the succeeding year. Curio had made his mark early, as an orator in the 90s—despite a woeful memory and the absence of formal training. Political turmoil followed in 90, and a threat of prosecution drove Curio from Italy to Sulla's camp. In the 80s he was given major military responsibilities by his commander, and returned to Rome in Sulla's entourage—

[4] For the elections of 79, see Plut. *Sulla*, 34.4–5; *Pomp.* 15.1–2; criticism and discussion of the account in Syme, *Sallust*, pp. 184–186; Gruen, *Roman Politics*, pp. 272–277. Badian, *Studies*, pp. 232, 234, n.17, suggests that Sulla backed Mam. Lepidus for the consulship; followed by Sumner, *JRS*, 54 (1964): 45. There is no evidence. We know only that Mamercus suffered defeat—probably in 79; Cic. *De Off.* 2.58. On Catulus and M. Lepidus in the 80s, see Badian, *Studies*, pp. 217–219; Gruen, *AJP*, 87 (1966): 391–393; the death of Catulus senior: Gruen, *Roman Politics*, pp. 233–234; Lepidus and the proscriptions: Sallust, *Hist.* 1.55.18, Maur. And see now, in general, Criniti, *MemIstLomb*, 30 (1969): 340–371.

[5] Sallust, *Hist.* 1.86, Maur.; Cic. *De Off.* 2.58.

[6] For his conservatism, see the anecdote in Val. Max. 7.7.6: as consul Mamercus dismissed the civil case brought by a eunuch on the grounds that his very presence would pollute the magisterial tribunal. Cf. also Asconius, 60, 79, Clark, with Sumner, *JRS*, 54 (1964): 41–48. Lepidus was in the company of Hortensius, Catulus, Metellus Pius, and M. Lucullus.

[7] Cic. *Brutus*, 175: *multum etiam in causis versabatur isdem ferre temporibus D. Brutus, is qui consul cum Mamerco fuit, homo et Græcis doctus litteris et Latinis.*

[8] Sallust, *Hist.* 1.55.2–3, Maur.

to obtain a prætorship and a share in the proscriptions.[9] Lengthy and loyal service lay behind Curio's accession to consular dignity in 76. It was not an untypical case.

The brothers Luculli could also boast of distinguished military records under the command of Sulla. L. Lucullus' association with him stretched back to the Social War. Later, during the contest with Mithridates, he was Sulla's most trusted and devoted officer. The dictator's regard for him was attested again in his will—not that anyone had doubts. Lucullus assumed the guardianship of Sulla's orphaned son. His brother, M. Lucullus, fought for the Sullan cause at least during civil war in 83. The service may go farther back. Marcus and Lucius were close, almost inseparable. Political activities, even from their youth, generally found them performing in tandem.[10] It was fitting that one should follow the other in Rome's highest magistracy: L. Lucullus in 74, M. Lucullus in 73.

Similar rewards went to the Cottæ brothers, Caius and Marcus, consuls in 75 and 74. Military service under Sulla is unattested. But C. Cotta was probably with Sulla in the East during the 80s and returned with him to Rome. His career closely paralleled that of his friend C. Curio. Like Curio, the meticulous and cerebral Cotta was registered among Rome's leading young orators in the 90s. Like Curio too, Cotta faced political prosecution in 90, departed into exile, and obtained restoration upon Sulla's triumphant conclusion of the civil war.[11] The earlier career of his brother Marcus escapes record. He may also have spent the difficult years of the 80s abroad. His political allegiance in the 70s is clear, in any case. He collaborated closely with his consular colleague, L. Lucullus, both during their year of office and during their joint enterprise against Mithridates in the following years. The Cottæ were at the center of the establishment.[12]

The machinations of familial politics show themselves again and again in

[9] On Curio's intellectual failings and oratory, see Cic. *Brutus*, 210–220; cf. 192, 305; *De Orat.* 2.98; his threatened prosecution and departure, Asconius, 74, Clark; Cic. *Brutus*, 227; service for Sulla, Broughton, *MRR,* II:56, 59; return, Cic. *Brutus,* 311; cf. Sallust, *Hist.* 2.47.4, Maur.; gains from the proscriptions, Schol. Bob. 89, Stangl.

[10] See, e.g., Plut. *Luc.* 1.1, 1.6, 37.1, 43.3; Cic. *Verr.* 2.4.147; *Acad. Quæst.* 2.1; *De Off.* 2.50; *P. Red. in Sen.* 37; *P. Red. ad Quir.* 6; Quint. *Inst. Orat.* 12.7.4. On L. Lucullus, see further above, chap. 2. For M. Lucullus' activities in 83, see Plut. *Sulla*, 27.7; cf. *Luc.* 37.1.

[11] See above, chap. 1, n.60. On Cotta's oratory, see, esp., Cic. *Brutus*, 202–203, 317; *De Orat.* 3.31; cf. Sallust, *Hist.* 2.47.4, Maur.; for his absence in the 80s and return after civil war, Cic. *Brutus,* 227, 311. Cotta was also most adept at electioneering techniques; [Q. Cic.] *Comm. Petit.* 47; cf. Cic. *De Off.* 2.59.

[12] Cf. Sallust, *Hist.* 3.48.8, Maur.: *ex factione media consul*, on C. Cotta. Lucullus' intrigues with P. Cethegus paralleled those of M. Cotta; cf. Ps. Ascon. 259, Stangl: *gratia Cottæ consulis et Cethegi factione in senatu*; and see above, chap. 1, n.118. For the service of Lucullus and M. Cotta against Mithridates, see Broughton, *MRR*, II:101–102. Plutarch's story of their rivalry for *gloria* in the East, even if true, carries no political relevance; *Luc.* 8.1–3.

the 70s. Two Octavii, cousins, held successive consulships: Cn. Octavius in 76, L. Octavius in 75. The sources, unfortunately, preserve little of note on these men: Cn. Octavius was gentle and harmless, afflicted with a severe case of gout; L. Octavius was sluggish and indifferent.[13] Whether there was direct connection with Sulla is indiscernible. But the hypothesis is not without plausibility. L. Octavius was the son or brother of Cn. Octavius, who succeeded Sulla in the consulship in 87 and suffered execution at the hands of Sulla's *inimici.* His kinsmen received recompense through high magistracies in the mid-70s. Their abilities were undistinguished, but their politics were dependable. The Octavii worked closely with their consular colleagues, C. Curio and C. Cotta.[14]

The pattern continues. Two Lentuli held consulships in 72 and 71: Cn. Cornelius Lentulus Clodianus and P. Cornelius Lentulus Sura. Were there Sullan credentials here also? No military activities are recorded for them in the previous decades. Both men are noticed by Cicero among the ambitious young orators of the 90s. Neither could claim exceptional competence: Cn. Lentulus was obtuse and vainglorious; P. Lentulus was a man with illustrious forebears and lofty aims, but an evil reputation for licentiousness and intrigue.[15] Where were they in the 80s? If not in Sulla's camp, then at least away from Rome. They too, like Curio, Cotta, and others, found the atmosphere uncongenial and received welcome again only after Sulla had established a new regime.[16] It is a reasonable conclusion that both Clodianus and Sura embarked on political careers with the blessing of Sulla. In Sura's case, the evidence is specific: he was awarded a quæstorship under Sulla the dictator.[17] The electorate did not forget. A Sullan background probably helped the Lentuli to realize consular ambitions by the end of the decade.[18]

[13] On Cn. Octavius, Sallust, *Hist.* 2.26, Maur.: *Octavium mitem et captum pedibus;* cf. Cic. *Brutus*, 217; *De Fin.* 2.93; Quint. *Inst. Orat.* 11.3.129. On L. Octavius, Sallust, *Hist.* 2.42, Maur.: *Octavius languide et incuriose fuit.*

[14] Cooperation between Cn. Octavius and C. Curio: Cic. *Brutus*, 217; L. Octavius and C. Cotta: Sallust, *Hist.* 2.45, Maur.; cf. Cic. *Verr.* 2.1.30, 2.3.18–19.

[15] On the characters of the two men, see Cic. *Brutus,* 234–235; cf. 230; *Cat.* 3.16; Sallust, *Hist.* 4.1, Maur. For Sura's reputation, see Plut. *Cic.* 17.1. He was later to be expelled from the senate and eventually executed as one of Catiline's collaborators.

[16] Cic. *Brutus*, 308, 311.

[17] Plut. *Cic.* 17.2. His performance in office was not auspicious. Extravagance with public funds, perhaps bordering on embezzlement, earned him the rebuke of Sulla himself. Note that Sura's father was a P. Lentulus; Broughton, *MRR*, II:121–probably identifiable with a legate in the Social War and one of the murdered victims of Sulla's enemies in 87; Appian, *BC*, 1.72.

[18] The two men, to be sure, may have had little love for each other. Sura's transgressions and reputation cost him expulsion from the senate by the censors of 70, one of whom was Clodianus; Plut. *Cic.* 17.1.

For only three consuls in the 70s are no Sullan connections discoverable: C. Cassius Longinus, L. Gellius Publicola, and Cn. Aufidius Orestes, the chief magistrates in 73, 72, and 71. And even here, the absence of testimony, rather than positive refutation, stands in the way. Evidence of any meaningful sort exists only for the prior career of L. Gellius. It was a lengthy one. Gellius lived to a ripe old age and belonged almost to a previous generation. His public service dated back to 120, as a youthful assistant to C. Carbo, the consul of that year. Gellius' rise was not exactly meteoric. Though he possessed all the tools of an orator, he lacked those indefinable qualities which could rank him with the best of his contemporaries. More than two decades elapsed between his prætorship and his consulship. The intervening years are largely blank. We know only of employment in the East after his prætorship in 94, when Gellius sardonically summoned Athenian intellectuals and offered to settle all philosophical debate.[19] Delay in attaining the consulship does not imply the disfavor of Sulla or the Sullani. Gellius' lack of consular ancestors affords sufficient explanation. That he achieved it at all, even in old age, is remarkable. The patronage of Pompeius Magnus may be the key. Gellius had been a leading officer under Pompey's father during the Social War. It is then no coincidence that he sponsored measures on the general's behalf during his consulship and later took a place on his staff in the eastern wars.[20] Information on Cassius and Aufidius is quite limited and speculation would be rash.[21]

The decade closed with the consulship of M. Crassus and Pompey the Great. Their claims, of course, were irresistible. Achievements, influence, cash, and prestige overawed any potential competitors. But memories of Sulla were not altogether irrelevant. Pompey had been Sulla's most effective and successful lieutenant, and Crassus had commanded his right wing at the pivotal battle of the Colline Gate. That background provided indispensable preliminaries for their rapid rise to authority.

The electorate displayed predictable consistency in the 70s. Of the eighteen consuls chosen between 78 and 70, six, at least, had performed military service for Sulla: Mam. Lepidus, C. Curio, the Luculli, Pompey, and Crassus; four were demonstrable beneficiaries of Sulla: M. Lepidus, Q. Catulus, D. Brutus,

[19] Gellius' service with the consul of 120: Cic. *Brutus*, 105; his shortcomings as an orator: Cic. *Brutus*, 174: *L. Gellius non tam vendibilis orator, quamvis nescires quid ei deesset*; his sojourn in Athens: Cic. *De Leg.* 1.53; cf. *SIG*[3] 732. On his personality, see also Val. Max. 5.9.1.

[20] For Gellius' position under Pompeius Strabo, see *ILLRP*, II:30, no. 515; cf. Cichorius, *Röm. Stud.*, p. 139. For his connection with Pompeius Magnus, see above, chap. 1.

[21] Cassius is identifiable, perhaps, with a *monetalis* of the 80s; Broughton, *MRR*, II:435. Not much is to be learned from the few isolated references to Aufidius' early career; Cic. *Pro Planc.* 52; *De Off.* 2.58; Val. Max. 7.7.6.

and P. Lentulus; and five show familial connections that point in the same direction: Cn. Lentulus, the Cottæ, and the Octavii. The dictator's system was perpetuated, not only in structure but in personnel.

Another feature exhibits clear continuity. *Nobiles* dominate the consular *fasti* of the 70s. Sixteen out of eighteen chief magistrates could point to consular ancestors, most of them to multiple consular ancestors. Patrician clans, like the Aemilii Lepidi and the Cornelii Lentuli, enhanced the lists, as did leading plebeian *gentes,* like the Lutatii Catuli, the Cassii Longini, the Aurelii Cottæ, the Junii Bruti, and the Licinii Crassi. Only two consuls in the 70s, C. Scribonius Curio and L. Gellius Publicola, possessed no forebears in that office.[22] Few could quarrel, however, with the choice of Curio. His was a distinguished prætorian family, with men of some prominence since the early second century. Curio's father was a figure of high repute and talent; the fact that he never reached the consulship was later remarked on with surprise.[23] The office could not be denied to his son. The younger Curio's record of prolonged service to Sulla assured his victory. Gellius alone is anomalous. The name does not appear before on the consular or prætorian lists. But the latter are far from complete in our records. L. Gellius doubtless had senatorial ancestry. No source speaks of his low birth, a conspicuous omission. In 63 Cicero could boast that he was himself the first *novus homo* to reach the consulship for a very long time: living memory could hardly adduce another.[24] The vaunt is hyperbolic. Yet even Cicero could have commanded no credence if L. Gellius, consul only nine years before, were not of senatorial family. As a youth Gellius had been *contubernalis* of the consul C. Carbo. That suggests familial connections of some substance.[25] The *gens* was inconspicuous but respectable. For Gellius, association with Pompeius Magnus paved the way to consular dignity.

The *fasti consulares* of the 70s, it is clear, contained an eminent array of names. Ties of patronage, which bound the voting populace to the dominant

[22] One will not include Cn. Aufidius Orestes, consul 71, in this company. Though the Aufidii show no previous consuls, Orestes was born an Aurelius Orestes, the fourth successive generation of that family to hold the chief magistracy. Aufidius was an adopted, not an inherited name. Aufidius the elder arranged the adoption in extreme old age, presumably to secure an heir to his name and property; Cic. *De Domo,* 35. It was Orestes' ancestral connections, however, which gained him a consulship. On the Aufidii, cf. Syme, *Historia,* 4 (1955): 55–56.

[23] Cic. *Brutus,* 124: *ut eum mirer, cum et vita suppeditavisset et splendor ei non defuisset, consulem non fuisse*; cf. *Brutus,* 110, 122; *De Orat.* 2.98.

[24] Cic. *De Leg. Agrar.* 2.3: *me perlongo intervallo prope memoriæ temporumque nostrorum primum hominem novum consulem fecistis.*

[25] Cic. *Brutus,* 105. In Ps. Asconius, 251, Stangl, Gellius is even termed *consularis et nobilis vir.*

clans of the aristocracy, remained unbroken. These *necessitudines,* hereditary bonds and obligations created by *beneficia,* continued to be a principal element in determining the behavior of the electorate.[26] Leading patrician and plebeian houses were consistently victorious. *Nobiles* with consular predecessors retained a massive advantage at the polls. The ghost of Sulla smiled.

SENATORIAL RIVALRIES AND ELECTORAL CONTESTS

The decade of the 60s marked the heyday of Pompeius Magnus. In 69 he was himself a *consularis,* in a position to occupy the front benches of the *curia* and provide direction to senatorial debate. From 67 to 62 he served abroad, exercising extensive commands and pushing Roman frontiers to new distances. None could match his fame or his influence. One might expect the consular elections to reflect his impact. But Pompey possessed no monopoly on Roman politics. The circle of Lucullus and Catulus was potent, and had little love for Pompey. Their interests were perpetuated by the group of younger politicians centered upon Cato. Several electoral contests engaged the energies of those rival forces. And numerous other *nobiles,* without connection to Cato or Pompey, relied on distinguished names and ancestral clients to gain high office. M. Crassus was more interested in the lower ranks of the senate, and Julius Cæsar was too young to exert serious effect. But *gentes* like the Metelli, Pisones, Cottæ, Lepidi, and Antonii were active and prominent. The 60s show no sharp break with the past.

Inspection of the consular lists for that decade offers a striking fact. The stature and reputation of Pompey could not easily be translated into success with the voters of the *comitia centuriata.* His political foes exhibit greater and more consistent strength. The consuls of 69 exemplify the situation. Q. Metellus Creticus could count thirteen progenitors who had achieved consular office. His colleague, Q. Hortensius, had a less illustrious family, but a more distinguished career. His ringing oratory had dominated the law courts for more than two decades. The two men enjoyed a harmonious relationship.[27] And they shared bitter antipathy toward Pompey. Hortensius objected sharply

[26] It is the great merit of Meier's *Res Publica Amissa* to have demonstrated this with clarity and persuasion; esp., pp. 7–41, 174–200. But Meier presses the case too far. By dwelling on private *necessitudines* to the exclusion of all other elements, he underrates the effect political quarrels among the *nobilitas* might have upon electoral outcomes. The starkly atomistic structure postulated by Meier allows little scope for the ingenuity and resourcefulness of Roman politicians.

[27] As consuls-elect they collaborated in support of Verres; Cic. *Verr.* 1. *passim*; esp. 1.18–19, 1.23, 1.26, 1.29. And Hortensius resigned his province of Crete to Metellus; Dio, 36.1a; Schol. Bob. 96, Stangl.

to Pompey's command against the pirates in 67; it was not irrelevant that Metellus Creticus was one of those slated to be replaced by Pompey. The irascible Creticus did not take his supersession lightly. He harried Pompey's agents and heatedly denounced the general.[28] The arrogance of Hortensius and the ruthlessness of Metellus do not win admiration. But Roman elections depended on status and connections. Those advantages were possessed in abundance by the consuls of 69.

Inimici of Pompey obtained success also in the immediately subsequent years. L. Metellus, brother of Q. Metellus Creticus, succeeded his brother in 68. And C. Calpurnius Piso, one of Pompey's most redoubtable adversaries, followed in 67. Of L. Metellus we gain only a small glimpse from the sources: a man of no great consequence.[29] But he had the proper credentials for the consulship. C. Piso was a more formidable figure. A renowned family buttressed his ambitions: six Pisones had graced previous consular lists. And among his friends were Lucullus, Hortensius, and Bibulus. Resolute and relentless in opposing Pompeian schemes, Piso feared no one; and his year of office was memorable.[30]

The general's political opponents garnered further electoral victories in the closing years of the decade. Both consulships of 62 were captured by men who show close connection to Lucullus and Cato. D. Junius Silanus, the husband of Cato's sister, after an unsuccessful bid in 65, offered himself again in 63–a man of some intelligence, but lacking in industry or forceful leadership.[31] His consular ancestry, however, and the backing of Cato weighed heavily. In addition, there was L. Licinius Murena, boasting a distinguished military record and a respected prætorian family. Murena had served with his father in the Sullan ranks and went on to become a trusted legate of his relative Lucullus in the Mithridatic wars of the 70s. In 63 Lucullus celebrated a triumph; his veterans were back in Rome–a heavy source of votes and

[28] On Hortensius' opposition to the pirate law, see Cic. *De Imp. Pomp.* 51–53; the clash between Creticus and Pompey, Plut. *Pomp.* 29; Dio, 36.18–19, 36.45.1; Livy, *Per.* 99. Creticus' triumph was delayed as a consequence; Sallust, *Cat.* 30.3–4. On Creticus generally, see now Van Ooteghem, *Les Cæcilii Metelli de la République* (Brussels, 1967), pp. 220–239.

[29] Cf. his embarrassed and conflicting actions as governor of Sicily in 70; Cic. *Verr.* 2.2.63, 2.2.138–140, 2.2.161–163, 2.3.43–46, 2.3.144, 2.3.152–153, 2.3.156. For a kinder appraisal, see Ooteghem, *Metelli*, pp. 240–244.

[30] Discussion and references in Gruen, *CSCA*, 1 (1968): 156–159. On Piso's legislative activity in 67, see below, chap. 6.

[31] Cic. *Brutus*, 240: *studi ille quidem habuit non multum sed acuminis et orationis satis.* Cf. his wishy-washy indecision in the Catilinarian debate; Sallust, *Cat.* 50.4; Plut. *Cato*, 22.3–23.1; *Cic.* 20.3–21.3; Suet. *Iul.* 14. On his previous attempt at the consulship, see Cic. *Ad Att.* 1.1.2.

influence for L. Murena.[32] Their challengers proved ineffectual. L. Catilina was in the lists, despite earlier failure, as was the learned but priggish jurist Ser. Sulpicius Rufus. But Catiline, it seems, had tried the patience of the voters. And the pedantic airs of Sulpicius won few friends; his unpropitious canvass consisted more in threatening *ambitus* prosecutions than in wooing electors. Cicero's support helped him little.[33] The elections duly returned Silanus and Murena: Lucullus' friends could count the results satisfactory.[34]

In 61 and 60 Pompey's plans met with frustration, partly through the efforts of recalcitrant consuls. M. Valerius Messalla Niger held that office in 61. His political connections elude research. But a patrician had natural advantages with the Roman electorate. And Messalla may have been among those patricians patronized by Sulla.[35] Friction developed between Messalla and his consular colleague, M. Piso, a friend of Pompey's. At the trial of Clodius, Messalla stood with Lucullus, Hortensius, and C. Piso.[36] Matters got worse for Pompey in the following year. Q. Metellus Celer, once Pompey's legate and his brother-in-law, reached the chief magistracy in 60. He could have been a substantial proponent of Pompeian aims. But the general let the opportunity slip. When he divorced his wife, Mucia, he alienated her brother Celer irrevocably. Familial pride and straitlaced morals impelled Celer toward a sharp

[32] See, esp., Cic. *Pro Mur.* 37–39, 53, 69. On his father's service with Sulla, Broughton, *MRR,* II:56, 61, 64, 70, 77; Murena's service with Lucullus, Broughton, *MRR,* II:113, 119, 134. The close connection with Lucullus: Cic. *Ad Att.* 13.6.4.

[33] On Catiline's hopes, see Cic. *Pro Mur.* 49; Sallust, *Cat.* 26.1; Sulpicius' abortive campaign; Cic. *Pro Mur.* 7–8, 43–52; cf. Dio, 37.29.1–5; Plut. *Cic.* 14.1–2, 14.5–6.

[34] That Cato, shortly after the elections, stood with Sulpicius in his *ambitus* prosecution of Murena should not be given political significance. Cato had been no supporter of Sulpicius in the canvass, but both were firm advocates of stricter *ambitus* legislation. A test case might help the cause and Cato had sworn to bring proceedings against any offending candidate, excluding his brother-in-law Silanus; Plut. *Cato,* 21.2–3. The threat was meant primarily for Catiline; Cic. *Pro Mur.* 51. As Cicero makes clear in his defense speech, there had never been friction between Cato and Murena; Cic. *Pro Mur.* 56: *accusat M. Cato qui cum a Murena nulla re umquam alienus fuit.* The advocacy of greater controls on electoral practices had put Cato in an awkward political plight. Q. Hortensius was on the other side in the Murena case, as was M. Crassus; Cic. *Pro Mur.* 10, 48; Plut. *Cic.* 35.3. But the prosecution opened no irreparable breach. Murena and Cato are seen in political cooperation within a short time after Murena's acquittal; Plut. *Cato,* 28.2–3. The two consuls of 62 also sponsored legislation that had been advocated by Cato; see below, p. 254.

[35] He had been appointed to the pontificate by 73; L. R. Taylor, *AJP,* 63 (1942): 394–395. And he was a close friend of P. Sulla's; Cic. *Pro Sulla,* 20.

[36] Cic. *Ad Att.* 1.13.2–3, 1.14.5–6. Two years later he was to serve on the agrarian commission that implemented Cæsar's law; *ILS,* 46. Obviously, that cannot be taken to define his position in 61.

reaction.[37] As consul he took the lead in obstructing Pompey's bills on the eastern arrangements and on allotments for veterans.[38]

By contrast, Pompeian supporters gained but few victories in the consular balloting of the 60s. One such victor was M'. Acilius Glabrio, consul in 67. By 68 Pompey was beginning to work toward a new overseas command. It would be useful to have a friendly consul in the ensuing year, especially in view of the imminent election of C. Piso. Sluggishness and torpor made Glabrio a pliant individual.[39] And Pompey could count also on familial ties. Glabrio's wife was Aemilia, sister of M. Scaurus and stepdaughter of Sulla the dictator. Pompey had close connections with that family and had once been the husband of another of Sulla's stepdaughters.[40] In 68 Lucullus lost the province of Cilicia to Q. Marcius Rex. The following year saw his major provinces of Bithynia and Pontus snatched away and awarded to M'. Acilius Glabrio. The latter move was clearly designed as a holding operation for Pompey. A. Gabinius, the tribune of 67 who promoted Pompey's command against the pirates, also sponsored the measure that sent Glabrio to succeed Lucullus. The master plan worked without a hitch. Glabrio duly dawdled in Asia, absorbing many of Lucullus' old soldiers but performing no feats of magnitude. In the following year, with the pirates disposed of, Pompey took over the reins from Glabrio and went on to conduct the war against Mithridates.[41]

Pompey no doubt hoped for congenial consuls again in 66 and 65. But he could not so easily work his will when abroad. His favored candidate for 66, we may judge, must have been the garrulous and demagogic M. Lollius Palicanus, a man despised by the *nobilitas.* Palicanus was from Picenum, the home of Pompey's hereditary connections; the two had collaborated on tribuni-

[37] Dio, 37.49.3: Μέτελλος δὲ ὀργῇ, ὅτι τὴν ἀδελφὴν αὐτοῦ, καίτοι παῖδας ἐξ αὐτῆς ἔχων, ἀπεπέπεμπτο, και πάνυ πρὸς πάντα ἀντέπραξεν. On his familial pride, Cic. *Ad Fam.* 5.1.1; his public morals, Val. Max. 7.7.7. Celer was less effective in private life–he was the cuckolded husband of Clodius' wayward sister, Clodia; Cic. *Ad Att.* 2.1.5. Catullus' famous poem, 83, may refer to Celer's marital ineffectiveness and obtuseness; but see Wiseman, *Catullan Questions* (Leicester, 1969), pp. 42–60. On Celer generally, see Ooteghem, *Metelli*, pp. 245–279.

[38] Dio, 37.49–50. In this he clashed dramatically with the Pompeian tribune L. Flavius. Shackleton Bailey, *Cicero's Letters*, I:334, suggests that Flavius may have impeded Celer's hopes to obtain the province of Gaul. In light of all this evidence, it is difficult to credit Dio's assertion, 37.49.1, that Pompey supported the consular canvass of both Afranius and Metellus Celer in 61–*pace* Syme, *Rom. Rev.*, p. 33; Meier, *Res Pub.*, p. 19, n.70.

[39] Cic. *Brutus,* 239: *M'. Glabrionem . . . socors ipsius natura neglegensque tardaverat.*

[40] For Glabrio's marriage, see Asconius, 28, Clark; on Pompey's association with the house of Sulla, see Gruen, *Historia*, 18 (1969): 75–77.

[41] That Gabinius' measure gave Glabrio his command is clear from Sallust, *Hist.* 5.13, Maur. Lucullus was most displeased with his successor; Dio, 36.14.4, 36.17.1. Other references in Broughton, *MRR*, II:143, 154.

cian reform in the late 70s.[42] Fawning speeches to the populace and public demonstrations enflamed the urban crowd on Palicanus' behalf. But the urban crowd did not control consular elections. C. Calpurnius Piso stiffened himself in opposition to popular furor. That Palicanus was an adherent of Pompey's was bad enough; worse yet, he came from a family of no distinction or record. Piso, who administered the *comitia*, refused to acknowledge Palicanus' candidacy and effected his rejection in advance.[43] Among the candidates in the following year was Pompey's brother-in-law P. Sulla, a relative of the dictator's. Gains during the proscriptions brought him wealth and prompted extravagance. Sulla would not shun the use of cash to secure endorsement from the voters.[44] That endorsement came, but only temporarily. Criminal charges followed swiftly, and the consuls-elect suffered conviction *de ambitu*. P. Sulla never did get his consulship.[45] None of the successful candidates for 66 and 65, M'. Lepidus, L. Volcacius, L. Cotta, and L. Torquatus, carried the Pompeian banner.

In 62 Pompey was preparing his long-awaited return to Rome.[46] Successes abroad had been unbroken; at home they might not come so easily. Hence, it is no accident that Pompey played an active and vigorous role in the consular elections for 61 and 60. The general's choice fell first upon M. Pupius Piso, a trusted lieutenant throughout the eastern wars and a man whose friendship with Pompey may stretch back to the 80s. And Piso was not merely a military figure. In addition to his family's *dignitas*, he possessed a wry and caustic wit, attained some repute as an orator, and was steeped in Greek learning

[42] See above, chap. 1, n.57. Palicanus may also have reckoned on the support of the Pompeian tribune Gabinius, who was married to a Lollia; Suet. *Iul.* 50.

[43] The story is told in full by Val. Max. 3.8.3. For Palicanus' low birth, see Sallust, *Hist.* 4.43, Maur.: *M. Lollius Palicanus, humili loco Picens.* The elections were postponed for some time; Cic. *De Imp. Pomp.* 2; *Ad Att.* 1.11.2. That was due to the struggle over *ambitus* legislation between Piso and C. Cornelius; see below, chap. 6. Dio's reference to violence in the campaign is probably also an outgrowth of that legislative contest; 36.39.1.

[44] On P. Sulla's connection with the dictator, see Cic. *Pro Sulla*, 72; *De Off.* 2.29; cf. Gellius, 12.12; the relationship to Pompey, Cic. *Ad Q. Frat.* 2.3.3; Syme, *Sallust*, p. 102, n.88.

[45] Full references in Broughton, *MRR*, II:157. The elections of 66 and the so-called "first Catilinarian conspiracy" have been endlessly discussed. It should no longer be necessary to refute hypotheses about the schemes of Cæsar and Crassus, which have no place in this period, if at all. Nor is it clear that the interests of Pompey were engaged in the outcome of this electoral contest. Attention to untainted evidence provides a less complex and more plausible picture. Bibliographical references may be found in H. Frisch, *ClMed*, 9 (1948): 21–29, and Gruen, *CP*, 64 (1969): 20–24. Add also W. Wimmel, *Hermes*, 95 (1967): 192–221, and R. Seager, *Hommages Renard* (1969), II:680–686.

[46] If Schol. Bob. 134, Stangl is to be believed, there was an attempt at the beginning of the year to permit Pompey's candidacy in absence for the consulship of 61; cf. Meier, *Athenæum*, 40 (1962): 103–125. The effort, in any case, was not pursued.

and Peripatetic philosophy. In 62 Pompey dispatched Piso to Rome ahead of the returning forces as his candidate for the consulship. The elections, it seems, were postponed at Pompey's request to permit Piso's candidacy. Cato, as might be expected, stood in stern opposition. But Piso's canvass achieved success.[47] Another Pompeian officer was available for the next year. L. Afranius had been with Pompey in both the Sertorian and Mithridatic campaigns. But undistinguished origins stood against him. Afranius had hoped for the consulship in 62, but, on the advice of Pompey, had stepped aside for M. Piso. It was wiser not to overextend the patience of the voters. But in the following year both Pompey and Piso engaged in strenuous efforts to promote Afranius' candidacy. The fact that he lacked ability, energy, and ancestry proved this time to be of secondary importance. Political pressure prevailed. The opposition of Catonians, including electoral postponement, was again of no avail. Afranius attained his consulship for 60.[48]

The harvest was not a rich one. Only three consuls in the 60s can be decisively claimed as Pompeians. Of these, Glabrio served his turn dutifully. But the electoral triumphs of M. Piso and Afranius proved to be of small value for Pompey. Their efforts, as we have seen, were effectively stymied by uncongenial and uncooperative colleagues, M. Messalla and Q. Metellus Celer. The *inimici* of Pompey earned the greater share of electoral satisfaction.

But factional rivalry tells only a part of the story. Candidates rarely ran as Pompeians or anti-Pompeians. Familial ties, connections, wealth, and aristocratic heritage counted heavily with the voters. The three Metelli and two Pisones who won consular office in the 60s were elevated by their ancestors' prestige and only secondarily (if at all) by their political stance. The same may safely be said of most of the other men elected to the chief magistracy in that decade.

The consuls of 65, L. Manlius Torquatus and L. Aurelius Cotta, had exhibited high ability, as well as distinction. Torquatus boasted an ancient patrician lineage. His own career included military service under Sulla in the East and presence even at the battle of the Colline Gate: yet another example of men

[47] On Piso's character and background, see the references and discussion in Gruen, *CSCA*, 1 (1968): 167–169. For the election of 62, Dio, 37.44.3; Plut. *Pomp.* 44.1-2; *Cato*, 30.1-2; and see above, ch. 3, n.9.

[48] On the elections, see Cic. *Ad Att.* 1.16.12-13; Dio, 37.49.1; Plut. *Pomp.* 44.3-4; *Cato*, 30.5; cf. Schol. Bob. 87, Stangl. For Afranius' expectations in the previous year, see Plut. *Præc. Rei Pub. Ger.* 11.6; his lengthy service under Pompey, Plut. *Sert.* 19; Orosius, 5.23.14; Plut. *Pomp.* 34.1, 36.2, 39.2; Dio, 37.5.3-5; his personality and consulship, see above, chap. 3, n.11. Afranius' victory demonstrates the impact that politics could occasionally have upon electoral results. *Pace* Meier, *Res Pub.*, pp. 7–23, they cannot be reduced entirely to the operation of private *necessitudines*.

with Sullan backgrounds who achieved the consulship in later years.[49] Contemporaries recognized him as a leader of exceptional acumen, patriotism, and integrity: Torquatus was elegant in speech, prudent in judgment, and altogether civilized.[50] The family of L. Cotta, also linked to Sulla, occupied particular prominence in this period. Cotta himself, brother of the consuls of 75 and 74, had in 70 moved that most statesmanlike measure which reformed the structure of the juries. A fondness for wine only added to his charm. Cotta is consistently described by Cicero as a man of the highest capacity and intelligence.[51] He also enjoyed the signal honor of elevation to the censorship only a year after his tenure as consul.[52]

Personal merit was no guarantor of election. Cotta and Torquatus, in fact, obtained their posts only after *ambitus* convictions had eliminated the original winners, P. Sulla and P. Autronius Pætus. But noble lineage could override other considerations. C. Antonius serves as an appropriate example. A son of the great orator M. Antonius, he had been a ruthless lieutenant of Sulla's, an exploiter of provincials, and generally opprobrious. Violent in speech and deed, though afraid of his own shadow, Antonius had once been expelled from the senate for heavy debts and licentiousness.[53] But political connections and the Sullan background returned him to prominence in the 60s. Antonius, whatever his failings as a human being, was a politician to be reckoned with. In 63 he acquired consular rank. M. Valerius Messalla, the consul of 61, had also shaken off the effects of an earlier expulsion from the senate. Diligent activity in the law courts brought him back into the good graces of the voters. He was eventually to attain the censorship.[54] Q. Marcius Rex possessed multifarious connections and a stubborn and cross-grained character. A marriage to Clodia Tertia gave him familial ties to the Claudii, the Metelli,

[49] References on his career in Broughton, *MRR*, II:61, 70, 146. There may also have been service with Pompey, Broughton, *MRR*, II:151, n.16. Not that he is to be reckoned simply as an agent of Pompey. Torquatus had many influential friends, including Q. Hortensius; Cic. *Pro Sulla*, 12.

[50] Cic. *Brutus*, 239: *L. Torquatus elegans in dicendo, in existimando admodum prudens, toto genere perurbanus*; Cic. *Pro Sulla*, 34: *homo amantissimus patriæ, maximi animi, summi consilii, singularis constantiæ*; cf. *Pro Sulla*, 11, 30, 49; *In Pis.* 44, 47. Note also his life-long friendship with Atticus; Nepos, *Att.* 1.4.

[51] Cic. *De Domo*, 84: *vir prudentissimus; De Leg.* 3.45: *vir magni ingenii summaque prudentia, L. Cotta; Phil.* 2.13: *L. Cotta, vir summo ingenio summaque prudentia*; cf. *Pro Sest.* 73. On his fondness for wine, Plut. *Cic.* 27.2.

[52] Cic. *De Domo*, 84; Plut. *Cic.* 27.2.

[53] See, esp., [Q. Cic.] *Comm. Petit.* 8–9; Asconius, 84, Clark.

[54] Val. Max. 2.9.9: *M. Valerius Messala censoria nota perstrictus censoriam postmodum potestatem impetravit; quorum ignominia virtutem acuit*; Cic. *Brutus*, 246: *M. Messalla . . . prudens, acutus, minime incautus patronus, in causis cognoscendis componendisque diligens, magni laboris, multæ operæ multarumque causarum.*

and Lucullus. The associations were vital in obtaining the consulship of 68. But no group could rely on Rex's loyalty. He clashed with his brother-in-law Lucullus in Asia. When P. Clodius made himself a nuisance in Lucullus' ranks, Rex ostentatiously gave him refuge and appointed him to command of his fleet. It was a gesture of defiance toward Lucullus, not of friendship toward Clodius; with equal ostentation Rex later left Clodius out of his will. Nor did these maneuvers entail collaboration with Pompey. Q. Marcius Rex was one of those eastern commanders unceremoniously superseded by Pompey and then obliged to await his triumph for years–a triumph he apparently never received.[55]

Factional labels are best avoided also for the remaining consuls in this decade. The victors for 66 were M'. Æmilius Lepidus and L. Volcacius Tullus. The career of neither man shows clear political allegiance or significant activity. Both consuls presided over senatorial rejection of a bill moved by Manilius, the Pompeian tribune of 66. But both seem to have interceded on behalf of C. Cornelius, another friend of Pompey's.[56] Lepidus and Volcacius were prudent and inconspicuous. Two safe and relatively innocuous candidates were returned for 64 as well: L. Julius Cæsar and C. Marcius Figulus. Figulus' previous *cursus* escapes record. But he could point to an ancestor in the consulship, three generations before. And the family possessed opulence: Figulus' descendants constructed for him an elaborate and expensive funerary monument.[57] L. Cæsar was also of consular family, and married well–into the Fulvii Flacci, a *gens* of great prominence in previous generations. Collaboration with his younger and more illustrious kinsman, C. Cæsar, is attested for subsequent years, but need not be invoked to explain the election. A reflective and religious man, who composed a lengthy work on augury, L. Cæsar represented a reliable choice for the voters.[58] No information subsists on Servilius Vatia, who was chosen as successor to L. Metellus in 68 and who died before formal investiture with office.[59] Important connections doubtless stood behind him. His relative P. Servilius Vatia, consul in 79, had been an associate of Sulla's at least since 88; and there were close familial ties to the Metelli.[60]

Electoral competitions in the 60s cannot be reduced to a simplistic pattern.

[55] For Rex's family connections, see Münzer, *RE*, 14: 1583–1584, "Marcius," n.92; his conflict with Lucullus, Dio, 36.2.2, 36.15.1, 36.17.2; the disinheriting of Clodius, Cic. *Ad Att.* 1.16.10; the postponed triumph, Sallust, *Cat.* 30.3–4; for further references on his service abroad, see Broughton, *MRR*, II:146, 154.

[56] Dio, 36.42.3; Asconius, 59–60, Clark; cf. Sumner, *JRS*, 54 (1964): 41–42.

[57] Cic. *De Leg.* 2.62.

[58] Macrob. *Sat.* 1.16.29. For collaboration between the two Cæsares, see Dio, 37.27.2; Cæs. *BG*, 7.65.1.

[59] Dio, 36.4.1. The successor of L. Metellus is given by the Chronographer of 354 as Vatia.

[60] Cf. Gruen, *Roman Politics*, pp. 178, 238, 266.

Some involved political rivalries, with major stakes, such as the conflicts between Pompeian and anti-Pompeian candidates, which revolved around the general's eastern commands or his proposed settlement. Others reveal personal friction, clashing ambitions among *nobiles* to attain high office. The friction could erupt into fierce bitterness, as in the confrontations of 66. But a consistent strand is discernible in the results. To the battles of politicians the voters were generally indifferent; their decisions were made on other grounds. With few exceptions, they persisted in returning men of family, lineage, and pedigree.

An exception came in 64. On that election we are especially well informed—naturally. It was the year of Cicero's consular campaign and his most remarkable triumph. The *novus homo,* with no consular or senatorial antecedents, scored a memorable upset. The campaign will repay scrutiny.

Several competitors could already be foreseen in 65. Cicero registers eight names in a letter to Atticus during July of that year. But when candidates actually presented themselves a year later, four of those individuals had dropped out. Lack of consular ancestry stood against all four, and in three of the cases humble backgrounds rendered them virtually ineligible.[61] Their withdrawal is strong evidence for the importance of birth and blood in the making of a serious candidate. The surviving contenders provided stiff competition. Two patricians offered themselves. L. Catilina escaped conviction on a *repetundae* charge and was now running hard. P. Sulpicius Galba possessed an unassailable character, but he damaged his chances by the premature selling of his wares—Galba suffered from overexposure.[62] Further, there were two plebeian *nobiles:* the disreputable but politically formidable C. Antonius and the future Catilinarian L. Cassius Longinus, a man branded as more stupid than wicked, who was thrust forward by a host of illustrious forebears.[63] Finally, two sober and estimable *candidati* from senatorial families stood for the office: Q. Cornificius and C. Licinius Sacerdos.[64]

[61] Namely, M. Cæsonius, T. Aufidius, and M. Lollius Palicanus. The fourth, C. Aquillius Gallus, was of prætorian stock, but ill health and absorption in legal matters removed him from the running; Cic. *Ad Att.* 1.1.1. None is given in the list of actual candidates recorded by Asconius, 82, Clark.

[62] Cic. *Ad Att.* 1.1.1: *prensat unus P. Galba sine fuco ac fallaciis more maiorum negatur; ut opinio est hominum, non aliena rationi nostræ fuit illius hæc præpropera prensatio*; cf. [Q. Cic.] *Comm. Petit.* 7; Cic. *Pro Mur.* 17. On Galba's character, cf. Asconius, 82, Clark; Cic. *Pro Mur.* 17. On Catiline's candidacy, see Asconius, 82, 83, Clark.

[63] Asconius, 82, Clark: *Cassius quamvis stolidus tum magis quam improbus videretur, post paucos menses in coniuratione Catilinæ esse eum apparuit ac cruentissimarum sententiarum fuisse auctorem.* His corpulence was also notorious; Cic. *Cat.* 3.16: *L. Cassi adipes.* Cicero had a more favorable judgment on Cassius earlier; *Pro Cluent.* 107. On Cassius' career, see Münzer, *RE,* 3:1738–1739, "Cassius," n.64. Antonius' candidacy is registered by Asconius, 82–83, Clark.

[64] Asconius, 82, Clark: *duos qui tantum non primi ex familiis suis magistratum adepti erant, Q. Cornificium et C. Licinium Sacerdotem . . . Sacerdos nulla improbitate notus.* On Cornificius'

Cicero, by contrast, was a *novus homo,* son of an *eques:* no Tullius Cicero had ever sat in the Roman senate. Unkind comments about his *municipalis origo* haunted him throughout his career. A new man, in the eyes of the nobility, was little better than a foreigner or a resident alien. The great families of Rome shuddered at the prospect of an *inquilinus* in the consulship: it threatened a pollution of that office.[65] Cicero would have to confront ingrained prejudice. *Consulares* would be jealous, *novi homines* who never progressed beyond the prætorship even more jealous.[66] Yet, as is well known, Cicero not only gained election, he came in at the head of the poll, in his first try for the office, with the unanimous vote of all the centuries.[67] How had it happened?

The ancients had an explanation. Cicero, if not wellborn, was at least conservative and reliable. If he failed, there would be worse. Catiline and Antonius had linked themselves in candicacy. Their aim was not simply consular office, but revolutionary upheaval, and, perhaps, a coup d'etat. The aristocracy preferred a *novus homo* to *novæ res.*[68]

But a doubt supervenes. The information derives from Sallust, and Sallust, as is notorious, predated the conspiratorial designs of Catiline. No one, in 64, could have forecast the events that were to rock the city in the following year. Cicero's *In Toga Candida,* pronounced prior to the consular elections, delivered a savage attack on Catiline and Antonius, implying even that Antonius might stir his herdsmen to revolt.[69] But how many Romans would be persuaded by that speech? Political invective was commonplace, and hyperbole would be recognized for what it was. The reputation of Antonius had not prevented resumption of a senatorial career or election to a prætorship. And Catiline's questionable activities in the past provided no hindrance to

later wealth, see Cic. *Ad Att.* 12.17. The Cornificii hail from Lanuvium; Syme, *Historia*, 4 (1955): 61. Cicero thought little of Q. Cornificius' chances in 65; *Ad Att.* 1.1.1. Sacerdos had recently done yeoman service as legate of Metellus Creticus; Cic. *Pro Planc.* 27. Other references in Münzer, *RE*, 13:458–459, "Licinius," n.154.

[65] Sallust, *Cat.* 23.6: *namque antea pleraque nobilitas invidia æstuabat, et quasi pollui consulatum credebant, si eum quamvis egregius homo novus adeptus foret*; Sallust, *Cat.* 31.7: *quom eam servaret M. Tullius, inquilinus civis urbis Romæ*; Cic. *Pro Sulla*, 22: *et me tertium peregrinum regem esse dixisti*; cf. *De Har. Resp.* 17; Asconius, 93–94, Clark. For the electoral difficulties of the *novus homo* in general, see Wiseman, *New Men*, pp. 100–107.

[66] [Q. Cic.] *Comm. Petit.* 13.

[67] See, e.g., Cic. *In Vat.* 6; *In Pis.* 3; *De Leg. Agrar.* 2.4, 2.7; *De Off.* 2.59; Asconius, 94, Clark.

[68] Sallust, *Cat.* 23.4–24.1; cf. 21.3; Appian, *BC*, 2.2; Plut. *Cic.* 10–11. The analysis is accepted by, e.g., Mommsen, *Röm. Gesch.*, III:178–180; Rice Holmes, *Rom. Rep.*, I:236–241; Meyer, *Cæsars Monarchie*, pp. 23–24.

[69] Cic. *In Tog. Cand., apud* Asconius, 87, Clark: *pastores retinet. ex quibus ait se cum velit subito fugitivorum bellum excitaturum.* See the fragments of Cicero's speech quoted in Asconius, 82–93, Clark.

high office. In 65 Cicero had considered defending him on an extortion charge, in the hopes that they might collaborate in the consular canvass.[70] Moreover, Antonius was successful in 64 itself, finishing second to Cicero in the *comitia.* If the voters had been convinced by the *In Toga Candida,* they could have fastened not only on Cicero, but on Galba or another candidate. As it was, Antonius gained victory and Catiline finished a close third.[71] Fear of Cicero's competitors does not explain his election.

Perhaps there were more hidden fears and suspicions. M. Crassus and C. Julius Cæsar, it is often asserted, lay behind Catiline and Antonius: elevation of Cicero was meant to checkmate the schemes of those politicians.[72] The assertion finds no basis in contemporary testimony. Only Asconius notes the involvement of Crassus and Cæsar, and his information probably has its source in Cicero's scandalous secret memoir, not published until after his death. Its purpose was posthumous denunciation of Cæsar and Crassus. Prudence forbids citation of that document as firm evidence for the 60s.[73] Crassus had no reason to love Catiline, the friend and protégé of Q. Catulus. In the previous year Crassus and Catulus had engaged in heated rivalry during their joint censorship.[74] As for Cæsar and Antonius, few will have forgotten that Cæsar, a decade before, brought criminal proceedings against Antonius for his extortionate activities in Greece.[75]

The truth, as so often, is probably simpler. Cicero was a *novus homo,* but no ordinary *novus homo.* A spectacular career at the bar had kept him in the public eye for nearly two decades. More important, it earned numerous political credits, which he could now hope to cash in. Many admirers and beneficiaries were expected to cast favorable votes. "A man considered worthy of defending *consulares* cannot be unworthy of the consulate."[76] Equestrian and municipal

[70] Cic. *Ad Att.* 1.2.1: *hoc tempore Catilinam, competitorem nostrum, defendere cogitamus . . . spero, si absolutus erit, coniunctiorem illum nobis fore in ratione petitionis.*

[71] Asconius, 94, Clark: *Antonius pauculis centuriis Catilinam superavit.*

[72] See, e.g., Heitland, *Rom. Rep.,* III:77–81; Cary, *CAH,* IX:482–484; R. E. Smith, *Cicero,* pp. 92–98.

[73] Asconius, 83, Clark: *coierant enim ambo* [Catiline and Antonius] *ut Ciceronem consulatu deicerent, adiutoribus usi firmissimis M. Crasso et C. Cæsare . . . ei enim acerrimi ac potentissimi fuerunt Ciceronis refragatores cum petiit consulatum . . . et hoc ipse Cicero in expositione consiliorum suorum significat.* On the secret memoir, see Cic. *Ad Att.* 2.6.2, 14.17.6; Dio, 39.10.1–3; Plut. *Crass.* 13.2–3; cf. P. A. Brunt, *CR,* 71 (1957): 193–195.

[74] The censorship of 65: Dio, 37.9.3; Plut. *Crass.* 13.1; Catiline's connection with Catulus: Orosius, 6.3.1; Sallust, *Cat.* 34.3–35.6; Schol. Bern. Lucan, 2.173.

[75] Plut. *Cæs.* 4.1; Asconius, 84, Clark; cf. [Q. Cic.] *Comm. Petit.* 8. Cicero, in fact, made reference to the affair in 64; *In Tog. Cand. apud* Asconius, 83–84, Clark.

[76] [Q. Cic.] *Comm. Petit.* 2: *non potest qui dignus habetur patronus consularium indignus consulatu putari.* This tract is ostensibly a memorandum on electioneering written for Cicero by his brother in 64. Its authenticity has been much disputed; among recent works, see M. I. Hender-

background might be an advantage as well as a liability. There were voters of substance in the *equester ordo* and among the *municipales.* For some, Cicero was a "favorite son." The success of a *novus homo* would be an encouragement to other men in that category. And a new generation of aspiring orators also found Cicero attractive.[77]

But success in the consular *comitia* would require more powerful backing. Cicero had carefully cultivated the favor of Pompeius Magnus in 66 and 65, supporting the general's Mithridatic command and defending his friends Cornelius and Manilius. He took pains to remind the electorate of those facts.[78] And Cicero did not stop there. The *novus homo* would need support everywhere. While advocating Pompeian causes, he was careful not to alienate other powerful interests. So, in the speech that urged Pompey's Mithridatic command, he included warm praise of the general's predecessor L. Lucullus.[79] As a consequence, Cicero, in 64, was able to hope for the aid of men like C. Piso and L. Domitius Ahenobarbus.[80] Thorough work in the wards and political organizations of the city paid dividends, as did trips to leading figures in the *municipia.*[81] Cicero had mastered the techniques of electioneering.

The canvass of Cicero is not to be taken as typical. Men with more distin-

---

son, *JRS,* 40 (1950): 8–21; R. G. M. Nisbet, *JRS,* 51 (1961): 84–87; R. Till, *Historia,* 11 (1962): 315–338; Balsdon, *CQ,* 13 (1963): 242–250; J. S. Richardson, *Historia,* 20 (1971): 436–442; R. E. A. Palmer, *RivFilol,* 99 (1971): 385–393. The author's knowledge of the political situation in 64 is considerable and the avoidance of anachronism scrupulous. That does not, however, establish contemporaneity; only that the author had good sources, such as the *In Toga Candida* and the *Pro Murena.* No defender of the tract has yet met the most serious objection: why should Cicero need the advice of his younger, less experienced brother, who had not even stood for the prætorship? The debate, in any event, does not affect the document's value. It is exceptionally well informed on matters in the 60s.

[77] [Q. Cic.] *Comm. Petit.* 3: *habes enim ea quæ qui novi habuerunt? omnis publicanos, totum fere equestrem ordinem, multa propria municipia, multos abs te defensos homines cuiusque ordinis, aliquot conlegia, præterea studio dicendi conciliatos plurimos adulescentulos, cottidianam amicorum adsiduitatem et frequentiam*; cf. also *Comm. Petit.* 50; Cic. *Pro Cæl.* 10; and Cic. *Ad Att.* 1.1.1: *nam illi* [Galba] *ita negant vulgo ut mihi se debere dicant.*

[78] [Q. Cic.] *Comm. Petit.* 51: *iam urbanam illam multitudinem et eorum studia qui contiones tenent adeptus es in Pompeio ornando, Manili causa recipienda, Cornelio defendendo . . . efficiendum etiam illud est ut sciant omnes Cn. Pompei summam esse erga te voluntatem et vehementer ad illius rationes te id adsequi quod petis pertinere;* also *Comm. Petit.* 5, 14. Cicero's request to Atticus to gain Pompey's favor is only half joking; Cic. *Ad Att.* 1.1.2. That Cicero also advocated the *lex Gabinia* in 67 has been held by some scholars; J. A. Davison, *CR,* 44 (1930): 224–225; Ward, *CW,* 63 (1969): 8–10. But the orator's silence in the *De Imp. Pomp.* is decisive against that hypothesis.

[79] Cic. *De Imp. Pomp.* 5, 10, 20–21, 26.

[80] Cic. *Ad Att.* 1.1.2–4. Domitius had assisted Cicero in his prætorian canvass three years earlier; *Ad Att.* 1.1.3.

[81] [Q. Cic.] *Comm. Petit.* 18–19, 30–31.

guished names and *gentes* could eschew many of these activities. But Cicero's success, in light of the evidence discussed, no longer appears incongruous.[82] He was not an "optimate" candidate or a "popularis" candidate. By scrupulously expanding his contacts, the orator gained a host of varied backers: *publicani, equites* generally, grateful beneficiaries from the law courts, admirers from the younger generation, men from the *municipia,* and several of Rome's political leaders.[83] The aggregate was perhaps not enough to make Cicero a power in his own right, much though he would have liked to believe it. But it was enough for consular *dignitas* and the ennobling of his family.

A brief retrospect is now possible on the 60s. It is plain that the Roman voter found no turning point in the year 70. Continuity again transcends the vicissitudes. The number of available ex-Sullan officers naturally diminished as the date of Sulla's death receded. Even so, three consuls of the 60s fall into that category: L. Torquatus, C. Antonius, and L. Murena. Another former lieutenant, L. Catilina, narrowly missed the consulship, as did P. Sulla, a relative of the dictator's. And one may note M'. Acilius Glabrio, Sulla's son-in-law and successful candidate for 67. Even more striking are the links, familial or political, between most of the consuls in the 60s and their predecessors in the previous decade. Under this heading come no fewer than ten holders of the chief magistracy: Q. Hortensius, Q. Metellus Creticus, L. Metellus, Q. Marcius Rex, Servilius Vatia, C. Piso, M'. Lepidus, L. Cotta, L. Cæsar, and L. Murena.

The claims of blood were not to be denied. Seventeen of twenty-one consuls in the period 69–60 had ancestors in the consulship, a proportion very close to that of the previous decade.[84] Four of them were patricians: Lepidus, Torquatus, Cæsar, and Valerius Messalla; and there were six representatives from the great plebeian houses of the Metelli, Pisones, and Cottæ. Successes won by the four non-*nobiles* are all explicable. L. Murena stemmed from distinguished prætorian ancestry, his record showed service for Sulla, and his backers included the adherents of Lucullus. Volcacius Tullus, apparently, possessed a family with some connections in the senate.[85] Afranius secured office through strenuous efforts by Pompey and the Pompeians. And Cicero's meticulous canvassing had the support of numerous varied interests, including powerful

[82] On the electoral campaign generally, see Ciaceri's careful analysis; *Cicerone*, I:168–194; and cf. Wiseman, *New Men*, pp. 134–142.

[83] [Q. Cic.] *Comm. Petit.* 50: *dicendi laus, studia publicanorum et equestris ordinis, hominum nobilium voluntas, adulescentulorum frequentia, eorum qui abs te defensi sunt adsiduitas, ex municipiis multido eorum quos tua causa venisse appareat.* Cf. Plut. *Cic.* 10.1: ἐπὶ δὲ τὴν ὑπατείαν οὐχ ἧττον ὑπὸ τῶν ἀριστοκρατικῶν ἢ τῶν πολλῶν προήχθη.

[84] Vatia, the suffect consul of 68, though he did not actually live to take office, is included in this number.

[85] Cf. Cic. *Pro Planc.* 51.

elements in the aristocracy. Consistency and conservatism in the electorate endured in the 60s. Dominated, as it was, by the well-to-do from Italian towns and property owners in the countryside, its conservatism does not surprise. The Roman *nobilitas* remained unchallenged.

CONSULAR ELECTIONS AND THE "TRIUMVIRATE"

C. Julius Cæsar was consul in 59. It was a memorable and pivotal chief magistracy: the "consulship of Julius and Cæsar" cynical wags termed it.[86] The year ushered in the last decade of the free state and marked the gathering of that coalition which moderns have known as "the first triumvirate." Does this mean that the triumvirs thereafter twisted institutions to their own ends, overawed rivals, and controlled the process of government?[87] Consular elections in the Republic's last decade seem to point in a different direction. They disclose the abiding strengths of the traditional system—which was not easily shaken.

Pompeian consuls in 61 and 60 had been ineffectual. Uncooperative colleagues accounted largely for their failure to push through the claims of Pompey and his veterans. Julius Cæsar, a more forceful and determined personality, offered a better hope. He had been a useful advocate of the general in the past and could be relied on again. Better, however, that he should hold office with another individual amenable to Pompey's interests. A promising choice emerged: Pompey's friend L. Lucceius, the learned scholar and historian.[88] After some dickering he joined forces with Cæsar. Lucceius' claims on the electorate were inferior, but his financial resources formed a valuable asset.[89]

[86] Suet. *Iul.* 20.2.

[87] As, e.g., Mommsen, *Röm. Gesch.*, III:207–219, 305–340.

[88] The friendship with Pompey: Cic. *Ad Fam.* 13.41, 13.42. Lucceius composed a history of the Italian and civil wars; Cic. *Ad Fam.* 5.12.2. On his reputation as a scholar, see also Cic. *Pro Cæl.* 54: *ille vir illa humanitate præditus, illis studiis, illis artibus atque doctrina illius ipsius.* The recent effort by W. C. McDermott, *Hermes*, 97 (1969): 233–246, to distinguish Lucceius the historian from the friend of Pompey is conjectural and unconvincing. McDermott cannot believe that the "honorable" scholar could be identical with the "unscrupulous" consular candidate. But on his own analysis, that honorable scholar retailed the most scandalous stories about Catiline; Asconius, 91–92, Clark. And Asconius explicitly identifies the prosecutor of Catiline with the consular candidate. None of the ancient references to the man show inconsistency. The Lucceius noted in some letters of late 51 and 50 is, of course, to be distinguished from the historian. But Cicero avoids confusion by explicit reference to him as son of Marcus; *Ad Att.* 5.21.13; cf. 5.20.8, 6.1.23, 7.3.6. The historian was son of Quintus; Cic. *Ad Fam.* 5.12–15.

[89] Suet. *Iul.* 19.1: *e duobus consulatus competitoribus, Lucio Lucceio Marcoque Bibulo, Lucceium sibi* [Cæsar] *adiunxit, pactus ut ii, quoniam inferior gratia esset pecuniaque polleret, nummos de suo communi nomine per centurias pronuntiaret.* Cf. Cic. *Ad Att.* 1.14.7, 1.17.11, 2.1.9; Asconius, 91, Clark.

The collaboration ran into difficulties. Political groups unsympathetic to Pompey frowned on the prospect of two Pompeian consuls in office. In M. Calpurnius Bibulus they had a strong candidate of their own. The *cognomen* does not appear earlier in the *fasti,* but the Calpurnii were *nobiles,* and Bibulus' branch may be an offshoot from the Calpurnii Pisones. C. Piso backed his canvass, as did Cato. Tenacious and unyielding, Bibulus had a long feud with Cæsar, and he did not blench at vigorous solicitation of the voters. Many aristocrats contributed to his campaign coffers.[90]

Cæsar emerged with a smashing victory at the polls, unanimous assent from the voting centuries.[91] But the combine of Pompey's enemies had also gained success. Bibulus finished second in the voting and served as Cæsar's colleague in 59. For the third successive year Pompey's influence prevailed only sufficiently to carry one candidate into office. The unhappy Lucceius, who had provided much of the financial contribution, failed in his personal quest.

It is of importance here to distinguish between the aims of the participants and the motives of the electorate. The political contest between Pompeians and anti-Pompeians stimulated the candidacies and provoked the vigorous character of the campaigning in 60. It does not follow, however, that the average voter calculated his choice in those terms. Personal patronage, ancestral connections, distribution of favors, and the glamor of noble *nomina* supplied the decisive elements in determining the cast of an individual ballot in most instances. Cæsar and Lucceius may have combined their resources in a joint campaign. But the Roman electoral system did not permit official "tickets." There is no reason to doubt that many electors opted for both Cæsar and Bibulus. Indeed, the outcome of the *comitia* virtually demands that conclusion.[92] The Roman voter did not choose Cæsar because he would support Pompeian veteran benefits nor Bibulus because he would oppose them. Campaign promises and overt political stances rarely played a role in the elections.

[90] Suet. *Iul.* 19.1: *optimates . . . auctores Bibulo fuerunt tantundem pollicendi, ac plerique pecunias contulerunt, ne Catone quidem abnuente eam largitionem e re publica fieri.* On support by C. Piso, see Cic. *Ad Att.* 1.17.11.

[91] Dio, 37.54.3.

[92] This important feature is cogently argued by Meier, *Res Pub.*, pp. 15, 197–200. The traditional attitudes of the voters, however, do not obviate the political content of the campaign itself. Nor did familial relationships necessarily determine one's stance in the campaign. A certain Servilius Cæpio, though a relative of Cato's, supported Cæsar in his canvass and used his influence against Bibulus; Suet. *Iul.* 21: *Servilio Cæpione, cuius vel præcipua opera paulo ante Bibulum impugnaverat.* Münzer, *Röm. Adelsp.*, pp. 338–339, identifies that individual with young M. Brutus, nephew of Cato and adopted son of a Servilius Cæpio. The identification has not met with universal consent; cf. Shackleton Bailey, *Cicero's Letters*, I:400. But Cato's relations with the Cæpiones are clear: his mother married a Servilius Cæpio; Plut. *Cato,* 1.1.

The prudent candidate would shy away from them altogether.[93] The electorate endorsed men, not platforms.

The exasperation of truncated victories drove Pompey into a new alliance. A coalition with Crassus and Cæsar would bring results unattainable in previous years. The potent character of that alliance gave Cæsar the confidence to override Bibulus' obstructionism and to implement the Pompeian program—and much else besides. Strength of the backing spelled the difference between the failures of M. Piso and Afranius and the successes of Cæsar.

The triumvirate's impact made itself felt also on the immediately subsequent elections. Pompey pushed the candidacy of yet another ex-officer and lieutenant, A. Gabinius.[94] Ciceronian invective has blackened his reputation and character, but Gabinius deserves a more sober judgment. The private vices, exploited and magnified by Cicero, were overmatched by public service. Gabinius' family did not lack distinction in the senate, and his father, apparently, had been a legate of Sulla's. Activities in his tribunate of 67 had demonstrated a genuine interest in administrative and constitutional reform.[95] Of even greater stature was L. Calpurnius Piso Cæsoninus, whose house could count eight previous holders of the consulship. Sometime in 59 he became the father-in-law of Julius Cæsar. That markedly improved his connections and his chances. But L. Piso is not to be regarded as Cæsar's pliant tool. Cæsar had as much to gain from marriage alliance with Piso as Piso with Cæsar. The candidate's family had long been a conspicuous force in Roman politics; L. Piso himself carried considerable weight in senatorial circles. The move forged still another link in Cæsar's lengthening chain of associations with powers in the Roman oligarchy. Cicero's frantic diatribes have left as twisted a picture of Piso as of Gabinius: Piso's frowning and solemn airs concealed his inner corruption, lewdness, and dissipation; his Epicureanism and philosophic learning provided screens for self-indulgence and vice. The invective was standard and would have little impact on an electorate which did not assess those qualities. Cicero had reason to complain of Piso later. But in 59 the orator himself was an active supporter of Piso's canvass, as were several scions of the aristocracy. Cæsar had made a shrewd choice in his new father-in-law.[96]

[93] Cf. [Q. Cic.] *Comm. Petit.* 53: *nec tamen in petendo res publica capessenda est neque in senatu neque in contione.*

[94] In the process, the triumvirs threw over Crassus' friend Q. Arrius; Cic. *Ad Att.* 2.5.2, 2.7.3. An insignificant family and mediocre talent would make him difficult to elect. One need not postulate an overt break between Crassus and his triumviral partners, as Rowland, *Historia*, 15 (1966): 220–221.

[95] For Gabinius' candidacy, backed by both Pompey and Cæsar, see Cic. *Ad Att.* 2.5.2; Plut. *Pomp.* 48.3; *Cato*, 33.4; Appian, *BC*, 2.14. On A. Gabinius, the legate of Sulla, see Appian, *Mithr.* 66. He was probably father of the consul of 58. On Gabinius and his family, see Badian, *Philologus*, 103 (1959): 87–99; cf. E. M. Sanford, *TAPA*, 70 (1939): 64–92.

[96] The discussion summarized here may be found in greater detail, with references, in Gruen,

The elections passed without incident. Piso and Gabinius were duly returned by the voters. The results cause no surprise. Nor do they suggest revolutionary change or shocking new development. Gabinius' record was strong and his backers were influential. Piso had the support of Cæsar. And, more important, he was a man of substance in the oligarchy, regarded not as a Cæsarian, but as a leader of the *boni*.[97]

The cement of the triumvirate, which had never quite hardened, soon began to disintegrate. Piso and Gabinius, lumped together as twin monsters by Cicero, did not enjoy harmony throughout their tenure of office. When P. Clodius turned his thunder on Pompey in 58, Gabinius came to the defense of his former chief. But Piso had no reason to be beholden to Pompey. He encouraged Clodius' attacks and relished Pompey's difficulties.[98] The rift boded ill for the unanimity of the dynasts. Their successes in the elections of 59 were not repeated thereafter.

Pompey and Cæsar found one candidate on whom they could agree in 58. P. Cornelius Lentulus Spinther seemed safe and reliable. The Cornelii Lentuli carried enormous prestige. Patrician blood flowed through their veins, and the oligarchy was honeycombed with their relatives. L. Lentulus Niger had sought in vain to challenge the candidates of the triumvirate in 59.[99] His relative Spinther behaved with greater circumspection in the following year. Atticus could describe him in 58 as wholly answerable to Pompey.[100] And in the consular elections he received the strong endorsement of Julius Cæsar as well. Cæsar had been cultivating Spinther's favor for several years, promoting his claims for a pontifical post and for the province of Spain

---

CSCA, 1 (1968): 163–167. For Cæsar's motives in supporting Piso, see, esp., Dio, 38.9.1. His initial choice, apparently, was C. Octavius, husband of his niece and father of the future emperor Augustus. But Octavius perished in 59, before he could submit his *professio*; Cic. *Phil.* 3.15; Suet. *Aug.* 4. On the personality of Piso, consult further the sources collected in Münzer, *RE*, 3:1387–1390, "Calpurnius," n.90; cf. Syme, *Rom. Rev.*, pp. 135–136; Nisbet, *Cicero, In L. Calpurnium Pisonem Oratio* (Oxford, 1961), pp. v–xvii, 192–197; P. Grimal, *Ciceron, Discours contre Pison* (Paris, 1966), pp. 44–65.

[97] That is clear in Cic. *Pro Sest.* 20: *erat hic omnium sermo: "est tamen rei publicæ magnum firmumque subsidium . . . habebit senatus in hunc annum, quem sequatur; non deerit auctor et dux bonis."* Bibulus' postponement of the *comitia* in that year was a mere demonstration; Cic. *Ad Att.* 2.15.2, 2.20.6, 2.21.5; cf. Linderski, *Historia*, 14 (1965): 423–442; L. R. Taylor, *Historia*, 17 (1968): 188–193. No recorded violence or intimidation accompanied the campaign, though an attempted prosecution of Gabinius after his victory was turned away by a show of force; Cic. *Ad Q. Frat.* 1.2.15. On the elections of 59, see also W. C. Grummel, *CJ*, 49 (1954): 351–355.

[98] Cic. *In Pis.* 27–28; *De Domo*, 66; cf. *In Pis.* 16; Dio, 38.30.2; see Gruen, *CSCA*, 1 (1968): 166.

[99] Cic. *In Vat.* 25.

[100] Cic. *Ad Att.* 3.22.2: *sæpe enim tu ad me scripsisti eum totum esse in illius* [Pompey] *potestate.*

after his prætorship.[101] Once again, the mutual benefit of an association needs to be stressed. Spinther was not an instrument of the triumvirs, shoved into the consulship over the objections of a reluctant populace. The connection should be approached from the other side. The standing of the patrician Lentuli with the aristocracy and the voters made Spinther worth cultivating by the triumvirs.

The dynasts were not so fortunate in the voters' choice as Spinther's colleague for 57. Q. Metellus Nepos, volatile, opportunistic, and unpredictable, had nonetheless been a valuable associate of Pompey's in the past.[102] But Pompey's divorce of Nepos' sister Mucia delivered an unpardonable blow to the pride of the Metellan clan. Metellus Celer's strenuous opposition to Pompey in his consulship of 60 has already been noted. In 59, Nepos, we are told, expressed fierce hatred of the triumvirate.[103] Relations with Pompey were severed. But a Cæcilius Metellus did not require superfluous backing for consular aspirations. Sixteen previous Metellan consuls gave Nepos sufficient credentials.[104]

Neither consul proved amenable to the interests of the triumvirate. Nepos defied Pompey in promoting the machinations of his cousin P. Clodius against the general's friend and political ally T. Annius Milo.[105] And, more disconcerting, the hitherto pliable Lentulus Spinther proved to have ambitions of his own. Friction developed with Pompey over the task of restoring Ptolemy Auletes to Egypt. Spinther advocated a corn commission for the general in the fall of 57. The purpose was to take Pompey out of the running for the Egyptian venture.[106] Lentulus persisted and nagged friends and partisans to uphold his own interests in the matter. Though unsuccessful in the end, he and others had managed to thwart the aims of Pompey. The dynasts, it is clear, could not determine the actions of elected officials in Rome. Their frustrations are betokened further in the results of the ensuing elections.

[101] Cæs. *BC*, 1.22: *veteremque amicitiam commemorat Cæsarisque in se beneficia exponit; quæ erant maxima: quod per eum in collegium pontificum venerat, quod provinciam Hispaniam ex prætura habuerat, quod in petitione consulatus erat sublevatus.*

[102] Sources on Nepos' career in Münzer, *RE*, 3:1216–1218, "Cæcilius," n.96; Ooteghem, *Metelli*, pp. 280–294. On his role in late 63 and 62, see, esp., Meier, *Athenæum*, 40 (1962): 103–125. Plutarch's description is appropriate, *Cic.* 26.7: αὐτὸς δέ τις εὐμετάβολος.

[103] Cic. *Ad Att.* 2.12.2. It is possible that the dynasts offered Nepos an augurate as appeasement, to no avail; Cic. *Ad Att.* 2.5.2.

[104] No evidence buttresses the conjecture of Syme, *Rom. Rev.*, p. 43, that Pompey may have backed the canvass of Nepos; also Meier, *Res Pub.*, p. 19, n.70.

[105] Cic. *Ad Att.* 4.3.3–4; *Pro Sest.* 89; Dio, 39.7.4; Gruen, *Historia*, 18 (1969): 83.

[106] Plut. *Pomp.* 49.5. The same motive may explain Nepos' acquiescence in that grain commission; Cic. *Ad Att.* 4.1.7. Or, perhaps, he hoped to undermine another bill, which would have awarded Pompey even larger authority; Cic. *Ad Att.* 4.1.7. Further references and discussion in Gruen, *Historia*, 18 (1969): 81.

Two more *nobiles* entered office in 56, Cn. Cornelius Lentulus Marcellinus and L. Marcius Philippus. The dynasts could not have been pleased. Marcellinus opposed their schemes with unrestrained vehemence. A powerful speaker, with high intelligence and firm convictions, he wrecked proposals that would honor Cæsar and lashed out viciously against the provincial ambitions of Pompey.[107] His colleague, Philippus, was more subdued and less conspicuous. He preferred to follow the lead of Marcellinus.[108] Philippus too had much to recommend him to the electorate. His family was old and prestigious, his father the celebrated consul and censor of the previous generation, one of the most powerful men of his day. And not the least of Philippus' assets was the fact that Cato was his son-in-law.[109] Both consuls advocated signal honors for Cato, both criticized extension of Cæsar's Gallic command, and both resisted the aims of Pompey and Crassus.[110]

The facts stand out with clarity. A conservative electorate, impervious to pressure from military men or demagogues, continued to elevate candidates from the traditional ruling class. The four victors for 57 and 56, the Lentuli, Q. Metellus Nepos, and L. Philippus, all derived from the most blue-blooded of families. Had they stood a generation before, the results would have been no different.

By early 56, the coalition of Pompey, Crassus, and Cæsar was in a shambles. Stubborn and independent consuls in 57 and 56 had contributed heavily to their discomfort. And a new candidate, with even more potent backing, emerged for 55. L. Domitius Ahenobarbus, cousin of Catulus and brother-in-law of Cato, submitted his name and announced his intention to replace Cæsar in Gaul. The nobility of his family had guaranteed a consulship from birth, and ancestral *clientelæ* in Gaul made him a logical choice for that post. Pompey, frustrated and disconsolate, could endure no further defeats in the electoral *comitia*. The forthcoming campaign in 56 helped to catalyze the conference of Luca.

An initial plan envisioned support of candidates sympathetic to the triumviral interests. But the experience of previous years had shown that even success

[107] Discussion and sources in Gruen, *Historia*, 18 (1969): 82, 98. On Marcellinus' abilities, see, esp., Cic. *Brutus*, 247: *Cn. autem Lentulus Marcellinus nec umquam indisertus et in consulatu pereloquens visus est, non tardus sententiis, non inops verbis, voce canora, facetus satis.*

[108] Cic. *Ad Q. Frat.* 2.4.4: *consul est egregius Lentulus, non impediente collega.*

[109] Plut. *Cato,* 25.1.

[110] Honors to Cato, Plut. *Cato,* 39.3–4; Cæsar's command, Cic. *De Prov. Cons.* 18, 21; opposition to Pompey and Crassus, Dio, 36.26.1, 39.27.3. Philippus was later to contract a marriage alliance with Cæsar; but that has no relevance for his stance in 56; cf. Taylor, *Party Politics*, pp. 228–229, n.12; Gruen, *Historia*, 18 (1969): 97–98. Further on Philippus, Münzer, *RE*, 28:1568–1571, "Marcius," n.76; Ooteghem, *Lucius Marcius Philippus et sa famille* (Brussels, 1961), pp. 173–185.

at the polls could not guarantee the loyalty of supporters once a candidate took office. Hence, Crassus and Pompey determined to submit their own names, and Cæsar pledged active support.[111] The unabashed power play did not meet with favorable reaction in Rome. Even when the triumvirs were operating in solid conjunction, they could not run roughshod over Roman politics. The consuls of 56, Philippus and Marcellinus, stoutly resisted the syndicate, the senate organized demonstrations to protest the candidacies, and popular feeling ran high against the dynasts. No possibility existed for success at the *comitia* in 56. Only by desperate postponement of the elections into the following year, when an *interregnum* would weaken the leadership of the opposition, could Crassus and Pompey hope for more favorable results. And even then the problems were substantial. Other candidates had withdrawn, but Domitius remained in the field, his courage steeled by the indomitable Cato. Strong-arm techniques were required to effect the intimidation of Domitius and the Catonians. Julius Cæsar finally broke the deadlock by releasing numbers of his troops on furlough; their votes and, perhaps, their menacing presence tipped the scales. Crassus and Pompey at last entered office in late January 55.[112]

The striking events of 56 and 55 affirm the importance of that election. But they are striking precisely because they are unusual. No other electoral campaign in the late Republic had been marred by similar pyrotechnics. Few had had so much at stake. The triumviral combine was faced with political extinction. Experience of the immediately preceding years had underlined the central role of the consulate. The dynasts could not allow it to slip from their grasp in 55. Hence, the extraordinary vehemence and the violations of standard procedures for that year.

Temporary advantage accrued to the dynasts. But the costs in prestige and popularity were high. The propaganda of the Catonians and their conscious posture as wronged victims were more effective in the long run. By branding the triumvirs as would-be tyrants and revolutionaries, they struck responsive chords among the basically conservative Roman voters. Crassus and Pompey proved unable to transmit their hold on the chief magistracy to others. The elections for 54 ran a normal course.

[111] Dio, 39.27.2; Plut. *Pomp.* 51.4; *Crass.* 14.6; *Cæs.* 21.3; *Cato*, 41.1; Appian, *BC*, 2.17; Suet. *Iul.* 24. Pompey and Crassus had not had their candidacies accepted as late as November; Cic. *Ad Att.* 4.8a.2; cf. Shackleton Bailey, *PCPS*, 183 (1954–5): 27–28; *Cicero's Letters*, II:236–237.

[112] The events are described in numerous sources: Cic. *Ad Att.* 4.8a.2; *Ad Q. Frat.* 2.4.6; Dio, 39.27–31; Plut. *Pomp.* 51–52; *Crass.* 14–15; *Cæs.* 21; *Cato*, 41–42; *Comp. Nic. et Crass.* 2.1; Val. Max. 6.2.6; Livy, *Per.* 105; Appian, *BC*, 2.17–18; Vell. Pat. 2.46.1; see further Neuendorff, *Die römischen Konsulwahlen*, pp. 50–54; Afzelius, *ClMed*, 4 (1941): 162–170; Meier, *Res Pub.*, pp. 294–295; Gruen, *Historia*, 18 (1969): 95–99.

L. Domitius Ahenobarbus, persistent and undaunted, revived his candidacy. This time he was not to be denied that consulship predicted from the cradle. And another weighty competitor presented himself. Ap. Claudius Pulcher, vaunting family pride and supreme self-confidence, could summon *clientelæ* gathered by generations of *beneficia* bestowed by the Claudii. Self-serving and self-indulgent, he could scorn the claims of lesser men.[113]

The triumvirs did not repeat methods adopted in the previous year's campaign. Jealous of their standing with the populace, they reverted to conventional politics. Pompey canvassed vigorously for an old and loyal adherent, T. Ampius Balbus.[114] It was to no avail. In the company of the distinguished candidates of 55, Balbus could not compete. The electorate, in predictable fashion, endorsed Domitius Ahenobarbus and Ap. Claudius. Their activities in 54 spelled continued embarrassment for the dynasts. Obviously, there was no "triumviral regime."[115]

The pattern repeated in the following year. Cæsar and Pompey actively championed favored candidates, the electorate reacted coldly, and the enemies of the triumvirate were returned at the polls. The confused and devious machinations of that campaign need not be recounted in detail. The story has been told elsewhere.[116] Triumviral support went to M. Æmilius Scaurus and C. Memmius. The former paraded considerable wealth and a host of familial associations. Among other things, he was the stepson of Sulla the dictator and related by marriage to Pompey the Great. Scaurus' vanity, greed, and reputation for living beyond his means would not stand in the way. C. Memmius had earned his spurs as a vocal opponent of Cæsar and the Cæsarian legislation in 59 and 58. But his mocking wit found a number of targets. Memmius contracted a feud with the Luculli, attacked both L. and M. Lucullus, and even haunted the boudoir of M. Lucullus' wife. Like Scaurus he had close links to the house of Sulla and to Pompey. The connections among Scaurus, the Sullæ, the Memmii, and Pompey were intertwined and multiple.

[113] On Claudius' career and character, see above, pp. 59, 97–98. References in Münzer, *RE*, 3:2849–2853, "Claudius," n.297.

[114] Cic. *Pro Planc.* 25; Schol. Bob. 156, Stangl. Cf. Balbus' actions on Pompey's behalf in 63; Vell. Pat. 2.40.4. There was, apparently, prolonged postponement of the elections in 55; Cic. *Ad Att.* 4.13.1. But the circumstances are unknown, and there is no evidence for any upheavals.

[115] The oft-repeated notion that Ap. Claudius entered office as an advocate of the triumvirs should now be set at rest. Opportunism dictated a marriage alliance with Pompey. But that was yet to come. In 54, Appius served his own interests, and they were not those of Pompey or his associates; see Gruen, *Historia*, 18 (1969): 100–103. Cf., esp., the attacks by Appius and Domitius on Crassus and Gabinius; Cic. *Ad Fam.* 5.8.1; *Ad Q. Frat.* 2.13.2, 3.2.3; Dio, 39.60.3.

[116] Gruen, *Hommages Renard* (1969), II:311–321.

Julius Cæsar, on sound political grounds, was willing to forget the past. In 54 Cæsar and Pompey expended considerable energy on behalf of Memmius and Scaurus.[117]

In opposition stood two potent candidates. The patrician M. Valerius Messalla Rufus, also a relative, by marriage, to Sulla and nephew of Hortensius, ran for office, sponsored by the consortium of Pompey's enemies.[118] The other contestant, equally formidable, was Cn. Domitius Calvinus, whose *gens* could trace consulships back to 332. Mercurial and ambitious, he had been a loud foe of the triumvirs in 59, an effective collaborator of Bibulus. Conservative elements backed his canvass for the prætorship in 57 and again for the consulship in 54. Calvinus had powerful friends.[119]

The lines were firmly drawn in the summer of 54. But the lure of consular office provoked new combinations, shady deals, and shifting arrangements among candidates and supporters. The men endorsed by the dynasts exposed themselves as inept and irresponsible. Pompey suffered acute embarrassment; Cæsar stamped about in helpless anger. Public outrage and political manipulation produced a seemingly endless string of postponements. The elections did not take place until July of 53, a full year behind schedule. M. Messalla and Cn. Domitius emerged victorious. The triumvirate had been turned back again by the Roman voter.[120]

It is clear that the dynasts could not manipulate electoral results to their taste in the 50s. The coalition was itself too shaky to institute a permanent ascendancy. When aims were common and efforts were united, they could

[117] Cic. *Ad Att.* 4.15.7, 4.16.6; Suet. *Iul.* 73. On the variegated familial associations, see Gruen, *Historia*, 18 (1969): 75–77; *Hommages Renard* (1969), II:313–314. References on the personalities and careers of Scaurus and Memmius are collected in Klebs, *RE*, 1:588–590, "Aemilius," n.141; Münzer, *RE*, 15:609–616, "Memmius," n.8. Further on Memmius, see the lengthy study by G. Della Valle, *RendLinc*, 14 (1938): 731–886, whose conclusions must be judged with caution.

[118] Cic. *Ad Att.* 4.15.7. Pompey had expressed nervous anxiety over Messalla's candidacy in the previous year; Cic. *Ad Att.* 4.9.1: *nihil minus velle mihi visus est quam Messallam consulatum petere.* On Messalla's relation to Sulla, see Plut. *Sulla,* 35.3; to Hortensius, Val. Max. 5.9.2; and cf. Syme, *JRS*, 45 (1955): 158. He held the augurate for fifty-five years; Macrob. *Sat.* 1.9.14; it was evidently attained under Sulla; see Cichorius, *Röm. Stud.*, p. 234.

[119] Cic. *Ad Att.* 4.16.6: *Domitius ut valeat amicis.* On his earlier career, see Cic. *Pro Sest.* 113; *In Vat.* 16, 38; Schol. Bob. 135, 146, 151, Stangl; cf. Dio, 38.6.1. The prevailing notion that Cæsar supported Calvinus should now be abandoned; Shackleton Bailey, *Cicero's Letters,* II:203; Gruen, *Hommages Renard* (1969), II:314–315.

[120] The events are outlined in detail, with references, in Gruen, *Hommages Renard* (1969), II:315–321. Cf. also Neuendorff, *Die römischen Konsulwahlen*, pp. 56–65. There is no reason to believe that the turmoil was cynically arranged by Pompey to provoke demand for a dictatorship; as, e.g., Drumann-Grœbe, *Geschichte Roms*, II:4–8; Mommsen, *Röm. Gesch.*, III:334–336; Meyer, *Cæsars Monarchie*, pp. 191–197, 207–211. The affair underlines not Pompey's shrewdness but his ineptitude.

exercise effect, as in the elections for 58. But the electorate was generally intractable. Even the conference of Luca brought no *dominatio*. Crassus and Pompey were forced to great lengths to obtain their own consulships in 55. Thereafter, their stock with the voters rapidly depreciated. Republican political traditions stood in the way.

THE SOLE CONSULSHIP OF POMPEIUS MAGNUS

The year 52 introduced sharp change–or so it has seemed. Chaos provoked a radical departure from convention. A solitary figure was named to the consulship–a virtual contradiction in terms. Did that signal the collapse of the constitution, a herald of the new order? Analysis of the background will suggest a very different conclusion.

The turmoil of the previous campaign set an unwholesome precedent. A half-year without consuls in 53 meant an unstable government, an insecure populace, and a paralysis of public business. Worse still, the new chief magistrates, freshly installed in July, had to worry immediately about arrangements for the next set of elections. Canvassing would have to be done in haste, a concentration of frantic electioneering by the hopefuls for 52. Given only a short compass of time, candidates could not afford to be gentle. Unrest stirred by the previous campaign offered examples of useful techniques, on which the next candidates improved.

T. Annius Milo submitted his *professio*, rousing violent passions, both pro and con. The rugged and brutal politician from Lanuvium already had much experience in situations of turbulence. His campaign had been calculated for a long time. Pompey had proffered the hope of a consulship as early as 57.[121] In November of 54 Milo began pressing the general to carry out that promise. But Pompey, unfortunate in his choice of adherents in recent years, was persuaded that Milo was a declining asset. The conference of Luca had shuffled some earlier alignments. The fickle but powerful P. Clodius transferred allegiance to Pompey, but the bitterness with Milo remained unaffected.[122] That must have strained relations between Milo and Pompey. When Milo asked for encouragement in 54, Pompey promised nothing–and offered support to another candidate.[123] Milo was not to be headed off. He could reckon

[121] Appian, *BC*, 2.16.

[122] Cic. *De Har. Resp.* 50–52; *Ad Att.* 4.8a.3; Schol. Bob. 170, Stangl; cf. Cic. *Pro Mil.* 21, 79.

[123] Cic. *Ad Q. Frat.* 3.8.6: *Pompeius ei* [Milo] *nihil tribuit, et omnia Guttæ, dicitque se perfecturum, ut illo Cæsar incumbat.* "Gutta" is unknown and unidentifiable. Some have suggested "Cottæ" as an emendation, perhaps a reference to M. Cotta who later fought for Pompey in 49; cf. Shackleton Bailey, *PCPS*, 187 (1961): 3. But no further evidence is available for Pompey's electoral support for that individual.

on many other friends and backers. Cicero, who owed him much, was strong in support, as were numerous young men, like Cælius and Curio, and no small number of aristocrats who would welcome the opportunity to promote a candidate over Pompey's objections. Milo had advanced his claims by sponsoring elaborate entertainments. And he contracted marriage with Fausta, the promiscuous daughter of Sulla. Her faithlessness as a spouse would not matter much; the political advantage counted. Finally, Milo attained the backing of M. Cato, not the least of his assets. Milo's chances for victory were by no means insignificant.[124]

Pompey had his own candidate in 53, P. Plautius Hypsæus. The Plautii possessed long-standing affiliations with Pompey, several of their number turning up as his supporters in the past two decades.[125] Plautius Hypsæus had been Pompey's quæstor in the East and enjoyed close relations with the general. His political loyalty was reliable and had already been demonstrated in the senate, as well as in the field.[126] Pompey, thwarted in two previous elections, campaigned industriously for Plautius.[127]

A third hopeful entered the lists, the most prominent of the *candidati.* No man in Rome could boast a more illustrious name than Q. Cæcilius Metellus Pius Scipio Nasica. He was head of the great Metellan clan, and through his veins flowed the blood of the patrician Scipiones, the Licinii Crassi, and the Mucii Scævolæ.[128] But the quality of the pedigree did not correspond with the character of its possessor.[129] Metellus Scipio was dull and uninspired, lacking in ability, possessed with a fondness for pornographic displays.[130] His political career had been independent and unencumbered. Along with other Metelli, he appeared in defense of Verres in 70. But further

[124] Cic. *Ad Fam.* 2.6.3: *habemus hæc omnia: honorum studium conciliatum ex tribunatu . . . vulgi ac multitudinis propter magnificentiam munerum liberalitatemque naturæ, inventutis et gratiosorum in suffragiis studia*; cf. Cic. *Ad Q. Frat.* 3.9.2; *Pro Mil.* 25, 34, 95–96; Asconius, 31, 33, Clark. For Cato's support, see Asconius, 53–54, Clark; the marriage to Fausta in November, 55, Asconius, 28, Clark; Cic. *Ad Att.* 4.13.1; her promiscuity, Macrob. *Sat.* 2.2.9. Milo had gone deeply in debt; Pliny, *NH*, 36.104. Wiseman, *JRS*, 56 (1966): 108–114, argues that Q. Cicero had earlier hoped to stand with Milo for the consulship of 52. The evidence is inconclusive. Quintus did not, in any event, offer himself when the time came.

[125] See above, chap. 3, n.65.

[126] Asconius, 35, Clark; Cic. *Ad Fam.* 1.1.3; *Pro Flacco*, 20; Schol. Bob. 100, Stangl.

[127] Asconius, 35, Clark: *Hypsæo summe studebat.*

[128] Cic. *Brutus*, 212: *etenim istius genus est ex ipsius sapientiæ stirpe generatum; nam et de duobus avis . . . Scipione et Crasso, et de tribus proavis, Q. Metello . . . P. Scipione . . . Q. Scævola augure . . . o generosam . . . stirpem et tamquam in unam arborem plura genera, sic in istam domum multorum insitam atque innatam sapientiam!*

[129] Cic. *Pro Corn. apud* Asconius, 74, Clark: *summa nobilitate, eximia virtute prædito.*

[130] His dullness: Cic. *Ad Att.* 6.1.17. An elaborate and lewd entertainment was prepared for him as consul; Val. Max. 9.1.8. All the relevant evidence on Metellus is collected and discussed by Ooteghem, *Metelli*, pp. 298–327.

collaboration with the clan is unattested. Metellus Scipio was no favorite of the Catonian group. He married an Aemilia Lepida, abruptly dislodging her from a betrothal to the indignant M. Cato. And Cato's ape, M. Favonius, conducted an unsuccessful prosecution of Metellus Scipio in 60.[131] Political *inimici*, however, need not be of great concern to a man who could summon the voting *clientela* of the Metelli and the Scipiones.

It was a turbulent contest, with few scruples. The model of the previous campaign was imitated and eclipsed. P. Clodius shuddered at the prospect of his vindictive foe in the consulship. Hence he threw the weight of his influence–and his gangs–behind the candidacies of Plautius Hypsæus and Metellus Scipio. Those two saw the advantage of a collaboration to shut off Milo and conducted a joint campaign. The involvement of Clodius brought escalation on the other side. Electioneering was fraught with bribery and street fights.[132] The consuls of 53, responsible for overseeing the election, allowed events to slip from their control. Both were caught in the riots and felled by stones.[133] As a consequence, the *comitia* could not be summoned, and the disturbances again postponed decision beyond the end of the year.[134]

The confusion was climaxed by a brutal struggle between the gangs of Milo and Clodius on January 18. Clodius himself was slain, and there followed street riots culminating in the burning of the senate house. The events at last induced Roman authorities to take decisive action. A *senatus consultum ultimum* gained passage: the *interrex,* the tribunes, and Pompeius Magnus were instructed to enforce order. The inclusion of Pompey, of course, came for obvious reasons. As proconsul with *imperium* he could levy troops to guarantee the suppression of disturbances.[135]

[131] Defense of Verres: Cic. *Verr.* 2.2.79–81; friction with Cato: Plut. *Cato,* 7.1–2; prosecution by Favonius: Cic. *Ad Att.* 2.1.9; cf. Taylor, *Studies in honor of Ullman* (1964), I:79–85. A marriage connection with M. Crassus may be noted. Metellus' daughter was married to the son of Crassus; Plut. *Pomp.* 55.1. But no evidence attests to political cooperation between the two men; and nothing to justify the statement that Metellus "had been in Crassus' orbit"; Taylor, *Party Politics,* p. 150.

[132] See especially Asconius, 30, 48, Clark. References to the riots are many: Plut. *Cæs.* 28.3–4; *Cato,* 47.1; Livy, *Per.* 107; Dio, 40.46.3; Schol. Bob. 169, 172, Stangl. Cicero, as usual, goes too far in asserting that the defeat or death of Milo would have put Clodius' own creatures in the consulship; *Pro Mil.* 89: *Milone occiso habuisset suos consules.* But Clodius' violent support for Plautius and Metellus is clear and frequently attested; Cic. *Pro Mil.* 25, 34, 43; Dio, 40.48.2; Asconius, 30, 48, Clark; Schol. Bob. 169, 172, Stangl; Schol. Gronov. 322, Stangl.

[133] Dio, 40.46.3; Schol. Bob. 172, Stangl.

[134] Asconius, 30, 31, 33, Clark; Dio, 40.46.1, 40.48.1; Schol. Bob. 169, 172, Stangl.

[135] Asconius, 34, Clark: *itaque primo factum erat s.c. ut interrex et tribuni plebis et Cn. Pompeius, qui pro cos. ad urbem erat, viderent ne quid detrimenti res publica caperet, dilectus autem Pompeius tota Italia haberet*; also 51–52, Clark; Cæs. *BG,* 7.1; Dio, 40.49.5, 40.50.1. Further on the senatorial action, Cic. *Pro Mil.* 12–13, 31, 70; Asconius, 44, Clark; Schol. Bob. 116, Stangl.

As for the elections, the senate had lost patience with unchecked campaign excesses. And they had no use for the three candidates, all of whom had disgraced themselves. To restore order, a dramatic step was necessary. The *patres* canceled elections for 52 and installed a temporary authoritarian rule. The recourse to emergency government possessed antecedents in Roman history. Indeed the antique institution of the dictatorship had existed for just such purposes: an interlude of authoritarianism until normal processes could be resumed. Pompey alone merited consideration for such a post. The general's partisans clamored for his elevation as dictator. Others suggested that Cæsar be recalled and share power with him. That prospect was anathema to the senatorial majority. But further paralysis could not be tolerated. The faction of Cato was prepared with an answer to break the stalemate. M. Bibulus moved in the senate that Pompey be given full authority–not, however, as dictator, but as consul without colleague. Cato subscribed to the motion, and dissent fell silent. Pompey entered his sole consulship by March 52.[136]

The political and constitutional implications of this development have generally been misconstrued. Many take the action of Cato and Bibulus, tendering sole power to Pompey, as a signal of reconciliation between the factions, a new league arranged against Cæsar.[137] It was nothing of the kind. The Catonians sought a restoration of order in the city; Pompey had the authority and troops to effect it. As the sources make clear, the senatorial decree was framed to forestall cries for a dictatorship or, even worse, a joint regime

---

Milo, facing an upsurge of hostile public opinion, for the first time appeared subdued and contrite. He offered to withdraw his candidacy. That did not soften Pompey's antipathy; Asconius, 35, Clark.

[136] Asconius, 36, Clark: *visum est optimatibus tutius esse eum consulem sine collega creari, et cum tractata ea res esset in senatu, facto in M. Bibuli sententiam s.c. Pompeius ab interrege Servio Sulpicio V Kal. Mart. mense intercalario consul creatus est statimque consulatum iniit.* For Cato's role, see Plut. *Pomp.* 54.4; *Cæs.* 28.4–5; *Cato*, 47.2–3; Appian, *BC*, 2.23. On the pressure for a dictatorship and for inclusion of Cæsar, see Asconius, 33, 35, Clark; Dio, 40.45.5, 40.46.1, 40.50.3–4; Plut. *Pomp.* 54.3; *Cæs.* 28.4–5; Appian, *BC*, 2.23; Suet. *Iul.* 26. There had been some suggestion even for election of consular tribunes; Dio, 40.54.4. Other references on the appointment of Pompey: Vell. Pat. 2.47.3; Livy, *Per.* 107; Val. Max. 8.15.8; Plut. *Cato*, 48.1; Tac. *Ann.* 3.28; Appian, *BC*, 2.28. For a summary of the evidence and brief discussion, see Neuendorff, *Die römischen Konsulwahlen*, pp. 66–73.

[137] Such is the retrospective judgment of Vell. Pat. 2.47.3: *tertius consulatus soli Cn. Pompeio etiam adversantium antea dignitati eius iudicio delatus est, cuius ille honoris gloria veluti reconciliatis sibi optimatibus maxime a C. Cæsare alienatus est.* Cf. Dio, 40.50.5. The formulation has been adopted by several scholars, who see Pompey as playing a double game, solidifying his support with senatorial conservatives, while awaiting the proper moment for a break with Cæsar; cf. Meyer, *Cæsars Monarchie*, pp. 221–222; Syme, *Rom. Rev.*, pp. 39–40; Taylor, *Party Politics*, pp. 149–152; Gelzer, *Pompeius*, pp. 172–175; Carcopino, *César*, pp. 336–343.

of Cæsar and Pompey.[138] The intractable Cato had no interest in a new political ally. When Pompey made overtures to him, he was coolly rebuffed.[139] At the trial of Milo, Pompey pressed hard for conviction; Cato, Hortensius, Favonius, and others were active on the defense benches.[140] Cato balked Pompey in other trials of that year and did not hesitate to criticize certain features of the general's judicial legislation.[141]

Pompey, to be sure, angled for further alliances with the *nobiles*. That represented conventional tactics and had been consistent Pompeian policy for three decades. But his new affiliation brought him no closer to the circle of Cato. At some time in 52 Pompey wed the daughter of Q. Metellus Scipio, personal *inimicus* of Cato and Favonius. It was a good match. Cornelia, recently widowed by the death of P. Crassus, was charming and cultivated, with suitable feminine diffidence. More important, Pompey now had attachment to the noblest families of Rome. But not to the allies of Cato.[142]

A consulship without colleague was anomalous and unprecedented. And Pompey's position strained precedent in other ways. He was technically proconsul of Spain, while serving as chief magistrate in Rome; and only three years had elapsed since his last consulship, a violation of Sulla's law enforcing a gap of ten years. Was that a confession of the failure of Republican institutions? Authoritarian rule, it could be argued, had replaced traditional procedures. And many have noted the similarities between Pompey's status and the later principate of Augustus. Again, however, the superficial can too easily be confused with the essential. Romans would not have described the events of 52 as a breakdown of the Republic. Suspension of constitutional practices to meet a crisis is an experience common to all states. Rome had resorted to such suspensions in the past. It was one of the virtues of her system that provisions for emergency measures were actually built into the constitution. The dictatorship had served that function in the early and middle Republic, and the *senatus consultum ultimum* in more recent years. The third consulship of Pompey stood in that tradition. It involved no permanent change in the

[138] Dio, 40.50.4; Plut. *Pomp.* 54.3; *Cæs.* 28.4–5.

[139] Plut. *Pomp.* 54.5–6.

[140] Cic. *Pro Mil.* 1–2, 26, 44; *Ad Fam.* 15.4.12; Asconius, 34, 37–38, 53–54; Vell. Pat. 2.47.5; Schol. Bob. 117, Stangl. See below, chap. 8.

[141] At the trial of Munatius Plancus: Dio, 40.55.2; Plut. *Pomp.* 55.5–6; *Cato*, 48.4; Val. Max. 6.2.5; criticism of Pompey's *ambitus* bill: Plut. *Cato*, 48.3.

[142] On Cornelia's qualities, see Plut. *Pomp.* 55.1–2. Precise date of the marriage is uncertain. Plutarch puts it after Pompey's appointment as consul, which is entirely plausible. Asconius, 31, Clark, refers to Metellus as Pompey's father-in-law during his campaign for the consulship. But that may simply be sloppy writing. There is no evidence that Pompey supported Metellus' campaign in 53. It is noteworthy that Asconius describes Pompey's electoral activities solely in terms of support for Plautius; 35, Clark.

structure—quite the reverse. The purpose was explicit and limited: Pompey was chosen to restore the city to health and normality.[143]

The general performed his task with dispatch and success. We shall examine later his administrative legislation of 52. It proved to be sober, firm, and conservative. An additional fact, generally brushed over, is in reality central. The "sole consulship" received sanction consciously and overtly as a temporary position. The senate directed Pompey to choose a colleague at any time after the first two months, whenever the situation was in hand. Pompey adhered dutifully to that stipulation. His new father-in-law was the beneficiary. For the last five months of the year Metellus Scipio and Pompeius Magnus served as joint consuls. Like all consuls, they would step down when the year closed, to be held accountable for all actions during their term of office. The sole consulship had been of brief duration, as planned.[144]

THE CONSISTENCY OF THE ELECTORATE

A return to normality is no better exemplified than in the conduct of elections during the final three years before the civil war. Pompey's unique position in 52 was obviously regarded as an expedient and an interlude. The electorate felt free to operate in traditional fashion thereafter—and they did. The six consuls of 51, 50, and 49 epitomize the continuing force of familial politics and the attachment of voters to hereditary patrons. The great plebeian house of the Claudii Marcelli, with an antique record of service to the state, vaulted back into prominence at the end of the Republic. Deftly promoting one another's claims, the Marcelli attained consulships in each of the three years. Their colleagues, Ser. Sulpicius Rufus, L. Aemilius Lepidus Paullus, and L. Cornelius Lentulus Crus, all possessed attachments, by kin or marriage, to that family. It was a striking illustration of conventional electoral politics.[145] The elections of those three years may be a better guide to the tenor of the times than the extraordinary circumstances of 52.

[143] Cic. *Pro Mil.* 68: *sed quis non intellegit omnis tibi rei publicæ partis ægras et labantis, ut eas his armis sanares et confirmares, esse commissas*; Appian, *BC* 2.28: ἐς θεραπείαν τῆς πόλεως ἐπικληθεὶς; Plut. *Pomp.* 55.3: ὧν ἐκεῖνον ἰατρὸν ᾕρηται καὶ μόνῳ παραδέδωκεν αὑτήν; Tac. *Ann.* 3.28: *tum Cn. Pompeius tertium consul corrigendis moribus delectus*; Livy, *Per.* 107: *cum seditiones inter candidatos consulatus . . . ad comprimendas eas Cn. Pompeio legato.*

[144] On the senatorial decree: Plut. *Pomp.* 54.5; the choice of Metellus Scipio: Plut. *Pomp.* 55.7; Dio, 40.51.2–3; Appian, *BC*, 2.25.

[145] M. Marcellus, consul 51, and C. Marcellus, consul 49, were brothers; their cousin, C. Marcellus, was consul in 50. On the family's relations with the Cornelii Lentuli, see above, p. 102. There was a connection with Sulpicius Rufus through the Junii Bruti; Münzer, *Röm. Adelsp.*, pp. 404–407. And L. Lepidus Paullus was brother-in-law of a Junia; Münzer, *RE*, 10:1110–1111, "Junia," n.193.

Pompeius Magnus, sole consul though he was, proved unable or unwilling to determine electoral results for 51. M. Cato himself offered his candidacy and employed it as a showcase for proper electioneering. He ostentatiously scorned stratagems and pandering to the populace. Cato would distribute no cash and promise no favors. The campaign seems to have been designed to win admiration rather than votes. Cato, in any case, had reason to be satisfied with the politics of the victorious candidates, Ser. Sulpicius Rufus and M. Claudius Marcellus.[146] The erudite lawyer Sulpicius, after two previous failures, at last attained the consulship consonant with his patrician heritage. His was not to be a forceful chief magistracy. But, as a stickler for legality and tradition, he could be relied upon to maintain constitutional standards. M. Marcellus' political posture was unambiguous. Already in 52 he defied Pompey by coming to the defense of Milo against the general. And Romans knew him as an intense foe of Julius Cæsar. Marcellus was an orator of great power and a man of tenacious convictions.[147] Obviously the dynasts had no friends in the consulship of 51.[148]

Their fortunes did not improve in the succeeding elections. Marcellus' cousin C. Claudius Marcellus stood for office in 51, evidently with the backing of the consul. It was a source of family pride.[149] C. Marcellus was committed to pursuing the policies of his cousin.[150] L. Aemilius Lepidus Paullus, it ap-

[146] On the campaign for 51, see Plut. *Cato,* 49.1–4; Dio, 40.58.1–3; cf. Livy, *Per.* 108. Cæsar, *BC,* 1.4.1, alleged, perhaps disingenuously, that Cato was vexed at his defeat. Cato and Sulpicius had collaborated in the past: both had urged stringent electoral controls in 63; and Cato backed Sulpicius in his prosecution of Murena; see below, pp. 220–221, 273. In 52, Marcellus, along with Cato, was among the supporters of Milo; Asconius, 34, 39, 40, Clark. A certain Marcellus is depicted by Plutarch as one of Cato's most intimate friends; *Cato,* 18.3–4. He is usually identified with the consul of 51. Perhaps. But in describing the campaign for 51, Plutarch notes only Cato's association with Sulpicius; *Cato,* 49.2. The intimate friend is more likely the consul of 50 or the consul of 49. *Amicitia* with the Marcelli is, in any case, clear.

[147] On Marcellus' hatred for Cæsar, see Plut. *Cæs.* 29.1. His anti-Cæsarian activities in 51 are well known–and they roused the displeasure of Pompey; Cic. *Ad Att.* 5.11.2, 8.3.3; Appian, *BC,* 2.26; cf. Cic. *Ad Fam.* 4.7.2, 4.9.2; *Pro Marc.* 16; Cæl. *Ad Fam.* 8.8; Cæs. *BC,* 1.2. On Marcellus' oratory, see Cic. *Brutus,* 249–250; Dio, 40.58.3.

[148] Sulpicius, to be sure, resisted Marcellus' efforts to recall Cæsar from Gaul; Suet. *Iul.* 28–29; cf. Livy, *Per.* 108. His grounds, however, were purely legal, not political; Dio, 40.59.1. Sulpicius and the Marcelli were *propinqui*; Cic. *Ad Fam.* 4.12.3. On Sulpicius' consulship, see also C. Saunders, *CR,* 37 (1923): 110–113; Meloni, *Ann. Univ. Cagliari,* 13 (1946): 132–150.

[149] In September, Cicero wrote to M. Marcellus to congratulate him on the election of his cousin; *Ad Fam.* 15.9.1: *te et pietatis in tuos et animi in rempublicam et clarissimi atque optimi consulatus, C. Marcello consule facto, fructum cepisse, vehementer gaudeo.*

[150] Appian, *BC,* 2.26; Suet. *Iul.* 29: *insequenti quoque anno Gaio Marcello, qui fratri patrueli suo Marco in consulatu successerat, eadem temptante.* Dio's statement, 40.59.4, that Pompey promoted Marcellus' election because he was hostile to Cæsar, is obvious hindsight. The break between

peared, had similar commitments. A son of M. Lepidus, the consul of 78, Paullus inherited a blood feud with Pompey the Great. In 59 he could already be characterized as a bitter foe and potential assailant of Pompey. A public appearance is recorded also in 56 when Paullus threatened prosecution of Cæsar's adherent P. Vatinius. And, most recently, he attained the prætorship in 53, much to the dismay of P. Clodius, now Pompey's ally.[151] A third candidate, the gifted orator M. Calidius, presented himself. But his genealogical credentials could not bear comparison with those of his rivals. The ancestors of Marcellus and Paullus carried them to victory in 51.[152] In the year 50 itself, of course, the political horizon clouded perceptibly. When relations between Cæsar and Pompey began to strain to the breaking point, many Roman politicians were compelled to make unwelcome choices. The two consuls of 50 ended on opposite sides. That, however, could not have been predicted in 51. Marcellus and Paullus had both been elected as bitter enemies of Julius Cæsar.[153]

The coalition of Cæsar's enemies in Rome was growing. So long as his opponents controlled the chief magistracies, demands for his recall would continue to mount. The proconsul of Gaul saw the value of having a strong candidate on the ballot in the elections for 49. Ser. Sulpicius Galba was Cæsar's choice, a man of distinguished stock and a former legate of Cæsar's, one of the few patricians who had served under him in Gaul.[154] Galba's prospects,

---

Cæsar and Pompey did not come until 50. At that time, Marcellus was with Pompey; but not before. Dio, in the same passage, asserts that Pompey backed Curio's tribunician canvass on similar grounds–which is transparently false.

[151] The accusation in 59: Cic. *Ad Att.* 2.24.2–3; *In Vat.* 25; the attack on Vatinius; Cic. *Ad Q. Frat.* 2.4.1; the prætorship: Cic. *Pro Mil.* 24.

[152] Cæl. *Ad Fam.* 8.4.1; cf. Cic. *Ad Fam.* 15.7, 15.8, 15.9.1, 15.12.1. On Calidius, see Cic. *Brutus*, 274–278; cf. Val. Max. 8.10.3. Cicero refers to a candidate in 51 in whose defeat he rejoices; *Ad Att.* 5.19.3; cf. 6.8.3. That individual is sometimes identified with Calidius. But the elections are not necessarily consular. Nor is there any reason for Cicero to have hoped for Calidius' defeat. Calidius had promoted his recall from exile; Cic. *Post Red. in Sen.* 22; and the two had recently collaborated at the trial of Milo; Asconius, 34, Clark. W. S. Watt, *Mnemosyne*, 16 (1963): 373–375, revived the argument that Lucilius Hirrus, ædilician candidate, is meant. That has now been decisively refuted by Shackleton Bailey, *Cicero's Letters*, III:314–315. But Shackleton Bailey's case for Calidius remains unconvincing.

[153] Appian, *BC*, 2.26: οἱ μάλιστα ἐχθροὶ τοῦ Καίσαρος ἐς τοὐπιὸν ἡρέθησαν ὕπατοι, Αἰμίλιός τε Παῦλος καὶ Κλαύδιος Μάρκελλος. That Paullus' change of front came as a surprise is clear from Cic. *Ad Att.* 6.3.4: *sed mehercule Curionis et Pauli, meorum familiarium, vicem doleo;* cf. Cæl. *Ad Fam.* 8.11.1: *furore Paulli.*

[154] Hirtius, *BG*, 8.50.4. Cæsar also had his eye on T. Labienus for a future consulship, probably for 48; Hirtius, *BG*, 8.52; cf. Syme, *JRS*, 28 (1938): 121–123. The vexed question of Cæsar's personal plans for the consulship will be discussed below. C. Considius Longus, who left a proconsulship of Africa later in 50 to canvass for office, was doubtless aiming for 48 as well; Schol. Gronov. 291, Stangl.

in any ordinary year, would have been favorable. In 50, however, he faced determined opposition. C. Marcellus, cousin and brother of the two preceding consuls, presented his candidacy, pledged to carry out the anti-Cæsarian policies of his kinsmen. And with him was L. Cornelius Lentulus Crus, the sixth Lentulus to stand for the consulship in little more than two decades. Dissolute and indebted, Crus relied on a multitude of hereditary *clientelæ* to offset deficiencies of character.[155]

Nothing suggests that Pompey openly backed the anti-Cæsarian candidates against Sulpicius Galba. Among other considerations, Galba had cooperated with Pompey as recently as 52, M. Marcellus had acted at cross-purposes with him in 51, and the Lentuli possessed a recent history of opposition to the general.[156] The Pompeian lineup against Cæsar in the civil war is not to be projected back even into 50. In the elections of that year, Galba's attachment to Cæsar proved to be a liability rather than an asset. But the voters were not choosing between Pompeians and Cæsarians. Lentulus and Marcellus—*nobiles, adfines* of each other, and relatives of the four preceding consuls—had strong and traditional claims on the electorate. Their success at the polls requires no unusual hypotheses. The standard conventions of Republican politics were still in force.[157]

The campaign in 50 was the last election of the free state. In 49 civil war engulfed Italy, and Julius Cæsar dictated future magisterial appointments. But the stubborn tenacity of Roman institutions receives no better illustration than in the electoral results of the Republic's last years. In the three campaigns that preceded civil war, the voters returned three patricians and three Claudii Marcelli. It is easy in retrospect to wax eloquent about the gathering storm. It would be more accurate to acknowledge that contemporary Romans were not obsessed by it. Electoral politics remained largely unaffected.

[155] On Lentulus' character, see Cæs. *BC*, 1.4.2; Cic. *Ad Att.* 11.6.6; cf. Cic. *Brutus*, 268; Cæl. *Ad Fam.* 8.4.1; Vell. Pat. 2.49.3. Cæsar later sought to play on Lentulus' greed by offering a deal; Cic. *Ad Att.* 8.9a.2, 8.11.5, 8.15a.2. On C. Marcellus, the sources preserve little. But Cicero in 49 characterized both Marcellus and Lentulus as uninspiring and unstable; *Ad Att.* 8.15.2: *nec me consules movent, qui ipsi pluma aut folio facilius moventur.* On the career of Galba, see Münzer, *RE*, 4A:769–772, "Sulpicius," n.61.

[156] On Galba and Pompey in 52, see Val. Max. 6.2.11; cf. Cic. *Ad Fam.* 6.18.4; on M. Marcellus, see above, n.147; on the Lentuli, see above, pp. 94, 102–103.

[157] Cæsar's opponents naturally rejoiced at the defeat of Galba. They would characterize it as a political victory; Hirtius, *BG*, 8.50.4: *insolenter adversarii sui gloriarentur L. Lentulum et C. Marcellum consules creatos qui omnem honorem et dignitatem Cæsaris spoliarent, ereptum Ser. Galbæ consulatum, cum is multo plus gratia suffragiisque valuisset, quod sibi coniunctus et familiaritate et consuetudine legationis esset.* Yet later in 50, there was talk that the venal Lentulus might be won over by Cæsar; Cic. *Ad Att.* 6.8.2. In the end both Lentulus and Marcellus proved to be ardent foes of the proconsul: Cæs. *BC*, 1.1–2, 1.4; Suet. *Iul.* 29; Plut. *Pomp.* 59.1–4; Dio, 40.66.2–3; Appian, *BC*, 2.33.

A summary of the results in the 50s reinforces earlier conclusions. Domination by the *nobilitas* persisted. Twenty-one individuals held consular office between 59 and 49. Twenty of them were *nobiles.*[158] The consistency of that record after the Sullan era is unmistakable. A. Gabinius is the lone anomaly and he barely affects the generalization. Gabinius' forebears were prætorian, with Sullan connections; he had himself compiled a notable record–and an influential backing. There were no fewer than eight patrician consuls in that decade. And a ninth, Metellus Scipio, was born a patrician and was adopted into a plebeian family. Nine of the chief magistrates had had relatives in that office during the 70s and 60s: the three Lentuli, the two Metelli, Cæsar, Piso, Messalla, and Æmilius Paullus Lepidus. And that does not even include Pompey and Crassus, who had themselves held the office in 70. The continuity is striking. Amidst the rapid and dizzying events of the late Republic, the tastes of the electorate were unaltered.

Did the "triumvirate" control Roman politics after 60? Electoral results supply a clear answer in the negative. Only when the dynasts themselves stood could they have real impact. And even then they faced difficulty. Crassus and Pompey had an arduous struggle in 55; Pompey's consulship in 52 came under a senatorial directive. As for their adherents, only Piso and Gabinius in 59 and Lentulus Spinther in 58 were successful at the polls; Metellus Scipio was a Pompeian appointee at a time when normal procedure was suspended. And their behavior in office did not necessarily bear out the expectations of their backers. Many campaigns must have found the triumvirs without candidates. In others, their choices were explicitly rebuffed: Lucceius in 60, T. Balbus in 55, Memmius and Scaurus in 54, Galba in 50. Roman voters proved to be conservative and consistent. No individual or group could effect a stranglehold on the electoral process. Hereditary patrons, aristocratic lineage, and past *beneficia* furnished the most substantial determinants in the *comitia.* That was as true in 50 as it had been in 78.

Thirty years have here been surveyed, the last generation of the Republic. There were sixty-one consuls, fifty-eight different individuals. Only seven of them came from non-consular families. And the victories of those seven are, in every case, readily explicable through connections or background. In this central respect, the late Republic maintained and perpetuated antique tradition.

But the breakdown lay elsewhere, so it can be argued: the electorate was no longer free; strong men imposed their own candidates, wholesale bribery dominated campaigns, and escalating disruptions turned the voting process into a farce. The validity of those generalizations needs to be challenged. The evidence examined here will not bear them out.

[158] Pompey, of course, held two consulships–in 55 and in 52.

None will deny that bribery was an instrument of electioneering. But "bribery" was a slippery term then, as it is now. Solicitation of votes in any form runs a fine line between proper and offensive behavior. In Rome it was not always easy to distinguish between favors tendered to clients and corrupt practices.[159] As we shall see, legislators wrestled with difficulty over that issue in the framing of *ambitus* measures. Can one be sure that the late Republic sinned with greater frequency in this area than did earlier periods? Prosecutions *de ambitu* do not prove it. They were generally inspired by politics rather than moral indignation. And the late Republic had no monopoly on *ambitus* trials. That men of wealth possessed distinct advantages in consular campaigns is, of course, true. But in that respect also the late Republic shows no difference from the past.[160] The sources attest to corruption, or attempted corruption, of the voters in the Ciceronian age. But it is useful to be precise. The attestations are limited to nine of the thirty years between 78 and 49, and many of them derive from tendentious informants. One may note also that in four of those nine years, innuendos notwithstanding, no formal charges grew out of the campaigns.[161] We own much fuller information on the late Republic than on previous eras; hence, perspective may be warped. Dubious practices in the canvass were not an invention of the Ciceronian age. The deplorable activities that reached their peak in 53 ought not to be adjudged as typical. In fact they were highly unusual, as the accounts for that year make abundantly clear. What is more important–and more neglected–is the absence of any attested bribery in the three years that followed, the last years of the Republic. The system did not perish from an overdose of electoral bribery.

What of turmoil and disruptions at the *comitia*? Were voters deprived of free choice by intimidation and force? Some striking examples exist. Pompey and Crassus were elected for 55 by postponing the vote and driving opponents from the field. The turbulence of 54 and 53 culminated in cancellation of the *comitia* and a consul without colleague. But twenty-six of the thirty campaigns under discussion were free of serious disruption.[162] Surely that is the significant statistic. Of course, one may point to several instances of postponed elections. But postponements reflect politics, not upheaval. Machinations by

[159] The problem emerges forcefully in Cic. *Pro Mur.* 68–77.

[160] See Polyb. 6.57.

[161] The years are 70, 68, 66, 64, 63, 61, 60, 54, 53. Even if the evidence is accurate, that progression hardly suggests escalation.

[162] There were disturbances in 75, but they are attested only for the prætorian, not the consular elections; Sallust, *Hist.* 2.45, Maur. Apart from 56, 54, and 53, the evidence for electoral upheaval is clear only for 67; Dio, 36.39.1; cf. Val. Max. 3.8.3. But even then it seems to have grown out of a legislative contest, rather than the consular campaign; see below, chap. 6.

presiding officers to promote favored candidates or push through legislation account for the delays.[163] That kind of obstructionism was a feature common to periods much earlier than the Ciceronian age. It does not suggest breakdown of order in the late Republic. The routine campaigns far outnumbered the disturbed. It is time that they received the attention customarily accorded to the more spectacular but more anomalous events.

Candidates were endorsed for office, not as politicians, but as patrons, benefactors, and heirs of illustrious *gentes.* Politics might sometimes intervene. Factional contests, personal feuds, and attempts by leading figures to promote their own adherents occasionally dictated the list of *candidati.* But the electorate's choice, with few exceptions, was determined by traditional considerations. Their roots were in rural Italy and their interests were linked to the existing order.

[163] Apart from 56, 54, and 53, delays are attested for the campaigns in 67, 63, 62, 61, 59, and 55. Whenever details are known, they indicate political manipulation.

V

THE SENATE

THE STRUCTURE of Roman society was hierarchical—fixed not by law or caste but by tradition. Leadership by a self-perpetuating aristocracy went unquestioned by a populace addicted to political orthodoxy. The ruling class fastened its hold through a system of patronage and clientage, a pattern of mutual obligations. For members of the privileged orders, the senate was a prime focus of activity. The august body symbolized status and prestige: a collection of Rome's ex-magistrates. Hierarchy permeated all levels, including the ruling class itself. The Roman senate contained discernible gradations, with varied levels of *dignitas.* Consular rank afforded preeminence, an elevated station in the *curia,* and principal control of senatorial business: the *nobilitas* of former consuls stood in ascendancy. Consular elections to the end of the Republic, as we have seen, returned families with lengthy records of service and conspicuous pedigrees. Below the *consulares* were the ex-prætors, then the former ædiles, tribunes, and quæstors. The gradations were firmly observed in senatorial discussion. *Consulares* delivered their *sententiæ* first, followed by prætorians, *ædilicii, tribunicii,* and ex-quæstors. The presiding officer could exercise some discretion in calling upon individuals within each rank, but would rarely break the order of the ranks themselves. Senators who had not passed beyond the quæstorship seldom uttered a syllable in the *curia.* Romans possessed a strong sense of ascending *dignitas.*

The enormous collective prestige of the senate rested on a simple principle: its membership consisted of men who had been elected to magisterial office. The magistracy was but a year in duration; senatorial membership was lifetime, subject only to periodic and minor revision by the censors. After Sulla, election to the quæstorship, lowest rung on the magisterial ladder, provided automatic enrollment in the senate. Movement up through the ranks depended on successive election to higher offices. The senate was not bogged down with a seniority system. An aging ex-quæstor enjoyed no accumulation of *auctoritas* if he failed to attain higher magistracies. Hence, the increase of a senator's prestige and authority was tied closely to his hold on the electorate. In that enterprise, the ancient houses of the *nobilitas,* with an intricate web of associations through the social structure, retained an imposing advantage. The persistent dominance of consular houses, regardless of changing issues and political contests, has already been demonstrated in detail. What of the men elected to the prætorship, the ædileship, and the tribunate? Is it possible to detect a shift in the social status of the men attaining office and rising through the levels of the senate establishment? Does the Ciceronian age betoken a change in the composition of Roman leadership? Available evidence is by no means complete. But careful scrutiny will yield some results.

THE PRÆTORS

The prætorship ranked just below the consulate. Tenure of that office conferred power and prominence. Responsible duties in the law courts attached to prætors; they presided over the *quæstiones perpetuæ,* in which so much of Roman politics took place. Apart from the consuls, they alone possessed *imperium* in the city. Prætors and ex-prætors could expect important and sometimes lucrative provinçial assignments. And the prætorship was a final prerequisite for consular eligibility. In the post-Sullan era eight prætors were chosen annually. Only one-quarter of them could realistically anticipate attainment of the consulship. But without the prior step the magisterial summit was closed. It will pay dividends to examine the prætorian lists of the late Republic.

Testimony is extensive, though not exhaustive. In the thirty years between 78 and 49, two hundred forty prætors were returned by the electorate. Assiduous research by scholars has uncovered a large proportion of the names. One may identify—with certainty, or a very high degree of probability—nearly 75 percent of the prætors in this period: one hundred seventy-eight persons.[1] What were their origins?

[1] The indispensable work, of course, is Broughton's *MRR*. Inevitably, there are some errors, perpetuated or perpetrated. But the monumental labors involved in that production cannot receive sufficient praise. On the prætorian lists, Broughton employed, with care and intelligence, some earlier studies, now superseded but by no means valueless: P. Wehrmann, *Fasti prætorii ab A. U. DLXXXVIII ad A. U. DCCX* (Berlin, 1875); M. Hölzl, *Fasti Prætorii ab A. U. DCLXXXVII usque ad A. U. DCCX* (Leipzig, 1876); F. Stella Maranca, *MemLinc*, 6.2 (1927): 277–376. The prosopographical compilation in L. R. Taylor's *Voting Districts*, pp. 184–269, is an important supplement. And mention must be made of certain key articles,

Consular ancestry was virtually indispensable for aspirants to the chief magistracy. The same could not hold for the prætorship. With eight places available each year, there was additional elbowroom for candidates outside the ranks of the *nobilitas.* That makes all the more remarkable a revealing statistic: close to half of the known prætors in the Ciceronian age derived from consular families. The number of annual offices prevented the *nobiles* from monopolizing the prætorship as they did the consulship. But the overwhelming advantage possessed by men of consular stock is clear. Given the statistics, it appears that few of them failed in a quest for the prætorship.

One will not claim unqualified precision in the figures. *Nobilitas* attaches to several of the prætorian names in the late Republic only by conjecture and plausibility. In other instances men who attained the prætorship late in this period could not trace consular kinsmen back beyond the Sullan dictatorship. Firmer conclusions will come through rigorous application of criteria. Only families who could boast of pre-Sullan consuls will here be reckoned as *nobiles.* And the *nomen* alone will not be presumed to be decisive. Not all of the Cornelii or the Valerii or the Claudii belong to consular branches of those *gentes.* The combination of *nomen* and *cognomen* is more reliable indication. When the latter is missing, *prænomina* often supply important clues.

Even the most conservative of estimates, however, discloses an extensive proportion of consular houses who supplied successful candidates for the prætorship. On this reckoning seventy-seven of the one hundred seventy-eight known prætors possessed verifiable consular forebears in pre-Sullan generations.[2]

---

filling in gaps or clarifying material in Broughton and Taylor: Syme, *CP*, 50 (1955): 127–138; *Historia*, 4 (1955): 52–71; *Historia*, 13 (1964): 105–125; Badian, *Historia*, 12 (1963): 129–143; Wiseman, *CQ*, 14 (1964): 122–133. On *novi homines*, see now the very useful study of Wiseman, *New Men, passim.* The availability of his careful researches permits us to leave aside lengthy discussion of the geographical origin of new senators; see esp., *New Men*, pp. 13–32.

[2] Included in this number are M. Juventius Laterensis, prætor in 51, and M'. Juventius Laterensis, who reached the office some time in the Ciceronian age. No previous Juventius Laterensis appears on the consular *fasti.* But the consular ancestry of M. Laterensis is explicitly affirmed; Cic. *Pro Planc.* 15, 18. No doubt it was traceable to M. Juventius Thalna, consul in 163. On M'. Laterensis, see Syme, *Historia*, 4 (1955): 63–64. Similarly, L. Sergius Catilina, who reached the prætorship in 68. The sources describe him as a *nobilis*; Sallust, *Cat.* 5.1; [Q. Cic.] *Comm. Petit.* 9. Evidently, he could claim descent from the Sergii Fidenates who supplied consuls in the late fifth and early fourth centuries. P. Lentulus Sura is here counted twice. He held prætorships in 74 and 63, expulsion from the senate having occurred in the interim. References to the sources can be readily found in Broughton's *MRR* and will be cited here only when necessary to the argument. Add also C. Cœlius Caldus, son of the consul of 94, not listed in Broughton's text, but given in the *Supplement*, p. 17. The prætorship is certain from his description as *imperator* on coins. And T. Manlius Torquatus, whom Broughton lists only as a senator; *MRR*, II:493. Cicero's text makes it most likely that he reached the prætorship; *Brutus*, 245: *si vita suppeditavisset . . . consul factus esset.* For a full list of magistrates arranged by status, see Appendix I below.

That is a minimum number. It may be expanded somewhat through reasonable hypothesis. Two Terentii Varrones obtained prætorships in the late Republic, the great scholar and author M. Terentius Varro, and A. Terentius Varro, cousin of Hortensius. The family had not been of prominence in recent generations. But a C. Terentius Varro appears on the consular *fasti* for 216, the ill-fated general defeated by Hannibal at Cannæ. There is no reason to doubt that the Varrones of Cicero's era stemmed from that *consularis*—and there is positive evidence in support.[3] M. Calpurnius Bibulus, prætor in 62 and consul in 59, was the first of that name in curule office. But the distinction of his career and connections make it impossible to reckon him a *novus homo.* A derisive nickname probably accounts for the *cognomen.* Bibulus surely belongs to a consular branch of the Calpurnii, perhaps the Calpurnii Pisones.[4] Q. Pompeius Bithynicus seems to have reached prætorian rank sometime in the early 60s. Again the *cognomen* should not mislead. It was conferred for service in Bithynia. The family descends, almost certainly, from Q. Pompeius, the consul of 141.[5] P. Cælius (or Cœlius), prætor in 74, is registered but once in the sources. The *prænomen,* however, evokes another P. Cœlius, senator and legate in 87—surely from the house of the Cœlii Caldi, which attained consular status in the 90s.[6] C. Licinius Macer, the annalist and friend of M. Crassus, was prætor in 68. The *cognomen* does not elsewhere stand on record. But Macer's son was named C. Licinius Calvus, an obvious echo of the Licinii Calvi who furnished two consuls in the fourth century. The annalist's celebration of the Licinii in his history exposes his connection, or assumed connection, with the ancient house.[7]

Further additions can be made, though with less assurance. C. Sulpicius, who aided Cicero in gathering evidence against the Catilinarians during his praetorship of 63, is otherwise unknown. But the *prænomen* "Gaius" is frequently employed by several branches of the distinguished Sulpicii, all consular and patrician houses, stretching back to the early Republic. The prætor of 63 may well belong to one of them, most probably the Sulpicii Galbæ, who

[3] Serv. *Ad Æn.* 11.743; see the arguments of Cichorius, *Röm. Stud.*, pp. 189–191. The date of M. Terentius Varro's prætorship is uncertain, but was possibly in the early 60s; Cichorius, *Röm. Stud.,* pp. 203–204. The Varrones were related not only to Hortensius but to Lucullus. Lucullus' brother, M. Lucullus, was adopted by a Terentius Varro.

[4] See above, p. 142.

[5] See Miltner, *RE*, 21:2050, "Pompeius." The effort of Miss Taylor, *Voting Districts*, pp. 244–245, to associate him with the family of Pompeius Magnus has been refuted by Badian, *Historia*, 12 (1963): 138–139. Not that it would matter for our purposes. Magnus' father was consul in 89. That Q. Pompeius Bithynicus attained prætorian office was seen by Willems, *Le Sénat*, I:457. Broughton fails to list the prætorship, though he acknowledges its probability in his index; *MRR*, II:603.

[6] On the Cœlii Caldi, see the persuasive arguments of Badian, *Studies*, pp. 92–93.

[7] Cf. R. M. Ogilvie, *A Commentary on Livy, Books 1-5* (Oxford, 1965), pp. 7–12.

remained prominent through the end of Republican history and beyond. A similar inference may apply to Cn. Manlius, prætor in 72. The Manlii comprised several branches, patrician and plebeian. But "Gnæus" is found only among the patricians: the great consular clans of the early and middle Republic. Cn. Manlius very likely came of illustrious stock. Still another possible candidate deserves notice: Q. Publicius, prætor ca. 67. The Publicii Malleoli show a consul in 232. And "Quintus" was a *prænomen* employed by that *gens.*[8] Finally, one may include P. Servilius Vatia Isauricus, prætor in 54 and future consul of 48, the staunch friend and emulator of M. Cato. Servilius' father reached the consulship in 79—not, to be sure, in the pre-Sullan era. But the elder Servilius, prætor no later than 90, would surely have attained his consulship in the 80s were it not for civil war and disruption. Though he is the first Servilius Vatia on the consular *fasti,* he was no *novus homo.* Numerous branches of the Servilii supplied Roman consuls throughout Republican annals. The Vatiæ derived, unquestionably, from one of them.[9]

With the inclusion of these ten names, all more than likely from consular *gentes,* the total reaches eighty-seven. That is just short of half the known prætors from 78 to 49. Caution, however, must be exercised. The proportions are not to be extrapolated and made to apply to all the missing names. Men with consular forebears wielded authority, and are more likely to find place in extant records than colleagues of lesser station. In fact, forty-seven of this number went on to achieve consulships. In several instances their prætorships are postulated only on the grounds of the higher office. The evidence, it must be repeated, is not complete. But even if none of the missing sixty-two or so prætors were of consular houses, the *nobiles* will still have attained a third of the prætorian posts—and the proportion may be closer to one-half. Although those results might have been expected, it is reassuring to have them confirmed by statistics. The voting populace had not altered its tastes or its habits. The patterns that held in an earlier era continued to hold in

[8] Observe Q. Mall. on a Sicilian coin of the late Republic, perhaps the prætor of 67 himself; Broughton, *MRR,* II:478. Wiseman, *CQ,* 15 (1965): 158–159, conjectures Transpadane origins for Q. Publicius on the basis of an inscription, now lost, from Verona. That any Transpadani reached the prætorship as early as this, however, is most dubious. Two other names, registered by Broughton, have here been excluded. Their prætorships are, at best, dubious. A certain Domitius was scheduled to be presiding officer at Cælius' trial in 54; Cic. *Ad Q. Frat.* 2.13.2. Münzer, *RE,* 5:1316–1318, "Domitius," n.11, makes him a prætor in 54, a man nowhere else recorded. More likely he is Domitius Calvinus, the prætor of 56, serving here as a *quæsitor.* The Postumius mentioned as assigned to Sicily in 49 need not have been an ex-prætor; Cic. *Ad Att.* 7.15.2. The Ciceronian passage implies no more than quæstorian rank; cf. Shackleton Bailey, *Cicero's Letters,* IV:310–311.

[9] The elder Servilius was already a consular candidate in 88; Plut. *Sulla,* 10.3. It was the determined opposition to Sulla which blocked his way, until the dictator could himself install Servilius for 79.

the Ciceronian age. Men whose ancestors had exercised high office in Rome's past and who inherited a legacy of political credits and connections rarely met with failure in the prætorian elections. At that level *nobilitas* was an unchallengeable credential.[10]

Factional allegiance was generally of small account in consular elections, although pointed political battles occasionally determined a result. In prætorian contests, their effect is barely discernible. A notable exception came in early 55 when Pompey and Crassus overtly pushed their candidates through—to the detriment of political rivals.[11] Stray references reveal a few other instances in which partisan implications found play in the prætorian *comitia:* so C. Alfius Flavus, endorsed by Cæsar in 57, failed of election, defeated by an outspoken enemy of Cæsar's.[12] And, of course, there was the turbulent campaign of 53, partly revolving about Clodius' bid for the prætorship.[13] But such contests were rare. Prætorian elections were usually untroubled by tumult or political clash. Family background, patronage, and inherited connections sufficed to assure victory for individuals who possessed those qualifications. The Cornelii Lentuli attained eight prætorships in this period, the Cæcilii Metelli six, the Aurelii Cottæ, Manlii Torquati, and Calpurnii Pisones four each, the Æmilii Lepidi, Claudii Marcelli, and Sulpicii Galbæ three each; two prætorships were obtained by the families of the Antonii, Luculli, Terentii Varrones, Pompeii, Julii Cæsares, Junii Silani, Claudii Pulchri, Cassii Longini, Valerii Messallæ, Licinii Crassi, Juventii Laterenses, and Minucii Thermi. Patrician houses and old plebeian *gentes* predominate. Their names and their families' associations determined the results. Intra-senatorial rivalry played only a minor and intermittent role. Traditional allegiance to the *nobilitas* remained the principal influence at the balloting.

Consular background brought guaranteed success for aspirants to the prætorship. If that were not available, the next best credential was possession of ancestors in the prætorship. The electorate recognized those names as well.

[10] There is no discernible shift in the last three decades of the Republic, even taken individually. Of the eighty-seven prætors with consular forebears, twenty-five came in the 70s, thirty-two in the 60s, and twenty-four in the 50s. Six others, Q. Pompeius Bithynicus, M. Terentius Varro, C. Cœlius Caldus, T. Manlius Torquatus, M'. Juventius Laterensis, and Ti. Claudius Nero, held prætorships at an undetermined time within this period. Excluded here is M. Claudius Marcellus, a senior *prætorius* in 73; Broughton, *MRR*, II:114. His prætorship almost certainly preceded 78.

[11] Dio, 39.32; Plut. *Pomp.* 52.2; *Cato*, 42.

[12] Cic. *In Vat.* 38: *dixisse* [Cæsar] *se C. Alfium præteritum permoleste tulisse . . . graviterque etiam se ferre prætorem aliquem esse factum, qui a suis rationibus dissensisset.* The victorious candidate referred to was either Cn. Domitius Calvinus or Q. Ancharius; cf. Cic. *Pro Sest.* 113–114; *In Vat.* 16; Schol. Bob. 151, Stangl.

[13] See above, chap. 4. One might observe also the prætorian canvass of Metellus Creticus in 75, backed openly by both consuls; Sallust, *Hist.* 2.45, Maur.

They would not readily advance them to the consulate; but prætorian office was a plausible expectation for men who boasted forebears of that rank. The testimony here is more fragmentary and problematic. But at least twenty holders of the office in the Republic's last generation can be demonstrably tied to prætorian families of pre-Sullan date.

Some claimed distinguished ancestry, with several precursors in the prætorship. So Cn. Tremellius Scrofa, the friend of Varro, took pride in the fact that members of his *gens* attained prætorian rank in seven successive generations.[14] L. Licinius Murena was the fourth in a direct line of prætors stretching back to his great-grandfather. Murena himself finally ennobled that estimable family from Lanuvium with a consulship in 62.[15] At least four prætors adorned the family tree of C. Memmius, the mercurial orator, versifier, and patron of Lucretius. He duly followed the path of his antecedents, securing the office in 58.[16] A more distant antiquity could be claimed by L. Ælius Tubero, a close friend and relative of Cicero's, who shared similar tastes in literature and learning. An Ælius Tubero earned prætorian standing as long ago as 201. There were doubtless others in the interim, though details and dates are wanting. Random anecdotes reveal two prætorian Ælii Tuberones, perhaps predecessors of L. Tubero. The last obtained his office sometime in the 50s.[17] An unbroken string of prætorships in the family also backed the claims of M. Fonteius, prætor ca. 75 and Cicero's client in 69.[18] How far back they went is uncertain—at least to 166.[19] The house of L. Cornelius Sisenna, prætor in 78 and the finest historian of his generation, shows a prætor as far back as 183. Other men who reached the office in the 50s could point to a lineage dating from the third or early second centuries: L. Villius Annalis, whose forefather authored a landmark measure on magisterial candidacy in 180; Sex. Quinctilius Varus, whose prætorian pedigree carried back to 203; and the annalistic writer L. Scribonius Libo, Pompey's *adfinis* and counselor, who had an ancestor in the prætorship of 204.[20] From at least the mid-second

[14] Varro, *De Re Rust.* 2.4.2.

[15] For Murena's prætorian stock, see Cic. *Pro Mur.* 15.

[16] On the Memmii, a vexed and perplexing problem, see, most recently, Wiseman, *CQ*, 17 (1967), pp. 164–167.

[17] On the Ciceronian prætor, Broughton, *MRR*, II:259–260; his intimacy with Cicero, Cic. *Pro Lig.* 12, 21; the two undated prætors, Broughton, *MRR*, II:462.

[18] Cic. *Pro Font.* 41: *continuæ præturæ*.

[19] The Fonteius mentioned by Cicero in 54 may also have been a prætor; *Ad Att.* 4.15.6; Broughton, *MRR*, II:221. The family tradition was maintained.

[20] Libo's own prætorship, to be sure, is not quite certain; cf. Broughton, *MRR*, II:248. L. Villius Annalis is very likely the senator in 55 who engaged in fisticuffs with M. Crassus; Plutarch terms him Λεύκιον Ἀννάλιον; *Comp. Nic. et Crass.* 2.2. He is given a separate entry, however, by Wiseman, *New Men*, p. 212, no.27.

century stem the prætorian kinsmen of Rubrius and C. Cosconius.[21] Bellienus' *gens* produced two prætors at the end of that century.[22] And, finally, there are five men in the prætorian lists of the 60s and 50s whose progenitors achieved that rank in the previous generation: Sextilius, A. Gabinius, C. Cæcilius Cornutus, Q. Ancharius, and M. Nonius Sufenas.[23]

Thus far, we have eighteen names in the category of late Republican prætors who followed their ancestors into that office. Conjecture can swell the number somewhat. T. Aufidius shed his background as a businessman to reach a prætorship ca. 67 and conduct a praiseworthy governorship of Asia. It would be rash to conclude that his antecedents were equestrian. Perhaps an earlier generation had fallen on hard times. But the second century exhibits at least three senatorial Aufidii, one of them a prætor. Their *imagines* stood behind a descendant's claim.[24] The same may be said of the era's preeminent juridical scholar, C. Aquillius Gallus, who acquired prætorian office in 66. Pliny the Elder registers him as an *eques*. But if that is an accurate description of Gallus, it need not apply to earlier members of his *gens*. L. Aquillius Gallus, prætor in 176, should be brought into the reckoning: probably a distant kinsman.[25] Another learned man, P. Nigidius Figulus, obtained the post in 58. Of prætorian progenitors we are ignorant. But C. Nigidius, prætor in 145, may be relevant. And two final names deserve inclusion: men with prætorian relatives on the margins of the Sullan era–and possibly earlier. The worthy orator M. Calidius won his prætorship in 57 and entertained consular aspirations. A predecessor, Q. Calidius, perhaps his parent, was prætor in 79. The office might have been attained earlier but for political enmities: Q. Calidius

[21] Rubrius' prætorship was, apparently, in 68, C. Cosconius' in 63. The prætorship of a second Cosconius in 54 is conjectural and best left out of account; Syme, *CP*, 50 (1955): 130. On the ancestor of Rubrius, a senator and probably a prætorian in 129, see Taylor, *Voting Districts*, p. 251; Broughton, *MRR Suppl.*, p. 54.

[22] The name is variously spelled. But C. Billienus in 107 and L. Bellienus in 105 should be associated with the prætor of ca. 68, given as Bellinus by Plut. *Pomp.* 24.6. The first of this series evidently inaugurated the family's prominence; Cicero describes him as a self-made man; *Brutus*, 175. Bellienus may, of course, be a *cognomen* rather than a gentile designation; observe C. Annius Bellienus, a legate in the 70s; Cic. *Pro Font.* 18; cf. Broughton, *MRR*, I:558, n.4. He could be identical with the prætor of 68, a possibility not canvassed by Broughton. But Bellienus as a *nomen gentilicium* is well attested, and is here the better alternative; cf. Shackleton Bailey, *PCPS*, 185 (1958–59): 11–13.

[23] For Sextilius, the lineage is probably longer. A P. Sextilius is discoverable before the mid-second century; Broughton, *MRR*, II:465.

[24] Note the prætor of 107. There is also a Cn. Aufidius T.f., demonstrating that family's use of the *prænomen* Titus; cf. Syme, *Historia*, 4 (1955): 55–56. T. "Ofidius," a senator ca. 165, is surely an Aufidius: Broughton, *MRR*, II:494; perhaps father of the previous. On the prætor of 67, see Val. Max. 6.9.7; cf. Cic. *Pro Flacco*, 45; *Brutus*, 179.

[25] On the jurist as *eques*, see Pliny, *NH*, 17.2. He was a consular candidate for 63, along with–it might be observed–T. Aufidius; Cic. *Ad Att.* 1.1.1.

had been tribune as long before as 98 when his actions roused strong personal backlash.[26] Lastly, there was Claudius Glaber, who fought unsuccessfully against Spartacus as prætor in 73. His older brother (it seems), C. Claudius Glaber, was already *prætorius* by that time, perhaps reaching the post in the previous decade.[27]

These five additions, more or less plausible, expand the sum to twenty-three. The statistic is fluid rather than firm; absence of documentation, not contrary evidence, prevents an increase in the total. Prætorian progenitors of many other late Republican prætors have very likely escaped record. The data fall off sharply before the Ciceronian age. Minimum figures only are here transmitted. But the combination of men with known consular or prætorian ancestors has now reached one hundred ten.

At the same time, the late Republic shows no noticeable increase in social mobility through the upper strata. Prætorian ancestry brought respectability and influence, but rarely access to the consulship. Of the twenty-three men here registered only three went on to the chief magistracy: L. Murena, A. Gabinius, and L. Scribonius Libo. The successes of Murena, a man of military repute and formidable endorsement, and Gabinius, Pompey's lieutenant, have been explored earlier. Scribonius Libo, an astute operator, was connected by marriage to both Pompeius Magnus and Octavianus, and eventually became an adherent of M. Antonius. Even so, he had to wait two decades for a consulship—until late in the triumviral period.[28] The hierarchical barriers remained high to the end of the Republic. The *populus Romanus* would have it no other way. At the upper reaches of society, distinctions of hereditary station were unyielding.

A third category of prætors demands attention: men of senatorial origins, though without forefathers in the higher magistracies. That there should be some such is inescapable. Sulla had increased the number of annual prætors from six to eight. That immediately augmented opportunities for clans whose members had not previously exceeded tribunician or ædilician standing. Twenty-eight attested late Republican prætors seem to fall into that bracket.

[26] Cic. *Pro Planc.* 69; Val. Max. 5.2.7. There may have been an even earlier Calidius in the prætorship; *IG*, 7.18; cf. Wiseman, *CQ*, 14 (1964): 123. The prætorian descent of Nigidius is doubted, for no discernible reason, by Wiseman, *New Men*, p. 244, no. 271.

[27] See on this Taylor, *Voting Districts*, pp. 176, n.22, 204; Badian, *Historia*, 12 (1963): 133. Prudence forbids inclusion of L. Appuleius, prætor 59, in this company. The *cognomen* Saturninus, usually attached to him, has been decisively removed by the arguments of Syme, *Historia*, 13 (1964): 111, 121–122. Hence, he will not stem from the prætorian Appuleii Saturnini. One should remove also C. Licinius, allegedly a prætor before 75; Broughton, *MRR*, II:115. His name is the consequence of an apparent dittography; see the arguments of Badian, *Historia*, 12 (1963): 134–135.

[28] On Scribonius Libo, see Münzer, *RE*, 2A:881–885, "Scribonius," n.20.

Here inference and surmise must play a larger role. The genealogy of most of the relevant individuals cannot be demonstrated with decisiveness. But balance of probability turns up a number of reasonably certain names.

Several of them show progenitors in a pre-Sullan tribunate. Among these were Sex. Peducæus and his son C. Curtius Peducæanus, prætors in 77 and 50 respectively, close friends of Cicero's. They doubtless derived from Sex. Peducæus, the tribune of 113. The father of Cicero's client P. Sestius is specifically designated as a tribune, probably in the 90s.[29] C. Vergilius, a prætor in 62, very likely belongs to the family of Sulla's enemy M. Vergilius, who harassed Sulla during a tribunate of 87. Two Titii obtained prætorships in the late Republic. That family was certainly tribunician: a Sex. Titius appears as tribune in 99 or 98; and the sources reveal two other Titii as authors of legislation, both perhaps pre-Sullan.[30] Less certainty can be claimed for Q. Fufius Calenus, a Cæsarian collaborator in 59 and a thorn in the side of Cicero. *Cognomen* suggests familial origins in Cales. But perhaps the mid-second-century Fufius who sponsored a reform bill on legislative procedure was a distant ancestor. Tribunician lineage is ascribable also to Q. Voconius Naso and his son (?), both prætors in the late Republic. A Q. Voconius Saxa held the tribunate in 169. The rarity of the *nomen* and the identity of the *prænomina* argue for the connection.[31]

Senatorial extraction is clear for various other prætors. The *senatus consultum* of 129 lists several senators of that date, among them an Antistius, a Silius, an Appuleius, and a Plætorius. All show descendants of the same *gentilicia* in late Republican prætorships.[32] M. Cæsius, prætor in 75, and L. Lucceius, prætor in 67, were probably not the first of their clans to reach the senate. The Cæsii can claim a *monetalis* in the late second century, the Lucceii, a legate in Macedon in 92.[33] Attestation of senatorial forebears is direct for two

[29] Cic. *Pro Sest.* 6.

[30] Cf. Broughton, *MRR*, II:473. C. Titius Rufus, prætor in 50, was son of a Lucius. That may be L. Titius noted as a prætor some time in the Ciceronian period; Val. Max. 8.3.1; cf. Pliny, *NH*, 31.11. Relationship of C. Vergilius to the tribune of 87 depends, of course, on the latter's name. The tradition is not unanimous–it could be "Verginius"; cf. Badian, *Studies*, p. 100.

[31] It is possible, but not likely, that the two Ciceronian Voconii are identical; Broughton, *MRR Suppl.*, p. 70. The family of Fufius Calenus, not specifically attested as senatorial, was obviously of some substance; Cic. *Verr.* 2.2.23; *Phil.* 8.13; cf. Shackleton Bailey, *CQ*, 10 (1960): 263.

[32] On the *s.c.* of 129, see Taylor, *Voting Districts*, pp. 170–175. Note also a M. Plætorius, senator in 82; Broughton, *MRR*, II:494.

[33] Broughton, *MRR*, II:20 n.8, 434. Cæsius is surely the same man noted in the *consilium* of 73 as Μάαρκος Κάσιος; *SIG*,[3] 747. There is no need to conjecture an unknown "M. Cassius"; see Badian, *Historia*, 12 (1963): 134–135; R. K. Sherk, *Roman Documents from the Greek East* (Baltimore, 1969), p. 137.

more prætors: C. Licinius Sacerdos and Q. Cornificius.[34] Accident only, we may be sure, fails to preserve the progenitors of L. Volcacius Tullus, consul in 66, and L. Afranius, consul in 60. Similarly, P. Autronius Pætus, elected to the consulship of 65, but disqualified by an *ambitus* conviction. Those three would hardly have entertained such lofty aspirations without predecessors in the senate.[35]

Eight further names require inclusion, though there can be no claim of irrefutable proof. C. Verres, the notorious governor of Sicily, is nowhere termed a *novus* in Cicero's *Verrines*—an eloquent omission. In fact, Verres' father sat in the senate in the late 70s. Our records do not pinpoint the date of his entrance into the *ordo senatorius.* But it presumably predated that of his son, who attained the quæstorship in 84.[36] A. Plautius, urban prætor in 51, was son of an *eques.* But numerous Plautii grace the magisterial *fasti* from the fourth century on. Of direct pertinence is another A. Plautius, a senatorial legate during the Social War. His namesake may safely be reckoned as carrying senatorial blood.[37] So also may M. Junius, prætor ca. 67, and C. Fabius, prætor in 58. The *cognomina* are missing, therefore barring certainty. Reasonable inference can be substituted. "Marcus" was a common *prænomen* among the Junii Bruti and Junii Silani, both consular clans. The prætor of 67 may belong to one or the other of them. If not, there are also frequent appearances of Junii without attested *cognomen* in earlier generations. C. Fabius probably did not carry the patrician blood of the great Fabian clans that went back to Rome's antique past. But alternate Fabii offer themselves as possibilities: he may be a Fabius Hadrianus; if so, perhaps a son of C. Fabius Hadrianus, prætor in 84. Senatorial background, in any case, may be legitimately assumed. Illustrious *gentilicia,* combined with obscure *cognomina,* mark P. Servilius Globulus, prætor in 64, and L. Cæcilius Rufus, prætor in 57. The Servilii had various branches, with four centuries of membership in the *curia.* Globulus' family was doubtless an offshoot from one of them.[38] Cæcilii appear with equal frequency on the magisterial lists. No Cæcilius Rufus, apart from the prætor of 57, is attested. But that worthy, half-brother or cousin of P. Sulla,

[34] Asconius, 82, Clark.

[35] The lowly origins of Afranius are exaggerated by hostile propaganda. One may observe a C. Afranius Stellio, prætor 185, though probably not of the direct line of L. Afranius. That Volcacius' family was senatorial is clear from Cic. *Pro Planc.* 51.

[36] On Verres the elder, see Cic. *Verr.* 2.2.95–96, 2.2.102.

[37] Cicero designates the prætor of 51 as a *homo ornatissimus*; Cic. *Pro Planc.* 17, 54. Notice, too, M. Plautius Silvanus, tribune in 89 or 88. His descendant, the consul of 2 B.C., was grandson of an A. Plautius—probably the prætor of 51; Taylor, *Voting Districts*, p. 243. Cf. also Wiseman, *New Men*, p. 252, no. 324.

[38] Cf. Cic. *Pro Flacco, apud* Schol. Bob. 96, Stangl: *P. Servilio, gravissimo et sanctissimo cive.*

was evidently of distinguished lineage.[39] M. Considius Nonianus, prætor ca. 54, was, it seems, born a Nonius. The latter family had attained senatorial rank by the 80s. Finally, one possibility, perhaps just short of probability: Q. Valerius Orca, prætor in 57, could not boast a family of great antiquity; but his parent may well have been Q. Valerius Soranus, an ill-fated tribune in the late 80s.[40]

The preceding survey has gathered twenty-eight names of ostensible senatorial ancestry. Specific attestation is rare; of necessity, conjecture must be summoned to assistance. The total here may be too high, rather than too low. Not that many of these individuals should be removed to a status of *novitas:* the movement should probably be upward. If evidence were fuller, several in this category might show prætorian predecessors. It bears repeating that the *fasti prætorii* of pre-Sullan days are sparse indeed. Our cumulative sum now encompasses one hundred thirty-eight men. It would be foolhardy to claim precision for that figure: some names can be challenged; others might be added. But revision of the list would not destroy its approximate accuracy. Senatorial families of prior generations predominate overwhelmingly among the late Republican prætors.

There remain the personages for whom no pre-Sullan magisterial forebears are discoverable. At best, they are a small minority. Not that the men themselves were insignificant—capturing of prætorian office without precursors in the *curia* was no mean feat. Hence one might expect some individuals with talent, accomplishments, or loyalty to politicians with influence. Some of these *novi homines* went on to play prominent and conspicuous roles, belying their obscure origins.

The Tullii Cicerones spring immediately to mind. Quintus was carried to political success in large part by his brother's repute. The elder Cicero abandoned a municipal background to acquire renown through oratorical performances and an astute fostering of connections. Political courage and a penchant for the spectacular would call some *novi homines* to the attention of more powerful figures, thereby earning patronage and advance. So, for example, one may note T. Annius Milo, of Lanuvine family, whose exploits in the streets won the support of Pompeius Magnus; or Vatinius, perhaps from a recently enfranchised Marsian house, whom Cæsar found to be a loyal and effective adherent; or M. Favonius, who attached himself to Cato and rose from municipal origins in Terracina to attain prætorian rank at the end of

[39] Cic. *Pro Sulla*, 62: *ornatissimum virum.*

[40] See Cichorius, *Hermes*, 41 (1906): 59–68; Taylor, *Voting Districts*, p. 261. It is best to leave out of account "P. Valerius" cited as a prætor in 73 by Appian, *BC*, 1.116. He is probably a phantom, a mistake for P. Varinius who did exercise a prætorship in that year; Münzer, *Philologus*, 55 (1896): 387–389.

the Republic.[41] The benefactions of an imposing politician also explain the emergence of the Arrii, prætors in 73 and ca. 64; the resources of M. Crassus stood behind them. And they may have stood behind C. Coponius, prætor in 49, a former officer under Crassus.[42] Others made their reputations through activist tribunates. Energetic holders of that office could win popular credit or appeal to special-interest groups. One may notice L. Quinctius and M. Lollius Palicanus, ardent reformers as tribunes in the 70s, the successful prætorian candidates in the 60s. Lowly derivations are attested for both; conscious catering to popular interests enabled them to overcome that handicap. Similarly, L. Roscius Otho, as tribune in 67, sponsored legislation to enhance the *dignitas* of the *equester ordo,* a posture that no doubt smoothed a path to his prætorship of 63. A relative (perhaps), L. Roscius Fabatus, reached the office in 49. He may be associated with an agrarian measure during his tribunate of 55; and of equal relevance were years of service in Gaul under Julius Cæsar. A. Allienus enjoyed a parallel career: colleague of Roscius Fabatus in the tribunate and praetorship and cosponsor of the *lex agraria;* he later served Cæsar in the civil war. L. Flavius' tribunician bill for land distribution in 60 failed of passage. But the gesture gave him useful backing for a prætorship in 58. And notice T. Labienus, who advocated *popularis* and Pompeian causes as tribune in 63 and rose to a prætorship by 59.[43] Exceptional military qualities might bring a few men from modest beginnings to a senatorial career and even to prætorian station: for example, the old soldier M. Petreius, who carried a lengthy record in war to his prætorship in 64, and beyond; and C. Pomptinus, a legate of Crassus' in the 70s, prætor in 63, and a man praised for martial prowess. The sources know them as *homines militares.*[44]

[41] On the origins of these men, see Taylor, *Voting Districts,* pp. 190, 213, 262–263, Milo is not to be associated with the consular Annii of the second century, *pace* Wiseman, *New Men,* p. 213, no. 30. Such a connection would hardly have been omitted by Asconius, 53, Clark–or in Cicero's *Pro Milone*; Taylor, *Voting Districts,* p. 190.

[42] There were Coponii in the senate of the second century, but with different *prænomina.* C. Coponius comes from a Latin family enfranchised late in that century; Cic. *Pro Balbo,* 53. On the Arrii, see, esp., Cic. *Brutus,* 242–243, and above, chap. 2, n.113. The family may stem from Formiæ; cf. Taylor, *Voting Districts,* p. 193. Some have urged that these two Arrii are the same man; cf. Syme, *CP,* 50 (1955): 133; Wiseman, *New Men,* p. 214, no. 37. But that requires rejection of the explicit evidence of Schol. Gronov. 324, Stangl.

[43] See Broughton, *MRR,* under the relevant years. Inadvertently, he leaves out Labienus; but see his index, II:578. Labienus certainly reached the prætorship before going to Gaul; see Hirtius, *BG,* 8.52. On the humble origins of Quinctius and Lollius Palicanus, see Cic. *Pro Cluent.* 112; Sallust, *Hist.* 4.43, Maur. Further on Lollius, cf. the remarks of Badian, *Historia,* 12 (1963): 137–138, and Wiseman, *New Men,* pp. 237–238, no. 231. The Roscii may derive from Lanuvium; Taylor, *Voting Districts,* p. 251. On Allienus, cf. Wiseman, *New Men,* p. 211, no. 21.

[44] Sallust, *Cat.* 45.2, 59.6; cf. on Petreius, Cic. *Pro Sest.* 12: *mirificus usu in re militari.* On qualities generally demanded of *novi homines* who hoped for office, cf. Wiseman, *New Men,* pp. 116–122, 173–181.

For the *novus homo,* however, even visible endowments and industry were rarely sufficient. High office demanded patronage. Most of the prætors who could point to no senatorial predecessors may be associated with one or another of Rome's leading politicians or political families. Pompeian supporters abound in this crew. We have noticed already Milo, Labienus, Lollius Palicanus, L. Flavius, and M. Petreius. Add also T. Ampius Balbus, Pompey's unsuccessful consular candidate in 55,[45] and perhaps the otherwise unknown C. Attius Celsus, prætor in 65, who urged Cicero to take up the cause of Pompey's tribune C. Manilius.[46] And there is Gutta, to whose consular aspirations Pompey gave hope in late 54.[47] Finally, a connection with Pompey is attested for L. Culleolus, prætor ca. 60.[48] Cæsar was active as well in promoting *novi homines.* Among his prætorian partisans one may list Vatinius, Allienus, and Roscius Fabatus. There were others. Cæsar's brother-in-law M. Atius Balbus rose from municipal origins to prætorian rank by 59. C. Octavius, heir to a respectable and wealthy equestrian family from Velitræ, married Cæsar's niece, achieved a prætorship in 61, and was balked of a consulate, so later reports had it, only by premature death.[49] The obscure C. Alfius Flavus had Cæsar's backing in his prætorian canvass of 57. That effort miscarried, but Alfius seems to have been successful in a second effort for 54.[50] And perhaps we should include P. Attius Varus, prætor ca. 53. His kinsman Q. Attius Varus was serving as Cæsar's *præfectus equitum* at about the same time.[51] M. Crassus did not normally push his clients as far as the prætorship. But Q. Arrius reached it; C. Pomptinus and L. Quinctius had begun military careers under Crassus in the campaign against Spartacus, and C. Coponius in the Par-

[45] There is a C. Ampius listed as a prefect in 201; Broughton, *MRR*, I:322; but no reason to postulate a connection. L. Flavius had backing from both Pompey and Cæsar; Cic. *Ad Q. Frat.* 1.2.11.

[46] Asconius, 65, Clark. For his origin, perhaps from Amiternum, see Syme, *Historia*, 13 (1964): 113. He may be the man mentioned by Varro as enrolled into the senate; Nonius, 199, L; Wiseman, *New Men*, p. 279, no. 522.

[47] Cic. *Ad Q. Frat.* 3.8.6. There is no need to emend to "Cotta" here. Gutta did have a predecessor in the senate of the 70s. But the family cannot be traced beyond Sulla.

[48] Cic. *Ad Fam.* 13.41, 13.42. Culleolus is perhaps a Cornelius Culleolus; Cicero attests to such a man in 87; *De Div.* 1.4. Whether the family was senatorial, however, remains uncertain.

[49] On Octavius, see Vell. Pat. 2.59.2; Suet. *Aug.* 2–4. Suetonius' statement, *Aug.* 4.1, that Atius Balbus possessed several senatorial predecessors is evidently based on a mistaken interpretation of Cic. *Phil.* 3.16; see Wiseman, *Historia*, 14 (1965): 333.

[50] He presided over two criminal courts in that year, no doubt as prætor; Broughton, *MRR*, II:227, n.3. For Cæsar's support in 57, see Cic. *In Vat.* 38. On Alfius' municipal origins, see Wiseman, *New Men*, p. 211, no. 20.

[51] That P. Attius Varus served the Pompeian cause against Cæsar in 49 is not to the point. That conflict shattered many previous attachments.

thian war. The associates of Lucullus and Cato consisted primarily of *nobiles.* But M. Favonius was an exception. And notice should be taken of C. Valerius Triarius, a prætor in 78 who aided the government's cause–and that of Q. Catulus–against the rebel M. Lepidus. Triarius, despite his rank, went on to serve under the younger L. Lucullus in Asia until 67. His family also had close ties with that of M. Cato.[52]

Evidence on the few remaining prætors is too flimsy to permit conclusion on associations or background. Only two of them, so far as is known, L. Turius and M. Cæsonius, were bold enough to seek consulships–in vain.[53] Two others were clients of Cicero in the mid 60s, C. Orchivius from Præneste and Q. Gallius.[54] M. Juncus, the prætor of 76, later prosecuted by Cæsar, probably belongs to the Junii Junci, a senatorial house in the early Empire.[55] But no prior member of the clan shows up in our records. Modest backgrounds may be assumed for two prætors of 73, P. Varinius and L. Cossinius. The latter hailed from Tibur, the first of his family to attain Roman franchise.[56] The *cognomen* of T. Vettius Sabinus, possibly a prætor in 59, need not reflect his origins. And testimony fails altogether on the derivations of C. Megabocchus, C. Septimius, C. Considius Longus, P. Orbius, and C. Sosius. The latter won his prætorship only in the last year before civil war.[57] Finally, there is M. Mummius, prætor in 70. The *gentilicium* is known in senatorial families, but not with that *prænomen.* Caution prohibits assigning him forebears in the senate.

So much for prætors whose senatorial ancestry was lacking–or unattested. Forty individuals have been placed under that heading. Again the number may be too high. Express evidence for *novitas* exists for some; but for most it is only the silence of the sources which has relegated them to that category. Several of the latter may have had precursors in the *curia,* traces of whose presence have vanished. Even if one retains the maximum figure, however, it constitutes a small minority of the one hundred seventy-eight prætors known.[58]

[52] Asconius, 18–19, Clark. Triarius is not, of course, to be linked to the patrician Valerii. The family may originate from Fundi; cf. Taylor, *Voting Districts,* pp. 261–262. On connections and interrelationships between senatorial houses and municipal families generally, see Wiseman, *New Men,* pp. 33–64.

[53] Cic. *Ad Att.* 1.1.1–2; *Brutus,* 237; cf. Shackleton Bailey, *Cicero's Letters,* I:290, 292–293.

[54] On Orchivius' provenance, see Taylor, *Voting Districts,* p. 240.

[55] Cf. Broughton, *MRR,* II:100, n.6.

[56] Cic. *Pro Balbo,* 53–54.

[57] On the hazards of employing *cognomina* to deduce provenance, see Badian, *JRS,* 52(1962): 209; and note Cic. *Ad Fam.* 15.20.1. Vettius' prætorship is by no means certain; see Gruen, *Latomus* (forthcoming). On Megabocchus, evidently a prætor some time before 54, see Cic. *Pro Scauro,* 40. Syme, *Rom. Rev.,* p. 200, supports Picene origins for C. Sosius.

[58] The total of one hundred seventy-eight is not, of course, sacrosanct. To arrive at the

Statistics can be deceptive for any period, and especially when there is much that is uncertain. But we are better informed on the Ciceronian age than on any other comparable era in antiquity. It is open to anyone to shift certain individuals from one category to another; effect on the general totals cannot be significant. A few important conclusions may be safely drawn. Though the number of annual prætors received an increase after Sulla, access to the office remained restricted by traditional criteria. Consular ancestry virtually guaranteed election to the prætorship; prætorian ancestry was only slightly less useful. If both qualifications were lacking, senatorial precursors afforded eligibility. Those three groups account for nearly 80 percent of the attested prætors in the Republic's last generation. Of the purported *novi homines* who secured the post, a few owed success to capacity and industry, most to association with prominent political leaders. Only a tiny proportion of men from non-consular families moved from the prætorship into the chief magistracy: eight, to be precise—and three of them had to await the Cæsarian or triumviral periods.[59] The narrowness of the aristocratic bottleneck was unchanged. The established hierarchy shows no discernible shift in structure or personnel.

THE ÆDILES

Analogous documentation is unavailable on the ædiles. One can hardly make a pretense at statistical evaluation here. Four ædiles were elected each year: two curule ædiles and two plebeian ædiles. In the thirty years under consideration, therefore, one hundred twenty men acquired the office. Scrappy testimony—with several *incerti*—turns up only forty-eight of that number. The ædileship was not a requisite part of the *cursus honorum*. Men of some wealth would often seek the post, employing it to sponsor games and shows and thereby to procure added popularity in the quest for higher office. But many *nobiles* chose to avoid it altogether, relying on their names or husbanding their resources for prætorian campaigns. Analysis of ædilician personnel will tell us only a little of the aristocratic social structure, especially in view of gaps in the evidence. The results may be briefly surveyed.

---

figure one must excise some dubious individuals on Broughton's lists: "P. Valerius" in 73 is almost certainly a mistake for P. Varinius. For "Q. Curius" in 67 should be substituted L. Turius, consular candidate in 65. And three alleged prætors in 54 should be removed: "Domitius" is best identified with the prætor of 56, Postumius' military service in 49 does not imply a prior prætorship, and C. Cosconius is based on the questionable reading of an inscription which is itself probably post-Republican; on the last, see Syme, *CP*, 50 (1955): 130. Among the prætors of uncertain date listed by Broughton, *MRR*, II:462–466, it has been thought safest to include only three, Ti. Claudius Nero and M. Terentius Varro, who certainly fall in this period, and L. Titius, who very probably does.

[59] Namely, Volcacius Tullus, cos. 66, M. Cicero, cos. 63, Murena, cos. 62, Afranius, cos. 60, Gabinius, cos. 58, Vatinius, cos. 47, Fufius Calenus, cos. 47, and Scribonius Libo, cos. 34.

Preserved ædilician names are too few to allow substantial conclusions. But the proportions are worth recording. They provide revealing parallels with the prætorian *fasti.* Over 40 percent of the known or conjectured ædiles derive from families of the consular *nobilitas.* Fifteen men are certain in this list; another six may be reckoned as possibilities, but no more than possibilities.[60] Some old and distinguished clans show representatives on the ædilician *fasti* of the Ciceronian age: a Sulpicius Galba, a Calpurnius Piso, a Cornelius Lentulus, a Licinius Crassus, a Cæcilius Metellus, a Fabius Maximus, a Claudius Marcellus, and two Æmilii Lepidi. The lists also contain some of the most prominent politicians of the era: Cæsar, Hortensius, Bibulus, Domitius Ahenobarbus, Clodius. Twelve of them went on to consulships, four others to the prætorship. Only five did not advance to higher office: murder terminated P. Clodius' career, judicial condemnation that of L. Bestia; Visellius Varro died prematurely not long after his ædileship; and M. Octavius may have perished in the civil war. Not all *nobiles* bothered with ædilician *comitia.* But it is clear that those who did were generally winners, and could proceed swiftly beyond.[61]

[60] Consular names in the ædileship, culled from Broughton's collection, total twenty-two. But Q. Metellus Celer, allegedly ædile in 67, is best dropped. The story in Val. Max. 6.1.8 need not imply an ædileship. Nor is it entirely clear that he refers to the future consul of 60. One must also remove a L. Calpurnius Bestia. Broughton gives two of them: ædiles in 59 and 57. But even if these are two separate individuals, only one is an attested ædile; Cic. *Phil.* 13.26. Four other men must remain questionable entries. P. Licinius Crassus Dives is inserted in 60 on the grounds that he was *iudex quæstionis* in the following year. That such posts normally went to ex-ædiles has been argued with plausibility. But it cannot be regarded as an inflexible rule; cf. the remarks of J. Seidel, *Fasti ædilicii von der Einrichtung der plebejischen Ädilität bis zum Tode Cæsars* (Breslau, 1908), pp. 50–51. A postulated ædileship for Q. Metellus Scipio rests only on his sponsorship of gladiatorial games in 57; Cic. *Pro Sest.* 124; Schol. Bob. 137, Stangl. Seidel, *Fasti ædilicii*, pp. 84–85, is properly skeptical. L. Æmilius Paullus Lepidus began work on the Basilica Æmilia ca. 55; Cic. *Ad Att.* 4.16.8–the reference is wrongly recorded by Broughton, *MRR,* II:216. That may, but need not, suggest an ædileship. Ædilician office for M. Æmilius Lepidus ca. 53 depends on his role as *interrex* in the following year; Willems, *Le Sénat*, II:10–14; Seidel, *Fasti ædilicii*, p. 70. Probabilities are in its favor, but that is all. Among the ædiles of consular family one must include M. Octavius, who attained the office in 50. But not C. Octavius, ædile ca. 64. The former was son of a Cnæus, doubtless the consul of 76. Consular Octavii go back to the mid-second century. The forebears of C. Octavius, Cæsar's *adfinis*, however, were equestrian. C. Flaminius, ædile ca. 67, is here reckoned of consular stock. The *prænomen* indicates connection with the C. Flaminii of the late third and early second centuries. Wiseman, *New Men*, p. 231, no. 179, lists him as a *novus*–but without argument. Also, C. Visellius Varro, a learned jurisconsult and a cousin of Cicero's. The Visellii do not appear in earlier magistracies, but the *cognomen* suggests adoption by the Terentii Varrones; cf. Taylor, *Voting Districts*, p. 266. On Visellius, see Cic. *Brutus*, 264; cf. *De Orat.* 2.2; *De Prov. Cons.* 40.

[61] Cicero's *Pro Plancio* should be read in the light of these statistics. Though the speech is devoted to justifying the election of an *eques* to the ædileship, it does not disguise the

Our sparse data can disclose only four ædiles of prætorian lineage. Two of them are certain. C. Licinius Murena, younger brother of the consul of 62, whose ancestors included three prætors, acquired ædilician rank ca. 59. And C. Cosconius, ædile in 57, could look back to prætorian kinsmen in the second century. A third man, Nonius, is described as holder of a curule office. That could mean a prætorship, though more probably an ædileship. He was, no doubt, a Nonius Sufenas. A precursor had been prætor in 81.[62] The fourth was P. Nigidius Figulus, future prætor of 58. His activity in 60 indicates an ædileship in that year.[63] Again, we may be sure, the number would rise appreciably if information revealed more than a fraction of the personnel.

Nine more men can claim senatorial pedigree. For five of them ædileships are specifically recorded: C. Junius, M. Plætorius, C. Vergilius Balbus, L. Appuleius, and A. Plautius. Four others appear also to have held the office in this period: Q. Curtius, Q. Voconius Naso, Q. Marcius Crispus, and C. Vibius Pansa.[64]

We are left with fourteen *novi homines* who gained ædilician station in the late Republic: less than 30 percent of the preserved total of forty-eight names. That proportion is not far different from figures calculated on the prætorship. And, once again, the emergence of most of the new men can be tied to associations with prominent politicians. M. Crassus' patronage accelerated the early careers of Cn. Plancius and M. Cælius Rufus.[65] Connections with the family of Julius Cæsar help explain the rise of C. Octavius and C. Toranius.[66] Powerful support also lay behind the triumviral adherent C.

---

fact that *nobiles* and men of senatorial families usually possessed an inside track to the office. See, esp., Cic. *Pro Planc.* 10: *eos, qui suffragium ferant, quid cuique ipsi debeant, considerare sæpius, quam, quid cuique a re publica debeatur*; 50: *numquam enim fere nobilitas, integra præsertim atque innocens, a populo Romano supplex repudiata fuit.* Cf. also 7, 12, 15, 17, 18, 23, 51–53, 59.

[62] On Nonius, see Catullus, 52; and below, chap. 8, n.24. Note also the Nonius, candidate for the tribunate in 101 and described by Appian as ἐπιφανὴς ἀνήρ; *BC*, 1.28.

[63] So, rightly, Kroll, *RE*, 17:201, "Nigidius"; now accepted by Broughton, *MRR, Suppl.*, p. 42. But see Badian, *Studies*, p. 143.

[64] Curtius and Voconius served as *iudices quæstionis* in 70 and 66; hence, probably, ex-ædiles. Marcius Crispus was very likely *ædilicius* by the time of his service in Macedon in the mid-50s; Syme, *CP*, 50 (1955): 135. His ancestry is unknown. But Q. Marcii are attested in the second century; Broughton, *MRR*, II:587. On Pansa's postulated ædileship in 49, see Broughton, *MRR*, II:258. A Cæsarian officer and adherent, he was son of a moneyer in the 80s; Gundel, *RE*, 8A:1954, "Vibius," n.16; Taylor, *Voting Districts*, p. 265.

[65] On these associations, see above, p. 74. Cicero's claim, *Pro Planc.* 60, that countless others of Plancius' background had attained similar office is standard hyperbole.

[66] Octavius, as noted earlier, was Cæsar's nephew by marriage and father of the future *princeps* Augustus. Toranius, of obscure origins, was Augustus' tutor and guardian; Suet. *Aug.*

Messius, Cato's friend M. Favonius, and the brothers Cicero, all of whom reached the ædileship in this period. Six men lack recorded patrons among key senatorial figures: L. Voluscius (or Volscius), L. Lartius, C. Annæus, M. Seius, M. Cæsonius, and Q. Gallius. Gaps in our evidence prevent reconstruction of what may have been influential backing in those cases also.[67]

It bears repetition that our testimony on ædiles is distressingly flimsy: forty-eight (more or less) known office holders out of the one hundred twenty elected in the Ciceronian era. But examination of their social ancestry produces results not very different from those discovered among the far more numerous prætors. Nearly half stemmed from consular families; that background was a certain passport to success with the voters. And, overall, senatorial lineage accounts for approximately 70 percent of the ædiles. *Novi homines* required assiduous and important patronage, for this office as for the prætorship. For most of the attested new men who secured it, that patronage is demonstrable. The Ciceronian age shows no easier entrance to ædilician posts than previous periods. Conventional criteria for the higher levels of senatorial rank remained firmly in force.

THE TRIBUNES

The tribunate was a different matter—or so one might expect. It played no official role in the *cursus honorum.* Technically, the tribunate was not even a magistracy, rather an institution created by the *plebs,* designed to protect and promote the interests of the commons. It gave scope for progressive, even radical legislation, or, at least, pronouncements. The character of the post led many politicians to shun it. M. Tullius Cicero, aiming to project an image of respectability, avoided the tribunate and sought ædilician office instead.

---

27. That he proceeded to a prætorship is possible but unlikely; see Broughton, *MRR, Suppl.*, p. 63; contra: Willems, *Le Sénat*, II:466–467.

[67] Volscius, Lartius, and Annæus appear on a *consilium* of 73, all apparently of ædilician rank; Broughton, *MRR*, II:115. On Annæus, cf. Syme, *Historia*, 13 (1964): 110–111. He is doubtless identical with Annæus Brocchus mentioned in Cic. *Verr.* 2.3.93, and perhaps also with the senator named as Ἀμναῖος by Plut. *Cato*, 19.5; cf. Wiseman, *New Men*, p. 211, no. 22. Volscius is probably to be identified with a certain Volscius, legate in Bithynia in 73; Sallust, *Hist.* 3.59, Maur. On the name, see Badian, *Gnomon*, 33 (1961): 498. One other alleged ædile, M. Aufidius Lurco, has here been excluded. Willems, *Le Sénat*, I:491, inserts him in 52, followed by Broughton, *MRR*, II:235. But Willems' arguments had already been countered by Seidel, *Fasti ædilicii*, pp. 87–88. Plut. *Cato*, 46.4, records a certain Δουριων in the ædileship of that year. Seidel emends to Κουρίων. In that case, reference is doubtless to C. Curio, tribune in 50. Since Curio was in Asia in 53, he is not likely to have been ædile in 52. Seidel's conjecture still seems best: Curio sponsored lavish funeral games in honor of his father, who had recently perished, from which Plutarch erroneously inferred that he was ædile; cf. Pliny, *NH*, 36.116–120.

Here, if anywhere, there should have been a haven for men without illustrious genealogy, an avenue for *novi homines* to acquire popular favor and advance to positions of influence in the ruling class. The tribunician college numbered ten men annually. And Romans of patrician blood were ineligible for the office. Hence there was room–and inducement–for scions of lesser families and *gentes* new to the political arena. Such men, one might anticipate, should have dominated the tribunician lists. That is not the case. Examination of available data will dispose of the notion.

The record once again is incomplete. If all were known, we could list three hundred tribunes in the Ciceronian age. But the sources vouchsafe us only somewhat more than one-third of that sum. Still, the sample is not insignificant. One hundred thirteen names can be culled from the evidence, almost all certain.[68] The proportion of *nobiles,* senatorial families, and *novi homines,* for reasons noted above, do not follow closely the lines of prætors and ædiles. But the differences, one may learn with surprise, are far less striking than the similarities.

Consular pedigree would not necessarily predispose a young aristocrat toward the tribunate. But, though the office was closed to patricians, there is no lack of plebeian *nobiles* on the tribunician lists between 78 and 49. As many as thirty-three can be discovered, most with assurance. That represents almost 30 percent of the recorded tribunes.

As a group they do not possess the luster of the late Republican prætors and ædiles. Several men, it seems, sought the post to revive the political fortunes of families whose consulates were already dimmed by antiquity. Others were from houses which had acquired consular *dignitas* for the first time in the previous generation. For example, C. Licinius Macer, a reformist tribune in 73, claimed descent from consuls of the fourth century–but his line had produced none since then. A single consulship had ennobled the house of Q. Minucius Thermus, tribune in 62, and that was four generations earlier. Similarly, Ælius Ligus: well over a century elapsed between his sole consular ancestor and his own career.[69] Note also C. Visellius Varro the jurist–a cousin of Cicero's–if, as is likely, he was adopted by a Terentius Varro. Other tribunes resuscitated clans that were powerful in the Gracchan era but lacking in members of prominence since then: Q. Opimius, C. Popillius, and C. Fannius.[70]

[68] In addition to Broughton's *MRR,* one should consult, especially, G. Niccolini's *Fasti dei Tribuni della Plebe* (Milan, 1934).

[69] Ligus, as tribune in 58, was an adherent of Clodius and a bitter opponent of Cicero. Hence, one will not take literally the orator's vindictive remark that Ligus wrongly appropriated his ancestry; *Pro Sest.* 69: *cognomen sibi ex Æliorum imaginibus arripuit.* There is no good reason to doubt his descent from the consul of 172.

[70] That C. Popillius, tribune in 68, was a Popillius Lænas is not certain but probable. He is perhaps identical with the Popillius Lænas registered as a senator in 44; Plut. *Brut.*

Among those whose houses achieved *nobilitas* only in the previous generation were C. Antonius, P. Rutilius Lupus, and C. Scribonius Curio.[71]

Scions of more prestigious lines, however, are also to be found in the tribunate. The eminent Cæcilii Metelli certainly did not scorn the post. There may have been as many as four Metelli among late Republican tribunes.[72] The Cassii Longini contributed three men to the tribunician lists. Two of them came in 49: C. Cassius Longinus, a bitter enemy of Cæsar's and his future assassin, and Q. Cassius Longinus, an ardent Cæsarian. Obviously, those individuals were not elected for their politics. The fact reemphasizes once more that down to the very eve of civil war elections operated on conventional lines. The cousins split irrevocably in 49; that was of no concern to the voters, who endorsed both men: the prestige of the Cassian *gens* was sufficient.[73] Similarly, both M. Cato and C. Cato, who had no common ground politically, served in tribunician office: the history of their *gens* provided requisite credentials. Other clans of lofty prominence supplied tribunes in the Ciceronian age: the Cornelii Lentuli, Papirii Carbones, Mucii Scævolæ, Atilii Serrani, Domitii, Licinii Crassi, Pompeii, Aurelii Cottæ, and Marcii Philippi–and, of course, P. Clodius Pulcher, who doffed his patrician status to gain eligibility

15–16; Appian, *BC*, 2.115–116. The last consular Popillius came in 132. One should include here also L. Calpurnius Bestia, tribune in 62, a descendant, perhaps a grandson, of the consul of 111, though the latter was his *gens'* only representative in the chief magistracy.

[71] Antonius was son of the consul of 99, Lupus probably son of the consul of 90. Curio's father was consul in 76; therefore not, strictly speaking, pre-Sullan. But the elder Curio's career was somewhat delayed by civil strife and exile. One may note too C. Antonius' nephew, M. Antonius, the future triumvir, who obtained his tribunate in 49.

[72] We can be definite about two: Metellus Nepos, a volatile tribune in 62, and L. Metellus who boldly defied Cæsar in 49, denying him access to the *ærarium*. The other two are less certain. Cic. *De Imp. Pomp.* 58 lists four men who served as legates in the year following their tribunates. One was a Q. Metellus. Wiseman, *CQ*, 14 (1964): 122–123, identifies him with Q. Metellus Creticus, consul in 69, and suggests a tribunate in 82 or 81–therefore just outside the period of concern here. But Wiseman may place too much emphasis on the order of names given by Cicero. They need not have been in order of seniority. More likely, reference is to Q. Metellus Celer, who can be amalgamated with the Q. Cæcilius on an inscription evidently recording the tribunician college of 68; *ILS*, 5800; cf. Syme, *JRS*, 53 (1963): 55–60. The fourth Metellus is Q. Metellus Scipio, whom Broughton places in 59–without a query; *MRR*, II:189. The only evidence is Cic. *Ad Att.* 2.1.9, which speaks of an electoral contest between Metellus and Favonius. It was, apparently, a supplementary election, possibly for the tribunate, but perhaps for the ædileship; so Taylor, *Studies Ullmann* (1964), I:79–85. Other references cited by Broughton–Val. Max. 9.1.8; Cic. *In Vat.* 16–are not to the point.

[73] There is a third Cassius, evidently a tribune, mentioned as a Clodian supporter in 56; Cic. *Ad Q. Frat.* 2.1.2. Shackleton Bailey, *PCPS*, 187 (1961): 1, wishes to emend him out of existence, suggesting Caninius as a substitute–for no good reason. Note, e.g., the L. Cassius who later appears as a prefect in 48; Broughton, *MRR*, II:283.

for the post.[74] Lastly, one may take note of the agrarian reformer, P. Servilius Rullus, tribune in 63. Cicero's character assassination notwithstanding, Rullus publicly boasted of his *nobilitas,* a claim not to be taken lightly.[75]

The total of thirty-three *nobiles* is not so impressive as comparable figures for the prætorship and ædileship. But the reasons are clear. Patricians were barred from the post. Other men of noble ancestry did not need it, or chose to stay away from the image it represented. But aristocrats whose line had been ennobled only in the previous generation or whose ancestors had lacked consulships for a century and more found it a useful vehicle whereby to advance their public careers. *Nobiles* from more prominent stock appear less frequently in the tribunate than in curule office. But numerous examples have been noted. The tribunate did not lack distinguished representatives.

Tribunes of prætorian descent also turn up in the lists; thirteen are discoverable. Most seem to have employed the office as a stepping-stone toward prætorian rank themselves. One only, A. Gabinius, rose as high as the consulship. Others emulated their forefathers in winning prætorships: C. Memmius, the tribune of 66, C. Cæcilius Cornutus, Q. Ancharius, and M. Nonius Sufenas. Each of these found the tribunate suitable for conspicuous activity, which kept him in the public eye. Gabinius advocated progressive legislation; Memmius became involved in judicial actions; Ancharius was a vociferous opponent of the triumvirate in 59, Nonius an energetic adherent in the turbulent electoral maneuvering of 56; and Cornutus seems to have been a staunch and rigid

[74] Some comments are necessary on a few of these individuals. Cn. Lentulus is another of those ex-tribunes who became legates, mentioned, without date, in Cic. *De Imp. Pomp.* 58. He too should be linked to the tribunician college of 68, which includes a Cn. Cornelius; *ILS*, 5800. The man is, very likely, Cn. Lentulus Marcellinus, future consul of 56; Syme, *JRS*, 53 (1963): 55–56. Cotta, listed by Broughton as tribune in 49, should be marked with a query. Lucan, 3.114–168, gives him a speech restraining L. Metellus from foolhardy action against Cæsar. Possibly he was a tribune–like L. Metellus–but no more than possibly. No Aurelius Cotta is ready at hand with whom to identify him. But note "Aurelius," an officer, perhaps a legate, in the Cæsarian forces in 45; Cic. *Ad Att.* 14.9.3. Q. Mucius Scævola, tribune in 54, certainly came from the distinguished clan which had already produced six Roman consuls. So, surely, did Q. Mucius Orestinus, tribune in 64. No other Mucii are known in the Republic but Mucii Scævolæ. Orestinus was evidently adopted into the family. And the *cognomen* suggests that he was born an Aurelius Orestes, also a consular *gens.* Sex. Atilius Serranus Gavianus, tribune in 57 and opponent of Cicero's recall, was defamed by the orator, apparently with slurs on his parentage; Cic. *Pro Sest.* 72. But the text is corrupt, and little should be made of the tendentious remark. In any case, Atilius' career was promoted by the house into which he was adopted–the Atilii Serrani, who produced three consuls in the second century.

[75] Cic. *De Leg. Agrar.* 2.19. Perhaps he derived from the Servilii Gemini, a prominent family since the late third century. Rullus' father was a man of means; Pliny, *NH*, 8.210–possibly the *monetalis* of ca. 100; see Syme, *Hermes*, 92 (1964): 410; Sumner, *TAPA*, 97 (1966): 571–572.

conservative—a "Pseudo-Cato," Cicero termed him.[76] Of the remainder, some may also have gone on to the prætorship: L. Hostilius Dasianus, a restive character; C. Cosconius; Q. Terentius Culleo; L. Caninius Gallus; P. Aquillius Gallus; C. Memmius, the tribune of 54; and Rubrius. But absence of testimony forbids the citing of particulars.[77] In this number too belongs Cn. Sicinius, a vocal and energetic advocate of tribunician reform in 76, whose career was terminated by political opponents. The family had vanished into obscurity since the eminent Cn. Sicinius of the early second century, who had twice won election to the prætorship.[78] For purposes of advancement through senatorial ranks, men of prætorian extraction found the tribunate an eminently serviceable institution.

Evidence becomes less tractable thereafter. Another sixty-seven tribunes are variously registered in the sources. To distinguish between the *novi homines* and the men with predecessors in the *curia* is not always easy. Conclusions must often rest on conjecture and probabilities. But a rough reckoning is possible.

For twenty-nine of this number senatorial genealogy is, at least, a reasonable surmise. In several instances the family may be better than merely senatorial—possibly prætorian, or even consular. Ambiguous data, however, do not permit secure application of the latter labels. Various individuals fall into this marginal category. Among them are two Fabii, tribunes ca. 64 and 55.[79] Obviously, they do not belong to the patrician Fabii, but there may be relation to C. Fabius Hadrianus, the prætor of 84.[80] Possibly too the otherwise unknown Terentius who was tribune in 54. It would be rash to insist that he was a Terentius Varro. But several other Terentii sat in the Roman senate, including three prætors from the early second century. Mamilius, known only as co-author of an agrarian bill ca. 55, may have had eminent ancestors in the distant past. The *gens* shows plebeian consuls and prætors in the third century.

[76] On Cornutus, see Cic. *Ad Att.* 1.14.6: *Cornuto vero Pseudocatone.* References on the others are collected by Broughton, *MRR*, under the appropriate years.

[77] Of this group, only Rubrius' tribunate is uncertain, though probable; Broughton, *MRR*, II:259. He very likely stems from the prætorian Rubrius of 129; Taylor, *Voting Districts*, p. 251. The connection is implicitly denied by Wiseman, *New Men*, pp. 256–257, no. 363. Caninius Gallus' ancestry is not attested. But association with the Caninii Rebili, who show a prætor in 171, is a reasonable possibility; cf. Syme, *Historia*, 13 (1964): 114. On Dasianus, see Sallust, *Hist.* 4.55, Maur. Though born a Dasius, he was evidently adopted by the Hostilii Catones, a prætorian family of the third and second centuries; Münzer, *RE*, 8:2505–2506, "Hostilius," n.13.

[78] On Sicinius, see above, chap. 1, n.52. It is noteworthy that no imputations of low birth stand against him, as they do against other militant tribunes of the 70s, L. Quinctius and Lollius Palicanus.

[79] The dates are not certain; cf. Broughton, *MRR*, II:162, 164, n.4, 217.

[80] The *prænomen* "Gaius" is attested for the tribune of 55.

His connection with those *nobiles* is speculative; more likely he is associated with the Mamilii Limetani, senators in the late second and early first centuries. A similar conjecture is possible for P. Cornelius, registered as tribune in 51. The patrician Cornelii, naturally, cannot be considered, but the Cornelii Sisennæ, a prætorian house, employed the *prænomen* "Publius."[81] C. Herennius, a tribune in 60, was son of a Sextus, and therefore not immediately connected to the consul of 93, M. Herennius. But he may be adjudged at least of senatorial heritage.[82] Finally, there is L. Marius, a reformist tribune and collaborator with Cato in 62. He was certainly not in the direct line of the great C. Marius. But other branches of the Marii had also attained prominence in earlier generations. For none of the preceding can one assert with conclusiveness that forebears are to be found on the consular or prætorian lists. But they ought not, in any case, be denied senatorial background.

Several others fall into this bracket. Some moved from tribunates to prætorships, thereby further elevating families that had already possessed senatorial standing: Q. Cornificius, P. Servilius Globulus, L. Cæcilius Rufus, Q. Fufius Calenus, C. Curtius Peducæanus, P. Sestius, A. Plautius, and C. Vibius Pansa. The remainder show demonstrable antecedents in the *curia.* L. Volcacius, tribune in 68, surely belongs to the Volcacii Tulli, a respected clan, which two years later produced its first consul.[83] His colleague C. Fundanius achieved little prominence. But the family could already boast senators by the time of Sulla, and perhaps much earlier. Two Antistii held tribunates in the mid-50s. That clan shows several senators in the preceding periods. Cicero's friend Sex. Peducæus was son of a prætor in the 70s and descendant of another tribune from the late second century. C. Lucilius Hirrus, a cousin of Pompey's and advocate of his dictatorship in 53, stemmed from a senatorial family prominent already in the second century. Another Pompeian tribune, T. Munatius Plancus Bursa, was turbulent and disruptive in office in 52. His ancestors were more respectable. The clan was Tiburtine, but a Munatius, probably Bursa's parent, was a Sullan officer during the eastern wars of the 80s. Still other friends of Pompey appear on the tribunician lists: Plautius, possibly a tribune in 70, and D. Lælius, who held the office in 54. The latter is probably not heir to the consular Lælii of the second century. But his father, a legate of Pompey's in 76, was a respected figure and may have had senatorial status

[81] Cf. Taylor, *Voting Districts*, p. 207.

[82] Cic. *Ad Att.* 1.18.4. Despite Nicolet, *L'Ordre Equestre*, p. 262, the passage does not suggest that Herennius' father was an *eques.* Wiseman, *New Men*, p. 235, no. 204, takes Cicero's outburst, *homo nequam atque egens*, to imply *novitas; Ad Att.* 1.19.5. But there was a C. Herennius in the senate in 129; Taylor, *Voting Districts*, p. 173.

[83] The effort of Syme, *JRS*, 53 (1963): 59–60, to identify the tribune of 68 and the consul of 66 is unconvincing.

before the Sullan dictatorship.[84] Finally, there is Q. Manlius, tribune in 69, whom Cicero, depending on his immediate purpose, describes either as a man of outstanding integrity or as a shameless scoundrel.[85] The *prænomen* "Quintus" is rare among Manlii. But the tribune may, without duress, be claimed as a son of A. Manlius, Q.f., a *monetalis* at the end of the second century.[86]

A few more names call for inclusion, though with considerably less assurance. Note first Q. Marcius, tribune in 68, possibly identical with Q. Marcius Rufus, a legate in the servile war of 71.[87] He may have been a new man, another protégé of M. Crassus, under whom he served against Spartacus. No earlier Marcii Rufi grace the magisterial *fasti* of the Republic. But senatorial progenitors cannot be ruled out. Two Q. Marcii, without *cognomina*, do put in an appearance, a *tribunus militum* in 193 and a moneyer ca. 103. They may illuminate the origins of Crassus' legate. Likewise, C. Papius, author of a restrictive bill on citizenship in 65; his lineage is not disclosed; even if he is related to L. Papius, a *monetalis* in the 70s, this does not push the family beyond Sulla. But one may observe two other Papii to whom legislation is ascribed; they were therefore magistrates, and possibly pre-Sullan.[88] That brings us to the notorious tribunes of 67 and 66, C. Cornelius and C. Manilius, adherents of Pompey, sponsors of controversial enactments, and future defendants on *maiestas* charges. The sources are fuller on these individuals, but convey no information on their parentage. An argument from silence may be invoked. If their derivation were humble, the hostile aristocratic tradition would surely not have passed over the fact. Senatorial ancestors are correspondingly probable. Manilii are attested in the *curia* of the second century. Plebeian Cornelii are few, but not unknown.[89]

The residuum can now be surveyed: thirty-eight tribunes for whom senatorial predecessors cannot be found. Again the list is fluid. It may be sparseness of evidence alone that restricts many to this category. An example is M. Valerius, tribune in 68, on whom the sources vouchsafe no information. There are innumerable senatorial Valerii, almost all of them patrician. The origins of this individual remain hidden. So do those of two Cœlii who held tribunician office in the period: Q. Cœlius Latiniensis and M. Cœlius Vinicianus. The Cœlii Caldi were a recent senatorial clan; but no positive data associate them with the Ciceronian tribunes, and the *prænomina* differ. Unless unsuspected items turn up, they cannot be adjudged to be of senatorial descent.

[84] Cf. Cic. *Pro Flacco,* 2: *D. Lælium, optimi viri filium.* Plautius is postulated on the basis of *leges Plautiæ,* which apparently came in 70. He might conceivably have passed them as prætor; more probably as tribune.

[85] Cic. *Verr.* 1.30; *Pro Cluent.* 38–39.

[86] Cf. Taylor, *Voting Districts,* pp. 229–230.

[87] Syme, *JRS,* 53 (1963): 59.

[88] Broughton, *MRR,* II:471–472.

[89] Taylor, *Voting Districts,* p. 207.

As might be anticipated, the majority of *novi homines* attached themselves to one or another of the leading political figures. Among Pompeian tribunes may be reckoned the loquacious agitator from Picenum, M. Lollius Palicanus, who pressed for institutional reform in 71. Also, two tribunes in 63, T. Ampius Balbus and the Picentine military man T. Labienus, who actively promoted Pompey's interests in that year. L. Flavius in 60 sponsored an abortive land measure to provide for Pompeian veterans. The actions of T. Milo and C. Messius in 57 on the general's behalf are well known. His influence may lie behind their election and careers. And M. Cœlius Vinicianus in 53 joined in the clamor to elevate Pompey to a dictatorship. Cæsarian tribunes are also discoverable: notably, P. Vatinius, author of the bill that gave Cæsar his Gallic command; and Vatinius' colleague in 59, C. Alfius Flavus. We might add, perhaps, Q. Numerius Rufus, L. Roscius Fabatus, and C. Trebonius, all of whom moved into positions of authority in the Gallic armies after termination of their tribunates. A. Allienus, co-author of an agrarian law on Cæsar's behalf in 55, later held Sicily for Cæsar during the civil war. And among the pro-Cæsarian tribunes in 51 were two men, C. Cælius Rufus, probably from Tusculum, and L. Vinicius from Cales.[90] Crassus too had friends in the tribunate. The volatile L. Quinctius was his legate in the crushing of Spartacus. Cn. Plancius, tribune in 56, possessed an ancestral connection with Crassus and his family. A possible connection existed also with L. Roscius Otho, who held office in 67. Roscius opposed military commissions for Crassus' foe Pompeius Magnus. And two Roscii are later found among Crassus' officers in the Parthian war. If Roscius was acting for Crassus in 67, so, presumably, was L. Trebellius, who joined him in vetoing the *lex Gabinia.* We may include as well M. Cælius Rufus, whose political start came with Crassus' patronage, though he did not acquire his tribunate until after Crassus' death. *Novi homines* were not conspicuous in the opposition to the triumvirate. But at least two tribunes were active in that role: L. Ninnius Quadratus and C. Ateius Capito, who provided obstruction to the *lex Trebonia* in 55; the latter harried Crassus in particular, calling down fearful curses upon him.[91] Both may have been sponsored by the Catonian circle or by other *nobiles* antagonistic to the dynasts.

The rest are not readily linked to any individual or group. Most receive mention only in passing or because unusual circumstances brought them fleetingly to the attention of the sources. The struggle over Cicero's recall in

[90] On Cælius' origin, see Wiseman, *CQ*, 14 (1964): 126; *contra*: Taylor, *Voting Districts,* pp. 199–200. Cf. Linderski, *Eos*, 56 (1966): 146–150. Trebonius' father is specifically attested as an *eques*; Cic. *Phil.* 13.23.

[91] Ninnius' tribunate had come in 58; but he joined Ateius in his attacks on the triumvirs in 55; Dio, 39.35.5.

57 discloses four tribunes, C. Cestilius, M. Cispius, T. Fadius, and Q. Fabricius, who happen to be registered only because of the orator's later gratitude. Q. Cœlius Latiniensis and C. Falcidius appear in a list of tribunes who became legates, and nowhere else.[92] As for the others, we know little more than that they held the tribunate: M. Terpolius, M. Valerius, C. Antius, L. Fabricius, M. Aufidius Lurco, L. Novius, L. Racilius, Manilius Cumanus, and C. Furnius.[93] Only one went on to a memorable career: C. Sallustius Crispus, a troublesome tribune in 52, rose to political prominence through the patronage of Cæsar the dictator–and then to literary eminence through disillusionment.

Results can now be recapitulated: they are not negligible. One must, as always, exercise caution. The one hundred thirteen names gathered here represent 38 percent of the tribunes elected in the Ciceronian period. And one cannot regard it as an altogether random sample. Identities of tribunes are often preserved only because the individual was sufficiently active or notorious to arouse the interests of the sources. It is rare that an entire tribunician college is known. Chance alone, a single inscription, reveals the college of 68; and the special interests of Cicero convey the names of all tribunes in 57. By contrast, only seven tribunes altogether are recorded for the decade of the 70s, where our evidence is at its most fragmentary. But that decade is unusual in other ways. Limitations placed upon the tribunate by Sulla may have discouraged many aristocrats who might otherwise have stood for the office. In effect, our statistical sample is almost wholly limited to the 60s and 50s. That, however, engenders greater confidence in the results. For that period we possess one hundred six names out of a possible two hundred, better than 50 percent.

The survey discloses that tribunician office was somewhat more open to *novi homines* than was the ædileship or prætorship. Approximately one-third of the known tribunes chosen in the late Republic appear to have had no progenitors in senatorial ranks. And the tribunate could serve as a springboard for more prestigious posts. Nearly half of those new men went on to curule office: sixteen obtained the prætorship, and three of them even acquired consular rank, though not until after 49.[94] In that respect, the tribunate did

[92] Cic. *De Imp. Pomp.* 58. The dates of their tribunates precede 66 and were recent enough to be remembered, but cannot be further specified. See the attempt of Wiseman, *CQ*, 14 (1964): 122–123.

[93] L. Fabricius' tribunate, in fact, is not certain; Broughton, *MRR*, II:141, n.8, 174. Lurco, despite Suet. *Cal.* 23, is not to be associated with Alfidius, the maternal grandfather of Livia Augusta; so, rightly, Wiseman, *Historia*, 14 (1965): 335–336; *contra*: Shackleton Bailey, *Cicero's Letters*, I:323. On Terpolius, see Wiseman, *New Men*, p. 265, no. 424. For reasons to be discussed in another context, L. Procilius, whom Broughton places in a tribunate of 56, should be removed from the lists; see below, chap. 8, n.25.

[94] The three consuls are P. Vatinius, C. Trebonius, and L. Vinicius. Vinicius' consulship did not come until 33–if indeed he is identical with the tribune of 51. The *novi homines*

provide some conveyance for social mobility within aristocratic ranks. But, from a larger prespective, the differences in personnel between that office and the prætorship or ædileship are minor. And they are more than adequately accounted for by simple explanation: there were ten annual tribunes, as opposed to eight prætors and four ædiles, and the office was not open to patricians. Once those factors are taken into consideration, the differences vanish. Roughly 30 percent of the attested tribunes were *nobiles,* and two-thirds of the total came from senatorial stock. Some were vocal, even radical, in their year of office, but almost all settled down to perfectly conventional careers—a long-standing characteristic of *tribunicii.* The late Republican tribunate attracted few wide-eyed rabble-rousers from humble backgrounds and obscure families. The conservative nature of the Roman electorate extended also to that post.[95]

THE PEDARII

The higher offices remained a restrictive preserve. Romans possessed a tidy sense of proper hierarchical arrangements. Infusion of new blood into the magistracies, even the tribunate, was slow, limited, and largely controlled by the interests of powerful gentes and major politicians. But *consulares, prætorii, ædilicii,* and *tribunicii* did not constitute the entire senatorial class. The rank and file require consideration. Their numbers were much larger in the Ciceronian age than before. Their influence on policy making was rarely direct. Discussion and debate in the *curia* did not normally evoke their participation. Unless a man achieved the upper rungs of the magisterial ladder, he would remain, in effect, a "freshman senator" throughout his career, seldom called upon to address the House, almost never in a position to act as a spokesman of senatorial policy. But the lesser senators were by no means invisible. Their functions were exercised by foot rather than by voice—*pedarii,* they were called—that is, they voted in all divisions of the House. And, one might add, they could lobby, grumble, urge, or sulk. They had interests to protect, friends to support, measures to approve or disapprove. It will be of value to gather what information exists on the *pedarii.*[96]

---

who went from tribunate to prætorship are L. Quinctius, M. Lollius Palicanus, L. Roscius Otho, T. Ampius Balbus, L. Flavius, T. Annius Milo, L. Roscius Fabatus, A. Allienus, M. Cispius, M. Cœlius Vinicianus, M. Cælius Rufus, C. Sallustius Crispus, and C. Furnius—the last five after 49.

[95] Observe, for example, the last tribunician election before the civil war. Seven men are known in that college: six of them were from consular *gentes,* the seventh from a prætorian house.

[96] On the term *pedarii,* see Gell. 3.18; cf. Cic. *Ad Att.* 1.19.9, 1.20.4. And see the discussion by R. T. Scott and L. R. Taylor, *TAPA,* 100 (1969): 548–557.

The dictatorship of Sulla was a watershed. The Roman senate underwent a process of regeneration and substantial expansion. Three hundred was the customary total in the pre-Sullan era. Crisis, war, and civil strife in the 80s thinned its number to a distressing degree. Perhaps as many as two hundred senators perished in that decade.[97] That was far more than could be made up by normal additions, through election or censorial enrollment. Sulla set his hand to the task of restoration with energy and vision. He did not stop at replacing numbers up to their older level. The new judicial responsibilities which the dictator assigned to the senatorial class demanded a *curia* of much larger size. The usual complement in the post-Sullan period comprised approximately six hundred men.[98] Actual figures, no doubt, fluctuated. Censorial purges might occasionally reduce the *curia;* alternately, the censors might be generous in their enrollment. Sixty-four names were expunged from the rolls in 70; in 61, by contrast, a new censorship brought in members, which transcended the customary total.[99] But it is clear that the Ciceronian senate contained roughly twice the membership of its pre-Sullan predecessors. That, in itself, is a fact of critical importance. Whence came the influx?

Sulla's enrollments have engendered widespread discussion. Favorable sources declare that the dictator drew on the equestrian classes and brought in eminently respectable men who in the past had been just short of senatorial rank. Many of them may indeed have been sons of senators, too young to enter the *curia* before, or older men cheated of their senatorial seats because of a hostile government in the 80s.[100] The anti-Sullan tradition furnishes a contrasting version: the dictator enrolled common soldiers, military men, and supporters from any social level.[101] It is easy and proper to decry the extreme positions. Sulla could hardly have doubled senatorial numbers by incorporating only men who already belonged to the class. And the evidence does not support a notion of Sulla's swamping the senate with lowly *milites.* Only a single such individual can be cited: L. Fufidius, a fawning associate of the dictator's, who rose from the centurionate to senatorial rank.[102] There cannot

[97] So, Orosius, 5.22.4; Eutropius, 5.9.2. The accuracy of their estimates cannot, of course, be guaranteed; cf. Syme, *PBSR*, 14 (1938): 10–11.

[98] Willems, *Le Sénat*, I:404–406.

[99] Livy, *Per.* 98; Dio, 37.46.4.

[100] Appian, *BC*, 1.100; Livy, *Per.* 89. H. Hill, *CQ*, 26 (1932): 170–177, takes Sulla's senators as holders of the *equus publicus*; hence, men who would have been senators in due course anyway; cf. also Gabba, *Athenæum*, 29 (1951): 262–270. That, however, makes it difficult to account for an expansion to six hundred members.

[101] So Sallust, *Cat.* 37; Dion. Hal. 5.77. That hostile judgment is adopted by Willems, *Le Sénat*, I:407–415, and Carcopino *Sylla ou la Monarchie Manquée* (Paris, 1931), p. 65.

[102] See the sneering comment of Sallust, *Hist.* 1.55.22, Maur. That he was previously a *primipilaris* is given by Orosius, 5.21.3; cf. Florus, 2.9.25; Plut. *Sulla*, 31.3. Hence, he would

have been many. Sulla, no doubt, turned to men of experience: *equites* who had served on the juries, the business classes, leading figures from Italian municipalities, and officers of rank who had served him loyally in the civil wars.[103]

Generalized statements and hunches are insufficient. Efforts have also been made to identify the Sullan appointees.[104] It is an enterprise fraught with hazard, for the sources do not specify any individual enrollees of Sulla. Guesswork has created lists drawn up by moderns based on men known to be senators in the 70s. But in few instances only can we be confident that those men were installed by Sulla and did not reach the *curia* through election to the quæstorship. It is not our purpose here to distinguish these groups, a hypothetical undertaking at best. The importance of Sulla's reform lay in the expansion itself of the senatorial class. Whoever were the particular individuals enrolled in 81, the senate maintained its numbers at approximately six hundred to the end of the Ciceronian period through quæstorian elections. Sulla raised the annual complement of quæstors to twenty, who would automatically enter the senate upon election.[105] The body would now perpetuate itself without further need for ad hoc supplementation. Our concern is with the composition of the *curia* in the Republic's last generation, not just with Sulla's direct beneficiaries, even if they could be satisfactorily singled out. Holders of the consulate, prætorship, ædileship, and tribunate have already been discussed. To obtain fuller understanding of the senate's makeup in terms of social class, it will be necessary to identify the *pedarii,* insofar as that is possible.

The following pages will survey those men who may reasonably be said to have entered the senate between the dictatorships of Sulla and Cæsar, but who did not, at least in our evidence, rise beyond the quæstorship in that period. Three groups of men are included in this compilation: those whose quæstorships are attested with no indication of higher office, those specifically

---

probably have acquired equestrian standing; Syme, *PBSR*, 14 (1938): 13. He is presumably not identical with the Fufidius who served as governor of Spain in 80; Plut. *Sert.* 12.3; Sallust, *Hist.* 1.108, Maur.; see Nicolet, *REL*, 45 (1967): 297–301. There were also equestrian Fufidii—not necessarily related; cf. Nicolet, *L'Ordre Equestre*, p. 584.

[103] Among numerous scholarly discussions, one may note Syme, *PBSR*, 14 (1938): 22–25; Gabba, *Athenæum*, 34 (1956): 124–133; *App. BC Lib. Prim.*, 343–345; E. Valgiglio, *Silla e la crisi repubblicana* (Florence, 1956), pp. 94–99; Meier, *Res Pub.*, pp. 256–258; Nicolet, *L'Ordre Equestre*; pp. 581–591.

[104] Hill, *CQ*, 26 (1932): 174–177, produces a list of eighty-one names. It is expanded to one hundred and two, probables and possibles, by Gabba, *Athenæum,* 29 (1951): 267–270. Neither is accompanied by much argument. Certain names on both lists are justly questioned by Nicolet, *L'Ordre Equestre*, pp. 581–588.

[105] Tac. *Ann.* 11.22.

noted as senators by the sources and for whom no particular magistracy is known, and those who served as legates abroad and do not appear otherwise in magisterial lists. Employment of these criteria will add two hundred names to the Ciceronian senate. Again firm precision cannot be claimed. Several of these individuals may indeed have gone on to further office unrecorded in the extant evidence. But the compilation will permit a clearer picture than has hitherto been available of the rank and file of the late Republican senate.[106]

Investigation must begin once more with the men of consular ancestry. It is possible to produce forty-six names. At first blush, that causes considerable surprise. Is it likely that so many *nobiles* failed to proceed beyond the quæstorship? Closer analysis affords some explanation. Several of these men perished before they could stand for higher office. Among them were the two sons of M. Crassus the triumvir. Both attained quæstorships in the mid-50s. One of them, M. Crassus, joined Cæsar's forces in Gaul, remained a firm Cæsarian in the civil war, and was evidently in line for rapid promotion. He vanishes after 49, obviously a victim of the war. His brother, P. Crassus, a devoted disciple of Cicero's, also served with Cæsar in Gaul, then transferred to his father's staff for the Parthian campaign, where, despite gallant heroism, he fell at Carrhæ.[107] Faustus Sulla, ill-fated son of the dictator, a *quæstorius* in 49, welcomed civil war as an opportunity to recoup his debts. But he fought with little success on the side of Pompey and was slain as a prisoner in 46.[108] Cn. Calpurnius Piso, a proquæstor in Spain in 64, was murdered there by Spanish cavalrymen.[109] Cut off well before his time also was Cicero's promising son-in-law, C. Calpurnius Piso. As quæstor in 58, the loyal Piso postponed personal ambitions to work diligently and exhaustingly for his father-in-law's recall from exile. Untimely illness swept him off in the following year, before Cicero could express his gratitude in person.[110] Three others, perhaps of noble birth, perished in the course of their service abroad. C. Malleolus, a quæstor in 80, indulged in greedy speculation in Cilicia, but did not live to return to Rome. His activities reflected no credit upon a consular house long in

[106] It will be prudent to exclude men who reached the upper magistracies after inception of Cæsar's dictatorship in 48. Some may have been of prior senatorial rank, but Cæsar was not bound by traditional practices in his appointments. Similarly with legates. Prior to 49, men with that title were almost certainly senators. After civil war began, however, commanders could not afford to observe technicalities in choosing their staffs. The legates of this period are collected (but not exhaustively) by Bartsch, *Die Legaten.*

[107] Münzer, *RE,* 13:268–269, "Licinius," n.56; Münzer, *RE,* 13:291–294, "Licinius," n.63.

[108] Broughton, *MRR,* II:297; on his debts and hopes in wartime, cf. Cicero's indignant remark; *Ad Att.* 9.11.4.

[109] Sallust, *Cat.* 19.3–5; Asconius, 92, 93, Clark; Dio, 36.44.5.

[110] Münzer, *RE,* 3:1391, "Calpurnius," n.93.

decline and hoping for revival.[111] Among the victims of the Mithridatic war was "L. Mallius," a senator and legate in 74. The name is so given in the Greek.[112] The Latin may be "Manlius" or "Manilius," possibly designating consular background. The question of his origin remains open. Censorinus, a younger senator who fell in hand-to-hand combat at Carrhæ, was probably a Marcius Censorinus, a consular clan since the mid-second century. He succumbed together with his friend and comrade P. Crassus.[113]

Other misfortunes lay in the path of young *nobiles.* A few were felled by political prosecution. M. Atilius Bulbus and C. Popillius, allegedly venal jurors at Oppianicus' trial in 74, were shortly thereafter convicted, though on charges other than judicial corruption.[114] A third juror on that bench, M'. Aquillius, was evicted from the senate by the censors of 70, and was evidently unable to resume a political career.[115] Unmasking of the Catilinarian conspiracy terminated other careers, notably the violent young patrician C. Cornelius Cethegus, who was executed as a plotter in 63.[116] And two Sullæ, perhaps relatives of the dictator, suffered condemnation as Catilinarians in the following year.[117]

Certain men of noble birth acquired their quæstorships late in the 50s. Though technically *pedarii* within the limits of this inquiry, they went on to higher office after 49. That category includes the two Antonii, Gaius and Lucius, brothers of the future triumvir, whose quæstorships came in 51 and 50. They chose the right side in civil war, and obtained curule office after the conflict. Also the brilliant young intellectual M. Brutus, a quæstor in 53 and eventually a prætor and *consul designatus* before he met death at Philippi. Cæsar's legate in Gaul, M. Junius Silanus, also belongs here; he may be identical with the future consul of 25. Three more should be cited in this company: Q. Marcius Philippus, proconsul in 47 and evidently *senatorius* earlier; Cn. Calpurnius Piso, a proquæstor in the Pompeian ranks of 49; and A. Pompeius Bithynicus, quæstor in Sicily in the late 50s.[118] And one may add young

[111] Broughton, *MRR,* I:80. He was, in all probability, a Publicius Malleolus, from a family that had once attained the consulship, a century and a half earlier.

[112] Appian, *Mithr.* 71.

[113] Plut. *Crass.* 25.3, 25.12.

[114] Cic. *Pro Cluent.* 71–73; *Verr.* 1.39. That Popillius derived from the consular Popillii Lænates is uncertain but possible. An Atilius Bulbus stands in the *fasti* as twice consul in the third century.

[115] Cic. *Pro Cluent.* 127.

[116] On his senatorial rank at the time, see Sallust, *Cat.* 17.3; his character, Sallust, *Cat.* 43.4. Cethegus' brother even cast a vote against him in the senate; Ampelius, 31. But some of the discredit may have rubbed off. The brother is not heard from again.

[117] Cic. *Pro Sulla,* 6; Sallust, *Cat.* 17.3.

[118] On Philippus, see Broughton, *MRR,* II:289; on Piso, Broughton, *MRR,* 100, n.7, 261; the latter is probably identifiable with the consul of 23. Bithynicus, attested as prætor in

Q. Hortensius, unworthy son of the great orator, who seems to have been quæstor in 51. He later embraced the cause of Cæsar, obtaining the prætorship as a reward.[119]

These individuals having been subtracted, we are left with twenty-three *nobiles* who achieved senatorial rank in the Ciceronian age but secured no recorded office beyond the quæstorship. Most receive but the barest mention in the sources, a reference or two indicating their status and no more. Several of them may also have perished before age rendered them eligible for further posts. Nine legates or quæstors who served abroad in this period warrant mention here. We possess only their names and little further information: P. Lentulus Marcellinus, quæstor in Cyrene ca. 75; Mam. Æmilius Lepidus, an officer under Antonius and Lucullus in the 70s; Fulvius, perhaps a Flaccus or a Nobilior, who was legate in Greece in 73; M. Aurelius Scaurus, a quæstor in Asia before 70; Censorinus, legate or prefect in 70; L. Octavius and M. Pomponius, officers of Pompey in the pirate war; and two legates of 53, Q. Fabius Vergilianus and C. Valerius Flaccus.[120] Four more acquired quæstorships late in the period and vanish thereafter, perhaps victims of the civil war: C. Cœlius Caldus, Sex. Quinctilius Varus, M'. Acilius, and a certain Varro, possibly a Terentius Varro.[121]

The rest are noted in passing only—as senators within this period—and never again. Three of them are included here for the sake of completeness, but may actually have entered the senate before Sulla's dictatorship: Q. Petillius, a senator by 78; L. Valerius, part of a senatorial commission in 76; and Juventius, father of the prætor of 51.[122] No useful information survives

---

the mid-40s may be the "A. Pom." on bronze coinage in Sicily; hence a quæstor before 50; Broughton, *MRR*, II:479.

[119] Cic. *Ad Att.* 6.3.9; Broughton, *MRR, Suppl.*, p. 29. One ought not to place under this heading Q. Fabius Sanga, a senator in 63. As chief patron of the Allobroges, he must be a Q. Fabius Maximus; Sallust, *Cat.* 41. Hence, identifiable with the ædile of 57, already noted earlier; cf. Shackleton Bailey, *CQ*, 10 (1960): 259.

[120] For references, see Broughton, *MRR*, under the appropriate years. Not all of these men are certifiable *nobiles*. M. Pomponius may, or may not, stem from the consular Pomponii of the late third century. Fulvius' ancestry is a matter of guesswork. Similarly, Q. Fabius Vergilianus—but the *prænomen* may suggest a patrician Fabius, adopted from the Vergilii. Only the name "Mamercus" survives for the officer of Antonius and of Lucullus; Broughton, *MRR*, II:105. They are probably identical—perhaps son of the consul of 77; Sumner, *JRS*, 54 (1964): 47. One can hardly attach to this company M. Marius, an officer of the rebel Sertorius in Spain; Broughton, *MRR*, II:93. His post, we may be sure, was not obtained through election in Rome.

[121] This last is certainly to be distinguished from the celebrated scholar; Broughton, *MRR*, II:100, n.7, 264. On M'. Acilius, whose identity remains uncertain, see Broughton, *MRR*, II:285, n.8, 478; *Suppl.*, p. 1.

[122] Broughton, *MRR*, II:95, 494; *Suppl.*, p. 32. The Petillii could claim a consul in 176. Valerius' origins are not attested. But the *prænomen* "Lucius" was common among the consular Valerii.

on M. Bæbius, L. Cassius, and T. Quinctius Crispinus, senators in the 70s, nor on T. Annius, who was in the *curia* by 66.[123] Finally, there is L. Volumnius, a friend and correspondent of Cicero's in 50, and two senators, Licinius Crassus Damasippus and Ser. Sulpicius, who turn up in Africa in 49 as advisers of the Numidian prince Juba.[124] They too may not have survived the civil war.

There is little point in speculation on the foregoing names where data are minimal in the extreme. In certain instances, consular ancestry is no more than probable. It is clear, in any case, that there were few *nobiles* who remained in the lower ranks of the senate for long. The number twenty-three might be reduced further if we possessed obituary notices for those individuals. Several may have fallen in war or from illness while still junior senators. And one cannot rule out higher magistracies that escaped the notice of our sources. Or, perhaps, for some, senatorial status sufficed for their purposes. Observe, for example, the devious manipulator and wire-puller P. Cornelius Cethegus, restored to the senate by Sulla and a potent author of senatorial intrigues in the 70s. Lack of curule office did not forestall his operations.[125] But Cethegus was exceptional, an assiduous student of "inside" politics. The general proposition holds: men from consular families were *pedarii* only until age permitted them to stand for higher magistracies.

Next, the *pedarii* of prætorian stock: seventeen names, with varying degrees of certitude, fall under this rubric. For a few only does any information exist beyond the mere notice of a quæstorship, a legateship, or senatorial standing. Among them was C. Memmius, brother-in-law of Pompey and his quæstor in 76. A devoted friend to his chief, Memmius fought valiantly and perished in the campaign against Sertorius during the subsequent year.[126] Furius Crassipes, second husband of Cicero's daughter Tullia and heir to a prætorian family from the second century, reached the quæstorship in 51. His relations

[123] For Bæbius, see Cic. *Pro Cluent.* 47, 53; Cassius, Cic. *Verr.* 1.30; Crispinus, Cic. *Pro Font.* 1; Annius, Cic. *Pro Cluent.* 78, 182. Again consular ancestry is not conclusively demonstrable in each case. But the Bæbii show two consuls in the second century, the Quinctii Crispini one in the late third century. And Annius may derive from the consular Annii of the late second century.

[124] On Volumnius, see Cic. *Ad Fam.* 7.32.1. He may be the senator noted by Varro, *De Re Rust.* 2.4.11; wrongly cited in Broughton, *MRR*, II:498. That he descends from L. Volumnius, consul in 307, must remain conjectural. Badian, *Historia*, 12 (1963): 142, denies it, perhaps rightly, but without evidence. More dubious, and best left out of the reckoning, is P. Volumnius, recorded as a *iudex* in 66; Cic. *Pro Cluent.* 198. After the *lex Aurelia* of 70, jury service does not necessarily imply senatorial status. And there was at least one equestrian P. Volumnius; Cic. *Ad Fam.* 7.32.1; Nepos, *Att.* 12.4. But note also the pontiff P. Volumnius, perhaps identifiable with the *iudex*; Macrob. 3.13.11; L. R. Taylor, *AJP*, 63 (1942): 388–389. For Damasippus and Sulpicius, see Cæs. *BC*, 2.44.

[125] See above, chap. 1, n.118.

[126] Münzer, *RE*, 15:608–609, "Memmius," n.7.

with Cicero were generally strained: the orator had no high opinion of his son-in-law's intelligence.[127] A more unsavory character was M. Porcius Læca, who opened his house to Catilinarian plottings in 63 and suffered conviction for his crimes in 62.[128] And there is the unlucky L. Rubrius, a senator captured in 49 by Cæsar, an event which evidently terminated his political career.[129] A more fortunate choice was made by C. Caninius Rebilus, who served as a Cæsarian legate in Gaul and was eventually promoted to a consulship in 45.[130] The same might have been in store for L. Aurunculeius Cotta, a dutiful and intrepid lieutenant of Cæsar's, who was cut down in the thick of battle.[131] Other senators of prætorian family are little more than names to us: C. Annius Bellienus and C. Fonteius, legates in Gaul in 74; T. Mænius and L. Claudius, *quæstorii* by 73; M. Fabius Hadrianus, who saw long service under Lucullus in the Mithridatic wars; P. Atilius, a Pompeian officer in the pirate campaign; and Cornelius Sisenna, adopted son (or stepson) and legate of Gabinius' in 57. Finally, two Sextilii belong on the list, a legate under Lucullus in 69 and a quæstor of 61; and two Sentii, a legate or quæstor in 68 and a senator in 49.[132] The total is not large. Men of prætorian lineage, with few exceptions, could also expect to move out of the junior ranks of the senate fairly rapidly.

One may anticipate a rather larger number of *pedarii* whose line was senatorial but whose kinsmen had not reached the prætorship or consulship. Investigation discloses thirty-eight individuals who seem to fit into this bracket. Once more prior warning is salutary. In most cases, senatorial ancestry is postulated rather than demonstrable; given the state of the evidence, that is inescapable. As with our previous discussions of magistrates, nomenclature must be the

[127] See, esp., Cic. *Ad Att.* 9.11.3. For the quæstorship, see Cic. *Ad Fam.* 13.9.

[128] Cic. *Pro Sulla,* 6. His senatorial status is affirmed by Sallust, *Cat.* 17.3; cf. Florus, 2.12.3. Citations in Broughton, *MRR,* II:495 are inaccurate. A Porcius Læca appears as prætor in 195.

[129] Cæs. *BC,* 1.23. Rubrius' family included a *prætorius* in 129 and a prætor in 68.

[130] Cæs. *BG,* 7.83, 7.90. He is doubtless descended from the prætor of same name in 171.

[131] Broughton, *MRR,* II:225.

[132] On Cn. Sentius Saturninus, the legate or quæstor of 68, see Cic. *Pro Planc.* 19, 27, 29; correctly explained by Syme, *Historia,* 13 (1964): 121–122; *ibid.*: 157–158. He derives from a prætor in 94, the first of his family to attain that rank. C. Sentius, a senator in 49, is very likely also a Saturninus; Joseph. *Ant.* 14.229. Syme, *Historia,* 13 (1964): 161–162, wishes to expunge this Sentius altogether, but his arguments are not decisive. The two Sextilii must be kept separate. A legate in 69 would hardly have needed to stand for the quæstorship of 61. They are also to be distinguished from Sextilius, the prætor of 68. The family was prætorian since the mid-second century. On the other individuals mentioned above, see Broughton, *MRR,* under the relevant years. Fabius Hadrianus' antecedents are unknown. But another Fabius Hadrianus, probably his brother, had achieved prætorian rank in the 80s. L. Claudius is not of the patrician Claudii, who shunned that *prænomen.* But a L. Claudius shows up as prætor in 174. On Sisenna, see Badian, *Philologus,* 103 (1959): 97.

principal guide. Placement of certain personages on this list may be reasonably questioned; the list, as a whole, however, will not be far off the mark.

The decade after Sulla's dictatorship serves as a starting point. A number of otherwise unknown senators turn up there, either Sullan appointees or men elected to the quæstorship before 70. On this decade, Cicero's *Verrines* and *Pro Cluentio* provide valuable assistance, denoting several jurors and other senators present at the trials of Oppianicus and Verres. Among the respectable *iudices* at Oppianicus' hearing in 74 were M. Juventius Pedo and M. Minucius Basilus. Both had had long experience on the bench, perhaps even pre-Sullan. They earn high praise from Cicero.[133] Less admirable was C. Herennius, who, it was said, allowed himself to be bought and was later found guilty on a charge of peculation.[134] Similar information exists on Cn. Egnatius, another venal *iudex* in 74. That miscalculation cost him the family's fortunes: Egnatius' self-righteous father disinherited his son. Not that Egnatius *pater,* also a senator, was any better; in 70 he was himself expelled from the *curia* for his objectionable manner of life.[135] Two more jurors are registered for the trial of Verres in 70: M. Lucretius and Q. Titinius. Both, it seems, were from lesser branches of senatorial families, perhaps examples of Sullan appointees. Titinius, a man of wealth and business connections, had equestrian relatives, but may derive from the senatorial Titinii of the second century. Neither rose to higher magistracies.[136]

[133] Cic. *Pro Cluent.* 107: *Qualis vir, M. Iuventius Pedo fuit ex vetere illa iudiciorum disciplina? . . . M. Basilius?* Nicolet, *L'Ordre Equestre,* pp. 583–584, 587, argues from this passage that Juventius and Basilus were equestrian jurors before 81, brought into the senate by Sulla. The conclusion is tenable, but not certain. The juries were not exclusively equestrian prior to Sulla's reform; cf. Gruen, *Roman Politics,* pp. 221, 236, 255–256. In any case, both probably possessed senatorial kinsmen: Juventius is to be associated with the Juventii who show several members in the senate, perhaps even with the consular branch of that *gens*; and a L. Minucius Basilus was a legate of Sulla's in 88. On the Basili, cf. Wiseman, *New Men,* pp. 241–242, no. 258.

[134] Cic. *Verr.* 1.39; cf. Syme, *Historia,* 4 (1955): 63. That he was a direct descendant of M. Herennius, consul in 93, is dubious. But the family was quite probably senatorial; cf. the senator C. Herennius in 129.

[135] Cic. *Pro Cluent.* 135. The family was senatorial at least since the mid 2nd century. It may be Etruscan or Samnite in origin; Syme, *Historia,* 4 (1955): 61; Taylor, *Voting Districts,* p. 211.

[136] Cic. *Verr.* 2.1.18, 2.1.128. Similarly, M. Lucrctius' background is uncertain. Men of that name appear in tribunician lists of the late third and early second centuries, but the consular Lucretii, of earlier date and different *prænomina,* are to be kept separate. For Titinius' wealth, cf. Cic. *Ad Att.* 7.18.4; his equestrian brother, Cic. *Verr.* 2.1.128. The family is closely connected with Minturnæ; cf. Taylor, *Voting Districts,* p. 259. That Titinius was equestrian by origin is possible. But there are prior senatorial Titinii; Broughton, *MRR,* II:626, and see Badian, *Historia,* 12 (1963): 141. Nicolet, *L'Ordre Equestre,* pp. 257–258, regards him as a Sullan appointee, then later contradicts himself; *L'Ordre Equestre,* 586. There were Titinii who fell

Isolated references bring to light other *pedarii* with senatorial background in the 70s. Two elderly senators receive mention under the year 76: Q. Lucilius and T. Manilius. The former was an interlocutor in Cicero's dialogue *De Natura Deorum,* set in that year. Son of a senator in 162, he himself was obviously in extreme old age by the mid-70s. The family shows no other Republican senators and was evidently of small weight in the *curia.* T. Manilius is cited as a respected and affluent senior senator in 76. His forebears are unrecorded, but it is not likely that he was a *novus homo.*[137] Lucilius and Manilius are here included in the interests of thoroughness; given their age, however, they may have entered the senate well before Sulla's dictatorship. So also, perhaps, did D. Lælius, a Pompeian legate who perished in the Sertorian campaign in 76.[138] Certain younger men, on the other hand, cited as quæstors or legates, definitely did attain senatorial status within the 70s: P. Rutilius Nudus, quæstor and legate during the 70s; L. Plætorius Cestianus, quæstor ca. 74; M. Postumius, quæstor in Sicily in 73; Furius, an officer vanquished by Spartacus in 73; and Q. Marcius Rufus, one of Crassus' legates in the gladiatorial war.[139] Note too the young and promising orator C. Sicinius, who died a *quæstorius* some time in the 70s.[140] Finally, there is the disreputable Q. Curius, expunged from the senate rolls in 70, later an adherent of Catiline's, and then an informer against his accomplices.[141]

---

in the proscriptions; [Q. Cic.] *Comm. Petit.* 9. But Sulla's wrath need not have fallen on all branches of that *gens.*

[137] On Manilius, see Cic. *Pro Rosc. Comm.* 43–44. There are no attested T. Manilii among the *consulares* of that *gens.* But observe the senator Manilius in 184; Plut. *Cato Maior,* 17.7; and another unattached Manilius, prætor before 82; Pliny, *NH,* 33.21. For Lucilius Balbus, Cic. *De Nat. Deor.* 2.11, 2.14–15; cf. *De Orat.* 3.78; and see Syme, *Historia,* 4 (1955): 64.

[138] Broughton, *MRR,* II:95. He is not of the consular Lælii; Cic. *Pro Flacco,* 18; Shackleton Bailey, *CQ,* 10 (1960): 256; probably from another senatorial branch of that family.

[139] For P. Rutilius Nudus, see Syme, *CP,* 50 (1955): 137. The *cognomen* is not otherwise attested among Republican Rutilii. But Nudus was surely no *novus homo.* The *prænomen* is used by consular branches of the family. And Nudus himself was father-in-law of L. Piso, the consul of 58; Asconius, 5, Clark; and see Münzer, *RE,* 1a:1:1268, "Rutilius," n.30. Plætorius, given high marks by Cicero, was still in the senate in 66; *Pro Cluent.* 165. But there is no evidence for curule magistracies. He is doubtless a descendant of the L. Plætorius, senator in 129, possibly from Tusculum; Taylor, *Voting Districts,* p. 243. Postumius' lineage is uncertain. The *prænomen* "Marcus" is attested among the Postumii Albini, but very rarely. That he was at least of senatorial ancestry, however, is a safe conjecture. On Furius, see Plut. *Crass.* 9.4. He is not to be identified with the prætor of 75 who is almost certainly a L. Turius. Connections with the patrician Furii can hardly be asserted. But one may confidently suppose senatorial lineage. No prior Marcius Rufus is known. But "Quintus" is common among senatorial Marcii. The legate of Crassus was surely from a minor branch of that *gens.*

[140] Cic. *Brutus,* 263–264. Various Sicinii turn up in earlier magistracies, including a consular branch. The *prænomen* "Gaius" is attested among them only for a tribune in 449.

[141] That Curius came of senatorial stock may tentatively be surmised from Sallust's description; *Cat.* 23.1: *natus haud obscuro loco.*

So much for the *pedarii* of the 70s who can claim senatorial extraction. The preserved names do not, of course, exhaust the list. But they may be representative of men with that background who entered the senate in the decade after Sulla's dictatorship. The families are respectable but not distinguished. Some, like M. Lucretius, may have recovered senatorial rank for *gentes* that had not possessed it for many generations. Others, like Q. Titinius, stemmed from clans many of whose members were equestrians. And most belonged to lesser and relatively obscure branches of senatorial houses. That they did not rise to upper magistracies will not cause surprise.

Six more names crop up in the 60s. Only one has left any meaningful mark on the tradition. L. Vargunteius, a senator by the early 60s, succumbed to an *ambitus* prosecution, then joined Catiline's ring of plotters, for which he was convicted and eliminated from public life in 62.[142] P. Sulpicius obtained the quæstorship in 69 and then drops out of sight. He is possibly a P. Sulpicius Rufus, connected with the plebeian side of that house which produced the notorious tribune of same name in 88.[143] M. Lollius appears once in the sources, as a colleague of Cato's in the quæstorship of 64. His origins are discoverable: Lollius was, very likely, son of an aged Roman knight, Q. Lollius, whose humiliation was among the atrocities of Verres in Sicily. But the family also shows senators in the past, including another M. Lollius, Q.f., senator in 129.[144]Among quæstors in the 60s ought perhaps to be listed C. Considius Nonianus, who produced coinage ca. 63. The Nonii, whence the quæstor was adopted, were a senatorial family, albeit of only recent emergence.[145] Add

[142] See below, chap. 7, n.81. In view of the infrequency of the name, it is reasonable to link Vargunteius to the *monetalis* of the late second century; Broughton, *MRR*, II:455.

[143] He is best dissociated, however, from P. Sulpicius Rufus, a Cæsarian legate in the 50s and future prætor of 48. The latter was a younger man; Broughton, *MRR*, II:136, n.8; *Suppl.*, 61-62; Sumner, *Phoenix*, 25 (1971):249-250. There is another problem about the quæstor of 69. He was already a senator in 70, yet stood for the quæstorship of the following year; see Cic. *Verr.* 1.30, and the comments of Schol. Gronov. 337, Stangl. Another scholiast gets around that problem by asserting that Sulpicius' magistracy was a tribunate; Ps. Asconius, 216, Stangl. But that will not do. Cicero states that he will take office on the Nones of December, the opening of the quæstorian year, and distinguishes him from the tribunes-elect. Sulpicius must then have been enrolled in the senate by Sulla, but sought the quæstorship anyway–for purposes unfathomable to us; cf. Nicolet, *L'Ordre Equestre*, p. 585. Hill, *CQ*, 26 (1932): 173, wrongly identifies him with P. Sulpicius Galba. Galba was rejected as a juror by Verres; Cic. *Verr.* 2.1.18.

[144] On the quæstorship, see Plut. *Cato*, 16.6. For the humiliation of Q. Lollius, see Cic. *Verr.* 2.3.61-63. His son, M. Lollius, is described by Cicero as *adulescens* in 70; hence, readily identifiable with the quæstor of 64.

[145] Sex. Nonius Sufenas was prætor in 81; and two Nonii, perhaps senators, appear on the *consilium* of 89; Cichorius, *Röm. Stud.*, p. 170; Criniti, *L'Epigrafe di Asculum*, pp. 152-155.

also C. Plotius, a senator and legate of Asia some time before 60.[146] Finally, there is M. Gratidius, from the Arpinate house, closely linked in blood and marriage to the Marii and the Cicerones, who saw service with Q. Cicero in the latter's proconsulship of 61.[147]

Evidence is fuller on the 50s. Here one can unearth another fifteen individuals in this category. Cæsar, especially, made good use of lesser-rank senators on his staff in Gaul. At least six such men are identifiable. Three of them benefited enormously in prestige and *honores* from their service, bringing their families for the first time into the upper magistracies during the Cæsarian dictatorship: L. Minucius Basilus, a Picene landowner, obtained a prætorship in 45; L. Munatius Plancus, from Tibur, rose to a consulate in 42 with a lengthy variegated career to follow; and P. Sulpicius Rufus scaled the heights of *dignitas* to a censorship in 42. All had been legates of Cæsar during the later 50s.[148] Three more Cæsarian officers in Gaul show no later augmentation in status; they may not have outlived the Gallic campaigns or the civil war: C. Antistius Reginus, M. Sempronius Rutilus, and C. Volcacius Tullus.[149] To those individuals we may add Marcius Rufus, a quæstor in the Cæsarian forces in 49, and Q. Cornificius, an officer, perhaps a quæstor, in 48. Cornificius, at least, went on to secure prætorian status during the dictatorship.[150] Julius Cæsar did well by his subordinates.

A few more personages with similar credentials appear in the 50s. In the entourage of Crassus in Syria was a certain Vargunteius, kinsman of the ill-fated Catilinarian Vargunteius. He is not heard from again, nor are T. Titius, legate in an unidentifiable province in 51, and L. Marius, quæstor in Syria during 50.[151] The unlucky T. Antistius was proquæstor in Macedon in 49, caught

[146] Cic. *Pro Flacco*, 50.

[147] Cic. *Ad Q. Frat.* 1.1.10. The Gratidii reached the senate in the previous generation under the sponsorship of Marius.

[148] Basilus was born a Satrius and was adopted by his uncle; Münzer, *RE*, 15:1948, "Minucius," n.38; Wiseman, *New Men*, pp. 241–242, no. 258. The Satrii are of no consequence, but the adoptive family produced a legate in the previous generation. Munatius Plancus, friend and admirer of Cicero, was no doubt related to the Sullan legate in the 80s; Wiseman, *New Men*, p. 242, no. 261.

[149] Volcacius Tullus was still alive in 48, but is not heard from thereafter; Cæs. *BC*, 3.52. His family was consular, but only acquired that status in the Ciceronian age with the consul of 66. The Antistii Regini show a tribune in 103, and the Sempronii Rutili one in 189.

[150] Broughton, *MRR*, II:259, 276.

[151] See Broughton, *MRR*, under the appropriate years. The Titii produced more than one senator in the pre-Sullan era, though T. Titius is the first known individual of that *prænomen*. Still, the family is rare enough to suggest a relationship. For L. Marius, no evidence is available. He was doubtless related to the tribune of 62, though descent from the great Marius whose family did not use the *prænomen* "Lucius" is most dubious. Senatorial background is a safe assumption. The L. Marius who prosecuted Scaurus in 54 is probably identifiable with the quæstor of 50.

in the midst of a civil war for which he had little taste. He evaded the wrath of Pompey by flight, later obeyed Cæsar's order to return home, but perished of a lengthy illness while en route—one of the more poignant victims of that fratricidal conflict.[152] More fortunate was the crafty Q. Lucretius Vespillo, senator and Pompeian officer in 49 and 48, who managed to survive the war and retribution and who eventually obtained a consulship in 19.[153] Two last senators crop up momentarily in the sources in the late 50s: P. Cornificius, who denounced Milo at a session of the *curia* in 52, and M. Servilius, a figure of low repute and disarrayed life-style, who underwent *repetundæ* prosecution in 51.[154]

The foregoing compilation has now assembled one hundred and one names: forty-six of consular families, seventeen of prætorian, and thirty-eight with lesser senatorial background. The first group, as we have seen, is misleading. Many of them ascended to the consulship or prætorship under Cæsar the dictator; for others, premature death or judicial conviction terminated careers at the junior level. Few *nobiles* lingered in the ranks of the *pedarii.* That is only slightly less true of the men with prætorian ancestry. Among the remainder, access to higher office was more difficult. Only Cæsar's officers and men who deserted to him could hope for promotion. Individuals from lesser senatorial families or minor branches of prominent houses show a larger proportion among the *pedarii* than was evident in surveys of the *tribunicii, ædilicii, prætorii,* and *consulares.* Admission to the *curia* was available to them, but mobility within it was still restricted.

Attention may now be directed to the *pedarii* who lacked senatorial predecessors. Here the facts stand out in bold relief. Fully ninety-nine such personages are discernible in the Ciceronian senate, a number nearly equivalent to all other categories combined. It is here, in the less prestigious strata of the *curia,* that the real change in personnel is most apparent. The post-Sullan era expanded the senate dramatically. It was now open to *novi homines* on an unprecedented scale. The identifiable individuals require some scrutiny.

A large percentage of known senators come in the 70s—thanks again to the *Verrines* and the *Pro Cluentio.* The trial of Oppianicus once more furnishes several names—names unattested before in the Roman senate. Among the

[152] Cic. *Ad Fam.* 13.29.3–4.

[153] Miltner, *RE,* 13:1691, "Lucretius," n.47. He is, no doubt, a descendant of Lucretius Vespillo, ædile in 133.

[154] On Cornificius, see Asconius, 36, Clark; cf. Syme, *Historia,* 4 (1955): 60–61. On Servilius, Cæl. *Ad Fam.* 8.8.2–4. His identity is not recoverable: perhaps the Servilius who was prefect under Pompey in 65, or the legate under Gabinius in 57. Certainly not of the consular Servilii among whom the *prænomen* "Marcus" is attested only once. There are several earlier Servilii without known associations, including a M. Servilius, *monetalis* in the early first century, and a prætor in 88.

honorable jurors in that case were C. Caudinus, L. Caulius Mergus, Q. Considius, Cn. Heius, L. (or P.) Octavius Balbus, and P. Saturius.[155] All were evidently *novi homines,* no doubt of equestrian stock, and perhaps Sullan appointees.[156] Some of the appointments were less judicious: C. Fidiculanius Falcula, Ti. Gutta, P. Popillius, and P. Septimius Scævola, who were accounted corrupt jurors and suffered criminal prosecutions on that and other grounds in subsequent years.[157] The *novitas* of three of those individuals is transparent in their names.[158] Nor can one forget the notorious C. Ælius Staienus, who pocketed cash from Oppianicus meant to purchase most of the bench itself. He succumbed to a *maiestas* condemnation shortly thereafter.[159] More names are revealed in the *Verrines: iudices* and other senators in the late 70s. Among them two Octavii Ligures, senators by 75, perhaps from Forum Clodi; Calidius, son of a respected and popular Roman *eques,* one of Verres' Sicilian victims; M. Crepereius, heir to an equestrian house of rigorous standards and traditions, a juror in 70; Q. Junius, rejected as a juror by Verres because, so Cicero alleges, he was too independent of mind; and C. Gallus, a senator in Sicily in 70, whose purposes were thwarted by Verres and his associates.[160]

[155] Cic. *Pro Cluent.* 107. The text gives P. Octavius Balbus. But in *Verr.* 2.2.31, one reads L. Octavius Balbus. The correct *prænomen* is uncertain, but the two men are surely to be amalgamated; cf. Wiseman, *CQ*, 14 (1964): 124. On Considius, see now Wiseman, *New Men*, pp. 225-226, no. 132. Broughton, *MRR*, II:489, suggests that Caudinus may be a Cornelius Lentulus Caudinus; hence, a patrician from a most eminent consular house. The conclusion is implausible. No Lentulus is found with the name since the beginning of the second century; and the *prænomen* "Gaius" is never attested among the Cornelii Lentuli at any time. Note the same conclusion now in Wiseman, *New Men*, p. 223, no. 111.

[156] On some of these individuals, see Nicolet, *L'Ordre Equestre*, pp. 384-385, 587-588.

[157] On their trials, with references, see below, Appendix II. Popillius is not to be confused with the Popillii Lænates. He was, in fact, the son of a freedman; Cic. *Pro Cluent.* 132.

[158] Cf. Cicero's fiercely contemptuous sneer at Falcula in *Pro Cæc.* 28.

[159] See below, Appendix II. Cicero asserts that Staienus illegitimately arrogated to himself the name Ælius Pætus, which belonged to a distinguished consular clan; *Pro Cluent.* 72; *Brutus,* 241. In this instance, his allegation is credible. The Ælii Pæti had, it seems, long since died out.

[160] Verres, father of the rapacious governor of Sicily, has here been excluded. His entrance into the senate doubtless preceded the Sullan dictatorship. For the Octavii Ligures, see Cic. *Verr.* 2.2.21, 2.2.23; cf. Wiseman, *CQ*, 14 (1964): 128. On Calidius, see Cic. *Verr.* 2.4.42. He probably does not belong to the senatorial Calidii, Marcus and Quintus, of the early first century. Calidius' father was a knight–and a Cn. Calidius. On M. Crepereius, see Cic. *Verr.* 1.30: *ex acerrima illa equestri familia et disciplina.* Q. Junius is registered by Cic. *Verr.* 2.1.18. He surely did not belong to the consular Bruti or Silani, who show no use of the *prænomen* "Quintus." There is a L. Junius, Q.f., on Pompeius Strabo's *consilium* in 89; Cichorius, *Röm. Stud.*, p. 168; Criniti, *L'Epigrafe di Asculum*, pp. 141-142–but no evidence for senatorial status. For C. Gallus, see Cic. *Verr.* 2.3.152. Badian, *Gnomon*, 33 (1961): 495-496, suggests that he is identical with C. Aquillius Gallus, the jurist and prætor of 66. If so, the name should be excised in this category–but the matter is too uncertain.

Legates and quæstors in the 70s swell the list. A number of *novi homines*, for example, are to be found on the staff of C. Verres in Sicily. The fact is not surprising: he was himself of recent senatorial family. And Verres was not anxious to have many young *nobiles* about who might exercise surveillance over his dubious activities. He needed more trustworthy officers: hence, his own brother-in-law T. Vettius, and young Q. Cæcilius Niger, from a Roman family in Sicily, who was later suborned as Verres' prosecutor in order to forestall Cicero's efforts.[161] There were also three other legates from obscure and previously unrecorded families: P. Cæsetius, P. Cervius, and P. Tadius. Not all of them proved to be as reliable as Verres anticipated. Vettius' brother brought evidence for the prosecution in 70, as did a certain Q. Tadius, and Verres felt it necessary to reject Cervius as one of his *iudices*.[162] Further provincial officers are registered for the 70s: P. Oppius, for example, quæstor and an officer of M. Cotta's in Bithynia, later dismissed by his commander to face charges of mutiny in Rome. His family, so it would seem, was equestrian.[163] The campaign against Sertorius produced a number of *novi homines* who served in Spain. Most notably, the mysterious and artful L. Fabius Hispaniensis, a quæstor in government forces against Sertorius in 81, who later transferred allegiance to the rebel, and eventually seems to have been leagued with his assassins.[164] Also, C. Tarquitius, L. Thorius Balbus, Aquinus, Titurius Sabinus, and C. Urbinius.[165] Others saw service in the eastern wars of the 70s, under M. Antonius or L. Lucullus: L. Marcilius, C. Salluvius Naso, Barba, Manius, C. Gallius, and Sornatius.[166] And mention should be made also of Mummius, an inept officer of Crassus' in the gladiatorial war of 72.[167]

[161] On Vettius, Cic. *Verr.* 2.3.168, 2.5.114; Cæcilius Niger, Cic. *Div. in Cæc. passim*; cf. Nicolet, *L'Ordre Equestre*, pp. 256–257, 259. Syme, *Historia*, 4 (1955): 71, identified Vettius with the moneyer T. Vettius Sabinus and the prætor of 59; so also Taylor, *Voting Districts*, p. 265. But the brother of Verres' quæstor was named P. Vettius Chilo, a wealthy and influential equestrian businessman; Cic. *Verr.* 2.3.166. It is best to keep them separate.

[162] Cic. *Verr.* 2.1.128, 2.3.166–168, 2.5.114. On Cæsetius and Tadius, see Cic. *Verr.* 2.2.49, 2.4.146, 2.5.63. Tadius was related to Verres' mother; Cic. *Verr.* 2.1.128. The family was equestrian; Nicolet, *L'Ordre Equestre*, p. 342.

[163] There are prior Oppii in senatorial ranks, including some *prætorii*. But P. Oppius' equestrian connections are clearly implied in Cicero's defense speech; Quint. *Inst. Orat.* 5.13.21.

[164] On the quæstorship, Broughton, *MRR*, II:77. Sallust, *Hist.* 3.83, Maur., describes Fabius as *ex proscriptis*. That may suggest that he joined the insurrection of Lepidus in 77, and perhaps escaped to Spain with Perperna, there to link with Sertorius. Perperna's plotters against Sertorius in 72 apparently included Fabius; Sallust, *Hist.* 3.83, Maur. Gabba, *Athenæum*, 32 (1954): 305–307, argues from the *cognomen* "Hispaniensis" that Fabius came from a family of Romans resident in Spain in the pre-Sullan era.

[165] Evidence collected by Broughton, *MRR*, II:77, 84, 87, 100, 103. On Tarquitius, cf. J. Heurgon, *Latomus*, 12 (1953): 407–408.

[166] Broughton, *MRR*, II:105, 112–113, 120. Barba is possibly a Cassius Barba, progenitor of the later Cæsarian; Syme, *CP*, 50 (1955): 133; or else identical with Sornatius; Syme,

Lastly, a few senators without aristocratic forebears are randomly attested in the 70s. A certain Postumus, Murena's prosecutor in 63, was candidate for the prætorship in that year; hence, evidently a *quæstorius* by the late 70s.[168] The brothers Cæpasii, from humble origins and sporting municipal accents, rose through diligence and energy to the quæstorship.[169] One may note further L. Valerius Triarius, urban quæstor in 81; L. Faberius, a senator by 78; C. Velleius, an intellectual with philosophical interests registered in 76; C. Luscius Ocrea, an elderly senator mentioned in that year as well; P. Annius Asellus, who perished without male heirs in 75; Q. Axius, the legal expert; A. Cascellius, M. Publicius Scæva, and Q. Rancius, four *quæstorii* listed in 73; and L. Rutilius, recorded in the senate in 72, probably identical with the *monetalis* L. Rutilius Flaccus.[170] Perhaps too the Samnite warrior of wealth and station, Statius, who was an enemy of Rome in the Social War, but who later obtained citizenship, honors, and senatorial status.[171] The unfortunate senator Attidius

---

Historia, 13 (1964): 123; Wiseman, *New Men*, pp. 262, no. 406, 280, no. 525. He is not to be amalgamated with the Voconius also listed on Lucullus' staff. The latter seems to have been a prefect, perhaps not of senatorial rank; Plut. *Luc.* 13.1–2. C. Gallius may be identical with "C. Gallus," a senatorial juror in 70; see above, n.160. "Manius," legate of M. Antonius, it could be argued, is a *prænomen*, rather than a *nomen*; Wiseman, *New Men*, pp. 239–240, no. 245. But not likely in this case: Sallust, *Hist.* 3.6, Maur. identifies him as *Manio legato*, evidently his first mention of the man—which would hardly be by his *prænomen* alone.

[167] Plut. *Crass.* 10.1–3. He surely does not derive from Mummius Achaicus, the conqueror of Greece, but is doubtless related to, though probably not identical with, M. Mummius, prætor in 70.

[168] Cic. *Pro Mur.* 57. He may (or may not) be a Curtius Postumus, a family later ardently pro-Cæsarian. There is no specific evidence; cf. Syme, *CP*, 50 (1955): 134. Sumner, *Phoenix*, 25 (1971): 254, reckons him a Postumius Albinus—but this requires four emendations in Cicero's text.

[169] Cic. *Brutus*, 242.

[170] On Triarius, Cic. *Verr.* 2.1.37; Faberius, *CIL*, I.^{2}588; Velleius, Cic. *De Nat. Deor.* 1.15; cf. *De Orat.* 3.78; Luscius Ocrea, Cic. *Pro Rosc. Com.* 43–44; P. Annius Asellus, Cic. *Verr.* 2.1.104; Q. Axius, A. Cascellius, Publilius Scæva, and Q. Rancius, *SIG*,^{3} 747; Rutilius Flaccus, Cic. *Pro Cluent.* 182; Broughton, *MRR*, II:451. Axius is perhaps related to the *eques* L. Axius, a breeder of pigeons; Varro, *De Re Rust.* 3.7; Pliny, *NH*, 10.37. Cascellius derives, so it can be argued, from Sora; Wiseman, *New Men*, p. 222, no. 106.

[171] Appian, *BC*, 4.25. Syme, *PBSR*, 14 (1938): 23, suggests that Statius was recruited for the senate in 88. But it is not likely that Sulla brought a Samnite leader into the senate directly after the Social War. The occasion of recruitment is better placed during the dictatorship. Syme also, *loc. cit.*, notes another Samnite, Minatus Magius, who chose the Roman side in the allies' revolt and earned prætorships for his two sons. But if Vell. Pat. 2.16.2–3 is accurate, those prætorships preceded the reconstitution of the senate in 81: *cum seni [prætores] adhuc crearentur.* Broughton, *MRR*, II:489, lists one other senator in the 70s, a C. Claudius noted by Cicero in 71; *Pro Tullio*, 14. But he may well be C. Claudius Glaber, a *prætorius* by 73, and probably should not have a separate entry. The ex-centurion L. Fufidius, discussed above, evidently was a Sullan appointee; see above, n.102.

fled to Mithridates to escape judicial condemnation, but was eventually detected in conspiracy and executed on the Pontic king's orders. And, finally, one may observe Licinius Bucco, senatorial husband of a domineering and imposing *femina*.[172] The names, unfamiliar and undistinguished, betray the influx of new men into the *curia*. Sulla's dictatorship and the decade that followed it constituted the turning point. Romans from the *municipia* and *equites* of varied background were now filling up the "back benches" of the senate.

The process continued in the 60s. Evidence, unfortunately, is less plentiful here and fewer individuals can be itemized. But some obvious *novi homines* emerge from the extant material. They may be swiftly reviewed. In almost every instance they appear but once or twice in the sources. So, for example, Q. Annius Chilo, who joined in the schemes of Catiline, tampered with the loyalty of the Allobroges, and was later executed by the state in 63.[173] Another Catilinarian was personally eliminated by his father, the senator A. Fulvius.[174] In 63 also one may note L. Sænius, who delivered evidence against Catiline in the senate, and Cn. Terentius, who was charged with custody of one of the prisoners.[175] Among legates and officers abroad in the 60s were L. Lollius and Manlius Priscus, members of Pompey's staff in the East, L. Bassus, Manlius Lentinus, T. Varius Sabinus, and P. Septimius.[176] Other senators come fleetingly to attention, in varied contexts: the genial horse-breeder Q. Lucienus, a friend of Varro's; Cn. Tudicius, who delivered testimony for Cluentius in 66; and C. Albinius, worthy and admired father-in-law of P. Sestius.[177]

More plentiful data on the 50s permit us to expand the list considerably. In Cæsar's entourage in Gaul was Q. Pedius, the proconsul's nephew. His

[172] Appian, *Mithr.* 90, puts Attidius' execution in 67, prior to which he had spent a long time at Mithridates' court. Date of his indictment and flight is unknown; perhaps in the early 70s. He may have been a Sullan appointee. On Licinius Bucco, see Val. Max. 8.3.2.

[173] Cic. *Cat.* 3.14; Sallust, *Cat.* 17.3, 50.4. Neither the *prænomen* nor the *cognomen* is attested among the senatorial Annii.

[174] Sallust, *Cat.* 39.5; Val. Max. 5.8.5; Dio, 37.36.4. Again, the *prænomen* is not in use by the earlier senatorial houses of the Fulvii.

[175] Sallust, *Cat.* 30.1, 47.4. Terentii are present in the pre-Sullan senate, but no prior Cn. Terentius.

[176] On Lollius, see Appian, *Mithr.* 95. There were, of course, senatorial Lollii, as noted before–but no L. Lollii. The officer of Pompey is probably to be associated with another Pompeian adherent, Lollius Palicanus, a man of undistinguished birth. For Manlius Priscus, Broughton, *MRR*, II:160; L. Bassus, Dio, 36.19.1; Manlius Lentinus, Dio, 37.47–48. Bassus, perhaps, is a Lucilius Bassus; cf. Syme, *Historia*, 13 (1964): 161. Septimius is recorded as a quæstor to M. Terentius Varro, evidently during Varro's promagistracy; Broughton, *MRR*, II:477. That service probably came in the mid 60s; Cichorius, *Röm. Stud.*, pp. 203–205. Varius Sabinus was in Greece with M. Plætorius, evidently the governor of 63; Syme, *Historia,* 5 (1956): 207.

[177] On Lucienus, see Varro, *De Re Rust.* 2.5.1, 2.7.1–16; Tudicius, Cic. *Pro Cluent.* 198; Albinius, Cic. *Pro Sest.* 6; *Ad Fam.* 13.8.1–3.

uncle's patronage was insufficient to gain him even an ædileship in the 50s; but civil war and Cæsar's triumph changed all that: Pedius went on to consular rank in 43.[178] Further, there was the military historian A. Hirtius, of municipal origins, eventually Cæsar's choice for the consulship of 43, and Q. Titurius Sabinus, an impulsive soldier whose career was terminated by death at the hands of the Gauls.[179] A few other *novi homines,* active or latent supporters of Cæsar in the 50s, moved into loftier posts after the civil war; L. Ateius Capito, son of a centurion, who was in the senate by 51 and later rose to a prætorship; the Ostian T. Sextius, who became prætor and proconsular governor of Africa in the 40s; T. Furfanius Postumus, apparently quæstor in Sicily forced out by the Pompeians, eventually promoted to curule office by Cæsar; C. Rabirius Postumus, the shrewd banker and longtime friend of Cæsar's, who was raised to the prætorship and entertained hopes for consular rank.[180]

Cicero's subordinates in Cilicia included L. Mescinius Rufus, a lightfingered and untrustworthy quæstor, the veteran military man M. Anneius, and Atticus' friend L. Tullius.[181] Obscure figures turn up also in the service of M. Crassus during the ill-fated Parthian expedition: Megabocchus and a certain Octavius, both of whom proved their mettle at Carrhæ, but did not live to tell the tale.[182] Shadowy too are Servianus, a legate of Gabinius' in 57; L. Sestius Pansa, an Asian proquæstor in 54; M'. Sabidius, a legate in Sicily; and Sallustius and Veiento, officers of Bibulus in Syria at the end of the decade.[183] And

[178] On his ædilician defeat, see Cic. *Pro Planc.* 17, 54. Further on Pedius, see Münzer, *RE*, 19:38–40, "Pedius," n.1.

[179] On Hirtius, vonder Mühll, *RE*, 8:1956–1962, "Hirtius," n.2; Titurius Sabinus, Münzer, *RE*, 6A:1575–1577, "Titurius," n.3. He may have been son of L. Titurius Sabinus, the Pompeian legate of 75. But the family does not seem to have been in the senate before Sulla.

[180] For L. Ateius Capito, see Cæl. *Ad Fam.* 8.8.6; Tac. *Ann.* 3.75; Furfanius, Cic. *Ad Att.* 7.15.2; *Ad Fam.* 6.8.3, 6.9–perhaps from Spoletium, Syme, *Historia*, 13 (1964): 116–117; Rabirius Postumus, Cic. *Ad Att.* 12.49.2; cf. Broughton, *MRR*, II:481; *Suppl.*, p. 53. But cf. on Furfanius and Postumius the discussion of Sumner, *Phoenix*, 25 (1971):254–255, 268–269. On the family of T. Sextius, see Wiseman, *CQ*, 14 (1964): 130–131.

[181] Broughton, *MRR*, II:242, 244–245. Anneius may be the young man who contested the will of his father; Val. Max. 7.7.2. If so, he is son of a Roman *eques*, but adopted by a Sufenas, perhaps a Nonius Sufenas. The brother of Mescinius Rufus was also an *eques*; Nicolet, *L'Ordre Equestre*, pp. 258–259. Tullius will have been of similar stock, possibly son of L. Tullius, a *magister scripturæ* noted in the 70s; Cic. *Verr.* 2.3.167.

[182] Plut. *Crass.* 25, 27–31. There is nothing to suggest that Octavius derived from the senatorial branches of that *gens.* He may be the loose-tongued and light-headed Octavius who mocked Cæsar and Pompey in 59; Suet. *Iul.* 49. Megabocchus was presumably a relative of the C. Megabocchus convicted after governing Sardinia some time before 54; Cic. *Pro Scauro*, 40.

[183] On Servianus, see Broughton, *MRR*, II:204. The name is sometimes emended to "Servilius"; perhaps identical with the prefect of Pompey's fleet in 65; Broughton, *MRR*, II:160.

the 50s witness the emergence of another new house, the brothers Ligarii: Titus, a quæstor in 54, and Quintus, legate of Africa and later the subject of Cicero's compelling *Pro Ligario,* which earned him a pardon from Cæsar.[184] With somewhat less confidence we may register Canidius, an official of Cato's in Cyprus during the early 50s, perhaps an ex-quæstor.[185]

Various and sundry other *novi homines* are discoverable in the senate of the 50s. Information permits only the itemizing of their names. Observe, for example, Cæcilius, an unknown quæstor of 59; Cn. Oppius Cornicinus, an elderly senator in 57; L. Procilius, recorded at a senatorial meeting of 56; M. Eppius, witness to a senatorial decree in 51; and Cn. Nerius, a *quæstor urbanus* in 49.[186] Further, some men are noted under unusual circumstances: C. Vibienus, slain in domestic riots of 58; Sex. Teidius, the lame senator who discovered Clodius' mangled body in 52; and the unhappy Q. Calpenus, a former senator reduced to the humiliating status of a gladiator during Cæsar's dictatorship.[187] Also in the senate by the late 50s were Servæus, convicted *de ambitu* in 50 after campaigning for the tribunate; the obscure Tuticanus Gallus; Postumius, a subordinate officer of Cato's in 49; and Licinius Lenticula (or Denticula), who was restored from exile in 49.[188] Finally, M. Aquinus,

---

But "Servianus" is not impossible; cf. the moneyer L. Servius Rufus in the 40s or Servius Cordus, a quæstor ca. 48; Syme, *Historia*, 4 (1955): 69. For Sestius Pansa, see Broughton, *MRR*, II:224; Sabidius, Broughton, *MRR*, II:483. Veiento may be a Fabricius Veiento, ancestor of the convicted author under Nero; Cic. *Ad Att.* 7.3.5; Tac. *Ann.* 14.50; cf. Cic. *Ad Att.* 4.17.3. The *cognomen*, however, or a variant thereof, is also found among the Perpernæ, a consular clan. But caution forbids listing Veiento among the *nobiles*. On Sallustius, certainly not the historian, see Cic. *Ad Fam.* 2.17; cf. Syme, *Sallust*, p. 11.

[184] On T. Ligarius, Cic. *Pro Lig.* 35-36; on Q. Ligarius, Cic. *Pro Lig. passim.*

[185] Cf. Wiseman, *CQ*, 14 (1964): 123.

[186] For Cæcilius, Cic. *Ad Att.* 2.9.1, perhaps a relative of Atticus' uncle, or of the C. Cæcilius mentioned in Cic. *Pro Flacco*, 89; M. Oppius Cornicinus, Cic. *Ad Att.* 4.2.4; *P. Red. ad Quir.* 12; Procilius, Cic. *Ad Q. Frat.* 2.8.1; Eppius, Cæl. *Ad Fam.* 8.8.5; Nerius, Broughton, *MRR*, II:259; Wiseman, *New Men*, p. 244, no. 270. Oppius can hardly be regarded as an authentic descendant of Sp. Oppius Cornicen, the decemvir of the mid fifth century. Procilius is identifiable with the man convicted in 54; Cic. *Ad Att.* 4.15.4. But there is no reason to reckon him a tribune in 56; see below, chap. 8, n.25.

[187] On Vibienus, see Cic. *Pro Mil.* 37; cf. Wiseman, *Mnemosyne*, 16 (1963): 275-283. Broughton, *MRR*, II:498, wrongly places his death in 52; see Clark, *Cic. Pro Mil.*, 34. On Teidius, Asconius, 32, Clark; cf. Plut. *Pomp.* 64; Calpenus, Suet. *Iul.* 39.

[188] Servæus' conviction is given by Cæl. *Ad Fam.* 8.4.2. On Tuticanus, see Cæs. *BC*, 3.71. Cichorius, *Röm. Stud.*, pp. 79-81, offers the ingenious conjecture that Lucilius plays on the name P. Tuticanus Gallus with his *Publius Pavus Tubitanus quæstor* (XIV.467-468)-hence the family would already be senatorial in the second century. It will be prudent, however, not to reckon Tuticanus of aristocratic ancestry on the basis of that speculation. Postumius is identifiable with T. Postumius, an orator slain in the civil war; Cic. *Ad Att.* 7.15.2; *Brutus*, 269. The *prænomen* dissociates him from the senatorial Postumii; cf. Shackleton Bailey, *Cicero's Letters*, IV:310-311. On Licinius, see Cic. *Phil.* 2.56; Dio, 45.47.4.

epitomized as the *novus homo* of humble derivation who rose to magisterial rank in Rome.[189]

Thus the *pedarii.* Scrappy documentation prevents a fleshing-out of the skeleton. It is only the rare personage in this cast for whom we can pinpoint background, family, and associations. Yet it seems clear that even the lower ranks of the *curia* were not recruited from lowly artisans, foreigners, or the proletariate. The *equester ordo* was a prime source of personnel; men of status and wealth from business, from the land, and from the *municipia.* For many of the *novi homines,* equestrian origins are specifically attested: fathers, brothers, or other relatives in the class of knights—for example, M. Anneius, Q. Axius, Cæcilius, Q. Cæcilius Niger, Calidius, L. Mescinius Rufus, P. Oppius, Q. Pedius, C. Rabirius Postumus, P. Tadius, L. Tullius, T. Vettius. The same may be assumed for the bulk of the remainder. Their presence will not have demeaned the senate. As has recently—and properly—been observed, barriers between the senatorial and equestrian *ordines* were far from impenetrable. The image of *equites* as tawdry businessmen should long since have been exploded. They included influential men of affairs, landowners, bankers, and tax farmers, many of them representatives of the municipal aristocracy throughout Italy. In wealth and even in influence, individual *equites* might often surpass their senatorial counterparts. The area of natural opposition between the two *ordines* was narrow, the area of common interest very large. Insofar as there had been friction, it revolved primarily around control of the courts; after the Sullan era, that bone of contention was a thing of the past. Senators and *equites* were united in support of a social and economic order in which they were the controlling forces. The difference rested in *dignitas* and access to *honores.* The *equester ordo* constituted essentially that part of the Roman upper classes which had not served in the halls of the senate. For some, that was a matter of choice; for others, it was due to the restrictive traditions of the senatorial class. But here too the Ciceronian period witnessed a change of policy. Sulla's expansion of the senate opened up positions that enabled numerous individuals to abandon equestrian origins and take on senatorial status. In itself, that was no radical innovation—except in numbers. Boundaries between the *ordo senatorius* and the *ordo equester* had grown gradually more indistinct. Several *gentes* included both senatorial and equestrian branches; and members of even the same family could be found both in the senate and among the *equites.* The Ciceronian age accelerated and encouraged the process, bringing into the *curia* major equestrian houses and representatives of the Italian aristocracy.[190] But the gates swung wide only at a certain level. The bulk of the new men spent their senatorial careers among the *pedarii.*

[189] *BAfr.* 57.3: *homo novus parvusque senator.*

[190] On the *equester ordo,* see Nicolet, *L'Ordre Equestre, passim*; esp., pp. 253–464; also Brunt,

Review of the Ciceronian senate sheds some needed light. Statistics can deceive: bold and clear in expression, they are tentative and vulnerable in fact, a stimulus for reflection rather than a fixed and finished product. When reduced to particulars, the imprecision is evident–and inescapable: many individuals perch on various borderlines. Categorization here (like all categorization) is ultimately arbitrary. But patterns emerge, disputable in detail, firmer in the outline. It is possible to draw certain conclusions.

The names gathered include all known magistrates elected for the years 78 through 49, plus every individual who may reasonably be said to have entered the senate between Sulla's dictatorship and the civil war. Structure of the senate takes on discernible shape. The conventional hierarchy, taut and pyramidal, was unshaken; if anything, it was more rigid than in the past. There is no sign of a breakdown in well-established patterns of deference.

The consulship was claimed as a birthright by the *nobilitas.* Their control of the office during the Republic's last generation amounted to a near exclusivist monopoly: fifty-four of sixty-one consular posts. That discovery is neither new nor surprising. More telling are analogous configurations found on each rung of the magisterial ladder. Men with consular ancestors in pre-Sullan Rome possessed every advantage also in prætorian contests. Nearly half of all known prætors elected in the Ciceronian age were *nobiles* and almost 80 percent possessed precursors in the senate. The prætorship was hardly more open to *novi homines* than was the consulate. The new men who reached that rank had in almost every instance been demonstrably advanced by powerful politicians or political groups for their own purposes. Documentation drops off sharply on the ædiles, but the proportions show no marked change. *Nobiles* account for more than 40 percent of the recorded number, men of senatorial blood for more than 70 percent. Even more striking are figures on the tribunate. That office was nominally an organ of the *plebs,* a voice of the common man. Patricians were debarred from offering themselves, and some other aristocrats avoided the post lest they be tainted with radical coloration. But analysis of the preserved names reveals that conventional standards applied here as well. Approximately 30 percent of the tribunes derived from consular houses, two-thirds of the total from senatorial houses. Activist posturing was common during the year of a man's tribunate; it was usually followed by a sober and conservative career. There can be little doubt that Roman adherence to a standard hierarchy was unchanged–perhaps even tightened–in the later years of the Republic. No need to postulate intimidation or heavy-handed control of the electoral processes. There are but few examples of disruption in the

---

Second Int. Conf. of Econ. Hist., 1962 (Paris, 1965), I:117–137. On the influx of Italians, cf. the remarks of Syme, *PBSR,* 14 (1938): 22–25; Gabba, *Athenæum,* 32 (1954): 102–114.

magisterial *comitia*. The Roman voter performed in habitual ways. A practiced aristocracy, relying on patronage and heritage, remained secure.

At the same time, however, a safety valve existed. The aristocracy was secure, but not frozen or petrified. The Ciceronian senate contained twice as many members as its predecessors. Into its ranks came former *equites*, municipal leaders, representatives from minor branches or lesser offshoots from senatorial houses. It formed a logical and proper corollary to the enfranchisement of Italy after the Social War and the expansion of empire witnessed by the late Republic. The change is best observed among the *pedarii*, men installed by Sulla or elected to the quæstorship but remaining within the lower echelons of the senate during the Ciceronian era. In this company, the *nobiles* constitute only a small proportion. The recorded names account for about 23 percent of the number; but many of them did move to higher levels after the civil war, and many others were prevented only by death or conviction from attaining further magistracies. By contrast, one-half of the *pedarii* whose names have come down to us were new men without ancestors in the senate. The recruits, it must be stressed, differed little from the old aristocrats in economic position or social temperament. There was small risk that they would alter the conservative and conventional attitudes of the ruling class. And few of them could expect elevation to posts higher than junior magistracies without the patronage and backing of the mighty. But the drawing-in of such groups permitted the senate to be more responsive to wider elements in Italian society; and, no less important, it served to co-opt those individuals and families whose wealth and influence might otherwise have presented a challenge to the established powers. Far from showing signs of crumbling, the traditional structure gained a broader perspective and firmer stability.

VI

LEGISLATIVE ACTIVITY: CRIMINAL AND ADMINISTRATIVE LAW

THE REPUBLICAN ruling class has suffered much abuse. Sallust's moralizing branded it with idleness, selfish ambition, and greed. Modern historians have continued the denunciations with even greater vehemence: Roman senators in the late Republic betrayed the principles of their ancestors; concerned only with preservation of its privileges, the ruling class ignored responsibilities to the community, became an ever more closed corporation, and inexorably undermined its own authority; corruption and self-indulgence proved to be a cancer in the aristocracy; by neglecting internal reform, the aristocrats brought on revolution.[1] This depressing tale has too long gone unchallenged. Was it, in fact, true that the *nobiles* overlooked or perpetuated abuses, and narrowed themselves into a tight and irresponsible oligarchy? Did they yield the initiative to popular demagogues and military leaders, thereby forfeiting respect and sealing their own doom?

It will not be easy to issue a definitive answer. But the censure rests too much on moral pronouncements, not enough on facts. Enlightenment may come from examination of the proposals, decrees, and legislation attested in the late Republic. Despite countless volumes on the period, this central aspect has yet to receive systematic analysis. So, for example, it has been assumed that bills which proposed reform or institutional change were submitted almost exclusively by tribunes acting in the interests of the people or of certain

[1] The thunderous pronouncements of Mommsen set the tone for almost all subsequent analyses; see, esp., *Römische Geschichte* (Berlin, 1903–1904), III:461–569. For typical examples, see Gelzer, *Cicero* (Wiesbaden, 1969), pp. 14, 63, 152; R. E. Smith, *The Failure of the Roman Republic* (Cambridge, 1955), pp. 108–119; and, most recently, Meier, "Ciceros Consulat," in G. Radke, *Cicero, ein Mensch seiner Zeit* (Berlin, 1968), pp. 64–78.

politicians.[2] In fact, reform measures initiated in the senate were more than twice as numerous as tribunician proposals. And not all of the latter met with senatorial resistance. The image of hidebound conservatives reacting in reflex against every suggestion for change does not correspond to the evidence.

Several charges stand against the senate in the area of governmental administration: corruption in the electoral process, inequities in the judiciary, unwillingness to countenance administrative or institutional amendment, and inability to maintain internal order. Profit will accrue from examination of each of these aspects. For it is striking that the bulk of the known legislative proposals and enactments fall precisely in those areas.

THE ATTACK ON ELECTORAL CORRUPTION

Electoral abuses did not originate in the Ciceronian age. Measures dealing with *ambitus* (electoral corruption) are attested from the days of the early Republic. At some time, ca. 120, Rome instituted a permanent court to deal with such violations. The *quæstio de ambitu* had considerable business in subsequent years. Vigorous campaigning could easily slide into shady practices. Competitors would keep a sharp eye on their rivals in anticipation of potential prosecution.[3] Sulla, in reorganizing the courts, directed his attention to the problem of *ambitus.* A *lex Cornelia* stands on record, sharpening the penalty for conviction on this charge. Henceforth, a candidate found guilty of illegal canvassing would be prohibited for a decade from resuming his candidacy.[4] That the measure served as a deterrent may be doubted. No *ambitus* cases are attested for the decade after Sulla's dictatorship. But our evidence falls well short of completeness. A number of trials receive only the briefest mention in passing and remain without date or without charge.[5] In any event, the absence of *ambitus* prosecutions would not prove the absence of illegal canvassing. Filing of formal charges, more often than not, depended on political circumstances and the influence wielded by prospective participants. There was much talk, for example, of voter bribery in the elections of 70.[6] Yet none of the victorious candidates suffered prosecution.

[2] Cf. L. R. Taylor, *Party Politics*, pp. 71–75.

[3] Cf. Q. Cicero's advice to his brother; *Comm. Petit.* 52: *cura ut . . . si qua possit ratione, competitoribus tuis exsistat aut sceleris aut libidinis aut largitionis accommodata ad eorum mores infamia.*

[4] Schol. Bob. 78, Stangl: *superioribus temporibus damnati lege Cornelia hoc genus pœnæ ferebant, ut magistratuum petitione per decem annos abstinerent.* On measures against *ambitus* from the early Republic, see A. W. Zumpt, *Das Criminalrecht der römischen Republik* (Berlin, 1869), II:2.218–222. For the institution of the *quæstio de ambitu*, see Gruen, *Roman Politics*, pp. 120–125; 260–261.

[5] So, for example, an *ambitus* case, apparently in the early 60s, is alluded to, as an aside, by Cicero in *Pro Cluent.* 132.

[6] Cf. Cic. *Verr.* 1.17–29.

Chicanery in the electoral process remained a problem. The censors of 70 struck numerous Romans off the senate rolls. Those who were ousted needed election to office to recover senatorial status. That provided even greater heat in the electoral scramble of subsequent years.[7] To those desperate for office, felonious methods lay at hand. It is no coincidence that agitation for greater controls came a short time thereafter.

The year 67 witnessed pressures for an *ambitus* bill with more teeth. A fractious contest ensued. Principal antagonists were a tribune, C. Cornelius, and the consul C. Calpurnius Piso. Rival bills were offered, tribunician veto intervened, and mob violence threatened chaos, before a measure finally secured passage. The affair is commonly misunderstood. Temptation is great to see a contest between the popular, reformist tribune, eager to correct abuses, and a conservative senate headed by the consul, who resisted change. That antithesis, however, misleads. Politics were indeed involved. Cornelius had been quæstor of Pompey the Great's in the Spanish wars of the 70s. And Piso, friend of Lucullus, Hortensius, and Bibulus, was a bitter foe of Pompey's. His opposition to Cornelius formed but part of his activity during a vigorous consulship. Piso also clashed with A. Gabinius and Lollius Palicanus, both of whom had associated themselves with Pompey. And he attacked the general directly, throwing all possible obstacles in the way of his command against the pirates.[8] But friction between reformers and reactionaries would be an improper conclusion. As so often in Roman history, when change seemed necessary, politicians contended to secure credit for sponsoring the innovation. Cornelius initiated the pressure, but when an *ambitus* bill eventually passed, it was that of C. Calpurnius Piso: the *lex Calpurnia.*

What happened precisely is unclear. Our sources leave something to be desired. Dio Cassius' account is brief and does not preserve all details. Cicero's speech at Cornelius' trial in 65 exists only in fragments, supplemented by Asconius' sometimes disjointed commentary. But reconstruction is possible. The evidence lends itself to a new approach: events take shape as a jockeying for position and rivalry between men anxious to gain recognition as sponsors of reform.

The content of Cornelius' proposal is unknown. Senatorial discussion, however, found it too severe: excessive penalties, so it was claimed, would not act as a deterrent to *ambitus* because the courts would be unwilling to convict. The consuls were therefore instructed to frame a more moderate measure for

[7] Dio, 36.38.2: *ἐπειδὴ . . . πολλοὶ τῶν ὑπὸ τῶν τιμητῶν διαγεγραμμένων ἀναλαβεῖν τρόπον τινὰ τὴν βουλείαν ἐσπούδαζον, συστάσεις καὶ παρακελευσμοὶ παμπληθεῖς ἐφ' ἁπάσαις ταῖς ἀρχαῖς ἐγίγνοντο*. Wiseman, *JRS*, 59 (1969): 65–67, suggests that enrollment of new voters by the censorship of 70–69 encouraged an increase in electoral malpractice.

[8] Discussion and references in Gruen, *CSCA*, 1 (1968): 156–159.

presentation to the assembly.[9] There was evidently no question of rejecting the demand for new *ambitus* legislation. The issue at stake involved the form of the *lex.* Piso constructed his bill and urgently pressed for passage. Magisterial elections were at hand, and under Roman law, no legislation could be proposed after the date for the elections had been announced. Piso required special dispensation to present his measure to the people; the senate acquiesced.[10] The unusual procedure is explicable only by Piso's need for haste. He had to preempt Cornelius' bill lest it be passed and render his own bill otiose.

Cornelius was not easily circumvented. He now directed his fire at the inappropriateness of senatorial action, urging that no release from the laws could be granted except by the people themselves.[11] If this approach were to prove successful, Piso's bill would be postponed and Cornelius could push his own proposal through. The maneuver set a chain of rapid events in motion. A tribune emerged to veto Cornelius' effort; Cornelius pressed on, reading aloud his own bill against dispensations; rioting ensued, Piso was attacked directly, his *fasces* were broken, and Cornelius dismissed the assembly.[12] The result, it appears, was postponement of the elections by Piso.[13] That gave the consul renewed opportunity to present his *ambitus* bill to the assembly.

The *populus,* goaded by Cornelius and other tribunes, found fault with Piso's *rogatio.* It provided penalties for offending candidates, but did not address itself to other offenders, notably the *divisores,* bribery agents who distributed cash through the tribes. Popular reaction insisted that, unless *divisores* were subject to prosecution, *ambitus* could not be curbed. Hence, Piso's bill met with disfavor; the people clamored for Cornelius' proposal.[14] The immediately subsequent events do not receive treatment in the sources. But it is possible to effect a reconstruction. Piso was no fool; nor was he an inveterate reactionary. Passage of a *lex* in his name constituted the principal aim. He evidently modified his proposal and included provisions directed against the activities of the *divisores.* Such, at least, is a logical inference from the fact that the professional bribery-agents now vented their wrath upon

[9] Dio, 36.38.4–5.

[10] Dio, 36.39.1. The prohibition on legislative bills between the announcement and the holding of elections was contained in the *leges Ælia et Fufia;* cf. Schol. Bob. 148, Stangl.

[11] Asconius, 58, Clark; Dio, 36.39.2.

[12] Asconius, 58, 60–61, Clark; Cic. *In Vat.* 5; Dio, 36.39.3–4; Quint. *Inst. Orat.* 4.4.8.

[13] There were, in fact, two postponements of the elections in 67; Cic. *De Imp. Pomp.* 2; cf. *Ad Att.* 1.11.2.

[14] Cic. *Pro Corn. apud* Asconius, 74–75, Clark: *qua re cum hæc populus Romanus videret et cum a tribunis plebis doceretur, nisi pœna accessisset in divisores, exstingui ambitum nullo modo posse, legem hanc Corneli flagitabat, illam quæ ex s.c. ferebatur repudiabat.*

the consul, attacking him in force and driving him from the forum.[15] Piso retreated, only to return the stronger. By posing as the wronged champion of reform, he had successfully isolated the *divisores* as the source of violent opposition. Piso could now call upon all patriotic citizens to support his cause. The senate provided a bodyguard, and at the succeeding *comitia* the bill was passed.[16] Piso had effectively neutralized and outbid Cornelius.

If Piso's measure originally seemed more moderate than that of Cornelius, it could hardly have been so in final form. His bill prescribed penalties considerably stiffer than those of any previous *ambitus* legislation. The *lex Calpurnia* swiftly got the reputation of extreme severity.[17] Sulla's law had banned convicted candidates from canvassing for a decade. The *lex Calpurnia* excluded them from office altogether, expelled them from the senate, and imposed a financial penalty.[18] The nature of the provisions against *divisores* are not known. But extension of *ambitus* legislation against those who actually distributed the cash was a change of real substance.[19] The *nobiles* had not proved to be an obstacle to reform. Piso earned credit for a sweeping *lex de ambitu.* That effected, his friends settled for a compromise measure on the other issue raised by Cornelius: dispensations from the law could be granted by the senate, so long as a quorum of two hundred was present, and *intercessio* was forbidden

[15] Asconius, 75, Clark: *C. Piso . . . cum legem de ambitu ex s.c. graviorem quam fuerat antea ferret et propter multitudinem divisorum qui per vim adversabantur e foro eiectus esset.* Best discussion of these complex events is by W. McDonald, *CQ*, 23 (1929): 196–208, if one leaves aside his identification of the combatants as "popular party" and "senatorial party." Cf. also Nicolet, *RevHistDroitFrEtr*, 36 (1958): 262–266.

[16] For Piso's summons to the people, see Cic. *Pro Corn. apud* Asconius, 75, Clark: *qui rem p. salvam esse vellent, ut ad legem accipiendam adessent*; cf. Dio, 36.39.1.

[17] Cic. *Pro Mur.* 46: *erat enim severissime scripta Calpurnia.*

[18] Dio, 36.38.1: μήτ' ἄρχειν μήτε βουλεύειν σφῶν μηδένα, ἀλλὰ καὶ χρήματα προσοφλισκάνειν; Schol. Bob. 78, Stangl: *aliquanto postea severior lex Calpurnia et pecunia multavit et in perpetuum honoribus iussit carere damnatos*; Asconius, 69, Clark: *lex hæc Calpurnia de ambitu erat . . . in qua præter alias pœnas pecuniaria quoque pœna erat adiecta*; cf. Asconius, 88, Clark.

[19] Mommsen, *Römisches Strafrecht* (Leipzig, 1899), 870, denies that Piso's bill encompassed the *divisores.* But that ignores the obvious implications of Asconius, 75–76, Clark, discussed above. *Divisores* were certainly liable for prosecution by the mid 50s; Cic. *Pro Planc.* 55. Zumpt, *Criminalrecht*, II:2.225–226, rightly points to Cic. *Pro Mur.* 47: *pœna gravior in plebem tua voce efflagitata est.* If, in 63, a heavier penalty was demanded against the *plebs*, it follows that the *lex Calpurnia* was directed against other than just senatorial offenders. Zumpt, however, as he so often does, presses his case too far in insisting that the clause against *divisores* was contained not in Cornelius' proposal but only in Piso's. The evidence of Asconius, 74–75, Clark, excludes that notion. The reconstruction of W. E. Heitland, *The Roman Republic* (Cambridge, 1923), III:53, that the *lex Calpurnia* offered lesser penalties for candidates and *divisores* than Cornelius' bill, is undemonstrable. McDonald's view, *CQ*, 23 (1929): 204–205, that the final version of Piso's law differed little from Cornelius' original proposal, is probably closer to the mark.

if the matter was brought to the people.[20] The Roman ruling class had acted with circumspection.

Other practices connected with canvassing now became subject to senatorial scrutiny. Those who sought office customarily surrounded themselves with large throngs of clients and ostensible supporters. The routine displayed influence and popularity. Candidates wishing to exude confidence and attract the independent voter would not appear in public without an impressive array of attendants.[21] But the practice could lend itself to abuse. Genuine loyalty or enthusiasm need not be the only motives drawing men to the retinue of a candidate. Suspicious minds detected inducements: gladiatorial shows, generous banquets, free seats at the games, perhaps even financial compensation for those who would attend the office seeker. Such activities had not previously been tampered with. But in the post-Sullan era, pressure for governmental regulation increased.

Evidence on the matter is skimpy in the extreme. A single reference in passing informs us of the *lex Fabia,* which restricted the number of attendants permitted to accompany a candidate.[22] Date and sponsor of the legislation go unreported. The early 60s, however, when electoral practices were undergoing review, provide the appropriate occasion. A pertinent piece of evidence lends confirmation. Young M. Cato, carefully cultivating a reputation for rectitude, embarrassed his rivals when he stood for the military tribunate: he alone scrupulously obeyed a recent law that forbade candidates to employ *nomenclatores.*[23] The latter were retainers who performed the useful task of keeping the candidate informed of voters' names.[24] Purists regarded use of *nomenclatores* as promoting deception. It would not be rash to suggest that this prohibition was part of the *lex Fabia.* Cato served as military tribune in 67 or 66. The measure may therefore be placed not far in time from that of C. Piso, whose friends and associates included Cato's circle.[25]

The proliferation of legislative enactments could not always curb long-standing practices. Humble clients persisted in accompanying their patrons in the

[20] Asconius, 59, 72, Clark; cf. Dio, 36.39.4.

[21] Cf. [Q. Cic.] *Comm. Petit.* 34–37; Cic. *Pro Mur.* 70.

[22] Cic. *Pro Mur.* 71.

[23] Plut. *Cato,* 8.2.

[24] Cf. Cic. *Ad Att.* 4.1.5; *Pro Mur.* 77.

[25] On the date of Cato's military tribunate, see Broughton, *MRR,* II:147, 150, n.12. The *lex Fabia* must predate 63 when it is cited by Cicero. G. Niccolini, *I Fasti dei Tribuni della Plebe* (Milan, 1934), p. 266, puts it in 64, on the grounds that the *Commentariolum Petitionis* knows of no restrictions on attendants for candidates. But the authenticity of that tract is in dispute; see above, chap. 4, n.76. Cicero's solitary reference to the *lex Fabia,* in fact, suggests that the law is earlier than 64; *Pro Mur.* 71: *Itaque et legi Fabiæ quæ est de numero sectatorum, et senatus consulto quod est L. Cæsare consule* [64] *factum restiterunt.*

canvass. It was one of their few means of discharging obligations to benefactors.[26] Nor did the *nomenclator* disappear. That convenient institution, which enabled candidates to greet voters by name, was too useful to be dropped. Legislation violating accepted standards proves generally unenforceable. Even Cato recognized its futility and resumed employment of *nomenclatores*.[27] The year 66, which followed passage of the stringent *lex Calpurnia de ambitu*, nonetheless witnessed a notorious electoral scandal. The *consules designati* were both convicted of bribing the electorate, and new elections had to be held.[28] Even penalties assessed against *divisores* did not prevent their activities in that campaign.[29] The ousted candidates refused to acknowledge the results and organized disturbances aimed at the new consuls in the beginning of 65.[30] The problem of electoral malpractice remained unresolved.

Senatorial leaders who sought to eliminate *ambitus* must have urged further restrictions after the scandals of 66. Debate and discussion on the matter persisted in subsequent years. Although details cannot be reconstructed, activity in the senate, with a view to new legislation, is clear. In 65 a *senatus consultum* authorized amendment of the *lex Calpurnia* in some respect, probably tightening its provisions.[31]

Further action followed in 64. It was the year of Cicero's consular canvass. His chief rivals, C. Antonius and L. Sergius Catilina, bore unsavory reputation, and there were suspicions of a deal that might involve bribery of the electorate. C. Antonius had been expelled from the senate by the censors of 70 because of a career marked by greed, extortion, and ruthlessness. It might be expected that he would not shrink from bribery to recover his position through a consular post.[32] Catiline was under a cloud on more than one count. Acquitted of extortion in 65, allegedly through collusion with the prosecutor, he would

[26] Cic. *Pro Mur.* 71: *nulla est enim pœna qui possit observantiam tenuiorum ab hoc vetere instituto officiorum excludere.*

[27] Cic. *Pro Mur.* 77: *Quid, quod habes nomenclatorem? In eo quidem fallis et decipis . . . Quid, quod cum admoneris, tamenne per monitorem appellandi sunt cum petis, quasi incertus sis?* The evidence of *Comm. Petit.* 34–37 reflects the practice of the 60s, regardless of what laws may have been on the books.

[28] Sources in Broughton, *MRR*, II:157.

[29] Such, at least, is the implication of Cic. *Pro Corn. apud* Asconius, 74–75, Clark.

[30] Cf. Gruen, *CP*, 64 (1969): 20–24.

[31] Cic. *Pro Corn. apud* Asconius, 69: *Tertium est de legum derogationibus: quo de genere persæpe s.c. fiunt, ut nuper de ipsa lege Calpurnia cui derogaretur.* Whether one should read *obrogationibus*, instead of *derogationibus*, is uncertain. The former would imply an addition to the original law, the latter a subtraction from it. Zumpt, *Criminalrecht*, II:2.249–250, regards the *lex Fabia* as the outcome of this *senatus consultum.* If so, one might have expected Cicero to refer to the *lex*, not simply to senatorial action.

[32] For a summary of Antonius' career and character, see Asconius, 84, Clark.

soon be indicted for murders committed during the Sullan proscriptions.[33] The two men collaborated in their canvass, and rumors spoke of big money and perhaps powerful politicians behind them.[34]

The situation provided occasion for a new senatorial measure increasing the penalties for *ambitus*. Sources, unfortunately, are silent on the substance of the bill, beyond the intensification of punishment. It may have contained a provision cracking down further on the use of attendants by candidates.[35] But reaction was swift. It could be argued that the *senatus consultum* was illegitimate because it was directed *ad hominem* at Catiline. A tribune, Q. Mucius Orestinus, therefore exercised his veto, and the measure was shelved. Political alignments on the issue, if any, are indiscernible. Orestinus may have acted because of personal connections with Catiline. Cicero, though denouncing his rival candidates in the *In Toga Candida* speech, apparently did not press for the new *ambitus* law.[36] The affair revolved around attack and defense of Catiline, rather than the merits of the bill. Orestinus delivered verbal assault on Catiline's rival Cicero.[37] The orator responded with the *In Toga Candida*, but as far as *ambitus* legislation was concerned, he pronounced himself satisfied with the *lex Calpurnia*.[38]

Not everyone was satisfied. Though we are ignorant of the details, it is possible to discern the outlines of debate. *Ambitus* infractions brought predictable response. In 67 Cornelius and Piso had engaged in outbidding one another with the severity of their measures. Subsequent senatorial actions moved in the same direction: the closing of loopholes and the compounding of penalties. But the consequences were not all salutary. Some provisions, like the elimination of *nomenclatores* and the restriction on *adsectatores* (attendants), proved unenforceable. And increased penalties brought criticism that the harshness was no longer commensurate with the offense. The latter argument may have inspired Orestinus' veto in 64. It was, in any case, dramatized at the beginning of 63.

[33] For alleged chicanery in the extortion trial, see Cic. *De Har. Resp.* 42; [Q. Cic.] *Comm. Petit.* 10; Asconius, 86–87, Clark. The trial in 64 took place shortly after the elections; Asconius, 91, Clark.

[34] Asconius, 82–83, Clark.

[35] On the increase of penalties, see Asconius, 83, Clark: *cum in dies licentia ambitus augeretur propter præcipuam Catilinæ et Antoni audaciam, censuerat senatus ut lex ambitus aucta etiam cum pœna ferretur.* The *s.c.* of 64, resisted because of limitations on attendants, may be identical with this measure; Cic. *Pro Mur.* 71. *Contra*: T. E. Kinsey, *RevBelg*, 43 (1965): 57–59.

[36] For the veto and the shelving of the law, see Asconius, 83, 85–86, 88, Clark. Catiline was married to an Aurelia Orestilla; hence perhaps a personal connection with Mucius Orestinus; cf. Münzer, *RE*, 16:423–424, "Mucius," n.12.

[37] Cic. *Pro Corn. apud* Asconius, 86, Clark.

[38] Cic. *Pro Corn. apud* Asconius, 88, Clark: *sed ego ea lege contentus sum qua duos consules designatos uno tempore damnari vidimus.*

The *lex Calpurnia de ambitu* provided that convicted offenders be expelled from the senate and excluded from further office. Among the victims of that legislation was P. Sulla, Pompey's brother-in-law and one of the convicted *consules designati* of 66. The demonstration organized against his successors at the outset of the following year may have been in part a protest against the severity of the law. Sulla's status remained for the moment unaltered. But one of the tribunes elected for 63 was his half-brother L. Cæcilius Rufus. Cæcilius' first order of business was the reinstatement of Sulla. He did not propose to criticize the judgment of the court that convicted his brother. Cæcilius essayed a more fundamental approach: he called the law itself into question. Mitigation of Sulla's punishment was the goal. To effect it, Cæcilius had to argue for the law to be amended and the penalty retroactively reduced.[39] The *acerbitas* of the *lex Calpurnia* was now under challenge. The argument had some merit: exclusion from public office for electoral indiscretions could put a heavy damper on political activities. This was especially true if, as seems the case, the *lex Calpurnia* was more specific in assessing the penalty than in defining the offense. Cæcilius could muster some support.[40] But the implications of his proposal caused misgivings. Amendment of the law was, of course, proper, but retroactive reversal of a judicial decision raised problems that many senators did not want to face. And, in the light of recent events, the *patres* were in no mood to emasculate *ambitus* legislation by reduction of punishment. Sulla acknowledged the futility of pushing a measure against the senatorial majority and instructed his supporters to desist. The bill perished in the senate and never reached the assembly.[41]

Excessive speculation on the politics of this affair would be imprudent. Yet the involvement of Pompey's friends bears notice. It will be remembered that an ex-officer of Pompey's first broached the issue of *ambitus* legislation in 67, only to be outbid by Pompey's *inimicus* C. Piso. In 63, when criticism emerged against the harshness of Piso's *lex,* it came on behalf of Pompey's brother-in-law. Resistance to the motion, we may surmise, was led by Piso and his associates. P. Sulla ordered the bill withdrawn, and the request was transmitted to the senate by another brother-in-law of Pompey's, Q. Metellus

[39] Cic. *Pro Sulla,* 63–64: *nihil de iudicio ferebat, sed pœnam ambitus eam referebat quæ fuerat nuper superioribus legibus constituta. Itaque hac rogatione non iudicum sententia, sed legis vitium corrigebatur. Nemo iudicium reprehendit, cum de pœna queritur, sed legem . . . semper Cæcilius in calamitate fratris, sui iudicum potestatem perpetuandam, legis acerbitatem mitigandam putavit.*

[40] Dio, 37.25.3, suggests that the consul C. Antonius was sympathetic to the proposal. But his account is tendentious and probably ought not be pressed.

[41] Cic. *Pro Sulla,* 62: *promulgarit impulsus amore fraterno, destiterit fratris auctoritate deductus*; 65: *lex dies fuit proposita paucos, ferri cœpta numquam, deposita est in senatu.*

Celer.[42] The general evidently wished to avoid another political defeat on this issue.

The advocates of stringent penalties carried the day. And in the course of 63 they sought to press their advantage by promoting even more restrictive legislation. That effort paralleled the abortive attempt of the previous year. Once again a consular candidacy by Catiline provided the occasion. This time the movement for a sharper *ambitus* law had the *auctoritas* of a distinguished jurist and expert in civil law, Ser. Sulpicius Rufus. Only one consular post in any particular year was open to a patrician. Sulpicius, in advancing his own candidacy for that position, reaffirmed the dangers that an election of Catiline might bring.[43] Sulpicius' repute carried weight. He was the most learned of jurists, the only man, so Cicero affirmed, who transformed the science of civil law into an art. Sulpicius was at the top of his profession, one of the few men who could combine profound erudition and penetrating acumen.[44] But the expert in jurisprudence did not necessarily make the competent politician. Cicero poked good-natured fun at the jurist bogged down in legalistic minutiæ. Men of action, not phrasemongers, won consular elections.[45] Sulpicius recognized his disadvantages: hence his electoral campaign was conducted with denunciations of his rivals, rumors of bribery, and threats of prosecution. Part and parcel of this strategy was the demand for a new and more severe bribery law.[46] He could hope to carry with him that large portion of the senate which had been frustrated by Orestinus' veto in the previous year and was prepared to sanction harsh legislation.

The provisions that Ser. Sulpicius sought to urge upon the senate are not altogether clear. But the bill certainly possessed a sweeping and extreme character. Convicted candidates were not only to be excluded from public life; they were to suffer exile. Punishment for the *plebs* was to be increased. This refers probably to *divisores,* not to recipients of bribes. It would hardly be possible to garner evidence for indictment of the latter. A further clause provided penalties for those who pleaded ill health. That would apply, one may surmise, to jurors and witnesses in *ambitus* cases.[47] Sulpicius also sought

[42] Cic. *Pro Sulla,* 65: *et id mandatu Sullæ Q. Metellus prætor se loqui dixit Sullam illam rogationem de se nolle ferri.*

[43] Cic. *Pro Mur.* 48.

[44] Cic. *Brutus,* 150–156; *De Leg.* 1.5.17; Gellius, 2.10. There are, of course, numerous references to Sulpicius in later jurists. On his career generally, see the biography by P. Meloni, *Ann. Univ. Cagliari,* 13 (1946): 67–245.

[45] Cic. *Pro Mur.* 38: *Imperatores enim comitiis consularibus, non verborum interpretes, deliguntur*; Cicero's prolonged mockery is in *Pro Mur.* 19–30.

[46] Cic. *Pro Mur.* 43–47.

[47] Cic. *Pro Mur.* 47: *pœna gravior in plebem tua voce efflagitata est . . . exsilium in nostrem ordinem . . . morbi excusationi pœna addita est*; cf. Zumpt, *Criminalrecht,* II:2.226–228; 259–260.

to place every advantage with the prosecutor: he would have the right of selecting jury panels.[48] Beyond that, the proposed clauses are obscure. Cicero denounces the remainder as leveling all distinctions in the voting process, on the model of the *lex Manilia*. The text, however, is corrupt and interpretation difficult. Most probably, the orator alludes to a tribunician bill of Manilius in 66, which authorized freedmen to vote with their ex-masters, hence spreading them among all tribes. Precisely how and why Sulpicius expected to revive that measure is unclear. Perhaps it was a maneuver to gain passage of his *ambitus* bill in the assembly.[49]

The radical proposal must have stirred considerable senatorial debate. Much depended on the reaction of the consul, M. Cicero, who would be called upon to present the bill to the *populus*. Cicero's attitude may be divined. A year before, he had occupied Sulpicius' position, delivering fiery diatribes against rival candidates. But he had not advocated more severe *leges de ambitu:* the *lex Calpurnia* was quite severe enough. At the same time he was reluctant to see changes in the law that would reduce the penalty.[50] Cicero maintained that stance during his consulship, advising Sulpicius that the *lex Calpurnia* was sufficiently potent for his purposes.[51] But the consul found himself in an awkward position. Sulpicius was pushing ahead, and a senatorial majority was inclined toward legislation that would enact heavier penalties. Politics may also have played a role. The interests of Cato, it can be inferred, coincided with the Sulpician proposal. Cato joined with Sulpicius in attacks on Catiline and threatened to bring a charge against the alleged conspirator. Cato was also at Sulpicius' side in the later accusation of L. Murena, who had obtained election.[52] By contrast, a rigorous *ambitus* law would probably not have been to the liking of Pompeius Magnus. The general was soon to return to Italy from the eastern wars. He had his own favorites in mind for future consular posts and would have had reservations about restrictive legislation that might excessively tie his hands. Cicero professed to be serving Pompey's interests during his consulship, and his own election was in large part influenced by

[48] Cic. *Pro Mur.* 47: *editicios iudices esse voluisti.* That *editicii iudices* were panels of jurors chosen by the prosecutor may be inferred from Cic. *Pro Planc.* 36, 41; and see Schol. Bob. 152, Stangl.

[49] Cic. *Pro Mur.* 47: *confusionem suffragiorum flagitasti, prærogationum legis Maniliæ æquationem gratiæ, dignitatis, suffragiorum.* "*Prærogationum*" makes no sense; the emendation "*perrogationem*" may be proper. Reference to *suffragia* must be to votes in the assembly, not in the *iudicia*. On Manilius' proposal in 66, see Asconius, 45, 64, 65, Clark; Dio, 36.42.1–4.

[50] Cic. *Pro Sulla*, 62–66; *De Leg. Agrar.* 2.10.

[51] Cic. *Pro Mur.* 46: *legem ambitus flagitasti, quæ tibi non deerat; erat enim severissime scripta Calpurnia.* For Cicero's stance in 64, see Asconius, 88, Clark.

[52] For Cato's threatened prosecution of Catiline, see Cic. *Pro Mur.* 51; for his accusation of Murena, Cic. *Pro Mur.* 3, 13, 58, 62, and *passim*; Plut. *Cic.* 35.2; *Cato*, 21.3–6.

his association with Pompey.[53] Pressures on the consul were not readily reconcilable.

In the end, Cicero did sponsor and secure the passage of a new *ambitus* measure. Given the forces acting upon him, the resultant law possessed intelligence and appeal. The *lex Tullia de ambitu* has not received the credit it warrants. Its provisions take on meaning in light of the previous discussion. Senatorial sentiment for stricter penalties could not be gainsaid. The steering of any bill through the *curia* would have to cater to that mood. Cicero's *lex*, on senatorial instruction, contained Sulpicius' recommendations on exile for convicted candidates and stiffer sanctions for their agents among the *plebs*. *Exilium* for the victims was specified as ten years in duration. The clause prohibiting fabricated excuses for absence from court also found its way into the new law.[54] But Cicero succeeded in persuading the senate to reject the more radical aspects of Sulpicius' proposal, namely the altering of voting procedures and the selection of jury panels by prosecutors.[55]

The particularly enlightened portions of Cicero's law, however, lay elsewhere. The deficiencies of earlier *ambitus* legislation consisted not so much in the leniency or harshness of their sanctions. Excessive senatorial energy had been consumed in debating that issue. The real problem arose from the ill-defined nature of *ambitus* itself. Previous *leges* had been specific on penalties but vague on the crime. Hence, candidates had been encouraged to threaten rivals on flimsy pretexts, construing conventional acts like favors to clients as ostensible grounds for an *ambitus* charge. More pointed legislation, which curtailed attendants or *nomenclatores*, did not help matters, for they were largely unenforceable. More clearly than most of his contemporaries, Cicero recognized these liabilities and addressed himself to them. His law drew sharply defined distinctions. Customary attentions paid to clients were naturally expanded in an electoral campaign. The *lex Tullia*, however, spelled out the lines between innocent acts and conscious violations. The use of *adsectatores* was punishable only if men were paid to greet or accompany the candidate; reserved places for the populace at games financed by the candidate were outlawed; and

[53] Cf. [Q. Cic.] *Comm. Petit.* 5, 51. Cicero stressed his advocacy of Pompey's interests in the *De Lege Agraria, passim.*

[54] Cic. *Pro Mur.* 47, 89; *Pro Planc.* 83; Schol. Bob., 79, Stangl. Dio, 37.29.1, provides the information that exile was fixed at ten years. The Bobbiensian scholiast reports that the law was formally sponsored by both consuls; 79, 140, 151, 166, Stangl. Cicero was, in any case, the prime mover.

[55] Cic. *Pro Mur.* 47. Cicero elsewhere alludes to a proposal on *editicii iudices*, which may refer to Servius' efforts; *Pro Planc.* 41; cf. on this passage, Schol. Bob. 161, Stangl: *commemorationem videtur facere Tullius eius temporis quo Se* [rvius ?] . . . See Zumpt, *Criminalrecht*, II:2.261–263; *contra*: J. L. Strachan-Davidson, *Problems of the Roman Criminal Law* (Oxford, 1912), II:103–108.

a ban was placed on public banquets sponsored by office seekers.[56] The production of gladiatorial shows need not be eliminated. Cicero's law concerned itself only with abuse of the practice: it forbade politicians from organizing such shows within two years of their candidacy for office.[57] Such are the attested clauses of the Ciceronian bill.[58] The measure bore marks of care and moderate compromise. While strengthening the penalties against genuine offenders, both candidates and their agents, it closed the loopholes of earlier legislation. Cicero distinguished between harmless favors bestowed by patrons upon clients and criminal solicitation of votes. He tightened the language and the particulars of the law to provide firm guidelines for judicial process.[59] The senate showed itself capable of profiting from past mistakes and of tailoring legislation to meet current needs.

Cicero skillfully shepherded his bill through. The *severitas* of the penalties circumvented any opposition from Cato, Sulpicius, and others who urged rigor. And the measure's clarity would facilitate a more rational implementation. The *lex Tullia de ambitu* could expect a better fate than its predecessors.

Not that the circle of Cato professed itself satisfied. An attempt at amendment or substitute was made in 61. Pompeius Magnus had returned to Rome, anxious to guarantee a succession of supporters in the chief magistracy. M. Pupius Piso, together with his former commander, worked energetically to assure the election of another ex-officer of Pompey's, L. Afranius, for the year 60. The general's political enemies seized the occasion to spread rumors and insinuate charges. Cato and his brother-in-law Domitius Ahenobarbus were in the forefront, alleging that Pompey was distributing cash for Afranius and that Piso was actually harboring the *divisores* at his home as a headquarters for payment. The allegation may be doubted. Cicero, in any case, gave no

[56] Cic. *Pro Mur.* 67: *senatus consultum me referente esse factum, si mercede obviam candidatis issent, si conducti sectarentur, si gladiatoribus vulgo locus tributim et item prandia si vulgo essent data, contra legem Calpurniam factum videri.* One may safely assume that this *senatus consultum* was incorporated into the *lex Tullia.* It came with the approval of all the consular candidates; *Pro Mur.* 68. Contra: T. E. Kinsey, *Mnemosyne*, 19 (1966): 272–273.

[57] Cic. *Pro Sest.* 133–135; *In Vat.* 37; Schol. Bob. 140, Stangl; cf. Cic. *De Har. Resp.* 56. The *lex Tullia* is mentioned also in Cic. *Pro Mur.* 3, 5.

[58] It has been conjectured that the *lex Tullia* also required candidates to submit their *professiones* in person; see, e.g., G. Rotondi, *Leges Publicæ Populi Romani* (Milan, 1912), p. 379. That requirement did not hold in early 63 (Cic. *De Leg. Agrar.* 2.24), but was in effect by 60 (Plut. *Cæs.* 13; Suet. *Iul.* 18; Appian, *BC*, 2.8). Cicero's *ambitus* bill is the only known law in the interim with which one might associate the provision. But the orator's scorn for such a restriction in early 63 (*De Leg. Agrar.* 2.24) makes it most unlikely that he would have placed it in his own bill a few months later. On the question of *ratio absentis*, see Balsdon, *JRS*, 52 (1962): 140–141; criticized by J. Linderski, *Mélanges Michalowski* (1966), pp. 523–526.

[59] Cicero could later contrast the charge of *ambitus* in respect to clarity with the more ambiguous and obscure charge of *maiestas*; *Ad Fam.* 3.11.2.

credence to the reports about Piso's activities.[60] And neither Afranius nor his backers suffered any indictments. But the Catonian pair used the opportunity to press for more restrictive legislation. Two senatorial decrees were sponsored by Cato and Domitius: to permit the searching of magistrates' houses, and to ban the harboring of *divisores.* The pressure went further. A tribune, Lurco, proposed a new and curious *ambitus* law. Those who promised cash for voters in a tribe but failed to deliver were exempt from penalty; but a man convicted of carrying through on the promise would be obliged to pay 3,000 sesterces to each tribe for life.[61] The wording of that provision suggests that it was directed principally against the *divisores,* not the candidates. Its purpose, so it would seem, was to encourage informers, playing upon the greed of the *plebs* itself. The sponsors doubtless regarded it as a powerful deterrent to electoral corruption. But cooler heads will have foreseen more reprehensible consequences: the bill might stimulate a rash of accusations, clogging the courts with cases based on flimsy pretexts. Cicero, whose *lex* would be amended or replaced, found no merit in the proposal. A campaign against adoption, we may assume, was launched. The Roman people rejected the measure.[62] The *lex Tullia* remained the operative legislation on *ambitus.* Further measures were not discussed, to our knowledge, before 56. By that time electoral abuses had become ensnared in the problem of violence and intimidation. It is to that issue that attention must now be directed.

MEASURES ON VIOLENCE AND COMBINES

The problem of violence did not confine itself to the late Republic. Recorded instances of *vis* are numerous, well before the Ciceronian age. It could be argued that it lay deep in Roman character, traceable to the earliest history of the Republic: the use of private force was based on a fundamental principle of self-help, characteristic of a society without sophisticated legal institutions.[63] Yet no *quæstio de vi* was instituted until the last generation of the Republic. Even Sulla's relatively comprehensive reorganization of the criminal judiciary found no place for a court on violence. The failure to cope with violent activity constitutes another charge often leveled by moderns against the senate

[60] Cic. *Ad Att.* 1.16.12: *consul autem ille* δευτερεύοντος *histrionis similis suscepisse negotium dicitur et domi divisores habere; quod ego non credo.* The stories of Pompey's bribery on Afranius' behalf are repeated, no doubt without independent evidence, by Plutarch; *Cato,* 30.5; *Pomp.* 44.3–4; cf. Dio, 37.49.1.

[61] Cic. *Ad Att.* 1.16.13: *novi est in lege hoc, ut qui nummos in tribu pronuntiarit, si non dederit, impune sit, sin dederit, ut quoad vivat singulis tribubus HS CIƆ CIƆ CIƆ debeat.* For the identification of Lurco, perhaps a M. Aufidius Lurco, see Shackleton Bailey, *Cicero's Letters,* I:323.

[62] Cic. *Ad Att.* 1.18.3.

[63] So A. W. Lintott, *Violence in Republican Rome* (Oxford, 1968), pp. 6–66.

of Cicero's day. But it is precisely that period, and not before, which witnessed the enactment of legislation *de vi.*

Sulla's oversight on the matter can be explained. He regarded it, perhaps, as covered by two other *leges* passed under his authority. The *lex Cornelia de sicariis et veneficiis* sufficed for cases of homicide. And the *lex Cornelia de maiestate* addressed itself to attacks against public safety and the security of the state.[64] But the very year of Sulla's death saw the creation of a new law, the first directed specifically against the crime of *vis.* The consul of 78, Q. Lutatius Catulus, sponsored the measure. The description retailed by Cicero makes it clear that Catulus' *lex* was aimed at the violent insurrection raised in Italy by Lepidus, which threatened the very fabric of the state.[65] It is not immediately evident why the Sullan *maiestas* law was not brought into operation. Wherein lay the need for new legislation? A reasonable conjecture is possible. *Leges de maiestate* in the past, so far as our evidence goes, applied only to public officials and members of the senate. It was their abuse of power and their violation of entrusted duties which impaired the *maiestas* of the *res publica.*[66] The widespread extent of the Lepidan *seditio* roused considerable fears. The movement might best be checked and similar movements discouraged by making all citizens liable for punishment under the law on offenses of public violence–hence the creation of the *lex Lutatia de vi* and a new category of Roman criminal law.[67]

Reference to the *lex Lutatia* occurs only once, in Cicero's *Pro Cælio.* By contrast, several prosecutions *de vi* are recorded in the period 63–52, all of them under a certain *lex Plautia.* The latter must have been the operative legislation on violence during those years and earlier. What was the relationship between the *lex Lutatia* and the *Lex Plautia?* The matter has been endlessly discussed. All that is needed here is a brief review. Cicero's allusion to the measure of Catulus is rhetorical and strained: he associates it directly with

[64] On the Sullan murder law, see Zumpt, *Criminalrecht,* II:2.1–38; Gruen, *Roman Politics,* pp. 261–262; the *maiestas* law, Zumpt, *Criminalrecht,* II:1.376–392; Gruen, *Roman Politics,* pp. 259–260. Most recently, J. D. Cloud, *ZSS,* 86 (1969): 258–286, has argued that Sulla's *lex de sicariis* was designed primarily not to punish murder but to protect citizens from private gangsters and hoodlums. If so, however, this makes it more difficult to understand the need for the *lex Plautia de vi.*

[65] Cic. *Pro Cæl.* 70: *de vi quæritis; quæ lex ad imperium, ad maiestatem, ad statum patriæ, ad salutem omnium pertinet, quam legem Q. Catulus armata dissensione civium rei publicæ pæne extremis temporibus tulit.*

[66] Cf. R. A. Bauman, *The Crimen Maiestatis in the Roman Republic and Augustan Principate* (Johannesburg, 1967), pp. 87–88, 281–282.

[67] Such would seem to be the implication of Cic. *Pro Cæl.* 1: *esse legem, quæ de seditiosis consceleratisque civibus, qui armati senatum obsederint, magistratibus vim attulerint, rem publicam oppugnarint.*

the law under which the Catilinarian conspirators were charged. Yet we know that the Catilinarians were condemned under the *lex Plautia de vi.*[68] Consequently, some have identified the two measures: Catulus urged the reform and a Plautius actually sponsored it. But the phrase *Catulus tulit* will hardly permit that conclusion. Other inferences are possible. Perhaps the *lex Lutatia* was an ad hoc bill, setting up a special *quæstio* to deal only with Lepidus' insurrection; the *lex Plautia* followed sometime later and inaugurated a permanent court on violence. Or else both operated simultaneously, and were directed at different types of offenses: the *lex Lutatia* punished *vis contra rem publicam,* the *lex Plautia* punished *vis contra privatos.* Either solution presents difficulties. In view of Sulla's careful enactments on permanent courts, it is unlikely that Catulus would have thought in terms of a *quæstio extraordinaria.* Nor would that easily suit the context of Cicero's statement, which ties together *vis* legislation in a direct line from 78 to 56. Roman legislators were thinking now in terms of permanent institutions, not makeshift solutions. A similar objection would hold against the conjecture that both laws rested simultaneously on the books. Sulla's tendency was to combine separate and related offenses into a single *lex,* not to confuse matters by a plethora of *quæstiones.* His immediate successors would hardly have reversed that development. Not a single recorded trial after 78 fell under the *lex Lutatia.* Moreover, several of the cases heard under the *lex Plautia* clearly involved offenses against the *res publica.* Cicero's allusion to Catulus is to the originator of legislation *de vi,* and that is all.[69]

It will be more plausible to imagine that the *lex Lutatia* constituted a *quæstio perpetua.* All citizens who engaged in *seditio* against the state would be held liable. Since acts of private violence, especially when directed against public figures or involving public issues, also concerned the state, need was found for further, more comprehensive legislation. That will explain passage

[68] Cicero's association of the Catilinarian trials with Catulus' law: *Pro Cæl.* 70: [following immediately after the passage quoted above, n.65] *quaque lex sedata illa flamma consulatus mei fumantis reliquias coniurationis exstinxit.* For use of the *lex Plautia* against Catiline in 63 and his followers in 62, see Sallust, *Cat.* 31.4; Ps. Sallust, *Inv. in Cic.* 2.3; Schol. Bob. 84, Stangl.

[69] For the view that the two laws are identical, see Mommsen, *Strafrecht*, p. 654; W. Kunkel, *RE*, 24:747, "quæstio"; W. Vitzthum, *Untersuchungen zum materiellen Inhalt der lex Plautia und lex Iulia de vi* (Diss. Munich, 1966), pp. 38–42. That the *lex Lutatia* created a special *quæstio*, later replaced by a permanent court under the *lex Plautia*, was conjectured by J. N. Hough, *AJP*, 51 (1930): 135–147; cf. Niccolini, *Fast. Trib. Pleb.*, p. 378. On the two laws as simultaneously operative and covering different offenses, see J. Cousin, *Rev. Hist. Droit* (1943), pp. 88–94. The theory of Zumpt, *Criminalrecht*, II:1.266–281, that the *lex Plautia* predates the *lex Lutatia*, has nothing to recommend it. Cicero would not then have pointed to Catulus as the originator, nor would Sulla have ignored legislation *de vi.*

of the *lex Plautia,* which probably replaced Catulus' measure, incorporating its provisions on *seditio* but authorizing the *quæstio de vi* to deal with cases of private violence as well.[70] The date of Plautius' law can be fixed no more firmly than prior to 63, when Catiline was charged under it. Consensus now seems to have moved toward the year 70, a reasonable suggestion. The author may then be identified with the magistrate who sponsored agrarian legislation for Pompey and issued the proposal to recall the remnants of Lepidus' following.[71] An important political fact emerges. The Plautii were steady supporters of Pompeius Magnus.[72] Whatever the identity of this particular Plautius, an association with Pompey is a plausible hypothesis. That makes 70, the year of Pompey's first consulship, all the more appropriate. The general sponsored or encouraged other reform legislation in that year. Advocacy of a measure that expanded and replaced that of his rival Catulus was no doubt welcome. But, political motives aside, the continuity and the growing sophistication of criminal legislation stand out the more clearly. Pompey himself would later urge changes in the criminal law and the judiciary system. The Roman senate remained alive and active on the issue of maintaining internal order.

Organized collections of men could prove dangerous. The government began to consider measures for dispersal of suspected or suspicious groups. A single source makes reference to the *lex Gabinia,* which forbade clandestine gatherings in the city, under pain of capital penalty.[73] It will be prudent not to lay heavy stress upon that information. The author of the law is unidentified. But A. Gabinius, tribune in 67 and a supporter of Pompey, cannot be ruled out. He sponsored a number of measures in his tribunate, and the action would be consistent with Pompey's interest in curbing opportunities for violence. The 60s, moreover, provide a suitable occasion for measures of this sort.[74]

[70] The conclusion expressed here is similar to that recently argued by Lintott, *Violence,* pp. 109–123. But Lintott's theory that violence *contra rem publicam* had to be proved for conviction under the *lex Plautia* is unnecessary. Such would not seem to be the case in the trials of Camurtius and Cæsernius; Cic. *Pro Cæl.* 71. Nor would it readily explain citations of the *lex Plautia* in later jurists referring only to violent invasions of private property; *Digest,* 41.3.33.2; Justinian, *Inst.* 2.6.2.

[71] See, e.g., Broughton, *MRR,* II:128, 130, n.4; Gelzer, *Cæsar,* p. 29; Syme, *JRS,* 53 (1963): 57–58; Lintott, *Violence,* pp. 111, 122–123.

[72] See above, chap. 3, n.65.

[73] Porcius Latro, *Decl. in Cat.* 19: *coitiones clandestinas in urbe.*

[74] The sponsor of this *lex Gabinia* is usually identified with the tribune of 139 who promulgated Rome's first *lex tabellaria*; Rotondi, *Leges Publicæ,* p. 297; Niccolini, *Fast. Trib. Pleb.,* p. 140; Broughton, *MRR,* I:483, n.3. No positive evidence supports the identification. The tribune of 67 is a more likely candidate.

Clear evidence, in any case, attests to senatorial action in this area in 64. A *senatus consultum* ordered the disbanding of several of the *collegia* that operated in various districts of the city. These groups had a long history, organized either as trade guilds or as religious and social clubs. In the late Republic, however, they consisted largely of freedmen and slaves. Government officials evidently became wary of them as a potential source of disturbance. Hence, their dissolution was authorized on the grounds of danger to the state.[75] Not all were removed by that particular action. A series of measures, both senatorial decrees and *leges,* took aim at *collegia* and suspicious organizations in subsequent years.[76] The repressive activity was perhaps too extreme. The breaking-up of social clubs and religious groups, some of them probably harmless, could not have appealed to popular sentiment. P. Clodius, as is well known, capitalized on that sentiment in his tribunate of 58. His tribunician law canceled previous legislation, renewed the legitimacy of the old *collegia,* and authorized the creation of new ones.[77] In this instance, senatorial restrictive legislation had brought justifiable reaction. One need not regard Clodius' motives simply as a desire to recruit gangs for street warfare. The demand for law and order had brought unnecessary curtailment of civil liberties, as it so often does. Clodius was here backing a proper cause.

The issue of controlling potentially dangerous organizations became increasingly tied to the problem of electoral corruption. *Collegia* could themselves serve as vehicles for soliciting votes.[78] More significant and more pertinent were the *sodalitates,* clubs organized within tribes and attached to particular leaders. They were especially potent instruments in electoral contests. And

[75] Cic. *In Pis.* 8; Asconius, 7, Clark: *L. Iulio C. Marcio consulibus quos et ipse Cicero supra memoravit senatus consulto collegia sublata sunt quæ adversus rem publicam videbantur esse constituta.* On the *collegia,* see F. M. De Robertis, *Il Diritto Associativo Romano* (Bari, 1938), pp. 71–162; S. Accame, *Bull. Mus. Imp. Rom.,* 13 (1942): 13–48; Taylor, *Voting Districts,* pp. 76–77; Lintott, *Violence,* pp. 78–83; S. Treggiari, *Roman Freedmen during the Late Republic* (Oxford, 1969), pp. 168–177; and especially Linderski, in M. N. Andreev, et al., *Gesellschaft und Recht im Griechisch-Römischen Altertum* (Berlin, 1968), pp. 94–132, with references to earlier literature. Linderski argues cogently that the *s.c.* was directed against both trade guilds and religious associations that had proved troublesome.

[76] Asconius, 75, Clark: *frequenter tum etiam cœtus factiosorum hominum sine publica auctoritate malo publico fiebant; propter quod postea collegia et s.c. et pluribus legibus sunt sublata.* Linderski, *op. cit.*, pp. 96–101, believes that the *plures leges* refer to measures stretching from 64 to Asconius' own day.

[77] Cic. *Pro Sest.* 55; *In Pis.* 9; Asconius, 7, 8, Clark; Dio, 38.13.2; Plut. *Cic.* 30.1; cf. Cic. *P. Red. in Sen.* 33; see Lintott, *Greece and Rome,* 14 (1967): 157–169, who, however, stresses too much the strict organization on which Clodius could rely.

[78] Cf. [Q. Cic.] *Comm. Petit.* 30: *deinde habeto rationem urbis totius, conlegiorum omnium, pagorum, vicinitatum.*

they could be employed for the purpose of arranging and distributing bribes.[79] Naturally, groups of men active in channeling cash to voters through the tribes might also serve to intimidate and threaten. The difficulty lay in formulating legislation to grapple with the problem.

Senatorial action came in 56. It represents yet another instance in which the government profited from previous errors and developed a more intelligent approach. The dispersal of organized clubs by decree had offended popular sensibilities and violated civil liberties. Clodius' law of 58 had reversed that process. A more legitimate avenue was found in 56. The senate could apply to established procedures and acknowledged *crimina* covered by the *leges de vi* and *de ambitu.* Disruptions and organized demonstrations in early February provided the occasion.[80] A resolution was passed in the *curia* authorizing a law to disband the *sodalitates;* refusal to disperse would be punishable as *vis.*[81] The import of that measure should not be missed. It was not simply a directive to break up political and social clubs. Such an order would have fallen afoul of the *lex Clodia,* which was the law of the land. The senate was calling attention to the activities of the *sodalitates,* which not only violated legislation *de vi* but fell also in the category of *ambitus.* By April 56 one could speak of *crimina* linking bribery agents and members of *sodalitates* in the context of *ambitus* offenses. Reference must be to the *senatus consultum* of 56.[82] The senate, it is plain, was moving toward a rational means of curbing the illicit actions of organizations without infringing freedom of assembly.

Passage of a *senatus consultum* did not entail passage of the *lex* that it promoted. Nothing demonstrates the enactment of this measure into law in 56. Political considerations may have intervened. The sponsor of the senatorial decree, it seems, was Q. Hortensius.[83] The stance would be perfectly consistent

[79] [Q. Cic.] *Comm. Petit.* 19: *nam hoc biennio quattuor sodalitates hominum ad ambitionem gratiosissimorum tibi obligasti, C. Fundani, Q. Galli, C. Corneli, C. Orchivi*; Cic. *Pro Planc.* 37: *cuiuscumque tribus largitor esset per hanc consensionem, quæ magis honeste quam vere sodalitas nominaretur, quam quisque tribum turpi largitione corrumperet.*

[80] See Cic. *Ad Q. Frat.* 2.3.2–4.

[81] Cic. *Ad Q. Frat.* 2.3.5: *eodem die senatus consultum factum est, ut sodalitates decuriatique discederent; lexque de iis ferretur, ut, qui non discessissent, ea pœna, quæ est de vi, tenerentur.*

[82] Cic. *Pro Cæl.* 16: *quod haud scio an de ambitu et de criminibus istis sodalium ac sequestrium, quoniam huc incidi, similiter respondendum putem.* The connection is discussed and elucidated in the excellent article of Linderski, *Hermes*, 89 (1961): 106–119. The *s.c.* should not be regarded simply as directed at *ambitus*; so Mommsen, *Strafrecht*, pp. 871–872; nor was it limited to the question of *vis* and the dispersal of clubs; as Zumpt, *Criminalrecht*, II:2.373–375, 382–391; De Robertis, *Diritto Associativo*, pp. 101–109; Taylor, *Party Politics*, p. 210, n.101. The *ambitus* offense charged against Cælius in April, 56, may have been connected with violence at pontifical elections; Cic. *Pro Cæl.* 19: *aiebant enim fore testem senatorem, qui se pontificiis comitiis pulsatum a Cælio diceret.*

[83] That inference was persuasively presented by Linderski, *PP*, 79 (1961): 304–311. The

for Hortensius and the friends of Cato who were pressing for restrictions on violence and for extension of *ambitus* legislation. But restrictions at that time would not have been welcome to the enemies of the Catonian cause. Cato's brother-in-law Domitius Ahenobarbus had announced his candidacy for the consulship with the avowed intention of replacing Cæsar in Gaul. That fact and others lay behind the conference of Luca in April and the renewal of active cooperation among the triumvirs. Their first order of business was to secure the election of Pompey and Crassus for 55 by whatever means necessary. In that process they must have endeavored to prevent passage into law of any measure that cracked down further on electoral practices. Disorder and disruption marked the campaign. Intimidation of voters and bribery were alleged. The elections themselves were postponed into the year 55 before Pompey and Crassus at last attained office.[84] Under the circumstances, it may be assumed that the legislation contemplated in February did not see fruition in 56.

Implementation of the senatorial decree came, however, in the following year. The consuls, Pompey and Crassus, had employed unsavory means to gain election. The urgency of their political situation demanded it. But they were not interested in making these techniques permanent or legitimate. It was Crassus himself who sponsored the law that culminated the reform movement of the past several years. His *lex Licinia de sodaliciis* made it a formal crime to employ organized groups of men for the purpose of corrupting or intimidating voters in the tribes.[85] The measure bore marks of prudence and care. It did not, so far as is known, disband the *sodalitates;* it simply declared illegal certain of their activities. Nor did it attempt to curtail proper solicitation of votes or the genuine energies expended in electoral campaigns. Traditional ties of patronage and the repayment of political *beneficia* were not interfered with. The *lex Licinia* attacked the artificial garnering of support through cash and fear.[86] Crassus' law, in effect, sharpened the notion of *ambitus,*

---

argument is based on a senatorial speech by Hortensius urging the decree that lay behind the *lex Licinia de sodaliciis* of 55; Cic. *Pro Planc.* 37: *an et agitata tum, cum ista in senatu res agebatur, et disputata hesterno die copiosissime a Q. Hortensio, cui tum est senatus assensus?* There can be little doubt that the *lex Licinia* grew out of the *s.c.* of February, 56.

[84] Cic. *Ad Att.* 4.8a.2; Suet. *Iul.* 24; Plut. *Pomp.* 51–52; *Cato,* 41–42; *Crass.* 14–15; Dio, 39.27; 39.30–32; Appian, *BC,* 2.17; see Gruen, *Historia,* 18 (1969): 91–92, 95–96.

[85] Cic. *Pro Planc. passim*; esp. 45–48; and see Schol. Bob. 152, Stangl: *qui reus de sodaliciis petitus est lege Licinia, quam M. Licinius Crassus, Cn. Pompei Magni collega, in consulatu suo pertulit, ut severissime quæreretur in eos candidatos qui sibi conciliassent* [*sodales*] *ea potissimum de causa, ut per illos pecuniam tribulibus dispertirent ac sibi mutuo eadem suffragationis emptæ præsidia communicarent.*

[86] Cic. *Pro Planc.* 44–45: *noli enim putare, Laterensis, legibus istis, quas senatus de ambitu sancire voluerit, id esse actum, ut suffragatio, ut observantia, ut gratia tolleretur. Semper fuerunt boni viri, qui apud tribules suos gratiosi esse vellent; neque vero tam durus in plebem noster ordo fuit, ut eam coli nostra modica liberalitate noluerit.*

bringing within its purview the objectionable practices, such as organized distribution of bribes and intimidation associated with the *sodalitates.*

The law had additional teeth. Strict clauses and heavy penalties were of no account if juries were to make them a pretext for acquittals. Some had raised that point against Cornelius' bill a dozen years before. In 63, consequently, Ser. Sulpicius Rufus attempted to tip the scales against the defendant. His proposal espoused some form of jury selection in which the accuser would have the advantage. The effort foundered. Individual challenges by prosecutor and defendant remained the customary means of reducing the *iudices* to the number who would actually sit on a particular case. A law of Vatinius in 59 modified that practice somewhat.[87] For the crime *de sodaliciis,* however, Crassus found another method. A general list of *iudices* was drawn up annually, probably by tribes. From that pool came the jurors for any particular case. Under the *lex Licinia* there were to be no individual challenges. The law permitted the *accusator* to choose four tribes, of which the *reus* could reject only one; the remaining three would hear the case. Hence the removal of particular jurors was no longer possible. Jury selection was largely taken out of the hands of the principals involved in any trial. They would have to take their chances with the *iudices* impaneled in the tribes. The solution was clever and appealing. Crassus retained the principle of *reiectio,* enshrined in criminal procedure. But the *reiectio* would have to address itself to a tribe en bloc and could not single out specific jurors, or even panels produced by the prætor. Prosecutors had the initiative and the advantage. But the whole process aimed at a more impartial bench, one not readily manipulable by the advocates.[88]

In the same spirit came a bill from Crassus' consular colleague and political ally, Pompeius Magnus. Details of the measure are obscure, but the thrust is clear. It fixed procedure for framing the annual *album* of jurors for all criminal cases. Hitherto, the urban prætor discharged that task, with few

[87] See below, p. 243.

[88] Description of the process in Cic. *Pro Planc.* 36–37; Schol. Bob. 152, 160, Stangl. Cicero, acting as defense counsel, had reason to be critical and perhaps disingenuous. One need not believe that the framers of the law expected prosecutors to choose tribes which the defendant had allegedly corrupted. And even Cicero is critical, not of the *lex*, but of the *accusator*'s violation of its spirit; *Pro Planc.* 42: *neque ego nunc legis iniquitatem queror, sed factum tuum a sententia legis doceo discrepare.* And he inadvertently puts his finger on the real substance of the measure: *iudices* are selected not individually but indiscriminately; *Pro Planc.* 41: *nos neque ex delectis iudicibus, sed ex omni populo, neque editos ad reiiciendum, sed ab accusatore constitutos iudices ita feremus, ut neminem reiiciamus?* Modern discussions generally grapple with the technical aspects, without satisfactory analysis of motives and purposes; so, e.g., Zumpt, *Criminalrecht*, II:2.392–404; Mommsen, *Strafrecht*, pp. 214–217; Strachan-Davidson, *Problems*, II:103–110; Greenidge, *Legal Procedure*, pp. 453–456; Nicolet, *L'Ordre Equestre*, p. 620.

restrictions. Political intrigue or mutual favors might affect the names actually chosen. Some men received places on the list through influence or connections; others begged off through similar means. The *lex Pompeia,* by contrast, provided a rational mechanism which canceled the arbitrary whims of magistrates and manipulations by their friends. *Iudices* would be determined by the law, not by men.[89] The mechanism itself is nowhere described. But Asconius notes one feature of the law: jurors were still to be drawn from the three *ordines* defined by the *lex Aurelia* of 70: *senatores, equites,* and *tribuni ærarii.* But henceforth they would come only from the highest census classes within those groups. The consequence, or at least the intent, was to staff the courts with men less susceptible to bribery and temptation.[90] The two consular measures dovetailed nicely: Pompey's reduced magisterial powers generally in the choice of *iudices;* Crassus' correspondingly reduced the power of advocates in specific cases of *sodalicium.* It was no small gesture. Political affiliations and other extraneous motives were inconsistent with equitable selection of juries.

Whether the *lex Licinia de sodaliciis* replaced the *lex Tullia de ambitu* is uncertain. It did not, of course, supplant the *lex Plautia de vi,* which endured to the end of the Republic and covered a wider area of offenses. No prosecutions are recorded under Cicero's *ambitus* law after 55. And it is noteworthy that when Vatinius was accused *de ambitu* in 54 for, among other things, employing gladiatorial shows in violation of the *lex Tullia,* the formal charge against him came under the *lex Licinia de sodaliciis.*[91] It appears then that Cicero's measure remained on the books. But the *lex Licinia* evidently incorporated the provisions of earlier laws and added that form of *vis,* so prevalent of late, the violence perpetrated by political clubs in elections. The penalties adduced are unspecified; we hear only that they were increased. If Crassus adopted the formulation of the *senatus consultum* of 56, the new sanction was equal to that of *vis,* that is, a capital penalty enforced by permanent exile.[92]

[89] Cic. *In Pis.* 94: *neque legetur quisquis voluerit, nec quisquis noluerit non legetur . . . iudices iudicabunt ei quos lex ipsa, non quos hominum libido delegerit.*

[90] Asconius, 17, Clark: *rursus deinde Pompeius in consulatu secondo, quo hæc oratio dicta est, promulgavit ut amplissimo ex censu ex centuriis aliter atque antea lecti iudices, æque tamen ex illis tribus ordinibus, res iudicarent*; cf. Cic. *Phil.* 1.20. A less favorable estimate, as one might expect, is given in the Pseudo-Sallustian *Ep. ad Cæsarem,* 3.3: *iudicia tametsi, sicut antea, tribus ordinibus tradita sunt, tamen idem illi factiosi regunt, dant, adimunt quæ lubet, innocentis circumveniunt, suos ad honorem extollunt*; cf. 7.10–11. For modern discussions, see Zumpt, *Criminalrecht,* II:2.352–361; Greenidge, *Legal Procedure,* p. 448; Hill, *Roman Middle Class,* pp. 178, 212; Nicolet, *L'Ordre Equestre,* pp. 605–607, 618–620. On selection of the *album* under the *lex Aurelia,* see Cic. *Pro Cluent.* 121.

[91] For Vatinius' violation of Cicero's law, see Cic. *In Vat.* 37; *Pro Sest.* 135; for the formal charge, Schol. Bob. 160, Stangl. See the discussion in Gruen, *HSCP,* 71 (1966): 218–220.

[92] That the penalty was increased is reported by Dio, 39.37.1. Exile of some sort was certainly

Again senatorial application rather than somnolence is manifest. The measures of 55 addressed themselves to a number of issues: proper judicial procedure, the problem of electoral corruption, the transformation of social clubs into political organizations, and the use of violence. It will obviously not do to describe the "first triumvirate" as despots or thugs bent on the destruction of traditional institutions. In the electoral contest of 56 they were fighting for their political lives. But once the candidacies of Crassus and Pompey proved successful, they turned, in fact, to the strengthening of Republican institutions. A pattern discerned before is repeated yet again. Q. Hortensius had advocated a curtailment of the *sodalitates* in 56. His political foes rendered it impossible. But in the following year those same foes brought the legislation into effect under their own auspices. Jockeying for position and credit traditionally characterized Roman politics. It need not disturb a more fundamental unanimity on preservation of the electoral process and maintenance of order.[93]

THE POMPEIAN LAWS OF 52

Revision of the *leges de vi* and *de ambitu* was called for again in 52. Electoral contests for that year had been especially fierce. Much cash changed hands, so it was alleged, and violent disturbances made the streets unsafe. The elections were postponed, and the year 52 opened without consuls. Bitterness continued, as did disruptions. The death of P. Clodius at the hands of Milo's attendants brought tensions to a peak. Clodius' mourners took revenge, sending the *curia* itself up in flames as their patron's funeral pyre. The absence of executive officials meant continued insecurity and threat of increased anarchy. The senate finally acted with firmness. Extraordinary circumstances brought extraordinary measures. Political differences evaporated again when restoration of order was necessary. On the prompting of Cato and Bibulus, the senate appointed Pom-

---

involved; Cic. *Pro Planc.* 8, 79. On the penalty *de vi,* see Cic. *Pro Sulla,* 89–90; *Pro Sest.* 146. For the *lex Licinia* as incorporating earlier *ambitus* legislation, see Cic. *Pro Planc.* 36: *in qua tu nomine legis Liciniæ, quæ est de sodaliciis, omnis ambitus leges complexus es.*

[93] No further legislation *de ambitu* or *de vi* is recorded between 55 and 52. There were heated senatorial discussions in 54 during the electoral scandals of that year. But that was an ad hoc proceeding aimed at the consular candidates to apply pressure for fair electoral practices. It did not aim at permanent change in the *ambitus* law. In any case, tribunician veto canceled the effort; nothing came of it; Cic. *Ad Att.* 4.17.3; *Ad Q. Frat.* 2.16.2; Plut. *Cato,* 44; and see the commentary of Shackleton Bailey, *Cicero's Letters,* II:215–216. Similarly, the *s.c. de ambitu* of February, 55, was an ad hoc measure aimed at the long-delayed prætorian elections for that year. We know of it only because of the political contest between the triumvirs and the Catonians. The decree, moved by Afranius and backed by Pompey and Crassus, secured senatorial approval after an abortive effort by Cato to introduce amendment; Cic. *Ad Q. Frat.* 2.9.3; Plut. *Cato,* 42. There is no suggestion that it proposed alteration in the existing *lex de ambitu.*

pey to the chief magistracy, and for the time being, at least, he would be without colleague. The purpose, quite clearly, was to reestablish the force of law.[94]

Pompey's response was vigorous and firm. Electoral corruption and violence had exceeded endurable bounds in recent months. Existing legislation had proved insufficient in circumstances of heated rivalry and explosive emotions. The *lex Plautia de vi* and the *lex Licinia de sodaliciis* remained on the books. But Pompey created additional legislation aimed directly at the events which had threatened to paralyze governmental operations. Two separate enactments, *de vi* and *de ambitu,* secured passage under his ægis. Speed and dispatch were essential; and there was to be no ambiguity. Pompey's laws, backed by *senatus consulta,* were designed to provide efficient procedure and to impose weighty penalties. But the two measures possessed different characters. It will be of value to maintain clarity on the distinctions.

The *lex Pompeia de vi* instituted an ad hoc proceeding. The purpose was a clear and definitive stance on recent disturbances. An example needed to be made. The best way to pronounce conditions intolerable and to prevent their repetition was to single out the men responsible for those conditions. Such, at least, seems to have been Pompey's approach. His measure left no doubts about intentions. It included explicit mention of Clodius' murder, the burning of the senate house, and the riots that followed.[95] There was some discomfort in the senate when the proposal came under discussion. None doubted the need for swift prosecution and stringent penalty. The senate declared itself unambiguously on the facts: the murder of Clodius and subsequent chaos were acts *contra rem publicam.*[96] But extraordinary, ad hoc proceedings did not suit everyone's taste. Hortensius voiced senatorial reluctance. He was prepared to have the trials take place outside the regular order and schedule; but it was better to operate by existing legislation than to create a special court for the occasion. Whatever the merits of the immediate proposal, it might set an unfortunate precedent.[97]

Pompey clearly wished to go further than the senatorial majority. Though he would not disturb existing statutes, he persuaded himself that present

[94] On the events, covered in all standard works, see, e.g., Rice Holmes, *Rom. Rep.*, II:164–168.

[95] Cic. *Pro Mil.* 15: *tulit enim de cæde, quæ in Appia via facta esset, in qua P. Clodius occisus esset*; Asconius, 36, Clark: *duas ex s.c. promulgavit, alteram de vi qua nominatim cædem in Appia via factam et incendium curiæ et domum M. Lepidi interregis oppugnatam comprehendit, alteram de ambitu*; cf. Schol. Bob. 112, 117, Stangl.

[96] Cic. *Pro Mil.* 12–13, 31; Asconius, 44, Clark; Schol. Bob. 116, Stangl.

[97] Cic. *Pro Mil.* 13: *hanc vero quæstionem, etsi non est iniqua, numquam tamen senatus constituendam putavit; erant enim leges, erant quæstiones vel de cæde vel de vi, nec tantum mærorem ac luctum senatui mors P. Clodii adferebat, ut nova quæstio constitueretur*; Asconius, 44, Clark; Schol. Bob. 117, Stangl.

conditions required a special court, a conspicuous display of governmental authority. A senator demanded that Hortensius' motion be divided and that separate votes be taken. The portion asking for proceedings *extra ordinem* passed without dissent; the portion requesting that they be held under present laws, presumably the *lex Plautia de vi* and *lex Cornelia de sicariis*, was vetoed by two tribunes. Pompey would have his way. Milo and others charged with public disturbances were to be prosecuted by a *quæstio extraordinaria* set up by the *lex Pompeia de vi*.[98] A tribune favorable to Milo made a final effort to block the new proceeding. But Pompey was committed. He announced his readiness to defend the state with arms, thereby overbearing any efforts at obstruction. After vigorous harangues, the law received popular endorsement.[99]

Trials held under the new law were to be models of efficiency, and sanctions were severe.[100] The cumbersome procedure of the regular courts became streamlined. Advocates for defense and prosecution were reduced in number, and a strict time limitation was placed on all speeches. The tiresome exercises that characterized and prolonged most judicial hearings would play no part under the *lex Pompeia de vi*: written testimony from absent advocates was banned, as were laudatory orations and character witnesses. The whole procedure was not to outrun five days.[101] A clause in the law provided for immediate selection of an ex-consul as presiding officer for the court, by popular vote. But there can be no doubt that Pompey controlled the course of events. He nominated a candidate for the post, who was forthwith elected. He also drew up the list of jurors from which the bench for each case would be chosen.[102] There were to be no loopholes in this special process.

[98] Cic. *Pro Mil.* 14: *quod si per furiosum illum tribunum senatui quod sentiebat perficere licuisset, novam quæstionem nullam haberemus; decernebat enim, ut veteribus legibus, tantum modo extra ordinem, quæreretur; divisa sententia est postulante nescio quo . . . sic reliqua auctoritas senatus empta intercessione sublata est*; Asconius, 44–45, Clark: *cum Hortensius dixisset ut extra ordinem quæreretur apud quæsitorem . . . invenimus Fufium, qui diceret "divide"; reliquæ parti sententiæ ego et Sallustius intercessimus*; Schol. Bob. 117, Stangl: *nam duo conplectebatur: ut et veteribus legibus et extra ordinem quæreretur; huic sententiæ dicit M. Tullius intercessum atque ita factum ut extra ordinem quidem quæreretur, non tamen vetusta, sed nova lege Pompeia.* Cf. Meyer, *Cæsars Monarchie*, p. 231. Others believe, despite the Bobbiensian scholiast, that the only *s.c.* passed was that which declared the murder and subsequent disorders *contra rem publicam*; A. C. Clark, *Cicero. Pro Milone* (Oxford, 1895), pp. 13–14; Stein, *Senatssitzungen*, pp. 53–54.

[99] Asconius, 36, 49–50, Clark.

[100] Asconius, 36, Clark: *pœna graviore et forma iudiciorum breviore.*

[101] Asconius, 36, 39, Clark; Cic. *Brutus*, 324; *De Fin.* 4.1.1; Val. Max. 6.2.5; Dio, 40.52.1–2; Plut. *Cato*, 48.4; Tac. *Dial.* 38.

[102] Cic. *Pro Mil.* 21–22: *delegit ex florentissimis ordinibus ipsa lumina . . . vero te, L. Domiti, huic quæstioni præesse maxime voluit . . . tulit ut consularem necesse esset . . . ex consularibus te creavit potissimum;* Asconius, 38, Clark: *perlata deinde lege Pompei, in qua id quoque scriptum*

Previous criminal laws remained in force. It was not Pompey's object to replace them. That is demonstrable from the fact that Milo was prosecuted under the *lex Pompeia,* and was then charged again under the *lex Plautia de vi.* Others also suffered the same fate.[103] The measure was conceived as a temporary expedient. *Quæstiones extraordinariæ* possessed drama and focused public attention in a fashion impossible for normal processes. That will explain Pompey's motivation. Preservation of public order, so seriously menaced in previous months, required a spectacular display and drastic example.

By contrast, Pompey's *lex de ambitu* was projected for a longer future. The distinction has not always been recognized, understandably. The assembly promulgated both bills at the same time and established similar procedural rules for both.[104] But their objects were quite different. The *lex de vi,* instituting a special, temporary *quæstio,* overtly aimed at offenses committed in the immediate past, offenses specified in the law itself. The *lex de ambitu* contained no such limitations.[105] It was not simply the present candidates for office who were subject to its provisions. Pompey made the law retroactive; office seekers who had committed violations in the past but had escaped prosecution could still face charges under the new legislation.[106] Cato objected to the retroactive character of the law; so, no doubt, did others, who feared the raking-up of old and half-forgotten abuses.[107] But clauses of that sort were by no means unknown in criminal legislation. Opponents would point out the injustice, and supporters would issue disclaimers, but the provisions remained.

More important, Pompey designed the *lex de ambitu* to be the operative statute on electoral bribery. Not that it replaced the *lex Licinia de sodaliciis:* both measures saw application in 52. The unhappy Milo, who was charged under the two *leges de vi,* the Plautian and the Pompeian, was also prosecuted

---

erat ut quæsitor suffragio populi ex iis qui consules fuerant crearetur, statim comitia habita, creatusque est L. Domitius Ahenobarbus quæsitor; album quoque iudicum qui de ea re iudicarent Pompeius tale proposuit ut numquam neque clariores viros neque sanctiores propositos esse constaret.

[103] Asconius, 54–55, Clark.

[104] Zumpt, *Criminalrecht,* II:2.419–420, conjectured that the Pompeian enactments on *vis* and *ambitus* were actually two clauses of the same measure. That is decisively refuted by Asconius, 36, Clark: *de legibus novis ferendis rettulit; duas ex s.c. promulgavit, alteram de vi . . . alteram de ambitu.*

[105] The contrast is clear in Asconius, 36, Clark; see above, n.95.

[106] Appian, *BC,* 2.23, asserts that the law was retroactive back to Pompey's first consulship in 70. The statement is unverifiable, imbedded as it is in a dubious story. None of the known defendants was prosecuted for crimes that stretched back beyond 54. Clark, *Cic. Pro Mil.,* xii–xiv, suggests that Appian erroneously substituted Pompey's first consulship for his second in 55. In all probability, no date was specified in the *lex* itself.

[107] Plut. *Cato,* 48.3; cf. Appian, *BC,* 2.23, 2.25.

under both the *lex Licinia de sodaliciis* and the *lex Pompeia de ambitu.*[108] But whereas Pompey's *lex de vi* pointed only at the disturbances prompted by Milo, his supporters, and his rivals, and lapsed when those offenders were tried, the *ambitus* law endured. A case stands on record in 51 involving electoral corruption that dated back to 54 and had no connection with the events of late 53 and 52: M. Valerius Messalla was accused and acquitted *de ambitu,* only to be convicted shortly thereafter *de sodaliciis.*[109] Crassus' law, so it seems, had incorporated earlier legislation on electoral abuses and combined it with provisions on the *sodalitates.* Pompey's reasons for again separating out the crime of *ambitus* and providing an independent *quæstio* are not readily discernible. The need for clarity and sharp distinctions may suffice as explanation. Pompey had shown a similar attitude in a somewhat parallel instance during his second consulship of 55. He reviewed the crime of parricide from Sulla's general homicide measure and established a separate enactment for it.[110] The Pompeian *lex de vi* was ephemeral and was intended to be so; its purpose was to make a conspicuous example of the worst offenders against public order. But the *lex de ambitu* represents a solid achievement, recalled by writers of much later eras as a milestone in the war against electoral corruption.[111]

The sources attach most of Pompey's new procedural arrangements to the *lex de vi.* Should one infer then that they were fashioned only for the *quæstio extraordinaria* and were to carry no further implications? That would be a hasty conclusion. The bulk of the extant evidence concerns itself with *de vi* procedure and particularly with the trial of Milo; hence, perhaps, an overbalanced picture. The procedural rules framed in 52 were detailed and complex. It is not likely prima facie that they were intended only for the temporary tribunal of that year. Asconius, in fact, cites certain regulations that were to apply both to the *quæstio de vi* and to the *quæstio de ambitu,* namely, that advocates' speeches would observe a strict time limit and would take place on the same day on which the decision was rendered.[112] The *ambitus quæstio* was a permanent court. Possibly, then, the new rules applied to all the criminal *quæstiones.* That, in any case, is what Dio Cassius specifically

[108] Asconius, 54–55, Clark.

[109] Cic. *Ad Fam.* 8.2.1; 8.4.1; Val. Max. 5.9.2. Messalla's case renders unacceptable the view of Zumpt, *Criminalrecht,* II:2.419–434, and of Greenidge, *Legal Procedure,* p. 392, that Pompey's judicial arrangements were operative only to the end of 52.

[110] See below, pp. 246–247.

[111] Pliny, *Pan.* 29.1: *huius aliquando cura Pompeio non minus addidit gloriæ quam pulsus ambitus campo, exactus hostis mari, Oriens triumphis Occidensque lustratus*; Vell. Pat. 2.47.3: *sed eius consulatus omnem vim in cœrcitionem ambitus exercuit*; cf. Cic. *Brutus,* 245; Cæs. *BC,* 3.1; Tac. *Dial.* 38; Plut. *Pomp.* 55.4; Dio, 40.52.3–4.

[112] Asconius, 36, Clark: *utraque enim lex prius testes dari, deinde uno die atque eodem et ab accusatore et a reo perorari iubebat, ita ut duæ horæ accusatori, tres reo darentur.*

affirms. Having noted the limitations on speeches and the abolition of character witnesses, he adds that these and other reforms were framed by Pompey for all the courts.[113] Tacitus offers the same interpretation.[114] There is no reason to doubt these statements. Presumably, not all the regulations have been recorded. So, for example, only a chance comment informs us that the *lex Pompeia* required a fixed day, determined in advance, for each trial. The enactment perfectly suits Pompey's general aim to bring order and pattern to the whole system of criminal courts. It fits with the provisions, noted earlier, that streamlined procedure and reduced the wasteful machinations that had plagued the courtroom.[115]

Most significant was a new arrangement for the selection of jurors. Asconius describes the process for the trail of Milo. The taking of testimony and the organization of details consumed four days. But it was only on the fifth and last day that the bench of *iudices* who were to pass judgment was selected by lot. The *sortitio* produced 81 jurors, 27 from each *ordo.* Accuser and defendant were allowed five challenges in each *ordo.* That left a final number of 51 who would cast the verdict. One cannot minimize the effect of that change. It meant that the jurors themselves would not be identified until the very day of the trial. Bribery of the bench was thereby rendered immeasurably more difficult.[116] That safeguard did not pertain merely to the trial of Milo, nor even to the *quæstio extraordinaria de vi.* That Pompey intended it as a general feature for criminal cases is demonstrable. Reduction of the final

[113] Dio, 40.52.3: καὶ ταῦτα μὲν ἄλλα τέ τινα κατὰ πάντων ὁμοίως τῶν δικαστηρίων ἐτάχθη.

[114] Tac. *Dial.* 38: *primus hæc tertio consulatu Cn. Pompeius adstrinxit, imposuitque veluti frenos eloquentiæ, ita tamen ut omnia in foro, omnia legibus, omnia apud prætores gererentur.*

[115] On the fixing of dates for trials, see Cic. *Ad Att.* 13.49.1; for other procedural changes, see above, n.101.

[116] Asconius, 39, 53, Clark. Cæsar later complained that under the *lex Pompeia* one set of jurors heard the evidence, another delivered the verdict; *BC,* 3.1. Exact relationship between the bench that sat in the first four days and the 81 selected on the last day is unclear. The figure of 360 *iudices* is recorded more than once for the year 52; Cic. *Ad Att.* 8.16.2; Vell. Pat. 2.76.1; Plut. *Pomp.* 55. That this was a number particularly chosen for 52 is indicated by the fact that in the following year 300 senators alone were reckoned for jury service; Cic. *Ad Fam.* 8.8.5. Strachan-Davidson, *Problems,* II:110–111, believes that the 360 were assigned only for the *quæstio de vi,* and that the entire group heard evidence until the last day, when 81 were selected out of their number. Nicolet, *L'Ordre Equestre,* pp. 620–623, limits them to the *quæstiones de vi* and *de ambitu.* More likely, the 360 constituted the entire *album* available for criminal cases in that year. We know that Pompey drew up a careful and selective list; Cic. *Pro Mil.* 21–22; Asconius, 38, Clark. Zumpt's thesis, *Criminalrecht,* II:2.455–461, that various jurors heard testimony and that the final 81 had access to the written record is ingenious but unverifiable. Further speculation would be pointless. The crucial fact is that the final bench could not be known until the day of decision.

jury to 51 applied not only in Milo's case but in another trial in the same year, this one under the *lex Plautia*. And the practice of selecting jurors unknown to the participants until the last moment is attested for cases *de ambitu* as well.[117] Pompey's genuine, even obsessive, concern for judicial institutions cannot be gainsaid. Later writers might dwell upon the general's troops, which ringed about the courtroom at Milo's trial. That demonstration was memorable, but exceptional. Pompeius Magnus showed abiding interest in the stability and improvement of the *iudicia*.

MORE CRIMINAL LAWS

It had been the hope of Sulla the dictator to establish a rational and comprehensive system for the criminal judiciary. The Sullan laws reorganized the *quæstiones*, defined crimes with greater precision, combined offenses under new headings, strengthened earlier courts, and created new ones where necessary.[118] Apart from measures *de ambitu* and *de vi*, there was little legislative tampering with the Sullan code in the late Republic. Most of the dictator's enactments endured. But where it proved desirable to expand on or add to the *leges Corneliæ*, Roman statesmen and legislators were not found wanting.

The most notable measure in this category was the *lex Julia repetundarum*. Cæsar's consulship of 59, marked as it is with turmoil and disruption, seems to symbolize breakdown. The political situation, as explored earlier, produced certain unconventional behavior on all sides in that year. But it was not the intention of Cæsar and his associates to weaken or discard Republican institutions, much less to perpetuate the rule of force. The *lex Julia repetundarum* stands as a most telling document of Cæsar's priorities.

It will serve little purpose to rehearse the history of *repetundæ* legislation. Basically, it concerned itself with extortionate activities by Roman provincial governors abroad. The *quæstio de rebus repetundis* originated as long ago as 149. Successive laws on the subject endeavored, at least in theory, to protect against mistreatment of provincials, foreigners, or subjects by Roman officials through exaction of criminal penalties and civil recovery of damages. An extortion law by Sulla receives notice, but little evidence remains on its precise provisions. It may have made only minor changes in existing legislation.[119] By contrast, the measure of Julius Cæsar was extensive, detailed, and had a lasting effect. It continued to be cited by jurists well into the imperial period.

[117] The jurors who sat on the case of Saufeius under the *lex Plautia* numbered 51; Asconius, 55, Clark. And Cæsar's distinction between jurors who heard testimony and those who passed verdicts has reference to trials *de ambitu; BC*, 3.1: *nonnullos ambitus Pompeia lege damnatos . . . quæ iudicia aliis audientibus iudicibus, aliis sententiam ferentibus.*

[118] Cf. Gruen, *Roman Politics*, pp. 258–265.

[119] Cf. Gruen, *Roman Politics*, pp. 258–259.

The *lex Julia de repetundis*, it is clear, was no hastily conceived, makeshift bill put together for political purposes. Considerable preparation and careful drafting preceded its implementation. The measure contained over one hundred clauses.[120] Of these only a few are known, though enough to give some index of its character. Cæsar employed the *lex Cornelia* as a basis, but went well beyond it, encompassing a wider variety of abuses and spelling out the offenses and procedures in meticulous detail. Activities of Roman officials abroad were hemmed about with manifold restrictions. The *lex Julia* set rigorous limits to the expenses which any provincial governor could claim from the *ærarium* or from the provincials.[121] A strict accounting was enforced. The financial records of a governorship had to be deposited in two cities of the province, and a duplicate was to be dispatched to Rome. Provision existed also for the sealing of accounts in the public records, lest there be any opportunity for falsification.[122] Occasions for exploitation of provincials were numerous. The *lex Julia* enumerated illegitimate exactions in detail: the requisitioning of ships, the levying of grain, the demand of cash for a gold crown.[123] Many others no doubt received specification, but the precise clauses do not survive. The law did not confine itself to pecuniary offenses. Cæsar borrowed provisions from the Sullan *lex de maiestate*: governors were held liable *de repetundis* for leaving their province, waging war, or entering any other realm without express permission of the senate and the people.[124] Cæsar apparently proposed to incorporate within his measure all manner of offenses likely to be committed by officials with power abroad. Promagistrates with *imperium* did not represent the only targets; any official on public business or exercising public authority was to be held responsible under the law.[125]

That the *lex Julia* was broad and comprehensive is plain. Just how comprehensive, one cannot altogether discern. A measure with over one hundred divisions must have covered a staggering range of topics. Some were procedural, such as a time limit on the trial proceedings, the number of witnesses a participant could summon, or the specification that a majority of votes among the jurors sufficed for decision.[126] More important, the law went beyond the punishment of offenses committed in the provinces. It encompassed the unauthorized taking of monies in virtually every imaginable performance of

[120] Cælius cites the one hundred and first clause; *Ad Fam.* 8.8.3.

[121] Cic. *Ad Att.* 5.10.2, 5.16.3, 5.21.5. This was, it seems, an expansion upon similar provisions in the Sullan law; Cic. *Ad Fam.* 3.10.6.

[122] Cic. *Ad Att.* 6.7.2; *Ad Fam.* 2.17.2, 5.20.2; *In Pis.* 61; *Pro Flacco*, 21.

[123] Cic. *In Pis.* 90.

[124] Cic. *In Pis.* 50.

[125] *Digest*, 48.11.1: *lex Iulia repetundarum pertinet ad eas pecunias, quas quis in magistratu, potestate, curatione, legatione vel quo alio officio munere ministeriove publico cepit*; cf. 48.11.3; 48.11.9.

[126] Cic. *Pro Flacco*, 82; Val. Max. 8.1.10; Cælius, *Ad Fam.* 8.8.3.

public duties: rendering judgments, bearing witness, delivering opinions in senate or *consilium*, enrolling or releasing men in military service, contracting for public works, distributing public grain.[127] How many of these provisions were adopted from previous enactments cannot be known, nor does it matter. Cæsar's law provided precision and detail that eclipsed its predecessors, and it endured.

Leges repetundarum, from their inception, had been directed exclusively against magistrates, senators, and members of senatorial families.[128] These were principally the men in a position to exercise authority and thereby to abuse it. Reformers had made efforts in the past to extend liability to *equites*, particularly in respect to their service as jurors. Political considerations consistently thwarted the attempts.[129] The senate actually promulgated a decree to that effect in 74, but the consuls cautiously refrained from bringing it to a vote of the people.[130] In 61 the issue was raised once again. Cato urged upon his colleagues a measure that would make all jurors, regardless of class, subject to prosecution for judicial bribery. The *curia* acquiesced and framed the bill. Cicero, though recognizing the propriety of the measure, correctly divined the hostile reaction of the *equites* and argued against it—better to preserve harmony among the orders than to aggravate relations unnecessarily. The proposal was rejected in the popular assembly.[131] Cæsar's law came into effect only two short years later. As we have seen, its provisions encompassed not only provincial governors, but legates, ambassadors, and every official responsi-

[127] *Digest*, 48.11.3: *lege Iulia repetundarum tenetur, qui cum aliquam potestatem haberet, pecuniam ob iudicandum decernendumve acceperit*; 48.11.6: *eadem lege tenentur, qui ob denunciandum vel non denunciandum testimonium pecuniam acceperint . . . lege Iulia repetundarum cavetur, ne quis ob militem legendum mittendumve æs accipiat, neve quid ob sententiam in senatu consiliove publico dicendam pecuniam accipiat, vel ob accusandum vel non accusandum*; 48.11.7: *illud quoque cavetur ne in acceptum referatur opus publicum faciendum, frumentum publice dandum, probandum, apprehendendum.* Cf. also *Digest*, 1.9.2, 22.5.13; Paul. *Sent.* 5.28. The recently edited papyrus fragment of Paulus' *Sententiæ* at Leiden, 1–8, also makes reference to the *lex Julia;* see the commentary by G. G. Archi, *Pauli Sententiarum Fragmentum Leidense* (Leiden, 1956), pp. 81–84, 94–102, 106–110.

[128] *Lex repet.* 2 = *FIRA*, I:85–86.

[129] Livius Drusus in 91 sought in vain to make *equites* liable for judicial corruption; Cic. *Pro Rab. Post.* 16; *Pro Cluent.* 153; Appian, *BC*, 1.35; see U. Ewins, *JRS*, 50 (1960): 104–106; Gruen, *Roman Politics*, pp. 208–209; E. J. Weinrib, *Historia*, 19 (1970): 419–426.

[130] Cic. *Pro Cluent.* 136–137.

[131] Cic. *Ad Att.* 1.17.8: *promulgatum ex senatus consulto fuisse ut de eis qui ob iudicandum accepissent quæreretur; qua in re decernenda cum ego casu non adfuissem sensissemque id equestrem ordinem ferre molestè neque aperte dicere, obiurgavi senatum; Ad Att.* 2.1.8: *quid verius quam in iudicium venire qui ob rem iudicandum pecuniam acceperit? censuit hoc Cato et adsensit senatus: equites curiæ bellum—non mihi, nam ego dissensi; Ad Att.* 1.18.3: *facto senatus consulto de ambitu. de iudiciis, nulla lex perlata; exagitatus senatus, alienati equites Romani quod erat "qui ob rem iudicandam."*

ble for performing public functions. In addition, the *lex Julia* included judicial corruption under the heading of *repetundæ*. On the matter of equestrian liability, however, Cæsar was prudent. Unwilling, it seems, to risk failure of so important a bill through obstruction, he skirted the issue. If *equites* were not specifically exempted under the *lex Julia,* they were, at least, not mentioned.[132]

The omission may be labeled inequitable. But Cæsar can hardly be charged with oversight or prejudice. He wanted to assure passage of an otherwise comprehensive law by avoiding entanglement in political dissension. It is revealing to note that, when the question of equestrian responsibility received a hearing again in 55, Cæsar's political ally Pompeius Magnus raised it. By that time the senate itself preferred to rest on the existing legislation rather than to risk alienation of the *equites.*[133] A continuity of attitude on legislative reform, which transcended political differences, appears again in this instance. The proposal mooted by M. Cato in 61 without success was introduced six years later by his political foe Pompey. That, as we have seen, was no isolated phenomenon.

The *lex Julia repetundarum* endured as a monument to the insight and industry of Cæsar. Credit need not go, however, to the consul alone. A sweeping measure to control abuses by public officials was no doubt welcomed by the senate as a whole. Many of its members may have participated in the drafting and framing of the complex legislation. Nothing in the sources suggests any opposition to its passage. The argument from silence is here especially strong. In a year when other Cæsarian actions roused so much dissent and disruption, the absence of objection to the *repetundæ* law stands out the more markedly. The scrupulous character of the law, its strictness, and its severity appealed to the temperaments of *nobiles* who were moving in the same direction in *ambitus* and *vis* legislation.[134] Cæsar's *lex* received high praise

[132] Cic. *Pro Rab. Post.* 12: *qua lege? Iulia de pecuniis repetundis; quo de reo? de equite Romano; at iste ordo lege ea non tenetur.* Imperial jurisconsults, to be sure, affirmed that the *lex Julia* covered not only public officials but their *cohortes*, and even asserted that *iudices pedanei* were liable for judicial corruption under its provisions; *Digest*, 48.11.1; Paul. *Sent.* 5.28; cf. the Leiden fragment of Paulus, 5. The references, however, must be to extensions of the law under the Empire; they will not have been in Cæsar's original measure; Mommsen, *Strafrecht*, p. 712. The tortuous arguments of Zumpt, *Criminalrecht,* II:2.269–302, cannot get around the explicit testimony of Cicero. Cf. also E. Fallu, *LEC*, 48 (1971): 196–204.

[133] Cic. *Pro Rab. Post.* 13: *nam cum . . . Cn. Pompeio de hac ipsa quæstione referente existerent non nullæ . . . sententiæ, quæ censerent . . . ut comites omnes magistratuum lege hac tenerentur, vos, vos, inquam, ipsi et senatus frequens restitistis*; cf. *Pro Rab. Post.* 18.

[134] Cicero labeled it, with praise, a *lex acerrima*; *In Vat.* 29. On the date of its passage, see S. I. Oost, *AJP*, 77 (1956): 19–28; Fallu, *LEC*, 48 (1971): 194–196. This is not the place for extended discussion of that most vexed problem, the *pœna legis repetundarum.* Penalties had been successively increased in *repetundæ* laws, and there is no reason to believe that Cæsar's

from his contemporaries.[135] It placed control over magisterial abuse of power at home and abroad upon a rational footing. Exhaustive definitions marked its format. The state now possessed full machinery to hold its own officials to account.

Other minor judicial legislation in 59 warrants mention in passing. The sponsors, it may be noted, were associates and allies of Cæsar. The tribune, P. Vatinius, damned by Cicero as an agent of disorder, nonetheless interested himself in judicial reform. His measure obtains but brief notice in the evidence; its content is correspondingly elusive. Evidently it instituted change in the procedure for challenging jurors. Cicero designates it a *lex de alternis consiliis reiciendis*.[136] Reference to *consilia* rather than to *iudices* is suggestive. *Consilium* is the term for a prætor's bench of jurors in a particular hearing. Vatinius' law seems to have authorized accuser and defendant to reject whole panels. The prætor, one may surmise, would produce three alternate panels, the principals in the trial each rejecting one, and the remaining crew would hear the case. If that interpretation is correct, the procedure would curtail elimination of particular jurors and compel advocates to challenge men in preselected groups.[137] *Accusator* and *reus* would have to deal with blocs of *iudices*, not with individuals. This development, as we have seen, was carried further by Crassus' *lex de sodaliciis* in 55, which restricted advocates' *reiectio* to tribal divisions of the annual *album*, a stage even earlier than the prætor's formation of panels. Vatinius' measure evidently sought to reduce last-minute manipulation in jury selection.

A statute on the courts in 59 is also attributed to another supporter of Cæsar, the prætor Q. Fufius Calenus. Fufius' bill was straightforward and useful: the three *ordines* that sat on any case, senators, *equites,* and *tribuni ærarii*, were to have their votes tabulated and recorded separately.[138] The secret

---

was an exception; Cic. *De Off.* 2.75: *tot leges et proximæ quæque duriores.* The evidence would suggest that, at least for some of the offenses covered by the law, a capital penalty was to be exacted; Cic. *Pro Rab. Post.* 11, 41, 48; Paul. *Sent.* 5.28. For others, *infamia* resulted, the loss of certain political and civil privileges; cf. *Digest*, 1.9.2; 22.5.13; 48.11.6. A full discussion of the evidence may be found in Sherwin-White, *PBSR*, 17 (1949): 5–25. Zumpt, *Criminalrecht*, II:2.329–346, argues, unconvincingly, that a defendant's *caput* was not in jeopardy during the Republic.

[135] Cic. *Pro Sest.* 135: *optima lex; In Pis.* 37: *lege Cæsaris iustissima atque optima*; cf. *In Vat.* 29; *De Prov. Cons.* 7; *Pro Rab. Post. 8; Schol Bob.* 140, 149, Stangl.

[136] Cic. *In Vat.* 27. The scholiast is unable to add elucidation; Schol. Bob. 149, 150, Stangl.

[137] Zumpt, *Criminalrecht*, II:2.289–291, and Mommsen, *Strafrecht*, p. 216, believe that individual challenges would follow the *reiectio* of the panels. But no evidence can be cited to buttress that conjecture; cf. Strachan-Davidson, *Problems*, II:110. See also Greenidge, *Legal Procedure*, pp. 451–452.

[138] Dio, 38.8.1. Cf. C. MacDonald, *CR*, 7 (1957): 198. For Fufius' connection with Cæsar in 59, see Cic. *Ad Att.* 2.18.1.

ballot, of course, remained. But the *lex Fufia* would afford some measure of control. Bribery of jurors was less likely when responsibility for acquittal or conviction could be fixed, at least in terms of the *ordines*.

The year 59 made no small contribution in the area of judicial legislation: a major restructuring of the *repetundæ* law, a reform of jury selection, and a tightening of voting procedure.[139] Enemies might rail against Cæsar and his associates for political excesses and unseemly methods. But examination of legislative activity tells a different story. The drive to strengthen institutions was a characteristic common to many Roman statesmen.

Criticism leveled against the "triumvirate" for its actions in 59 is matched only by that directed against the tribunate of P. Clodius in the following year. Clodius emerges in the sources as archdemagogue, rabble-rouser, and mob leader. Yet Clodius, like Cæsar, was the author of a criminal law of no mean significance: the *lex Clodia de capite civis*. That his methods were unpalatable to many aristocrats should not preclude an acknowledgment of his achievement. The "sources" on Clodius, after all, reduce themselves essentially to Cicero, his bitter *inimicus*. The tribune's measure deserves a more impartial verdict.

None will deny the personal motivation involved in Clodius' bill. The law was framed deliberately to assure that Cicero would be its first victim. As is notorious, the orator was forced into exile and deep humiliation. But personal pique and spite do not supply full explanation. Behind this measure lay a lengthy history of debate stretching back for three-quarters of a century. At stake was a fundamental question: the state's right to suspend law during public emergencies and to authorize extralegal actions by its representatives.

Emergency powers traditionally came to consuls or other officials through the mechanism of a senatorial decree, the *senatus consultum ultimum*. That maneuver surfaced for the first time in 121 when forces organized by the consul effected the assassination of C. Gracchus and his associates. Subsequent occasions were not infrequent. The *s.c.u.* saw employment in crises or alleged crises, and involved the slaying of Roman citizens. The practice could be defended on the ground that extralegal authority was essential in times of internal threat to the state. But objectors could also make out a case. A law of C. Gracchus himself had outlawed capital condemnation of citizens without sanction of the people. Gracchus' slayer was charged on that count in 120 and acquitted. Specious argument held that the men killed were enemies

[139] Reference is made also to a provision fixing the number of men who could accompany an advocate soliciting information abroad; Cic. *Pro Flacco*, 13. The scholiast is unsure whether that clause belongs in the *lex Vatinia* or the *lex Fufia*; Schol. Bob. 97–98, Stangl. Since the provision applies foremost, if not exclusively, to *repetundæ* investigations, it may, in fact, have been in Cæsar's *lex*.

of the state and hence no longer citizens. Precedent was powerful in Rome. The *s.c.u.* received no further challenge for over half a century. In 63 the issue was aired again. At the trial of Rabirius, accusers challenged the *s.c.u.*, claiming that it could not authorize private citizens to take the law into their own hands. The case ended without resolution. But Cicero's actions in the same year against the Catilinarian conspirators thrust the debate into high relief. The consul had enjoyed senatorial backing in organizing resistance to plots that menaced the state. None could quarrel with military operations against *hostes* in the field. But the disposal of captured and unarmed conspirators was a more difficult matter. With Catiline still at large and the crisis unsettled, Cicero determined upon the execution of the prisoners. A senatorial meeting bolstered his confidence, but responsibility belonged to the consul. Naturally, subsequent criticism was keen, and the whole question of senatorial and consular suspension of due process was very much in the air. It is in that context that the force of Clodius' measure must be understood.[140]

Cicero, on innumerable occasions, made reference to Clodius' illegitimate actions against him. He branded the bill unconstitutional because it took the form of a *privilegium*; that is, it was an *ad hominem* measure, naming Cicero specifically, a procedure judged illegal ever since the Twelve Tables.[141] That charge is tendentious and misleading. In fact, there were two *leges Clodiae*. The first and by far the more important made no mention of Cicero. It was directed at those offenses, so often shielded by the *s.c.u.*, that resulted in violation of constitutional procedure. The *lex Clodia* affirmed or reaffirmed the principle that anyone who executed Roman citizens without trial would be subject to conviction and exile.[142] Of course, the enactment, as everyone knew, had Cicero as its primary target. It was retroactive in application; the execution of the Catilinarians was still fresh in mind. Cicero had no illusions. After soliciting support in vain, the orator withdrew into exile before any formal proceedings began.

It was only at that point that Clodius passed his second bill, declaring Cicero an outlaw, confiscating his property, and fixing the territorial limits

[140] On the history of the *s.c.u.* and the debates which it engendered, see G. Plaumann, *Klio*, 13 (1913): 321–386; Lintott, *Violence*, pp. 149–174; B. Rödl, *Das Senatus Consultum Ultimum* (Bonn, 1969). Most recently, Th. N. Mitchell, *Historia*, 20 (1971): 47–61, argues that the senate, not the consul, bore final responsibility under the *s.c.u.* But it was the consul who came under judicial attack in 58—and in 121.

[141] See, e.g., Cic. *Ad Att.* 3.15.5; *De Domo*, 43–45, 80, 110; *Pro Sest.* 64–65; *In Pis.* 30.

[142] Vell. Pat. 2.45.1: *P. Clodius . . . legem in tribunatu tulit, qui civem Romanum indemnatum interemisset, ei aqua et igni interdiceretur;* Dio, 38.14.4: ὁ δὲ δὴ νόμος ὃν μετὰ ταῦτα ὁ Κλώδιος ἐσήνεγκεν, ἄλλως μὲν οὐκ ἐδόκει ἐπ' αὐτῷ [Cicero] τίθεσθαι, οὐδὲ γὰρ τὸ ὄνομα αὐτοῦ εἶχεν ἀλλὰ κατὰ πάντων ἁπλῶς τῶν πολίτην τινὰ ἄνευ τῆς τοῦ δήμου καταγνώσεως ἀποκτενούντων ἢ καὶ ἀπεκτονότων ἐσήγετο; cf. Livy, *Per.* 103; Plut. *Cic.* 30.4; Appian, *BC*, 2.15.

which he could no longer cross. This, of course, specified Cicero by name, but it was simply a formal *interdictio,* made possible by the orator's own implicit admission of guilt through self-exile. By denouncing the *lex Clodia* as a *privilegium*, Cicero deliberately telescoped the two measures and obfuscated the issue. In private correspondence, however, he could acknowledge the fact: two enactments were involved and the first made no *ad hominem* reference.[143] An important consequence follows. When Cicero was recalled from exile in 57, the *interdictio* was lifted and Clodius' second law was repealed. That law could be faulted on several grounds, though repeal resulted more from political pressure than from legal deficiencies. The initial *lex Clodia*, however, was not affected. Interpretation and enforcement would always be subject to political contingencies. But the principle lodged in the bill had broad significance. Magistrates armed only with senatorial directives would not be so ready to contravene the laws of the people. The effect of the *lex Clodia* transcended the dubious motives of its author.

One other alteration of the criminal law, of minor import, can be briefly noticed. Imperial jurists preserve record of a *lex Pompeia de parricidiis*. Although no date is given, Pompey's second consulship in 55 would be suitable; it was the year in which he addressed himself particularly to judicial matters. The crime of parricide had been punishable by the assembly down to the end of the second century B.C. Shortly thereafter it came under the jurisdiction of the jury courts, and Sulla in 81 incorporated the charge within his general measure on homicide, the *lex Cornelia de sicariis et veneficiis*.[144] What prompted Pompey to delineate *parricidium* once again and institute a separate enactment for it is unclear. It may have been the same tendency toward greater precision that marked Cæsar's extortion law. The *lex Pompeia* enunciated in detail the acts that would fall under the heading of parricide rather than murder. Identity of the victim, of course, determined the charge. Pompey included within the category the murder of parents, grandparents, brothers, sisters, uncles, aunts, cousins, spouses, in-laws, and even patrons. All were spelled out in the text of the legislation.[145] The punishment exacted was identical with that of the Sullan homicide law, namely, a capital penalty. Need for a separate enactment may have had legal justification. Premeditation, perhaps, had to be established

[143] Cic. *Ad Att.* 3.15.5: *quod te cum Culleone scribis de privilegio locutum, est aliquid, sed multo est melius abrogari . . . nec quicquam aliud opus est quam abrogari; nam prior lex nihil lædebat*; cf. *Pro Sest.* 25, 53. For fuller references on both laws, see Broughton, *MRR*, II:196. The exposure of Cicero's tendentiousness was made long ago by W. Sternkopf, *Philologus*, 59 (1900): 272–304; cf. also Greenidge, *Legal Procedure*, pp. 359–366.

[144] References and discussion in Gruen, *Roman Politics*, pp. 261–262.

[145] *Digest*, 48.9; Paul. *Sent.* 5.24. Discussion in Zumpt, *Criminalrecht*, II:2.361–367; Mommsen, *Strafrecht*, pp. 643–646; Rotondi, *Leges Publicæ*, pp. 406–407. The category of *patroni* presumably refers to the slaying by a freedman of his former master.

for conviction under the general homicide statute; but culpable slaying of a relative sufficed to determine guilt under the *lex Pompeia*.[146] The measure illustrates again the growing sophistication in matters of criminal law that was characteristic of the late Republic. It is revealing that no contemporary source makes reference to this measure; nor do any of the later ancient historians who wrote on the period notice it. The reason is plain: Pompey's *lex* had no political content. Hence modern historians pass over it without mention.[147] That typifies the tendency to concentrate on the fleeting events and neglect the more enduring enactments of the late Republic.

Unusual circumstances might sometimes provide the occasion for new criminal law. But what stands out from this discussion is that legislators did not, on the whole, think in terms of ad hoc measures. They endeavored to establish principles of general application and lasting import. In this respect the Ciceronian period forms a sharp contrast to the pre-Sullan era, in which criminal legislation was still in embryonic formation. Trial and error, rather than systematic development, marked the process. Some statutes set up permanent courts and procedures. But many offenses remained without juristic definition. They had to be dealt with as the occasion arose, generally in a political context. The available machinery was either trial before the assembled citizenry or a special court, *quæstio extraordinaria*, created for the particular event. The first, of course, was cumbersome in the extreme and subject to the temporary whims and pressures playing upon the populace. The second invariably became entangled in politics, rendering impartial jurisdiction virtually impossible. Insecurity and discontinuity marked the practice—hence, the development of fixed procedures through permanent courts, *quæstiones perpetuæ*. Sulla's dictatorship structured and systematized that development. Criminal offenses and procedures acquired definition in statutes that authorized standing courts to pass judgment. There should no longer be need for makeshift arrangements or *ad hominem* proceedings.[148] The legislators of the late Republic acknowledged and perpetuated that system. Criminal laws passed after Sulla either revised and expanded earlier legislation or defined new offenses and created new, fixed procedures. The *leges de ambitu,* the *lex Julia de repetundis,* and the *lex Clodia* fall in the first category, the *leges de vi* and *de parricidiis* in the second. Each was meant to have general applicability and permanent status.

Pompey's *lex de vi*, of course, was an exception. The highly charged situation surrounding that measure has already been discussed. And even then most

[146] So Zumpt, *Criminalrecht*, II:2.361–363. For the penalty, see *Digest*, 48.9.1: *ut pœna ea teneatur, quæ est legis Corneliæ de sicariis.*

[147] It does not appear even in Broughton's *MRR.*

[148] The development is traced in Gruen, *Roman Politics, passim.*

senators balked at the ad hoc proceeding. Apart from that episode, the evidence discloses only a single special tribunal in the Ciceronian age.

A *quæstio extraordinaria* tried P. Clodius in 61. The offense was exceptional in every regard. Clodius had allegedly participated *incognito* in the feast of the *Bona Dea*, a ritual open only to female celebrants. The violation constituted an affront to the gods. Nothing resembling a precedent for such a case could be uncovered, and no guidelines to determine proceedings.[149] The question was referred to the Vestals and to the priests, as stewards of the state religion. They pronounced simply that an offense against the gods had been committed.[150] Under other circumstances that might have been the end of the matter. No compelling reason demanded secular intervention. But Clodius was a politician of note, with a dubious reputation and a host of enemies in the senate. Hence, pressure arose for a judicial proceeding. No standing court existed, of course, with jurisdiction over such offenses. A senatorial decree, therefore, instructed the consuls to bring a bill to the assembly instituting a *quæstio extraordinaria.*[151] Debate and dissension ensued in the senate, and the contest spilled over into public meetings and the streets.

The intensity of the political clash engulfed any impartiality on the legal question.[152] The *senatus consultum* called for a special court, for which the prætor would handpick a jury. Its object was little short of inquisitorial procedure. Feelings ran high against Clodius, and the measure received overwhelming senatorial backing. Clodius' supporters objected; M. Piso and Curio fought against the decree, and a tribune, Q. Fufius Calenus, exercised his veto against it. Matters reached an impasse.[153] A way out was found by Hortensius. He persuaded Fufius to drop his veto and to introduce a new bill himself. It was identical with the consular measure except for the constitution of the jury. The prætor would not have a free hand in appointing jurors; presumably, the customary and impartial operation of the lot would select the bench. Fufius' proposal passed.[154]

The affair produced the one known *quæstio extraordinaria* directed at a

[149] Cic. *De Har. Resp.* 37–38: *quod quidem sacrificium nemo ante P. Clodium omni memoria violavit . . . quis enim ante te sacra illa vir sciens viderat, ut quisquam pœnam quæ sequeretur id scelere scire posset?*

[150] Cic. *Ad Att.* 1.13.3; Dio, 37.46.1.

[151] Cic. *Ad Att.* 1.13.3: *deinde ex senatus consulto consules rogationem promulgasse*; Asconius, 53, Clark: *s.c., decretumque ut extra ordinem de ea re iudicium fieret*; Suet. *Iul.* 6; Schol. Bob. 85, 89, Stangl.

[152] The politics of the affair are discussed below, chap. 7.

[153] Cic. *Ad Att.* 1.14.1, 1.14.5; *Pro Mil.* 13; Asconius, 45, Clark; Schol. Bob. 115, Stangl.

[154] Cic. *Ad Att.* 1.16.2; *Parad.* 4.32; Asconius, 45, Clark. On the penalty, a capital one envisioning enforced exile, see Strachan-Davidson, *Problems,* II:40–47; on the political aspects, Ciaceri, *Cicerone,* II:20–25; Balsdon, *Historia*, 15 (1966): 65–73.

single individual in the Ciceronian age. Explosive political motives kept this case out of the realm of traditional criminal legislation from the beginning. Reluctance to establish permanent procedure in a matter that belonged more properly in the religious sphere may also help to explain the ad hoc proceeding.[155] The exception, in fact, throws the rule into relief. For even this instance, enmeshed as it was in politics and personal enmities, produced a tribunal constituted by traditional regulations governing the standing courts. The Romans tended to eschew ephemeral arrangements. Criminal statutes were designed for the future as well as the present.[156]

Crime is not readily legislated out of existence. Societies other than Rome have experienced that unhappy fact. None will pretend that the criminal laws enacted in the late Republic wiped out all abuses. Electoral bribery, for example, continued, perhaps increased, despite a series of *leges de ambitu*. But the situation is not to be traced to senatorial indolence. The record shows a government persistently grappling with the problem, framing and reframing legislation, with an eye to tightening statutes and curbing offenses. It is not the case that vigor was exhibited only by tribunes and popular leaders while the aristocracy slumbered in luxury. In almost every instance criminal statutes were consular, based on declarations issued from the *curia*.[157]

Roman politicians did not divide themselves into reformist and conservative camps. As we have noted over and again, measures propounded by one individ-

[155] Zumpt, *Criminalrecht*, II:2.268–277, in fact, argues that the *lex Fufia* did institute a permanent *quæstio de religione*. It was this which distinguished it from the abortive consular *rogatio*. But the hypothesis is refuted by Cicero's explicit statement that the two measures differed only in the provision for constituting the jury; *Ad Att.* 1.16.2: *Hortensius excogitavit ut legem de religione Fufius tribunus pl. ferret, in qua nihil aliud a consulari rogatione differebat nisi iudicum genus*. That no permanent process was intended is indicated also by the varied terminology used to describe the offense: *de religione*: Cic. *Ad Att.* 1.13.3, 1.14.1, 1.16.2; *De Har. Resp.* 37; *de incesto*: Cic. *Pro Mil.* 13; *In Pis.* 95; Asconius, 45, Clark; Vell. Pat. 2.45.1; Val. Max. 4.2.5, 8.5.5, 9.1.7; Schol. Bob. 85, 89, 115, 173, Stangl; *de pollutis sacris*: Suet. *Iul.* 6; *pollutarium cæremonarium*: Suet. *Iul.* 74; ἀσέβεια: Plut. *Cic.* 28.3; *Cæs.* 10.5; Appian, *BC*, 2.14.

[156] On one other occasion a proposal was mooted for a *quæstio extraordinaria*. When Vettius in 59 alleged a conspiracy against Pompey, P. Vatinius, so Cicero claims, urged proceedings against all those named. But the proposal received no support and perished without issue; Cic. *In Vat.* 26: *promulgarisne . . . quæstionem de tot amplissimis et talibus viris . . . quibus rebus omnium mortalium non voluntate, sed convicio repudiatis fregerisne in carcere cervices ipsi illi Vettio, ne . . . in te ipsum quæstio flagitaretur?* Cf. Cic. *Ad Att.* 2.24.3.

[157] The only certain exception is Clodius' *lex de capite civis*. The *lex Gabinia* forbidding secret meetings is possibly, but not definitely, to be assigned to the tribune of 67. Otherwise, we known only of Cornelius' abortive *ambitus* proposal in 67 and Cæcilius' equally abortive attempt to modify the *ambitus* law in 63. The bills of Vatinius and Fufius in 59 were concerned with judicial procedures, rather than criminal statutes. And both were cooperating closely with the consul C. Cæsar.

ual or group could later be promulgated by their enemies. Politics might determine the timing, but divisions on principle played little role. No group was committed to the defense and perpetuation of abuses. Nor did the "triumvirs" rely on extra-constitutional techniques and scorn traditional institutions. Their activities in the area of criminal law proved to be serious and significant. Crassus' measure *de sodaliciis* afforded an intelligent approach to the control of violations by political clubs. The *lex repetundarum* of C. Cæsar was a carefully conceived statute, which was to have enduring import. And Pompey engaged himself industriously and persistently in judicial matters ranging from procedural rules to legislation on *ambitus, vis,* and even *parricidium*. Special conditions, often political in character, might provide impetus for new enactments. But legislators could see beyond the immediate occasion. They preferred general statutes to makeshift solutions. The late Republic was a pivotal period in the fashioning of Roman criminal law.

ADMINISTRATIVE LEGISLATION

Considerable legislation is recorded on administrative matters. In this area again no party lines can be discovered, nor should any be expected. Some of the measures called forth opposition and proboked struggles. But, as so often, it was reflex politics. Competing politicians would not passively permit rivals to gain the recognition afforded by enactments passed under their names. Several political groups and individuals were active in the area of administrative reform.

Partisans of Pompeius Magnus showed conspicuous energy on this score. Two tribunes of 67, C. Cornelius and A. Gabinius, officers and friends of Pompey, promoted a battery of measures. The contest between Cornelius and C. Piso over *ambitus* legislation in 67 has already been noted. In the course of it, Piso's senatorial friends had sought to promote his own bill by enabling him to promulgate it even after the elections had been announced. That transparent political move provoked Cornelius' important proposal reaffirming that exemptions from the law could be allotted only by the *populus*, not the senate. Veto and conflict greeted the bill, and Cornelius framed it anew–in more palatable form. The senate was authorized to grant dispensations, but only if a minimum of two hundred members were present. And if the matter came before the assembly, no *intercessio* was permissible. Hence, senatorial *auctoritas* was preserved, but ultimate popular sovereignty received reaffirmation. The political *inimici* of Cornelius frowned, but the measure, in that form, gained passage without difficulty.[158]

[158] Asconius, 58–59, Clark: *Tum Cornelius ita ferre rursus cœpit ne quis in senatu legibus solveretur nisi cc adfuissent, neve quis, cum solutus esset, intercederet, cum de ea re ad populum ferretur. Hæc sine tumultu res acta est. Nemo enim negare poterat pro senatus auctoritate esse eam legem; sed*

Of even greater significance was Cornelius' law on the *edictum perpetuum*. It had been the customary practice for incoming prætors to announce the procedural guidelines that they would follow in issuing judicial decisions during their year of office. Administrative convenience was the purpose, but no legal obligation lay upon the prætor to abide by his own edict. Some magistrates violated the guidelines, thereby causing confusion and insecurity. The *lex Cornelia* imposed on all future prætors the requirement of adhering strictly to their *edicta*. Arbitrary deviations were now ruled out, and litigants were no longer at the mercy of partisan judicial officers. Again Cornelius' enemies muttered in discomfort, but no one ventured to raise objection to an intelligent and desirable reform.[159]

Cornelius addressed himself to still another abuse in 67. Envoys from foreign states were vulnerable figures in Rome. Their presence in the city generally looked to favor or advantage for their home constituency. The object might require some peddling of influence. If ready cash were not available, Roman moneylenders would usually oblige. Usurious rates were not uncommon, and repayment on the debts could only fall on the treasuries of the states that had dispatched the *legati*. Cornelius properly denounced the practice as an excessive drain on the financial resources of Roman provinces. He urged upon the senate a proposal to ban all lending of money to foreign envoys. That step, it seems, proved too extreme for senatorial tastes. Ad hoc decrees forbidding loans to certain envoys had been sufficient in the past, when called for. The senate showed itself reluctant to countenance a general measure abolishing all such transactions. Cornelius' effort foundered in the *curia*, and although he complained in a public meeting, as tribunes were wont to do, he did not, apparently, press the matter further.[160] His tribunician colleague, A. Gabinius, however, took up the cudgels, and with greater success. By 56 a *lex Gabinia* stood on the books, forbidding loans in Rome to representatives of foreign communities. One might ascribe that law to 67, when the issue was under discussion. Yet the failure of Cornelius to promulgate such a bill

---

tamen eam tulit invitis optimatibus, qui perpaucos amicis gratificari solebant; 72, Clark; cf. 60–61, Clark; Dio, 36.39.1–4; Cic. *In Vat.* 5; Quint. *Inst. Orat.* 4.4.8; and see above. Miss Taylor, *CP*, 36 (1941): 128–130, attributed to Cornelius only the narrow motive of trying to obstruct certain electoral candidates. That is a view which she later generously retracted; *JRS*, 52 (1962): 23.

[159] Asconius, 59, Clark: *Aliam deinde legem Cornelius, etsi nemo repugnare ausus est, multis tamen invitis tulit, ut prætores ex edictis suis perpetuis ius dicerent; quæ res studium aut gratiam ambitiosis prætoribus qui varie ius dicere assueverant sustulit*; Dio, 36.40.3. For a previous instance of deviation from the edict, see Cic. *Verr.* 2.1.119. Cornelius' law, of course, still left prætors free to issue *decreta* on matters not covered in their *edictum perpetuum*; see A. Metro, *Iura*, 20 (1969): 500–524.

[160] The account is contained in Asconius, 57–58, Clark.

suggests that it was premature and makes it unlikely that Gabinius could have succeeded in the same year. One need not doubt that the two tribunes collaborated on the effort in 67 and that Gabinius' law grew out of the abortive proposal of Cornelius. But the passage of the measure is more properly placed in Gabinius' consulship of 58 or, less likely, his prætorship in 61.[161] By that time the aristocracy was prepared to acknowledge the virtue of a general enactment aimed at the abuse.

Gabinius also promulgated a law obliging the senate to hear deputations from abroad during the month of February. Reception of envoys was, therefore, to take precedence over all other senatorial business in the early part of the year. The measure should be taken in connection with Gabinius' other enactment on foreign *legati*. The former too is customarily assigned to his tribunate of 67. Yet a problem arises. Our sources record a *lex Pupia* which apparently forbade the holding of senatorial sessions on *dies comitiales,* at least for the months of January and February. Gabinius' bill modified that pronouncement and permitted meetings in February for the presentation of foreign ambassadors.[162] Ostensibly, the author of the *lex Pupia* is M. Pupius Piso, consul in 61, the only Pupius known to hold high office in the late Republic. Placement of the Gabinian law in 67 has caused some scholars to shift the *lex Pupia* back to the presumed prætorship of M. Piso in 72 or 71.[163] In light of our previous discussion, that solution is unnecessary. Gabinius' law on loans to envoys belongs, most probably, in his consulship of 58. It is reasonable to put the measure on senatorial hearings in the same year. The two form a coherent combination. Gabinius proposed to eliminate manipulation of foreign ambassadors by Roman officials and moneylenders. Audiences for these legations were now fixed on the senatorial calendar and were not subject to arbitrary shifts by men in a position to sell their influence. The ban on loans further reduced pressure on foreign representatives. Their business

[161] Reference to the law comes only in Cic. *Ad Att.* 5.21.12, 6.2.7. Nothing shows that it applied to all provincial loans rather than just to loans for official representatives. The reconstruction of Heitland, *Rom. Rep.,* III:48–50, requires that Cornelius' moderate bill be defeated while Gabinius' more radical measure secure passage in 67, a most unlikely notion followed by many moderns. Mommsen, *Strafrecht,* pp. 885–886, more plausibly, puts the *lex Gabinia* in 58, though without argument.

[162] Cic. *Ad Fam.* 1.4.1: *senatus haberi ante Kalendas Febr. per legem Pupiam, id quod scis, non potest, neque mense Febr. toto, nisi perfectis aut reiectis legationibus; Ad Q. Frat.* 2.13.3: *comitialibus diebus, qui Quirinalia sequuntur, Appius interpretatur, non impediri se lege Pupia, quo minus habeat senatum, et quod Gabinia sanctum sit, etiam cogi, ex Kal. Febr. usque ad Kal. Mart. legatis senatum quotidie dare.* Cf. *Ad Q. Frat.* 2.3.3; *Pro Sest.* 74.

[163] The most recent discussion of the evidence and the literature is by A. Michels, *The Calendar of the Roman Republic* (Princeton, 1967), pp. 42–45. She retains the *lex Pupia* in 61, but gives no date for the *lex Gabinia.*

could now be handled under a more rational and impartial system. The *leges Gabiniae,* we may conclude, were not the enactments of a rabble-rousing tribune, but consular measures authorized by *senatus consulta.* The *lex Pupia* also takes its rightful place as a consular law in 61. One may note that M. Piso, author of that legislation, was also a close associate of Pompey's. The *amici* of Pompey show persistent concern for administrative and institutional reform.

Another misuse of authority caused added burdens to provincial communities. The senate traditionally granted *liberæ legationes* to its members, that is, nominal commissions to visit the provinces. The practice was insidious. Senators went abroad on private, not official, business. But because they received overt authorization from the *curia,* they had claims to be treated as representatives of Rome and thereby to demand privileges and expenses from the provincials. It was a custom much lamented and complained of by the *provinciales.* Here again, however, the senate was willing to countenance internal reform. In 63 the consul M. Cicero introduced a measure to abolish *liberæ legationes.* If we may believe his own reflections penned many years later, he received solid backing from his senatorial colleagues. The proposal failed of passage through a tribunician veto. But a compromise solution took effect: *liberæ legationes,* previously unrestricted, were now to be limited to a year's duration.[164] Though the offense was not thoroughly eradicated, Cicero's bill represented a salutary step in the right direction.

Institutional reform, it is already clear, did not reflect the party line of a particular group. T. Labienus, a vigorous and popular tribune in 63, brought about repeal of a Sullan law and restored the election of priestly colleges to the people. In this he received the enthusiastic support of Julius Cæsar, who cooperated with Labienus on more than one occasion in that year. The measure is normally portrayed as a political move. And one need not doubt that the authors aimed at popular approbation and advancement of their own careers. But observe that no opposition is recorded to the proposal. Cicero resisted other efforts of Labienus and Cæsar that were patently political, but popular election of priests denoted a reasonable and acceptable change. In a year when political conflict was keen, the absence of evidence for a struggle on this issue is noteworthy.[165] Cæsar's interest in administrative reform has already been instanced in these pages. We may notice also, in passing, his

[164] Cic. *De Leg.* 3.18: *quod quidem genus legationis ego consul, quamquam ad commodum senatus pertinere videbatur, tamen adprobante senatu frequentissimo, nisi mihi levis tribunus plebis tum intercessisset, sustulissem; minui tamen tempus et, quod erat infinitum, annuum feci.* For provincial complaints on this practice, see Cic. *De Leg. Agrar.* 1.8, 2.45; *Pro Flacco,* 86; cf. *Ad Fam.* 12.21.

[165] The measure is noted only by Dio, 37.37.1–2. His linking of it with Cæsar's election as *pontifex maximus,* however, is erroneous; see above, chap. 2, n.138.

first enactment as consul in 59: Cæsar established the requirement that all acts of the senate and of the popular assemblies be recorded and published.[166] The change would enforce greater responsibility and more systematic governmental operation.

M. Cato has traditionally been associated with obstructionism and reaction. The interpretation misses the essential dynamism of that statesman. Among other things, it neglects his activity in the interest of progressive reform. That interest manifested itself as early as his quæstorship of 64. Cato supervised with sternness the clerks and assistants who, as permanent employees, had been accustomed to deceiving and manipulating the quæstors, their inexperienced superiors. Cato rigorously scrutinized public accounts and fashioned the quæstor's task into a systematic order. Cato's virtue, it was said, elevated the quæstorship to the dignity of a consulship.[167] Among the quæstor's functions was the supervision of senatorial decrees regularly deposited for safekeeping in the state treasury. That process too was subject to abuse. Quæstors, through favor or intimidation, had, on occasion, included false decrees at the behest of friends and patrons in the senate. Cato, of course, could not be imposed on in that fashion, and he brought the practice conspicuously to the attention of the public.[168] As quæstor he was in no position to sponsor legislation. But the hand of Cato is surely discernible in a consular law of 62 on the subject. The *lex Licinia Junia*, promoted by L. Murena and D. Silanus, the latter being Cato's brother-in-law, seems to have concerned itself generally with proper modes of legislative procedure. Its one reported clause, however, outlawed any clandestine deposit of laws in the *ærarium*. Presumably, every legislative act would henceforth be formally and openly attested before its placement in the archives. The law evidently contained a criminal sanction, and offenders were to be prosecuted in the courts.[169] Cato's efforts had borne substantial fruit. The evidence shows again and again that the acknowledgment of reform transcended political considerations. For it was in this same spirit that Cato's *inimicus* Julius Cæsar three years later promulgated his measure on the publication of all acts of the senate and assemblies. The common attitudes, not the divisions, of the ruling class force themselves ever more strikingly upon our attention.[170]

[166] Suet. *Iul.* 20.1: *inito honore primus omnium instituit, ut tam senatus quam populi diurna acta confierent et publicarentur.*

[167] Plut. *Cato,* 16.2–3, 17.1–2.

[168] Plut. *Cato*, 17.3. On the falsification of senatorial decrees, cf. Gabba, *StudClassOrient*, 10 (1961): 90–96.

[169] Schol. Bob. 140, Stangl: *Licinia vero et Iunia consulibus auctoribus Licinio Murena et Iunio Silano perlata illud cavebat, ne clam ærario legem inferri liceret, quoniam leges in ærario condebantur.* Other references collected in Broughton, *MRR*, II:173.

[170] The indefatigable Cato also sponsored intelligent reform in his tribunate of 62. He and

A minor and obscure instance provides further illustration. Cato had no more intense political foe than P. Clodius. Sources on the late Republic have conveyed stereotypical portraits: Cato a throwback to antique Roman virtue, Clodius the reckless demagogue. Hence, one is not surprised to learn of Cato's strict regulation of lax practices associated with quæstors' clerks. More interesting is the fact that Clodius carried that very policy a step further. A law, evidently of his tribunate, sharply restricted the private business activities of quæstors' scribes. No source on the late Republic, naturally, divulges that information. It appears only as an aside in Suetonius' *Life of Domitian* and rarely receives discussion in modern works.[171] The enactment, to be sure, was not itself of great moment. It may serve, however, as yet another check on the schematic designs and selective silences contained in the ancient testimony. On this issue of administrative reform Cato and Clodius were at one: state regulation of public employees to prevent conflict of interest. Again a small item exposes homogeneity of policy as perhaps more basic than political friction.

Clodius, indeed, showed considerable interest in administrative matters. The smokescreen of Ciceronian invective has prevented proper recognition of the fact. A *lex Clodia* of 58 relieved legislative assemblies of certain restrictive limitations on their activity. Precise content of the law remains elusive despite incessant and ingenious modern conjectures. The area of certainty is here quite narrow. Clodius' measure introduced some modification of earlier legislation that had been on the books for a century. Unfortunately, evidence on the previous laws, the *leges Ælia et Fufia,* depends largely on reconstruction of the Clodian measure. Of the Ælian and Fufian laws we may say with confidence only that they regulated certain proceedings in the popular assemblies. They forbade some, if not all, legislation between the announcement and the holding of elections, and they permitted *obnuntiatio*, that is, the blocking of comitial action by magistrates and augurs through appeal to unfavorable divine signs.[172]

---

a fellow tribune, L. Marius, attacked the false statements of returning *imperatores*, who customarily exaggerated their exploits in order to secure triumphs. Cato's new measure obliged generals to attest under oath to the number of enemies slain abroad; a minimum of 5,000 was necessary to justify a triumph; Val. Max. 2.8.1. And notice too Cato's interest in denying official sanction to debts incurred by provincial cities to Roman citizens. Cato and his *æmulator* P. Servilius Isauricus sponsored a clause to that effect in an *s.c.* of 60; Cic. *Ad Att.* 1.19.9, 1.20.4, 2.1.10. The measure discloses an attitude not dissimilar to that of Gabinius and Cornelius in their bills restricting loans to provincials.

[171] Suet. *Dom.* 9: *scribas quæstorios negotiantis ex consuetudine sed contra Clodiam legem.*

[172] References in Broughton, *MRR*, I:452-453. For bibliography see Weinrib, *ZSS*, 87 (1970): 395. Sumner's effort, *AJP*, 84 (1963): 337-358, to distinguish various clauses in the two laws, is unnecessary and largely unconvincing. The view of A. E. Astin, *Latomus*, 23 (1964): 421-445, that the measures involved a comprehensive treatment of all legal conditions governing the assemblies, is attractive, though unverifiable.

In both these areas Clodius' bill lifted some restrictions. The rantings of Cicero are predictable. For him Clodius abolished all restraints, destroyed ritual observances, canceled vetoes and *obnuntiatio*, permitted legislation on all *dies fasti*, and eliminated every safeguard; in a word, the *lex Clodia* repealed altogether the provisions of the *leges Aelia et Fufia*.[173] One need not pause over the rhetoric. Cicero's statements are flamboyant and demonstrably false. *Obnuntiatio*, at least in some form, was still permissible after 58, and *intercessio* certainly endured, as did the reporting of *auspicia*. Clodius' law introduced modification, not repeal, of earlier regulations.[174]

Confusion remains. But the occasion for Clodius' bill is not in dispute. The previous year had seen repeated attempts by the consul Bibulus to obstruct the legislation of Cæsar. Bibulus' use of *obnuntiatio* through "watching the skies" was within the law, but consciously contrived and politically motivated. The Aelian and Fufian laws had confirmed the practice of *obnuntiatio*, no doubt to provide a restraint upon reckless legislative sessions. But Bibulus had twisted it to the purpose of his own cause. It was careful strategy designed to drive Cæsar to excess and discredit. Clodius had a cogent case for reform. Not that he was concerned for the Cæsarian legislation—indeed, he was among its critics and threatened its repeal. But the tribune did not want to face the same kind of obstructionism; he was preparing an extensive legislative program of his own. And, more important, he could argue that the tactics of Bibulus, if unchallenged, would set a precedent and hamstring all future activities of the popular assemblies. Restriction of *obnuntiatio* and extension of available days for legislative meetings constituted the substance of Clodius' measure.[175] Ciceronian excess can be safely jettisoned. The *lex*

[173] Cic. *Pro Sest.* 33: *lata lex est, ne auspicia valerent, ne quis obnuntiaret, ne quis legi intercederet, ut omnibus fastis diebus legem ferri liceret, ut lex Aelia, lex Fufia ne valeret; Pro Sest.* 56; *P. Red. in Sen.* 11; cf. *De Har. Resp.* 58; *In Vat.* 18; *In Pis.* 9-10; *De Prov. Cons.* 46.

[174] This has long been recognized, though scholars differ on the precise changes. McDonald, *JRS*, 19 (1929): 164-179, conjectured that Clodius prevented magisterial *obnuntiatio* in legislative assemblies, but not in electoral *comitia*. Sumner, *AJP*, 84 (1963): 337-358, goes further and applies the restriction to tribunes as well. Yet *obnuntiatio* in respect of legislation seems implied in Cic. *Pro Sest.* 78. Hence, Balsdon, *JRS*, 47 (1957): 15-16, and Astin, *Latomus*, 23 (1964): 421-445, reconstruct a more moderate bill that simply allowed the people to cancel *obnuntiatio* on ad hoc occasions. That, however, conflicts not only with Ciceronian exaggerations, but with the more precise statements of Asconius, 8, Clark: *ne quis per eos dies, quibus cum populo agi liceret, de cælo servaret*; and of Dio, 38.13.6: ἐσήνεγκε μηδένα τῶν ἀρχόντων ἐν ταῖς ἡμέραις ἐν αἷς ψηφίσασθαί τι τὸν δῆμον ἀναγκαῖον εἴη, τὰ ἐκ τοῦ οὐρανοῦ γιγνόμενα παρατηρεῖν. S. Weinstock, *JRS*, 27 (1937): 215-222, cut the knot by arguing that Clodius did repeal the Aelian and Fufian laws but that his own measure was annulled shortly thereafter. That solution founders on the resounding silence of Cicero. Better to confess ignorance on the precise details of Clodius' law.

[175] The latter feature cannot be any more specifically defined than the former. For the most recent discussion, without clear conclusion, see Michels, *Calendar*, pp. 94-97.

Clodia warrants a fairer hearing. Safeguards remained, and abuse was checked. By voting the bill, the Roman people had yielded not to demagoguery but to sound administrative reform.

Similar analysis is applicable to Clodius' law restricting the power of the censors. Once again, if reliance were placed only on the railings of Cicero, the measure would appear extravagant and irrational: Clodius swept away the censorship, eradicating all the powers attaching to that office.[176] The facts are considerably less drastic. The censors had long exercised the privilege of reviewing senatorial and equestrian lists and of removing unsuitable individuals from those *ordines*. That privilege could be, and no doubt often had been, abused for political purposes. The *lex Clodia* did not abolish censorial authority in this area but applied salutary limitations to it. Henceforth, no one could be expelled from the ranks of the senate or the *ordo equester* except after full and fair hearing and only with the concurrence of both censors.[177] The bill does not have the stamp of irrationality or excess. Even the most flamboyant of Roman politicians enacted measures with a view to proper institutional change.

A summary is in order. Legislation in the late Republic was full and frequent. Roman legislators showed remarkable energy, care, and ingenuity. Certain areas received particular attention: electoral reform, judicial procedure, criminal laws, and administrative regulations. The preceding survey has confirmed a number of conclusions. Nearly fifty *leges* and decrees are recorded in these fields, and fewer than a third are ascribable to tribunes. The proposition that tribunician initiative was the principal source of reform may now be decisively discarded. Of the tribunician laws almost all belong to just two tribunes, Cornelius in 67 and Clodius in 58. And their measures, while possessing popular appeal, also effected sound and sensible change. One may cite Cornelius' bills on the prætorian edict, electoral bribery, and exemptions from the law, or Clodius' enactments on due process in capital trials, unwarranted obstructionism, and the censorship. Analysis of the evidence also refutes any efforts to discern a "reform party." Pompeius Magnus, Julius Cæsar, and M. Crassus all sponsored serious legislation; and the same can be said of men like C. Piso, Hortensius, and Cato. Political differences often engendered friction over proposed bills. But measures offered by one individual or group frequently turn up again later in similar form with the endorsement of their own rivals. Certain

[176] Cic. *De Har. Resp.* 58: *censuram exstinxit; In Pis.* 9: *vetus illa magistra pudoris et modestiæ censura sublata est; Pro Sest.* 55; *De Prov. Cons.* 46.

[177] Asconius, 8, Clark: *ne quem censores in senatu legendo præterirent, neve qua ignominia afficerent, nisi qui apud eos accusatus et utriusque censoris sententia damnatus esset*; Dio, 38.13.2; cf. Schol. Bob. 132, Stangl. The measure was repealed or altered in 52 by the consul Metellus Scipio; Dio, 40.57.1–3. Circumstances and details, however, are unknown.

years stand in the textbooks as emblematic of disruption and decay: 59, 58, 55, 52. Yet those very years produced solid legislation aimed at stability and progressive reform: the Julian extortion law, Clodius' legislative program, the *lex Licinia de sodaliciis*, and a series of careful enactments by Pompey on judicial procedure and criminal law.[178]

A legislative flood marks the generation of Cicero. The staggering number of measures dwarfs by comparison all previous eras of Roman history. Is that a sign of health or disease? The question is not easily answered. Legislative enactments alone cannot effect fundamental reform, if that be needed. The foregoing analysis has endeavored to show that Rome's ruling class exhibited concern and energy in seeking solutions for problems through legislation. A blanket verdict is best avoided. Some of the solutions proved temporary and ineffective, others earned a more enduring success. The fact that Rome required a succession of *leges de ambitu* attests to the difficulty of framing a definitive measure that could finally curb that abuse. Enactments like the *lex Plautia de vi* or the bills on *collegia* and *sodalicia* proved insufficient when internal disturbances rocked the city. On the other hand, more permanent contributions were made by Cæsar's *lex de repetundis*, Cornelius' bill on the prætorian edict, and numerous changes in procedural and administrative matters.

Through it all, the bulk itself of the legislative activity stands out. That fact is impressive, but disturbing. It may be that it proved more damaging than advantageous. Rome had not needed such activity in the past. The *mos maiorum* had sufficed; express regulations could be kept to a minimum. But the period that ran from the Gracchi to Sulla undermined confidence in established traditions. Sulla sought to restore that confidence. But in so doing he adopted the premises of the Gracchi themselves: that desired ends are best enforced by overt legislation. The generation that followed Sulla accepted that principle. The aim of securing reform and preventing infractions issued in a stream of new *leges*. The movement edged toward a firmer structure, but the result allowed less freedom for maneuver. A more informal but more secure age in the past could absorb change and overlook abuse without severely shaking the system. But when malleable traditions were hardened into laws, even minor offenses had to be regarded as illegal violations. The consequence

[178] It is possible that Pompey even conceived a project involving codification of Roman public law. The project is noted only by a single–and very late–source; Isidorus Hispalensis, *Origines*, 5.1.5: *Leges autem redigere in libris primus consul Pompeius instituere voluit, sed non perseveravit obtrectatorum metu*. But the report is not implausible. Its authenticity is defended by E. Pólay, *Acta Antiqua*, 13 (1965): 85–95. On the later reputation of Pompey's third consulship generally, see Cic. *Phil.* 1.18; Appian, *BC*, 2.25.

was a mania for fashioning and refining statutes, and a mounting succession of judicial prosecutions. The direction of post-Sullan society moved from flexible institutions toward strictly defined practices. The structure was tighter but more brittle. Roman statesmen were, on the whole, sincere and assiduous in attacking contemporary problems. But the means employed, a proliferation of statutory law, may have contributed to the Republic's undoing.

VII

CRIMINAL TRIALS: THE IMPLICATIONS

WAGING OF political warfare in the criminal courts had a long history. The *quæstiones perpetuæ* were born in politics. From their inception the interests of justice were tempered with a generous mixture of politics. Two generations prior to the Ciceronian age established that pattern. It persevered to the end of the Republic.

Not that every criminal trial was manipulated. Political significance resided in the opportunities available for prominent individuals or groups to gain ground on rivals and competitors. Electoral defeat was only temporary embarrassment; legislative failure could subsequently be reversed; but conviction on a criminal charge might entail permanent exclusion from the public scene. The criminal docket was full in the late Republic. Well over a hundred cases are reported in the 60s and 50s. Many involved individuals of small significance, noted only in passing somewhere in the Ciceronian corpus. But a healthy number engaged the activities of Roman *principes* or their *amici.* Those events could have telling political consequences. Contending senatorial interests found the *iudicia* convenient vehicles whereby to resolve or to compound their friction. Private feuds among *nobiles* were also frequently on exhibit. And criminal trials offered occasion for aspiring orators and politicians to display their gifts and advance their careers. The combination of elements assured a continuing stream of judicial proceedings, which contributed markedly to the course of late Republican politics.

The structure examined in previous chapters takes on fuller shape through analyses of criminal trials. Contests for power among leading political groups can be further illustrated. So also can the fragmenting of noble *gentes* through private quarrels in the courts, and the emergence of new figures attaining prominence or notoriety. Larger issues too were raised in the *iudicia.* Or they could be seized upon as pretexts to embarrass and attack political *inimici.*

POMPEIUS AND THE TRIALS OF THE 60s

Pompeius Magnus was in the East in the mid-60s, not subject to the call of the *iudicia.* But friends and adherents at home offered appropriate targets for his competitors. C. Cornelius, an ex-quæstor of Pompey's, was a reformist tribune in 67, sponsoring legislation and rousing the violent enmity of the consul C. Piso. The following year witnessed the activity of another energetic tribune, C. Manilius, who sponsored the bill for Pompey's Mithridatic command, over the objections of Catulus, Hortensius, and others. It comes as no surprise, therefore, that indictments were brought against Cornelius and Manilius in 66 and that both men sustained full-scale prosecutions in 65. Pompey's foes were unable to impede his military commissions; hence, best attack the general indirectly by hauling his confederates before the bar. The political character of these cases is clear.

Manilius, it seems, had earlier felt the wrath of Pompey's enemies. Young Cn. Piso, inspired by bitter hostility toward Pompey, brought Manilius to trial in 69 or 68. When Pompey himself exercised influence on Manilius' behalf, the outspoken Piso turned his fire on the general and threatened still another prosecution. The outcome of that affair does not stand on record.[1] But the events of Manilius' tribunate offered further fuel for prosecutors. An action was brought *de repetundis* in December 66, shortly after Manilius' tenure as tribune.[2]

The substance of the accusation is unknown. Manilius had certainly not been engaged in provincial administration of late. Minor clauses in the Sullan *repetundæ* law might have been invoked to frame an indictment.[3] Grasping for a suitable charge suggests all the more strongly a purely political proceeding. M. Cicero, prætor in 66, was in charge of the *quæstio repetundarum.* It was not an enviable position. The orator was anxious to show his favor to Pompey and to Pompey's friends. He had already spoken eloquently on behalf of Manilius' Mithridatic bill. But now tempers ran high and popular demonstrations impeded the proceedings. Cicero fixed the last day of 66 for the trial, that he might be able to oversee the case as presiding officer. But

[1] Val. Max. 6.2.4. Discussion in Gruen, *CSCA*, 1 (1968): 160–162.

[2] Cic. *Pro Corn. apud* Asconius, 62 Clark: *postulatur apud me prætorem primum de pecuniis repetundis*; cf. Plut. *Cic.* 9.4: ἔτι δ' ἡμέρας δύο ἢ τρεῖς ἔχοντι τῆς ἀρχῆς αὐτῷ προσήγαγέ τις Μανίλιον εὐθύνων κλοπῆς.

[3] Like the provision *quo ea pecunia pervenerit*; Cic. *Pro Rab. Post.* 8.

disturbances prevented any formal hearings. Cicero promised instead to serve as defense counsel when the trial resumed.[4]

Manilius' prosecutors were not through with him yet. The *repetundae* charge may have been tenuous and flimsy. But disruptions in late 66 provided grounds for another accusation. Manilius was now indicted *de maiestate.*[5] The prosecutor was Cn. Minucius, an obscure and insignificant figure. But the friends of Catulus and Cato had a major interest in the discomfiture of Pompeius Magnus. When Manilius attempted to upset judicial process by employing bands of hirelings to intimidate Minucius, the effort was counteracted by a force under the leadership of L. Domitius Ahenobarbus, the swaggering brother-in-law of Cato.[6] Cicero's support for Manilius earned credit with Pompey, but was to no avail. A *senatus consultum* instructed both consuls to stand guard over the trial to curb any further demonstrations. Manilius was convicted and disappears from history.[7]

Cornelius' association with Pompey brought him similar difficulties. There was much that could be alleged against him. A turbulent tribunate in 67 had involved confrontation with the consul C. Piso; and the passage of legisla-

[4] Plut. *Cic.* 9.4–6; Dio, 36.44.1–2. The disturbances may have been initiated by Pompey's enemies. That is especially likely if, as Asconius reports, Cn. Piso and Catiline were involved; Asconius, 66, Clark; cf. Cic. *Cat.* 1.5. See the discussion in Gruen, *CP*, 64 (1969): 20–24. A possible reference to these events lurks in Cic. *De Leg. Agrar.* 2.49; see B. Rawson, *CP*, 66 (1971): 26–29.

[5] Schol. Bob. 119, Stangl: *causam de maiestate.* The statement is dismissed as a mistake by E. J. Phillips, *Latomus*, 29 (1970): 603–605, but his arguments are inconclusive. Ciaceri, *Cicerone*, I:153–156, has no grounds for the assertion that Manilius was tried twice in 65, once *de repetundis* and once *de maiestate.* Nothing attests to the resumption of *repetundae* proceedings, which were impeded in 66. Asconius knows of only one trial of Manilius in 65; 60, 66, Clark.

[6] Schol. Bob. 119, Stangl: *Nam cum C. Manilius post annum tribunatus sui quem turbulentissime gesserat causam de maiestate dicturus esset accusante Cn. Minucio, id egit, ut per multitudinem conspiratam obsideret eundem Cn. Minucium accusatorem suum. Cui obsesso auxilium tulit adgregata bonorum multitudine L. hic Domitius.* Further on the disruptions at the trial: Asconius, 60, 66, Clark.

[7] Asconius, 60, Clark: *ex s.c. ambo consules . . . praesidebant ei iudicio, non* [Manilius] *respondisset atque esset damnatus*; cf. 76, Clark. That Cicero actually served as defense counsel for Manilius is disputed. Gelzer, *Cicero*, p. 60, denies it; so also Phillips, *Latomus*, 29 (1970): 606–607. Ciaceri, *Cicerone*, I:154, argues that, if Cicero appeared, it was at the *repetundae* hearing, not the *maiestas* trial. The language of [Q. Cic.] *Comm. Petit.* 51 is ambiguous: *urbanam illam multitudinem et eorum studia . . . adeptus es in Pompeio ornando, Manili causa recipienda, Cornelio defendendo.* But a fragment exists of Cicero's *Pro Manilio*; Nonius, p. 235, M. There is no decisive reason to associate this with a *contio* in 66 rather than the trial in 65; much less to postulate a speech later published but never delivered; R. Heinze, *AbhLeipz*, 27 (1909): 997. We know, in any case, that a praetor of 65, C. Attius Celsus, strenuously urged Cicero to take up the defense of Manilius; Asconius, 65, Clark. Reconstruction of Cicero's motives by Ward, *TAPA*, 101 (1970): 545–556, is highly speculative and implausible.

tion through dubious tactics had evoked the hostility of many *principes*. In 66 Cornelius was arraigned *de maiestate*. The *accusatores* were two brothers, P. and L. Cominius, young *equites* from Spoletium, who had already made a modest reputation as prosecutors. The effort came to naught in that year. There was collusion—or perhaps blundering. The presiding officer, L. Cassius Longinus, failed to appear on the appointed day. Some alleged collaboration with the defense. The accusers were driven from the field by organized mobs and fled the city by scrambling over rooftops. When Cassius resumed proceedings on the following day, no prosecutors were in evidence. Rumor reported that they had been bribed into silence. Cassius could then, with impunity, dismiss the case.[8]

That was not to be the end of it. The fate of Manilius revived the courage of P. Cominius. Anxious to dispel rumors of his corruption in 66, he renewed the action against Cornelius.[9] The case stirred considerable interest and drew large crowds. Cornelius avoided the errors of Manilius. Few attendants accompanied him to court; he would not risk upheavals which might provide his prosecutors with additional grounds for accusation. And he engaged the services of M. Cicero. The orator's efforts for Manilius may have been ineffective and fruitless. But the defense of Cornelius was a source of pride. Cicero argued the case for four full days and eventually wrote up his defense in two separate orations. The speeches were cited with admiration by later authorities.[10] Only fragments remain now, with Asconius' extended commentary, but enough to give some indication of the issues involved.

The crime of *maiestas* was slippery and ambiguous. "Damaging the majesty of the Roman people" was a charge subject to varied interpretations. The Sullan *maiestas* law, under which Cornelius was charged, had added many provisions to earlier legislation and had introduced a precision that was previously lacking. But ambiguity lay in the very nature of *maiestas*. It was an ineradicable feature that endured well into the imperial period. Manilius had been charged *de maiestate* on the basis, apparently, of disruptive activity that wrecked a public proceeding. With Cornelius, the actions of his tribunate offered scope for the *accusatores*. When presenting his measures on exemptions from the law, he had been met with tribunician veto. The interposing tribune forbade the herald to read out Cornelius' *rogatio*. But Cornelius ignored the *intercessio* and read out the bill himself, thereby precipitating riots and a cessa-

[8] The story is recounted by Asconius, 59–60, Clark. On the Cominii, see further Cic. *Pro Cluent.* 100–102; *Brutus*, 271.

[9] Asconius, 60, Clark: *Manilius . . . damnatus, recreavit se Cominius, ut infamiam acceptæ pecuniæ tolleret, ac repetiit Cornelium lege maiestatis*; cf. Cic. *Pro Corn. apud* Asconius, 62, Clark; Cic. *Brutus*, 271.

[10] See, e.g., Quint. *Inst. Orat.* 8.3.3: *nec fortibus modo sed etiam fulgentibus armis prœliatur in causa Cicero Cornelii*; also Asconius, 62, Clark; Pliny, *Ep.* 1.20.8–9.

tion of public business. Those events were raked up by the prosecution in 65 to authorize a charge of *maiestas.*[11]

The ambiguity of *maiestas,* of course, permitted manipulation by both defense and prosecution. Cornelius, it could be argued, had doubly impaired the dignity of the tribune's office. He had ignored the veto of his colleague, and though a tribune himself, he had read out the provisions of a bill at a public *contio.* The prosecution provided prominent witnesses to the facts—which Cicero could not deny.[12] But they were unable to cite particulars in the law which could clinch the charge. Cicero seized upon that opportunity: the actions of Cornelius did not coincide with anything spelled out as an offense in *maiestas* legislation. The *accusatores* resorted to the spirit of the law, urging a liberal interpretation of its ambiguity.[13] That, of course, could also be turned to Cicero's advantage. Ambiguity cuts both ways, and the "spirit of the law" is generally interpreted to the tastes of the pleader. If Cicero could not deny the facts, he could deny their implication: Cornelius had read out his measure only for the sake of reexamining it; as for tribunician veto, he had complied with it by canceling the meeting thereafter; there was no *tribunicia potestas imminuta.*[14] Legal sophistries abounded on both sides; the slippery character of *maiestas* encouraged them.

[11] On the events of 67, see Asconius, 58, Clark; and see above, chap. 6.

[12] Bauman, *Crimen Maiestatis,* pp. 71–75, argues that the charge of impairing tribunician dignity relates not to the overriding of a veto, but to Cornelius' reading of his own bill. Hence, the diminished *tribunicia potestas* was not that of Globulus, the interceding tribune, but of Cornelius himself. That would seem, at first glance, to be the import of Quint. *Inst. Orat.* 4.4.8: *maiestatem minuit C. Cornelius; nam codicem tribunus pl. ipse pro contione legit:* cf. 5.13.18, 5.13.25, 10.5.13. Cornelius' action was, so far as men knew, unprecedented. What made it subject to a *maiestas* charge, however, was not simply that Cornelius read the bill, but that it was done in violation of a veto. That seems clear in Asconius, 60–61, Clark: *Dixerunt autem hoc: vidisse se cum Cornelius in tribunatu codicem pro rostris ipse recitaret, quod ante Cornelium nemo fecisse existimaretur. Volebant videri se iudicare eam rem magnopere ad crimen imminutæ maiestatis tribuniciæ pertinere; etenim prope tollebatur intercessio, si id tribunis permitteretur.* Cf. also Cic. *Pro Corn. apud* Asconius, 71, Clark: *neque enim maius est legere codicem, cum intercedatur, quam sitellam ipsum coram ipso intercessore deferre*; Cic. *In Vat.* 5. The point is that violation of the veto consisted precisely in the reading of the bill; Asconius, 58, Clark. Bauman is led into a false distinction by his own assumption that earlier *maiestas* legislation had specified overriding of *intercessio* as a fixed offense; *op. cit.*, pp. 54–55. But there is no evidence for such an explicit clause, and the continued ambiguity of *maiestas* militates strongly against it. Meier, *MusHelv*, 25 (1968): 87–88, argues that Cornelius' reading of his measure suspended, rather than violated, an *intercessio.* Sources cited above would seem to point in the other direction.

[13] Asconius, 62, Clark: *cum sit Cornelius reus maiestatis legis Corneliæ, utrum certæ aliquæ res sint ea lege comprehensæ quibus solis reus maiestatis teneatur, quod patronus defendit; an libera eius interpretatio iudici relicta sit, quod accusator proponit.* Cf. Quint. *Inst. Orat.* 7.3.35.

[14] Cic. *In Vat.* 5: *Codicem legisse dicebatur; defendebat testibus conlegis suis non se recitandi causa*

But it would be a mistake to dwell on the legal arguments. Politics was the central issue in this case, as in that of Manilius. Five distinguished *consulares* served as witnesses for the prosecution: Q. Catulus, Q. Hortensius, M. Lucullus, Q. Metellus Pius, and Mam. or M'. Lepidus.[15] The anti-Pompeian flavor of that assemblage stands out sharply. Cicero had no illusions about the political implications. He included warm praise of Pompey in the defense speech. The fact that Cornelius had been Pompey's quæstor was well known–and relevant.[16]

Manilius had succumbed to his prosecutors. But Cornelius had more to recommend him–not just Ciceronian rhetoric and Pompeian endorsement. Cornelius' tribunate, despite the strictures of his enemies, had produced intelligent and welcome legislation. His reputation for integrity remained high. The *accusatores* produced awesome witnesses. But the most impressive testimony came from the defense bench. P. Servilius Globulus, the tribune whose veto had been ignored by Cornelius in 67, refused to condemn that act and spoke up instead on Cornelius' behalf. The case for the prosecution suffered irreparable damage. Cornelius, whose decorum at the trial was impeccable, could not simply be branded a reckless demagogue. When the votes were tallied, he had been handsomely acquitted: *equites* and *tribuni ærarii* were for him, so we are told, and a good portion of the senatorial jurors.[17] Politics had inspired the accusations against both Manilius and Cornelius in 65. The outcomes, however, were strikingly different. It is a feature worthy of remark. Whatever the political machinations behind the scenes, Roman jurors might still render verdicts on the merits of the case.

---

legisse, sed recognoscendi. Constabat tamen Cornelium concilium illo die dimisisse, intercessioni paruisse; Asconius, 61, Clark: *non poterat negare id factum esse Cicero, is eo confugit ut diceret non ideo quod lectus sit codex a tribuno iniminutam esse tribuniciam potestatem*; cf. Quint. *Inst. Orat.* 6.5.10. The fragments of Cicero's *Pro Cornelio* are collected in Asconius, 62–81, Clark; cf. the sensible discussion in Ciaceri, *Cicerone*, I:156–163.

[15] Asconius, 60, 79, Clark; cf. Sumner, *JRS*, 54 (1964): 41–48, on the question of Mam. or M'. Lepidus. The list given by Val. Max. 8.5.4 includes L. Lucullus. He is, almost certainly, to be excised.

[16] Asconius, 61, Clark; Quint. *Inst. Orat.* 4.3.13, 9.2.55; cf. [Q. Cic.] *Comm. Petit.* 51.

[17] Asconius, 61, Clark: *Adiumen tum autem habuit quod, sicut diximus, Cornelius præter destrictum propositum animi adversus principum voluntatem cetera vita nihil fecerat quod magnopere improbaretur; præterea quod et ipse Globulus qui intercesserat aderat Cornelio, et–quod ipsum quoque diximus–quod Cornelius Pompeii Magni quæstor fuerat, apud duas decurias profuit equitum Romanorum et tribunorum ærariorum et ex tertia quoque parte senatorum apud plerosque exceptis eis qui erant familiares principum civitatis*; 81, Clark: *magno numero sententiarum Cornelius absolutus est.* Exact voting figures could not be given, for the votes of the three *ordines* were not tallied separately before 59. M. Crassus was one of the senatorial jurors; Asconius, 76, Clark. Other references to the trial: [Q. Cic.] *Comm. Petit.* 19; Schol. Bob. 144, Stangl; Quint. *Inst. Orat.* 5.13.18, 5.13.25, 6.5.10, 7.3.35, 10.5.13. See also Ciaceri, *Cicerone*, I:159–163; Gelzer, *Cicero*, pp. 62–66.

Friends of Pompey were not the only men under judicial fire in the 60s. Counterattacks are attested also against his adversaries. Information is less full; but the pattern stands forth with clarity. So, C. Calpurnius Piso was twice indicted, in 68 and 63. The first instance involved an *ambitus* charge, in connection with his consular canvass. Piso managed to rebut it, through influence and cash; the case never came to court.[18] His turbulent consulship roused the ire of Pompey's adherents. And a proconsulship in Gaul during the ensuing years provided further material for criminal charges. In 63 Piso was prosecuted *de repetundis*. Among the complainants was C. Julius Cæsar, fervent in his advocacy of Pompeian causes. Cæsar was also advancing his own stock, declaring sympathy with the Transpadane Gauls, one of whom Piso had allegedly executed during his governorship. Cicero, serving out his consular year, was induced to take the case—not, of course, out of hostility to Pompey. The orator had solicited Piso's aid in his consular campaign. His defense brief represented acknowledgment of the obligation. Piso's backers stood firm; they obtained a verdict of not guilty.[19]

The Luculli also faced arraignment in the courts during the mid-60s. The instigator here was C. Memmius, the quarrelsome and pleasure-loving *adfinis* of Pompey. In his tribunate of 66, Memmius leveled accusation against M. Lucullus, finding fault with Lucullus' behavior as quæstor in the Sullan era a decade and a half before. The digging up of old offenses betrays political motivation. Memmius was unable to make the charges tell and turned his fire instead on the defendant's brother L. Lucullus. The latter had recently returned from Asia, looking now for a triumph to compensate for his loss of the Mithridatic command to Pompey. Memmius blocked the triumph, raised doubts about Lucullus' fiscal integrity, and accused him of prolonging the eastern campaigns for purposes of self-aggrandizement. The move was calculated to secure Pompey's favor. Lucullus underwent a formal trial, so Plutarch asserts, though Cato later intervened, causing the case to be dismissed without issue.[20] That neither M. nor L. Lucullus was convicted would not have worried Memmius much. The purpose was served: the maintenance of steady judicial pressure on the *inimici* of Pompey. Cæsar's indictment of Q. Catulus in 62 possessed similar incentive. His aim was to transfer the honor of reconstructing the temple of Jupiter Capitolinus from Catulus to Pompey: hence, a prosecution of Catulus for embezzlement of the funds with which

[18] Dio, 36.38.3: **ὅ γε Πίσων καὶ γραφεὶς ἐπὶ τούτῳ** [ambitus] **καὶ πρὸς ἑνὸς καὶ πρὸς ἑτέρου τινὸς εξεπρίατο τὸ μὴ κατηγορηθῆναι**. cf. Sallust, *Hist.* 4.81, Maur.

[19] Cic. *Pro Flacco*, 98; Sallust, *Cat.* 49.2. For Cicero's solicitation of Piso's support in 65, see Cic. *Ad Att.* 1.1.2.

[20] The trial of M. Lucullus: Plut. *Luc.* 37.1; the attacks on Lucullus: Plut. *Luc.* 37.1–2; *Cato*, 29.3–4. See Gruen, *Athenæum*, 49 (1971): 56–58.

he was entrusted.[21] We are uninformed as to the outcome. Perhaps the case was not pressed to a conclusion. Again the object was less to secure conviction than to employ the courts as a vehicle for embarrassment of political foes.

In the same category belongs the trial of the Greek poet from Antioch, A. Licinius Archias, in 62. The indictment maintained that Archias had falsely claimed Roman citizenship and was subject to prosecution under a law directed against aliens, passed three years before. Archias, of course, was not the primary target. The gentle and aged poet was harmless—and no political figure. He had laid claim to Roman citizenship in 89, more than a quarter of a century before. None had challenged the claim till now. Politics dictated the move. Archias was a showpiece of the Lucullan circle. The poet had recently completed a noble work extolling the exploits of L. Lucullus in Asia.[22] That was a calculated retort to Pompey, who was soon to demand a triumph for completing Lucullus' unfinished task. The poet had been a client and protégé of Roman *nobiles* from his arrival in Rome forty years earlier. The group that took him under its wing and continued to exercise patronage in ensuing years included Metellus Pius, Q. Catulus, Hortensius, Cato, and, especially, the Luculli. The list reads very much like the roster of names that offered hostile testimony against Cornelius in 65.[23] M. Lucullus appeared at the trial on Archias' behalf, and the intimate friendship with Metellus Pius and L. Lucullus is stressed again and again. The poet's *gentilicium* is, of course, adopted from the Luculli themselves.[24] There can be little doubt that the trial was designed as a pointed thrust at the coterie that had patronized Archias.

Again M. Cicero served as defense counsel. It was a delicate role—with divided loyalties. The orator was not anxious to offend Pompeius Magnus. But he prized good relations also with men like the Luculli, C. Piso, and Domitius Ahenobarbus, who had assisted in his elevation to the consulship. And there was an older debt to Archias. The poet had been one of Cicero's earliest teachers. Cicero could imagine himself immortalized in verse, like Lucullus: Archias had already begun a work celebrating the consulship of 63.[25] The defense speech was unusual, perhaps a reflection of Cicero's awkward plight. The implicit political struggle is, of course, ignored. There is much praise for Lucullus, but also a passing reference—with respect—to Pompey the Great. And a healthy portion consists of a pæan to the delights and value of literary study. Since Pompey was away and an insignificant prosecutor was

[21] Dio, 37.44.1.

[22] Cic. *Pro Arch.* 21; *Ad Att.* 1.16.15.

[23] Cic. *Pro Arch.* 6.

[24] Cic. *Pro Arch.* 5–9, 11, 21, 26, 31.

[25] Cic. *Pro Arch.* 28, 31. It was, evidently, never completed; cf. Cic. *Ad Att.* 1.16.15. On Archias as Cicero's teacher, see Cic. *Pro Arch.* 1–2.

present, it was easy to evade allusion to the general's interest in the case and to transform the speech into an innocuous eulogy of a poet. It was also prudent.[26] Whatever Cicero's difficulties, however, the trial of Archias takes its proper place in the list of judicial clashes between Pompey and his principal *inimici* headed by Lucullus, Catulus, and Hortensius.

One other case fits this context. In 60, Valerius Messalla, evidently the *adfinis* of Sulla and nephew of Hortensius, was prosecuted and acquitted on a charge unspecified in the evidence. Messalla was known in the mid-50s for enmity toward Pompey, who strove mightily to prevent his election to the consulship. The antagonism is duly reflected in his trial of 60. Hortensius acted as defense counsel. And some cryptic remarks by Cicero reveal a strong concern in the case expressed by Pompey and his confederate L. Afranius.[27]

The stunning rise to power and authority of Pompey the Great constituted the single most important political fact of the 60s. Its effects have been noted in several areas. Not the least of them was the persistent number of criminal cases pitting Pompeian partisans and antagonists against one another. Decisive results were still wanting. Of the cases discussed, only Manilius suffered condemnation. But criminal trials provided a dramatic forum. They guaranteed that public attention would not lag.[28]

[26] It defies reason to imagine that Cicero's defense of Archias signals a transfer of allegiance to Pompey's enemies; as Heitland, *Rom. Rep.*, III:113–114. The encomium of Lucullus is proper in the context; *Pro Arch.* 21. But Pompey's accomplishment is also registered; *Pro Arch.* 24. Similarly, in celebrating Pompey's virtues in the *De Imperio Pompei*, Cicero had also heaped praise on Lucullus. His posture was consistent. In 63 he had urged the granting of a triumph to Lucullus; Cic. *Acad. Prior.* 3.2. At the same time he sponsored a ten-day *supplicatio* for Pompey's victories; Cic. *De Prov. Cons.* 27. Cicero was anxious to burn no bridges. His defense of Archias fits the pattern; cf. J. H. Taylor, *AJP*, 73 (1952): 62–70; T. A. Dorey, *Orpheus*, 2 (1955): 32–35. The prosecutor, a certain Gratius, is unknown; Cic. *Pro Arch.* 8, 12.

[27] Cic. *Ad Att.* 2.3.1: *Valerius absolutus est Hortensio defendente. Id iudicium Auli filio condonatum putabatur; et Epicratem suspicor, ut scribis, lascivum fuisse.* The remarks are perhaps ironic; so Shackleton Bailey, *Cicero's Letters*, I:355. On Messalla, see Cic. *Ad Att.* 4.9.1; Val. Max. 5.9.2.

[28] Some scholars have seen the extortion trial of M. Fonteius in 69 as another example of judicial attack on Pompey's friends; Carcopino, *Hist. Rom.*, II:579; Ward, *Latomus*, 27 (1968): 802–805; cf. Ooteghem, *Pompée*, p. 157. The hypothesis lacks substantive support. Fonteius, of prætorian ancestry, had engaged in high-handed activities as governor of Gaul—an unhappy blunder. Gallic provincials had important patrons in Rome, notably the patrician family of the Fabii Maximi. One of the *accusatores* was M. Fabius, upholding the claims of his *gens*; Cic. *Pro Font.* 36. No further implications need be read into the case. The principal prosecutor, M. Plætorius, is unknown, though a Plætorius, perhaps the same man, is elsewhere mentioned; Cic. *Ad Fam.* 1.8.1; *Ad Att.* 5.20.8. Cicero spoke for the defense in order to keep faith with the *equites*; cf. Cic. *Pro Font.* 32. There is nothing to suggest connection with Pompeius; see Gruen, *AJP*, 92 (1971): 12–13. Fonteius' fate is uncertain. The M. Fonteius mentioned in 68 may or may not have been the same man; Cic. *Ad Att.* 1.6.1. Gelzer, *Cicero*, p. 52, is too positive; cf. also Ciaceri, *Cicerone*, I:93.

FEUDS AND RIVALRIES

The political contest revolving about Pompeius Magnus was a dominant feature in the 60s. But it does not, by any means, exhaust the criminal trials of the decade. Many of them involved personal feuds among Roman *nobiles* or rivalries between houses. A few examples will suffice to illustrate that theme.

M. Aurelius Cotta, consul in 74, offered a vulnerable target. He had engaged in political intrigue during his consulship and was then assigned the province of Bithynia during the Mithridatic war, where his blunders and incompetence caused serious damage to the Roman cause and considerable difficulty for L. Lucullus.[29] Disgruntlement and defeat provoked near mutiny in the ranks. Cotta reacted sharply and sought scapegoats. A subordinate officer, the proquæstor P. Oppius, was singled out, dispatched to Rome and charged, in a letter of Cotta's, with mutiny and attempted murder. The case reached court, apparently, in 69. Cicero, coming to the defense of a man who, like himself, was an *eques* by origin, attacked the prosecutor's brief as insufficient and inconsistent, though with due apologies to M. Cotta. The outcome is unknown and political implications ought not to be read into the affair. Cotta simply contrived to divert attention away from his own inadequacies.[30] The maneuver proved unsuccessful. When Cotta returned, sometime in the early 60s, he was himself put on trial, probably for *peculatus* or *res repetundæ*. Representatives from Heraclea, which had been plundered and brutalized by Cotta, appeared in order to deliver hostile testimony. The accuser was an ambitious ex-tribune, C. Papirius Carbo, anxious to make a killing at the bar. Carbo succeeded and earned his reward: Cotta's place among *consulares* in the senate.[31] The feud persisted. Carbo went on to become governor of Bithynia himself at the end of the decade, performing no more admirably than had his victim. Cotta's young son, on the very day that he assumed the *toga virilis,* avenged his father by prosecuting C. Carbo. Conviction followed and the family's honor had been salvaged.[32] The sequence affords a pointed illustration of private quarrels in the *iudicia.*

The same applies to judicial contests between M. Calidius and the Gallii. Calidius, the eminent and accomplished orator, brought a charge of *ambitus* against Q. Gallius in 64 for illegal canvassing in his prætorian campaign.

[29] Sources in Broughton, *MRR,* II:101.

[30] The reconstruction of Ward, *Latomus,* 27 (1968): 805–808, is imaginative but without foundation. Cf. the discussion, with full references, in Gruen, *AJP,* 92 (1971): 13–15.

[31] Dio, 36.40.4: Γάιον Κάρβωνα τὸν κατηγορήσαντα αὐτοῦ τιμαῖς ὑπατικαῖς καίπερ δεδημαρχηκότα μόνον ἐσέμνυναν; Val. Max. 5.4.4; Memnon, 59 = *FGH,* 3B.366–367. On rewards for prosecutors, see L. R. Taylor, *Party Politics,* pp. 112–116.

[32] Dio, 36.40.4; Val. Max. 5.4.4.

Deep bitterness ensued. Gallius, it was alleged, actually tried to fend off the prosecution by hiring men to poison his accuser. Calidius brought documentary evidence to that effect into the trial. But the prosecutor's calm and methodical manner was turned against him by Cicero, who appeared for the defense: if Calidius is so relaxed, he can't be serious.[33] Whether Gallius suffered conviction is not reported. But the vendetta continued. After Calidius himself stood for the consulship in 51, he faced an *ambitus* action engendered by the Gallii brothers. The jury found for the defendant: Calidius' capacities as prosecutor may have left something to be desired, but he was supremely eloquent in his own defense.[34] The endurance of the family rivalry is clear. The courts were handy instruments for the working-out of *inimicitiæ*.

Another example may be adduced. In 65 came the celebrated extortion trial of L. Sergius Catilina. The name had already earned notoriety in Rome's political circles. Catiline's early career gained impetus from nimble maneuvering and resourceful and unscrupulous tactics. Tradition registers a catalogue of perversities, several drawn from Cicero's venomous *In Toga Candida* and the *Commentariolum Petitionis:* adulterous activities, incest, sacrilege, and domestic homicide.[35] Many of the claims are grotesque, some doubtless unfounded. A later judgment by Cicero himself acknowledges Catiline's abilities: martial prowess, endurance, devotion to friends, and remarkable charisma.[36] Paradoxical qualities made him a figure of repute and gossip, with powerful *amici*

[33] Cic. *Brutus,* 277–278: *Tu istuc, M. Calidi, nisi fingeres, sic ageres?* Also Val. Max. 8.10.3; Quint. *Inst. Orat.* 11.3.155. Further quotes from the speech: Quint. *Inst. Orat,* 8.3.66, 11.3.165. That the charge was *ambitus,* growing out of the prætorian campaign, is stated by Asconius, 88, Clark. The trial is customarily dated to 66; Drumann-Grœbe, *Geschichte Roms,* V:398–399; Ciaceri, *Cicerone,* I:139–140; Gelzer, *Cicero,* pp. 59–60; H. Malcovati, *Oratorum Romanorum Fragmenta*² (Turin, 1955), pp. 435–436. Wrongly. Gallius, to be sure, was prætor in 65, and therefore campaigned in 66; Asconius, 62, Clark. But Asconius says explicitly that Cicero's defense of Gallius took place after delivery of the *In Toga Candida* in 64; see 88, Clark: *Q. Gallium, quem postea reum ambitus defendit.* One cannot cavalierly employ Asconius against himself. The two passages are not mutually exclusive: the *ambitus* trial awaited the expiry of Gallius' office. [Q. Cic.] *Comm. Petit.* 19 does state that Cicero could reckon on the adherents of Gallius in his consular attempt because of taking up his defense. But even if that document is authentic, it need not imply that the trial had already taken place; cf. Balsdon, *CQ,* 13 (1963): 248–249.

[34] Cæl. *Ad Fam.* 8.9.5: *Calidius in defensione sua fuit disertissimus, in accusatione satis frigidus; Ad Fam.* 8.4.1. Ps. Asconius, 219, Stangl, actually extends the feud back another generation, asserting that Calidius' father, Q. Calidius, had been prosecuted by Gallius. But that is confusion. The prosecutor was actually Q. Lollius; Cic. *Verr.* 2.3.63.

[35] Sources on the actions under Sulla are given by Broughton, *MRR,* II:72. The relevant portions of *In Toga Candida* are in Asconius, 83–93, Clark; buttressed by [Q. Cic.] *Comm. Petit.* 8–10; and see Sallust, *Cat.* 5, 15; Cic. *Cat.* 1.14.

[36] Cic. *Pro Cæl.* 12–14.

and embittered foes. Catiline's prosecution had unquestioned political overtones.

But personalities and private antagonisms may have been more central. Catiline was indicted *de repetundis* for purported felonies in Africa. Identity of the prosecutor stimulates interest: P. Clodius Pulcher. Cicero, in retrospect, could not bring himself to believe that those two persons were anything but confederates in villainy. His version of the trial gained ascendancy: corruption of the jurors and connivance by the prosecutor guaranteed Catiline's acquittal.[37] It was not necessarily so. Catiline obtained weighty endorsements. The consul L. Manlius Torquatus spoke in his defense, as did several eminent *consulares.* Even Cicero contemplated for a time the political advantages of appearing as Catiline's *advocatus.*[38] Collusion by Clodius is an unnecessary hypothesis. An earlier judicial encounter bears relevance here. In 73 the young Clodius first put his talents on show, denouncing a number of Rome's religious officials and leveling charges of *incestum* against the Vestal Virgin Fabia. The trial itself came to naught; Fabia, in any case, was absolved. Of greater pertinence, however, is the fact that Catiline was implicated in those charges as well. The event sheds light on his subsequent prosecution in 65. *Inimicitia* between Clodius and Catiline endured. The *accusatio de repetundis* takes its place in the register of private feuds and enmities.[39]

The fierce hostility between P. Vatinius, the Cæsarian tribune of 59, and young C. Licinius Calvus may stem from the 60s. Vatinius, a *novus homo* from Reate, stood for the quæstorship in 64 and secured election, though only barely—at the bottom of the list. His reputation for barbarity and perversity, cloaked by professed Pythagoreanism, is a construct of Cicero's, who had reason to vilify him later. But a prosecution *de ambitu* in 64 is not impossible. Calvus, an erudite and gifted orator as well as a neoteric poet, brought the charge, so it is reported. That event is the first notice of an *inimicitia* which issued in venomous attacks by Calvus during the 50s when Vatinius was an agent of the triumvirate.[40]

[37] Cic. *De Har. Resp.* 42; *In Pis.* 23; [Q. Cic.] *Comm. Petit.* 10; Asconius, 87, Clark. The acquittal is attested also by Cic. *Ad Att.* 1.16.9; *In Pis.* 95; Asconius, 9, 86–87, 89, 92, Clark; cf. 66, Clark. The remark of Cic. *Ad Att.* 1.2.1 need not imply *prævaricatio*; cf. Gruen, *Athenæum,* 49 (1971): 59–62. Initial indictment had come in 66; Asconius, 85, 89, Clark; Sallust, *Cat.* 18.2; Cic. *Pro Cæl.* 10.

[38] Cic. *Ad Att.* 1.2.1; *Pro Cæl.* 14; *Pro Sulla*, 81; Asconius, 85–87, Clark; cf. Cic. *Ad Att.* 1.1.1.

[39] On the *incestum* trial of 73 evidence is scattered but consistent; Plut. *Cato*, 19.3; Asconius, 91, Clark; Orosius, 6.3.1; cf. [Q. Cic.] *Comm. Petit.* 10; Sallust, *Cat.* 15.1, 35.1; Cic. *Cat.* 3.9. A fuller discussion in Gruen, *Athenæum*, 49 (1971): 59–62. And note Clodius' ardent support for Cicero against the machinations of Catiline in 63; Plut. *Cic.* 29.1; cf. Asconius, 50, Clark.

[40] Schol. Bob. 145, Stangl: *honorem quæsturæ post omnes novissimo loco datum et adhuc damna-*

Personal friction between Metellus Scipio and Cato has already been noted: Metellus had seized Cato's betrothed to make her his own wife. The antagonism is further illustrated in 60 when Cato's disciple M. Favonius suffered electoral defeat at Metellus' hands and sought to recover position by prosecuting him for *ambitus*. Cicero took the case, much to Favonius' annoyance. The latter's inept pleading won him no credit and gained Metellus an acquittal.[41] Conflict between Metellus Scipio and the Catonians persisted in the 50s and eventually brought Metellus into the camp of Pompeius Magnus.

Prosecutions *de ambitu* need not, of course, imply personal feuds. Growing, as they did, out of electoral contests, they often represented efforts by defeated candidates to displace their conquerors in court and thereby to regain the magisterial posts themselves. That was clearly the case in the notorious prosecutions of P. Autronius and P. Sulla by L. Torquatus and L. Cotta in 66. The events, following upon the consular elections, resulted in the conviction of Autronius and Sulla and the subsequent appointment of their prosecutors to the consulship. The scramble for office dictated those proceedings, not political or personal *inimicitia*.[42] But the case itself provoked considerable bitterness–with later repercussions. The reckless and violent Autronius had sought to break up the trial by organizing gladiators and slaves to stir rioting. And both Sulla and Autronius arranged demonstrations at the beginning of 65 to undermine the positions of their successful rivals.[43] Those activities

---

tionis eius nutare fortunam; reus postulatus erat accusatore C. Licinio Calvo. Cf. Cic. *In Vat.* 11. The scholiast's comment does not, of course, command implicit faith; see Gruen, *HSCP*, 71 (1966): 228–229, n.28. On Cicero's vilification of Vatinius, see, esp., *In Vat.* 10–14. He was also involved in a judicial hearing of some sort in 66; Plut. *Cic.* 9.3. On the later contests between Vatinius and Calvus, see Gruen, *HSCP*, 71 (1966): 215–233.

[41] The charge is not specified, but was evidently *ambitus*, for Cicero puts it in the context of the electoral campaign; *Ad Att.* 2.1.9: *Favonius meam tribum tulit honestius quam suam, Luccei perdidit. Accusavit Nasicam* [Metellus Scipio Nasica] *inhoneste, ac modeste tamen; dixit ita ut Rhodi videretur, molis potius quam Moloni operam dedisse. Mihi quod defendissem leviter suscensuit.* Cicero, as he so often did, was hedging his bets. He supported Favonius in the canvass, and then defended Metellus against Favonius. He had, of course, done precisely the same in 63, backing Sulpicius Rufus for the consulship and then opposing his prosecution of the victorious candidate Murena. The campaign in 60 occurred no later than May; hence, probably, a supplementary election to fill a vacancy, either for the tribunate or the ædileship; M. Alford, *CR*, 41 (1927): 216–217; L. R. Taylor, *Studies Ullman* (1964), I:79–85. Miss Taylor's view that Cicero and Lucceius supported the candidacy of Metellus is not a natural inference from the text; see Shackleton Bailey, *Cicero's Letters*, I:350–351.

[42] So, for example, Torquatus' close friends had no qualms about defending and supporting the case of Sulla in court; Cic. *Pro Sulla*, 49: *sapientissimus vir* [Torquatus] *familiarissimis suis non suscensuit, pater tuus, cum Sullam et defenderent et lauderent.*

[43] On rioting at the trial, see Cic. *Pro Sulla*, 15, 71. The demonstrations in 65 are frequently discussed. They have been much exaggerated by later traditions; cf. Gruen, *CP*, 64 (1969): 20–24. Further evidence on the trials and their outcome: Cic. *Pro Sulla*, 1, 49–50, 88–90;

left a legacy of hatred. When opportunity presented itself again, in 62, young L. Torquatus, son of the consul of 65, brought P. Sulla to court once more, this time on a charge of violence.[44]

The *ambitus* trial of L. Murena in 63 belongs in a similar category. No prior enmity existed between Sulpicius Rufus and Murena. But Sulpicius, turned back at the polls in that year, saw no better way to attain consular office than to press an *ambitus* case against the victorious Murena. Previous ties or commitments played no role in this affair. Implications from the evidence are clear on that point. Cicero had been active in Sulpicius' electoral campaign, but espoused the cause of Murena in the trial, whereas Murena's prosecutors included some of his own family friends and neighbors. Sulpicius was motivated by ambition.[45] That was a common feature in cases *de ambitu.* Nothing further need be hypothesized.

Other hearings involved notable figures, with political connotations, such as the *repetundæ* prosecution of C. Licinius Macer in 66. Macer, a historian and an intellectual, had also been a fiery tribune in 73, an advocate of tribunician reform, and a critic of the established oligarchy. His activities in the interval are not registered. Popular sympathies were no longer with him by the time of his trial. But a larger personage may stand in the background. Macer carried great political weight; but more important, he had the resources of M. Crassus behind him.[46] The trial of Macer may represent indirect attack by the *inimici* of Crassus. It proved fatal for Macer. The jurors found him guilty, and the defendant perished shortly after the announcement.[47]

The *incestum* trial of P. Clodius Pulcher in 61 supplied high political drama. The offense was minor, so it would appear: violation of the sacred rites of the Bona Dea. It might easily have been handled by religious authorities.

Sallust, *Cat.* 18.2; Asconius, 75, 88, Clark; Suet. *Iul.* 9; Dio, 36.44.3; Livy, *Per.* 101; Schol. Bob. 78–79, 83, 84, Stangl. Torquatus' son evidently participated in the prosecution as well; Cic. *De Fin.* 2.62.

[44] Cic. *Pro Sulla, passim;* cf. Schol. Bob. 84, Stangl.

[45] Cic. *Pro Mur.* 56: *Nam ut omittam Servium Sulpicium quem intellego non iniuria L. Murenæ sed honoris contentione permotum, accusat paternus amicus, C. Postumus, vetus, ut ait ipse, vicinus ac necessarius, qui necessitudinis causas compluris protulit, simultatis nullam commemorare potuit.* The motives of Cato in appearing for the prosecution have already been discussed. They did not involve a break with Murena; see above, chap. 4, n.34. On Cicero's speech *Pro Murena,* see R. W. Husband, *CJ,* 12 (1916): 102–118; J. Humbert, *Les plaidoyers écrits et les plaidoiries réelles de Ciceron* (Paris, 1925), pp. 119–142; Ciaceri, *Cicerone,* I:281–283; D. M. Ayers, *CJ,* 49 (1954): 245–253. Other references to the trial: Plut. *Cic.* 35.3; *Cato,* 21.3–6; Schol. Bob. 96, 151, Stangl.

[46] Plut. *Cic.* 9.1: Λικίννιος Μάκερ, ἀνὴρ καὶ καθ' αὑτὸν ἰσχύων ἐν τῇ πόλει μεγα καὶ Κράσσῳ χρώμενος βοηθῷ.

[47] Cic. *Ad Att.* 1.4.2; Plut. *Cic.* 9.1–2; Val. Max. 9.12.7; cf. Gruen, *HSCP,* 71 (1966): 215–217.

But the political influence of Clodius and the Claudii turned the affair into a scandal and produced a trial of major proportions. The confusing scramble over form and judicial procedure has already been delineated. A *quæstio extraordinaria* was eventually instituted, but one which employed the customary means of jury selection.[48] It was politics that converted the episode into a cause célèbre.

Clodius' frenetic but appealing career had won popularity with the *plebs*. That provided a considerable political advantage. And Clodius boasted important connections in the aristocracy. The great house of the Scribonii Curiones cooperated with him and offered support at the trial.[49] In addition, one of the consuls of 61, M. Pupius Piso, and one of the tribunes, Q. Fufius Calenus, were active in his behalf. Clodius' brother, Ap. Claudius Pulcher, also proved useful.[50] Numerous allegations were aired at the trial: among them, a complaint that Clodius had seduced the wife of the *pontifex maximus* C. Julius Cæsar. Not that Cæsar himself pressed charges. Anxious to retain his reputation as a popular champion, he did not risk confrontation with Clodius. Cæsar declined to appear in court. The *pontifex maximus* contented himself with divorcing his spouse.[51] Clodius' influence was appreciable.

But he also had made numerous enemies, who would not let the opportunity slip. A private feud with the Cornelii Lentuli came to the fore. The principal *accusator* was L. Lentulus Crus, the future consul of 49; his *subscriptores* were Lentulus Marcellinus and Lentulus Niger. And a fourth member of the *gens*, Lentulus Spinther, sat on the jury and delivered a negative vote. Personal *inimicitia* is specified as the motive.[52] Political considerations supervened as well. Lucullus had clashed with Clodius in the past. Now the allies of Lucullus seized the occasion to eliminate a formidable political rival. They were the prime movers in urging a public trial *extra ordinem:* not just Lucullus,

[48] See above, chap. 6.

[49] Cic. *Ad Att.* 1.14.5, 1.16.1; Schol. Bob. 85, Stangl.

[50] Cic. *Ad Att.* 1.13.3, 1.14.1, 1.14.5–6, 1.16.1–2, 1.16.8; Schol. Bob. 85, Stangl. On Ap. Claudius' assistance, see Schol. Bob. 90–91, Stangl. C. Causinius Schola from Interamna, who testified to establish Clodius' alibi, is not a figure of any significance; Cic. *Pro Mil.* 46; Asconius, 49, Clark; cf. Quint. *Inst. Orat.* 4.2.88.

[51] That Cæsar's refusal to testify came from fear of Clodius' popularity, not from political connection, is the unanimous affirmation of the sources: Dio, 37.45.1–2, 38.12.1; Plut. *Cæs.* 10.5; Appian, *BC*, 2.14; cf. Plut. *Cic.* 28.3; Suet. *Iul.* 6; Schol. Bob. 90, Stangl. Cæsar's reluctance did not prevent his mother and sister from testifying against Clodius; Suet. *Iul.* 74; Schol. Bob. 89, Stangl. The initiative for prosecution came from Q. Cornificius, who may have been acting for Cæsar; Cic. *Ad Att.* 1.13.3; cf. Plut. *Cic.* 28.3; Gruen, *Phoenix*, 20 (1966): 121.

[52] On Spinther, see Dio, 39.6.2: *ἰδίας ἔχθρας τὸν Κλώδιον ἀμυνόμενος, ὑφ' ἧς καὶ τὴν μοιχείαν αὐτοῦ δικάζων κατεγνώκει*. On the Lentuli as prosecutors, see Cic. *De Har. Resp.* 37; Val. Max. 4.2.5; Schol. Bob. 85, 89, Stangl.

but Catulus, Hortensius, Cato, Favonius, C. Piso, and Valerius Messalla.[53] Numerous others brought testimony against Clodius. Among them was Cicero, whose deposition punctured the defendant's alibi. The orator later in the year mocked Clodius in the senate and denounced both Clodius and his adherent Scribonius Curio.[54] One other *subscriptor* to the charge is named: C. Fannius. He turns up later as a controversial tribune in 59, vigorously opposing the schemes of Julius Cæsar.[55] Clodius' *inimici* embraced a broad range of Roman politicians.

The concerted efforts of various groups to terminate Clodius' career proved to be abortive. The vote was close, but definitive: thirty-one for acquittal, twenty-five for conviction.[56] Clodius' opponents did not take defeat with good grace. Cicero and Catulus charged that the jurors were corrupted, and later tradition enshrined the fact.[57] That was standard invective. Whatever the truth of the insinuations, the acquittal brought a thunderous political triumph for Clodius. His following, already large and clamorous, continued to grow. The prosecution had backfired. The affair served to thrust Clodius all the more into the center of Roman politics.[58]

It is clear that a single pattern is not to be imposed upon criminal prosecutions in the 60s. Judicial combats between Pompey's friends and enemies form only one of many themes. More prevalent were private quarrels, often stretching over generations, which saw outlet in the courts. Competition for office might also be settled through judicial proceeding; charges of *ambitus* were frequent companions of electoral campaigns. The courts afforded springboards for aspiring aristocrats, ordeals for established leaders. Varied elements brought

[53] Cic. *Ad Att.* 1.13.3, 1.14.2, 1.14.5–6, 1.16.2–5; *Pro Mil.* 73; Dio, 37.46.3; Plut. *Cic.* 29.4, 29.6.

[54] On Cicero's testimony, see Cic. *Ad Att.* 1.16.4–5; Plut. *Cic.* 29.1; Appian, *BC*, 2.14; Val. Max. 8.5.5; Schol. Bob. 85, 86, Stangl; Schol. Gronov. 322, Stangl. The *altercatio*: Cic. *Ad Att.* 1.16.8–10; Plut. *Cic.* 29.6. The fragments of Cicero's *In Clodium et Curionem* are preserved by Schol. Bob. 86–91, Stangl; cf. Cic. *Ad Att.* 3.12.2, 3.20.2; Quint. *Inst. Orat.* 3.7.2. Numerous other prominent *nobiles* appeared for the prosecution; Dio, 37.46.1.

[55] Cic. *Ad Att.* 2.24.3. On Fannius' activities in 59, see Cic. *Pro Sest.* 113; *In Vat.* 16; Schol. Bob. 35, 146, Stangl; cf. Dio, 38.6.1.

[56] Cic. *Ad Att.* 1.16.5; Schol. Bob. 85, 90, 91, Stangl. Plut. *Cic.* 29.6 gives thirty to twenty-five. The acquittal is noted also in Cic. *Ad Fam.* 1.9.15; *Pro Sest.* 89; *In Pis.* 95; Plut. *Cæs.* 10.5–7; Val. Max. 8.5.5, 9.1.7.

[57] Cic. *Ad Att.* 1.16.5; *De Har. Resp.* 36–38; Dio, 37.46.3; Plut. *Cic.* 29.5–6; Val. Max. 9.1.7; Schol. Bob. 86, 90, 91, 173, Stangl.

[58] There is no longer any reason to credit the view that Crassus' cash was behind Clodius' acquittal; cf. Gruen, *Phoenix*, 20 (1966): 121–122; Wiseman, *CQ*, 18 (1968): 297–299. The old *communis opinio* is reiterated, without argument, in J. O. Lenaghan, *A Commentary on Cicero's Oration De Haruspicum Responso* (The Hague, 1969), pp. 12, 88, 152; and see now P. W. Fulford-Jones, *CQ*, 21 (1971): 183–185.

into the *iudicia* not only lesser individuals like Calidius and the Gallii, but *nobiles* of the highest rank like P. Sulla and Metellus Scipio, and major politicians like Catiline and Clodius. The criminal trial was not an aberration but an institution.[59]

THE FACADE AND THE REALITY

Political trials could appear under numerous guises. Sometimes issues of significant public import might serve as a vehicle. Politicians would not hesitate to capitalize on what seemed the tide of public opinion. The issues themselves could be employed as a facade behind which to work out personal and factional rivalries.

Such, for example, was the campaign in the mid-60s to redress grievances produced by the Sullan proscriptions. The victims of confiscations and brutality by Sullan hirelings a decade and a half before had received no compensation. Now it became politically profitable to stir up that question. In the mid-60s there arose demands to recover and restore the bounty seized by the Sullani, to punish the executioners of the Sullan era, to bring back political exiles, and to reinstate the civil rights of the proscribed and their sons. Legitimate claims lay behind these endeavors. But shrewd politicians could also exploit them for their own, unrelated purposes.

Two cases in 66, discussed elsewhere, appropriately suit this context. Faustus Sulla, son and heir of the dictator, was indicted for possession of property appropriated by his father and rightfully belonging to the state. The fact that Faustus was closely connected to Pompeius Magnus was surely not irrelevant in a year when other associates of Pompey, Cornelius and Manilius, were attacked in the courts. And another case lends confirmation. The tribune C. Memmius, *adfinis* of Pompey and brother-in-law of Faustus Sulla, brought to light misdemeanors allegedly committed by M. Lucullus. Those too involved embezzlement of state funds during the regime of Sulla the dictator. It was evidently an instance of political retaliation. Neither Faustus Sulla nor M. Lucullus suffered condemnation. Roman aristocrats, whatever their political predilections, shrank from the social consequences of throwing into question all the dispensations of the Sullan era. But the trials themselves exemplify

[59] The murder trial of the knight A. Cluentius, though filled with fascinating problems and of great importance to the principals involved, possessed only marginal relevance to contemporary Roman politics. Cicero's *Pro Cluentio* has inspired a large modern literature; see, e.g., G. Hoenigswald, *TAPA*, 93 (1962): 109–123, with references to earlier studies; most recently, Ooteghem, *Hommages Renard* (1969), II:777–788.

use of the judiciary as a platform for internecine senatorial quarrels. Friction between Pompey and the friends of Lucullus loomed in the background.[60]

The raking up of old Sullan abuses went a step further in 64. Hired executioners had earned rewards by eliminating victims on Sulla's proscription lists. Some of those assassins were still around–and identifiable. M. Cato, as he so often did, called the fact to public attention. Publicity and pressure were applied to force the disgorging of the ill-gotten gains, thereby assisting a needy state treasury.[61] There followed criminal complaints and trials for murder. The issue was popular, with considerable notoriety. Hence, Julius Cæsar, among others, grasped the occasion to prosecute a number of Sulla's henchmen.[62]

The names of two convicted murderers have come down to us. They are both small fry: L. Luscius, an ex-centurion who became a man of opulence as a consequence of his Sullan activities; and L. Bellienus, uncle of Catiline and assassin of Lucretius Ofella who had stood for the consulship in defiance of Sulla's wishes.[63] The conviction of Bellienus, however, opened the door to a prosecution of greater political import. Catiline himself was brought to book for his involvement in the proscriptions. His *inimici* had seen their opportunity. The prosecutor was L. Lucceius, the erudite historian and a friend of Pompey's, who was later to combine with Cæsar in the consular campaign of 60. But Catiline remained too powerful. The ex-consuls who had come to his assistance in the extortion trial of 65 backed him again in 64. Despite alleged boasts of his exploits in the Sullan period, Catiline was exonerated once more.[64]

Political prosecutions under the guise of questions of state were standard fare in the 60s. The trial of C. Rabirius in 63 presents a prime example. In this instance the defendant himself was not the principal object. The trial constituted a platform for the *accusatores.*

Rabirius' crime was murder of the tribune Saturninus thirty-seven years

[60] On the indictment of Faustus Sulla, see Cic. *Pro Cluent.* 94; *De Leg. Agrar.* 1.12; *Pro Corn. apud* Asconius, 73, Clark; and Asconius' commentary, *loc. cit.* On M. Lucullus' trial, see Plut. *Luc.* 37.1. And note too the prosecution of C. Orchivius in 65–the man who had presided over Faustus Sulla's hearing in the previous year; [Q. Cic.] *Comm. Petit.* 19. A fuller discussion on all these matters in Gruen, *Athenæum,* 49 (1971): 56–58.

[61] Plut. *Cato,* 17.4.

[62] Cic. *Pro Lig.* 12; Schol. Gronov. 293, Stangl; Dio, 37.10.1–2. The notice in Suet. *Iul.* 11, that Cæsar presided over the *quæstio de sicariis,* is less plausible; see above, chap. 2, n.124.

[63] Asconius, 90-91, Clark; Dio, 37.10.1–2.

[64] The prosecutor is named by Asconius, 90-91, Clark. Lucceius later published his speeches, which included slanderous comments on Catiline's adulteries and incest; Asconius, 91–92, Clark. On the ex-consuls who defended Catiline, see Cic. *Pro Sulla,* 81. The acquittal is also noted elsewhere; Cic. *Ad Att.* 1.16.9; *In Pis.* 95; Dio, 37.10.3.

before. His own stature was of no account in 63. The aged and obscure Roman *eques* carried no political weight. But the principle at stake possessed broad significance. Saturninus had been slain in the midst of a political disturbance, under the authority of a *senatus consultum ultimum.* That action had gone unchallenged for a generation. But in the mid-60s, when old and half-forgotten abuses were being brought to the fore, it seemed appropriate to revive the matter. It was obviously a test case, as had been that of Faustus Sulla. The purpose, it seems, was not to question the legitimacy of the *s.c.u.* as such, but rather to set firm limits to it. Publicly appointed magistrates, it was conceded, could act under senatorial declaration of martial law. But if any common citizen could commit murder with impunity under such circumstances, all due process would be wiped out. Such was the principle advocated by the prosecutors: a good *popularis* line. Hence it is logical to find Julius Cæsar behind the proceedings. And with him was another friend of Pompey's, T. Labienus, the activist tribune of 63. Labienus had a solid claim to his role: among those who had been slain with Saturninus was Labienus' uncle.[65]

An ordinary trial before the *quæstio de sicariis* would not adequately fulfill the purpose. Cæsar sought to capture public attention with drama and spectacle. The accusation issued forth under antiquated and obsolete procedure. Rabirius would be tried for *perduellio,* a proceeding that had no precedent since the monarchical period, if at all. All the rusty paraphernalia of a forgotten age was assembled: the cross itself for crucifixion, the somber executioner with the tools of his trade, the cruel language of a distant antiquity.[66] Two *duumviri perduellionis* were appointed by the prætor to pass sentence. No accident dictated their appointment: they were Cæsar himself and his kinsman L. Cæsar, the consul of 64. The two men immediately announced a verdict of condemnation.[67]

The spectacle was a farce—and designedly so. Cæsar and his associates concerned themselves with demonstration and display rather than conviction. The consul Cicero stepped in to reaffirm the state's authority and Roman traditions. The procedure was quashed.[68] But that was not to be the conclusion of the matter. The elaborate staging had been too well set to go entirely by default. Labienus as tribune now brought formal charges against Rabirius before the entire assembly of the people. It was the first known instance of trial before

[65] Cic. *Pro Rab. Perd.* 20.

[66] Cic. *Pro Rab. Perd.* 10–11, 15–17, 28.

[67] Dio, 37.27.2; Cic. *Pro Rab. Perd.* 12: *hic popularis* [Labienus] *a IIviris iniussu vestro non iudicari de cive Romano sed indicta causa civem Romanum capitis condemnari cœgit.* Suetonius states that Cæsar was chosen by lot, but that refers perhaps only to announcement of the decision; *Iul.* 12. One can hardly credit the conjecture of Hardy, *Some Problems,* pp. 112–113, that selection of Cæsar was a coincidence!

[68] Cic. *Pro Rab. Perd.* 10: *de perduellionis iudicio, quod a me sublatum;* cf. 11, 15, 17.

the *populus* since the Sullan dispensations. Cicero involved himself again, this time as defense counsel, trumpeting his case as an assertion of senatorial privilege. Q. Hortensius, swift to counter the moves of Pompeian adherents, spoke for the defense as well. The argument centered on the state's right of self-protection in circumstances of national emergency. What decision might have been rendered is unknown and unimportant. The men who arranged the anomalous proceeding had also prepared a dramatic conclusion. Q. Metellus Celer, prætor in 63 and brother-in-law of Pompey, ran up the red flag on the Janiculan hill. The action marked a distress signal, which in the early days of Rome's history indicated invasion from the city's enemies. The assembly was forthwith dismissed and the proceedings were canceled. That afforded an appropriately ludicrous termination.[69] The aims of Julius Cæsar and Labienus had been achieved: they had put on exhibit their advocacy of a popular cause. It was of no concern to them that the harassed *senex* Rabirius would live out his remaining days in Rome rather than in exile. The entire affair had been a transparent political demonstration.

The conspiracy of Catiline followed in subsequent months. That too would provide occasion for criminal charges. Catiline had already twice escaped conviction, in trials of 65 and 64. The subtle and devious conspirator did not readily supply a handle for his *inimici.* In 63, shortly before the elections at which Catiline stood, M. Cato threatened him with prosecution. It was bluster, without substance. Catiline had made no overt move by that time. He could afford to answer Cato with arrogance and contempt.[70] Nothing further came of it.

[69] The sequence given here is admittedly a reconstruction. A baffling variety of alternatives have also been proposed; see Strachan-Davidson, *Problems,* I:188–204, for a summary of opinions up to his own day. Since then one may note Hardy *Some Problems,* pp. 99–125; Meyer, *Cæsars Monarchie,* pp. 549–563; Rice Holmes, *Rom. Rep.,* I:452–455; E. H. Renkema, *Mnemosyne,* 55 (1927): 395–400; Lengle, *Hermes,* 68 (1933): 328–340; Gelzer, *Cicero,* pp. 76–79; Ooteghem, *LEC,* 32 (1964): 234–246; Bauman, *The Duumviri in the Roman Criminal Law and in the Horatius Legend* (Wiesbaden, 1969), pp. 9–21. Dio's account, 37.26.1–37.27.3, 37.28.4, telescopes events. His notion that trial before the people came on appeal from the duumvirs' decision is refuted by Cicero's evidence that those proceedings were quashed; *Pro Rab. Perd.* 10–11, 17. Cicero's speech was delivered at a second and separate trial, that initiated by Labienus. It is commonly held that the second proceeding provided for the penalty of a fine. The idea rests, however, only on a single statement of Cicero; *Pro Rab. Perd.* 8. And he refers there, apparently, to earlier charges brought against Rabirius, involving a number of other alleged offenses. Elsewhere, Cicero makes clear that Rabirius was being tried on a capital charge; *Pro Rab. Perd.* 1: *in hac defensione capitis, famæ fortunarumque omnium C. Rabiri;* 5, 26, 31, 37; cf. *In Pis.* 4; *Orat.* 102; Quint. *Inst. Orat.* 5.13.20. On the defense by Hortensius, see Cic. *Pro Rab. Perd.* 18. Despite Dio, 37.27.3, Metellus Celer's intervention was surely prearranged with Cæsar and Labienus; cf. Syme, *JRS,* 28 (1938): 118.

[70] Cic. *Pro Mur.* 51; Plut. *Cic.* 14.3. The threatened charge was, perhaps, *ambitus.* Shackleton Bailey, *Phoenix,* 24 (1970): 164, confidently asserts it; the sources do not specify.

By October, Cicero had amassed considerable data through informants. News arrived from Etruria concerning the armed preparations of Catiline's confederate C. Manlius. And the consul received letters regarding Catiline's plans from most reputable *nobiles:* M. Crassus, Metellus Scipio, and M. Marcellus. A senatorial meeting was summoned and the *senatus consultum ultimum* was passed.[71] That emboldened Catiline's enemies. As was so often the case, a young aristocrat, anxious to establish his reputation at the bar, stepped forward to initiate proceedings. L. Æmilius Paullus Lepidus, son of the ill-fated consul of 78, laid an action against Catiline under the *lex Plautia de vi.*[72] Again, however, it proved hasty and premature. No hard evidence was available. Catiline countered with a canny move. He disarmed his foes by offering to go into voluntary custody in the home of a prominent senator. But who would have him? Catiline suggested M'. Lepidus, consul in 66 and relative of the prosecutor. He was met with refusal. Other audacious suggestions followed: perhaps Cicero himself, or the prætor Q. Metellus Celer. Both men declined. Catiline turned to a fourth possibility, who agreed to harbor him—perhaps a certain M. Marcellus.[73] The maneuver seems to have succeeded. It allotted Catiline additional time to mature his plans. The sources contain no suggestion that any formal hearings were undertaken. Again hard evidence was lacking. Cicero's *First Catilinarian Oration,* delivered shortly thereafter, in early November, is filled with bravado and obloquy, but no sign of evidence that would stand up in court. Catiline departed from Rome on schedule—his own schedule. He shrewdly turned the indictment to his own purposes. Masking his intention of joining Manlius in Etruria, Catiline dispatched letters and reports that he chose voluntary exile in Massilia. The scheme might throw his opponents off guard and cast upon them the odium of driving an uncondemned man into exile.[74] No judgment of a court was ever passed against L. Catilina.[75]

[71] For the sequence of events, see any standard account; e.g. Rice Holmes, *Rom. Rep.,* I:259–260.

[72] Sallust, *Cat.* 31.4; Dio, 37.31.3; Schol. Bob. 149, Stangl, adds that Paullus indicted Catiline's ally C. Cethegus as well. That is his comment on Cic. *In Vat.* 25: *L. Paullum . . . qui duo nefarios patriæ proditores domesticos hostes legibus exterminarat.*

[73] Cic. *Cat.* 1.19. The fourth name is muddled in the manuscripts. They give either "M. Marcellus" or "Metellus." Cf. Quint. *Inst. Orat.* 9.2.45. Editors' combination "M. Metellus" is unwarranted, though there is an unidentifiable M. Metellus mentioned in the year 60; Cic. *Ad Att.* 2.1.1. Cicero's description of the man as Catiline's *sodalis* points elsewhere. Two Marcelli, father and son, are registered among Catiline's adherents in the conspiracy; Orosius, 6.6.7. One was C. Marcellus; Cic. *Pro Sest.* 9; the other, perhaps, M. Marcellus. Dio, 37.32.1–3, wrongly states that Catiline found refuge with the prætor Metellus Celer. The suggestion of W. E. Gwatkin, *TAPA,* 65 (1934): 271–281, that he was Metellus Nepos, recently returned from Pompey's camp, has little to recommend it.

[74] Cic. *Cat.* 2.14, 2.16; Sallust, *Cat.* 34.2; cf. Diodorus, 40.5a.

[75] Dio, 37.33.3 does say that the "Romans" voted him guilty of violence. That, however,

The arrest and execution of the conspirators in December is not to be reckoned in the class of judicial proceedings. Formal discussion took place in the senate alone. To be sure, the consul introduced witnesses and documents, and examined the accused. There was full-scale debate and a vote for execution. But the Roman senate had no authority to sit as a court. Cicero summoned the *patres* in order to bolster his stance and gain moral stimulus. But the *Fourth Catilinarian,* delivered in the *curia* on December 5, makes no secret of the fact that the decision is the consul's alone. And in the following year, Cicero accepted full responsibility for the deed.[76]

The senatorial debate has received interminable scholarly analysis; this is not the place for reexamination. But a relevant point may be noted. Some discussion and at least one proposal seem to have contemplated a future trial. Julius Cæsar, maintaining his *popularis* posture, objected to summary execution of the captured conspirators. He offered the alternative suggestion that their property be confiscated and that they be held in custody in the *municipia.* Sources are divided on the import of that proposal. Cicero was not happy with it. In his response, the consul implies that Cæsar was advocating lifetime imprisonment with no hope of succour. That formulation was adopted by some later authorities.[77] Yet Cæsar prided himself in his speech on hewing to a constitutional and traditional line. Lifetime imprisonment was not a penalty under Roman criminal law. Officials customarily resorted to incarceration of the accused only as a safeguard against their escape.[78] It is possible then that Cæsar suggested just a temporary measure, to be applied until the uprising in Italy could be crushed and a trial held under normal circumstances. That is certainly the interpretation placed on it by more detached sources.[79]

---

refers not to a judicial decision, but to a senatorial declaration in mid-November that Catiline and his compatriots be adjudged *hostes;* cf. Sallust, *Cat.* 36.2.

[76] Cic. *Pro Sulla,* 33: *ego vitam omnium civium . . . quinque hominum amentium ac perditorum pœna redemi;* cf. *Cat.* 4, *passim.* It has sometimes been claimed, on the basis of Polybius, 6.13.4, that the senate did have judicial authority with regard to *hostes;* cf. G. W. Botsford, *CW,* 6 (1913): 130–132. But reference to a period before standing courts existed is of no account on this question. Clodius' law in 58 barring the execution of Roman citizens without trial could not be challenged by Cicero; see above, chap. 6.

[77] Cic. *Cat.* 4.7–8: *sancit* [Cæsar] *ne quis eorum pœnam quos condemnat aut per senatum aut per populum levare possit; eripit etiam spem quæ sola homines in miseriis consolari solet;* cf. *Cat.* 10. Sallust follows that interpretation; *Cat.* 51.43: *ita censeo* [Cæsar] . . . *ipsos in vinculis habendos per municipia . . . neu quis de eis postea ad senatum referat neve cum populo agat;* also Dio, 37.36.1–2.

[78] Cf. Mommsen, *Strafrecht,* pp. 960–963.

[79] Plut. *Cic.* 21.1; Appian. *BC,* 2.6: προσετίθει διαθέσθαι τοὺς ἄνδρας Κικέρωνα τῆς Ἰταλίας ἐν πόλεσιν αἷς ἂν αὐτὸς δοκιμάσῃ μέχρι Κατιλίνα καταπολεμηθέντος ἐς δικαστήριον ὑπαχθῶσι καὶ μηδὲν ἀνήκεστον ἐς ἄνδρας ἐπιφανεῖς ᾗ πρὸ λόγου καὶ δίκης

The proposal, of course, failed. The senate, convinced by Cato's militant rhetoric, voted the execution of the plotters. There was no judicial process.

When the conspiracy had spent itself, however, normal procedures could be restored. A wave of prosecutions followed in the early months of 62.[80] The *lex Plautia de vi* was available, and it was used. Some of those accused were obviously culpable. As men of small consequence they were also readily disposed of. A few names survive in the sources. C. Cornelius and L. Vargunteius were allegedly hirelings of Catiline, engaged to murder Cicero. The consul had foiled that plot. Now both men sustained prosecution, confronted with Cicero's testimony and that of others. Cornelius was an *eques,* otherwise unknown. Vargunteius had reached the senate, with high magisterial ambitions. But a conviction *de ambitu* had meant demotion–and desperation. He had once had important contacts: Hortensius had defended him on the *ambitus* charge. In 62 there was no one to come to his aid.[81] Associated with them in the prosecution was M. Porcius Læca, at whose home, so some alleged, the conspiracy itself was hatched.[82] Two other names register no recognition: Servius and Publius Sulla.[83]

A bigger catch would be P. Autronius Pætus. Successful as a consular candidate in 66, Autronius had been deposed by *ambitus* conviction and gave vent to baser instincts. Violence was his frequent companion. He engaged in it at his *ambitus* trial, at demonstrations against his consular successors,

---

ἐξειργασμένος· Suet. *Iul.* 14 is consistent with their accounts. For this view, see Hardy, *The Catilinarian Conspiracy in Its Context* (Oxford, 1924), pp. 93–94. Appian, *BC,* 2.5 adds that a formal motion to this effect was put by Ti. Claudius Nero. The fact is confirmed by Sallust, who states that Dec. Silanus altered his original motion because of Cæsar's speech and then voted for the proposal of Nero; *Cat.* 50.4: *permotus oratione C. Cæsaris pedibus in sententiam Ti. Neronis iturum se dixerat.*

[80] Cic. *Pro Sulla,* 92. The venomous charges of Ps. Sallust, *Inv. in Cic.* 3–4, that Cicero himself conducted such trials in 63 for the purpose of levying fines and pocketing the cash, deserve no credit. Monetary penalties were not assessed under the *lex Plautia de vi.* Dio, 37.36.3–4, does suggest that the consuls of 63 conducted hearings on charges against conspirators. But he can cite no cases. Reference may be to the wild allegations made against Crassus and Cæsar. They were quashed before coming to court; Sallust, *Cat.* 48.3–9, 49.1.

[81] The trials in 62: Cic. *Pro Sulla,* 6. On the plot to kill Cicero, see Sallust, *Cat.* 28.1; Cic. *Cat.* 1.9; *Pro Sulla,* 18, 52. Vargunteius' trial *de ambitu;* Cic. *Pro Sulla,* 6. Conviction and demotion are safe conjectures; see Linderski, *Historia,* 12 (1963): 511–512. Cornelius is not to be confused with the tribune of 67.

[82] Sallust, *Cat.* 27.3; Cic. *Cat.* 1.8–9, 2.13; *Pro Sulla,* 52.

[83] Cic. *Pro Sulla,* 6: *Quis nostrum Serv. Sullam, quis Publium, quis M. Læcam, quis C. Cornelium defendendum putavit, quis iis horum adfuit?* Cf. Sallust, *Cat.* 17.3: *P. et Ser. Sullæ Ser. filii.* Publius is not, of course, the same P. Sulla whom Cicero defended in that year. That the charge came under the *lex Plautia de vi* is affirmed by Schol. Bob. 84, Stangl; cf. Cic. *Pro Cæl.* 70; Ps. Sallust, *Inv. in Cic.* 3. The conviction of Catilinarians is noted also in Cic. *Pro Sest.* 66; *Pro Flacco,* 96.

and as one of Catiline's chief lieutenants. There were political scores to settle with P. Autronius. Ancient comments are not kind: he was reckless, truculent, and licentious, with a predilection for foul language and brutality.[84] The evidence weighed heavily against Autronius. He had organized supplies, arms, and other implements for Catiline's army. Gallic envoys contributed hostile testimony; incriminating letters and reports were used by the prosecution. Autronius scrambled in desperation to cash in on old obligations. His relatives, the Marcelli, pleaded for him. Autronius himself begged Cicero to defend him, recalling a time when they had been schoolboys together and adolescent companions. The appeals were in vain. Cicero, in fact, testified for the prosecution. Autronius' old friends and comrades, many of high station, deserted en masse. Political *inimici* took pleasure. The guilt was also plain.[85] As Cicero could boast, shortly thereafter, all the Catilinarians against whom he testified were condemned.[86]

After Autronius a logical target offered: P. Sulla, who had been elected with him in 66 and deposed with him in the same year. Political machinations and private feuds both came into operation here, under the guise of weeding out a Catilinarian. Conviction under the *lex Calpurnia de ambitu* in 66 had entailed for P. Sulla the loss of his senate seat and exclusion from further office. But he did not lack prominence and influence. Wealth meant power. P. Sulla had attained opulence during the regime of his kinsman Sulla the dictator. More important, he had married the sister of Pompey the Great, who was soon to return from the East. It was an ideal occasion for Pompey's political foes to score an indirect hit. And there existed personal friction as well. Sulla and L. Manlius Torquatus had clashed in the *comitia* and the courts in 66. Now, in 62, it was Torquatus' son who brought the charge of violence against P. Sulla.

But a case against Sulla was more difficult to prove. Powerful friends and money came to his aid. The same men whose testimony had damaged Au-

[84] See, esp., Cic. *Pro Sulla,* 71: *semper audax, petulans, libidinosus; quem in stuprorum defensionibus non solum verbis uti improbissimis solitum esse scimus verum etiam pugnis et calcibus.* A voice with loud and piercing tones added to the image; Cic. *Brutus,* 241.

[85] Cic. *Pro Sulla,* 7: *Autronio nonne sodales, non collegæ sui, non veteres amici quorum ille copia quondam abundarat, non hi omnes qui sunt in re publica principes defuerunt?* On Autronius' role in the conspiracy: Cic. *Pro Sulla,* 17; the appeals to Cicero from Autronius and the Marcelli: Cic. *Pro Sulla,* 18–19; Schol. Bob. 79, Stangl. Cicero appeared against him in court, alleging that Autronius had dispatched the assassins instructed to murder him; *Pro Sulla,* 10, 18.

[86] Cic. *Pro Sulla,* 21, 48, 83. The names of no other *damnati* are known. L. Sergius, Catiline's lowly armor-bearer, is sometimes included in this company; cf. Drumann-Groebe, *Geschichte Roms,* V:573; Hoy, "Political Influence," pp. 94–95. That cannot be substantiated by Cicero's vague phrase *"damnatus iniuriarum"*: *De Domo,* 13. Sergius was still around in 56; hence, obviously not convicted *de vi.*

tronius' cause showed willingness to speak in Sulla's behalf. Defense benches glittered with the luminaries of the state.[87] The Marcelli vouched for him, as did M. Messalla, presumably the consul of 61.[88] And Cicero himself argued the brief for the defense: a potent ally, and not just because of his oratorical talents. The dramatic shift by the man who had unmasked the conspiracy and had testified against other defendants in 62 was bound to make a powerful impression. The fact that P. Sulla lent Cicero a handsome sum with which he purchased a home on the Palatine added to the orator's enthusiasm.[89] Finally, Q. Hortensius agreed to argue for Sulla's innocence of an earlier connivance with Catiline. He had personal knowledge of the affair and could refute it.[90] Against that formidable array the prosecutor could summon but few weapons. Only a single *subscriptor* backed L. Torquatus, and he added small adornment to the cause: C. Cornelius, son of the conspirator tried previously, perhaps expecting to help his father by turning state's evidence. Young Torquatus was erudite and scholarly, with wide learning even on abstruse matters, and an expert on Epicureanism. But the feud with Sulla was bitter. He took care to select jurors who would be most severe toward the defendant.[91]

Numerous charges emerged at the trial. The defense was able to counter. Sulla, it was said, had engaged in an abortive scheme with Catiline and Autronius to murder the consuls of 65. Hortensius handled that matter. The plot was, in any case, a phantasmagoria.[92] A troop of gladiators had been rounded up in 63, allegedly to assist in Catilinarian rioting. Cicero responded that their purchase had in view the games sponsored by Sulla's relative Faustus Sulla. For this the orator could employ documentary evidence from other friends and *adfines* of Pompey: Faustus Sulla, C. Memmius, and Q. Pompeius; also Cæsar's kinsman, the consul of 64.[93] An uprising in Spain, the prosecution charged, was to occur in conjunction with Catiline's endeavor: Sulla masterminded that plan, dispatching his friend P. Sittius to Spain. Cicero had an appropriate rejoinder: Sittius went to Spain for business reasons, and he left a full year before the machinations of Catiline; besides, Sittius was not the

[87] Cic. *Pro Sulla,* 5: *in quibus subsellis hæc ornamenta ac lumina rei publicæ; Pro Sulla,* 13, 82.

[88] Cic. *Pro Sulla,* 20.

[89] Gellius, 12.12.2.

[90] Cic. *Pro Sulla,* 3–6, 13–14, 22, 51; Schol. Bob. 77, Stangl.

[91] On Torquatus' learning, see Cic. *Brutus,* 265; *De Fin.* 1.13, 1.25; the *reiectio* of jurors: Cic. *Pro Sulla,* 92; Schol. Bob. 84, Stangl; C. Cornelius as *subscriptor:* Cic. *Pro Sulla,* 51–52.

[92] Cic. *Pro Sulla,* 11, 14, 68.

[93] Cic. *Pro Sulla,* 54–55.

sort to engage in revolution.[94] As for a claim that Sulla had stirred the inhabitants of Pompeii to insurrection, Cicero brought those citizens themselves to testify for Sulla. Pompeii had never declared for Catiline.[95] Finally, to the main charge—that Sulla had actively conspired with Catiline, Autronius, and the others to overthrow the state in 63—Cicero affirmed that amidst the voluminous information brought to him in that year none related to P. Sulla. Confessed conspirators who incriminated others did not name Sulla. The defendant was not even in Rome when the conflagration burst.[96] How far was the defense speech disingenuous? That will never be known. Cicero may well have made alterations in the published version, excising some matters and adding others that could not have been uttered in 62.[97] But Sulla's participation in the conspiracy, if there was any participation, can only have been marginal; the charge amounted essentially to guilt by association. Political weight behind Sulla's defense proved, in any event, too potent for conviction. The blood feud between Sulla and the Torquati continued. But the defendant escaped, to live on in Italy and resume political activity.[98]

The aftermath of the conspiracy was utilized also to hunt even larger game. In December 63, an obscure informer, L. Tarquinius, ventured to raise the name of M. Crassus and to implicate him in Catilinarian intrigues. None would allow himself to believe it. At least none would profess to believe it. Rumors circulated rapidly. Some suspected that P. Autronius had put Tarquinius up to his revelations so that Crassus might protect the true conspirators through his immense influence. Others adjudged Cicero to be the instigator. Crassus himself, no friend of the orator, subscribed to the latter theory,

[94] Cic. *Pro Sulla,* 56–59. Sittius came under fire himself. But not necessarily a formal indictment; he was safely absent abroad. Cicero makes reference to this portion of the *Pro Sulla* later; *Ad Fam.* 5.17.2: *cum in tui familiarissimi iudicio ac periculo tuum crimen coniungeretur, ut potui accuratissime, te tuamque causam tutatus sum.* The same passage records an actual trial of Sittius, in which Cicero served as defense counsel. But the order of events as given makes it clear that this occurred some time earlier: *primis temporibus.* Sallust subscribes to the view that Sittius was actually in league with Catiline; *Cat.* 21.3; perhaps mendaciously; cf. Syme, *Sallust,* pp. 100–101, 133. The stigma of Catilinarian associations clung to Sittius, however. He was prosecuted again and, apparently, convicted in 57; Cic. *Ad Fam.* 5.17.2; cf. J. Heurgon, *Latomus,* 9 (1950): 369–377. Heurgon conjectures that the charge, even then, came under the *lex Plautia de vi.* That is unattested. The high price of grain put Sittius in bad odor. He had invested heavily in Africa; Cic. *Pro Sulla,* 56; *Ad Fam.* 5.17.2; cf. *De Domo,* 11.

[95] Cic. *Pro Sulla,* 60–62.

[96] Cic. *Pro Sulla,* 14, 36–39, 53, 86.

[97] So Meyer, *Cæsars Monarchie,* p. 21; Humbert, *Les plaidoyers,* pp. 142–153, both excessively skeptical.

[98] On continued friction between Sulla and the Torquati, see Cic. *Ad Att.* 4.18.3; *Ad Q. Frat.* 3.3.2. Sulla is mentioned again in 57; Cic. *Ad Att.* 4.3.3.

at least in subsequent years. In 63 he promptly collected political debts. The senate, in plenary session, threw out the testimony of Tarquinius and ordered him to be put in custody. No charges could be lodged against M. Crassus.[99]

At the same time a corresponding effort materialized to include Julius Cæsar among the conspirators. The political inspiration was transparent. The men behind it were acknowledged foes of Cæsar and long-standing rivals of Pompeius Magnus: Q. Catulus and C. Piso. Both had clashed with Cæsar earlier in the year. Catulus had sustained defeat by him in the race for the chief pontificate; and Piso had recently been prosecuted, with Cæsar as *accusator.* Both now put pressure on Cicero to arrange for hearings and to collect or fabricate testimony through his cooperative informants. The consul, disbelieving or too cautious to risk a clash with the strong popular following of Cæsar, shrank from the task. He would hear no information against Cæsar. Catulus and Piso persisted, spreading rumors and tales to undermine Cæsar's reputation. No formal proceeding, however, was instituted.[100]

In 62, when Catilinarian confederates were being prosecuted and convicted, the enemies of Cæsar tried again. This time they suborned two notorious informers to present the complaints: L. Vettius and Q. Curius. Both men, an *eques* and a senator respectively, had been useful to Cicero in bringing information in 63.[101] The deceitful Vettius laid Cæsar's name before the presiding magistrate of the *quæstio de vi.* Curius included it in a list of conspirators given to the senate. Curius claimed the authority of Catiline himself; Vettius even threatened to produce a letter from Cæsar to Catiline. It was a clumsy and inept case, with incompetent principals. The *inimici* of Cæsar cannot seriously have expected a conviction. The purpose was simply character assassination. The prospective defendant made an immediate and forceful rejoinder. He turned up senatorial records to show that Cicero had cleared him of any conspiratorial suspicions in 63. Cæsar proceeded then, in his capacity as prætor, to impound Vettius' property and have him jailed; and the same for Novius Niger, the *quæsitor* who had been willing to hear the charges.[102] Julius Cæsar was never brought to book. Exploitation of the Catilinarian affair by politicians through the courts, however, is exposed again and again.[103]

[99] The story is in Sallust, *Cat.* 48.3–9.

[100] Sallust, *Cat.* 49.1–4; Plut. *Cic.* 20.4; *Cæs.* 7.3–4; 8.1–2; Appian, *BC,* 2.6. Cato's speech was also not free of anti-Cæsarian innuendo; Sallust, *Cat.* 52.16; cf. Plut. *Cato,* 23.1–2; *Cæs.* 7.1.

[101] On Vettius, see Cic. *Ad Att.* 2.24.2: *Vettius ille, ille noster index;* on Curius, an original member of the conspiracy, see Sallust, *Cat.* 17.3, 23.1–4, 26.3, 28.2.

[102] The course of events is given in Suet. *Iul.* 17.

[103] No further names of victims are recorded, though Vettius made numerous other allegations, and, we are told, there were additional convictions; Dio, 37.41.2–4. Vettius brought information about an uprising among the Pæligni and implicated two Marcelli, father and

The cases discussed illuminate an important feature of late Republican politics. Serious issues of public concern often gained hearing not so much for their own sake as for the political advantage of certain groups. Not that the feature was unique to the Ciceronian age. But information on that era allows for fuller insight. Three matters of magnitude were prominently manipulated in the later 60s: the Sullan proscriptions, the *senatus consultum ultimum,* and the Catilinarian conspiracy. Each provoked criminal prosecutions–with unfortunate consequences. Politicians found opportunities for their own purposes. But the effect was to divert attention away from the more basic problems of state.

THE TRIUMVIRATE AND THE OPPOSITION

Catilinarian echoes lingered in the years that followed. They severely damaged the cause of C. Antonius as late as 59, when he was at last brought to trial. That case is most revealing, on a number of counts.

A variegated career and an unsavory reputation lay in Antonius' past. Brutality, misdeeds, and dissolute habits had brought him prosecution in the 70s and expulsion from the senate in 70. He worked his way back up the magisterial ladder to a consulship in 63, with no corresponding gain in character. His consular campaign had been conducted in tandem with Catiline. That called forth Cicero's denunciations in the *In Toga Candida*–in vain. The two consuls of 63 had little use for each other.[104]

Antonius' behavior in his consular year was ambiguous and disconcerting. The "conspiracy" of Catiline proved a source of grave embarrassment. Antonius shrank from insurrectionist schemes, but he was also ill at ease as commander of the Republic's troops against his former associate. His campaigns were marked by indecisiveness; the final battle found him nursing an alleged illness. A lieutenant finished the job on Catiline. As *imperator,* Antonius became official victor in the *bellum Catilinæ,* a fact which Catiline's surviving friends

---

son; Orosius, 6.6.7. Whether anything came of that is unknown. Lintott, *Violence,* p. 119, suggests, on the basis of Cic. *Pro Cæl.* 71, that the trials of M. Camurtius and C. Cæsernius may have grown out of Vettius' accusations in 62. The evidence refutes him. Cicero's phrase *Vettiano nefario stupro* indicates a moral offense, not a charge *de vi.* And he states specifically that the defendants were not liable under the violence law: *lege de vi certe non tenebantur.* As for the date, it can hardly be as late as 62: *tanti flagitii memoriam non exstinctam illam quidem, sed repressam vetustate.* The obscure case of Camurtius and Cæsernius is best left in obscurity. A certain senator, A. Fulvius, perished as a consequence of involvement with the conspirators. But he was condemned by his father in a domestic tribunal, not in a public court; Sallust, *Cat.* 39.5; Val. Max. 5.8.5; Dio, 37.36.4.

[104] On Antonius' early career and misdeeds; [Q. Cic.] *Comm. Petit.* 8; Asconius, 84, Clark; the election for 63, see above, chap. 4.

did not forget. But the consul's hesitancy also stimulated rumors about his complicity in the designs of Catiline himself.[105]

Antonius' ineptitude during his consulship was further compounded by felonies committed as governor of Macedon in the immediately succeeding years. Important personages showed an interest in engineering Antonius' downfall, among them Pompeius Magnus and Julius Cæsar. A dossier of indictments began to take shape in 61. A year later Antonius was summoned home and in 59 he underwent formal trial. Three young men handled the prosecution–a splendid opportunity for public display and personal advancement. The fiery and gifted M. Cælius Rufus took the chief role among the *accusatores,* joined by Q. Fabius Maximus, heir to a prestigious patrician house, and by Caninius Gallus. Their political associations disclose a notable pattern: links can be detected with M. Crassus, C. Cæsar, and Cn. Pompeius respectively. It was the year of the "first triumvirate." Antonius' prosecution marks the first instance of triumviral collaboration in the *iudicia.* The fact is confirmed by the activities of the Cæsarian P. Vatinius, who modified his judiciary law in order to deny its benefits to Antonius. The defendant offered a convenient target.[106]

The technical charge against C. Antonius, it seems, was *res repetundæ,* in connection with alleged misbehavior in Macedon.[107] But the technical charge was a minor issue. The prosecutors, as in all Republican trials, had a free hand to raise any matter that might bring discredit upon the defendant. Antonius' supposed sympathies with Catiline were stressed to good effect in the accusers' brief.[108] And another extraneous item played a role of no mean significance in this trial. Debate over execution of the Catilinarians had plagued Roman politics since December 63. Remaining adherents of Catiline or men who objected to the principle of the executions saw symbolic value in Antonius' prosecution. Conviction would mean demise of the man officially proclaimed as conqueror of Catiline.[109]

The latter element determined Cicero's otherwise reluctant and ill-humored decision to take up Antonius' cause. The orator had long been under fire for his slaying of the conspirators. The propagandistic use that could be made of a conviction stimulated his already sensitive antennæ. And Cicero had no

[105] See, esp., Cic. *Pro Sest.* 8, 12; *In Pis.* 5; Dio, 37.30.3; Plut. *Cic.* 12.3; Schol. Bob. 126, Stangl.

[106] On the prosecutors, see Cic. *Pro Cæl.* 15, 18, 47, 74, 78; *In Vat.* 28; Val. Max. 4.2.6; Quint. *Inst. Orat.* 4.2.123–124, 9.3.58; Schol. Bob. 94, 149, Stangl. Vatinius' machinations: Cic. *In Vat.* 27–28; Schol. Bob. 149, Stangl. The direct involvement of Pompey is attested by Cic. *Ad Att.* 1.12.1. On the political associations, see Gruen, *Latomus* (forthcoming).

[107] Schol. Bob. 94, Stangl. See Gruen, *Latomus* (forthcoming).

[108] Cic. *Pro Cæl.* 15, 74, 78.

[109] Cic. *Pro Flacco,* 5, 95.

reason to feel comfortable with the involvement of the triumvirs in this case. The chief critics of his *annus mirabilis* had been the partisans of Pompeius Magnus in 63: Julius Cæsar and Metellus Nepos. Cicero excogitated the elements of a crisis. He not only defended Antonius in court, but utilized the forum to castigate Cæsar and deprecate the triumvirate. That turned out to be a grievous personal miscalculation. The dynasts shortly thereafter authorized Clodius' *transitio ad plebem.* Cicero's exile in the following year can be traced to that miscalculation.[110]

C. Antonius was duly convicted, and departed into exile.[111] The verdict was difficult to avoid in view of the varied interests lined up against him. But the trial carries import well beyond Antonius' personal discomfiture. A confluence of disparate political issues conspired to transform it into a cause célèbre. Antonius' prosecution was the last of those directed against men tainted with a Catilinarian background—and the first to engage the united efforts of the triumvirate. At the same time it brought into focus the ominous implications of Cicero's deeds in 63. The political overtones in Antonius' trial set the stage for a series of subsequent developments. The issue of Catilinarian executions, the prestige of the triumvirate, and the judicial battles of Cicero's advocates and adversaries would become increasingly enmeshed in the years that followed.[112]

These elements are already evident in another *repetundæ* case, later in 59. Cicero ventured the defense of L. Valerius Flaccus, recently returned from a governorship of Asia. Depredations abroad again formed the substance of the charge. The peoples of Asia Minor flocked to Rome to testify on the exploitation: Lydians, Mysians, and Phrygians—"Asiatic Greeks," sneered Cicero, unworthy of belief, especially if they speak under oath.[113] For the orator, one item took on paramount importance. Flaccus had been prætor in the *annus mirabilis.* At that time he had worked loyally for Cicero, aiding in the arrest of witnesses and the rounding-up of testimony against the Catilinarians. Cicero's blinders were on again. He openly lamented the fall of Antonius. His enemies had already claimed one victim. Flaccus was next. The men who had contributed to Catiline's demise were picked off, one by one. Cicero himself was the ultimate object.[114]

[110] Cic. *De Domo,* 41; Suet. *Iul.* 20; Dio, 38.10.1, 38.10.4.

[111] Cic. *Pro Flacco,* 5, 95; *In Vat.* 28; *Pro Cæl.* 74; Val. Max. 4.2.6; Dio, 38.10.3; Schol. Bob. 94, Stangl; cf. Strabo, 10.2.13; Cic. *Phil.* 2.56, 2.98–99.

[112] The trial of Antonius and its background, summarized here, is discussed in detail, with full references, in Gruen, *Latomus* (forthcoming). Add also Vitzthum, *Untersuchungen,* pp. 5–7.

[113] Cic. *Pro Flacco,* 3, 6–26, 60–66.

[114] Cic. *Pro Flacco,* 5: *Condemnatus est is qui Catilinam signa patriæ inferentem interemit*

The orator surmised that motive for Flaccus' trial, as he had for Antonius'—wrongly. But he had reason for insecurity. The triumvirs had assisted in Clodius' transfer to the *plebs.* And Clodius was clamoring for Cicero's head. The latter's uneasiness is explicable: Pompeius Magnus stood behind the prosecution. Chief *accusator* was D. Lælius, family friend and partisan of Pompey. The Greeks of Asia had been stirred to action by the report that Pompey was a determined foe of Flaccus, had urged Lælius to the prosecution, and was backing him with all his prestige, influence, and resources.[115] At least one of the *subscriptores* to the charge is also identifiable as an adherent of the triumvirs: L. Cornelius Balbus, the canny Spanish businessman, a client of Pompey's and an agent of Cæsar's.[116] Several other men contributed to the *accusatio,* lesser lights with personal or financial grievances. Such, for example, was Appuleius Decianus, portrayed by Cicero as a devious Roman *negotiator* in Asia, with a penchant for shady deals and a fondness for young boys. His father had been prosecutor of L. Flaccus the elder and was himself condemned to exile in Asia. The family feud, as was so often the case, perpetuated itself.[117]

The source of Pompey's enmity toward L. Flaccus remains unknown. Flaccus, of old patrician stock, had been a Pompeian legate in the Mithridatic war.[118] There had evidently been a falling-out. In the year of the triumvirate that fact contained political implications. The opponents of the triumvirs turned out in force to buttress Flaccus' defense. P. Servilius Isauricus and Q. Metellus Creticus came forth to testify for him. So did Cn. Domitius Calvinus, a tribune in 59, who launched vigorous assaults on the dynasts. And Q. Hortensius joined Cicero in presenting the defense brief.[119] That

. . . *rapitur ad pœnam qui indicia communis exitii cepit . . . socii consiliorum, ministri comitesque vexantur; quid auctores, quid duces, quid principes sibi exspectent?* So also *Pro Flacco,* 95–97, 103–105; Schol. Bob. 93, 94, 107, Stangl. Cicero seems to put in this same category his two successful defenses of A. Minucius Thermus, on unknown charges, earlier in the year; *Pro Flacco,* 98. But that will be further exaggeration. No additional evidence exists on this individual; and nothing to associate him with the events of 63.

[115] Cic. *Pro Flacco,* 14: *sermo est tota Asia dissipatus Cn. Pompeium, quod L. Flacco esset vehementer inimicus, contendisse a Lælio, paterno amico ac pernecessario, ut hunc hoc iudicio arcesseret, omnemque ei suam auctoritatem, gratiam, copias, opes ad hoc negotium conficiendum detulisse.* On Lælius, see above, chap. 3, n.71.

[116] Val. Max. 7.8.7; Schol. Bob. 93, Stangl.

[117] Cic. *Pro Flacco,* 77. On Decianus, see Cicero's lengthy recital of charges; *Pro Flacco,* 51, 70–83. Other witnesses against Flaccus are not identifiable: M. Lurco, P. Septimius, M. Cælius, Falcidius, and Cætra; Cic. *Pro Flacco,* 10–11, 86–87, 90, 100; Schol. Bob. 95, Stangl. M. Cælius, noted only briefly, is surely not M. Cælius Rufus, the accuser of Antonius. He may be a relative of the *eques* in Sicily; Cic. *Verr.* 2.4.37. Falcidius is possibly son of an ex-tribune; Cic. *De Imp. Pomp.* 58.

[118] Dio, 36.54.3–4.

[119] Cic. *Ad Att.* 2.25.1; *Pro Flacco,* 31, 41, 54, 100; Schol. Bob. 96, Stangl.

is of more than passing interest. In his lengthy military career, Flaccus had served not only with Pompey, but with Servilius Isauricus, Metellus Creticus, and M. Pupius Piso.[120] At his trial, Pompey was hostile; Pupius Piso, who remained a Pompeian partisan, was nowhere in evidence; but Servilius and Creticus, who had broken with the general, were now testifying for Flaccus. The case mirrors accurately the new political lineup inspired by the coming of the triumvirate.

With C. Antonius the triumvirs had had an easy mark. The defendant was evidently culpable. And his earlier career had created even greater odium. Apart from Cicero, who had his own reasons, the sources record no *patroni.* But Flaccus' trial was a different matter. Opposition to the triumvirate had grown in force by the summer of 59. The defense bench reflects that fact. Flaccus, whatever his crimes, enjoyed acquittal.[121] The case heralds that great struggle between the dynasts and their adversaries which was to dominate the ensuing years.

At least one other effort to strike at the triumvirs through the courts stands on record for 59. An *ambitus* prosecution was set in motion, aimed at A. Gabinius, who had been elected to the consulship through the resources and assistance of Pompeius Magnus. An outspoken young politician, C. Cato, initiated the action. But technical difficulties barred his way. The prætor in charge of the *quæstio de ambitu* was an adherent of the dynasts. He carefully dodged Cato and granted him no hearing; the accusation was never put on the docket. Cato ranted with fury at a *contio,* labeling Pompey's tactics dictatorial. The effort was unavailing. Forceful demonstration drove him from the rostra. Gabinius did not have to undergo prosecution.[122]

The following year saw further abortive attempts to bring the triumvirs and their confederates to book. At the beginning of 58 Cæsar himself became vulnerable. His consulship had expired and the strong-arm tactics he had employed in ramming through his legislation gave ample scope for judicial action. Cæsar's enemies were ready to pounce. Two prætors, C. Memmius and L. Domitius Ahenobarbus, raised questions in the senate about the legitimacy of Cæsar's consular activities. But that assemblage shrank from a formal

[120] Cic. *Pro Flacco,* 6.

[121] Macrob. *Sat.* 2.1.3. One may note that he went on to serve under L. Piso in Macedon in 57; Cic. *In Pis.* 54. That is further indication that Piso, now father-in-law of Cæsar, had no great love for Pompeius Magnus.

[122] Cic. *Ad Q. Frat.* 1.2.15; *Pro Sest.* 18. Identity of the prætor is not specified. Perhaps T. Ampius Balbus, a protégé of Pompey's; or Q. Fufius Calenus, who collaborated with the dynasts. For sake of completeness, one might recall again the mysterious affair of L. Vettius, the disreputable informer who alleged a massive plot against Pompey. He was, in fact, indicted *de vi.* His enemies proposed a special *quæstio;* Cic. *Ad Att.* 2.24.4; *In Vat.* 26. But the matter died there. Vettius was found strangled in prison; see above, pp. 95–96.

inquiry. Judicial procedures would attract wide public attention. Charges were leveled against a quæstor of Cæsar's and then against Cæsar himself. No private individual, rather a tribune of the people, L. Antistius, emerged to bring the accusation: the syndicate's foes aimed at maximum publicity. Julius Cæsar, however, was technically immune; as proconsul of Gaul he could not be held liable for prosecution. The *inimici* of Cæsar were certainly familiar with the principle. Their purpose was not to force the matter to court but to tarnish Cæsar's image and raise public doubts about his integrity. The proconsul could have ignored the assault. But he too recognized the value of public opinion. Cæsar shrewdly induced the tribunician college to reaffirm officially the principle of promagisterial immunity: a man absent in the service of the state was not subject to trial. The propaganda battle ended in a standoff.[123]

Opponents of the triumvirate, however, resumed the assault. Their next object was P. Vatinius, who shared responsibility with Cæsar for the tumultuous legislation of 59. Vatinius faced charges of violating the *lex Licinia Junia,* which regulated legislative procedure. Parallels with the attack on Cæsar are close. Vatinius too was absent *rei publicæ causa*—as legate to Cæsar. And Vatinius, like his chief, asked for tribunician affirmation of his rights. Political propaganda was again the objective, on both sides. Vatinius dramatized his case further by waiving judicial immunity and returning to Rome, thereby, presumably, to underline the illegitimacy of the indictment. The hearing itself dissolved in turbulence. Vatinius had the support of the boldest of tribunes, P. Clodius Pulcher. When his *inimici* pressed ahead with the charges, thus forcing Vatinius to make the next move, Clodius resorted to violence. The proceedings were disrupted and judicial inquiry was canceled. Vatinius returned to Julius Cæsar. But his adversaries had scored a telling point. The dynasts had once more been compelled to employ discreditable methods. Their reputation with the *populus* dwindled further.[124] Utilization of the courts represented another weapon—and an effective one—in the propaganda campaign against the triumvirate.

CICERO, CLODIUS, AND POMPEIUS

Cicero had blundered badly at the trial of Antonius. Outspoken comments pushed Pompey and Cæsar into temporary cooperation with P. Clodius. The

[123] The affair is recounted in Suet. *Iul.* 23. On the *lex Memmia,* which forbade prosecution in the *quæstiones* of an official *rei publicæ causa absens,* see Val. Max. 3.7.9; and the recent discussion by E. J. Weinrib, *Phoenix,* 22 (1968): 37–46. The effort of Badian, *CQ,* 19 (1969): 200–204, to transfer this trial to 56 is unpersuasive. For a more detailed examination of the case summarized here, see Gruen, *Athenæum,* 49 (1971): 62–65.

[124] The facts are given in Cic. *In Vat.* 33–34; cf. *Pro Sest.* 135; Schol. Bob. 140, 150, Stangl. And see the reconstruction in Gruen, *Athenæum,* 49 (1971): 65–67.

orator had unwittingly involved himself in growing controversy swirling about the triumvirate. His prospects became increasingly bleak in succeeding months. A new and vigorous defense of his policies surfaced at Flaccus' trial. But the future did not look brighter. Clodius had become a member of the *plebs* and secured election to the tribunate. He would not delay satiation of his vengeance. And as tribune he could press his attack on the illegality of Cicero's actions in 63. A prosecution loomed in the offing–and perhaps the termination of Cicero's political career. His brother Quintus was absent, in Asia, where his governorship had been something less than exemplary. Quintus was due to return in 58. Political enemies prepared charges against him as well. It would help prejudice the case against Cicero himself.[125] The orator had drawn the wrath of Cæsar and Pompey through his stance at Antonius' trial and again with Flaccus' acquittal. And the haughty *nobilitas* of Rome could not be reckoned upon to stand by the *novus homo.*

P. Clodius, with an extensive political following of his own, did not need the backing of the triumvirate. He had already broken with them in 59. But nothing would deflect his plans for Cicero.[126] A massive legislative program in 58 augmented his popularity–and his power. His law *de capite civis* leveled a proper rebuke to misuse of the *senatus consultum ultimum.* It also aimed point-blank at Cicero. The dynasts could not prevent it; Clodius had stolen Cæsar's own thunder. And the *nobilitas* showed reluctance to intervene. The prosecution was prepared and conviction was certain. None could deny the facts. Cicero had executed Roman citizens without trial. The question whether the deed was justified would not readily be determined by legal argumentation. It was strictly a matter of politics. And for M. Cicero the political climate in 58 was not propitious. The case never came to court. Cicero, in anticipation of the verdict, withdrew into exile.[127]

In 58 Clodius was unassailable. The exile of Cicero marked only his most dramatic triumph. Clodius' political machine operated virtually without challenge, so long as his tribunate endured. Among Cicero's tortured agonies abroad was nagging fear that his brother too would be prosecuted upon his return from Asia.[128] He need not have worried. Clodius had had his revenge.

[125] Cicero is already anxious about Quintus' lot in the spring of 59; *Ad Att.* 2.4.2, 2.18.3.

[126] Cf. Gruen, *Phoenix,* 20 (1966): 120–128.

[127] The story need not be retold in detail here. For full discussion and references, see Drumann-Groebe, *Geschichte Roms,* V:624–647; Ciaceri, *Cicerone,* II:46–64; Gelzer, *Cicero,* pp. 135–147. On Clodius' law, see above, chap. 6. On the chronological problems of Cicero's departure and journey, see, esp., C. L. Smith, *HSCP,* 7 (1896): 65–84; Sternkopf, *Philologus,* 59 (1900): 272–304; Shackleton Bailey, *Cicero's Letters,* II:227–232.

[128] The worried concern crops up again and again in the letters from exile, throughout 58; Cic. *Ad Att.* 3.8.2–4, 3.9.1, 3.11.2, 3.13.2, 3.17.1, 3.17.3, 3.19.3, 3.23.5; *Ad Q. Frat.* 1.3.5, 1.3.8–9, 1.4.5; cf. *De Domo,* 69, 76; and see Fallu, *LEC,* 48 (1971), 180–204.

He could ignore political small fry: no prosecution was lodged against Quintus. The tribune turned to larger game: attacks on the triumvirate, criticism of Cæsar's legislation, and physical assaults on Pompey the Great. Specific criminal indictments in the latter part of 58 go unrecorded. But there were some. Plutarch affirms that Clodius brought several of Pompey's friends to court, as a test of political strength. The notice bears the stamp of plausibility.[129]

Clodius' machinations bedeviled and complicated Roman politics. The year 59 had witnessed a vigorous propaganda contest, partly played out in the courts, between aristocratic leaders, notably the Catonian faction, and the triumvirate. Clodius muddied those waters. An enemy of the Catonians, as was amply demonstrated by his trial of 61, he had now turned on the dynasts as well. The exile of Cicero had been watched by both groups in silence or concealed pleasure. But the growing authority of Clodius was unwelcome. When the tribune's term of office expired, counter moves began. On the matter of humbling Clodius there could be agreement among dynasts and senatorial conservatives. The principal object was the recall of Cicero. Not that everyone had suddenly come to love the *novus homo.* His recall was strictly a symbolic gesture: the administration of a political defeat to Clodius. Pompeius Magnus, whose prestige had suffered most at Clodius' hands, led the way, mobilizing his resources and organizing supporters like Milo and Sestius to collect bands and defy his *inimicus.* A heavy majority of public officials in 57 helped to promote the return of Cicero. The friends of Cato were not themselves conspicuous in the venture. But they had no reason to oppose it. The orator's arrival in August 57 was greeted with acclamation. That too was largely a gesture. It would rub salt in Clodius' wounds.[130]

The unity exhibited in effecting Cicero's return did not, of course, endure. The demonstration had served its purpose—the chastening of Clodius. But Pompey's relations with the *nobilitas* continued to deteriorate. Cicero, filled with renewed zeal, hoped to draw Pompey away from his triumviral partners. And Clodius remained recalcitrant and influential.

Bitter confrontation over the recall of Cicero engendered an intense feud between Milo and Clodius. As part of the campaign to emasculate the latter, Milo resorted to the courts. Early in 57, well before Cicero's return, he lodged an indictment under the *lex Plautia de vi.*[131] It was, of course, the pot calling the kettle black, but in politics that detail bothered no one. Elimination of Clodius through an adverse judicial verdict would have smoothed the path

[129] Plut. *Pomp.* 48.6: τοῖς φίλοις δίκας ἐπῆγε πεῖραν ἐν ἐκείνοις τῆς Πομπηίου λαμβάνων δυνάμεως·

[130] On the events, see Ciaceri, *Cicerone,* II:64–70; Gelzer, *Cicero,* pp. 147–150.

[131] On the charge, see Cic. *P. Red. in Sen.* 19; *Pro Mil.* 35.

for Pompey and Cicero. But Clodius summoned political resources of his own. One of the consuls, a prætor, and a tribune intervened. A magisterial edict was passed, blocking and canceling judicial proceedings. Two of the individuals are readily identifiable. Ap. Claudius, prætor in 57, stood by his brother, defying those elements which sought to terminate his career. The consul was Q. Metellus Nepos, Clodius' cousin and brother of Pompey's estranged wife, Mucia. Nepos made his anti-Pompeian stance clear. Identity of the tribune is a matter of guesswork. Two candidates are possible: Sex. Atilius Serranus and Q. Numerius Rufus, who engaged strenuously in efforts to hamper Cicero's recall. Clodius' allies were still serving him well. Milo's prosecution collapsed.[132] The deadlock triggered brutal consequences. Pompey's mounting despair drove him to more radical techniques. The bands of Milo now entered the streets, to engage in violent encounters with the Clodiani. The tumult paralyzed many governmental operations; among other things there was a suspension of all judicial activity. But the show of force and the gathering of a temporary, but effective, political coalition brought about Cicero's return. It was only in the fall of 57 that normal procedures could be resumed. There followed shortly a renewal of Milo's indictment against Clodius.[133]

The case provides an important reflection of the new political constellation. Cicero's return had terminated the brief unity of senatorial groups against Clodius. Numerous machinations entered into the affair. Clodius was standing for the ædileship of 56. Once he assumed office there would be immunity and escape from judicial attack. Hence, Milo, as tribune, persistently stood in the way of ædilician elections. Successive postponements would permit

[132] Cic. *Pro Sest.* 89: *Ecce tibi consul, prætor, tribunus pl. nova novi generis edicta proponunt. ne reus adsit, ne citetur, ne quæratur, ne mentionem omnino cuiquam iudicum aut iudiciorum facere liceat;* cf. *Pro Sest.* 92; *P. Red. in Sen.* 19; *Pro Mil.* 38; Plut. *Cic.* 33.3. Nepos is named specifically by Dio, 39.7.4–39.8.1. And both Nepos and Ap. Claudius came to Clodius' defense later in the year; Cic. *Ad Att.* 4.3.3–4. On the activities of Serranus and Numerius Rufus, see Broughton, *MRR,* II:201–202.

[133] It has not always been recognized that there were two separate prosecutions of Clodius in 57. So, Dio, apparently, amalgamates them; 39.7.4–39.8.1. The strands are properly disentangled by Clark, *Cic. Pro Mil.,* 37; see also the careful discussions of Meyer, *Cæsars Monarchie.* pp. 109–112, n.3, and Stein, *Senatssitzungen,* p. 37. Cicero explicitly notes two indictments; *Pro Mil.* 40: *Milo continuit et P. Clodium in iudicium bis;* cf. *Ad Att.* 4.3.2 (Nov. 57): *antea, cum iudicium nolebat;* Plut. *Cic.* 33.3: Μίλων πρῶτος ἐτολμησε τὸν Κλώδιον εἰς δίκην απάγειν βιαίων. The orator affirms also that Milo's use of armed bands occurred only after failure of the initial prosecution; *P. Red. in Sen.* 19; *Pro Sest.* 88, 92; *Pro Mil.* 38. Cf. Metellus Nepos' assertion that he had twice rescued Clodius; *Ad Fam.* 5.3.2. On the suspension of judicial activity, see Cic. *P. Red. in Sen.* 6; *P. Red. ad Quir.* 14; *Pro Sest.* 85.

trial before Clodius had the protection of a magistracy.[134] Scuffles in the street resumed, to inflame the issue in November, followed by a senatorial meeting to debate it.

The personnel involved demand attention. Clodius' gangs were led by Gellius and a certain Decimus. The former was an *eques,* brother of Gellius Publicola, previously an associate of Pompey's but ranged with the opposition in 59. "Decimus" is unidentifiable, the name perhaps a corruption in the manuscripts. But a case can be made for Dec. Junius Brutus, a young *nobilis* with diverse connections who was soon to join Cæsar in Gaul. More interesting, Clodius himself made his headquarters in the home of P. Sulla. That item is worthy of note. Sulla, the brother-in-law of Pompey, was now harboring Pompey's *inimicus.* It further illustrates the exodus of Roman *nobiles* from the general's circle after 59. At the senatorial session, consul-designate Lentulus Marcellinus took Milo's part, moving that elections be postponed until the trial of Clodius had passed. His antagonism to Clodius was not dictated by Pompey: Marcellinus opposed schemes of the triumvirate as well. Metellus Nepos and Ap. Claudius, Clodius' kinsmen, tried the tactic of filibuster. But Marcellinus held his ground. A senatorial resolution was passed, along the lines of his motion: trial would take place before the ædilician *comitia.*[135]

The Roman *nobilitas,* it is clear, was split on the issue. The vote in the senate in November must have been close, for the whole matter was reopened in the following month. The divisions became even more apparent. A tribune, L. Racilius, a friend of Cicero's, sought reaffirmation of electoral delay to allow for the prosecution. Marcellinus obliged, as did his colleague, L. Marcius Philippus. Cicero, of course, supported that resolution. And an eloquent speech for it was delivered by the tribune Antistius Vetus, a former quæstor of Julius Cæsar's. But C. Porcius Cato, who had clashed with Pompey over Gabinius' trial in 59, raised strenuous objection, backed by a certain Cassius, perhaps from the noble *gens* of the Cassii Longini. A clamorous demonstration by Clodius' adherents broke up the meeting. When discussion resumed, the senate reversed its decision: elections were to be held; there would be no trial.[136]

[134] Cf. Dio, 39.7.3, 39.18.1.

[135] Cic. *Ad Att.* 4.3.2–5; *De Har. Resp.* 15; see Stein, *Senatssitzungen,* p. 36. For the conjecture on Dec. Brutus, see Wiseman, *CQ,* 18 (1968): 299–302. Cicero names also a Q. Flaccus who headed Milo's bands. He too was ostensibly a *nobilis,* perhaps a Fulvius Flaccus; cf. Shackleton Bailey, *Cicero's Letters,* II:176. There were men of rank on both sides.

[136] The initial meeting and its indeterminate conclusion: Cic. *Ad Q. Frat.* 2.1.2–3; the new resolution: Cic. *Pro Sest.* 95: *accusare eum moderate . . . per senatus auctoritatem non est situs.* If *senatus auctoritas* is here used in its technical sense, the decree was vetoed, which is to be expected. But the new mood of the senate is clear. Part of the problem may have been constitutional. Jury panels were normally allotted by the quæstors; Dio, 39.7.4; Lengle, *ZSS,* 66 (1933): 291–292. The quæstors of 57 terminated their year of office on December

Cicero laments the fact later and provides a telling analysis: the same aristocrats who had voted for his recall turned about and saved Clodius from prosecution.[137]

Cicero's statement tells much. The data just examined stand in support. And they permit reconstruction of the political shift in late 57. The power of Clodius had reached its peak in 58. Alienation of key groups in the aristocracy and defiance of the triumvirs did not impede his progress. Clodius sponsored important and attractive legislation, and successfully rode the tide of popular enthusiasm. When Milo attempted to bring him to court in early 57, friends in authority stepped in and canceled the litigation. But something happened thereafter. It was not simply the organization of rival bands and defeat in street brawls. Turmoil in the city and the interruption of public business, especially judicial business, was intolerable to the *nobilitas.* A new unity emerged to break the power of Clodius. The campaign to recall Cicero encountered hardly a ripple of dissent in the senatorial class. That demonstration having been effected, the need for a united front became less urgent. One can discern the changing picture in the fall of 57. The humbling of Clodius was welcome to most aristocratic groups, but not if it meant the revived authority of Pompeius Magnus. Pompey had expected to be chief beneficiary of the events. And in September he obtained a new command to supervise Rome's grain supply throughout the Mediterranean. Roman senators, cautious and wary, began to rethink their positions. The second indictment of Clodius proves it. The senate wavered in division. Some of its members pressed ahead in the prospect of eliminating Clodius for good. But Milo's triumph would be Pompey's triumph. The balance shifted. More and more *nobiles* moved to protect the mercurial ex-tribune from prosecution. A chastened Clodius could be a useful ally. Better that than enhanced *potentia* for

5. And until ædilician elections could be held, there would be no quæstorian elections either. Internal divisions within the *curia* may be illustrated in more than one instance. Most strikingly: Gellius Publicola was an active agent for Clodius; his half-brother, the consul Marcius Philippus, pressed for Clodius' prosecution. The two brothers were not on particularly warm terms; cf. Cic. *Pro Sest.* 110–111. The "Cassius" noted in Cic. *Ad Q. Frat.* 2.1.2 is otherwise unknown. Shackleton Bailey, *PCPS*, 187 (1961): 1, suggests emendation to "Caninius," a known tribune in 56.

[137] Cic. *Ad Fam.* 1.9.15: *impunitatem est illorum sententiis adsecutus . . . qui me homines quod salvum esse voluerunt, est mihi gratissimum; sed vellem non solum salutis meæ, quemadmodum medici, sed, ut aliptæ, etiam virium et coloris rationem habere voluissent.* Clark, *Cic. Pro Mil.*, 37, argues that Milo attempted yet a third prosecution in 56. But the passage cited in support, Cic. *De Har. Resp.* 7, referring to Clodius as Milo's *reus*, is nontechnical and indicates intent only. Clodius was ædile in 56. If Milo could prosecute him anyway, what was all the fuss about in late 57? The thesis is decisively refuted by Cic. *Pro Mil.* 40: *P. Clodium in iudicium bis . . . vocavit.*

Pompey the Great. Milo was stymied, Cicero dismayed and disappointed. And the aristocracy proceeded to spur on Clodius, so long as he directed his fire at Pompey and his *amici.*[138] Once again, analysis of criminal indictments serves to illuminate the whole complex political fabric.

The shifting momentum is clear in early 56. Clodius had gained election to the ædileship–and judicial immunity. That, of course, coincided with a lapse of immunity for the magistrates of 57 who had sponsored Cicero's recall. The orator himself did not need to fear a repetition of his personal ordeal. But his friends and associates were vulnerable. Clodius had a free hand here, and encouragement from the *nobilitas.* Judicial attacks upon the men who brought Cicero back would afford an embarrassment not only to the orator but to Pompey. It is hardly an accident that the early months of 56 saw no fewer than four prosecutions of men who had been in office or active in 57: three tribunes, Milo, Sestius, and Cispius, and a former ædile, Calpurnius Bestia.

Milo, naturally, was the initial target and the most desirable. In January, Milo's magisterial term had expired and Clodius' had begun. The situation, consequently, had come full circle. Milo was arraigned *de vi* for having employed armed mobs, including slaves and gladiators, in the struggle over Cicero's exile.[139] Clodius took the occasion to deliver boisterous harangues against Milo in public *contiones.* Pompey, of course, came to his defense, as

[138] Cic. *De Har. Resp.* 50: *Etiamne in sinu atque in deliciis quidam optimi viri viperam illam venenatam ac pestiferam habere potuerunt? Quo tandem decepti munere? Volo, inquiunt, esse qui in contione detrahat de Pompeio; De Har. Resp.* 52; *Ad Fam.* 1.9.10; *Ad Q. Frat.* 2.3.4.

[139] It has been unanimous scholarly assumption that Clodius planned to prosecute Milo in a *iudicium populi;* so again, most recently, Lintott, *Violence,* pp. 96, 98, 100, 218. That is perhaps hasty. To be sure, Cicero records three separate *contiones* before the people; *Ad Q. Frat.* 2.3.1-2. And later still a fourth date was set for the trial; *Ad Q. Frat.* 2.5.5. But there is nothing to show that these were the three *anquisitiones* and the *quarta accusatio* of a popular trial. Clodius was simply using the *contiones* as an informal means of castigating Milo before trial. Cicero's description of formal procedure for a *iudicium populi* prescribes a *trinum nundinum* between the third *anquisitio* and the final hearing; *De Domo,* 45. By contrast, Clodius' third *contio* against Milo was on Feb. 17, and the trial was not scheduled until May 7. Why the long delay? The evidence is clear that Milo was indicted *de vi;* Cic. *Pro Sest.* 95; Asconius, 48, Clark; cf. Schol. Bob. 122, Stangl. Since the *lex Plautia de vi* was in force, governing a regularly constituted *quæstio,* there was no reason for a *iudicium populi.* Ædiles may once have had such powers. But there is no instance of an ædilician prosecution before the people in the late Republic. Cf. G. Dignös, *Die Stellung der Ædilen im römischen Strafrecht* (Diss. Munich, 1962), pp. 86-95. Cicero, as ædile in 70, threatened one against Verres; *Verr.* 2.1.14. But that was bluster, and issued in no practical result. If Clodius actually planned to bring Milo before a popular court, the move would have been highly unusual, and unprecedented in recent history. In that event Cicero would hardly have refrained from adverse comment.

did Cicero. Their policies were at stake. A third spokesman for Milo is named: Marcellus, very likely M. Marcellus, future consul of 51. There may have been a personal tie. M. Marcellus defended Milo again some years later, at his trial in 52. At that time Pompey was estranged, but Marcellus stuck with Milo. In 56 Clodius pressed his attack with customary abandon. Other politicians with flamboyant styles joined him: C. Cato who had helped prevent Clodius' own trial, and P. Vatinius, the Cæsarian tribune of 59, who was repaying Clodius for services rendered during his arraignment in 58. Vatinius' activities betoken a growing chasm between Cæsar and Pompey. Clodius had exploited that division successfully in 58. The tactic was now revived.[140]

Verbal confrontation came on February 2, then physical confrontation on February 6. Milo was under indictment, but Pompey was the object of most of Clodius' abuse. Clodius cynically played to the prejudices of anti-Pompeian elements in the aristocracy. Violent rowdies filled the forum and took the part of either Clodius or Milo. A melee ensued and the gathering dissolved in disorder. The senate assembled to survey matters. As Clodius anticipated, many senators expressed hostility toward Milo–and toward Pompey. The allies of Cato were especially vocal: Bibulus, Favonius, Servilius, and Curio. M. Crassus kept a prudent silence, but he showed no sympathy for the cause of Milo. Pompey grew more nonplussed. Frustrated by the Catonians and assaulted by Clodius, he convinced himself that Crassus also had turned against him, and he even feared an assassination plot. But with all the internal tergiversations, a real consistency endured in the *curia.* On that score Clodius had miscalculated. Roman aristocrats enjoyed the discomfiture of Pompey, even added to it; but they did not take violence lightly. Clodius, once again, had gone too far–to his cost. A senatorial resolution was passed, condemning his actions at the *contio* and branding them as inimical to the interests of state.[141] The preliminaries to Milo's prosecution had served their purpose: humiliation and embarrassment for Pompey and his adherents. The senate would not indulge Clodius further. The trial itself was now postponed to May. In fact, it never took place.[142]

[140] Pompey was most conspicuous on Milo's behalf; Cic. *Ad Q. Frat.* 2.3.1–4; *Ad Fam.* 1.5b.1; *Pro Mil.* 40, 68; Asconius, 48, Clark; Dio, 39.18.1–2. Marcellus and Cicero were also active; Cic. *Ad Q. Frat.* 2.3.1. For Marcellus' later defense of Milo, Asconius, 34, 39, 40, Clark. On C. Cato's aid to Clodius, see Cic. *Ad Q. Frat.* 2.3.4; *Ad Fam.* 1.5b.1; on Vatinius, Cic. *In Vat.* 40; Schol. Bob. 151–152, Stangl. For Clodius at Vatinius' trial in 58, see above, n.124.

[141] For the events, see Cic. *Ad Q. Frat.* 2.3.1–4; cf. *Ad Fam.* 1.5b.1; *Pro Mil.* 40; Dio, 39.19.1–2; Plut. *Pomp.* 48.7. On the senatorial decree, Cic. *Ad Q. Frat.* 2.3.3: *senatus consultum factum est, "ea, quæ facta essent a.d. viii Id. Febr. contra rempublicam esse facta."*

[142] Trial was fixed for May 7; Cic. *Ad Q. Frat.* 2.5.5. The conference of Luca, however, intervened, and Clodius changed political coloration. There is no evidence that proceedings were resumed against Milo.

But other prosecutions, with similar purposes, were already in the works. Calpurnius Bestia was arraigned *de ambitu* on February 11. Cicero appeared as defense counsel and an interested party. His speech recalled the defendant's services in 57: Bestia had risked life and limb in the bloody skirmishes that punctuated the issue of Cicero's restoration.[143] He had obviously been active, in conjunction with tribunes and others, in relieving Cicero of his exile. That made him a suitable prey in 56. The prosecutor was young M. Cælius Rufus, who had already contended with Cicero in court, at the trial of Antonius in 59. Precocious and avid for high office, Cælius did not select his victims for their politics. Personal rivalry, ardor, and ambition determined his moves.[144] A trial *de ambitu* in early February presumably had reference to the previous year's campaigning, when Bestia sought the prætorship.[145] But the political implications of the case stand forth with clarity. The issue of Cicero's exile and recall and the prestige of Pompey were central elements, as in Milo's arraignment. Cicero's defense speech evidently proved to be potent. Bestia gained acquittal.[146]

P. Sestius was the next intended victim. As tribune in 57, he, along with Milo, had been most responsible for the armed bands that challenged Clodius' *operæ* in the streets. And he had borne the brunt of much of the fighting, sustaining physical wounds for his efforts. Cicero had no great personal love for the man. Sestius was high-strung, stubborn, and peevish–and Cicero had found fault even with the bill Sestius had drafted for his recall from exile.[147] But in 56 those petty complaints were set aside and Sestius' cause was Cicero's.

[143] Cic. *Ad Q. Frat.* 2.3.6. This Bestia is probably to be distinguished from the tribune of 62, with like name. See now Gruen, *Athenæum,* 49 (1971): 67–69, with references to earlier literature.

[144] Cf. Cic. *Pro Cæl.* 76: *de impetu animi loquor, de cupiditate vincendi, de ardore mentis ad gloriam.*

[145] Bestia already possessed ædilician rank; Cic. *Phil.* 11.11, 13.26; on his campaign for the prætorship, see Cic. *Pro Cæl.* 26. He was condemned before reaching it; Cic. *Phil.* 11.11.

[146] Though the trial ended in acquittal, Cælius was preparing a new *ambitus* indictment against Bestia; Cic. *Pro Cæl.* 1, 16, 56, 76, 78; cf. *Pro Cæl.* 7, 45; *Brutus,* 273; Pliny, *NH,* 27.4. The latter case concerned the prætorian campaign of 56, for which Bestia was at last convicted; Cic. *Phil.* 11.11: *quam absurdum autem, qui prætor fieri non potuerit, petere eum consulatum? Nisi forte damnationem pro prætura putat;* cf. *Pro Cæl.* 26; Gruen, *Athenæum,* 49 (1971): 67–69.

[147] For Cicero's private opinion of Sestius, see Cic. *Ad Q. Frat.* 2.4.1: *illius perversitatem . . . ferremus . . . in defendendo moroso homini;* cf. *Ad Q. Frat.* 2.3.5–6; *Ad Att.* 4.3.3. There is some truth in Ps. Sallust, *Inv. in Cic.* 7: *de Sestio male existimas;* and Ps. Cic. *Inv. in Sall.* 12: *Sesti insolentiam repressi.* On Sestius' bill in 57, see Cic. *Ad Att.* 3.20.3: *rogatio Sesti neque dignitatis satis habet nec cautionis.* Cicero sneered at his prose style, Cic. *Ad Att.* 7.17.2; cf. *Ad Fam.* 7.32.1. Sestius even attempted, with habitual clumsiness, to interfere in his own case; for which he was sarcastically rebuked by Cicero; Plut. *Cic.* 26.5.

As quæstor in 63, he had helped steel the shaky resolve of C. Antonius and showed himself an effective lieutenant in military operations against the Catilinarians. Moreover, the hazardous exploits of his tribunate, in the teeth of Clodius' gangs, transformed his trial into a symbolic test of Cicero's prestige and policy.[148]

Sestius' opponents contemplated a double prosecution. On February 10 two indictments were lodged, *de ambitu* and *de vi.* The first doubtless had reference to Sestius' tribunician campaign in 58, analogous to the charge leveled against Bestia. The second concerned the collecting of gangs in 57, putting Sestius' case in the same category as that of Milo. The connection among these three trials is plain. *Ambitus* charges generally followed disputed elections, often brought by defeated candidates to reverse the results. When they did not come until after tenure of office, one may be sure that political considerations, rather than electoral rivalry, supplied the determining element. The prosecutions of Bestia and Sestius conform to that principle. In Sestius' case a single reference to the indictment *de ambitu* survives; there is no evidence for proceedings or issue. It may be that prosecutors felt chances for conviction were better on the violence count; hence, the *ambitus* charge evaporated. In any event, all remaining testimony applies to the prosecution *de vi.* That was brought through to conclusion.[149]

Complications in the political scene multiplied. The personages engaged in Sestius' trial illustrate the fact. The formal prosecutors, as so often happened, were small fry, only their names being recorded and those names relatively uninformative.[150] P. Clodius, of course, stood behind the *accusatio*–but well

[148] On the quæstorship, Cic. *Pro Sest.* 8–11; the tribunate, Cic. *Pro Sest. passim.* Sestius' family was undistinguished but ambitious. He himself had married into the Albinii and the Cornelii Scipiones; Cic. *Pro Sest.* 6–7; *Ad Fam.* 13.8.1.

[149] On the double indictment, see Cic. *Ad Q. Frat.* 2.3.5. The prosecutors *de ambitu* are named, but unidentifiable. Cn. Nerius brought the charge, a man not otherwise attested. He produced as corroborating witnesses a Cn. Lentulus Vatia and a C. Cornelius. Excessive speculation on these men would be foolish, especially as the prosecution, so far as we know, came to naught. But Lentulus Vatia, as a witness against Sestius, the collaborator of Milo and Pompey, would fit the political context. He was evidently born into the Cornelii Lentuli, a family now hostile to Pompey, and was adopted by the Servilii Vatiæ, who followed the same anti-Pompeian course. That would militate strongly against identification of C. Cornelius as the Pompeian tribune of 67. The assertion of Shackleton Bailey, *CQ,* 10 (1960): 258, that Vatia and Cornelius "must have been *populares* to attack that staunch champion of the *boni.* P. Sestius," shows an unwonted blindness to the complexities of Roman politics.

[150] The names themselves are unclear. Cicero gives a certain "M. Tullius" as the man who made the *postulatio; Ad Q. Frat.* 2.3.5. Elsewhere, he names the principal prosecutor as "Albinovanus"; *In Vat.* 3, 41. The scholiast supplies a *prænomen:* "P. Albinovanus"; Schol. Bob. 125, Stangl. Scholars have combined them: "P. Tullius Albinovanus." Perhaps. But that necessitates emendation in Cicero's text. Possibly M. Tullius was replaced as prosecutor by P. Al-

behind. His overt presence against Milo had alienated many *nobiles* and wrecked the possibility of a trial. It was better to remain in the background this time. But Clodius' interest in Sestius' case was well known.[151] More conspicuous was P. Vatinius, a close confederate of Clodius in the trials of both Milo and Sestius. Vatinius delivered venomous and damaging testimony against the defendant and against his counsel.[152] Another hostile witness, as might be expected, was the extravagant gourmand and pseudointellectual Gellius Publicola, a leader of Clodius' bands.[153] Finally, we may note the young aristocrat L. Æmilius Paullus Lepidus. His purpose was not assault on Cicero. Paullus had indicted Catiline *de vi* in 63, and later supported Cicero's recall in 57. But he carried on a family feud with Pompeius Magnus. Paullus' father had been slain by Pompey, and the son was known as a fierce enemy of the general. Paullus had little in common with Vatinius, whom he despised. The aim of his testimony was, no doubt, to increase difficulties for Pompey.[154]

The lineup for Sestius, however, was impressive. Cicero, of course, delivered the principal speech, utilizing the occasion for a broad defense of his own policy. Present also, as moral support for Sestius, were Milo and P. Lentulus Spinther, who had been the chief agents of Cicero's restoration. And Pompey himself delivered a *laudatio,* in praise of Sestius' character.[155] The vigorous and somewhat drastic activities of 57 in Cicero's behalf were on trial here. Sestius, Milo, Lentulus, and Pompey all bore responsibility for those activities. The conjunction of their efforts, together with Cicero, at Sestius' trial provided a natural corollary. In addition, Sestius secured three other defense speeches from significant personages: Q. Hortensius, M. Crassus, and C. Licinius Calvus.[156] The fiery young Calvus, we may assume, was carrying out his embittered feud with P. Vatinius. Crassus' motives, as ever, are more obscure. Love for Pompey did not inspire him. But Crassus had gone on record as approving Cicero's actions of 63; and he supported restoration of the exile's property in 57.[157] At Sestius' trial he took the opportunity to reiterate that

---

binovanus in a *divinatio.* The subscriptor was T. Claudius, nowhere else mentioned; Cic. *In Vat.* 3. Not, apparently, a *nobilis.* The Claudii Nerones employed the *prænomen* "Tiberius," but not "Titus."

[151] See Cic. *In Vat.* 41: *illo* [Clodius] *tamen adiuvante.* The scholiast goes further; Schol. Bob. 125, Stangl: *accusare de vi P. Clodius Sestium cœpit.*

[152] Cic. *Ad Fam.* 1.9.7; *Pro Sest.* 135; *In Vat.* 1, 40–41; Schol. Bob. 125, 139, 152, Stangl.

[153] Cic. *Pro Sest.* 110–112; *In Vat.* 4; Schol. Bob. 135, Stangl.

[154] Paullus testified against Sestius, but threatened prosecution of Vatinius; Cic. *Ad Q. Frat.* 2.4.1. On his services for Cicero, see Sallust, *Cat.* 31.4; Cic. *In Vat.* 25; Schol. Bob. 149, Stangl; Cic. *Ad Fam.* 15.13.2; the enmity with Pompey: Cic. *Ad Att.* 2.24.2; *In Vat.* 25.

[155] Cic. *Ad Fam.* 1.9.7; *Pro Sest.* 144.

[156] Cic. *Pro Sest.* 3, 14, 48; *Ad Q. Frat.* 2.4.1; Schol. Bob. 125, Stangl.

[157] Cic. *Ad Att.* 1.14.3, 4.2.3; *De Har. Resp.* 12.

position. Hortensius' appearance is more revealing. The attitude of senatorial conservatives, as we have seen, had maintained an internal consistency, despite ostensible wavering, in previous months. Hatred in the Catonian group for Pompey was matched only by that for P. Clodius. Hence, the Catonians had been neutral or sympathetic in the campaign to recall Cicero. But with Clodius humbled, they felt no qualms about encouraging him, so long as he was making matters difficult for Pompey in late 57 and early 56. But no more–senatorial leaders did not permit a conviction of Milo. Nor, apparently, did they approve the attack on Sestius. Many *principes,* in addition to Hortensius, backed Sestius' defense.[158]

Multiple motives impelled the participants in Sestius' case, as in most cases. Personal rivalries played a role: feuds between Æmilius Paullus and Pompey, between Vatinius and Licinius Calvus. Defense of past actions mobilized Cicero, Pompey, Milo, and Lentulus Spinther. Obligations to Clodius influenced Vatinius and Gellius, while the need to keep Clodius in harness supplied motives for Hortensius and his friends on the other side. The trial not only reveals divisions in the ruling class; it also gives pointed illustration of the crumbling of the triumvirate. Crassus had spoken for Sestius, for his own reasons. But Cæsar's *adsecula* Vatinius was active in the prosecution. And Cicero's vicious reply to Vatinius' testimony included unmistakable reflections on Cæsar's consulship.[159] Pompey had good cause to distrust his triumviral partners. Widening of that breach was deliberate policy on the part of Cicero and, perhaps, others. The triumvirate reached its lowest ebb in early 56. Sestius' trial confirms the fact.

The attack on Sestius ended in failure. Vatinius had foreseen it. A charge *de vi* which had failed against Milo would stand equally small chance against Sestius. The oligarchy continued to associate violence with Clodius rather than with his antagonists. Prosecutors tried to dodge that difficulty. They dissociated Milo's actions from Sestius', even praised the former, in the hopes of concentrating odium on Sestius.[160] The attempt misfired. As Cicero insisted–with justice–the cases of Milo and Sestius were inseparably intertwined. Both were brought into court for the same reasons and by the same mis-

[158] Cf. Cic. *In Vat.* 10: *his principibus civitatis, qui adsunt P. Sestio.*

[159] Cic. *Ad Fam.* 1.9.7; *Ad Q. Frat.* 2.4.1; *In Vat.* 5, 13–18, 21–32, 35–36. The published version of Cicero's *In Vatinium* perhaps softened the references to Cæsar. But none could have mistaken the implications even then; cf. Pocock, *Comm. Cic. In Vat.*, pp. 1–9; contra: U. Albini, *PP,* 66 (1959): 172–184. On Vatinius as Cæsar's *adsecula,* see Cic. *Pro Sest.* 135.

[160] Cic. *Pro Sest.* 86–87, 90; *In Vat.* 40. Vatinius had hoped that the prosecutors might press a charge other than *vis;* perhaps *ambitus.* And he even suspected Albinovanus of collusion with the defense when he chose the *vis* count to make his case; Cic. *In Vat.* 3, 41. See the elucidation by Pocock, *Comm. Cic. In Vat.*, pp. 134–145.

creants.[161] The jury concurred. Sestius gained acquittal on March 11, by unanimous vote.[162]

The friends of Clodius, it seems, made still one further effort. M. Cispius, another tribune of 57, obscure and insignificant, but resolutely loyal to Cicero in that difficult year, endured prosecution *de ambitu.* No specific date is given, nor are prosecutors named. But Cispius' trial fits snugly in the context of early 56. Like Milo and Sestius, he had held office in 57, promoted Cicero's cause, and was then defended by the orator. The charge *de ambitu,* probably with reference to his tribunician campaign in 58, also puts Cispius' trial in a category with those of Bestia and Sestius. Cicero was urged to his defense by young M. Juventius Laterensis, one of the orator's staunchest proponents in 58 and 57. The same issues were at stake in Cispius' case. The prosecution belongs, surely, in the first months of 56.[163] It was the only one of the four, however, that ended in conviction. Cispius was a minor figure, without the battery of *nobiles* behind him that Milo or Sestius had commanded. Even Cicero's defense may have been less than enthusiastic. There had once been personal friction between the two men.[164] But the victory was a small one for the Clodiani. Their principal targets had escaped.

The judicial war could be carried on by the other side as well. In March Milo brought an indictment, doubtless *de vi,* against Sex. Clœlius, an unsavory creature of Clodius. Cicero never mentions that individual without heaping the vilest abuse: Clœlius was lecherous, gluttonous, and murderous, a prime agent in the worst excesses of Clodius' mobs.[165] The attack was unsuccessful, though a near miss. Clœlius attained acquittal by three votes. Cicero laments the ineptitude of the prosecution: Milo relied on a feeble crew of *accusatores.* Division in the jury is revealing. *Tribuni ærarii* voted against Clœlius, *equites* split evenly, but senatorial jurors were heavy for acquittal. The reason could

[161] Cic. *In Vat.* 41: *in re publica administranda T. Annio cum P. Sestio consiliorum omnium societas fuerit . . . est enim reus uterque ob eandem causam et eodem crimine, alter die dicta ab eo, quem tu unum improbiorem esse quam te numquam soles confiteri, alter tuis consiliis, illo tamen adiuvante.*

[162] Cic. *Ad Q. Frat.* 2.4.1.

[163] It can come no later than 54, when it is mentioned in Cicero's *Pro Plancio,* 75–76; cf. Schol. Bob. 165, Stangl. Most scholars place it in 54; e.g., Lange, *Röm. Alterth.* III:347–348; Gelzer, *Cicero,* p. 195. But without evidence. The matter of Cicero's exile and recall was of considerably less interest at that point. For Juventius Laterensis' activity for the orator, see Cic. *Pro Planc.* 2, 73, 86. He was no friend of the triumvirate; Cic. *Ad Att.* 2.18.2, 2.24.3; *In Vat.* 26. Cispius had been a strong opponent of the Clodiani in 57; Cic. *P. Red. in Sen.* 21; *Pro Sest.* 76.

[164] Cic. *P. Red. in Sen.* 21.

[165] Esp., Cic. *De Domo,* 25–26, 47–48; *Pro Cæl.* 78; cf. *In Pis.* 23: *tu, Clodiane canis.* On the man's name, see the irrefutable arguments of Shackleton Bailey, *CQ,* 10 (1960): 41–42.

readily be divined: hostility to Pompey in the aristocracy determined the vote.[166] Other battles in the courts proved more propitious. Cicero records with glee that several convictions of his *inimici* occurred in March, including a certain Servius. One may imagine that these were all lesser hirelings of P. Clodius.[167]

The cascade of prosecutions in early 56 arose, first and foremost, from the intense *inimicitia* between Milo and Clodius. But involved in every one were the policy and actions of Cicero and the prestige of Pompey the Great. The senatorial aristocracy found itself caught in the middle, endeavoring to keep Clodius under control and at the same time diminish Pompey's stature and weaken his ties with fellow triumvirs. The policy enjoyed apparent success. Clodius was thwarted in the important cases, like those of Milo and Sestius. But Pompey too got pointed reminders, as in the acquittal of Sex. Clœlius. Condemnations were returned only for the lesser figures, like M. Cispius and Servius, defeats for Cicero and Clodius respectively. Both Clodius and Pompey suffered frustration. The trials of these months elucidate in large measure what was soon to come: the conference of Luca and the defection of Clodius to the triumvirate.

One last trial deserves comment in this connection. The prosecution of M. Cælius Rufus in early April 56 grew out of a personal quarrel. There is no need to question that fact. Young Cælius, as was noted, had broken a friendship with L. Bestia and had prosecuted him *de ambitu* earlier in the year. Beaten in that effort, he prepared a new *ambitus* indictment, which was now hanging fire. In retaliation, Bestia's son, L. Sempronius Atratinus, hauled his family's tormentor before the court. The formal arraignment came under the *lex de vi*. But Atratinus and his *subscriptores* raked up every dubious episode in Cælius' brief but colorful career. Cælius' personal life received special abuse. His former association with Catiline was mentioned, and there were coarse references to his philandering, profligacy, indebtedness, lechery, and general dissoluteness. Cælius' reputation as a carefree man-about-town and indis-

[166] Cic. *Ad Q. Frat.* 2.4.6: *Unum accidit imprudentia Milonis incommode, de Sex. Clœlio, quem neque hoc tempore, neque ab imbecillis assusatoribus mihi placuit accusari; ei tres sententiæ teterrimo in consilio defuerunt . . . ea ipsa in re Pompei offensio nobis obstitit; senatorum enim urna copiose absolvit, equitum adæquavit, tribuni ærarii condemnarunt.* The acquittal is noted also in Cic. *Pro Cæl.* 78.

[167] Cic. *Ad Q. Frat.* 2.4.6: *quotidianæ damnationes inimicorum, in quibus me perlubente Servius allisus est, ceteri conciduntur.* Servius is customarily identified with a Servius Pola who turns up again in 54, where he is specifically registered as a client of the *gens Clodia;* Cic. *Ad Q. Frat.* 2.13.2. But a man convicted in 56 would not be around to engage in politics in 54. Given the political associations, the two individuals are very likely related. That is all that can be said with confidence.

criminate lover could be damaging. The defense was obliged to excuse his excesses as a sowing of wild oats.[168]

Such were the incidental insinuations. Cicero chose to deal with them at length in his defense speech. Not one of them amounts to *vis*. The legal charges were evidently handled by other speakers, in orations no longer preserved. Substance and basis for a *vis* prosecution remain obscure. But hints survive to provide at least a skeletal reconstruction. Cicero reports that Cælius was accused of involvement in seditious activities at Naples, assault on Alexandrines at Puteoli, forcible seizure (it seems) of property belonging to a certain Palla, and the murder of Dio.[169] Of these Cicero addressed himself only to the last. But elucidation comes also from another source. The affair revolved about the notorious Ptolemy Auletes. Extravagant and corrupt, Auletes sought Roman recognition and assistance for his restoration to the throne of Egypt. The Alexandrines who had deposed him resisted. They sent their own delegation to Rome, headed by the Academic philosopher Dio. Clandestine intrigue followed. Through agents and cash, Auletes arranged intimidation of the envoys and a number of murders, including that of Dio himself.[170] The nature of Cælius' participation is unknown. But the accusations against him are clearly linked with these episodes: the assassination of Dio, assault on the envoys at Puteoli, and, doubtless, the sedition at Naples.[171]

It is pertinent to observe that Pompeius Magnus had a large stake in the fate of Auletes. The triumvirs in 59 had effected Roman recognition of the king, and accepted a handsome sum in compensation. Auletes had been deposed in the interim and was now pressing for restoration. The man who would restore him could expect considerable authority and cash. Now it was precisely in early 56 that a furious political contest issued over that question. And Pompey's partisans were in the forefront, seeking to obtain the commis-

[168] On these incidental accusations, see, e.g., Cic. *Pro Cæl.* 6–7, 10, 15, 17, 20, 25, 27, 29–30, 35. There was also a suggestion that he was involved in electoral bribery; Cic. *Pro Cæl.* 16; Schol. Gronov. 323, Stangl. On Cælius' prosecution of Bestia, see above, n.146. None of these attacks, however, were relevant to the legal charge, which was definitely *de vi;* Cic. *Pro Cæl.* 1, 70, 72; Quint. *Inst. Orat.* 4.2.27, 11.1.51; Suet. *Rhet.* 2. On the date of the trial, see Austin, *Cic. Pro Cæl.*, p. 121.

[169] Cic. *Pro Cæl.* 23: *de seditionibus Neapolitanis, de Alexandrinorum pulsatione Puteolana, de bonis Pallæ . . . de Dione;* cf. Quint. *Inst. Orat.* 4.2.27: *narret de bonis Pallæ totamque de vi explicet causam.* On the charges, see Austin, *Cic. Pro Cæl.*, pp. 152–154.

[170] Cic. *Pro Cæl.* 23–24, 51–55; Dio, 39.12–14.

[171] Connection with the goods of Palla is too obscure for speculation. Palla, it can be surmised, was the stepmother of L. Gellius Publicola, consul in 36, who was married to Sempronia Atratina, adoptive sister of Cælius' prosecutor; Dio, 47.24.3–6; so Austin, *Cic. Pro Cæl.*, pp. 74, 155. Hence, perhaps, another instance of the familial quarrel between Cælius and the Atratini.

sion for him.[172] Removal of the Alexandrine envoys would be in Pompey's interest, as well as Auletes'. Rumors had already circulated that Pompey, who sheltered and entertained Ptolemy Auletes, had connived at the murder of Dio and the Egyptian envoys.[173]

The trial of Cælius thereby fortuitously took on political connotations. The friends of Cato endeavored to implicate Pompey and to wreck his aspirations for an Egyptian command. One may observe that Cato's *amicus* Favonius pressed for senatorial investigation of the whole Alexandrine affair.[174] And the adherents of Clodius were equally anxious to destroy Pompey's standing. They lurked behind the accusation of Cælius.

The two *accusatores* had personal incentive: Sempronius Atratinus because his father was prosecuted by Cælius, and L. Herennius Balbus because of intimate friendship with the family. Yet it may not be irrelevant to note a marriage connection between Sempronius and Gellius Publicola, one of Clodius' most prominent lieutenants. And Herennius, who was later among the prosecutors of Milo in 52, can also be associated with C. Herennius, a political ally of Clodius.[175] One need not press those connections. Prominence of the Clodiani in the prosecution is affirmed by the damaging evidence delivered by Clodia. That infamous lady, sister of Clodius and widow of Metellus Celer, cut a striking figure in Rome and at aristocratic resorts in Campania. Her festive parties and literary salon were celebrated, as were her amours.[176] Cælius had been among her lovers. The aftermath of that liaison evidently left bitterness. The accusers themselves asserted that Clodia supplied them with much of their information. For Cicero, she was the moving force behind the whole trial.[177] In addition to Clodia's testimony, a certain P. Clodius inveighed solidly against Cælius' moral shortcomings. That will not have been the tribune of 58, about whom Cicero would have had much more to say; it was more likely a lesser member of the *gens* or a client.[178] Clodius himself,

[172] See Meyer, *Cæsars Monarchie,* pp. 126–131; Ooteghem, *Pompée,* pp. 368–376; P. T. Eden, *RhMus,* 105 (1962): 352–358; Gruen, *Historia,* 18 (1969): 81.

[173] Dio, 39.14.3; Strabo, 17.1.11.

[174] Dio, 39.14.1.

[175] On Sempronius and Gellius, see above, n.171. For Herennius' friendship with Sempronius' father, Cic. *Pro Cæl.* 56; cf. 26. His prosecution of Milo's adherents is given by Asconius, 34, Clark. The text offered by Clark in his *Cic. Pro Mil.,* 99 is preferable to his later thoughts in the edition of Asconius. On C. Herennius, see Cic. *Ad Att.* 1.18.4, 1.19.5. Cf. on these matters Austin, *Cic. Pro Cæl.,* pp. 78, 154–157.

[176] Cf., esp., Cic. *Pro Cæl.* 49.

[177] Cic. *Pro Cæl.* 50: *crimen accusatores abs te et testem eius criminis te ipsam dicunt se habere; Pro Cæl.* 75: *tantumque abest ab illius familiaritatis infamia, ut eiusdem nunc ab sese inimicitias odiumque propulset; Pro Cæl.* 78: *ne patiamini . . . M. Cælium libidini muliebri condonatum.*

[178] Cic. *Pro Cæl.* 27; Austin, *Cic. Pro Cæl.,* pp. 155–156.

as in the case of Sestius, found it more prudent to stay in the background. But the involvement of his clan is clear.[179]

Clodia's evidence referred particularly to an attempt on the life of Dio. That furnished the most explosive political issue. It had already been linked, in popular report, to the name of Pompeius Magnus. Clodia charged that Cælius had taken gold from her in order to turn it over to L. Lucceius, who would then arrange for the assassination. And she added one further allegation: an elaborate story about Cælius' plans to poison her.[180] As was well known, Lucceius was counted among the close friends of Pompey. The dragging in of his name exposes the political motivation. It no longer causes surprise that Cicero took up the case despite having clashed twice before with Cælius in the law courts. The orator would resist any machinations by the *gens Clodia,* especially if they might redound to the discredit of Pompey the Great. Similar motives had probably inspired him when he defended P. Asicius, an agent of Ptolemy Auletes, who had been formally prosecuted for the slaying of Dio.[181] Cicero devoted the bulk of his speech to a scathing attack on Clodia and an encomiastic defense of Cælius' character. The official charge, *de vi,* linked in some way to intimidation of the Alexandrines at Puteoli and Naples, had been dealt with by another advocate, M. Crassus.[182] Crassus' presence here parallels his appearance for P. Sestius. Crassus was no friend of the Clodiani. It will be recalled, too, that M. Cælius had been his political protégé.[183] As with Milo and Sestius, the effort of the Clodiani was abortive. Cælius escaped conviction.[184]

[179] One other hostile witness is mentioned, a senator who was to claim that Cælius had attacked him physically at the pontifical elections; Cic. *Pro Cael.* 19. The marginalia to one of the manuscripts give here *De Teste Fufio.* If that is accurate, it may be reference to Q. Fufius Calenus the tribune of 61 who was of assistance to Clodius at his trial; cf. Austin, *Cic. Pro Cæl.*, p. 70. His presence against Cælius would be fitting.

[180] On Lucceius' involvement, Cic. *Pro Cæl.* 51–55; the poisoning allegation, Cic. *Pro Cæl.* 56–59. Austin, *Cic. Pro Cæl.*, pp. 77, 113, rightly points out that the charge refers to an earlier attempt to murder Dio, rather than the actual assassination. Nor was it the formal charge. Murder would come under the *quæstio de sicariis et veneficiis.*

[181] Asicius was acquitted; Cic. *Pro Cæl.* 23–24. The prosecutor in that case, apparently, had been C. Licinius Calvus; Tac. *Dial.* 21. Dio, 39.14.4, reports that many Alexandrines were also accused in this connection, but few were convicted.

[182] Cic. *Pro Cæl.* 18, 23. Cælius also delivered at least one speech in his own defense; Cic. *Pro Cæl.* 45; *Brutus,* 273; Quint. *Inst. Orat.* 1.6.29, 4.2.27, 8.6.53, 11.1.51; Suet. *Rhet.* 2; see Malcovati, *ORF,* pp. 485–486.

[183] Cic. *Pro Cæl.* 9. In this connection it is worth noting that two young intellectuals, T. and C. Coponius, were cited as character witnesses for Cælius; Cic. *Pro Cæl.* 24. One of them was soon to accompany Crassus as a prefect in the Parthian war; Plut. *Crass.* 27.7–8.

[184] That is proved by his continued presence in Rome; Cic. *Ad Q. Frat.* 2.13.2.

Once again a plethora of considerations moved the participants in Cælius' trial. That feature seems common to every case for which sufficient information survives. It is a healthy corrective to simplistic interpretations of criminal trials in this period. But whatever the origins of Cælius' prosecution and the truth or falsity of the allegations, the case took on significant political overtones. It belongs in the context of indirect attacks on Pompeius Magnus and the bitter feud between Clodius' circle and their enemies, which dominated Roman politics in 57 and early 56.[185]

The information provided by criminal trials is rich and revealing. Several strands are isolable in the 60s. Clashes between the interests of Pompey and Lucullus constituted a prevailing element. Though the outcome was indecisive, since convictions were few, the judicial war embittered relations and helped to determine Pompey's move into the triumvirate. At the same time familial feuds and the scramble for magisterial office received outlet in the courts. A number of such cases permeated the 60s, exposing increased dissensions and divisions within the ruling class. And larger issues came to the fore in that decade: the compensation of Sulla's victims, the question of the *senatus consultum ultimum,* the Catilinarian uprising. Each of them was manipulated by politicians or political groups as an instrument to attack *inimici* and rivals in the *iudicia.*

The creation of the triumvirate in 59 injected a new item into the reckoning. Judicial hearings presented an ideal forum for aristocratic propaganda against the dynasts. And then the emergence of Clodius fragmented the political scene once more. Senatorial groups were caught in the crossfire between Clodius and the dynasts. The ensuing struggle dominated criminal prosecutions in 57 and early 56. Trials increase in number and significance during those months. Personal animosity between Clodius and Milo supplied a basic stimulus. But political overtones were inescapable. The courts were employed by Cicero for self-justification, by Pompey as defense of his policies and partisans, by the aristocracy to maintain a balance and to curb the ambitions of both Clodius and the triumvirate. Stalemate and miscarried efforts featured the

[185] The trial of Cælius and Cicero's *Pro Cælio* have engendered a multitude of scholarly discussions, wth varied results. The political overtones are acutely pointed out by Heinze, *Hermes,* 60 (1925): 193–258, and Ciaceri, *Atti Accad. Arch. Nap.,* 11 (1930): 1–24; cf. F. Lovera, *Mondo Classico,* 6 (1936): 167–178; G. Pacitti, *Atti Congr. Int. Stud. Cic.* (1959), II:67–79. Dorey, *Greece and Rome,* 27 (1958): 175–180, rightly stresses the personal motives involved, though he unduly ignores the political implications. On the *Pro Cælio,* one may also consult with profit E. Norden, *SBBerl* (1913), pp. 2–32; R. Reitzenstein, *NAkG* (1925), pp. 25–32; Humbert, *Les plaidoyers,* pp. 153–167. Indispensable is the excellent edition by Austin, *Cic. Pro Cæl., passim;* though his conclusion, p. viii, that "society reasons prompted the case, and the issue was the social disappearance of either Clodia or Cælius," will not convince many.

judicial contests. Clodius' once powerful position crumbled; Pompey's prestige was under constant attack; his friends were cool or hostile; the triumvirate was in a state of collapse. The tactics of Cato and Bibulus had gained the major successes. But those successes proved costly. The frustrating results of political prosecutions in early 56 forced a new and unexpected coalition: the revival of the triumvirate and a union with the Clodiani.

Some general observations may be pertinent. More than fifty criminal cases of some political import, between the years 69 and 56, have here been examined. The criminal trial formed a conspicuous feature of the age. Simplistic analysis will not do. There is no single or consistent pattern. Where evidence is full, it is possible to discern a multiplicity of motives that induced men to engage in the *iudicia:* private quarrels, familial rivalries, ambition to put one's talents on display, personal obligations, political contests, and public issues. Results also varied. More prominent individuals generally secured acquittal. But there were exceptions. Defendants who had roused widespread hostility did not escape, such as Manilius, P. Autronius Pætus, or C. Antonius. Minor figures often made convenient scapegoats–they would be easier to convict. So, some of the Sullan executioners were condemned, but not Catiline; some of the Catilinarians were condemned, but not P. Sulla. But even small fry received favorable verdicts when powerful defenders came to their aid, witness Archias, or L. Flaccus, or Cælius. The political climate at any particular point had much to do with the outcome of prosecutions. It enforced Cicero's exile in 58, and brought him back in 57. It enabled Clodius and Milo to circumvent trial, but convicted some of their adherents. The verdict in any individual case was not crucial. The trial itself was the important event: a forum for propaganda and a vehicle for political ambition and rivalry.

VIII

CRIMINAL TRIALS: THE CONTINUITIES

A MEETING at the small town of Luca in northern Italy threatened to alter the course of Roman history. Pompeius Magnus forced the issue. His prestige had plummeted at an alarming rate in early 56. He had been assaulted by the Clodiani and deserted by aristocratic allies; the sullen hostility of M. Crassus was disquieting, and there were grave uncertainties over the attitude of Julius Cæsar. Pompey made his move at last. Through the unwitting assistance of M. Cicero, he put pressure on Cæsar and temporarily halted the decline in his fortunes. The conference of Luca in April, 56 brought renewal of the syndicate that had been formed in 59.[1]

Long-term success for the new coalition depended, however, on the attitude of the Roman oligarchy. Pedigreed senators were not given to meek submission. The propaganda campaign undertaken in 59 redoubled with vigor after Luca. The triumvirs had no designs on the constitution. Their aim was traditional: power in the senate and magistracies through combines of influential individuals and groups. In that struggle aristocratic leaders were able to compete more than adequately. We have already seen their continued ascendancy in the electoral contests. They could also make effective use of the courts. Direct judicial attacks on the triumvirs would be to no avail. Both Cæsar and Pompey possessed *imperium* and immunity; Crassus was elusive and formidable. But in the months after Luca an increasing number of triumviral adherents were brought before the bar. As always, the technique afforded a most useful means of puncturing the prestige of one's *inimici.*

[1] On the conference of Luca and its immediate consequences, cf. Gruen, *Historia,* 18 (1969): 89–96.

THE REACTION TO LUCA

In the autumn of 56, the canny Spanish financier L. Cornelius Balbus underwent prosecution. He seemed an inviting target. Balbus was a noted manipulator—in matters financial and political. The inordinate wealth accumulated by a foreigner aroused envy and resentment. Slanderous gossip and backbiting circulated against him. It became a favored topic of conversation at aristocratic dinner parties.[2] But when Balbus was brought to court none doubted the real objects of attack. Balbus was close to both Pompey and Cæsar. He had performed distinguished service for Pompey in the Sertorian war of the 70s. Rewards included bestowal of Roman citizenship under Pompey's auspices, suburban gardens and a country home at Tusculum, gifts from the general.[3] Julius Cæsar also recognized the merits of Balbus. As governor of Spain in the late 60s, he made valued use of the Gaditane's abilities in administrative affairs.[4] Balbus' diplomatic talents proved to be equally serviceable. He acted as intermediary in the delicate negotiations that led to the formation of the triumvirate.[5] Links among the three men were strengthened further. When Pompey wed the daughter of Cæsar, Balbus was adopted by Pompey's literary friend and client, the Greek intellectual Theophanes.[6] The prosecution in 56 was manifestly directed against the triumvirs. Cicero exposed that fact openly in court.[7]

The case against Balbus charged illegal arrogation of citizenship. It was an offense covered by the *lex Papia* of 65, a bill aimed at coercion and intimidation of aliens.[8] Balbus' claim to Roman franchise had gone unquestioned for a decade and a half. As in the case of Archias, prosecuted under the same *lex Papia* in 62, timing and purpose of the trial were dictated by political considerations alone. A fellow Gaditane acted as *accusator.* The principals behind him are unnamed.[9] But the defense bench was redoubtable. It conspicuously displayed the new unity of the dynasts. Both Pompey and Crassus delivered impassioned pleas on behalf of Balbus. Cæsar, as proconsul of Gaul, could not, of course, be present. But his patronage and close relations with the defendant were referred to on more than one occasion.[10] The triumvirs

[2] Cic. *Pro Balbo,* 18, 56–59.

[3] Cic. *Pro Balbo,* 5–7; *Ad Att.* 7.7.6, 9.13a; Pliny, *NH,* 5.36.

[4] Cic. *Pro Balbo,* 43, 63.

[5] Cic. *Ad Att..* 2.3.3.

[6] Cic. *Pro Balbo,* 57; *Ad Att.* 7.7.6.

[7] Cic. *Pro Balbo,* 59: *non igitur a suis, quos nullos habet, sed a suorum, qui et multi et potentes sunt, urgetur inimicis.*

[8] Cic. *Pro Balbo,* 52.

[9] Cic. *Pro Balbo,* 32.

[10] For Pompey and Crassus, see Cic. *Pro Balbo,* 2, 17, 50, 59; references to Cæsar, Cic. *Pro Balbo,* 43, 63–64; cf. 58. There were representatives from Gades there also, to submit a deposition in support of Balbus; Cic. *Pro Balbo,* 39–40.

took no chances in this case. Pompey brought pressure to bear on M. Cicero and induced him to deliver the culminating speech. The orator had another motive as well: Balbus had been most sympathetic and useful while Cicero was in exile. But prodding from the triumvirs supplied the decisive element in Cicero's appearance.[11] One need not dwell on the elaborate legal argumentation. The political factor was the determinant. A sympathetic jury confirmed Balbus' privileges. His trial represented the opening shot in a judicial campaign against hangers-on of the triumvirate.

An abortive effort is attested at the beginning of 55. Pompey and Crassus had just obtained appointment to the consulship. Their purpose now was to steer friends to success in the prætorian elections. As was expected, Cato stood in opposition. And he had a double strategy. If adherents of the triumvirate could not be beaten at the polls, perhaps the results could be reversed in court. Cato pressed for amendment to a senatorial resolution. The Catonian rider would fix a gap of sixty days after the *comitia*, which, of course, would allow space for *ambitus* proceedings. The attempt foundered and the consuls had their way. The victorious candidates, Vatinius among them, were safe for another year.[12] But other victims were available.

Evidence discloses three cases in 55 which feature attacks on *amici* of Pompeius Magnus. L. Caninius Gallus, tribune in 56, sustained prosecution. The charge is unknown; perhaps *ambitus*, on the analogy of cases in the previous year. Of the trial little is reported, except that Cicero was constrained to defend him. In a private letter, the orator laments his lack of options.[13] The pressure, we may be sure, came, here as in the case of Balbus, from Pompey. Caninius Gallus had been an active agent for Pompey during his tribunate, an advocate of the Egyptian commission.[14] The trial, it appears, ended in conviction—perhaps not an event of great importance, but rather a signal to the dynasts of continued influence by their opponents in the *iudicia*.[15]

[11] Cic. *Pro Balbo*, 4: *sed mos est gerundus non modo Cornelio, cuius ego voluntati in eius periculis nullo modo deesse possum, sed etiam Cn. Pompeio, qui sui facti, sui iudicii, sui benefici voluit me esse . . . et prædicatorem et actorem;* cf. *Pro Balbo*, 59. For Balbus' services to Cicero, see *Pro Balbo*, 58.

[12] Cic. *Ad Q. Frat.* 2.9.3; Plut. *Cato*, 42.1–2.

[13] Cic. *Ad Fam.* 7.1.4: *ne forte videar tibi non modo beatus, sed liber omnino fuisse, dirupi me pæne in iudicio Galli Canini.*

[14] Sources in Broughton, *MRR*, II:209.

[15] The conviction of Caninius Gallus by a certain M. Colonius is specifically recorded by Val. Max. 4.2.6. There is no evidence for the customary identification of this defendant with Caninius Gallus, consul in 37 and son of the tribune. Better to see this as a reference to the trial in 55. It is noteworthy that Caninius does not turn up in the sources again until 51, when he was to be found in Athens, perhaps an exile; Cic. *Ad Fam.* 2.8.3.

In the same year may be placed the trial of T. Ampius Balbus, who had promoted the general's interests during his tribunate of 63 and who had recently suffered defeat at the consular elections despite vigorous backing from Pompey. Only a single notice survives on the trial: both Pompey and Cicero delivered orations on Ampius' behalf.[16] Finally, an accusation came before the censors against the annalist L. Scribonius Libo. Again, the sally was directed primarily against Pompey. Libo was his *adfinis*, a trusted adviser, and a loyal confederate. Pompey himself appeared at the censorial hearing to take his part. The *accusator*, Helvius Mancia from Formiæ, son of a freedman though he was, brazenly trained his fire on the general, raking up crimes committed in the civil war a quarter-century before.[17] The string of events form a pattern. Enemies of the triumvirate had taken the offensive. Cicero recognized the fact. He would have preferred to remain out of it; but his oratorical talents were conscripted by Pompey. Cicero complied, with reluctance and resignation.[18]

The offensive continued. It reached fever pitch in the summer and early fall of 54. At least a half-dozen trials were crammed into that short space, all with the same purpose. The opponents of the triumvirate owned considerable material with which to institute criminal proceedings. Turbulence and conflict had marked the electoral campaigns of 56. The syndicate had met with stiff resistance: hence deliberate disruptions, which caused postponement of the *comitia* into 55. Crassus and Pompey at last attained the consulship early in the year. They proceeded to carry favored candidates for the prætorian and ædilician posts, but again only after violence and intimidation made a mockery of standard procedures.[19] In 54 Cato and his allies launched political reprisals in earnest. The men under prosecution in the middle of that year fit a collective picture. They were either magistrates of 56 and agents of the triumvirs who had provoked disturbances and delays in the elections, or magistrates of 55, elected by virtue of those disturbances.

One may note initially the fiery but unstable C. Porcius Cato, brought to trial at the beginning of the summer. Earlier, he had been a vehement critic of Pompey, a would-be prosecutor of both Gabinius and Milo. The conference of Luca, however, found him pliable. As tribune in 56, he was prominent in forcing postponement of the electoral *comitia*, thereby putting

[16] Cic. *De Leg.* 2.6; cf. Quint. *Inst. Orat.* 3.8.50. On Ampius' tribunate, Vell. Pat. 2.40.4; the consular candidacy, Cic. *Pro Planc.* 25; Schol. Bob. 156, Stangl.

[17] Val. Max. 6.2.8. On Scribonius Libo, see above, chap. 3, n.63. The censors are not named; but 55 was the only censorial year between 61 and 50. It is surely the proper year.

[18] Cic. *Ad Fam.* 7.1.4: *neque enim fructum ullum laboris exspecto, et cogor nonnumquam homines non optime de me meritos rogatu eorum, qui bene meriti sunt, defendere.*

[19] On the consular elections, see above, chap. 4, n.112; for the prætorian and ædilician elections, see, esp., Dio, 39.32.1-3; Plut. *Pomp.* 52.2, 53.3; *Cato,* 42.1-5; Val. Max. 4.6.4; Appian, *BC,* 2.17.

his new loyalty to the dynasts on show.[20] Evidently, there was legislation involved, either sponsored or sabotaged by C. Cato. When prosecution came in 54, there were two counts against him, under the *lex Licinia Junia* and the *lex Fufia*. Those measures were concerned with improper passage of legislation. Cato's tumultuous activities in his tribunate obviously furnished basis for the charges.[21] Once again, a young man embarking on a political career applied as prosecutor: the future historian Asinius Pollio, a member of Rome's youthful smart set and the circle of Catullus. But C. Cato had impressive defense counsel. The triumvirs saw to that. The patrician M. Scaurus, Pompey's *adfinis* and former lieutenant, spoke on Cato's behalf. So did the flashy young poet and orator Licinius Calvus. Calvus, like others, had become reconciled with Julius Cæsar after Luca. His defense of Cato attests to that. For both Cicero and Calvus such tasks were burdensome and unwelcome. But Cicero knew the forces behind C. Cato. He could confidently predict acquittal on both counts, and he was right.[22]

In conjunction with this trial came another, the prosecution of a certain Sufenas. Cicero links them closely. Both involved disrupted elections, corruption, and violence to the state.[23] Reference is obviously to the events of 56. Sufenas, one may safely surmise, had been a colleague and collaborator of C. Cato's in the tribunate of that year. Like Cato, Sufenas–presumably a Nonius Sufenas–was found innocent.[24] The dynasts were protecting their adherents.[25]

[20] Livy, *Per.* 105; Dio, 39.27.3. On his earlier activities, as enemy of the dynasts, see Cic. *Ad Q. Frat.* 1.2.15, 2.1.2, 2.3.1–3, 2.4.5; *Ad Fam.* 1.2.4, 1.4.2, 1.5.2, 1.5b.1; Dio, 39.15.3–4.

[21] Cic. *Ad Att.* 4.16.5, 4.15.4. Linderski, *Studi in onore di E. Volterra* (1969), II:298–302, suggests that a charge deriving from the *lex Fufia* may indicate that Cato had employed *obnuntiatio* illegally in blocking the elections.

[22] Cic. *Ad Att.* 4.16.5: *lege Iunia et Licinia scis absolutum; Fufia ego tibi nuntio absolutum iri, neque patronis suis tam libentibus quam accusatoribus.* The reluctant *patroni* include, no doubt, Calvus himself. The involvement of Calvus and Asinius Pollio is given by Seneca, *Controv.* 7.4.7; see the discussion in Gruen, *HSCP,* 71 (1966): 222–225. For Scaurus' testimony, see Asconius, 18, Clark. Cato's acquittal is noted also in Cic. *Ad Att.* 4.16.6, 4.15.4; Asconius, 19, Clark.

[23] Cic. *Ad Att.* 4.15.4: *ambitum, comitia, interregnum, maiestatem.* The rhetoric here does not entail that Cato and Sufenas were formally charged *de maiestate* and *de ambitu* respectively, *pace* Linderski, *Studi Volterra* (1969), II:295–302.

[24] Cic. *Ad Att.* 4.15.4. He may have been the son of Sex. Nonius Sufenas, a Sullan prætor in 81. L. R. Taylor, *Athenæum,* 42 (1964): 17–22, wants to identify him also with a Nonius Struma (or *struma*) mentioned as holding a curule seat in a line of Catullus, 52. He is associated there with Vatinius' consular expectations: *sella in curuli struma Nonius sedet/ per consulatum perierat Vatinius.* Hence, it is assumed, he occupied curule office in 55, the year of Vatinius' prætorship. Broughton, *MRR,* II:216, makes him curule ædile; Miss Taylor conjectures a prætorship. One cannot rule out either possibility. But identity with the tribune of 56 is unproved and doubtful; cf. now Shackleton Bailey, *Cicero's Letters,* III:246.

[25] A certain Procilius, prosecuted at the same time, is generally placed in the same category,

Acquittals did not slow down opponents of the triumvirate. In midsummer they turned to some elected officials of 55 who had been nominees of Pompey and Crassus. C. Messius was ædile in 55, chosen in the turmoil of those elections. Pompey counted him an *amicus*, one of his clients from Campania; Messius had advocated elaborate powers for the general when he was tribune in 57.[26] Messius knew what was coming. His ædileship at an end, he hastily took a post on Cæsar's staff in Gaul, an appointment engineered by Ap. Claudius, now cooperating with the dynasts. But the allies of Cato were not to be put off. P. Servilius Isauricus, Cato's nephew by marriage and a dutiful partisan, issued a prætorian edict instructing Messius to return for trial. The charge, it seems, came under the *lex Licinia de sodaliciis*, with reference to Messius' disputed appointment as ædile. Pompey made haste to arrange for the defense. Cicero was again recruited. He could comfort himself with the recollection that Messius had once advocated his recall from exile. And Licinius Calvus also spoke for Messius, perhaps at the behest of Cæsar. No evidence survives on the result. Cicero anticipated a tough struggle. But Messius turns up again in Italy in 49; perhaps, then, the jurors had rendered a favorable verdict.[27] The pressure on supporters of the syndicate, however, did not let up.

---

even registered (without a query!) as a tribune in 56 and ally of Cato and Sufenas; Broughton, *MRR*, II:209. That is, at best, a conjecture–and not a very good one. Cicero pointedly distinguishes Procilius' case from those of Cato and Sufenas. Not only was Procilius convicted, whereas the others gained acquittal. The crimes of Cato and Sufenas involved electoral turmoil; Procilius, apparently, was charged with murder; Cic. *Ad Att.* 4.15.4: *Sufenas et Cato absoluti, Procilius condemnatus; ex quo intellectum est* τρισαρειοπαγίτας *ambitum, comitia, interregnum, maiestatem, totam denique rem publicam flocci non facere, patrem familias domi suæ occidi nolle;* cf. *Ad Att.* 4.16.5. Clodius was the prosecutor; Cic. *Ad Att.* 4.15.4: *Publius . . . criminans.* Shackleton Bailey, *Cicero's Letters*, II:208, emends to *lacrimans.* But that is forced by his view that Procilius was attacked as a partisan of the dynasts. Banish that assumption, and the need for emendation disappears. Cicero goes on to note that Hortensius was "his usual self" in Procilius' trial: *cuius modi solet.* That should mean he was defense counsel, a posture one might expect if Clodius were accusing, less likely if he were defending. If the Procilius case has political import, we cannot ferret it out. It may safely be dissociated from Cato, Sufenas, et al. So, rightly, Linderski, *Studi Volterra* (1969), II:290–295.

[26] The friendship with Pompeius: Cic. *Ad Att.* 8.11D.2: *tuus familiaris;* the tribunate: Cic. *Ad Att.* 4.1.7; the ædileship: Broughton, *MRR*, II:216.

[27] Principal evidence on all this is in Cic. *Ad Att.* 4.15.9: *Messius defendebatur a nobis de legatione revocatus; nam eum Cæsari legarat Appius; Servilius edixit ut adesset; tribus habet Pomptinam, Velinam, Mæciam; pugnatur acriter; agitur tamen satis.* Cf. Münzer, *RE*, 29.1243, "Messius," n.2; Shackleton Bailey, *Cicero's Letters*, II:211–212. Calvus' speech is noted by Seneca, *Controv.* 7.4.2; cf. Gruen, *HSCP*, 71 (1966): 222. The charge is unspecified, but reference to the three tribes selected by the prosecutor clearly suggests the *lex Licinia de sodaliciis;* see above, pp. 230–231. On Messius' services for Cicero, see Cic. *P. Red. in Sen.* 21. On the right to recall legates for trial, see *Dig.* 5.1.2. For mention of Messius in 49, see Cic. *Ad Att.* 8.11D.2.

The next object was no less a figure than P. Vatinius. Advancement of Vatinius' career was one of the most conspicuous effects of Luca. His clashes with Pompey in 56 were conveniently forgotten, swept aside by the new unity of that conference. Vatinius obtained the prætorship of 55 through the efforts of Pompey and Crassus. Dubious machinations by the consuls effected the defeat of Vatinius' chief competitor, M. Cato. And Vatinius had employed gladiators in his campaign, in violation of *ambitus* statutes. Plenty of material was available to justify charges after Vatinius' prætorship had expired.[28] As with Messius, the official accusation was covered by the *lex Licinia de sodaliciis*, which had now superseded previous *ambitus* laws.[29] Again the triumvirate took steps to protect their *adsecula*. M. Cicero was the unhappy agent. Cæsar interceded directly, with an urgent request that Cicero take the case. The orator consented, but with heavy misgivings. Only two years had elapsed since he cut Vatinius to ribbons at the trial of Sestius; and only a year and a half since he had supported Cato's candidacy against Vatinius. The speech *Pro Vatinio* must have been tortured indeed. Naturally, the written version never saw the light of day. Cicero suffered a drumfire of criticism, for which only agonized apologies could be offered. His political impotence was dramatically on exhibit.[30] The volatile C. Calvus, however, could not be coerced. His feud with Vatinius stretched back for several years. He had assailed him on more than one occasion in the past and had vowed prosecution. Opportunity came in 54. Calvus engaged in the *accusatio* with relish. His brilliance, however, was overmatched by the experienced talents of Cicero. With the triumvirs standing united in the background, Vatinius evaded condemnation.[31]

Another beneficiary of the syndicate stood trial at the same time. M. Livius

[28] On the intimidation of Cato and Vatinius' election, see Dio, 39.32.1–2; Plut. *Pomp.* 52.2; *Cato,* 42.3–5; cf. Val. Max. 7.5.6; Livy, *Per.* 105. On the use of gladiators, Cic. *Pro Sest.* 133–135; *In Vat.* 37.

[29] Cic. *Pro Planc.* 40; Schol. Bob. 160, Stangl; Hieron. *Adv. Rufin.* 3.39; cf. Schol. Bob. 150, Stangl.

[30] Cic. *Ad Fam.* 1.9.19: *De Vatinio autem, primum reditus intercesserat in gratiam per Pompeium . . . post autem Cæsaris, ut illum defenderem, mira contentio est consecuta;* cf. Plut. *Cic.* 26.1. On the criticism, see also Ps. Sallust, *Inv. in Cic.* 7; Ps. Cic. *Inv. in Sall.* 12; cf. Quint. *Inst. Orat.* 11.1.73. Cicero's defense of Vatinius is noted, as well, in Cic. *Ad Q. Frat.* 2.16.3; *Ad Fam.* 5.9.1; Schol. Bob. 160, Stangl; cf. Val. Max. 4.2.4, with Gruen, *HSCP,* 71 (1966): 229, n.33.

[31] For the confrontation of Calvus and Cicero, see, esp., Seneca, *Controv.* 7.4.6. The fragments of Calvus' speech are collected by Malcovati, *ORF,* pp. 494–498; see the discussion in Gruen, *HSCP,* 71 (1966): 218–221. On Calvus' earlier threat to prosecute, see Cic. *Ad Q. Frat.* 2.4.1. The acquittal is affirmed in Cic. *Ad Fam.* 5.9.1. Cicero had predicted it in advance; *Ad Q. Frat.* 2.16.3: *ea res facilis est.* Vatinius, though acquitted, had not grown any fonder of Cicero; cf. Cic. *Ad Q. Frat.* 3.9.5.

Drusus Claudianus, despite impressive genealogical credentials, remains an obscure figure. But he is identified in 59 as a man looking to Julius Cæsar for patronage, associated in that context with P. Vatinius.[32] The connection presumably continued, and the trials of Drusus and Vatinius may be conjoined. Further suggestion comes from the fact that Licinius Calvus, the *inimicus* of Vatinius, also delivered a speech against Drusus Claudianus. Formal prosecutor was a certain Lucretius, who appears later as a foe of Cæsar. M. Cicero, with a begrudging sigh of resignation, took Drusus' part.[33] The two trials hang together. One might suspect that Drusus, like Vatinius, had been a magistrate, even a prætor, in 55. But speculation would be rash. Drusus was not charged with electoral tampering. His crime was *prævaricatio*, collusive prosecution. Perhaps he had served as a phony prosecutor in one of the other trials in 54. Like his accomplices, he obtained release, though by a narrow margin.[34]

The pattern can be further documented. Dio reports that Pompey and Crassus in 55 effected the election of congenial prætors, ædiles, and all but two tribunes.[35] The two curule ædiles were Cn. Plancius and A. Plotius. In 54 Plotius came in for attack; Plancius was formally prosecuted.[36] Accusers invoked the *lex Licinia de sodaliciis* against Plancius, probably in late August 54. The charge, under the circumstances of those months, suggests a magistracy in 55 attained with the assistance of the triumvirs. Vatinius and Messius had been indicted on the same count; both were men forced on the electorate by the dynasts. That Plotius and Plancius had received similar favors is a safe assumption.[37]

[32] Cic. *Ad Att.* 2.7.3: *illa opima ad exigendas pecunias Druso, ut opinor, Pisaurensi an epuloni Vatinio reservatur.*

[33] Cic. *Ad Att.* 4.15.9: *deinde me expedio ad Drusum, inde ad Scaurum; parantur orationibus indices gloriosi.* Cicero elsewhere laments the excessive number of trials with which he was burdened in the summer of 54; Cic. *Ad Q. Frat.* 2.16.1. On Lucretius as prosecutor, Cic. *Ad Att.* 4.16.5. He is very likely Q. Lucretius, the friend of Cæsar's assassin Cassius; Cic. *Ad Att.* 7.24; Cæs. *BC,* 1.18.1; Orosius, 6.15.4; cf. Cæs. *BC,* 3.7.1; so Drumann-Groebe, *Geschichte Roms,* VI:29; Münzer, *RE,* 26:1657–1658, "Lucretius," n.12; Shackleton Bailey, *Cicero's Letters,* II:202. Calvus' speech against Drusus is noted by Tac. *Dial.* 21.2.

[34] Cic. *Ad Q. Frat.* 2.16.3: *Drusus erat de prævaricatione a tribunis ærariis absolutus, in summa quattuor sententiis, cum senatores et equites damnassent;* also *Ad Att.* 4.17.5. Taylor, *Athenæum,* 42 (1964): 23, suggests that Drusus was prætor in 55. The question should be left open.

[35] Dio, 39.32.2–3.

[36] That Plotius was not actually brought to trial is clear from Cic. *Pro Planc.* 17. But he was implicated with Plancius in the same offense; Cic. *Pro. Planc.* 54: *A. Plotium, virum ornatissimum, in idem crimen vocando.*

[37] The dates of their ædileships were established by Taylor, *Athenæum,* 42 (1964): 12–28, to whose article the following account is much in debt. Her argument withstands the highly conjectural suggestions of Sumner, *Phoenix,* 25 (1971): 249. Plancius' trial is discussed also

Additional evidence points in the same direction. The Plautii (or Plotii) had intimate associations with Pompeius Magnus in the 60s and 50s. A. Plotius himself was a loyal adherent. As tribune in 56 he acted as intermediary for Pompey and Ptolemy Auletes to secure an Egyptian command for the general. He was later to govern Bithynia for Pompey in the civil war.[38]

Plancius' ties were not so clear-cut. An *eques* and a *novus homo* interested in a senatorial career, he would seek support where he could. Plancius' youthful military service had come under A. Manlius Torquatus, later a legate of Pompey's, and then under Q. Metellus Creticus, the general's fervid foe.[39] But there were other, older connections. Plancius' father was a highly successful and influential businessman. Bold and outspoken in his views, he rose to the top of his profession, manager and director of several tax-farming companies. The elder Plancius became a *princeps* among *publicani*.[40] An early contact with P. Crassus, father of the triumvir, is on record. Plancius had headed the equestrian contingents that served in the legions of Crassus. And later, in 60, when the *publicani* of Asia sought reduction of their tax contract, the elder Plancius represented them as leader and spokesman. One may observe that M. Crassus was most interested in that effort, and probably had money invested in the venture. And Julius Cæsar, as consul in the following year, granted the request, a boon conspicuously acknowledged by Plancius.[41] Support of the triumvirate for the candidacies of Plotius and Plancius falls into place. And Plancius was to suffer the consequences in 54.

That Plancius' trial was merely another thrust by the Catonian faction would be a hasty conclusion. More evidence exists on this case: in particular, Cicero's defense speech. And, as we have seen so often, where documentation is fuller the complexities are exposed. In contrast to the other cases discussed (so far as one can make out), the prosecutor here was an unsuccessful competitor in the election. M. Juventius Laterensis brought the charge, a youth of distinguished consular family, furious at and disbelieving in his defeat by a knight's

---

by Drumann-Groebe, *Geschichte Roms,* VI:39–56; Ciaceri, *Cicerone,* II:127–133; W. Kroll, *RhMus,* 86 (1937): 127–139; all without recognition of the political elements involved. Evidence for the trial exists solely in Cicero's *Pro Plancio* and the commentary in Schol. Bob. 152–169, Stangl.

[38] The tribunate: Dio, 39.16.2; service in Bithynia: Cic. *Ad Fam.* 13.29.4. On relations between Pompey and the Plautii, see above, chap. 3, n.65.

[39] Cic. *Pro Planc.* 27. On A. Torquatus, see now Mitchell, *Historia,* 15 (1966): 23–26.

[40] Cic. *Pro Planc.* 24: *erat pater is, qui est princeps iam diu publicanorum;* on his business dealings and character, see Cic. *Pro Planc.* 31–35.

[41] On the elder Plancius' service with P. Crassus, see Cic. *Pro Planc.* 32; his involvement in the Asian tax contract, Cic. *Pro Planc.* 34–35. For M. Crassus' interest in the affair, see Cic. *Ad Att.* 1.17.9. The connections are acutely pointed to by Taylor, *Athenæum,* 42 (1964): 22.

son. Laterensis was a firm aristocrat, solid in his convictions, with jealous concern for his lineage. Prosecution of a victorious candidate by his disappointed rival was, of course, a commonplace. Plancius, like other magistrates elected in the turmoil of early 55, entered upon office immediately after announcement of the results. He could not, therefore, be brought to court in 55. But Laterensis aimed at vindication of his *dignitas* in the following year. He required no triumvirate and no public contest for senatorial supremacy to furnish inspiration. Aristocratic *dignitas* was sufficient incentive. Personal rivalry for office and honor endured as continuous counterpoint to public issues of the day.[42]

In the heated political conflicts of mid-54, however, the trial of Plancius cannot have been altogether irrelevant. Cicero spoke for the defense, as he had for Messius, Vatinius, and Drusus Claudianus.[43] The orator, embarrassed no doubt by the electoral scandals of early 55, deftly leaves them out of account. His speech pursues a familiar line: the now wearisome refrain of his actions against the Catilinarians and his unjustified exile. Plancius had come to Cicero's aid in troubled times. As quæstor in Macedon he sheltered and protected the exile, accepting hazards that were shunned by his superior officers. It was a service that Cicero did not forget.[44] Hence, the orator's opening remarks attempt to set the trial in a context of assault on his own policy and career: Plancius' accusers are really Cicero's accusers; the defendant is the superficial victim, the defense counsel the real target.[45] That tired chant may have had some force in 57 or 56, hardly in 54. Juventius Laterensis was not the man to deliver a tirade on Cicero's previous career. As the orator himself concedes, Laterensis had lent him significant assistance in his hour of need, even protecting his wife and children during the exile. And it was Laterensis again who

[42] On Laterensis, see, esp., Cic. *Pro Planc.* 6, 9–13, 17–18, 50–53. The trial in 54 refutes definitively the older notion that Plancius was serving as ædile in that year. Magisterial immunity would have foreclosed prosecution. The case is argued at length by Miss Taylor, *op. cit.*, though she unduly neglects the personal elements involved in the accusation.

[43] That Hortensius also spoke for Plancius is an unwarranted assumption. His speech concerned only the technicalities of the *lex Licinia de sodaliciis,* for he had urged a similar measure in 56; Cic. *Pro Planc.* 37; cf. Taylor, *Athenæum,* 42 (1964): 41–42; *contra:* Kroll, *RhMus,* 86 (1937): 136; Linderski, *PP,* 79 (1961): 304–311. If Hortensius had actually defended Plancius, Cicero would have made more of that fact than a single brief allusion.

[44] Cic. *Pro Planc.* 26, 99; *P. Red. in Sen.* 35; *Ad Att.* 3.14.2; *Ad Fam.* 14.1.3. Not that Plancius' motives were altogether altruistic. He hoped to earn plaudits by accompanying Cicero back from exile; Cic. *Ad Att.* 3.22.1: *spes homini est iniecta . . . posse nos una decedere, quam rem sibi magno honori sperat fore.* In his tribunate of 56 Plancius was somewhat less than enthusiastic in Cicero's cause, a fact which the orator endeavors, with awkwardness, to excuse; Cic. *Pro Planc.* 28, 77; cf. *Ad Q. Frat.* 2.3.3.

[45] Cic. *Pro Planc.* 1: *cum autem audirem meos partim inimicos partim invidos, huic accusationi esse fautores . . . dolebam, iudices, et acerbe ferebam, si huius salus ob eam ipsam causam esset infestior, quod is meam salutem atque vitam sua benevolentia, præsidio, custodiaque texisset.*

in 56 collaborated with Cicero in the defense of M. Cispius, at whose prosecution Ciceronian policy had indeed been on trial.[46] In 54 that matter was no longer relevant.

Cicero, to be sure, felt the accusers' barbs at the trial of Plancius. The criticism, however, was leveled not at his past but at his present. That fact is central and illuminating. Laterensis' references to the past questioned Cicero's lack of fortitude, rather than his policy: the orator should have stood and fought in 58 instead of slinking off into exile.[47] And Laterensis gave voice to the exasperation of many in Cicero's audiences who had lost patience with his self-justifications: "How long must we hear the same old obsolete strains?"[48] But the major barrage of criticism found another track: Cicero's subservience to the triumvirs. That, of course, was pertinent and timely. Laterensis had joined the chorus of detractors who judged Cicero's defense of triumviral agents contemptible. The orator was forced into a labored apologia.[49] The significance of that attack should not have been missed by historians. That it came at Plancius' trial was hardly accidental: Cicero's defense furnished another example of obligations performed for the dynasts.

Laterensis' conscience was clear. He had been a stalwart opponent of the triumvirate since 59, even abandoning his candidacy for the tribunate rather than swear allegiance to Cæsar's agrarian law.[50] His attack on Cicero as a toady of the dynasts now fits the larger perspective. The trial of Plancius, originating in electoral rivalry, took on political coloration as part of the senatorial propaganda against the triumvirs.[51]

The fierce judicial struggle had taken its toll. Six adherents of the triumvirs were put in the dock in the summer of 54. Of the six defendants none can be said with certainty to have been convicted. C. Cato, Sufenas, Vatinius,

[46] Cic. *Pro Planc.* 73, 75–77; cf. 2, 86.

[47] Cic. *Pro Planc.* 86: *dixisti enim, non auxilium mihi, sed me auxilio defuisse.* Cicero replies at some length; *Pro Planc.* 86–90.

[48] Cic. *Pro Planc.* 75: *atque etiam clamitas, Laterensis: "quousque ista dicis? . . . obsoletæ iam sunt preces tuæ."*

[49] Cic. *Pro Planc.* 91–94. Cicero's justifications here parallel closely his reply to similar criticism from his friend Lentulus Spinther later in the year; *Ad Fam.* 1.9.4–22.

[50] Cic. *Ad Att.* 2.18.2; *Pro Planc.* 13, 52. His hostility to Pompey is clear also from Cic. *Ad Att.* 2.24.3. One may note, in addition, that Laterensis' *subscriptor* in the trial of Plancius was the youthful L. Cassius Longinus, brother of Cæsar's future assassin. His speech too was punctuated with sarcastic jibes at Cicero; Cic. *Pro Planc.* 58.

[51] The outcome of the trial is not registered. That Plancius does not turn up again in the evidence until the mid-40s, when he lived in Corcyra as a Pompeian exile, may be suggestive; Cic. *Ad Fam.* 4.14, 4.15, 6.20.1. Cicero was willing to publish his *Pro Plancio* shortly after the trial; Cic. *Ad Q. Frat.* 3.1.11. Gelzer, *Cicero,* 200, infers acquittal from that fact. It is better to leave the matter uncertain.

and Drusus Claudianus were definitely acquitted; Messius and Plancius may have been. Not that one should infer triumphant vindication of the coalition's policy. The battles in court were keen; some of the verdicts no doubt were very close. Drusus, at least, had but a narrow escape. Caninius Gallus had probably been convicted in the previous year. Of greater importance was the fact that criminal trials gave scope for the dissemination of political propaganda. By trumpeting in public the misdemeanors of the triumvirs and forcing them to defend acts of dubious constitutionality, the *boni* strengthened their own moral and political position. The judicial attacks generated increasing discomfort in the ranks of the syndicate.

TRIALS AND TRIBULATIONS OF A. GABINIUS

The biggest prize was still to come. In September 54 A. Gabinius returned to Rome from a lengthy governorship of Syria. The proceedings against him were long in preparation, framed as a dramatic climax to the judicial offensive of the last several months. Other defendants had been, for the most part, minor hangers-on of the dynasts. Gabinius, by contrast, was an ex-consul, the most prominent *amicus* of Pompey the Great, author of significant legislation, a governor of Syria, and the man who had installed Ptolemy Auletes on the throne of Egypt. His return aroused eager expectations. It was to be the year's great cause célèbre.

Gabinius' most embittered foe, M. Cicero, had been calling attention to his real or alleged transgressions abroad for over two years. The orator registered dismay at Gabinius' vast devastations, extortions against provincials, and crushing of Roman *publicani*; a somber tale of avarice and perfidy.[52] In 55 Cicero pointed to Gabinius' high-handed actions, including an unwarranted invasion of Egypt, and warned that he had violated both *maiestas* and *repetundae* statutes.[53]

The prognostication proved to be accurate. In February 54 preliminaries were already under way. Representatives of Syrian provincials and of the *publicani* came to Rome to present depositions. Gabinius was fiercely assailed.[54] By the fall, the venomous campaign of character assassination reached large proportions. Gabinius, beleaguered and insecure, crept into the city under cover of night. He chose a sparsely attended meeting for his first appearance in the senate. Not that it made any difference. He was shouted down by his colleagues and abused by the *publicani*.[55]

[52] See, e.g., Cic. *De Prov. Cons.* 9–12; *De Domo*, 60; *Pro Sest.* 93; *In Pis.* 48–50.

[53] Cic. *In Pis.* 50.

[54] Cic. *Ad Q. Frat.* 2.13.2: *eodem igitur die Syriis est senatus datus frequens; frequentes contra Syriaci publicani; vehementer vexatus Gabinius.*

[55] Cic. *Ad Q. Frat.* 3.1.24, 3.2.2; Dio, 39.62.1.

An army of anxious prosecutors contended with one another to bring Gabinius to court. This was to be the real test of the triumvirs' position in the *iudicia.* No fewer than three separate indictments, for three separate *quæstiones*, stood against Gabinius. *Maiestas* and *res repetundæ* offered natural avenues. But no possible item was overlooked. Gabinius was also to be charged *de ambitu.* Reference must be to his consular campaign of five years before. As consul and proconsul since that time, he remained immune until 54–but no more. Gabinius had been earlier arraigned on an *ambitus* count in 59, but machinations by his political allies blocked the proceedings.[56] The *accusator* at that time was C. Cato, who subsequently transferred allegiance to the triumvirate. But there was no lack of prosecutors in 54. And the triumvirate could no longer control events. P. Sulla applied for the job of prosecuting Gabinius *de ambitu.* Backing Sulla with equal vigor were his stepson C. Memmius, tribune in that year, his brother Cæcilius, and his son.[57] The identity of those persons reveals the breakup of Pompey's old faction. P. Sulla was Pompey's brother-in-law; C. Memmius was his nephew. The general's fortunes had shifted drastically. Sulla had supported Clodius against Pompey in 57; now he was setting upon Pompey's chief lieutenant. Memmius railed against Gabinius at a public *contio*, with unrestrained vituperation.[58] Sulla's claim did not go unchallenged. His longtime foe L. Torquatus also coveted the task of impugning Gabinius in court. A *divinatio* was necessary. Sulla gained selection as the official prosecutor.[59] That is the last we hear of the *ambitus* charge. Perhaps it was lost in the shuffle of the other, more serious indictments, or held in abeyance to be used against Gabinius at a later time, if needed. The *maiestas* and *repetundæ* cases proceeded on schedule.

Numerous candidates presented themselves also as prospective *accusatores* on the extortion count. C. Memmius, Sulla's *subscriptor*, wanted the principal role in the trial *de repetundis*. Backing him was young L. Ateius Capito, whose brother (or cousin) had been a bitter critic of Pompey and Crassus as tribune in the previous year.[60] They had stiff competition: the patrician Ti. Claudius

[56] Cic. *Ad Q. Frat.* 1.2.15; *Pro Sest.* 18.

[57] Cic. *Ad Q. Frat.* 3.3.2; *Ad Att.* 4.18.3.

[58] Cic. *Ad Q. Frat.* 3.2.1. Gabinius was supported here by the celebrated orator M. Calidius. But Calidius could not get a word in edgewise.

[59] Cic. *Ad Q. Frat.* 3.3.2; *Ad Att.* 4.18.3. The bitter feud between Sulla and Torquatus stretched back to the consular campaign of 66. Torquatus twice prosecuted Sulla, in 66 and 62; see above, pp. 283–285. Part of Sulla's motive may have been a desire to regain access to *honores* which had been denied him ever since his own conviction *de ambitu;* cf. Cic. *Pro Cluent.* 98. If so, it helps to explain Torquatus' interest in blocking Sulla's involvement as prosecutor.

[60] Cic. *Ad Q. Frat.* 3.1.15. On C. Ateius Capito, tribune in 55, see Broughton, *MRR*, II:216.

Nero, son of a former legate of Pompey's. He represents another example of Pompey's breach with a *nobilitas* which had once found him attractive. And there were the Antonii brothers, Gaius and Lucius, inaugurating political careers. Once again a *divinatio* was required: Memmius got the job.[61] No contest emerged for the *maiestas* prosecution. L. Lentulus Niger had a strong claim. The Lentuli carried a record of enmity toward Pompey. And Niger's father had been shunted aside by triumviral machinations when competing with Gabinius for the consulship in 59. The younger Niger was bursting for vengeance.[62] Finally–a surprise, according to Cicero–the consul Ap. Claudius Pulcher joined the chorus against Gabinius, hurling accusations of *maiestas* at him in the senate. Defection by the opportunistic Appius provides a good index of the triumvirate's slipping hold on former allies.[63] By mid-October the lineups were set. Gabinius would face a battery of charges and accusers.

The *maiestas* trial came first. The prosecution had a strong prima facie case, revolving about Gabinius' restoration of Ptolemy Auletes. Ptolemy's fate had been the subject of a fearful wrangle in early 56. Senatorial debate and conflict produced a stalemate, hampering especially the ambitions of Pompey the Great. The matter, we may be sure, was discussed at Luca. As a consequence, Gabinius, on Pompey's instructions, carried out the job in early 55.[64] The act directly violated Sulla's *lex de maiestate*, which forbade a Roman governor to leave his province, wage war, or enter another realm without express permission of the senate or the people.[65]

Pompey scurried about desperately to drum up support for Gabinius. He made use of cash and solicited jurors. The *auctoritas* of Pompey was Gabinius'

[61] Cic. *Ad Q. Frat.* 3.1.15, 3.2.1. That Memmius was the eventual prosecutor is clear from Cic. *Pro Rab. Post.* 7, 20–21.

[62] Cic. *Ad Q. Frat.* 3.1.15, 3.4.1; *Ad Att.* 4.18.1. On the elder Niger's rivalry with Gabinius, see Cic. *In Vat.* 25. His son was also accused of a plot against Magnus; Cic. *Ad Att.* 2.24.2. And one may observe that a kinsman, P. Lentulus Spinther, was balked of the task of restoring Ptolemy Auletes, a task later assumed by Gabinius.

[63] Cic. *Ad Q. Frat.* 3.2.3: *qui* [Appius] *quidem mirificus illo die . . . fuit in Gabinium; accusavit maiestatis.* Ap. Claudius did not conduct the prosecution itself, which was left to Lentulus. Probably he confined his attacks to the preliminaries. Dio, 39.60. 2–4, also affirms that Appius worked against Gabinius, in conjunction with his colleague Domitius Ahenobarbus; cf. Cic. *Ad Q. Frat.* 3.2.1.

[64] Sources in Broughton, *MRR,* II:218.

[65] Cic. *In Pis.* 50. Gabinius replied that his act was authorized by law; Cic. *Pro Rab. Post.* 20: *lege etiam id sibi licuisse dicebat.* The *lex* referred to is doubtless Clodius' measure giving Gabinius the province of Syria, with large powers; Broughton, *MRR,* II:193–194. It is highly unlikely, however, that there was any explicit sanction for leaving the province; see Ciaceri, *Processi politici e relazioni internazionali* (Rome, 1918), pp. 227–234.

one chance.[66] As in other key cases of 54, the employment of Cicero as defense counsel would be eminently desirable. Pompey sought to apply pressure–but not too much. The humiliation would have been drastic indeed. No man was more fiercely hated by Cicero than the ex-consul of 58, who had stood by while Clodius worked his will. Cicero's ringing abuse of Gabinius had filled the forum for three years. Only a month before, the orator had inserted another brutal aside against Gabinius at the trial of Plancius.[67] And on Gabinius' initial appearance in the senate after his return, there had been a sharp exchange between them, precipitating a near riot.[68] Some men indeed urged Cicero to take the prosecution; others felt it was a foregone conclusion.[69] The orator was caught in a squeeze. Defending Gabinius was out of the question. But his serving as prosecutor would implacably alienate Pompey, an unwelcome prospect, especially in view of Milo's impending consular candidacy.[70] Cicero chose a middle course. He testified for the prosecution, but avoided vehemence and rancor. Gabinius expressed immense relief and gratitude.[71]

What is one to make of the outcome? Gabinius obtained a narrow acquittal, thirty-eight votes to thirty-two.[72] Cicero was moderate during the trial, but furious at the result. Hysterical comments followed in the letters: the law courts have collapsed, the Republic is no more.[73] But Cicero spoke too soon –and to excess. Reasons for acquittal may be divined. Lentulus Niger, out of excessive zeal or inexperience, botched the prosecution. His *subscriptores* were even worse. That cannot have helped matters.[74] Whether the jury was actually tampered with remains dubious. Pompey had certainly pulled every string available to him. Yet, paradoxically, it was not so much the persuasive power of Pompey as the fear of a potential dictatorship which induced fainthearted jurors to vote acquittal. The image fixed upon the triumvirate by

[66] Cic. *Ad Q. Frat.* 3.2.1: *probe premitur, nisi noster Pompeius, dis hominibusque invitis, negotium everterit; Ad Q. Frat.* 3.3.3: *Pompeius vehemens in iudicibus rogandis;* cf. Dio, 39.55.4–6, 39.60.2–4, 39.62.1–3.

[67] Cic. *Pro Planc.* 86–87.

[68] Cic. *Ad Q. Frat.* 3.2.2.

[69] Cic. *Ad Q. Frat.* 3.4.2–3, 3.6.5.

[70] Cic. *Ad Q. Frat.* 3.1.15: *Pompeius a me valde contendit de reditu in gratiam: Ad Q. Frat.* 3.2.2: *nolo cum Pompeio pugnare; satis est, quod insta* de Milone.*

[71] Cic. *Ad Q. Frat.* 3.4.2–3, 3.9.1; cf. 3.3.3. Dio wrongly states that Cicero prosecuted; 39.62.2.

[72] Cic. *Ad Att.* 4.18.1; *Ad Q. Frat.* 3.4.1. The acquittal is noted also in Cic. *Ad Att.* 4.19.1; *Ad Q. Frat.* 3.9.3; Dio, 39.55.4–5, 39.62.2–3.

[73] E.g., Cic. *Ad Q. Frat.* 3.4.1, 3.9.3.

[74] Cic. *Ad Q. Frat.* 3.4.1: *omnino nihil accusatore Lentulo subscriptoribusque eius infantius: Ad Att.* 4.18.1. Lentulus' poor showing was predictable in advance; Cic. *Ad Q. Frat.* 3.3.3.

their enemies had taken hold–with ironical consequences.[75] One may add also that *maiestas*, as ever, was vague and ambiguous, slippery in definition, difficult to establish. The obstacles were many; but Gabinius' margin was slim. The fact encouraged rather than discouraged his enemies. Public indignation mounted. The prosecutors had marshaled an even more potent dossier on the *repetundae* charge. This time they were not to be turned back.[76]

A defiant signal of what was to come occurred an hour after Gabinius' acquittal on the *maiestas* count. His Greek freedman Antiochus was promptly convicted under the *lex Papia* for illegal arrogation of citizenship. Antiochus himself was a personage of little consequence. But the jurors, enraged at his patron's escape, vented their wrath on the client.[77] That set the stage for full vengeance.

Manifold *repetundae* charges loomed against Gabinius. His activities in Syria, over three years, gave sufficient scope. The governor had returned a wealthy man. Lavish sums, it was said, had been extorted from the provincials. And Roman *publicani* had come to the senate with tales of Gabinius' interference with their activities.[78] Nor was that all. Gabinius, by restoring Ptolemy Auletes, had made himself eligible for an extraordinary financial gain. The king promised ten thousand talents to the man who put him back on the

[75] Cic. *Ad Att.* 4.18.3: *est non nullus odor dictaturae, sermo quidem multus: qui etiam Gabinium apud timidos iudices adiuvit;* also *Ad Q. Frat.* 3.4.1. Cicero reports also that Domitius Calvinus, though an enemy of Pompey's, voted for acquittal–conspicuously. And a certain *praetorius* Cato rushed to bring the first announcement of acquittal to Pompey; *Ad Q. Frat.* 3.4.1. That can hardly be M. Cato, as often assumed. Linderski, *Studi Volterra* (1969), II:281–289, opts for C. Cato, conjecturing a praetorship in 55. But C. Cato was tribune in 56 and still an *adulescens* in 59; Cic. *Ad Q. Frat.* 1.2.15. Perhaps there should be emendation; cf. Shackleton Bailey, *PCPS*, 187 (1961): 3.

[76] Cf. Cic. *Ad Q. Frat.* 3.4.1: *est omnino tam gravi fama hoc iudicium, ut videatur reliquis iudiciis periturus, et maxime de pecuniis repetundis; Ad Att.* 4.18.1; Dio, 39.63.1.

[77] Cic. *Ad Att.* 4.18.4: *absoluto Gabinio stomachantes alii iudices hora post Antiochum Gabinium . . . lege Papia condemnarunt.* Antiochus' comment on the verdict is garbled in a hopelessly corrupt text. There was some reference to the *lex maiestatis*, perhaps a lament that Gabinius' acquittal on that charge redounded unfavorably upon himself; cf. Shackleton Bailey, *Cicero's Letters*, II:223. The inference of Bauman, *Crimen Maiestatis*, pp. 77–79, that cases under the *lex Papia* were heard in the *quaestio maiestatis* is entirely without foundation. Among other things, Bauman ignores the fact that the verdict against Antiochus was delivered on the same day as that of Gabinius' *maiestas* trial. Two cases would not be heard simultaneously by a single court.

[78] Dio, 39.55.5; cf. Cic. *De Prov. Cons.* 9; *Pro Sest.* 93; *In Pis.* 48–50. On the *publicani*, see Cic. *Ad Q. Frat.* 2.13.2, 3.2.2. Ciaceri, *Processi*, pp. 215–222, argues that Dio followed a fabricated tradition and that no extortion against provincials had taken place. Certainly it would not be easy for a governor to offend both the tax gatherers and the provincials. But anything was fair game at a *repetundae* trial. Whether the allegations were true or not, prosecutors would hardly have refrained from raising them in court.

throne. That unsavory affair did not sit well with the Roman populace. Whether Gabinius actually received the cash is doubtful. But the allegations would place his actions within the purview of the *lex Julia repetundarum*. Cæsar's extortion law had adopted a provision from the Sullan *lex de maiestate* with regard to unauthorized foreign invasions by governors. Inclusion of such a clause within a *repetundæ* measure could only have been justified by reference to monetary gain by the offending governor. Hence, though Gabinius was discharged by the *maiestas* court, he could be had up again for the same offense, under the *lex Julia de repetundis*. It was the Egyptian venture which had placed Gabinius in particularly bad odor. And his accusers were pressing that fact once again, this time with reference to the defendant's financial earnings.[79]

Pompey acknowledged the gravity of the situation. Cicero's integrity could be sacrificed. Pompey would not accept a negative response on this occasion. He reminded the orator pointedly of past obligations and arranged a shamefaced reconciliation; Cicero duly appeared for the defense. Criticism of Cicero's turnabout reached fervid proportions; and his apologia was weak indeed.[80] The triumvirs staked their prestige on this case. Pompey delivered a speech to the assembled populace on Gabinius' behalf, and Cæsar dispatched a letter from Gaul to the same purpose. Envoys from Alexandria heeded Pompey's summons to provide testimony for the defense.[81] Gabinius pled that his Egyptian adventure was in the interests of state; depositions from Pompey, Auletes, and the Alexandrines maintained that he received no funds except for military purposes.[82] It was all futile. The jurors proved unyielding this time: Gabinius sustained conviction and ignominy. He sought refuge in exile.[83]

[79] On the *lex Julia*, see Cic. *In Pis.* 50; cf. Zumpt, *Criminalrecht*, II:2.317–319. Ciaceri, *Processi*, pp. 227–230, believes that the law concerned only moneys taken from provincials. But that is refuted by Gabinius' case itself, which Ciaceri must weakly label an "exception." It is doubtful that Gabinius ever received the 10,000 talents. The prosecutor refers only to the king's "promise"; Cic. *Pro Rab. Post.* 21; cf. Dio, 39.56.3; Plut. *Ant.* 3.2; rightly, Ciaceri, *Processi*, p. 217. The *litis æstimatio* assessed 10,000 talents against Gabinius; Cic. *Pro Rab. Post.* 30; Schol. Bob. 177, Stangl. But even sale of Gabinius' goods did not realize that amount; Cic. *Pro Rab. Post.* 8, 37.

[80] Cic. *Pro Rab. Post.* 19: *quem* [Gabinius] *enim ex tantis inimicitiis receptum in gratiam summo studio defenderim, hunc adflictum violare non debeo; quocum me si ante Cn. Pompei auctoritas in gratiam non reduxisset, nunc iam ipsius fortuna reduceret; Pro Rab. Post.* 33; Dio, 39.63.2–5; Val. Max. 4.2.4; Quint. *Inst. Orat.* 11.1.73.

[81] Cic. *Pro Rab. Post.* 31–33; Dio, 39.63.1–5.

[82] Cic. *Pro Rab. Post.* 20, 34–36.

[83] Cic. *Pro Rab. Post.* 20, 38; Dio, 39.55.5–6, 39.63.1–5; Val. Max. 8.1.abs.3; Schol. Bob. 177, Stangl. Appian, *BC*, 2.24, wrongly puts the conviction and exile in 52; cf. Appian, *Syr.* 51. Zumpt, *Criminalrecht*, II:2.336–337, accepts the statement and postulates yet another trial and conviction of Gabinius. The theory has not found other advocates.

The case provided a dramatic culmination of the political trials in 54 and exposed burgeoning resentment against the dynasts. The umbrella of triumviral patronage served to protect other defendants. And Gabinius himself had eluded condemnation in the *maiestas* court–but no more. The *maiestas* acquittal had produced stormy protest; the jurors themselves barely escaped violence.[84] And when M. Cicero was then pulled in as defense counsel, the machinations of Pompey had become intolerable. The move boomeranged badly. Cicero encountered torrents of abuse. The hypocrisy and sham of his posture alienated public opinion irrevocably. Rome was not prepared to submit to the dictates of a particular clique.[85] The conviction of Gabinius was worth several acquittals of lesser men.

The trial had an immediate corollary. Enemies of the triumvirate, having gained the advantage, capitalized on it. An assessment of ten thousand talents was fixed against Gabinius. That was the sum allegedly promised him by Ptolemy Auletes. But the state could not realize it, even after sale of Gabinius' worldly possessions. The attack moved elsewhere. Another clause of the *lex Julia repetundarum* was exploited: *quo ea pecunia pervenerit.* Accusers maintained that Gabinius had turned over funds to C. Rabirius Postumus. And Rabirius now faced trial.[86]

Rabirius Postumus was notorious and vulnerable. A businessman of fabulous wealth, he earned repute as a shrewd financial speculator, with international holdings of staggering extent. Rabirius manipulated private and public enterprises; foreign states, provinces, and kings were beholden to him. Among other transactions, he stood in the center of the most infamous financial affair of the period. When Ptolemy Auletes sought Roman recognition and reinstatement to his throne, he delivered or pledged vast sums to the triumvirs. The bulk of the money came as a loan from Rabirius Postumus. It seemed a sound investment. Ptolemy obtained his kingdom again in 55, with the cooperation of Gabinius and his *patroni.* But the debt had to be repaid. Auletes found a novel way. Rabirius Postumus was made financial minister of Egypt itself. He would recover what was owed by fleecing the subjects of the king.[87]

[84] Dio, 39.63.1.

[85] Ciaceri, *Processi,* pp. 222–226, rightly sees politics as the determining element in the outcome. But he may stress too much the effect of the *publicani*'s resentment upon jurors of their class, *equites* and *tribuni ærarii.* Those groups did not always vote together anyway. Ciaceri suggests also that Cicero's speech was defeatist and reluctant. To be sure, Dio has Fufius Calenus say later that Cicero defended Gabinius in such a way as to get him condemned; 46.8.1. But at the time Cicero asserted that his defense was delivered with the utmost zeal; *Pro Rab. Post.* 19: *summo studio defenderim;* cf. Val. Max. 4.2.4. Cicero's appearance alone was enough to provoke rage–and enthusiasm for the prosecution; Dio, 39.63.5.

[86] Cic. *Pro Rab. Post.* 8–12.

[87] Cic. *Pro Rab. Post.* 1–7, 28. On Rabirius, irrefutably identified with the Cæsarian Curtius Postumus, see H. Dessau, *Hermes,* 46 (1911): 613–620.

The venture was not an altogether happy one. Resentment among the Egyptian populace against their monarch was transferred to his minister. A national uproar ensued; Rabirius suffered imprisonment and humiliation, and had to flee for his life to Rome.[88] Enemies of the triumvirate could now tap the widespread indignation against that arrogant financier.[89]

The hearing formed an appendage to the conviction of Gabinius: the same accuser, defense counsel, and *iudices.*[90] And once again, the prestige of the triumvirs was at stake. Pompeius Magnus had arranged the original loan from Rabirius to Auletes. And Rabirius was an old friend of Julius Cæsar, who sustained and protected him after his ignominious flight from Alexandria. Cicero rightly complains that the attack on Rabirius was part of the continuing campaign to undermine the position of Cæsar.[91]

The accusers, as was customary, threw in every possible item to evoke prejudice against the defendant. They called attention to various financial dealings, included Rabirius in a general indictment of public corruption, alleged that he had goaded Gabinius into restoring Ptolemy, brought up his exactions in Egypt, asserted that he had raised money for himself over and above the original loan, and even mocked his foppish affectation of Egyptian manners. The Alexandrine envoys themselves, who had testified for Gabinius, were willing to turn against Rabirius Postumus in court.[92] All of those insinuations were, of course, immaterial to the case in point, that is, Rabirius' receipt of moneys from Gabinius. And Cicero has no difficulty in demonstrating their irrelevance.[93] But the orator too indulged in special pleading. He conjoined the cases of Gabinius and Rabirius Postumus, thereby producing the impression that both were charged on the same count. It was a clever artifice. The *lex Julia repetundarum,* like earlier extortion laws, did not hold *equites* liable for prosecution. Hence, Cicero argues, Rabirius is immune, and the accusers have no business bringing him to court. It formed the central portion of his case.[94] But the claim was fallacious. *Equites*, to be sure, could not

[88] Cic. *Pro Rab. Post.* 22, 39.

[89] Cf. Cic. *Pro Rab. Post.* 40: *sermo illius temporis . . . tum subinvisum apud malivolos Postumi nomen, propter opinionem pecuniæ nescio quam æstatem unam, non pluris, auris refersit istis sermonibus.*

[90] Cic. *Pro Rab. Post.* 8: *est enim hæc causa, quo ea pecunia pervenerit, quasi quædam appendicula causæ iudicatæ atque damnatæ.* Cicero again spoke for the defense, Memmius was prosecutor, and the jurors remained in place; Cic. *Pro Rab. Post.* 7, 10.

[91] Cic. *Pro Rab. Post.* 44: *videtis hos quasi sumptos dies ad labefactandam illius dignitatem.* For Cæsar's friendship and patronage of Rabirius, see Cic. *Pro Rab. Post.* 41–43, 48; on Pompey's involvement, *Pro Rab. Post.* 6.

[92] Cic. *Pro Rab. Post.* 6, 19, 22, 25, 30–36, 39–40..

[93] See the intelligent account of Ciaceri, *Processi*, pp. 203–214. That the Alexandrines could testify for Gabinius and against Rabirius involved no contradiction; cf. Ciaceri, *Processi*, pp. 211–213.

[94] Cic. *Pro Rab. Post.* 12–19.

be charged *de repetundis*. But that restriction did not apply to the relevant clause in Cæsar's law: *quo ea pecunia pervenerit.* It was for the recovery of money that Rabirius was brought before the bench.[95]

What was the result of the hearing? Moderns have generally assumed an acquittal. But the grounds for that assumption are weak and unpersuasive. The influence of Cæsar, it is asserted, must have sufficed to save his client. And Rabirius turns up again in 49, evidently not a condemned exile.[96] But reference to Cæsar's *gratia* is of small account. If the triumvirs were unable to save Gabinius, they would hardly have been more persuasive in Rabirius' behalf. As for Rabirius' status in 49, it does not affect the argument. His trial concerned the recovery of cash assessed against Gabinius. There is nothing to show that conviction under that clause carried a penalty of exile.[97] In the political atmosphere of October 54, Rabirius Postumus had little chance to escape. The same jurors who condemned A. Gabinius would not likely have spared his despised collaborator. Opposition to the triumvirate had made effective use of the *iudicia.*

For two solid years, following the trial of Cornelius Balbus, judicial attacks upon adherents of the syndicate had been steady and unceasing. Thirteen men identifiable as *amici* or *clientes* of the triumvirs faced prosecution within that space of time. There may have been more. Most were acquitted, but the triumvirs could not reckon the results as successes. Public exposure of their less savory tactics and undue pressures provoked growing resentment and alienation. Open abuse of their leadership swelled in vehemence. Pompey was defiantly lacerated at the trial of Scribonius Libo. Cæsar came in for attack at Vatinius' trial. And the consular actions of Pompey and Crassus were under heavy fire during at least half a dozen prosecutions in 54. Their reluctant agents, notably M. Cicero, suffered vitriolic opprobrium. The momentum of the opposition built with increasing force and culminated in the convictions of Gabinius, Antiochus, and Rabirius Postumus.

[95] That is clear, despite Cicero's disclaimer, from Cic. *Pro Rab. Post.* 12: *Qua lege? "Iulia de pecuniis repetundis." Quo de reo? "De equite Romano." At iste ordo lege ea non tenetur. "Immo illo," iste, "capite, quo ea pecunia pervenerit."*

[96] Cic. *Ad Att.* 9.2a.3, 9.3.2, 9.5.1, 9.6.2; *Ad Fam.* 2.16.7. The case is argued by Dessau, *Hermes,* 46 (1911): 613–620, followed, e.g., by Drumann-Groebe, *Geschichte Roms,* VI:70, n.7; vonder Mühll, *RE,* 1A(1): 27–28, "Rabirius," n.6; Gelzer, *Cicero,* p. 204. Ciaceri does not find Dessau's arguments convincing, but nonetheless believes in Rabirius' acquittal; *Processi,* p. 214; *Cicerone,* II:138.

[97] Cf. Cic. *Pro Rab. Post.* 46: *etiam optat miser ut condemnetur a vobis; ita bona veneant, ut solidum suum cuique solvatur; nihil iam aliud nisi fidem curat; nec vos huic . . . quicquam præterea potestis eripere.* Cicero's dramatic plea, at the close of his speech, *Pro Rab. Post.* 48, is conventional rhetoric. Cf. Quint. *Inst. Orat.* 4.1.46: *nam se quoque moveri interim finget, ut pro Rabirio Postumo Cicero.* Suet. *Claud.* 16, in fact, reports that Rabirius was convicted, though he wrongly ascribes it to a *maiestas* charge.

The conference of Luca proved to be a mighty catalyst. Some may have feared that it provided the alliance of Cæsar, Pompey, and Crassus with a power base which could render their adversaries impotent. In fact, it stimulated a stronger and more determined resistance. Public opinion could be a priceless ally; the opponents of the triumvirate mobilized it with consummate skill. The dynasts were induced to draw in their horns. The electoral fiasco of early 55 was not repeated. Candidates of the syndicate sustained firm rejection in subsequent years; their influence in senatorial circles suffered correspondingly. Pompey and Crassus made haste to demonstrate good faith by sponsoring legislation on electoral bribery and violence. Their public image remained a prime consideration. The trials of 55 and 54 were carefully calculated to tarnish that image.

THE CASE OF M. ÆMILIUS SCAURUS

Political combat between the triumvirs and their antagonists after Luca casts other matters in the shade. Few prosecutions outside that context even survive on record. But the scrappy available testimony discloses that private hostilities still kept the *iudicia* busy. Whatever the change in political issues or climate, long-standing practices died hard.

Some examples may be registered. Bitterness between M. Cælius Rufus and the family of Clodius is illustrative. A brief notice informs us that the *gens Clodia* prepared a new charge against Cælius in 54. Servius Pola was instructed to bring the accusation–a man characterized as loathsome in appearance and barbaric in manner. His relative had been among the Clodiani convicted in 56.[98] Nothing more is heard of the affair. It may never have come to court. A brief mention, in passing, reports the conviction of a certain M. Fulvius Nobilior in the autumn of 54. But we have no further data.[99]

The bewildering electoral scramble of 54 also produced prosecutions. Again the clash of individual ambitions supplied the principal element. That was customary in the mutual hurling of *ambitus* charges among rival candidates. But other factors may have supervened. The triumvirs had backed certain hopefuls in that campaign, M. Scaurus and C. Memmius. Their competitors were Domitius Calvinus and M. Messalla. Scandalous deals and flagrant outlays

[98] Cic. *Ad Q. Frat.* 2.13.2: *vereor ne homo teter et ferus, Pola Servius, ad accusationem veniat: nam noster Cælius valde oppugnatur a gente Clodia.* On the Servius condemned in 56, see Cic. *Ad Q. Frat.* 2.4.6.

[99] Cic. *Ad Att.* 4.18.3; perhaps a relative of the *eques* named among Catiline's supporters; Sallust, *Cat.* 17.3. One other possible trial is hinted at in 54; Cic. *Ad Att.* 4.15.6. But reference to *Fontei causa* does not necessarily imply a criminal prosecution, and the context of the statement rather tells against it.

of cash, however, confused the picture. All four candidates were indicted *de ambitu*. Pompey and Cæsar, unfortunate in their choices, had drawn back. But the residue of their political struggles in 54 may have had some impact on the personnel engaged in the accusations. Domitius Calvinus was arraigned by his fellow candidate C. Memmius, who had the endorsement of Pompey and Cæsar. Messalla's defense counsel was Hortensius, his prosecutor Q. Pompeius Rufus, a political adherent of Pompey's. Two men competed for the right to accuse Pompey's relative M. Scaurus: P. Valerius Triarius, a close friend of Cato and his family, and young L. Cæsar, a man who did not follow the politics of the Cæsares. The accuser of Memmius, Q. Acutius, a high-minded and learned youth, is not otherwise identifiable.[100] As usual, political conflict and personal ambitions were intertwined. But the former ought not to be excessively stressed here. Pompey and Cæsar had already expressed disappointment in the maneuvers of their candidates. Cicero felt free to encourage all four contenders, and eventually offered his services as defense counsel to Valerius Messalla.[101] Disorder and confusion, in any event, produced lengthy delay. None of the trials was brought to conclusion before 52. It is best to regard them as the conventional consequence of heated electoral rivalry and the aristocratic drive for office.

Electoral rivalry underlay another trial in the late summer of 54. *Res repetundæ* was the charge; but the consular *comitia* were the prize. M. Æmilius Scaurus returned from a governorship of Sardinia, with an eye on the chief magistracy. His father before him had held it—and much else besides. The elder Scaurus had been censor and *princeps senatus*, the most powerful figure in the senate for two decades. His son inherited not only a handsome financial estate but a vast network of connections. Scaurus had a packet of political promissory notes. And he was prepared to reclaim the debts. A voting populace harbored fond memories of his father and also of Scaurus' own generosity.[102] Stepson of Sulla the dictator, former officer and *adfinis* of Pompey the Great, M. Scaurus carried impressive credentials. Weakness of character and objectionable personal habits would not have slowed his advance.[103] But there was a larger obstacle: a prosecution *de repetundis*, instituted prior to the elections.

Ap. Claudius Pulcher arranged the affair. Familial interests provided initial

[100] The personnel in the trials is given by Cic. *Ad Att.* 4.17.5; *Ad Q. Frat.* 3.2.3, 3.9.3; cf. *Ad Att.* 4.18.3. On the electoral campaign, see Gruen, *Hommages Renard* (1969), pp. 311–321, and above, chap. 4.

[101] Cic. *Ad Q. Frat.* 3.1.16, 3.3.2.

[102] Cic. *Ad Att.* 4.16.6: *ædilitas eius memoriam non ingratam et est pondus apud rusticos in patris memoria.*

[103] On Scaurus, see above, p. 148.

impetus: Appius' brother, C. Claudius, coveted the consulship. Only one patrician could succeed at the polls; hence, it was smart politics to damage Scaurus' prospects, even better to eliminate him altogether with a conviction. That accounts for the inception of the case.[104] There was a change shortly thereafter. C. Claudius withdrew his candidacy, preferring a longer tenure as governor of Asia–or, perhaps, prorogued by political foes in the senate.[105] But Ap. Claudius did not lose interest in the case. That devious manipulator concocted a scheme in collusion with two other candidates, Memmius and Domitius Calvinus. Their election would guarantee a proconsular command desired by Appius.[106] Accordingly, he pressed ahead with the case, to sabotage Scaurus' candidacy. Young prosecutors, of small repute but eager, were readily found: P. Valerius Triarius, L. Marius, Q. and M. Pacuvius. Triarius was a gifted and industrious orator, a friend of M. Cato's and the son of a former legate under L. Lucullus. He kept faith with the Sardinian victims of M. Scaurus; Sardinia had once been governed by Triarius' father. The Pacuvii brothers were clients of Ap. Claudius; so perhaps was L. Marius.[107] They cooperated dutifully. The prosecution received an allotment of thirty days to collect evidence in Sardinia. But the privilege was waived. The *accusatores* would brook no delay; their purpose was to bring Scaurus to court before the consular elections, else the whole trial would lose its political force.[108] No one could be deceived on that point. The prosecution's goal of influencing the electoral assembly was an open secret.[109]

M. Scaurus was prepared–more than prepared. His defense bench included a most extraordinary array of names. No other trial in the Republic evoked the participation of so many distinguished and diverse individuals. Six men delivered formal speeches for the defense; that in itself was a most unusual

[104] Cic. *Pro Scauro,* 31–37; Schol. Ambros. 275, Stangl.

[105] Cic. *Pro Scauro,* 35.

[106] Cic. *Ad Att.* 4.17.2; see Gruen, *Hommages Renard* (1969), pp. 315–318.

[107] Asconius, 18–19, Clark. Asconius notes that the Pacuvii bore the *cognomen Claudii.* Some have emended to *Caldi,* unnecessarily. A kinsman of L. Marius' had been tribune in 62, cooperating at that time with M. Cato; Val. Max. 2.8.1. And Cato was thought to be unsympathetic to Scaurus' case; Asconius, 19, Clark. But, as presiding officer at the trial, he maintained a scrupulous neutrality; Asconius, 20, 29, Clark; Val. Max. 3.6.7.

[108] Asconius recognizes the motivation, 19, Clark: *cuius rei hanc causam reddebant, quod interea comitia consularia.* Cicero suggests other reasons in his defense speech; *Pro Scauro,* 23–28. But he puts his finger on the principal aim in a private letter; *Ad Att.* 4.15.9: *fortasse accedent etiam consules designati; in quibus si Scaurus non fuerit, in hoc iudicio valde laborabit.* Despite Shackleton Bailey, *Cicero's Letters,* II:212, there is nothing in that passage to suggest that *consules designati* were immune from prosecution; rather the reverse. On the question of immunity for magistrates-elect, see now Weinrib, *Phoenix,* 25 (1971): 145–150.

[109] Cic. *Pro Scauro,* 30: *quod occultum tamen non erat, non esse hoc iudicium iudicii, sed comitiorum consularium causa comparatum.*

practice. Four of them were at the top of the oratorical profession: M. Cicero, Q. Hortensius, M. Calidius, and M. Marcellus. In addition, no fewer than nine ex-consuls uttered testimony to Scaurus' character, including even the ancient M. Perperna, a miracle of longevity, consul thirty-eight years before, who outlived all his contemporaries.[110] As if that were not enough, special pleas came to the jurors, with tears and lamentations, from men of the younger generation, aristocrats and *novi homines*, up to ten in number.[111] How does one explain so imposing a lineup?

Customary political analyses will not do. Pompey came to the aid of Scaurus, his former legate and brother-in-law. But some of Pompey's most intransigent foes also stood with the defense: Servilius Isauricus, Æmilius Paullus Lepidus, Lentulus Niger. Other anomalous combinations presented themselves. P. Clodius delivered a long-winded speech for Scaurus. And at his side were his implacable enemies, M. Cicero and T. Annius Milo.[112] No other occasion, before or after, saw those individuals in league. Apart from the young men who pleaded for Scaurus, there appeared several senior statesmen for whom this was the sole recorded appearance as judicial advocates: Perperna, Servilius Isauricus, L. Volcacius Tullus, L. Piso, L. Philippus. It was a remarkable assemblage. Obviously the case did not have the political connotations of other prosecutions in 54. The triumvirs and their adversaries had temporarily suspended their contest.[113]

Partial explanation may be found in the widespread net of M. Scaurus' connections. A number of the men who spoke for the defense were his relatives. Among the younger pleaders, M'. Acilius Glabrio and C. Memmius were both nephews of Scaurus. Milo had recently become his brother-in-law. Pompey himself had once been wed to another sister of Scaurus'; the general's children were half-brothers to Scaurus' son. And Scaurus' own half-brother, Faustus Sulla, was most active in his cause, engaging in violent scuffles before the trial and heartrending appeals during it.[114] The influence of Pompeius Magnus,

[110] On Perperna's longevity, see Val. Max. 8.13.4; Pliny, *NH*, 7.156; Dio, 41.14.5.

[111] The names are given by Asconius, 20, 28, Clark. They constitute twenty-three individuals in all, in addition to Scaurus himself, who also pled on his own behalf.

[112] On Clodius' speech, see Cic. *Pro Scauro*, 37: *qui multa dixit*.

[113] Ciaceri, *Cicerone*, II:112–127, tries mightily to read political connotations into the case. For him, Cæsar and Pompey backed Ap. Claudius in his prosecution; enemies of the triumvirate supported Scaurus. The analysis makes no sense and is contradicted by the evidence. Ciaceri does not know what to make of Clodius, who, in his view, must now have abandoned the dynasts once again. The hypothesis is, in any case, refuted by Pompey's overt testimony for Scaurus. Meier, *Res Pub.*, p. 18, sees the trial as evidence for the basic unanimity of the Roman ruling class. That will not help. In the year 54, as we have seen, the case of Scaurus was exceptional, not typical.

[114] On all this, see Asconius, 19–20, 28, Clark.

who had endorsed Scaurus for the consulship, may account for some of the individuals on the defense bench. M. Cicero had yielded to Pompeian pressure before. Clodius and C. Cato had attached themselves to Pompey after Luca. His request perhaps underlies their collaboration with Cicero. Cato had recently been acquitted at his own trial, having had the support of Scaurus.[115] And one may observe other associations, of longer standing. The defendant's mother had been married in turn to Rome's most formidable senators, M. Scaurus, the *princeps senatus*, and L. Sulla, who inherited Scaurus' mantle upon his death in 89. Many men owed *beneficia* to Scaurus the elder, many more to Sulla the dictator. Some of them, or their sons, turn up among supporters of the defendant in 54: P. Servilius Isauricus, Q. Hortensius, Q. Metellus Nepos, M. Messalla Niger, L. Marcius Philippus, L. Calpurnius Piso.[116]

But links to an earlier generation do not provide complete satisfaction. The fluidity of Roman politics, noted so often, would have softened their impact.[117] The motives of certain advocates remain unexplained—for example, M. Marcellus and L. Paullus, future consuls of 51 and 50, and the obscure youths L. Æmilius Burca and M. Lænas Curtianus. For some others, the ties to Scaurus the elder or to the Sullan dictatorship were tenuous and distant. A quarter-century had elapsed since Sulla's death, another decade since Scaurus' death. In Roman politics that was a long interval indeed. Ap. Claudius, the consul of 79, had been restored to public life by Sulla. Yet his two sons were on opposing sides in the case of M. Scaurus. And what could induce

[115] Asconius, 18, Clark. One can add that personal friction developed between the brothers Clodius and Ap. Claudius, which may illuminate their appearance on opposite sides at Scaurus' trial; Cic. *Pro Mil.* 75.

[116] Servilius was Sulla's choice for the consulship of 79. Hortensius had close links from his youth to the circle of the Metelli, in which both Scaurus and Sulla played central roles. The family of Metellus Nepos, of course, belongs in this company as well. Messalla's sister became Sulla's bride in the dictator's declining years; Plut. *Sulla,* 35.1–3. The father of L. Philippus, a shrewd and devious politician, had moved to Sulla's side in the civil war and served as his legate; Livy, *Per.* 86. As for L. Piso, he could recall an occasion when his grandfather had been defended *de repetundis* by M. Scaurus the elder; Cic. *De Orat.* 2.265. Two of the younger supporters of Scaurus in 54, P. Lentulus and C. Peducæus, may also fit in this category, though the associations are more tenuous. A certain P. Lentulus was assassinated by the enemies of Sulla in 87; Appian, *BC,* 1.72. And a Sex. Peducæus obtained the prætorship in the last year of Sulla's life; Broughton, *MRR,* II:92, n.2.

[117] E. Courtney, *Philologus,* 105 (1961): 151–156, sees the entire trial as a throwback to the struggles between Marius and Sulla in the previous generation, though he misses most of the important connections. That the defendant could count on some contacts made by his father and stepfather is doubtless true. But to read the trial solely in terms of the past is excessive. The evidence will not support it. L. Paullus Lepidus defended Scaurus; his father had led a revolt against the Sullan system. The venerable M. Perperna, another supporter of Scaurus, had been no friend of Sulla and the Metelli in his prime. And M. Marcellus' ancestor had been a legate of Marius himself.

the tottering M. Perperna, now in his nineties, to emerge from retirement and bear witness for Scaurus?

Perhaps enlightenment may come through a fresh approach. In July, when Scaurus was first indicted, Cicero remarked that there was very little sympathy for the cause. The orator expected considerable difficulty in the defense.[118] Prosecutors assembled damaging evidence. They included character assassination, as was customary: allegations of poisoning in Sardinia and of unbridled lust culminating in suicide by a lady whose virtue was compromised.[119] More to the point were charges of extortionate activities in the province. Numerous Sardinians attested to those depredations. Cicero's only response was a conventional one, employed also in other *repetundae* cases, a disparaging of Sardinian national character: most Sardinians are liars and their evidence is accordingly worthless.[120] Resort to that line discloses the weakness of the defense case. Scaurus' guilt was plain.[121] Yet between July and September virtually the whole Roman *nobilitas* rallied around the defendant. And the verdict provided a thunderous vindication: sixty of sixty-eight votes were for acquittal.[122]

Only an extraordinary cause could have brought together so many individuals of such varied political attitudes. Perhaps anxiety about the consequences produced this hybrid assemblage. Scaurus had offered his candidacy for the consulship. The motives of the prosecutors were transparent. By rushing through a *repetundae* accusation before the election, they could cancel Scaurus' ambitions. The same had been done to Catiline in 66 and 65. And it is noteworthy that at his trial *de repetundis*, Catiline could also summon the support of numerous distinguished *consulares*, a fact which turned an almost certain conviction into an acquittal.[123] Not that the aristocracy was necessarily concerned with the personal fate of Scaurus, much less with his election. After the triumphant acquittal, Scaurus' backers swiftly melted away and he encountered sound defeat at the elections. The trial alone brought a unanimity in the ruling class. One will not ascribe that solely to Scaurus' associations, and certainly not to his character. Fear of a dangerous precedent may have been more telling.

Ambitus prosecutions among rival competitors were traditional and relatively

[118] Cic. *Ad Att.* 4.16.6: *Scaurum Triarius reum fecit; si quaeris, nulla est magnopere commota* **συμπάθεια**; also *Ad Att.* 4.15.9; cf. *Ad Q. Frat.* 2.16.3.

[119] Cic. *Pro Scauro,* 1–13.

[120] Cic. *Pro Scauro,* 14–20, 38–45.

[121] Val. Max. 8.1.10: *M. quoque Aemilius Scaurus repetundarum reus adeo perditam et conploratam defensionem in iudicium attulit.*

[122] Asconius, 28, Clark. The acquittal is noted also in Cic. *Ad Att.* 4.17.4–5; *Ad Q. Frat.* 3.1.16; Val. Max. 8.1.10.

[123] Cic. *Ad Att.* 1.1.1; *Pro Sulla,* 81.

harmless. They generally took place after the electoral *comitia* or even after the term of office. But accusation on other charges, designed to knock a candidate out of the race even before the voting, would have more serious consequences. What happened to Scaurus could happen to any aristocrat. The *nobilitas* jealously guarded access to high magisterial posts. If political trials were to interfere with the competition for office, it would severely cramp the style of potential candidates. Better to keep criminal accusations entirely apart from electoral campaigns. That issue brought the ruling class out in full force against the prosecutors of M. Scaurus. It helps to explain the unusual gathering which made that case in every regard exceptional.[124]

IMPLEMENTATION OF THE *Leges Pompeiae*

The furious succession of trials in 54 had left even Cicero breathless and the Roman public exhausted.[125] Some relief from the courts would be welcome. The judicial battles had served their political purpose: a salient challenge to the position of the triumvirate. A lull set in thereafter. Even the scandalous electoral campaign, which stretched well into the year 53 and produced indictments of all candidates, did not issue in actual prosecutions for some time to come. Perhaps the solidity of aristocratic opinion, so dramatically manifested at Scaurus' trial, had put a damper on further accusations, even those *de ambitu*. The year 53, notably, is devoid of recorded prosecutions.

A new set of events altered the picture. Milo's explosive canvass for the consulship evoked an unprecedented level of violence and turmoil in late 53 and early 52. The situation passed the point of Roman tolerance. The murder of Clodius in January 52, urban riots, and the burning of the senate house finally engendered vigorous reaction. It culminated, as we have seen, in the sole consulship of Pompeius Magnus, with the blessing of senatorial conservatives. Pompey took his "law and order" role most seriously. A series of firm judicial measures took hold–to suppress lawlessness and to reestablish governmental authority.[126] There followed a lengthy sequence of criminal trials, under the new legislation, beginning in April of 52. Pompey was determined to cleanse the city of the disruptive elements that had produced the chaos

[124] An immediate sequel was organized to drive the point home. Cicero urged that the unsuccessful *accusatores* be charged with calumnious prosecution. But enough was enough. The prætor M. Cato conducted the hearing, and his *consilium* absolved the prosecutors: Triarius unanimously, the Pacuvii with but ten dissenting votes, and Marius with but three; Asconius, 29, Clark.

[125] Cf. Cic. *Ad Q. Frat.* 2.16.1: *sic enim habeto, numquam me a causis et iudiciis districtiorem fuisse.*

[126] On the electoral campaign, see above, chap. 4; on Pompey's laws in 52, see above, chap. 6.

of recent months. Unlike the cases of previous years, these prosecutions took the form of a state campaign against the authors of public disorder.

The principal malefactor, of course, was T. Annius Milo. His had been the most brutal and unscrupulous canvass, and his was the chief responsibility for Clodius' assassination. Against Milo, Pompey directed most of his energies. Milo had once been the general's most effective ally. But his enterprise had exceeded the bounds of acceptability. Pompey had grown cool after Luca and, to all intents and purposes, had renounced his friendship in subsequent years.[127] As a showcase for his new judicial structure, the general had decided to make an example of Milo. Pompey conspicuously poisoned public opinion against the defendant. He professed fear for his life, remained in his gardens with an armed guard, and alleged that Milo was plotting his murder.[128] No one could be uncertain about the consul's intentions. Milo was to be prosecuted under the new *lex Pompeia de vi*, in a *quæstio extraordinaria* designed for the occasion–with Milo specifically in mind. The *quæsitor* and jurors were Pompeian nominees. Although Pompey himself was officially neutral, it was common knowledge that he hoped for a conviction.[129] Lest there be any doubt about the display of state power, Pompey had the courtroom surrounded with armed soldiers. Cicero, of course, maintained that it was done to prevent interference by the frenzied mobs of Clodiani. And there may be truth to that. Pompey would brook no disruption of proceedings from whatever source. But the effect–perhaps the intent–was also to overawe the defense.[130]

There was no dearth of eager prosecutors. The charge of violence referred particularly to the bloody clash in January and the slaying of P. Clodius. The family and friends of Clodius sought satisfaction. Two young men named Ap. Claudius were the principal *accusatores*, both nephews of Clodius, sons of his brother C. Claudius. Youth did not stand in their way. They conducted a vigorous prosecution.[131] Clodius' widow, Fulvia, was there also, and his

[127] Cf. Cic. *Ad Q. Frat.* 3.8.6.

[128] Cic. *Pro Mil.* 64–68; Asconius, 36, Clark: *timebat autem Pompeius Milonem seu timere se simulabat;* also 38, 50–52, Clark.

[129] Cicero does his best to evade that embarrassing fact, but his own evidence puts it out of doubt; Cic. *Ad Fam.* 3.10.10: *qua denique ille facilitate, qua humanitate tulit contentionem meam pro Milone adversante interdum actionibus suis;* cf. *Pro Mil.* 1–2, 15, 21, 22, 65–71. See also Vell. Pat. 2.47.4: *Milonem reum non magis invidia facti quam Pompei damnavit voluntas;* and Schol. Bob. 112, Stangl: *Pompeius obnixe studens in damnationem Milonis;* cf. Schol. Bob. 125, Stangl; Schol. Gronov. 323, Stangl.

[130] Cic. *Ad Fam.* 3.10.10; *Pro Mil.* 1–3, 71; Asconius, 30, 38, 40, 41–42; Hirtius, *BG,* 8.52; Quint. *Inst. Orat.* 4.2.25; Dio, 40.53.2–3, 40.54.2–4; Plut. *Cic.* 35.1–4; Suet. *Iul.* 30; Schol. Bob. 112, 124, Stangl; Schol. Gronov. 323, Stangl.

[131] Cic. *Pro Mil.* 59; Asconius, 34, 38, 39, 41, and esp. 54, Clark: *damnatum autem opera maxime Appi Claudi pronuntiatum est.* The younger of the two was evidently adopted by his uncle Ap. Claudius Pulcher; hence the *prænomen.*

mother-in-law, Sempronia, to move the jurors with tearful testimony.[132] *Subscriptores* included two obscure personages, P. Valerius Nepos and P. Valerius Leo, as well as a more interesting figure, the future triumvir M. Antonius. Antonius' relations with Clodius had fluctuated–not surprisingly, in view of the latter's vagaries. But, after Clodius' death, he was prepared to take his part. A former cavalry officer under Gabinius and soon to join Cæsar in Gaul, Antonius may have been acting in the interests of the triumvirs–and certainly in his own. Joining with those *accusatores* was L. Herennius Balbus, formerly a prosecutor of Cælius in 56, also with the connivance of Clodius. His family had close connections with the slain politician.[133] In addition, hostile testimony came from C. Causinius Schola, an old friend of Clodius' from Interamna; C. Clodius, perhaps a freedman from Clodius' household; and Q. Arrius, presumably the former henchman of M. Crassus.[134]

More important than the actual participants in the trial loomed the attitude of public officials. The stage was carefully set and the fury of the populace sufficiently aroused to guarantee conviction even before the case itself was heard. We have noted already the machinations of Pompeius Magnus, the sole consul and head of government. Three tribunes of 52 collaborated with him, friends and supporters of Clodius: Q. Pompeius Rufus, T. Munatius Plancus, and C. Sallustius Crispus. They were clamorous and inflammatory. Their public harangues and violent speeches were aimed not only at Milo but at his proponent M. Cicero. Cicero himself endured threats of prosecution and exile. Clodius' tactics were used to good effect after his death. The state's representatives had turned popular sympathies decisively against T. Annius Milo.[135]

The clear-cut character of the case did not prevent it from becoming a partisan issue. The sole consulship of Pompey, authorized by a motion of Bibulus and Cato, should no longer be seen as a moratorium on previous political wars, designed to effect coalition against Julius Cæsar.[136] Milo's trial

[132] Asconius, 40, Clark.

[133] For the *subscriptores*, see Asconius, 34, 41, Clark. Cicero speaks of a close friendship between Antonius and Clodius in 58; *Phil.* 2.48. But there was friction later, and a violent scuffle; Cic. *Pro Mil.* 40; *Phil.* 2.21, 2.49; cf. Dio, 40.45.2. Another link associated them. Antonius was eventually to marry Clodius' widow Fulvia. On relations among Antonius, Clodius, and Fulvia, see C. L. Babcock, *AJP*, 86 (1965): 1–32. There is no reason to doubt that the M. Antonius who prosecuted Milo is the future triumvir; cf. Clark, *Cic. Pro Mil.*, 106. On L. Herennius Balbus, see above, chap. 7, n.175.

[134] Cic. *Pro Mil.* 46; Asconius, 40, Clark. On Arrius, see above, chap. 2, n.113.

[135] Asconius, 37–38, 40, 42, 49, 50–51, 52, Clark; Dio, 40.49.1–2; Schol. Bob. 115, Stangl; cf. Cic. *Pro Mil.* 12, 45; Appian, *BC*, 2.21.

[136] The view appears again in the most recent works; e.g., D. C. Earl, *Historia*, 15 (1966): 310–311, who gives no indication of the abundant evidence on Milo's trial. Also, E. Wistrand, *Sallust on Judicial Murders in Rome* (Göteborg, 1968), pp. 5–55.

gives the lie to that analysis. The Catonian faction looked upon Pompey as a necessary but temporary evil, a policeman to curb disorder, but not a political ally. They welcomed the strict legislation (though even in that respect there were objections to certain clauses and procedures). But they were not prepared to engage in witch-hunts against Pompeian *inimici*. Pompey's relentless campaign to eliminate Milo met with resistance.

Cicero was Milo's chief counsel. Past obligations dictated that posture.[137] Milo's role in effecting the orator's recall from exile could not be forgotten, nor their intimate collaboration in the political trials of 56. It was not a happy choice for Cicero, especially in the face of Pompey's grim soldiers. But considerable assistance came from the friends and allies of M. Cato. His circle was committed to thwarting the aims of Pompey. Order having been restored in the city, the Catonian group returned to the partisan activities of 54.

Cato himself delivered a strong speech in the *curia* after Clodius' death, condoning the actions of Milo. At the trial he was open in his sympathies for Milo and supported the cause of his defenders.[138] Cato, in fact, sat on the bench of *iudices*; it was taken for granted that he would cast his vote for acquittal.[139] Cato's bosom companion M. Favonius bore witness before the court that Milo's deed was a justifiable act of self-defense. Cicero relied heavily upon his information.[140] The powerful rhetoric of Q. Hortensius, Cato's brother-in-law, was also enlisted on Milo's behalf: a few words only, but his presence alone would be effective.[141] Finally, there was Cato's nephew, the brilliant young intellectual M. Brutus. Though Brutus did not himself speak at Milo's trial, he advised Cicero on the defense, and shortly thereafter composed his own *Pro Milone* for publication and dissemination.[142]

Other impressive figures worked on Milo's behalf: Faustus Sulla, Milo's brother-in-law, spoke for the defense, thereby defying Pompey as did the accomplished orator M. Calidius. And M. Marcellus, who had supported Milo in 56, did so again in 52, with great skill, especially effective in cross-examining prosecution witnesses. Marcellus would reach the consulship in the following year and pursue political conflict with Pompey.[143] Milo also enjoyed assistance

[137] Cic. *Ad Att.* 9.7.3: *beneficium sequor . . . non causam, ut in Milone.*

[138] Cic. *Ad Fam.* 15.4.12: *cuius* [Clodius] *etiam interitum . . . Milonis causa in senatu defendenda, approbaris;* Asconius, 34, 53–54, Clark.

[139] Asconius, 53–54, Clark; Vell. Pat. 2.47.5; cf. Cic. *Pro Mil.* 26, 44.

[140] Cic. *Pro Mil.* 26, 44; Asconius, 54, Clark.

[141] Asconius, 34, Clark; Schol. Bob. 117, Stangl.

[142] Asconius, 41, Clark; Schol. Bob. 112, Stangl; Quint. *Inst. Orat.* 3.6.93, 10.1.23, 10.5.20.

[143] Asconius, 34, 39, 40, Clark. For Marcellus' earlier defense of Milo, see Cic. *Ad Q. Frat.* 2.3.1.

from two tribunes, Manilius Cumanus and M. Cælius Rufus, who endeavored to checkmate Clodius' friends in the college. Cælius even staged an elaborate pretense with Milo, in the hopes of having charges promptly dismissed before they came to a formal hearing.[144] Of Manilius Cumanus no further information survives. But the colorful M. Cælius performed as was expected. He had not forgotten the efforts of the Clodian *gens* to convict him in 56 and 54. More recently, he had objected, in vituperative language, to Pompey's *quæstio extraordinaria*, restrained only by the general's show of force.[145] There had been senatorial agreement on Pompey's appointment as sole consul, but no unanimity beyond that. The trial of Milo exemplified "politics as usual."

It was not easy to devise a strategy for the defense. The slaying of Clodius by Milo's retainers, under instructions from their chief, was well known and thoroughly witnessed. Milo entered no plea of innocence: the deed was admitted.[146] Brutus urged Cicero to take the line that Clodius' death was in the interests of the state. But that would be risky and double-edged. Cicero preferred to argue the case as one of self-defense: it was Clodius, not Milo, who planned the ambush; the defendant simply reacted out of protective instincts.[147] How well that approach would sit with the jurors is uncertain. Powerful elements strained in the opposite direction. Popular passions had already turned against Milo. A healthy portion of senatorial opinion must also have been ranged against a man responsible for so much tumult. And the ring of Pompeian soldiers, in full view of the proceedings, considerably dampened the spirit of the defense. Cicero avers, in the published version of his speech, that he would not be put off by the menacing presence of armed men around the courtroom. His ingratiating commentator, Asconius, adds that Cicero was undeterred by popular hostility, Pompeian displeasure, or open show of force.[148] But even Asconius must admit that the orator spoke with something less than his customary force.[149] Later authors supply a more vivid portrait: Cicero was dumbfounded with fear and anguish; he was barely able to utter a few trembling phrases and yielded the floor in a hurry.[150] Copies of that abortive talk circulated in antiquity. But Cicero,

[144] Asconius, 34, 37, Clark; Appian, *BC*, 2.22.

[145] Asconius, 36, Clark: *et cum pertinacius leges Cælius vituperaret, eo processit iræ Pompeius ut diceret, si coactus esset, armis se rem publicam defensurum.*

[146] Cic. *Pro Mil.* 7, 15, 23, 57, 81.

[147] Cic. *Pro Mil.* 24-56. Of course, Cicero does not fail to add, at least in the published speech, that Clodius' death was, in fact, in the public interest; *Pro Mil.* 72-91. On Brutus' line of defense, see above, n.142.

[148] Cic. *Pro Mil.* 1-3; Asconius, 38, Clark.

[149] Asconius, 42, Clark: *non ea qua solitus erat constantia dixit.*

[150] Dio, 40.54.2; Plut. *Cic.* 35.2-4; Schol. Bob. 112, Stangl: *nam metu consternatus et ipse Tullius pedem rettulit.*

shortly after the trial, wrote up a new speech of appreciably greater power and conviction. It was never delivered, but stands today among his finest literary works.[151] Under the circumstances of enmity and intimidation, there need be no surprise that Milo was decisively convicted. To Milo in his retreat at Massilia Cicero later sent a copy of his speech composed after the fact. Milo responded with a bitter quip: had the spoken oration been as compelling, he might never have enjoyed the mullets of Massilia.[152]

The conviction and exile of Milo did not suffice for Pompey's purposes; he sought a telling demonstration that the electoral practices of 53 and 52 would not be tolerated again in Rome. On that score he was at one with the senatorial aristocracy. Milo, *in absentia*, faced three further indictments: *de ambitu, de sodaliciis,* and *de vi.* The last came under the *lex Plautia*, for Milo had already been convicted under Pompey's special *lex de vi.* They would, of course, be of no practical effect; Milo had already vacated the city. But the aim was to discourage definitively any further violators. It offered a fresh opportunity for young men to address the bar, even though no defense would be forthcoming. The two Appii Claudii came forth once more as *accusatores* in the *ambitus* hearing; L. Cornificius and C. Ateius had apparently been turned away at the *divinatio.*[153] P. Valerius Leo, who had assisted at the initial prosecution, emerged again as a *subscriptor*, as did a certain Cn. Domitius.[154] P. Fulvius Neratus, a man of considerable learning, served as *accusator* in the

[151] Asconius, 42, Clark; Dio, 40.54.2–3; Schol. Bob. 112, Stangl; Quint. *Inst. Orat.* 4.2.25, 4.3.17, 9.2.54, 11.3.47; cf. Cic. *De Opt. Gen. Orat.* 10. Ciaceri, *Cicerone*, II:149–157, believes that the published and delivered speeches did not differ substantially in content. That is not buttressed by Asconius, 42, Clark: *scripsit vero hanc quam legimus ita perfecte ut iure prima haberi possit.* On the *Pro Milone* generally, one may consult the valuable and informative edition of Clark, *Cic. Pro Mil., passim.* The discussion by Husband, *CW*, 8 (1915): 146–150, 156–159, is faulty and unreliable.

[152] Dio, 40.54.3–4. The vote for conviction was thirty-eight to thirteen; Asconius, 53, Clark. The conviction is recorded also in Dio, 40.53.2, 40.54.1; Plut. *Cic.* 35.4; Vell. Pat. 2.47.4; Appian, *BC*, 2.24; Livy, *Per.* 107.

[153] Asconius, 38–39, Clark; cf. Clark, *Cic. Pro Mil.*, 103–104. The manuscripts give C. Ceteius; emendation to Ateius is plausible. A C. Ateius Capito was tribune in 55 and an outspoken opponent of the triumvirs; Broughton, *MRR*, II:216. Whether the two are identical cannot be established. The tribune of 55 later became a firm friend of Julius Cæsar's; Cic. *Ad Fam.* 13.29.6. L. Cornificius is similarly unidentifiable–perhaps the later consul of 35; cf. Syme, *Historia*, 4 (1955), 60–61. The Cornificii were also adherents of Cæsar; see Shackleton Bailey, *CQ*, 10 (1960): 263.

[154] Asconius, 54, Clark. Domitius may be the man who later served as cavalry officer under Cæsar in 49; Cæs. *BC*, 2.42.3. He is not likely to have been an Ahenobarbus, despite Münzer, *RE*, 5:1317, "Domitius," n.11. Perhaps a son of Domitius Calvinus, consul in 53. The elder Calvinus had moved toward Pompey in 54; Cic. *Ad Q. Frat.* 3.4.1. He was later with Cæsar in the civil war; Broughton, *MRR*, II:227. It appears that Cæsarian partisans, as well as friends of Pompey, were engaged in the attack on Milo.

trial *de sodaliciis.* And L. Cornificius, rejected in the *ambitus* case, returned to prosecute Milo *de vi.*[155] Obviously, there was no lack of men eager for an easy killing. The results, of course, could be easily forecast. Jurors returned condemnatory verdicts on all counts. The friends of Cato had picked a poor battleground on which to challenge Pompey. Popular sentiment had abandoned those responsible for lawlessness and disruption. Milo's conviction was to be an *exemplum.* Few lamented his departure.

A corollary followed directly upon the heels of Milo's exile. M. Saufeius had commanded Milo's armed bands at the climactic battle in which Clodius lost his life. He was now charged twice *de vi,* once under Pompey's law and once under the *lex Plautia.* Saufeius himself was a figure of small consequence. Nor should political implications be read into the case. Nothing suggests that Pompey showed any interest in it, much less that his principal adversaries were concerned. The explanation is simpler. In the wake of Milo's conviction, the captain of his bodyguard seemed a logical target. He supplied yet another occasion for eager novices to display their wares in the courtroom. Saufeius would appear an even easier victim than his patron. Three *accusatores* spoke on the first count, three others on the second. They were all young or obscure individuals, hoping for some public prestige.[156] The case proved to be more difficult than was expected. Cicero appeared for the defense in both trials. With him in the first case was M. Cælius, again resisting the vengeance of the Clodiani, and in the second M. Terentius Varro Gibba, a young *eques* who was a pupil and an admirer of Cicero's.[157] The orator's motive need not have been continued loyalty to the friends of Milo. Cicero had personal associations with the family of M. Saufeius.[158] With formidable

[155] Asconius, 54, Clark. On Fulvius Neratus, see Cic. *Pro Flacco,* 46. Cornificius' *subscriptor* was the obscure and otherwise unknown Q. Patulcius. Clark, *Cic. Pro Mil.,* 117, has no warrant for stating that the trial *de vi* came under Sulla's *lex de sicariis.*

[156] The accusers were L. Cassius, L. Fulcinius, and C. Valerius under the *lex Pompeia,* C. Fidius, Cn. Aponius, and M. Seius under the *lex Plautia;* Asconius, 54–55, Clark. Of these, only L. Cassius may be of some prominence. He is customarily identified with the future tribune of 44, brother of Cæsar's assassin; perhaps also the L. Cassius who was *subscriptor* to the prosecution of Plancius in 54; Cic. *Pro Planc.* 58. Even here, however, certainty is impossible. The other prosecutors were *novi homines* and unknowns. Information survives only on M. Seius, perhaps the *eques* and businessman who cultivated friendships with influential figures, such as Ap. Claudius, D. Junius Brutus, Terentius Varro, and Atticus; Münzer, *RE,* 2A(2):1121–1122, "Seius," n.4. A connection with Ap. Claudius may help explain interest in prosecuting Milo's client.

[157] Asconius, 55, Clark. On Terentius, see esp. Cic. *Ad Fam.* 13.10. He is not to be confused with the great scholar and polymath Terentius Varro, from whom, at a critical moment, he was at pains to distinguish himself; Dio, 47.11.3–4.

[158] Cf. Cic. *Ad Att.* 1.3.1, 2.8.1, 4.6.1, 6.1.10, 6.9.4. There may be a connection also between Cælius and the Saufeii; *CIL,* 14.2624; cf. Münzer, *RE,* 2A(1):257, "Saufeius," n.6.

defense counsel, Saufeius escaped the fate of Annius Milo. The margin of a single vote earned him acquittal on the first count, a rather larger difference on the second.[159] Pompey evidently did not exert pressure.

The pressure moved in the opposite direction. Milo was not the only man responsible for the convulsions of recent months. Clodius' murder had triggered even greater disturbances, climaxed by the burning of the senate house. Senatorial action and Pompeian legislation in early 52 took those deeds very much into consideration. Milo had been a necessary sacrifice. But that involved no rise in Clodius' stock. Acquittal of Milo's lieutenant Saufeius, despite obvious guilt, was due, so it was said, to lingering hatred for the memory of Clodius.[160] And now the judicial processes turned decisively against the Clodiani. Saufeius' counterpart on the other side, the notorious Sex. Clœlius, found that his slippery fortunes had at last run out. The ringleader of Clodius' satellites, Clœlius had incited the mobs which set the *curia* ablaze.[161] He had narrowly eluded condemnation on a charge *de vi* in 56. But under the tighter and more stringent *lex Pompeia* in 52, the state exacted its penalty: Clœlius was condemned by an overwhelming vote.[162] The remainder of Clodius' minions suffered a similar fate. Asconius reports a series of prosecutions and convictions.[163] The *leges Pompeiæ* were geared to stamp out lawlessness of whatever political origin. Their application was systematic and relentless. Pompey had exerted his energies especially against Milo. That was to be the model. He left the initiative to others thereafter. But he would not have barred the way to attacks on Sex. Clœlius and his associates. The general had no reason to protect the *epigoni* of Clodius.

The attacks broadened, however, and in such a way as to provoke discomfort for Pompey. Among the men active in the previous electoral campaign were Pompeian friends and supporters. Some of them, in rendering opposition to Milo, had themselves engaged in dubious and disruptive machinations. They too were eminently vulnerable. The Catonian group and other *inimici* of Pompey had committed a tactical error in seeking to thwart the general through defense of Milo. A more promising approach now offered itself. By prosecuting allies of Pompey under his own laws, they could steal his thunder and usurp his role as defender of public order. Pompey confronted

[159] Asconius, 55, Clark.

[160] Asconius, 55, Clark: *manifestumque odium Clodi saluti Saufeio fuit, cum eius vel peior causa quam Milonis fuisset.*

[161] Cic. *Pro Mil.* 33, 90: *qui mortuus uno ex suis satellitibus Sex. Clœlius duce curiam incenderit.*

[162] Asconius, 55–56, Clark: *magno consensu damnatus est.* The accusers were again obscure figures, C. Cæsennius Philo and M. Alfidius, the defense counsel even more obscure, T. Flacconius.

[163] Asconius, 56, Clark: *multi præterea et præsentes et cum citati non respondissent damnati sunt, ex quibus maxima pars fuit Clodianorum.*

the awkward predicament of either sacrificing his friends or abandoning his cultivated image.

Milo had had two principal challengers for the consulship of 52. P. Plautius Hypsæus and Q. Metellus Scipio combined in a forceful campaign to obstruct Milo and to capture the chief magistracies for themselves. Their methods, however, were little better than Milo's own. Extensive bribery and deployment of armed retainers featured in the canvassing on both sides. Plautius and Metellus shared responsibility for the chaos which brought on senatorial reaction and the *senatus consultum ultimum*.[164] In 52 they would have to answer for their actions. Both men were indicted under the new *lex Pompeia de ambitu*. That posed a perplexing dilemma for Pompeius Magnus. Plautius Hypsæus was a longtime friend and the man for whom Pompey himself had ardently campaigned. Metellus Scipio had recently become the general's father-in-law. His own legislation was being pressed into service against his partisans. The enemies of Pompey had shrewdly resumed the political initiative.

Pompey faced a troublesome choice. He attempted to hedge his bets. The new alliance with Metellus Scipio was too valuable to forgo. It gave the general a foothold in the ruling class, an area where his support had progressively eroded. The fact was brought home once again by Metellus' prosecutor, C. Memmius, an *adfinis* of Pompey and previously his choice for a consulship in 54, but now irrevocably hostile.[165] The backing of Metellus Scipio, with his glittering pedigree and substantial connections, would give Pompey a standing in the senate that he had long coveted. The general determined to intervene. There were pleas to the jurors, even the adoption of mourning posture, so it is reported. Those may be embellishments. An easier way was found. Pompey put an end to his solitary position as consul; he named Metellus Scipio as his colleague in August to fill out the rest of the year. The maneuver entailed judicial immunity and a dropping of the charges.[166] That saved Metellus but earned Pompey considerable ill will: "author and subvertor of his own laws."[167]

[164] On the electoral campaign, see above, chap. 4.

[165] The prosecutor is given by Appian, *BC,* 2.24. Dio, 40.53.2, states that there were two *accusatores,* but gives no names.

[166] Dio, 40.51.2–3, 40.53.1–2, tells the most sober and plausible story. Val. Max. 9.5.3 adds that Pompey importuned the jurors; Plut. *Pomp.* 55.4 even has him invite the entire body of 360 *iudices* to his home, whence they left in the company of the defendant. Appian, *BC,* 2.24, gives the putting-on of mourning, not only by Pompey but even by certain jurors, thereby inducing Memmius to give up the case. The embellishments are dubious. Metellus' appointment to the consulship foreclosed any proceedings.

[167] Tac. *Ann.* 3.28: *suarumque legum auctor idem ac subversor;* also Plut. *Pomp.* 55.4: πάλιν οὖν ἤκουε κακῶς.

The attempt on Metellus Scipio had misfired, but not without a propaganda victory. Pompey's reputation suffered. He could not afford further loss of public esteem: Plautius Hypsæus had to be sacrificed. The defendant looked to Pompey for assistance, but Pompey looked the other way. He severed their long-standing connection. Plautius demeaned himself to the point of groveling at his patron's feet—to no avail. Pompey's brusque reply ended all hopes: "You are spoiling my dinner!" Plautius was shortly thereafter condemned *de ambitu*.[168] Pompey's effort to have it both ways, however, did not sit well with his constituents. Heavily criticized, on the one hand, for having gotten Metellus Scipio off, he was now attacked for abandoning an old friend.[169]

The *inimici* of Pompey did not forfeit their advantage. Criminal proceedings followed against two boisterous and demagogic tribunes of 52, T. Munatius Plancus Bursa and Q. Pompeius Rufus. Both men had cooperated with Pompey in efforts to block Milo's election, both had conducted noisy harangues before and during Milo's trial, and both had joined in the clamor that led to destruction of the senate house.[170] Pompeius Rufus was Clodius' most intimate friend, Plancus his imitator.[171] They were logical targets for a prosecution *de vi*, no doubt—for added effect—under Pompey's *lex de vi*. Trials would have to await the expiry of their tribunates. They proceeded shortly thereafter, in early 51.[172]

The groups that had failed in their defense of Milo combined once again, this time to prosecute the men who had harassed him. Pompeius Rufus was accused by M. Cælius, the foe of Clodius and Pompey, who had defended both Milo and Saufeius. Cælius had encouragement, we may be sure, from the Catonian faction. Pompeius Rufus, in addition to attacking Milo, had arrogantly thrown M. Favonius into jail on some trifling pretext.[173] Retaliation was not long delayed. As for Plancus Bursa, his *accusator* was M. Cicero himself, on one of the very rare occasions in which Cicero stood on the

[168] On Pompey's scornful rebuff, see Val. Max. 9.5.3; Plut. *Pomp.* 55.6. The conviction is noted also by Dio, 40.53.1; Appian, *BC,* 2.24.

[169] Cf. Plut. *Pomp.* 55.6.

[170] Sources in Broughton, *MRR,* II:235–236.

[171] Asconius, 50, Clark; Cic. *Ad Fam.* 7.2.3.

[172] Dio, 40.55.1: ἐπειδὴ πρῶτον ἐκ τῆς ἀρχῆς ἐξῆλθον. Clark, *Cic. Pro Mil.,* 129–133, places the trials in mid-52, in conjunction with those of Milo, Plautius, and Metellus Scipio. But Plutarch's statement, *Pomp.* 55.6, that Plancus' case preceded that of Plautius, is surely an error. Plutarch is not noted for chronological accuracy. Clark's theory requires a tribunate running from mid-53 to mid-52, an extraordinary exception which would surely have been noted in the sources. One should point out also that Pompey was unable to appear in person at Plancus' trial and sent a written deposition instead. That is strong indication that he was proconsul, rather than consul. Hence, the trials are almost certainly in early 51.

[173] Dio, 40.45.4. On Cælius as Pompeius Rufus' prosecutor, see Val. Max. 4.2.7.

prosecution's side of a case. The orator had a personal score to settle with Plancus, whom he had once defended and who repaid the kindness by assaulting his patron and threatening him with legal action during the tumults of 52. Cicero's hatred for Plancus, so he remarked, surpassed even that for Clodius.[174] Support for the accusation came also from the *boni*, including especially the friends of Cato. Cato himself was there as a juror, throwing out of court depositions in favor of the defendant.[175] And one further item completes the picture. The relatives of Milo's lieutenant M. Saufeius rejoiced in Cicero's onslaught on Plancus Bursa.[176] The assemblage of men pressing for conviction of the two tribunes is solid and consistent. Former defenders of Milo and Saufeius had now taken the offensive. As Cicero noted, his prosecution would convert the fall of Milo into a triumph.[177]

Pompey found himself once more in a quandary. His legislative measures were being exploited to bring to justice his own adherents. Having wavered in the trials of the consular candidates, he wavered again in the cases of the ex-tribunes. He offered no assistance to Pompeius Rufus. Rufus was reduced to appeals to his mother, Cornelia, the daughter of Sulla—without success. The jury returned a verdict of guilty.[178] But Pompey did work energetically to obtain acquittal for Munatius Plancus Bursa. He could not compromise his *fides* further and witness the elimination of his partisans, one by one. The general composed an elaborate eulogy and entreaty on Plancus' behalf, dispatching it to be read at court. It was that written testimony which Cato ruled inadmissible, ostentatiously stopping up his ears when an attempt was made to introduce it. Pompey had landed himself in a dilemma again. As proconsul, he could not appear in person. To honor his obligations to Plancus he had to send his *laudatio* in writing. But a *laudatio* violated the provisions of his own measure, which forbade written depositions. Cato made good use of that contradiction to turn the jury against the defendant.[179] Another verdict of condemnation was announced. It was an overt and stinging rebuff to Pompeius Magnus.[180]

[174] Cic. *Ad Fam.* 7.2.3: *oderam multo peius hunc quam illum ipsum Clodium; illum enim oppugnaram, hunc defenderam;* Asconius, 38, Clark. Plut. *Cic.* 25.1 contains, perhaps, another reference to that earlier defense of Plancus. Cicero may also have assisted in the case against Pompeius Rufus. Rufus, in any event, was a bitter enemy, later suspected of plotting Cicero's murder; Cic. *Ad Fam.* 8.1.5.

[175] See Cic. *Ad Fam.* 7.2.2: *tantum studium bonorum in me exstitisse;* on Cato's actions, see Val. Max. 6.2.5; Plut. *Pomp.* 55.5–6; *Cato,* 48.4; Dio, 40.55.2.

[176] Cic. *Ad Att.* 6.1.10.

[177] Cic. *Ad Fam.* 7.2.2: *gloria potius amici quam calamitate.*

[178] Val. Max. 4.2.7; Dio, 40.55.1, 40.55.3; cf. Cic. *Ad Fam.* 8.1.5.

[179] Val. Max. 6.2.5; Plut. *Pomp.* 55.5–6; *Cato.* 48.4; Dio, 40.55.2.

[180] Cic. *Ad Fam.* 7.2.2–3: *In primisque me delectavit, tantum studium bonorum in me exstitisse*

In no other known case was Pompey able or willing to protect malefactors, even when they had acted in his interests. The way was clear for a determined and relentless governmental campaign against the transgressors. The new Pompeian legislation *de ambitu* had a retroactive clause. And it was applied with strictness. Prosecutions under that and other measures crowded the courts and received considerable publicity. The sources report a plethora of cases, which filled the docket and kept advocates constantly on the run. Orators like Cicero and Hortensius were called upon almost daily to plead before the bar for some litigant or other.[181]

Details survive for only a few instances. So, for example, the consular candidates for 53, who had engaged in shameless bribery and manipulations, were at last brought to book. M. Scaurus, who had had a multitude of defenders in 54, was practically deserted in 52. Cicero, it seems, still came to his aid–but without effect. Pompey, who had once been his patron and advocate, now turned his back. When popular clamor rose for Scaurus, Pompeian troops dispersed the crowd in order to let the court work its will. Scaurus was condemned and withdrew to ignominious exile.[182] With him fell another consular candidate of 54, C. Memmius. Memmius too had once been backed by Pompey. Political estrangement followed after 54; the general would certainly not have come to the aid of that individual.[183] Messalla Rufus was the next victim. Unlike Scaurus and Memmius, Messalla had been a successful contender for the consulship of 53–not, however, without elaborate expenditure of cash and dubious deals. Implementation of his indictment encountered

---

contra incredibilem contentionem clarissimi et potentissimi viri . . . Numquam ulli fortiores cives fuerunt quam qui ausi sunt eum contra tantas opes eius, a quo ipsi lecti iudices erant, condemnare. The rebuff of Pompey is noted also by Dio, 40.55.3–4; Plut. *Pomp.* 55.6; cf. Cic. *Phil.* 6.10, 13.27. Earl, *Historia,* 15 (1966): 310–311, suggests that Pompey and the *boni* had entered into a bargain: Pompey was willing to sacrifice Plancus and Pompeius Rufus in return for the conviction of Milo. That is decisively refuted not only by Pompey's ardent plea for Plancus, but by the remarkable assemblage of defenders for Milo, notably from the faction of Cato. The complexities and crosscurrents involved in the trials of 52 vitiate the attempt of Wistrand, *Judicial Murders,* pp. 5–55, to see them all as a conscious campaign by Pompey and the Catonians to crush Cæsarian adherents and intimidate Cæsar. Wistrand, unfortunately, neglects to examine the cases themselves and relies instead on the obviously tendentious, if not spurious, statement of Ps. Sallust, *Ep. ad Cæs.* 2.3.3. Of course, Cæsar later, after outbreak of the civil war, took advantage of the situation to advocate restoration of the exiles; Cæs. *BC,* 3.1; Cic. *Ad Att.* 7.11.1, 9.14.2, 10.4.8, 10.8.2, 10.13.1, 10.14.3. And he did eventually have them recalled; Cic. *Phil.* 2.56; Appian, *BC,* 2.48; Dio, 41.36.2. But Cæsar's attitude had been very different in 52; cf. Appian, *BC,* 2.25.

[181] Cic. *Brutus,* 324; *Ad Fam.* 7.2.4; Asconius, 56, Clark; Cæs. *BC,* 3.1; Dio, 40.52.1, 40.55.1; Plut. *Cato,* 48.4–5; Appian, *BC,* 2.24; cf. Cic. *Brutus,* 243: *iudicialis annus.*

[182] Appian, *BC,* 2.24; Cic. *De Off.* 1.138. On Cicero's defense, cf. Quint. *Inst. Orat.* 4.1.69.

[183] Appian, *BC,* 2.24; cf. Cic. *Ad Fam.* 13.1.1.

lengthy delays; but the trial came to fruition in 51. Messalla, endorsed by the enemies of Pompey, proved a more difficult target. A poignant speech by his uncle Q. Hortensius and active support from M. Cælius brought him an acquittal *de ambitu*. It was only temporary reprieve. The verdict did not find favor, which surprised even Messalla's defense counsel. Compliant jurors were roundly criticized; Hortensius himself was hissed in public, the first such occasion in his long and distinguished career.[184] A second arraignment of Messalla followed, under the *lex Licinia de sodaliciis*. There was no escape this time: he sustained conviction and banishment.[185] Offenders against the law were not to elude justice, whatever their politics.

The sources record still another case under the *lex Pompeia*: an indictment of Cicero's old client P. Sestius, with the orator again as defense counsel. Action against him may have been *de ambitu*, perhaps deriving from a campaign for the prætorship.[186] And a final instance warrants mention. T. Fadius, a former quæstor of Cicero's, suffered judicial condemnation in 52. There is no indication of the charge. But one may note that Cicero ascribes the verdict, by one vote, to the influence of a "certain someone"–Pompeius Magnus, no doubt. Pompey, it seems, was now enforcing rigid application of his laws.[187] Criminal prosecutions in 52 were burdensome for the advocates but salutary for the *res publica*. The government and its *iudices* had reestablished control.

Pompeian legislation proved eminently effective. Many of the men who participated in and contributed to the anarchic conditions of previous months had now been brought to justice. In that fact Pompey could take pride. The judicial system possessed a more solid footing. The worst effects of internal dissension had been alleviated. But the political aspect of these events deserves reiteration. The opportunities to play politics were not overlooked. Once the crisis passed, divisions reappeared–as they did so often. The courts were again

[184] The fullest account, such as it is, is in Cæl. *Ad Fam.* 8.2.1; also Cic. *Ad Att.* 5.12.2; *Brutus*, 328; Val. Max. 5.9.2.

[185] Cæl. *Ad Fam.* 8.4.1. A fourth candidate in 54, Domitius Calvinus, had also been indicted *de ambitu;* Cic. *Ad Att.* 4.17.5, 4.18.3; *Ad Q. Frat.* 3.2.3, 3.3.2. No further word exists on resumption of that case.

[186] Cic. *Ad Att.* 13.49.1; *Ad Fam.* 7.24.2. Shackleton Bailey's suggestion, *Cicero's Letters*, V:392, that it was a revival of the earlier *ambitus* charge of 56, is less likely; cf. Cic. *Ad Q. Frat.* 2.3.5. Appian, *BC*, 2.24, records the conviction *de ambitu* of a certain Σέξστος. But Sestius, it seems, was acquitted. He served as a provincial governor in 49; Broughton, *MRR*, II:264. Appian's notice may be an inadvertent reference to Sex. Clœlius, who was, of course, convicted in 52, though on a different charge.

[187] Cic. *Ad Fam.* 5.18.1-2: *potentiæ alicuius condonatum*. On the name T. Fadius, not T. Fadius Gallus, see Shackleton Bailey, *CR*, 12 (1962): 195-196. He had been Cicero's quæstor in 63; Cic. *P. Red. in Sen.* 21; and an advocate of his recall in 57; Cic. *Ad Q. Frat.* 1.4.3; *Ad Att.* 3.23.4.

utilized by Pompey's senatorial adversaries to remove his clients and to expose his own inner contradictions. These were not mere pinpricks designed to discomfit the general. By demonstrating the continued strength and influence of his adversaries they guaranteed that Pompey would not use his sole consulship as a springboard for personal ascendancy.

THE TENACITY OF CONVENTION

Only two years elapsed between these events and the outbreak of civil war. It is tempting to see breakdown and collapse, the abandonment of customary procedures, the gloomy specter of armed strife. Better, however, to let the evidence speak for itself. It tells a very different story. Firm reassertion of order and stability in 52 would have provoked optimism rather than despair. Strict and detailed legislative enactments had strengthened the hand of the government. Stern penalties had been exacted against ringleaders and agents of disruption. Pompeius Magnus had served his turn, checking upheaval and restoring normal process. And even he could not protect adherents who had engaged in turmoil. Pompey stepped down at the close of his official term. It could now be assumed that the chaos of late 53 and early 52 would not be repeated. The mood in immediately subsequent years reflects that public confidence. As we have seen, electoral contests were untroubled, and candidates and victors were very much as expected. The same character of normality applies to criminal prosecutions in 51 and 50. There were no extraordinary confrontations that presaged civil war, and no overturning of regular routines. The trials involved conventional and familiar matters: rivalries for office, personal feuds, clashes between individuals and *gentes* for *dignitas* and *gloria*.

In the consular elections for 50, C. Marcellus gained one of the posts. A disappointed rival, the orator M. Calidius, promptly put him on trial for electoral corruption. None would have found that operation surprising. Calidius' family did not carry the ancient prestige of the Marcelli. His hope lay in reversal of the voting results—through use of forensic talent. It was a common tactic. Even more common was its failure. Calidius' repute stood high as a courtroom speaker, and he was much in demand by litigants of all political persuasions. But in his own behalf he proved weak and ineffective. There was too much at stake personally.[188] Calidius himself faced prosecution *de ambitu*. The consular seat, of course, was no longer at issue here. The defendant had already been rejected at the polls. But personal *inimici* saw an opening to obtain satisfaction. The brothers Gallii undertook the accusation. They recalled with rancor Calidius' prosecution of Q. Gallius thirteen years

[188] Cæl. *Ad Fam.* 8.9.2, 8.9.5.

before. It was judicial retaliation, a standard feature in Roman politics.[189] There were, no doubt, numerous instances of like character, for which the sources have not vouchsafed details. Note, for example, the conviction of a certain Servæus, elected to the tribunate in 51 but promptly thereafter prosecuted and cheated of office.[190] Of similar import was the judicial battle in the same year between C. Sempronius Rufus and M. Tuccius. Tuccius initiated the matter with a prosecution. Sempronius, a politician and businessman of dubious repute, returned the favor, bringing a charge *de vi* against his *accusator*. The attempt backfired. Sempronius was himself condemned, amidst much applause, on grounds of calumnious prosecution.[191] Men like Servæus, Tuccius, and Sempronius were small-time politicians of little weight, practically unknown. That their judicial contests should hold the stage in 51 is eloquent documentation for the continuity of routine politics. Obviously, fear of cataclysm did not absorb Roman attentions even in the last months of the Republic.[192]

The trials of the Claudii attracted considerable interest in 51 and 50. They too belong in the category of conventional political warfare. That family of arrogant time-servers provoked a large array of *inimici*. The death of P. Clodius removed their most conspicuous and obnoxious member. Focus shifted to his two patrician brothers. C. Claudius Pulcher served as proconsul of Asia in the later 50s, Ap. Claudius as proconsul of Cilicia. Neither had conducted a model governorship. Both were haled into court upon their return to the city. Their unorthodox careers had not spared them prosecution.

C. Claudius confronted a charge *de repetundis* in 51. With characteristic impudence, he expected to manipulate events. A brazen effort to corrupt the jury marked his defense preparations. It was a sad miscalculation. The court found Claudius guilty and added a heavy assessment of damages, which his holdings proved insufficient to cover. The defendant departed to exile and disgrace. The case continued, however, to the further ignominy of C. Claudius. Recovery of money due the state was insisted on. The burden shifted

[189] Cæl. *Ad Fam.* 8.4.1, 8.9.5. On the trial in 64, see above, chap. 7, n.33. Calidius evidently escaped conviction. He was more convincing as defender than as prosecutor; Cæl. *Ad Fam.* 8.9.5.

[190] Cæl. *Ad Fam.* 8.4.2.

[191] Cæl. *Ad Fam.* 8.8.1. Cælius spoke for the prosecution, bringing up all of Sempronius' shady transactions of the past. On Sempronius, see Münzer, *RE*, 2A(2):1436–1437, "Sempronius," n.79.

[192] Cicero, to be sure, reproves Cælius for reporting only trivialities, and asks for information on more important matters. But the more important matters are only those which concern himself; Cic. *Ad Fam.* 2.8.1: *ne illa quidem curo mihi scribas, quæ maximis in rebus reipublicæ geruntur cotidie, nisi quid ad me pertinebit.*

to M. Servilius, who was arraigned as recipient of Claudius' excess gains. The intricacies of the complex proceedings that followed need not detain us. Servilius not only was required to yield funds obtained from Claudius but sustained an extortion charge himself. Several other individuals became involved. An inexperienced prætor misunderstood the legal niceties; and the affair dragged into multiple hearings. Among the prosecutors was Q. Pilius Celer, a man more accomplished in speech than in intelligence, an *adfinis* of Atticus and recently returned from service with Cæsar in Gaul. More striking was the testimony of young Ap. Claudius, son of the convicted governor of Asia. Appius denounced Servilius and even contended for the prosecution. Servilius, it seems, had been C. Claudius' intermediary in his attempted corruption of the jury. With a keen eye for gain, he had pocketed much of the cash himself. Through audacious and shameless pronouncements, Ap. Claudius disclosed all the details, including his father's own felonious machinations. A fitting climax capped the events: young Appius was himself indicted *de repetundis* by the Servilii and *de vi* by his own agent. The entire affair reflected sharp discredit upon the *gens Claudia*, a fact suitably exploited by their rivals.[193]

Ap. Claudius Pulcher, elder brother of Publius and Gaius, was next to come under fire. The devious politician had constructed and shed alliances with dizzying frequency throughout his career. With his own brother P. Clodius there was alternate cooperation and conflict. Appius moved toward the triumvirate after Luca and then harassed them during his consulship in 54. He utilized marital links with other noble houses when they were profitable, discarded them when they were inconvenient. Double-dealing was his stock in trade, most visibly instanced by his scandalous electoral pact in 54. A rapacious tenure in Cilicia followed. The list of transgressions was long.

Ap. Claudius was twice indicted in 50: of *maiestas* and of *ambitus*.[194] But

[193] The sordid tale is recounted by Cæl. *Ad Fam.* 8.8.2–3: cf. Cic. *Ad Fam.* 11.22.1. Discussion of the confused details may be found in Tyrrell and Purser, *Correspondence*, III:109–110; How, *Select Letters*, II:260–263; cf. Shackleton Bailey, *Philologus*, 105 (1961): 86. On Q. Pilius Celer, see Cic. *Ad Att.* 4.18.5, 6.3.10, 10.1A. Ap. Claudius is the same youth who prosecuted Milo in 52–with greater success. The identity of M. Servilius is uncertain. He may be the individual mentioned by Cicero among those who spoke too much–to too little purpose; *Brutus*, 269. Shackleton Bailey, *Cicero's Letters*, III:264, identifies him with the future tribune of 43. How's note on Servilius, *Select Letters*, II:260, is valueless; the tribune M. Servilius Geminus of 60 B.C. is entirely fictitious.

[194] Cic. *Ad Fam.* 3.11.1–3, 3.12.1. Broughton, *MRR*, II:229, 242, wrongly says extortion. *Repetundæ* is mentioned only in *Vir. Ill.* 82.4. It was a natural inference, but bears no credence in view of the Ciceronian evidence. The *maiestas* charge was used against Appius as it had been against Gabinius after his proconsulship. Cf. Cic. *Ad Fam.* 3.6.3. *Ambitus* referred probably to his infamous electoral agreement in 54; less likely to the censorial elections of 50. In May, it was not yet certain that there would be censors; Cic. *Ad Fam.* 3.10.3; but Appius was already under indictment: cf. Shackleton Bailey, *PCPS*, 185 (1958–59): 6–7.

he would not be so easy a mark as his brother. Appius' good fortune gave him a convenient prosecutor: the dissolute and prodigal young patrician P. Cornelius Dolabella. That was not a man likely to evoke the respect of the jurors. Dolabella, having recently discarded an elderly wife, was angling for a new marriage and for the fame of a successful prosecution.[195] Appius came into court well prepared. Patrician and consular rank stood to his advantage, and his connections encompassed a wide circle. His consulship in 54 had brought Appius closer to Domitius Ahenobarbus and to some of the friends of Cato. A daughter was given in marriage to M. Brutus, the nephew of Cato. A second daughter, somewhat later, wed the son of Pompeius Magnus.[196] The latter alliance offered mutual advantage: another example of Pompey's efforts to rebuild contacts with the old aristocracy, a complement to his new marriage link with Metellus Scipio. It proved equally beneficial for Ap. Claudius. Both of his sons-in-law, Pompey and Brutus, were diligent in soliciting support for his defense. Pompey, as proconsul, could not appear in court; but Brutus could, and so could Q. Hortensius. It was the last appearance at the bar for the great orator, who perished a few days later.[197] Appius' canny knack of making opportune associations at proper times had come to his assistance once again.

The prospects and influence of Ap. Claudius may be read in the correspondence of Cicero. Clodius' brother had, of course, long been a foe of the orator, a sponsor of his exile, an opponent of his recall. Reconciliation had come, however, in 54, uneasy but superficially cordial.[198] Cicero succeeded Appius as governor of Cilicia in 51. Their formal relations fluctuated. Appius pointedly snubbed the orator, avoiding a meeting in the province. Cicero wrote with unrestrained vehemence to Atticus of his predecessor's extortionate activities in Cilicia.[199] To Appius himself Cicero's missives were at first proper and friendly, later strained and sharp, with unconcealed indignation.[200] After mid-50, however, one discerns a marked change in tone. Appius was now under indictment. Pompey, Brutus, and others interceded with Cicero on his behalf. And the orator had his own interests in mind. Unhappy and impatient

[195] On Dolabella, see M. Polignano, *RendLinc,* 1 (1946): 240–275, 444–501.

[196] See Münzer, *RE,* 3:2850, "Claudius," n.297. The marriage alliance with Pompey should not be put as early as 54; cf. Gruen, *Historia,* 18 (1969): 101–103.

[197] For solicitations by Pompey and Brutus, see Cic. *Ad Fam.* 2.13.2, 3.10.2, 3.11.3; *Ad Att.* 6.2.10; Cæl. *Ad Fam.* 8.6.3; defense by Brutus and Hortensius: Cic. *Brutus,* 230, 324.

[198] Cic. *Ad Fam.* 1.9.4, 1.9.19, 3.10.8; *Ad Q. Frat.* 2.12.2–3; *Pro Scauro,* 31.

[199] Cic. *Ad Att.* 6.1.2.

[200] The letters through July of 51 express feigned cordiality; Cic. *Ad Fam.* 3.1–3.5. Thereafter, the bitterness is plain; Cicero did not forgive Appius' effrontery; *Ad Fam.* 3.6–3.8. Appius' own letters blew hot and cold, some remonstrances and some compliments; cf. Cic. *Ad Att.* 6.1.2; *Ad Fam.* 3.9.1, 3.11.5.

in Cilicia, he wanted no prorogation of command. The stature of Ap. Claudius is reflected in Cicero's excessively generous letters promising every sympathy and support: Appius could be a valuable ally in guaranteeing the orator's swift return.[201] It was a source of grave embarrassment and surprise that the prosecutor P. Dolabella, in the course of the proceedings, became Cicero's own son-in-law. The match had been arranged without Cicero's knowledge or consent. Letters from Cilicia express his acute discomfiture, his protestations and disclaimers, his assurances of continued support.[202] Cicero spared no demeaning comment: he claims to have embraced Appius in his thoughts, even to have smothered his letters with kisses.[203] The exaggerated compliments do not redound to Cicero's credit. But they indicate the power and influence of Ap. Claudius.

The trials should not be taken as foreshadowing the coming conflict between Pompey and Cæsar. To be sure, the flighty and fickle Dolabella eventually joined Cæsar. But there were no premonitions of that fact at the time of the prosecution. Another opportunistic youth, M. Cælius Rufus, would also move into the camp of Cæsar. But he backed Claudius in his trial, importuning Cicero for his support.[204] The assistance of Brutus, Hortensius, and Pompey testifies to Appius' connections, not to a struggle with Cæsar. His trial takes its place as part of the judicial attacks upon the *gens Claudia*, evidenced in 51 and 50. Old feuds and the family's arrogance lay in the background. Appius, with substantial assistance, obtained clearance on both the *ambitus* and *maiestas* counts, followed by triumphant election to the censorship.[205]

It was not the end of Appius' tribulations. By the early fall of 50, he became censor, basking in authority and indulging in rancor. He imitated the shades of greater ancestors, and expelled numerous individuals from the senate. Among his intended victims was M. Cælius. Conveniently forgetting Cælius' support at his trial, Appius preferred to remember the older bitterness between his clan and the young orator. The censor promoted a charge of unnatural vice against Cælius, summoning up Servius Pola as prosecutor, the same man who had threatened an accusation of Cælius in 54.[206] Cælius, enraged

[201] The letters to Appius are, of course, contrived and strained. But see also a letter to Cælius at the same time; Cic. *Ad Fam.* 2.13.2: *quid est causæ cur mihi non in optatis sit complecti hominem florentem ætate, opibus, honoribus, ingenio, liberis, propinquis, adfinibus, amicis.*

[202] Cic. *Ad Fam.* 3.10.1, 3.10.5, 3.12.2; cf. *Ad Fam.* 2.13.2, 2.15.2: *Ad Att.* 6.6.1; Cæl. *Ad Fam.* 8.6.2.

[203] Cic. *Ad Fam.* 3.11.2: *complexus igitur sum cogitatione te absentem; epistulam vero osculatus, etiam ipse mihi gratulatus sum.*

[204] Cæl. *Ad Fam.* 8.6.1–3, 8.6.5; Cic. *Ad Fam.* 2.13.1–2.

[205] Cic. *Ad Fam.* 3.11.1–2, 3.12.1; Dio, 40.63.2.

[206] Cæl. *Ad Fam.* 8.12.1–3. For the threat in 54, see Cic. *Ad Q. Frat.* 2.13.2.

and bitter, retaliated by bringing the same charge against his tormentor. It was a shrewd move. The allegation fitted the character of Appius at least as well as Cælius, as all men knew.[207]

The trials probably never reached court. There is no reason to doubt that their origin was personal pique and long-standing enmity. But the consequences carried larger political implications. In the fall of 50, matters were coming to a head between Julius Cæsar and the senatorial aristocracy. Ap. Claudius, now the close friend of Domitius Ahenobarbus and the *adfinis* of Pompey the Great, had become a central figure in the new and growing coalition. His heavy-handed censorial activities inadvertently created new friends for Cæsar. They included ambitious and offended young aristocrats like Dolabella, Curio, Sallust–and now M. Cælius.[208]

One may discern the fruit of that conflict in the later part of 50. Many intellectuals and politicians of the younger generation were moving toward Cæsar. The fact emerges in a fierce contest for a seat in the augural college, left vacant by the recent death of Q. Hortensius. Domitius Ahenobarbus, longtime friend and *adfinis* of Hortensius, expected election to the post. Connections, background, and influence spoke for him. Ap. Claudius, already in the college, unquestionably sponsored him. The Cæsarian candidate was M. Antonius, recently returned from a legateship in Gaul. His contemporaries were strong in support: notably M. Cælius and C. Curio. The office itself carried little power. But it offered prestige and *auctoritas*. The campaign was adjudged a symbolic test of strength between interests in the new political constellation. Cælius remarks the unusual character of the election: men forgot old obligations and voted along strict party lines.[209] That this feature evoked notice demonstrates its extraordinary character. It was a sign of the passing of the old order. Zealous–perhaps overzealous–campaigning by Antony's friends earned him the victory: a stunning blow to Domitius Ahenobarbus, reminiscent of Cæsar's pontifical election over Q. Catulus thirteen years before. The haughty *nobilis* and ex-consul did not take defeat by a rank newcomer lightly: Antony had not yet held even the tribunate. Domitius sought retaliation through the courts. The men who had audaciously solicited votes through intimidation were brought to trial *de vi*. Cælius and Curio could not themselves be prosecuted, for they occupied magisterial office, the ædileship and tribunate respectively. But their collaborators were tried, and many of them were found

[207] Cæl. *Ad Fam.* 8.12.3; cf. 8.14.4. The crime was covered by a *lex Scantinia* of uncertain date. There is no clear reference to the law before 50, but several thereafter. The evidence is collected, with citation of scholarly discussions, in Rotondi, *Leges Publicæ*, p. 293.

[208] See, esp., Cæl. *Ad Fam.* 8.12.1; Dio, 40.63.3–5; cf. Syme, *Rom. Rev.*, p. 41.

[209] Cæl. *Ad Fam.* 8.14.1: *magna illa comitia fuerunt, et plane studia ex partium sensu apparuerunt; perpauci necessitudinem secuti officium præstiterunt;* cf. Meier, *Res Pub.*, pp. 12–14.

guilty. Ahenobarbus' son, Cn. Domitius, was active in the prosecutions, avenging the honor of his *gens*.[210] Even here, one may conclude, where the larger political issues were coming to the fore, it was family pride, a staple item in Roman history, which provoked the final criminal trials of the Republic.

A staggering number of prosecutions are attested in the Republic's last years. The sources provide some detail on at least fifty cases in the brief period between Luca and the outbreak of civil war. On occasion, as in mid-54 and mid-52, the court calendar was clogged with cases that could hardly be handled by the *iudicia*. The confusing mass has previously discouraged systematic inquiry.

The foregoing pages, however, suggest that the trials break down conveniently into analyzable patterns. For two years after Luca a mounting judicial campaign was waged against allies and beneficiaries of the triumvirate. Convictions were rare, but the continuous pressure caused distress, expense, and unwelcome labor to the dynasts. By mid-54 their adversaries had generated a new climate of opinion pronouncedly favorable to their own interests. The spectacular trials and condemnation of Gabinius and his accomplices provided a suitable climax. The conference of Luca had threatened to establish political ascendancy by a single coalition. That it did not do so may be traced, in large part, to that persistent judicial campaign.

The seemingly endless series of trials in 52 also possessed a consistent rationale. They exemplified reestablishment of state authority and official renunciation of anarchic tactics. New legislation and a string of convictions cracked down on the authors of disorder. The results revived confidence in Republican institutions. At the same time they offered a platform for political groups that wished to keep a tight rein on Pompeius Magnus. His sole consulship would not be a mechanism for prolonged personal power: condemnations of his more zealous adherents saw to that.

Another element requires emphasis. *Haute politique* by no means determined the origin or issue of every criminal case. Nor was the appearance of an individual for the prosecution or defense necessarily a political act. Certain orators of particular skill and competence made courtroom advocacy into something approaching a profession. Persuasive speakers like Cicero, Hortensius, and M. Calidius were almost constantly on call. Political import may have attached to no more than a minority of their judicial activities. The

[210] Convictions of Curio's friends *de vi* are noted by Cic. *Phil.* 2.4. Only one name is preserved: a certain Cn. Saturninus accused by Cn. Domitius: Cæl. *Ad Fam.* 8.14.1. Cælius mentions here also the acquittal of a Sex. Peducæus; but no reason to suspect connection with the aftermath of the augural elections. Dio, 40.64.3, should not be taken as referring to an actual prosecution of Curio. He is speaking of Marcellus' attacks on Curio in the senate.

interests of the sources and the accident of transmission have produced an imbalance of political cases. But it is possible to see, even in the preserved evidence, the frequency of suits growing out of private enmities, familial conflicts, and lingering feuds. Those were abiding features, sometimes separate from, often involved in, cases of larger political significance. The theme persisted to the very end. The *ambitus* trials and the attacks on the Claudii in 51 and 50 exemplify it even in the last months before civil war.

Recurrent motifs prevail. The three decades between the Sullan and Cæsarian dictatorships show not so much change as repetition. Struggles between Pompey and his foes for senatorial supremacy evoked criminal prosecutions in the mid-60s; the same contest marked the trials of 52. The filtering of propaganda through the courts was a tactic used against the triumvirate in 59 and 58; it was also the tactic employed after the conference of Luca. Exploitation of public issues against political rivals was prominent in the attack on Sulla's proscriptions; it came up again in the aftermath of the Catilinarian conspiracy; and it reappeared in the trials of rabble-rousers in 52. Hindsight has caused modern obsession with the background of civil war. It has too long clouded perception of a central fact: the remarkable conventionality of Roman behavior.

THE PLEBS AND THE ARMY

THE ROMAN *plebs* does not loom large in accounts of the Republic's history. Ancient authors paid it little heed. The writing of history was a luxury of the upper classes: when they deigned to take note of their social inferiors, it was with scorn and derision. The commons generally emerge in literary sources as a "crowd," a "mob," or "the rabble," capable of occasional disturbances but basically without influence. Nor is epigraphic evidence of much assistance. Members of Rome's humbler orders have left little more than their names on funerary epitaphs as a tangible token of their earthly existence. Yet the *plebs* cannot be left out of the reckoning. Agitation for and by the populace plays an intermittent and conspicuous role in the late Republic. Agrarian problems plagued the government at various times throughout the period. The rural poor–tenants, agricultural laborers, and small farmers–filled the ranks of the Roman army, creating a potentially explosive force. And increased urban violence has often been pointed to as a prime factor in the demise of the free state. The aims of the proletariate and their impact on the course of events remain elusive. Although accessible documentation on these matters is limited in the extreme, an effort to ferret it out may bring some tentative results.

THE URBAN PLEBS

Population statistics on the city of Rome are unavailable. Only guesswork can be substituted. In the year 46 B.C., 320,000 names were on the lists of those eligible to receive grain from the state.[1] The figure refers to free adult

[1] Suet. *Iul.* 41.3.

males. Computations from that basis are hazardous. Three years of civil war preceded, and a considerable reduction of the citizen body.[2] Perhaps the number of grain recipients exceeded 400,000 in the last decade of the Republic. Evidence on women and children is entirely wanting. Female offspring were less desirable than male and a smaller percentage of them would have survived. If one adds the families of men on the grain lists, the total probably falls short of one million free inhabitants. That comprises the heaviest bulk of urban dwellers. Members of the upper classes were doubtless of small numerical significance and many of them would have been domiciled outside the city.

The servile population is even more difficult to estimate. Large numbers of slaves were brought in during the German wars at the end of the second century, and many more were added during the Gallic campaigns of Cæsar. The slave trade in the East, at least until Pompey's reduction of piracy in the 60s, must have swelled the number. But a liberal policy of manumission provided a steady check on the total. No general figures exist. Modern estimates range from 100,000 to about 300,000 slaves. The entire population of the city, slave and free, in the Ciceronian age may have exceeded one million, but probably not by much.[3]

The urban *plebs* was a mixed lot. Ancient observers depicted them as a conglomerate of many nations and peoples. Immigration and a commingling of the races gave rise to disdain and lamentation by aristocratic sources: foreign elements debased the populace and corrupted the citizenry. That analysis has attracted some moderns as well—those who find in the growing number of men with eastern backgrounds the source of Rome's decline and an increased disrespect for Republican institutions.[4] What was the composition of the *plebs urbana?*

[2] Appian, *BC*, 2.102, reports that the citizenry had been depleted by one half—doubtless a confusion with Cæsar's reduction of the grain rolls. A similar confusion exists in Plut. *Cæs.* 55.3 and Livy, *Per.* 105. But the decline in citizens by 46 was marked, as a census of that year discovered; Dio, 43.25.2. For contemporary testimony, see Cic. *Pro Marc.* 23. The evidence is doubted by Wiseman, *JRS*, 59 (1969): 62–63, 72, but without compelling arguments. Brunt attributes the reduction not so much to war losses as to a steady demographic decline in previous decades; *Italian Manpower*, pp. 100–112, 381.

[3] The classic study is that of K. J. Beloch, *Die Bevölkerung der griechisch-römischen Welt* (Leipzig, 1886), pp. 392–412; cf. Rice Holmes, *Rom. Rep.*, I:360–363; W. J. Oates, *CP*, 29 (1934): 101–116; Brunt, *Past and Present*, 35 (1966): 8–9; *Italian Manpower*, pp. 376–388. On slave numbers, see the discussion of W. L. Westermann, *The Slave Systems of Greek and Roman Antiquity* (Philadelphia, 1955), pp. 63–69.

[4] [Q. Cic.] *Comm. Petit.* 54: *Roma est civitas ex nationum conventu constituta. in qua multæ insidiæ, multa fallacia, multa in omni genere vitia versantur*; Appian, *BC*, 2.120: διεφθαρμένης ἐκ πολλοῦ τῆς πολιτείας; παμμιγές τε γάρ ἐστιν ἤδη τὸ πλῆθος ὑπο ξενίας. For the argument on race mixture as a contributing factor to Rome's ills, see T. Frank, *AHR*, 21 (1916): 689–708;

The influx of slaves and concomitant manumission produced a large number of freedmen in the city. Servile origins generally meant foreign origins. Some of the slaves may have been homebred, offspring of slave households, and a few perhaps were abandoned infants or men sold to pay off debts. But little evidence exists for the latter two categories: testimony on infant exposure is largely confined to the imperial period and to areas outside Italy; debt slavery was illegal in the late Republic and instances of evasion of the laws were probably rare.[5] The vast majority of slaves had doubtless been war captives, with a smaller number derived from the slave trade and piracy. Almost all were non-Italians. The freeing of urban slaves was easy and regular—less so for the servile populace of the countryside. There were numerous reasons for the frequency of manumission in the city. Recognition of ability or loyal service might prompt the act, or genuine affection between master and slave. Political motives also came into play: freed slaves would become clients of the master, attending him in public, and supporting him in politics. And an economic aspect cannot be overlooked: the liberated slave was eligible for grain subsidies from the state and would no longer be a financial burden on his owner—but might still owe services to him.[6]

Manumission entailed automatic access to Roman franchise. Hence, the practice appreciably increased the number of foreign-born admitted into the citizenry. But the notion that Greeks or Orientals constituted a heavy majority is incapable of substantiation. The argument depends on a preponderance of Greek names in the sepulchral inscriptions of freedmen and slaves. But servile nomenclature does not necessarily disclose provenance. Other elements explain the imbalance: slave-names were generally applied by the masters, and Romans would prefer Greek *nomina* to less familiar barbaric names; many appellations were no doubt fixed by slave traders who operated primarily in Greek-speaking areas; and the relative poverty of the Latin language in

---

accepted by L. R. Taylor, *AJP,* 82 (1961): 113–115. The notion has led to extreme and unfounded assertions; cf., e.g., J. W. Heaton, *Mob Violence in the Late Roman Republic* (Urbana, Illinois, 1939), p. 18: "Italy received great crowds of Greeks, Syrians, Phoenicians, Jews, Egyptians, Gauls, Germans, and others. . . . It was they who gradually replaced the patient, dogged, and rugged peasants of the early Republic with the nervous, excitable, and unbalanced proletariate of the first century."

[5] On exposure, see Westermann, *Slave Systems*, pp. 85–86. Brunt, *JRS*, 48 (1958): 167–168, argues that the sale of self and children may have been more common than generally supposed. Štaerman, *Blütezeit der Sklavenwirtschaft*, pp. 36–70, stresses domestic breeding as a principal source for the replenishment of slaves. But the evidence is skimpy and inconclusive.

[6] Note the implication of Cic. *Phil.* 8.32 that slave captives who were frugal and diligent normally obtained their *libertas* within six years. On the motives for manumission, see now the careful study of S. Treggiari, *Roman Freedmen during the Late Republic* (Oxford, 1969), pp. 11–20.

nomenclature naturally called for the frequent use of Greek names.[7] The captives of war came largely from the West–Spain, Gaul, and North Africa. Slaves of eastern provenance were acquired primarily through the mart. If anything, they were probably in a minority. The view that they "debased" the populace rests on ancient statements which betray the aristocratic snobbery of the tradition. In fact, the Hellenic and eastern nations supplied Rome with many of her physicians, teachers, artisans, small merchants, tradesmen, architects, clerks, and minor administrators. Nationality and background did not stand in their way. The ready emancipation of slaves is a revealing fact. Rome had long been a melting pot of Italian peoples. In the late Republic the same process of assimilation was well under way for men of foreign origins.[8]

The proportion of freed slaves or heirs of freed slaves in the urban populace cannot be decisively determined. Estimates have ranged as high as 90 percent. That is surely too high. Epigraphic evidence has been called into account: funerary inscriptions attesting the names of members of the lower orders, men who attained no social distinctions or magisterial titles. Servile names predominate, though not by nine to one. The ratio is closer to three to one. But it is faulty methodology to extrapolate from that statistic alone. Freedmen may have been more likely to record their names than *ingenui* from the urban *plebs*. The *libertus* took pride in his enfranchisement and would be anxious to commemorate it for posterity. And the majority of sepulchral epitaphs probably came from relatively successful tradesmen and artisans, occupations largely dominated by freedmen. Poorer members of the city populace, whether freeborn or not, would not often have the wherewithal to set up epigraphic monuments. Hence, apparently useful statistical evidence turns out to be of small value.[9]

[7] See the excellent article of M. L. Gordon, *JRS*, 14 (1924): 93–111, as against Frank, *AHR*, 21 (1916): 689-708. Cf. also Westermann, *Slave Systems*, pp. 96–98; Treggiari, *Roman Freedmen*, pp. 5–8.

[8] So, rightly, Gordon, *JRS*, 14 (1924): 110-111. Her evidence is primarily early Imperial; but the conclusion would hold–at least for the beginnings of the process–for the late Republic.

[9] The extreme view of freedmen dominance in the urban *plebs* was propounded by Frank, *AHR*, 21 (1916): 689-708. See the corrective applied by Taylor, *AJP*, 82 (1961): 113-132, and Treggiari, *Roman Freedmen*, pp. 32-34. Again the evidence is mostly Imperial, rather than Republican. Brunt, *Italian Manpower*, pp. 386-387, guesses that freedmen and slaves comprised between two-thirds and three-quarters of the city's population–but that is sheer speculation. For some healthy skepticism on the use of statistics that do not offer representative samples, see F. G. Maier, *Historia*, 2 (1954): 318-351. Observe that Cicero's remarks to the urban *plebs* in his *De Lege Agraria* consistently stress their Roman and Italian heritage; 2.9, 2.16, 2.21, 2.49-50, 2.69, 2.73, 2.81-82, 2.84. Elsewhere *libertini* are portrayed merely as a part–and evidently not an overwhelming part–of the urban populace; Cic. *Cat.* 4.16; [Q. Cic.] *Comm. Petit.* 29. The preponderance of freedmen in the city remains unverifiable–and questionable.

Proportions are not discernible. But there are certain areas of civic life in which freedmen commonly participated. Cultivated Romans, at least in principle, looked down their noses at handicrafts, retail trade, and manual labor. That kind of prejudice, of course, was an upper-class luxury. Lesser Romans, even those of free birth, could not always afford to shun such occupations.[10] But the prevailing attitude left a clear field for *liberti,* who consequently had open access to most livelihoods in the city. They constituted many of the *tabernarii,* the shopkeepers and retail businessmen. Some rose to positions as *mercatores* and *negotiatores,* merchants and traders. The skills of freedmen from Hellenic areas permitted them to obtain almost a monopoly in occupations like medicine, education, clerical work, and the professions generally. Domestic positions were beneath the dignity of *ingenui,* hence were dominated by slaves and freedmen. And the latter engaged also in architecture and various arts and crafts. By contrast, the freeborn lower classes were more frequently to be found in unskilled occupations, in the building trades, dock labor, and seasonal or temporary work.[11]

Rome was a bustling metropolis, the center of a vast empire. The attractions of the city had seduced immigrants from the Italian countryside since the early second century—and from abroad, in even larger numbers, during the Republic's last few generations.[12] Opportunities were extensive in the capital of an empire: work and advancement for skilled and unskilled alike. The city absorbed freedmen and slaves, rustics and provincials, western barbarians and Hellenic intellectuals. All enriched the talents and character of the citizenry. The variety of backgrounds and abilities gave the late Republic advantages not available in previous generations.

Nonetheless, a rosy portrait of the proletariate's lot would be a distortion. The Roman *plebs* suffered under limitations and handicaps: their political power was minimal, their economic situation often unstable, the relief of their complaints rarely easy. Some of the problems may be briefly sketched.

The slave, of course, lacked political rights altogether and possessed only

[10] See the evidence collected and discussed by F. M. De Robertis, *Lavoro e Lavorati nel Mondo Romano* (Bari, 1963), pp. 21–97. For the attitude of the upper classes in the late Republic, see esp. Cic. *De Off.* 1.150–151: *illiberales autem et sordidi quæstus mercennariorum omnium . . . sordidi etiam putandi, qui mercantur a mercatoribus, quod statim vendant . . . opificesque omnes in sordida arte versantur; nec enim quicquam ingenuum habere potest officina.*

[11] See the discussions of M. E. Park, *The Plebs in Cicero's Day* (Diss. Cambridge, Mass., 1918), pp. 51–90; M. Maxey, *Occupations of the Lower Classes in Roman Society as Seen in Justinian's Digest* (Diss. Chicago, 1938), *passim*; and Treggiari, *Roman Freedmen*, pp. 87–161; cf. Brunt, *Past and Present*, 35 (1966): 13–16.

[12] For immigration from the Italian countryside in the late Republic, see Sallust, *Cat.* 37.4–9; Varro, *De Re Rust.* 2.pr.3; cf. Appian, *BC*, 2.120; Dio, 38.1.3.

a minimum of civil rights.[13] His treatment was heavily dependent upon the mercy, humanity, and self-interest of his owner. The urban *servus,* generally in closer contact and more personally valuable to the master, could expect a better lot than his more anonymous counterpart in the countryside. And he could look forward to manumission. The freedman automatically obtained full citizenship rights–an institution of unusual generosity, in which the Romans took pride. But the law and the fact did not always coincide. Freedmen were regularly enrolled only in the four urban voting tribes, thereby markedly reducing the effectiveness of any individual *libertus'* vote in the tribal assembly.[14] The wealthier members of that class had some influence in the *comitia centuriata,* which elected the higher magistracies.[15] But the *ordo libertinus* as a whole possessed scant political weight. Technically, they were eligible for magistracies and the senate–or so it would appear. But social prejudice in the ruling class assured that few, if any, would attain that distinction. The path was easier for sons of freedmen, but not much easier. Those who managed to reach the senate afforded ready targets for expulsion by the censors.[16] *Liberti* were excluded from the *equester ordo* and, except in emergencies, from the military service. Their freedom was, in practice, heavily circumscribed by obligations still due their former masters, now their patrons–enforced in some cases by law, in most by the powerful concept of *fides.*[17]

The freeborn urban *plebs* suffered under no legal handicaps. But practical limitations were many. Their low economic status permitted them little influence in the centuriate assembly. A larger role would be played in the *comitia tributa,* but only by those members of the *plebs* who happened to be enrolled in rural tribes. What proportion they represented cannot be known; very likely the majority of the masses were registered in urban tribes where their votes would have small force.[18] Not all were destitute, to be sure. Small

[13] Cf. Westermann, *Slave Systems*, pp. 80–84; A. Watson, *The Law of Persons in the Later Roman Republic* (Oxford, 1967), pp. 173–184.

[14] See Asconius, 52, Clark: *rusticis tribubus quæ propriæ ingenuorum sunt.* But, occasionally, men enrolled in urban tribes might be transferred to a rural tribe for a particular vote if there were no representatives present from that tribe; Cic. *Pro Sest.* 109; cf. L. R. Taylor, *Hommages Bidez et Cumont* (1948), II:325; and, in general, Taylor, *Voting Districts*, pp. 132–149. Freedmen manumitted informally would not possess voting rights of any kind; Treggiari, *Roman Freedmen*, pp. 29–31.

[15] [Q. Cic.] *Comm. Petit.* 29.

[16] Cf. Cic. *Pro Cluent.* 131–132; Dio, 40.63.4.

[17] On all this, see the thorough and sensible treatment of Treggiari, *Roman Freedmen*, pp. 37–86; cf. also Watson, *Law of Persons*, pp. 226–236.

[18] Cf. Taylor, *Party Politics*, pp. 50–62; contra: Brunt, *Past and Present*, 35 (1966): 6–7. Uncertainty beclouds the question of how far immigrants from the country were re-registered into urban tribes. No pair of censors between 69 and 28 completed their task. But unfinished work may well have been taken into account–involving many transfers from rural into urban tribes; cf. Brunt, *Italian Manpower*, pp. 104–106.

shops and family-owned businesses were often in the hands of *ingenui.* But since freedmen occupied many of the trades and professions, numerous *ingenui* may have depended on casual jobs which provided neither security nor consistent income. A minimum grain requirement was supplied by the state, and after Clodius' measure of 58, it was distributed free of charge. That cannot have been sufficient for all needs. Allotments went to males alone–no provision existed for wives and families–and the grain supply was liable to interruption or reduction when piracy was rife or wars disturbed the grain routes.[19]

Living conditions for those with slender means left much to be desired. The *principes* might dwell in luxurious quarters, but many in the lower classes were crowded into *insulæ,* blocks of flats and tenement houses, where rents were often high and absentee landlords not very generous. Cicero–and others–demanded prompt payment from tenants, but showed little promptness in authorizing repairs. Collapse of buildings was a frequent occurrence and the danger of fire was ever present, a boon for shrewd speculators like M. Crassus, a potential calamity for the urban poor. Earthquakes and floods are also recorded in the late Republic, rendering some men homeless and desperate. Rome possessed no organized fire department in the Republic. And, even apart from natural disasters, the menance of eviction always hung over the tenant who was uncooperative or tardy with the rent.[20]

Finally, another matter is often overlooked. What chance might the common man have before the bar? Criminal *quæstiones* with elaborate procedural regulations governed charges like electoral bribery, extortion, embezzlement, treason. Those were major crimes, not likely to be committed by any but men of means and standing. And indeed the recorded criminal trials almost all involved notable figures with political connections. But what of violations like petty larceny, vagrancy, or minor assault which might be expected among the lower classes? The *quæstiones* were not geared for such offenses; and it is inconceivable that the assembly of the people would be summoned to hear cases of that sort. In all probability, lower-class violators were dealt with summarily, through magisterial *cœrcitio,* with no opportunity for appeal and little concern for procedural safeguards or civil liberties. Unless a powerful

[19] On the grain distribution, see below, pp. 384–386; and cf. Brunt, *Past and Present,* 35 (1966): 17–18.

[20] On Cicero's attitude, see Cic. *Ad Att.* 14.9.1: *tabernæ mihi duæ corruerunt reliquæque rimas agunt . . . hanc ceteri calamitatem vocant, ego ne incommodum quidem*; cf. *Ad Att.* 15.17.1, 15.20.4. For Crassus' exploitation of collapsed buildings and fires, see Plut. *Crass.* 2.3–4. Earthquakes and floods: Dio, 37.58.3, 39.20.2, 39.61.1–2; Orosius, 6.14.4–5; the threat of eviction: Cic. *Pro Flacco,* 22. The subject is discussed, with references, by Z. Yavetz, *Latomus,* 17 (1958): 500–517. Cf. also F. Schulz, *Classical Roman Law* (Oxford, 1951), pp. 542–549.

patron were found, the accused from the humbler orders had little chance at court.[21]

The urban proletariate could list any number of serious grievances. But did these grievances–or efforts to redress them–produce disruption which contributed to the Republic's fall? It would be wise not to exaggerate their role. The nature of periodic disorders in the city will be examined more thoroughly later. For the moment, suffice it to say that, whatever their discontents, the commons lacked power or will to create a genuine threat to the establishment. They had neither homogeneity nor unity. That fact is fundamental. One cannot speak of the *plebs* as if it were a separate bloc operating in unison and motivated by class consciousness. A large percentage of its number comprised clients and dependents of Rome's aristocratic families.[22] For most, their welfare was tied more closely to relations with powerful patrons than to members of their own class. The result was an enduring fragmentation. Without means, influence, or solidarity, the proletariate was in no position to create real difficulty for the government. And, more important, it possessed little inclination to upset the social structure. As Cicero properly remarked, the *plebs* did not engage in hazardous struggles to advance its own interests.[23]

THE ARMY

Principal agent in the destruction of the Republic, so it would appear, was the Roman army. Disturbances in the city, discontents among the urban populace, could not readily shake the ruling class so long as the army remained loyal. But if Roman soldiers could be turned against the state by their own generals, preservation of the existing order was no longer possible. In a strict sense, of course, that is irrefutably true. The Republic perished when large armies clashed in Italy and abroad in a contest that endured for nearly twenty

[21] Cf. W. Kunkel, *AbhMünch*, 56 (1962): 71–79, who believes that these matters were treated as mere police actions by the *tresviri capitales*. The situation was probably little better in civil cases. Plaintiffs stood small chance against defendants with *gratia, potentia*, and *pecunia*; cf. Cic. *Pro Cæc.* 73. See the discussion of J. M. Kelly, *Roman Litigation* (Oxford, 1966), *passim*; esp. pp. 1–68.

[22] Cf., e.g., Cic. *Pro Mur.* 70–71: *homines tenues . . . a quibus si domus nostra celebratur, si interdum ad forum deducimur . . . diligenter observari videmur et coli; tenuiorum amicorum et non occupatorum est ista adsiduitas, quorum copia bonis viris et beneficis deesse non solet . . . atque hæc a nobis petunt omnia neque ulla re alia quæ a nobis consequuntur nisi opera sua compensari putant posse.* Note also the remark of Cæsar quoted by Gellius, 5.13.6: *neque clientes summa infamia deseri possunt.*

[23] Cic. *De Leg.* 3.24: *plebes de suo iure periculosas contentiones nullas facit.* Meier, *Res Pub.*, pp. 107–115, rightly stresses the fragmentation and impotence of the *plebs urbana*, but fails to acknowledge the authentic grievances which they must have felt.

years and swept away the prior governmental system. But the fact itself demands explanation. What converted the military, traditional defender of the state and architect of empire, into an instrument of destruction? Historians have not lacked for answers. The late Republic, it is argued, witnessed profound changes in the character of the soldiery. Once recruited from property owners and men with a stake in the established structure, it now consisted of lower-class elements anxious for personal gain and stimulated by economic inequities. Once a citizen militia with a basically civilian mentality, it had become a professional army promoting warfare as a way of life. Once imbued with patriotic ardor, it had transferred its loyalty from the state to its own generals and leaders, producing, in effect, a series of private, client forces with no abstract attachments to the Republic.[24]

Such judgments have not always received serious analysis. On the face of it alone there is inconsistency in the conceptualization. Creation of a professional army, devoted to the military life and given to the warrior's mentality, is not readily reconcilable with the idea of client forces recruited by individual leaders and mobilized for private purposes. The former suggests militarization of the citizenry, the latter politicization of the soldiery. One cannot easily have it both ways. And there are other problems. Why should professionalism, if such there was, entail disloyalty? Professional armies, as often as not, have served to promote and defend the interests of established regimes. Personal recruitment and utilization of private clients in the army was not a new phenomenon; it had occasionally been a positive element in Rome's expansion and domination of foreign foes. As for the composition of the military from lower social levels, the fact is undeniable. That, however, need not make the army an agent of revolution. Indeed, by providing for the unemployed and poor a source of livelihood, a career, and the expectation of economic gain, the army may have reduced the risk of uprising from below. The whole issue might profit from a rethinking.

A golden haze of idealization surrounded the theoretical underpinnings of the early Roman army. Allegedly, it was restricted only to men of substance and property, men with roots in Italian soil who served in defense of home and hearth: a genuine citizen militia.[25] If the theory ever had any basis in fact, it had long since lost it by the late Republic. C. Marius abolished the property qualification in 107, in order to obtain needed volunteers for the Jugurthine War. Later writers branded the act as infamous, a betrayal of Roman traditions, an opening of the ranks to the poor and homeless, who had no natural feelings of patriotism. Anti-Marian sources lie behind that formulation. In fact, there had been a gradual reduction of property requirements for military

[24] Cf. the formulation by Gabba, *Athenæum*, 29 (1951): 178–188.

[25] Val. Max. 2.3.1; Plut. *Mar.* 9.1; Gellius, 16.10.11.

personnel beginning well before Marius. The development dates back perhaps to the Hannibalic war and continued through the second century, when the demands of continuous foreign wars were imposing a more realistic system. The "proletarianization" of the military had been in process for a long time. Marius simply wiped away a *de iure* arrangement that was already obsolete *de facto.* The change was not without significance. It unquestionably opened up the service to some volunteers who were ineligible for conscription even under the most relaxed criteria. But there was no sudden and massive onrush of destitute proletarians into the military at the end of the second century.[26] Nor can one speak of a sharp change from a conscript army to a system of volunteers. The *dilectus* had always been the theoretical basis of Rome's forces. But volunteers are attested, on occasion, from the late third century. The government would not discourage them–especially in dangerous and difficult wars. And the Marian reforms, though they removed all property barriers, did not abolish the levy. Conscription continued, over and above the enlisted volunteers, to the end of the Republic.[27] Draftees had grumbled with resentment in the second century; they were equally resentful in the Ciceronian age.[28] The differences between the pre- and post-Marian armies appear considerably less substantial than has often been believed.

Whence came the recruits for the late Republican army? Apart from rare emergency situations, only freeborn citizens were enrolled in the legions. That meant, in practice, exclusion of much of the urban proletariate, that is, the *liberti* and men of servile orgins. But a large portion of the populace dwelled in the countryside. The decline of the small farmer provides a consistent theme in Roman literature. Yet it will not do to imagine vast estates stretched over all of Italy. There were still numerous free peasants who tilled the soil on their own possessions. And many others remained on the land, even after losing their property, to work as laborers on the farms and as hired hands on the ranches, or as tenants for absentee proprietors.[29] Among such hardy men the military might find able personnel.

[26] The careful researches of Gabba, *Athenæum*, 27 (1949): 173–209, have put this conclusion beyond doubt. See now also, with full bibliography, Harmand, *L'Armée*, pp. 11–20, and Brunt, *Italian Manpower*, pp. 403–408.

[27] R. E. Smith, *Service*, pp. 4–5, 44–47. On volunteers in the early second century, see, e.g., Livy, 42.32.6. Further examples are in Brunt, *Italian Manpower*, pp. 393–396. On the levy in the first century, see sources cited by Smith, *Service*, p. 46, n.1; Brunt, *Italian Manpower*, pp. 408–410, 635–638.

[28] The evidence is noted by Brunt, *Italian Manpower*, pp. 396–398.

[29] Cf. Varro, *De Re Rust.* 1.17.2: *omnes agri coluntur hominibus servis aut liberis aut utrisque: liberis aut ipsi colunt, ut plerique pauperculi cum sua progenie, aut mercennariis, cum conducticiis liberorum operis res maiores . . . administrant.* Further references in Brunt, *JRS*, 52 (1962): 71–72. Cf. K. D. White, *BICS*, 14 (1967): 62–79.

When Marius removed the last legal obstacles, the troops who followed him in the African and German wars were preponderately rustics: not farm owners, on the whole, but men who labored in the fields of the Italian countryside.[30] There is no reason to doubt that rural areas and the *municipia* supplied the bulk of the legionaries in subsequent years. The Social War in 90–89 represents a milestone. Upon its conclusion, Roman citizenship extended throughout the Italian peninsula. Thereafter, a distinction between Roman and allied contingents vanished. All of Italy served as recruiting ground for the legions. In the civil war of the 80s, both Marius and Sulla drew forces from landed districts. By the late 70s a popular orator could complain that Rome's rural population was being drained off to the provinces to fight in conflicts promoted by potentates.[31] Pompey's troops in the eastern wars of the 60s are described as *rustici ac milites.* A large bloc of Crassus' army in Syria came from Lucania. For the Gallic wars Cæsar drew heavily on conscripts from Cisalpine Gaul. His veterans were properly depicted as *homines rustici* and *homines agrestes.* To quell the Catilinarian uprising, the government called up levies, especially in northern Italy. The evidence is consistent throughout. The countryside afforded the principal recruiting ground for the Roman army.[32] Some may have come from the working classes and tradesmen of the *municipia.* But the greater part doubtless consisted of farm laborers, insecure smallholders, seasonal employees, and the rural poor. For such men, the army offered a more steady employment and, in many instances, a more lucrative prospect. Military service, viewed from this angle, may be said to have reduced rather than increased any penchant for revolutionary activites. And it served

[30] Appian, *BC*, 1.29: τοῖς οὖσιν ἀνὰ τοὺς ἀγρούς, οἷς . . . ὑπεστρατευμένοις Μαρίῳ. Cf. Sallust's description of the men who supported Marius for the consulship of 107; *Iug.* 73.6: *opifices agrestesque omnes, quorum res fidesque in manibus sitæ erant, relictis operibus frequentarent Marium.*

[31] Marius got recruits from the farmers and free shepherds of Etruria; Plut. *Mar.* 41.2; Appian, *BC*, 1.67. Sulla scoured the entire countryside to build up his forces; Appian, *BC*, 1.81, 1.86. And see Licinius Macer's remark in 73, as reconstructed by Sallust, *Hist.* 3.48.27, Maur.: *atque hæc eadem non sunt agrestibus, sed cæduntur inter potentium inimicitias donoque dantur in provincias magistratibus*; rightly stressed by Harmand, *L'Armée*, p. 253.

[32] On Pompey's eastern troops, see Cic. *Pro Arch.* 24. Lucullus' forces doubtless had similar rural origins; cf. Horace, *Ep.* 2.2.39. For the Lucanian contribution to Crassus' army, see Pliny, *NH*, 2.57.147. Cæsar's recruitment in the Cisalpina: Cæs. *BG*, 2.2, 6.1; the description of his veterans as rustics: Cic. *Ad Fam.* 11.7.2; *Phil.* 7.9; the government levies in 63 from *agrum Picenum et Gallicum*: Cic. *Cat.* 2.5; Sallust, *Cat.* 30.2. Rural origins for the legionaries is now generally recognized. See the evidence collected in Brunt, *JRS*, 52 (1962): 73–75, 85–86; additional references and discussion in Harmand, *L'Armée*, pp. 245–258. Promagistrates abroad might also call upon Romans resident in the provinces or even, occasionally, recruit provincials, awarding them the franchise in recompense; Smith, *Service*, pp. 48–49, 54–57; Harmand, *L'Armée*, pp. 248–249, 254–255.

another significant purpose. After the Social War and Italian enfranchisement, the gathering of men from all over the peninsula into the legions enabled them to play a key role in unifying the peoples of Italy.

There is, however, a darker side, stressed by ancients and moderns. Lower-class elements joined the army to improve their economic situation. Hence, ambition for gain rather than patriotism dominated.[33] Conscripts presumably came to share the same aims. A dismal conclusion might be drawn from that fact: the soldiery would as lief turn against the state as against its enemies in the interests of economic advantage. Consequently, even if the army's rank and file harbored no revolutionary ideology, it might readily become the instrument for overthrow of the government. The issue deserves careful consideration.

That the rural poor enlisted into military service for economic advantage cannot be doubted. But regular receipts did not always meet needs or expectations. The Marian reforms which eliminated all financial qualifications for the service made no change in the rate of army pay. A soldier received five *asses* per day—a bare subsistence, with deductions for food and arms.[34] And even that was not always forthcoming. If the government at home was short of funds, the troops might have to wait for recompense; arrears often piled up. Pompey faced that difficulty during the Sertorian war; L. Piso encountered a hostile soldiery in the mid-50s whose pay was overdue; and Cicero in 51 took over troops in Cilicia who were still awaiting back pay.[35] Mutinous activities over such matters were evidently not infrequent.[36]

But there existed other sources of gain, less regular but more lucrative. To loyal and successful soldiers the general would often make generous grants of cash. Sulla was free with *donativa.* Sertorius showed similar gratitude to his *milites.* The profitable wars in the East enabled both Lucullus and Pompey to provide handsome rewards to their troops. And Julius Cæsar too did not refrain from distributions of donatives in Gaul on a large scale.[37] But the

[33] Cf. Sallust on the Marian reform, *Iug.* 86.3: *homini potentiam quærenti egentissimus quisque opportunissumus, quoi neque sua cara, quippe quæ nulla sunt, et omnia cum pretio honesta videntur.* And, on Sulla's reliance upon the basest men who would do anything for the smallest *beneficia*, Dio, fr. 108.1–2.

[34] G. R. Watson, *Historia*, 7 (1958): 113–120; Harmand, *L'Armée*, pp. 262–272. Brunt, *PBSR*, 18 (1950): 50–56, less plausibly, calculates three and one-third *asses* per day.

[35] On Pompey's difficulties, see Sallust, *Hist.* 2.98.2–3; Piso's problems, Cic. *In Pis.* 92–93; the Cilician troops, Cic. *Ad Att.* 5.14.1.

[36] Cf. Cic. *Ad Q. Frat.* 1.1.5: *nullam seditionem exercitus pertimescimus, quæ persæpe sapientissimis viris acciderunt.*

[37] Sulla: Plut. *Sulla*, 12.9; Sertorius: Plut. *Sert.* 10.3; Lucullus: Plut. *Luc.* 37.4: Pompey: Plut. *Pomp.* 45.3; Appian, *Mithr.* 116; Cæsar: Hirtius, *BG*, 8.4; Plut. *Cæs.* 15.3, 17.1; Suet. *Iul.* 68. See Harmand, *L'Armée*, pp. 468–470; Brunt, *Italian Manpower*, p. 412.

practice was not new. It would be foolish to infer that rewards for troops implied a moral decay of the military. Instances abound of similar grants for victorious soldiers from at least the fourth century.[38] Again the Ciceronian age marks no shocking reversal of form.

Beyond *donativa* there was booty—an especially attractive inducement. Almost every major commander in the late Republic for whom sufficient evidence exists indulged his forces in pillage. The practice was accepted—and expected. Sulla's soldiers enriched themselves by plundering Athens and then devastating the wealthy towns and countryside of Asia Minor. In the civil war in Italy, Sulla trod more cautiously at first. He bound the troops with an oath to abstain from any damage to the homeland—unless he gave the orders. Those orders evidently came, and the Sullani continued to reap their gains from defeated enemies in the peninsula.[39] Their opponents were little better: the Marians in Asia and the Sertorians in Spain also knew the value of booty.[40] Sulla's successors in Asia continued the practice of looting that area's treasures. L. Murena the elder overran Cappadocia and returned laden with plunder. Lucullus professed regret at his troops' pillaging and, at times, attempted to restrain them; but not very often. Generally he stood aside while his men profited handsomely from the spoils.[41] M. Crassus also engaged in plunder during the Mesopotamian campaign. And even Cicero himself turned over booty to his soldiers in Cilicia. For him, as for all others, that routine was simply a matter of course.[42] Julius Cæsar, naturally, says little about pillage and booty in his *Bellum Gallicum*. But Suetonius offers a different picture: Cæsar plundered temples all over Gaul and sacked towns more often because of the wealth of their inhabitants than because of their hostility to Rome. That notice may well be exaggeration, stemming from anti-Cæsarian sources. But one can hardly imagine that Cæsar's soldiers abstained from the riches of Gaul through eight long years of hard fighting and numerous victories.[43]

[38] E.g., Livy, 7.37, 10.46, 28.9, 39.7, 45.40, 45.42, 45.43. References from Harmand, *L'Armée*, p. 468. And see the table in Brunt, *Italian Manpower*, p. 394.

[39] For the plunder in Greece and Asia, see Appian, *Mithr.* 38–39, 55, 61; Plut. *Sulla*, 25.2; cf. Appian, *BC*, 1.57; the soldiers' oath, Plut. *Sulla*, 27.3; the devastations in Italy, Appian, *BC*, 1.51, 1.86, 1.88, 1.94; Florus, 2.9.28.

[40] Dio, fr. 104; Diod. 38.39.8.1–4; Plut. *Sert.* 19.4; *Pomp.* 19.3.

[41] On Murena, Appian, *Mithr.* 64–65; on Lucullus, Cic. *De Imp. Pomp.* 22; Plut. *Luc.* 14.2–3, 17.6–7, 19.3–4, 24.8, 29.3, 30.4, 31.8; Dio, 36.2.4, 36.7.4, 36.16.3; Plut. *Crass.* 18.4; Appian, *Mithr.* 78, 82, 85–86, 90.

[42] Cic. *Ad Att.* 5.20.5: *hilara sane Saturnalia militibus quoque, quibus exceptis + captivis + reliquam prædam concessimus.* For Crassus' behavior, see Plut. *Crass.* 17.3. On the whole question of booty in the late Republic, see Harmand, *L'Armée*, pp. 283–286, 409–417.

[43] Suet. *Iul.* 54.2: *in Gallia fana templaque deum donis referta expilavit, urbes diruit sæpius ob prædam quam ob delictum.* That Cæsar's soldiers were well-heeled at the end of the Gallic wars may be inferred also from Suet. *Iul.* 68. Harmand, *L'Armée*, pp. 412–415, eager to dissociate

The practice was widespread. Once more, however, the abundance of testimony on the late Republic should not mislead us into thinking that it was a creation of that era. Distribution of the spoils of war to soldiers by their commanders had a hoary pedigree by the late Republic. It already was an established institution in the fifth century—at a time when the state allegedly possessed only a citizen militia. And it continued throughout.[44] The Ciceronian age had no monopoly on soldiers with designs on gain.

Enrollment of the *proletarii* and obsession with economic profit lead one to expect an unreliable and undisciplined army. The assumption has provoked much moralizing: Rome's soldiery in the late Republic was no more than a mercenary force, prepared to go with the highest bidder, unaccountable to and unconcerned with the traditions of the state.[45] Certainly examples of insubordination, even mutiny, are frequent and usually prompted by the selfish avarice of the troops. Pompey encountered it during the African campaign of 81. His troops ceased all military operations for several days in a mad scramble for fabled treasures reportedly hidden away by Carthaginians many generations before.[46] Lucullus' forces in Asia a decade later were so avid for gain that they often neglected the object of their campaign. Once within an ace of capturing Mithridates himself, they turned aside to seize, plunder, and quarrel over the mule that bore gold from the royal coffers; Mithridates safely slipped away. Again, when Lucullus ordered the capture alive of the king's secretary, who was in possession of key documents, the soldiers found that he carried five hundred gold pieces, murdered him, and sequestered the cash, ignoring the private papers. Lucullus hoped to spare the city of Amisus; his soldiers, in outright defiance, ruthlessly sacked the town, pillaging everything that was valuable and destroying the rest. So long as enrichment was forthcoming they followed their commander further into Asia. But, softened by luxury and successes, they balked at the prospect of a lengthy and unprofitable campaign against the Parthians and compelled Lucullus to abandon the idea.[47] An important precedent lurked behind this behavior. It was the

---

Cæsar from the practices of his contemporaries, rejects Suetonius' evidence, but without good grounds. To be sure, Plutarch's assertion that Cæsar captured over eight hundred towns is a wild exaggeration; *Cæs.* 15.3. As Harmand points out, no more than twenty-five can be discovered in the pages of Cæsar's *Commentaries*. But that does not disprove the occasional or, more likely, the frequent, distribution of booty. Cæsar's reference in *BG*, 7.28, is to an unusual situation, even if the remark is not disingenuous: *nec fuit quisquam qui prædæ studeret.*

[44] See, e.g., Livy, 4.34, 5.21, 7.27, 10.31, 24.16, 43.19.

[45] Cf. Mommsen, *Röm. Gesch.*, III:497–499.

[46] Plut. *Pomp.* 11.3–4.

[47] Dio, 36.16.3: **καὶ διὰ τοῦθ' οἱ στρατιῶται, ἕως μὲν εὖ τε ἐφέροντο καὶ τὰς ἁρπαγὰς ἀνταξίας τῶν κινδύνων εἶχον, ἠκροῶντο αὐτοῦ, ἐπεὶ δὲ ἔπταισαν καὶ ἐς φόβον ἀντὶ τῶν ἐλπίδων ἀντικατέστησαν, οὐδὲν ἔτι προετίμησαν**; Plut. *Luc.* 30.3–4. On the failure to capture

fear of being replaced by other forces and losing the chance of great profits in Asia that had induced Sulla's soldiers to march on Rome and inaugurate the civil war in 88.[48]

Desertions too—and recalcitrance in the face of battle—are recorded in the late Republic. The four legions of Scipio Asiagenus abandoned their commander en masse in 83 and transferred to the side of Sulla.[49] In the following year, Carbo was deserted by his cavalry, who preferred to serve with Sulla, and C. Marcius lost a whole legion in a mutiny.[50] The so-called Valerian or Fimbrian troops pursued a remarkable career of treachery and insubordination. Enrolled for the Asian campaign by L. Valerius Flaccus in 86, they soon overthrew their chief and elevated his subordinate officer Flavius Fimbria to command. But Fimbria proved to be no more successful in retaining their devotion. When the opportunity presented itself, the Fimbriani changed allegiance to Sulla and continued to serve in Asia during subsequent years. Lucullus took charge of them in the 70s and met the same fate as his predecessors. The Fimbriani led the sedition against him in 67 and left the service, only to rejoin when Pompey assumed command of the Mithridatic war.[51] No better example can be imagined of the fickleness of the troops. And there are other instances. Sertorius could not control all of his soldiers, many of whom left him and joined the ranks of Metellus Pius.[52] Lucullus' whole effort in Asia collapsed when his weary and indignant forces rebelled in mutiny.[53] Pompey too was not immune from desertions in the Mithridatic war.[54] L. Piso, if one can believe Cicero, was besieged by his soldiers at Dyrrachium in 56 when their pay was in arrears: the mutineers burned down his headquarters and compelled him to flee under cover of night. Crassus found his army reluctant and terrified in the face of Parthia's unfamiliar warfare. Even Julius Cæsar had to quell panic in the Gallic legions, who preferred to abandon their standards and return home rather than encounter the warriors of Ariovistus. And in 49 he suffered a sullen mutiny from forces who claimed that

Mithridates, Plut. *Luc.* 17.4-6; cf. Cic. *De Imp. Pomp.* 22; murder of the king's secretary: Plut. *Luc.* 17.7; the sacking of Amisus: Plut. *Luc.* 19.1-5.

[48] Appian, *BC*, 1.57.

[49] Appian, *BC*, 1.85; Plut. *Sulla*, 28.1-3.

[50] Appian, *BC*, 1.89-90.

[51] Appian, *Mithr.* 51-53, 59-60, 64, 72; Plut. *Luc.* 7.1-2, 34-35; *Sulla*, 25.1; Livy, *Per.* 82-83, 98; Vell. Pat. 2.24.1; Dio, fr. 104, 36.14-16, 36.46.1; Diod. 38-39.8.1-4.

[52] Appian, *BC*, 1.112.

[53] Plut. *Luc.* 33-35; Appian, *Mithr.* 90; Cic. *De Imp. Pomp.* 23-24; Dio, 36.14-16; Livy, *Per.* 98.

[54] Dio, 36.47.2; cf. 36.45.4; Appian, *Mithr.* 110. Sulla seems to have faced similar problems earlier against Mithridates; cf. Front. *Strat.* 2.3.17.

he had reneged on a promised donative and had disappointed their hopes for plunder.[55]

Nor did angry *milites* shrink from the ultimate crime: murder of their officers. The Social War was especially brutal in this regard. A consular legate, A. Postumius Albinus, who had alienated his troops by harsh punishments, was clubbed to death by them; his superior officer, Sulla, winked at the crime to appease the murderers. The consul L. Cato narrowly escaped stoning: his soldiers could find no stones and had to settle for clods of earth. In 88, the army of Pompeius Strabo refused to accept his replacement by Q. Pompeius and expressed their discontent by murdering the successor. Strabo's son, the young Magnus, barely foiled a plot aimed at his assassination in the same year. When Cinna tried to induce his troops to cross the Adriatic in 84 he was met with open revolt and was stabbed to death. The treacherous Fimbriani murdered their initial commander Valerius Flaccus and later, after abandoning Fimbria, induced him to commit suicide.[56] The record is a sorry one.

But what does it all amount to? The vast majority of these examples belong to the grisly period of the Social and civil wars in the 80s. It makes little sense to cite desertions from one side to another as disloyalty to the state, when the whole question of the government's legitimacy was at issue. As rival forces contended for control of the Republic, the enlisted man, not unnaturally, gravitated toward potential victors. No wider explanation is required for the desertions from Scipio, Carbo, and Marcius to Sulla, or from Sertorius to Metellus Pius—nor for the murders of Q. Pompeius and Cinna. Any party, with equal legitimacy—or lack of it—will brand deserters as traitors when the government is the object of dispute. Even the peregrinations of the Fimbriani are explicable in the context of a bewildering and fluid situation during which rival commanders each claimed the right to bear the standards of the state.[57] The dissipation of Lucullus' forces came when it appeared that Pompeius Magnus was prepared to take over the eastern wars. Most of those who abandoned Lucullus reenlisted under Pompey, who promised greater

[55] On the mutiny against Piso: Cic. *In Pis*. 92–93; Crassus' troops: Plut. *Crass*. 18.3–5; Cæsar's problems in Gaul: Cæs. *BG*, 1.39–41; Dio, 38.35–47; in the civil war: Appian, *BC*, 2.47; Dio, 41.26.1.

[56] On Albinus, see Plut. *Sulla*, 6.9; Livy, *Per*. 75; Val. Max. 9.8.3; Polyænus, 8.9.1; L. Cato: Dio, fr. 100; Q. Pompeius: Vell. Pat. 2.20.1; Val. Max. 9.7.ex.2; Livy, *Per*. 77; Appian, *BC*, 1.63; Pompeius Magnus: Plut. *Pomp*. 3.1–3; Cinna: Vell. Pat. 2.24.5; Livy, *Per*. 83; Appian, *BC*, 1.78; Flaccus: Plut. *Luc*. 7.2; Appian, *Mithr*. 52; Vell. Pat. 2.24.1; Livy, *Per*. 82; Fimbria: Appian, *Mithr*. 60; Livy, *Per*. 83; Vell. Pat. 2.24.1; Plut. *Sulla*, 25.1.

[57] The effort of E. Wiehn, *Die illegalen Heereskommanden in Rom bis auf Cæsar* (Marburg, 1926), pp. 75–95, to systematize and categorize the military anomalies of the 80s and 70s is singularly pointless.

success; they did not desert to the enemy. And one may go further: apart from some men who were attracted by the gold of Mithridates, there are no clear instances of actual defection to the foes of Rome.[58] The seeking after profit did not necessarily entail lack of patriotism.

Broad statements about the army's disloyalty to the Republic are inappropriate and misguided. As for military mutinies, a by now familiar refrain is here suitable once more: the practice was no novelty in the age of Cicero. Despite conventional idealizations of antique martial virtue, insubordination, in fact, had a long history. Occasions can be discovered as early as the fifth century and in all succeeding eras. Note, for example, the soldiers' rebellion against no less a general than Scipio Africanus in 206. Even Scipio's popularity and successes could not ward it off: arrears of pay overbore other considerations.[59] The problem–and the reaction–knew no particular period.

It was in the late Republic, moreover, that a major step was taken toward stabilizing the situation. Julius Cæsar doubled the regular pay of his legionaries. The receipts from Gaul made it possible.[60] None will claim that all problems vanished thereupon. But a more substantial earning reduced dependence on chance donations or windfalls of booty. There would now be fewer occasions for discontent.

What of the oft-repeated charge about client armies in the late Republic? Many explanations of the Republic's fall dwell on this feature as central: armies had become the personal possessions of individual commanders, who bent them to their own will; soldiers looked with gratitude for *beneficia* to their generals and had little to expect from the state; hence, the passing of national loyalty and the inevitability of the government's collapse.[61] The starkness of that portrait is considerably overdrawn, as we shall see.

The image of Cæsar's crossing the Rubicon dominates retrospective speculation too much. An unusual situation has been transformed into a typical one. Scholars point to a famous passage as representative: soldiers regarded

[58] Appian, *BC*, 1.117, does speak of αὐτομόλων τε πολλῶν who were rejected by Spartacus during the servile war in 72. But that may be reference to runaway urban slaves, rather than to deserters from the army. *Contra*: Z. Rubinsohn, *RivFilol*, 99 (1971): 294–295.

[59] Polyb. 11.25–30; Livy, 28.24–29; Appian, *Iber.* 34–36. Other instances of early mutinies are collected by W. S. Messer, *CP*, 15 (1920): 158–171.

[60] Suet. *Iul.* 26.3. The date of this change is not given, but it was undoubtedly during the later part of the Gallic wars; cf. Harmand, *L'Armée*, 266–268. There were precedents here too. Legionaries had occasionally been rewarded with double pay in the past, after successful campaigns or conspicuous virtue; data collected by Brunt, *Italian Manpower*, p. 411.

[61] Cf. K. von Fritz, *The Theory of the Mixed Constitution in Antiquity* (New York, 1954), pp. 296–300; Smith, *Failure*, pp. 127–128.

themselves as Cæsarians or Pompeians rather than servants of the state.[62] But application of that assertion to the armies of the Ciceronian age is illegitimate. The reference pertains to a period in which civil war had been raging for four years throughout the empire. It goes without saying that *milites* would reckon themselves Cæsarians or Pompeians at that point. Devastations of warfare, waged on both sides by Romans, eradicated the authority of civil government. Loyalty to the state lacked substance when the state itself was a phantom. The situation was not always thus. On the eve of civil war in December 50, Pompey encountered stubborn opposition when he attempted to recruit forces. The majority of eligible men clamored for a settlement of the controversy and an avoidance of armed conflict. Evidently, even at that late stage, they did not regard themselves as either Cæsarians or Pompeians.[63]

Much has been made of the military oath sworn by soldiers to their general. The *sacramentum* bound men in obedience and discipline. It did not, apparently, contain a specific time limit in the Republic. Hence, there was a personal quality involved: troops were expected to follow their commander for the duration of a war.[64] Does this mean, however, that generals now had control of nearly private armies, obliged in religion and morality to follow commands without concern for the interests of state? That deduction is unwarranted. Naturally, time limits were avoided. The length of a particular contest could not generally be determined in advance, especially from the second century on, when foreign wars often consumed several years. But individual commanders were sometimes replaced before the fighting was concluded. Some soldiers might be simultaneously discharged, but others would renew their oath to the succeeding general—as undoubtedly occurred when Pompey took charge of the Mithridatic war. Lucullus' troops did not feel any obligation to follow him forever.[65] Note also that Pompey readily turned over to Cæsar one of the legions sworn in by him as consul in 55.[66] Such instances tell against the personal force of the *sacramentum*.

A late source records the form of the oath: soldiers vow not to retire until their service is complete by order of the consul.[67] Reference to the

[62] *BHisp.* 17: *utinam quidem dii immortales fecissent; ut tuus potius miles quam Cn. Pompei factus essem et hanc virtutis constantiam in tua victoria, non in illius calamitate præstarem*; see H. Drexler, *Hermes*, 70 (1935): 208–227; Gabba, *Athenæum*, 29 (1951): 186–188.

[63] Plut. *Pomp.* 59.2.

[64] See Smith, *Service*, pp. 29–33, with references to earlier literature. On the contents of the oath, see Polyb. 6.21.2; Dion. Hal. 10.18, 11.43.

[65] Plut. *Luc.* 35.6: ἀπεχώρησαν ἐκ τοῦ χάρακος, ἐπιμαρτυράμενοι πεπληρῶσθαι τὸν χρόνον, ὃν ὡμολόγησαν τῷ Λουκούλλῳ παραμένειν.

[66] Cæs. *BG*, 6.1: *ab Gnæo Pompeio proconsule petit . . . quos ex Cisalpina Gallia consulis sacramento rogavisset, ad signa convenire ut ad se proficisci iuberet.*

[67] Serv. *Ad Æn.* 7.614: *sacramentum, in quo iurat unusquisque miles se non recedere, nisi præcepto consulis post completa stipendia, id est militiæ tempora.*

consul almost certainly dates back to the Republican era. Ultimate authority, therefore, as acknowledged by the *sacramentum* itself, resided in the civil government and its representatives.[68] To be sure, one can find examples of personal oaths taken to commanders outside the regular processes. Cinna persuaded an army to swear fealty to him in 87. Fimbria attempted to extort a similar oath from his forces in 85. When Sulla was on the point of transferring his army to Italy in 83, he obliged them with a vow not to abandon him. And Julius Cæsar, in an identical situation in 49, bound his troops to obedience before leading them into Italy.[69] But none of these situations can be in any way regarded as typical. All took place in conditions of civil war. The demand for a special oath betrays the insecurity of the general in circumstances when his legitimacy was in doubt. Far from reflecting normal processes, it exposes their absence. Nor did the oath solidify the commander's personal following. Cinna was later murdered by his soldiers, and Fimbria was abandoned by his. Only the successes of Sulla and Cæsar enabled them to escape a similar fate. And both profited handsomely from desertions by *milites* who had earlier sworn allegiance to others. The events of civil war cannot be used to establish norms. More significant is the fact that no extraordinary personal *sacramenta* are recorded between 83 and 49. The regular oath does not buttress any theory about private armies.

Generals authorized by the state to recruit armies might indeed draw on their own clients. The practice was entirely logical and hardly novel. It is attested well before the Ciceronian era. Scipio Æmilianus in 134, when Rome was overburdened with military demands, enrolled five hundred of his own friends and clients for the Numantine campaign. And there are further instances in the late Republic. During the Social War, Pompeius Strabo was given responsibility in Picenum. He unquestionably employed personal dependents in that area. Those clients were inherited by Strabo's son Pompey the Great, who gathered them into an armed force when he fought for Sulla in 83. At the same time, Q. Metellus Pius and M. Crassus enrolled recruits, in Africa and Spain respectively, to bring them onto Sulla's side. They may well have made use of foreign *clientelæ*. Domitius Ahenobarbus, in summoning

[68] Smith, *Service*, pp. 31–33, argues that, since Servius specifies a twenty-five-year term of service, his evidence refers to the early Empire or later and is inappropriate for the Republic. But observe that Servius makes no mention of the twenty-five-year term in the passage noted above. It occurs elsewhere: Serv. *Ad Æn.* 2.157. And Isidore, *Orig.* 9.3.53, who also records that minimum term, does not include reference to the consul's authority: *sacramentum, in quo post electionem iurat unusquisque miles non recedere a militia, nisi post completa stipendia, id est militiæ tempora; et hi sunt qui habent plenam militiam; nam viginti et quinque annis tenentur.* Cf. the critique of Smith's argument by Harmand, *L'Armée*, pp. 299–302.

[69] On Cinna, Appian, *BC*, 1.66; Fimbria: Appian, *Mithr.* 59; Sulla: Plut. *Sulla*, 27.3; Cæsar: Appian, *BC*, 2.47; cf. 2.140.

forces in 49, called upon his own tenants and retainers. In all these instances, however, the troops would be limited to relatively small contingents. Roman generals did not construct major armies out of their own families' *clientelæ*.[70] Crassus' famous boast that no man could call himself wealthy unless he equipped his own legion does not mean that men actually did so. Crassus himself may have used cash and other inducements to assist in enrolling forces for the Spartacus war. But that situation was brought about by the absence of Rome's regular armies abroad. And Crassus made no use of his troops other than to quell the servile rebellion.[71]

Rome's generals were her magistrates and promagistrates–politicians all, not professional military men. Naturally they saw in their armies a source of potential political advantage. Although they could not fill up recruitment quotas with clients alone, they might make the army itself a means of conferring *beneficia* and accumulating *clientelæ*. Pompey's long years of command in Spain and the East meant vast numbers of legionaries who would remember his bounty and generosity. Cæsar's lengthy term in Gaul had similar objects in view. Lucullus was faced with mutinies and desertions in his eastern campaigns. But some, at least, of his veterans returned with friendlier feelings. The army of Lucullus, Cicero reports, was in Rome to celebrate his triumph in 63 and to lend support for his protégé L. Murena's electoral campaign.[72] The practice of adding to one's *clientelæ* through the service was not confined to the most major figures alone. Murena himself recruited troops in Umbria for his Gallic promagistracy; his liberality to them had in view future electoral backing.[73] The political fruits are often visible. Pompey's veterans were instrumental in promulgating the triumvirate's measures in 59. Cæsar dispatched some of his troops on furlough to Rome in 55 in order to assist in the consular elections of Crassus and Pompey. And M. Antonius' chances for the augurate in 50 were appreciably boosted by Cæsar's canvassing in northern Italy, whence he had recruited most of his forces.[74]

None of this, however, was revolutionary. Efforts by Rome's politicians to convert soldiers into political assets represented conventional behavior. And

[70] So, rightly, Brunt, *JRS*, 52 (1962): 76–77. On Scipio Æmilianus, see Appian, *Iber.* 84. For Picenum and the Pompeii, see Vell. Pat. 2.29.2; Appian, *BC*, 1.80; Plut. *Pomp.* 6.1–2. On Metellus and Crassus, Plut. *Crass.* 4.1, 6.1–2; Appian, *BC*, 1.80; cf. Badian, *For. Client.*, pp. 266–267. Domitius' retainers: Cæs. *BC*, 1.17, 1.34, 1.56.

[71] Crassus commanded six new legions in 71; Appian, *BC*, 1.118. Whether he recruited them himself is not specifically recorded.

[72] Cic. *Pro Mur.* 37, 69.

[73] Cic. *Pro Mur.* 42: *habuit proficiscens dilectum in Umbria; dedit ei facultatem res publica liberalitatis, qua usus multas sibi tribus quæ municipiis Umbriæ conficiuntur adiunxit.*

[74] On Pompey's veterans in 59, Plut. *Pomp.* 48.1; *Luc.* 42.6; *Cæs.* 14.6; Cæsar's soldiers in 55, Dio, 39.31.1–2; Plut. *Crass.* 14.6; Antony's election, Hirtius, *BG*, 8.50.

it will not do to assert, as is often done, that the *milites* of the late Republic automatically became the private *clientelæ* of their commanders.[75] Assistance and loyalty to their patron depended on his *beneficia;* there were few moral or hereditary bonds. Donatives and booty in the service would win favor—and land grants after return to Italy. But the gratitude did not always endure. One hears nothing again of Metellus Pius' troops after they were promised agrarian lots in 70, nor of Lucullus' soldiers after his triumph. Pompey's veterans secured land in 59 through the machinations of their general and his political allies. Yet they showed no inclination to support his projects in subsequent years. In 56, when Pompey was under assault from Clodius' mobs, he called up assistance from Picenum and Cisalpine Gaul, presumably his old clients, not his veterans.[76] When the triumvirs backed candidates for election in the late 50s, Cæsar could send soldiers to cast their votes; they were still under his command and receiving benefits. Pompey evidently had no such control over ex-soldiers.[77] And in 49, when civil war erupted, Pompey turned to the *coloni* settled in Campania, many of them doubtless his veterans; the response was decidedly unenthusiastic.[78] And concentration on the leading generals ignores those dozens of proconsuls who commanded armies abroad but never, so far as we know, developed any patron-client relationships with them. Cicero speaks often and proudly of his military accomplishments in Cilicia; yet there is no sign that the soldiers became part of his *clientela.* The whole notion of soldiers as private instruments of their generals in both the military and political realms needs drastic revision.[79]

Common presumption holds that the armies of Cicero's day developed a "professional" character absent in previous eras. One of the by-products, some have argued, was the emergence of a military mentality, a homogeneity in

[75] As, e.g., A. von Premerstein, *AbhMünch*, 15 (1937): 22–26; Taylor, *Party Politics*, pp. 47–48; Gabba, *Athenæum*, 29 (1951): 183–188.

[76] Cic. *Ad Q. Frat.* 2.3.4.

[77] Cic. *Ad Att.* 4.16.6.

[78] Cic. *Ad Att.* 7.14.2: *me Pompeius Capuam venire voluit et adiuvare dilectum; in quo parum prolixe respondent Campani coloni*; cf. *Ad Att.* 7.21.1, 7.23.3. Acutely noted by Meier, *Res Pub.*, pp. 104–105.

[79] There is little warrant, for example, for Smith's statement that personal relations between general and army were close and retained in the political arena; *Service*, pp. 41–42; still less for Gabba's insistence that military leaders were also heads of popular factions and democratic groups; *Athenæum*, 29 (1951): 189–202. The importance of the client relationship is rightly questioned by Brunt, *JRS*, 52 (1962): 76–77; Harmand, *L'Armée*, pp. 442–455. For Harmand, only Cæsar was able to establish that relationship with his forces. Perhaps so—he certainly had the longest continuous period abroad with which to develop it. But since civil war supervened upon his return we shall never know how devoted his troops might have been in politics had they been discharged in 49.

the ranks, which produced soldiers alien to civil traditions and indifferent to Republican institutions.[80] Precisely what is meant by "professional," however, remains unclear. That many *municipales, agrestes,* country laborers, marginal subsistence farmers, and the rural poor enlisted to obtain a better livelihood is unquestionably true. It does not follow that they all saw in the army a permanent career. Testimony on men in the ranks is, of course, most scanty–as it is on the common man throughout history. Only indirect evidence is available for speculation.

There can be no doubt that the military demands upon the late Republic required a revision of earlier presuppositions. It no longer sufficed to call up soldiers on an ad hoc basis for brief campaigns after which they would be discharged to their homes. Wars became lengthy, distant, and difficult. Provincial holdings were extensive in both the western and the eastern Mediterranean. And it was dangerous to leave those provinces devoid of forces. Invasions from without or revolts from the subject populace within could hardly be met if Rome relied on emergency recruitments at home for each crisis. In fact, by the era of Cicero garrison armies existed in all provinces where neighbors were hostile or subjects potentially restless. Extent of the forces varied, depending on the situation and the character and importance of the province. But the institution of a standing army was acknowledged *de facto,* if not *de iure.*[81] Yet it is hazardous to equate a standing army with a professional army. The retention of forces abroad at a certain level and on a permanent basis does not mean that the personnel was permanent. Release of part of the garrison when replacements were available would maintain total numbers without requiring indefinite service for individuals.

Did soldiers enlist for lengthy terms in the late Republic? Polybius remarks that in the second century infantrymen were expected to serve for a fixed number of years. The precise number, unfortunately, is corrupt in the text: evidently six, but some editors have read sixteen.[82] Whatever the figure may be, the practice may have been different in the Ciceronian period. Augustus, we are told, initiated a new system wherein the length of *stipendia* was specified at sixteen years. If so, the change implies that fixed terms were not regularly observed in the preceding era.[83] And that is the conclusion which the evidence, such as it is, would also seem to demand. The Fimbriani, the nearest instance

[80] Cf. Gabba, *Athenæum,* 29 (1951): 178–182, 202–211, 249–250; Smith, *Service,* pp. 11–26, 59–69.

[81] Smith's discussion, *Service,* pp. 11–26, is essential reading on this point. Cf. now, for more detail, Brunt, *Italian Manpower,* pp. 446–472.

[82] Polyb. 6.19.2; see F. W. Walbank, *A Historical Commentary on Polybius,* I (Oxford, 1957): 698.

[83] Dio, 54.25.5–6; Suet. *Aug.* 49.

to what may be regarded as professional *milites,* enlisted in 86 and, through a succession of commanders, seem to have remained in Asia for over twenty years. But the example is unusual, perhaps unique. The majority of Sulla's forces, disbanded after the civil war, had been acquired by him in Italy only two years before. Veterans of the Sertorian war retired after a maximum of ten years' service in Spain, many of them probably with less time there. Pompey discharged his troops in 62; though some had been inherited from Lucullus, most had served no more than six or seven years. The soldiers called up by L. Piso in 58 were dismissed by him three years later. Cæsar's legions stayed with him in Gaul; but he had to do much recruiting during the 50s; not all had been there from the beginning. And there was talk of war-weariness by the end of the decade.[84] It is clear that there were no standard norms. The extent of the war or the desires of commander and troops dictated the length of service. An individual recruit did not necessarily obligate himself to a protracted tenure in the ranks. Some doubtless spent the better part of a lifetime abroad and preferred it that way. They can hardly have constituted a majority. The larger armies of the late Republic returned to Italy. And most of them sought landed property in the countryside to resume civilian life. The "military mentality" is unattested, and "professional army" is a misnomer.

One can cite certain individuals designated by the sources as *homines militares*: men who spent long years in fighting and who developed a high degree of martial skills.[85] Note, for example, P. Considius, an expert in war, who saw duty in the armies of Sulla, M. Crassus, and Cæsar successively–a career that must have spanned at least a quarter-century.[86] One of Pompey's soldiers in the pirate war of 67, L. Septimius, was still in the service in 48, at which time he betrayed his former commander and engineered his murder.[87] M. Petreius had been a military man for thirty years by 63. Nor did that satiate his appetite for war; Petreius resumed activity as a Pompeian subordinate in Spain after 55 and was still fighting there in 49, only to perish during

[84] On all this, see the perceptive remarks of Brunt, *JRS,* 52 (1962): 75, 80–81, with references. Accepted by Harmand, *L'Armée,* pp. 258–260. Note also that in 67 the government ordered disbandment of part of Lucullus' forces who claimed that their term had expired; Cic. *De Imp. Pomp.* 26. Lucullus had been in the East for seven years. Some of his troops had been there since Servilius Vatia's campaigns in 78, but few, apart from the Fimbriani, any longer than that.

[85] Gabba, *Athenæum,* 29 (1951): 202–211, stresses their importance as evidence for professionalism in the army; so also Smith, *Service,* pp. 62–69.

[86] Cæs. *BG,* 1.21: *P. Considius, qui rei militaris peritissimus habebatur et in exercitu L. Sullæ et postea in M. Crassi fuerat.*

[87] Cæs. *BC,* 3.104; Plut. *Pomp.* 88.1.

the civil war while in his sixties.[88] Long military experience also marked L. Valerius Flaccus and C. Pomptinus who headed government forces against Catiline in 63.[89] Similarly, there were Q. Marcius Crispus, who served in Macedon during the mid-50s, and M. Anneius, one of Cicero's subordinates in Cilicia, both of whom are depicted as masters of military science.[90]

Exaggerated conclusions ought not to be drawn from these examples. Broad military experience did not necessarily make men unsuited or indifferent to civil careers. The very men noted above may serve as illustrations. Despite his penchant for the battlefield, M. Petreius was also a senator and rose to the prætorship by 64. Far from scorning Republican traditions, he was conspicuous in 59, opposing the schemes of Cæsar and taking a political stand with M. Cato.[91] L. Valerius Flaccus and C. Pomptinus were delegated responsibilities against Catiline in 63, not simply because of their martial talents, but because both held prætorian office in that year. Evidently they found no inconsistency between service in the army and high office in Rome. Q. Marcius Crispus, after a distinguished military career, went on to attain a prætorship by 46. M. Annæus' position in Cilicia was that of a *legatus,* which implies senatorial rank, a status unattainable except through election to civil office.[92] Other senators who spent much of their adult lives in warfare never lost sight of their political station in Rome. Q. Sertorius made his name on the battlefield and eventually perished there. But he had also risen through the ranks of civil magistracies to the prætorship. Only the divisive contests of civil war forced him to end his life as a declared outlaw rather than an esteemed senator. Long service at the front did not make L. Murena a professional soldier; he capped his career with consular office, thereby ennobling a prætorian family.

[88] Sallust, *Cat.* 59.6: *homo militaris, quod amplius annos triginta . . . cum magna gloria in exercitu fuerat*; Vell. Pat. 2.48.1; Broughton, *MRR*, II:268, 302. His death came in Africa in 46.

[89] Sallust, *Cat.* 45.1-2: *homines militares.*

[90] Cic. *In Pis.* 54: *belli ac rei militaris peritum . . . Q. Marcium*; Cic. *Ad Fam.* 13.57.1: *M. Anneium . . . eius opera, consilio, scientia rei militaris vel maxime intellego me et rempublicam adiuvari posse.*

[91] Dio, 38.3.2.

[92] Cf. the sober remarks of Harmand, *L'Armée*, pp. 387-389. Smith's references, *Service*, pp. 62-64, to legates who did not pursue further political careers prove nothing. Those men must have been senators–and politicians–to have received appointment as *legati* in the first place. Absence of testimony on their later careers may simply reflect the skimpiness of our sources. And some of Smith's entries are illegitimate: C. Memmius and Q. Marcius Crispus did hold office after their military service; T. Labienus would almost certainly have done so, but for the civil war. The inclusion of C. Volusenus Quadratus depends on identification of the military tribune in 56 with the *præfectus equitum* of 51–which is uncertain; cf. Harmand, *L'Armée*, pp. 356-357.

L. Afranius endured many campaigns with Pompey in Spain and in the East from the 70s through the 50s. But in the interim he had attained all official posts in Rome, including the consulship itself. T. Labienus earned notoriety first as a politician, an active tribune in 63, and eventually a prætor. It was only later that he established his reputation as Cæsar's principal lieutenant in the Gallic wars. Even then, however, Labienus kept his gaze fixed on senatorial *honores:* he was aiming for a consulship in 48.[93] Similarly, Ser. Sulpicius Galba, a legate in Gaul in the 60s and again under Cæsar in the 50s, returned from Cæsar's camp to obtain a prætorship in 54, and was Cæsar's candidate for the consulship of 49. P. Sulpicius Rufus' dutiful service in the Gallic wars earned him a prætorship in 48 and, eventually, the censorship in 42.[94]

Additional instances could be cited. It is by now evident that even those individuals singled out as *homines militares* had not abandoned the forum for the camp.[95] The known examples are, of course, almost all officers–hence politicians and senators. For men in the ranks there were few opportunities to pursue *honores* in Rome. And, for the most part, they remain faceless and nameless. But wealth accumulated abroad might permit a higher social status at home. Centurions especially–however lowly their origins–were in a position to enrich themselves on profitable campaigns. Some might attain equestrian rank, as did L. Petronius, who perished by his own hand at the side of his benefactor in 87.[96] Perhaps also P. Cæsius, a non-Roman from Ravenna, whose services in the Social War gained him the franchise and eventually classification as an *eques.*[97] At least one ex-centurion, L. Fufidius, actually entered the senate, promoted by L. Sulla during his dictatorship.[98] Advancement such as the latter instance must have been rare. But many centurions certainly retired

[93] Hirtius, *BG*, 8.50; cf. Syme, *JRS*, 28 (1938): 121–123.

[94] Cf. Cicero's famous contrast of the legal and military careers, both rendering successful men eligible for the highest civil offices; *Pro Mur.* 22–30; esp. 30: *duæ sint artes igitur quæ possint locare homines in amplissimo gradu dignitatis, una imperatoris, altera oratoris boni; ab hoc enim pacis ornamenta retinentur, ab illo belli pericula repelluntur.*

[95] Cicero's assertion that much of the senatorial youth in his day shunned military service may apply to the old aristocracy, but hardly to the senate's rank and file; *Pro Font.* 42–43.

[96] Val. Max. 4.7.5: *L. quoque Petronius . . . admodum humili loco natus ad equestrem ordinem et splendidæ militiæ stipendia P. Cæli beneficio pervenerat.* The passage does not, of course, prove that Petronius had been a centurion; cf. Gelzer, *Kleine Schriften*, I:20. But it was evidently military service which enabled him to obtain equestrian rank.

[97] Cic. *Pro Balbo*, 50; cf. Nicolet, in J. P. Brisson, *Problèmes de la guerre à Rome* (Paris, 1969), p. 148.

[98] Sallust, *Hist.* 1.55.22, Maur.; Orosius, 5.21.3. Perhaps he should be distinguished from the propraætor in Spain in 80; Sallust, *Hist.* 1.108, Maur.; Plut. *Sert.* 12.3; cf. Nicolet, *REL*, 45 (1967): 297–301; Wiseman, *New Men*, p. 232. See also Plut. *Sulla*, 31.3; Florus, 2.9.25. We need not take literally Sallust's tendentious remark about *gregarii milites* in the Sullan senate; *Cat.* 37.6.

from service with earnings that qualified them as *equites.* That opened to them important positions in civilian life. We are told specifically that centurions who attained equestrian status frequently sat on the benches of Rome's judicial tribunals.[99] The civil career retained its attractiveness to those equipped to pursue it–including those who gained that equipment through military *stipendia.* Of the common rankers, some may have remained in the service for long periods; most returned home with additional revenues or expectations of landed property. Military service did not alienate the soldier from the Republic.

Julius Cæsar crossed the Rubicon with his army in 49. The event has been taken as emblematic, the culmination of a steady and relentless development. But where are the precedents? One may point to L. Sulla's march on Rome in 88, forty years before. But the parallel is far from exact. Sulla marched on Rome, but not against Rome. Sulla was consul in 88, the official head of government, duly awarded the province of Asia and control of the Mithridatic war. He returned in arms when political *inimici* ventured to snatch that commission from him. Not that the act was in any way defensible. Almost all of Sulla's officers abandoned him rather than partake in the move. His troops, however, followed, looking to profits in the eastern wars and unwilling to be replaced by other soldiers. But before one lapses into rhetoric about private armies and military *clientelæ*, it is pertinent to recall an obvious fact. The soldiers took orders, not from a rebel chief bent on overthrowing the Republic, but from a Roman consul, the head of state, challenging those who had usurped his authority. The civil war of 83–81 represented but a logical corollary: a struggle over legitimacy, not for a new order. Sulla's subsequent reforms were conservative and solidifying.

Sulla's march does not explain the actions of Julius Cæsar. A generation intervened, with no emulators of Sulla's deed–not Pompey, who had all the necessary resources; not Lucullus; not the numerous other commanders who were in charge of sizable armies in the Ciceronian age, like Metellus Pius, Servilius Vatia, C. Curio, M. Crassus, M. Lucullus, C. Piso, L. Murena, C. Antonius, L. Piso, and A. Gabinius.[100] Nor did Julius Cæsar appeal to the example

[99] Cic. *Phil.* 1.20: *At quæ est ista tertia decuria? "Centurionum," inquit. Quid? Isti ordini iudicatus lege Iulia, etiam ante Pompeia, Aurelia non patebat? "Census præfiniebatur," inquit. Non centurioni quidem solum sed equiti etiam Romano; itaque viri fortissimi atque honestissimi qui ordines duxerunt res et iudicant et iudicaverunt.* On the centurionate, see Harmand, *L'Armée*, pp. 334–336, 477–479; Nicolet, in Brisson, *Problèmes*, pp. 146–153.

[100] Excluded here are Q. Sertorius and M. Lepidus. Both, of course, were rebels in the government's eyes. But Sertorius in Spain was simply carrying on the remnants of the civil war, rejecting the legitimacy of Sulla's regime. Lepidus probably did not intend armed insurrection at the outset, but was driven into it by the victims of Sulla's proscriptions; see above, chap. 1. On *imperia extraordinaria,* see below, Appendix III.

of Sulla. Far from it. Sulla had narrowed the privileges of Roman tribunes; Cæsar went to war in defense of their time-honored rights–such, at least, was his claim.[101] A complex swirl of events triggered the crossing of the Rubicon, most of them emerging only in the immediately preceding months.[102] No lengthy string of precedents clarified and sanctioned Cæsar's decision. It is unwarranted foreshortening to leap blithely from Sulla to Cæsar, branding their acts as representative and ignoring a whole generation that produced no analogous examples. The Roman army consisted of individuals interested in profit and social betterment; it was not a source of revolutionary sentiment. Not even the soldiers of Julius Cæsar marched into Italy with the intent or the desire to bring down the Roman Republic.

THE GRAIN DISTRIBUTION

What response was forthcoming from Rome's leaders to the needs of the *proletarii?* If one credits Sallust, the whole of the late Republic consumed itself in a struggle between rich and poor, between the mighty and the lowly, the *nobilitas* and the populace.[103] But that embittered historian was writing in the wake of a brutal and disillusioning civil war. The portrait is overdrawn and misleading. Traditional links between noble *patroni* and their *clientelæ* cannot be left out of the reckoning. They produced countless vertical slices into the social structure, which prevented hardening of the horizontal lines. The trumpetings of Cicero about *concordia* among the classes may have been largely wishful thinking. But it would be equally mistaken to represent his age as dissolved by class conflict. The aristocracy, alert to its own welfare, did not turn an entirely deaf ear to the claims of Rome's lower orders.[104]

The economic conditions of the *plebs*, as we have seen, were hardly enviable. That was especially true after the civil war and dictatorship of the Sullan era. Small farmers who found themselves on the wrong side would not have been spared retaliation; nor would residents of the Italian municipalities who had opposed Sulla. And neutrals, we may be sure, endured irreparable losses when armed strife devastated the countryside in the 80s and during the Lepidan

[101] Cf. Cæs. *BC*, 1.7, where the contrast with Sulla is explicitly affirmed.

[102] On this, see below, chap. 11.

[103] Cf. Sallust, *Iug.* 41.5–6: *Namque coepere nobilitas dignitatem, populus libertatem in lubidinem vortere, sibi quisque ducere, trahere, rapere. Ita omnia in duas partis abstracta sunt, res publica, quæ media fuerat, dilacerata. Ceterum nobilitas factione magis pollebat, plebis vis soluta atque dispersa in multitudine minus poterat*; cf. also Sallust, *Cat.* 37.10–39.2; *Hist.* 1.12, Maur.

[104] Terms like "aristocracy" or "ruling class" must here be understood to include not simply the so-called (by moderns) *optimates*, such as Lucullus, Cato, or Hortensius, but *nobiles* and upper-class politicians generally, including Cæsar, Clodius, Crassus; i.e., men in a position to exercise political power. There was no fundamental ideological cleavage between *optimates* and *populares*. See above, chap. 2.

insurrection.[105] Abandonment or destruction of property reduced many former landowners to the status of rural laborers and tenant farmers. And others must have sought a livelihood in Rome in the course of the following decades, thereby gradually swelling the freeborn component of the *plebs urbana*. Since the professions and crafts remained largely the province of freedmen, the dislocated ex-farmers were often limited to unskilled jobs and, perhaps, prolonged periods of unemployment. Sulla had done nothing to make their lot easier. In 81 the dictator abolished an institution practiced in Rome for two generations: state purchase and distribution of grain at cheap prices for the urban populace.[106] It was not one of his happier or more prescient enactments.

But the government in subsequent years proved to be more sensitive to the urban situation. Lepidus' demand for a *lex frumentaria* in 78 was premature and abortive. The internal and external strife that followed delayed any official action on this score. But a new measure, sponsored by the consuls of 73, revived grain distributions once more.[107] Straitened financial circumstances limited the benefaction. The sources imply that there were 40,000 recipients under this bill. But there may have been more, many more. In any case, there is no reason to doubt the government's sincerity in dealing with the problem. Whatever the humanitarianism—or lack of it—in Roman officials, a contented *plebs* would be in the interest of the state.[108]

Of equal significance, not to be overlooked, were private benefactions. The patron relationship continued to be fundamental in Roman society. And politicians could add significantly to their repute and following by providing grain for the proletariate below the market price. Cicero made certain to ship extra supplies to Rome during his Sicilian quæstorship of 75. Q. Hortensius and M. Seius utilized their ædileships of 75 and 74 respectively to make corn available at rates which the *plebs* could afford. And M. Crassus fed the populace for three months in 70 out of his own resources.[109] The public interest was served—as were the private ambitions of Roman politicians.

Sponsorship of *leges frumentariæ* was a traditional demagogic device—but

[105] Cf., e.g., Florus, 2.6.11–14, 2.9.22; Appian, *BC*, 1.86.

[106] Sallust, *Hist.* 1.55.11, Maur.; Gran. Licin. 34, Flem.

[107] Sallust, *Hist.* 3.48.19, Maur.; Cic. *Verr.* 2.3.163, 2.3.173, 2.5.52; cf. Asconius, 8, Clark. For Lepidus' proposal, see Gran. Licin. 34, Flem.; cf. Criniti, *MemIstLomb*, 30 (1969): 397–399.

[108] The figure of 40,000 is derived from combination of Sallust, *Hist.* 3.48.19, Maur. and Cic. *Verr.* 2.3.72; discussed by J. Van Berchem, *Les Distributions de blé et d'argent à la plèbe romaine sous l'empire* (Geneva, 1939), pp. 15–16, and Brunt, *Past and Present*, 35 (1966): 17. Rowland, *Acta Antiqua*, 13 (1965): 81–83, argues for a much higher figure on the basis of Cic. *Verr.* 2.3.163: perhaps as many as 180,000. That is certainly excessive; cf. Brunt, *Italian Manpower*, pp. 378–379.

[109] On Cicero's quæstorship, Broughton, *MRR*, II:98; Hortensius: Cic. *Verr.* 2.3.215; Seius: Cic. *De Off.* 2.58; cf. Pliny, *NH*, 15.2; Crassus: Plut. *Crass.* 12.2; *Comp. Nic. et Crass.* 1.4.

not of demagogues alone. The Catilinarian conspiracy, even though successfully crushed, had raised the specter of urban revolt. The government, as a consequence, evinced increased concern for the welfare of the hungry and restless *plebs*. In 62, a new grain bill secured passage, appreciably increasing the recipients of public bounty, probably to over 200,000. Its sponsor was that most undemagogic of Roman politicians, M. Porcius Cato. Obviously, the advocacy of corn distribution knew no party. The measure averted what might have been an ugly situation and at least dissipated, if it did not eliminate, popular discontent.[110]

A final and logical step awaited execution. The broad *popularis* program of P. Clodius in 58 could not leave the proletariate out of account. Clodius' *lex frumentaria* put the seal on a lengthy development: henceforth, grain was to be allocated absolutely free of charge to adult males on the lists of the *plebs frumentaria*.[111] Moralists might deplore the debilitating effects of the "dole." And Clodius' contemporary detractors stressed the added financial burden on the state's resources, a standard complaint against frumentary laws.[112] But in the economic circumstances of Republican Rome it offered important benefits. The roster of eligible recipients increased as well, partly because shrewd masters freed some of their slaves to take advantage of the new generosity.[113] It may have climbed beyond 400,000 in the Republic's last decade.

The fact that Clodius brought to fruition a development furthered also by M. Cato is worthy of note. We have had occasion to remark on several instances where reform proposals received the endorsement of various figures who were otherwise at odds politically. A more minor example involving Cato and Clodius was discussed earlier: both, at different times, sponsored measures to restrict and regulate activities of public employees.[114] The continuity is even more striking on the matter of grain distribution. That issue engaged the activities of men as different as Cicero, Crassus, Hortensius, Cato, and Clodius: popular demagogues, enterprising politicians, and conservatives alike. It was smart politics, and it spared the state much misery. One did not have to subscribe to a particular political persuasion to acknowledge that fact. Not that the problem of feeding the urban poor was altogether alleviated. Temporary food shortages caused by external crisis or piracy occasionally provoked riot in the city, as we shall see. But public and private actions by the establishment betray continued concern, if not sympathy, for the plight of the *plebs*.

[110] Plut. *Cæs.* 8.4; *Cato*, 26.1. Plutarch puts Cato's action in the context of his political rivalry with Julius Cæsar—a not unreasonable analysis. But he makes it clear that impetus came from the potentially dangerous aftermath of the Catilinarian movement.

[111] Cic. *Pro Sest.* 55; *De Domo*, 25; Asconius, 8, Clark; Dio, 38.13.1; Schol. Bob. 132, Stangl.

[112] Cf. *Ad Herenn.* 1.21; Cic. *Pro Sest.* 103; *Tusc. Disp.* 3.48; *De Off.* 2.72.

[113] Dio, 39.24.1; Dion. Hal. 4.24.5; cf. Brunt, *Italian Manpower*, pp. 379–381.

[114] See above, pp. 254–255.

LAND DISTRIBUTION

Bread for the masses, however, was insufficient. Since the dole applied only to free males, no man could expect to support a family without other sources of livelihood. Agriculture was still by far the most important occupation in Italy—and, for a free man, the most respectable means of earning a living.[115] The rank and file of returning veterans encompassed men reared in rural Italy and anxious to acquire or reacquire landed property. And there is no reason to doubt that the freeborn component of the urban commons also aspired to land in the countryside, especially those whose roots were in the soil and whose recent migration to the city had been forced by civil war and devastation. Government purchase and dispensing of plots in Italy could have provided needed relief in the city. But on this score the state often proved reluctant and difficult to budge. Expense offered a principal obstacle, or so, at least, it was claimed.[116] Also, a commitment to the rights of private property and a traditional abhorrence of egalitarianism stood in the way.[117] Most important, however, one may assume, was the fear that redistribution of land would mean removal of tenants installed under the dictatorship and would stir up again all the passions and violence of the civil war. That represented a risk which many in the aristocracy were unwilling to run.

Others saw it differently. There was a good conservative argument for land allotments. By providing lots in Italy, the government could repopulate the countryside and restore the rural yeomanry. Not the least of the benefits from such a policy would be removal from the city of its less desirable and potentially inflammatory elements. It was precisely that motive which impelled Ti. Gracchus in the first major agrarian reform in 133. And it persisted as a theme throughout the Ciceronian era. *Leges agrariae*, when proposed, normally had returning veterans first in view. But the element of relieving urban stress played its part in most of the bills. Within the aristocracy, those two conflicting considerations needed to be weighed constantly: the advantage of reducing proletariate numbers in the capital and the risk of provoking social upheaval in the countryside. And the dilemma was complicated by factional strife in the senate: *beneficia* for veterans would enhance the prestige and increase the adherents of returning generals; their political foes would not readily consent.

[115] Cf. Cic. *De Off.* 1.151: *omnium autem rerum, ex quibus aliquid acquiritur, nihil est agri cultura melius, nihil uberius, nihil dulcius, nihil homine libero dignius.* See De Robertis, *Lavoro*, pp. 52–63.

[116] Cf. Cic. *De Leg. Agrar.* 2.10, 2.15; *Ad Att.* 2.16.1; and see Brunt, *JRS*, 52 (1962): 84.

[117] Cf. Cic. *De Off.* 2.73: *in primis autem videndum erit ei, qui rem publicam administrabit, ut suum quisque teneat neque de bonis privatorum publice deminutio fiat*; also *De Off.* 2.78; *De Rep.* 1.43.

Hence, a variety of complications bedeviled agrarian legislation throughout the late Republic.

The first recorded measure after Sulla's dictatorship came in 70. The end of the Sertorian war and the return of triumphant generals motivated it. Initiative came from the Roman senate, which authorized the setting aside of land for veterans of the Spanish campaigns, the soldiers of both Pompeius Magnus and Metellus Pius. Nothing revolutionary was contained in that proposal. Agrarian rewards for loyal and victorious soldiers had a long history, dating back to the early second century. The Gracchan program surely had in mind, at least in part, the returning veterans of the Numantine war. And the tradition was broadened by legislation at the end of the second century, for the benefit of Marius' troops, men of lower-class origins, survivors of the Jugurthine and German wars.[118] Of the measure in 70, too little is known to permit detailed discussion. None could deny honors due the troops of Pompey and Metellus, who had stamped out the last embers of civil war and preserved the regime from armed rebels. The senate approved a measure for land grants, an act then translated, so it seems, into a law of the people–the *lex Plotia agraria*. Implementation, however, was another matter. Some of the Pompeian servicemen were apparently settled on landed property. But full distribution to the troops suffered delay and postponement. Pretext stressed insufficient resources in the treasury. In fact, the postponement may reflect political opposition to the triumphant commanders. Since Pompey drew on many of his former soldiers to mount the eastern expeditions of the 60s, the senate could defer execution of the *lex* without fear of volatile consequences.[119]

Nothing in the (very sketchy) evidence on the *lex Plotia* suggests that it had in view any but veterans of the Spanish campaigns and the servile war. Surplus population in the city had evidently not yet become a serious issue. And since the major conflicts in the East drained off much manpower, no immediate pressure existed for land distribution on a large scale. By 63, however, the Mithridatic war, now more than a decade old, was drawing to a close. Pompey would soon be home, faced with a massive demobilization

[118] On the earlier agrarian measures or proposals, see G. Tibiletti, *Athenæum*, 28 (1950): 183–266; Gabba, *Athenæum*, 29 (1951): 211–225; cf. Gruen, *Roman Politics*, pp. 50–51, 99–102.

[119] The *lex Plotia* is mentioned but once, without elucidation; Cic. *Ad Att.* 1.18.6. The author, however, may well be the same Plautius or Plotius who sponsored the bill on amnesty for the Lepidani in 70 and the *lex Plautia de vi*. If so, his *lex agraria* is best regarded as a follow-up to the *s.c.* on land allotments to the Spanish veterans. Dio, 38.5.1, speaks of delay in the measure's implementation. But the settlement of some Pompeian soldiers is affirmed by Plut. *Luc.* 34.3–4. On these matters, see the illuminating discussions of Gabba, *PP*, 13 (1950): 66–68; R. E. Smith, *CQ*, 7 (1957): 82–85.

problem. And increasing numbers of freeborn poor in Rome were causing discomfort among the ruling class. Such matters formed the background for the most sweeping of agrarian proposals in the city's history: the *rogatio Servilia*, brought before the senate and the people at the beginning of 63.

Sponsor of the bill was P. Servilius Rullus, a shadowy character. Rullus is unnoticed by the sources before his tribunate of 63–and unnoticed thereafter. Hence, it is normally assumed that he was a mere front man for more powerful figures. Several hints in Cicero's speeches against the measure allude to machinations in the background, politicians who stood behind the tribune, prepared to capitalize on the events.[120] Moderns have seen it as a plot of Crassus and Cæsar.[121] The conjecture is hasty and ill-founded. Cicero's references are studiously nebulous. There may or may not have been powerful *nobiles* behind Rullus. Cicero probably had little evidence; but it was in his interests to let his audience imagine the worst.[122] Perhaps Rullus merits more credit than is usually accorded him. In any case, the bill itself requires attention. Our information is defective–wholly dependent on three Ciceronian orations, all contrived to undermine it.[123] Despite the rhetoric, however, one can discern a blueprint, intelligent in design and farsighted in conception.

Extensive care had gone into the framing of the bill. At least forty clauses were contained therein, outlining the supervision, purchase, and distribution of land assignments.[124] Responsibility was to fall to a commission of ten men, who would hold office for five years. A full administrative staff would be theirs, duly detailed in the bill: clerks, surveyors, scribes, architects, and attendants, and all manner of supplies.[125] The decemvirs were subject to popular election, by seventeen of the thirty-five tribes. Rullus himself was to supervise the procedure, presiding over the allotment to choose the participating tribes, and he would himself be eligible for appointment to the commission. Cicero, of course, imputes sinister and self-seeking motives to the tribune,

[120] Cic. *De Leg. Agrar.* 1.11, 1.16, 1.22, 2.20, 2.23, 2.46, 2.63, 2.98.

[121] Hardy, *Some Problems*, pp. 68–98; Meyer, *Cæsars Monarchie*, pp. 13–14; Gelzer, *Cæsar*, pp. 42–45; Rice Holmes, *Rom. Rep.*, I:242–249; Ciaceri, *Cicerone*, I:195–215; Afzelius, *ClMed*, 3 (1940): 214–235; E. J. Jonkers, *Social and Economic Commentary on Cicero's De Lege Agraria Orationes Tres* (Leiden, 1963), pp. 7–8.

[122] Cf. Sumner, *TAPA*, 97 (1966): 572–573.

[123] There were four altogether; one has perished. The first addressed itself to the senate, the other two to the *populus*; see Cic. *Ad Att.* 2.1.3. The account in Plut. *Cic.* 12.2–5 is wholly derivative from Cicero. So, rightly, L. Agnes, *RivFilol*, 21 (1943): 41–45; it ought never to have been doubted. Other references are brief and add nothing: Cic. *In Pis.* 4; *Pro Rab. Perd.* 32; *Pro Sulla*, 65; *Ad Fam.* 13.4.2; Dio, 37.25.3–4; Pliny, *NH*, 7.117, 8.210; Quint. *Inst. Orat.* 2.16.7; Gellius, 7.16.7.

[124] Cic. *De Leg. Agrar.* 3.4.

[125] Cic. *De Leg. Agrar.* 2.32.

and denounces the undemocratic character of those provisions. His tendentious account need not be followed. Selection of voting tribes by lot just prior to the election had a proper end in view: removal of incentive to bribery. Since no one could know in advance who the actual electors would be, there was little point in soliciting or intimidating voters. As for the other provisions to which Cicero reacts in horror–limitation of candidates to men present in Rome; Rullus' role as *rogator*, presiding officer, and candidate; the possibility of combining the decemvirate with ordinary magistracies; and the use of a *lex curiata*, with ban on tribunician veto, to sanction the proceedings–all, in fact, had good precedents in previous legislation. The bill aimed at impartial proceedings, coupling dispatch in implementation with sufficient constitutional safeguards.[126]

The novelty and importance of the *rogatio Servilia* lay not in its procedural regulations but in its scope. Distribution of public land, of course, stayed within the government's province. How much was available by 63 is uncertain; but there remained the rich agricultural territory of the *ager Campanus* and the *ager Stellas*. Those lands had been untouched by the Gracchan assignations and even by the Sullan redistribution; let out at rent, they had provided a steady income to the state for several generations. The Rullan bill proposed to forgo that income: the public land would be turned over to private citizens in lots of ten or twelve *iugera*, enough to support five thousand new settlers. Cicero sheds bitter tears over the break with long-established tradition and the loss of revenue for the public coffers.[127] The hyperbolic lamentation ought not to be overvalued. Increased receipts from the provinces, especially with the suppression of piracy and the prospective end of the Mithridatic war, would more than compensate for the revenue loss.

But allocation of public land would not suffice for all needs. More property in Italy needed to be made available for consignment. The Rullan bill specifically eschewed confiscation of property or forcible seizures. The state would purchase land, and only from landowners willing to sell. Cicero, naturally, puts the worst construction upon the legislator's motives: the measure creates a dumping-ground for land whose owners could not otherwise find a purchaser; hence, there would be room for considerable jobbery between the decemvirs and the sellers; and land thus realized would be of the worst quality, uncultivable, sandy wastes or marshy swamps.[128] The rhetoric was pungent

[126] On the election procedure contained in the *rogatio*, see Cic. *De Leg. Agrar.* 2.16–17, 2.20–21, 2.24, 2.26, 2.28–30. That the use of seventeen tribes would reduce extraneous influence on the voter was properly noted by Hardy, *Some Problems*, p. 83; cf. Afzelius, *ClMed*, 3 (1940): 224–226. On precedents for Rullus' other electoral clauses, see Gabba, *Mélanges Piganiol* (1966), II:769–776.

[127] Cic. *De Leg. Agrar.* 1.20, 2.76–86, 2.96, 3.15.

[128] Cic. *De Leg. Agrar.* 1.14–15, 2.63–72, 2.98.

and effective, but misleading in the extreme. Cicero could not possibly know, nor could Rullus be expected to specify in advance, which lands would be purchased. Consequently, the orator's denunciatory flights are altogether fanciful. It is true that many Sullan colonists, unpopular with their neighbors and unsuccessful as farmers, were anxious to sell. Individual purchasers were hard to find; and the Rullan bill gave the frustrated seller a customer in the state. But nothing shows that the property involved would be worthless. And the bill provided numerous advantages both for individuals and for the public. It gave legal title, once for all, to the Sullan beneficiaries, thereby closing a running sore and a potential source of controversy. If they wished to dispose of their holdings, the state would give full compensation.[129] For some, of course, that would be an unexpected and undeserved boon. But it was better to give blanket endorsement to their claims than risk endless legal wrangles and possible disruption. Those who had been ousted from their farms in the Sullan period would presumably constitute a large proportion of the recipients under the new law. They were to recover land at state expense, but without confiscation and terrorizing. The agriculture of Italy could only benefit with skilled farmers replacing frustrated ex-soldiers. And one might anticipate gains for the economy generally. Unsuccessful cultivators, recompensed in cash, could invest it in other, more congenial ventures. That entailed increased opportunities and transactions for financiers and businessmen.[130] Numerous groups stood to profit; and so, not least, did the economy as a whole. Rullus' proposal was perspicacious and thoughtful.

Of course, all depended on the government's ability to finance this venturesome project. The point was not ignored by the *rogatio Servilia*. Framers of the measure dwelled in detail on new or increased sources of revenue. First, it authorized the sale of public sites in the city, as well as other items and properties in Italy belonging to the state. Nothing revolutionary here: it was simply implementation of a senatorial decree that dated back to 81.[131] That, probably, would not realize a large return. Of greater significance, Rullus' bill directed the decemvirs to offer for sale foreign dominions that had fallen into Roman hands since 88. Here was prospect of lucrative revenue indeed, for the clause encompassed wealthy areas in Asia Minor, Cyprus, and, perhaps, Egypt. Not that one should follow Cicero's imaginative speculations about decemvirs' auctioning off whole provinces, nations, or kingdoms. More likely, the proposal envisioned selling of certain portions of the *ager publicus* which would bring in the most profit; it hardly involved the disposal of actual

[129] Cic. *De Leg. Agrar.* 2.68–70, 3.3, 3.6–14.

[130] Cf. the remarks of Afzelius, *ClMed*, 3 (1940): 230–232.

[131] Cic. *De Leg. Agrar.* 1.3–4, 2.35–37.

Roman provinces.[132] Additionally, the law specified areas of public land abroad, in Sicily, Greece, Africa, and Asia, most of it long in Roman possession, which would be subject to immediate sale to provide ready cash.[133] And further avenues of financing were to be explored: the imposition of taxes upon those public lands which had not been authorized for sale, and the use of booty, spoils, and crown-gold from foreign conquests.[134] From the gains appropriated through these various means, the government was to buy and allot real estate in Italy, dispatching colonists throughout the peninsula.[135]

For whose benefit? Conjectures about murky figures in the background plotting political manipulation are best left aside. The evidence will not support them. Cicero's frantic claims that the bill was directed against Pompeius Magnus warrant no credit. To be sure, a clause limited eligible candidates for the agrarian commission to men actually present in Rome, thereby excluding Pompey. But that provision would also exclude other promagistrates outside the city, among them Pompeian *inimici*. Authors of the bill hoped for immediate implementation; it would involve lengthy and unnecessary delay to await the return of Pompey, who had not yet completed his conquests and who had a massive task of provincial reorganization ahead of him. Moreover, there is little reason to suppose that the conqueror of the East and Rome's foremost citizen was eager to acquire a post in which he would be but one of a board of ten and where the duties were largely administrative. In fact, Pompey, to our knowledge, received mention by name in only one connection in the Rullan *rogatio*, and that with honor: he alone was to be exempt from the provision directing Roman generals to turn over the spoils of war to the state treasury.[136] Cicero's line of reasoning can be abandoned.

Another explanation has also found favor: promoters of the legislation never expected it to be adopted; their purpose was simply to drive Cicero and the conservatives into a position of opposing a popular measure. The move would discredit their policies and advance the ambitions of other politicians.[137] That cynical view allows little merit to the *rogator* and his supporters. And, more important, it ignores the elaborate care and research that went into a measure so scrupulous in its provisions and detailed in its expression.

[132] Cic. *De Leg. Agrar.* 1.1–2, 2.38–46; see Hardy, *Some Problems*, pp. 74–77.

[133] Cic. *De Leg. Agrar.* 1.5–6, 2.47–58, 3.15.

[134] On the imposition of a *vectigal*, see Cic. *De Leg. Agrar.* 1.10, 2.56–57, 2.62; on booty and spoils of war, Cic. *De Leg. Agrar.* 1.12–13, 2.59.

[135] Cic. *De Leg. Agrar.* 1.16–17, 2.31, 2.33–34, 2.73, 2.75.

[136] Cic. *De Leg. Agrar.* 1.13, 2.60; see the astute remarks of Sumner, *TAPA*, 97 (1966): 580–581.

[137] Cf. E. T. Sage, *CJ*, 16 (1921): 230–236; Agnes, *RivFilol*, 21 (1943): 35–41; Syme, *Sallust*, pp. 98–99.

It seems hardly likely that such effort was invested in drafting an enactment which its sponsors knew would be abortive.

The Rullan bill may well have aimed at genuine social reform. Distribution of landed property on a large scale to the otherwise unemployed or underemployed capable of making good use of it would be of pronounced advantage to the state as a whole. The veterans of Pompey's eastern campaigns, whose return could already be anticipated, were unquestionably the men to whom the statute was, at least in part, directed. The timing makes it almost certain. And the scope could hardly be otherwise justified.[138] That Julius Cæsar was behind the proposal has often been surmised. It would not be inappropriate. As we have seen, other acts of that individual, in 63 and before, exhibit efforts to curry favor with Pompey. And several features of the bill parallel those later advocated in Cæsar's own agrarian legislation. But hypothesis is best suspended here. It took no extraordinary shrewdness to see the political value in espousing the cause and interests of Pompey. Others, apart from Cæsar, took that route in the 60s. Servilius Rullus was one of them. Passage of his *lex* would be most welcome to Pompeian servicemen–and politically advantageous to Rullus.

But veterans were not the only men for whom benefits waited in the *rogatio Servilia.* The measure looked to immediate settlements, well before the troops far off in Asia could be expected to return. Ready cash was to be supplied without delay.[139] And the bill outlined explicitly the number of colonists who were to be dispatched: five thousand, with each decemvir selecting five hundred men. Since the purchase of property in Italy would take considerable time, the initial settlers were marked out for land already owned by the state, that is, the *ager Campanus et Stellas.*[140] The men in view were obviously the *plebs urbana.* Cicero brands them as Rullus' ragged band of impoverished criminals: shiftless and indigent scoundrels eager for a chance at newfound opulence. Even more significant, Rullus himself advocated his proposal as a means of clearing the city of undesirable elements: the masses had too much influence; best that they be drained off to the countryside. That line, of course, appeared in a speech delivered in the senate, not to the populace, contrived for appeal to the ruling class and underlining the solid conservative reasons for agrarian reform.[141] The urban proletariate was

[138] That Pompey's troops expected landed benefits is clear from Cic. *De Leg. Agrar.* 2.54.

[139] Cic. *De Leg. Agrar.* 1.2: *nunc præsens certa pecunia numerata quæritur.*

[140] Cic. *De Leg. Agrar.* 1.20, 2.76, 2.85, 2.96.

[141] Cic. *De Leg. Agrar.* 2.70: *et nimirum illud est, quod ab hoc tribuno plebis dictum est in senatu, urbanam plebem nimium in re publica posse; exhauriendum esse*; cf. *De Leg. Agrar.* 1.22: *Rullum timetis, cum omni egentium atque improborum manu; De Leg. Agrar.* 2.97: *hi ex summa egestate in eandem rerum abundantiam traducti.* Brunt, *JRS*, 52 (1962): 72, unduly minimizes the role of the city *plebs* in this measure; also *Italian Manpower*, pp. 312–313.

a chief object of this proposal.[142] If passed, it might relieve the aristocracy of some unwelcome elements in the city, help to enrich the countryside, and pump new life into the economy.

Yet the *rogatio Servilia* failed of enactment–that much is incontrovertible. A tribune, L. Cæcilius Rufus, threatened to interpose his veto. Perhaps the bill was withdrawn at that point. Or else, if it reached the assembly, it was evidently rejected.[143] How had it happened? The measure ought, by all rights, to have appealed to both senate and *populus*. Here one can resort only to inference. Threat of tribunician *intercessio* might not have intimidated a more influential politician. But Servilius Rullus and his backers possessed insufficient *gratia* to press their fight to a conclusion.[144] Whatever the bill's merits, lack of *auctoritas* could be a decisive factor in the outcome, as it was so often.

The attitude of the populace is, at first blush, puzzling. Why should it turn away from an enactment which seemed to be in its own interests? Much of the credit (or blame) was ascribed to Cicero.[145] Perhaps rightly so. The gross misrepresentations and deliberate distortions in his speeches against Rullus have been exposed by moderns. They may not have been so obvious to his audience. With consummate skill, Cicero drew his lurid portraits of decemvirs acting as tyrants, controlling the treasury, lording it over citizens, provinces, and foreign potentates, and converting their office into an instrument of despotism. Add to that the fervid allegations that allotted land would be of the poorest quality–a fraud perpetrated on the settlers–and the insistence that the bill's authors were *inimici* of Pompey the Great. Cicero's version became enshrined in the tradition. Presumably, that version proved at least equally persuasive to his hearers. It is well to recall who constituted the audience for Cicero's popular harangues. The soldiers of Pompey, prospectively the chief recipients of the measure's bounty, were abroad and in no position to refute arguments or to vote on enactments. The urban *plebs* was interested–but only a part of the urban *plebs*. A sizable proportion of the city's population consisted of freedmen, the shopkeepers and retailers, artisans, members of the professions, and retainers of noble houses. Those individuals

[142] The fact is clear in Cic. *De Leg. Agrar.* 2.71; cf. 2.65. Rural tribesmen were to be the first beneficiaries of the measure; Cic. *De Leg. Agrar.* 2.79. These were, very likely, ex-country dwellers and dispossessed farmers who had moved into the city and were eager to return to the land.

[143] For Cæcilius' veto, see Cic. *Pro Sulla*, 65. The populace, in any case, seems to have signified its disapproval of the measure; Cic. *Pro Rab. Perd.* 32; Plut. *Cic.* 12.5; Pliny, *NH*, 7.117.

[144] Later sources suggest that the consul C. Antonius was initially attracted by the measure and then won over by Cicero; Plut. *Cic.* 12.3–4; Dio, 37.25.3–4. Be that as it may, the fact remains that Antonius played no recorded role in the discussion of the bill.

[145] Cic. *In Pis.* 4; *Ad Fam.* 13.4.2; Plut. *Cic.* 12.5; Dio, 37.25.4.

were foreign-born or bred in Rome. Committed and secure in the city, they had small interest in land grants.[146] Of the freeborn *plebs*, for whom the *rogatio Servilia* was intended, many may well have been led astray by the obfuscating rhetoric of M. Cicero. It is not difficult to understand why Rullus' statute found little favor with the populace.

The aristocracy was another matter. Their stance will have been based on hard calculation, not readily swayed by Cicero's grotesque prognostications. Some may indeed have been sympathetic to a proposition that would remove the poor to the land and offer other advantages to the economy. But politics was always a prime consideration with the ruling classes. It did not require unusual prescience to foresee the political capital that Pompey could make of a measure promising settlement for his vast assemblage of veterans. Additionally, *principes* in the senate might well look askance at a provision which removed from commanders the right to dispose of the spoils of war. That had traditionally afforded a means of dispensing patronage–and it must have been especially galling to many aristocrats that Pompey was exempt from the provision.

Apart from politics, more basic considerations came into play. The doling out of the Campanian land would be a break with long-standing tradition, a prospect that doubtless made many aristocrats uncomfortable. So also did the loss of revenue from that territory, counted on for so many generations. Redistribution of land on an unprecedented scale must have terrified the conservatives. Rullus' measure did not permit confiscations or forceful expulsions. But the prospect of massive dislocations, even though voluntary, was enough to provoke nervousness in the ruling class. And another key feature of the bill must have drawn mixed reactions from the senate. The elaborate provisions for securing cash–sale of public property at home and abroad, imposition of new taxes in the provinces, disposal of booty–were perfectly sound features. But by placing these responsibilities in the hands of an agrarian commission elected by the people, the Rullan bill menaced a fundamental tenet of the constitution: the control of public finances and foreign policy by the Roman senate. That argument will have weighed heavily with the *nobilitas*.[147] On balance, they turned against the proposal. Servilius Rullus, faced with strong opposition in the *curia* and insufficient support in the *populus*, allowed the matter to drop.

Rejection of the *rogatio Servilia* was not the senate's most sagacious decision. Its passage might have been a major step toward solution of the city's problems–and a safety valve for the restless. As it was, failure of the bill played no

[146] Cf. Cic. *De Leg. Agrar.* 2.71.

[147] Cf. Cic. *De Leg. Agrar.* 1.27: *huius ordinis auctoritas*.

small part in stirring recruits for Catiline's insurrection, which followed shortly. On that we shall have more to say. But there were others prepared to take up the cause of agrarian reform. The return of Pompey's veterans brought the issue into sharp focus.

Pompey arrived in Italy in December 62. As we have seen, his first act was to discharge and dismiss his troops, a dramatic advertisement that he would not use intimidation or unconstitutional tactics. Pompey fully expected that his presence and prestige would guarantee legislation to provide for his soldiers and implement his promises. It was not to be so easy.

A year went by, filled with political jockeying and preparations for the general's spectacular triumph. In January 60, at last, a new *lex agraria* was offered, sponsored by the tribune L. Flavius on Pompey's behalf.[148] Without benefit of an extant Ciceronian speech, we cannot reconstruct the bill's details. The *rogatio Servilia* very likely served as a model, at least in part. Flavius' proposal rendered available Italian public land undistributed from the time of the Gracchi. But it went further, into more controversial matters. The bill encompassed the Sullan assignations, even including territory that Sulla had declared public but did not reallocate. That might indeed lay open the path for confiscation and serious disruption. For the rest, there would be state purchase, financed for five years by the new revenues coming in from Pompey's recent conquests. Further provisions are not reported.[149] But more than sufficient ground existed for opposition. For the aristocracy the same objections which had held against the Rullan measure still held–only more so. There was greater risk of forceful dislocation and perhaps violence. And this bill represented an overt move in Pompey's interests. The general's *inimici* turned out in force: the consul Metellus Celer, backed energetically by M. Cato and L. Lucullus. A sharp altercation between Celer and Flavius resulted in the arrest of the consul, embarrassment for Pompey, and a humiliating withdrawal of the measure.[150]

Politics decided the fate of this bill. But the soldiers of Pompey were not the only ones thwarted of their aims. Flavius' *rogatio*, like that of Rullus, also had in view the relocation of the urban poor and the revival of the

[148] Cic. *Ad Att.* 1.18.6.

[149] Our knowledge of the bill is confined largely to those portions which Cicero found objectionable–though he did approve the means of financing; Cic. *Ad Att.* 1.19.4.

[150] The story is told in Dio, 37.49.2–37.50.6; cf. Plut. *Luc.* 42.6; *Cato*, 31.1. That political opposition to Pompey dictated the resistance is affirmed by Cic. *Ad Att.* 1.19.4: *huic toti rationi agrariæ senatus adversabatur, suspicans Pompeio novam quandam potentiam quæri.* By June of 60 the bill was already dead; Cic. *Ad Att.* 2.1.6: *quod de agraria lege scribis, sane iam videtur refrixisse.*

countryside.[151] Those aspects have too often been overlooked. Agrarian legislation did not point simply to the benefit of returning veterans, though the conclusion of a major war would often provide the stimulus. The problem of the city, of overpopulation and underemployment, was very much in the minds of the legislators. But the political opposition to Pompey, by frustrating the claims of the veterans, also closed off an avenue of hope for the urban poor.

The obstacle proved to be temporary. As was noted earlier, Pompey's defeats in the senate drove him to alliance with Cæsar and Crassus and to more forceful methods. In 59 Cæsar himself at last successfully promulgated agrarian laws of significant proportions.

The procedure, if possible, was to be traditional and unprovocative. Cæsar duly submitted his first measure to the senate for approval. As might have been expected, he could not obtain a majority. Senators who had resisted any increase in Pompey's *auctoritas* would take no more kindly to the machinations of what was now a triumvirate. The *curia* dragged its feet through filibuster and obstruction—and then rejected the proposal.[152] But this time the sponsors of agrarian reform were not to be headed off. The *lex agraria* was brought to the people. Bibulus, Cato, and others objected, employing vetoes and invoking religious bans—to no avail. There followed some scuffles in the street, in which the conservatives were conspicuously worsted. Pompey and Crassus declared publicly their strong backing for the Cæsarian statute. Some Pompeian veterans in the city formed a menacing presence; and Pompey himself declared readiness to use force, if it should become necessary. The *lex Julia* gained passage probably in late January, to be followed by a supplementary bill a few months later.[153] Not that the triumvirs could settle back in smug self-satisfaction. As we have seen, Cato's tactics had made their victory a costly one. The dynasts had been pushed toward extremism, unconstitutional behavior, and even threats of violence to secure their ends. Their actions weakened ties and support in the *nobilitas*. And enemies of Cæsar could later challenge the legality of his measures—which they did.[154]

[151] Cic. *Ad Att.* 1.19.4: *qua constituta diligenter et sentinam urbis exhauriri et Italiæ solitudinem frequentari posse arbitrabar*; also Dio, 37.50.1, who may imply that Flavius added this aspect as an afterthought, in order to assist in the bill's passage.

[152] Dio, 38.1.2, 38.3.1–3; Plut. *Cæs.* 14.1–2; Appian, *BC*, 2.10; Schol. Bob. 146, Stangl.

[153] Dio, 38.4–7; Plut. *Pomp.* 47.4–48.2; *Cæs.* 14.2–3; *Cato*, 31–32; *Luc.* 42.6; Livy, *Per.* 103; Appian, *BC*, 2.10–12; Suet. *Iul.* 20; Schol. Bob. 133, Stangl. The tribunician college was split: P. Vatinius and C. Alfius supported Cæsar; Cn. Domitius Calvinus, Q. Ancharius, and C. Fannius opposed him; Schol. Bob. 135, 146, 147, 151, Stangl; cf. Dio, 38.6.1.

[154] Cic. *De Har. Resp.* 48; *Pro Sest.* 40, 135; *De Domo*, 40; *In Pis.* 79; *De Prov. Cons.* 43, 45–46; Suet. *Iul.* 23; Schol. Bob. 130, Stangl.

But we are concerned here with the substance of those measures. The first attests to the shrewdness of Julius Cæsar—or of the drafters of the law. Our knowledge is skimpy, but the bill seems to have adopted the more salutary features of the Rullan and Flavian *rogationes*, while avoiding their errors. The *lex Julia* directed the distribution of public land in Italy, but specifically exempted the *ager Campanus*, which had caused such hostility to the Rullan proposal. Remaining property for allotment would be purchased by the state only from those willing to sell; there was no suggestion of confiscation or disputed titles, which had helped effect the downfall of Flavius' measure. And to eliminate the possibility of chicanery, which Cicero had criticized in the *rogatio Servilia,* the new law asserted that there would be no haggling over prices: property would be bought by the state at prices fixed by a previous assessment. An agrarian commission was to be set up consisting of twenty men, and Cæsar explicitly ruled out his own eligibility, thereby avoiding charges of personal graft like those leveled against Rullus. Financing, as previously suggested in Flavius' bill, would come from the wealth and new taxation accruing from Pompey's eastern conquests.[155] The *lex Julia* incorporated nothing which had not been part of previous agrarian proposals. But Cæsar, it is clear, took special care to dodge the pitfalls exposed by his predecessors' failures. As Dio Cassius properly remarked, no one could find anything of substance to criticize in the statute. Opposition was purely a matter of politics: fear of the consul's growing prestige and popularity.[156]

Cæsar's initial optimism, however, proved unjustified. The *lex agraria* did not suffice for all needs.[157] A supplementary enactment was called for. In late April, Cæsar produced his *lex Campana*, proposing, as the Rullan bill had proposed before him, that the Campanian land be divided up and allotted to new settlers. That move alienated additional members of the senate. But no serious opposition mounted this time. There would be little point to it, in view of previous experience; and obviously the new legislation was needed if genuine agrarian settlement was to be made. The board of twenty installed by the first *lex* would also govern distribution of the *ager Campanus*.[158]

[155] The source followed here is Dio, 38.1.4-7, who affords the most incisive and informative account. Cf. Cic. *Ad Fam.* 13.4.2; *De Domo*, 23. On the commission of twenty, see further Cic. *Ad Att.* 2.6.2, 2.7.3; Schol. Bob. 161-162, Stangl. Cicero mentions also a board of five, perhaps a subcommittee of the whole; *Ad Att.* 2.7.4; cf. *ILS*, 46. The orator's support for the bill was solicited by Cæsar in vain; Cic. *Ad Att.* 2.3.3-4, 2.4.2. And he was offered a post on the commission, which he refused; Cic. *Ad Att.* 2.19.4, 9.2a.1; *De Prov. Cons.* 41; Vell. Pat. 2.45.2; Quint. *Inst. Orat.* 12.1.16.

[156] Dio, 38.2.1-3. Also Plut. *Cato*, 31.5.

[157] Cf. Cic. *Ad Att.* 2.15.1.

[158] Cic. *Ad Att.* 2.16.1-2, 2.17.1; Dio, 38.7.3; Vell. Pat. 2.44.4; Appian, *BC*, 2.10; Suet.

Such, basically, represents the sum of our information on the agrarian legislation of 59. Details are wanting, but the general thrust seems clear.

Who would be the beneficiaries of these measures? The obvious answer would seem to be Pompey's veterans. Yet a remarkable fact emerges from examination of the ancient testimony. With regard to the first *lex agraria*, only a single source makes reference to Pompeian troops as potential recipients of land grants.[159] As for the *lex Campana,* one finds again only an isolated remark about *milites,* and that apparently alludes to the troops of Cæsar, not Pompey.[160] To be sure, we can hardly doubt that Pompey's veterans were, in fact, provided for. Some of them were present in Rome and helped to assure passage of the legislation, and surely not for altruistic motives.[161] But the purpose, or at least the avowed purpose, of Cæsar's agrarian statutes was rather different.

The sources unanimously assert that the *leges agrariæ* aimed at settlement of the urban poor onto the land.[162] Dio Cassius' statement is the most explicit: Cæsar's bill would make property available to the whole populace, in order to reduce swollen numbers in the city and restore labor in the countryside.[163] Other references to the first agrarian measure point in the same direction: it was designed for the indigent, the impoverished, the "multitude."[164] More precise statements exist on the *lex Campana*: a clause therein specified that

---

Iul. 20. There was grumbling and discontent; Cic. *Ad Att.* 2.16.1; Plut. *Cic.* 26.3. But only Cato ventured open resistance–without success; Plut. *Cato,* 33.1–2; Suet. *Iul.* 20. Pompey stood firmly behind the measure; Vell. Pat. 2.44.4. Cicero even imagined that the general might threaten the use of *exercitus Cæsaris*; *Ad Att.* 2.16.2; perhaps metaphorical; so Gelzer, *Hermes,* 63 (1928): 115–117; *contra*: Meier, *Historia,* 10 (1961): 79–84. The oath contained in the bill was sworn to by all candidates for office but Juventius Laterensis, who thereby forfeited his candidacy; Cic. *Ad Att.* 2.18.2. The commission of twenty would be utilized also in Campania, as is clear from Varro, *De Re Rust.* 1.2.10; Vell. Pat. 2.45.2; Suet. *Aug.* 4. That Cæsar passed two separate agrarian laws in 59 ought never to have been doubted; see Cary, *JP,* 35 (1920): 174–190; rightly followed by subsequent scholars. The chronology of these measures and of Cæsar's consulship generally has been endlessly discussed; see, e.g., Gelzer, *Hermes,* 63 (1928): 113–137; L. R. Taylor, *AJP,* 72 (1951); 254–268; Meier, *Historia,* 10 (1961): 68–98; Linderski, *Historia,* 14 (1965): 423–442; Shackleton Bailey, *Cicero's Letters,* I:406–408; Taylor, *Historia,* 17 (1968): 173–193.

159 Dio, 38.5.1–2, puts a speech into Pompey's mouth, supporting the *lex Julia* as fulfillment of a promise made to his soldiers. Cf. also Dio, 38.1.3, 38.1.7.

160 Plut. *Cic.* 26.3.

161 Plut. *Pomp.* 48.1–2; *Luc.* 42.6; *Cæs.* 14.6, 14.8; Appian, *BC,* 2.10; cf. Cic. *Ad Att.* 2.16.2.

162 Even Pompey's speech, as imagined by Dio, claims that benefits will go not only to his troops, but to other citizens as well: 38.5.2: *προσήκει καὶ ἐκείνοις τὴν ὑπόσχεσιν καὶ τοῖς ἄλλοις τὴν ἐπικαρπίαν τῶν κοινῶν πόνων ἀποδοθῆναι.*

163 Dio, 38.1.2–3.

164 Cic. *Ad Att.* 2.3.4: *pax cum multitudine*; Plut. *Pomp.* 47.3; *Cæs.* 14.1; *Cato,* 31.4; Appian, *BC,* 2.10.

men with three or more children were eligible for lots in Campania. That, obviously, did not include many veterans of the eastern wars. And Cicero scornfully affirms that the land was to be distributed to the *multitudo.*[165]

The unanimity of our evidence is striking. Not that the soldiers were overlooked–many, if not most of them, must have received allotments. But it is reasonable to conclude that the Julian laws were advertised primarily as solutions to the urban problem. Good politics induced the sponsors to mute the claims of the veterans, thereby blunting some of the political opposition to Pompey, and to stress the social aspects of the legislation. Those tactics were better calculated to appeal to conservative opinions, as well as to win the favor of the masses. But whatever the motives of the triumvirs, benefits promised in the statutes had to be delivered. Some, at least, of the proletariate must have found new livelihood in the countryside.

On the effects of the legislation we possess little information. Extant testimony refers only to the *lex Campana.* When the law was first propounded, Cicero sneered that no more than five thousand men could be accommodated; and he expected that Cæsar would face the antagonism of those who were left out.[166] In fact, twenty thousand farmers eventually obtained settlement under Cæsar's measures–no small number.[167] The sources ascribe that figure to the Campanian law alone. But the *ager Campanus* could hardly have accommodated such numbers. And a good part of it was still undistributed in 51, evidently meant for Cæsar's forces in Gaul.[168] A total of twenty thousand men, however, may well have received allotments as a consequence of both *leges*; many of them settled outside Campania.[169] The agrarian commission was hard at work soon after the passage of the first bill. Their accomplishments were surely not negligible.[170]

[165] Cic. *Ad Att.* 2.16.1; also Vell. Pat. 2.44.4; Plut. *Cato*, 33.1. For the clause on fathers of three, see Dio, 38.7.3; Suet. *Iul.* 20; Appian, *BC*, 2.10.

[166] Cic. *Ad Att.* 2.16.1.

[167] Vell. Pat. 2.44.4; Suet. *Iul.* 20.3; Appian, *BC*, 2.10. Both Suetonius and Appian believe that the 20,000 consisted only of fathers with at least three children. But some Pompeian veterans were also settled in Campania, as may be inferred from Cæs. *BC*, 1.14; cf. Cic. *Phil.* 2.101. M. A. Levi, *Atene e Roma*, 3 (1922): 251–252, accepts Cicero's figure of 5,000, arguing that it accurately designates the number of colonists dispatched from Rome; the remaining 15,000 were prior inhabitants now permitted to hold their possessions as private property. But the language of Velleius and Appian distinctly implies that all 20,000 were new settlers.

[168] Cæl. *Ad Fam.* 8.10.4.

[169] Cf. Brunt, *Italian Manpower*, pp. 314–319, who, however, needlessly assumes that nearly all recipients of land obtained lots outside Campania. If that were so, the necessity for the *lex Campana* itself becomes more difficult to explain. That 20,000 new settlers were impossible in Campania was demonstrated by Levi, *Atene e Roma*, 3 (1922): 239–252.

[170] Cic. *Ad Att.* 2.6.2, 2.7.4. Valerius Messalla Niger took pride in his role as agrarian

An irksome question remains. If the Campanian land were made available for distribution, what would become of the resident farmers who had rented their property from the state? The sources are entirely silent. Some moderns have inveighed mightily against Cæsar for evicting the Campanian populace wholesale and replacing sturdy yeomen with idle paupers. Or else, it has been suggested, the farmers remained and became tenants of the new owners rather than of the state. Most scholars, oddly, have ignored the question altogether.[171] But the *argumentum ex silentio* is here particularly strong. Had there been severe dislocation we should surely have heard of it. To imagine that settlers were dispatched from the city to Campania and that ex-farmers took their place as unemployed proletariate argues not only inhumanity but foolishness. The notion of massive expulsions is sheer speculation, akin to the horrors conjured up by Cicero on the Rullan bill.[172] Nor would it have afforded any solution to convert the farmers into tenants of absentee landlords. A simpler answer may be the proper one. Cæsar's law parceled the *ager Campanus* into lots of ten *iugera* each.[173] In all likelihood, that meant smaller divisions, perhaps considerably smaller divisions, than the previous arrangement—enough to accommodate not only the prior tenants but also the new colonists. Although individual property would now be of less extent, it would be private property.[174] A clause in Cæsar's *lex* enforcing inalienability of the land grants for twenty years must be seen in this context. By banning sale of the new lots, it guarded against remigration of settlers into the city.[175] Whatever the political motives of the triumvirs, they had promulgated undeniably constructive legislation. The *leges agrariæ* of 59 provided land for the city's underemployed and without dislocation in the country.

A further enactment demands comment: the shadowy *lex Mamilia Roscia Peducæa Alliena Fabia*. It goes unmentioned by contemporary sources; but three of its clauses, dealing with boundary questions, are preserved in the

---

commissioner; the post is recorded on his *elogium; ILS*, 46. Other known commissioners were Pompey and Crassus themselves, the agricultural experts M. Terentius Varro and Cn. Tremellius Scrofa, Cæsar's *adfinis* M. Atius Balbus, and C. Cosconius; Broughton, *MRR*, II:191–192.

[171] That the farmers were expelled is assumed by Rice Holmes, *Rom. Rep.*, I:316. Meyer, *Cæsars Monarchie*, pp. 64–65, suggests that they tilled the lands for new absentee owners. Both possibilities—and no others—are canvassed by Cary, *CAH*, IX:517.

[172] Cic. *De Leg. Agrar.* 2.84. Cf. the wild and unfounded statements of Tyrrell and Purser, *Correspondence of Cicero*, I:427.

[173] Cic. *Ad Att.* 2.16.1.

[174] Comparison with the Rullan bill is useful. That too proposed to divide the Campanian land into lots of ten *iugera*; Cic. *De Leg. Agrar.* 2.78–79. And it is clear that such division would permit a great many more landholders than before; see Cic. *De Leg. Agrar.* 2.85, who, of course, puts the worst construction on this plan. The fact is confirmed by Cic. *Pro Sest.* 9, who speaks of the old inhabitants of Capua, still residents but now called *coloni*.

[175] Appian, *BC*, 3.2, 3.7.

corpus scriptorum gromaticorum, perhaps deriving from Frontinus.[176] The date has engendered much dispute, but a plausible case can be made for a tribunician law in the year 55. Two of the bill's authors were prætors in 49 and a third was a promagistrate in 48; hence 55 would be appropriate for their tribunates. And, more important, one may discern a connection with Julius Cæsar. The *lex MRPAF* repeated a clause already contained in Cæsar's agrarian law of 59.[177] L. Roscius Fabatus and C. Fabius both served as Cæsarian legates in Gaul after 54; A. Allienus and Sex. Peducæus fought for him in 48. The measure evidently supplemented the *leges agrariæ* of 59.[178]

Import of the bill remains mysterious. The extant clauses deal with boundaries and landmarks. Perhaps then it was called for because of disputes arising out of assignations under the *leges Juliæ*.[179] But that cannot have been its sole purpose. The nature of our source explains the preservation of these particular provisions. In fact, the *lex MRPAF* was longer, perhaps much longer, with as many as fifty-five subdivisions, or even more.[180] Reference is contained therein to the founding of colonies and the establishment of municipalities and lesser forms of incorporated communities.[181] The relationships of new settlements and settlers to the older communities probably required a municipal reorganization not covered by the legislation of 59. That may account for much of the *lex MRPAF.*

But there is more. The new statute seems to have prescribed additional land grants.[182] It should take its place in the series of late Republican agrarian

[176] The extant text may be most conveniently consulted in S. Riccobono, *Fontes Iuris Romani Anteiustiniani* (Florence, 1941), I:138–140.

[177] See *Dig.* 47.21.3.

[178] Literature on the law is long and tedious. See the summary, with full references, by F. T. Hinrichs, *Historia*, 18 (1969): 521–537. Identification with the *lex Mamilia*, mentioned in Cic. *De Leg.* 1.55, has been rightly rejected; Hinrichs, *op. cit.*, pp. 521–523. On the date of 55, see, esp., Willems, *Le Sénat*, I:497–498; Cary, *JRS*, 19 (1929): 113–116; H. Rudolph, *Staat und Stadt im römischen Italien* (Leipzig, 1935), pp. 186–207; Taylor, *Studies in Honor of A. C. Johnson* (1951), pp. 70–73. In the most recent discussion, Hinrichs argues for a prætorian law in 49—unconvincingly. No other evidence exists for joint legislation by prætors. Moreover, Hinrich's reconstruction requires a prætorian college of ten in 49, which is unlikely and unattested. His allegation that L. Roscius Fabatus could not have been tribune in 55 because he was quæstor in 54 is entirely without foundation.

[179] So Taylor, *Studies Johnson* (1951), p. 76.

[180] The extant divisions are given under the rubrics KLIII, KLIV, and KLV. That may mean K(aputu)l(um) III, IV, and V, in which case we have the third, fourth, and fifth clauses. More likely, the abbreviations signify K(aput) LIII, LIV, and LV, which means the measure contained at least fifty-five clauses.

[181] KLIII: *quæ colonia hac lege deducta quodve municipium præfectura forum conciliabulum constitutum erit*; KLV: *qui hac lege coloniam deduxerit, municipium præfecturam forum conciliabulum constituerit*; Riccobono, *FIRA*, I:138–139.

[182] KLIV: *qui ager hac lege datus adsignatus erit*; Riccobono, *FIRA*, I:139.

bills. Details are wanting and conjecture must be substituted. It is doubtful that further public land was still available for allocation. Probably the Mamilian law authorized purchase of property for distribution on a scale larger than that anticipated by the *leges agrariæ* of 59. The reason is not far to seek. Use of the Campanian land for allotments came under sharp political attack once more in 56.[183] Prospective land grants for Cæsar's Gallic forces were in jeopardy. The conference of Luca, of course, intervened and dissipated the threat. But it would be wise to increase the territory marked out for land assignation. Cæsar expanded his forces steadily through recruitment. And Crassus enrolled new armies for the Parthian war, armies which would eventually have to be provided for. The need for additional property was manifest. Tribunician elections for 55, so we are told, resulted in a heavy majority of men favorable to the triumvirate.[184] The evidence and probabilities conjoin neatly. A tribunician measure in 55 sanctioning added agrarian distribution is appropriate and intelligible.

Evidently, the *lex Mamilia Roscia Peducæa Alliena Fabia* aroused no dispute or hostile reaction. The reason cannot be that the triumvirate ran roughshod over helpless opposition. As we have seen, in other areas, political *inimici* of the dynasts continued to resist their designs, often successfully. But land reform no longer stirred passions.

The fact is significant. The struggles in 63 and 59 had been politically inspired on both sides. They reflected a contest for prestige within the ruling class. By the mid-50s agrarian distributions to the needy and deserving seemed to have gained common consent; the triumvirs' enemies would have to campaign on other fronts. One should not conclude that the aristocracy had been bludgeoned into reluctant submission. No wild melee or grave disturbances shook the state on this issue. Defeat of the Rullan *rogatio* did not produce violent reaction, though it doubtless helped to stimulate some of Catiline's recruits. And, it is often forgotten, Pompey's eastern veterans returned to Italy more than two years before any provision was made for them. Yet they provoked no uprising, threatened no march on the *curia*, even after the collapse of Flavius' bill. The approach was to be constitutional and traditional. Cæsar himself attempted to steer his measures through the senate before offering them to the populace. Only when his carefully drafted *lex agraria*, a sound and unprovocative statute, met with obstruction by intransigent political foes did the veterans and some of the *plebs* make their views felt. Thereafter, there was little dissent over land distribution. The ruling class as a whole,

[183] See esp., Cic. *Ad Q. Frat.* 2.5.1: *vehementer actum de agro Campano clamore senatus prope contionali.*

[184] Dio, 39.32.3.

one may suggest, had come to acknowledge its utility. Conservatives could afford to drag their feet when the need was not urgent. But Rome's population swelled in the post-Sullan period. And the problem was complicated by the large armies required for overseas wars in the 60s and 50s: if sites in the country could not be found for those soldiers upon their return, they might fill the city to overflowing. There were still conventional objections to *leges agrariæ:* concern for the state of the treasury, commitment to the principle of private property, a dread of rural dislocation. But the legislation of 59 quieted most of those fears. It provided for sound financing, respected property titles, and eschewed forcible expulsions. Opposition was reduced to a purely political level. And that soon vanished.

None can pretend that the agrarian measures of the late Republic re-created the rural yeomanry of pre-Hannibalic Italy. It would be folly to believe that a plot was provided for every veteran and every applicant from the city. And few will conclude that the grain dole relieved all economic discomfort in the urban proletariate. Nor did the ruling class exhibit a surplus of sagacity. The measures taken were generally ad hoc, provoked when conditions demanded, often delayed by and embroiled in politics. There were no sweeping reforms or long-term changes—no sharp rise in standard of living for the *plebs urbana,* no agricultural innovations to assure success for the new peasant farmers. On these grounds the Republican government cannot receive high marks; but no lower than those of most governments throughout history. The ruling class shrank from drastic change that might tamper with the social structure—again a characteristic of almost all ruling classes. But the evidence suffices to show that it did not confine itself to obstinate reaction. Legislative enactments betoken recognition of the problems and authentic efforts to deal with them. Expediency, rather than humanitarianism, may underlie the actions. But the effect was the same. Hereditary ties that crossed class lines had not been severed.

DISCONTENTS AND VIOLENCE

A VIOLENT and tumultuous era is the standard description of the Ciceronian age. Certainly it had its share of disruption—perhaps more than its share. That characteristic, however, need not be taken as demonstration of a deep-seated malaise pointing irreversibly to disaster.

The Roman *plebs,* as we have seen, had reasons to be malcontent. But outlets also existed. Application to patrons for private benefactions constituted a built-in feature of the system. And the *plebs* cherished a long-standing tradition: the right to demonstrations, even disorderly demonstrations, as an expression of popular feelings. Public meetings, theatrical performances, circuses, and political events often stirred up the passions of the crowd. Out of such occasions grew a large proportion of the turbulence in the late Republic. Excessive weight should not be placed on it. The practice is common in preindustrial societies. That it was more heated and more frequent in the Ciceronian age than in earlier periods may be attributed to growth of population in the city. Riotous activities afforded a convenient means to bring popular grievances to the attention of the officialdom. They in no way imply a desire to tear down the government or to destroy the social fabric. It would be a mistake to equate turbulence with revolution. The Romans knew better. Instances of disruption need to be placed in proper perspective. The Republic, it will be seen, was not seriously menaced from below.

SLAVES, FREEDMEN, and *PEREGRINI*

The men of lowest social status might be expected to provide revolutionary material. The *servi* were devoid of all power and privileges. Freedmen stood but a short step beyond in prestige, generally scorned and despised by their betters, at least as a class. They might hear the term "slaves" hurled at themselves in derision. And aliens, lacking the prerogatives of Roman citizens, were also kept from the centers of authority. Did these groups furnish sources of insurrectionist activities in the late Republic? The available evidence would not support such a theory.

Of slave revolts as such we hear nothing—at least not in the city. The rebellion of slaves and gladiators under Spartacus in the late 70s constitutes the only event of its kind in the Ciceronian age. And its participants were drawn principally from the maltreated herdsmen of the countryside or the potential victims of the arena. These men derived, for the most part, from rough and uncultivated origins, Thracian backwoodsmen or Celtic barbarians who toiled on the large estates and ranches of Italy.[1] Their bitterness is clear—as is the instinct for revenge upon their former masters. Spartacus butchered his captives and forced Roman prisoners to engage in gladiatorial combat for the sport of his own followers.[2] But no suggestion emerges anywhere in the sources that the rebels were motivated by idealistic dreams of the equality of slave and free; still less that they aimed at an overthrow and reconstruction of the social order. Their activities pointed toward self-liberation and escape from Italy.

The brutality of the struggle was inevitable: there could be no negotiation in a servile war, no hope for clemency or rehabilitation. Spartacus raised the most serious slave insurrection in Rome's history. His courage and ability are beyond question. But perhaps one ought not to overrate his accomplishments. The gladiators owed their temporary success principally to the fact that Rome took the rebellion too lightly and that the bulk of government forces happened to be abroad.[3] It was in no way a rising of the masses—the freeborn poor had little, if any, involvement. Analogies with a class struggle or socialistic goals are misleading and off the point.

Spartacus' abortive effort found no emulators in the Republic's final decades. The desperate men who joined his ranks cast a lurid light on the harsh

[1] Plut. *Crass.* 9.3–5. Rubinsohn, *RivFilol*, 99 (1971): 290–299, points to evidence that may imply the involvement of free elements in the uprising; cf. Cic. *Verr.* 2.5.158–170; Appian, *BC*, 1.116; *Mithr.* 109; Florus, 2.8.1–2. But it is wildly excessive to see the affair as generated by Italian nationalism.

[2] Florus, 2.8.9; Appian, *BC*, 1.117. Cf. Sallust, *Hist.* 3.98, Maur.: *neque sanctum aut nefandum quicquam fuit iræ barbarorum et servili ingenio.* That slaves were resentful and chafed under harsh masters none can deny; cf. Sallust, *Iug.* 31.11; *Ad Herenn.* 23; Varro, in Non. Marc. 122, 563, Lindsay. On one occasion, so we are told, *servi* burned down the villa of Sulla's stepson M. Æmilius Scaurus, destroying invaluable works of art; Pliny, *NH*, 36.24.

[3] See above, chap. 1. On the devastations, cf. Brunt, *Italian Manpower*, pp. 287–289.

conditions and hopelessness of *servi* in the countryside. Whether conditions improved to any significant degree thereafter we have no way of telling. But rural slaves did not again engage in rebellion. And the event does not bear at all on the urban proletariate. Slaves in the city were too useful, on the whole, to be mistreated. Their occupations consisted largely of domestic service and labor in small shops; and the prospect of manumission and citizenship was always dangled before them. Economic and personal relationships between masters and slaves reinforced the status quo. None will be so naive as to deduce that the *servi* were content with their lot. But incentive and ability to revolt were absent. We encounter no instance of insurrection among urban slaves as a group in the late Republic.[4]

The same holds for freedmen–no sign of serious agitation in the Ciceronian era. Only a single political issue mooted during the period affected the *ordo libertinus* as such: the matter of voting rights. Freedmen possessed the franchise. There was no movement to eradicate that privilege. But, as was noted before, they were usually registered in the four urban tribes, units already overpopulated, in which the individual vote counted for little. Efforts had been made in earlier generations to alter that arrangement, always by ambitious and prominent politicians seeking to expand their *clientelæ* amidst the freedmen population. Each of the changes, however, proved to be fleeting and temporary, followed by more restrictive measures. Rome's ruling classes looked with disfavor upon increased voting power for ex-slaves. Attempts to redistribute *liberti* among all thirty-five tribes occurred in the 80s, in connection with the enfranchisement of Italy. But Sulla's dictatorship, while accepting the general enrollment of new citizens, confined freedmen once again to the urban tribes. And there they remained during the Ciceronian age.[5]

The matter was aired twice more, to our knowledge, in the Republic's last generation. The activist tribunes of 67 and 66, C. Cornelius and C. Manilius, saw it as a needed area of reform. Cornelius raised the issue; Manilius

[4] On Spartacus, see now–against Marxist interpretations–the cogent arguments of J. Vogt, *AbhMainz* (1957), pp. 7–57; esp. pp. 7–18, 25–27, 37–38, 48–57; similarly, Štaerman, *Blütezeit der Sklavenwirtschaft*, pp. 261–269. Rome had an intermittent problem with fugitive slaves through much of the later Republic; references in Štaerman, *op. cit.*, pp. 238–242. That, however, is a very different matter from insurrection. Clodius' riotous activities in the 50s involved the use of slaves, among others; cf., e.g., Cic. *Pro Sest.* 53, 75, 81, 85; *De Domo*, 54, 79, 89; *In Pis.* 23; *Pro Planc.* 86; *Pro Mil.* 26, 36–37; see H. Kühne, *Helikon*, 6 (1966): 95–113, who, however, takes Cicero's fulminations too seriously. The orator, naturally, harped on this element to excess. Clodian riots did not, in any real sense, entail a rising of slaves as a class; see below, pp. 444–446. On relations between slaves and masters in the late Republic, see Štaerman, *Blütezeit der Sklavenwirtschaft*, pp. 171–213.

[5] For sources and discussion of the pre-Ciceronian efforts to expand freedmen's voting privileges, see L. R. Taylor, *Voting Districts*, pp. 132–144; Treggiari, *Roman Freedmen*, pp. 37–50.

actually promulgated a bill. The measure provided for the enrollment of freedmen into the same tribes as their former masters and patrons. That, of course, would have the effect of general distribution into all thirty-five voting units. It need not be taken as a radical or disruptive move. Many aristocrats may have preferred a new arrangement whereby they could make better voting use of their own clients. But competitors naturally branded it as revolutionary, and the affair became entangled in politics. Manilius was seen with a following of freedmen and slaves, and Domitius Ahenobarbus gathered a band in opposition. The bill obtained passage, but only through some tumult and violence. As a consequence, the senate annulled it shortly thereafter, on the grounds that it was passed *per vim,* or perhaps *contra auspicia.*[6]

The question lay dormant subsequently, until Clodius pushed it once more in 52. That demagogue had, in his tribunate of 58, effected abolition of all charge for state grain subsidies. The result was to encourage increased instances of manumission, as masters preferred to have their slaves on the state rolls.[7] Clodius sought now to make further political capital out of the growing freedmen population. In his campaign for the prætorship of 52, he promised to revive the abortive enactment of Manilius and to distribute *liberti* among rural as well as urban tribes.[8] After Clodius' death in early 52 the project was dropped. No one else picked it up.

It seems clear that freedmen did not particularly exercise themselves over restrictions on their voting power. On each occasion that the cry was raised for more equitable enrollment in the tribes it was raised by a Roman politician, usually for his own purposes. The two isolated attempts in the Ciceronian age both proved abortive; yet no rumblings or threats emanated from the *liberti.* The wealthier among them already possessed some influence in the *comitia centuriata;* for the rest, weight in the assemblies was of relatively small concern. The voice of the mob could be heard on less formal occasions, through popular demonstrations or at *contiones.*[9] Freedmen doubtless engaged in these demonstrations, but as individuals, not as representatives of a class. No grievances united them as a whole or organized them into a bloc. Varied occupations

6 Asconius, 45, 64, 65, Clark; Dio, 36.42.1–4. On the grounds for annulment, see Lintott, *Violence,* pp. 134, 143. It is possible that Sulpicius Rufus sought to revive the measure in 63, without success; Cic. *Pro Mur.* 47. But corruption in the text makes it difficult to arrive at a definitive conclusion; see above, chap. 6, n.49.

7 Cf. Dio, 39.24.1.

8 Asconius, 52, Clark; Schol. Bob. 173, Stangl. Cicero's tirades against the proposition are, of course, tendentious and exaggerated; *Pro Mil.* 25, 87. The orator suggests even that Clodius promised to liberate the slaves; *Pro Mil.* 89; accepted by Kühne, *Helikon,* 6 (1966): 110. One need not take that claim literally. See now the recent and more sober assessment by Treggiari, *Historia,* 19 (1970): 121–122.

9 Cf. Cic. *Pro Flacco,* 17, 66–67.

kept them divided, increased economic opportunities lay at hand, and attachments to diverse aristocratic patrons obviated the need for amalgamation along class lines. Some political influence was attained by individual *liberti*: those who had accumulated means in business enterprises or those who were trusted agents and advisers to prominent *nobiles*. But their tendencies will have been conservative, not seditious.[10] The *ordo libertinus* never acted as a group, indeed can hardly be said to have had an existence as a group.[11] Late Republican problems cannot be laid to their charge.

What of the aliens? One recorded measure suggests trouble. A *lex Papia* gained passage in 65 expelling from Rome all *peregrini* who were not permanently domiciled in Italy. Should that be taken as evidence for disruption or potential disruption from foreign elements in the capital? A brief discussion is in order.

Agitation for the franchise had rocked the government and plunged Italy into a civil war in 90. It drove home a bitter lesson for Rome–and one well learned. After the conclusion of that conflict Roman citizenship extended to the entire peninsula south of the Rubicon. The generation of Cicero was spared venomous rivalry between Roman and Italian. The new citizens were swiftly absorbed into Roman social and political life. Although, as we have seen, traditional conservatism restricted high offices primarily to the old families, leaders from Italian communities and municipalities gradually rose to the officer ranks of the Roman army and filled the back benches of the Roman senate. The source of this discontent which had plagued the pre-Sullan generation was now erased.

But enfranchisment for the inhabitants of Italy did not encompass the whole of the area known as Cisalpine Gaul, whose southern frontier probably stood at the Rubicon. The boundary was artificial and irrational. No significant difference of race, culture, or level of civilization divided men on the two sides of the river. Yet the government continued to regard Cisalpine Gaul as foreign territory, assignable as a *provincia,* and not part of Italy. The Cisalpina itself comprised a patchwork of citizen and noncitizen communities. Under a measure of 89, dwellers north of the Po, the Transpadani, acquired the *ius Latii,* a recognition of their affinity with Romans, but still short of the full franchise.[12] There may have been greater generosity to sites in Cisalpine Gaul south of the Po, where a larger number of Roman citizens already resided. That line too was not absolutely rigid. Latin colonies north of the Po became *municipia,* and there were areas south of the river where men

[10] Cf. Cic. *Pro Sest.* 97: *sunt etiam libertini optimates.*

[11] Cf. the comments of Treggiari, *Roman Freedmen*, pp. 162–168, 177–193.

[12] Asconius, 3, Clark.

still lacked the franchise.[13] But basically the Transpadani represented the one major group in the peninsula without direct access to citizen rights.

A shrewd politician could turn the situation to his advantage by urging extension of the franchise to the Alps. It would entail a considerable addition to his *clientela.* Julius Cæsar, it seems, recognized that opportunity. One source reports that he encouraged Latin colonists, presumably in the Transpadana, to agitate for citizenship as early as 69 or 68.[14] He certainly kept his sympathies for the Transpadani before the public eye. In 63 Cæsar prosecuted C. Piso, charging, among other things, that he had illegally executed a Transpadane.[15] The *lex Vatinia* of 59, which awarded Cæsar the province of Cisalpine Gaul, also authorized him to install a new citizen foundation in the area, the fruit of which was the colony of Novum Comum. The Cisalpina presented a constant source of recruitment for the proconsul, who gained many supporters there and continued to press for full enfranchisement. Eventually, in 49, Cæsar implemented his plans through legislation which brought Roman citizenship all the way to the Alps.[16]

It happens that the issue had also been a matter of particular dispute in 65, the year of the *lex Papia.* Cæsar was not the only politician to concern himself with the claims of the Transpadani. In that year the two censors, M. Crassus and Q. Catulus, quarreled over the admission of Transpadane Gauls to citizen rights. The struggle paralyzed censorial activities and ended with the premature resignation of both men from office.[17] Although we are not told which censor took which position, it is probable that the ambitious Crassus, always on the lookout for expanded *clientelæ,* initiated the contest by advocating enfranchisement. In this context, surely, we must place the *lex Papia,* passed in the same year and sponsored by an otherwise unknown tribune, C. Papius. The bill provided for the expulsion of foreigners from the city, and set up judicial proceedings against all those who had been illegally enrolled on the citizen lists.[18] Timing of the law suggests that there was

[13] Cf. U. Ewins, *PBSR,* 23 (1955), 75–83; Taylor, *Voting Districts,* pp. 124–125; Brunt, *Italian Manpower,* pp. 166–172.

[14] Suet. *Iul.* 8. The statement that he was stirring them to insurrection can be doubted: that will be the product of later anti-Cæsarian propaganda. So also the remark that Cæsar was connected with alleged plans for conspiracy and uprisings among the Transpadani in 65; Suet. *Iul.* 9.3; cf. Strasburger, *Cæsars Eintritt,* pp. 96–97. But the stories are evidence for Cæsar's avowed interests in the inhabitants of northern Italy.

[15] Sallust, *Cat.* 49.2.

[16] On the *lex Vatinia,* see Suet. *Iul.* 28.3; Cæsar's continued interest in the rights of the Transpadani: Cæl. *Ad Fam.* 8.1–2; Cic. *Ad Att.* 5.2.3; Hirtius, *BG,* 8.50, 8.52. On the eventual enfranchisement of Cisalpine Gaul, see the discussion of Ewins, *PBSR,* 23 (1955): 83–95.

[17] Dio, 37.9.3–4.

[18] Dio, 37.9.5: κἀν τούτῳ πάντες οἱ ἐν τῇ Ῥώμῃ διατρίβοντες πλὴν τῶν τὴν νῦν Ἰταλίαν

some clamor in Rome among *peregrini*, perhaps especially Transpadani. Papius' *lex* will not have named the latter specifically, but they were doubtless the men uppermost in mind.[19]

The event, however, is notable in its isolation. It forms no part of a pattern of agitation by aliens or Latins. Apart from this one instance, we hear of no campaigns in the city for extension of citizen privileges.[20] As in the case of freedmen, the issue comes to the fore only when Roman politicians employed it to foster their own ambitions. The *lex Papia* is best explained, not as an effort to remove unwanted elements from the city, but as a counter to the political aims of M. Crassus. The same concern lest any individual gain credit for the broadening of the franchise prevented any change in the status of the Transpadani until the dictatorship of Cæsar. The attitude of Scribonius Curio may be taken as representative: full enfranchisement was a proper and just goal, but politically inexpedient.[21]

THE VICTIMS OF SULLA

Discontented elements with more serious grievances must be sought elsewhere. One group needs analysis: the victims of Sulla. Civil war in the 80s had claimed many lives and fortunes. And the immediate aftermath was equally grim. Sulla the dictator instituted large-scale proscriptions to reward his followers at the expense of conquered political foes. In his name—and partly behind his back—murders and confiscations wrought havoc in 82 and 81.[22]

οἰκούντων, ἐξέπεσον Γαίου τινὸς Παπίου δημάρχου γνώμῃ. That this was an expulsion law is clear too from Cic. *De Off.* 3.47: *male etiam, qui peregrinos urbibus uti prohibent eosque exterminant, ut Pennus apud patres nostros, Papius nuper.* Cf. Cic. *De Leg. Agrar.* 1.13: *illa lege, qua peregrini Roma eiciuntur.* But it also allowed for judicial proceedings: Archias, Balbus, Gabinius Antiochus, among others, were charged under the law; cf. Cic. *Pro Arch.* 10; *Pro Balbo*, 52; *Ad Att.* 4.18.4; Schol. Bob. 175, Stangl. We need not follow the confused account of R. W. Husband,, *CP*, 11 (1916): 323-333, who believes that Papius promulgated two separate measures. The *lex Papia* is mentioned also by Val. Max. 3.4.5, who evidently mistook it for a much earlier piece of legislation.

[19] The argument was propounded with cogency by Hardy, *Some Problems*, pp. 43-67. That the Transpadani were concerned is often denied on the basis of Dio's language: πλὴν τῶν νῦν Ἰταλίαν οἰκούντων. The Italy of his day encompassed what had once been Cisalpine Gaul, and hence, on that ground, the Transpadani ought to have been exempt from the *lex Papia*. But it is possible that Dio—or his source—is quoting the terms of the *lex* itself; so Hardy, *Some Problems*, pp. 62-63. "Those now [i.e., in 65] dwelling in Italy" would not include the Transpadani.

[20] Wiseman, *JRS*, 59 (1969): 59-75, believes that the lengthy gap between the censorial *lustra* of 69 and 28 represents successful attempts by the *nobilitas* to block additional enrollments on the voting lists. But the total absence of any agitation tells against the theory.

[21] Cic. *De Off.* 3.88: *male etiam Curio, cum causam Transpadanorum æquam esse dicebat, semper autem addebat: "vincat utilitas!"*

[22] Sources collected in Broughton, *MRR*, II:69.

Those scars were slow to heal. Sulla's actions cast a pall over the succeeding generation. Not content with punishment of his foes, the dictator contrived to penalize their heirs. The deprivations were economic and political. Hostile municipalities were stripped of territory, some of citizenship. Sullan colonists, the loyal and victorious troops, settled in various parts of Italy—on land seized from Sulla's enemies and denied to their sons. The latter lost not only their ancestral property but many of their political rights: Sullan legislation denied to the heirs of the proscribed the privilege of standing for office and imposed other civil disabilities.[23] The victims must have had to resort to tenant-farming or to seek jobs as casual rural laborers. Resentment was keen against Sullan colonists lording it over lands snatched from political opponents.[24] And the rural problem had urban repercussions. Some of the men who lost their holdings and found subordination difficult gradually began to drift into the city. Improvement of their lot cannot have been easy, especially with their political rights curtailed.[25] Hence, there was a pool of resentful and potentially dangerous individuals. Did they have a serious effect on the stability of the late Republic?

The fruits of Sulla's actions were discernible immediately upon his death. Armed outbreak erupted in Etruria: evicted settlers assaulted the strongholds of Sulla's veterans and beneficiaries. Some politicians in Rome, notably M. Lepidus, the consul of 78, sought to exploit the situation. The logic of Lepidus' position drove him from propagandistic pronouncements to the leadership of open rebellion. It was revival—or better, continuation—of the civil war. Lepidus' revolt presented a threat not only to "conservatives" but to all the beneficiaries of Sulla, including the new senators from the municipalities and the *equester ordo,* and the veterans who had now become landowners. Naturally, the ranks closed. Political support melted away in Rome, and Lepidus' insurrection was crushed within a year.[26]

[23] For Sulla's treatment of Italian towns, see, esp., Cic. *De Domo,* 79; Appian, *BC,* 1.96, 1.100; Florus, 2.9.27; the Sullan colonists, Sallust, *Hist.* 1.55.12, Maur.; Cic. *Cat.* 2.20; *Pro Mur.* 49; Sallust, *Cat.* 28.4; the penalties imposed on heirs of the proscribed, Sallust, *Hist.* 1.55.6, Maur.; Plut. *Sulla,* 31.4; Livy, *Per.* 89; and, esp., Vell. Pat. 2.28.4: *adiectum etiam, ut bona proscriptorum venirent, exclusique paternis opibus liberi etiam petendorum honorum iure prohiberentur simulque, quod indignissimum est, senatorum filii et onera ordinis sustinerent et iura perderent.*

[24] Cic. *Cat.* 2.20; *De Leg. Agrar.* 2.70.

[25] On the presence of Sullan victims in the city, see Sallust, *Cat.* 37.4–9; Cic. *Pro Mur.* 49.

[26] On the revolt as a continuation of civil war, see Orosius, 5.22.16: *Sylla mortuo Lepidus, Marianæ partis adsertor, adversus Catulum Syllanorum ducem surgens redivivos bellorum civilium cineres suscitavit.* And see Cicero's linking of the wars of Cinna, Marius, Sulla, and Lepidus; *Cat.* 33.24–25: *non illi nullam esse rem publicam sed in ea quæ esset se esse principes, neque hanc urbem conflagrare sed se in hac urbe florere voluerunt.*

Survivors of the rebellion moved into Spain, there to join the forces of Q. Sertorius. That area was a bastion of anti-Sullan sentiment. Sertorius' adherents consisted of implacable enemies of Sulla, exiles driven out by the proscriptions, and now the remnants of Lepidus' movement.[27] But Sertorius advocated no social revolution, though success would surely have entailed reverse proscriptions and the reinstallation of exiles and ousted landowners. He offered a challenge to the legitimacy of the Sullan regime. The defeat of Sertorius represented, in effect, the closing battle in the civil war which had begun ten years before with Sulla's march on Italy.[28] Sertorius' target was the government in Rome, the government of his political enemies. Had he been victorious, there would have been a change in leadership, not in social or political system.

The failures of Lepidus and Sertorius permitted the establishment to breathe easier. And, as we have seen earlier, the regime, having obtained greater security, could also take steps to placate former enemies. In 70 a senatorial decree, followed by a law of the people, offered amnesty to the survivors of the insurrection. Adherents of Lepidus and Sertorius were once more welcomed into the Roman fold. The government recalled exiles and restored most of their civil and political rights.[29] That move placed a conspicuous seal on fratricidal strife: the era of civil war had ended; Rome was to be whole again. Such, at least, was the intention. Of course, there were limits to the government's generosity. Return of confiscated property obtained no consideration. The recipients of Sulla's bounty had now dwelt on their plots for a decade. Redistribution of the land would involve a social upheaval, which the government would not face, and would produce a loss of confidence, which might bring about its fall. Former exiles once again had free access to the city and political rights, but some of the proscribed were still debarred from public office. Those limitations presaged further troubles. But the state was now free from military insurrection and more stable than it had been for two decades.

The issue of Sulla's proscriptions and his victims lay dormant for a time. When it was raised again in the mid-60s, it came in an overtly political context, at the instigation of politicians. Genuine redress of grievances was

[27] See, esp., Florus, 2.10.1; Plut. *Sert.* 6.2, 22.1, 25.1–2.

[28] The fact was clear to the victorious generals, who sought to portray Sertorius as a foreign foe only in order to acquire triumphs in Rome; Florus, 2.10.9: *victores duces externum id magis quam civile bellum videri voluerunt, ut triumpharent.* On Sertorius' aims, see Plut. *Sert.* 22.3–7. It was no accident that Sertorius kept in close touch with certain political figures in Rome; Plut. *Pomp.* 20.4; *Sert.* 27.3; Appian, *BC*, 1.115.

[29] Sallust, *Hist.* 3.47, Maur.; Cic. *Verr.* 2.5.151–152; Suet. *Iul.* 5; Dio, 44.47.4; Gellius, 13.3.5. A similar offer had previously been made by Metellus Pius, to encourage treachery against Sertorius; Plut. *Sert.* 22.1.

at best a secondary concern. The dictator's son Faustus Sulla was prosecuted *de peculatu* in 66, in order to force disgorgement of illicit funds inherited from his father. In the same year, M. Lucullus underwent trial for mismanagement of finances during the Sullan era. Authentic social reform played little part in those proceedings. Political motivation dominated. It represented another stage in the contest for power between the partisans of Lucullus and Pompeius Magnus. A similar pattern prevails in the trials in 64 of Sullan hirelings and assassins who had profited during the proscriptions by executing men marked out on the proscription lists. The murders and terror of the dictator's administration could now be safely denounced fifteen years later. But the matter was used primarily as a stick with which aspiring politicians could beat their political opponents.[30] Agitation over Sulla's gifts and the beneficiaries of his favor persisted in the mid-60s. But there was no thought of compensation for the men who had suffered under the dictatorship. If funds were to be recovered, they would go to the state treasury in order to shore up public finances. Even at that, however, juries proved reluctant to convict the heirs or beneficiaries of Sulla, lest the way be thus paved for further demands. It was best not to open that Pandora's box.[31]

In 63 a new issue confronted the senate. For the first time a movement surfaced to restore eligibility for office to sons of the proscribed. That in itself causes surprise. Nearly twenty years had passed since the disabilities were imposed. Yet there had been no previous clamor to remove them, so far as is known. The timing may, of course, mean that the men affected had recently attained or were soon to attain the age at which they would normally be eligible for magistracies. But that will not be a full explanation. Not only had the relevant parties been silent on the matter before 63, but they took no action after that date, even though their claims went unanswered. The fact suggests that extraneous political motivation inspired the airing of this grievance as well. It was yet another harmless attack on Sulla's ghost, an opportunity for demagogic posturing. The dated sins of the dictator now offered popular targets. As we have noted in other contexts, Julius Cæsar was especially active in 63, advancing his *popularis* reputation through advocacy of positions congenial to the commons.[32] Restoration of political rights to the victims of Sulla would have an appropriately *popularis* ring. A tribune

[30] On these trials, see above, chap. 7.

[31] Cic. *Pro Corn. apud* Asconius, 73, Clark; and Asconius' commentary *ad loc.* See also Cic. *Pro Mur.* 42. Similarly, in 72, when a *lex* required Sullan profiteers to return sums remitted them by the dictator, the purpose was to assist the treasury, not to ease the plight of those whose property had been seized and put on the market; Cic. *Verr.* 2.3.81–82; Sallust, *Hist.* 4.1, Maur.

[32] See above, chap. 2.

(unnamed) actually brought the proposal to the populace. But evidence exists for Cæsar's involvement, perhaps inspiration; undoubtedly he advertised his sympathy for the measure.[33]

Other supporters escape record. But there was considerable discussion and debate.[34] The issue exercised the attention of the eloquent consul of that year. Cicero delivered a potent speech, no longer extant, on the bill. He expressed sympathy with its aims–none could do otherwise. The Sullan enactments on this score no longer found favor with the *populus.* But Cicero took the same line here that he had taken three years before in support of Faustus Sulla. The dictator's actions had been cruel and unreasonable; but better not to rock the boat: the stability of the state required preservation of the Sullan constitution.[35] The conservative argument rang true with the voters. That certain individuals, through no crime of their own, were denied the *ius honorum* was a glaring inequity. But to open magistracies to men burning with resentment, however justified, would run the risk of disruption and intemperance in the higher realms of government. That prospect was abhorrent not only to the senate but evidently to the commons as well. The basically conservative character of the Roman populace evinced itself once more. The bill perished in the assembly.[36]

A revealing feature is worth attention. We hear of no violence or agitated activity in connection with this measure on the *ius honorum.* The cause had attracted no supporters since Sulla's death. And when it was finally proposed–without success–no repercussions followed. Apparently it offered just another vehicle for standard *popularis* posturing. Its advocates allowed it to die without undue concern. Its potential beneficiaries were either too few or too impotent

[33] The evidence is not altogether above suspicion. Cæsar did eventually restore the sons of the proscribed to full political privileges during the dictatorship; Dio, 44.47.4. Hence, perhaps his sympathy for their condition was predated by the sources; so Strasburger, *Cæsars Eintritt*, p. 117. Vell. Pat. 2.43.4 is the only direct testimony to Cæsar's interest in the matter during the 60s, and he believes, wrongly, that the disabilities were, in fact, removed at that time. But Cæsar had been active earlier, in 70, on behalf of amnesty for the Lepidani; Suet. *Iul.* 5; Gellius, 13.3.5. His sympathies were surely for the proposal in 63; and he would have no reason to hold his tongue. On the tribunician initiative, see Dio, 37.25.3.

[34] Dio, 37.25.3, may imply that the consul C. Antonius approved the bill, but his reference is vague and, on this score, perhaps tendentious.

[35] Quint. *Inst. Orat.* 11.1.85: *Cicero de proscriptorum liberis fecit: quid enim crudelius quam homines honestis parentibus ac maioribus natos a republica summoveri? Itaque durum id esse summus ille tractandorum animorum artifex confitetur, sed ita legibus Sullæ cohærere statum civitatis adfirmat, ut iis solutis stare ipsa non possit.*

[36] Cic. *In Pis.* 4: *ego adulescentis bonos et fortis, sed usos ea condicione fortunæ, ut, si essent magistratus adepti, rei publicæ statum convolsuri viderentur, meis inimicitiis, nulla senatus mala gratia, comitiorum ratione privavi*; also Cic. *De Leg. Agrar.* 2.10; *Ad Att.* 2.1.3; Pliny, *NH*, 7.117; Plut. *Cic.* 12.1.

to raise a clamor. The tribune who proposed it—and perhaps Julius Cæsar as well—had made their point; there was no need to force matters. It is clear that the political victims of Sulla did not constitute a significant pressure group which could seriously threaten the peace of the city. In general, efforts to reverse injustices perpetrated in the Sullan era played but a small part in the succeeding generation. And those efforts were themselves provoked usually by considerations marginal to the interests of the injured.

The question of the *ius honorum,* of course, can only have affected scions of the more prominent anti-Sullan families. Access to high office was not a realistic aspiration for the common man. Similarly, the political trials of the 60s involving former adherents and henchmen of the dictator would have had little impact on the *plebs.* Even if convictions had been forthcoming, the resultant cash would have gone into public coffers, not into the pockets of Sulla's victims. It is little cause for wonder, therefore, that no mass disturbances accompanied the failure of anti-Sullan measures in the mid-60s.

But one disturbance did engage the energies of lesser men damaged in the Sullan era, and of many others besides. It is that to which attention must now be turned.

THE CONSPIRACY OF CATILINE

A single armed insurrection afflicted Rome in the post-Sullan generation.[37] That event, of course, was the conspiracy of Catiline. Few episodes in Roman history have provoked more passionate and more voluminous literature throughout the centuries. Catiline has been described either as an archvillain, purveyor of every imaginable vice, bent on nothing but destruction and nihilism; or as Rome's one genuine reformer, champion of the downtrodden, advocate of a new social order. Other commentators have adopted different approaches: Catiline emerges as an instrument of certain prominent politicians, or, alternatively, as a man aiming at personal, dictatorial power, a precursor of Julius Cæsar. A more sober assessment is required. It is not our purpose here to dwell on details of the conspiracy—the chronology, detection, and punishment—items which have been thoroughly, even excessively, discussed.[38]

[37] The insurrections of Lepidus and Sertorius were, of course, armed revolts, but they were both outgrowths of and essentially continuous with the civil wars of the Sullan era. Spartacus' uprising was not an attack on Rome, but rather a desperate attempt by slaves and gladiators to obtain freedom by escaping from Italy.

[38] The classic account is still that of C. John, *JahrbClPhil*, Supp. VIII (1876): 703–819. See also Hardy, *The Catilinarian Conspiracy in Its Context* (Oxford, 1924). For a succinct review of the modern tradition, see the useful remarks of Yavetz, *Historia*, 12 (1963): 485–487. A full and valuable bibliography is compiled by Criniti, *Ævum,* 41 (1967): 370–395.

Other matters, of more basic import, need attention: the composition and aims of the conspiracy, the social and economic problems that called it forth, and the impact it had on Roman government and society.

Evidence on L. Sergius Catilina derives very largely from two sources: Cicero's orations and Sallust's monograph. Both are hostile, almost unrelievedly so. Catiline, so it is asserted, was a born conspirator, driven inescapably to revolution by his own reckless passions and lust for power.[39] The portrait is distorted and misleading. On Catiline's earlier career we have already had occasion to speak. A profiteer in the Sullan proscriptions, he had earned repute both for military prowess and for ruthlessness. Darker rumors were spread about domestic crimes, including incest and even murder. The reliability of those stories does not stand high. Catiline's political career, in any event, seems to have been unaffected. He was a *nobilis,* a patrician, albeit one whose family had enjoyed little prominence in the previous several generations. And he possessed other advantages. Catiline could claim important friends in the aristocracy, including the eminent Q. Catulus. Several ex-consuls spoke up in his behalf at the extortion trial of 65 and again in a prosecution of 64. On both occasions Catiline obtained acquittal. The repeated attacks themselves argue for his political influence. The consulship was his aim, an office denied his family since the fifth century. Three times Catiline stood for that post: in 66 a technicality barred his candidacy; in 64 he finished a narrow third in a strong field; and in 63 he failed again–for the last time. In all this there is nothing to suggest revolutionary schemes. Cicero himself had considered a joint candidacy with Catiline in 65. None before 63 could have imagined what would occur in that year. Sallust, to be sure, puts conspiratorial designs in Catiline's mouth in 64. That is transparent retrospection, duly exposed by modern scholars. The man who entertained hopes of Rome's highest office had no cause to plot sedition.[40]

Catiline was an aristocrat, proud of his patrician lineage, sensitive about his *dignitas.* His clan dated back to the early Republic, with a lengthy record of service to the state. Catiline sneered with condescension at Cicero, whose family bore no comparison with his own and who was little better than a resident alien.[41] All his energies and resources had been utilized in a quest

[39] Cf. Sallust, *Cat.* 5.6–7; Cic. *Cat.* 1.13–16.

[40] Cf. Sallust, *Cat.* 16.4: *ipsi consulatum petenti magna spes*; also *Cat.* 20.17, 21.3, 26.1; Plut. *Cic.* 11.1. On Sallust's predating, see John, *JahrbClPhil*, Supp. VIII (1876): 763–777. For Catiline's earlier career, see above, pp. 270–271.

[41] Sallust, *Cat.* 31.7: *ne existumarent sibi, patricio homini, cuius ipsius atque maiorum pluruma beneficia in plebem Romanam essent, perdita re publica opus esse, cum eam servaret M. Tullius, inquilinus civis urbis Romae*; Appian, *BC*, 2.2.

for the consulship. Only after his third defeat and the obvious disenchantment of the voters did Catiline react in violent indignation: his *dignitas* was impaired, his toil had been for naught, unworthy men had been preferred to him. Those are very much the sentiments of the Roman aristocrat.[42] Catiline would not be thwarted of his ambition. After the elections of 63, plans for a coup began to materialize. If disruption and conspiracy be required, then so be it. Catiline scorned the electoral results which had rebuffed him. He retained the hope of preeminence within the state–but, it should be noted, as consul, not as dictator.[43] Long after Cicero acquired damaging reports on Catiline's activities, he was unable to move against him. The conspirator still had too many friends and sympathizers in the senate–or perhaps simply fellow *nobiles* who would not credit the reports.[44] The notion that Catiline proposed to pull down the whole structure of government and society may be unwarranted. Like Lepidus before him, he unleashed forces which probably went far beyond his original intentions.

The motives of the conspirators were, very likely, as varied as their number. Of Catiline's accomplices we have several names, but little more than that. Some belonged to the senatorial class, willing to risk all in a coup. Their characters or fortunes may explain their involvement. First and foremost was P. Cornelius Lentulus Sura, whose resplendent family outshone all his allies. Lentulus, in fact, was an ex-consul, grandson of a *princeps senatus*. But immoral and disreputable behavior had cost him his senate seat in 70. Fiery ambition brought him back on the political scene in the 60s, and he worked his way to a prætorship again in 63. But a dubious career and low reputation made it unlikely that he would move higher. Lentulus did not rest content with that status. Illustrious lineage and a host of *adfines* in high office inspired him with limitless aims. He was fond, so it was said, of quoting the Sybilline Oracles that promised *regnum* and *dominatio* to three Cornelii: Cinna and Sulla had attained that peak; Lentulus expected to step into their shoes. Here was a proper colleague for L. Catilina.[45] Another patrician of prominent family joined the crew: C. Cornelius Cethegus. A young man practiced in insurrection, he had once, so it seems, been a sympathizer of Sertorius. Cethegus was given to fury and impetuosity, and railed at his comrades for dilatoriness; eager for arson and murder, he stored a cache of weapons in his home. Patrician blood had permitted him to reach the senate, but Cethegus found little favor

[42] Sallust, *Cat.* 35.3–4: *iniuriis contumeliisque concitatus, quod fructu laboris industriæque meæ privatus statum dignitatis non optinebam . . . non dignos homines honore honestatos videbam*; cf. Syme, *Sallust*, pp. 71–72.

[43] See Sallust, *Cat.* 20.17: *hæc ipsa, ut spero, vobiscum una consul agam*; cf. Plut. *Cic.* 14.1–2.

[44] Cic. *Cat.* 1.30, 2.3–4, 2.14; *Pro Mur.* 51.

[45] On Lentulus Sura, see Münzer, *RE*, 4:1399–1402, "Cornelius," n.240.

even with his own family.[46] P. Autronius Pætus also had personal grievances. Elected to the consulship in 66, he was convicted *de ambitu,* deposed from office, and expelled from the senate. Autronius did not suffer adversity lightly. Violent in speech and deed, he offered himself as an agent of supplies for the conspiracy.[47] Two other men with analogous complaints participated in the plot, ex-senators who had been ejected from the *curia.* L. Vargunteius, a would-be assassin of Cicero, had lost his senate seat through condemnation *de ambitu.* And Q. Curius, a man of respectable family but disreputable habits, had suffered expulsion in 70. Loose-tongued and untrustworthy, he later became an informant for Cicero.[48]

Additional individuals of noble birth can be found in Catiline's entourage. The corpulent L. Cassius Longinus, a prætor in 66 and unsuccessful candidate for the consulship of 63, evidently took his defeat hard. Cassius arrogated to himself the task of burning the city.[49] L. Calpurnius Bestia, a tribune-elect in 63, allegedly was assigned to deliver a verbal attack on Cicero, which was to be the signal for armed uprising.[50] Two men named Sulla are registered by Sallust: Publius and Servius, both sons of a Servius Sulla. Apart from the connection with Catiline, they go unmentioned. But the name itself and senatorial rank point indubitably to relationship with the house of Sulla the dictator. Lack of advancement consistent with their background may have provoked their discontent.[51] Two final senators receive mention, with no indication as to why they were drawn into the conspiracy: Q. Annius Chilo, who intrigued among the Allobroges, and M. Porcius Læca, who offered his home as a headquarters for the plotters.[52]

[46] Cicero alleges that Cethegus had gone to Spain during the Sertorian war to murder Metellus Pius; *Pro Sulla,* 70; cf. Sallust, *Cat.* 52.33. On his character, see Sallust, *Cat.* 43.3–4: *Cethegus semper querebatur de ignavia sociorum . . . natura ferox, vehemens, manu promptus erat;* Cic. *Cat.* 3.16: *C. Cethegi furiosam temeritatem;* also Cic. *Cat.* 3.8, 3.10, 4.11, 4.13; *Pro Sulla,* 53; Sallust, *Cat.* 32.2, 50.2; Plut. *Cic* 18.2, 19.1. Cethegus was a senator in 63; Sallust, *Cat.* 17.3. His own brother voted for his execution; Ampelius, 31.

[47] On Autronius, see above, pp. 282–283.

[48] For Vargunteius, Sallust, *Cat.* 17.3, 28.1; Cic. *Cat.* 1.9; *Pro Sulla,* 6, 67; cf. Linderski, *Historia,* 12 (1963): 511–512; on Curius, Sallust, *Cat.* 23.1: *Q. Curius, natus haud obscuro loco, flagitiis atque facinoribus coopertus, quem censores senatu probri gratia moverant;* also *Cat.* 26.3, 28.2; cf. [Q. Cic.] *Comm. Petit.* 10.

[49] On his character, see, esp., Asconius, 82, Clark; his eagerness for arson, Cic. *Cat.* 3.14, 4.13; *Pro Sulla,* 53. Other references in Münzer, 3:1738–1739, "Cassius," n.64.

[50] Sallust, *Cat.* 17.3, 43.1; Appian, *BC,* 2.3. The story is doubted by Syme, *Sallust,* pp. 132–133, who regards it as a malicious invention by Sallust.

[51] Sallust, *Cat.* 17.3, 47.1; Cic. *Pro Sulla,* 6.

[52] The Q. Annius of Sallust, *Cat.* 17.3, 50.4, is surely identifiable with Q. Annius Chilo mentioned in Cic. *Cat.* 3.14; cf. [Q. Cic.] *Comm. Petit.* 10. On Porcius Læca, see Cic. *Cat.* 1.8, 2.13; *Pro Sulla,* 6, 52; Sallust, *Cat.* 17.3, 27.3–4; Florus, 2.12.3.

Such were the members of the *ordo senatorius* recorded among Catiline's accomplices. Some of them stemmed from most distinguished families, causing shock and surprise: a Lentulus, a Cethegus, a Cassius Longinus, two Sullæ.[53] What was their motivation? Habitual luxury and licentiousness that produced debts of enormous magnitude is the usual answer: Catiline was the champion of the indebted aristocracy. But the conclusion is unproved and insufficient. Catiline himself appears to have been in no financial straits.[54] The problem of debt, to be sure, contributed to the strength of the conspiracy, as we shall see. But monetary obligations alone will not account for everything. Wounded pride and fierce ambition thwarted by their peers fired the men who constituted leadership in the plot. Catiline, Autronius, and Cassius Longinus had been cheated of the consulship–or so at least they persuaded themselves. Lentulus, Vargunteius, and Curius had been ousted from the senate. Cethegus and the Sullæ had not obtained the *honores* of their ancestors. Disgruntlement, indignation, and avaricious political appetite, rather than economic pressure, seem to have been characteristic of the conspiracy's *principes.*[55]

Sallust singles out four men of equestrian rank among those who hatched the *coniuratio:* M. Fulvius Nobilior, L. Statilius, P. Gabinius Capito, and C. Cornelius.[56] Nobilior, so it would appear, sprang from illustrious stock. The family had been of the highest eminence until the mid-second century, but of no consequence thereafter. Political frustration suffered by the clan may lie behind Nobilior's participation.[57] The equestrian status of P. Gabinius Capito perhaps suggests frustration as well; his family was prætorian–and he showed ardor for disruption.[58] Senatorial connections may also be hypothesized for C. Cornelius, one of those to whom was delegated the task of murdering Cicero.[59] Statilius remains a shadowy figure. No relatives are known

[53] Cf. Florus, 2.12.3: *ipse* [Catiline] *patricius; sed hoc minus est: Curii, Porcii, Sullæ, Cethegi, Autronii, Varguntei atque Longini, quæ familiæ! quæ senatus insignia! Lentulus quoque tum cum maxime prætor.*

[54] So, at least, Catiline averred; Sallust, *Cat.* 35.3. But see Cic. *Pro Mur.* 50. Sallust claims that the conspirator was oppressed by poverty; *Cat.* 5.7; cf. Florus, 2.12.1. But it is clear that his credit was good–even on the eve of conspiracy; Sallust, *Cat.* 24.2.

[55] Cf. Cic. *Cat.* 2.19: *eorum qui, quamquam premuntur ære alieno, dominationem tamen exspectant, rerum potiri volunt.*

[56] Sallust, *Cat.* 17.4.

[57] A certain Fulvius, son of a senator A. Fulvius, is also registered by Sallust as following Catiline in battle; *Cat.* 39.5; cf. Val. Max. 5.8.5; Dio, 37.36.4. He is sometimes wrongly identified with Nobilior; cf. E. Schwartz, *Hermes*, 32 (1897): 563. The senator's son is specifically distinguished from the original plotters. And "Aulus" is not a *prænomen* known among the Nobiliores. See Münzer, *RE*, 7:267–268, "Fulvius," n.94; Syme, *Sallust*, p. 129.

[58] Cf. Cic. *Cat.* 3.6: *horum omnium scelerum improbissimum machinatorem*; cf. *Cat.* 3.12, 4.12, 4.13; Sallust, *Cat.* 43.2. Further on Capito, see Badian, *Philologus*, 103 (1959): 97–99.

[59] Sallust, *Cat.* 28.1; Cic. *Pro Sulla*, 6, 18, 51–52.

in the Republican senate. But he exercised a position of leadership in the inner councils of the conspiracy.[60]

Sallust vouchsafes no further names among those who helped concoct the scheme. But other men turn up later in the story. A few were individuals of some substance, perhaps included in the category of home-town leaders from the colonies and municipalities of Italy.[61] The Campanian man of affairs, P. Sittius, who had his estates sold to resolve debts, was abroad in Africa, ostensibly to supervise his financial investments. But some alleged later that he was raising an army and creating mischief in Mauretania and Spain, on Catiline's instructions.[62] Additional *municipes* receive mention: the Camertine Septimius, dispatched to stir uprising in Picenum; M. Cæparius from Terracina, who was to organize the slaves in Apulia; and T. Volturcius from Croton, a go-between with the Allobroges, who eventually turned informer and delivered decisive evidence on the promise of immunity.[63] Further, there were Publicius and Minucius, perhaps both *equites,* burdened by debt, who accompanied Catiline when he abandoned Rome; Fulvius, son of a senator, who joined the ranks of Catiline's army; C. Mevulanus, military tribune in 63, who engaged in conspiracy in Pisaurum and the Cisalpina; and P. Umbrenus, the enterprising freedman whose business interests in Gaul and connections with leaders of the Allobroges made him a useful ally.[64] Obscure beyond recovery are a certain C. Julius, instructed to tamper with discontented elements in Apulia; L. Tarquinius, who turned state's evidence against the plotters; and Tongilus, one of Catiline's favorites from boyhood.[65] Military leadership in Etruria, a strong-

[60] Cf. Sallust, *Cat.* 47.4, 52.34; Cic. *Cat.* 3.6, 3.9, 3.14; Appian, *BC,* 2.4.

[61] Sallust, *Cat.* 17.4: *multi ex coloniis et municipiis.*

[62] Sallust, *Cat.* 21.3; Cic. *Pro Sulla,* 56. On Sittius, see Münzer, *RE,* 3A:409–411, "Sittius," n.3.

[63] On Septimius, Sallust, *Cat.* 27.1; Cæparius, Sallust, *Cat.* 46.3–4, 47.1; Cic. *Cat.* 3.14; Volturcius, Sallust, *Cat.* 44.3, 45.3–4, 47.1; Cic. *Cat.* 3.4, 3.8, 4.5; Florus, 2.12.9; Appian, *BC,* 2.4.

[64] For Publicius and Minucius, see Cic. *Cat.* 2.4. They are not identifiable. But note the *eques* Publicius, an infamous manager of electoral bribery; Ps. Asconius, 212, Stangl. And a Q. Minucius turns up as a respected *eques* in Sicily in the 70s; Cic. *Verr.* 2.2.69, 2.2.80, 2.3.148. Conjecture on associations would be futile. There are too many unknown figures with those names; e.g., the freedman Publicius who resembled Pompey; Val. Max. 9.14.1; Pliny, *NH,* 7.53; or the Cn. Minucius who prosecuted Manilius in 65; Schol. Bob. 119, Stangl. On Fulvius, see above, n.57; Mevulanus, Cic. *Pro Sest.* 9; Umbrenus, Cic. *Cat.* 3.14; Sallust, *Cat.* 40.1–6.

[65] C. Julius: Sallust, *Cat.* 27.1; Tarquinius: Sallust, *Cat.* 48.3–8; Tongilus: Cic. *Cat.* 2.4. C. Flaminius, at whose home near Arretium Catiline stayed briefly, is not specifically designated as a conspirator; Sallust, *Cat.* 36.1. He may be identical with the ædile of 67. Obscurity and uncertainty surround the Marcelli, father and son, recorded as stirring insurrection among the Pæligni; Orosius, 6.6.7. One of them may be C. Marcellus who consorted with gladiators in Capua; Cic. *Pro Sest.* 9.

hold of Catilinarian sentiment, rested in the hands of C. Manlius and P. Furius, ex-soldiers of Sulla who had obtained land there under the dictatorship. Manlius had risen from the ranks, a former centurion in Sulla's army, later a landowner, but an unsuccessful one, and now in desperate straits.[66] Finally, one ought not to forget the notorious Sempronia, a woman of noble birth, cultured tastes, and considerable charm. Wife of an ex-consul and daughter of a distinguished house, she had now passed her prime and exhausted her resources. Indebtedness and appetite for pleasure led her to indulge in intrigue. Sempronia combined feminine wiles with masculine audacity–a valuable contribution to conspiratorial designs.[67]

It was a mixed lot. Single-minded purpose cannot readily be ascribed to this group, and it would be wrong to try. Some were senators balked of lofty aspirations and prepared for a coup to attain positions previously denied them. Others were *equites* anxious for political power; or scions of decayed aristocratic houses, desirous of emulating the station of their ancestors; or even businessmen with means and connections, gambling perhaps on the possibilities for financial speculation which a period of disruption might bring. Frustrated office seekers may also account for some of the men from the *municipia* who had suffered setbacks analogous to the disgruntled politicians in Rome. To this group were added those whose debts, stemming from indiscretions or incompetence, had deprived them of their accustomed standard of living. Such was the leadership–not social outcasts, but men whose families had tasted power and who wanted more.[68]

That assemblage, however, could have accomplished little by themselves. It would be a grave mistake to dismiss the Catilinarian conspiracy merely as a movement of corrupt and debauched aristocrats. Whatever the aims of its leaders, there was no hope of fulfillment without stirring a wider pool of discontent. Insofar as any real threat was posed to the government, it came less from Catiline and his accomplices than from those faceless participants whose names escape record but whose grievances can be divined.

Propaganda and invective pollute the tradition. Catiline, of course, professed

[66] For Furius, see Cic. *Cat.* 3.14; Sallust, *Cat.* 50.4. On Manlius' background, see Cic. *Cat.* 2.14, 2.20; Sallust, *Cat.* 28.4; Asconius, 50, Clark; Dio, 37.30.5; Plut. *Cic.* 14.1–2; Appian, *BC*, 2.2.

[67] The description is in Sallust, *Cat.* 25. Sempronia was married to Dec. Brutus, consul in 77, still alive but absent from Rome in 63; Sallust, *Cat.* 40.5. That she was a daughter of C. Gracchus is unlikely. More probably, she belongs to the Sempronii Tuditani; Ciaceri, *Atti Accad. Arch. Nap.*, 11 (1930): 219–230; Syme, *Sallust*, pp. 134–135; *contra*: A. Pastorino, *GiornItalFilol*, 3 (1950): 358–363.

[68] Cic. *Cat.* 2.19: *honores quos quieta re publica desperant perturbata se consequi posse arbitrantur*; Sallust, *Cat.* 37.10: *quicumque aliarum atque senatus partium erant conturbari rem publicam quam minus valere ipsi malebant.*

to be championing a righteous and needed cause. His was an attack, so Sallust has him claim, upon the monopolistic control of government and society by a few potentates at the top: the remainder of the populace is without influence, authority, or dignity.[69] He would strike a blow for *libertas:* a more equitable share of political power, of honor, of glory–and of wealth.[70] Catiline affirmed the cause of the wretched as his own. The masses, he asserted in the senate, required only leadership to enforce their just demands, and he would supply it.[71] Catiline's associate C. Manlius dispatched a message from his camp in Etruria. He eschewed all material aims: the goal was simply *libertas,* the opportunity to get out from under the oppression of the magistrate and the moneylender. The restoration of justice, not the overthrow of society, defined the avowed objective.[72]

The view from the other side, naturally, was quite different. Hyperbolic statements from Cicero, on which so much of the later tradition rests, offer the blackest imaginable descriptions of the conspiracy's participants. They were criminals and reprobates, ruined and reckless men, parricides and assassins, barely to be regarded as human beings–wild beasts parading in men's clothing.[73] Cicero's storehouse of vituperation was inexhaustible. To the plotters he denied all semblance of morality: they were gluttonous, wanton, lascivious, steeped in debauchery and lust, heedless squanderers of wealth and patrimonies.[74]

It requires no profound insight to recognize propaganda for what it is. Altruistic aims proclaimed for the Catilinarian movement concealed the self-serving motives of vindictive and ambitious leaders. On the other hand, depiction of lower-class unrest as stimulated by criminal elements and degenerates constitutes standard invective, not only in Rome but throughout the centuries.[75] Exposure of the propaganda, however, is but an initial step. The fact remains that Catiline attracted support from varied elements, who were

[69] Sallust, *Cat.* 20.7: *nam postquam res publica in paucorum potentium ius atque dicionem concessit . . . volgus fuimus sine gratia, sine auctoritate*; also *Cat.* 58.11. Sallust himself, though holding no brief for Catiline's motives, agrees with the social analysis; *Cat.* 39.1–2.

[70] Sallust, *Cat.* 20.14, 58.8.

[71] Sallust, *Cat.* 35.3: *miserorum causam pro mea consuetudine suscepi;* Cic. *Pro Mur.* 50–51: *eum qui esset futurus dux et signifer calamitosorum . . . tum enim dixit duo corpora esse rei publicæ. unum debile infirmo capite, alterum firmum sine capite; huic, si ita de se meritum esset. caput se vivo non defuturum*; Plut. *Cic.* 14.4.

[72] Sallust, *Cat.* 33.4–5: *at nos non imperium neque divitias petimus . . . sed libertatem . . . te atque senatum obtestamur, consulatis miseris civibus, legis præsidium. quod iniquitas prætoris eripuit. restituatis.*

[73] Cic. *Cat.* 1.23, 1.25, 1.27, 1.33, 2.22; *Pro Mur.* 83; *Pro Sulla*, 76; Sallust, *Cat.* 14.1, 14.3.

[74] Cic. *Cat.* 2.5, 2.7–10, 2.22–23; Sallust, *Cat.* 14.2, 24.3, 37.5.

[75] Cf. G. Rudé, *The Crowd in History* (New York, 1964), pp. 7–8, 198–208.

not interested in the political aims of the leaders and who did not comprise scum, felons, and the dregs of society. What were the social grievances which Catiline's undertaking permitted to surface in a dramatic fashion?

The evils wrought by Sulla were showing their effects. Dislocation in the countryside, created by the proscriptions, took its toll: landless men unable to find a steady living as rural laborers, veterans with no property to return to, heirs of the proscribed lacking political or economic means to recover their position. Such men were naturally encouraged by the prospect of upheaval; other avenues did not seem open to them.[76] Of at least equal significance in Catiline's ranks, however, were the Sullan veterans and colonists themselves. They had reaped the benefits of the proscriptions; but those benefits did not in every case endure. Farming proved to be a more difficult task than some had bargained for. Land was sometimes of poor quality, and ex-soldiers who had been abroad for several years did not always become successful or contented tillers of the soil. A bad harvest would force them to borrow, and a succession of such harvests might put them hopelessly in arrears. The alternative was sale of the land; but for confiscated property, with dubious titles, few buyers could be found.[77] The plight of some of the colonists was causing them to sink to the level of the dispossessed. One need not follow the sources in branding these individuals as reckless spendthrifts who had dissipated their resources with excessive spending and ostentatious luxury.[78] But it is likely that many of them had contracted heavy financial obligations which could no longer be discharged. An added element aggravated the situation. These men were ex-soldiers who had once profited handsomely in a period of civil upheaval. They recalled the days of swift promotions and lucrative gains. The solution of the sword was, for them, attractive and appropriate.[79]

[76] Sallust, *Cat.* 28.4: *Manlius in Etruria plebem sollicitare, egestate simul ac dolore iniuriæ novarum rerum cupidam, quod Sullæ dominatione agros bonaque omnia amiserat*; *Cat.* 37.9: *quorum victoria Sullæ parentes proscripti bona erepta, ius libertatis imminutum erat*; Cic. *Pro Mur.* 49: *homines perculsi Sullani temporis calamitate*; cf. Sallust, *Cat.* 58.13.

[77] Cf. Cic. *De Leg. Agrar.* 2.68: *quam multos enim, Quirites, existimatis esse, qui latitudinem possessionum tueri, qui invidiam Sullanorum agrorum ferre non possint, qui vendere cupiant, emptorem non reperiant, perdere iam denique illos agros ratione aliqua velint?*

[78] Cic. *Cat.* 2.5, 2.20; Sallust, *Cat.* 16.4, 28.4; Appian, *BC*, 2.2. Brunt, *Italian Manpower*, pp. 310–311, argues that many of the Sullan veterans had received pestilential wasteland, thereby helping to explain their economic plight. But Cicero specifically distinguishes the holdings of the Sullani from the unprofitable and uncultivable land; *De Leg. Agrar.* 2.70; cf. 1.15.

[79] Sallust, *Cat.* 37.6: *multi memores Sullanæ victoriæ, quod ex gregariis militibus alios senatores videbant, alios ita divites ut regio victu atque cultu ætatem agerent, sibi quisque, si in armis foret, ex victoria talia sperabat*; also *Cat.* 16.4: *victoriæ veteris memores civile bellum exoptabant*; *Cat.* 21.4, 57.1; Cic. *Cat.* 2.20. Despite Harris, *Rome in Etruria and Umbria*, pp. 289–294, the evidence is strong and consistent.

Such were the rustics–dispossessed or indebted, captained by determined men like C. Manlius and P. Furius–who formed the backbone of Catiline's support in the countryside.[80] It need never have been. The measure drafted by Servilius Rullus for presentation in early 63 addressed itself to precisely those problems. Its enactment would have placed the state in a position to purchase property from men who were otherwise unable to dispose of it or to liquidate their debts. And plots would have been available for the dispossessed, as well as for the city *plebs* anxious for a new start on the land. The bill raised legitimate hopes. Its defeat must have seemed to many the foreclosing of a last avenue to personal economic recovery. The coming of the Catilinarian conspiracy in the months that followed was no coincidence.

The timing may also shed light on another matter of more sweeping import. No theme runs more consistently through the sources than the problem of indebtedness generally. It was an affliction felt not only in Rome, but everywhere in Italy, and even in the provinces.[81] The situation seems to have been especially urgent in 63.[82] Early in the year a tribune actually proposed a formal reduction or abolition of debts.[83] Nothing, presumably, came of that motion. Catiline could, therefore, make *tabulæ novæ* one of the watchwords of his platform.[84] Cicero later adjudged the principal effect of his consulship to have been the salvation of public credit and the successful defense of the creditor class.[85]

Who were the indebted groups to whom Catiline directed his appeal? As has been noted, the Sullan colonists, who had borrowed on security of their land and who were unsuccessful or dissatisfied with farming but were unable to sell their property, formed part of his following. Additionally, there were men of more elevated backgrounds, who had indulged in heavy outlays to finance electoral campaigns or promote their political standing. For such individuals disposal of landed property, even if a market could be found, was unthinkable. Real estate brought income in the form of rents, and it represent-

[80] Cic. *Cat.* 3.14; *Pro Mur.* 49; Plut. *Cic.* 14.1; Appian, *BC,* 2.2. Etruria was not the only locus of discontent. Catiline had expectations of uprisings throughout the peninsula; cf. Brunt, *JRS,* 52 (1962): 73. See also S. L. Mohler, *CW,* 29 (1936): 81–84.

[81] Sallust, *Cat.* 16.4: *æs alienum per omnis terras ingens erat*; Cic. *Cat.* 2.8: *nemo non modo Romæ sed ullo in angulo totius Italiæ oppressus ære alieno fuit quem non ad hoc incredibile sceleris fœdus asciverit.* Cf. the complaints of the Allobroges in Gaul; Sallust, *Cat.* 40.1, 40.4, 41.2; and debts in Spain and Africa; Cic. *Pro Sulla*, 58.

[82] Cic. *De Off.* 2.84: *numquam vehementius actum est quam me consule, ne solveretur . . . numquam . . . maius æs alienum fuit.* And cf. the anecdote in Val. Max. 4.8.3.

[83] Dio, 37.25.4.

[84] Sallust, *Cat.* 21.2; Cic. *Cat.* 2.18; *De Off.* 2.84; Dio, 37.30.2.

[85] Cic. *Ad Att.* 2.1.11: *me illum ipsum vindicem æris alieni*; *Ad Fam.* 5.6.2: *qui ex obsidione feneratores exemerit*; *Ad Q. Frat.* 1.1.6; *De Off.* 2.84.

ed an indispensable accouterment of the aristocrat. A period of insecurity, moreover, caused a sharp decline in property values.[86] But indebtedness did not exist only among the landowning classes. Small businessmen too would contract loans, and even the *plebs,* faced with high rents, might have to turn to the moneylender in order to keep a roof over their heads.[87] For the little man, lacking political influence and financial means, recourse was difficult when he fell into arrears. Debt slavery was officially illegal. But private arrangements sometimes brought the debtor into temporary bondage in order to pay off his obligations. Magistrates' judgments were not normally kind to the insolvent.[88] Catiline had an extensive field from which to draw adherents.

But why should the debt problem have come to a head in Cicero's consulship? The aristocratic practice of borrowing capital to finance political campaigns was nothing new. The plight of the Sullan colonists did not suddenly come to light in 63. And high rents, with concomitant hardships on the urban *plebs,* had a longer history as well. The answer must lie in events closely preceding the year of the conspiracy.

The large numbers and varied types of men in debt suggest that the extension of credit had been easy in Rome—perhaps too easy. The practices of the moneylender seem to have produced an inflated financial structure, and also a fragile one. A quarter-century earlier bankers and financiers had much of their money tied up in investments abroad, especially in the wealthy province of Asia. When Mithridates slaughtered Italian businessmen and seized Roman property in Asia, the repercussions were severe: a financial crash in Rome.[89] Mithridates remained a threat in the 70s and early 60s. And the prevalence of piracy in the Mediterranean made overseas investments hazardous. Money-

[86] Cicero divides these debtors into two classes, both evidently of aristocratic standing; *Cat.* 2.18–19: *unum genus est eorum qui magno in ære alieno maiores etiam possessiones habent quarum amore adducti dissolvi nullo modo possunt . . . alterum genus est eorum qui, quamquam premuntur ære alieno, dominationem tamen exspectant.* On debts in the upper classes, cf. M. W. Frederiksen, *JRS,* 56 (1966): 128–131; J. P. Royer, *RevHistDroit,* 45 (1967): 191–240, 434–450. On the decline in property values, see Val. Max. 4.8.3: *Catilinæ furore ita consternata re publica ut ne a locupletibus quidem debitæ pecuniæ, propter tumultum pretiis possessionum deminutis, solvi creditoribus possent.*

[87] Such men may be included in the category described by Cic. *Cat.* 2.21: *qui iam pridem premuntur, qui numquam emergunt . . . qui vadimoniis, iudiciis, proscriptione bonorum defetigati permulti et ex urbe et ex agris se in illa castra conferre dicuntur*; cf. *Pro Mur.* 50; Sallust, *Cat.* 20.13; Yavetz, *Latomus,* 17 (1958): 514–517; *Historia,* 12 (1963): 485–499.

[88] Sallust, *Cat.* 33.1, 33.5; Cic. *Pro Flacco,* 48; *Cat.* 2.5; cf. F. v. Woess, *ZSS,* 43 (1922): 485–529; Brunt, *JRS,* 48 (1958): 168; Frederiksen, *JRS,* 56 (1966): 129–130.

[89] Cic. *De Imp. Pomp.* 19: *nam tum, cum in Asia res magnas permulti amiserunt, scimus Romæ solutione impedita fidem concidisse.* Cf. Jonkers, *Social and Economic Commentary on Cicero's De Imperio Cn. Pompei* (Leiden, 1959), pp. 34–35.

lenders were in no hurry to press claims; it was better to let the interest accumulate. But the situation changed sharply when Pompey took charge of the eastern wars. His appointment alone created a wave of new confidence.[90] Defeat of the pirates followed in short order in 67. And Mithridates' position rapidly worsened under the pressure of Pompey's attacks. By 63 Roman control in Asia was secure and in the process of extension. The creditor class would naturally hasten to reinvest sums in the East, where returns were most profitable. The fact is demonstrable. Money was flowing abroad in such quantities that the senate felt compelled to issue a decree in 63 banning, at least temporarily, the export of gold and silver.[91]

The prospect of lucrative gain in the East far outweighed profits that had been made by lending money and by investments in Italy. Since the race for a monetary foothold abroad must have been keen, creditors doubtless cracked down hard on outstanding debts in order to obtain necessary capital. And they would be reluctant to lend out cash for any but the most secure returns. Interest rates were consequently fluctuating and unstable.[92] The calling-in of debts and the tight money situation had serious consequences. It will have been felt by *nobiles* accustomed to borrowing for political purposes, by farmers who could no longer obtain loans on the security of their property, by small businessmen and laborers for whom the interest rates were prohibitive, and by provincials in the West whose promissory notes had to be converted into cash for investments in the East. Men who had previously enjoyed easy credit found that the situation had changed dramatically.[93] That the crisis came during Cicero's consulship is thereby explicable.[94]

The Catilinarian movement touched sensitive chords among the urban *plebs* as well as among the rustics. Those plagued by high rents, poor living conditions, and underemployment, and frustrated by government refusal of land grants must have caught eagerly at propaganda suggesting a change of regime. Men without means or hope had little to lose.[95] Cicero and Sallust, of course, depict them as the "dregs" of society, the "cesspool" of the city. Sallust's claim that the *plebs* as a whole flocked to a revolutionary banner is an obvious

[90] Cic. *De Imp. Pomp.* 44.

[91] Cic. *Pro Flacco*, 67; *In Vat.* 12.

[92] Cic. *Ad Att.* 1.12.1; *Ad Fam.* 5.6.2. That creditors were calling in their debts is clear from Val. Max. 4.8.3.

[93] Cic. *Cat.* 2.10: *res eos iam pridem, fides nuper deficere cœpit*; *De Leg. Agrar.* 2.8: *sublata erat de foro fides*; cf. *Cat.* 1.14; Sallust, *Cat.* 35.3.

[94] On the debt problem and Catiline's conspiracy, see W. Allen, *CJ*, 34 (1938): 70–85; R. Scalais, *LEC*, 8 (1939): 487–492.

[95] Sallust, *Cat.* 21.1: *homines quibus mala abunde omnia erant, sed neque res neque spes bona ulla*; cf. *Cat.* 36.4.

exaggeration.[96] But it is clear that the most destitute and poverty-stricken of the proletariate became ready recruits for Catiline.[97]

The possibility of upheaval naturally attracted certain marginal elements as well. In the city, young men, some even from wealthy and noble families, joined out of restlessness, boredom, or a desire to prove their manhood.[98] In the country there came brigands, anxious for pillage and gain.[99] Leaders of the conspiracy would welcome any sort of following to obtain their ends: not only citizens, but men of all backgrounds and provenance. The ranks of the discontented extended well beyond Italy.[100]

Slaves, however, were another matter. Were they utilized by the conspirators? That has sometimes been believed.[101] Cicero, of course, would do his best to persuade his hearers that slaves were being recruited. The horror of a servile rebellion would help solidify the cause of the establishment. Yet careful perusal of the evidence refutes the presumption. The most that Cicero–or Sallust–can say is that Catiline "hoped" to attract slaves or "was in the process" of stirring servile insurrection.[102] "Reports" circulated concerning slave unrest in Capua and Apulia; an adherent of Catiline was allegedly "about to go" to Apulia to rouse slave herdsmen and shepherds; Cicero even asserted that Catiline had intimate friends in the gladiatorial schools.[103] The rumors were enough to frighten the city; the senate ordered gladiatorial troops to be shut up in the municipalities for safe-keeping.[104] But rumors, "reports," "intentions," and allegations should not be mistaken for facts. They are the traditional recourse of propagandists. Had there been actual participation by slaves, the speeches of Cicero would have harped ceaselessly upon it. In fact, the orator, once the conspirators were safely placed in custody, proudly affirmed that

[96] Sallust, *Cat.* 37.1: *omnino cuncta plebes novarum rerum studio Catilinæ incepta probabat.* Sallust puts the statement in a general moralizing context about the behavior of the lower classes at all times and places: they always hate the good, love the evil, and await opportunities for revolution–a typical aristocratic portrait; *Cat.* 37.2-3.

[97] Cic. *Cat.* 1.12: *sin tu, quod te iam dudum hortor, exieris, exhaurietur ex urbe tuorum comitum magna et perniciosa sentina rei publicæ*; *Cat.* 2.7-8: *o fortunatam rem publicam, si quidem hanc sentinam urbis eiecerit . . . non solum ex urbe verum etiam ex agris ingentem numerum perditorum hominum conlegerat*; Sallust, *Cat.* 37.4-5: *omnes, quos flagitium aut facinus domo expulerat, ei Romam sicut in sentinam confluxerant.*

[98] Sallust, *Cat.* 14.5-7, 17.6, 43.2; Cic. *Cat.* 1.13, 2.22-23.

[99] Sallust, *Cat.* 28.4.

[100] Sallust, *Cat.* 24.3, 39.6; Cic. *Cat.* 4.6; *Pro Mur.* 78.

[101] So, most recently, Yavetz, *Historia*, 12 (1963): 494.

[102] Cic. *Cat.* 1.27: *evocatorem servorum*; *Cat.* 4.4: *servitia excitantur*; Sallust, *Cat.* 24.4: *Catilina credebat posse servitia urbana sollicitare.*

[103] Reports of slave unrest: Sallust, *Cat.* 30.2; Cæparius' alleged mission to Apulia, which never took place; Cic. *Cat.* 3.14; Sallust, *Cat.* 46.3; Catiline and gladiators: Cic. *Cat.* 2.9.

[104] Sallust, *Cat.* 30.7.

no *servus*, whose condition was even barely tolerable, sympathized with plans for disruption.[105] To be sure, some of Catiline's accomplices, notably Lentulus Sura, argued for the inclusion of slaves. But Catiline himself rejected the proposition unequivocally: servile elements were to have no part in a cause which belonged to Roman citizens alone.[106]

The cause was varied and multifaceted–as varied as the groups of Roman citizens involved. Leadership at the top came from disappointed and malcontented aristocrats, envious of their more successful peers and eager for a shakeup in government which would give them the controlling hand.[107] They aimed for a political coup and the creation of a new dominant faction in the state. That purpose had little in common with the social and economic grievances felt by the lower classes. And it is extremely doubtful that Catiline, who had concentrated all his energies on securing the consulship, had laid long-range plans for a social revolution.[108] If there were to be any hope of success, however, the strike would have to come immediately. Pompeius Magnus, with the bulk of the Roman army, was still abroad; but his victory was already in sight. A delay of any extent in the conspirators' plans would be fatal. That too helps to explain the timing of the insurrection.[109] Catiline now resolved to exploit the discontents felt in other segments of society, through propaganda and slogans: freedom from oppressive rulers, abolition of debts, a more equitable distribution of wealth.[110] Hence, aspirations and expectations rose in

[105] Cic. *Cat.* 4.16.

[106] Sallust, *Cat.* 56.5: *alienum suis rationibus existumans videri causam civium cum servis fugitivis communicavisse.* For Lentulus' vain attempts to persuade Catiline, see Cic. *Cat.* 3.8, 3.12; Sallust, *Cat.* 44.5–6. Only secondary sources suggest that slaves actually took part in the insurrection; Dio, 37.33.2; Appian, *BC*, 2.2; and cf. Suet. *Aug.* 3. Their evidence cannot stand in view of the primary authorities. It is true that when Lentulus, Cethegus, and others were jailed, attempts were made to arouse slaves and freedmen for their rescue; Sallust, *Cat.* 50.1–2; Dio, 37.35.3; Appian, *BC*, 2.5. But the men solicited were apparently personal retainers and dependents of the incarcerated *nobiles*. That has no relevance for any general servile uprising.

[107] Cic. *Cat.* 2.19; Sallust, *Cat.* 37.10; cf. Cic. *Cat.* 4.12. Sallust speaks also of certain *nobiles*, secretive and hidden, lurking in the background and hoping for *dominatio*; *Cat.* 17.5. It was once an article of faith that Cæsar and Crassus manipulated the conspiracy from behind the scenes. Cf., e.g., E. T. Salmon, *AJP*, 56 (1935): 302–316. The view has long been discredited and requires no further refutation here; cf. the succinct discussion of Rice Holmes, *Rom. Rep.*, I:470–473; also Strasburger, *Cæsars Eintritt*, pp. 120–125; E. D. Eagle, *Phoenix*, 3 (1949): 15–30. On the charges leveled against Cæsar and Crassus, which, properly, came to naught, see above, pp. 285–286.

[108] When the uprising came, there were few men even equipped with implements of warfare; Sallust, *Cat.* 56.3, 59.5.

[109] Sallust, *Cat.* 16.4; Florus, 2.12.1; Plut. *Cic.* 10.1–2.

[110] Only Dio, 37.30.2, mentions land distribution as part of Catiline's program. Hence, the proposal should be labeled as dubious–Cicero would not have missed the opportunity to dwell on it.

various groups that were otherwise little inclined to cooperate: evicted farmers, Sullan colonists, oppressed debtors, restless youths, the urban poor. Each had its own grievances, each its own ends. That Catiline was able to control this miscellaneous assemblage is dubious. It was not his intent to destroy a social structure over which he expected to preside as consul and leader of the prevailing faction. His resolute refusal to enroll slaves, his letters and speeches to the senate, emphasize the posture of a wronged aristocrat and champion of just causes. And even the message of C. Manlius stresses the need to restore justice, not to overthrow society. The majority of participants doubtless shared that general goal. But once violent passions were unleashed, none could predict what consequences might follow.

How serious a menace did the Catilinarian uprising in fact pose to the establishment? Manlius, who organized the forces in Italy, began with two thousand men. The addition of volunteers and sympathizers, we are told, brought his total up to the equivalent of two full legions.[111] Whether that literally means twelve thousand men may be doubted. When Catiline eventually perished in battle, only three thousand men fell with him; the remainder were swiftly rounded up, offering little effective resistance.[112] In Rome, the supporters are not calculable. Catiline's plan in the city, however, seems to have rested on surprise rather than numbers: arson, key assassinations, sudden disruption, and panic. It is revealing that after the conspiracy's unmasking only five men were executed, four others were condemned *in absentia*, and another six were convicted in the following year.

Evidently the number of rebels proved to be insufficient–grossly insufficient. Support in the countryside materialized to a small extent, mostly among ex-soldiers for whom resort to arms was second nature. But the total force was hopelessly insignificant, even in the face of government troops that did not include the vast armies in the East. In the city, lack of response to Catiline's call was even more striking. Whatever sympathy there may have been at the outset, reports of planned fires, murders, and pillage caused it to evaporate. The upper classes, senators and *equites*, as one might expect, stood united against any riot or disruptive activity.[113] More interesting, however, is the attitude of the urban *plebs*. Originally attracted by the prospect of debt relief and improved conditions, they were not prepared to countenance actual vio-

[111] Sallust, *Cat.* 56.1–2.

[112] The number is given by Dio, 37.40.1. On capture of the stragglers, see Dio, 37.41.1. Appian, *BC*, 2.7, gives the total as twenty thousand, a grossly inflated figure. At an earlier stage, despite government offers of rewards and immunity, there were no deserters; Sallust, *Cat.* 36.5; cf. 30.6–7. But that changed after arrest of the conspirators in Rome: Catiline's forces swiftly lost personnel; Sallust, *Cat.* 57.1; Plut. *Cic.* 22.5.

[113] Cf., e.g., Cic. *Cat.* 1.21, 2.25, 4.22; *Pro Flacco*, 96; *Ad Att.* 2.1.7.

lence and destruction. In any serious urban tumult, they would themselves have been the chief victims, their meager properties and possessions the first casualties. Hence, the *plebs* applauded, with enthusiasm and undoubted sincerity, the capture of the conspirators.[114] Cicero proudly lists the categories of men who rallied to his aid and turned their backs decisively on Catilinarian schemes: not simply senators, *equites*, and *principes*, but the whole class of freeborn proletariate, even those of the most slender means, lowly clerks, *liberti,* slaves, shopkeepers, and small businessmen, to whom peace and order in the city was indispensable and inviolable.[115] The language may be excessive, but there is no reason to doubt the essential accuracy of the statement. The city populace had legitimate complaints, but like most Romans, they feared the consequences of radical change and social upheaval.[116]

The conspiracy of Catiline collapsed. Some sympathy existed for its ends, almost none for its means. That it looms so large in both ancient and modern literature is principally a matter of accident. It was Cicero's consular year—and his greatest triumph. Discovery and suppression of the plot accrued largely to the consul's credit.[117] And he never allowed his countrymen to forget it. Ciceronian orations elevated the deed into the removal of a horrific menace and the salvation of the state itself. To be sure, much of the rhetoric came in response to strident criticism over execution of the prisoners, which forced the orator into somewhat excessive self-justification. But the fact remains that Cicero's own speeches and writings form the basis of most of the tradition. Coupled with Sallust's monograph, they provide information of a richness almost unparalleled in ancient history. The significance of the Catilinarian affair emerges with undue and misleading proportions.

It is evident, in retrospect, that the event did not shake the foundations of the state.[118] The government was in no real danger of toppling; the conspiracy, in fact, strengthened awareness of a common interest in order and stability.

[114] Sallust, *Cat.* 48.1-2: *plebs, coniuratione patefacta . . . mutata mente Catilinæ consilia execrari, Ciceronem ad cælium tollere . . . incendium vero crudele, immoderatum, ac sibi maxume calamitosum putabat, quippe cui omnes copiæ in usu cotidiano et cultu corporis erant*; Plut. *Cic.* 22.3-5.

[115] Cic. *Cat.* 4.14-17; cf. Yavetz, *Historia*, 12 (1963): 496-497.

[116] Cf. Sallust, *Cat.* 31.1-3; Dio, 37.10.4.

[117] The fact was duly acknowledged by Sallust in his monograph. A once prevalent notion that the historian was biased against Cicero no longer finds favor—rightly. See, e.g., Broughton, *TAPA*, 67 (1936): 34-46; A. La Penna, *StudItalFilClass*, 31 (1959): 16-32; Syme, *Sallust*, pp. 105-111.

[118] Little value attaches to the notion that Catiline's plot foreshadowed the civil war of the 40s; so, e.g., W. Hoffman, *Gymnasium*, 66 (1959): 459-477. It would be hazardous, however, to vault to the opposite extreme, as does K. H. Waters, *Historia*, 19 (1970): 195-215, who regards the conspiracy as the personal creation of Cicero and almost all of its details as the product of the orator's fertile imagination.

It is not, however, to be dismissed as a minor and meaningless episode. Motives of the leaders may have been personal and less than admirable. But the movement itself called to notice a number of authentic social ills which had previously lacked effective expression: the plight of the ex-farmer now landless and dislocated, the precarious existence of the rural laborer, the discontent of the unsuccessful Sullan colonist without a market for his property, the injustice and fragility of the financial structure, the broad extent of the debt problem, the oppressive conditions facing some of the city masses. Few men, it must be stressed again, were willing to revolt to correct those ills. The shape of the social structure remained basically unaffected by the Catilinarian uprising. But the grievances had been brought to public attention.

Nor did the government sit back idly, content and secure with the successful dispersal of the insurrection. Those whose hopes had been raised by Catiline, though unwilling to engage in armed revolt, were still prepared to press their case. Some looked forward to Pompey's homecoming, expecting that he might reenact Sulla's return and initiate a new round of confiscations and land distributions. Their expectations were dashed: Pompey fired off a missive in early 62 announcing that he would not disturb the civil peace. That afforded a relief of large proportions for the ruling class.[119] No threat to public order seemed likely to materialize in the near future. But legislation in subsequent years shows that prominent leaders recognized the utility of responding to needs exposed in the Catilinarian affair. The grain bill sponsored by Cato in 62 obviously belongs in this context: a significant expansion of benefits for the urban poor, to be followed four years later by Clodius' even more generous *lex frumentaria*. Politics, as we have seen, delayed palliation of the agrarian problem. But not for long. Two major bills in 59 and another in 55 went a long way toward relief. Dissatisfied landowners could now sell their property to the state, resolve their debts, and perhaps even invest elsewhere; many displaced farmers in the city and in the countryside would once again obtain lots of their own.

At the same time, the government maintained and increased the security of the creditor class. There were to be no *tabulæ novæ*; contractual obligations would be enforced. Otherwise financial stability and the whole economic structure would be perpetually unstable.[120] Businessmen benefited, especially the commercial interests. In 60, a prætorian measure, sponsored by Metellus Nepos, eradicated all customs dues on ports in Italy. That will have accommodated not only traders, but prosperous landowners who exported products,

[119] Cic. *Ad Fam.* 5.7.1; see Gruen, *Phoenix*, 24 (1970): 237–243.
[120] Cic. *De Off.* 2.84.

and in general, the wealthy consumer of luxury imports.[121] In the short run, the advantage of the creditor might not be good news to the little man. But security for the financial classes, buttressed by firm government support and considerably enhanced by the new stability in Asia, was bound to benefit the Roman economy as a whole. It would be absurd to suppose that permanent solution had been found for all the complaints of the lower orders. But Roman leaders had learned much from the Catilinarian agitation. They did not retreat into inactive conservatism, standing pat and hastening their doom.

URBAN VIOLENCE

The Catilinarian episode was an aberration. But violence was not. The history of the Ciceronian age is laced with instances of urban violence. It is tempting to see in that feature a crucial element for explaining the Republic's fall. Frequent outbursts and agitation, so it might appear, discredited the machinery of government and weakened the fabric of the community. The matter needs reconsideration. Recorded examples of turbulence abound in the late Republic as never before in Roman history. That fact is incontrovertible. But what does it mean?

The exceptional abundance of information for the Ciceronian age accounts in part for the imbalance. More important, it is a function of the growth of population in the city, the dislocation and fluidity that marked the *plebs urbana* in this era. But violence was not new to Rome. The two generations that preceded Sulla show numerous examples. And roots go back to early Roman history: the notions of popular justice and self-help were deeply ingrained in Roman character, sanctioned by ritualized practices, acknowledged and adopted even in the legal structure. The lack of an organized police force in the Republic possesses significance. It does not stem from oversight or miscalculation. Roman leaders wanted no part of such an institution. A harsh and repressive instrument in the wrong hands could exacerbate discontents and rend the social fabric on which the aristocracy relied. And the absence of professional law enforcement officials is suggestive also on another count. It discloses the prevalence of the idea, dating back to Rome's less sophisticated past, that recourse to private force could often be a legitimate means of expressing grievances and correcting injustice. That idea was exploited with greater frequency by politicians, demagogues, and others in the late Republic. But it did not itself involve anything novel.[122]

[121] Cic. *Ad Att.* 2.16.1; *Ad Q. Frat.* 1.1.33; Dio, 37.51.3–4. Metellus' measure, of course, reduced profits for the *publicani.* But the tax-farmers of Asia gained relief in 59; Suet. *Iul.* 20.3; Appian, *BC,* 2.13; Dio, 38.7.4.

[122] See the illuminating discussion of Lintott, *Violence,* pp. 6–66, who, however, does not

The meaning of violence in the Ciceronian era requires analysis, not presumption. It is an easy leap to make from intermittent disruptions to the fall of the Republic. But is it warranted? That the episodes of private *vis* led inexorably to the collapse of the government constitutes an assumption rather than a demonstration. Only recently has serious attention been paid to the history of violence in the United States. "Violence is as American as cherry pie"—so we are now told. The rhetorical artifice is not without substance. Outbursts of violence, for noble or ignoble motives, minor or serious, resulting in constructive change or repression, run as a persistent thread throughout American history.[123] Yet none entailed the overthrow of government or the destruction of civil society. No necessary connection exists between urban tumult and the downfall of authority.

Certain key questions will be investigated here. What motivated eruptions of violence in the city? How far were they directed against the established social structure? What effect did they have on the strength and stability of the government? Answers, if there be any, can come only through examination of the recorded instances.

---

recognize fully the implications for the late Republic. On the absence of a police force, cf. the remarks of Meier, *Gött. Gel. Anz.*, 216 (1964): 44–48; *Res Pub.*, pp. 157–159. There were, of course, examples of violent quarrels between private individuals, especially in the countryside. Disputes over land titles or boundaries could produce feuds, sometimes resulting in bloody clashes of armed retainers. Scope for private action was wide here. The government did not normally intervene. *Leges de vi* dealt with political violence affecting the state. Disputes between individuals, even when bloodshed was involved, were a matter for the civil law. And the notion of self-help to assert rights permitted loose interpretation. The practice only began to get out of hand after the civil wars of the 80s—understandably so. Dislocation and resort to force had become a habit with some. Quarrels over landed property induced certain claimants to arm slaves and clients—with deleterious consequences; Cic. *Pro Tull.* 8–11, 18–22; *Pro Cæc.* 1, 20–23. Steps were taken to tighten the law. A prætorian edict of 76 cracked down on the use of armed men, facilitated procedures for the plaintiff in any legal action, and prescribed heavier penalties for offenders. Subsequent prætors seem to have issued similar injunctions; Cic. *Pro Tull.* 8–11; *Pro Cæc.* 23, 89–93. How effective they were is unknown. We are told that forceful struggles over pastureland were common; Cic. *Pro Cluent.* 161: *ut solet*. Allegations about violence on the land were made also against Crassus, Autronius, and C. Rabirius; Cic. *Parad.* 46; *Pro Sulla*, 71; *Pro Rab. Perd.* 8. All these occasions may have come in the decade or so after the civil wars. Later allegations connected Clodius with ejection of men from landed property; Cic. *Pro Mil.* 26, 50, 74, 75, 87. No formal proceedings, so far as is known, were undertaken in any of these cases. The prætorian edicts, in any event, indicate official willingness to deal with serious outbreaks which might affect the public interest. But it is noteworthy that the Republic never regarded them as within the province of criminal law. *Vis* involving private individuals in the countryside had no discernible impact on the affairs of state. On this whole question, see Lintott, *Violence*, pp. 27–29, 125–131; Brunt, *Italian Manpower*, pp. 551–557.

[123] See now R. M. Brown, in H. D. Graham and T. R. Gurr, *Violence in America: Historical and Comparative Analysis* (New York, 1969), pp. 45–84.

The urban *plebs*, as we have seen, was no monolith. It comprised slaves, freedmen, shopkeepers, craftsmen, professionals, skilled and unskilled laborers, displaced farmers, and the poor generally. To imagine that they were all of one mind would be far from the mark. A central feature of Roman political life bears repeated emphasis: the system of patronage and clientage. A large proportion of the proletariate possessed closer bonds to individual houses of the *nobilitas* than to others of their own social class. This held true particularly for the freedmen, grateful for their manumission and still tied in *fides* to their former masters. And freedmen constituted no small percentage of the city's resident population. Hence, we can expect to find that common action among the *plebs* marked the exception rather than the rule. And that is indeed the case. But certain issues could arouse the passions of the proletariate as a whole, or, at least, a significant part of it, cutting across the traditional lines of personal or political connections.

Acute grain shortage would, of course, affect most members of the *plebs urbana*. It might even provoke riot. An instance stands on record in 75. When the people were hungry, they found it natural to strike out against officials who could conveniently be held responsible. During the electoral campaign of 75 the consuls appeared in public; a crowd gathered and launched an assault, forcing them to scurry ignominiously for shelter.[124] That the disruption was widespread would be a hasty judgment. Attack on the consuls is the only known fact. And positive results followed: private benefactions on a large scale in 75 and 74, and a new grain bill in 73.[125]

Precariousness of the grain supply also explains actions of the mob in 67. Piratic descents upon Roman shipping had played havoc with imports of food. The situation reached grave proportions in the early 60s. Scarcity produced hoarding and exorbitant prices.[126] In 67 Gabinius presented his measure awarding wide powers to Pompeius Magnus to conduct a sweeping campaign against the privateers. Resistance came in the senate, naturally. Political opponents did not look kindly upon increased prestige for Pompey. But this time, the interests of the *plebs* were directly involved. When Gabinius was manhandled in the senate, a mob attacked the *curia* itself, causing the panicked senators to scatter for safety. The consul C. Piso, who maintained resistance, was nearly killed by the angry crowd.[127] Opposition melted away, and the *lex Gabinia*

[124] Sallust, *Hist.* 2.45, Maur.; cf. 2.44, Maur.: *immane quantum animi exarsere*; 2.46, Maur.: *festinantibus in summa inopia patribus*. If the latter passage is correctly associated with the food riot, it suggests that the senate as well as the magistrates were under fire.

[125] See above, p. 385.

[126] Cic. *De Imp. Pomp.* 44.

[127] Dio, 36.24.1–3; Plut. *Pomp.* 25.3–4.

secured passage. The *plebs* knew what it was doing. An immediate consequence of Pompey's appointment was a substantial fall in grain prices, to the unrestrained joy of the populace.[128]

Serious food shortage occurred again a decade later.[129] Reasons are not readily discernible. Clodius' *lex frumentaria* of 58, which distributed corn free and to larger numbers, may have contributed to a temporary shortage. For those not on the distribution lists, prices were much higher than before. Manumission of slaves added to the crisis; so also, perhaps, did the influx of people from the countryside to demonstrate for Cicero's recall in 57. When the orator returned, Clodius was anxious to shift the blame, charging Cicero himself with responsibility for the shortage. Cicero offered different reasons: a lack of corn surplus in the provinces, exportations elsewhere than to Italy, hoarding by corn dealers in order to raise market prices, and, of course, the ill effects of Clodius' grain law.[130] Whatever the causes, the *plebs* indulged in violent protest. A mob flocked into the theater, dispersed spectators, and created a mass demonstration. There followed an attack on the senate and the consul, stoning and rioting. No meeting of the *patres* could be held for a day or two, for fear of personal safety.[131] Cicero naturally stressed the machinations of Clodius, arguing that his hired rowdies and assassins instigated the tumult. And there is no reason to doubt that Clodius took advantage of the situation and vented his wrath upon the orator and Pompeius. But a shortage of food prompted the uprising; men were hungry and desperate. This was no mere political device. Cicero himself admits as much.[132] Once again, results were forthcoming. A senatorial decree, followed by a consular *lex*, authorized a five-year commission for Pompey to supervise and guarantee the grain supply throughout the Mediterranean.[133] The psychological effect was potent, and the crisis passed.[134] Not that grain shortages vanished–problems arose again in 56.[135] But the senate swiftly allocated more cash for the corn supply. We hear of no further popular uprisings on the issue.[136]

[128] Cic. *De Imp. Pomp.* 44: *tanta repente vilitas annonæ ex summa inopia et caritate rei frumentariæ consecuta est unius hominis spe ac nomine*; Plut. *Pomp.* 27.2: ἐποίει δὲ τὴν χαρὰν τὸ παρ' ἐλπίδα τῆς μεταβολῆς τάχος, ὑπερβάλλουσαν ἀφθονίαν τῆς ἀγορᾶς ἐχούσης.

[129] Cic. *De Domo*, 10–12; *P. Red. in Sen.* 34; *Ad Att.* 4.1.6; Asconius, 48, Clark; Plut. *Pomp.* 49.5.

[130] Cic. *De Domo*, 11, 14, 25; *Ad Att.* 4.1.6; Plut. *Pomp.* 49.5.

[131] Cic. *De Domo*, 5–6, 11–14; *Ad Att.* 4.1.6; Asconius, 48, Clark.

[132] Cic. *De Domo*, 12: *difficultatem annonæ summamque inopiam rei frumentariæ, ut homines non iam diuturnam caritatem, sed ut famem plane timerent, nemo negat*; *Ad Att.* 4.1.6: *annonæ summa caritas*; cf. Brunt, *Past and Present*, 35 (1966): 25–26.

[133] Sources in Broughton, *MRR*, II:203–204.

[134] Cf. Plut. *Pomp.* 50.2–undoubtedly, however, an exaggeration.

[135] Cic. *De Har. Resp.* 31; *Ad Q. Frat.* 2.3.2.

[136] Cic. *Ad Q. Frat.* 2.5.1.

Other matters could also occasion disturbances in the city: notably, legislation proposed in the interests of the *plebs*. Sponsorship of "popular" measures was a standard device of demagogic politicians. It would be rash to ascribe purely altruistic motives to the sponsors. Politicians who could not rely on substantial hereditary *clientelæ* often espoused bills designed to appeal to large segments of the populace. And, at times, the struggle over those bills might invite disruptive participation from the proletariate.

Violence accompanied one such proposal in 67. C. Cornelius, absorbed in a heated legislative contest with C. Piso, offered a bill prohibiting any exemption from the laws except by express approval of the people. Piso intervened to block proceedings. When a menacing crowd gathered, the consul ordered arrests to be made. That fired the mob. Piso's *fasces* were broken and he was pelted with stones. Cornelius feared a riot, withdrew his motion, and substituted a more moderate one, which gained passage.[137] The issue, obviously, was not one of great moment. But popular passions, as this episode shows, could also be aroused over an extension of the people's constitutional prerogatives.

In this category too come the agrarian laws of 59. It is noteworthy that no tumult or demonstrations accompanied the proposals of 63 and 60. But the *plebs*, stiffened by impatient Pompeian veterans, showed itself ready to use muscle in 59. Bibulus' opposition was overborne–and Cato's. The consul was thrust from the rostra, his *fasces* were smashed, and a bucket of manure was dumped on his head. The crowd hurled some objects, and a few suffered wounds. There were no widespread riots. But further threat of force assured enactment of the *leges agrariæ*.[138] Politics may have inspired Cæsar and Pompey. But the *plebs* looked forward to solid benefits and was prepared to insist.

The same may be said of Clodius' statutes in 58. Opponents railed at him for organizing gangs of thugs. But some of his measures, at least, possessed popular appeal: the *lex frumentaria*, the removal of certain restrictions on legislative assemblies, revival of the *collegia*, reduction of the censors' powers, and the prohibition on capital punishment without due process. Strong-arm methods, threats, and roaming mobs assisted promulgation of these *leges*.[139] But there is no reason to believe that all the agitators had to be bribed or hired by Clodius. His proposals appealed to a broad cross section of the urban populace concerned with civil rights and economic benefits. That Clodius engaged some ruffians need not be doubted. But he also successfully

[137] Asconius, 58, Clark; Dio, 36.39.2–4.

[138] Cic. *In Vat.* 5; *P. Red. ad Quir.* 14; Suet. *Iul.* 20; Dio, 38.5.4–38.6.3; Plut. *Cato*, 32.2; *Luc.* 42.6; *Pomp.* 48.1–2; *Cæs.* 14.6–7.

[139] Sources in Broughton, *MRR*, II:196.

mobilized a large segment of the *plebs* with an attractive program that short-circuited the usual lines between humble clients and their noble patrons.

The urban crowd was sometimes volatile, but not usually irrational. When outbreaks occurred, the perpetrators had definite objects in mind. That is obvious in the case of food riots, and also in the case of desirable legislation just noted. And there were other instances. C. Cornelius had been a popular tribune in 67. When political enemies put him on trial in the following year, angry bands chased off the prosecutors, forcing them to flee for safety.[140] That may have been out of genuine enthusiasm for the defendant. Similar motives provoked the commotions at the trial of Rabirius in 63. The populace knew full well that the issues at stake there involved personal rights and the extra-legal authority of the senate.[141] Display of popular indignation at Gabinius' acquittal in 54 was perhaps also spontaneous.[142] And the same may hold for the loud and negative response in the forum and theater to Messalla's acquittal in 51.[143] A long and respected tradition in Rome assured that the *plebs* could shout and demonstrate at public meetings, the *contiones*, at the circus, and at the theater. The outbursts betokened conventional and generally harmless means of expressing popular attitudes. Occasionally they might degenerate into disorder, as in 63 when the crowd at a theatrical performance exposed its ire at L. Roscius Otho, whose tribunician bill had awarded reserved seats for the *equites* but not for any other segment of the public.[144] Note also the tumult at C. Pomptinus' triumph in 54, which even produced some bloodshed.[145] Such instances, however, were rare, and caused no serious disturbance of normal processes.

It should be stressed that these periodic outbursts did not aim at overthrow of the establishment—quite the contrary. The *plebs* was expounding legitimate grievances or airing genuine feelings. Demands involved reaffirmation of civic rights, redress of economic ills, or protection for popular champions. Such appeals denoted claims on the government, not assaults on the existing order. The phenomenon is common to preindustrial crowds in most periods of history. They utilized what means they had to focus public attention upon their needs: shouts, demonstrations, and sometimes force. In mob action, the poor would often seize the opportunity to harass the rich, destroy property,

[140] Asconius, 59–60, Clark.

[141] Dio, 37.26–27.

[142] Dio, 39.62.2–39.63.1.

[143] Cæl. *Ad Fam.* 8.2.1.

[144] Plut. *Cic.* 13.2–3. On Roscius' bill, passed four years earlier, see Broughton, *MRR*, II:145. At the time of passage Roscius had the backing of the *plebs*, or so we are told; Cic. *Pro Corn. apud* Asconius, 78, Clark.

[145] Dio, 39.65.2.

take out frustrations against their economic betters. The practice was natural and was repeated in most other times and places. But the *plebs* showed no desire to topple the social structure; they took it for granted. It was the ruling class indeed to whom they turned for correction of injustice and relief of economic distress.[146] And Roman political leaders proved to be responsive. Actions taken to alleviate food shortages, distribute grain, allocate land, or pass measures on civil and political rights did not eliminate all of Rome's social problems. But they helped to promote confidence in the government and to maintain the communal fabric.

In fact, those episodes of violence in the late Republic which involved claims of the *plebs* as a whole were in a distinct minority. By far the bulk of disorderly outbursts had no relevance to social grievances. Rather, they grew out of demonstrations arranged by politicians and political factions, mobilizing clients, retainers, and personal followers for their own purposes. Agitation revolved around legislative proposals, criminal trials, and electoral contests.[147] The engagement of the *plebs* remained marginal rather than central. These were struggles among Roman leaders—or would-be leaders.

A number of legislative matters provoked temporary disorders. The contest between Cornelius and Piso in 67 over *leges de ambitu* was manifestly a jockeying for political position. But Piso's efforts to preempt the tribune's law with a measure of his own produced a tumult in which some men were killed.[148] And Piso himself, induced by popular outcry to modify his bill, succeeded only in outraging the *divisores*, who put upon him by force and cast him from the forum. The consul returned with a larger force and pushed his measure through.[149] That the public at large had much interest in precise formulation of the rival *leges* is dubious. The men who were engaged surely comprised personal adherents of the contending politicians. In a similar category was C. Manilius' *rogatio* on distributing freedmen among all voting tribes, presented on the last day of 67. Manilius assembled a band of freedmen and slaves to bolster support for the measure. Resistance came from Domitius Ahenobarbus, who gathered a group of his own. Violent clashes ensued, and many of the tribune's followers lost their lives. The *rogatio* was passed into law, only to be annulled later. Description of the events shows that Manilius'

[146] Cf. the illuminating analyses of preindustrial urban crowds in later periods by E. J. Hobsbawm, *Primitive Rebels* (New York, 1965), pp. 108–125, and Rudé, *Crowd in History*, esp. pp. 47–65, 135–148, 195–269.

[147] Cf. Cic. *Pro Sest.* 77: *nam ex pertinacia aut constantia intercessoris oritur sæpe seditio, culpa atque improbitate latoris commodo aliquo oblato, imperitis aut largitione, oritur ex concertatione magistratuum.*

[148] Dio, 36.39.1.

[149] Asconius, 74–76, Clark.

adherents were a picked band, not independent representatives of the *liberti* clamoring for class privileges.[150]

Struggles over extraordinary commands for the triumvirs also occasioned some outbursts on the streets. Metellus Nepos in 62 sought to have Pompey recalled to take over operations against Catiline. Political opponents objected. Metellus employed armed men, gladiators, and slaves. But a crowd was produced on the other side as well; the *rogatio* failed and Metellus escaped to Pompey.[151] In 59 Vatinius broke through resistance on Cæsar's Gallic commission by muscular tactics, permitting Bibulus and his allies to play the role of political martyrs.[152] And again in 55, the *lex Trebonia* on commands for Pompey and Crassus gained passage only after a violent fracas in which several men were injured and some actually killed. The culprits, however, were not the *plebs* generally, but attendants of the tribunes who backed the bill.[153]

Violence on a larger scale erupted in 57, again prompted by a tribunician bill. Clodius had obtained widespread popular favor in 58. Support for his *lex Clodia de capite civis* may have been largely genuine and spontaneous. The expulsion of Cicero was a consequence, a prime object for Clodius but hardly for the *plebs* as a whole. When efforts commenced for Cicero's recall in 57, Clodius determined to resist at all costs. That he carried the populace with him on this issue is most doubtful. It was a matter of political face. Personal dependents had to be relied on, and Clodius had assembled a large group of loyal and rugged followers. Q. Fabricius in January presented a formal resolution for Cicero's return. Riot and disorder followed; terrorist activities of Clodius' bands dominated the streets. Cicero's reports after the fact paint lurid scenes of chaos and destruction: stones, swords, clubs, even pieces of railing used; massacres in the forum; the Tiber stuffed with corpses, sewers clogged, and gore mopped from the street with sponges; men saved from slaughter only by feigning death or crawling under a mounting pile of bodies. Exaggeration and distortion are patent. Cicero would spare no horror in depicting Clodius' activities. For him, as usual, the mobs consist essentially of salaried hoodlums, riffraff, professional assassins, gladiators, runaway slaves, and the

[150] Asconius, 45, Clark: *C. Manilius tribunus plebis subnixus libertinorum et servorum manu perditissimam legem ferret . . . idque per tumultum ageret et clivum Capitolinum obsideret, discusserat persuperatque cœtum Domitius ita ut multi Manilianorum occiderentur.*

[151] See, esp., Cic. *Pro Sest.* 62; Dio, 37.43.1–3; Plut. *Cato*, 26–29; Suet. *Iul.* 16.

[152] Cic. *In Vat.* 5, 21–23; Schol. Bob. 147, Stangl; cf. Plut. *Cæs.* 14.6–8. It is possible that the Ciceronian passages refer here to clashes over the agrarian laws, rather than to Vatinius' own *lex* on the Gallic command; cf. Pocock, *Comm. Cic. Vat.*, pp. 82, 101–102.

[153] Dio, 39.34–36; esp. 39.35.5: οἱ ὑπηρέται τῶν δημάρχων; also Plut. *Cato*, 43.1–4. Dio's account shows that Cato deliberately provoked sponsors of the enactment into extreme methods.

city scum.[154] However gross the description, we need not doubt that the active agitators were largely retainers of Clodius and his allies. The proletariate in general had no cause for violent resistance to Cicero's return. In fact, at the theater and the assemblies popular approval for the recall was strong and vociferous.[155] But the existence of disorder, from whatever cause, always offered opening for the poor and desperate to indulge passion against the well-to-do. That feature evidently played a role in extending some of the chaos.[156] The basic issue, however, was a political one. Clodius utilized his forces, after Cicero's return, to attack the orator, his family and friends, especially Pompey and Milo. Retaliation took analogous form. Milo and Sestius organized retainers of their own to engage Clodius in the streets and eventually to overcome him. Their methods proved to be no more gentle or more admirable. Cicero's praise for their actions arises out of transparent partisanship: force is justifiable if it is exercised in a proper cause; Milo championed the cause of the *boni* and all right-thinking men. In fact, the men they gathered were a private retinue drawn mainly from personal clients.[157] The issue was not one to awaken the basic interests of the *plebs urbana*.

Outbursts associated with criminal trials belong in a similar category. The clamor for Cornelius in 65 may have been an exception. But most instances betray manipulation by political figures. P. Autronius, bitter and explosive by nature, endeavored to disperse the court at his *ambitus* trial of 66 by loosing slaves and gladiators and creating a tumult; the effect was only to hasten his conviction.[158] The same fate was suffered by C. Manilius, convicted *de maiestate* in 65, despite, or rather because of, his use of roughnecks to upset the tribunal.[159] In 61 Clodius employed some young toughs to threaten and intimidate during the discussion of his sacrilege trial and at the trial itself. But no actual violence resulted. Again this was a private band, rounded up

[154] Endless and highly colored descriptions primarily in Cic. *Pro Sest.* 75–92; cf. Cic. *P. Red. ad Quir.* 14; *Pro Mil.* 38; Dio, 39.7.2; Plut. *Cic.* 33.3.

[155] Cf. Cic. *Pro Sest.* 108–109, 120–125; Dio, 39.7.2; Plut. *Cic.* 33.3–4.

[156] Cf. Cic. *Pro Sest.* 85: *omnia hominum cum egestate tum audacia perditorum clamore, concussu, vi, manu gerebantur*; *Pro Planc.* 86: *egentes in locupletes, perditi in bonos, servi in dominos armabantur*; *De Domo*, 61.

[157] Cf. on Sestius, Cic. *P. Red. in Sen.* 19–20: *cuius ego clientibus, libertis, familia, copiis, litteris . . . sum sustentatus.* Further on the violent clashes, see, e.g., Cic. *Pro Sest.* 78–79, 84–92; *Ad Att.* 4.3.2–3; Schol. Bob. 125, Stangl.

[158] Cic. *Pro Sulla*, 15, 71.

[159] Asconius, 60, Clark. These *duces operarum* were doubtless drawn from the *libertinorum et servorum manus* which Manilius had employed in advocating his voting bill; Asconius, 45, Clark. Manilius' enemies also seem to have employed some muscle at the trial; Cic. *Pro Corn. apud* Asconius, 66, Clark. Demonstrations at Manilius' earlier hearing in 66 did not, apparently, involve any violence, though there was disruption; Dio, 36.44.1–2; Plut. *Cic.* 9.4–6.

and headed by Clodius' political friends.[160] The coming of the triumvirate produced a spate of political trials. During the intense struggles of 59 and 58, two prosecutions of triumviral adherents were broken up by disorder. C. Cato's attempt to indict Gabinius *de ambitu* failed when the prosecutor was chased from the forum and barely escaped serious injury. Vatinius' trial in 58 also erupted in chaos. The defendant had appealed to tribunes for assistance. When that proved insufficient, he had the *quæsitor* hurled from his tribunal, the benches upset, and the voting urns cast away. Presiding officer and *accusatores* fled the scene; the case collapsed by default.[161]

The bitter personal and political quarrel between Clodius and Milo also spilled over into the courts. Clodius was indicted *de vi* in 57, Milo in 56. Neither case came to fruition; both involved rowdyism and physical confrontation. Clodius' gangs went on a rampage in November 57, assaulting the persons and homes of Cicero, his brother, and Milo. The latter's followers were equally obstreperous, driving their enemy to cover. Senatorial deliberations on arrangements for Clodius' trial were disrupted by shouting crowds assembled on the steps of the *curia*.[162] When Clodius in turn put Milo under indictment, he utilized the opportunity not only to attack his *inimicus* but to organize followers in demonstrations, vicious abuse, and assaults on Pompeius Magnus.[163] The clashes were obviously political in context and meaning. Disorder arose from political demonstration, not as a feature of popular unrest. An aristocratic defendant's career was in jeopardy in every major criminal case. Active support by his clients, even to the point of intimidating the prosecutors, was a commonplace.[164]

The same immoderate zeal exhibited itself in electoral campaigns, especially for the major offices. It was customary for candidates to parade about with a large entourage. That practice naturally increased the likelihood of stormy clashes between rivals. Such was the case, for example, in 67, when excessive enthusiasm at the canvassing resulted in some deaths.[165] Again in 66 a bitter contest seems to have induced at least one candidate to enroll bands of toughs. And the frustrated hopefuls, returned at the polls and rejected in the courts,

[160] Cic. *Ad Att.* 1.14.5: *concursabant barbatuli iuvenes, totus ille grex Catilinæ duce filiola Curionis*; *Ad Att.* 1.16.4–5; Schol. Bob. 85, Stangl.

[161] On Gabinius' indictment, Cic. *Ad Q. Frat.* 1.2.15; *Pro Sest.* 18; Vatinius' trial: Cic. *In Vat.* 33–34; *Pro Sest.* 135; Schol. Bob. 140, 150, Stangl.

[162] Cic. *Ad Att.* 4.3.2–5; *Ad Q. Frat.* 2.1.2–3; Dio, 39.7.4–39.8.1.

[163] Cic. *Ad Q. Frat.* 2.3.1–4; *Ad Fam.* 1.5b.1; *Pro Mil.* 40; Dio, 39.19.1–2; Plut. *Pomp.* 48.7. For a time, there was suspension of all judicial business; Cic. *Pro Sest.* 85.

[164] Cf. the actions of C. Cato's retainers against his *accusator* Asinius Pollio in 54; Seneca, *Controv.* 7.4.7: *a clientibus Catonis rei sui Pollionem Asinium circumventum in foro cædi.*

[165] Dio, 36.39.1.

may have organized a demonstration against their rivals upon the opening of the consular year.[166] A decade passed without serious incidents at the *comitia*. Cicero's dramatic appearance with a breastplate and a bodyguard in 63 was obvious sham. Nothing in fact occurred.[167] In 56, however, the triumvirs, thwarted in recent electoral contests, mobilized all their resources to obtain sympathetic magistrates for the following year. Their provincial commands and political futures were at stake. Delay was needed in order to postpone the *comitia* and create an *interregnum*. In that effort adherents of the triumvirs ran into stiff opposition: senatorial enemies threatened them with force, and an angry crowd in retaliation menaced the senate house.[168] The postponement was effected. But Domitius Ahenobarbus, prodded by Cato, pressed his candidacy against Pompey and Crassus until he was driven off by force, his attendant was slain, and Cato was wounded.[169] The intimidation continued at the prætorian and ædilician elections. The dynasts shoved most of their favorites through, but only at the cost of some violence; Pompey returned home, his toga bespattered with blood.[170] Again politics predominated. There was no popular rising. The faction of Cato had deliberately goaded the triumvirs into excesses in order to strengthen its own moral position.[171]

The scramble for office in 54 involved outlays of cash on an unprecedented scale. Of actual violence we possess little evidence. But the brother of one of the candidates claimed to have been attacked and his slaves wounded; he promised to return force with force. And there was evidently some hurling of missiles, even the use of swords.[172] Cato, when he attempted to enforce financial accounting upon the magistrates-elect, was put upon by a mob, and restored order only with great difficulty.[173] Political rivalry once more stimulated violence in the electoral campaigns for 52. With Milo canvassing for the consulship, Clodius for the prætorship, and Pompey actively supporting other candidates, an especially volatile atmosphere permeated the city. Various armed bands backing each hopeful engaged in brutal, sometimes bloody clashes. Because elections suffered delay and no executive officials were in office, the

[166] P. Sulla, so it was alleged, gathered forces to use against Torquatus; Cic. *Pro Sulla*, 68: *contra patrem tuum operas et manum comparasse*. The plot, designed for January 65, much exaggerated by later sources, may have been no more than a political demonstration against the new consuls; cf. Sallust, *Cat.* 18.5–6; Dio, 36.44.4–5; Gruen, *CP*, 64 (1969): 20–24.

[167] Cic. *Pro Mur.* 52; *Pro Sulla*, 51; Dio, 37.29.2–5; Plut. *Cic.* 14.5–6.

[168] Dio, 39.28–29.

[169] Dio, 39.31.1–2; Plut. *Pomp.* 52.1–2; *Crass.* 15.2–5; *Cato*, 41.2–5; Appian, *BC*, 2.17.

[170] Dio, 39.32.1–3; Plut. *Pomp.* 53.3; *Cato*, 42.3–5; Appian, *BC*, 2.17; Val. Max. 4.6.4.

[171] Cf. Plut. *Cato*, 41.5.

[172] Asconius, 20, Clark; Appian, *BC*, 2.19; cf. Dio, 40.45.1.

[173] Plut. *Cato*, 44.2–4.

disorder could not readily be controlled. The slaying of Clodius, followed as it was by mob riots and burning of the *curia*, brought unendurable chaos. It also brought Pompey's one-man consulship and the imposition of vigorous reaction.[174] Legislative enactments in 52 eliminated the crisis and restored order. Electoral campaigns were calm and untroubled in subsequent years.[175]

Violence, it is clear, was not an unfamiliar occurrence in Rome.[176] But it would be a mistake to regard it as evidence for serious unrest among the urban *plebs* as a whole. By far the majority of disruptive outbreaks stemmed from machinations by Roman politicians. Riots over economic deprivation or civil rights might mobilize a large number of the *plebs*. But those eruptions were rare and brief, and they usually obtained at least formal satisfaction. Most occasions of violence arose from political struggles in which the proletariate had only marginal concern. Legislative contests, criminal trials, and electoral rivalries were, on the whole, aristocratic matters. Mobs participated as adherents of politicians, not as advocates of class interest. The *plebs* was divided and fragmented, not a unit.[177]

Clients and retainers formed the bulk of strong-armed men in these clashes. Where gladiators and slaves appear in the sources, they were probably troops owned by the politicians who employed them or by their *amici*. To be sure, the frequency of violence may have encouraged some unemployed proletarians to hire themselves out as bully-boys to the highest bidder.[178] But Cicero's incessant sneers at his enemies' "hirelings" and "mercenaries" convey routine propaganda. It would be rash to infer that Rome spawned a whole class of professional ruffians available to any politician with sufficient cash.[179] One may notice, for example, that when Pompey came under assault from Clodius' gangs, he summoned men from the countryside to his aid; that is, his old

[174] On riots in the canvassing, see, esp., Cic. *Pro Mil.* 37, 41; Asconius, 30, 31, 33, 43, 48, Clark; Dio, 40.46.3, 40.48.1–2; Plut. *Cæs.* 28.3–4; *Cato*, 47.1; Livy, *Per.* 107; Schol. Bob. 116, 169, 172, Stangl.

[175] A minor exception was the augural campaign in 50, during which M. Antonius was returned through the assistance of some rather overzealous supporters; Cic. *Phil.* 2.4; cf. *Ad Fam.* 8.14.1. That practice, as we have seen, was hardly unusual.

[176] For a list of violent episodes in the Republic, see the very useful compilation of Lintott, *Violence*, pp. 209–216.

[177] Sallust, *Iug.* 41.6: *ceterum nobilitas factione magis pollebat, plebis vis soluta atque dispersa in multitudine minus poterat.* Cf. Meier, *Res Pub.*, pp. 107–115, who, however, is too extreme in dismissing any common interests among the *plebs*.

[178] Cf. Sallust, *Cat.* 50.1: *duces multitudinum qui pretio rem publicam vexare soliti erant.*

[179] Lintott, *Violence*, pp. 74–77, exaggerates this element in the gangs of the 60s and 50s; cf. also Brunt, *Past and Present*, 35 (1966): 23, who offers a useful catalogue of Ciceronian references to *operæ* and *mercenarii*.

clients from the *ager Picenus et Gallicus.*[180] And when Cicero expected trouble in 59, his supporters offered assistance in the form of their own families, friends, clients, freedmen, and slaves.[181] The personal and political quality of these events predominates. Struggles in the streets were basically extensions of struggles among Rome's prominent figures.

Clodius alone seems to have made a serious attempt to cut across the traditional lines and organize mass support in the populace. His broad program in 58 aroused considerable enthusiasm and earned him a wide following. But Clodius was not content with temporary popularity, to be followed by a more conventional career—the usual fate of demagogic tribunes. He endeavored to institute more permanent bases of support, ready-made groups of proletarian adherents to further his political aspirations. Reconstitution of the *collegia* was a central part of the plan. These trade guilds and religious associations included both laborers and shopkeepers among their numbers: slaves, freedmen, and the working poor. The *collegia* brought together proletariate without regard to their individual connections with noble clans. Gratitude to Clodius gave him a very effective political machine in 58. And he appears to have utilized the *collegia* in part as a recruiting ground and as a system of organization for mobilizing his supporters. That it was a "para-military" organization, as is often claimed, may be excessive. But the guilds themselves, associated with districts of the city, provided convenient structures whereby to call up men for demonstrations or conflicts in the streets.[182]

Cicero, as we have seen, dwells on Clodius' use of runaway slaves, gladiators, and hirelings. A more sober judgment is possible. Gladiatorial corps might be bought, but not readily hired, and Clodius could probably not afford a large number. Runaway slaves would certainly not identify themselves as such; references to *fugitivi* usually betray invective. Where Cicero alleges slaves, he often means ex-slaves, that is, freedmen. And there is evidence that freeborn citizens were also involved in Clodius' entourage.[183] This kind of support

[180] Cic. *Ad Q. Frat.* 2.3.4: *itaque se comparat, homines ex agris arcessit . . . magna manus ex Piceno et Gallia exspectatur.*

[181] Cic. *Ad Q. Frat.* 1.2.16: *omnes et se et suos liberos, amicos, clientes, libertos, servos, pecunias denique suas pollicentur.*

[182] Cic. *P. Red. ad Quir.* 13; *P. Red. in Sen.* 33; *Pro Sest.* 34; *De Domo*, 13, 54, 129; *Pro Mil.* 76. See discussions by Lintott, *Violence*, pp. 77–85; Treggiari, *Roman Freedmen*, pp. 168–177; Kühne, *Helikon*, 6 (1966): 95–113.

[183] Cic. *De Domo*, 54: *non modo liberos, sed etiam servos*; *De Domo*, 79: *conductis operis non solum egentium, sed etiam servorum*; cf. *De Domo*, 13, 89–90; *Ad Att.* 4.3.2. Clodius' following certainly included voters; Cic. *Pro Sest.* 57; *De Domo*, 89. Freedmen, in any case, would hardly engage in the destruction of public records and censorial registers, which attested to their own manumissions; Cic. *Pro Cæl.* 78; *Pro Mil.* 73.

from a cross section of the urban populace suggests that Clodius made good use of the *collegia*. One may note, however, that most of the passages cited refer to the tribune's activities in 58. At that time he was riding the crest of the wave, his legislative program having won the sympathy of a good slice of the *plebs urbana*. It is not likely that Clodius retained equally broad backing in subsequent years, which were dominated by his vindictiveness toward Cicero and his consuming feud with Milo. The urban populace will have found little to interest them in those ventures. Cicero's strictures in 57 and 56 may have more substance. Clodius was compelled to employ gladiators and to turn to experienced roughnecks in order to bolster a following which had lost most of the more respectable enthusiasts of 58.[184]

Hence, it appears that not even Clodius was able to weld any large proportion of the *plebs* into a united mass for very long. The fragmentation of the proletariate persisted through the Republic. That feature prevented any serious concerted action. But it also had its advantages. The ties of patron to client meant that the interests of many lower-class personages received a hearing from individual *nobiles* and aristocratic clans, who were kept apprised of their needs and for whom conferral of *beneficia* meant political advantages in return. Movements of the *plebs* as a whole were scarce, and they usually gained some results. Men like Cicero might brand common laborers, artisans, and shopkeepers as the "dregs of the city" or the "wretched rabble."[185] But governmental officials, as has been noted, frequently found it expedient to answer cries of distress.

Incidents of violence, it is now plain, were not aimed at destroying the social structure or overturning the state. They involved either claims on the government for benefits due the people or, more commonly, political struggles among aristocratic leaders. The pent-up emotions of hungry or depressed men often gained release during periods of disorder. Their targets, not unnaturally, included property and possessions of the wealthy—the usual casualties in urban riots. But their quarrel was not directly with the government.

A further question, however, remains. Whatever the intent of the rioters, did the increasing occurrence of violence in fact weaken the authority of government and make it easier for military leaders to seize control? The logic

[184] Cf. Cic. *Ad Att.* 4.3.2: *post has ruinas, incendia, rapinas desertus a suis . . . servorum consiliis utitur.* Observe that public expressions of support for Cicero, while in exile, came (so he avers) from all the *collegia* and *societates*; *De Domo*, 74, 142; *Pro Sest.* 32; *In Pis.* 41. The populace did not, however, forget Clodius' achievements on their behalf in 58, as is attested by the demonstrations after his death; see, esp., Asconius, 32–33, Clark; Dio, 40.49.2–3; cf. Val. Max. 3.5.3.

[185] Cf. Cic. *Pro Flacco*, 18: *opifices et tabernarios atque illam omnem fæcem civitatem*; *Ad Att.* 1.16.11: *misera ac ieiuna plebecula.*

of that connection should not be assumed. Food riots and clamor for civic privileges were few in number and short in duration; favorable, if not altogether satisfactory, responses from the powers that be promoted a general faith in the existing order. Violent outbursts inspired by politicians actually influenced the course of events very rarely. Of electoral contests in the Ciceronian age, only the results for the year 55 can be said to have been determined by intimidating tactics. And the intimidators paid a large political price. The effect was not much greater in criminal trials. Popular outcry may have helped in the acquittal of Cornelius; but violence did not save Autronius or Manilius. Gabinius and Vatinius escaped conviction through strong-arm devices; but both men were prosecuted again under calmer circumstances, and Gabinius, at least, suffered condemnation. Violence attended the cases of Clodius and Milo, but political considerations produced a stalemate. In the vast majority of criminal cases no disorder is recorded. Similarly, legislative proposals which provoked popular enthusiasm and demonstrations would obtain passage sometimes for that very reason—for example, Cornelius' bills in 67, the *leges agrariæ* of 59, and Clodius' program in 58. And, at times, intimidation proved successful, as with extraordinary commands for the triumvirs. But it was of no avail in Manilius' measure on freedmen, Nepos' effort to promote a special command for Pompey, or Clodius' attempt to block the recall of Cicero. And here again the great bulk of legislation in the period passed without incident.

Rome lived with violence through much of the late Republic. A large and volatile urban population made that nearly inescapable, as almost all societies have discovered. The foundations of the state did not crumble as a consequence, any more than they did in the riots of eighteenth- and nineteenth-century England or nineteenth- and twentieth-century America. Absence of a police force made it difficult to nip disturbances in the bud. But that absence also betokened a recognition that demonstrations and vociferous actions were legitimate expressions of popular desires. The theater, the circus, and the forum provided traditional arenas for such expressions. When matters threatened to get out of hand, magistrates would intervene, or in serious political situations, the *senatus consultum ultimum* was invoked to restore control. A series of *leges de vi*, discussed earlier, further disclose the government's concern for more definitive controls. But the use of military force to suppress dissent in the city was rigorously eschewed by the establishment. Only once, in 52, when prolonged disorder and lack of executive officials created havoc, were troops employed to restore stability. The situation was extraordinary and the solution unprecendented. But the effect in no way delivered Rome into military occupation or set the stage for military conflict. Pompeius

Magnus, the military leader par excellence, used the occasion to reestablish order with civil enactments and comprehensive legislation. His tenure as sole consul was effective but brief. Regular procedures followed–and calm. When war came in 49, it emerged from entirely unrelated conditions.[186]

The circumstances under which Rome's lower classes lived were not often pleasant–again a situation familiar to almost all big cities throughout history. Some of the recorded violence may be attributed to that fact; most of it grew out of politics. What is noteworthy, however, is that the establishment did not normally crush urban dissent by force. Outlets for popular discontent existed. The ruling class generally tolerated rather than suppressed outbursts. Demonstrations, even violence, were extensions of the *plebs'* prerogatives to voice its needs; they did not present a challenge to the state's authority. The Roman aristocracy recognized that fact better than have its modern critics. When the Republic fell, it was not the proletariate that brought it down.

[186] The connection so frequently asserted by scholars is nowhere demonstrated. Cf., most recently, Lintott, *Violence*, p. 1: "There can be little doubt that the conflicts within the city were the first steps in civil war. . . . The transition from fighting with gangs in the streets to fighting with armies in the field is essentially one of scale, and . . . it is not difficult to understand why it should have occurred." Yet nothing in the pages of his book shows that that transition is either natural or obvious.

XI

THE COMING OF CIVIL WAR

THE WRITING of history is forever plagued by the temptations of hindsight. Knowledge of the issue invariably, if unconsciously, becomes the starting point of the search for antecedents. The method is hazardous and delusive. It is not easy to erase from the mind an image of Cæsar the triumphant conqueror of Pompey, the victor in civil war, the successful survivor of the Republic's ruin. Armed strife destroyed the fabric of the Republican state. Explanation of that cataclysm has allowed little scope for accident or inadvertence. Not that it was necessarily the deliberate scheme of Julius Cæsar—though that view has been expounded, with vigor and authority, by eminent scholars.[1] Rather, the accumulation and concentration of power in the hands of two personages, so it has been affirmed, rendered any other result impossible. Cæsar and Pompey could not long maintain a harmonious coexistence: the falling-out was inevitable and with it the war that would force all Romans to select sides. The analysis entails an inescapable march of events. It is a discomforting solution—and a suspicious one.

Ancients were no less prone to the approach than moderns. The quest for causes of the fratricidal contest centered on the personalities of the principals: Cæsar's power evoked the suspicions of Pompey, Pompey's eminence stirred the envy of Cæsar; Pompey could endure no equal, Cæsar no superior.[2] Cæsar, it was reported, had remarked that he could more readily be dislodged

[1] The classic formulation, of course, is that of Mommsen, *Röm. Gesch.,* III:461–569. Cf. also Carcopino, *César,* pp. 471–514.

[2] Florus, 2.13.14: *Iam Pompeio suspectæ Cæsaris opes et Cæsari Pompeiana dignitas gravis. Nec ille ferebat parem, nec hic superiorem.* Also, Lucan, 1.125–126; cf. Vell. Pat. 2.33.3; Plut. *Ant.* 6.

from a second-rank position to obscurity, than from preeminence to second fiddle.[3] The sources emphasize two events that formed a point of no return for the dynasts: the deaths of Julia and of M. Crassus. Julia, the daughter of Cæsar and wife of Pompey, perished in childbirth in 54, thereby snapping the personal bonds between the two men. Crassus fell on the battlefield of Carrhæ in 53, thus breaking the three-cornered relationship and leaving Pompey and Cæsar to confront each other directly without an intermediary or a balance wheel. Thereafter, the ultimate struggle was only a matter of time; it was already foreordained. Such constitutes the favored ancient explanation.[4] And it has obtained the endorsement of numerous scholars.[5]

The interpretation is singularly unsatisfactory. Pompey's marriage to Julia in 59 had been a contractual arrangement for political purposes. It conspicuously sealed the bargain for public cooperation between the dynasts. That a relationship of genuine warmth developed between husband and wife was merely a fortuitous dividend, welcome but unanticipated. Julia's death involved sore bereavement for both father and husband, but did not make the political reasons for continued collaboration any less cogent.[6] Nor should Crassus be regarded as the man who had held the coalition together. That shrewd manipulator had entered the compact for his own purposes, participating actively when it suited his interests, remaining in the background otherwise. There had never been any personal amity between Crassus and Pompey. Their compact depended on politics, not mutual admiration.

It remains to examine the evidence itself, without preconception born of hindsight, for the relations between Pompey and Cæsar from 54 to 49. There is little in their actions which presaged future conflict, let alone civil war. Far from severing their alliance after the death of Julia, the dynasts, it can be documented, cooperated politically until well into the year 50.

[3] Suet. *Iul.* 29.1: *quod sæpe ex eo auditum ferunt, "difficilius se principem civitatis a primo ordine in secundum quam ex secundo in novissimum detrudi."*

[4] See, e.g., Vell. Pat. 2.47.2; Val. Max. 4.6.4; Lucan, 1.98–120; Florus, 2.13.13; Plut. *Pomp.* 53.4–7; *Cæs.* 28.1; Dio, 40.44.2–3.

[5] E.g. Mommsen, *Röm. Gesch.*, III:353–356; Rice Holmes, *Rom. Rep.*, II:154, 163–164; Heitland, *Rom. Rep.*, III:235, 239–240; Adcock, *CAH*, IX:622–623; Carcopino, *César*, pp. 290, 300; Ooteghem, *Pompée le Grand*, pp. 427–428, 436; C. Wirszubski, *Libertas as a Political Idea at Rome during the Late Republic and Early Principate* (Cambridge, 1950), p. 78; Scullard, *Gracchi to Nero*, p. 124.

[6] Julia was given a public funeral and was buried in the Campus Martius. Plutarch, characteristically, introduces a rift here, stating that the honor was meant more for Cæsar than for Pompey; *Pomp.* 53.4–5. Pompey had originally planned to bury her at his own villa. But he would certainly not have objected to a public funeral. The decision was clearly a political act—and was opposed as such by Domitius Ahenobarbus, enemy of Pompey and Cæsar alike, and by some tribunes; Dio, 39.64; Plut. *Cæs.* 23.4; Livy, *Per.* 106.

THE COALITION INTACT

The joint consulship of Crassus and Pompey in 55 had produced welcome benefits for their clique: a renewal of Cæsar's tenure in Gaul and similar long-term commands for his triumviral partners. There was more glory to be won in Gaul and in Syria, but also greater danger. Pompey's position must have appeared potentially the most powerful of the three. His provinces were the two Spains, where no serious fighting was required. In addition, he retained his function as superintendent of Rome's grain supply, an authority invested in him since 57. And Pompey adopted the unorthodox practice of dispatching legates and officers abroad to oversee his provinces. He himself remained in Italy, in the environs of Rome, where he could keep his finger on the pulse of domestic politics. The arrangements were, no doubt, foreshadowed at Luca. There is nothing to suggest that Julius Cæsar disapproved. The installation of Crassus and Pompey in office in 55 had required disruption and unsavory tactics; it also involved the inclusion of their partisans in other magistracies. But with their immediate aims effected, the triumvirs preferred to adhere to traditional practices. Solid and conservative legislation issued from the consuls of 55. They backed supporters for offices of the subsequent year, but proved unable to prevent election of candidates hostile to their interests. Crassus departed for Syria in November, amidst much abuse. Conventional politics had resumed.

The year 54 betokened no friction between Pompeius Magnus and Julius Cæsar. Both men campaigned for the same aspirants to consular office: C. Memmius and M. Scaurus. The choices did not prove felicitous. Private bargains and illicit machinations got in the way. Pompey's maneuvers recoiled badly, and his candidates fell through, to the annoyance of Cæsar. The Roman electorate again showed itself impervious to the desires of the triumvirate.[7] But Cæsar's reaction to his partner's ineptitude did not involve any lapse in their cooperation. Common interests bound them closely in 54. Friends of both men, ex-magistrates of 55, were in the dock almost without cease in that year. M. Cicero answered the call of the dynasts frequently: to defend not only Pompeian *amici* like C. Messius but also Cæsarian adherents like P. Vatinius and Drusus Claudianus.[8] Pressure was applied from both men, in tandem.

Julia's death came in the late summer of 54. If it opened a breach between Pompey and Cæsar, there is no sign of it in subsequent months. The trial of Gabinius followed. Pompey, of course, solicited assistance for his former officer. The affair presented a critical test case for the strength of his position.

[7] On these events, see above, pp. 148–149.

[8] On the trials, see above, chap. 7.

And the proconsul of Gaul did his part. Unable to attend in person, he made certain to have his views transmitted to Rome: his letter in Gabinius' behalf was read aloud at the trial.[9] Domestic turbulence in the later months of the year spurred rumors of an impending dictatorship. There were men prepared to offer such a motion, friends of Pompey: and he was the logical recipient of the post. Whether Pompey wanted it was unclear. He disavowed it publicly; but the denials were not so adamant in private.[10] Considerable opposition manifested itself, and the matter was dropped. Even had it materialized, however, Pompey's powers would doubtless have been brief in duration and limited in scope. The suggestion came only because of delays in the consular election and the distastefulness of an *interregnum.*[11] There was nothing for Cæsar to fear. Indeed, had Pompey been awarded such a post, he would most likely have utilized it to facilitate the election of the triumviral candidates, and perhaps also to influence Gabinius' jury. Resistance to the proposal, as Cicero makes clear, came, not from the friends of Cæsar, but from the *boni.*[12] Failure to have it implemented entailed a defeat for the coalition as a whole. The nobility had maintained a firm stance; and the triumvirate could stir no enthusiasm among the populace.[13] Anti-triumviral candidates obtained election to the consulship; A. Gabinius suffered conviction and exile. Cæsar and Pompey could hardly afford a split when their adversaries were gaining political ground. The compact remained very much in force. In the winter of 54–53, Cæsar required larger forces to overawe imminent Gallic rebellions. A levy in Cisalpine Gaul did not suffice, and the proconsul asked Pompey to supply one of his own legions. The request was granted, so Cæsar gratefully reported in the *Bellum Gallicum,* both for the *res publica* and for their personal *amicitia.*[14]

The evidence indicates no change in the relationship during 53. Cæsar demonstrated his good faith with the proposal of a new marriage alliance to fill the void left by Julia's death. There were no other daughters available, but Cæsar could produce a grandniece: Octavia, already married to C. Marcellus, the future consul of 50. For the sake of politics a hasty divorce could be arranged. And Cæsar went further. He offered to divorce his own wife,

[9] Dio, 39.63.4.

[10] Cic. *Ad Q. Frat.* 3.8.4: *Pompeius plane se negat velle; antea ipse mihi non negabat . . . velit, nolit, scire difficile est.*

[11] Talk of a dictatorship is connected, in every instance, with the possibility of an *interregnum;* Cic. *Ad Att.* 4.18.3; *Ad Q. Frat.* 2.15a.5, 3.8.4, 3.9.3.

[12] Cic. *Ad Q. Frat.* 3.8.4: *rumor dictatoris iniucundus bonis; Ad Q. Frat.* 3.9.3: *de dictatore tamen actum nihil est . . . principes nolunt.*

[13] Cic. *Ad Q. Frat.* 3.9.3: *populus non curat.*

[14] Cæs. *BG,* 6.1: *et rei publicæ et amicitiæ.* See also Plut. *Cato,* 45.3. The loan is incorrectly recorded in Plut. *Pomp.* 52.3; *Cæs.* 25.1.

the daughter of L. Piso, and take the hand of Pompey's daughter, though she was betrothed—perhaps already wed—to Faustus Sulla.[15] Pompey declined the arrangement—on what grounds we are uninformed. The fact should not be taken as a sign of strain in the relationship. Cæsar's generous offer was a gesture, a mark of the continuation of their alliance. The refusal by Pompey may have been equally generous; as he knew, Cæsar did not really want to divorce Calpurnia.[16] And there were good political reasons for maintaining the status quo. Pompey perhaps considered it prudent not to alienate influential and independent *nobiles* like L. Piso and C. Marcellus. Their support could be valuable in senatorial contests. Moreover, Pompey no doubt preferred to keep his marital options open. He would soon forge links with aristocrats of similar weight and *gratia:* Ap. Claudius Pulcher and Q. Metellus Scipio. It can be seen as part of the effort to strengthen the dynasts' connections within the *nobilitas* where they had, of late, been losing ground.[17] Cæsar's *amicitia* was secure. The syndicate had to expand its contacts elsewhere.

Another piece of information, often overlooked, reinforces the argument. When Pompey married Julia in 59, Cæsar framed a will naming his new son-in-law as principal heir to his estate. The provision was a matter of public knowledge, and Cæsar made a point of reading it aloud to his assembled troops. Julia's death provoked no change in the contract. Cæsar did not cut Pompey out of his will until the outbreak of civil war.[18]

Crassus' death in the summer of 53 left a great many Romans to cast about for new political alliances. Some joined the camp of Cæsar; others perhaps drifted into the circle of his enemies. But there is no discernible

[15] The report is in Suet. *Iul.* 27, our only source for this arrangement. The date, unfortunately, is not given. Suetonius' account makes no pretense at chronology, and its placement in his text is no help. Gelzer, *Cæsar,* p. 151, puts it in 52; so also Meyer, *Cæsars Monarchie,* p. 228. Rice Holmes, *Rom. Rep.,* II:163–164, dates it after the death of Crassus in 53. None provides any discussion. Carcopino, *César,* p. 338, suggests the end of 53 when Cæsar had returned to Ravenna for recruiting purposes. But it seems unlikely that Cæsar would have waited so long after Julia's death to offer a new marriage compact. Perhaps the winter of 54–53 is more reasonable. But it is all guesswork. Cæsar's playing fast and loose with Octavia may help to explain the hostility of her husband, C. Marcellus, in his consulship of 50. A like reaction perhaps helps to account for the behavior of Faustus Sulla, who went on to oppose Pompey at the trial of Milo in 52; Asconius, 34, Clark.

[16] The marriage with Calpurnia endured until Cæsar's death. It is noteworthy that Suetonius, our one informant on Cæsar's offer, does not even mention Pompey's non-acceptance, let alone suggest any annoyance on Cæsar's part. Evidently the gesture itself was the important fact.

[17] Cf. the sensible remarks of R. Sealey, *ClMed,* 18 (1957): 97.

[18] Suet. *Iul.* 83.1: *Quintus Tubero tradit heredem ab eo scribi solitum ex consulatu ipsius primo usque ad initium civilis belli Cn. Pompeium, idque militibus pro contione recitatum.* Tubero was a contemporary witness.

effect on the relationship between the syndicate's surviving partners. Ancient testimony on the later months of 53 and early 52 is preoccupied with the stormy consular elections. Pompey engaged in vigorous activity, primarily to block the candidacy of T. Annius Milo. That Cæsar played any role in the contest is nowhere recorded. But one stray item should be noted. Cicero reveals that the proconsul of Gaul had once ridiculed his excessive protestations on Milo's behalf.[19] Cæsar, we may infer, found no fault with Pompey's opposition to the candidacy of Milo. The campaign, as was discussed previously, degenerated into tumultuous conflict, extending beyond the onset of the new year and paralyzing government operations. Urban riots produced temporary chaos and revived the clamor for a dictatorship. Once again, lack of executive officers evoked the demand for an unorthodox remedy. Nothing in the sources suggests that Julius Cæsar had any discomfort with the idea. Indeed, there was some talk, especially from the tribunes, that there be a joint consulship of Cæsar and Pompey to repress disturbances and restore order in the city. For Cæsar it was premature; much work remained to be done in Gaul. But the common assumption in Rome—and a proper assumption—held that the dynasts were still operating as a team. Fear of a joint office helped persuade the senate to award Pompey a sole consulship. For the opponents of the syndicate, that offered a much more satisfactory alternative.[20]

Many of Pompey's activities in his consulship of 52 have been scrutinized earlier. It should now be clear that they involved no reconciliation with the followers of Cato or the enemies of the dynasts. Pompey shrewdly extended his ties with leading families of the aristocracy: hence his marriage to the daughter of Q. Metellus Scipio and the wedding of Cn. Pompeius the younger to the daughter of Ap. Claudius Pulcher. Those connections strengthened the hand of the coalition within the senate's upper echelons. They do not represent a Pompeian move toward the Catonians. Neither Metellus Scipio nor Ap. Claudius possessed any obligations to that coterie.[21] Pompey's foes remained unrelenting in their opposition, as has been demonstrated in the political trials of that year. But his consulship was a decided success in the restoration of urban stability. Julius Cæsar made no secret of his admiration for Pompey's accomplishment.[22]

[19] Cic. *Ad Fam.* 7.5.3: *illo vetere verbo meo, quod cum ad te* [Cæsar] *de Milone scripsissem, iure lusisti.*

[20] On the move for a dual consulship, see Suet. *Iul.* 26.1; Dio, 40.50.3–4.

[21] On the marriage link with Metellus Scipio, see above, chap. 4, n.142. The tie with Ap. Claudius is customarily placed in 54, perhaps wrongly; cf. Gruen, *Historia,* 18 (1969): 101–103, where it is erroneously stated that Pompey himself married Appius' daughter. It was, of course, Pompey's son. Both marriages fit appropriately in 52.

[22] Cæs. *BG,* 7.6: *cum iam ille urbanas res virtute Cn. Pompei commodiorem in statum pervenisse intellegeret;* cf. also Appian, *BC,* 2.25.

We may turn now to the measures of 52 that directly or indirectly affected Cæsar's status in Gaul. They have too often been regarded as Pompeian maneuvers to undermine his partner's position. Careful examination will suggest a very different conclusion.

Julius Cæsar desired and expected to cap his triumphant campaigns in Gaul with a consulship in Rome. It would be a fitting climax and would provide a suitable stage on which to advertise his *dignitas* and *gloria*. But constitutional problems presented obstacles. A candidate for office had to be present in the city to submit his *professio* before he could be legitimately considered by the electors. Cæsar had experienced that difficulty before. In 60, after his governorship of Spain, he asked leave of the senate to offer his candidacy in absence in order to celebrate a triumph. The request was stubbornly resisted by Cato, among others, and the proconsul had to foresake triumphal honors so as to render himself eligible for the chief magistracy.[23] Cato could be counted on again to filibuster against any similar proposal in 52. And Cæsar, whose Gallic campaigns were still incomplete, entertained no thoughts of a return to Rome and forfeiture of his *imperium*. His influence with officials at home would determine the prospects of an exemption from the standard practice. And that, of course, depended on the attitude of Pompeius Magnus. Fortunately, the sources are here clear and unambiguous: Pompey exerted himself strenuously to obtain the concession for his partner. Cæsar initiated the negotiations in the winter of 53–52, while he was at Ravenna. Joining him there was M. Cicero, very likely as an emissary from Pompey. Cæsar desired a tribunician bill that would award him the right to stand for office *in absentia*. Cicero, it appears, contracted to use his influence on M. Cælius, scheduled for the tribunate in that year.[24] Pompey would take care of the rest. Once installed as sole consul, he applied considerable pressure on the tribunician college to sponsor a bill on Cæsar's *ratio absentis*. As expected, Cato objected at length, and his supporters attempted to stall the enactment.[25] But the importunings of Pompey held the day. The proposal passed into law with unanimous endorsement by the tribunician college.[26] Pompey had kept faith with his fellow dynast.

[23] Suet. *Iul.* 18; Plut. *Cato*, 31.2–3; *Cæs.* 13.1; Dio, 37.54.1. On the question of candidacies in absence, see Balsdon, *JRS*, 52 (1962): 140–141; Linderski, *Mélanges Michalowski* (1966), pp. 523–526. The latter's argument is cogent and consistent, but perhaps too strict in its exegesis of the sources.

[24] Cic. *Ad Att.* 7.1.4: *nam ut illi hoc liceret adiuvi, rogatus ab ipso Ravennæ de Cælio tribuno pl.*

[25] Cæs. *BC,* 1.32; Livy, *Per.* 107; Plut. *Pomp.* 56.3.

[26] That the bill came at the insistence of Pompey is clear in the sources: Cic. *Ad Fam.* 6.6.5: *quoniam ipso consule pugnante populus iusserat; Ad Att.* 8.3.3: *contendit ut decem tribuni pl. ferrent ut absentis ratio haberetur.* Similarly, Cic. *Ad Att.* 7.3.4; Florus, 2.13.16; Appian,

Another doubt must be cleared away. The sources report that Pompey himself, shortly thereafter, enacted a law that apparently canceled the provisions of the tribunician measure: the *lex Pompeia de iure magistratuum.* The latter reaffirmed the older convention that no one seeking office could be considered unless he presented himself in person. How does one reconcile this with Pompey's own behavior in urging an exemption for Cæsar just before? The ancient tradition essayed an explanation: Pompey was absentminded! Forgetting about the law of the ten tribunes (though only a short interval had passed since its adoption), he proceeded, in oblivion, to sponsor the new measure that invalidated it. The friends of Cæsar objected strenuously, reminding Pompey of the exemption granted their chief. The consul then hastily reversed himself, withdrawing the statute from the *ærarium* and inserting a correction that permitted those previously exempted to retain that privilege.[27] A tissue of improbabilities, surely. Standard explanations suggest either that Pompey was genuinely forgetful or that he sought to remove Cæsar's privilege surreptitiously and was caught in the act; therefore he was forced to append a corrective clause.[28] The time is long past due for that erratic version to be expunged from the textbooks. An anti-Pompeian tradition has foisted it upon the sources. That Pompey could have been such an oblivious bumbler as to forget the import of a bill which he had himself advocated so urgently only weeks before surpasses all belief. And the alternative is no less incredible. Could Pompey seriously have expected to deceive Cæsar's partisans in Rome by expressly annulling his *ratio absentis* and then hoping no one would notice? That interpretation clears him of absentmindedness but posits an even more colossal ineptitude. The story, in this form, cannot stand.[29]

Perhaps the *lex de iure magistratuum* was called for precisely because previous practice had been waived on Cæsar's behalf. It acknowledged a need to reiterate

BC, 2.25. Dio Cassius, committed to the view that there was already a breach between the dynasts, has to interpret the fact as a Pompeian concession to forestall other ambitions of Cæsar; 40.51.1–2. Cicero later claimed that his support for the measure was reluctant and that he had advised Pompey against it; Cic. *Ad Att.* 7.7.6; *Phil.* 2.24. But there is no doubt that he advocated it at the time; Cic. *Ad Fam.* 6.6.5; *Ad Att.* 7.1.5; cf. *Ad Att.* 7.18.2. The bill is noted also by Cæs. *BC,* 1.9.2; Livy, *Per.* 107–108; Suet. *Iul.* 26.

27 Suet. *Iul.* 28; Dio, 40.56.1–3. It is reported by Plut. *Cato,* 49.3, that Cato moved a *senatus consultum* requiring candidates to solicit voters in person rather than employ intermediaries. That proposal is to be dissociated from the *lex de iure magistratuum.* Though Plutarch discusses it in the context of Cato's consular campaign in 52, it more properly belongs in the 60s, when such measures were central topics of debate; cf. Cic. *Pro Mur.* 71; and see above, chap. 6. Perhaps it is identical with the *s.c.* of 65; Cic. *Pro Corn. apud* Asconius, 69, Clark.

28 See, e.g., Meyer, *Cæsars Monarchie,* pp. 243–244; Heitland, *Rom. Rep.,* III:247; Rice Holmes, *Rom. Rep.,* II:237; Syme, *Rom. Rev.,* p. 40; Carcopino, *César,* p. 347; Gelzer, *Pompeius,* p. 178, *Cæsar,* p. 153.

the general principle: candidacies *in absentia* were not to be a regular part of Roman institutional practice. But Cæsar's privilege, awarded by a law of the people, remained unaffected. The new measure may have contained specific reference to that exemption; one need not believe it was hastily added to correct an oversight. A remark of Cicero's, our one contemporary allusion to the enactment, supports that conclusion: Pompey urged the tribunes to grant Cæsar a *ratio absentis* and then confirmed the prerogative in his own statute.[30] Julius Cæsar had no complaint to make of his ally's behavior.

Attention must turn now to the *lex Pompeia de provinciis* of 52. This has supplied the touchstone for most argumentation that Pompey endeavored to upset Cæsar's tenure in Gaul and his plans for the future. The measure provided for a five-year gap between the exercise of a magistracy in Rome and the governing of a province abroad. Consuls and prætors had customarily moved off to their provincial assignments during or immediately after their magisterial year, so as to avoid lapse of *imperium.* Under the new legislation, they would have to wait five years after expiry of office before their *imperia* could be renewed and their provinces assigned by senate and people.[31] Prior to 52, a law of C. Sempronius Gracchus, in force since 123, governed the allocation of consular provinces. Under that *lex Sempronia* the senate was required to name the consular provinces for the following year before the electoral *comitia.* The law (or a subsequent measure) permitted no tribunician veto on the allocation. Successful candidates would then draw lots to determine which of the two provinces would fall to each. They were free to proceed to their *provinciæ* at any time after the opening of their consular year, though, in the normal course of events, they would await its expiry. Similar procedures evidently did not apply to the prætors. Their provinces were determined by senatorial decree sometime after they took office.[32] The *lex Pompeia* rendered those practices otiose. The need no longer existed for an allocation prior to the consular elections, since the new consuls could not hold provincial command for five years. The assignments would be made annually to ex-consuls and ex-prætors whose magistracies had long since concluded.

[29] So, rightly, Balsdon, *JRS,* 52 (1962): 141.

[30] Cic. *Ad Att.* 8.3.3: *contendit ut decem tribuni pl. ferrent ut absentis ratio haberetur. quod idem ipse sanxit lege quadam sua.* To be sure, *quadam* appears to be a sneer at the validity of the exemption, but it leaves no question as to Pompey's intent or as to the effect of the law.

[31] Dio, 40.56.1. That the new assignments required both a *senatus consultum* and a *lex* is implied in Cic. *Ad Fam.* 2.7.4, 15.9.2, 15.14.5.

[32] On the *lex Sempronia,* see the sources cited in Broughton, *MRR,* I:514. That tribunician veto was forbidden is stated by Cic. *De Prov. Cons.* 17. Orthodox scholarly opinion once postulated a law of Sulla's requiring all magistrates to remain in Rome during their year of office before they could take up provincial command. The notion was exploded by Balsdon, *JRS,* 29 (1939): 57–73. The numerous exceptions to that practice make it impossible to believe in the rule, which is itself nowhere attested.

In what way would this affect Cæsar's situation? The prevailing view warrants brief summary. In 55 a consular law of Pompey and Crassus renewed Cæsar's tenure in Gaul for another five years.[33] Whatever the terminal date fixed in that statute (if terminal date there was), the proconsul could assume that normal operation of the *lex Sempronia* would afford him sufficient notice of senatorial plans on disposition of the Gallic provinces. Time would be available to wind up affairs in Gaul and perhaps, if desirable, to prepare for another consular candidacy. The *lex Pompeia,* however—so it is averred—undermined those plans. By canceling, in effect, the law of C. Gracchus, it opened up disquieting possibilities. There would no longer be advance notice on the Gallic succession. The senate could, at whatever point Cæsar's term was due to run out, declare the Gauls to be consular provinces and immediately dispatch new governors from among the eligible ex-magistrates. Cæsar would be obliged to relinquish command and armies directly and to return to Rome to face his enemies as a *privatus.* Worse still, it assured that, even if he should gain election to the consulship, he could look forward to no immediate provincial command after his office. Pompey, therefore, had revealed his true colors and had thrown down the gauntlet to his erstwhile collaborator.[34]

Reassessment is necessary. The foregoing interpretation does not stand up to scrutiny. An obvious prima facie difficulty emerges directly. Pompey had, shortly before, advocated Cæsar's *ratio absentis* and then affirmed it in his own law. Is it plausible that he would go on to sponsor a measure whose purpose was to assure a sudden supersession of Cæsar and perhaps render the *ratio absentis* useless? Weighty evidence would be required to establish that hypothesis. None is forthcoming. Cæsar's proconsular situation, in fact, does not seem to have been at issue when the *lex Pompeia* secured passage. A crucial piece of information has too often been neglected. The bill did not emerge *de novo* in Pompey's consulship of 52. Its provisions had already been anticipated in a senatorial decree of the previous year—when, surely, no reference to Cæsar was expressed or intended. Pompey simply adopted that decree and made it the basis of his own law of 52. The object is plainly stated in the sources and is entirely plausible. Electoral tumults and bribery had constituted Rome's chief problem in recent months. Candidates indulged

[33] Broughton, *MRR,* II:215.

[34] The theory stems from Mommsen, *Die Rechtsfrage zwischen Cæsar und dem Senat* (Breslau, 1857), pp. 1–58. Though many have taken issue with him on the terminal date, most have followed his analysis of the *lex Pompeia.* E.g., Rice Holmes, *CQ,* 10 (1916): 49–56; Hardy, *Some Problems,* pp. 150–206; Meyer, *Cæsars Monarchie,* p. 243; C. G. Stone, *CQ,* 22 (1928): 193–201; E. T. Salmon, *CJ,* 34 (1939): 388–395; L. R. Taylor, *Party Politics,* p. 151; Gelzer, *Pompeius,* pp. 178–179. The careful and original thesis of P. J. Cuff, *Historia,* 7 (1958): 464–468, also assumes that the *lex Pompeia* marks the breach between Pompey and Cæsar.

in excesses and in lavish outlays of cash, buoyed by the prospect of provincial assignment and a lucrative post abroad. The temptation would be removed by enforcing a lengthy gap between magistracy and promagistracy. That was expressly the aim of the senatorial decree and of Pompey's steering it into law.[35]

The enactment had an intelligent and worthy purpose. Not simply to create an effective deterrent to electoral misbehavior. It furnished the first clear sign that Rome had begun to look upon provincial government as something more than an appendage to an urban magistracy. Overseas administration, as well as management of the electoral process at home, would benefit. The measure fits suitably within the context of Pompeian legislation in 52, designed to effect smoother and more efficient governmental operations. Narrow interpretation of the *lex Pompeia* as an anti-Cæsarian move not only misjudges the politics of that year but seriously undervalues the scope and aims of Pompey's legislative program.

It is not impossible, of course, that Pompey considered the adverse effects which his *lex* might have on Cæsar's position. But there was a ready avenue of escape for the proconsul of Gaul. The *lex Pompeia* affected all regular provincial assignations in the future. It was already in operation in 51, calling out for foreign duty some rather reluctant ex-magistrates like M. Bibulus and the very unmilitary M. Cicero. But Cæsar's command was an extraordinary one, sanctioned by a law of the people. Pompey may well have felt that Cæsar's proconsulship was not subject to the new legislation. As if to underscore the fact, Pompey had his own tenure in Spain renewed for an additional five-year term. If his command was unaffected by the *lex Pompeia*, so presumably was Cæsar's. Both depended on prior legislation passed by the people in 55.[36] The notion that Pompey's extended *imperium* represented a direct threat to Cæsar rests again on hindsight, looking back from the civil war. The governorship of Spain would no more pose a threat to Cæsar as *privatus* than did Cæsar's Gallic command to Pompey as *privatus* in the early 50s.

[35] On the *s.c.* of 53, see Dio, 40.46.2–3; cf. 40.30.1. That Pompey's bill was a reaffirmation of the decree is asserted also by Dio, 40.56.1: **τό τε δόγμα τὸ μικρὸν ἔμπροσθε γενόμενον ὥστε τοὺς ἄρξαντας ἐν τῇ πόλει μὴ πρότερον ἐς τὰς ἔξω ἡγεμονίας, πρὶν πέντε ἔτη παρελθεῖν, κληροῦσθαι, ἐπεκύρωσεν**. To be sure, Cæsar later complained that the law was used against him in 49, for it enabled handpicked officers to be sent to Gaul instead of men who had just completed prætorship or consulship; Cæs. *BC*. 1.85.9–10; cf. *BC*. 1.6. But there is nothing to suggest that the measure had that in view from the beginning.

[36] On the renewal of Pompey's command, see Dio, 40.44.2, 40.56.2; Appian, *BC*. 2.24. Plutarch, probably incorrectly, states that the renewal would endure for four years; *Pomp*. 55.7; cf. *Cæs*. 28.5. It is sometimes assumed that the second term would run from 52 to 47; Adcock, *CAH*, IX:628. More likely, it was scheduled to begin after expiry of the *lex Trebonia* and would therefore run to 45.

Finally, Pompey had inserted a safeguard into the *lex Pompeia,* in the event that Cæsar's enemies did hope to employ it against him. Under the previous system tribunician *intercessio* was banned for the senatorial disposition of consular provinces. That restriction had now fallen, together with the *lex Sempronia.* Pompey's new measure permitted the exercise of a tribune's veto on assignation of provinces. Hence, if attempts were made to compromise Cæsar's position in Gaul, a tribune could readily be found to cancel the proceedings.[37]

The sources betray no hint that anyone regarded Cæsar's situation as menaced by Pompey in 52—quite the contrary. The activities of Pompey had assured his ally of a right to stand for office *in absentia* and had denied the privilege to all others. The extraordinary character of the Gallic campaigns and Cæsar's achievements made that concession eminently proper. The loophole of tribunician veto seemed to guarantee the proconsul exemption from any ill effects of the otherwise estimable *lex Pompeia de provinciis.* And the people of Rome could not deny the splendor of his accomplishments. When Cæsar had successfully concluded the siege of Alesia, late in 52, a public thanksgiving of twenty days was ordered.[38] The proconsul of Gaul could with justice and satisfaction praise the activities of Pompey's third consulship.

THE CONSERVATIVE OFFENSIVE

The *inimici* of Cæsar began their campaign against him in earnest in 51. The long tenure in Gaul was drawing to a close, and anxious politicians sought means to discredit the proconsul before he could make a triumphant return. Cæsar had no friends in the consulate of 51, and there was a growing hostility among envious members of the *nobilitas.* Ser. Sulpicius Rufus remained placid, but his consular colleague, M. Marcellus, whose anti-Cæsarian sympathies were well known, could be reckoned on to force matters to an issue. Much hinged on the actions of Pompeius Magnus. His position and attitudes in 51 warrant close analysis.

Cæsar's activities in the Cisalpina were especially disquieting to his political foes. He had advocated Roman franchise for the Transpadane Gauls as early as 69 or 68, so it is reported.[39] In the course of his campaigns he had won more friends in that area; Cisalpine Gaul had been a fruitful recruiting ground for the Cæsarian forces. The *lex Vatinia,* it appears, contained a clause empower-

[37] That tribunician veto was permitted under the *lex Pompeia* is clear from the frequent exercise of that right in 51 and 50. The law evidently posed no menace to Cæsar; so, rightly, Adcock, *CAH,* IX:627–628; Balsdon, *JRS,* 29 (1939): 173–174.

[38] Cæs. *BG,* 7.90. Dio, 40.50.4, no doubt erroneously, reports that the *supplicatio* was to endure for sixty days.

[39] Suet. *Iul.* 8.

ing Cæsar to institute a Roman colony in the territory, a clause which he implemented at Novum Comum.[40] In 51 further rumors circulated about the Transpadani–perhaps that the proconsul intended to bestow full Roman citizenship everywhere in the area.[41] If so, Cæsar's *clientela* would be immeasurably increased and his influence in the *comitia* correspondingly more powerful. The prospect was uncomfortable indeed to his *inimici*. It causes no surprise that M. Marcellus chose this issue on which to launch a direct attack. He challenged the legitimacy of Cæsar's enfranchisement grants and moved that the colonists at Novum Comum be stripped of their citizenship.[42] And Marcellus went further. To dramatize his stance, he arranged the public flogging of a prominent citizen of Novum Comum. The act demonstrated his scorn for Cæsar's grants; a Roman citizen could not be so treated. Marcellus bade the humiliated victim to convey his scars as a message to Julius Cæsar.[43] The outcome of this affair oddly escapes record. But Pompey's posture may be divined–and that is the central item. As Cicero properly observed, the foul behavior of Marcellus delivered a blow felt as much by Pompey as by Cæsar.[44] Their fortunes, in July 51, were still coupled.

Marcellus had other avenues of attack. A movement was now under way to obtain Cæsar's recall from his proconsular command. The agitation, it seems, began in the spring of 51. Marcellus pounced on the news of Alesia and the capitulation of Vercingetorix to claim that Cæsar's task in Gaul was complete: the governor's term should be concluded and his armies disbanded.

[40] Suet. *Iul.* 28.3; cf. Strabo, 5.1.6. See the careful discussions of Hardy, *Some Problems,* pp. 126–149; Rice Holmes, *Rom. Rep.,* II:317–320. Appian, *BC,* 2.26, wrongly states that Cæsar bestowed Latin rights upon Novum Comum. In fact, most Transpadani possessed *Latinitas* since the Social War; Asconius, 3, Clark.

[41] Cf. Cic. *Ad Att.* 5.2.3; Cæl. *Ad Fam.* 8.1.2.

[42] Suet. *Iul.* 28.3: *rettulit etiam, ut colonis, quos rogatione Vatinia Novum Comum deduxisset, civitas adimeretur, quod per ambitionem et ultra præscriptum data esset.* The fate of the motion is unknown. Cic. *Ad Att.* 5.2.3 mentions an *auctoritas perscripta,* presumably a vetoed senatorial decree. But there is no reason to connect that with Marcellus' motion. Cicero, in fact, seems to distinguish it from the Transpadane affair.

[43] Plut. *Cæs.* 29.2; Appian, *BC,* 2.26. Plutarch states that the victim was a decurion, a more plausible version than Appian's reference to him as an ex-magistrate, which should unquestionably have entailed Roman citizenship. Cicero's account is ambiguous; *Ad Att.* 5.11.2: *etsi ille magistratum non gesserit, erat tamen Transpadanus*; cf. Shackleton Bailey, *Cicero's Letters,* III:207. Miss Taylor, *Voting Districts,* pp. 125–126, argued that the man flogged by Marcellus was a citizen of Comum, the old Latin colony, rather than of Cæsar's new citizen colony, since he is described as *Comensis,* not *Novocomensis;* cf. Cic. *Ad Fam.* 13.35.1. That, however, contradicts both Plutarch and Appian, and, if true, would make Marcellus' action a less effective demonstration against Cæsar.

[44] Cic. *Ad Att.* 5.11.2: *Marcellus fœde de Comensi . . . ita mihi videtur non minus stomachi nostro* [Pompey] *quam Cæsari fecisse.*

As a corollary, so Marcellus urged, there was no longer any reason for Cæsar's candidacy *in absentia.* If he wished to offer himself for the consulship, he should return to Rome directly.[45] The maneuver was shrewd and calculated. As Marcellus–and other foes of Cæsar–must have known, the siege of Alesia did not end matters in Gaul. Cæsar still feared further insurrection, and the whole task of provincial organization lay before him. More important, arrangements for his soldiers' rewards were as yet incomplete. To disband the army at this point might inspire new tribal revolts and permit Cæsar's enemies to disparage the effectiveness of his achievement. His successor would have the opportunity of finishing the job and earning the credit. An immediate recall would also place the proconsul at a disadvantage in consular elections scheduled for the immediate future and for which he had made no preparations. Such, it appears, was the plan of Cæsar's senatorial adversaries.

Marcellus delayed formal presentation of his motion. Mooted first in the early spring, it was then postponed to June 1. That date came and went. Marcellus became more restrained in his attacks. In late July a senatorial decree proclaimed that no action would be taken until Pompey himself was present to participate in the discussions. The matter was expected to come before the House on August 13. But a judicial proceeding intervened, requiring additional delay. September 1 was set for the hearing, again in vain; some felt that nothing would be done until the following year.[46] Marcellus' dilatoriness, however, did not reflect inertia; it was a matter of policy.[47] He was evidently canvassing senatorial support before making a formal move–and was encountering resistance. Though there existed pressure to have Cæsar succeeded, little enthusiasm manifested itself; Marcellus could not get a quorum in the senate.[48]

[45] Marcellus' arguments are given in Suet. *Iul.* 28.2. Gelzer, *Cæsar,* pp. 172–173, incorrectly believes that he had actually framed a senatorial resolution to that effect in the spring, adducing Cic. *Ad Att.* 5.2.3 and Hirt. *BG,* 8.53.1. But Cælius states unequivocally that Marcellus made no formal motion before June 1; *Ad Fam.* 8.1.2: *nihil rettulit de successione provinciarum Galliarum, et in Kalendas Iun., ut mihi ipse dixit, eam distulit relationem.* It is clear, however, that Marcellus had already expressed his intentions in public by that time. The consul's argument is not to be taken to imply that the *lex Pompeia Licinia* of 55 actually contained a clause saying Cæsar could be recalled when Gaul was pacified; see G. R. Elton, *JRS,* 36 (1946): 19–20; Cuff, *Historia,* 7 (1958): 457–458; *contra:* Balsdon, *JRS,* 29 (1939): 167–172. Cæsar held a provincial command, not an assignment for a specific task.

[46] For the postponement to June 1, see Cæl. *Ad Fam.* 8.1.2; Marcellus' restraint: Cæl. *Ad Fam.* 8.2.2; the *s.c.* of July and the date of August 13: Cæl. *Ad Fam.* 8.4.4; further delay in August: Cæl. *Ad Fam.* 8.9.2.

[47] Cæl. *Ad Fam.* 8.2.2: *Marcelli impetus resederunt, non inertia, sed, ut mihi videbantur, consilio.*

[48] Cæl. *Ad Fam.* 8.5.3: *Marcellus idem illud de provinciis urget, neque adhuc frequentem senatum efficere potuit.* Cf. Cæl. *Ad Fam.* 8.9.2. On the phrase *frequens senatus,* see Balsdon, *JRS,* 47 (1957): 19–20.

The reasons are not far to seek. Opposition to Cæsar mounted, but a recall at this stage was difficult to justify. The *lex Pompeia Licinia* of 55 allotted Cæsar a five-year command in Gaul. Whatever was stated therein about a terminal date, the year 51 would be too early on any reckoning. Marcellus' arguments regarding completion of the task fell flat, especially after rumors in the late spring that the Gauls were stirring again.[49] An attempt, sometime in September, to obtain senatorial sanction for the removal of Cæsar was stillborn. Marcellus had modified his tactics and moved that the Gallic command be terminated on March 1, 50. Opinion in the House was sharply divided. Marcellus' proposal met resistance from several tribunes and from his consular colleague, Ser. Sulpicius. The conservative lawyer branded the move as illegitimate, as well as premature. A majority in the *curia* told against Marcellus' motion.[50]

The effort to unsettle Cæsar had foundered. But the issue of the consular provinces was in the air, and some decision seemed called for. Consequently, a milder form of the original motion was presented at the end of September. This time the senate acted, at last. Four resolutions secured passage in the *curia* on September 30. The first proclaimed that discussion on the consular provinces would not be held until March 1, 50, and would then take precedence over all other public business. The second declared that obstructionism or vetoes against those dispositions would be adjudged in violation of the public interest. A third decree took specific aim at Cæsar, providing for senatorial inspection of the discharge claims of any of his soldiers. The purpose, presumably, was to encourage defection and weaken the commander's hold on his troops. And the fourth set aside the eight prætorian provinces and one other—Cilicia—currently governed by an ex-consul (Cicero) to be reserved for *prætorii*

[49] Cæl. *Ad Fam.* 8.1.4.

[50] Hirtius, *BG,* 8.53: *sententiisque dictis discessionem faciente Marcello . . . senatus frequens in alia omnia transiit.* That the motion named March 1 as the end of the proconsular command is reported by Cic. *Ad Att.* 8.3.3. That is surely March 1, 50. Date of the meeting itself is unrecorded—and not mentioned at all by Cælius. Rice Holmes, *Rom. Rep.,* II:308, puts it in September 1. Wrongly. Cælius states specifically that no quorum was attainable on that day; *Ad Fam.* 8.9.2: *in Kalend. res reiecta re, ne frequentiam quidem efficere potuerant.* The session referred to by Hirtius was a *senatus frequens; BG,* 8.53. It evidently came some time later in the month. For the opposition of Sulpicius Rufus, see Suet. *Iul.* 28–29; Dio, 40.59.1; Livy, *Per.* 108; cf. Cic. *Ad Fam.* 4.4.3. Marcellus' effort is referred to also by Appian, *BC,* 2.25–26, and, in confused fashion, by Plut. *Cæs.* 29.1. Hirtius stated that the move was *ante tempus,* in violation of the *lex Pompeia Licinia;* so also Suet. *Iul.* 28.2: *rettulit ad senatum, ut ei succederetur ante tempus.* That is unquestionably correct. But it does not prove that the *lex Licinia Pompeia* contained an express terminal date, nor that it forbade discussion before a particular date. Else the series of debates in 51 could hardly have taken place; cf. Adcock, *CQ,* 26 (1932), 20–23; C. E. Stevens, *AJP,* 59 (1938): 169–172; Balsdon, *JRS,* 29 (1939): 167–180.

again in 50. That would leave just Syria, the Spains, and the Gauls. Since Pompey's Spanish command had already been renewed, this decree guaranteed that the Gallic provinces would be up for distribution the following spring. The latter three resolutions were transparently anti-Cæsarian; friendly tribunes accordingly vetoed all three. More noteworthy, however, is the fact that no *intercessio* was applied against the initial *senatus consultum.* Cæsar's partisans were content to allow discussion on provincial assignments after March 1, 50. The proconsul, it appears, felt that that allowed sufficient breathing space.[51] There is no reason to believe that he evinced displeasure at this outcome. The offensive resolutions had been vetoed. Delay was in his interest. When debate resumed there could always be more *intercessiones,* if such should be needed.[52]

A pivotal question must now be confronted directly. What hand did Pompey have in these varied machinations? Orthodox opinion finds him engineering moves in the background against Cæsar, while taking care to avoid overt offense which might damage his own position. The evidence itself does not easily support that contention.

Pompeius Magnus, of course, was rarely given to revealing his own feelings. A penchant for ambiguous remarks kept his contemporaries off balance. The "credibility gap" between his public professions and private aims has already been noted on several occasions. It was still there to baffle and annoy observers in the summer of 51.[53] Discussions with Pompey at Tarentum in May convinced Cicero that the general would be a vigilant and steadfast defender of the public order.[54] Vague formulations of that sort were typical Pompeian expressions. Cicero may have taken them to mean that Pompey would resist the claims of Cæsar. But that would be an unwarranted reading of the general's mind.

In fact, Pompey was playing a delicate and difficult political game. The compact with Cæsar had served him well in the past, and he had no reason to seek its dissolution. At the same time, Pompey's aristocratic pretensions remained unchanged. New contacts with prominent *nobiles* in 52 revived hopes that he could recover the position of a *princeps* within the senatorial order

[51] The resolutions are given in full by Cæl. *Ad Fam.* 8.8.5–8. See the discussion by M. van den Bruwæne, *LEC,* 21 (1953): 19–27, who, however, sees Pompey behind the entire anti-Cæsarian maneuver.

[52] Cælius foresaw delaying tactics that might drag matters out for another two years; *Ad Fam.* 8.5.2.

[53] Cæl. *Ad Fam.* 8.1.3: *solet enim aliud sentire et loqui, neque tantum valere ingenio, ut non appareat, quid cupiat.*

[54] Cic. *Ad Fam.* 2.8.2: *civem egregium esse Pompeium, et ad omnia, quæ providenda sunt in republica, et animo et consilio paratum; Ad Att.* 5.7: *civem illum egregium relinquebam et ad hæc quæ timentur propulsanda paratissimum;* cf. *Ad Att.* 5.5.2, 5.6.1; Cæl. *Ad Fam.* 8.1.3.

that he had once held in the 60s. But matters were more difficult and complicated now. The envy and resentment of his peers had cost him much influence in the *curia* during the previous decade. Of late, that envy and resentment directed itself more and more against Julius Cæsar, whose martial exploits caused growing discomfort within aristocratic ranks. Pompey's commitments to his old ally were not readily reconcilable with the attitudes of his new associates. That may account for much of the general's ambiguity and apparent wavering in 51 and early 50. Yet it will not be rash to postulate a logical policy underlying his actions. Pompey aimed perhaps at a coalition encompassing not only supporters of the triumvirate but also prestigious clans of the *nobilitas*. The resultant combination would erode the power of the Catonians and other foes of the dynasts, leaving the field clear for political ascendancy. It was a perfectly conventional goal in the tradition of Roman politics. Hindsight can tell us, of course, that the project proved to be beyond the capacity of Pompey. Internal jealousies and suspicions within the ruling class made it impossible for the general to balance successfully the conflicting interests which he sought to reconcile. But the hypothesis of such a plan can render intelligible his actions and statements in these pivotal months.

Inimici of the coalition sought to exploit its ambiguities in July of 51. Pompey, as was noted above, had generously lent Cæsar one of his own legions a year and half before. By now, however, so some could claim, the dangers in Gaul had passed. Ought Cæsar not to relinquish that legion? And why was Pompey not demanding its return? The raising of that issue represents a manifest effort to embarrass the dynasts. If Pompey declined to press his partner, his enemies could sow suspicions of a military buildup in Gaul. If, on the other hand, he yielded to senatorial insistence here, it might provoke a premature strain in the alliance. Pompey responded with prudent circumspection: he would withdraw the legion from Gaul, but in his own time, and not under the hostile pressure of his detractors.[55]

The affair is illuminating in more than one way. It exposes the tactics of Pompey's antagonists. They intended to probe the weaknesses of his alliance, hoping either to compel a precipitate break with Cæsar or to place the dynasts in the position of appearing to threaten the *res publica*. The former would splinter much of Pompey's own support; the latter would permit a new campaign of vilification against the coalition. Those tactics have a familiar ring. It was precisely the scheme put into operation by the Catonians after formation of the triumvirate almost a decade before. Their success at that time warranted repetition. Pompey's response is similarly revealing. A promise to recall the legion would allay suspicions and dampen the propaganda of

[55] Cæl. *Ad Fam.* 8.4.4: *coactus est dicere Pompeius, se legionem abducturum, sed non statim, sub mentionem et convicium obtrectatorum.*

his adversaries. But he would not offend Cæsar by a hasty or blustering act. If a shift in the forces were required, it would come when he and his partner had agreed upon the appropriate occasion.

Efforts to divide the dynasts met with little success. As we have seen, Marcellus' dramatic onslaught on Cæsar's enfranchisement of Novum Comum raised Pompey's hackles. Hence, the matter seems to have been dropped. And there are other indications that the triumvirs continued to have friends and enemies in common. T. Munatius Plancus Bursa had been convicted in early 51, a sore embarrassment for Pompey, who had exerted mighty efforts to procure his acquittal. Plancus next turns up in Ravenna, the recipient of a handsome bounty from Julius Cæsar.[56] The consular elections of 51 returned two foes of Cæsar, C. Marcellus and L. Æmilius Paullus. Marcellus was prepared to continue the policies of his cousin, the consul of 51. And Paullus carried on a hereditary feud with Pompey, which overbore all other considerations.[57] Of similar interest is C. Scribonius Curio, elected tribune for the year 50. A precocious and sharp-tongued young orator, he had been an outspoken assailant of the triumvirate as early as 59. He had not altered that posture in the meanwhile. Cicero solicited his assistance for Milo's campaign in 53, a fact that would not have met with Pompey's approval. Curio's successful tribunician campaign in 51 came despite opposition from friends of both Pompey and Cæsar.[58] He was expected to carry on the schemes hatched by enemies of the dynasts to discredit and divide them. Cælius conjectured that Curio would attempt to remove some of Cæsar's authority while offering a paltry sop to Pompey.[59] That, of course, concided precisely with the propaganda campaign of 51. Cæsar and Pompey were still dual targets.

The issue of the Gallic succession, however, was the crucial matter. It fits suitably in the context of this campaign. By July 51 Marcellus' efforts to obtain Cæsar's recall dominated much of senatorial discussion. And once more Pompey was pressed for some public statement on the controversy, in the

[56] Cæl. *Ad Fam.* 8.1.5. Rightly noted by Stevens, *AJP,* 59 (1938): 179. On Plancus' trial see above, pp. 346–347.

[57] See above, pp. 156–157.

[58] Cæl. *Ad Fam.* 8.4.2: *Curio . . . ratione et insidiis usus videretur in evitandis eorum consiliis, qui se intenderant adversarios is eius tribunatum; Lælios et Antonios, et id genus valentis dico.* The "Lælii" were friends of Pompeius; Cic. *Pro Flacco,* 14. "Antonii" is doubtless reference to the Cæsarian officer M. Antonius; cf. W. K. Lacey, *Historia,* 10 (1961): 320–321. Shackleton Bailey, *Philologus,* 105 (1961): 85–86, prefers "Lollios" to "Lælios." But his reduction of politics to *optimates* and Cæsarians is inappropriate for 51. For Curio's attacks on the triumvirate in 59, see Cic. *Ad Att.* 2.18.1, 2.19.3; Suet. *Iul.* 50.1; cf. Cic. *Ad Att.* 2.24.2–3. For Cicero's request to him on Milo's behalf, see Cic. *Ad Fam.* 2.6.4–5.

[59] Cæl. *Ad Fam.* 8.10.3: *Curionem video se dupliciter iactaturum; primum, ut aliquid Cæsari adimat, inde ut aliquid Pompeio tribuat, quodvis quamlibet tenue munusculum.*

hopes that his response could be used against him. The general, as he did so often, retreated into harmless platitudes, evading the challenge of his foes: "all men must render respect to the judgments of the senate."[60] And Pompey's next move was a journey to Ariminum. That, we may be sure, was no random trip. Ariminum bordered the limits of Cæsar's *provincia*, Cisalpine Gaul. He could not, of course, have met with Cæsar directly; the proconsul was elsewhere.[61] But it provided a convenient location for parleys with his ally's agents and messengers. One may properly conjecture a negotiation regarding their common stance on the Gallic succession.

Debate came to a head in Rome in the late summer. When Marcellus actively lobbied for termination of Cæsar's command as of March 50, Pompey stood ready to resist the proposal directly. He offered his own opinion in the senate: any *senatus consultum* at that time would be premature and unjustifiable. His action was no doubt instrumental in senatorial rejection of Marcellus' motion.[62] Cælius reports a public statement of Pompey's in this connection, which needs comment. The general announced that he would not countenance the possibility of Cæsar's exercising both provincial command and the consulship simultaneously.[63] That has been taken as an overt stand by Pompey against the aspirations of the proconsul, decisive evidence for the break in their compact. But in light of the previous discussion we may suspect that this was yet another Pompeian response to a malicious and leading question by enemies of the dynasts. It in no way implies that Cæsar in fact sought to retain his army and hold the consulship at the same time, much less that Pompey had severed relations with his ally. Hostile senators, preparing a propaganda case, had suggested revolutionary aims on Cæsar's part and endeavored once again to discomfit Pompey with embarrassing questions. The general's retort represents a typical evasion. He could not agree to a tampering with Cæsar's command at this point; but he upheld the principles of the constitution. Nothing could be more "Pompeian."

The raising of the Gallic question, however, had provoked concern—and

[60] Cæl. *Ad Fam.* 8.4.4: *inde interrogatus est de successione C. Cæsaris . . . "omnis oportere senatui dicto audientes esse."*

[61] See Hirtius, *BG,* 8.46. On Pompey's trip to Ariminum, see Cæl. *Ad Fam.* 8.4.4; Cic. *Ad Att.* 5.19.1.

[62] Cæl. *Ad Fam.* 8.9.5: *hanc sententiam dixit, nullum hoc tempore senatus consultum faciendum;* Cic. *Ad Att.* 8.3.3: *Marcoque Marcello consuli finienti provincias Gallias Kal. Mart. die restitit.* The fact is attested also by Appian, *BC,* 2.26, and Dio, 40.59.3, both of whom, as might be expected, impute hypocrisy to Pompey. Cf. also Plut. *Pomp.* 56.2. That, of course, is retrospective judgment demanded by their own interpretations—or those of their sources.

[63] Cæl. *Ad Fam.* 8.9.5. The text, in fact, is corrupt. Mss read: *Pompeius tuus aperte Cæsarem et provinciam tenere cum exercitus et consul.* Plausible emendation restores the following: *Pompeius tuus aperte Cæsarem non vult et provinciam tenere cum exercitu et consulem esse.*

public suspicion. To that extent Marcellus and his backers had been successful. The dynasts could not evade the matter altogether. Marcellus' proposal to oust Cæsar on March 1 found insufficient favor. A less extreme *sententia* was put forth by Metellus Scipio, Pompey's father-in-law: debate on disposition of the Gauls should begin on March 1, no other item taking precedence. That motion was also not to the liking of Julius Cæsar. Cæsar's trusted agent L. Cornelius Balbus expressed his displeasure and remonstrated with Scipio in private. Their discussion seems to have had effect. Nothing more is heard of the proposal. But the event itself is noteworthy. Pompey obviously could not answer for all of his new allies. The expansion of his aristocratic ties also caused strains within his own alliance, a feature that we have seen to be recurrent throughout the Ciceronian period.[64] The enlargement of political combines always ran the risk of incorporating disparate members whose independence might weaken rather than strengthen the group's cohesion. That tension had numerous complications in the realignments of the 60s. It was still there to frustrate Pompey's schemes in 51 and would ultimately rend his coalition apart.

Cæsarian partisans would not accept their chief's precipitate removal, nor a firm decision to reassign his provinces on March 1. The latter would imply that the Gauls were categorized with all other provinces and subject to the *lex Pompeia de provinciis.* Cæsar, it seems, counted on the rationalization that his command had been authorized by the people and therefore evaded the provisions of the *lex Pompeia.* To endorse Metellus Scipio's proposal or one like it would involve yielding that claim. Tribunes sympathetic to Cæsar were not prepared to make the concession, and any such proposal was sure to be vetoed.[65] But they would not stand in the way of a senatorial decision to set debate on provinces generally for the following March. Their stance neatly removed steam from the opposition's propaganda campaign and still left room for *intercessio* if Gaul should come under discussion in March. As was already noted, the resolutions of late September reflected those lines exactly. The decree to open debate on provincial assignment in March encountered no veto. But the *senatus consultum* which attempted to place Cæsar's *provinciæ* into that debate by consigning almost all others to ex-prætors was nullified by tribunician *intercessio.*[66]

[64] On Balbus and Metellus Scipio, see Cæl. *Ad Fam.* 8.9.5: *Scipio hanc, ut Kalend. Martiis de provinciis Galliis, neu quid coniunctim referretur; contristavit sententia Balbum Cornelium et scio, eum questum esse cum Scipione.* Note also Pompey's cousin C. Lucilius Hirrus, who consistently cast his senatorial vote against Cæsar in 51; Cæl. *Ad Fam.* 8.8.5–6, 8.9.1. On Lucilius' connection with Pompey, see above, chap. 3, n.75.

[65] Cæl. *Ad Fam.* 8.9.2: *Galliæ, quæ habent intercessorem, in eandem condicionem quam ceteræ provinciæ vocantur.*

[66] Cæl. *Ad Fam.* 8.8.5, 8.8.8; see the incisive analysis of Stevens, *AJP,* 59 (1938): 188–191.

The postponement was now official. There could be no further attempts on Cæsar's position for five months. But foes of the coalition continued to hope for an advantage by asking pointed questions of Pompeius Magnus–questions obviously designed to sow the seeds of future dissension. Pompey was asked again about his attitude toward Cæsar and the possible prolongation of an already lengthy tenure. The general kept faith with his ally: there would be no discussion of Gaul before March 1 without injustice to Cæsar. But what about after that date? Here Pompey felt compelled to appease Metellus Scipio and other skeptical members of the *nobilitas* whose support he was reluctant to lose: he saw no reason to delay debate beyond March 1.[67] The interrogators pressed on, in the hope of inducing Pompey to commit himself irrevocably. What if there should be tribunician *intercessio* at that time? Magnus confronted the query directly: there was no difference between refusing to obey a *senatus consultum* and using others to obstruct a *senatus consultum*.[68] And if Cæsar should wish to be consul while retaining his army? To that question Pompey responded by scoffing: that was no more likely than a son taking a club to his father.[69]

Pompey's series of answers persuaded his audience that a bargain had been effected between himself and Julius Cæsar.[70] The impression was not unwarranted. Pompey had doubtless contracted to employ his influence toward postponing any debate on consular provinces until the following spring. That charge was carried out; Cæsar had no grounds for complaint. To fend off hostile questioners and allay senatorial suspicions, Pompey took up a proper constitutional posture: no delay after March 1; no further *intercessio*; and, of course, Cæsar would not wish to be consul and provincial commander simultaneously.

Whether Cæsar had also contracted privately to meet those conditions cannot be known. The words and actions of Pompey are, in any case, explicable. He had upheld the interests of his ally and, at the same time, had blunted

[67] Cæl. *Ad Fam.* 8.8.9: *ut diceret se ante Kalend. Mart. non posse sine iniuria de provinciis Cæsaris statuere, post Kal. Mart. se non dubitaturum.* Cælius' statement in *Ad Fam.* 8.8.4 is evidently based on that remark of Pompey's: *plane perspecta Cn. Pompei voluntate in eam partem, ut eum decedere post Kalendas Martias placeret.*

[68] Cæl. *Ad Fam.* 8.8.9: *cum interrogaretur, si qui tum intercederent, dixit hoc nihil interesse, utrum C. Cæsar senatui dicto audiens futurus non esset, an pararet qui senatum decernere non pateretur.*

[69] Cæl. *Ad Fam.* 8.8.9: *Quid si, inquit alius, et consul esse, et exercitum habere volet? At ille, quam clementer! Quid si filius meus fustem mihi impingere volet?* The question, expressly recorded here by Cælius, suggests that it was a similar query to which Pompey responded in Cæl. *Ad Fam.* 8.9.5.

[70] Cæl. *Ad Fam.* 8.8.9: *His vocibus, ut existimarent homines, Pompeio cum Cæsare esse negotium, effecit.* The term *negotium* must mean "bargain" or "deal" here–as it usually does; cf. Stevens. *AJP*, 59 (1938): 177–179; Balsdon, *JRS*, 29 (1939): 175–177; Elton, *JRS*, 36 (1946): 39–41.

the effectiveness of his adversaries' propaganda. The dynasts would worry about March 1 when the time came. By then events in Gaul or elsewhere might justify reconsideration and perhaps even additional delay. Cæsar's options were open. If the situation augured well, he would return and seek election; if not, pretext could be found to prolong his command.[71] For the moment, the foes of the dynasts had been stymied. Political fencing, of course, would continue, as it had continued throughout Roman history. But there were few who could reasonably have forecast a civil war.[72]

C. CURIO AND THE INCREASE OF TENSIONS

Rome, in late 51 and early 50, as always, bubbled with politics, intrigue, and machinations. As we have seen, electoral rivalry and judicial contests proceeded apace with little hint that storm clouds were gathering. Far from contemplating a clash between the dynasts, public attention focused elsewhere. Menace seemed to loom from the East. Crassus' ignominious defeat weakened Rome's eastern position and caused considerable insecurity at home. Fears of a Parthian invasion into Roman provinces marked debates in the senate and among the populace. In the late summer and fall of 51, numerous suggestions and alternatives were mooted. Some recommended that Pompey be dispatched to the Parthian front, others that Cæsar be commissioned to take his army there, still others that the consuls should go. The varied opinions issued in no decision. Most of the discussion centered on Pompey; but there was substantial sentiment that he should remain in Italy, lest there be opportunity for new urban unrest.[73] The debate dragged on into the year 50. Pompey himself seemed inclined to go, and Cicero expected his appointment as late as February. But a senatorial majority overruled his wishes. At the same time they were unwilling to grant any further dignity to Julius Cæsar.[74] Politics obviously blocked any decision. The aristocracy would not enhance the prestige

[71] Cæl. *Ad Fam.* 8.8.9: *Itaque iam, ut video, alteram utram ad condicionem descendere vult Cæsar, ut aut maneat, neque hoc anno sua ratio habeatur, aut, si designari poterit, decedat.* Only an a priori hypothesis can see in *hoc anno* anything but a reference to the year 50.

[72] Sulpicius Rufus may have been one; Cic. *Ad Fam.* 4.3.1. But Cicero's remark here was penned in 46, well after the fact. Even if it is accurate, it ascribes only general warnings to Sulpicius. There is nothing in that passage to show that Sulpicius foretold conflict between Pompey and Cæsar. He may indeed have warned against the armed force controlled by their combination.

[73] Cic. *Ad Att.* 5.18.1: *vereor ne senatus propter urbanarum rerum metum Pompeium nolit dimittere;* Cæl. *Ad Fam.* 8.10.2: *alius enim Pompeium mittendum, alius ab urbe Pompeium non removendum, alius Cæsarem cum suo exercitu, alius consules, nemo tamen ex senatus consulto privatos.*

[74] Cic. *Ad Att.* 5.21.3: *cum Pompeius propter metum rerum novarum nusquam dimittatur, Cæsari nullus honos a senatu habeatur; Ad Att.* 6.1.14: *erit ad sustentandum quoad Pompeius veniat, qui litteris quas ad me mittit significat suum negotium illud fore.*

or forces of either of the dynasts. It was Rome's good fortune that Parthia proved less aggressive than had been feared. Of concern for prospective hostilities between Pompey and Cæsar there is here no trace. Pompey scrupulously maintained a pacific posture.[75]

The arrangement, however, was soon to receive a serious test. The first of March was approaching and with it a time of reckoning. Many awaited with eagerness a discussion of the consular provinces, which could not readily be postponed further. Cæsar, it appeared, was not yet prepared to resign his post, and there was worry lest he attempt another delay.[76] The Marcelli and the Catonians could be counted on to force the issue. They hoped for immediate supersession and the dispatching of a successor. At that time Pompey would have less room to maneuver. He himself had approved the senatorial resolution that fixed March 1 as the day of decision. An awkward dilemma lay ahead. Pompey had the alternative of supporting Cæsar's recall and provoking a breach in their relations, or of advocating postponement and compromising fidelity to his own pronouncements. Pressure from senatorial conservatives was pushing matters to a head. That was expected. But the unity of the dynasts suffered strains also from an entirely different and unexpected quarter: the tribunician activities of C. Scribonius Curio.

The gifted but erratic and unpredictable Curio secured appointment, through a supplementary election, to the tribunate of 50.[77] His personality and behavior contributed in no small part to the friction that developed in that year. For those historians who reckon the civil war as long foreordained, Curio represents no more than a minor instrument of large forces sweeping to an inevitable calamity. But it would be rash to underrate the importance of individual personality and unanticipated events. The activities of Curio, so one might argue, provided an indispensable ingredient in generating the civil war.[78] Time is ripe for a reassessment of that tribunate.

As was noted before, Curio's election came over the opposition of Pompeians and Cæsarians. But few could reckon on the consistency of that volatile individual. Curio was brilliant and talented, but reckless, ambitious, and perverse. It was hazardous to predict his behavior; some claimed that Curio did

[75] Though Atticus had his doubts about Pompey's sincerity, Cicero was convinced that the general was a man of peace; *Ad Att.* 6.1.11: *in Pompeio te spem omnem oti ponere non miror; ita res est, removendumque censeo illud "dissimulantem."*

[76] Cic. *Ad Att.* 5.20.7, 6.1.24.

[77] The vacancy was created by the conviction *de ambitu* of Servæus, a tribune-designate; Cæl. *Ad Fam.* 8.4.2.

[78] Cf. Vell. Pat. 2.48.3: *bello autem civili . . non alius maiorem flagrantioremque quam C. Curio tribunus plebis subiecit facem;* Lucan, 4.819 ff.

not know his own mind.[79] Cicero was properly concerned when he learned of Curio's election. He sent prompt congratulations, but tempered them with solemn warnings about the perilous character of the times and the need for caution and deliberation.[80]

The concern proved to be well founded. Curio swiftly moved to the center of the stage, upsetting the calculations of many politicians from all parts of the political spectrum. From Curio's attacks, as tribune-designate, upon the dynasts, Cælius expected that he would take the part of senatorial conservatives. The effort to recall Cæsar, which M. Marcellus had generated in 51, would be resumed, so it was anticipated, by Curio.[81] In November, a month before taking office, Curio was still sniping at Pompey and Cæsar.[82] But his activities did not confine themselves to barbed jibes. Curio had a program of his own. He announced preparation of a new measure on the Campanian land. Although sources do not specify its content, the purpose can be divined. Evidently some territory was to be set aside and made available for distribution—for soldiers or for the *plebs*. Pompey felt aggrieved; he had evidently planned to employ the land for his own veterans or prospective veterans. Cæsar took the news calmly.[83] When the tribunate opened, Curio bided his time. He continued to assault the dynasts verbally. But otherwise December and January seem to have been spent in drafting measures and preparing the ground for them. Some observers were misled into thinking that Curio's tribunate would be uneventful.[84]

In February, however, Curio burst into a flurry of activity. A series of bills bearing his name came before the populace. The law on the Campanian land does not receive further mention. Perhaps it was held in abeyance. But Curio advocated the deposition of King Juba in Numidia and the use of his land for allotments. In addition, there was a *lex viaria*, which proposed

[79] Vell. Pat. 2.48.3: *vir nobilis, eloquens, audax, suæ alienæque et fortunæ et pudicitiæ prodigus;* Cæl. *Ad Fam.* 8.4.2: *Curio qui nihil consilio facit;* cf. Cæl. *Ad Fam.* 8.6.5. Further on Curio's character, see Cic. *Brutus,* 280–281.

[80] Cic. *Ad Fam.* 2.7.1–2.

[81] Cæl. *Ad Fam.* 8.4.2, 8.5.3.

[82] Cæl. *Ad Fam.* 8.10.3.

[83] Cæl. *Ad Fam.* 8.10.4: *illud addo ad actiones C. Curionis, de agro Campano; de quo negant Cæsarem laborare, sed Pompeium valde nolle, ne vacuus advenienti Cæsari pateat.* The implication here is that Cæsar was not expected to be pleased with the measure.

[84] Cæl. *Ad Fam.* 8.6.4; Cic. *Ad Fam.* 2.13.3. For attacks on the dynasts, see Vell. Pat. 2.48.4, though Velleius, knowing what came later, judges these attacks as hypocritical: *simulatione contra Pompeium et Cæsarem, sed animo pro Cæsare stetit.* So also Dio, 40.61.1–2; Livy, *Per.* 109. Much of Curio's overt activity at the outset of the tribunate was directed toward inserting an intercalary month. It would allow additional time for legislation; Cæl. *Ad Fam.* 8.6.5; cf. Cic. *Ad Att.* 5.21.14; Dio, 40.62.1–2.

a five-year commission to superintend the building and repair of roads in Italy; Curio himself would be in charge of operations. Further, he offered a *lex alimentaria*, evidently for grain distribution—perhaps to undercut the popularity of Pompey, who had previously exercised that responsibility. Finally, we have reference to a measure of Curio's of which one provision instituted a luxury tax on travelers. Presumably, it was part of a *lex sumptuaria*—that too would find favor with the populace.[85]

The program was consistent and appealing. Secondary sources, judging Curio's motivations from his later pro-Cæsarian activities, have distorted the picture: Curio proposed radical legislation in the hopes that it would be rejected, thereby providing pretext for open espousal of Cæsar's cause.[86] That is transparent inference of motives from results. In fact, Curio's set of measures reads like the standard demagogic posture of an activist tribune. Agrarian bills, a grain law, road-building projects, and restrictions on luxury are all familiar devices. Curio had been the darling of the populace before—notably in 59, when his blistering oratory earned widespread public applause. The tribunate afforded an ideal vehicle for his talents—and his ambitions. A broad *popularis* program advocated with energy and decisiveness would win plaudits for its proposer, as well as a substantial following. Clodius had demonstrated that in 58. And Clodius had been a good friend of Curio's; his widow, moreover, was now Curio's wife. No matter if the proposals stirred resistance or even failed of passage—the advocacy itself could elevate a shrewd and determined tribune to the level of a popular hero. Even in the year 50 the prospect of civil war, if such there was, did not alter familiar political behavior.

To classify Curio as a puppet of Julius Cæsar's is oversimplification. Of course, later tradition alleged that the tribune received an enormous bribe to serve Cæsar's interests. That, we may be sure, derives from anti-Cæsarian sources. There is no trace of it in any of the contemporary evidence.[87] Nor

[85] Cælius notes the *lex viaria* and the *lex alimentaria; Ad Fam.* 8.6.5. On the former, see also Appian, *BC*, 2.27. For the bill to seize Juba's land, see Cæs. *BC*, 2.25; Dio, 41.41.3; Lucan, 4.688–692. The tax on traveling expenses is recorded in Cic. *Ad Att.* 6.1.25. Despite Shackleton Bailey, *Cicero's Letters*, III:255, there is no reason to see that provision as part of the *lex viaria*; cf. Tyrell and Purser, *Correspondence*, III:203; Lacey, *Historia*, 10 (1961): 323. Curio added another pinprick for Pompey. He advocated the restoration from exile of C. Memmius, convicted under the *lex Pompeia de ambitu*; Cic. *Ad Att.* 6.1.23. On Curio's feverish legislative activity, see also Dio, 40.61.2–40.62.1.

[86] Cf. Dio, 40.61–62; Appian, *BC*, 2.27.

[87] Allegations of bribery are preserved by Dio, 40.60.2; Plut. *Pomp.* 58.1; *Cæs.* 29.2–3; *Ant.* 5.1; Appian, *BC*, 2.26; Val. Max. 9.1.6; Suet. *Iul.* 29.1; Lucan, 4.819–820. The story was known to Velleius Paterculus, but he reserved judgment; 2.48.4. It is decisively refuted by Lacey, *Historia*, 10 (1961): 318–319. No imputation of bribery need be read in Cic. *Brutus*, 280.

does anything in Curio's legislative proposals suggest direction from Cæsar. To be sure, agrarian measures might have in view the prospective return of veterans from Gaul. But Curio intended to obtain credit for arranging their settlement–and perhaps even administering it–thereby stealing Cæsar's thunder and laying claim to some of his *clientelæ*. Cælius describes the *lex viaria* as similar to the Rullan land bill of 63. He refers to parallel procedural arrangements, notably a governing commission that would hold office for five years to implement the law. But there is another important parallel. Rullus' enactment looked toward the imminent return of Pompey's troops from the East. The sponsor or his backers would be in a good position to provide for the veterans and earn political credit. Curio's statutes, if adopted, would give him a similar role and central position in the post-Gallic war settlement. Curio professed to speak for Cæsar, but worked in his own cause.[88]

Curio was no more an "instrument" in 50 than Clodius had been in 58. Indeed, he had learned much from his now deceased *amicus*. Clodius' remarkably successful popular legislation had cut neatly across the political contests between the triumvirs and their senatorial adversaries. He outmaneuvered the Catonians by addressing himself to the tastes of the populace; and he fostered splits in the triumvirate by directing assaults on Pompey while scrupulously avoiding offense to Crassus and occasionally claiming the backing of Cæsar. As we shall see, this same strategy best explains the actions of C. Curio, a strategy which he, like Clodius, hoped to utilize as a springboard for his own authority.[89]

As March 1 approached, Cæsar felt an increasing need to shore up his political position. He had for some time been sending Gallic gold to Rome to finance public spectacles and building programs, thus cultivating a mass of grateful beneficiaries among the populace. At the same time he used appropriate occasions to indulge his soldiers through a generous distribution of booty and by increases of pay.[90] Those moves take on particular meaning in light of Curio's actions and promises. Cæsar would not easily yield to another his claims as patron of the legions and benefactor of the urban *plebs*.

[88] Cæl. *Ad Fam.* 8.6.5: *legemque viariam, non dissimilem agrariæ Rulli.* The suggestion of Lacey, *Historia*, 10 (1961): 325–326, that this proposal intended a commission with *imperium* for Cæsar is entirely without supporting evidence. In view of the attitude of our sources, the *argumentum ex silentio* is here particularly strong. In fact, Appian, *BC*, 2.27, states that Curio himself would head that commission.

[89] Curio's independence and demagogic program is rightly stressed by C. L. Babcock, *AJP*, 86 (1965), 9–10, 28–31. Babcock's notion that Fulvia inspired and advised the tribune is attractive but undemonstrable. Curio had ideas of his own. And Babcock's purposes did not enable him to explore fully the situation in 50.

[90] Cæs. *BG*, 7.89; Hirtius, *BG*, 8.4; Suet. *Iul.* 26.

It would be equally useful, however, to win friends among the magistrates of 50. The two consuls, C. Marcellus and L. Æmilius Paullus, had been elected as known *inimici* of Cæsar. Marcellus' kinship to the proconsul by marriage did not alter his implacable hostility. Paullus, however, might be more amenable. He needed money to build the Basilica Æmilia, a monument to his family. And he was angling for a provincial assignment, an ambition that could only be realized by exemption from the *lex Pompeia de provinciis*. That Cæsar purchased his services with a lavish donation was later alleged, but it cannot be proved. More likely, the promise of support for a provincial command determined Paullus' switch of allegiance. In any event, he soon publicly espoused the cause of Julius Cæsar.[91] More striking still was the new posture of C. Curio. In February, he left off his attacks on Cæsar and began to speak on the proconsul's behalf. Cælius attributed it to his fickleness; Cicero professed in retrospect that he could have predicted it, but was nonetheless most disturbed by the report.[92]

The issue at stake, of course, was termination of Cæsar's command. It was to be discussed in a matter of weeks. By February both Curio and Paullus signified their determination to block it. Some pivotal questions must now be squarely faced. Pompey had successfully postponed discussion in 51 in Cæsar's interests. Why could he not be reckoned on to do the same again? Why did Cæsar go to such lengths to enlist the aid of former enemies rather than rely on Pompey's assistance? What induced Curio to espouse the Cæsarian cause on this issue? Where did Pompeius Magnus now stand vis-à-vis his collaboration with the proconsul of Gaul? If satisfactory answers can be obtained for these questions, they will shed considerable light on the friction that culminated in civil war.

First, the machinations of Cæsar. In 52 the law of the ten tribunes, passed at Pompey's urging, had granted Cæsar the right to stand for consular office

[91] Even Lacey, who disproves the bribe to Curio, takes for granted the purchase of Paullus; *Historia*, 10 (1961): 319, 327; as do all other commentators; e.g. Syme, *Rom. Rev.*, p. 69. Yet the evidence for Paullus is no better or earlier than that for Curio. The two are linked together in the secondary sources: Appian, *BC*, 2.26; Plut. *Pomp.* 58.1; *Cæs.* 29.2–3; Suet. *Iul.* 29; cf. Dio, 40.63.5. There is nothing in Cæl. *Ad Fam.* 8.4.4 to support the notion that Paullus had already been bribed in late 51. Paullus' transfer to Cæsar obviously came as a surprise to Cicero in May of 50; *Ad Att.* 6.3.4. For Paullus' provincial aspirations, see Cæl. *Ad Fam.* 8.10.3; Cic. *Ad Att.* 6.1.7. He evidently hoped for Cilicia, perhaps seeking exemption from the *lex Pompeia* because of the Parthian menace; cf. Mommsen, *Rechtsfrage*, p. 47; Lacey, *Historia*, 10 (1961): 327.

[92] Cæl. *Ad Fam.* 8.6.5: *levissime enim, quia de intercalando non obtinuerat, transfugit ad populum et pro Cæsare loqui cœpit;* Cic. *Ad Fam.* 2.13.3: *Quid ais? Cæsarem nunc defendit Curio? Quis hoc putaret præter me? Nam, ita vivam, putavi;* Cic. *Ad Att.* 6.3.4: *huc enim odiosa adferebantur de Curione, de Paulo.*

in absentia. In what year would he have expected to exercise that prerogative? Cæsar himself later claimed that he had been authorized to offer his candidacy in the year 49 for the consulship of 48–naturally. The proconsul's concern in that passage is to justify his invasion of Italy; the statement is imbedded in an apologia charging his enemies with violating his rights and forcing him to resort to arms.[93] Some scholars have accepted that assertion at face value: the *ratio absentis* was specified for 49, and Cæsar was later deprived unlawfully of a privilege awarded him by the people.[94] Yet it is in the highest degree unlikely that the law of 52 would have fixed 49 as a date for Cæsar's candidacy. Debate on the official terminus of the Gallic command continues in scholarly journals. But whether the five-year extension under the *lex Pompeia Licinia* began in 55 or 54, the command–on any theory–would have run out before the elections of 49. Hence, the ten tribunes in 52 could hardly have stipulated a *ratio absentis* for those elections. Cæsar would not require the prerogative after his command expired–nor could a case be made out for it. The law doubtless mentioned no particular date for the candidacy.[95] Cæsar later exploited that ambiguity in self-justification. But his interpretation would not have been in view in 52. At that time the proconsul preferred flexibility. Cæsar, it was assumed, would offer his name in the year 50. For that we have the explicit testimony of Cælius.[96] The dynasts were evidently pointing for those elections. Pompey's obstruction of the attempted recall in 51 allowed his ally to remain in Gaul, where he could use the *ratio absentis* in the following year.

This background is essential to a comprehension of the events of the spring

[93] Cæs. *BC*, 1.9: *doluisse se, quod populi Romani beneficium sibi per contumeliam ab inimicis extorqueretur, ereptoque semestri imperio in urbem retraheretur, cuius absentis rationem haberi proximis comitiis populus iussisset*; cf. Livy, *Per*. 108.

[94] E.g. Elton, *JRS*, 36 (1946): 37–39. Sealey, *ClMed*, 18 (1957): 87–101, goes further and argues that the law of the ten tribunes not only specified 49 for the *ratio absentis* but extended Cæsar's *imperium* through the elections of that year. That scholar is not usually misled by apologetic propaganda.

[95] Apart from Cæsar's statement noted above, no source suggests that the *lex* marked any specific elections for exercise of the *ratio absentis*.

[96] Cæl. *Ad Fam*. 8.8.9: *ut aut maneat, neque hoc anno sua ratio habeatur, aut, si designari poterit, decedat*. To be sure, Sulla's *lex annalis* required a ten years' gap between consulships for a single individual; Broughton, *MRR*, II:75. Cæsar later employed that argument too to justify a candidacy in 49, after his term had expired; Cæs. *BC*, 1.32, 3.1; followed by Dio, 40.51.2. But it would have had little force in 52. Pompey had just obtained two consulships within four years. And, perhaps, for the elections of 50 Cæsar counted on an inclusive reckoning of the *decennium* (i.e. 59–49). See also Suet. *Iul*. 26.1, who suggests that the law of the ten tribunes anticipated a Cæsarian candidacy shortly before his term was due to conclude. On this, cf. the arguments of Stevens, *AJP*, 59 (1938): 172–175; also Salmon, *CJ*, 34 (1939): 388–395.

of 50. Cæsar evidently chose not to run in the elections of that year. The reason, unfortunately, eludes us. The proconsul probably sought more time in Gaul to undertake and complete a provincial organization as a lasting monument to his achievement. In any event, he did not submit his name, and backed instead another candidate, his former legate Ser. Sulpicius Galba.[97] For further delay Cæsar needed strong political assistance in Rome; the provinces were due for distribution on March 1. And he wanted more than delay. Having abstained from consular candidacy in 50, Cæsar now sought to have the *ratio absentis* extended beyond the point for which it was first intended. If the Gallic settlement were to take him well into the year 49, he required assurance that he could still stand in absence at that time.

But it was precisely on this matter that he could not altogether rely on the aid of Pompeius Magnus. In the previous fall Pompey had been maneuvered by senatorial conservatives into overt pronouncements on a similar question. Under prodding from hostile questioners, he rejected the possibility that Cæsar would be consul and provincial *imperator* simultaneously.[98] He could not easily back down on those public statements. Further prodding might elicit awkward responses on extension of the *ratio absentis*. And Cæsar may not have been altogether happy with his ally's new friends in Rome. Metellus Scipio had already shown reluctance to cooperate with Cæsar; Ap. Claudius was at all times unreliable, and was now related by marriage to M. Cato. Cæsar recognized the utility of soliciting added political support among Roman magistrates, in order to obtain extension of his privileges. Hence, the stepped-up *beneficia* to the populace, and the representations to Æmilius Paullus and Scribonius Curio.

Next, Curio. Why did that mercurial character emerge as a spokesman for Julius Cæsar? The notion of a cash transaction is most dubious. Nor is it likely that Curio suddenly found attractive the man whom he had been lacerating for years. The temperament of the tribune makes it difficult to regard him as anyone's lackey. Curio was playing his own game and building his own political base. A principal avenue to success lay in weakening those elements which might bar the way. It was very much in Curio's interest to drive a wedge between Pompey and Cæsar, to shatter their coalition and reduce their political weight. The job had been made easier for him by the schemes of the Marcelli and the Catonians. The tactics of those groups, as we have seen, had been to force Pompey into positions where he must either strain relations with Cæsar or adopt postures that would render him vulnerable to propaganda assault. Curio now exploited that advantage from the other side. His advocacy of agrarian legislation and other popular bills put him

[97] Hirtius, *BG*, 8.50.4.

[98] Cæl. *Ad Fam.* 8.9.5, 8.8.9.

in a position to bargain politically with Julius Cæsar. And by taking Cæsar's part on the matter of the consular provinces, he would aggravate tensions between the dynasts and further impair their relationship. As we shall see, Curio's excessive and deliberate stridency supplied a key element in hastening the break, which neither Cæsar nor Pompey had contemplated a few months before.[99]

And what of Pompeius Magnus? Through the end of the year 51, he had carefully kept faith with his triumviral partner. And no evidence suggests that he was eager to sever relations in the early months of 50. But his situation grew increasingly complicated, and the varied interests with which he was connected appeared increasingly incompatible. Pompey's long-cherished aim for acceptance by the *nobilitas* seemed close to realization. But many of his aristocratic friends balked at collaboration with Julius Cæsar; their efforts aimed at splitting Pompey off from his ally. Other senatorial groups, hostile to both dynasts, were forcing Pompey into a corner, thus exposing the fragile character of the coalition, which he had hoped to hold together. Internal aristocratic rivalries continued to plague such combinations, as they did throughout Roman history. And Pompey was further embarrassed when Cæsar elected not to stand for the consulship in 50; the proconsul sought added time in Gaul and a postponement of his *ratio absentis*. Pompey would cooperate in finding pretexts for a longer stay in Gaul. But his own public pronouncements made it awkward in the extreme for him to approve an extended tenure that would go beyond the elections of 49 and violate the spirit, if not the letter, of the law of the ten tribunes. The requests of the proconsul must have made more plausible the propaganda of Cato and the Marcelli: Cæsar's aims were limitless and incompatible with the constitution. Another factor added to Pompey's uneasiness: the activities of Curio and Paullus on Cæsar's behalf. Curio had long been a critic of Pompey, and his attacks now increased in frequency and intensity. And Paullus nursed an inherited enmity toward the general; his hostility too was unabating. Cæsar, like Pompey, felt the need of expanding his connections with accommodating aristocrats. But, as happened so often in other political combines, the addition of new allies hampered rather than fortified the collaboration.

A variety of elements, it is clear, contributed to the growing tensions in the dynasts' alliance. By the spring of 50 those tensions were soon to burst the restraints of civility and undermine the convenience of concord. But another fact should also now be clear. One cannot divide Roman politics into Cæsarians and Pompeians even as late as the year 50. Several groups

[99] Cf. Pompey's complaint in Cæl. *Ad Fam.* 8.11.3: *ait Curionem quærere discordias*; a revealing passage too often passed over in discussions on these events.

and groupings, each promoting its own interests and pursuing its own tactics, share responsibility for the aggravation of conflict. Senatorial conservatives helped force the issue. The Catonians threatened Cæsar and harassed Pompey. The Marcelli and their allies embarrassed the coalition, vexing Pompey and challenging Cæsar's privileges. Pompey's aristocratic friends, like Metellus Scipio, distrusted Cæsar and urged Pompey to choose between them, a choice he much preferred not to make. Curio adopted a *popularis* line, skirting the other combines, but advocated Cæsarian interests while assaulting Pompey, in order to widen a breach between the dynasts. Cæsar himself pressed for further *honores*, which strained Pompey's patience, and cultivated *amici*, which heightened Pompey's suspicions. And Pompey allowed himself to be drawn into statements that limited his flexibility and into combines that splintered his loyalties. Once again the complexities of Roman politics need to be reiterated and reemphasized. The dualism enforced by civil war cannot be read back even to the very year which preceded that conflict.

We are in a position now to understand the course of events in 50. March 1 came, and with it the scheduled debate on consular provinces. But Curio interposed his veto, forbidding discussion of the matter. The proffered excuse is not recorded. Very possibly, Curio urged the priority of his own bills, which had still to be examined and judged.[100] Postponement of the provincial debate served Cæsar's needs and helped to polarize opinion in Rome. It was also in Curio's interest: he could use the occasion to publicize his popular program. Retaliation came from the conservatives. Quite apart from the issue of Cæsar and the Gauls, they frowned upon a broad legislative scheme with radical overtones. Hence, the aristocracy limited Curio's opportunities: his effort to intercalate had already been rejected; now the senate reduced the number of comitial days on which he might offer his bills.[101] Obviously, the struggle over Cæsar's provinces was not the only item exercising public attention. An old-fashioned contest over *popularis* legislation still held the political stage.

But Cæsar's enemies would not countenance an indefinite delay of provincial distribution. Curio had the cooperation of L. Æmilius Paullus.[102] But the other consul, C. Marcellus, did not permit matters to drag on. In March or April he took the lead in demanding decisive action. Cæsar's commission, he maintained, was drawing to a conclusion; it was perfectly legitimate to

[100] Cic. *Ad Att.* 6.2.6: *habebam acta urbana usque ad Non. Mart.; e quibus intellegebam Curionis nostri constantia omnia potius actum iri quam de provinciis.*

[101] Cæl. *Ad Fam.* 8.11.1: *Curio . . . cui omnibus rationibus comitiales dies eripiebantur.* On the intercalation, see Cæl. *Ad Fam.* 8.6.5; Dio, 40.62.1–2.

[102] Cic. *Ad Att.* 6.3.4; Cæl. *Ad Fam.* 8.11.1; see the sound arguments of Lacey, *Historia*, 10 (1961): 327–328.

designate successors and provide for direct supersession.[103] Procrastination had caused swelling resentment. And now Pompey could no longer evade the issue. Goaded into delivering an opinion, he attempted, as in 51, to strike a balance between the conflicting pressures operating on him. Extension of the Gallic command beyond the consular elections of 49 could not be condoned. But Pompey still hoped to retain his ties with the proconsul. If Cæsar wished more time to complete the organization of the conquered province, he should have it. Pompey proposed an additional seven months: Cæsar could remain in Gaul until November, but must depart thereafter. It was a reasonable offer, eminently fair to his ally, so Pompey thought. It set a definite terminus to the command, a move that would undermine conservative propaganda. And it allotted Cæsar extra time to complete needed arrangements in Gaul. Perhaps Pompey might yet be able to save his scheme for a grand coalition.[104]

The prospect filled C. Curio with alarm. A compromise that might reinforce the combine of the dynasts would seriously impair his plans. Curio was determined to establish his own political base on the wreckage of that combine. It can now be understood why the tribune suddenly abandoned all his legislative proposals and concentrated his activity on resisting this scheme. If Pompey and Cæsar should solidify their cooperation, there would be much less room for Curio to maneuver. Hence, he not only attacked the proposal with vehemence, claiming that Cæsar would defend his veto, but indulged in loud

[103] Appian, *BC*, 2.27: Κλαύδιος δ' εἰσηγεῖτο πέμπειν Καίσαρι διαδόχους ἐπὶ τὰ ἔθνη; καὶ γὰρ 'έληγεν ὁ χρόνος. Appian's chronology is not altogether trustworthy; he includes events and proposals that properly belong later in the year. But there is no reason to doubt that Marcellus was pressing for Cæsar's recall in the spring. Cf., on this, Hardy, *Some Problems,* pp. 169–172; Rice Holmes, *Rom. Rep.*, II:309–310.

[104] Cælius transmits the information, though he is skeptical of Pompey's sincerity; *Ad Fam.* 8.11.3: *in unam causam omnis contentio coniecta est, de provinciis; in quam adhuc incubuisse cum senatu Pompeius videtur, ut Cæsar Id. Novemb. decedat . . . Pompeius, tamquam Cæsarem non impugnet, sed, quod illi æquum putet, constituat.* The Ides of November must refer to the year 50. If they were still nineteen months away, Cælius would surely have mentioned the fact. Suggestion that November 49 is meant depends on the a priori and unfounded assumption that Cæsar's legal term in Gaul extended to March 49; as, e.g., Mommsen, *Rechtsfrage*, p. 53; Hardy, *Some Problems,* pp. 194–198; Rice Holmes, *CQ*, 10 (1916): 49–56; T. Frank, *CR*, 33 (1919): 68–69; M. Cary, *CR*, 33 (1919): 109; Elton, *JRS*, 36 (1946): 30–32. Adcock, *CQ*, 26 (1932): 23–26, sees November 13 as the terminal date specified in the *lex Pompeia Licinia.* But it is mentioned nowhere else than in this passage, and Cælius' language does not support the contention. No more plausible is the theory that Pompey proposed deferment of the consular elections until after November 50, to permit Cæsar's candidacy for 49; so Stone, *CQ*, 22 (1928): 200; Balsdon, *JRS*, 29 (1939): 173–174. There is nothing in the sources to indicate any discussion on electoral postponement–nor that Cæsar was any longer interested in his own candidacy for 49.

verbal assaults on Pompey, including a heavy indictment of his second consulship in 55.[105]

The assumption that Curio was here serving as Cæsar's mouthpiece misconstrues the situation. The proconsul was no more anxious for a precipitate break than was Pompey, That Cæsar preferred a conciliatory policy is demonstrated by his actions in the following month. The senate decreed that each of the dynasts supply one legion to be sent to the East to ward off the Parthian menace. Pompey agreed, and he designated as his contribution the legion that he had lent Cæsar two years before. In effect, this meant that the Gallic army would be supplying both legions. Yet Cæsar made no objection, complying with the request and displaying his good faith.[106] He cannot have approved Curio's vituperative onslaughts against Pompey. And there is further evidence. At this same time, Cæsar's agent Cornelius Balbus had to expostulate with Curio on another matter, lest he act against the proconsul's interests. There was considerable public doubt about the sincerity of Curio's representations on Cæsar's behalf.[107] Quite properly did Pompey complain that Curio was stirring up quarrels where none need exist.[108] The tribune was determined to shatter any effort that might hold Cæsar and Pompey together.[109]

Curio successfully exacerbated tensions. Pompey's proposal that Cæsar withdraw from Gaul in November was blocked by his efforts and made to seem an aggressive act against the proconsul. Like Clodius before him, Curio claimed Cæsar's backing while he engaged in virulent criticism of Pompey. He knew the issue on which the dynasts' alliance was most vulnerable, and he hammered it home: the *ratio absentis*. The tribune insisted that Cæsar be allowed to remain in Gaul and to exercise his candidacy in absence when it was appropri-

[105] Cæl. *Ad Fam.* 8.11.3: *Curio omnia potius subire constituit quam id pati; ceteras suas abiecit actiones . . . accipitur* [Pompey] *satis male a Curione, et totus eius secundus consulatus exagitatur.* The consulship is sometimes taken to be that of 52. Appian, *BC*, 2.27, does say that Curio exploited public hostility against Pompey for his bribery prosecutions, evidently a reference to the judicial activity of 52; so Wistrand, *Sallust on Judicial Murders*, pp. 32–33. But Cælius specifies the "second consulship." And the electoral machinations and bullying tactics of 55 also gave considerable scope for criticism. Curio was taking up a line espoused by the Catonians and others in the mid-50s.

[106] Hirtius, *BG*, 8.54; Dio, 40.65.1–4; Appian, *BC*, 2.29; Plut. *Cæs.* 29.3–4; *Pomp.* 56.3; cf. Cæs. *BC*, 1.4, 1.32; Cic. *Ad Fam.* 2.17.5.

[107] Cæl. *Ad Fam.* 8.11.2: *Nam cum Curione vehementer locutus est* [Balbus], *et eum, si aliter fecisset, iniuriam Cæsari facturum dixit; tum eius fidem in suspicionem adduxit.* The issue here concerned a *supplicatio* for Cicero's achievements in Cilicia.

[108] Cæl. *Ad Fam.* 8.11.3.

[109] Cf. Vell. Pat. 2.48.5: *saluberrimas coalescentis condiciones pacis, quas et Cæsar iustissimo animo postulabat et Pompeius æquo recipiebat, discussit ac rupit.*

ate, presumably in 49. Pompey consented to the first but could not back down on his opposition to the second. Curio pressed the matter in full knowledge of that fact and (no doubt deliberately) roused fears that if his veto were overriden, Cæsar would defend him with force.[110] The belligerence was surely unwelcome to Cæsar, but Curio had preempted his options by advocating his ends. Once again, the example of Clodius in 58 may well have served as a model.

The Marcelli conveniently took up the bait and played into Curio's hands. From opposite sides and for different reasons they, in fact, shared the same goal: the breakup of the dynastic coalition. The Marcelli hoped to dislodge Pompey from Cæsar; Curio, to dislodge Cæsar from Pompey.[111] The tribune's obstructive tactics reinforced the conservatives' claim that Cæsar paid no heed to senatorial opinion. In May or June they resumed the political offensive. C. Marcellus, we may be sure, initiated the activity. It was his cousin M. Marcellus, consul in the previous year, who now delivered the motion in the senate: tribunes who blocked senatorial disposition of the provinces should be severely dealt with. Justification for this move rested presumably on the *senatus consultum* of 51 that branded such obstruction as inimical to the interests of the state. The resolution had, of course, been vetoed, but the Marcelli did not allow that detail to stand in their way.[112] Curio's *intercessio* against provincial discussions was now under fire and with it Cæsar's claim to an extension of his *ratio absentis*. On this question the Marcelli could expect to carry Pompey with them and thereby to force an overt fissure in the coalition. They might also hope to call Curio's bluff about Cæsar's defense of his veto.

But the Marcelli had miscalculated the tenor of senatorial opinion. Despite the intrigues among principal aristocratic interests, the bulk of the *curia* preferred not to see matters pushed to a confrontation. It is too easy to overlook the attitudes of the lesser nobility and the *pedarii* who, in fact, constituted the major proportion of the House. Many of them were the first of their families to enjoy senatorial privileges. They showed no desire to be drawn into a struggle that might provoke military intervention and the destruction of their newly won station. Cæsar, it could be argued, had been awarded the *ratio absentis* by a law of the people. Extension of the privilege seemed of no great moment. Why cater to the wishes of an extremist group, which

[110] Cæl. *Ad Fam.* 8.11.3: *valde autem non vult* [Pompey], *et plane timet, Cæsarem consulem designari prius quam exercitum et provinciam tradiderit . . . hoc tibi dico, si omnibus rebus prement Curionem, Cæsar defendet intercessorem.*

[111] Cf. Balbus' remark in March 49 after the break was complete; Cic. *Ad Att.* 8.15a.1: *Cæsarem et Pompeium perfidia hominum distractos.*

[112] Cæl. *Ad Fam.* 8.13.2. For the resolution of 51, see Cæl. *Ad Fam.* 8.8.6.

might drive the proconsul to desperation and run the risk of bloodshed? The senatorial majority was not to be rushed into hasty action by belligerent conservatives. When Marcellus proposed the censure of Curio, the motion was overwhelmingly rejected. The House now put itself on record as approving postponement of the provincial question and an absent candidacy for Cæsar in 49.[113]

Pompeius Magnus was nonplussed. He had been maneuvered into an intractable stance on the *ratio absentis* by Cæsar's enemies. And now he saw that stance rejected by a large senatorial majority. Assaulted by popular leaders like Curio and rebuffed by moderate sentiment in the *curia*, he found himself gradually isolated on the "right," which had long been dominated by his *inimici*. It is not hard to imagine that the illness into which Pompey now sank was in part psychosomatic.[114] The Marcelli had failed to discredit C. Curio, and had been decisively outvoted in the senate. But they achieved a more foreboding aim. By forcing the issue in stark terms they opened a public split between the dynasts which could not readily be healed. Curio's tactics had been shrewd and masterful. His actions were now vindicated by a vote of the senate. And his aggressive stance had helped drive Cæsar's claims into a position where they could no longer be regarded as compatible with Pompeian pronouncements. The alliance of Pompey and Cæsar was sorely strained and on the verge of collapse. By the late summer of 50 civil war could actually be regarded as a possibility.[115] That development was not fostered or desired by the dynasts themselves, and certainly not by the senatorial majority, let alone the Roman populace. The division had been sedulously cultivated by Curio on the one side and the Marcelli on the other. Not that those individuals aimed at armed conflict–which would be as detrimental to their goals as to anyone else's. But their intrigues effected polarization of the political community. It was the critical step toward Rome's fratricidal struggle.

THE BREAK

Events in the late summer and fall increased the difficulties. Two censors entered office–not the most congenial of colleagues: L. Calpurnius Piso and

[113] Cæl. *Ad Fam.* 8.13.2: *primaque M. Marcelli sententia pronuntiata esset, qui agendum cum tribunis plebis censebat, frequens senatus in alia omnia iit . . . transierant illuc, rationem eius habendam, qui neque exercitum neque provincias traderet.* Also Cic. *Ad Att.* 7.7.5. Cælius had accurately predicted the attitude of the senate: they did not wish to bring matters to a crisis; *Ad Fam.* 8.11.3: *nostri porro, quos tu bene nosti, ad extremem certamen rem deducere non audent.*

[114] Cæl. *Ad Fam.* 8.13.2; Vell. Pat. 2.48.2; Plut. *Pomp.* 57.1; Appian, *BC*, 2.28.

[115] Cæl. *Ad Fam.* 8.14.4.

Ap. Claudius Pulcher. Piso, now a senior statesman, was Cæsar's father-in-law and a man of independent political tastes. The wily Claudius had recently obtained links through marriage to Pompeius and to the Catonians, and he counted Cæsar's bitter enemy Domitius Ahenobarbus among his close friends. Piso proved to be relatively inactive, unwilling to become enmeshed in the approaching struggle. But Appius exercised his office with vigor and without discretion. Several senators were expelled from their seats by that censor, among them the future historian Sallust and C. Ateius Capito, an opponent of the triumvirs during his tribunate of 55.[116] In addition, Appius quarreled with several other young aristocrats, engaging P. Dolabella and M. Cælius Rufus in the courts, and attempting in vain to oust C. Curio from the senate. In the latter effort the otherwise lethargic Piso emerged to resist his colleague; Curio obtained assistance also from the consul L. Paullus; Appius' censure was thwarted. Ap. Claudius had taken his job seriously, rather too seriously. The blustering activity of his censorship earned him little credit. Appius' victims, or intended victims, edged toward the camp of Julius Cæsar. The proconsul of Gaul began to collect some of Rome's more talented young intellectuals and politicians.[117]

The elections produced mixed results. Cæsar's friend and former legate, Ser. Sulpicius Galba, fell through in the consular *comitia*. L. Cornelius Lentulus Crus and C. Marcellus, the third consecutive member of that family to hold the office, were returned. Neither would look kindly upon Cæsar's aspirations. Of the eight prætors elected, some, at least, were expected to favor the Cæsarian cause.[118] But the bulk of the higher magistrates were evidently hostile. The tribunate might be of greater importance, as Curio had shown. Cæsar could use a strong man in the office—one he could trust. M. Antonius was the proconsul's choice, an experienced officer in Gaul and scion of an influential family. Antony entered still another electoral contest in that year, one of less practical significance though of considerable symbolic value: a place in the augurate to succeed the recently deceased Q. Hortensius. As was noted earlier, Cato's brother-in-law Domitius Ahenobarbus coveted the post; a challenge from the much younger Antony was regarded as a blatant test of political strength for the Cæsarian faction. In this election men voted along political

[116] Cic. *De Div.* 1.29; Ps. Sallust, *Ep. ad Cæs.* 4.2; Ps. Cic. *Inv. in Sall.* 16; Dio, 40.63.3–4.

[117] On the judicial contests with Dolabella and Cælius, see above, pp. 353–355. Appius' actions helped solidify Cælius' resolve to opt for Cæsar; Cæl. *Ad Fam.* 8.17.1. On the clash with Curio, see Dio, 40.63.5. Ateius Capito also became an admirer of Cæsar; Cic. *Ad Fam.* 13.29.6.

[118] Cic. *Ad Att.* 6.8.2. The names are not given. Very likely, M. Lepidus, brother of L. Paullus, and A. Allienus and L. Roscius Fabatus, who had sponsored an agrarian bill for Cæsar in 55; cf. Shackleton Bailey, *Cicero's Letters*, III:273.

lines and not in accordance with familial obligations. Cæsar himself arrived in northern Italy to solicit colonists and municipalities on Antony's behalf. No effort was spared. Heavy contributions from Gaul financed the campaign; vigorous, even excessive, canvassing occurred in Rome by men like Cælius and Curio. Antony was a fortunate beneficiary, obtaining both the tribunician and augural posts.[119] Cæsar had demonstrated that he was not without electoral influence—when he set his mind to it. And the augural election, of unprecedented character in many ways, exemplified the polarity that was now about to shatter conventional Roman politics.

After midsummer of 50, positions had been hardened, and events progressed irreversibly toward cataclysm. Mutual suspicion, carefully implanted by extremists on both sides, rendered any genuine communication between Cæsar and Pompey impossible. Pompey now asserted that Cæsar's consular aspirations were unacceptable until he yielded up his army and provinces. Pompey could argue, with some justice, that he had made several adjustments in the past for his ally's sake, even offering another seven months of command as late as April 50. But he drew the line at the *ratio absentis*. Still another concession would be an affront to his own *dignitas*. Cæsar was not the only man who held his honor dear. The determined stance of Pompey found no favor with the proconsul of Gaul, who could only regard it as obstinacy and as a sign that his erstwhile collaborator had joined with the most rabid anti-Cæsarians.[120] Rumors of military preparations began to plague the city. Some spread reports that Cæsar planned to bring four legions into northern Italy. And Pompey, it was said, might join his forces in Spain.[121] Talk of civil war was in the air.[122]

In July or August, Curio, evidently with Cæsar's blessing, offered what appeared to be a way out of the impasse: both of the *imperatores* should dismiss their armies in order to relieve Rome of unnecessary anxiety.[123] The proposal naturally appealed to moderate sentiment in the senate and populace. But in the atmosphere of suspicion, Pompey and conservative aristocrats found it unacceptable. To their minds, the Cæsarians were offering an informal

[119] Cæl. *Ad Fam.* 8.14.1; Hirtius, *BG*, 8.50; Cic. *Phil.* 2.4; Plut. *Ant.* 5.1. At least one other Cæsarian gained election to a tribunate: Q. Cassius Longinus, a former quæstor of Pompey's; Cic. *Ad Att.* 6.8.2, 7.3.5.

[120] Cæl. *Ad Fam.* 8.14.2: *Cn. Pompeius constituit non pati C. Cæsarem consulem aliter fieri, nisi exercitum et provincias tradiderit: Cæsari autem persuasum est se salvum esse non posse, si ab exercitu recesserit.* Cf. Cæsar's later assessment, *BC*, 1.4.4: *totum se* [Pompey] *ab eius amicitia averterat et cum communibus inimicis in gratiam redierat.* Also Cæs. *BC*, 1.7.

[121] Cic. *Ad Att.* 6.8.2, 6.9.5, 7.1.1.

[122] Cæl. *Ad Fam.* 8.14.2-4; Cic. *Ad Att.* 7.1.3.

[123] Cæl. *Ad Fam.* 8.14.2; Hirtius, *BG*, 8.52; Vell. Pat. 2.48.1; Appian, *BC*, 2.27-28; Dio, 40.62.3-4.

settlement that violated statutory law. Cæsar's term was expiring (or had expired); Pompey had gained a five-year renewal in 52. Acceptance of the proposal would mean that Pompey's was far the greater concession. He had made his share of concessions in the past; there would be no further compromise of his *dignitas*. The rejection was inevitable–and was, no doubt, anticipated by Cæsar and Curio. With much of the moderate opinion in Rome, they would now have a propaganda advantage.[124]

The *boni* had held off their formal attacks after April. They too were maneuvering for propaganda advantage. Cæsar could have until November in Gaul, as Pompey had requested. That was generous, so it might be claimed, more than generous: Cæsar had ample opportunity to wind up affairs in Gaul. After the Ides of November, political offensive could resume–and with greater apparent justification. C. Marcellus moved that successors be appointed to take over the Gallic provinces, labeling Cæsar as a brigand and urging that he be declared a *hostis* if the senate's will were ignored. But resistance emerged once more. Curio, in the waning days of his tribunate, still had cards to play. Since the issue of Cæsar's *imperium* had been raised again in the House, Curio managed to frame a formal resolution embodying the line he had been advocating for months: both dynasts should resign their commands. M. Antonius and L. Piso lent strong support. The motion endeavored to circumvent Marcellus' aggressive proposal and to appeal to the rank and file of the Roman senate. Curio knew the general temper of his colleagues. The *patres* had in the spring overriden an effort to censure the tribune and had ratified Cæsar's desires in order to prevent confrontation and crisis. The pacific attitude remained unchanged in December. For that we have the testimony of Cicero, recently returned from Cilicia and everywhere testing public opinion. Aristocratic leaders were divided, so he reports, but sentiment otherwise was plain: senators, *equites, publicani,* farmers, *municipales,* all craved peace; any political settlement, regardless of legal niceties, was preferable to armed conflict. Those groups had little to gain and much to lose from a general conflagration.[125]

Curio's proposal struck most responsive chords. Given an opportunity to vote, the senate made its wishes abundantly clear. Unconcerned with the legal termini that exercise scholarly disputants, they carried the motion by a vote of three hundred seventy to twenty-two: Cæsar and Pompey should both resign their commissions and discharge their armies. Not only had the *patres*

[124] Appian, *BC,* 2.28, reports that Pompey actually did promise to give up his *imperium* before the time of its expiration. The move is nowhere else recorded. If true, it suggests that Pompey was attempting to counter Cæsarian propaganda by showing good faith. Curio attacked him for hypocrisy: a promise was of no value; dismissal of the army must take place immediately. To that demand Pompey remained impervious.

[125] Cic. *Ad Att.* 7.3.5, 7.5.4, 7.6.2, 7.7.5.

spoken decisively, but the populace too expressed its relief; Curio was hailed as a hero and a savior.[126] The tribune's strategy seemed to have borne fruit. He had successfully isolated Pompey, the Marcelli, and the Catonians as the sole obstacles to a peaceful arrangement and had markedly enhanced his own prestige in the bargain. The political influence of the conservatives appeared on the verge of collapse, and Pompey was about to be dragged down with them.

Politics, and nothing more, lit the fuse for this explosion. The *boni* could hardly acquiesce in this decision without consigning themselves to political oblivion. They had staked too much on the issue of Cæsar's recall to accept a rebuff with equanimity. The same was doubly true of Pompeius Magnus. Outmaneuvered and obstinate since the spring, he stood firm on principle. The senatorial vote, if unchallenged, would entail for Pompey considerable loss of face, perhaps even collapse of his hard-won prestige. Those facts must be understood if sense if to be made of the swift and aggressive acts that followed. Marcellus refused to heed the voice of the senatorial majority. A *senatus consultum* was advisory counsel, not a legal enactment. The consul had responsibility for the safety of Italy. Marcellus seized upon (or generated) rumors that Cæsar was on the point of invading Italy. With that as justification or pretext, he marched outside the *pomerium* and entrusted defense of the city to Pompey, authorizing him to employ the two legions under his command and to recruit others as necessary. Joining him were his cousin, also a C. Marcellus, and Lentulus Crus, the two consuls-elect, both virulent anti-Cæsarians. M. Cato, who had steadfastly opposed Curio, also approved—or so we may assume. And there need no longer be surprise that Pompey accepted the commission without reluctance.[127] The political future he had carefully sketched out for himself had crumbled in recent months. To salvage his *dignitas* required unbending resistance, whatever the cost.

Cæsar had not intended to push matters to the brink of war. The proposals of Curio were calculated to win senatorial approval of a peaceful compromise, for which the proconsul, of course, would gain the credit. But the Pompeians could not afford a reconciliation in which they would be reduced to the second rank. The letters of Cicero in December 50 expose the attitudes of the two sides. Cæsar hoped for negotiations and a settlement. Avoidance of war—given the sentiment of the senatorial majority, the upper classes, and the populace generally—could only have been to his advantage. Hence, Balbus arranged a meeting with Metellus Scipio, evidently in an attempt to resolve

[126] Appian, *BC*, 2.30; Plut. *Pomp.* 58.3–5; *Cæs.* 30.1–2.

[127] Hirtius, *BG*, 8.55.1; Dio, 40.64.4, 40.66.1–2; Appian, *BC*, 2.31; Plut. *Pomp.* 58.6–59.1; *Cato*, 51.5; *Ant.* 5.2; Orosius, 6.15.1; cf. Meyer, *Cæsars Monarchie*, pp. 271–275.

differences. And Hirtius too returned from the Cæsarian camp to organize private discussions. A large number of senators frowned on Pompey's taking over the two legions in Campania. The articulate classes preferred any settlement to civil war.[128] But Pompey was adamant. He spoke of nothing but war, even alleged that Hirtius' failure to visit him personally was proof of Cæsar's estrangement and bellicosity. He would no longer truckle to any request. Cæsar's consular aspirations he now rejected absolutely, whether or not the proconsul would yield up his army.[129] The Pompeians needed civil war to preserve their preeminence. Cæsar may not have wanted it, but he was prepared for it.[130]

Pompey's intransigence must have been reported to Cæsar by Hirtius before the middle of December. It is difficult to believe that the proconsul entertained any serious hopes for peace thereafter. Curio completed his last day as tribune with a bitter denunciation of Pompey, Marcellus, and the consuls-designate, and hastened to join Cæsar, urging him to prepare for war without delay.[131] Curio's successor, M. Antonius, took up the cudgels. On December 21, he delivered a lengthy tirade against Pompey, condemning his entire career, and openly issued threats of armed force.[132] With the new consuls due to take office on January 1, Cæsar knew that a declaration of war could not be far off. It was important to give himself every propaganda advantage in order to sway the minds of the uncommitted. Cæsar's supporters transmitted his willingness to give up provinces and armies and retain just two legions with Illyricum and Cisalpine Gaul, or even just Illyricum and one legion.[133] But the proconsul would brook no compromise of his *dignitas*. Curio was dispatched to Rome with a message stating Cæsar's position unambiguously:

[128] Cic. *Ad Att.* 7.4.2, 7.5.4, 7.6.2, 7.7.5. On Cæsar's efforts to negotiate, see also Hirtius, *BG*, 8.55.2.

[129] Cic. *Ad. Att.* 7.4.2: *de re publica autem ita mecum locutus est quasi non dubium bellum haberemus; nihil ad spem concordiæ; Ad Att.* 7.8.4–5: *quod quæris ecquæ spes pacificationis sit, quantum ex Pompei multo et accurato sermone perspexi, ne voluntas quidem est . . . non modo non expetere pacem istam sed etiam timere visus est.*

[130] Cf. Cicero's comment, written in retrospect; *Ad Fam.* 9.6.2: *vidi enim . . . nostros amicos cupere bellum; hunc autem non tam cupere, quam non timere.*

[131] Appian, *BC*, 2.31–32; Dio, 40.66.5.

[132] Cic. *Ad Att.* 7.8.5: *Antoni contionem habitam X Kal. Jan., in qua erat accusatio Pompei usque a toga pura, querela de damnatis, terror armorum*; cf. Plut. *Ant.* 5.2; *Cæs.* 30.2–3; *Pomp.* 59.2–chronologically inaccurate.

[133] Appian, *BC*, 2.32; Plut. *Cæs.* 31.1; Suet. *Iul.* 29.2; Vell. Pat. 2.49.4. Appian's statement that Pompey was willing to accede to this proposal, but was deterred by the consuls, may be legitimately doubted. It fits with no other evidence on Pompey's behavior and attitude at this juncture. Plutarch dates the proposal after the senatorial meetings in early January–probably wrongly; cf. Rice Holmes, *Rom. Rep.*, II:331–333.

he was still willing to resign his command if all other commanders would do likewise; but he would not endure any disparity in their forces.[134] He had prepared the ground carefully for self-justification.[135]

The remainder of the record is a sorry affair. *Pax*, so ardently desired by so many, became nonetheless a casualty of politics. Senatorial debate began promptly on January 1. The conservatives were in no mood to tolerate further delay. Having drawn Pompey into their camp, they hastened to authorize acts of war before the political situation slipped from their grasp. Cæsar's final messages were delivered to the *patres* by Curio. Antony and Q. Cassius urged them upon the House. Conflict ensued, for the consuls refused to put a motion along those lines. As they knew full well, the rank and file would still find it attractive. But they could not prevent senatorial discussion on the political situation generally. Sentiment in the *curia* was still pacific, leaning toward compromise. But events had proceeded too far. Pompey had already assumed command of forces in Italy. L. Lentulus and Metellus Scipio made it clear that if the senate opted for compromise, the consuls would go their own way in any event; war was certain; better to have a firm senatorial resolution and unite the populace. Moderate suggestions were overborne. The *pedarii* could not stem the tide when war loomed and Cæsar stood at the frontier. It was a classic example of a small minority stampeding the House through half-truths, slogans, and threats. The *senatus consulta* passed in the first week of January 49 were tantamount to a declaration of war.[136]

Decision was at last rendered on the Gallic provinces. The senate ruled that Cæsar must give up his post on or before a certain date of their fixing, else he would be judged an enemy of the state.[137] Sources do not specify the date; perhaps it was yet to be named. But the *curia* moved within days to implement the decision. Several resolutions followed. Cæsar was stripped

[134] Cæs. *BC*, 1.9.3; Suet. *Iul.* 29.2; Appian, *BC*, 2.32; Vell. Pat. 2.49.4; Dio, 41.1.1–4; cf. Gelzer, *Cæsar*, p. 190. It was this message which Cicero branded as menacing and bitter; *Ad Fam.* 16.11.2: *minacis ad senatum et acerbas litteras miserat.*

[135] On December 27, Cicero canvassed various possibilities: perhaps the senate might yet allow Cæsar's candidacy in absence, or he will himself give up his army and return to campaign in person; if not, he may allow the elections to go on without him, or attempt to obstruct them through tribunes. And Cicero does not rule out the likelihood that Cæsar will invade Italy if his candidacy is rejected; *Ad Att.* 7.9.2. It is a revealing reflection of the uncertainty in which Rome found herself at the end of the year.

[136] The sequence of debates and resolutions is given by Cæs. *BC*, 1.1–7. The secondary sources essentially corroborate: Appian, *BC*, 2.32–33; Plut. *Cæs.* 30.2–31.2; *Pomp.* 59.2–4; *Ant.* 5.2–4; Dio, 41.1–3. There is no cause to question the reported facts, though the account, of course, has a decided Cæsarian flavor.

[137] Cæs. *BC*, 1.2.6: *uti ante certam diem Cæsar exercitum dimittat: si non faciat, eum adversus rem publicam facturum videri*; Suet. *Iul.* 30.1; Plut. *Cæs.* 30.2; Dio, 41.3.4.

of his *ratio absentis*; if he wished to stand for the consulship, he would have to return as a *privatus*.[138] Domitius Ahenobarbus received official designation as Cæsar's successor in Gallia Transalpina.[139] Antony and Cassius, of course, interposed their veto. But this time the *intercessio* was ignored. A state of emergency existed, so it was asserted. The senate had recourse to a *senatus consultum ultimum*: consuls and other magistrates were empowered to take all steps necessary for public safety. The Cæsarian tribunes, along with Cælius and Curio, dramatized their plight and contributed to Cæsar's propaganda by fleeing to his camp.[140] There was no turning back. The blustering of Cato, the Marcelli, Lentulus, and Scipio, plus the menacing presence of Pompey's forces, had convinced the *patres*, if not of Cæsar's wickedness, at least of the inevitability of conflict. Cæsar required no further pretext. On the tenth or eleventh of January he crossed the Rubicon.

PRETEXTS AND MOTIVES

Rehearsal of the dismal events of late 50 does not produce a heartening picture. But it is possible now to draw more satisfactory conclusions about the origins and motivation for civil war. Notions of inevitability on the one hand or deliberate and lengthy calculation on the other are best discarded.

Did Cæsar march at the head of a social revolution? Cælius claimed in August 50 that all who lived in fear or without hope would join the proconsul's cause.[141] Cicero offered an equally sweeping judgment in December: Cæsar commanded the loyalty of desperate men, the entire youth of Rome, those condemned in the courts, stigmatized by the censors, or oppressed by debt; and, worse, the ruined *plebs urbana*.[142] The orator raised fearsome specters: cancellation of debts, recall of exiles, proscriptions, and devastation. Cæsar led a band of starved and impoverished scoundrels.[143]

The dire forecast, of course, proved largely false. But not only that—the

[138] Vell. Pat. 2.49.4: *privatus in urbem veniret et se in petitione consulatus suffragiis populi Romani committeret decrevere;* Florus, 2.13.15–16.

[139] Cæs. *BC*, 1.6.5–6; Suet. *Iul.* 34; Appian, *BC*, 2.32; Livy, *Per.* 109. Considius Nonianus was appointed to the Cisalpina; Cic. *Ad Fam.* 16.12.3; *Ad Att.* 8.11b.2.

[140] Cic. *Ad Fam.* 16.11.2; Cæs. *BC*, 1.5.5; Dio, 41.3.2–3; Appian, *BC*, 2.33; Plut. *Ant.* 5.4; *Cæs.* 31.2; Suet. *Iul.* 30.1; Livy, *Per.* 109.

[141] Cæl. *Ad Fam.* 8.14.3.

[142] Cic. *Ad Att.* 7.3.5: *omnis damnatos, omnis ignominia adfectos . . . omnem fere iuventutem, omnem illam urbanam ac perditam plebem . . . omnis qui ære alieno premantur.*

[143] References are many in the letters of early 49. See, e.g., Cic. *Ad Att.* 7.11.1: **χρεῶν ἀποκοπάς, φυγάδων καθόδους**; 7.13.1, 8.11.4, 9.1.3, 9.7.5: *egestates tot egentissimorum hominum*; 9.10.7: **νέκυιαν**; 9.12.3: *rerum novarum cupidi*; 9.18.2: *o copias desperatas*; 9.19.1: *perditis*; 10.8.2: *impetum in privatorum pecunias et exsulum reditum et tabulas novas et turpissimorum honores.*

analysis was erroneous. Cæsar did win the support of men who had suffered adverse judgments from the courts or the censors. But that has no relevance for the lower classes. The men involved were political exiles, mostly victims of Pompeian legislation in 52 or enemies of the censors of 50. These were aristocratic politicians, not down and out members of the proletariate. They would be useful as adornments of the Cæsarian faction.[144] That the *urban plebs* looked to Cæsar for salvation receives no support in the evidence. As it did in 63, the city populace preferred peace and order to violent disruption. Hence, their enthusiastic accolades for Curio and his proposal for mutual disarmament.[145] Despite Cæsar's victories in Italy, he faced hostile popular demonstrations in the theater in the spring of 49.[146]

Talk of debt cancellation was empty. Cæsar was not one to advocate *tabulæ novæ*. The creditor classes knew it all along. The *publicani* favored Cæsar from the beginning. *Equites* generally had hoped for a pacific resolution, but after the outbreak of hostilities they moved to the Cæsarian side, as did most of Italy's municipal leadership.[147] Cæsar dealt with the debt problem intelligently—and conservatively. By early 48, Cælius could maintain that the moneylenders alone were happy with Cæsar.[148] The exaggeration is patent. But more than a grain of truth lies therein. The crossing of the Rubicon in no way signaled a revolt of the masses.

The men who followed Julius Cæsar into Italy were, of course, the veterans of the Gallic wars. That constituted the sole common bond, and it proved sufficient. Personal courage and magnetism won the proconsul fanatical loyalty.[149] And he had been generous in bestowal of rewards.[150] His officers and legates were drawn from lesser senatorial families, the municipal aristocracy, and the equestrian class. These were not men eager to destroy the existing order. The troops themselves expected land grants upon their return. That tradition was now well established. The agrarian legislation of 59 and 55 had already made provision for the Cæsarian veterans. If more should be required, there might be overseas allotments, as Curio had suggested in 50. That is to say, the soldiers did not need to bring down the Republic in order to obtain such concessions. Cæsar's appeals to his forces, whether sincere or not, urged upon them the plea that he was defending the constitutional

[144] Cic. *Ad Att.* 7.8.5, 9.14.2, 10.14.3.

[145] Plut. *Cæs.* 30.1–2; *Pomp.* 58.5.

[146] Cic. *Ad Att.* 10.12a.3.

[147] Cic. *Ad Att.* 7.7.5, 8.13.2, 8.16.1–2, 9.5.3, 9.12.3, 9.13.4, 9.15.3; Plut. *Pomp.* 59.2.

[148] Cæl. *Ad Fam.* 8.17.2: *hic nunc præter fæneratores paucos nec homo nec ordo quisquam est, nisi Pompeianus.* On Cæsar's debt legislation, see now Frederiksen, *JRS*, 56 (1966): 132–141.

[149] Cf. Plut. *Cæs.* 16–17; Suet. *Iul.* 67–70.

[150] Cæs. *BC*, 3.6; Appian, *BC*, 2.47; Plut. *Cæs.* 17.1; Suet. *Iul.* 68.

system, the rights of tribunes, and conventional Roman *libertas* against a factious minority that sought monopolistic power and forced him into conflict. The troops followed Cæsar to protect his *dignitas* and to assure their own *beneficia* within the system.[151] The Republic perished in civil war. But that outcome had not been the object of its participants.

The legal terminus of Cæsar's command has been a fixation of scholars. A mountainous literature attests to this unhappy and fruitless endeavor. The ancients, by contrast, do not register an official time of expiry for the command. Nothing suggests that Cæsar's contemporaries came to blows over a legal terminus; indeed one may legitimately doubt that there was a specific date written into the law that authorized the proconsul's appointment. Not that the "Rechtsfrage" resolves itself simply into a "Machtfrage."[152] Quite the contrary: the Romans showed considerable concern for legal proprieties and authorized procedures on this issue as on others. An obvious conclusion has been mysteriously obscured: the existence of so much wrangling and dispute in 51 and 50 should mean that there was no stipulated terminus, rather than that there was one. Only a brief review of the various options which were discussed is needed. M. Marcellus raised the issue of Cæsar's provinces in 51 and proposed that he be recalled in that year. When opposition developed, he altered the suggested terminus to March 1, 50. That too met with resistance. Under the prodding of Pompeius and others, March 1 was designated a day for discussion rather than supersession. When it arrived, however, Pompey offered a new provision: Cæsar could stay until the Ides of November. And even after that time had elapsed and the breach in Rome proved to be irreparable, the *patres* decided in January 49 to fix yet another date for conclusion of the Gallic command. One can hardly escape the implication that no terminus was written into the *lex Pompeia Licinia.*

Provincial commands did not normally (if ever) contain terminal dates. They would conclude when the senate decided to reassign the provinces. It can be argued, of course, that Cæsar's provinces fell into another category—allotted not by senatorial vote but by a law of the people. And a length of time was specified: five years. But that need mean no more than that discussion on the redistribution would come in the fifth year after assumption of the command (or after passage of the enabling law). Presumably, one expected

[151] Cæs. *BC*, 1.7: *conclamant . . . sese paratos esse imperatoris sui tribunorumque plebis iniurias defendere; BC*, 1.22, 1.85, 3.57, 3.90–91: *Erat C. Crastinus evocatus in exercitu Cæsaris . . . "sequimini me," inquit, "manipulares mei qui fuistis, et vestro imperatori quam constituistis operam date. Unum hoc prœlium superest; quo confecto et ille suam dignitatem et nos nostram libertatem recuperabimus."* And see Cic. *Pro Lig.* 18: *quid egit tuus invictus exercitus, nisi ut suum ius tueretur et dignitatem tuam?*

[152] So Syme, *Rom. Rev.*, p. 48.

in 55 that such discussion would occur in 50. But there was no rigidity about it. So, Marcellus could initiate the debate in 51; and varied alternatives received consideration for almost two years thereafter. An incontrovertible fact stands out: no ancient source anywhere gives a precise date fixed by statute for Cæsar's supersession.[153] Understanding of the civil war is enhanced not at all by the assumption that Cæsar overstayed a legal term.

A rather different technicality created divisions in Rome and dominated debate in 50: the *ratio absentis*. Cæsar was accorded the privilege by a law of the people in 52. An ambiguity in that *lex*, so one may postulate, lay behind the dispute two years later.[154] It contained no reference to a particular election. Cæsar claimed the prerogative of a candidacy in absence for 49, though framers of the law had probably intended the year 50. In this he met with stiffer resistance than he may have bargained for. The issue was deliberated in late 51 and became more heated the next year when it was clear that Cæsar intended to postpone his candidacy. The conservatives remained adamant, and Pompey was entrapped by his own statements: Cæsar could have stood in absence in 50 but he had no right to the exemption in 49. But a senatorial majority, as we have seen, elected not to risk conflict over a triviality. In the late spring, they upheld Curio and gave their blessing to Cæsar's *ratio absentis* for 49.[155] Neither the *boni* nor Pompey, however, would

[153] So Balsdon, *JRS*, 29 (1939): 57–73, 167–180, still the best and most sensible account of the matter. That the *lex Licinia Pompeia* named no terminal date was a view expounded also by O. Hirschfeld, *Klio*, 4 (1904): 76–87; 5 (1905): 236–240. It is often argued, on the basis of Cic. *De Prov. Cons.* 36–37, that the *lex Vatinia* fixed March 1, 54, as the terminal date of Cæsar's initial five-year command. But March 1 may well have been a standard time for designation of consular provinces under the *lex Sempronia*. Whatever the intention of Vatinius' law, the wording was probably ambiguous, and Cæsar's enemies took March 1 as an opportunity to supersede him rather than simply to begin discussion. Marcellus tried the same thing in 51, with greater apparent justification in view of the *lex Pompeia* of 52. But Marcellus, like Cæsar's foes in 56, was rebuffed. See on this the cogent analysis of Cuff, *Historia*, 7 (1958): 445–471, though there is no need to follow him in believing that Pompey's law of 52 deliberately sought to make Cæsar's position difficult. Marcellus simply took advantage of the legislation for his own purposes. There are a few references in the sources which prima facie suggest a terminal date; Cic. *Ad Att.* 7.7.6, 7.9.4; Hirtius, *BG*, 8.39, 8.53; Suet. *Iul.* 26.1, 28.2; Dio, 40.59.3. None dwells on the matter and none specifies the day. All are explicable on the assumption that Cæsar's provinces were expected to be discussed some time in 50. The old Mommsenian view that Cæsar's time did not run out until March 1, 49, still commands a majority of scholarly support. But his arguments were demolished by Adcock, *CQ*, 26 (1932): 14–19. Much of the bibliography on this subject has already been registered. Add, among recent works, A. F. Stocker, *CJ*, 56 (1961): 242–248, C. A. Giannelli, *AnnPisa*, 35 (1966): 107–120, and S. Jameson, *Latomus*, 29 (1970): 638–660, which contribute nothing new. It is time to declare a moratorium on the Rechtsfrage.

[154] See above, pp. 475–476.

[155] Cæl. *Ad Fam.* 8.13.2.

yield on the issue. The sources make it clear that the *ratio absentis* still represented the principal sticking point in discussions as late as December.[156] The senatorial resolution in January which precipitated conflict expressly denied Cæsar's right to offer his candidacy except as a *privatus*.[157] In justifying his invasion of Italy, the proconsul complained that he was stripped of six months' *imperium*, which had been granted him by the people.[158] That, of course, is a case of special pleading, a part of Cæsar's self-vindication in retrospect. Nonetheless, it is plain that on this dispute turned most of the debates in the last months before war. And it was on this that Cæsar allowed his pride to become fatally involved.

Did Cæsar have a compelling reason for insistence on this privilege? Much scholarly opinion finds itself on his side. Common interpretation sees the proconsul forced into war by Pompeians and *boni* who refused his candidacy *in absentia*; Cæsar could not afford to return to Rome as a *privatus*, for he would be immediately prosecuted and eliminated from political life. That analysis has found its way into virtually every work on the subject, an article of faith unquestioned even by the keenest critics. Whence the origins of this theory? It rests on a famous statement ascribed to Cæsar as he ruminated over the corpse-strewn battlefield of Pharsalus: "They asked for it. I, Gaius Cæsar, would have been condemned in the courts despite my achievements, had I not resorted to arms."[159] But the source for that remark is not above suspicion: Asinius Pollio, historian, orator, and intellectual–and also a loyal member of Cæsar's forces from the Rubicon to the conclusion of civil war. Such a statement–whether or not Cæsar ever made it–was an obvious apologia for the massacre at Pharsalus.

To be sure, the proconsul's *inimici* had a judicial case prepared against him. Proceedings had already been initiated in 58 on the grounds of alleged violations in the passage of his legislation. But Cæsar escaped trial; he possessed *imperium* in the service of state and was not liable for prosecution.[160] Since that time his activities in Gaul provided additional levers whereby his enemies could institute criminal proceedings. Unconscionable slaughter of hostile tribes

[156] Cic. *Ad Att.* 7.7.6: *cum hoc aut depugnandum est aut habenda e lege ratio*; also *Ad Att.* 7.4.3, 7.6.2, 7.8.4, and especially Cicero's speculations in *Ad Att.* 7.9.2-3.

[157] Vell. Pat. 2.49.4; Florus, 2.13.16.

[158] Cæs. *BC*, 1.9.2: *doluisse se, quod populi Romani beneficium sibi per contumeliam ab inimicis extorqueretur, ereptoque semestri imperio in urbem retraheretur, cuius absentis rationem haberi proximis comitiis populus iussisset*; cf. *BC*, 1.32.

[159] Suet. *Iul.* 30.4: *hoc voluerent; tantis rebus gestis Gaius Cæsar condemnatus essem, nisi ab exercitu auxilium petissem*; the same in Plut. *Cæs.* 46.1-2.

[160] Suet. *Iul.* 23; cf. Suet. *Nero*, 2. For the attack on Cæsar's legislation of 59, see Cic. *Pro Sest.* 40, 135; *De Domo*, 40; *De Har. Resp.* 48; *De Prov. Cons.* 43; *In Pis.* 79; Schol. Bob. 130, 146, Stangl.

prompted Cato, at one point, to suggest that Cæsar himself be delivered up to the enemy as an expiatory offering.[161] And unauthorized departures from his province and widespread extension of the war laid Cæsar open to a charge under the *lex Cornelia de maiestate.* Cato had vowed for a long time that he would level an *accusatio* against the proconsul as soon as he returned.[162]

But the view that Cæsar feared the consequences of such a prosecution or was driven to civil war by that menace is dubious in the extreme. Nothing in the Ciceronian correspondence of this period hints at a prospective trial, let alone the probability of a conviction. And more telling is the absence of any reference to the matter in Cæsar's own *Bellum Civile,* where–if anywhere–it ought to have been cited in self-justification. Cicero's assumption throughout–and Pompey's–is that Cæsar would have no difficulty in gaining election to the consulship, whether or not he presented himself as a *privatus.*[163] That is suggested also by Cæsar's repeated offer to disarm, so long as Pompey would do the same. A criminal trial might indeed have been instituted. But far lesser men than Cæsar had eluded condemnation in the past. It is in the highest degree unlikely that his *inimici* could have obtained a conviction against the conqueror of Gaul and the benefactor of the state.[164] Cæsar had no reason to fear a lapse of *imperium.*

The Roman people found themselves puzzled and perplexed about the origins of this conflict.[165] And rightly so: motives for the civil war are nowhere to be found. Calamity had descended, catching men unawares; rational judg-

[161] Plut. *Cæs.* 22.3; *Cato,* 51.1–4; Suet. *Iul.* 24.3; Appian, *Celt.* 18.

[162] Suet. *Iul.* 30.3: *cum M. Cato identidem nec sine iure iurando denuntiaret delaturum se nomen eius, simul ac primum exercitum dimisisset*; cf. Ps. Sallust, *Ep. ad Cæs.* 4.2–3. Appian, *BC,* 2.23, 2.25, implies that the projected prosecution would be *de ambitu*–hardly a likely proposition. There is no evidence that Cæsar violated the *ambitus* statute; and numerous instances of breaches of the *lex maiestatis.* On this, see the compelling remarks of Bauman, *Crimen Maiestatis,* pp. 105–117.

[163] Cic. *Ad Att.* 7.4.3, 7.8.4, 7.9.3. The obvious implications of these statements have at last been drawn by Shackleton Bailey, *Cicero's Letters,* I:38–40, here a much better judge than most historians who have addressed themselves to the question. To be sure, Cælius postulates anxiety on Cæsar's part; *Ad Fam.* 8.14.2: *Cæsari autem persuasum est se salvum esse non posse, si ab exercitu recesserit.* But the context here shows that Cæsar's concern is with Pompey's army, not with political prosecution.

[164] Of course, Pompey's soldiers had surrounded the courtroom at Milo's trial in 52, a fact which Cæsar's apologists pointed to as a menacing precedent; Suet. *Iul.* 30.2. But Pompey was consul in 52, with the consent of a majority in the senate. Had Cæsar returned as *privatus* in 49, Pompey would have had no authority to use troops in the city–and would certainly have lacked the backing of senatorial sentiment.

[165] Cf. Cic. *Pro Marc.* 30: *diversæ voluntates civium fuerunt distractæque sententiæ; non enim consiliis solum et studiis, sed armis etiam et castris dissidebamus; erat enim obscuritas quædam, erat certamen inter clarissimos duces; multi dubitabant quid optimum esset, multi quid sibi expediret, multi quid deceret, non nulli etiam quid liceret.*

ments were overcome by the iron grip of events.[166] Pretexts, of course, abounded; most of them were issued after the fact as vindication: for example, defense of the state against a rebellious proconsul, or protection of the sacred rights of tribunes. But pretexts are not motives. Still less can one discern long-range plans or deliberate calculation to promote conflict.[167] Cæsar laid claim in 50 to additional time in Gaul in order to complete a thorough provincial organization. The *ratio absentis* presented a convenient vehicle for that claim: the proconsul could argue that it afforded him, by implication, an extended command through the elections of 49. And a second consulship upon his return would be most useful in facilitating acceptance of the new Gallic settlement. Nothing in that request implies plans for armed warfare or autocracy. And if Cæsar's offers for mutual disarmament were genuine, he was willing even to forego the *ratio absentis* in the later months of 50. But he would not yield submissively to the blusterings of the conservatives, much less to the bullying of Pompey. In the end it was a matter of personal *dignitas*. That was Cæsar's own explanation for the invasion of Italy. And we have no reason to doubt it.[168]

The same aristocratic pride impelled Pompeius Magnus. He had kept his bargain with Cæsar through the end of 51. And even in April of 50 he consented to a prolongation of the Gallic command. But he could not reverse his own stand on the *ratio absentis*. A communications barrier loomed thereafter, and mutual suspicion poisoned the atmosphere. Cæsar's proposals, delivered (or interpreted) by Curio, seemed like directives. And Pompey would not accede to directives.

The break between the dynasts need never have occurred.[169] It was consciously fostered by Curio for his purposes, by the Marcelli and the Catonians for theirs. The aim was not to generate civil war, but to split the combine, which had weighed so heavily in Roman politics for a decade. But their tactics created a situation that rapidly got out of hand. Pompey had no trust

[166] Cic. *Pro Lig.* 17: *fatalis quædam calamitas incidisse videtur et improvidas hominum mentis occupavisse, ut nemo mirari debeat humana consilia divina necessitate esse superata.* Cf. Cic. *Ad Att.* 7.3.5: [speaking of Cæsar's side] *causam solum illa causa non habet, ceteris rebus abundat.*

[167] There is nothing in Cæsar's behavior before civil war to substantiate Mommsen's portrait of a man bent on monarchy from the outset; *Röm. Gesch.*, II: *passim.* A similar case, with even less justification, has been made out for Pompey as the conscious creator of a military machine designed to provoke confrontation; cf., e.g., Pocock, *Greece and Rome*, 6 (1959): 68–81; and, most recently, D. W. Knight, *Latomus*, 27 (1968): 878–883.

[168] Cæs. *BC*, 1.7.7: *hortatur . . . ut eius existimationem dignitatemque ab inimicis defendant;* Cic. *Ad Att.* 7.11.1: *atque hæc ait omnia facere se dignitatis causa*; cf. Cæs. *BC*, 1.9.2: *sibi semper primam fuisse dignitatem vitaque potiorem*; but see Bauman, *Crimen Maiestatis*, pp. 128–130.

[169] As Cicero later lamented, if Pompey had heeded his advice and had not broken with Cæsar, the Republic would still be standing; *Phil.* 2.24: "*Utinam, Cn. Pompei, cum C. Cæsare societatem aut numquam coisses aut numquam diremisses!*" . . . *Hæc mea, M. Antoni, semper et de Pompeio et de re publica consilia fuerunt. Quæ si valuissent, res publica staret.*

in the spokesmen for Cæsar–his own enemies. And Cæsar felt increasing discomfort with the relatives and advisers of Pompeius. The distrust rendered genuine negotiation impossible. Pride and self-image brought the chief protagonists into positions where neither could yield to the other.[170] Of conscious desire for war there is no trace before the last weeks of 50. The senate enunciated its commitment to peace on more than one occasion. *Equites*, businessmen, farmers, and *municipales* displayed similar sentiments. And the urban populace expressed its stand by showering garlands on Curio after his proposal for disarmament. But the *boni* had entrapped themselves–and Pompey–in a political vise from which they could not emerge with dignity except by aggressive self-assertion–hence the escalating propaganda and bullying threats that issued in a *senatus consultum ultimum*. At that point no return from the brink was possible. Cæsar had spent a lifetime building his status and reputation. He could not permit them to collapse through submission. The rank and file followed their leaders, just as they had done through most of Roman history. It was not their purpose, any more than it was that of their commanders, to overthrow the state. The Gallic legions obeyed their patron and benefactor; he had deserved well of the *res publica*. Others followed Pompey and the consuls; they represented the *res publica*.[171]

Neither conscious choice nor inexorable fate determined the *bellum civile*. The same aristocratic drive for prestige and eminence that we have witnessed throughout the late Republic was still at work here. Pompey and Cæsar were by no means the only actors in that drama. Political conflict precipitated the crisis. That it culminated in war was the consequence of a polarization which briefly, but fatally, upset the traditional balance. The aggressiveness of Curio, the obstinacy of the *boni*, the mistrust of Pompey and Cæsar, can all be cited in the indictment. By December and January the *principes* had boxed themselves into a corner where threats of force were required to maintain *dignitas*. And the *dignitas* itself was empty until the threats became reality.

The fierce struggle for personal *dignitas* was not incompatible with the *res publica*. Indeed it was as old as the *res publica* itself. Julius Cæsar was not the first man to risk civil war in order to avenge wounded pride. A generation before, another patrician aristocrat had done the same. L. Sulla fought for himself and for the Republic. Cæsar had an identical vision. The Republic survived that earlier civil war, and it might have survived again. But this time the conflict touched off a chain of wars that endured, off and on, for nearly twenty years. When Augustus emerged triumphant, he was able to restore the veneer of the Republic; the substance was irrecoverable.

[170] Cf. Cic. *Ad Att.* 7.3.4: *De sua potentia dimicant homines hoc tempore periculo civitatis.*

[171] Cf. Cic. *Pro Lig.* 19: *secessionem tu illam existimavisti, Cæsar, initio, non bellum, neque hostile odium, sed civile discidium, utrisque cupientibus rem publicam salvam, sed partim consiliis, partim studiis a communi utilitate aberrantibus.*

CONCLUSION

"THE COLLAPSE of the Republic" is a convenient phrase—and a deceptive one. It conjures up a potent image: the disintegration of Roman society that purportedly set the stage for monarchy and a new order. Explanations can vary in approach and emphasis. Some discern a moral rot that ate at the vitals of society, a self-centered and divisive spirit that dispersed a once integrated community into warring component parts. The ruling class has come in for most of the criticism: narrow, selfish, and blind, they ignored the evils of their times; by hoarding their own privileges, they hastened catastrophe. Social upheaval is stressed by many: increased violence, the discontents of the urban masses and the rural poor, which splintered the Republic's unity and destroyed confidence in its institutions. The Ciceronian period witnessed, so it has been said, an age of individualism: the sense of communal attachment dissolved, to be replaced by an adherence to powerful and ambitious individuals who cared naught for the Republic except as an object for manipulation. A political realm was transformed into a cockpit for armies and their commanders. The once sedate and stable society gave way to a revolutionary era, which shattered the *mos maiorum* and left a divided populace grasping after a new structure. Finally, a glib pronouncement has condemned the Republic: the city-state was incapable of governing an empire. Imperial holdings had reached proportions that demanded a fundamental overhauling of government and society. The fall of the Republic was inevitable—and desirable.

A different approach has been essayed in this study. Its aim, in part, has been to suggest that the foregoing explanations are inadequate or, at best, insufficiently analyzed.

Moral decline is a slippery concept, useful propaganda in the hands of reformers, a convenient slogan for politicians or historians. The speeches of

Cicero abound in denunciations of vice, criminality, and corruption. But that is rhetorical invective, patent exaggeration, a part of the standard forensic vocabulary that Romans took for granted and not very seriously.[1] The orations of the elder Cato a century earlier, were they preserved, would show many of the same features. Moral degeneration is not to be measured by rhetorical hyperbole. It forms a major motif in Sallust's pessimistic reflections on the Republic. But Sallust, let it be recalled, penned his histories after the death of Cæsar, in the course of civil strife and despotism, a melancholy process that could sour any thinking man. Sallust dated the beginning of moral decline to 146 B.C., the time of the final destruction of Carthage: previously there had been *concordia* and unity, thereafter luxury, corruption, and destructive political ambition. The analysis, however, should not be confused with historical reality. Passing of the "golden age" formed a stock literary theme that had a long pedigree in both Greek and Latin literature. Condemnation of moral degeneracy had been a commonplace a century or more before Sallust. Fragments of the elder Cato prove it; and the same may be found in second-century historians like L. Piso, Polybius, and the annalistic writers consulted by Livy.[2] It was only too easy to ascribe a purer morality to the distant past while castigating the habits of one's contemporaries. In fact, political strife, restlessness in the army, discontents among the *plebs* and in the provinces, misconduct by Roman officials, and the effects of luxury and greed are all attested well before the Ciceronian age. Events of the late Republic are not explicable in terms of the collapse of antique virtue.

That the ruling class jealously guarded its prerogatives none will deny. But that attitude had deep roots in Roman history, and was in no way tantamount to a symptom of decline. Nor does it necessarily entail an abdication of responsibility. The image of Lucullus engulfed in torpor and the *piscinarii* idly tending their fishponds and game preserves has too long obscured the facts. Voluminous legislative activity in the Ciceronian age shows the aristocracy alert and industrious. The enactments covered a broad range of problems: political, administrative, social, and economic. Politics may have determined the timing or form of such enactments, and also the shifting lineups on advocacy or opposition. But neither stubborn resistance to change nor blindness to reality can be laid to the charge of the Roman ruling class.

Was this an age of "great individuals," who cast institutions in the shade and wrecked the corporate spirit of the state? That notion, of course, makes

[1] Cf. Syme, *Rom. Rev.*, pp. 149–152.

[2] See references and discussion in Earl, *The Political Thought of Sallust* (Cambridge, 1961), pp. 41–59. Also S. Uttschenko, *Der Weltanschaulich-Politische Kampf in Rom am Vorabend des Sturzes der Republik* (Berlin, 1956), pp. 88–106.

reference primarily to the "first triumvirate," and especially to Pompey and Cæsar. But concentration on those men can be overplayed to excess. To be sure, one may cite Ciceronian lamentations. The orator, more than once, spoke of the *regnum,* the despotism installed by the dynasts, who controlled all affairs, drew up their own lists of consuls, and forced all politicians to choose between servility and retirement. But Cicero's anxious reactions, hot-blooded and hasty, are confined largely to the years 59 and 55–54, to unusual occasions when the triumvirs successfully pooled political resources and intimidated opponents.[3] Electoral results, more often than not, went against the dynasts. If they concocted personal lists of favored candidates, the electorate does not seem to have paid heed. Criminal trials found many of their adherents in the dock, and several suffered condemnation. The presence of powerful individuals complicated politics, but did not revolutionize them. Cato's policy of reductionism proved to be no more permanent than the dynasts' machinations. The great families of the Republic–the Lentuli, Claudii, Metelli, Marcelli, Pisones, Lepidi, and others–went their own way, dominated neither by triumviral politics nor by Catonian ideology. There were divisions aplenty–as there always were in senatorial intrigues–but no neat categories of *optimates* and *populares,* of conservatives and radicals, of potent *militares* and cowed civilians. Pompeius Magnus himself sought acceptance and welcome in aristocratic circles; Cæsar moved appropriately through the proper ladder of offices, combining appeals to popular interests and patriotic sentiment with connections to the traditional aristocracy. The conspicuous figures should not be allowed to distort the general picture. As we have seen from several vantage points, politics operated very much as usual down to the eve of civil war.

Institutions remained intact: senatorial activity, electoral contests, legislative processes, political trials. The corporate sense of the ruling class survived internal squabbles and intrigues, indeed thrived on them, as it had throughout Roman history. Ranks of the aristocracy broadened in the late Republic, thereby subsuming and co-opting what might have been troublesome elements. Friction between the senatorial and equestrian orders had been exacerbated in the Gracchan era and its immediate aftermath. Control of the criminal juries was the prime source of conflict. But the issue evaporated in the age of Cicero. The *lex Aurelia* of 70 provided an equitable arrangement, which was not seriously challenged thereafter. Enfranchisement of the Italians automatically brought huge numbers of well-to-do municipal families into the *ordo equester.* Many remained outside the mainstream of Roman politics, by inclination and choice. Others, however, capitalized on their access to political involvement. Sulla's expansion of the senate opened the door. In the Republic's

[3] Cf., e.g., Cic. *Ad Att.* 2.9.1–2, 2.12.1, 2.14.1, 2.17.1, 2.18.1–2, 4.8a.2; *Ad Fam.* 1.8.1, 1.9.21; *Ad Q. Frat.* 2.9.3.

last generation numerous *equites* and municipal magnates entered the lower echelons of the *curia* and filled up the ranks of the *pedarii.* Distinctions between the average senator and the men of equestrian stock became fuzzy and unimportant. Both classes joined in cooperation and collusion for purposes of exploiting the provinces, amassing revenues and private wealth through business transactions and landed investments. In politics *equites* or former *equites* were, if anything, more conservative than their senatorial counterparts.[4] The late Republic witnessed a more extensive concert among the wealthy, the powerful, and the ascendant orders.

"Social upheaval" too is an overused and abused term. Incidents of violence occur with greater frequency in the Ciceronian age; or, to be more precise, we possess more abundant testimony on such incidents. Violence, in fact, was by no means absent in earlier and allegedly more stable periods. Careful scrutiny of disorders in the late Republic reveals little that smacks of social revolution. Riots for bread and for correction of injustice involved demands on the government, not a movement to overthrow it. Demonstrations of that sort were legitimate and tolerated, the grievances acted upon, if not altogether alleviated. And they remained a decided minority. The vast bulk of disorderly episodes concern matters unrelated to social inequities: they were planned political demonstrations prompted by legislative bills, electoral campaigns, or criminal prosecutions. Crowds were gathered by politicians for their own purposes and were composed largely of clients, retainers, and personal dependents. Aristocratic politics, not social unrest, promoted these affairs. And only rarely did they have any significant effect on the course of events. The masses were not driven by class solidarity or revolutionary aspirations. Sallust detects a sharp cleavage between *nobilitas* and *plebs,* a recurrent struggle that tore the Republic apart.[5] That broad and simplistic analysis dissolves upon confrontation with the evidence. Rome's proletariate had neither the will nor the means to overturn the social structure.

Military commanders and their armies possessed the means. But did they have the will? Detailed examination casts much doubt on that assumption. For displaced farmers, the rural poor, and the disadvantaged generally, military service offered a more continuous livelihood and the prospect of landed property after discharge. It was not in their interest to raise insurrection against

[4] The facts, now at last generally recognized, require no detailed treatment here; see Brunt, *Second Int. Conf. of Econ. Hist., 1962* (Paris, 1965), I:117–137; Meier, *Res Pub.*, pp. 64–95; Nicolet, *L'Ordre Equestre*, pp. 253–464; cf. Badian, *Rom. Imp.*, pp. 60–75. And one may consult now the convenient list of senators engaged in business and financial operations collected by Wiseman, *New Men*, pp. 197–202; cf. pp. 77–82.

[5] Cf. Sallust, *Iug.* 41.5; *Cat.* 37.10–39.3; *Hist.* 1.12, Maur. See La Penna, *Sallustio e la "rivoluzione" romana* (Milan, 1968), pp. 113–120.

the Republic. That loyalties shifted from the state to individual commanders is a misconception. *Milites* served their generals for gain and profit, but their attachments proved to be impermanent. "Client armies," if such there were, had no enduring existence in this period. Great military leaders sometimes exercised extraordinary commands abroad, but the commands were sanctioned by civil procedures, not as private ventures. Nor had soldiers and their officers become a "professional force." Rome's generals were elected officials and appointed promagistrates. They had no motive for turning their armies against the state. Civil war in the 80s disrupted and confused loyalties: the armies of Sulla and his enemies, however, contended for control of the government, rather than for its destruction. Similarly, in 49 both Cæsar and the senate advanced themselves as standard-bearers of the *res publica.* It is too easy to be bedazzled by Cæsar's triumphant march on Rome. The exceptional example cannot serve to define the era. Dozens of other promagistrates, including generals in charge of massive armies, served the state abroad, with never a move toward rebellion. Nor is there much likelihood that their forces would have followed them had they harbored such plans. Cæsar might have been branded a rebel by his foes, but not by his soldiers. The proconsul of Gaul, no less than his *inimici,* publicly advocated the defense of legitimacy—and of the *res publica.*

The city-state could not govern an empire. Such is the favored answer to the problem of the Republic's fall. A narrow oligarchy operating with restricted and outmoded institutions could no longer cope with vast territories containing multifarious populations. A republican structure created for a small community failed to meet the challenge of controlling a worldwide empire. Put in that form, the generalization has all the marks of logic and plausibility. It is illusory, however, to regard it as a solution.

That a republic possesses no competence to run an empire is not a self-evident proposition. Broad territorial holdings had been in Roman hands for nearly a century before the Republic's fall. The expanse, to be sure, had recently been increased, most dramatically through the conquest of Gaul. But the annexation of that province had only just been effected. If its administration were to stretch Republican resources beyond the breaking point, that consequence can hardly have been felt within a year of Gaul's subjugation. Provincial administration in the Republic, it can readily be admitted, left much to be desired. It was an amateur operation on the whole. Romans preferred it that way. Provincial governors were politicians, ex-magistrates on a temporary tour of duty. Their staffs too consisted of political appointees for the most part, arriving and departing with their chiefs. Financial exploitation of the provincials reached large proportions, filling the pockets of senators, *equites,* and Italians who had settled abroad, creating vast fortunes for the enterprising and the unscrupulous. Foreign territories were considered to be little more than ripe pickings for Rome's governing class.[6] But that is a different story. One may moralize forever on Roman greed and ruthlessness in the provinces without coming any closer to an answer for the Republic's fall. The fact remains that provincials, whatever their predilections, did not rise in revolt against the Roman Republic. The opportunity and the means were unavailable.

One may go further. Transformation of the Republic into a monarchy had nothing to do with a conviction–or even a realization–that provincial reform was a desideratum. The plans of Cæsar the dictator do not permit of secure specualtion. But on the administration of provinces he showed himself firmly conservative. A decree of the dictator limited tenure in the provinces to two years for ex-consuls, one year for ex-prætors.[7] Nothing could have been more in the spirit of Cornelius Sulla himself. The avoidance of professionalism in the governing of overseas territory remained a fixed principle. Matters improved under Augustus and his successors–or so it is often alleged. But political appointments continued, and predatory administrators still milked the subject populace. The lamentations and grievances of provincials persisted.[8] The passing of the Republic did not automatically bring an enlightened policy of overseas administration. The superficially comforting generalization on a city-state and an empire turns out to shed little or no light.

It is hazardous to place faith in the tortured exaggerations of Cicero. Of course, one may find numerous bemoanings of the Republic's fate in Cicero's correspondence: assertions that the state is about to go under, or, indeed, that it has already gone under, that the senate, courts, and institutions of government had been wrecked, that a fatal disease has left only the trappings of former glory.[9] Ciceronian hyperbole must be recognized for what it is. Once more, these statements belong almost exclusively to the years 59 and 54, and they reflect the orator's personal plight: the fear of Clodius' machinations in 59, the chagrin at having to defend adherents of the dynasts in 54. Cicero too readily equates his own problems with the ills of the Republic. When he was more secure and confident in his personal position, the letters brim with confidence–and the Republic is sound.[10] The orator, it is clear, can serve as no reliable weathervane for the condition of the *res publica*.

[6] See now Badian, *Rom. Imp.*, pp. 76–92.

[7] Cic. *Phil.* 1.19; Dio, 43.25.3; cf. Cic. *Phil.* 5.7, 8.27–28.

[8] Cf. Brunt, *Historia*, 10 (1961): 189–227.

[9] Cf., e.g., Cic. *Ad Att.* 2.1.8, 2.15.2, 2.19.1–5, 2.20.3–5, 2.21.1–2, 2.24.4, 2.25.2, 4.6.1–2, 4.18.2, 4.19.1; *Ad Fam.* 1.8.3–4; *Ad Q. Frat.* 1.2.15, 2.15a.5, 3.4.1–2, 3.6.4, 3.9.1.

[10] Cf., e.g., Cic. *Ad Att.* 4.1.3, 4.1.8, 4.2.6; *Ad Fam.* 1.7.8, 7.2.2, 7.2.4; *Ad Q. Frat.* 2.3.7, 2.4.6, 2.8.1.

The problem, it seems, has too long been put back to front. Civil war caused the fall of the Republic—not vice versa. The Republican machinery was not in a state of disrepair and collapse awaiting but a final push to kick away the remaining traces. Institutions, as we have seen, operated in customary fashion even in the years 51 and 50. And the war itself, far from being inescapable or premeditated, followed from a series of miscalculations in the last months before the opening of hostilities. Nor did the principals engage in conflict with the expectation, much less the aim, of putting an end to the Republic. It is unfair and misleading to claim that participants must have cared naught for the Republic, else they would not have taken up arms and turned it into a battleground. Civil strife and events beyond their control forced a great many to select sides and engage in conflict against their will. In the confusion of armed struggles, identification of the Republic's true champions was a matter of opinion—and of expediency.[11] Cæsar and Pompey, it bears repetition, both presented themselves as defenders of Roman traditions; and the same held true of leaders in the later rounds of the contest: Brutus and Cassius, M. Antonius, and even Octavianus. Matters had been no different during the civil war of the 80s. The Republic survived that conflict; Sulla's dictatorship aimed at guaranteeing its survival. And it might well have survived again. Little profit accrues from speculating on Cæsar's final aims; yet nothing in his securely attested reforms was inconsistent with a Republican system. The assassination of Cæsar, in any case, wiped his unfulfilled plans off the slate. The brutal and lengthy contest that followed made it impossible to pick up the pieces.

One may naturally object that if the Republic were still in a full state of health in 50 it ought not to have collapsed in the subsequent civil strife, any more than it did in the 80s. But the difference between these two struggles was vast—in extent, scale, and duration. It was not Italy alone that became engaged, but the resources and personnel of far-flung provinces. The foreign clients of Rome's leaders were brought into play, transforming a political battle into a Mediterranean war. The campaigns of Pompeius, of Cæsar, and of other Roman conquerors in previous decades had enormously increased the dependents and beneficiaries of leading *nobiles*. In Africa, Spain, Gaul, and the East countless numbers were dragooned into action by Roman patrons who summoned repayment on political debts and obligations.[12] The involvement of disparate elements in no way derived from attitudes toward the Roman

[11] Cf. Cic. *Pro Marc.* 20 [addressing Cæsar the dictator]: *noli igitur in conservandis viris bonis defetigari; non cupiditate præsertim aliqua aut pravitate lapsis, sed opinione offici stulta fortasse, certe non improba, et specie quadam rei publicæ.*

[12] Cf. Syme, *Rom. Rev.*, pp. 73–76.

Republic. But their participation gave to two decades of warfare a massiveness and destructiveness that rendered the old order irrecoverable.

The basic aim of this study, however, has been, not to explain the Republic's fall, but rather to explore the age of Cicero without the deceptive hindsight that stems from that fall. The results warrant reflection and, perhaps, provoke surprise. Roman behavior was conventional, on the whole, rather than novel. The continuities weighed more heavily than the innovations. The late Republic looked more to the past than to the future. Aristocratic politics had changed little. The noble houses remained at the center of affairs, exercising control through familial connections and expedient groupings. The old games were played not only by so-called conservatives but also by Pompey, by Crassus, and even by Cæsar. The jockeying for position and the rival ambitions were standard fare in Republican history. When Pompey amassed a potent lineup of senatorial connections, a reaction set in, as it had so often in the past: groupings re-formed and the Pompeian cause fragmented. Although the arrangement known as the "first triumvirate" gathered considerable influence, it evoked equally formidable opposition and split its own following. The faction of Cato boasted success in checkmating the triumvirs, but could not itself dominate senatorial politics. Overextension of political alliances generally brought greater divisions and splintering. The system itself resisted major groupings. Julius Cæsar hoped to circumvent the roadblocks by attracting adherents from among *novi homines, equites,* municipal families, and men from the lower ranks of the aristocracy. That fact and not any revolutionary designs prompted the senatorial stiffening against the proconsul of Gaul.

The continuities can be discerned in other aspects also. Electoral results demonstrate the tradition-oriented cast of the voters' mentality. Men of pedigree and noble lineage were consistently successful at the consular polls. The chief magistracy remained a virtual monopoly of the *nobilitas,* acknowledged and sanctioned by the electorate. Aristocratic names appear continuously on the prætorian lists as well, and in the ædileship. Even more significant, the tribunate itself, ostensibly an organ of the popular will, contained a preponderance of men whose families had sat in the senate during previous generations. The lower ranks of the *curia,* of course, included *novi homines* in larger numbers, which was inevitable in view of that body's expanded size. But the municipal magnates and former *equites* who filled the back benches were no less conservative and traditionalist in their sympathies than were their social superiors.

Criminal trials came in abundance during the late Republic. Most of those on record possessed political implications in one form or other, inescapably, since the principals were usually figures of some political standing. That feature too represented no new departure: the criminal courts as a vehicle for political warfare were a long-standing Roman institution. The cases served to highlight major senatorial struggles: the contest between Pompeius and the combine of his enemies in the 60s, the opposition campaign against the triumvirate, the aftermath of the Catilinarian conspiracy and execution of the conspirators, electoral rivalries, private enmities. Such characteristics underscore the continuities that gave a special flavor to aristocratic politics in the Roman Republic.

In the area of legislative procedure too there was continuity. The process had not been snatched out of the control of traditional organs. Senatorial discussion and *senatus consulta* preceded most enactments, duly promulgated by the *comitia.* Demagogic initiative and bypassing of the *curia* were the exception rather than the rule. Conservative but intelligent measures, on the whole, issued from the senate and magistrates, on a wide variety of matters: control of electoral abuses, maintenance of public order, clarification of judicial procedures, refinement of criminal legislation, more generous but responsible distribution of agrarian allotments, restructuring of administrative regulations. The legislation does not stand to the credit of a reformist pressure group. Bills were sponsored on different occasions by popular figures like Cornelius and Clodius, conservatives like Hortensius and Cato, senatorial leaders like M. Crassus, and even the so-called military men Cæsar and Pompey. Legislation, as always, was the business of Rome's ruling class.

It will not be inferred that all was sedate and untroubled in the Ciceronian era. The aim here has been neither whitewash nor apologia but an understanding of that era—in its own terms. Of course, there were elements that shared but little in the available benefits. We have already seen the grievances and plight of many of them: urban dwellers trapped in high-rent tenements, casual laborers dependent on insecure and underpaid employment, small farmers stripped of land and livelihood by civil strife and devastations of the countryside, the indebted classes victimized by an insecure financial structure. Employment in the army, increased pay, and the availability of *donativa* and booty relieved some of the distress; so also did governmental action in the areas of grain supply and distribution and the allocation of landed property. But that could not have solved all of the problems. Aristocratic patrons looked out for the interests of their clients—as was politically expedient—but not so as to alter significantly the living standards of the proletariate and the deprived. Economic exploitation of the provincials by Rome's governing class reached a peak of avarice and ruthlessness in the late Republic. Such features make the period rather less than an object of admiration or envy.

Fundamental change did not receive consideration. A reconstitution of the social and political structure was unthinkable for *nobiles* and *plebs* alike. Reforms, when they came, were generally piecemeal and unconnected, prompted by ad hoc situations, often induced by considerations of politics rather than humanity or justice. The result presented a patchwork of decrees, proposals, statutes, and administrative enactments–many of them ineffectual and of brief duration–but also some significant and enduring legislation. In a sense, the most arresting feature of the late Republic is not lawlessness but an obsession with legalisms. From the time of Sulla on, a mass of resolutions and statutory law interpreted and reinterpreted the *mos maiorum,* setting the context for many of the era's political struggles. A number of situations provide striking illustration: rivalries over passage of *ambitus* legislation, a burgeoning number of criminal trials for new or newly defined offenses, the ambiguities of conservative and liberal opinion on agrarian measures, debates on the validity of Catilinarian executions or the Cæsarian enactments of 59. Such matters stood at the very heart of late Republican politics.

It is fitting and instructive that the bewildering wrangle over Cæsar's *ratio absentis* and its technical ramifications should have precipitated the civil war itself. Both sides rested their public case on an allegedly strict interpretation of Roman law and proprieties. That fact points up all the more markedly the persistent attention–even when perverted–to constitutional principles and their interpretation. When a crisis developed, it came not from revolutionary action but from dispute about and divergence from traditional procedures. The conventions mattered–they were themselves the agents of tension and conflict that finally engulfed Rome in civil war.

Appendix I

COMPOSITION OF THE SENATE

For purposes of convenient reference there follows a list of Roman magistrates (other than consuls and censors) and senators in the period 78–49. Organization is by status and background: men of consular families, prætorian families, senatorial families, and *novi homines.* Magistrates include only those elected for the relevant years. The *pedarii* are those who entered the senate after Sulla's dictatorship and did not rise beyond the quæstorship (so far as is known) before 49. Many of the categorizations, of course, are uncertain. For a discussion of the *incerti,* see above on the senate. Numbers in parentheses are *RE* numbers.

I. The Prætors

A. Prætors of consular family

M'. Acilius Glabrio, pr. 70, cos. 67 (38)
M. Æmilius Lepidus, pr. 49, cos. 46, 42 (73)
M'. Æmilius Lepidus, pr. ca. 69, cos. 66 (62)
L. Æmilius Paullus, pr. 53, cos. 50 (81)
M. Æmilius Scaurus, pr. 56 (141)
C. Antonius, pr. 66, cos. 63 (19)
M. Antonius, pr. 74 (29)
Cn. Aufidius Orestes, pr. 77, cos. 71 (32)
C. Aurelius Cotta, pr. ca. 78, cos. 75 (96)
L. Aurelius Cotta, pr. 70, cos. 65 (102)
M. Aurelius Cotta, pr. ca. 77, cos. 74 (107)
M. Aurelius Cotta, pr. ca. 54 (109)
L. Cæcilius Metellus, pr. 71, cos. 68 (74)
M. Cæcilius Metellus, pr. 69 (78)

Q. Cæcilius Metellus Celer, pr. 63, cos. 60 (86)
Q. Cæcilius Metellus Creticus, pr. 74, cos. 69 (87)
Q. Cæcilius Metellus Nepos, pr. 60, cos. 57 (96)
Q. Cæcilius Metellus Pius Scipio, pr. ca. 55, cos. 52 (99)
M. Calpurnius Bibulus, pr. 62, cos. 59 (28)
C. Calpurnius Piso, pr. ca. 70, cos. 67 (63)
L. Calpurnius Piso, pr. 74 (98)
L. Calpurnius Piso Cæsoninus, pr. ca. 61, cos. 58 (90)
C. Cassius Longinus, pr. ca. 76, cos. 73 (58)
L. Cassius Longinus, pr. 66 (64)
C. Claudius Marcellus, pr. ca. 53, cos. 50 (216)
C. Claudius Marcellus, pr. ca. 52, cos. 49 (217)
M. Claudius Marcellus, pr. ca. 54, cos. 51 (229)
Ti. Claudius Nero, pr. before 63 (253)
Ap. Claudius Pulcher, pr. 57, cos. 54 (297)
C. Claudius Pulcher, pr. 56 (303)
C. Cœlius Caldus, pr. uncertain date (13)
P. Cœlius [Caldus], pr. 74 (2)
P. Cornelius Dolabella, pr. ca. 69 (140)
Cn. Cornelius Lentulus Clodianus, pr. ca. 75, cos. 72 (216)
Cn. Cornelius Lentulus Clodianus, pr. 59 (217)
L. Cornelius Lentulus Crus, pr. 58, cos. 49 (218)
Cn. Cornelius Lentulus Marcellinus, pr. 60, cos. 56 (228)
L. Cornelius Lentulus Niger, pr. ca. 61 (234)
P. Cornelius Lentulus Spinther, pr. 60, cos. 57 (238)
P. Cornelius Lentulus Sura, pr. 74 and pr. 63, cos. 71 (240)
P. Cornelius Sulla, pr. ca. 68 (386)
L. Domitius Ahenobarbus, pr. 58, cos. 54 (27)
Cn. Domitius Calvinus, pr. 56, cos. 53, 40 (43)
C. Fannius, pr. ca. 54 (9)
Q. Hortensius Hortalus, pr. 72, cos. 69 (13)
C. Julius Cæsar, pr. 62, cos. 59, 48, 46, 45, 44 (131)
L. Julius Cæsar, pr. ca. 67, cos. 64 (143)
D. Junius Silanus, pr. ca. 67, cos. 62 (163)
M. Junius Silanus, pr. 77 (170)
M. Juventius Laterensis, pr. 51 (16)
M'. Juventius Laterensis, pr. uncertain date (not in *RE*)
M. Licinius Crassus, pr. ca. 73, cos. 70, 55 (68)
P. Licinius Crassus Dives, pr. 57 (71)
L. Licinius Lucullus, pr. 78, cos. 74 (104)
M. Licinius Lucullus, pr. 76, cos. 73 (109)

C. Licinius Macer, pr. ca. 68 (112)
Cn. Manlius, pr. 72 (21)
A. Manlius Torquatus, pr. ca. 70 (70, cf. 13, 76)
L. Manlius Torquatus, pr. ca. 68, cos. 65 (79)
L. Manlius Torquatus, pr. 49 (80)
T. Manlius Torquatus, pr. uncertain date (85)
C. Marcius Figulus, pr. ca. 67, cos. 64 (63)
L. Marcius Philippus, pr. 62, cos. 56 (76)
Q. Marcius Rex, pr. ca. 71, cos. 68 (92)
[Minucius] Thermus, pr. ca. 67 (60)
Q. Minucius Thermus, pr. ca. 58 (67)
L. Octavius, pr. ca. 78, cos. 75 (26)
C. Papirius Carbo, pr. 62 (35)
P. Plautius Hypsæus, pr. ca. 55 (23)
Q. Pompeius Bithynicus, pr. uncertain date (25)
Q. Pompeius Rufus, pr. 63 (42)
M. Porcius Cato, pr. 54 (16)
Q. Publicius, pr. ca. 67 (13)
M. Pupius Piso, pr. ca. 72, cos. 61 (10)
P. Rutilius Lupus, pr. 49 (27)
L. Sergius Catilina, pr. 68 (23)
P. Servilius Isauricus, pr. 54, cos. 48, 41 (67)
C. Sulpicius, pr. 63 (10)
P. Sulpicius Galba, pr. ca. 66 (55, cf. 48)
Ser. Sulpicius Galba, pr. 54 (61)
Ser. Sulpicius Rufus, pr. 65, cos. 51 (95)
A. Terentius Varro, pr. ca. 78 (82)
M. Terentius Varro, pr. uncertain date (84, Supb. 6)
L. Valerius Flaccus, pr. 63 (179)
M. Valerius Messalla Niger, pr. ca. 64, cos. 61 (266)
M. Valerius Messalla Rufus, pr. ca. 62, cos. 53 (268)

B. Prætors of prætorian family
L. Ælius Tubero, pr. before 49 (150)
Q. Ancharius, pr. 56 (3)
C. Aquillius Gallus, pr. 66 (23)
T. Aufidius, pr. ca. 67 (12)
Bellienus, pr. 68 (1)
C. Cæcilius Cornutus, pr. 57 (43)
M. Calidius, pr. 57 (4)
Claudius Glaber, pr. 73 (165)

L. Cornelius Sisenna, pr. 78 (374)
C. Cosconius, pr. 63 (4)
Fonteius, pr. 54 (not in *RE*)
M. Fonteius, pr. ca. 75 (12)
A. Gabinius, pr. ca. 61, cos. 58 (11)
L. Licinius Murena, pr. 65, cos. 62 (123)
C. Memmius, pr. 58 (8)
P. Nigidius Figulus, pr. 58 (3)
M. Nonius Sufenas, pr. ca. 52 (52)
Sex. Quinctilius [Varus], pr. 57 (4)
Rubrius, pr. ca. 68 (4, cf. 10, 17)
L. Scribonius Libo, pr. before 49, cos. 34 (20)
Sextilius, pr. 68 (3)
Cn. Tremellius Scrofa, pr. ca. 58 (5)
L. Villius Annalis, pr. ca. 58 (7)

C. Prætors of senatorial family
L. Afranius, pr. 71, cos. 60 (6)
C. Antistius Vetus, pr. 70 (46)
L. Appuleius, pr. 59 (30)
P. Autronius Pætus, pr. ca. 68 (7)
L. Cæcilius Rufus, pr. 57 (110)
M. Cæsius, pr. 75 (9)
M. Considius Nonianus, pr. ca. 54 (13)
Q. Cornificius, pr. ca. 66 (7, Supb. 1.331)
C. Curtius Peducæanus, pr. 50 (23)
C. Fabius, pr. 58 (17)
Q. Fufius Calenus, pr. 59, cos. 47 (10)
M. Junius, pr. ca. 67 (25, cf. 23)
C. Licinius Sacerdos, pr. 75 (154)
L. Lucceius, pr. 67 (6)
Sex. Peducæus, pr. 77 (5)
M. Plætorius Cestianus, pr. ca. 64 (16)
A. Plautius, pr. 51 (8)
P. Servilius Globulus, pr. 64 (66)
P. Sestius, pr. ca. 54 (6)
P. Silius, pr. ca. 58 (8)
L. Titius, pr. uncertain date (14, cf. 15)
C. Titius Rufus, pr. 50 (37)
Q. Valerius Orca, pr. 57 (280)
C. Vergilius Balbus, pr. 62 (3)

C. Verres, pr. 74 (1)
Voconius, pr. ca. 54 (2)
Q. Voconius Naso, pr. ca. 61 (3)
L. Volcacius Tullus, pr. ca. 69, cos. 66 (8)

D. *Novi homines*

C. Alfius Flavus, pr. 54 (7)
A. Allienus, pr. 49 (1)
T. Ampius Balbus, pr. 59 (1)
T. Annius Milo, pr. 55 (67)
Q. Arrius, pr. 73 (7)
Q. Arrius, pr. ca. 64 (8)
M. Atius Balbus, pr. ca. 60 (11)
C. Attius Celsus, pr. 65 (not in *RE*)
P. Attius Varus, pr. ca. 53 (32)
M. Cæsonius, pr. ca. 66 (1)
C. Considius Longus, pr. ca. 58 (11)
C. Coponius, pr. 49 (3, cf. 9)
L. Cossinius, pr. 73 (2)
L. Culleolus, pr. ca. 60 (1)
M. Favonius, pr. 49 (1)
L. Flavius, pr. 58 (17)
Q. Gallius, pr. 65 (6)
Gutta, pr. ca. 55 (1)
M. Juncus, pr. 76 (4)
T. Labienus, pr. ca. 59 (6)
M. Lollius Palicanus, pr. ca. 69 (21, cf. 8)
C. Megabocchus, pr. uncertain date (1)
M. Mummius, pr. 70 (9, cf. 2)
C. Octavius, pr. 61 (15)
P. Orbius, pr. ca. 65 (3)
C. Orchivius, pr. 66 (2)
M. Petreius, pr. ca. 64 (3)
C. Pomptinus, pr. 63 (1)
L. Quinctius, pr. 68 (12)
L. Roscius Fabatus, pr. 49 (15)
L. Roscius Otho, pr. 63 (22)
C. Septimius, pr. 57 (7)
C. Sosius, pr. 49 (2)
M. Tullius Cicero, pr. 66, cos. 63 (29)
Q. Tullius Cicero, pr. 62 (31)

L. Turius, pr. 75 (2)
C. Valerius Triarius, pr. 78 (363)
P. Varinius, pr. 73 (1)
P. Vatinius, pr. 55, cos. 47 (3)
T. Vettius [Sabinus], pr. 59 (14)

II. The Aediles

A. Aediles of consular family

M. Aemilius Lepidus, æd. ca. 53, pr. 49, cos. 46, 42 (73)
L. Aemilius Paullus, æd. 55, pr. 53, cos. 50 (81)
M. Aemilius Scaurus, æd. 58, pr. 56 (141)
Q. Cæcilius Metellus Pius Scipio, æd. ca. 57, pr. ca. 55, cos. 52 (99)
L. Calpurnius Bestia, æd. ca. 59 (24)
M. Calpurnius Bibulus, æd. 65, pr. 62, cos. 59 (28)
L. Calpurnius Piso Cæsoninus, æd. ca. 64, pr. ca. 61, cos. 58 (90)
M. Claudius Marcellus, æd. ca. 56, pr. ca. 54, cos. 51 (229)
P. Clodius Pulcher, æd. 56 (48)
P. Cornelius Lentulus Spinther, æd. 63, pr. 60, cos. 57 (238)
L. Domitius Ahenobarbus, æd. 61, pr. 58, cos. 54 (27)
Q. Fabius Maximus, æd. 57, pr. ca. 48, cos. 45 (108)
C. Flaminius, æd. 67 (4)
Q. Hortensius Hortalus, æd. 75, pr. 72, cos. 69 (13)
C. Julius Cæsar, æd. 65, pr. 62, cos. 59, 48, 46, 45, 44 (131)
D. Junius Silanus, æd. ca. 70, pr. ca. 67, cos. 62 (163)
P. Licinius Crassus Dives, æd. ca. 60, pr. 57 (71)
M. Octavius, æd. 50 (33)
P. Plautius Hypsæus, æd. 58, pr. ca. 55 (23)
P. Sulpicius Galba, æd. ca. 69, pr. ca. 66 (55, cf. 48)
C. Visellius Varro, æd. ca. 59 (3)

B. Aediles of prætorian family

C. Cosconius, æd. 57, pr. before 47 (5)
C. Licinius Murena, æd. ca. 59 (119)
P. Nigidius Figulus, æd. ca. 60, pr. 58 (3)
Nonius Struma, æd. 55 (50)

C. Aediles of senatorial family

L. Appuleius, æd. ca. 61, pr. 59 (30)
Q. Curtius, æd. ca. 71 (12, cf. 25)
C. Junius, æd. 75 (15)
Q. Marcius Crispus, æd. ca. 58, pr. before 46 (52)

M. Plætorius [Cestianus], æd. 67, pr. ca. 64 (16)
A. Plautius, æd. 55, pr. 51 (8)
C. Vergilius Balbus, æd. 65, pr. 62 (3)
C. Vibius Pansa, æd. ca. 49, pr. ca. 48, cos. 43 (16)
Q. Voconius Naso, æd. ca. 67, pr. ca. 61 (3)

D. *Novi homines*
C. Annæus Brocchus, æd. ca. 73 (3)
M. Cælius Rufus, æd. 50, pr. 48 (35)
M. Cæsonius, æd. 69, pr. ca. 66 (1)
M. Favonius, æd. 52, pr. 49 (1)
Q. Gallius, æd. 67, pr. 65 (6)
L. Lartius, æd. ca. 73 (1)
C. Messius, æd. 55 (2)
C. Octavius, æd. ca. 64, pr. 61 (15)
Cn. Plancius, æd. 55 (4)
M. Seius, æd. 74 (3)
C. Toranius, æd. ca. 64 (4)
M. Tullius Cicero, æd. 69, pr. 66, cos. 63 (29)
Q. Tullius Cicero, æd. 65, pr. 62 (31)
L. Volscius, æd. ca. 73 (1)

III. The Tribunes
A. Tribunes of consular family
Aelius Ligus, tr. 58 (83)
C. Antonius, tr. 68, pr. 66, cos. 63 (19)
M. Antonius, tr. 49, cos. 44, 34 (30)
Sex. Atilius Serranus Gavianus, tr. 57 (70)
[Aurelius] Cotta, tr. 49 (not in *RE*)
L. Cæcilius Metellus, tr. 49 (75)
Q. Cæcilius Metellus Celer, tr. 68, pr. 63, cos. 60 (86)
Q. Cæcilius Metellus Nepos, tr. 62, pr. 60, cos. 57 (96)
Q. Cæcilius Metellus Pius Scipio, tr. 59, æd. ca. 57, pr. 55, cos. 52 (99)
L. Calpurnius Bestia, tr. 62 (24)
Cassius, tr. 56 (not in *RE*)
C. Cassius Longinus, tr. 49, pr. 44 (59)
Q. Cassius Longinus, tr. 49 (70)
P. Clodius Pulcher, tr. 58, æd. 56 (48)
Cn. Cornelius Lentulus Marcellinus, tr. 68, pr. 60, cos. 56 (228)
Cn. Domitius Calvinus, tr. 59, pr. 56, cos. 53, 40 (43, Supb. 3.394)

C. Fannius, tr. 59, pr. ca. 54 (9, cf. 16)
P. Licinius Crassus Dives, tr. 53 (75)
C. Licinius Macer, tr. 73, pr. ca. 68 (112)
L. Marcius Philippus, tr. 49, pr. 44, cos. 38 (77, cf. 74)
Q. Minucius Thermus, tr. 62, pr. ca. 58 (67)
Q. Mucius Orestinus, tr. 64 (12)
Q. Mucius Scævola, tr. 54 (23)
Q. Opimius, tr. 75 (11)
C. Papirius Carbo, tr. ca. 67, pr. 62 (35)
Q. Pompeius Rufus, tr. 52 (41)
C. Popillius, tr. 68 (4)
C. Porcius Cato, tr. 56 (6)
M. Porcius Cato, tr. 62, pr. 54 (16)
P. Rutilius Lupus, tr. 56, pr. 49 (27)
C. Scribonius Curio, tr. 50 (11)
P. Servilius Rullus, tr. 63 (80)
C. Visellius Varro, tr. ca. 69, æd. 59 (3)

B. Tribunes of prætorian family
Q. Ancharius, tr. 59, pr. 56 (3)
P. Aquillius Gallus, tr. 55 (25)
C. Cæcilius Cornutus, tr. 61, pr. 57 (43)
L. Caninius Gallus, tr. 56 (3)
C. Cosconius, tr. 59, æd. 57, pr. before 47 (5)
A. Gabinius, tr. 67, pr. ca. 61, cos. 58 (11)
L. Hostilius Dasianus, tr. 68 (13)
C. Memmius, tr. 66, pr. 58 (8)
C. Memmius, tr. 54 (9)
M. Nonius Sufenas, tr. 56, pr. ca. 52 (52)
Rubrius, tr. 49 (5)
Cn. Sicinius, tr. 76 (9)
Q. Terentius Culleo, tr. 58 (44)

C. Tribunes of senatorial family
L. Antistius, tr. 58 (13)
Antistius Vetus, tr. 56 (45)
L. Cæcilius Rufus, tr. 63, pr. 57 (110)
C. Cornelius, tr. 67 (18)
P. Cornelius, tr. 51 (44)
Q. Cornificius, tr. 69, pr. ca. 66 (7, Supb. 1.331)
C. Curtius Peducæanus, tr. 57, pr. 50 (23)

Fabius, tr. ca. 65 (1)
C. Fabius, tr. 55 (17)
Q. Fufius Calenus, tr. 61, pr. 59, cos. 47 (10)
C. Fundanius, tr. 68 (1)
C. Herennius, tr. 60 (8)
D. Lælius, tr. 54 (6)
C. Lucilius Hirrus, tr. 53 (25)
Mamilius, tr. 55 (not in *RE*)
C. Manilius, tr. 66 (10)
Q. Manlius, tr. 69 (34)
Q. Marcius [Rufus], tr. 68 (31, cf. 95)
L. Marius, tr. 62 (19)
T. Munatius Plancus Bursa, tr. 52 (32)
C. Papius, tr. 65 (5)
Sex. Peducæus, tr. 55 (6)
Plautius, tr. ca. 70 (3)
A. Plautius, tr. 56, æd. 55, pr. 51 (8)
P. Servilius Globulus, tr. 67, pr. 64 (66)
P. Sestius, tr. 57, pr. ca. 54 (6)
Terentius, tr. 54 (2, cf. 91, 92)
C. Vibius Pansa, tr. 51, æd. ca. 49, pr. ca. 48, cos. 43 (16)
L. Volcacius, tr. 68 (4)

D. *Novi homines*

C. Alfius Flavus, tr. 59, pr. 54 (7)
A. Allienus, tr. 55, pr. 49 (1)
T. Ampius Balbus, tr. 63, pr. 59 (1)
T. Annius Milo, tr. 57, pr. 55 (67)
C. Antius, tr. 68 (4)
C. Ateius Capito, tr. 55 (7)
M. Aufidius Lurco, tr. 61 (25, cf. 27)
C. Cælius Rufus, tr. 51 (7)
M. Cælius Rufus, tr. 52, æd. 50, pr. 48 (35)
C. Cestilius, tr. 57 (1)
M. Cispius, tr. 57, pr. uncertain date (4)
Q. Cœlius Latiniensis, tr. ca. 66 (20)
M. Cœlius Vinicianus, tr. 53, pr. ca. 48 (27)
L. Fabricius, tr. 62 (4)
Q. Fabricius, tr. 57 (7)
T. Fadius, tr. 57 (9)
C. Falcidius, tr. uncertain date (2)

L. Flavius, tr. 60, pr. 58 (17)
C. Furnius, tr. 50, pr. ca. 42 (3)
T. Labienus, tr. 63, pr. ca. 59 (6)
M. Lollius Palicanus, tr. 71, pr. ca. 69 (21)
Manilius Cumanus, tr. 52 (24)
C. Messius, tr. 57, æd. 55 (2)
L. Ninnius Quadratus, tr. 58 (3)
L. Novius, tr. 58 (7, cf. 12)
Q. Numerius Rufus, tr. 57 (5)
Cn. Plancius, tr. 56, æd. 55 (4)
L. Quinctius, tr. 74, pr. 68 (12)
L. Racilius, tr. 56 (2)
L. Roscius Fabatus, tr. 55, pr. 49 (15)
L. Roscius Otho, tr. 67, pr. 63 (22)
C. Sallustius Crispus, tr. 52, pr. 46 (10)
M. Terpolius, tr. 77 (1)
L. Trebellius, tr. 67 (3)
C. Trebonius, tr. 55, pr. 48, cos. 45 (6)
M. Valerius, tr. 68 (69)
P. Vatinius, tr. 59, pr. 55, cos. 47 (3)
L. Vinicius, tr. 51, cos. 33 (1)

IV. The *Pedarii*

A. *Pedarii* of consular family

M'. Acilius, quæst. before 50 (11)
Mam. [Æmilius Lepidus], leg. 74 (not in *RE*)
T. Annius, sen. 66 (21)
C. Antonius, quæst. ca. 51, tr. 46, pr. 44 (20)
L. Antonius, quæst. 50, tr. 44, cos. 41 (23)
M'. Aquillius, sen. 74 (not in *RE*)
M. Atilius Bulbus, sen. 74 (34)
M. Aurelius Scaurus, quæst. before 70 (216)
M. Bæbius, sen. 74 (18)
C. Calpurnius Piso, quæst. 58 (93)
Cn. Calpurnius Piso, quæst. 65 (69)
Cn. Calpurnius Piso, quæst. ca. 50, cos. 23 (95)
L. Cassius, sen. 70 (13)
C. Cœlius Caldus, quæst. 50 (14)
Cornelius Cethegus, sen. 63 (84)
C. Cornelius Cethegus, sen. 63 (89)
P. Cornelius Lentulus Marcellinus, quæst. ca. 75 (231)

Faustus Cornelius Sulla, quæst. 54 (377)
P. Cornelius Sulla, sen. 63 (385)
Ser. Cornelius Sulla, sen. 63 (389)
Q. Fabius Vergilianus, leg. 53 (154)
Fulvius, leg. 73 (1)
Q. Hortensius, sen. before 50, pr. ca. 45 (8)
M. Junius Brutus, quæst. 53, pr. 44 (53)
M. Junius Silanus, leg. 53, cos. 25 (171, cf. 172)
Juventius, sen. uncertain date (not in *RE*)
M. Licinius Crassus, quæst. 54 (56)
P. Licinius Crassus, leg. 54 (63)
Licinius Crassus Damasippus, sen. 49 (65)
L. Mallius, leg. 74 (8)
[Marcius] Censorinus, leg. 70 (47)
[Marcius] Censorinus, leg. 53 (42, cf. 43)
Q. [Marcius] Philippus, sen. before 48 (83)
L. Octavius, leg. 67 (27)
Q. Petillius, sen. 78 (6)
A. Pompeius Bithynicus, quæst. before 50, pr. ca. 45 (26)
M. Pomponius, leg. 67 (10)
C. Popillius, sen. before 70 (3)
C. [Publicius] Malleolus, quæst. 80 (19)
Sex. Quinctilius Varus, quæst. 49 (17)
T. [Quinctius] Crispinus, quæst. before 69 (39)
Ser. Sulpicius, sen. 49 (20, cf. 19)
[Terentius] Varro, quæst. before 49 (not in *RE*)
L. Valerius, sen. 76 (not in *RE*)
C. Valerius Flaccus, leg. 53 (169)
L. Volumnius, sen. 50 (4)

B. *Pedarii* of prætorian family
C. Annius Bellienus, leg. 74 (35)
P. Atilius, leg. 67 (23)
L. Aurunculeius Cotta, leg. 57 (6)
C. Caninius Rebilus, leg. 52, pr. ca. 48, cos. 45 (9)
L. Claudius, quæst. before 73 (23)
Cornelius Sisenna, leg. 57 (371)
M. Fabius Hadrianus, leg. 72 (83)
C. Fonteius, leg. 74 (7)
Furius Crassipes, quæst. 51 (54)
T. Mænius, quæst. before 73 (16)

C. Memmius, quæst. 76 (7)
M. Porcius Læca, sen. 63 (18)
L. Rubrius, sen. 49 (11)
C. Sentius [Saturninus], sen. 49 (4)
Cn. Sentius Saturninus, leg. 68 (Appuleius, 27)
Sextilius, leg. 69 (2)
P. Sextilius, quæst. 61 (13)

C. *Pedarii* of senatorial family
T. Antistius, quæst. 50 (22)
C. Antistius Reginus, leg. 53 (39)
C. Considius Nonianus, quæst. ca. 63 (12)
P. Cornificius, sen. 52 (6)
Q. Cornificius, quæst. before 48, pr. ca. 45 (8)
Q. Curius, quæst, before 71 (1, cf. 7)
Cn. Egnatius, sen. 74 (8)
Cn. Egnatius, sen. 74 (2)
Furius, leg. 73 (2)
M. Gratidius, leg. 61 (3)
C. Herennius, sen. 74 (7, no. 2)
M. Juventius Pedo, sen. 74 (18)
D. Lælius, leg. 76 (5)
M. Lollius, quæst. 64 (9)
Q. Lucilius Balbus, sen. 76 (20)
M. Lucretius, sen. 70 (9)
Q. Lucretius Vespillo, sen. 49, cos. 19 (36, 47)
T. Manilius, sen. 76 (10)
Marcius Rufus, quæst. 49 (94)
Q. Marcius Rufus, leg. 71 (95, cf. 31)
L. Marius, quæst. 50 (4)
L. Minucius Basilus, leg. 53, pr. 45 (38)
M. [Minucius] Basilus, sen. 74 (39)
L. Munatius Plancus, leg. 54, pr. ca. 45, cos. 42 (30)
L. Plætorius [Cestianus], quæst. ca. 74 (14)
C. Plotius, leg. before 60 (11)
M. Postumius, quæst. 73 (19)
P. Rutilius Nudus, leg. 74 (30)
M. Sempronius Rutilus, leg. 52 (82)
M. Servilius, sen. 51 (20)
C. Sicinius, quæst. ca. 70 (7)
P. Sulpicius, quæst. 69 (15, cf. 93)

P. Sulpicius Rufus, leg. 55, pr. 48 (93)
Q. Titinius, sen. 70 (17)
T. Titius, leg. 51 (26)
Vargunteius, leg. 54 (1)
L. Vargunteius, sen. 63 (3)
C. Volcacius Tullus, leg. 53 (7)

D. *Novi homines*

C. Aelius Staienus, quæst. 77 (Staienus, 1)
C. Albinius, sen. before 60 (1)
M. Anneius, leg. 51 (2)
P. Annius Asellus, sen. 75 (31)
Q. Annius Chilo, sen. 63 (18)
Aquinus, leg. 78 (1)
M. Aquinus, sen. uncertain date (2)
L. Ateius Capito, sen. 51, pr. uncertain date (9)
Attidius, sen. before 67 (2)
Q. Axius, quæst. before 73 (4)
Barba, leg. 73 (not in *RE*)
L. Bassus, leg. 67 (not in *RE*)
Cæcilius, quæst. 59 (1)
Q. Cæcilius Niger, quæst. 72 (101)
C. Cæpasius, quæst. before 70 (1)
L. Cæpasius, quæst. before 70 (1)
P. Cæsetius, quæst. 72 (3)
Calidius, sen. 73 (2)
Q. Calpenus, sen. uncertain date (1)
Canidius, quæst. ca. 58 (1)
A. Cascellius, quæst. before 73 (4)
C. Caudinus, sen. 74 (not in *RE*)
L. Caulius Mergus, sen. 74 (not in *RE*)
P. Cervius, leg. 73 (1)
Q. Considius, sen. 74 (7)
M. Crepereius, sen. 70 (1)
M. Eppius, sen. 51 (2)
L. Faberius, sen. 78 (2)
L. Fabius Hispaniensis, quæst. 81 (84)
C. Fidiculanius Falcula, sen. 74 (1)
L. Fufidius, sen. 78 (4)
A. Fulvius, sen. 63 (94)
T. Furfanius Postumus, quæst. 51, pr. ca. 46 (1)

C. Gallius, leg. 73 (3)
C. Gallus, sen. 70 (20)
Ti. Gutta, sen. 74 (1)
Cn. Heius, sen. 74 (3)
A. Hirtius, leg. 54, pr. 46, cos. 43 (2)
Q. Junius, sen. 70 (30)
Licinius Bucco, sen. uncertain date (39)
Licinius Lenticula, sen. before 49 (80)
Q. Ligarius, leg. 51 (4)
T. Ligarius, quæst. ca. 54 (5)
L. Lollius, leg. 67 (6)
Q. Lucienus, sen. ca. 67 (1)
C. Luscius Ocrea, sen. 76 (2)
Manius, leg. 74 (not in *RE*)
Manlius Lentinus, leg. 62 (58)
Manlius Priscus, leg. 65 (62)
L. Marcilius, leg. 74 (1)
Megabocchus, leg. 53 (1)
L. Mescinius Rufus, quæst. 51 (2)
Mummius, leg. 72 (2, cf. 9)
Cn. Nerius, quæst. 49 (3)
Octavius, leg. 54 (5)
P. Octavius Balbus, sen. 74 (46)
L. Octavius Ligus, sen. 75 (68)
M. Octavius Ligus, sen. 75 (69)
P. Oppius, quæst. 74 (17)
Cn. Oppius Cornicinus, sen. 57 (28)
Q. Pedius, leg. 58, pr. 48, cos. 43 (1)
P. Popillius, sen. 74 (17)
[T.] Postumius, leg. 49 (15, cf. 26)
Postumus, quæst. before 70 (Curtius, 21)
L. Procilius, sen. before 56 (1)
M. Publicius Scæva, quæst. before 73 (25)
C. Rabirius Postumus, sen. before 49, pr. ca. 48 (6)
Q. Rancius, quæst. before 73 (1)
L. Rutilius, sen. 72 (16)
M'. Sabidius, leg. uncertain date (3)
L. Sænius, sen. 63 (1)
Sallustius, leg. 51 (Caninius, 14)
C. Salluvius Naso, leg. 73 (1)
P. Saturius, sen. 74 (1)

P. Septimius, quæst. uncertain date (11)
P. Septimius Scævola, sen. 74 (51)
Servæus, quæst. before 50 (3)
Servianus, leg. 57 (not in *RE*)
L. Sestius Pansa, quæst. 54 (10)
T. Sextius, leg. 53, pr. ca. 45 (13)
Sornatius, leg. 72 (1)
Statius, sen. after 81 (1)
P. Tadius, leg. 73 (1)
C. Tarquitius, quæst. 81 (1)
Sex. Teidius, sen. 52 (2)
Cn. Terentius, sen. 63 (21)
L. Thorius Balbus, leg. 79 (4)
Titurius [Sabinus], leg. 75 (2)
Q. Titurius Sabinus, leg. 57 (3)
Cn. Tudicius, sen. 66 (1)
L. Tullius, leg. 51 (9, cf. 49)
Tuticanus Gallus, sen. before 48 (3)
C. Urbinius, quæst. 74 (2)
L. Valerius Triarius, quæst. 81 (366)
T. Varius Sabinus, leg. 63 (7c)
Veiento, leg. 50 (2)
C. Velleius, sen. 76 (1)
T. Vettius, quæst. 73 (11)
C. Vibienus, sen. 58 (3)

SUMMARY OF MAGISTRATES AND SENATORS, 78–49 B.C.

Consuls (61 elected, all known)

From consular families:	54 (88½%)
From prætorian families:	3 (5%)
From senatorial families:	3 (5%)
Novi homines:	1 (1½%)

Prætors (240 elected, 178 known)

From consular families:	87 (49%)
From prætorian families:	23 (13%)
From senatorial families:	28 (15½%)
Novi homines:	40 (22½%)

Aediles (120 elected, 48 known)	
From consular families:	21 (43¾%)
From prætorian families:	4 (8½%)
From senatorial families:	9 (18¾%)
Novi homines:	14 (29%)
Tribunes (300 elected, 113 known)	
From consular families:	33 (29%)
From prætorian families:	13 (11½%)
From senatorial families:	29 (25¾%)
Novi homines:	38 (33¾%)
Pedarii (200 known)	
From consular families:	46 (23%)
From prætorian families:	17 (8½%)
From senatorial families:	38 (19%)
Novi homines:	99 (49½%)

Appendix II

ADDITIONAL CRIMINAL TRIALS

Criminal trials proliferated in the Ciceronian age. More than one hundred had demonstrable political overtones. Most have received discussion above, so far as evidence permits. Countless others have escaped record, many, no doubt, of minor significance, others perhaps vanished through accident of transmission. For the remainder, only a reference or two survives, enough to provoke queries, not enough to allow discussion. A list follows. It makes no claim to completeness. If there is inducement for others to supply missing items, the purpose is served. The order is alphabetical by defendant, where the name is known. Thereafter, a few cases with unnamed defendants.

C. Ælius Staienus: Convicted *de maiestate,* in 74 or shortly thereafter. The charge involved mutinous activities as quæstor in the army of Mam. Æmilius Lepidus; Cic. *Pro Cluent.* 99–103; *Brutus,* 241; Ps. Asconius, 216, Stangl. Scandalous bribery at the trial of Oppianicus in 74 had destroyed Staienus' reputation, a matter employed to good effect by his accusers, the Roman *equites* P. and L. Cominius; Cic. *Pro Cluent.* 99–102; *Verr.* 2.2.79; Ps. Asconius, 219, Stangl; Schol. on Persius, *Sat.* 2.19.

L. Alenus: Charged with forgery of public documents. He had imitated the hand of six senior clerks in the record office. Notice comes in Cicero's *De Natura Deorum,* 3.74, whose dramatic date is 77 or 76. The crime evidently fell under Sulla's *lex testamentaria, nummaria;* cf. Cic. *Verr.* 2.1.108; Suet. *Aug.* 33; *Instit.* 4.18.7; *Digest,* 48.10.33. Hence, a date for the trial: sometime between 81 and 77. Cicero's language implies a conviction: *id quoque L. Alenus fecit.* The defendant's name cannot be vouched for; manuscripts give *aienus, lalenus,* and *asenus.* Perhaps one should read "Alfenus" or "Allienus." Cf. A.

S. Pease, *M. Tulli Ciceronis De Natura Deorum* (Cambridge, Mass., 1958), II:1160–1161.

M. Atilius Bulbus: Convicted *de maiestate,* sometime between 74 and 70. He was a juror in 74; Cic. *Pro Cluent.* 71–72; but was condemned by 70; Cic. *Verr.* 1.39. The offense involved tampering with a legion in Illyricum. A missive from the former governor, C. Cosconius, helped to produce conviction; Cic. *Pro Cluent.* 97; cf. *Pro Cluent.* 103.

Attidius: An exile at the court of Mithridates, after flight from judicial prosecution; Appian, *Mithr.* 90. Neither date nor charge is specified. But Attidius spent a number of years under Mithridates' protection before he conspired against his benefactor and suffered execution in 67: **διὰ δίκην φυγὼν ἐκ τῆς πατρίδος ἐς Μιθριδάτην πρὸ πολλοῦ καὶ φιλίας ἀξιούμενος ἑάλω τότε ἐπιβουλεύων αὐτῷ.** Flight from Rome may have come in the early 70s, but one can do no more than guess.

C. Cæsernius and M. Camurtius: Convicted on a morals charge. In 56 memory of the deed was already dimmed by time; Cic. *Pro Cæl.* 71. Perhaps the trials came in the 70s—or the early 60s. See above, chapter 7, n. 103.

M. Cæsonius: A juror at Oppianicus' trial in 74; Cic. *Verr.* 1.29. Other *iudices* were condemned for actions in that case, but Cæsonius was pronounced innocent. Moderns have overlooked his trial. But see Ps. Asconius, 216, Stangl: *hic ergo Cæsonius damnatis aliis iudicibus . . . innocens pronuntiatus est.*

Q. Calidius: Convicted *de repetundis* ca. 77. His parting shot to the courtroom alleged heavy judicial bribery; Cic. *Verr.* 1.38. The accuser was Q. Lollius; Cic. *Verr.* 2.3.63; not Gallius, as Ps. Asconius, 219, Stangl. The date is deduced from Calidius' propraetorship in Spain; cf. Broughton, *MRR,* II:86.

L. Calpurnius Piso: An intractable puzzle. Val. Max. 8.1.6 reports that L. Piso was prosecuted by a L. Claudius Pulcher for criminal acts against provincials; evidently, a trial *de repetundis.* Conviction was sure until Piso humbled himself, even groveled at the feet of the jurors: they granted him release. The individuals involved are not securely identifiable. The *prænomen,* at least, of the prosecutor must be wrong. No "Lucius" is attested among the many known Claudii Pulchri. Nor is it clear that the case even fell within the Ciceronian period. But a possible candidate exists for the defendant: L. Piso Frugi, prætor in 74. If so, the *accusator* could be any of the three Claudian brothers active in the decade of the 70s—perhaps C. Claudius Pulcher; cf. Gruen, *Athenæum,* 49 (1971): 55–56.

M. Canuleius: Defended on an unknown charge by Q. Hortensius and C. Aurelius Cotta. Cicero associates the case with that of Cn. Dolabella in 77; *Brutus,* 317. The two were perhaps not far distant in time.

M. Cassius: Indicted under the *lex Papia* for false arrogation of citizenship. The men who lodged complaints were Mamertini. But jurors were unsympathetic, and the Mamertini dropped their case; Cic. *Pro Balbo,* 52. The name suggests a client of the Cassii, probably the Cassii Longini. The date must fall between 65, the passage of the *lex Papia,* and 56, the occasion of the *Pro Balbo.*

Q. Cassius Longinus: Perhaps not a trial at all. Cicero reports in late 51 that Lucceius had some harsh words for Q. Cassius, a former quæstor of Pompeius'; Cic. *Ad Att.* 5.20.8. Not long before, the orator wrote to Cassius' cousin, C. Cassius, alluding to the burdens of his family; Cic. *Ad Fam.* 15.14.4: *onera tuorum.* Whether that amounts to a trial may be left to surmise.

P. Cornelius Dolabella: Twice defended by Cicero and acquitted on capital charges; Cic. *Ad Fam.* 3.10.5; cf. *Ad Fam.* 6.11.1. The cases were earlier than Cicero's departure for Cilicia in 51. Perhaps not much earlier. Dolabella was only a young man, even if one does not believe Appian that he was born in 69; *BC,* 2.129; cf. Shackleton Bailey, *Cicero's Letters,* III:269.

P. Cornelius Lentulus Sura: Twice acquitted; Cic. *Ad Att.* 1.16.9. The first occasion may have involved a charge of *peculatus* associated with his functions as quæstor in 81; Plut. *Cic.* 17.2. The second is undatable, but obviously earlier than 63, when Lentulus perished for Catilinarian crimes. There was bribery, so it was alleged, and a narrow margin of acquittal, by two votes; Plut. *Cic.* 17.3

Cornelius Lentulus: One of the three Lentuli who prosecuted Clodius in 61 was later defended by him *de ambitu;* Val. Max. 4.2.5 Principal prosecutor in 61 was L. Lentulus Crus, consul 49, his *subscriptores* Cn. and L. Lentulus, probably Marcellinus, consul 56, and Niger, prætor ca. 61, respectively; Ps. Asconius, 89, Stangl. Which of the three is meant cannot be divined.

Q. Curius: Convicted on an unknown charge. According to Asconius, 93, Clark, the prosecution came some time after Cicero's *In Toga Candida* of 64. A noted dice player and a friend of Catiline's, Curius turned informer against the Catilinarians in 63; Sallust, *Cat.* 17.3, 23.1–3, 26.3, 28.2; cf. [Q. Cic.] *Comm. Petit.* 10; Appian, *BC,* 2.3. Disreputable activities had caused his expulsion from the senate in 70; Sallust, *Cat.* 23.1. The giving of state's evidence would have provided immunity against conspiratorial charges. Hence, the trial probably postdates 63. If condemnation did not involve exile, 64 remains a possibility.

Cn. Decidius: Defended by Julius Cæsar on an unknown count. The manuscripts of Tac. *Dial.* 21.6 give *pro Decio Samnite.* Identification is probable with Cn. Decidius, a proscribed Samnite named in Cic. *Pro Cluent.* 161; see Münzer, *RE,* 4:2270–2271, "Decidius," n. 1. Did Cæsar perhaps plead for him during the proscriptions?

C. Fidiculanius Falcula: Twice indicted and acquitted for corrupt practices as juror in the Oppianicus trial of 74. The tribune L. Quinctius was prosecutor on the first occasion, alleging that Falcula had been unlawfully impaneled as a juror; Cic. *Pro Cluent.* 103, 113. The *lex repetundarum* was applied at the second trial: the charge was acceptance of bribes to condemn Oppianicus; Cic. *Pro Cluent.* 103–104, 108, 112–114; cf. Cic. *Pro Cæc.* 28–29; Ps. Asconius, 219, Stangl.

C. Fundanius: Defended by Cicero, sometime before Cicero's consular campaign in 64; [Q. Cic.] *Comm. Petit.* 19. Perhaps a *repetundæ* case? At any rate, there was a Greek witness for the prosecution; Quint. *Inst. Orat.* 1.4.14. On Fundanius, cf. Münzer, *RE,* 7:291–292, "Fundanius," n. 1.

Fuscinius: A most dubious entry. Charisius, 2.14, Keil, gives a fragment of C. Licinius Calvus' speech *de ambitu* against Fuscinius; cf. Zumpt, *Criminalprocess,* p. 535. But the name is otherwise entirely unattested. It is perhaps best to accept the emendation of "Vatinius"; Malcovati, *ORF,* 498, fr. 28. It will then be a quote from Calvus' speech against Vatinius in 54; see above, chapter 8, n. 31.

A. Gabinius: A red herring. In Cicero's *P. Red. ad Quir.* 11, there is an allusion to the orator's defense of Gabinius on a capital charge: *causam capitis receperam.* No other reference to the case exists, nor any evidence for a capital trial of Gabinius before 57. Cicero would hardly have avoided mention of Gabinius' ingratitude if he had, in fact, defended him in the past. The passage in *P. Red. ad Quir.* may be a later insertion; cf. E. Guerriero, *Mondo Classico,* 6 (1936): 160–166.

P. Gabinius: Condemned *de repetundis* between 76 and 70. *Terminus ante quem* is given by Cic. *Div. in Cæc.* 64. Gabinius was still a free man in 76; Lactantius, *Div. Inst.* 1.6.14. The *accusator* was L. Piso, who was given the task over Q. Cæcilius in a *divinatio;* Cic. *Div. in Cæc.* 64. The conviction is noted also in Cic. *Pro Arch.* 9. The prosecutor is identifiable with the prætor of 74; cf. Gruen, *CSCA,* 1 (1968): 162.

L. Gellius: Accused of adultery with his stepmother and of attempted parricide. The case was heard not in a court but by Gellius' father, L. Gellius Publicola, in his censorship of 70. The elder Gellius summoned the senate as an informal *consilium,* thereby receiving support for his judgment of not guilty; Val. Max. 5.9.1.

Ti. Gutta: Convicted *de ambitu;* Cic. *Pro Cluent.* 98; cf. *Pro Cluent.* 103; Ps. Asconius, 216, Stangl. Gutta was a juror in 74; Cic. *Pro Cluent.* 71, 75, 78, 127; Schol. on Persius, *Sat.* 2.19. Expulsion from the senate came in 70 because of alleged acceptance of bribes; Cic. *Pro Cluent.* 127. The *ambitus* trial should, therefore, be put sometime between 69 and 66; Zumpt, *Criminalprocess,* p. 528.

C. Herennius: Convicted *de peculatu* sometime before 70; Cic. *Verr.* 1.39. If he is the C. Herennius who was slain when serving under Sertorius in the mid-70s, the trial must predate 76; Sallust, *Hist.* 2.98.6, Maur.; Plut. *Pomp.* 18.3; Livy, *Per.* 91.

C. Hirtilius: Prosecuted by C. Rusius, a practiced *accusator,* defended by L. Cornelius Sisenna; Cic. *Brutus,* 259–260. Time, circumstances, and charge are not registered. But it was obviously before Sisenna's death in 67; Dio, 36.19.1. The name Hirtilius is unknown. The usual emendation to C. Hirtuleius may be right. Other Hirtuleii were supporters of Sertorius in the 70s; Broughton, *MRR Supp.,* p. 29.

M. Juncus: The fact is uncertain. Two fragments survive of a speech by Julius Cæsar *pro Bithynis;* Malcovati, *ORF,* pp. 395–396. In one, Cæsar addresses remarks to M. Juncus. That has led some to see Juncus as the presiding officer at a hearing in Bithynia, of which he was proconsul; sources in Broughton, *MRR,* II:98. More likely, it is a *repetundæ* case, Cæsar representing the Bithynians against their ex-governor. The trial will have followed Juncus' return to Rome in 74; cf. H. Dahlmann, *Hermes,* 73 (1938): 341–346. The reference in Gellius, 5.13.6, to Cæsar as *pontifex maximus* is not to be taken as having chronological import.

C. Junius: Presided over the much abused tribunal that tried Oppianicus in 74. Shortly thereafter he was convicted and fined on a charge of violating proper legal procedures. The tribune L. Quinctius brought the accusation, punctuating his attack by stirring up a crowd scene; Cic. *Pro Cluent.* 89–96, 103, 108, 113; Ps. Asconius, 255–256, Stangl; cf. Cic. *Verr.* 2.1.158. Junius was defended, it seems, by L. Piso Frugi; Schol. Gronov. 351, Stangl.

Licinius Lenticula: A notorious gambler and gamester, he was among the *calamitosi* restored to public life by M. Antonius in 49. Cicero reports that he had been condemned and, apparently, exiled on gambling charges; Cic. *Phil.* 3.56; cf. Dio, 47.45.4. Gambling was restricted by a series of measures, *lex Titia, lex Publicia,* and *lex Cornelia,* the last perhaps a Sullan enactment; *Dig.* 11.5.3. The defendant's name is uncertain: manuscripts of Cicero give *Lenticula* or *Denticula.* Dio calls him **Λεντίκουλον**.

L. Livineius Regulus: All is conjecture here. In a letter of uncertain date, Cicero refers to the *calamitas* of Regulus; *Ad Fam.* 13.60. That may indicate a conviction and exile. Regulus, it appears, was still in Rome in 58; cf. Cic. *Ad Att.* 3.17.1. That leaves a broad range of possibilities open for the date of his trial.

C. Megabocchus: Ex-governor of Sardinia, convicted, evidently, *de repetundis.* Several Sardinians spoke for him. But written testimony and other unimpeachable evidence was against him. The case occurred sometime before 54; Cic. *Pro Scauro,* 40.

Q. Mucius Orestinus: Indicted on a charge of theft by L. Calenus. Orestinus sought Cicero's assistance as defense counsel. An agreement with the prosecutor, however, terminated proceedings. The fact is mentioned in Cicero's *In Toga Candida;* Asconius, 86, Clark. Since Orestinus held the tribunate in 64, showing base ingratitude to Cicero in the process, the case is no later than 65. The prosecutor is, presumably, a Fufius Calenus, related to the prætor of 59 and perhaps identical with the L. Calenus who testified against Verres in 70; Cic. *Verr.* 2.2.23.

T. Munatius Plancus Bursa: Another example of ingratitude. Cicero defended him sometime before 52; Cic. *Ad Fam.* 7.2.3. Bursa turned about to link himself with Clodius and to deliver vituperative assaults on Cicero; see above, pp. 346–347. Plut. *Cic.* 25.1 speaks of Cicero's successful defense of a Munatius who repaid the act by prosecuting one of the orator's friends. That is doubtless the same Munatius and the same case. The charge is not recorded.

Pericles: An Ephesian nobleman who interfered with activities of a Roman quæstor, M. Aurelius Scaurus, in Asia. Scaurus dispatched him to Rome and leveled charges; Cic. *Verr.* 2.1.85. The hearing may have been only before the senate, rather than in court. The date is unspecified, but in 70 Cicero refers to it as *nuper;* hence, in the late 70s.

Phamea: Prosecuted for unknown reasons by the sons of Cn. Octavius in 52. Cicero had promised to appear for the defense, but had to beg off, for Sestius' trial was scheduled for the same day. The withdrawal caused resentment and anger; Cic. *Ad Att.* 13.49.1; *Ad Fam.* 7.24.2.

Plætorius: Not necessarily a trial. Cicero refers in late 51 to *incendio Plætoriano; Ad Att.* 5.20.8. If the "fire" is metaphorical, it could signify a prosecution. But the question must be left open; cf. Shackleton Bailey, *Cicero's Letters,* III: 230. Plætorius may be the M. Plætorius Cestianus who was prosecutor of Fonteius in 69; Cic. *Pro Font.* 36; cf. *Ad Fam.* 1.8.1.

C. Popillius: Condemned *de peculatu,* sometime before 70; Cic. *Verr.* 1.39. Allegations of judicial corruption were also introduced, though irrelevant to the main charge.

P. Popillius: Convicted *de ambitu;* Cic. *Pro Cluent.* 98. He was expelled from the senate by the censors of 70. Reasons for expulsion were his low birth—he was the son of a freedman—and alleged judicial corruption; Cic. *Pro Cluent.* 131–132; cf. *Pro Cluent.* 103. The trial *de ambitu* followed, evidently between 69 and 66. Lentulus Clodianus, one of the censors who expelled him in 70, testified for him in the *ambitus* case; Cic. *Pro Cluent.* 132.

C. Popillus Lænas: One of the murderers of Cicero in 43. He was earlier defended by Cicero on a charge of parricide and acquitted; Val. Max. 5.3.4; Plut. *Cic.* 48.1; Dio, 47.11.1; Seneca, *Controv.* 7.2. *init.* Some historians reported that Cicero's defense came in a civil case—probably wrongly; Seneca, *Controv.* 7.2.8. M. Cælius had urged Cicero to appear; Val. Max. 5.3.4. Hence, the trial precedes Cælius' death in 48. Any further specification would be sheer guesswork.

Procilius: Mentioned by Ps. Asconius, 236, Stangl, as an example of subordinate officials tried by provincial governors, rather than in Rome. There is no hint of a date. But the other example given is that of a certain Oppius, perhaps the P. Oppius who was prosecuted in 69; see above, p. 269.

Sex. Propertius: Arraigned in 58 by the tribune Ælius Ligus, friend and ally of Clodius; Cic. *De Domo,* 49. Ligus lost courage at the last moment, fearing a charge of calumnious prosecution. The case was dropped.

C. Rabirius: Acquitted on a charge of violating sacred groves and shrines; Cic. *Pro Rab. Perd.* 7. His accuser was C. Licinius Macer, whose death in 66 affords a *terminus ante quem.* The date usually given, 73, is based on no more than the fact that Macer was tribune in that year. Rabirius was later prosecuted for *perduellio* in 63; see above, chapter 7.

Sabinus: A friend of Cicero's, prosecuted by Munatius shortly after the latter was defended by Cicero; Plut. *Cic.* 25.1. The prosecutor was doubtless T. Munatius Plancus Bursa; the trial no later than 53; see above, pp. 346–347. Further speculation would be of small value.

Safinius: That Safinius was a defendant cannot be regarded as certain. Cicero reports that Ælius Staienus, prior to 74, took an enormous bribe in connection with a particular trial, comparable to that received at Oppianicus' trial; *Pro Cluent.* 99. Note the language: *quæ ille cum accepisset nomine iudicii Safiniani, sicut in Oppianici iudicio postea.* The phrase *iudicium Safinianum,* like *iudicium Iunianum,* may suggest that Safinius was the presiding magistrate rather than the defendant.

C. Sallustius Crispus: His trials are to be registered with doubt and caution. The source is a scandalous pamphlet attributed to Cicero, but probably of much later date and of dubious value. The author asserts that Sallust was twice prosecuted and twice narrowly acquitted by tainted jurors; [Cic.] *Inv. in Sall.* 14. The crime was sacrilege; Sallust was implicated with Nigidius, presumably the scholar P. Nigidius Figulus. No further information survives. The events are put just prior to Sallust's quæstorship, which, in his *cursus,* should have come ca. 55. But the quæstorship itself is not otherwise attested. Further scandals are reported in the pamphlet: Sallust openly confessed adulterous activities; [Cic.] *Inv. in Sall.* 15–16. That will not have been in court. Varro also wrote of Sallust's adulteries; Gellius, 17.18. The items cannot command implicit faith.

M. Seius: Ædile in 74; Broughton, *MRR,* II:102. At some earlier time he had suffered judicial condemnation; Cic. *Pro Planc.* 12; *calamitate iudicii.* That is the sum of the evidence.

P. Septimius Scævola: Condemned *de repetundis* in 72. At the *litis æstimatio* which followed there was reference to his transgressions as a bribed juror. But Scævola was officially condemned for other offenses, attested by witnesses from Apulia; Cic. *Verr.* 1.38; *Pro Cluent.* 115–116. The year is that of Q. Hortensius' prætorship; Cic. *Verr.* 1.38.

Q. Sergius: Convicted on a murder charge sometime after 90; Cic. *Pro Cluent.* 21. No better *terminus ante quem* can be given than 66, the date of the *Pro Cluentio.*

Cn. Sergius Silus: Attempted seduction of a *mater familiæ* got him condemned on a morals charge brought by Q. Metellus Celer; Val. Max. 6.1.8. The defendant may be identified with Cn. Sergius, a tax farmer attested in 72; Cic. *Verr.* 2.3.102. An approximate dating for the trial would be the late 70s or early 60s; cf. Gruen, *Roman Politics,* pp. 300–301.

Q. Sosius: A Roman *eques* from Picenum–and a confessed arsonist. He was convicted for burning down a record office; Cic. *De Nat. Deor.* 3.74. Nothing further is known. *Terminus ante quem* is supplied by the dramatic date of the *De Natura Deorum:* 77 or 76. The trial may well be pre-Sullan; cf. Cic. *Pro Rab. Perd.* 8. Münzer, *RE,* 5:1180, "Sosius," n. 3, puts the arson at time of the Social War, but without evidence. Pease, *Cic. Nat. Deor.,* II:1159–1160, suggests 83, time of the burning of the Capitol.

L. Varenus: Condemned under the *lex de sicariis,* evidently the Sullan *lex de sicariis.* His relatives were the victims. Varenus was indicted on three counts of murder; the deaths of C. Varenus and Salarius and the attempted killing of Cn. Varenus; Quint. *Inst. Orat.* 7.1.9. The prosecutor was a certain C. Ancharius Rufus. Cicero was defense counsel. The affair is known only from fragments of his speech quoted by Quintilian and Priscian; Quint. *Inst. Orat.* 4.1.74, 4.2.26, 5.10.69, 5.13.28, 7.2.22, 7.2.36, 9.2.56; Priscian, 7.14.70, 12.6.29, Keil. Oddly, it receives no mention in Ciaceri's *Cicerone* or Gelzer's *Cicero.* Gundel, *RE,* 8A:374–375, "Varenus," n. 3, suggests a date shortly after the Sullan proscriptions. The intrafamilial strife has certain parallels with the case of Sex. Roscius Amerinus in 80. But that is not evidence for a date. The only secure conclusion is that it was post-Sullan.

L. Vargunteius: Defended by Q. Hortensius *de ambitu,* and later condemned as a Catilinarian in 62; Cic. *Pro Sulla,* 6. The earlier trial is elucidated by Linderski, *Historia,* 12 (1963): 511–512. Vargunteius is described as a senator in 63 by Sallust, *Cat.* 28.1, as a knight by Cic. *Cat.* 1.9. That suggests conviction on the *ambitus* charge and expulsion from the senate, as specified in the *lex Calpurnia de ambitu.* The case should, therefore, be located between 67 and 63. Linderski suggests 66, in connection with the electoral scandals of that year; cf. Cic. *Pro Sulla,* 67.

C. Volcacius: A fragment of Cicero's *Pro Cornelio* is the only evidence; Asconius, 74, Clark: *non Cn. Dolabella C. Volcacium, honestissimum virum, com-*

muni et cotidiano iure privasset. As Asconius says, Cn. Dolabella is either the consul of 81 or the prætor of 81. The Ciceronian statement occurs between a reference to the Varian trials of 90 and allusion to a case involving L. Sisenna, who was particularly active in the 70s. The affair may have connection with the Sullan proscriptions.

The following cases receive brief mention in the sources, but without a record of defendants' names.

In 74 C. Verres was urban prætor. Cicero complains that Verres, as the presiding magistrate in a criminal case, once selected jurors who condemned a defendant without having heard the facts; *Verr.* 1.39.

As noted above, Ti. Gutta and P. Popillius were convicted *de ambitu* between 69 and 66. Their accusers had themselves earlier been found guilty on the same charge; Cic. *Pro Cluent.* 98.

When Verres was prosecuted in 70, his supporters concocted another extortion case, to be heard before Verres' own, thereby hoping to postpone the latter for another year. The defendant was apparently an ex-governor of Achæa; Cic. *Verr.* 1.6, 1.9, 2.1.30. Cicero, unfortunately, does not name the principals in the case. Later scholiasts report a plethora of names, based on muddled testimony and probably worthless. The prosecutor is variously given as Rupilius, Oppius, Q. Metellus, Piso, and Dasianus; other traditions made Oppius the defendant–or Scribonius Curio; Ps. Asconius, 207–208, Stangl; Schol. Gronov. 331–332, Stangl. The truth is not to be wrung from those jumbled statements. Nothing further is heard of the case, which may never have come to court.

Cicero records the conviction in 70 of a Roman senator whose financial resources were too meager to persuade the jurors on his behalf; *Verr.* 1.46. The scholiast's identification of the defendant with Dolabella is valueless; Ps. Asconius, 221, Stangl. Cn. Dolabella was convicted *de repetundis* seven years earlier; see Gruen, *AJP,* 87 (1966): 385–399.

Cicero, while defending Cluentius in 66, makes passing reference to a case *de ambitu* that was in process at the same time; *Pro Cluent.* 147. Any speculation would obviously be unwarranted.

M. Cato, as quæstor, pressed charges against one of his clerks, perhaps for embezzlement. Plutarch's term ῥᾳδιουργίας is imprecise and nontechnical; *Cato,* 16.3. The censor, Q. Lutatius Catulus spoke for the defense; a tie vote gained the defendant acquittal, but lost him his job; Plut. *Cato,* 16.4–6; *Præc. Reip. Ger.* 13; *De Vit. Pud.* 15. The date of Cato's quæstorship is uncertain: either 65 or 64; Broughton, *MRR,* II:165, n. 5; *MRR Supp.,* pp. 49–50.

The Gaditane L. Cornelius Balbus was awarded Roman citizenship in the late 70s. At some point thereafter he was enrolled into the Clustuminian tribe by virtue of a successful prosecution *de ambitu.* Balbus obtained the convicted defendant's tribe; Cic. *Pro Balbo,* 57. The case probably came after passage of the *lex Calpurnia de ambitu* in 67 and obviously before Balbus' own trial in 56.

The prosecutor of Balbus in 56 had himself earlier suffered conviction; Cic. *Pro Balbo,* 32. Since that individual was also an enfranchised Gaditane, his prosecution, like that of Balbus, probably fell under the *lex Papia.* That gives a date between 65 and 56.

P. Servilius Isauricus gave testimony against a defendant who was then convicted because of the immense authority of the witness; Val. Max. 8.5.6. Servilius is described, among other things, as a *censorius.* If that is accurate, the trial postdates 55, Servilius' censorial year; Broughton, *MRR,* II:215.

Three final cases, without date or defendant, are alluded to by Plutarch when he gives examples of Ciceronian witticisms: (1) the trial of a young man accused of poisoning his father; Plut. *Cic.* 26.5; (2) a case in which Cicero summoned a certain P. Consta as witness; Plut. *Cic.* 26.6; (3) a trial in which M. Appius (perhaps better, M. Oppius) and Cicero delivered opposing speeches; Plut. *Cic.* 26.8.

Appendix III

IMPERIA EXTRA ORDINEM

A POSTULATED dichotomy between civil authority and military power underlies many reconstructions of the late Republic. Officials and politicians might play their little games at home, but real *dominatio* belonged to the men who headed armies abroad. Military commands *extra ordinem* cleared a path that led directly to the Principate.[1] Such is the postulate. Proliferation of extraordinary commands creates a presumption that constitutional practices were increasingly set aside in favor of the unconstitutional. But the presumption itself can profit from reassessment.

In what sense were the great *imperia* of the late Republic really "extraordinary"? The term is often bandied about, rarely defined. One thinks naturally of Pompey's lengthy string of commissions, beginning when he was under age even for a civil magistracy: *imperium* was already his in 82, then the command of armies in Italy and Spain during the 70s; there followed mandates with sweeping powers against the pirates and against Mithridates in the subsequent decade, a new *imperium* and control of the Mediterranean grain supply from 57. No less significant was Cæsar's prolonged tenure in Gaul—nearly ten years at the head of Roman legions abroad. And in 55 came new legislation providing quinquennial terms in Spain and Syria for Pompey and Crassus respectively. But how seriously had the *mos maiorum* been breached? Conservatives, to be sure, might grumble—when it suited them. Cato made it a habit to protest against *potestates extraordinariæ*. But that did not prevent him from accepting a special commission of his own to secure the financial resources

[1] Mommsen, *Römisches Staatsrecht* (Leipzig, 1887), II:1.647–662; A. E. R. Boak, *AHR*, 24 (1918): 1–25. But cf. the rather different analysis of V. Ehrenberg, *AJP*, 74 (1953): 113–136.

of Cyprus for the Roman treasury.[2] Q. Catulus objected to the *rogatio Manilia,* which was to give Pompey his Mithridatic command, on the grounds that it set a new and dangerous precedent. Yet Catulus had consented to some of Pompey's earlier, equally dramatic appointments.[3] And even P. Clodius, not normally adjudged a stickler for constitutional niceties, protested the impropriety of extraordinary commissions in opposing Pompey's *cura annonæ.*[4] Obviously it was a conventional argument, trotted out whenever expedient –and otherwise ignored. Once should recall that some *consulares* and pillars of the aristocracy were open advocates of Pompey's command under the *lex Manilia.*[5] Such stands depended less on principle than on politics.

The flexibility of the Roman constitution is too often left out of the reckoning. Extraordinary commands are by definition unusual–which is not at all the same as unconstitutional. Wherein lay the dangerous innovations of late Republican *imperia extra ordinem?* Several aspects have been deemed troublesome: the appointment of *privati,* instead of duly elected magistrates, to important military tasks; the protracted tenure and broad powers accorded to the appointees; the increased involvement of the popular assemblies in provincial decisions previously disposed of by the senate. On all these matters, however, the *mos maiorum* had never been rigid or static. To Catulus' complaints about the Manilian law, Cicero renders the appropriate response: Romans have always conformed to convention in time of peace, to expediency in time of war–ever improvising policies to meet emergencies.[6] That is special pleading, of course, but not without substance. Further scrutiny will provide confirmation.

First of all, the matter of *privati cum imperio.* Instances in the late Republic are, in fact, few, most of them connected with the unusual career and abilities of Pompeius Magnus. Pompey, while still in his twenties, enrolled troops and brought them over to the side of Sulla in the late 80s, for which he received propraetorian *imperium.*[7] In the circumstances of civil war customary proprieties could not always be observed. Pompey's repute stood high. And he was called upon again to head government forces against Lepidus and

[2] Cic. *De Domo,* 22. On Cato's mission, see S. I. Oost, *CP,* 50 (1955): 98–112; Badian, *JRS,* 55 (1965): 110–121.

[3] Cic. *De Imp. Pomp.* 60: *in ipso Cn. Pompeio, in quo novi constitui nihil volt Q. Catulus, quam multa sint nova summa Q. Catuli voluntate constituta, recordamini.*

[4] Cic. *De Domo,* 18: *negat oportuisse quidquam uni extra ordinem decerni.*

[5] Cic. *De Imp. Pomp.* 68.

[6] Cic. *De Imp. Pomp.* 60: *maiores nostros semper in pace consuetudini, in bello utilitati paruisse, semper ad novos casus temporum novorum consiliorum rationes accommodasse.* On a later occasion, and with a different case to make, Cicero sought to soft-pedal this characteristic; *Phil.* 11.17–19.

[7] Sources in Broughton, *MRR,* II:70.

then Sertorius in 77. The state faced an emergency situation in both instances, a more than adequate motive for waiving the normal *cursus honorum.*[8] An analogous emergency explains the bestowal of proconsular *imperium* upon M. Crassus in 72, though he held no magistracy at the time. Several prætors and even two consuls had failed to check the servile insurrection of Spartacus. The government improvised in assigning Crassus to the task–and no one objected on constitutional grounds.[9] Similarly, when discussion arose in 67 over measures to be taken against Mediterranean pirates, Pompey was the obvious choice to organize the campaign. By this time, of course, he possessed consular rank and boasted military laurels unmatched by his contemporaries. The fact that he happened to be a *privatus* in 67 was unimportant and irrelevant. Pompey's enemies, of course, resisted the appointment with vigor. But their objections dwelled principally upon the danger of entrusting so much power to a single commander and not upon the alleged illegality of awarding *imperium* to a private citizen.[10] The same holds for Pompey's corn commission in 57. The bill that authorized it provided for *imperium pro consule* and a five-year term. Yet opposition was minimal–and no one suggested that Pompey's status as a *privatus* stood against him.[11]

The situation is readily explicable. Conferral of *imperium* upon a private citizen had a long history. The practice can be traced as far back as 295, during the darker days of the Third Samnite War. Four men, all ex-consuls, were invested with proprætorian *imperium* in order to facilitate the Roman effort. [12] Two generations later, the Hannibalic War brought danger unprecedented to Rome. The expedient of summoning ex-magistrates and *privati* to take over military commands was resorted to again and again during that conflict. Bestowal of proconsular *imperium* upon P. Scipio Africanus, at the age of twenty-five, constitutes only the most spectacular example. Other men too, like the great M. Marcellus, obtained promagisterial authority without

[8] On these events, see above, chap. 1.

[9] Sources in Broughton, *MRR*, II:118. That Crassus was a *privatus* at the time should no longer be doubted; see Shatzman, *Athenæum*, 46 (1968): 347–350.

[10] Cic. *De Imp. Pomp.* 52–53; Vell. Pat. 2.31.3–4; Plut. *Pomp.* 25.3–6. To be sure, Dio, in the fictitious speech that he puts in Catulus' mouth, includes a reference to the impropriety of bestowing *imperium* upon a private citizen; 36.33.1–3. That, however, is worth little. No other source alludes to it. And it is but one of several arguments offered in that speech; Dio, 36.31–36. Moreover, Catulus himself, if Dio is to be believed, was willing to authorize grants of *imperium*, so long as they went to several individuals and not to Pompey alone; Dio, 36.36.1–4. Some men suggested that, if Pompey should perish in his mission, Catulus–also a *privatus*–be appointed in his stead; Val. Max. 8.15.9; Dio, 36.36a.

[11] Sources in Broughton, *MRR*, II:203–204.

[12] Broughton, *MRR*, I:178; see W. Jashemski, *The Origins and History of the Proconsular and the Proprætorian Imperium to 27 B.C.* (Chicago, 1950), pp. 5–8.

currently occupying magistracies. A whole string of governors in Spain in the later part of the war and immediately thereafter fall into this category.[13] Expulsion of the invader and a subsequent increase in the number of annual magistrates with *imperium* reduced Rome's need to call upon *privati* for special assignments. But the senate and the people never forfeited their right to revive the expedient when the situation (military or political) called for it. That much is clear from the popular vote in 88 awarding the Mithridatic command to C. Marius, who was at that time a private citizen.[14] Use of *privati* for military mandates in the Ciceronian age had ample precedent. And Ciceronian instances were, in any case, quite rare. Julius Cæsar, in fact, professed shock that his senatorial enemies sent out *privati* to usurp his functions.[15] Cæsar's own command in Gaul followed his election to the consulship, as did the Syrian and Spanish governorships of Crassus and Pompey in 55, not to mention numerous other provincial posts and overseas assignments in the last decades of the Republic. The deleterious effect of *privati cum imperio* is a red herring.

Long-term commands permitted *imperatores* to develop or augment military reputations—and to solidify the adherence of their *milites*. The *lex Gabinia* specified a three-year term for Pompey's authority in the Mediterranean. Cæsar's proconsulship in Gaul was to run for five years, and later received renewal for another five. Pompey obtained the *cura annonæ* in 57, also for five years. The *lex Trebonia* of 55 gave five-year mandates to both Crassus and Pompey. And Pompey's governorship was extended for a second quinquennial term in 52. Those are the *imperia* customarily cited as undermining the traditional restraints of the constitution. Once again, however, an obvious question must be confronted: were lengthy commands an innovation of the late Republic?

The answer is not far to seek. Instances of prolonged military commissions abound in the Second Punic War. The Scipio brothers served for eight years in Spain, beginning in 218, and only death cut off their powers. Their successors stayed for five years, to be followed by two further governors, whose offices were prorogued for another six years until the end of the war. Nor was Spain exceptional in this regard. Sp. Lucretius exercised *imperium* in Liguria between 205 and 202 and Cn. Octavius commanded a fleet that operated off Sardinia and Sicily between 205 and 201.[16] The aftermath of the war saw no significant change. Governorships that ran four or five years were

[13] See the valuable discussion of Jashemski, *Origins and History*, pp. 20–39; on the governors of Spain, cf. now Sumner, *Arethusa*, 3 (1970): 85–102.

[14] Broughton, *MRR*, II:41. Observe that Scipio Æmilianus, though a *privatus*, was given consideration for the command against Aristonicus in 131; Cic. *Phil.* 11.18.

[15] Cæs. *BC*, 1.6.5; cf. 1.85.

[16] References in Broughton, *MRR*, I, under the appropriate years.

not at all unusual in the subsequent quarter-century.[17] Spain provided the site for most of the long-term promagistracies, as might be expected. Much hard fighting was required in the subjugation of that territory. And the Roman government was not to be hamstrung by any abstract principles about annual commands.

Instances aplenty can also be found in the later part of the second century and the early first century. Marius' spectacular achievements in Africa and against the Germans between 107 and 101 were, in one sense, unusual: he held five consulships during that period, the latter four designed for the German wars, in order to prevent possible conflicts with proconsuls. What needs stressing, however, is the fact that lengthy overseas assignments were by no means exceptional. In that regard Marius stood in an accepted tradition.[18] During the uncertainties of the Social and civil wars that followed, protracted commands were the rule rather than the exception. Unsettled conditions made the practice necessary as well as desirable.[19] And the precedents spilled over into the post-Sullan era as well. Foreign dangers in the 70s prompted a series of major overseas *imperia.* Among them, of course, were Metellus Pius' nine-year service against Sertorius in Spain, the lengthy Mithridatic commands of L. Lucullus and M. Cotta, and M. Antonius' broad commission against the pirates, as well as a number of other mandates enduring for four or five years.[20]

There is no need to belabor the point. Extended promagistracies were common well before their exercise by Pompey, Cæsar, and Crassus. And the triumvirs were not alone among their contemporaries in administering such commands.[21] Enemies of the coalition might argue that excessive powers were

[17] Note, for example, Cn. Cornelius Blasio and L. Stertinius in Spain from 199 to 196, T. Flamininus in Greece and Macedonia from 198 to 194, Q. Minucius Thermus in Liguria from 193 to 190, C. Flaminius in Spain from 193 to 190, L. Manlius Acidinus in Spain from 188 to 185, and M. Titinius Curvus in Spain from 178 to 175.

[18] Observe M'. Aquillius in Asia between 129 and 126, L. Aurelius Orestes in Sardinia between 126 and 122, M. Metellus in Sardinia between 115 and 111, M. Minucius Rufus in Macedonia and Thrace between 110 and 106, T. Didius in Spain between 98 and 93, and P. Crassus in Spain between 97 and 93. One should add also Q. Metellus Numidicus in Africa between 109 and 107. His removal, of course, was because of political rivalry with Marius and not because anyone felt that he had overstayed a proper term.

[19] C. Sentius' propraetorship in Macedonia from 93 to at least 87 is certain. Several other governors, it can be safely conjectured, remained at their posts for comparable or even longer periods in the late 90s and 80s. See the sound arguments of Badian, *Studies*, pp. 71–104.

[20] Cn. Dolabella governed Macedonia between 80 and 77, P. Servilius Vatia held forth in Cilicia from 78 to 74, and C. Curio was proconsul of Macedonia from 76 to 72.

[21] One might mention Q. Metellus Creticus in Crete between 68 and 65, C. Pomptinus in the Transalpina from 62 to 59, Q. Cicero in Asia from 61 to 58, C. Vergilius Balbus in Sicily from 61 to 58, A. Gabinius in Syria from 57 to 54, and P. Lentulus Spinther in Cilicia from 56 to 53.

awarded in their commissions. But political propaganda inescapably deals in exaggeration. The *lex Gabinia* gave Pompey authority anywhere on the Mediterranean coasts and fifty miles inland, the right to appoint legates, recruit forces, and employ money from the *ærarium*. Cæsar obtained similar powers for his Gallic proconsulate. The *lex Trebonia* contained provisions along these same lines, as did the measure for Pompey's corn commission in 57.[22] But none of these provisions was itself revolutionary. The very nature of a command against the Mediterranean pirates required widespread authority and had adequate precedent in the *imperium* of M. Antonius in the 70s. Appointment of legates by the commander was certainly no new phenomenon, nor was the recruitment of troops and the allocation of funds. The *leges* that authorized commands for the triumvirs simply made explicit the powers that naturally attached to their duties. In that sense, they put limits on authority rather than issued blank checks. If there was novelty in these enactments, it consisted in specifying the actual length of term awarded. That element had certainly not been customary earlier. The fact is worthy of note. Prolonged commands were hardly unusual; for the triumvirs, however, chronological limits were set. The Roman government recognized the value of extended and relatively untrammeled promagistracies. But when large powers were involved, it was best to set a time limit. Hence, the sponsors of these measures, far from setting aside the constitution, supplied their own constitutional checks–going their ancestors one better.

A final assumption requires correction: that involvement of the *populus* in these matters entailed usurpation of senatorial prerogatives. This notion too is a red herring. Certainly the determination of provincial assignments and the general supervision of foreign policy belonged in the hands of the senate. It was a matter of convenience and expertise. But the Roman people never yielded up its sovereignty in this area or any other. The assemblies exercised jurisdiction in provincial affairs when they saw fit. And occasions of popular intervention long predate the late Republic.

Once again precedents may be found in the Hannibalic conflict. The grim

[22] On the *lex Gabinia*, see Dio, 36.23.4, 36.36a, 36.37.1; Plut. *Pomp.* 25.2–3, 26.1–2; Appian, *Mithr.* 94; Vell. Pat. 2.31.2. That this measure gave Pompey *maius imperium* has been held by some; W. R. Loader, *CR*, 54 (1940): 134–136; S. Jameson, *Historia*, 19 (1970): 539–560. But the term does not appear in the sources, and Velleius is explicit: *imperium æquum in omnibus provinciis cum proconsulibus*. The right to appoint *legati* with propraetorian *imperium*, however, may have been an innovation dictated by the circumstances of the campaign; Appian, *Mithr.* 94; SIG^3, 750. On Cæsar's powers, cf. Cic. *In Vat.* 36; *De Prov. Cons.* 42; *Ad Fam.* 1.7.10; the *lex Trebonia*, Dio, 39.33.2; Plut. *Pomp.* 52.3, 53.1; *Cato*, 41.1, 43.1; *Cæs.* 28.5; Vell. Pat. 2.48.1; the corn commission, Cic. *Ad Att.* 4.1.6–7, 4.2.6; *Ad Q. Frat.* 2.5.1; Dio, 39.9.2–3; Plut. *Pomp.* 49.4–5; Appian, *BC*, 2.18.

situation faced by Rome after Cannæ no longer permitted the luxury of normal promagisterial appointments. In 215 the people expressed its will: M. Marcellus, the only man to have earned any success since Cannæ, received *imperium pro consule* by vote of the assembly.[23] Disaster in Spain in 211 carried off both of Rome's governors there. Once again an emergency situation meant reference to the *populus*—who then promoted young P. Scipio to the crucial post.[24] Decisions of the assembly with regard to *imperatores* in Spain seem to have been regular thereafter, at least to the end of the Second Punic War.[25] In less troubled times provincial business could be handled by the senate. But the *comitia* did not fail to discharge their authority when military crises or unusual political occasions demanded it. So, in 148 the people exempted Scipio Æmilianus from the laws, elected him to the consulship, and gave him charge of the war against Carthage. Seventeen years later, the *comitia tributa* determined Rome's commander in the war against Aristonicus. A *lex* in 107 set aside previous arrangements and sent Marius to salvage the Roman cause in Numidia. And another act of the assembly transferred the Mithridatic command from Sulla to Marius in 88.[26] What the people could give they could also take away. Q. Cæpio found that out in 105 when his *imperium* was revoked by vote of the assembly.[27] Political struggles might produce opposition to these enactments. But none could dispute the right of the *populus* to override and supersede the decisions of the senate.

In this regard the late Republic marked no constitutional innovation. The number of *leges* fixing promagisterial assignments became more plentiful: the *lex Gabinia* of 67, the *lex Manilia* of 66, the *lex Vatinia* of 59, Clodius' bills of 58 on the provinces for Piso and Gabinius, Pompey's *cura annonæ* of 57, the *lex Trebonia* and *lex Pompeia Licinia* of 55.[28] That may be a function of increased intensity in political contests—or simply a consequence of our more abundant information on the Ciceronian age. Excessive emphasis on these measures, however, beclouds an important fact. The engagement of popular authority in provincial appointments remained exceptional rather than normal in the late Republic, as in all other eras of Roman history.

[23] Livy, 23.30.19: *M. Marcello pro consule imperium esse populus iussit, quod post Cannensem cladem unus Romanorum imperatorum in Italia prospere rem gessisset;* cf. Jashemski, *Origins and History*, pp. 20–22.

[24] Livy, 26.2.5, 26.18; Appian, *Iber.* 18. Scipio's colleague, M. Junius Silanus, was probably also sent by vote of the people; Livy, 26.19.10.

[25] Cf. Livy, 29.13.7, 30.41.4–5, 31.50.11.

[26] Sources on these measures in Broughton, *MRR*, I:462, 500, 550, II:41.

[27] Asconius, 78, Clark; Livy, *Per.* 67.

[28] Cf. also the *rogationes* of C. Cato and Caninius on the restoration of Ptolemy Auletes in 56; Cic. *Ad Fam.* 1.4.1, 1.5a.2, 1.5b.2; *Ad Q. Frat.* 2.2.3, 2.3.1, 2.3.4, 2.4.4–5; Plut. *Pomp.* 49.6.

Senatorial action was the customary procedure in this sphere. Practices of the late Republic did not seriously affect it. All the special commands of the 70s were sanctioned by *senatus consulta.* They include, one may observe, Pompey's own commissions against Lepidus and Sertorius, as well as Crassus' *imperium* in the servile war.[29] It was the senate too which mobilized *imperatores,* still awaiting triumphs, against Catiline in 63.[30] Consular provinces, in accordance with the *lex Sempronia,* were chosen a year in advance, before the elections. But unforeseen military exigencies sometimes required improvisation; and the senate always possessed the power to make ad hoc arrangements, as it did in 60 when it instructed the consuls to draw lots for the two Gauls instead of the provinces previously selected.[31] The constitution was appropriately flexible on these matters, as on so many others. The important and potentially explosive question of restoring Ptolemy Auletes consumed months of debate–in the *curia.* It was only political stalemate on the issue that prevented effective action until 55.[32] A new ordinance on provincial arrangements was enacted in 54, once more on the basis of a *senatus consultum.*[33] It is clear that even decisions *extra ordinem* on the provinces remained generally within the domain of the senate.

The so-called extraordinary commands of the triumvirs may now be viewed in proper perspective. They had neither the purpose nor the effect of stripping the senate of its role in foreign affairs. A closer look will fortify that conclusion. The momentous Gallic command of Julius Cæsar was initiated by the *lex Vatinia* and passed by the assembly. The measure canceled earlier arrangements made by the senate for consular provinces in 59. But it is well to remember that Vatinius' law awarded Cæsar only the *provinciæ* of Cisalpine Gaul and Illyricum. The real battleground was Gallia Comata, the future source of Cæsar's triumphs and unparalleled prestige. And that was assigned to him by decree of the senate. The fact should not be glossed over; it gave the House an additional constitutional foothold whereby to review Cæsar's position and to keep the Gauls under surveillance in ensuing years.[34] A vote

[29] Broughton, *MRR,* II:90, 118. Note also that when Crassus requested the recall of Pompey and M. Lucullus from their provinces to provide further assistance in the Spartacus campaign his request went to the *curia*; Plut. *Crass.* 11.2.

[30] Sallust, *Cat.* 30.3.

[31] Cic. *Ad Att.* 1.19.2; cf. *Ad Att.* 1.16.8 for a similar instance in 61.

[32] Cic. *Ad Fam.* 1.1–7; *Ad Q. Frat.* 2.2–4.

[33] Cic. *Ad Att.* 4.16.5. Its contents, unfortunately, are unknown.

[34] On the *s.c.* for Transalpine Gaul, see Cic. *De Prov. Cons.* 36; *Ad Att.* 8.3.3; Suet. *Iul* 22; Dio, 38.8.5; Orosius, 6.7.1. Suetonius holds that the decree was passed under duress. Perhaps; but the senate had reasons of its own for maintaining official responsibility over Gaul. And passage of the decree further indicates Cæsar's concern for constitutional formalities.

of the assembly ratified Pompey's Mediterranean corn commission in 57. But the issue had been decided in the senate: a *senatus consultum* formed the basis for the assembly's measure. Far from undermining senatorial authority, Pompey received his post with the enthusiastic assent of the House.[35] The *lex Trebonia* awarded him a five-year command over both Spanish provinces in 55. But the senate's powers were not thereby abrogated. In 52, when Pompey's *imperium* was renewed for another quinquennium, the renewal came through a decision of the *curia*.[36] As is evident by now, the triumviral commands themselves rested in large part on senatorial resolutions. No sharp cleavage can be discerned between civil and military authority.

Increased numbers of special commissions, however, were potentially troublesome. The government was cognizant of the problem. In 53 a *senatus consultum* called for restructuring of the system: henceforth a hiatus of at least five years should be enforced between magistracy and promagistracy. The change would bring a measure of regularity back into the procedure. That resolution was enacted into law during the following year. Author of the legislative proposal was Pompeius Magnus himself.[37] Senatorial jurisdiction over provincial appointments was thereby reasserted. The House was to make all necessary assignments under the new law. And its general supervision of provincial matters endured to the outbreak of civil war.[38]

A brief retrospect is now possible. The idea that *imperia extra ordinem* eroded the structure of civil government is based on an unduly rigid view of the Roman constitution. In fact, procedures were supple and adhered to no fixed pattern.[39] When emergencies or unusual circumstances dictated it, private

[35] Cic. *Ad Att.* 4.1.6–7: *factum est senatus consultum in meam sententiam ut cum Pompeio ageretur ut eam rem susciperet, lexque ferretur . . . nihil Pompeio postulanti negarunt; De Domo*, 10: *ab universo senatu reclamatum est.* A grain shortage and popular unrest forced the issue. And political motives were also involved in Pompey's appointment; Cic. *De Domo*, 9–18; Asconius, 48, Clark; Plut. *Pomp.* 49.4–5. But the senate's formal authority is clear. Note too that another *senatus consultum* allocated the necessary funds for the task; Cic. *Ad Q. Frat.* 2.5.1. Further references to the bill: Cic. *Ad Att.* 4.2.6; *De Domo*, 3–4, 30; Dio, 39.9.2–3, 39.24.1; Livy, *Per.* 104; Plut. *Pomp.* 50.1; Appian, *BC*, 2.18.

[36] Plut. *Cæs.* 28.5; Appian, *BC*, 2.24; cf. Dio, 40.44.2, 40.56.2; Plut. *Pomp.* 55.7.

[37] Dio, 40.30.1, 40.46.1–3, 40.56.1; cf. Cæs. *BC*, 1.85.9.

[38] That much is abundantly clear from numerous Ciceronian references to his own situation in Cilicia; e.g. *Ad Att.* 5.4.2, 5.18.3, 6.4.1, 6.5.3, 6.6.3; *Ad Fam.* 2.17.7, 3.2.2, 3.3.1–2, 3.13.1, 15.1.4–5, 15.2.7–8, 15.4.2. Recurrent senatorial debates in 51 and 50 on Cæsar's Gallic command confirm the picture; see above, chap. 11. Observe also the senate's discussions on a prospective Parthian war and its instructions to Cæsar and Pompey to dispatch legions to that front; Cic. *Ad Att.* 5.18.1, 5.21.2–3; *Ad Fam.* 2.17.5, 3.3.1–2; Dio, 40.65.2–3; Appian, *BC*, 2.29.

[39] Even after consular provinces were allotted, there was nothing to prevent a consul from resigning his commission to his colleague. Hortensius did it in 69; Dio, 36.1a; Schol. Bob. 96, Stangl. And Cicero in 63; Cic. *Ad Fam.* 5.2.3–4, 5.5.2; *In Pis.* 5; *De Leg. Agrar.* 1.25–26, 2.103; Sallust, *Cat.* 26.4; Dio, 37.33.4; Plut. *Cic.* 12.4.

citizens could be appointed as *imperatores.* The late Republic had no monopoly on the practice. The same was true of long-term commands. Instances are discoverable well before the age of Cicero. The Roman senate customarily rendered decisions on provincial assignments, both regular and *extra ordinem.* But the right of the *populus* to override such arrangements on occasion was a long-established principle. Enactments of the assembly in the 60s and 50s stood in that tradition. If they awarded somewhat larger powers, they also supplied new checks on those powers: specified time limits for the exercise of *imperium.* The constitution had not been flouted. Senatorial management of provincial affairs remained the norm even to the end of the Republic. And it was reinforced in 52 by legislation sponsored by the very man who had made a habit of collecting "extraordinary commands." Cicero's pronouncement about the malleability of Roman institutions holds true. The dispatching of competent *imperatores* on special missions did not entail the crumbling of civil government.

BIBLIOGRAPHY

Accame, S. "La legislazione romana intorno ai collegi nel I secolo a.C." *Bull. Mus. Imp. Rom.*, 13 (1942): 13–49.

Adcock, F. E. "The Legal Term of Cæsar's Governorship in Gaul." *CQ*, 26 (1932): 14–26.

———. *Marcus Crassus, Millionaire.* Cambridge, 1966.

Afzelius, A. "Zur Definition der römischen Nobilität in der Zeit Ciceros." *ClMed*, 1 (1938): 40–94.

———. "Das Ackerverteilungsgesetz des P. Servilius Rullus." *ClMed*, 3 (1940): 214–235.

———. "Die politische Bedeutung des jüngeren Catos." *ClMed*, 4 (1941): 100–203.

Agnes, L. "Intorno alla *regatio Servilia.*" *RivFilol*, 21 (1943): 35–45.

Albini, U. "L'orazione contro Vatinio." *PP*, 66 (1959): 172–184.

Alford, M. "Notes on Cicero's Letters to Atticus, Book II." *CR*, 41 (1927): 215–218.

Allen, W. "In Defense of Catiline." *CJ*, 34 (1938): 70–85.

———. "The Vettius Affair Once More." *TAPA*, 81 (1950): 153–163.

Anderson, W. S. *Pompey, His Friends and the Literature of the First Century B.C.* Berkeley and Los Angeles, 1963.

Archi, G. G. *Pauli Sententiarum Fragmentum Leidense.* Leiden, 1956.

Astbury, R. "Varro and Pompey." *CQ*, 17 (1967): 403–407.

Astin, A. E. *"Leges Ælia et Fufia."* *Latomus*, 23 (1964): 421–445.

Austin, R. G. *M. Tulli Ciceronis Pro M. Cælio Oratio.* 3rd ed. Oxford, 1960.

Ayers, D. M. "Cato's Speech against Murena." *CJ*, 49 (1954): 245–253.

Babcock, C. L. "The Early Career of Fulvia." *AJP*, 86 (1965): 1–32.

Badian, E. *Foreign Clientelæ, 264–70 B.C.* Oxford, 1958.

———. "The Early Career of A. Gabinius (cos. 58 B.C.)." *Philologus,* 103 (1959): 87–99.
———. "Review of Broughton, *Supplement to The Magistrates of the Roman Republic.*" *Gnomon,* 33 (1961): 492–498.
———. "Forschungsbericht. From the Gracchi to Sulla (1940–1959)." *Historia,* 11 (1962): 197–245.
———. "Review of Taylor, *Voting Districts of the Roman Republic.*" *JRS,* 52 (1962): 200–210.
———. "Notes on Roman Senators of the Republic." *Historia,* 12 (1963): 129–143.
———. *Studies in Greek and Roman History.* New York, 1964.
———. "M. Porcius Cato and the Annexation and Early Administration of Cyprus." *JRS,* 55 (1965): 110–121.
———. *Roman Imperialism in the Late Republic.* 2nd ed. Oxford, 1968.
———. "Two Roman Non-Entities." *CQ,* 19 (1969): 198–204.
———. "Lucius Sulla, the Deadly Reformer." *Seventh Todd Memorial Lecture.* Sydney, 1970.
———. "Additional Notes on Roman Magistrates." *Athenæum,* 48 (1970): 3–14.
Balsdon, J. P. V. D. "Consular Provinces under the Late Republic." *JRS,* 29 (1939): 57–73, 167–183.
———. "Roman History, 58-56 B.C. Three Ciceronian Problems." *JRS,* 47 (1957): 15–20.
———. "Roman History, 65–50 B.C. Five Problems." *JRS,* 52 (1962): 134–141.
———. "The *Commentariolum Petitionis.*" *CQ,* 13 (1963): 242–250.
———. "*Fabula Clodiana.*" *Historia,* 15 (1966): 65–73.
Bartsch, B. *Die Legaten der römischen Republik vom Tode Sullas bis zum Ausbruche des zweiten Bürgerkrieges.* Breslau, 1908.
Bauman, R. A. *The Crimen Maiestatis in the Roman Republic and Augustan Principate.* Johannesburg, 1967.
———. *The Duumviri in the Roman Criminal Law and in the Horatius Legend.* Wiesbaden, 1969.
Beloch, K. J. *Die Bevölkerung der griechisch-römischen Welt.* Leipzig, 1886.
Beranger, J. "La date de la *lex Antonia de Termessibus* et le tribunat syllanien." *Mélanges d' archéologie et d'histoire offerts à André Piganiol* (1966), II:723–737.
Berchem, J. Van. *Les Distributions de blé et d'argent à la plèbe romaine sous l'empire.* Geneva, 1939.
Bersanetti, G. M. "La tradizione antica e l'opinione degli storici moderni sul primo triumvirato." *Riv. Indo-Grec.-Ital. Filol.,* 11 (1927): 1–20, 185–204.
———. "La tradizione antica e l'opinione degli storici moderni sul primo triumvirato." *Riv. Indo-Grec.-Ital. Filol.,* 12 (1928): 21–42.
Berve, H. "Sertorius." *Hermes,* 64 (1929): 199–227.

Bleicken, J. *Das Volkstribunat der klassischen Republik.* Munich, 1955.

Boak, A. E. R. "The Extraordinary Commands from 80 to 48 B.C." *AHR,* 24 (1918): 1–25.

Botsford, G. W. "On the Legality of the Trial and Condemnation of the Catilinarian Conspirators." *CW,* 6 (1913): 130–132.

Broughton, T. R. S. "Was Sallust Fair to Cicero?" *TAPA,* 67 (1936): 34–46.

———. "Notes on Roman Magistrates." *TAPA,* 77 (1946): 35–43.

———. *The Magistrates of the Roman Republic.* 2 vols. New York, 1951–1952.

———. *Supplement to the Magistrates of the Roman Republic.* New York, 1960.

Brunt, P. A. "Pay and Superannuation in the Roman Army." *PBSR,* 18 (1950): 50–71.

———. "Three Passages from Asconius." *CR,* 71 (1957): 193–195.

———. "Review of W. L. Westermann, *The Slave Systems of Greek and Roman Antiquity.*" *JRS,* 48 (1958): 164–170.

———. "Charges of Provincial Maladministration under the Early Principate." *Historia,* 10 (1961): 189–227.

———. "The Army and the Land in the Roman Revolution." *JRS,* 52 (1962): 69–86.

———. "The *Equites* in the Late Republic." *Second International Conference of Economic History, 1962* (Paris, 1965), I:117–137.

———. "The Roman Mob." *Past and Present,* 35 (1966): 3–27.

———. *Italian Manpower (225 B.C.–A.D. 14).* Oxford, 1971.

Bruwaene, M. Van den. "Precisions sur la teneur et l'importance du senatus-consulte d'octobre 51 av. J.C." *LEC,* 21 (1953): 19–27.

Burns, A. "Pompey's Strategy and Domitius' Stand at Corfinium." *Historia,* 15 (1966): 74–95.

Cadoux, T. J. "Marcus Crassus. A Revaluation." *Greece and Rome,* 3 (1956): 153–161.

Carcopino, J. *Sylla ou la Monarchie Manquée.* Paris, 1931.

———. *Histoire Romaine.* Vol. II. Paris, 1935.

———. *Jules César.* Paris, 1968.

Cary, M. "Pompey's Compromise." *CR,* 33 (1919): 109.

———. "The Land Legislation of Cæsar's First Consulship." *JP,* 35 (1920): 174–190.

———. "*Asinus Germanus.*" *CQ,* 17 (1923): 103–107.

———. "Notes on the Legislation of Julius Cæsar." *JRS,* 19 (1929): 113–119.

Ciaceri, E. *Processi politici e relazioni internazionali.* Rome, 1918.

———. "Il processo di M. Celio Rufo e l'arringa di Cicerone." *Atti Accad. Arch. Nap.,* 11 (1930): 1–24.

———. "La dama Sempronia nella congiura di Catilina." *Atti Accad. Arch. Nap.,* 11 (1930): 219–230.

———. *Cicerone e i suoi tempi.* 2 vols. Milan, 1939–1941.

Cichorius, C. "Zur Lebensgeschichte des Valerius Soranus." *Hermes*, 41 (1906): 59–68.

______. *Römische Studien.* Leipzig-Berlin, 1922.

Clark, A. C. *Cicero, Pro Milone.* Oxford, 1895.

Cloud, J. D. "The Primary Purpose of the *lex Cornelia de sicariis.*" *ZSS*, 86 (1969): 258–286.

Collins, J. H. "Porcia's First Husband." *CJ*, 50 (1955): 261–270.

Constans, L. A. *Un Correspondant de Ciceron, Ap. Claudius Pulcher.* Paris, 1921.

Cook, S. A., F. E. Adcock, and M. P. Charlesworth. *The Cambridge Ancient History.* Vol. IX. Cambridge, 1932.

Courtney, E. "The Prosecution of Scaurus in 54 B.C. " *Philologus*, 105 (1961): 151–156.

Cousin, J. "*Lex Lutatia de vi.*" *Rev. Hist. Droit* (1943): 88–94.

Criniti, N. "Studi recenti su Catilina e la sua congiura." *Aevum*, 41 (1967): 370–395.

______. "M. Aimilius Q.F.M.N. Lepidus 'ut ignis in stipula'." *MemIstLomb*, 30 (1969): 319–460.

______. *L'Epigrafe di Asculum di Gn. Pompeo Strabone.* Milan, 1970.

Cuff, P. J. "The Terminal Date of Cæsar's Gallic Command." *Historia*, 7 (1958): 445–471.

Dahlmann, H. "Cæsars Rede für die Bithynier." *Hermes*, 73 (1938): 341–346.

Davison, J. A. "Cicero and the *lex Gabinia.*" *CR*, 44 (1930): 224–225

Degrassi, A. *Inscriptiones Latinæ Liberæ Rei Publicæ.* Florence, 1965.

De Robertis, F. M. *Il Diritto Associativo Romano.* Bari, 1938.

______. *Lavoro e Lavorati nel Mondo Romano.* Bari, 1963.

Dessau, H. "Gaius Rabirius Postumus." *Hermes*, 46 (1911): 613-620.

______. *Inscriptiones Latinæ Selectæ.* 3 vols. Berlin, 1892–1916.

Deutsch, M. E. "Cæsar and Mucia." *Phil. Quart.*, 8 (1929): 218–222.

Dignös, G. *Die Stellung der Aedilen im römischen Strafrecht.* Diss. Munich, 1962.

Dorey, T. A. "Cicero, Pompey, and the *Pro Archia.*" *Orpheus*, 2 (1955): 32–35.

______. "Cicero, Clodia, and the *Pro Cælio.*" *Greece and Rome*, 27 (1958): 175–180.

Dragstedt, A. "Cato's *Politeuma.*" *Agon*, 3 (1969): 69–96.

Drexler, H. "Parerga Cæsariana." *Hermes*, 70 (1935): 203–234.

Drumann, W. *Geschichte Roms.* 2nd ed. by P. Groebe. Vols. I–VI. Berlin, 1899–1929.

Eagle, E. D. "Catiline and the *Concordia Ordinum.*" *Phoenix*, 3 (1949): 15–30.

Earl, D. C. *The Political Thought of Sallust.* Cambridge, 1961.

______. "The Early Career of Sallust." *Historia*, 15 (1966): 302–311.

Eden, P. T. "P. Cornelius Lentulus Spinther and Cn. Cornelius Lentulus Marcellinus. Cicero, *Ad Fam.* 1.1.2." *RhMus*, 105 (1962): 352–358.

Ehrenburg, V. "*Imperium Maius* in the Roman Republic." *AJP,* 74 (1953): 113–136.

Elton, G. R. "The Terminal Date of Cæsar's Gallic Proconsulate." *JRS,* 36 (1946): 18–42.

Ewins, U. "The Enfranchisement of Cisalpine Gaul." *PBSR,* 23 (1955): 73–98.

———. "*Ne quis iudicio circumveniatur.*" *JRS,* 50 (1960): 95–107.

Fallu, E. "La première lettre de Cicéron à Quintus et la *lex Julia de repetundis.*" *LEC,* 48 (1971): 180–204.

Frank, T. "Race Mixture in the Roman Empire." *AHR,* 21 (1916): 689–708.

———. "Pompey's Compromise: Cicero, *Ad Fam.* 8.11(3).68." *CR,* 33 (1919): 68–69.

Frederiksen, M. W. "Cæsar, Cicero, and the Problem of Debt." *JRS,* 56 (1966): 128–141.

Frisch, H. "The First Catilinarian Conspiracy. A Study in Historical Conjecture." *ClMed,* 9 (1948): 10–36.

Fritz, K. von. *The Theory of the Mixed Constitution in Antiquity.* New York, 1954.

Fulford-Jones, P. W. "Calvus 'ex Nanneianis'." *CQ,* 21 (1971): 183–185.

Gabba, E. "Le origini dell' esercito professionale in Roma. I proletari e la riforma di Mario." *Athenæum,* 27 (1949): 173–209.

———. "*Lex Plotia agraria.*" *PP,* 13 (1950): 66–68.

———. "Ricerche sull' esercito professionale romano da Mario a Augusto." *Athenæum,* 29 (1951): 171–272.

———. "Le origini della guerra sociale e la vita politica romana dopo l'89 a.C." *Athenæum,* 32 (1954): 41–114, 293–345.

———. "Il ceto equestre e il senato di Silla." *Athenæum,* 34 (1956): 124–138.

———. "Cicerone e la falsificazione dei senatoconsulti." *StudClassOrient,* 10 (1961): 89–96.

———. "Nota sulla rogatio agraria di P. Servilio Rullo." *Mélanges d'archéologie et d'histoire offerts à A. Piganiol* (1966), II:769–775.

———. *Appiani Bellorum Civilium Liber Primus.* 2nd ed. Florence, 1967.

Garzetti, A. "M. Licinio Crasso." *Athenæum,* 19 (1941): 1–37.

———. "M. Licinio Crasso." *Athenæum,* 20 (1942): 12–40.

Gelzer, M. "Die *lex Vatinia de imperio Cæsaris.*" *Hermes,* 63 (1928): 113–137.

———. "Hat Sertorius in seinem Vertrag mit Mithridates die Provinz Asia abgetraten?" *PhilWoch,* 52 (1932): 1129–1136.

———. *Pompeius.* Munich, 1949.

———. *Kleine Schriften.* Vols, I–II. Wiesbaden, 1962.

———. *Cæsar: Politician and Statesman.* Cambridge, Mass., 1968.

———. *Cicero. Ein Biographischer Versuch.* Wiesbaden, 1969.

Giannelli, C. A. "Le date di scadenza dei proconsolati di Giulio Cesare." *AnnPisa,* 35 (1966): 107–120.

Gordon, M. L. "The Nationality of Slaves under the early Roman Empire." *JRS,* 14 (1924): 93–111.

Graham, H. D., and T. R. Gurr. *Violence in America: Historical and Comparative Analysis.* New York, 1969.

Greenidge, A. H. J. *The Legal Procedure of Cicero's Time.* Oxford, 1901.

Grimal, P. *Ciceron, Discours contre Pison.* Paris, 1966.

Gruen, E. S. "Cicero and Licinius Calvus." *HSCP,* 71 (1966): 215–233.

———. "The Dolabellæ and Sulla." *AJP,* 87 (1966): 385–399.

———. "P. Clodius: Instrument or Independent Agent?" *Phoenix,* 20 (1966): 120–130.

———. *Roman Politics and the Criminal Courts, 149–78 B.C.* Cambridge, Mass., 1968.

———. "Pompey and the Pisones." *CSCA,* 1 (1968): 155–170.

———. "Pompey, the Roman Aristocracy, and the Conference of Luca." *Historia,* 18 (1969): 71–108.

———. "Notes on the 'First Catilinarian Conspiracy'." *CP,* 64 (1969): 20–24.

———. "The Consular Elections for 53 B.C." *Hommages à Marcel Renard* (1969), II:311–321.

———. "*Veteres Hostes, Novi Amici.*" *Phoenix,* 24 (1970): 237–243.

———. "Pompey, Metellus Pius, and the Trials of 70–69 B.C.: The Perils of Schematism." *AJP,* 92 (1971): 1–16.

———. "Some Criminal Trials of the Late Republic: Political and Prosopographical Problems." *Athenæum,* 49 (1971): 54–69.

———. "The Trial of C. Antonius." *Latomus* (Forthcoming).

Grummel, W. C. "The Consular Elections of 59 B.C." *CJ,* 49 (1954): 351–355.

Guerriero, E. "Di una supposta 'causa capitale' assunta da Cicerone in favore di Aulo Gabinio e nuovi dubbi intorno all' autenticità del discorso *post reditum ad Quirites.*" *Mondo Classico,* 6 (1936): 160–166.

Gwatkin, W. E. "Cicero *In Catilinam* I.19. Catiline's Attempt to Place Himself in 'libera custodia.'" *TAPA,* 65 (1934): 271–281.

Hanslik, R. "Cicero und das erste Triumvirat." *RhMus,* 98 (1955): 324–334.

Hardy, E. G. "The Catilinarian Conspiracy in Its Context: A Re-study of the Evidence." *JRS,* 7 (1917): 153–228.

———. *The Catilinarian Conspiracy in Its Context.* Oxford, 1924.

———. *Some Problems in Roman History.* Oxford, 1924.

Harmand, J. *L'Armée et la Soldat à Rome de 107 à 50 avant notre ère.* Paris, 1967.

Harris, W. V. *Rome in Etruria and Umbria.* Oxford, 1971.

Hathorn, R. Y. "*Calvum ex Nanneianis.*" *CJ,* 50 (1954): 33–34.

Hawthorn, J. R. "The Senate after Sulla." *Greece and Rome,* 9 (1962): 53–60.
Heaton, J. W. *Mob Violence in the Late Roman Republic.* Urbana, Illinois, 1939.
Heinze, R. "Ciceros politische Anfänge." *AbhLeipz,* 27 (1909): 945–1010.
______. "Ciceros Rede *Pro Cælio.*" *Hermes,* 60 (1925): 193–258.
Heitland, W. E. *The Roman Republic.* Vol. III. Cambridge, 1923.
Henderson, M. I. "De Commentariolo Petitionis." *JRS,* 40 (1950): 8–21.
______. "The Establishment of the 'equester ordo'." *JRS,* 53 (1963): 61–72.
Heurgon, J. "La lettre de Ciceron a P. Sittius (*Ad Fam.* 5.17)." *Latomus,* 9 (1950): 369–377.
______. "Tarquitius Priscus et l'organisation de l'ordre des haruspices sous l'empereur Claude." *Latomus,* 12 (1953): 402–417.
Heuss, A. *Römische Geschichte.* Braunschweig. 1960.
Hill, H. "Sulla's new Senators in 81 B.C." *CQ,* 26 (1932): 170–177.
______. *The Roman Middle Class in the Republican Period.* Oxford, 1952.
Hinrichs, F. T. "Das legale Landversprechen in Bellum Civile." *Historia,* 18 (1969): 521–544.
Hirschfeld, O. "Der Endtermin der gallischer Statthalterschaft Cæsars." *Klio,* 4 (1904): 77–88.
______. "Nochmals der Endtermin der gallischer Statthalterschaft Cæsars." *Klio,* 5 (1905): 236–240.
Hobsbawm, E. J. *Primitive Rebels.* New York, 1965.
Hoenigswald, G. "The Murder Charge in Cicero's *Pro Cluentio.*" *TAPA,* 93 (1962): 109–123.
Hoffman, W. "Catilina und die römische Revolution." *Gymnasium,* 66 (1959): 459–477.
Holmes, T. Rice. "Hirschfeld and Judeich on the *Lex Pompeia Licinia.*" *CQ,* 10 (1916): 49–56.
______. *The Roman Republic.* Vols. I–II. Oxford, 1923.
Hölzl, M. *Fasti Prætorii ab A.U. DCLXXXVII usque ad A.U. DCCX.* Leipzig, 1876.
Hough, J. N. "The *Lex Lutatia* and the *Lex Plautia de vi.*" *AJP,* 51 (1930): 135–147.
How, W. W. *Cicero, Select Letters.* Vols. I–II. Oxford, 1925–1926.
Hoy, L. P. "Political Influence in Roman Prosecutions, 78 to 60 B.C." Unpub. diss. Bryn Mawr, 1952.
Humbert, J. *Les plaidoyers écrits et les plaidoiries réelles de Ciceron.* Paris, 1925.
Husband, R. W. "The Prosecution of Milo." *CW,* 8 (1915): 146–150, 156–159.
______. "On the Expulsion of Foreigners from Rome." *CP,* 11 (1916): 315–333.
______. "The Prosecution of Murena." *CJ,* 12 (1916): 102–118.

Jameson, S. "Pompey's *Imperium* in 67: Some Constitutional Fictions." *Historia*. 19 (1970): 539–560.

———. "The Intended Date of Cæsar's Return from Gaul." *Latomus*, 29 (1970): 638–660.

Jashemski, W. *The Origins and History of the Proconsular and Propraetorian Imperium to 27 B.C.* Chicago, 1950.

John, C. "Die Entstehungsgeschichte der catilinarischen Verschwörung." *JahrbClPhil*, Supp. 8 (1876): 703–819.

Jonkers, E. J. *Social and Economic Commentary on Cicero's De Imperio Cn. Pompei.* Leiden, 1959.

———. *Social and Economic Commentary on Cicero's De Lege Agraria Orationes Tres.* Leiden, 1963.

Kelly, J. M. *Roman Litigation.* Oxford, 1966.

Kinsey, T. E. "Cicero, *Pro Murena*, 71." *RevBelg*, 43 (1965): 57–59.

———. "A *senatus consultum* in the *Pro Murena*." *Mnemosyne*, 19 (1966): 272–273.

Knight, D. W. "Pompey's Concern for Preeminence after 60 B.C." *Latomus*. 27 (1968): 878–883.

Kroll, W. "Ciceros Rede für Plancius." *RhMus*, 86 (1937): 127–139.

Kühne, H. "Die Stadtrömischen Sklaven in den *Collegia* des Clodius." *Helikon*. 6 (1966): 95–113.

Kunkel, W. "Untersuchungen zur Entwicklung des römischen Kriminalverfahrens in vorsullanischer Zeit." *AbhMünch*, 56 (1962): 1–149.

Lacey, W. K. "The Tribunate of Curio." *Historia*, 10 (1961): 318–329.

Laffi, U. "Il Mito di Silla." *Athenæum*, 55 (1967): 177–213.

Lange, L. *Römische Alterthümer.* Vol. III. Berlin, 1876.

La Penna, A. "L'interpretazione sallustiana della congiura di Catilina." *StudItalFilClass*, 31 (1959): 1–64, 127–168.

———. "Le *Historiæ* di Sallustio e l'interpretazione della crisi repubblicana." *Athenæum*, 51 (1963): 201–274.

———. *Sallustio e la "rivoluzione" romana.* Milan, 1968.

Lenaghan, J. O. *A Commentary on Cicero's Oration De Haruspicum Responso.* The Hague, 1969.

Lengle, J. "Die Auswahl der Richter im römischen Quæstionsprocess." *ZSS*. 66 (1933): 275–296.

———. "Die Staatsrechtliche Form der Klage gegen C. Rabirius." *Hermes*. 68 (1933): 328–340.

Levi, M. A. "Una pagina di storia agraria romana." *Atene e Roma*. 3 (1922): 239–252.

Linderski, J. "Two Speeches of Q. Hortensius. A Contribution to the Corpus Oratorum of the Roman Republic." *PP*. 79 (1961): 304–311.

———. "Ciceros Rede *Pro Cælio* und die Ambitus und Vereinsgesetzgebung der ausgehenden Republik." *Hermes,* 89 (1961): 106–119.

———. "Cicero and Sallust on Vargunteius." *Historia,* 12 (1963): 511–512.

———. "Constitutional Aspects of the Consular Elections in 59 B.C." *Historia,* 14 (1965): 423–442.

———. "Were Pompey and Crassus Elected in Absence to their First Consulship?" *Mélanges Offerts à K. Michalowski* (1966), pp. 523–526.

———. "The Surnames and the Alleged Affinity of C. Cælius Rufus." *Eos,* 56 (1966): 146–150.

———. "Der Senat und die Vereine," in M. N. Andreev, et al., *Gesellschaft und Recht in Griechisch-Römischen Altertum* (1968), pp. 94–132.

———. "Three Trials in 54 B.C.: Sufenas, Cato, Procilius and Cicero 'Ad Atticum,' 4.15.4." *Studi in onore di E. Volterra* (1969), II:281–302.

Lintott, A. W. "P. Clodius Pulcher. Felix Catilina?" *Greece and Rome,* 14 (1967): 157–169.

———. *Violence in Republican Rome.* Oxford, 1968.

Loader, W. R. "Pompey's Command under the *Lex Gabinia.*" *CR,* 54 (1940): 134–136.

Lovera, F. "Questioni riguardanti il processo *de vi* di Marco Celio Rufo e l'orazione di Cicerone." *Mondo Classico,* 6 (1936): 167–178.

Luibheid, C. "The Luca Conference." *CP,* 65 (1970): 88–94.

McDermott, W. C. "*Vettius ille, ille noster index.*" *TAPA,* 80 (1949): 351–367.

———. "De Lucceiis." *Hermes,* 97 (1969): 233–246.

MacDonald, C. "The *Lex Fufia* of 59 B.C." *CR,* 7 (1957): 198.

McDonald, W. "The Tribunate of Cornelius." *CQ,* 23 (1929): 196–208.

———. "Clodius and the *Lex Ælia Fufia.*" *JRS,* 19 (1929): 164–179.

MacMullen, R. *Enemies of the Roman Order.* Cambridge, Mass., 1966.

Maier, F. G. "Römische Bevölkerungsgeschichte und Inschriftenstatistik." *Historia,* 2 (1954): 318–351.

Malcovati, H. *Oratorum Romanorum Fragmenta Liberæ Rei Publicæ,* 2nd ed. Turin, 1955.

Maxey, M. *Occupations of the Lower Classes in Roman Society as Seen in Justinian's Digest.* Diss. Chicago, 1938.

Meier, C. "Zur Chronologie und Politik in Cæsars ersten Konsulat." *Historia,* 10 (1961): 68–98.

———. "Pompeius' Rückkehr aus dem Mithridatischen Kriege und die Catilinarische Verschwörung." *Athenæum,* 40 (1962): 103–125.

———. "Review of Adcock, *Roman Political Ideas and Practises.*" *Gött. Gel. Anz.,* 216 (1964): 37–52.

———. *Res Publica Amissa.* Wiesbaden, 1966.

______. "Die *Loca Intercessionis* bei Rogationen. Zugleich ein Beitrag zum Problem der Bedingungen der tribunischen Intercession." *MusHelv*, 25 (1968): 86–100.

______. "Ciceros Consulat." In G. Radke, *Cicero, ein Mensch seiner Zeit* (1968), pp. 61–116.

Meloni, P. "Servio Sulpicio Rufo." *Ann. Univ. Cagliari*, 13 (1946): 67–245.

Messer, W. S. "Mutiny in the Roman Army." *CP*, 15 (1920): 158–175.

Metro, A. "La *lex Cornelia de iurisdictione* alla luce di Dio Cass. 36.40.1–2." *Iura*, 20 (1969): 500–524.

Meyer, E. *Cæsars Monarchie und das Principat des Pompeius*. Stuttgart, 1922.

Michels, A. *The Calendar of the Roman Republic*. Princeton, 1967.

Mitchell, J. F. "The Torquati." *Historia*, 15 (1966): 23–31.

Mitchell, Th. N. "Cicero before Luca (September 57–April 56 B.C.)." *TAPA*, 100 (1969): 295–320.

______. "Cicero and the *Senatus consultum ultimum*." *Historia*, 20 (1971): 47–61.

Mohler, S. L. "*Sentina rei publicæ*. Campaign Issues, 63 B.C." *CW*, 29 (1936): 81–84.

Mommsen, T. *Die Rechtsfrage zwischen Cæsar und dem Senat*. Breslau, 1857.

______. *Römisches Staatsrecht*. 3 vols. Leipzig, 1887.

______. *Römisches Strafrecht*. Leipzig, 1899.

______. *Römische Geschichte*. Vol. III. Berlin, 1904.

Münzer, F. "Der erste Gegner des Spartacus." *Philologus*, 55 (1896): 387–389.

______. *Römische Adelsparteien und Adelsfamilien*. Stuttgart, 1920.

Neuendorff, A. *Die römischen Konsulwahlen von 78–49 v. Chr*. Breslau, 1913.

Neunheuser, J. E. *M. Æmilius Lepidus*. Münster, 1902.

Niccolini, G. *I Fasti dei Tribuni della Plebe*. Milan, 1934.

Nicolet, C. "Le Sénat et les mandements aux lois à la fin de la republique." *RevHistDroitFrEtr*, 36 (1958): 260–275.

______. *L'Ordre Equestre à l'Epoque Republicaine, 312–43 av. J.C.* Paris, 1966.

______. "Rome et les élections." *REL*, 45 (1967): 98–111.

______. "Arpinum, Æmilius Scaurus et les Tulli Cicerones." *REL*, 45 (1967): 276–304.

______. "Armée et société à Rome sous la République: A propos de l'ordre équestre." In J. P. Brisson, *Problèmes de la guerre à Rome* (1969), pp. 117–156.

Nisbet, R. G. M. "The *Commentariolum Petitionis*, Some Arguments against Authenticity." *JRS*, 51 (1961): 84–87.

______. *Cicero, In L. Calpurnium Pisonem Oratio*. Oxford, 1961.

Norden, E. "Aus Ciceros Werkstadt." *SBBerl* (1913): 2–32.

Oates, W. J. "The Population of Rome." *CP*, 29 (1934): 101–116.

Ogilvie, R. M. *A Commentary on Livy, Books 1–5*. Oxford, 1965.

Oost, S. I. "Cato Uticensis and the Annexation of Cyprus." *CP,* 50 (1955): 98–112.

———. "The Date of the *Lex Iulia de repetundis.*" *AJP,* 77 (1956): 19–28.

Ooteghem, J. Van. *Pompeé le Grand.* Brussels, 1954.

———. "Cicerón se défend." *LEC,* 25 (1957): 168–172.

———. *Lucius Licinius Lucullus.* Brussels, 1959.

———. *L. Marcius Philippus et sa famille.* Brussels, 1961.

———. "Pour une lecture candide du *Pro C. Rabirio.*" *LEC,* 32 (1964): 234–246.

———. *Les Cæcilii Metelli de la République.* Brussels, 1967.

———. "L'affaire Cluentius." *Hommages à Marcel Renard* (1969), II:777–788.

Pacitti, G. "Cicerone al processo di M. Celio Rufo." *Atti Congr. Int. Stud. Cic.* (1959), II:67–79.

Palmer, R. E. A. "Tre lettere in cerca di storico." *RivFilol,* 99 (1971): 385–409.

Park, M. E. *The Plebs in Cicero's Day.* Diss. Cambridge, Mass., 1918.

Pastorino, A. "La Sempronia della congiura di Catilina." *GiornItalFilol,* 3 (1950): 358–363.

Pauly, A., G. Wissowa, et al. *Real-Encyclopädie der Classischen Altertumswissenschaft.* Stuttgart, 1894–.

Pease, A. S. *M. Tulli Ciceronis De Natura Deorum.* Cambridge, Mass. 1958.

Perl, G. "Die Rede Cottas in Sallusts Historien." *Philologus,* 109 (1965): 75–82.

Phillips, E. J. "Cicero and the Prosecution of C. Manilius." *Latomus,* 29 (1970): 595–607.

Plaumann, G. "Das sogenannte *Senatus Consultum Ultimum,* die Quasi-diktatur der späteren römischen Republik." *Klio,* 13 (1913): 321–386.

Pocock, L. G. *Commentary on Cicero, In Vatinium.* London, 1926.

———. *"Pompeiusve Parem,"* *CP,* 22 (1927), 301–306.

———. "What Made Pompeius Fight in 49 B.C.?" *Greece and Rome,* 6 (1959): 68–81.

Pólay, E. "Kodifizierungsplan des Pompeius." *Acta Antiqua,* 13 (1965): 85–95.

Polignano, M. "Publio Cornelio Dolabella, uomo politico." *RendLinc,* 8.1 (1946): 240–275, 444–501.

Premerstein, A. von. "Vom Werden und Wesen des Prinzipats." *AbhMünch,* 15 (1937): 1–290.

Rawson, B. "*De lege agraria* 2.49." *CP,* 66 (1971): 26–29.

Reitzenstein, R. "Zu Ciceros Rede für Cælius." *NAkG* (1925), pp. 25–32.

Renkema, E. H. "De Iudicio perduellionis sublato." *Mnemosyne,* 55 (1927): 395–400.

Riccobono, S. *Fontes Iuris Romani Anteiustiniani.* Vol. I. Florence, 1941.

Richardson, J. S. "The *Commentariolum Petitionis.*" *Historia,* 20 (1971): 436–442.

Rödl, B. *Das Senatus Consultum Ultimum.* Bonn, 1969.

Rossi, R. F. "La congiura di Vettio." *Annali Triestini,* 21 (1951): 247–260.

———. "Sulla lotta politica in Roma dopo la morte di Silla." *PP,* 20 (1965): 113–152.

Rotondi, G. *Leges Publicæ Populi Romani.* Milan, 1912.

Rowland, R. J. "The Number of Grain Recipients in the Late Republic." *Acta Antiqua,* 13 (1965): 81–83.

———. "Crassus, Clodius, and Curio in the year 59 B.C." *Historia,* 15 (1966): 217–223.

Royer, J. P. "La problème des dettes à la fin de la république romaine." *RevHistDroit,* 45 (1967): 191–240, 407–450.

Rubinsohn, Z. "A Note on Plutarch, *Crassus,* X.1." *Historia,* 19 (1970): 624–627.

———. "Was the Bellum Spartacium a Servile Insurrection?" *RivFilol,* 99 (1971): 290–299.

Rudé, G. *The Crowd in History.* New York, 1964.

Rudolph, H. *Staat und Stadt im römischen Italien.* Leipzig. 1935.

Sage, E. T. "Cicero and the Agrarian Proposals of 63 B.C." *CJ,* 16 (1921): 230–236.

Salmon, E. T. "Catiline, Crassus, and Cæsar." *AJP,* 56 (1935): 302–316.

———. "Cæsar and the Consulship for 49 B.C." *CJ,* 34 (1939): 388–395.

Sanders, H. A. "The So-Called First Triumvirate." *Mem. Am. Acad. Rome,* 10 (1932): 55–68.

Sanford, E. M. "The Career of Aulus Gabinius." *TAPA,* 70 (1939): 64–92.

Saunders, C. "The Political Sympathies of Servius Sulpicius Rufus." *CR,* 37 (1923): 110–113.

Scalais, R. "Aspect financier de la conjuration de Catilina." *LEC,* 8 (1939): 487–492.

Scardigli, B. "Sertorio: Problemi cronologici." *Athenæum,* 49 (1971): 229–270.

Schulten, A. *Sertorius.* Leipzig, 1926.

Schulz, F. *Classical Roman Law.* Oxford, 1951.

Schur, W. "Homo Novus: ein Beitrag zur Sozialgeschichte der sinkenden Republik." *BonnJbb,* 134 (1929): 54–66.

———. *Sallust als Historiker.* Stuttgart, 1934.

Schwarz, E. "Die Berichte über die catilinarische Verschwörung." *Hermes,* 32 (1897): 554–608.

Scott, R. T., and L. R. Taylor. "Seating Space in the Roman Senate and the *Senatus Pedarii.*" *TAPA,* 100 (1969): 529–582.

Scullard, H. H. *From the Gracchi to Nero.* 3rd. ed. London, 1970.

Seager, R. "The First Catilinarian Conspiracy." *Historia,* 13 (1964): 338–347.

———. "Clodius, Pompey and the Exile of Cicero." *Latomus,* 24 (1965): 519–531.

———. "The Tribunate of Cornelius, Some Ramifications." *Hommages à Marcel Renard* (1969), II:680–686.

Sealey, R. *"Habe Meam Rationem." ClMed,* 18 (1957): 75–101.

Seidel, J. *Fasti ædilicii von der Einrichtung der plebejischen Ädilität bis zum Tode Cæsars.* Breslau, 1908.

Shackleton Bailey, D. R. "Emendations of Cicero, *Ad Atticum." PCPS,* 183 (1954–55): 26–31.

———. "On Cicero, *Ad Familiares." PCPS,* 185 (1958–59): 6–15.

———. "Sex. Clodius–Sex. Clœlius." *CQ,* 10 (1960): 41–42.

———. "The Roman Nobility in the Second Civil War." *CQ,* 10 (1960): 253–267.

———. "On Cicero, *Ad Familiares." Philologus,* 105 (1961): 72–89.

———. "Emendations of Cicero, *Ad Quintum Fratrem* and *Ad Brutum." PCPS,* 187 (1961): 1–7.

———. "Two Tribunes, 57 B.C." *CR,* 12 (1962): 195–197.

———. *Cicero's Letters to Atticus.* 6 vols. Cambridge, 1965–68.

———. "The Prosecution of Roman Magistrates-elect." *Phœnix,* 24 (1970): 162–165.

Shatzman, I. "Four Notes on Roman Magistrates." *Athenæum,* 46 (1968): 345–354.

———. "The Egyptian Question in Roman Politics, 59–54 B.C." *Latomus,* 30 (1971): 363–369.

Sherk, R. K. *Roman Documents from the Greek East.* Baltimore, 1969.

Sherwin-White, A. N. *"Pœna legis Repetundarum." PBSR,* 17 (1949): 5–25.

———. "Violence in Roman Politics." *JRS,* 46 (1956): 1–9.

Smith, C. L. "Cicero's Journey into Exile." *HSCP,* 7 (1896): 65–84.

Smith, R. E. *The Failure of the Roman Republic.* Cambridge, 1955.

———. "The *Lex Plotia Agraria* and Pompey's Spanish Veterans." *CQ,* 7 (1957): 82–85.

———. *Service in the Post-Marian Army.* Manchester, 1958.

———. *Cicero the Statesman.* Cambridge, 1966.

Štaerman, E. M. *Die Blütezeit der Sklavenwirtschaft der römischen Republik.* Wiesbaden, 1969.

Stein, P. *Die Senatssitzungen der Ciceronischen Zeit (68–43).* Münster, 1930.

Stella Maranca, F. "Fasti Prætorii dal 366 al 44 av. Cr." *MemLinc* 6.2 (1927): 277–376.

Sternkopf, W. "Über die 'Verbesserung' des Clodianischen Gesetzentwurfes *de exilio Ciceronis." Philologus,* 59 (1900): 272–304.

Stevens, C. E. "The Terminal Date of Cæsar's Command." *AJP,* 59 (1938): 169–208.

Stocker, A. F. "The *Legis Dies* of Cæsar's Command in Gaul." *CJ,* 56 (1961): 242–248.

Stockton, D. "Cicero and the *Ager Campanus.*" *TAPA*, 93 (1962): 471–489.
Stone, C. G. "March 1, 50 B.C." *CQ*, 22 (1928): 193–201.
Strachan-Davidson, J. L. *Problems of the Roman Criminal Law.* Vols. I–II. Oxford, 1912.
Strasburger, H. *Cæsars Eintritt in die Geschichte.* Munich, 1938.
Sumner, G. V. "*Lex Ælia, Lex Fufia.*" *AJP*, 84 (1963): 337–358.
______. "The Last Journey of L. Sergius Catilina." *CP*, 58 (1963): 215–219.
______. "Manius or Mamercus?" *JRS*, 54 (1964): 41–48.
______. "Cicero, Pompeius, and Rullus." *TAPA*, 97 (1966): 569–582.
______. "Proconsuls and *Provinciæ* in Spain, 218/7–196/5." *Arethusa*, 3 (1970): 85–102.
______. "The *Lex Annalis* under Cæsar." *Phoenix*, 2 (1971): 246–271, 357–371.
Suolahti, J. *The Junior Officers of the Roman Army in the Republican Period.* Helsinki, 1955.
Syme, R. "Cæsar, the Senate, and Italy." *PBSR*, 14 (1938): 1–31.
______. "The Allegiance of Labienus." *JRS*, 28 (1938): 113–125.
______. *The Roman Revolution.* Oxford, 1939.
______. "Review of Gelzer, *Cæsar.*" *JRS*, 34 (1944): 92–103.
______. "Review of Broughton, *Magistrates of the Roman Republic.*" *CP*, 50 (1955): 127–138.
______. "Review of A. E. Gordon, *Potitus Valerius Messalla.*" *JRS*, 45 (1955): 155–160.
______. "Missing Senators." *Historia*, 4 (1955): 52–71.
______. "Missing Persons (P-W.VIIIa)." *Historia*, 5 (1956): 204–212.
______. "Ten Tribunes." *JRS*, 53 (1963): 55–60.
______. *Sallust.* Berkeley and Los Angeles, 1964.
______. "The Historian Servilius Nonianus." *Hermes*, 92 (1964): 408–424.
______. "Senators, Tribes and Towns." *Historia*, 13 (1964): 105–125.
______. "The Stemma of the Sentii Saturnini." *Historia*, 13 (1964): 156–166.
Taylor, J. H. "Political Motives in Cicero's Defense of Archias." *AJP*, 73 (1952): 62–70.
Taylor, L. R. "Cæsar's Early Career." *CP*, 36 (1941): 113–132.
______. "Cæsar's Colleagues in the Pontifical College." *AJP*, 63 (1942): 385–412.
______. "Cæsar and the Roman Nobility." *TAPA*, 73 (1942): 1–24.
______. "Foreign Groups in Roman Politics of the Late Republic." *Hommages Bidez et Cumont* (1948), II:323–330.
______. *Party Politics in the Age of Cæsar.* Berkeley and Los Angeles, 1949.
______. "The Date and Meaning of the Vettius Affair." *Historia*, 1 (1950): 45–51.
______. "Cæsar's Agrarian Legislation and his Municipal Policy," *Studies in*

Roman Economic and Social History in Honor of Allan Chester Johnson (1951), pp. 68–77.

———. "On the Chronology of Cæsar's First Consulship." *AJP,* 72 (1951): 254-268.

———. *The Voting Districts of the Roman Republic.* Rome, 1960.

———. "Freedmen and Freeborn in the Epitaphs of Imperial Rome." *AJP,* 82 (1961): 113–132.

———. "Forerunners of the Gracchi." *JRS,* 52 (1962): 19–27.

———. "Magistrates of 55 B.C. in Cicero's *Pro Plancio* and Catullus, 52." *Athenæum,* 42 (1964): 12–28.

———. "The Office of Nasica recorded in Cicero *ad Atticum* 2.1.9." *Classical, Medieval, and Renaissance Studies in honor of Berthold Louis Ullman* (1964), I:79–85.

———. *Roman Voting Assemblies.* Ann Arbor, 1966.

———. "The Dating of Major Legislation and Elections in Cæsar's First Consulship." *Historia,* 17 (1968): 173–193.

Tibiletti, G. "Ricerche di storia agraria romana I: La politica agraria dalla guerra annibalica ai Gracchi." *Athenæum,* 28 (1950): 183–266.

Till, R. "Ciceros Bewerbung ums Konsulat." *Historia,* 11 (1962): 315–338.

Treggiari, S. *Roman Freedmen during the Late Republic.* Oxford, 1969.

———. "A New Collina." *Historia,* 19 (1970): 121–122.

Trencsényi-Waldapfel, I. "*Calvus ex Nanneianis* (di un luogo polo chiaro dell' Epistolaro Ciceroniano)." *Athenæum,* 42 (1964): 42–51.

Treves, P. "Sertorio." *Athenæum,* 10 (1932): 127–147.

Tyrell, R. Y., and L. C. Purser, *The Correspondence of M. Tullius Cicero.* 6 vols. Dublin, 1904–1933.

Uttschenko, S. *Der Weltanschaulich-Politische Kampf in Rom am Vorabend des Sturzes der Republik.* Berlin, 1956.

Valgiglio, E. *Silla e la crisi repubblicana.* Florence, 1956.

Valle, G. Della. "Gaio Memmio, Dedicatario del poema di Lucrezio." *RendLinc,* 14 (1938): 731–886.

Vitzthum, W. *Untersuchungen zum materiellen Inhalt der Lex Plautia und Lex Iulia de vi.* Diss. Munich, 1966.

Vogt, J. "Struktur der antiken Sklavenkriege." *AbhMainz* (1957), pp. 7–57.

Walbank, F. W. *A Historical Commentary on Polybius.* Vol. I. Oxford, 1957.

Ward, A. "Cicero's Support of Pompey in the Trials of M. Fonteius and P. Oppius." *Latomus,* 27 (1968): 802–809.

———. "Cicero's Support of the *Lex Gabinia.*" *CW,* 63 (1969): 8–10.

———. "Cicero and Pompey in 75 and 70." *Latomus,* 29 (1970): 58–71.

———. "The Early Relationship between Cicero and Pompey until 80 B.C." *Phoenix,* 24 (1970): 119–129.

———. "Politics in the Trials of Manilius and Cornelius." *TAPA*, 101 (1970): 545–556.

Waters, K. H. "Cicero, Sallust, and Cæsar." *Historia*, 19 (1970): 195–215.

Watson, A. *The Law of Persons in the Later Roman Republic.* Oxford, 1967.

Watson, G. R. "The Pay of the Roman Army. The Republic." *Historia*, 7 (1958): 113–120.

Watt, W. S. "Notes on Cicero, *Ad Atticum*, Books 5–8." *Mnemosyne*, 16 (1963): 364–399.

Wehrmann, P. *Fasti Prætorii ab A.U. DCLXXXVII ad A.U. DCCX.* Berlin, 1875.

Weinrib, E. "The Family Connections of M. Livius Drusus Libo." *HSCP*, 72 (1968): 247–278.

———. "The Prosecution of Roman Magistrates." *Phoenix*, 22 (1968): 32–56.

———. "The Judiciary Law of M. Livius Drusus (tr. pl. 91 B.C.)." *Historia*, 19 (1970); 414–443.

———. "*Obnuntiatio:* Two Problems." *ZSS*, 87 (1970): 395–425.

———. "The Prosecution of Magistrates-Designate." *Phoenix*, 25 (1971): 145–150.

Weinstock, S. "Clodius and the *Lex Ælia Fufia.*" *JRS*, 27 (1937): 215–222.

Westermann, W. L. *The Slave Systems of Greek and Roman Antiquity.* Philadelphia, 1955.

White, K. D. "*Latifundia.*" *BICS*, 14 (1967): 62–79.

Wiehn, E. *Die illegalen Heereskommanden in Rom bis auf Cæsar.* Marburg, 1926.

Willems, P. *Le Sénat de la république romaine, sa composition et ses attributions.* 2 vols. Louvain and Paris, 1878–1883.

Wimmel, W. "Die Zeitlichen Vorwegnahmen in Sallusts Catilina." *Hermes*, 95 (1967): 192–221.

Wirszubski, C. *Libertas as a Political Idea at Rome during the Late Republic and Early Principate.* Cambridge, 1950.

Wiseman, T. P. "The Potteries of Vibienus and Rufrenus at Arretium." *Mnemosyne*, 16 (1963): 275–283.

———. "Some Republican Senators and Their Tribes." *CQ*, 14 (1964): 122–133.

———. "Two More Senators." *CQ*, 15 (1965): 158–160.

———. "The Mother of Livia Augusta." *Historia*, 14 (1965): 333–334.

———. "The Ambitions of Quintus Cicero." *JRS*, 56 (1966): 108–115.

———. "Lucius Memmius and his Family." *CQ*, 17 (1967): 164–167.

———. "Two Friends of Clodius in Cicero's Letters." *CQ*, 18 (1968): 297–302.

———. *Catullan Questions.* Leicester, 1969.

———. "The Census in the First Century B.C." *JRS*, 59 (1969): 59–75.

———. "The Definition of 'eques Romanus' in the late Republic and early Empire." *Historia,* 19 (1970): 67–83.

———. *New Men in the Roman Senate, 139 B.C.–A.D. 14.* Oxford, 1971.

Wistrand, E. *Sallust on Judicial Murders in Rome.* Göteborg, 1968.

Woess, F.v. "Personalexekution und *cessio bonorum* im römischen Reichsrecht." *ZSS,* 43 (1922): 485–529.

Yavetz, Z. "The Living Conditions of the Urban Plebs in Republican Rome." *Latomus,* 17 (1958): 500–517.

———. "The Failure of Catiline's Conspiracy." *Historia,* 12 (1963): 485–499.

Zumpt, A. W. *Das Criminalrecht der römischen Republik.* Vol. II. Berlin, 1868–1869.

———. *Der Criminalprocess der römischen Republik.* Leipzig, 1871.

INDEX NOMINUM

INDEX RERUM